Theoretical
SOCIOLOGY

Other Authored Books by Jonathan Turner

Patterns of Social Organization (1972)
American Society: Problems of Structure (1972)
The Structure of Sociological Theory (1974)
Inequality: Privilege and Poverty in America (1976, with Charles Starnes)
Social Problems in America (1977)
Sociology: Studying the Human System (1978)
Functionalism (1979, with Alexandra Maryanski)
The Emergence of Sociological Theory (1981, with Leonard Beeghley)
Societal Stratification: A Theoretical Analysis (1984)
Oppression: A Socio-history of Black-White Relations in America (1985, with Royce Singleton and David Musick)
Herbert Spencer: A Renewed Appreciation (1985)
American Dilemmas: A Sociological Interpretation of Enduring Social Issues (1985, with David Musick)
Sociology: A Student Handbook (1985)
Sociology: The Science of Human Organization (1986)
A Theory of Social Interaction (1988)
The Impossible Science: An Institutional History of American Sociology (1990, with Stephen P. Turner)
The Social Cage: Human Nature and the Evolution of Society (1992, with Alexandra Maryanski)
Classical Sociological Theory: A Positivist's Perspective (1992)
Sociology: Concepts and Uses (1993)
Socjologia Amerykansa W. Posukiwaiou Tazamosci (1993, with Stephen P. Turner)
American Ethnicity: A Sociological Analysis of the Dynamics of Discrimination (1994, with Adalberto Aguirre)
Macrodynamics: Toward a Theory on the Organization of Human Populations (1995)
The Institutional Order (1997)
On the Origins of Human Emotions: A Sociological Inquiry into the Evolution of Human Affect (2000)
Face-to-Face: Toward a Sociological Theory of Interpersonal Behavior (2002)
Human Institutions: A Theory of Societal Evolution (2003)
The Sociology of Emotions (2005, with Jan E. Stets)
Incest: The Origins of the Taboo (2005, with Alexandra Maryanski)
Sociology (2006)
On the Origins of Society by Natural Selection (2007, with Alexandra Maryanski)
Human Emotions: A Sociological Theory (2008)
Theoretical Principles of Sociology, Volume 1: *Macrodynamics* (2010)
Theoretical Principles of Sociology, Volume 2: *Microdynamics* (2010)
Theoretical Principles of Sociology, Volume 3: *Mesodynamics* (2012)
The Problem of Emotions in Societies (2011)
Contemporary Sociological Theory (2012)
Ten Theoretical Perspectives in Sociology (2012)
The Problems of Discrimination in American Society (2012)

Edited Books by Jonathan Turner:
Theory Building in Sociology (1988)
Social Theory Today (1987, with Anthony Giddens)
Handbook of Sociological Theory (2001)
Handbook of the Sociology of Emotions (2007, with Jan E. Stets)
Handbook of Neurosociology (2012, with David Franks)

Theoretical
SOCIOLOGY
1830 TO THE PRESENT

Jonathan H. Turner
University of California, Riverside

Los Angeles | London | New Delhi
Singapore | Washington DC

Los Angeles | London | New Delhi
Singapore | Washington DC

FOR INFORMATION:

SAGE Publications, Inc.
2455 Teller Road
Thousand Oaks, California 91320
E-mail: order@sagepub.com

SAGE Publications Ltd.
1 Oliver's Yard
55 City Road
London EC1Y 1SP
United Kingdom

SAGE Publications India Pvt. Ltd.
B 1/I 1 Mohan Cooperative Industrial Area
Mathura Road, New Delhi 110 044
India

SAGE Publications Asia-Pacific Pte. Ltd.
3 Church Street
#10-04 Samsung Hub
Singapore 049483

Acquisitions Editor: David Repetto
Editorial Assistant: Lauren Johnson
Production Editor: Eric Garner
Copy Editor: QuADS Prepress (P) Ltd.
Typesetter: C&M Digitals (P) Ltd.
Proofreader: Susan Schon
Indexer: Jean Casalegno
Cover Designer: Gail Buschman
Marketing Manager: Erica DeLuca
Permissions Editor: Karen Ehrmann

Printed in the United States of America

Library of Congress Cataloging-in-Publication Data

Turner, Jonathan H.

Theoretical sociology : 1830 to the present / Jonathan H. Turner, University of California, Riverside.

pages cm
Includes index.

ISBN 978-1-4522-0342-3 (hbk. : alk. paper)
ISBN 978-1-4522-0343-0 (pbk. : alk. paper)

1. Sociology—History. I. Title.

HM445.T977 2013
301—dc23   2012031490

This book is printed on acid-free paper.

12 13 14 15 16 10 9 8 7 6 5 4 3 2 1

Brief Contents

Detailed Contents

Preface

This book started out to be an effort to combine materials from my two long-running theory texts, *The Emergence of Sociological Theory* (with Leonard Beeghley and Charles Powers) and *The Structure of Sociological Theory*. As I got into the project, however, it became increasingly clear that a new kind of book built around existing materials would be inadequate. New materials would be necessary. In the end, as much as 40% of the book is new, while the core goal of reviewing the older materials in depth and, where possible, formalizing past and present theories remains at center stage. So, as you can feel when lifting this book, it got away from me and became bigger than I had originally envisioned. Yet it was still great fun at this stage in my career to try to pull together the theorizing that has developed in sociology since 1830.

I have not covered everyone who has theorized, but I examine those theorists and theories that have endured and that still inform the sociological canon. My apologies to many others whose works are still an important part of a particular theoretical tradition but who only get footnotes or brief mentions here and there—there simply was not enough room in *one* book to cover all the important theorizing being done today. I had to focus on those who have been the most visible or who are the best exemplars of a particular theoretical perspective or tradition in sociology.

Inevitably, the book reflects my biases toward scientific theorizing, although many of the theories and theorists summarized in these pages do not share my scientific biases. Thus, I may have biases, but I am not a bigot about these, and I have done my best to represent the range of critical, if not antiscience, theories now in the discipline. But still, I have done what my students often call "turnerized" many theories by formalizing them and, in the eyes of my critics, "polluting" them with my desire to see theories formatted in ways that clarify the connections among forces driving some aspect of the social universe. Moreover, formalizing makes theories testable, which, in the end, is necessary if sociology is to be a science and, in my view, to be useful to the world.

In the 1980s and early 1990s, I had become depressed by what I felt was a movement away from science. But as I thought about the matter, I realized that I was blaming the wrong people; the antiscience rhetoric of many gave this impression, but in fact, scientific theorizing has accomplished a great deal in the almost fifty years that I have been a sociologist. The underlying cause of my despair is the overspecialization and compartmentalization of scientific theories into rather narrow and often balkanized theoretical research traditions. Much was going on, but it was narrow, filled with too many scope conditions. So the problem did not lie with the skeptics or critics of scientific sociology but, rather, with the way theoretical sociology was being developed. I cannot convince the critics about the prospects for a true science of society, but I hope that I can demonstrate the utility of breaking down some of the barriers that separate schools of theorizing in the discipline.

While formalizing theories and juxtaposing them, it became immediately obvious to me that many overlap, duplicate each other, or are complementary. Yet theoretical integration is much less common today than is theoretical differentiation. I have in my own work tried to integrate theories, but perhaps by putting such a large number of theories in one place, between the two covers of one book, others can see the need for more consolidation and integration of theories in sociology.

Even though this book has grown, it can still fulfill its initial purpose: to provide a text for students taking the classical and contemporary theories courses in universities. It can also be, I trust, a resource for those teaching these courses and for those needing summaries of theories for their own research. Whatever the fate of the book, it has been interesting to put together a great deal of material in one place.

Jonathan Turner

Murrieta, California

With gratitude and a new appreciation for life

**to Eric Sheperd, M.D., and Seth E. Anderson, M.D.,
and the staff of Cottage Hospital,
Santa Barbara, CA.**

CHAPTER 1

Theoretical Sociology

The Inevitability of Sociology

Long before sociology was given a name by Auguste Comte in 1830,[1] humans had thought about the social universe as they sought to adapt to their biophysical and sociocultural environments. Indeed, people have always been "folk sociologists," just as most people are today when they make a pronouncement on the causes of some social event or when they assert what should be done to resolve some problematic social condition. Also, very early in human history, but accelerating dramatically with the invention of writing, scholars began developing schools and systems of philosophical thought that had many of the elements of sociological analysis. So sociology has existed in one form or another for as long as we have been human.

The emergence of sociology and, hence, sociological theory was inevitable. If Auguste Comte had not been born, someone else would have articulated a name for the systematic and even scientific study of the social universe. Herbert Spencer's *The Study of Sociology*[2] might have become the new manifesto for the discipline, although, if such had been the case, sociology's official arrival might have been delayed for decades. The emergence of sociology was the culmination not only of a very long history of humans thinking about their creations—the social world—but of broader social and intellectual movements that began to bring Europe out of its "Dark Ages," after the collapse of the Roman Empire. This Renaissance also included new ways of thinking, which collectively are sometimes termed *The Enlightenment*. Once these new ways of thinking about the social world began to gain traction, it was inevitable that someone like Comte would come along to give a name to the

---

[1] Auguste Comte, *The Course of Positive Philosophy* (1830–1842); but the Harriet Martineau condensed translation, titled *The Positive Philosophy of Auguste Comte*, 3 vols. (London: Bell and Sons, 1898), is the more available and accessible source.

[2] Herbert Spencer, *The Study of Sociology* (London: Kegan Paul, Trench, 1873), made a strong case for viewing sociology as an explanatory science that could overcome human biases and develop laws explaining the dynamics of human social organization.

field. We should, therefore, briefly pause to see what The Enlightenment accomplished and why it set the stage for sociology to make its grand entrance before an often skeptical audience.

The Enlightenment and New Ways of Thinking

The Intellectual Revolution

When the Roman Empire finally collapsed, there followed a period often termed the Dark Ages. Much of the learning of Romans and, more important, of Greeks, Arabs, Persians, and Egyptians was lost; and only the faithful scribes of medieval monasteries kept the Eastern and Western intellectual traditions alive. The label *The Enlightenment* is obviously meant to connote a lighting of the dark, but in fact, the Dark Ages were not stagnant.[3] After the initial decline in Western civilization when the Roman Empire finally collapsed, living conditions for most people were miserable; and yet new inventions and new ideas were slowly accumulating, despite the oppressive poverty of the masses, the constant warfare among feudal lords, and the rigid dogma of religion. New forms and experiments in commerce, politics, economics, religion, art, music, crafts, and thinking were slowly emerging. As these elements of "the great awakening" were accumulating between the fifth and thirteenth centuries, a critical threshold was finally reached. Change came more rapidly as these innovations fed off of each other. As social structure and culture changed, so did human thinking about the world. Much of what had been lost from the Greeks and Romans, as well as from the early civilizations of the Middle East, was found (in dusty church libraries), rediscovered, and often improved upon. Nowhere is this more evident than in how scholars viewed science as a way of understanding the universe.

Francis Bacon (1561–1626) was the first to articulate clearly the new mode of inquiry: conceptualizations of the nature of the universe should always be viewed with skepticism and tested against observable facts. This sounds like scientific common sense today, but it was a radical idea at that time. This mode of inquiry stimulated great achievements in sixteenth- and seventeenth-century astronomy, including Isaac Newton's famous law of gravity. Thinking about the universe was now becoming systematic, but equally important, it was becoming abstract and yet empirical. The goal was to articulate fundamental relationships in the universe that could explain the many, varied ways these relationships can be expressed in the empirical world. To explain events thus required systematic and abstract thinking—in a word, it required theory. And this way of thinking literally transformed the world.

The Enlightenment was thus an intellectual revolution because it changed how we are to explain the universe, and, increasingly, it held out the vision that knowledge

---

[3]There is often a tendency to think that the Dark Ages were stagnant, but societies were slowly being rebuilt after the collapse of the Roman Empire. See Patrick Nolan and Gerhard Lenski, *Human Societies* (Boulder, CO: Paradigm Press, 2009) for a review of the technological changes that were occurring then; these would eventually drive societies toward modernity.

about how the universe operates can also be used to better the human condition. In fact, progress was not only possible but inevitable once science and rational thinking began to dominate how we explain the world, including the social world of our own creation. In England and Scotland, the Enlightenment was dominated by a group of thinkers who sought to justify the industrial capitalism that first appeared in the British Isles. Scholars like Adam Smith believed that individuals should be free of external constraints and should be free to compete, thereby creating a better society. While this might be considered a conservative philosophy today, it was liberal if not radical in its time. In France, the Enlightenment was dominated by a group of scholars known as the *philosophes*. Despite the fact that Adam Smith formulated one of the essential questions of sociology—How are increasingly specialized people working and living in different worlds to become integrated into a complex but coherent society?—it is the philosophes who had more influence on the emergence of sociology, although we should always remember that one of the most important thinkers of the nineteenth century, Karl Marx, saw himself as trying to improve upon Adam Smith's economic theory. Sociology thus has its major roots in the intellectual ferment generated by the French philosophes, but we must always remember that thinkers in the Anglo world also influenced the development of the new science of sociology.

The new thinking that drove The Enlightenment derived considerable inspiration from the scientific revolution of the sixteenth and seventeenth centuries. Newtonian physics is perhaps the symbolic peak of The Enlightenment because it broke what had been a philosophical dualism between the senses and reason. Reason and the world of phenomena *are not separate* but are part of a new way of knowing. Through concepts, speculation, and logic, the facts of the empirical world can be understood; and by accumulating facts, reason could sort through them and provide explanations for their existence and operation that were more than flights of intellectual fancy or impositions of religious dogma.

The world was no longer the province of the supernatural; it was the domain of the natural, and its complexity could now be understood by the combination of reason and facts. Newton's law of gravity was hailed as the exemplar of how scientific inquiry should be conducted. And gradually, the social universe was included in domains that science should explain. This gradual inclusion was a radical break from the past, where the social had been considered the domain of morals, ethics, and religion. The goal of the French philosophes, then, was to emancipate social thought from religious speculation; and while the philosophes were hardly very scientific, they performed the essential function of placing thought about the human condition in the realm of reason. As can be seen in the philosophes' statements about universal human rights, law, and natural order (ideas that are at the core of the U.S. Constitution), their work was seen as a radical attack on established authority in both the state and the church. From notions of natural laws, it is but a short step to thinking about the fundamental laws not only of human rights but also of human social organization. As will be evident in the next chapter, many of the less shrill and polemical philosophes actually made this short step and sought to understand the social realm through principles or laws that they felt were the equivalent of those developed by Newton for the physical realm.

Social conditions almost always affect how scholars think about the world, and such was the case for the philosophes, who were opposed to the Old Regime (monarchy) in France and supportive of the bourgeoisie in emphasizing free trade, free labor, free commerce, free industry, and free opinion. The growing and literate bourgeoisie formed the reading public that bought the books, papers, and pamphlets of the philosophes. These works are filled with seeming "laws" of the human condition, but these were mostly ideological or evaluative statements derived from moral, political, and social philosophies; they were not drawn from value-neutral reasoning or systematic empirical research and, hence, could not be considered scientific. Yet they implicitly supported the idea of systematic thought about the social universe, and in so doing, they heralded the view that a science of society could potentially be molded in the image of physics or biology. In fact, many argued that a science of the social world was not only possible but an inevitable outcome of human progress.

The basic thesis of all the philosophes—whether Voltaire, Rousseau, Condorcet, Diderot, or others—was that humans had certain "natural rights," which were violated by the institutional arrangements of the time. It was, therefore, necessary to dismantle the existing social order and substitute a new order that would be more compatible with the rights and needs of humans. This transformation was to occur through reasoned and progressive legislation. And it was one of the cruel ironies of history that the philosophes were forced to watch in horror as their names and ideas were used to justify the violent aftermath of the French Revolution of 1789—hardly the "reconstruction" of the social order that they had in mind.

In almost all of the philosophes' formulations was a vision of human progress. Humanity was seen to be marching in a direction governed by the law of progress, which was as fundamental as the law of gravitation in the physical world. Thus, the philosophes were clearly unscientific in their moral advocacy, but they offered at least the rhetoric of post-Newtonian science in their search for the natural laws of the human order in their formulation of the law of progress. These somewhat contradictory intellectual tendencies were to be merged together in Comte's advocacy of scientific sociology.

Comte did not have to reconcile these tendencies alone, because the most talented of the philosophes, scholars such as Montesquieu, Turgot, and Condorcet, had already provided Comte with the broad contours of reconciliation: the laws of human organization, particularly the law of progressive development, can be used as tools to create a better social world. With this mixture of concerns—morality, progress, and scientific laws—this new view of possibilities was carried into the nineteenth century.

New systems of thought do not appear only from heady intellectual debates; new ideas almost always reflect more fundamental transformations in the organization of the polity and production. Yet, once created, ideas have the capacity to stimulate new forms of politics and new modes of production. The Enlightenment was thus more than an intellectual revolution; its emergence was a response to changes in the patterns of social organization generated by new political and economic formations.

The Political and Economic Revolutions

For most of the eighteenth century, the last remnants of the old economic order were crumbling under the impact of the commercial and industrial revolutions. The expansion of free markets and trade eliminated much of the feudal order during the seventeenth century, but during the eighteenth century new restrictions were imposed by guilds controlling labor's access to skilled occupations and by charted (by the nobility) corporations controlling vast sectors of economic production. The cotton industry was the first to break the hold of the guilds and chartered corporations, and with each subsequent decade, other industries were subjected to the liberating effects of free labor, free trade, and free production. By the time larger-scale industrial production emerged—first in England, then in France, and later in Germany—the underlying economic reorganization had already been achieved. The new industrial base of manufacturing simply accelerated in the nineteenth century the transformations that had been at work for decades in the eighteenth century.

These transformations were profound: labor was liberated from the land; wealth and capital existed independently of the large noble estates; urbanization of the population was depopulating rural areas; competitive industries generated ever new technologies to stay a step ahead of competitors; markets expanded to distribute the finished goods produced by industry and to provide the basic resources needed for manufacturing; services increasingly became an important part of the economy; law became concerned with regularizing new economic processes, trade, and privilege for new and, often, old elites; the polity could no longer legitimate its leaders by "divine rights"; and religion was losing much of its influence in general but particularly in its capacity to legitimate polity. As these transformations methodically destroyed the old feudal order as well as the transitional mercantile order of guilds and chartered corporations, the daily lives of people also changed. Family structures began to shrink; new classes such as the urban proletariat and bourgeoisie expanded; people increasingly sold their labor as a commodity in markets; and many other former routines were changed. These changes, coupled with memories of the disorder caused by the revolution, provided the first French sociologists with their basic intellectual problem: how to use the laws of social organization to create a new, less volatile, and more humane social order.

By the time of the French Revolution, the old feudal system was a mere skeleton of its former self. Peasants had become landowners, although tenant farming was still practiced but subject to high rates of taxation. The landed aristocracy had lost much of its wealth through indolence, incompetence, and unwillingness to pursue occupations in the emerging capitalist order. In fact, many of the nobility lived in genteel poverty within the walls of their disintegrating estates, only to have their land purchased by the bourgeoisie or to seek out the bourgeoisie for loans and marital partners for their children. The monarchy was "diluted" or "polluted" by the selling of titles to the bourgeoisie and by the need to seek loans from those who had money. And so, by the time of the revolution, the monarchy was weak and in a fiscal crisis, increasingly dependent upon the bourgeoisie for support.

The structure of the state perhaps best reflects these changes. By the end of the eighteenth century, the French monarchy had become almost functionless. It had a centralized governmental system, but the monarch was now lazy, indolent, and incompetent. The real power resided in the professional administrators in the state bureaucracy, most of whom had been recruited from the bourgeoisie. The various magistrates were also recruited from the bourgeoisie, and the independent financiers, particularly the Farmers General, had assumed many of the tax-collecting functions of government. In exchange for a fixed sum of money, the monarch had contracted to the financiers the right to collect taxes, with the result that the financiers collected all that they could and, in the process, generated enormous resentment and hostility in the population. With their excessive profits, the financiers became the major bankers of the monarchy: the king, nobility, church, guild masters, merchants, and monopolistic corporate manufacturers often went to them for loans—thus increasing the abuse of their power. Thus, when the revolution came, it confronted a governmental system that had been in severe decline for a century; yet the violence of the revolution and the decades of instability in France that followed document that the bourgeoisie's assumption of power had been incomplete. True, the bureaucracies of the state, filled with bourgeoisie functionaries, kept the body of the state functioning, but often without a head. The ferment of ideas before and after the revolution only underscores a basic truth: change, and especially dramatic change, leads individuals to look for answers about "what to do."

In England, the changes were more evolutionary, with the result that sociology did not first emerge in the British Isles. The equivalent of the philosophes in the British Isles also thought about the nature of humans and their basic needs and rights, but they did so in a rather understated, almost passionless manner. The fire was in France because the abuses were greater and the transformation more revolutionary, leading people to think about how to reconstruct society. France was ready for sociology, and once it appeared, thinkers in the British Isles and Germany would find it an appealing way of dealing with the more evolutionary changes in their societies. Sociology was now ready to begin its long climb toward respectability.

The Controversy Over Science

Science as a Belief System

From the very beginning, when Auguste Comte proclaimed in 1830 that there could be a "social physics," there was immediate controversy over whether or not there could be a scientific sociology built around explanatory theories of the social universe. This controversy persists to the present day and, no doubt, will continue well into the future. One way to put the controversy into a broader perspective is to outline the fundamental beliefs of scientific theory in the broader context of other belief systems. Science is a belief system, but it is obviously not the only set of beliefs that influence people's perceptions and judgments. There are different types of knowledge possessed by humans, and science is only *one of several types,* which means, inevitably, that science as a way of knowing about the world will sometimes clash with the knowledge generated by other belief systems.

Social scientific theories begin with the assumption that the universe, including the social universe created by acting human beings, reveals certain basic and fundamental properties and processes that explain the ebb and flow of events in specific contexts. Because of this concern with discovering fundamental properties and processes, scientific theories are always stated abstractly, rising above specific empirical events and highlighting the *underlying forces that drive these events* in all times and places. In the context of sociological inquiry, for example, theoretical explanations are not so much about the specifics of a particular "economy" as about the underlying dynamics of production and distribution as social forces that drive the formation and change of economies. Similarly, scientific theories are not about a particular form of government but about the nature of power as a basic social force. Or, to illustrate further, scientific theories are not about particular behaviors and interactions among actual persons in a specific setting but about the nature of human interpersonal behavior in general and, hence, the forces that are always operative when people interact with each other. The goal, then, is always to see if the underlying forces that govern the particulars of specific empirical cases can be discovered and used to explain the operation of these empirical cases. To realize this goal, theories must be about the generic properties and processes transcending the unique characteristics of any one situation or case. Thus, scientific theories always seek to transcend the particular and the time-bound. Scientific theories are thus about the generic, the fundamental, the timeless, and the universal.

Another characteristic of scientific theories is that they are stated more formally than in ordinary language. At the extreme, theories are couched in another language, such as mathematics, but more typically in the social sciences, and particularly in sociology, theories are phrased in ordinary language. Still, even when using regular language, an effort is made to speak in neutral, objective, and unambiguous terms so that the theory means the same thing to all who examine it. Terms denoting properties of the world and their dynamics are defined clearly so that their referents are clear, and relationships among concepts denoting phenomena are stated in ways such that their interconnections are understood by all who examine the theory. At times, this attention to formalism can make theories seem stiff and dull, especially when these formalisms are couched at higher levels of abstraction. Yet without attention to what terms and phrases denote and connote, a theory could mean very different things to diverse audiences.

A final characteristic of scientific theories is that they are designed to be systematically tested with replicable methods against the facts of particular empirical settings. Despite being stated abstractly and formally, then, scientific theories do not stand aloof from the empirical. Useful theories all suggest ways in which they can be assessed against empirical events.

All scientific fields develop theories. For in the end, science seeks (a) to develop abstract and formally stated theories and (b) to test these theories against empirical cases to see if they are plausible. If a theory seems plausible in light of empirical assessment, then it represents *for the present time* the best explanation of events. If a theory is contradicted by empirical tests, then it must be discarded or revised. If competing theories emerge to explain the same phenomenon, they too must be empirically assessed, with the better explanation winning out.

Science is thus a rather slow process of developing theories, testing them, and then rejecting, modifying, or retaining them, at least until a better theory is proposed. Without giving attention to stating theories formally and then assessing them against the empirical world, they would become self-justifying and self-contained, reflecting personal biases, ideological leanings, or religious convictions.

Our biases and personal ideologies about what should occur and our commitment to dogmas articulated by religion are belief systems that stand in contrast to science as a belief system in one fundamental way: the theories of science are to be assessed empirically and, if necessary, rejected or at least revised in light of what the data say. These differences between scientific theory and other types of knowledge are presented in Figure 1.1.

The typology asks two basic questions:[4] (1) Is the search for knowledge to be evaluative or neutral? (2) Is the knowledge developed to pertain to actual empirical events and processes, or is it to be about nonempirical realities? In other words, should knowledge tell us what *should be* or *what is?* And should it refer to the observable world or to other, less observable realms? If knowledge is to tell us what should exist (and, by implication, what should not occur) in the empirical world, then it is *ideological knowledge*. If it informs us about what should be but does not pertain to observable forces but to hypothesized supernatural forces, then the knowledge is *religious* and, hence, about forces and beings in another realm of

Figure 1.1 Types of Knowledge

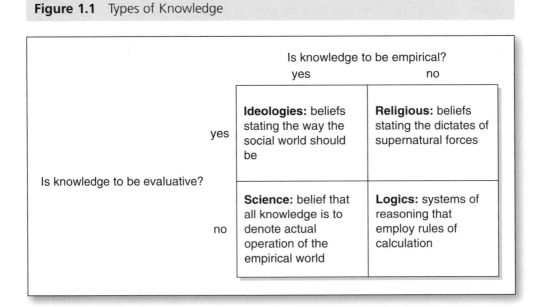

---

[4]I am borrowing the general idea from Talcott Parsons's *The Social System* (New York: Free Press, 1951).

existence. If knowledge is neither empirical nor evaluative, then it is a formal *system of logic,* such as mathematics, for developing other forms of knowledge, particularly science. And if it is about empirical events and is nonevaluative, then it is *science.*

This typology is crude, but it makes the essential point that there are different ways to look at, interpret, and develop knowledge about the world. Science is only one way. In its most developed form, science is based on the presumptions that theoretical knowledge (a) can be value-free, (b) can explain the actual workings of the empirical world in all times and places, and (c) can be revised as a result of careful observations of empirical events. These characteristics distinguish science from other belief systems that seek to generate understandings about the world.

The boundaries between these types of knowledge are often open, or at least permeable. Logics can be the language of science, as is the case when mathematics is used to state important relationships among forces driving the universe. The boundaries between these forms of knowledge can also be confrontational, as is evident today in the controversy between religious and scientific explanations for the evolution of humans. Within sociology proper, the most contentious and controversial relationship is between ideology and science. Many sociologists believe that theory must contain an ideological component; it must criticize undesirable conditions and advocate alternatives. Beliefs about "what should be" thus dominate the analysis of the social universe. This view of sociology contradicts the value-neutrality of science, where ideologies and other evaluative beliefs are not to contaminate analysis of social conditions. As noted earlier, the debate between those who advocate a scientific approach and those who argue for the infusion of ideology has been present for most of the history of sociology, and today this debate still rages. In Chapters 22, 23, and 24, I examine various strains of "critical theory" where the goal is to criticize existing conditions and to advocate potential alternatives.

These critical theories make a number of arguments. One is that no matter how hard scholars try to exclude ideology from their work, it will slip in. Every analyst is located at a particular position in society and will, therefore, have certain interests that guide both the problems selected for analysis and the mode of analysis itself. Inevitably, what people think should occur will enter their work; so it is only an illusion that statements about the operation of the social world are free of ideology. Another line of criticism is that when "scientists" study what exists, they will tend to see the way the social world is currently structured as the way things must be. As a result, theories about the world as it exists in the present can become ideologies legitimating the status quo and blinding thinkers to alternative social arrangements. And a third line of attack on the value-neutrality of science is that humans have the capacity to change the very nature of their universe; and as a result, there can be no immutable laws of human social organization because humans' capacity for agency allows them to alter the very reality described by these laws. As a result, a natural science of society is not possible because the very nature of social reality can be changed by the will of actors.

Those who advocate a scientific approach reject these arguments by critical theorists. While they see ideological bias as a potential problem, this problem can be mitigated, if not obviated, by careful attention to potential sources of bias. And even if one's position in the social world shapes the questions asked, it is still possible to answer these questions in an objective manner. Moreover, the notion that the objective study of the social world ensures that inquiry will support the status quo is rejected by those committed to science. Real science seeks to examine the forces driving the current world; and theories are about these underlying forces, which, in the very best theories, have operated in all times and places. Thus, science does not just describe the world as it presently is, but rather, it tries to see how forces operating in the past, present, and future work to generate the empirical world. These forces will thus change the present, just as they transformed the past into a new present, and will eventually bring about a new future. There is no reason, therefore, for theories to legitimate a status quo; indeed, theories are about the dynamic potential of the forces that change social arrangements. And finally, the contention of critics that humans can change the very nature of the forces driving the social world is rejected by scientists. Humans can, of course, change the social world as it exists, but this is very different from changing the fundamental forces that shape the organization of the social universe. Agency is thus constrained by the underlying forces that drive the social universe; indeed, for agency to be successful, it must be directed at changing the valences of the forces that drive the social universe, not the forces themselves. In fact, when people's concerted efforts to change certain arrangements consistently fail, this failure is often an indicator that they are fighting against a powerful social force. For example, humans can change the way they produce things, but they cannot eliminate production as a basic force necessary for the survival of the species; people can change political regimes, but they cannot eliminate the operation of power in social relations.

The debate over whether or not sociology can be a natural science will, no doubt, rage into the future because it has been a central part of the discipline since its founding. In Chapter 25, I review the various forms of theorizing in sociology, and then in Chapter 26, I will address the issue of scientific theory and its critics. For the present, let me outline how I will review the theories in the chapters of Parts I and II of the book.

Scientific Explanations

My goal in this book is to summarize the basic substantive arguments of various types of theories and theorists from the 1830s to the present. As I try to realize this goal, I will also formalize many theories into two formats: (1) abstract propositions and principles and (2) abstract analytical models. These are, I believe, the two most useful formats for formalizing scientific theories; and even when the theorists whom I review would not agree with this effort, I think that it is worthwhile because it makes the theories so formatted more precise. In Chapter 25, I will review the various formatting options for expressing the key dynamics in a theory; as I do so, I will also comment on their relative merits for developing cumulative theory in sociology. For the present, I should express my preference for two of these formats—the aforementioned propositions/principles and analytical models—because it will become evident that I formalize many of the theories into these formats, even if a classical theorist would turn over in his grave or a contemporary theorist would find such an exercise inappropriate. Not all theories can be easily converted into these formats, but where they can, I will do so in the interest of clarifying the inevitable ambiguities that accompany theories that are only stated in discursive text.

Principles and Propositions. Theories can be expressed as principles or abstract statements about the relations among social forces. For example, to take an idea from Karl Marx, one proposition is that "the likelihood that subordinate actors will mobilize for conflict against superordinate actors is a positive function of the degree of inequality in the system." This simplifies Marx, but it is the form of the statement that is important. Ideas are expressed more abstractly than in Marx, since there is no mention of capitalism, bourgeoisie, and proletariat but, instead, just actors who possess different levels of resources in a system of inequality. Conflict is not necessarily seen as "revolutionary" but simply varying by degree or other valences such as intensity. Marx would never have stated his theory in this manner, but the enduring qualities of Marx stem ultimately from his understanding of how inequalities translate into conflict, and so it is reasonable to express his and other theorists' ideas in this more abstract and formal format.

Analytical Models. Most theories view social processes as causally connected. One event causes another, as would be the case if Marx argued that inequality causes conflict via a series of additional causal connections related to how superordinates generate conditions that facilitate the mobilization of subordinates to pursue conflict. Rather than state these as propositions, it is also useful to specify the causal relations among these forces. To overly simplify Marx (see Chapter 4 for a more sophisticated model), Figure 1.2 gives a sense of what analytical models look like. First, variables in the model are stated more abstractly than is the case with a theorist. Second, time flows from left to right. Third, causal relations among forces are specified with arrows, which at times are signed. Fourth, and critical to many theories, there are reverse causal processes in which outcomes feed back and have causal effects on the very causal processes that caused these outcomes. The social world is recursive, folding back on itself, and analytical models can capture this type of causal relation. Also, by drawing a model, typically more complex than the illustration in Figure 1.2, we can gain a robust sense of the causal connections among the forces in play in a theory. Again, theorists may not develop such models, but where possible, I will translate their ideas into such models as a means of explicating the theory in more detail. Theories are best understood when formalized so that the forces in play are stated explicitly in either propositions or analytical models, or both. Thus, I will summarize the theories discursively in ordinary text, but where possible, I will also try to formalize them, often beyond what the theorists have actually done. Of course, at times, the theorists have already done at least some of this work, but in most cases, they have not; and so my goal is to formalize theories in ways that make them more explicit and powerful—at least by the criterion of science and scientific explanation. One need not accept the biases that inhere in my efforts, but it is always useful to determine exactly what theorists mean in their

Figure 1.2 Illustrative and Simplified Analytical Model of Karl Marx's Theory of Conflict

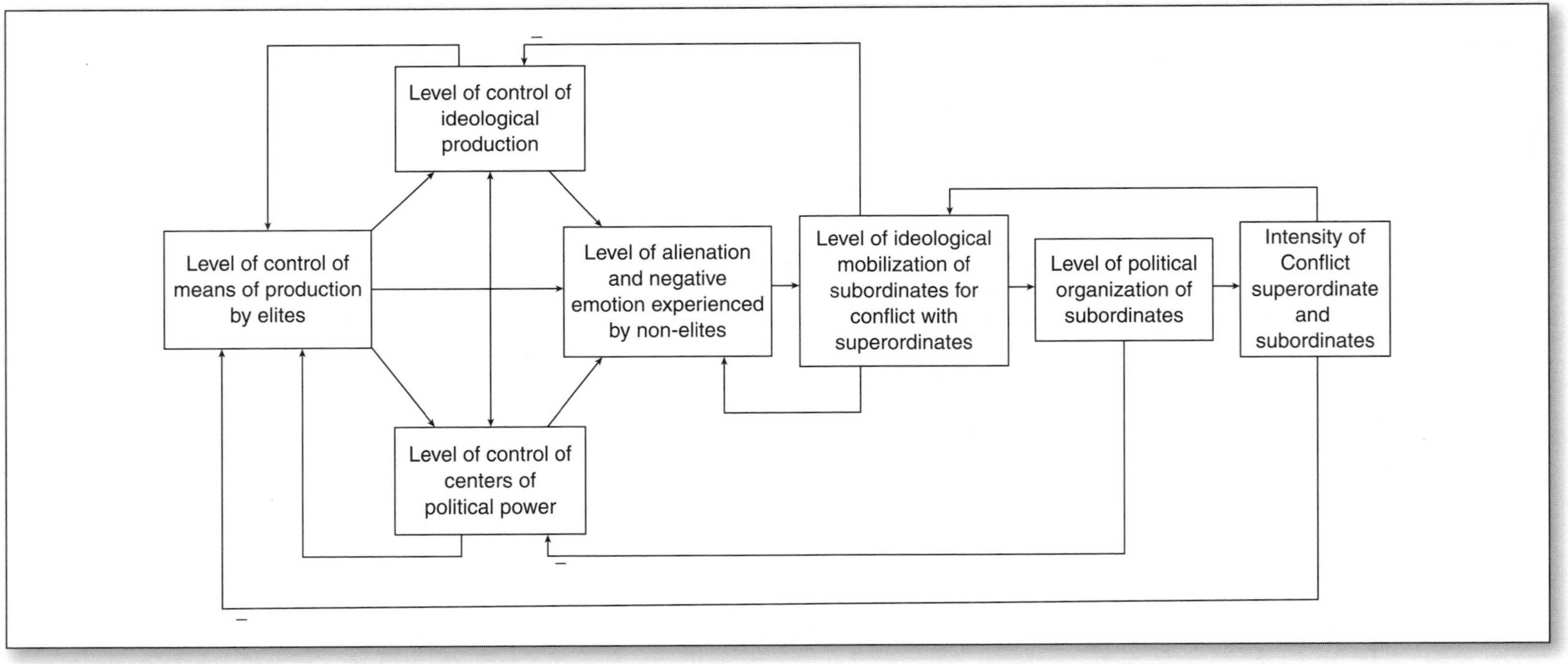

Note: Unsigned arrows denote positive effect; negatively signed arrows indicate a negative effect.

textual statements, and one way to make theories clear is to formalize them by trans-lating them into propositions and analytical models.

For our purposes, we simply must recognize that commitment to science varies among theorists in sociology. Yet in the pages to follow, my emphasis is on the con-tribution of theories to *the science of sociology.* Of course, those theories rejecting this orientation are also examined, but these alternatives will always be examined in terms of how they deviate from scientific sociology or, alternatively, how they con-tribute to scientific theory, even if those formulating such a theory have little faith in scientific sociology. For example, Max Weber certainly had doubts about sociol-ogy as a natural science, and yet his own work demonstrates that general models and laws of key processes can be articulated, and it is this aspect of Weber's work that I will emphasize in Chapter 5. Karl Marx did not reject science outright, but he did believe that the fundamental nature of the social universe changed over time and that theories could only be formulated for diverse historical efforts; but in fact, as I will emphasize, he developed a theory of conflict that is relevant for all times and places in human evolutionary history, not just the last great epoch before commu-nism (see Chapter 4). Thus, my analysis in this large book will be biased by my own commitment to scientific theory, but I will endeavor to be fair and to point out criticisms of such a bias.

Conclusion

Sociology, perhaps by another name, was inevitable as societies began to change rapidly. Social change always causes dislocations and disruption, and individuals will try to figure out what is going on. It was not until 1830 that sociology acquired its name and mission: to create a society of society and to use scientific knowledge to create better patterns of social organization. Thus, the original vision for the dis-cipline, as enunciated by Auguste Comte, did not separate science from active involvement in issues of what sociologists now call *practice;* science, Comte believed, made for the best sociological practice. Yet sociological practice, applied sociology, critical sociology, and scientific sociology are often seen as being in separate camps, but such need not be the case.

Still, there is, at best, an uneasy accommodation within theoretical sociology among these visions of what sociology should be and should do. This unease always existed in the discipline, and so we should not be surprised that it is still present today and, as I indicated earlier, well into sociology's future. Part I of this volume examines classical sociological theory, or the theoretical works of the first masters of the discipline—during sociology's first 100 years. These masters differed in their approaches. Some, like Auguste Comte, Herbert Spencer, and Émile Durkheim, were committed to a hard-science view of what sociology could and should be; others, like Georg Simmel and George Herbert Mead, leaned in this direction but were not as committed; Max Weber wanted sociology to be value-free and analytical, but the historian in him would not let him commit to the hard-science view of the disci-pline; and Karl Marx, though an activist, did believe that laws of sociology could be developed for distinct historical epochs, and so he too leaned toward a scientific view, but one devoted to revolutionary social change. Early American sociologists were much like the philosopher Mead and saw science in a positive light, but most were not trained in science; thus, their commitment to scientific theorizing was not strong, nor were they particularly interested in developing theories. The result is a rather conspicuous period between the death of the last of the great masters around 1930 and the beginning of the modern era of theorizing in the early 1950s. During this twenty-year gap, theorizing, especially more formal theorizing, was recessive. There *were* theorists, but none has endured, even giants in their time like Pitirim Sorokin; and so there is a break in theorizing that actually began by 1920, when functional theories and evolutionary approaches were discredited, only to reemerge some three decades later. But since the 1950s, theoretical sociology has expanded, specialized (at times too much), and significantly increased the explanatory power of the discipline to explain a wide range of phenomena. Thus, Part II of the book will document this renaissance of theorizing in the modern era. Then, in Part III, after examining the varieties of critical theories at the end of Part II, I will return to examining science and formal theorizing, with an eye to what critics and advocates have to say about the prospects for a science of the social universe that is much like the sciences of the physical and biotic universes.

PART I

The Classical Period, 1830–1935

CHAPTER 2

Auguste Comte and the Emergence of Sociology

Sociology existed long before Auguste Comte appeared on the intellectual scene. Indeed, as I emphasized in Chapter 1, humans have been thinking about themselves and their social relations from the dawn of *Homo sapiens*. Still, such reflection and inquiry did not have a name; nor did it have a method of inquiry in the turn into the nineteenth century. Even Auguste Comte's predecessors in France, who wrote voluminously about the state of society, did not have an explicit view of sociology as a distinctive kind of enterprise with a specific subject matter. And so, while we could move the beginnings of sociology back 100 years, if not thousands of years, it is best to begin when sociology was given a name and an outline of an explicit epistemology and methodology. By these criteria, sociology emerged with Auguste Comte, who gave the study of societies a name—at first *social physics* and then, rather reluctantly, *sociology*. And even more important, Comte championed an epistemology—the scientific study of the social universe—and even offered some guidelines about appropriate methodologies for studying this universe.

When the first volume of Comte's *Course of Positive Philosophy* was published in 1830, it created a sensation. Comte was proclaimed a genius, but unfortunately, he was a difficult genius. He was arrogant, often rude, defensive, and generally rather prickly; and over the next decade, he managed to alienate just about everybody, including his closest supporters. And by the time the last volume of *Course of Positive Philosophy* was published in 1842, not a single review appeared in the French press and journals. Comte was now widely regarded as a fool, and a crazy one at that. He was even seen to give a bad name to the very field of inquiry that he had named.

It is perhaps embarrassing to sociology that its founder was, by the end of his life, a rather pathetic man, calling himself the High Priest of Humanity and preaching to a ragtag group of disciples. Yet Comte's career had two phases: the early and happier scientific stage, when he argued persuasively for a science of society and was the toast of continental Europe for a brief time, and a later phase when he tried to make science a new religion for the reconstruction of society. The first phase culminated in his famous *Course of Positive Philosophy*, a monumental five-volume work that was published serially between 1830 and 1842. The second phase was marked by Comte's personal frustrations and tragedy, which found expression in *System of Positive Polity*, published between 1851 and 1854.[1] Even as Comte went off the deep end, he retained a firm belief that discovery of the laws governing the operation of human societies should be used to reconstruct society. For Comte, science did not oppose efforts to make a better world, but it was first necessary to develop the science half of this equation. For without a deep, scientific understanding of how society operates, it is difficult to know how to go about constructing a better society. This theme in Comte's work was simply an extension of the French philosophes' Enlightenment view that human society was progressing to ever better states of organization.

In this review of Comte's work, I will focus on the early phase, when Comte developed a vision for sociology. Indeed, he argued that sociology was to be the "queen science" that would stand at the top of a hierarchy of all sciences—an outrageous prediction but one that garnered a considerable amount of attention in his early writings. Comte's abrasive personality was eventually to be his undoing, however. By the time the last installment of *Course of Positive Philosophy* was published, he was a forgotten intellectual, but Comte's stamp on the discipline had already been achieved early in his career. Moreover, scholars in England were reading Comte again, and subsequent generations of French thinkers all had to come to grips with Comte's advocacy.

Comte's first essays signaled the beginning of sociology; his great *Course of Positive Philosophy* made a convincing case for the discipline. And his later descent can be ignored for what it was—the mental pathology of a once great mind. Let us begin with the early essays and then move to the argument in *Course of Positive Philosophy*.

Comte's Early Essays

It is sometimes difficult to separate Comte's early essays from those of Saint-Simon, because the aging master often put his name on works written by the young Comte. Yet the 1822 essay, "Plan of the Scientific Operations Necessary for Reorganizing Society,"[2] is clearly Comte's and represents the culmination of his thinking while working under Saint-Simon. This essay also anticipates, and presents an outline of, the entire Comtean scheme as it was to unfold over the succeeding decades.

In this essay, Comte argued that it was necessary to create a "positive science" based on the model of other sciences. This science would ultimately rest on empirical

---

[1]Auguste Comte, *System of Positive Polity*, 4 vols. (New York: Burt Franklin, 1875; originally published 1851–1854). I will use and reference Harriet Martineau's condensation of the original manuscript. This condensation received Comte's approval and is the most readily available translation. Martineau changed the title and added useful margin notes. My references will be to the 1896 edition of Martineau's original 1854 edition: Auguste Comte, *The Positive Philosophy of Auguste Comte*, 3 vols., trans. and cond. H. Martineau (London: George Bell and Sons, 1896).

[2]Auguste Comte, "Plan of the Scientific Operations Necessary for Reorganizing Society," reprinted in Gertrud Lenzer (ed.), *Auguste Comte and Positivism: The Essential Writings* (New York: Harper Torchbooks, 1975), 9–69.

observations, but like all science, it would formulate the laws governing the organization and movement of society, an idea implicit in Montesquieu's *The Spirit of Laws*, published a century earlier. Comte initially called this new science *social physics*. Once the laws of human organization have been discovered and formulated, Comte believed that these laws could be used to direct society. Scientists of society are thus to be social prophets, indicating the course and direction of human organization.

Comte felt that one of the most basic laws of human organization was the "law of the three stages," a notion clearly borrowed from French philosophers of the eighteenth century—figures such as Turgot, Condorcet, and Saint-Simon. He termed these stages the *theological-military, metaphysical-judicial,* and *scientific-industrial* or "positivistic." Each stage is typified by a particular "spirit"—a notion that first appeared with Montesquieu—and by temporal or structural conditions. Thus, the theological-military stage is dominated by ideas that refer to the supernatural while being structured around slavery and the military. The metaphysical-judicial stage, which follows from the theological and represents a transitional phase necessary for the emergence of the scientific or positivistic stage, is typified by new ideas that refer to the fundamental essences of phenomena and by new types of elaborations in political and legal forms. The scientific-industrial stage is dominated by the "positive philosophy of science" and industrial patterns of social organization.

Several points in this law of the three stages were given greater emphasis in Comte's later work. First, the social world reveals both cultural and structural dimensions, with the nature of culture or idea systems being dominant—an idea probably taken from Condorcet. Second, idea systems, and the corresponding structural arrangements that they produce, must reach their full development before the next stage of human evolution can occur. Thus, one stage of development creates the necessary conditions for the next. Third, there is always a period of crisis and conflict as systems move from one stage to the next because elements of the previous stage will inevitably come into conflict with the emerging elements of the next stage. Fourth, movement is always a kind of oscillation, for society "does not, properly speaking, advance in a straight line."

These aspects of the law of three stages convinced Comte that cultural ideas about the world were subject to the dictates of this law. All ideas about the nature of the universe must move from a theological to a scientific, or positivistic, stage. Yet some ideas about different aspects of the universe move more rapidly through the three stages than others do. Indeed, only when all the other sciences—first astronomy, then physics, later chemistry, and finally physiology or biology—have successively reached the positive stage will the conditions necessary for the emergence of social physics have been met. With the development of this last great science, it will become possible to reorganize society by scientific principles rather than by theological or metaphysical speculations.

Comte thus felt that the age of sociology had arrived. It was to be like Newton's physics, formulating the laws of the social universe. With the development of these laws, the stage was set for the rational and scientific reorganization of society. Many of the ideas from Comte's one-time mentor, Saint-Simon, can be seen in this advocacy, but Comte felt that Saint-Simon was too impatient in his desire to reorganize society without the proper scientific foundation. The result was a rather unpleasant break with Saint-Simon, as was to become ever more typical of Comte with others, and then the publication of the first volumes of Comte's *Course of Positive Philosophy,* which sought to lay the necessary intellectual foundation for the science of society.

Comte's *Course of Positive Philosophy*

Comte's *Course of Positive Philosophy* is more noteworthy for its advocacy of a science of society than for its substantive contribution to understanding how patterns of social organization are created, maintained, and changed. *Positive Philosophy* represents more a vision of what sociology can become rather than a well-focused set of theoretical principles. In reviewing this great work, then, I will devote most of my attention to how Comte defined sociology and how he thought it should be developed. Accordingly, I will divide the discussion into the following sections: (a) Comte's view of sociological theory, (b) his formulation of sociological methods, (c) his organization of sociology, and (d) his advocacy of sociology.

Comte's View of Sociological Theory

As a descendant of the French Enlightenment, Comte was impressed, as were many of the philosophes, by the Newtonian revolution. Thus, he argued for a particular view of sociological theory: all phenomena are subject to invariable natural laws, and sociologists must use their observations to uncover the laws governing the social universe, in much the same way as Newton had formulated the law of gravity. As Comte emphasized in the opening pages of *Positive Philosophy,*

> The first characteristic of Positive Philosophy is that it regards all phenomena as subject to invariable natural *Laws.* Our business is—seeing how vain is any research into what are called *Causes* whether first or final—to pursue an accurate discovery of these Laws, with a view to reducing them to the smallest possible number. By speculating upon causes, we could solve no difficulty about origin and purpose. Our real business is to analyse [*sic*] accurately the circumstances of phenomena and to connect them by the natural relations of succession and resemblance. The best illustration of this is in the case of the doctrine of Gravitation.[3]

Several points are important in this view of sociological theory. First, sociological theory is not to be concerned with causes per se but, rather, with the laws that describe the basic and fundamental relations of properties in the social world. Second, sociological theory must reject arguments by "final causes"—that is, analysis of the results of a particular phenomenon for the social whole. This disavowal is ironic because Comte's more substantive work helped found sociological functionalism, a mode of analysis that often examines the functions or final causes of phenomena (see Chapter 10). Third, the goal of sociological activity is to reduce the number of theoretical principles by seeking

---

[3]Comte, *Positive Philosophy,* vol. 1, 5–6 (emphasis in original).

only the most abstract and only those that pertain to understanding the fundamental properties of the social world. Comte thus held a vision of sociological theory as based on the model of the natural sciences, particularly the physics of his time. For this reason, he preferred the term *social physics* to *sociology.*[4]

The laws of social organization and change, Comte felt, will be discovered, refined, and verified through a constant interplay between theory and empirical observation. For, as he emphasized in the opening pages of *Positive Philosophy,* "if it is true that every theory must be based upon observed facts, it is equally true that facts cannot be observed without the guidance of some theory." In later pages, Comte became even more assertive and argued against what we might now term *raw empiricism.* The collection of data for their own sake runs counter to the goals of science:

> The next great hindrance to the use of observation is the empiricism which is introduced into it by those who, in the name of impartiality, would interdict the use of any theory whatever. No other dogma could be more thoroughly irreconcilable with the spirit of the positive philosophy. . . . No real observation of any kind of phenomena is possible, except in as far as it is first directed, and finally interpreted, by some theory.[5]

And he concluded,

> Hence it is clear that, scientifically speaking, all isolated, empirical observation is idle, and even radically uncertain; that science can use only those observations which are connected, at least hypothetically, with some law.[6]

For Comte, then, sociology's goal was to seek to develop abstract theoretical principles. Observations of the empirical world must be guided by such principles, and the abstract principles must be tested against the empirical facts. Empirical observations that are conducted without this goal in mind are not useful in science. Theoretical explanation of empirical events thus involves seeing how they are connected in law-like ways. For social science "endeavors to discover . . . the general relations which connect all social phenomena; and each of them is *explained,* in the scientific sense of the word, when it has been connected with the whole of the existing situation."[7]

---

[4]In Comte's time, the term *physics* meant study of the "nature of" phenomena; it was not merely the term for a particular branch of natural science. Hence, Comte's use of the label *social physics* had a double meaning: to study the "nature of" social phenomena and to do so along the lines of the natural sciences. He abandoned the term *social physics* when he realized that the Belgian statistician Adolphe Quételet was using the same term. Comte was outraged that his original label for sociology had been used in ways that ran decidedly counter to his vision of theory. Ironically, sociology has become more like Quételet's vision of social physics, with its emphasis on the normal curve and statistical manipulations, than like Comte's notion of social physics as the search for the abstract laws of human organization—an unfortunate turn of events.

[5]Ibid., vol. 2, 242. Comte, *Positive Philosophy,* vol.1, 4.

[6]Ibid., 243.

[7]Ibid., 240 (emphasis added).

Comte held a somewhat ambiguous view of how such an abstract science should be "used" in the practical world of everyday affairs. He clearly intended that sociology must initially establish a firm theoretical foundation before making efforts to use the laws of sociology for social engineering. In *Positive Philosophy,* he stressed,

> We must distinguish between the two classes of Natural science—the abstract or general, which have for their object the discovery of the laws which regulate phenomena in all conceivable cases, and the concrete, particular, or descriptive, which are sometimes called Natural sciences in a restricted sense, whose function it is to apply these laws to the actual history of existing beings. The first are fundamental, and our business is with them alone; as the second are derived, and however important, they do not rise to the rank of our subjects of contemplation.[8]

Comte believed that sociology must not allow its scientific mission to be confounded by empirical descriptions or by an excessive concern with a desire to manipulate events. Once sociology is well established as a theoretical science, its laws can be used to "modify" events in the empirical world. Indeed, such was to be the historic mission of social physics. As Comte's later works testify, he took this mission seriously, and at times to extremes. But his early work is filled with more reasoned arguments for using laws of social organization and change as tools for creating new social arrangements. He stressed that the complexity of social phenomena gives them more variation than either physical or biological phenomena have, and hence, it would be possible to use the laws of social organization and change to modify empirical events in a variety of directions.[9]

In sum, then, Comte believed that sociology could be modeled after the natural sciences. Sociology could seek and discover the fundamental properties and relations of the social universe, and like the other sciences, it could express these in a small number of abstract principles. Observations of empirical events could be used to generate, confirm, and modify sociology's laws. Once well developed laws had been formulated, they could be used as tools or instruments to modify the social world.

Comte's Formulation of Sociological Methods

Comte was the first social thinker to take methodological questions seriously— that is, how are facts about the social world to be gathered and used to develop, as well as to test, theoretical principles? He advocated four methods in the new science of social physics: (1) observation, (2) experimentation, (3) comparison, and (4) historical analysis.[10]

---

[8]Ibid., vol. 1, 23.

[9]See, for example, the relevant passages in Comte, *Positive Philosophy,* vol. 2, 217, 226, 234, 235, and 238.

[10]Ibid., vol. 2, 241–257.

Observation. For Comte, positivism was based on the use of the senses to observe *social facts*—a term that the next great French theorist, Émile Durkheim, made the center of his sociology. Much of Comte's discussion of observation involves arguments for the "subordination of Observation to the statical and dynamical laws of phenomena" rather than a statement on the procedures by which unbiased observations should be conducted. He argued that observation of empirical facts, when unguided by theory, will prove useless in the development of science. He must be given credit, however, for firmly establishing sociology as a science of social facts, thereby liberating thought from the debilitating realm of morals and metaphysical speculation.[11]

Experimentation. Comte recognized that artificial experimentation with whole societies, and other social phenomena, was impractical and often impossible. But, he noted, natural experimentation frequently "takes place whenever the regular course of the phenomenon is interfered with in any determinate manner." In particular, he thought that, much as is the case in biology, pathological events allowed "the true equivalent of pure experimentation" in that they introduced an artificial condition and allowed investigators to see normal processes reassert themselves in the face of the pathological condition. Much as the biologist can learn about normal bodily functioning from the study of disease, so social physicists can learn about the normal processes of society from the study of pathological cases. Thus, although Comte's view of natural experimentation was certainly deficient in the logic of the experimental method, it nonetheless fascinated subsequent generations of scholars.[12]

Comparison. Just as comparative analysis had been useful in biology, comparison of social forms with those of lower animals, with coexisting states, and with past systems could also generate considerable insight into the operation of the social universe. By comparing elements that are present and absent, and similar or dissimilar, knowledge about the fundamental properties of the social world can be achieved.

Historical Analysis. Comte originally classified historical analysis as a variation of the comparative method (i.e., comparing the present with the past). But his law of the three stages emphasized that the laws of social dynamics could ultimately be developed only with careful observation of the historical movement of societies.

In sum, then, Comte saw these four basic methods as appropriate to sociological analysis. His formulation of the methods is quite deficient by modern standards, but we should recognize that before Comte, little attention had been paid to how social facts were to be collected. Thus, although the specifics of Comte's methodological proposals are not always useful, their spirit and intent are important. Social physics was, in his vision, to be a theoretical science capable of formulating and testing the laws of social organization and change. His formulation of sociology's methods added credibility to this claim.

---

[11]Ibid., 245.

[12]Ibid., 246.

Comte's Organization of Sociology

Much as Saint-Simon had emphasized, Comte saw sociology as an extension of biology, which studies the "organs" in "organisms." Hence, sociology was to be the study of social organization, or the study of the organization of organisms. This emphasis forces the recognition that society is an "organic whole" whose component organs stand in relation to one another. To study these parts in isolation is to violate the essence of social organization and to compartmentalize inquiry artificially. As Comte emphasized, "There can be no scientific study of society, either in its conditions or its movements, if it is separated into portions, and its divisions are studied apart."[13]

Implicit in this mode of analysis is a theoretical approach that later became known as *functionalism* (see Chapter 10). As biology's prestige grew during the nineteenth century, attempts at linking sociological analysis to the respected biological sciences increased. Eventually, scholars began asking, What is the function of a structure for the "body social"? That is, what does a structure "do for" the maintenance of the social whole? Comte implicitly asked such questions and even offered explicit analogies to encourage subsequent organismic analogizing. For example, his concern with social pathology revealing the normal operation of society is only one illustration of a biological mode of reasoning. In his later work, Comte viewed various structures as analogous to the "elements, tissues, and organs" of biological organisms. In his early works, however, this organismic analogizing is limited to dividing social physics into statical and dynamical analysis.[14]

This division, I suspect, represents a merger of Comte's efforts to build sociology on biology and to retain his heritage from the French Enlightenment. As a scholar who was writing in the tumultuous aftermath of the French Revolution, he was concerned with order and stability. The order of biological organisms, with their interdependent parts and processes of self-maintenance, offered him a vision of how social order should be constructed or, in the case of France, reconstructed. Yet the Enlightenment had emphasized "progress" and the movement of social systems, holding out the vision of better things to come. For this reason, Comte was led to emphasize that "ideas of Order and Progress are, in Social Physics, as rigorously inseparable as the ideas of Organization and Life in Biology: from whence indeed they are, in a scientific view, evidently derived." Thus, he divided sociology into (a) social statics (the study of social order) and (b) social dynamics (the study of social progress and change).[15]

Social Statics. Comte defined social statics as the study of social structure, its elements, and their relations. He first analyzed "individuals" as the elements of social structure. Generally, he viewed the individual as a series of capacities and needs, some innate and others acquired through participation in society. He did not view the individual as a "true social unit"; indeed, he relegated the study of the individual to biology—an unfortunate oversight because it denied the legitimacy of psychology as a distinct social

---

[13]Ibid., 225.

[14]See, in particular, his *System of Positive Polity,* vol. 2, 221–276, on "The Social Organism."

[15]Comte, *Positive Philosophy,* vol. 2, 141.

science. The most basic social unit, he argued, is "the family." It is the most elementary unit, from which all other social units ultimately evolved:

> As every system must be composed of elements of the same nature with itself, the scientific spirit forbids us to regard society as composed of individuals. The true social unit is certainly the family—reduced, if necessary, to the elementary couple which forms its basis. This consideration implies more than the physiological truth that families become tribes, and tribes become nations: so that the whole human race might be conceived of as the gradual development of a single family. . . . There is a political point of view from which also we must consider this elementary idea, inasmuch as the family presents the true germ of the various characteristics of the social organism.[16]

Comte believed that social structures could not be reduced to the properties of individuals. Rather, social structures are composed of other structures and can be understood only as the properties of, and relations among, these other structures. Comte's analysis of the family then moves to descriptions of its structure—first the sexual division of labor and then the parental relation. The specifics of his analysis are not important because they are flawed and inaccurate. Far more important is the view of structure that he implied: social structures are composed of substructures and develop from the elaboration of simpler structures.

After establishing this basic point, Comte moved to the analysis of societal structures. His opening remarks reveal his debt to biological analysis and the functional orientation it inspired:

> The main cause of the superiority of the social to the individual organism is according to an established law; the more marked is the specialization of the various functions fulfilled by organs more and more distinct, but interconnected; so that unity of aim is more and more combined with diversity of means.[17]

Thus, as social systems develop, they become increasingly differentiated, and yet like all organisms, they maintain their integration. This view of social structure led Comte to the problem that Adam Smith had originally suggested with such force: How is integration among the parts maintained despite the increasing differentiation of functions? This question occupied French sociology in the nineteenth century, culminating in Durkheim's theoretical formulations. As Comte emphasized,

> If the separation of social functions develops a useful spirit of detail, on the one hand, it tends on the other, to extinguish or to restrict what we may call the aggregate or general spirit. In the same way, in moral relations, while each is in close dependence on the mass, he is drawn away from it by the

---

[16] Ibid., 280–281.
Ibid., 275–281.

[17] Ibid., 289.

expansion of his special activity, constantly recalling him to his private interest, which he but very dimly perceives to be related to the public.[18]

Comte's proposed solution to this problem reveals much about how he viewed the maintenance of social structure. First, the centralization of power in government counters the potentially disintegrating impact of social differentiation, which will then maintain fluid coordination among the parts of the system. Second, the actions of government must be more than "material"; they must also be "intellectual and moral." Hence, human social organization is maintained by (a) mutual dependence of system parts on one another, (b) centralization of authority to coordinate exchanges among the parts, and (c) development of a common morality or spirit among the members of a population. To the extent that differentiating systems cannot meet these conditions, pathological states are likely to occur. Figure 2.1 shows Comte's implicit model of social statics.

In presenting this analysis, Comte felt that he had uncovered several laws of social statics because he believed that differentiation, centralization of power, and development of a common morality were fundamentally related to the maintenance of the social order. Although he did not carry his analysis far, he presented both Herbert Spencer and Durkheim with one of the basic theoretical questions in sociology and the broad contours of the answer.

Social Dynamics. Comte appeared far more interested in social dynamics than in statics, for[19]

the dynamical view is not only the more interesting . . . , but the more marked in its philosophical character, from its being more distinguished from biology by the master-thought of continuous progress, or rather of the gradual development of humanity.[20]

Figure 2.1 Comte's Implicit Model of Social Statics

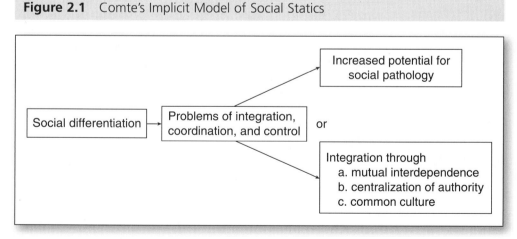

---

[18]Ibid., 293.

[19]Ibid., 294.

[20]Ibid., 227.

Social dynamics studies the "laws of succession," or the patterns of change in social systems over time. In this context, Comte formulated the details of his law of the three stages, in which idea systems, and their corresponding social structural arrangements, pass through three phases: (1) the theological, (2) the metaphysical, and (3) the positivistic. The basic cultural and structural features of these stages are summarized in Table 2.1.

Table 2.1 ignores many details that have little relevance to theory, but the table communicates, in a rough fashion, Comte's view of the laws of succession. Several points should be noted. First, each stage sets the conditions for the next. For example, without efforts to explain references to the supernatural, subsequent efforts at more refined explanations would not have been possible; without kinship systems, subsequent political, legal, and military development would not have occurred, and the modern division of labor would not have been possible. Second, the course of evolution is additive: new ideas and structural arrangements are added to, and build on, the old. For instance, kinship does not disappear, nor do references to the supernatural. They are first supplemented and then dominated by new social and cultural arrangements. Third, during the transition from one stage to the next,

Table 2.1 Comte's "Law of the Three Stages"

System	Stages		
	Theological	*Metaphysical*	*Positivistic*
1. Cultural (moral) system			
a. Nature of ideas	Ideas are focused on nonempirical forces, spirits, and beings in the supernatural realm	Ideas are focused on the essences of phenomena and rejection of appeals to the supernatural	Ideas are developed from observation and constrained by the scientific method; speculation not based on observation of empirical facts is rejected
b. Spiritual leaders	Priests	Philosophers	Scientists
2. Structural (temporal) system			
a. Most prominent units	Kinship	State	Industry
b. Basis of integration	Attachment to small groups and religious spirit; use of coercive force to sustain commitment to religion	Control by state, military, and law	Mutual dependence; coordination of functions by state and general spirit

elements of the preceding stage conflict with elements of the emerging stage, creating a period of anarchy and turmoil. Fourth, the metaphysical stage is a transitional stage, operating as a bridge between theological speculation and positivistic philosophy. Fifth, the nature of cultural ideas determines the nature of social structural (temporal) arrangements and circumscribes what social arrangements are possible. And sixth, with the advent of the positivistic stage, true understanding of how society operates is possible, allowing the manipulation of society in accordance with the laws of statics and dynamics.[21]

Although societies must eventually pass through these three stages, they do so at different rates. Probably the most important of the variable empirical conditions influencing the rate of societal succession is population size and density, an idea taken from Montesquieu and later refined by Durkheim. Thus, Comte felt that he had discovered the basic law of social dynamics in his analysis of the three stages, and that, coupled with the laws of statics, a positivistic science of society—that is, social physics or sociology—would allow for the reorganization of the tumultuous, transitional, and conflictual world of the early nineteenth century.

Comte's Advocacy of Sociology

Comte's *Positive Philosophy* can be viewed as a long and elaborate advocacy of a science of society. Most of the five volumes review the development of other sciences, showing how sociology represents the culmination of positivism. As the title, *Positive Philosophy*, underscores, Comte was laying a philosophical foundation and justification for all science and then using this foundation as a means for supporting sociology as a true science. His advocacy took two related forms: (1) to view sociology as the inevitable product of the law of the three stages and (2) to view sociology as the "queen science," standing at the top of a hierarchy of sciences. These two interrelated forms of advocacy helped legitimate sociology in the intellectual world and should, therefore, be examined briefly.

Comte saw all idea systems as passing through the theological and metaphysical stages and then moving into the final, positivistic stage. Ideas about all phenomena must pass through these phases, with each stage setting the conditions for the next and with considerable intellectual turmoil occurring during the transition from one stage to the next. Ideas about various phenomena, however, do not pass through these stages at the same rate, and in fact, a positivistic stage in thought about one realm of the universe must often be reached before ideas about other realms can progress to the positivistic stage. As the opening pages of *Positive Philosophy* emphasize,

> We must bear in mind that the different kinds of our knowledge have passed
> through the three stages of progress at different rates, and have not therefore

---

[21]Most of Comte, *Positive Philosophy,* vol. 3 is devoted to the analysis of the three stages. For an abbreviated overview, see vol. 2, 304–333.

arrived at the same time. The rate of advance depends upon the nature of knowledge in question, so distinctly that, as we shall see hereafter, this consideration constitutes an accessory to the fundamental law of progress. Any kind of knowledge reaches the positive stage in proportion to its generality, simplicity, and independence of other departments.[22]

Thus, thought about the physical universe reaches the positive stage before conceptions of the organic world do because the inorganic world is simpler and organic phenomena are built from inorganic phenomena. In Comte's view, then, astronomy was the first science to reach the positivistic stage, then came physics, next came chemistry, and after these three had reached the positivistic (scientific) stage, thought about organic phenomena could become more positivistic. The first organic science to move from the metaphysical to the positivistic stage was biology, or physiology. Once biology became a positivistic doctrine, sociology could move away from the metaphysical speculations of the seventeenth and eighteenth centuries (and the residues of earlier theological thought) toward a positivistic mode of thought.

Sociology has been the last to emerge, Comte argued, because it is the most complex and because it has had to wait for the other basic sciences to reach the positivistic stage. For the time, this argument represented a brilliant advocacy for a separate science of society, while it justified the lack of scientific rigor in social thought when compared with the other sciences. Moreover, though dependent on, and derivative of, evolutionary advances in the other sciences, sociology will study phenomena that are distinct from the lower inorganic phenomena as well as from the higher, organic world of biology. Although it is an organic science, sociology will be independent and study phenomena that "exhibit, in even a higher degree, the complexity, specialization, and personality which distinguish the higher phenomena of the individual life."[23]

This notion of hierarchy[24] represented yet another way to legitimate sociological inquiry: it explained why sociology was not as developed as the other highly respected sciences, and it placed sociology in a highly favorable spot (at the top of a hierarchy) in relation to the other "positive sciences." If sociology could be viewed as the culmination of a long evolutionary process and as the culmination of the positive sciences, its legitimacy could not be questioned. Such was Comte's goal, and although he was only marginally successful in his efforts, he was the first to see clearly that sociology could be like the other sciences and that it would be only a matter of time before the theological and metaphysical residues of earlier social thought were cast aside in favor of a true science of society. This advocacy, which takes up the major portion of *Positive Philosophy*, rightly ensures Comte's claim to being the founder of sociological theory.

---

[22]Ibid., vol. 1, 6–7.

[23]Ibid., vol. 2, 258.

[24]The hierarchy, in descending order, is sociology, biology, chemistry, physics, and astronomy. Comte added mathematics at the bottom because all sciences are ultimately built from mathematical reasoning.

Conclusions

Comte gave sociology its name, albeit reluctantly, because he preferred the label *social physics,* but he did much more—he gave the discipline a vision of what it could be. Few have argued so forcefully about the kind of science sociology should be, and he provided an interesting if somewhat quirky explanation for why this discipline should emerge and become increasingly important in the realm of science. Not all who followed Comte during the last two centuries would accept his positivism—that of a theoretically driven social science that could be used in the reconstruction of society—but he made several important points. First, theories must be abstract, seeking to isolate and explain the nature of the fundamental forces guiding the operation of society. Second, theories must be explicitly and systematically tested against the empirical world, using a variety of methods. Third, collecting data without the guidance of theory will not contribute greatly to the accumulation of knowledge about how the social universe operates. Finally, sociology should be used to rebuild social structures, but these applications of sociology must be guided by theory rather than by ideologies and personal biases.

Comte also anticipated the substantive thrust of much of early sociology, especially that of Herbert Spencer and Émile Durkheim. Comte recognized that as societies grow, they become more differentiated and the differentiation requires new bases of integration revolving around the concentration of power and around mutual interdependence. He did not develop these ideas very far, but he set an agenda. Comte also reintroduced the organismic analogy to social thinking, although many would not see this as a blessing. At the very least, however, he alerted subsequent sociologists that society is a system whose parts are interconnected in ways having consequences for the maintenance of the social whole. This basic analogy to organisms evolved into the functionalism of Spencer and Durkheim.

Still, there is much to criticize in Comte. He never really developed any substantive theory, apart from the relationship between social differentiation and new modes of integration. Most of Comtean sociology is a justification for sociology, and a very good one at that, but he did not explain how the social universe operates. He thought that his law of the three stages was the equivalent of Newton's law of gravity, but Comte's law is not so much a law as a rather simplistic view of the history of ideas. It made for an interesting way to justify the emergence of positivism and its queen science, sociology, but it did not advance sociology's understanding of the dynamics of the social universe.

Add Comte's personal pathologies, which made him a truly bizarre and pathetic figure by the time of his death, and we are perhaps justified in ignoring Comte as a theorist who contributed to our understanding of the social universe. We should remember him for his forceful advocacy of scientific sociology. No one has done better since Comte first began to publish his *Positive Philosophy.*

CHAPTER 3

Herbert Spencer

Sociologists in general and theorists in particular do not read Herbert Spencer today. They simply assume that there is little of interest to contemporary sociology in his works; and indeed, I have heard sociologists go on for quite some time talking about the faults of Spencerian sociology; and when I ask if they have ever read him, there is a stunned silence, followed by "Not much," which probably means "Not at all." Why does contemporary sociology shun the sociologist of the nineteenth century who was more famous than all other early sociologists, who wrote books that sold into the hundreds of thousands, who was the real father of the Human Area Relations Files, and who was widely considered an intellectual giant by fellow scientists? Part of the answer resides in Spencer's emphasis on evolution, which died in the first decades of the twentieth century; another part of the answer derives from his functionalisms, which—after their resurrection in the 1950s and 1960s in sociology—died again, and apparently Spencer with it; still another part, and I suspect the most important reason for contemporary sociology's self-imposed ignorance of Spencer's work, is that he was—by contemporary standards—a political conservative, although his ideas were liberal in his time. Whatever the reason, it is a mistake to dismiss Spencer, because his work contains many critical insights and, in fact, some of sociology's basic laws of social organization, as I hope to demonstrate in this chapter.

Herbert Spencer saw himself as a philosopher rather than as a sociologist. His grand scheme was termed *Synthetic Philosophy,* and it was to encompass all realms of the universe: physical, psychological, biological, sociological, and ethical. The inclusion of the ethical component makes this philosophy problematic because ideological statements do occasionally slip into Spencer's sociology. Spencer's philosophy was a grand, cosmic scheme, but when he turned to sociology, he made many precise statements and introduced a copious amount of empirical data to illustrate his theoretical ideas. Spencer was, at best, a mediocre philosopher, but he was a very accomplished sociologist, even though he took up sociology rather late in his career. We will begin with the moral philosophy, just to get it out of the way, and then we will turn to his important sociological contributions.[1]

Spencer's Moral Philosophy: *Social Statics* and *The Principles of Ethics*

In his later years, Spencer often complained that his first major work, *Social Statics*,[2] had received too much attention. He saw this book as an early and flawed attempt to delineate his moral philosophy and, hence, as not representative of his more mature thought. Yet the basic premise of the work is repeated in one of his last books, *Principles of Ethics*.[3] Despite his protests, his moral arguments have considerable continuity, although we should emphasize again that his more scientific statements can and should be separated from these ethical arguments.

Because Spencer's moral arguments did not change dramatically, we will concentrate on *Social Statics*. The basic argument of *Social Statics* can be stated as follows: human happiness can be achieved only when individuals can satisfy their needs and desires without infringing on the rights of others to do the same. As Spencer emphasized,

> Each member of the race . . . must not only be endowed with faculties enabling him to receive the highest enjoyment in the act of living, but must be so constituted that he may obtain full satisfaction for every desire, without diminishing the power of others to obtain like satisfaction: nay, to fulfill the purpose perfectly, must derive pleasure from seeing pleasure in others.[4]

In this early work, as well as in *Principles of Ethics*, Spencer saw this view as the basic law of ethics and morality. He felt that this law was an extension of laws in the natural

---

[1]Spencer's complete works, except for his *Descriptive Sociology* (see later analysis), are conveniently pulled together in the following collection: *The Works of Herbert Spencer,* 21 vols. (Osnabruck, Germany: Otto Zeller, 1966). However, our references will be to the separate editions of each of his individual works. Moreover, many of the dates of the works discussed span several years because Spencer sometimes published his works serially in several volumes (frequently after they had appeared in periodicals). Full citations will be given when discussing particular works. For a recent review of primary and secondary sources on Spencer, see Robert G. Perrin, *Herbert Spencer: A Primary and Secondary Bibliography* (New York: Garland, 1993).

[2]Herbert Spencer, *Social Statics: Or, the Conditions Essential to Human Happiness Specified, and the First of Them Developed* (New York: Appleton-Century-Crofts, 1888; originally published 1851). The edition cited here is an offset print of the original.

[3]Herbert Spencer, *The Principles of Ethics* (New York: Appleton-Century-Crofts, 1892–1898). An inexpensive and high-quality paperback edition of *The Principles of Ethics* has been published by the Liberty Press wing of the Liberty Foundation. *The Data of Ethics*, which is the first section of *The Principles* has recently been published by Transaction Publishers (2011), with a long introduction by Jonathan H. Turner.

[4]Spencer, *Social Statics,* 448.

world, and much of his search for scientific laws represented an effort to develop a scientific justification for his moral position. Indeed, he emphasized that the social universe, like the physical and biological realms, revealed invariant laws. But he turned this insight into an interesting moral dictum: once these laws are discovered, humans should obey them and cease trying to construct, through political legislation, social forms that violate these laws. In this way, he was able to base his laissez-faire political ideas on what he saw as a sound scientific position: the laws of social organization can no more be violated than can those of the physical universe, and to seek to do so will simply create, in the long run, more severe problems.[5] In contrast with Comte, then, who saw the discovery of laws as the tools for social engineering, Spencer took the opposite tack and argued that once the laws are ascertained, people should "implicitly obey them!"[6] For Spencer, the great ethical axiom, "derived" from the laws of nature, is that humans should be as free from external regulation as possible. Indeed, the bulk of *Social Statics* seeks to show how his moral law and the laws of laissez-faire capitalism converge and, implicitly, how they reflect biological laws of unfettered competition and struggle among species. The titles of some of the chapters best communicate Spencer's argument: "The Rights of Life and Personal Liberty," "The Right to the Use of the Earth," "The Right of Property," "The Rights of Exchange," "The Rights of Women,"[7] "The Right to Ignore the State," "The Limit of State-Duty," and so forth.

In seeking to join the laws of ethics, political economy, and biology, Spencer initiated modes of analysis that became prominent parts of his sociology. First, he sought to discover invariant laws and principles of social organization. Second, he began to engage in organismic analogizing, drawing comparisons between the structure of individual organisms and that of societies:

> Thus do we find, not only that the analogy between a society and a living creature is borne out to a degree quite unsuspected by those who commonly draw it, but also, that the same definition of life applies to both. This union of many men into one community—this increasingly mutual dependence of units which were originally independent—this gradual segregation of citizens into separate bodies, with reciprocally subservient functions—this formation of a whole, consisting of numerous essential parts—this growth of an organism, of which one portion cannot be injured without the rest feeling it—may all be generalized under the law of individuation. The development of society, as well as the development of man and the development of life generally, may be described as a tendency to individuate—*to become a thing*. And rightly interpreted, the manifold forms of progress going on around us, are uniformly significant of this tendency.[8]

---

[5]Ibid., 54–57.

[6]Ibid., 56.

[7]Spencer's arguments here are highly modern and, when compared with Marx's, Weber's, or Durkheim's, are quite radical. Spencer was a feminist long before the advent of "Feminism."

[8]Spencer, *Social Statics,* 497.

Spencer's organismic analogizing often goes to extremes in *Social Statics*—extremes that he avoided in his later works. For example, he at one point argued that "so completely . . . is a society organized upon the same system as an individual being, that we may almost say that there is something more than an analogy between them."[9]

Third, *Social Statics* also reveals the beginnings of Spencer's functionalism. He viewed societies, like individuals, as having survival needs, with specialized organs emerging and persisting to meet these needs. And he defined "social health" by how well various specialized "social organs" met these needs.

Fourth, Spencer's later emphasis on war and conflict among societies as a critical force in their development can also be observed. Although decrying war as destructive, he argued that it allows the more organized "races" to conquer the "less organized and inferior races"—thereby increasing the level and complexity of social organization. This argument was dramatically tempered in his later scientific works, with the result that he was one of the first social thinkers to see the importance of conflict in the evolution of human societies.[10]

In sum, then, *Social Statics* and *Principles of Ethics* are greatly flawed works, representing Spencer's moral ramblings. We have examined these works first because they are often used to condemn his more scholarly efforts. Although some of the major scientific points can be seen in these moral works, and although his scientific works are sprinkled with his extreme moral views, his ethical and scientific efforts nonetheless have a distinct difference in style, tone, and insight. Thus, we would conclude that the worth of Spencer's thought is to be found in the more scientific treatises, relegating his ethics to deserved obscurity. We will therefore devote the balance of this chapter to understanding his sociological perspective.[11]

Spencer's *First Principles*

In the 1860s, Spencer began to issue his general Synthetic Philosophy by subscription. The goal of this philosophy was to treat the great divisions of the universe—inorganic matter, life, mind, and society—as subject to understanding by scientific principles. The initial statement in this rather encompassing philosophical scheme was *First Principles,* published in 1862.[12] In this book, Spencer delineated the

---

[9]Ibid., 490.

[10]Ibid., 498.

[11]It should be remembered that this perspective was developed between 1873 and 1896. For a more complete and detailed review of Spencer's sociology during this period, see Jonathan H. Turner, *Herbert Spencer: A Renewed Appreciation* (Beverly Hills, CA: Sage, 1985).

[12]Herbert Spencer, *First Principles* (New York: A. L. Burt, 1880; originally published 1862). The contents of this work had been anticipated in earlier essays, the most important of which are "Progress: Its Law and Cause," *Westminster Review* (April 1857) and "The Ultimate Laws of Physiology," *National Review* (October 1857); moreover, hints at these principles are sprinkled throughout the first edition of *Principles of Psychology* (New York: Appleton-Century-Crofts, 1880; originally published 1855).

"cardinal" or "first principles" of the universe. Drawing from the biology and physics of his time, he felt that he had perceived, at the most abstract level, certain common principles that apply to all realms of the universe. Indeed, it must have been an exciting vision to feel that one had unlocked the mysteries of the physical, organic, and superorganic (societal) universe.

The principles themselves are probably not worth reviewing in detail; rather, the imagery they communicate is important. For Spencer, evolution is the master process of the universe, and it revolves around movement from simple to complex forms of structure. As matter is aggregated—whether this matter is the cells of an organism, the elements of a moral philosophy, or human beings—the force that brings this matter together is retained, causing the larger mass to differentiate into varying components, which then become integrated into a more complex whole. This complex whole must sustain itself in an environment, and as long as the forces that have aggregated, differentiated, and integrated the "matter" are sustained, the system remains coherent in the environment. Over time, however, these forces dissipate, with the result that the basis for integration is weakened, thereby making the system vulnerable to forces in the environment. At certain times, these environmental forces can revitalize a system, giving it new life to aggregate, differentiate, and integrate. At other times, these forces simply overwhelm the weakened basis of integration and destroy the system. Thus, evolution is a dual process of building up more complex structures through integration and the dissolution of these structures when the force integrating them is weakened.

This is all rather vague, of course, but it gives us a metaphorical vision of how Spencer viewed evolution. Evolution revolves around the process of aggregating matter—in the case of society, populations of human beings and the structures that organize people—and the subsequent differentiation and integration of this matter. The forces that aggregate this matter—forces such as immigration, new productive forms, use of power, patterns of conquest, and all those phenomena that have the capacity to bring humans together—are retained, and as a consequence, they also become the forces that differentiate and integrate the matter. For example, if war and conquest have been the basis for the aggregation of two populations, the coercive and organizational power causing their aggregation is also the force that will drive the pattern of differentiation and integration of the conquered and their conquerors. When this force is spent or proves ineffective in integrating the new society, the society becomes vulnerable to environmental forces, such as military aggression by another society.

This image of evolution helps explain the issues that most concerned Spencer when he finally turned to sociology in the 1870s. His view of evolution as the aggregation, differentiation, integration, and disintegration of matter pushed him to conceptualize societal dynamics as revolving around increases in the size of the population (the "aggregation" component), the differentiation of the population along several prominent axes, the bases for integrating this differentiated population, and the potential disintegration of the population in its environment. Evolution is, thus, analysis of societal movement from simple or homogeneous forms to differentiated or heterogeneous forms, as well as the mechanisms for integrating these forms in their environments. This is all we need to take from Spencer's *First Principles*.

Spencer moved considerably beyond this general metaphor of evolution, however, because he proposed many specific propositions and guidelines for a science of society. Ultimately, his contribution to sociological theorizing does not reside in his abstract formulas on cosmic evolution but, rather, in his specific analyses of societal social systems—what he called *superorganic* phenomena. This contribution can be found in two distinct works, *The Study of Sociology,* which was published in serial form in popular magazines in 1872, and the more scholarly *The Principles of Sociology,* which was published in several volumes between 1874 and 1896. The former work is primarily a methodological statement on the problems of bias in sociology, whereas the latter is a substantive work that seeks to develop abstract principles of evolution and dissolution and, at the same time, to describe the complex interplay among the institutions of society.

Spencer's *The Study of Sociology*

The Study of Sociology[13] was originally published as a series of articles in *Contemporary Review* in England and *Popular Science Monthly* in the United States. This book represents Spencer's effort to popularize sociology and to address "various considerations which seemed needful by way of introduction to the *Principles of Sociology,* presently to be written."[14] Most of *The Study of Sociology* is a discussion of the methodological problems confronting the science of sociology. At the same time, and in less well-developed form, a number of substantive insights later formed the core of his *Principles of Sociology.* We will first examine Spencer's methodological discussion and then his more theoretical analysis, even though this division does not correspond with the order of his presentation.

The Methodological Problems Confronting Sociology

The opening paragraph of Chapter 4 of *The Study of Sociology* sets the tone for Spencer's analysis:

> From the intrinsic natures of its facts, from our natures as observers of its facts, and from the peculiar relation in which we stand toward the facts to be observed, there arise impediments in the way of Sociology greater than those of any other science.[15]

He went on to emphasize that the basic sources of bias stem from the inadequacy of measuring instruments in the social sciences and from the nature of scientists who, by virtue of being members of society, observe the data from a particular vantage point. In a series of insightful chapters—far superior to any statement by any other sociologist of the nineteenth century—Spencer outlined in more detail what he termed *objective* and *subjective* difficulties.

Under objective difficulties, Spencer analyzed the problems associated with the "uncertainty of our data." The first problem encountered revolves around the

---

[13]Herbert Spencer, *The Study of Sociology* (Boston, MA: Routledge & Kegan Paul, 1873).

[14]Ibid., iv.

[15]Ibid., 72.

difficulty of measuring the "subjective states" of actors and, correspondingly, of investigators' suspending their own subjective orientation when examining that of others. A second problem concerns allowing public passions, moods, and fads to determine what sociologists investigate, because it is all too easy to let the popular and immediately relevant obscure from vision more fundamental questions. A third methodological problem involves the "cherished hypothesis," which an investigator can be driven to pursue while neglecting more significant problems. A fourth issue concerns the problem of personal and organizational interests influencing what is seen as scientifically important. Large-scale governmental bureaucracies, and the individuals in them, tend to seek and interpret data in ways that support their interests. A fifth problem is related to the second, in that investigators often allow the most visible phenomena to occupy their attention, creating a bias in the collection of data toward the most readily accessible (not necessarily the most important) phenomena. A sixth problem stems from the fact that any observer occupies a position in society and hence will tend to see the world in terms of the dictates of that position. And seventh, depending on the time in the ongoing social process when observations are made, varying results can be induced—thereby signaling that "social change cannot be judged . . . by inspecting any small portion of it."[16]

Spencer's discussion is timely even today, and his advice for mitigating these objective difficulties is also relevant: Social science must rely on multiple sources of data, collected at different times in varying places by different investigators. Coupled with efforts by investigators to recognize their bias, their interests, and their positions in society as well as their commitment to theoretically important (rather than popular) problems, these difficulties can be further mitigated. Yet many subjective difficulties will persist.

Spencer emphasized two classes of subjective difficulty: intellectual and emotional. Under intellectual difficulties, Spencer returned to the first of the objective difficulties: How are investigators to put themselves into the subjective world of those whom they observe? How can we avoid representing another's "thoughts and feelings in terms of our own"?[17] For if investigators cannot suspend their own emotional states to understand those of others under investigation, the data of social science will always be biased. Another subjective intellectual problem concerns the depth of analysis, for the more one investigates a phenomenon in detail, the more complicated are its elements and their causal connections. Thus, how far should investigators go before they are to be satisfied with their analysis of a particular phenomenon? At what point are the basic causal connections uncovered? Turning to emotional subjective difficulties, Spencer argued that the emotional state of an investigator can directly influence estimations of the probability, importance, and relevance of events.

After reviewing these difficulties and emphasizing that the distinction between subjective and objective is somewhat arbitrary, Spencer devoted separate chapters to "educational bias," "bias of patriotism," "class bias," "political bias," and "theological

---

[16]Ibid., 105.

[17]Ibid., 114.

bias." Thus, more than any other sociologist of the nineteenth century, Spencer saw the many methodological problems confronting the science of society.

Spencer felt that the problems of bias could be mitigated not only by attention to one's interests, emotions, station in life, and other subjective and emotional sources of difficulty but also by the development of "mental discipline." He believed that by studying the procedures of the more exact sciences, sociologists could learn to approach their subjects in a disciplined and objective way. In a series of enlightening passages,[18] he argued that by studying the purely abstract sciences, such as logic and mathematics, one could become sensitized to "the necessity of relation"— that is, that phenomena are connected and reveal affinities. By examining the "abstract-concrete sciences," such as physics and chemistry, one is alerted to causality and to the complexity of causal connections. By examining the "concrete sciences," such as geology and astronomy, one becomes alerted to the "products" of causal forces and the operation of law-like relations. For it is always necessary, Spencer stressed, to view the context within which processes occur. Thus, by approaching problems with the proper mental discipline—with a sense of relation, causality, and context—one can overcome many methodological difficulties.

The Theoretical Argument

The opening chapters of *The Study of Sociology* present a forceful argument against those who would maintain that the social realm is not like the physical and biological realms. On the contrary, Spencer argued, all spheres of the universe are subject to laws. Every time people express political opinions about what legislators should do, they are admitting implicitly to regularities that can be understood in human behavior and organization.

Given the existence of discoverable laws, Spencer stressed that the goal of sociology must be to uncover the principles of the morphology (structure) and physiology (process) of all organic forms, including the superorganic (society). But, he cautioned, we must not devote our energies to analyzing the historically unique, peculiar, or transitory. Rather, sociology must look for the universal and enduring properties of social organization.[19] Moreover, sociologists should not become overly concerned with predicting future events because unanticipated empirical conditions will always influence the weights of variables and, hence, the outcomes of events. Much more important is discovering the basic relations among phenomena and the fundamental causal forces that generate these relations.

In the early and late chapters of *The Study of Sociology,* Spencer sought to delineate, in sketchy form, some principles common to organic bodies. In so doing, he foreshadowed the more extensive analysis in *Principles of Sociology.* He acknowledged Auguste Comte's influence in viewing biology and sociology as parallel sciences of organic forms and in recognizing that understanding the principles of biology is a prerequisite for discovering the principles of sociology.[20] As Spencer

---

[18]Ibid., 314–326.

[19]Ibid., 58–59.

[20]Ibid., 328.

emphasized in all his sociological works, certain principles of structure and function are common in all organic bodies.

Spencer even hinted at some of these principles, on which he was to elaborate in the volumes of *Principles of Sociology*. One principle is that increases in the size of both biological and social aggregates create pressures for the differentiation of functions. Another principle is that such differentiation results in the creation of distinctive regulatory, operative, and distributive processes. That is, as organic systems differentiate, it becomes necessary for some units to regulate and control action, for others to produce what is necessary for system maintenance, and for still others to distribute the necessary substances among the parts. A third principle is that differentiation initially involves separation of regulative centers from productive centers, and only with increases in size and further differentiation do distinctive distributing centers emerge.

Such principles are supplemented by one of the first functional orientations in sociology. In numerous places, Spencer stressed that to uncover the principles of social organization, it is necessary to examine the social whole, to determine its needs for survival, and to assess the various structures by which it meets these needs. Although this functionalism always remained somewhat implicit and subordinate to his search for the principles of organization among superorganic bodies, it influenced subsequent thinkers, particularly Émile Durkheim.

In sum, then, *The Study of Sociology* is a preliminary work to Spencer's *Principles of Sociology*. It analyzes in detail the methodological problems confronting sociology; it offers guidelines for eradicating biases and for developing the proper "scientific discipline"; it hints at the utility of functional analysis; and, most important, it begins to sketch out what Spencer thought to be the fundamental principles of social organization. During the two decades after the publication of *The Study of Sociology*, Spencer sought to use the basic principles enunciated in his *First Principles* as axioms for deriving the more specific principles of superorganic bodies.

A Note on Spencer's *Descriptive Sociology*

Using his inheritance and royalties, Spencer commissioned a series of volumes to describe the characteristics of different societies.[21] These volumes were, in his vision, to contain no theory or supposition; rather, they were to constitute the "raw data"

---

[21]The full title of the work reads *Descriptive Sociology, or Groups of Sociological Facts*. The list of volumes of *Descriptive Sociology* is as follows: vol. 1: *English* (1873); vol. 2: *Ancient Mexicans, Central Americans, Chibchans, Ancient Peruvians* (1874); vol. 3: *Types of Lowest Races, Negritto, and Malayo-Polynesian Races* (1874); vol. 4: *African Races* (1875); vol. 5: *Asiatic Races* (1876); vol. 6: *North and South American Races* (1878); vol. 7: *Hebrews and Phoenicians* (1880); vol. 8: *French* (1881); vol. 9: *Chinese* (1910); vol. 10: *Hellenic Greeks* (1928); vol. 11: *Mesopotamia* (1929); vol. 12: *African Races* (1930); and vol. 13: *Ancient Romans* (1934). A revised edition of vol. 3, ed. D. Duncan and H. Tedder, was published in 1925; a second edition of vol. 6 appeared in 1885; vol. 14 is a redoing by Emil Torday of vol. 4. In addition to these volumes, which are folio in size, two unnumbered works appeared: Ruben Long, *The Sociology of Islam*, 2 vols. (1931–1933) and John Garstang, *The Heritage of Solomon: An Historical Introduction to the Sociology of Ancient Palestine* (1934). For a more detailed review and analysis of these volumes, see Jonathan H. Turner and Alexandra Maryanski, "Sociology's Lost Human Relations Area Files," *Sociological Perspectives* 31 (1988):19–34.

from which theoretical inductions could be made or by which deductions from abstract theory could be tested. These descriptions became the data source for Spencer's sociological work, particularly his *Principles of Sociology*. As he noted in the "Provisional Preface" of Volume 1 of *Descriptive Sociology,*

> In preparation for *The Principles of Sociology,* requiring as bases of induction large accumulations of data, fitly arranged comparison, I . . . commenced by proxy the collection and organization of facts presented by societies of different types, past and present . . . the facts collected and arranged for easy reference and convenient study of their relations, being so presented, apart from hypotheses, as to aid all students of social science in testing such conclusions as they have drawn and in drawing others.[22]

Spencer's intent was to use common categories for classifying "sociological facts" from different types of societies. In this way, he hoped that sociology would have a sound database for developing the laws of superorganic bodies. In light of the data available to Spencer, the volumes of *Descriptive Sociology* are remarkably detailed. What is more, the categories for describing different societies are still useful. Although these categories differ slightly from volume to volume, primarily because the complexity of societies varies so much, there is an effort to maintain a consistent series of categories for classifying and arranging sociological facts. Volume 1, *The English,* illustrates Spencer's approach.

First, facts are recorded for general classes of sociological variables. Thus, for *The English,* "facts" are recorded on the following:

1. Inorganic environment
   a. General features
   b. Geological features
   c. Climate

2. Organic environment
   a. Vegetable
   b. Animal

3. Sociological environment
   a. Past history
   b. Past societies from which the present system was formed
   c. Present neighbors

4. Characteristics of people
   a. Physical
   b. Emotional
   c. Intellectual

---

[22] *The English,* classified and arranged by Herbert Spencer, compiled and abstracted by James Collier (New York: Appleton-Century-Crofts, 1873), vi.

This initial basis of classification is consistent with Spencer's opening chapters in *Principles of Sociology.* (See his section on "Critical Variables.")

Second, most of *The English* is devoted to a description of the historical development of British society, from its earliest origins to Spencer's time, divided into the following topics:

Division of labor	Funeral rites	Arts
Regulation of labor	Laws of intercourse	Agriculture, rearing, and so forth
Domestic laws—marital	Habits and customs	Land—works
Domestic laws—filial	Aesthetic sentiments	Habitations
Political laws—criminal, civil, and industrial	Moral sentiments	Food
General government	Religious ideas and superstitions	Clothing
Local government	Knowledge	Weapons
Military	Language	Implements
Ecclesiastical	Distribution	Aesthetic products
Professional	Exchange	Supplementary materials
Accessory institutions	Production	

Third, for some volumes, such as *The English,* more detailed descriptions under these headings are represented in tabular form. *The English,* for example, opens with a series of large and detailed tables, organized under the general headings "regulative" and "operative" as well as "structural" and "functional." The tables begin with the initial formation of the English peoples around 78 CE and document through a series of brief statements, organized around basic topics (see previous list), to around 1850. By reading across the tables at any given period, the reader can find a profile of the English for that period. By reading down the columns of the table, the reader can note the patterns of change in this society.

The large, oversize volumes of *Descriptive Sociology* make fascinating reading. They are, without doubt, among the most comprehensive and detailed descriptions of human societies ever constructed, certainly surpassing those of Max Weber or any other comparative social scientist of the late nineteenth and early twentieth centuries. Although the descriptions are flawed by the sources of data (historical accounts and travelers' published reports), Spencer's methodology is sound, and because he employed professional scholars to compile the data, they are as detailed as they could be at the time. Had the volumes of *Descriptive Sociology* not lapsed into obscurity and had they been updated with more accurate accounts, modern social science would, we believe, have a much firmer database for comparative sociological analysis and for theoretical activity.

Spencer's *The Principles of Sociology*

The Principles of Sociology is a massive work—more than 2,000 pages.[23] It is filled with rich empirical details from *Descriptive Sociology,* but the book's importance resides in the theory that Spencer developed as the successive installments of this work were released between 1874 and 1896. In *The Principles of Sociology,* Spencer defined sociology as the study of *superorganic* phenomena—that is, of the relations among organisms. Thus, sociology could study nonhuman societies, such as ants and other insects, but the paramount superorganic phenomenon is human society. Spencer employed an evolutionary model; over the long haul of history, societies had become increasingly complex. Human societies had followed the basic principles, articulated in *First Principles,* of evolutionary movement from small, homogeneous masses to more complex and differentiated masses. Thus, for Spencer, evolution is the process of increasing differentiation of human populations as they grow in size.

Spencer argued that several important factors always influence this movement from small and homogeneous to large and complex social forms. One is the nature of the people involved, another is the effects of environmental conditions, and a third is what he termed *derived factors* involving the new environments created by the evolution of society. This last factor is the most important because the larger and more complex societies become, the more their culture and structure shape the environment to which people and groups must adapt. Of particular importance are the effects of (a) the size and density of a population and (b) the relations of societies with their neighbors. As the size and density of a population increase, it becomes more structurally differentiated, with the result that individuals live and adapt to highly diverse social and cultural environments. As societies get larger, they begin to have contact with their neighbors, and this contact can range from cordial relations of economic exchange to warfare and conquest. As we will see, these two derived factors are related in Spencer's scheme because the nature of internal differentiation of a population is very much influenced by the degree to which it is engaged in war with its neighbors.

The Superorganic and the Organismic Analogy

Part 2 of Volume 1 of *Principles of Sociology* contains virtually all the theoretical statements of Spencerian sociology. Employing the organismic analogy—that is, comparing organic (bodily) and superorganic (societal) organization—Spencer developed a perspective for analyzing the structure, function, and transformation of societal phenomena. Too often commentators have criticized Spencer for his use of the organismic analogy, but in fairness, we should emphasize that he generally

---

[23]Herbert Spencer, *The Principles of Sociology,* 3 vols., 8 parts (New York: Appleton-Century-Crofts, 1885; originally initiated in 1874). This particular edition is the third and is printed in five separate books; subsequent references are all to this third edition. Other editions vary in volume numbering, although part numbers are consistent across various editions. See also J. H. Turner's edited reprint of this edition, published by Transaction Publishers. This reprint contains a long summary and analysis of *The Principles of Sociology.*

employed the analogy cautiously. The basic point of the analogy is that because both organic and superorganic systems reveal organization among the component parts, they should reveal certain common principles of organization. As Spencer stressed, "Between society and anything else, the only conceivable resemblance must be due to *parallelism of principle in the arrangement of components*."[24]

Spencer began his analogizing by discussing the similarities and differences between organic and superorganic systems. Among important similarities, he delineated the following:

1. Both society and organisms can be distinguished from inorganic matter, for both grow and develop.

2. In both society and organisms, an increase in size means an increase in complexity and differentiation.

3. In both, a progressive differentiation in structure is accompanied by a differentiation in function.

4. In both, parts of the whole are interdependent, with a change in one part affecting the other parts.

5. In both, each part of the whole is also a microsociety or organism in and of itself.

6. And in both organisms and societies, the life of the whole can be destroyed, but the parts will live on for a while.[25]

Among the critical differences between a society and an organism, Spencer emphasized the following:

1. The degree of connectedness of the parts is vastly different in organic and superorganic bodies. There is close proximity and physical contact of parts in organic bodies, whereas in superorganic systems there is dispersion and only occasional physical contact of elements.

2. The nature of communication among elements is vastly different in organic and superorganic systems. In organic bodies, communication occurs as molecular waves passing through channels of varying degrees of coherence, whereas among humans, communication occurs by virtue of the capacity to use language to communicate ideas and feelings.

3. In organic and superorganic systems, there are great differences in the respective consciousness of units. In organic bodies, only some elements in only some species reveal the capacity for conscious deliberation, whereas in human societies all individual units exhibit the capacity for conscious thought.

---

[24]Spencer, *Principles of Sociology*, vol. 1, 448 (emphasis in original).

[25]This particular listing is taken from Jonathan H. Turner, *Contemporary Sociological Theory* (Newbury Park, CA: Sage, 2012).

The Analysis of Superorganic Dynamics

If Spencer had only made these analogies, there would be little reason to examine his work. The analogies represent only a sensitizing framework, but the real heart of Spencerian sociology is his portrayal of the dynamic properties of superorganic systems. We begin by examining his general model of system growth, differentiation, and integration; then we will see how he applied this model to societal processes.

System Growth, Differentiation, and Integration. As Spencer had indicated in *First Principles,* evolution involves movement from a homogeneous state to a more differentiated state. Spencer stressed that certain common patterns of movement from undifferentiated states can be observed.

First, growth in an organism and in a society involves development from initially small to larger units.

Second, both individual organisms and societies reveal wide variability in the size and level of differentiation.

Third, growth in both organic and superorganic bodies occurs through compounding and recompounding; that is, smaller units are initially aggregated to form larger units (compounding), and then these larger units join other units (recompounding) to form an even larger whole. In this way organic and superorganic systems become larger and more structurally differentiated. Hence, growth in size is always accompanied by structural differentiation of those units that have been compounded. For example, small clusters of cells in a bodily organism or in a small, primitive society initially join other cells or small societies (thus becoming compounded); then these larger units join other units (thus being recompounded) and form still larger and more differentiated organisms or societies, and so on for both organic and superorganic growth.

Fourth, growth and structural differentiation must be accompanied by integration. Thus, organic and societal bodies must manifest structural integration at each stage of compounding. Without such integration, recompounding is not possible. For instance, if two societies are joined, they must be integrated before they can, as a unit, become compounded with yet another society. In the processes of compounding—growth, differentiation, and integration—Spencer saw parallel mechanisms of integration in organisms and societies. For both organic and superorganic systems, integration is achieved increasingly through the dual processes of (1) centralization of regulating functions and (2) mutual dependence of unlike parts. In organisms, for example, the nervous system and the functions of the brain become increasingly centralized, and the organs become increasingly interdependent; in superorganic systems, political processes become more and more centralized, and institutions become increasingly dependent on one another.

Fifth, integration of matter through mutual dependence and centralization of control increases the "coherence" of the system and its adaptive capacity in a given environment. Such increased adaptive capacity often creates conditions favoring further growth, differentiation, and integration, although Spencer emphasized that dissolution often occurs when a system overextends itself by growing beyond its capacity to integrate new units.

These general considerations, which Spencer initially outlined in his 1862 *First Principles,* offer a model of structuring in social systems. In this model, the basic processes are (a) the forces causing growth in system size, (b) the differentiation of units, (c) the processes whereby differentiated units become integrated, and (d) the creation of a "coherent heterogeneity," which increases the level of adaptation to the environment.

Thus, for Spencer, institutionalization is a process of growth in size, differentiation, integration, and adaptation. With integration and increased adaptation, a new system is institutionalized and becomes capable of further growth. For example, a society that grows as the result of conquering another will tend to differentiate along the lines of the conqueror and the conquered. It will centralize authority; it will create relations of interdependence; and, as a result, it will become more adapted to its environment. The result of this integration and adaptation is an increased capacity to conquer more societies, setting into motion another wave of growth, differentiation, integration, and adaptation. Similarly, a nonsocietal social system such as a corporation can begin growth through mergers or expenditures of capital, but it soon must differentiate functions and then integrate them through a combination of mutual dependence of parts and centralization of authority. If such integration is successful, it has increased the adaptive capacity of the system, which can grow if some capital surplus is available.

Conversely, to the extent that integration is incomplete, dissolution of the system is likely. Thus, social systems grow, differentiate, integrate, and achieve some level of adaptation to the environment, but at some point, the units cannot become integrated, setting the system into a phase of dissolution. Figure 3.1 illustrates this process.

Thus, Spencer did not see growth, differentiation, and integration as inevitable. Rather, as differentiation increases, problems of integrating the larger social "mass" generate pressures to find solutions to these problems. For example, people will seek solutions if the roles people fill are poorly coordinated, if crime and deviance are high, if commitments to a society's values are weak, if people have no place to work, and if many other disintegrative pressures prevail. These disintegrative tendencies are

Figure 3.1 Spencer's General Model of Evolution

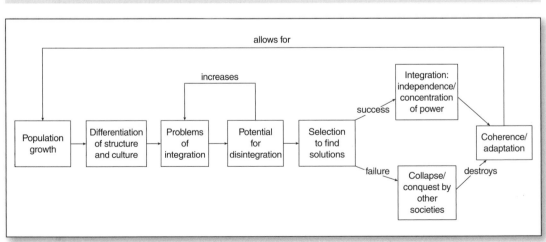

a kind of "selection pressure" because, as problems of integration mount, members of a population see the problems and attempt to do something about them. If members find ways to develop relations of mutual interdependence and to regulate their actions under a centralized authority, they can stave off these disintegrative pressures and prevent dissolution. Many societies, Spencer argued, had failed to respond adequately to pressures for integration, and as a result, they had collapsed or, more likely, had been conquered by a more integrated and powerful population. Indeed, Spencer argued that war has been an important force in human evolution because the more integrated and organized society will generally win wars against less integrated societies. As the conquered are integrated into the social structure and culture of their conquerors, the size and scale of society increase, and so, even as some societies dissolve or are conquered, the scale of societies had been slowly growing over the long course of human history. Spencer's famous phrase "survival of the fittest" was partly intended to communicate this geopolitical dimension of societal evolution.

Geopolitical Dynamics. Spencer's model of geopolitics is rather sophisticated for his time. As noted earlier, he argued that one of the most important forces increasing the size and scale of societies is war. Throughout *Principles of Sociology,* a theory of geopolitics is developed—a theory that, surprisingly, contemporary sociology ignores.

In this theory, Spencer posited that when power becomes centralized around its coercive base, leaders often use the mobilization of coercive power to repress conflicts within the society and, equally often, to conquer their neighbors. The reverse is also true: when leaders must deal with internal conflicts or external threats from other societies, they will centralize power to mobilize resources to deal with these sources of threat. So, for example, if there is class or ethnic conflict within a society, coercive power will be used to repress it, or if a neighboring society is seen as dangerous, political leaders will centralize coercive power to meet this perceived threat. Indeed, leaders will often use real or imagined internal and external threats as a way to legitimate their grabbing more power; once this power is consolidated, it can be used to centralize power even further.

The result is that once this cycle of threat and centralized power is initiated, it becomes self-fulfilling, for several reasons. First, when power is concentrated, it is used to usurp the wealth and resources of a population, with the result that inequality increases. Those with power simply tax or take resources from others to finance war-making and supplement their privilege. And as inequality increases, the sense of internal threat also escalates because those who have had their resources taken are generally hostile and pose a threat to the elites, who must then concentrate even more power to deal with this escalated threat, thereby increasing inequality and raising new threats. Over the long run, Spencer felt, this escalating cycle would potentially cause the disintegration of a society or make it vulnerable to conquest by other societies. Second, when power is concentrated and used to make war against other societies, resources must be extracted to pay for this military effort, thus potentially causing escalated inequality and internal threats, which would compound the problems of making war. As long as a society is successful in adventurism, the resentment of those who must pay for it often remains muted, but when external war-making does not go well, the resentment of those who have had their resources taken will increase and pose internal threats to the leaders, forcing them to mobilize more coercive power, if they can. Third, when power is concentrated to make war and such efforts at conquest are successful, it then becomes necessary to control those who have been conquered. The need to manage a restive and resentful population pushes political leaders to concentrate more power, thus extracting increasing resources for social control. As resources are channeled to social control, inequality increases, thereby escalating internal threats, which require even more usurpation of resources to maintain social control.

For Spencer, then, concentrating power is a double-edged sword. It allows one population to conquer another and to increase the size, scale, and complexity of human societies, but it also increases inequalities and internal threats that, unless the cycle of concentrating more power is broken, cause the disintegration of the new, larger, and more complex society. That is why Spencer argued that military adventurism in the industrial era is ill-advised; it drains a population's resources toward coercive and control activities and away from innovation and investment in domestic production. In essence, Spencer was arguing against the creation of what we would call today the *military-industrial complex.* Moreover, Spencer felt that once power is concentrated around the coercive base (military and police) of power, decision making by leaders in government is biased toward the use of coercion rather than toward negotiation, compromise, the use of incentives, and other alternatives to repression and tight control. For example, if Spencer had seen the rise of the Soviet Union through most of the twentieth century, his theory of geopolitics might have led him to predict its collapse in the 1990s.

Spencer's theory of geopolitics is woven throughout the pages of *Principles of Sociology,* and it is part of a much more general theory of the evolution of societies from simple to more complex forms. Spencer conceptualized these movements as a series of prominent stages.

Stages of Societal Evolution. Spencer argued that increases in the size of a social aggregate necessitate the elaboration of its structure. Such increases in size are the result of high birth rates, migrations, and populations joining through conquest and assimilation. Although Spencer visualized much growth as the result of compounding and recompounding—that is, successive joining together of previously separate social systems through treaties, conquest, expropriation, and other means—he also employed the concept of compounding in another sense: to denote successive stages of internal growth and differentiation of social systems.

Spencer employed the terms *primary, secondary,* and *tertiary compounding,* by which he meant that a society had undergone a qualitative shift in the level of differentiation from a simpler to a more complex form.[26] These stages of compounding marked a new level of differentiation among and within what Spencer saw as the three main axes of differentiation in social systems: (1) the *regulatory,* in which structures by mobilizing and by using power manage relations with the external environment, while engaging in internal coordination of a society's members; (2) the *operative,* in which structures

---

[26]Spencer, *Principles of Sociology,* 1:479–483.

meet system needs for production of goods and commodities and for reproduction of system members and their culture; and (3) the *distributive,* in which structures move materials, people, and information. In simple societies, these three great axes of differentiation are collapsed together, but as societies grow and compound, distinctive structures emerge for each of these axes. The subsequent course of evolution then occurs with further differentiation between and within these axes.

Primary compounding occurs when the simplest structures become somewhat more complex. At first, only a differentiation of regulatory and operative processes is evident. For example, the sexual division of labor between males and females might move to one where some males have more authority than do females (regulatory functions), while females begin to shoulder a greater burden in gathering food and in socializing the young (operative functions). Thus, the first big shift in the level of differentiation is along the regulatory and operative axes; only with further growth and differentiation of the population does a distinctive set of structures devoted to distribution of resources, people, and information emerge. Secondary compounding occurs, Spencer argued, when the structures involved in regulatory, operative, and distributive functions undergo further differentiation. For example, internal administrative structures might become distinguished from warfare roles in the regulative system; varieties of domestic activities, with specialized persons or groups involved in these separate activities, might become evident; or distinguishable persons or groups involved in external trade and internal commerce might become differentiated. Tertiary compounding occurs when these secondary structures undergo further internal differentiation, so that one can observe distinct structures involved in varieties of regulatory, operative, and distributive processes.

Figure 3.2 represents these dynamics diagrammatically as a model. This model outlines the stages of societal evolution in three respects. First, Spencer saw five basic stages: (1) simple without head or leadership, (2) simple with head or leadership, (3) compound, (4) doubly compound, and (5) trebly compound. Second, he visualized each stage as being denoted by (a) a given degree of differentiation *among* regulatory, operative, and distributive processes and (b) a level of differentiation *within* each process. Third, he suggested how the nature of regulation, operation, and distribution changes with each stage of compounding (as denoted by the descriptive labels in each box in Figure 3.2).

Contained within Spencer's view of the stages of evolution is a mode of functional analysis. By viewing social structures with reference to regulatory, operative, and distributive processes, Spencer implicitly argued that these three processes represent the basic "functional needs" of all organic and superorganic systems. Thus, a particular structure is to be assessed by its contribution to one or more of these three basic needs. But Spencer's functionalism is even more detailed, for he argued in several places that all social structures had their own internal regulatory, operative, or distributive needs, regardless of which of the three functions they fulfilled for the larger social whole in which they were located.[27] For example, the family might be viewed as an operative structure for the society as a whole, but it also reveals its own division of labor along regulatory, operative, and distributive functions.

---

[27]Ibid., 477.

Figure 3.2 Spencer's Stage Model of Societal Evolution

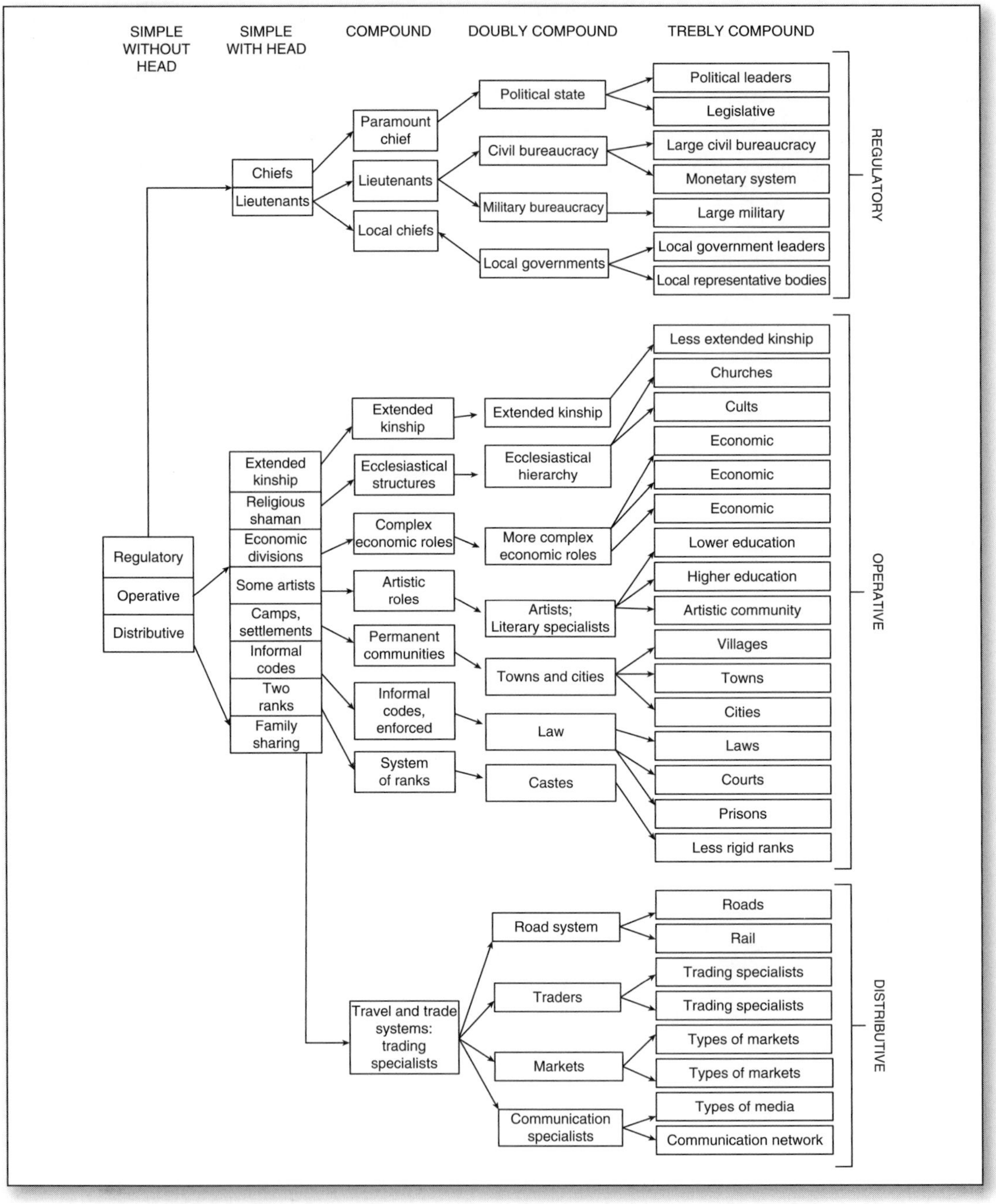

Sequences of Differentiation. Spencer devoted most of his attention to analyzing the regulatory system because he was primarily a theorist of power.[28] His discussion revolves around delineating those conditions under which the

___
[28]Ibid., part 2, 519–548.

regulatory system becomes (1) differentiated from operative and distributive processes and (2) internally differentiated. We can consider Spencer a political theorist because of this emphasis on the regulating system—that is, the center of power in society.

If we translate differentiation between regulatory and operative functions into more modern terminology, then the first phase of differentiation is between the emergence of a political system and the specialized structures involved in (a) production, or the conversion of resources into usable commodities, and (b) reproduction, or the regeneration of people as well as their culture. Most of Spencer's sociology is devoted to the regulatory system, especially the cause of centralized power and its consequences on operative and distributive processes. In general, Spencer posited the following conditions as increasing the concentration and centralization of power:

1. When productive processes become complex, they require some kind of external authority to coordinate activity to ensure that exchanges proceed smoothly, to maintain contractual obligations, to prevent fraud and corruption, and to ensure that the necessary productive activities are conducted. These pressures for external authority lead to the mobilization of power. Once this capacity to regulate the economy exists, the level of production can expand further, creating new pressures for expanded use of power to coordinate more complex levels of economic activity.

2. When there are internal threats, typically arising from conflicts over inequalities, centers of power will mobilize to control the conflict. Ironically, the use of power to control conflict often increases inequality because those with power begin to usurp resources for themselves. As a result, as more power is concentrated, further inequality and conflict will ensue in a cycle of conflict, use of power to control and usurp, increased inequality, and escalated potential for conflict.

3. When there are external threats from other societies arising from economic competition or military confrontations, centers of power will mobilize coercive forces to deal with such threats. Consequently, they will also set off the dynamics described under (2) above because when power is mobilized to deal with threats, it is also used to enhance the well-being of elites, thereby increasing inequality and the potential for conflict. Moreover, as noted for Spencer's theory of geopolitics, when a political system is mobilized for conflict with other societies, it will generally pursue war as the first option (rather than diplomacy), with the result that if it wins the war, this very success creates new internal threats, as specified in (2) above, revolving around the inequalities between the conquerors and the conquered.

As both regulatory and operative processes develop, Spencer argued, pressures for transportation, communication, and exchange among larger and more differentiated units increase. As a result of these pressures, new structures emerge as part of a general expansion of distributive functions. Spencer devoted considerable attention to the historical events causing increases in transportation, roads, markets, and communication processes, and by themselves, these descriptions make for fascinating reading. At the most general level, he concluded,

> The truth we have to carry with us is that the distributing system in the social organism, as in the individual organism, has its development determined by the necessities of transfer among inter-dependent parts. Lying between the two original systems, which carry on respectively the outer dealings with surrounding existences, and the inner dealings with materials required for sustentation [*sic*] its structure becomes adapted to the requirements of this carrying function between the two great systems as wholes, and between the sub-divisions of each.[29]

As the regulatory and operative systems expand, thereby causing the elaboration of the distributive system, this third great system differentiates in ways that facilitate increases in (1) the speed with which material and information circulate and (2) the varieties of materials and information that are distributed. As the capacities for rapid and varied distribution increase, regulatory and operative processes can develop further; as the latter expand and differentiate, new pressures for rapid and varied distribution are created. Moreover, in a series of insightful remarks, Spencer noted that this positive feedback cycle involved an increase in the ratio of information to materials distributed in complex, differentiating systems.[30]

In sum, then, Spencer's view of structural elaboration emphasizes the processes of structural growth and differentiation through the joining of separate systems and through internal increases in size. As an evolutionist, Spencer took the long-range view of social development as growth, differentiation, integration, and increased adaptive capacity; then, with this new level as a base, further growth, differentiation, integration, and adaptive capacity would be possible. His view of structural elaboration is thus highly sophisticated, and though flawed in many ways, it is the equal of any other nineteenth-century social theory.

System Dialectics and Phases. As we have emphasized, Spencer saw war as an important causal force in human societies. War pushes a society to develop centralized regulatory structures to expand and coordinate internal operative and distributive processes. Yet war can have an ironic effect on a society: once these operative and distributive processes are expanded under conditions of external conflict, they increasingly exert pressures for less militaristic activity and for less authoritarian centralization. For example, a nation at war will initially centralize along authoritarian lines to mobilize resources, but as such mobilization expands the scope of operative and distributive processes, those engaged in operation and distribution develop autonomy and begin to press for greater freedom from centralized control. In this way, Spencer was able to visualize war as an important force in societal development

---

[29]Ibid., vol. 1, 518.

[30]Of course, the absolute amounts of both increase, but the processing of information—credits, accounts, ideas, purchase orders, and so on—increases as a proportion of things circulated.

but, at the same time, as an impediment to development if concentrated power is used to concentrate even more power. And in an enlightening chapter on "social metamorphoses,"[31] he argued that the dynamic force underlying the overall evolution of the superorganic from homogeneous to heterogeneous states was the successive movement of societies in and out of the "militant" (politically centralized and authoritarian) and "industrial" (less centralized) phases. This cyclical dynamic is presented in Figure 3.3, which views these phases somewhat more abstractly than in Spencer's portrayal.

Figure 3.3 presents one of the most interesting (and often ignored) arguments in Spencerian sociology. For Spencer, there is always a dialectical undercurrent during societal evolution (and dissolution), revolving around the relationship between regulatory and operative processes. On the one hand, each of these initial axes of differentiation encourages the growth and development of the other in a positive feedback cycle, but on the other, there is an inherent tension and dialectic between the two. For example, war expands regulatory functions; increased regulatory capacity

Figure 3.3 Phases of Institutionalization

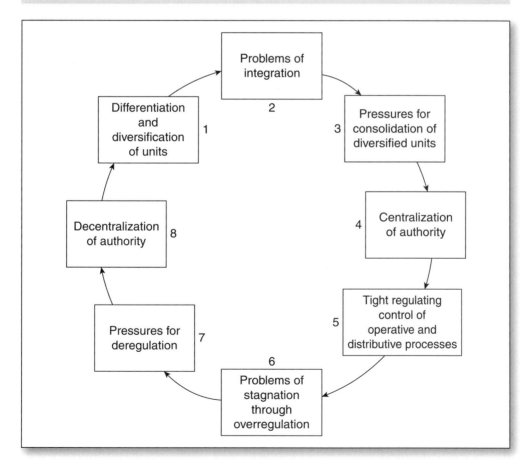

---

[31]Spencer, *Principles of Sociology,* vol. 1, 577–585.

allows for more extensive coordination of operative processes; and greater operative capacity encourages expanded war efforts and, hence, expansion of the regulatory system. But at some point in this cycle, the development of internal operative structures primarily for war-making becomes counterproductive, limiting the scope and diversity of development in operative processes. Indeed, Spencer argued that too much political control of production and reproduction causes economic stagnation and, in the reproductive sphere, arouses resentments. Over time, and under growing pressures from the internal sector as mobilization against tight control increases, the warlike profile of the regulatory system is reduced. Thus, as resentments against too much power arise, it is not inevitable that political elites will continue to concentrate power to manage such threats, as we examined earlier in Spencer's theory of geopolitics. Spencer saw an alternative: growing resentment leads political leaders to make concessions and to recognize that they must release some of their control. Spencer never specified the conditions under which leaders will give up power; he simply assumed that it had been an important dynamic in the evolution of human societies from simple to complex forms. When power is released, operative structures expand and differentiate in many directions, but over time, these structures become too divergent, poorly coordinated, and unregulated. A war can provide, Spencer believed, the needed stimulus for greater regulation and coordination of these expanded and diversified operative processes, thus setting the cycle into motion once again. Alternatively, problems of coordination become so acute that government must step in to restore order.

Such had been the case throughout evolutionary history, Spencer thought. Curiously, he also seemed to argue that modern, industrial capitalism made the need for war and extensive regulation by a central state obsolete. No longer would it be necessary, in Spencer's capitalistic utopia, for centralized government, operating under the pressures of war, to seek extensive regulation of operative and distributive processes. These processes were, in his vision, now sufficiently developed and capable of growth, expansion, and integration without massive doses of governmental intervention. Here, Spencer's ideology clearly distorts his perceptions because advanced capitalism requires the exercise of control by government; yet the analysis of the dialectic between militant and industrial societies allowed him to see how concentrated power could be lessened without disintegration.

Classifying Social Systems. Spencer also used these models of societal evolution (Figure 3.2) and system phases (Figure 3.3) as a basis for classifying societies. His most famous typology (Table 3.1) is of what he termed *militant* and *industrial* societies—a typology that commentators have frequently misunderstood. Too often, it is viewed as representing a unilinear course of evolutionary movement from traditional and militant to modern and industrial societal forms. Although Spencer often addressed the evolution of societies from a primitive to a modern profile, he did not rely heavily on the militant-industrial typology in describing types or stages of evolutionary change. Rather, as is emphasized in Figure 3.3, the militant/industrial distinction is primarily directed at capturing the difference between highly centralized authority systems where regulatory processes dominate and less centralized

Table 3.1 Spencer's Typology of Militant and Industrial Societies

Basic System Processes	Militant	Industrial
1. Regulatory processes		
a. Societal goals	Defense and war	Internal productivity and provision of services
b. Political organization	Centralized, authoritarian	Less centralized; less direct authority over system units
2. Operative processes		
a. Individuals	High degrees of control by state; high levels of stratification	Freedom from extensive controls by state; less stratification
b. Social structures	Coordinated to meet politically established goals of war and defense	Coordinated to facilitate each structure's expansion and growth
3. Distributive processes		
a. Flow of materials	From organizations to state; from state to individuals and other social units	From organizations to other units and individuals
b. Flow of information	From state to individuals	Both individuals to state and state to individuals

systems where operative processes prevail.[32] The term *industrial* does not refer to industrial production in the sense of modern factories and markets but, instead, to a reduction in centralized power and to the vitality and diversity of operative processes. Both the simplest and the most modern societies can be either militant or industrial; Spencer hoped that modern industrial capitalism would be industrial rather than militaristic. As we noted in the last section, however, Spencer saw societies as cycling in and out of centralized and decentralized phases. The typology is meant to capture this dynamic.

The distinction between militant and industrial societies emphasizes that during the course of social growth, differentiation, integration, and adaptive upgrading,[33]

[32]The misinterpretation of Spencer's intent stems from his introduction of the typology at several points in *Principles of Sociology.* From its usage in his discussion of political and industrial (economic) institutions, it would be easy to see the typology as his version of the stages of evolution. But if one reads the more analytical statement in the early chapter on social types and constitutions in vol. 1, paying particular attention to the fact that this chapter precedes the one on social metamorphoses, then our interpretation is clear. Because Spencer uses another typology for describing the long-run evolutionary trends, it seems unlikely that he would duplicate this effort with yet another typology on militant-industrial societies. See, in particular, *Principles of Sociology,* vol. 1, part 2, 569–580.

[33]I am using Talcott Parsons's terms here because they best connote Spencer's intent. See Parsons, *Societies: Evolutionary and Comparative Perspectives* (Englewood Cliffs, NJ: Prentice-Hall, 1966).

societies move in and out of the militant (dominance of regulatory) and industrial (operative) phases. Militant phases consolidate the diversified operative structures of industrial phases. The causes of either a militant or an industrial profile for a system at any given time are varied, but Spencer saw as critical (a) the degree of external threat from other systems and (b) the need to integrate dissimilar populations and cultures. The greater the threat to a system from external systems or the more diverse the system's population (an internal threat), the more likely it is to reveal a militant profile. Once external and internal threats have been mitigated through conquest, treaties, assimilation, and other processes, however, pressures for movement to an industrial profile increase. Such is the basic dynamic underlying the broad evolutionary trends from a homogeneous to a heterogeneous state of social organization.

Spencer's other typology, which has received considerably less attention than the militant/industrial distinction, addresses the major stages in the evolution of societies. Whereas the militant-industrial typology seeks to capture the cyclical dynamics underlying evolutionary movement, Spencer also attempts to describe the distinctive stages of long-term societal development, as modeled in Figure 3.2. This typology revolves around describing the pattern and direction of societal differentiation. As such, it is concerned with the processes of compounding. As was evident in Figure 3.2, Spencer marked distinctive stages of societal growth and differentiation: simple (with and without leadership), compound, doubly compound, and trebly compound.

In Table 3.2 we have taken Spencer's narrative and organized it in a somewhat more formal way. But the listing of characteristics for simple (both those with leaders and those without), compound, doubly compound, and trebly compound societies for regulatory, operative, and distributive as well as demographic (population characteristics) dimensions captures the essence of Spencer's intent. Several points need to be emphasized. First, although certain aspects of Spencer's description are flawed, his summary of the distinctive stages of societal evolution is equal, or superior, to any that recent anthropologists and sociologists have delineated.[34] Second, this description is far superior to any developed by other anthropologists and sociologists of Spencer's time.

Spencer sought to communicate what we can term *structural explanations* with this typology. The basic intent of this mode of explanation is to view certain types of structures as tending to coexist. As Spencer concluded,

> The inductions arrived at . . . show that in social phenomena there is a general order of co-existence and sequence; and therefore social phenomena form the subject-matter of a science reducible, in some measure at least, to the deductive form.[35]

Thus, by reading down the columns of Table 3.2, we can see that certain structures are likely to coexist within a system. And by reading across the table, the

---

[34]See, for example, Parsons, *Societies* and *The System of Modern Societies* (Englewood Cliffs, NJ: Prentice-Hall, 1971); Gerhard Lenski, Jean Lenski, and Patrick Nolan, *Human Societies* (New York: McGraw-Hill, 1991); and Morton H. Fried, *The Evolution of Political Society* (New York: Random House, 1967).

[35]Spencer, *Principles of Sociology,* vol. 1, part 2, 597.

patterns of change in structures with each increment of societal differentiation can be observed. Moreover, as Spencer stressed, such patterns of social evolution conformed to the general law of evolution enunciated in *First Principles*.[36]

The many facts contemplated unite in proving that social evolution forms a part of evolution at large. Like evolving aggregates in general, societies show integration, both by simple increase of mass and by coalescence and re-coalescence of masses. The change from homogeneity to heterogeneity is multitudinously exemplified; up from the simple tribe, alike in all its parts, to the civilized nation, full of structural and functional unlikenesses. With progressing integration and heterogeneity goes increasing coherence. We see the wandering group dispersing, dividing, held together by no bonds; the tribe with parts made more coherent by subordination to a dominant man; the cluster of tribes united in a political plexus under a chief with sub-chiefs; and so on up to the civilized nation, consolidated enough to hold together for a thousand years or more. Simultaneously comes increasing definiteness. Social organization is at first vague; advance brings settled arrangements which grow slowly more precise; customs pass into laws which, while gaining fixity, also become more specific in their applications to varieties of actions; and all institutions, at first confusedly intermingled, slowly separate, at the same time that each within itself marks off more distinctly its component structures. Thus in all respects is fulfilled the formula of evolution. There is progress toward greater size, coherence, multiformity, and definiteness.

In sum, then, Spencer provided two basic typologies for classifying societal systems. One typology—the militant/industrial distinction—emphasizes the cyclical phases of all societies at any stage of evolution. The second typology is less well-known but probably more important. It delineates the structural features and demographic profile of societies at different stages of evolution. Embedded in this typology is a series of statements on what structures tend to cluster together during societal growth and differentiation. This typology is, in many ways, the implicit guide for Spencer's structural and functional analysis of basic societal institutions, which constitutes Parts 3 through 7 in Volumes 1 and 2 of *Principles of Sociology*. We should, therefore, close our review of *Principles of Sociology* by briefly noting some of the more interesting generalizations that emerge from Spencer's description of basic human institutions.

The Analysis of Societal Institutions

Fully two-thirds of *Principles of Sociology* is devoted to an evolutionary description and explanation of basic human institutions.[37] For Spencer, institutions are enduring patterns of social organization that (1) meet the fundamental functional needs or requisites of human organization and (2) control the activities of individuals and groups in society. Spencer employed a "social selection" argument in his review of institutional dynamics. The most basic institutions emerge and persist because they provide a

---

[36]Ibid., 596.

[37]For a more detailed review of Spencer's institutional analysis, see Turner, *Herbert Spencer.*

Table 3.2   Spencer's Stages of Evolution

System Dimensions	Simple Society	
	Headless	*Headed*
1. Regulatory system	Temporary leaders who emerge in response to particular problems	Permanent chief and various lieutenants
2. Operative system		
a. Economic structure	Hunting and gathering	Pastoral; simple agriculture
b. Religious structure	Individualized religious worship	Beginnings of religious specialists: shaman
c. Family structure	Simple; sexual division of labor	Large, complex; sexual and political division of labor
d. Artistic–literary forms	Little art; no literature	Some art; no literature
e. Law and customs	Informal codes of conduct	Informal codes of conduct
f. Community structure	Small bands of wandering families	Small, settled groupings of families
g. Stratification	None	Chief and followers
3. Distributive system		
a. Materials	Sharing within family and band	Intra- and interfamilial exchange and sharing
b. Information	Oral, personal	Oral, personal
4. Demographic profile		
a. Size	Small	Large
b. Mobility	Mobility within territory	Less mobility; frequently tied to territory

Table 3.2   *(continued)*

Compound Society	Doubly Compound	Trebly Compound (Never Formally Listed)
Hierarchy of chiefs, with paramount chief, local chiefs, and varieties of lieutenants	Elaboration of bureaucratized political state; differentiation between domestic and military administration	Modern political state
Agricultural; general and local division of labor	Agricultural; extensive division of labor	Industrial capitalism
Established ecclesiastical arrangements	Ecclesiastical hierarchy; rigid rituals and religious observance	Religious diversity in separate church structures
Large, complex; numerous sexual, age, and political divisions	Large, complex; numerous sexual, age, and political divisions	Small, simple; decrease in sexual division of labor
Artists	Artists; literary specialists; scholars	Many artistic literary specialists; scholars
Informal codes; enforced by political elites and community members	Written law and codes	Elaborate legal codes; civil and criminal
Village; permanent buildings	Large towns; permanent structures	Cities, towns, and hamlets
Five or six clear ranks	Castes; rigid divisions	Classes; less rigid
Travel and trade between villages	Roads among towns; considerable travel and exchange; traders and other specialists	Roads, rail, and other nonmanual transportation; many specialists
Oral, personal; at times, mediated by elites or travelers	Oral and written; edicts; oracles; teachers and other communications specialists	Oral and written; formal media structures for edicts; many communications specialists
Larger; joining of several simple societies	Large	Large
Less mobility; tied to territory; movement among villages of a defined territory	Settled; much travel among towns	Settled; growing urban concentrations; much travel; movement from rural to urban centers

population with adaptive advantages in a given environment, both natural and social. That is, those patterns of organization that facilitate the survival of a population in the natural environment and in the milieu of other societies will be retained, or "selected"; as a consequence, these patterns will become institutionalized in the structure of a society. Because certain problems of survival always confront the organization of people, it is inevitable that among surviving populations a number of common institutions would be evident for all enduring societies—for example, kinship, ceremony, politics, religion, and economy. Spencer discusses more than these five institutions, but our review will emphasize only these, because they provide some of the more interesting insights in Spencerian sociology.

Domestic Institutions and Kinship

Spencer argued that kinship emerged to meet the most basic need of all species: reproduction.[38] Because a population must regulate its own reproduction before it can survive for long, kinship was one of the first human institutions. This regulation of reproduction involves the control of sexual activity, the development of more permanent bonds between men and women, and the provision of a safe context for rearing children.

Spencer's discussion of kinship was extremely sophisticated for his time. After making the previous functional arguments, he embarked on an evolutionary analysis of varying types of kinship systems. Although flawed in some respects, his approach was nonetheless insightful and anticipated similar arguments by twentieth-century anthropologists. Some of the more interesting generalizations emerging from his analysis are the following:

1. In the absence of alternative ways of organizing a population, kinship processes will become the principal mechanism of social integration.

2. The greater the size of a population without alternative ways of organizing activity, the more elaborate will be the kinship system and the more it will reveal explicit rules of descent, marriage, endogamy, and exogamy.

3. Those societies that engage in perpetual conflict will tend to create patrilineal descent systems and patriarchic authority; as a consequence, they will reveal less equality between the sexes and will be more likely to define and treat women as property.[39]

Ceremonial Institutions

Spencer recognized that human relations were structured by symbols and rituals.[40] Indeed, he tended to argue that other institutions—kinship, government, and

---

[38]Spencer, *Principles of Sociology,* vol. 1, part 3, 603–757. See also Leonard Beeghley, "Spencer's Analysis of the Evolution of the Family and the Status of Women: Some Neglected Considerations," *Sociological Perspectives* (formerly *Pacific Sociological Review*) 26 (August 1983):299–313.

[39]See Turner, *Herbert Spencer,* 115.

[40]Spencer, *Principles of Sociology,* vol. 2, part 4, 3–216.

religion—were founded on a "pre-institutional" basis revolving around interpersonal ceremonies, such as the use of (a) particular forms of address, (b) titles, (c) ritualized exchanges of greetings, (d) demeanors, (e) patterns of deference, (f) badges of honor, (g) fashion and dress, and (h) other means for ordering interactions among individuals. Thus, as people interact, they "present themselves" through their demeanor, fashion, forms of talk, badges, titles, and rituals, and in so doing, they expect certain responses from others. Interaction is thereby mediated by symbols and ceremonies that structure how individuals are to behave toward one another. Without this control of relations through symbols and ceremonies, larger institutional structures could not be sustained.

Spencer was particularly interested in the effects of inequality on ceremonial processes, especially inequalities created by centralization of power (as is the case in the militant societies depicted in Table 3.1). These interesting generalizations emerge from his more detailed analysis:

1. The greater the degree of political centralization that exists in a society, the greater the level of inequality there will be and, hence, the greater the concern for symbols and ceremonials demarking differences in rank among individuals.

2. The greater the concern over differences in rank, (a) the more likely people in different ranks are to possess distinctive objects and titles to mark their respective ranks and (b) the more likely interactions between people in different ranks are to be ritualized by standardized forms of address and stereotypical patterns of deference and demeanor.

3. Conversely, the less the degree of political centralization and the less the level of inequality, the less people are concerned about the symbols and ceremonies that demark rank and regulate interaction.[41]

Political Institutions

In his analysis of political processes in society, Spencer also developed a perspective for examining social class structures.[42] In his view, problems of internal conflict resulting from unbridled self-interest and the existence of hostility with other societies have been the prime causal forces behind the emergence and elaboration of government. Although governments reveal considerable variability, they all evidence certain common features: (a) paramount leaders, (b) clusters of subleaders and administrators, (c) large masses of followers who subordinate some of their interests to the dictates of leaders, and (d) legitimating beliefs and values that give leaders "the right" to regulate others. Spencer argued that once governmental structures come into existence, they are self-perpetuating and will expand unless they collapse internally for lack of legitimacy or are conquered from without. In particular, war and threats of war centralize government around the use of force to conquer additional territories and internally regulate operative processes, with the result that governmental structures expand. Moreover, the expansion of government and its

---

[41]See Turner, *Herbert Spencer,* 122.

[42]Spencer, *Principles of Sociology,* vol. 2, part 5, 229–643.

centralization create or exacerbate class divisions in a society because those with resources can use them to mobilize power and political decisions, which further enhance their hold on valued resources. Thus, Spencer developed a very robust political sociology, and although a listing of only a few generalizations cannot do justice to the sophistication of his approach, some of his more interesting conclusions are the following:

1. The larger the number of people and internal transactions among individuals in a society, the greater will be the size and the degree of internal differentiation of government.

2. The greater the actual or potential level of conflict with other societies and within a society, the greater will be the degree of centralization of power in government.

3. The greater the centralization of power, the more visible class divisions will be and the more these divisions create potential or actual internal conflict.

Religious Institutions

Spencer's analysis emphasized that all religions shared certain common elements: (a) beliefs about supernatural beings and forces, (b) organized groupings of individuals who share these beliefs, and (c) ritual activities directed toward those beings and forces presumed to have the capacity to influence worldly affairs.[43] Religions emerge in all societies, he argued, because they increase the survival of a population by (a) reinforcing values and beliefs through the sanctioning power of the supernatural and (b) strengthening existing social structural arrangements, especially those revolving around power and inequality, by making them seem to be extensions of the supernatural will.

Spencer provided an interesting scenario on the evolution of religion from primitive notions of "ancestor spirits" to the highly bureaucratized monotheistic religions that currently dominate the world. He saw the evolution and structural patterns of religion as intimately connected to political processes, leading him to propose the following generalizations:

1. The greater the level of war and conquest by a society, the greater are the problems of consolidating diverse religious beliefs, thereby forcing the expansion of the religious class of priests to reconcile these diverse religions and create polytheistic religions.

2. The greater the political centralization and the greater the level of class inequalities in a society, the more likely is the priestly class to create a coherent pantheon of ranked deities.

3. The more government relies on the priestly class to provide legitimation through a complex system of religious beliefs and symbols, the more this class

---

[43]Ibid., vol. 2, part 6, 3–159. We should note how close this view of religious functions is to that to be developed by Durkheim.

extracts wealth and privilege from political leaders, thereby consolidating their distinctive class position and creating an elaborate bureaucratic structure for organizing religious activity.

4. The more centralized a government is and the more it relies on religious legitimation by a privileged and bureaucratized class of priests, the greater the likelihood of a religious revolt and the creation of a simplified and monotheistic religion.

Economic Institutions

For Spencer, the long-term evolution of economic institutions revolves around (a) increases in technology or knowledge about how to manipulate the natural environment, (b) expansion of the production and distribution of goods and services, (c) accumulation of capital or the tools of production, and (d) changes in the organization of labor.[44] In turn, these related processes are the result of efforts to achieve greater levels of adaptation to the environment and to meet constantly escalating human needs. That is, as one level of economic adaptation is created, people's needs for new products and services escalate and generate pressures for economic reorganization. Thus, as new technologies, modes of production, mechanisms of distribution, forms of capital, and means for organizing labor around productive processes are developed, a more effective level of adaptation to the natural environment is achieved; as this increased adaptive capacity is established, people begin to desire more. As a result, economic production becomes less and less tied to problems of survival in the natural environment during societal evolution and is increasingly the result of escalating wants and desires among the members of a society.

Spencer further argued that war decreased advances in overall economic productivity because mobilization for war diverts the economy away from domestic production toward the development of military technologies and the organization of production around military products or services. For Spencer, war depletes capital, suppresses wants and needs for consumer goods, encourages only military technologies, and mobilizes labor for wartime production (while killing off much of the productive labor force). Only during times of relative peace, then, will economic growth ensue. Such growth in the domestic economy will be particularly likely to occur when there are increases in population size. In Spencer's view, escalating population size under conditions of peace creates pressure for expanded production while increasing needs for new products and services. These and many other lines of argument in his analysis of the economy have a highly modern flavor, but unlike his approach to other institutions, he presents few abstract generalizations, so we will not attempt to conclude with any here.

This brief summary of Spencer's analysis of basic institutions does not do justice to the sophistication of his approach. As much as any scholar of his time, or of today, he saw the complex interrelationships among social structures. One reason for this sophistication in his analysis is his in-depth knowledge of diverse societies, which he acquired through the efforts of researchers hired to construct descriptions

---

[44]Ibid., vol. 2, part 8, 327–608.

of historical and contemporary societies. Throughout his work, his ideas are illustrated by references to diverse societies. Such familiarity with many historical and contemporary societies came from his efforts to build a "descriptive sociology."

Spencer's Theoretical Legacy

As I stressed in Chapter 1 and have elaborated upon in Chapter 24, the power of a theory resides in the testable models and principles that it can generate. The theories of the early founders were, for the most part, stated discursively as text, whereas in science theoretical ideas are best stated in more precise formats, such as analytical models or elementary principles. Yet despite the lack of formalization by theorists of the classical era, their ideas are easily translated into models and abstract principles; and so for each of the major classical figures examined here in Part I, I will try to outline in more formal terms their enduring theoretical contributions. In Spencer's case, the core theoretical models and principles are readily extracted from more discursive text. Moreover, for all the vagueness of Spencer's cosmic view of evolution, it does provide a consistent metaphor that gives his theory continuity, unity, and coherence.

Spencer's Analytical Models of Societal Structures

Spencer was a functional theorist who often argued that structures exist to meet the basic requisites for regulation, operation (production and reproduction), and distribution. All such functional arguments obscure causality because they imply that needs for regulation, operation, and distribution somehow "cause" the structures that meet these needs to come into existence. But how does this occur? How can the outcome bring about the cause of this outcome? All functional theories encounter this problem; they assume that needs will magically bring about the necessary structures to meet these needs. As a result, the causal sequence of events is vague, if not somewhat mysterious. If this is the case, however, how do we draw a causal model of the processes involved?

There is a solution to this problem. Functional arguments need to be recast into *selection statements*. That is, we should view problems of regulation, operation (production and reproduction), and distribution not so much as the needs of the social system that must be fulfilled but as *selection pressures* placed on a population. A selection pressure is a problem of adaptation that people, as well as the structures organizing them, confront. For example, if there is not enough food to support a growing population, this crisis represents a selection pressure revolving around production and distribution. This pressure says, in effect: find a way to feed more people, or many people will soon be dead. Or if growth of the population creates problems of coordinating and controlling people's activities, this too is a selection pressure that forces individuals and collective units to search for solutions to these problems of regulation. Under these kinds of selection pressures, people and collective actors like groups and organizations try to find solutions. If by luck, invention, borrowing, or some other act they find a way to respond to the selection pressure, the population can remain viable in its environment. Thus, if a larger population cannot be coordinated or fed, these selection pressures send actors scrambling to find a way to increase the level of regulation or operation, to use Spencer's terms; and if they find a solution, then the population will maintain itself in its environment.

Functional statements, then, almost always contain an implicit appeal to selection processes. Many sciences use functional statements; for example, medical biologists often make functional arguments such as "The function of the heart is to distribute oxygen to parts of the body." By itself, this kind of argument obscures the causal processes whereby the heart evolved, but there is an implied selection argument in this statement: in the distant evolutionary past, natural selection worked to give larger organisms a pump to circulate blood to parts of the body, thereby increasing the chances that such organisms could survive in their environment. Similarly, all functional arguments in sociology can invoke the same selectionist argument. Although these kinds of selectionist statements do not fully resolve the problem of vagueness in the causal chain, they do avoid the problem of viewing the outcome as the cause of the processes producing this outcome.

To illustrate what selectionist causal arguments look like, Figure 3.4 translates Spencer's statements about the relationship between population size and differentiation along the regulatory, operative, and distributive axes into a complex analytical model. As the size of the population increases, problems of maintaining and regulating the members of the population intensify; these problems can be considered as escalating logistical loads or new burdens on a population that require a solution. These escalating logistical loads put selection pressure on the population to find new ways to manage the escalating burden. In Spencer's analysis of population growth and size, he argued that as logistical loads mount, selection pressures are placed on the population to consolidate and use power to coordinate more people, to expand production and reproduction so that members of the population can be sustained and regenerated, and to build new systems for distributing resources, people, and information. The positive signs on the arrows in Figure 3.4 indicate that increases in one causal force increase the values for others, whereas the negative signs indicate just the opposite. Therefore, growth of the population increases (via the positive signed arrow in the model) logistical loads, which, in turn, increases selection pressures that raise the potential for dissolution or, alternatively, cause actors to develop new regulatory, operative, and distributive structures.

An important aspect of complex analytical models is *reverse causal effects*, which are represented by the arrows flowing from right to left in the model in Figure 3.4. Analytical models typically address the recursive nature of social reality because the outcomes of one causal sequence generally feed back and affect the very forces that brought them about. Thus, in the model in Figure 3.4, as the potential for dissolution increases, this potential exerts a negative effect (symbolized by the negatively signed arrow) on the size of the population. In contrast, as new kinds of regulatory, operative, and distributive structures are generated, these structures have a positive effect on population size, allowing it to grow larger. As Spencer emphasized, with differentiation of new regulatory, operative, and distributive structures comes a greater capacity to support a larger "social mass."

Figure 3.4 Spencer's Implicit Selectionist Argument

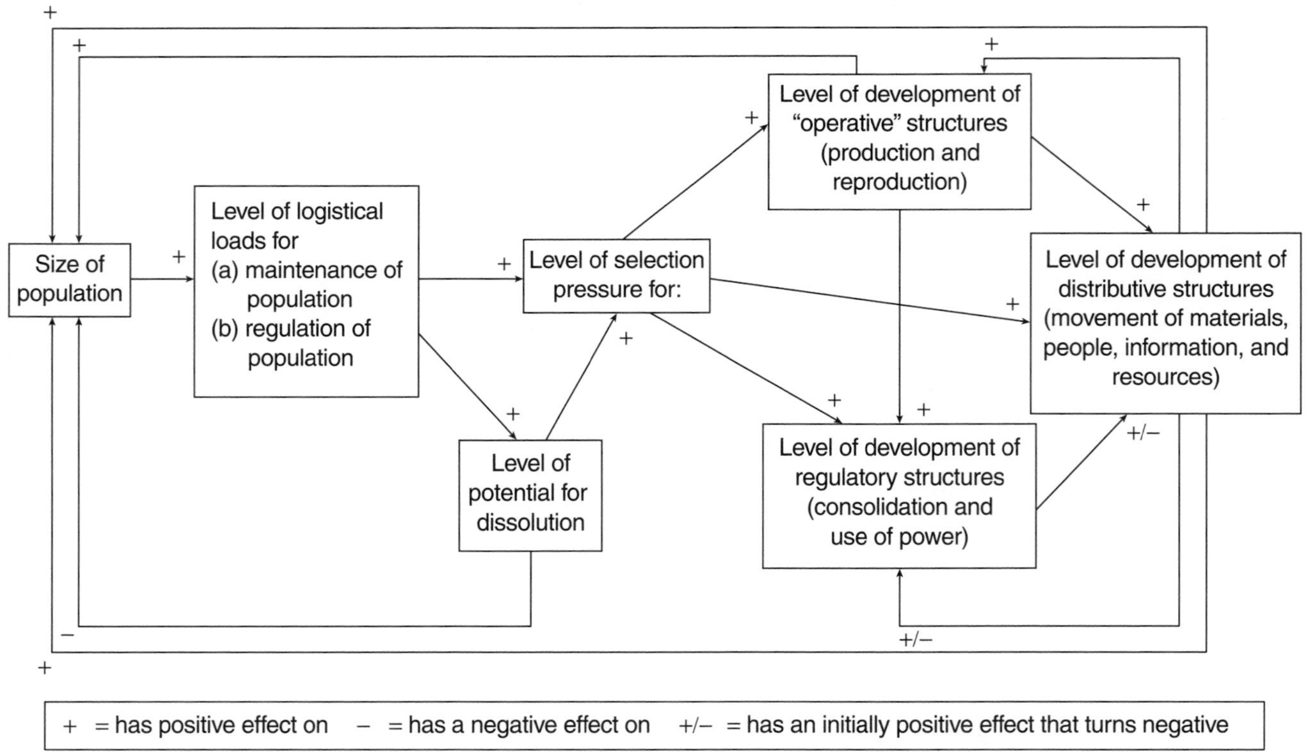

+ = has positive effect on   − = has a negative effect on   +/− = has an initially positive effect that turns negative

The model also reveals some mixed signs or arrows, such as the +/− sign of the direct causal path from development of regulatory to distributive structures as well as the reverse causal path back to regulatory from distributive processes. This sign denotes a positively curvilinear causal relation between these forces; that is, the causal relation is initially positive, with the development of regulatory structures causing the expansion of distributive processes (through building roads, ports, and other infrastructures as well as the coinage of money and enforcement of contracts in markets), but too much use of regulatory power turns the relationship negative, decreasing the dynamism of markets. Many processes in the social world are of this nature, with a force operating in one causal direction for a while, only to reverse the causal effect as the values for this force reach high levels. Spencer recognized that a certain amount of regulatory power had to be exerted on markets; and moreover, distribution requires government financing and building of infrastructures for moving people, information, and resources around. Consequently, the effects of the use of power on distribution are positive, until government begins to overregulate and stagnate market forces.

Figure 3.5 illustrates the basic elements of all complex analytical models by portraying Spencer's entire scheme in one causal model. The model starts, as Spencer intended, with those forces increasing the size of the population. At first, a growing population will simply create more structures of the same kind, or as the model highlights, the rate of "segmentation" will increase. For example, as a population of hunter-gatherers grows, it may simply create more bands of nuclear families as its first response to the increase in the logistical loads that come with growth. Segmentation can, for a time, manage the increasing logistical loads of growing size, but as the arrow indicates, this is a curvilinear effect. As is denoted by the −/+ sign of the arrow from segmentation to logistical loads, segmentation initially decreases logistical loads (the negative sides of the curvilinear relationship), but eventually, segmentation is insufficient to manage the escalation loads of growth. Thus, further segmentation begins to increase loads (the positive side of the curvilinear relationship). The larger size of the population and the declining effectiveness of segmentation increase logistical loads and selection pressures on the population to coordinate, control, and regulate the population and to distribute resources, information, and people about the society. Segmentation alone will no longer work; as logistical loads and selection pressures mount, the population must *differentiate* into new kinds of structures or face the possibility of dissolution (as denoted by the arrow from logistical loads to dissolution/disintegration). If these selection pressures are not met with an effective response, the likelihood of dissolution and disintegration of the population increases. If, however, differentiation of new kinds of regulatory, operative (productive and reproductive), and distributive structures can meet these selection pressures by managing the escalated logistical loads, then the potential for societal disintegration is reduced (as emphasized by the negatively signed reverse causal arrows from regulatory, operative, and distributive activity to selection pressures, which when reduced will travel along the positively signed arrows to lower the potential for dissolution). As the overall level of structural differentiation around new productive,

Figure 3.5 Spencer's General Theory of Societal Dynamics

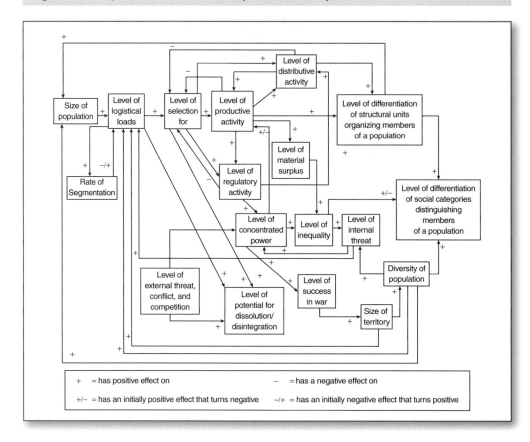

reproductive, regulatory, and distributive structures increases, this exerts a positive effect on population size (as denoted by the positive reverse causal arrow at the top of the model back to population size from structural differentiation). With increased differentiation, then the society can now support a larger "social mass," to use Spencer's terminology. This portion of the model thus summarizes Spencer's core evolutionary argument about size and differentiation, without all the baggage of evolutionary thinking. Spencer's model can be applied to any system—from a society to an organization, for example—because, as he argues, there is a fundamental set of causal relations between population size and structural differentiation.

We can now turn to the theory of power dynamics, that Spencer developed within this general theory of growth and differentiation. As regulatory processes expand, the level of concentrated power increases. Such an increase in mobilization of power, however, depends on expansion of production to generate the material surplus that can be used to finance the mobilization of power (as denoted by the positive signs on the arrows from productive activity to material surplus to concentrated power). It takes resources, after all, to support police, military, and administrative personnel, and as Spencer emphasized, without the expansion of production, the necessary material surplus cannot be generated to consolidate and concentrate power. Power will become even more concentrated, especially around the capacity for coercion and around the administrative structures monitoring conformity, under conditions of threat. Threats can be external, as is the case when societies engage in war or when they compete economically, or internal, especially as inequality and stratification increase. External threat and conflict increase mobilization of coercive power, as indicated by the positively signed arrow from threat, conflict, and competition to concentrated power. External threat also increases the potential for dissolution and disintegration, as emphasized by the positively signed arrow from external threat to dissolution. Turning to internal threats, inequality increases with concentrated power, as elites tax and usurp surplus for their own use and consumption. As inequality increases, people become resentful, which forces political elites to concentrate power even more, in a cycle that can ratchet itself up to the point of causing dissolution (as indicated by the reverse causal arrow from internal threat to logistical loads, back down to dissolution).

Whether from real sources of external threat or from manufactured external threats that political elites use to deflect attention away from inequalities that could generate internal threats, governments often go to war. Success in war often increases the size as well as the cultural diversity of the population and territory to be controlled. These changes—expanded territories to govern, increased size, and diversity of the consolidated populations—all increase the potential for dissolution because logistical loads are compounded: a larger population, per se, raises logistical loads (as denoted by the causal chain from size of territory to size of population to logistical loads). A larger territory presents entirely new logistical loads revolving around how to maintain control (as denoted by the arrow from size of territory to logistical loads). Finally, an increasingly diverse population, especially one that has been conquered and is resentful, poses logistical problems and internal threats (as indicated by the arrows from diversity of population to internal threat and logistical loads). As these logistical loads mount, the potential for dissolution also increases, as do the selection pressures to differentiate new regulatory, operative, and distributive structures. If new structures are differentiated and prove effective, the larger population can be more integrated and can remain viable in its environment. If, however, these structures cannot be generated or prove ineffective, then disintegration is more likely.

As we can see, then, Spencer's ideas can be translated without any real distortion into a complex analytical model. This model, which is more than 100 years old, can still provide new leads for sociological theory. And when converted into propositions or theoretical principles, the model offers many interesting hypotheses, if not laws of human organization.

Spencer's Abstract Theoretical Principles

Ultimately, it is desirable to express a theory as a series of propositions or principles. Spencer's major work is titled *The Principles of Sociology*, and it should not be surprising that the principles are easily extracted. Propositions emphasize key causal relations, and although we lose a sense of the robust direct and reverse causal effects among the forces in the theory, we gain parsimony with propositions. Indeed, as is evident, the model in

Figure 3.5 is complex—perhaps too complex. Translating key causal arguments into a smaller set of principles, as I do below, helps reduce this complexity.

1. The larger a population and the greater its rate of growth, the more intense are the logistical loads and the greater are the selection pressures for differentiation and elaboration of new productive, reproductive, regulatory, and distributive structures.

This law is the core of Spencer's theory; all else in his theoretical scheme follows from this statement of the relationship between population size and growth, on one side, and differentiation along the regulatory, operative (productive and reproductive), and distributive axes on the other. This is one of the basic laws of macro-sociology.

2. The development of new technologies and the differentiation of new structures for gathering resources and converting them into usable commodities (production) will increase with
    A. The size and rate of growth of a population
    B. The degree of access to natural resources, whether a society's own or those of another society
    C. The expansion of distributive capacities, especially those revolving around markets
    D. The consolidation of centers of power that are engaged in low to moderate levels of regulation of productive structures and that are able to avoid prolonged wars with neighboring societies.

This principle on production dynamics emphasizes that new modes of production and distribution as well as new forms of regulation are sought in order to support and coordinate the increased number of people in a society. Moreover, access to natural resources is also important, in two ways. First, the level of available resources is critical; societies without many natural resources will, in general, be less productive than will those with these resources. Second, societies with the power, technology, and distributive facilities to gather resources from afar can expand production, even with relatively few natural resources of their own. Thus, a society's distributive capacities within its own borders or with other societies are an important mediating factor in production. Moreover, Spencer felt that once markets develop to a threshold where they are free and open, encouraging competition and productive innovations, they would increasingly be the engine that drives production. Well developed and open markets, coupled with the infrastructure to move information, people (labor), and resources rapidly, will dramatically increase the demand for new kinds of productive outputs. In addition, this level of development in distributive structures will increase the volume, velocity, and scope of distribution in ways that create pressure to expand production. In Spencer's view, markets would no longer be a place where productive outputs are placed for distribution; rather, they would be the force that dictated how production would be conducted. Power is also very important in production, for, as Spencer consistently argued, low to moderate regulation of distributive and productive processes is conducive to the development of new technologies and productive structures. Too much centralization of power—what he termed "militant societies" (see Table 3.1)—would destroy incentives for new technologies and expansion of the distributive infrastructure as well as high-volume, high-velocity, and far-reaching markets. War is, he felt, the biggest inhibitor of production because it consumes productive capital, removes incentives to technological development outside of war-making machines, and inhibits investments in domestic production. Internal threats can similarly consume resources better devoted to the domestic economy, but never on the scale of war-making against other societies.

3. The differentiation of new reproductive structures for restocking the population, for socializing the population into a common culture, and for sustaining existing members of the population and the structures that organize them increase with

   A. The size and rate of growth of the population
   B. The level of differentiation of social structures
   C. The level of differentiation of culture.

Even though Spencer never directly addressed the question of reproduction, in the contemporary sense of this term, *The Principles of Sociology* is filled with analyses of reproductive structures. He tended to collapse these structures under what he termed "operative" or "sustaining" processes, so it is necessary to tease reproductive processes out of his analysis. For Spencer, differentiation of reproductive structures follows from the differentiation of social structures and culture. The more diverse the roles to be played in different kinds of structures and the more diverse the cultural symbols of a society, the greater are the logistical loads for reproduction and, hence, the more diverse and numerous will be distinctive kinds of reproductive structures.

4. The differentiation of centers of regulatory power will increase with

   A. The size and rate of growth of a population
   B. The material surplus from production
   C. The volume, velocity, and scope of exchange
   D. The level of inequality and internal threat
   E. The level of external threat from the environment, both biophysical and sociocultural
   F. The size of territories to be regulated.

Spencer argued that a larger population required new mechanisms for controlling and coordinating activities. Such structures can emerge, however, only with an increase in production to generate the material surplus to finance coercive and administrative structures engaged in regulation. Threats—whether internal, environmental (such as a natural disaster, famine, or decline in resources), or sociocultural (threats from other societies)—will also increase the level of differentiation of regulatory power, although these threats tend to centralize power (see the next proposition). Distributive structures also increase the differentiation of power because at least some of the infrastructures for markets must be financed and built by government, and although Spencer encouraged a "hands-off" policy by government toward production and markets, he recognized that distinctive power structures had to evolve to regulate many market aspects, such as coining money, enforcing contracts, and regulating crime and fraud. Thus, expanding distribution also will force the differentiation of new kinds of regulatory structures. Finally, Spencer recognized that extended territories pose special logistical loads for regulation, and as the amount of territory to be controlled increases, many distinctive levels and centers of power across the expanded territory will emerge, thus increasing the level of differentiation of government.

5. Power will increasingly be consolidated and centralized with

   A. Threat from any source, whether from biophysical or sociocultural environments, stratification and inequalities, or cultural and ethnic diversity
   B. Failure of existing regulatory structures to coordinate and control productive and distributive processes.

A good portion of Spencer's sociology concerns the degree of power, its causes, and its consequences. Threat will always lead to the mobilization of power, especially its coercive base as well as its administrative base for giving orders and monitoring conformity to directives. Also, when existing levels of power prove ineffective in coordinating and controlling activities, pressures will mount for increased centralization of power.

6. Power will be increasingly decentralized with

   A. High rates of political mobilization against overregulation, supported by liberal ideologies and large numbers of actors
   B. Increasing stagnation in productive and distributive structures.

The argument is that concentrated power, per se, will increasingly be resented, leading to mobilizations against such regulation. But, as Spencer's law on the centralization of power underscores, such mobilizations may be perceived as a threat, leading the political system to concentrate and centralize power even more. Spencer appears to see stagnation in production and markets as a key condition that explains when pressures for decentralizing power will be successful. When the economy is stagnant, the resources for tight regulation become ever more scarce, and Spencer appears to have assumed that political leaders will recognize the necessity to encourage innovation and investment in productive activities, especially when the population is mobilized to demand less regulation. This might have been simply wishful thinking on Spencer's part, but principles 3 through 6 on power give us a sense of the forces involved in the dynamics of consolidation and centralization/decentralization of power. Clearly much more work needs to be done in specifying the conditions under which power is consolidated, centralized, or decentralized, but for his time, Spencer's analysis is rather sophisticated.

7. The probability that a population will disintegrate and cease to be a coherent and distinctive system in its environment increases as logistical loads mount and selection pressures cannot be addressed. Logistical loads and selection pressures will increase with

   A. The size and rate of growth of a population
   B. The degree of cultural diversity in a population
   C. The size of the territory occupied by a population
   D. The level of inequality among members of a population, especially if strata are highly correlated with ethnic cultural diversity
   E. The rate and intensity of conflict with other societies
   F. The level of environmental crises, whether from natural disasters or depletion of resources.

From the publication of *First Principles*, Spencer emphasized that dissolution was part of the process of evolution. True, the long-term trend had been punctuated by collapse and conquests of populations. Thus, within *The Principles of Sociology* are several consistent lines of argument about the conditions under which populations disintegrate. Population size and rate of growth do not automatically lead to differentiation of effective regulatory, operative, or distributive structures. Population diversity, especially cultural and ethnic diversity, can push people away from each other or cause internal conflicts among diverse members of a population. Large territories are difficult to govern, and they pose constant problems of how to distribute information and resources. Populations spread out in space will develop cultural diversity, thus aggravating the logistical loads associated with this phenomenon. Inequalities stemming from too much concentrated power and usurpation of resources will eventually exceed government's capacity for coercive control. War and conflict with other societies always drain resources, lead to stagnation of production, and aggravate inequalities, to say nothing of the possibility of losing a war and being conquered. As Spencer always emphasized, populations must adapt to the natural environment, and moreover, populations can change their environments, often depleting resources and degrading the environment's ability to support productive activities. In addition to environmental depletion and degradation, episodic disasters can destroy a population.

Conclusions

Spencer clearly took seriously the emphasis on "principles" in his *The Principles of Sociology*. These principles are stated discursively in the text, but they are quite easy to spot if one is looking for them. Yet, as with the work of other early masters of theory such as Max Weber, where principles must be pulled from the text, we must be patient. Still, *Principles of Sociology* is not much longer than the collected works of Karl Marx, Max Weber, and Émile Durkheim, and so length alone cannot explain the reluctance of contemporary sociologists to read Spencer. Why, then, the disdain for Spencer?

As I suggested at the outset, Spencer's moral philosophy clearly stigmatized him, especially his view that government should not intervene too extensively to help the unfortunate. Such a view ran counter to the expansion of the welfare state in the twentieth century. This ideology taints Spencer's sociology, and it has clearly made scholars reluctant to give it a fair reading.

Spencer's coining of the phrase "survival of the fittest" and the use of this idea in much of twentieth-century conservative philosophy and, even worse, in the eugenics movement of the last century further stigmatized his sociology. Indeed, those advocating the selective breeding of humans or, alternatively, the natural death of the "less fit" have at times made appeals to Spencer, a fact that certainly has not helped our retrospective view of him.

Spencer also was the supreme generalist at a time when academic disciplines were beginning to specialize. Spencer's sociology is a part of a much larger, almost cosmic, vision of evolution in all domains of the universe. Twentieth-century sociologists were less likely to embrace such grandiose and rather vague pronouncements, and this is even more the case for the discipline today, when hyper-specialization is rapidly occurring.

Spencer's emphasis on evolution as the master societal process was also to get him into trouble. By the second decade of the twentieth century, evolutionary thinking was under heavy attack, and as the supreme evolutionary thinker in the social sciences, Spencer was under constant criticism. When the evolutionary paradigm collapsed and fell into obscurity in the 1920s, so did Spencer's sociology. Even with the revival of evolutionary thinking in sociology in the 1960s, Spencer was never resurrected, except by a few dedicated scholars.

Spencer probably wrote too much. The key ideas of Spencer's sociology must be extracted from thousands of pages, and most sociologists are unwilling to read all this material. Still, if scholars will have the patience to read through these many pages, they will find that Spencer's sociology had many strong points that deserve a rehearing. First, Spencer developed a very sophisticated theory of politics in his sociology. This theory emphasizes that the concentration of power dramatically transforms all other institutional systems, as can be seen by the propositions we have listed in the text, and it sets into motion both geopolitical and dialectical dynamics. Even by today's standards, this portion of Spencer's sociology is rather sophisticated. Indeed, Spencer should be considered a political theorist as much as a functionalist or evolutionary thinker, and if this fact were recognized, perhaps sociologists would be willing to give his work another reading. Second, Spencer's views on the dynamics of differentiation are worth revisiting. The basic relationships among system size, level of differentiation, and integration through interdependence and power do represent some of sociology's most powerful laws. Although more contemporary sociologists have worked with these ideas, they seem to forget from where they came. And third, even though the use of so much data from his *Descriptive Sociology* makes reading *The Principles of Sociology* an arduous task, much can be learned from these materials. Few sociologists have ever documented their arguments with so much ethnographic and historical detail. In some ways, Spencer can serve as a model for how this should be done.

CHAPTER 4

Karl Marx

Industrialization and capitalism destroyed patterns of feudal social relationships that had existed for a millennium, but in Karl Marx's view, these changes had produced a paradoxical result. Industrialization and capitalism meant that not only the means of sustenance but also new amenities could now be available for everyone, and yet only those who owned capital (income-producing assets) were actually benefiting from this increased productive capacity in industrial societies. These capitalists exploited the masses, who lived in great misery and depravity. To remedy this situation, Marx proposed new forms of social arrangements in which everyone's needs could be met. He argued that change was inevitable, with the only question being when it would occur. Throughout his life, Marx served as a participant, organizer, and leader of revolutionary groups dedicated to ending the exploitation of the masses.

Of all the classical sociologists, Marx was unique in that he acted as a revolutionary and a social scientist, a combination that constitutes the greatest weakness in his sociology. His orientation can be summarized in the following way. As a revolutionary, he sought to overthrow the existing order and substitute collective control of society by the people so that, in a cooperative context, they could be free to develop their potential as human beings. As a social scientist, he tried to show that such collective control was historically inevitable. According to Marx, history has a direction that can be observed. This direction, he and Engels wrote in *The Communist Manifesto,* will lead inevitably to a communist society in which "the free development of each is the condition for the free development of all."[1] In such a context, Marx believed, the few will no longer exploit the many.

Note: *Much of this chapter is coauthored with Leonard Beeghley.

[1]Karl Marx and Friedrich Engels, "The Communist Manifesto," in *The Birth of the Communist Manifesto,* ed. Dirk Struik (New York: International, 1971), 112.

The German Ideology

The German Ideology was completed in 1846, when Marx was twenty-eight years old and Engels was twenty-six. Much of this rather lengthy book is given over to heavy-handed and satirical polemics against various Young Hegelians, or the fanatical followers of Hegel. The publisher declined to accept the manuscript at the time, perhaps for political reasons, because Marx was already well-known as a radical and had been expelled from both Germany and France, or perhaps because of the arcane writing style. In any case, Marx later recalled, the manuscript was "abandoned to the gnawing criticism of the mice . . . since we had achieved our main purpose—self-clarification."[2]

Marx opened *The German Ideology* with a bitter attack on Young Hegelians, whom he described at one point as engaging in "theoretical bubble blowing."[3] For Young Hegelians, Marx observed, great conflicts and revolutions take place only in the realm of thought because no buildings are destroyed and no one is injured or dies. Conflicts revolve around the dialectics of mind games rather than the material world, where conflict really matters. Thus, despite their excessive verbiage, Marx believed, Young Hegelians merely criticized the essentially religious nature of Hegel's work and substituted their own negative religious canons. "It is an interesting event we are dealing with," he said caustically, "the putrescence of the absolute spirit."[4] In the process of debunking Young Hegelians' writings, however, Marx developed an understanding of social theory, a description of the characteristics of all societies, and a theoretical methodology for understanding those characteristics.

The Nature of Social Theory

As an alternative to the "idealistic humbug" of Young Hegelians, Marx argued that theoretical analyses should be empirically based. Social theory, he said, should be grounded on the "existence of living human individuals," who must survive, often in a relatively hostile environment.[5] This orientation is necessary because human beings are unlike other animals in that they manipulate the environment to satisfy their needs. They "begin to produce their means of subsistence, a step which is

---

[2]Karl Marx, "Preface," in *A Contribution to the Critique of Political Economy* (New York: International, 1970), 22.

[3]Karl Marx and Friedrich Engels, *The German Ideology* (New York: International, 1947), 3. Only Part 1 of the text is translated, and it is generally assumed that Engels' contribution to this portion of the book was minimal. This is mainly because the text appears to be an elaboration of Marx's "Theses on Feuerbach," which he outlined for himself in 1845; see *The Marx-Engels Reader,* ed. Robert C. Tucker (New York: Norton, 1978), 43–45. In addition, Engels stated repeatedly that Marx had already developed his conception of history before their collaboration. Therefore, in what follows, we will generally refer only to Marx.

[4]Marx and Engels, *German Ideology,* 3.

[5]Ibid., 7.

conditioned by their physical [that is, social] organization."[6] This idea implies that people are "conscious"—that is, they are capable of self-reflective thought. Thus, human beings are also unlike other animals in that they can look at themselves and their environment and then act rationally in their own interests. Consciousness thus arises from experience. Such an argument directly opposed Hegel's idealism, in which notions of morality, religion, and all other forms of awareness are considered to exist independently of human beings. Put in modern language, Marx was asserting that people produce their ideas about the world in light of the social structures in which they live and the experiences that they have in these structures. Further, as social structures change, the content of people's ideas (their consciousness) changes as well. In breaking with the idealists in this way, Marx did not imply a simple-minded materialist orientation. He did not see the human mind as a passive receptacle; rather, he saw it as active, both responding to and changing the material world.

According to Marx, then, social theory should focus on how people influence and are influenced by their material conditions: for example, their degree of hunger, degree of protection from the environment, opportunity to enjoy the amenities of life, and ability to realize their creative potential. This emphasis constitutes a fundamental epistemological break with idealism. In effect, Marx stood Hegel "right side up" by transforming philosophy into an empirical social science.

The Characteristics of All Societies

Based on this vision of social theory, Marx emphasized that theoretical analyses should be oriented to what he called "the real process of production."[7] The first characteristic of all societies is that human beings, unlike other animal species, produce sustenance from the environment to live and thereby "make history." Marx noted that human "life involves before anything else eating and drinking, a habitation, clothing, and many other [material] things."[8] Such needs are satisfied by employing technology to manipulate the environment in some socially organized manner. For Marx, this clearly implied that social theory has to deal with more than just ideas. It must be grounded in "the existence of living human individuals," who have material needs that must be satisfied through production. From this angle of vision, the task of social theory explains how people "produce their means of subsistence."

The second characteristic of all societies is that people create new needs over time. Need creation occurs because production (or work) always involves the use of tools or instruments of various sorts and these tools are periodically improved, yielding more and better consumer goods. Thus, Marx said, the processes of production and consumption always feed back on each other in a cumulative fashion, so that as one set of needs is satisfied, new ones emerge.[9] See Figure 4.1 for a graphic representation.

---

[6]Ibid., 8.

[7]Ibid., 18.

[8]Ibid., 16.

[9]Marx, "Introduction," in *A Contribution to the Critique of Political Economy,* 188–217.

Figure 4.1　Marx's View of Human Needs, Production and History

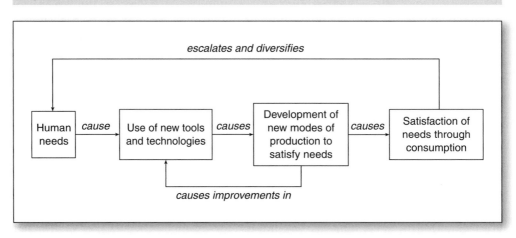

The process of need creation involves the desire not only for improved food, clothing, and shelter but also for the various amenities of life. Marx observed that in the production and consumption of goods beyond the minimum necessary for survival—what are called amenities—people become "civilized" in the sense that they can distinguish their uniquely human characteristics from those of other species. Thus, in *The Economic and Philosophic Manuscripts* (written in 1844), he described productive work as serving a dual purpose: (1) to satisfy physical needs and (2) to express uniquely human creativity. According to Marx, this duality is why other animals work only to satisfy an "immediate physical need, whilst man produces even when he is free from physical need and only truly produces in freedom therefrom."[10] Unfortunately, Marx believed, most people are prevented from expressing their human potential through work because the exploitation and alienation inherent in the division of labor prevent it.

The third characteristic of all societies is that production is based on a division of labor, which in Marx's writings always implies a hierarchical stratification structure, with its attendant exploitation and alienation. The division of labor means that the tasks that must be done in every society—placating the gods, deciding priorities, producing goods, raising children, and so forth—are divided among the members of that society. But Marx observed that in all societies the basis for this division was private ownership of land or capital, which he called the *means of production.* Private ownership of the means of production produces a stratification system composed of the dominant group, the owners, and the remaining classes arrayed below them in varying degrees of exploitation and alienation. Nonowners are exploited and alienated because they cannot control either the work they do or the products produced. For example, capitalists, not employees, organize a production line to produce consumer goods, and capitalists, not employees, own the finished products. But because employees, whom

---

[10]Karl Marx, *The Economic and Philosophical Manuscripts* (New York: International, 1964), 111.

Marx called *proletarians,* need these products to survive, they are forced to return their wages to the capitalists, who use the money to make more consumer goods and enrich themselves further. In this context, alienation takes the form of a fantastic reversal in which people feel themselves to be truly free only in their animal-like functions—such as eating, drinking, and fornicating, whereas in their peculiarly human tasks, such as work, they do not feel human because they control neither the process nor the result. On this basis, Marx concluded, in capitalism "what is animal becomes human and what is human becomes animal."[11] Thus, paradoxically, the division of labor means that proletarians continually re-create that which enslaves them: control of capital by the few.

In some form or another, Marx argued, exploitation and alienation occur in all societies characterized by private ownership of the means of production. That is, in all societies, members of the subordinate classes are forced to continuously exchange their labor power for sustenance and amenities so they can keep on producing goods to benefit the members of the dominant class. For Marx, this situation implied that social theory had to focus on who benefits from the existing social arrangements by systematically describing the structure of stratification that accompanies private ownership of the means of production. This situation also implied for Marx that only collective ownership could eliminate these problems.

The fourth characteristic of all societies is that ideas and values emerge from the division of labor. Put differently, ideas and values result from people's practical efforts at obtaining sustenance, creating needs, and working together. As a result, ideologies usually justify the status quo. ("Ideologies" are systematic views of the way the world ought to be, as embodied in religious doctrines and political values.) Thus, Marx argued, religious and political beliefs in capitalist societies state that individuals have a right to own land or capital; they have a right to use the means of production for their own rather than for the collectivity's benefit. It is perverse, he noted, for everyone to accept these values even though only a few people, such as landowners and capitalists, can exercise this right.

Marx believed that the values (or *ideologies,* to use his word) characteristic of a society are the tools of the dominant class because they mislead the populace about their true interests. This is why he described religion as "the opium of the masses."[12] He reasoned that religious belief functioned to blind people so they could not recognize their exploitation and their real political interests. Religion does this by emphasizing that salvation, compensation for misery and alienation on earth, will come in the next world. In effect, religious beliefs justify social inequality. For Marx, the fact that ideas and values emerge from the division of labor implies that social theory must focus on both the structural sources of dominant ideas and the extent to which such beliefs influence people.

---

[11]Ibid.

[12]Karl Marx, "A Contribution to the Critique of Hegel's Philosophy of Right," in *Marx Engels Reader,* 16–26, 53–66.

Marx's Theoretical Methodology

The exposition in *The German Ideology* is an early example of Marx's dialectical materialism. Although he did not use this phrase, it expresses the discontinuity and continuity between Hegel and Marx. Marx rejected Hegel by grounding social theory in the real world, where people must satisfy their physical and psychological needs. The term *materialism* denotes this. Having rejected the substance of Hegel's idealism, however, Marx continued to use the Hegelian method of analysis. The term *dialectical* denotes this. In Marx's hands, *dialectical materialism* transforms historical analysis.

Dialectical materialism has four characteristics. First, society is a social structure, or *system*. Marx did not use this modern term, but it means that societies can be seen as having interrelated parts, such as classes, social institutions, cultural values, and so forth. These parts form an integrated whole. Thus, the observer's angle is very important when viewing a society. In tracing the connections among the parts of the stratification system, for example, it can be seen that from one angle a specific label can be applied (e.g., bourgeoisie), whereas from another angle an opposing label can be applied (e.g., proletariat). But there is an inherent connection between the two classes, which is why Marx noted in *The Communist Manifesto* that it was tautologous to speak of wage labor and capital, for one cannot exist without the other. Similarly, this is why he described production and consumption as "identical," or as occurring "simultaneously." He meant that they were parts of a coherent structure, or system, and that there was an inherent connection between them. Furthermore, the process of production and consumption (which today would be called the economy) is connected to stratification. More generally, class relations are reflected in all arenas of social behavior: the economy, kinship, illness and medical treatment, crime, religion, education, and government. Although Marx emphasized the primacy of economic factors, especially ownership of the means of production, his work is not narrowly economic; it is, rather, an analysis of how social structures function and change.

Second, social change is inherent in all societies as people make history by satisfying their ever-increasing needs. For Marx, the most fundamental source of change comes from within societies rather than from outside them. The force behind these internally generated changes is the *contradiction* inherent in the system. Not only are all the parts of society connected, they also contain their own inherent contradictions, which will cause their opposites to develop. For example, as will be described in the next section, Marx argued that feudalism contained within itself the social relations that eventually became capitalism. Similarly, in the *Manifesto* and *Capital,* Marx contended that capitalism contained within itself the social relations that would inevitably engender a new form of society: communism.

Third, social change evolves in a recognizable direction. For example, just as a flower is inherent in the nature of a seed, so the historical development of a more complex social structure, such as capitalism, is inherent in the nature of a less complex one, such as feudalism. The direction of history is from less complex to more complex social structures, which is suggested by the pattern of need creation depicted earlier. Marx was a child of the Enlightenment, and he believed in the inevitability of human progress.[13] He had a vision of evolutionary development toward a utopian end point. For Marx, this end point was a communist society.

Fourth, freely acting people decisively shape the direction of history given the predictable patterns of opposition and class conflict that develop from the contradictions in society. As with all Marx's concepts, his use of the term *class* is sometimes confusing. The key to understanding this concept lies in the idea of opposition, for he always saw classes as opposed to one another. It should be remembered, however, that this opposition occurs within a stratification structure; classes are opposed but still connected.[14]

Thus, regardless of their number or composition, the members of different classes are enemies because they have opposing interests. This result was not a matter of choice but, rather, of location within the stratification structure. For example, if the position of an aggregate of people makes obtaining food and shelter a constant problem and if these people cannot control their own activities or express their human potential, they are clearly in a subordinate position in relationship to others. In their alienation, they have an interest in changing the status quo, whether they are aware of it or not. On the other hand, if the position of an aggregate of people is such that their basic needs are satiated, if they can control their daily activities, and if they can devote themselves to realizing their human potential, such people have an interest in preserving the status quo. Marx believed that these opposing interests cannot be reconciled.

Hence, given knowledge of the division of labor in capitalism, the differing interests and opportunities of the proletarians and capitalists are predictable, as is the generation of class conflict. The latter, however, is a matter of choice. History does not act, people do. From this point of view, Marx's theoretical task was to identify the social conditions under which people will recognize their class interests, unite, and produce a communist revolution. As will become clear later, Marx believed that he had achieved this goal. The important point to remember is that his theoretical methodology combines determinism, or direction, with human freedom: a communist revolution is a predictable historical event ushered in by freely acting people who recognize and act in their own interests.

Dialectical materialism can thus be summarized in the following way. Within any society, a way of producing things exists, both for what is produced and for the social organization of production. Marx called this aspect of society the *productive forces*.[15] In all societies, the productive forces are established and maintained through a division of labor. Those few who own the means of production make up the dominant class, which benefits from the status quo. The masses make up the

---

[13]Robert A. Nisbet, *Social Change and History* (New York: Oxford University Press, 1968).

[14]Bertell Ollman, "Marx's Use of 'Class,'" *American Journal of Sociology* 73 (March 1968):573–580.

[15]Sometimes Marx uses the phrase *forces of production* narrowly, so that it refers only to the instruments used in the productive process. Sometimes, however, he uses the phrase so that it refers to both the instruments used in production and the *social organization* that accompanies their use. By social organization is meant not only the organization of work (as in factories) but also family life, law, politics, and all other institutions. This tactic occurs with many of Marx's key concepts. See Bertell Ollman, *Alienation: Marx's Conception of Man in Capitalist Society* (New York: Oxford University Press, 1976).

subordinate class (or classes). They are exploited and alienated because they have little control over their lives, and hence they have an interest in change. Over time, new ways of producing things are devised, whether based on advances in technology, changes in the way production is organized, or both. Such new forces of production better satisfy old needs and stimulate new ones. They are in the hands of a new class, and they exist in opposition to current property relationships and forms of interaction. Over the long run, the tension between these opposing classes erupts into revolutionary conflict, and a new dominant class emerges.[16]

The end point of this continuum is a communist society, a communal social organization in which there is collective control of the means of production (in today's societies, this is capital) so that people, acting cooperatively, can be free. In such a social context, Marx argued, exploitation and alienation will not exist because the division of labor will not be based on private ownership of property.

The German Ideology constitutes the first presentation of Marx's theory. It is, however, incomplete. It does not, for example, raise one of the most crucial issues: How are the oppressed proletarians to become aware of their true interests and seize control of the society for the benefit of all? This and other problems of revolutionary action are dealt with in *The Communist Manifesto*.

The Communist Manifesto

In 1847, Marx and Engels joined the Communist League, which they soon dominated. Under their influence, the League's goal became the overthrow of bourgeois society and the establishment of a new social order without classes and private property. To this end, Marx and Engels decided to compose a manifesto that would publicly state the Communist League's doctrines. The result constitutes one of the greatest political pamphlets ever written.

The *Manifesto* opens with a menacing phrase that immediately reveals its revolutionary intent: "A specter is haunting Europe—the specter of Communism. All the Powers of old Europe have entered into a holy alliance to exorcise this specter." In a political context where opposition parties of all political orientations were called communist, Marx wrote, it was time for the communists themselves to "meet this nursery tale of the specter of Communism with a Manifesto of the party itself."[17] The remainder of the *Manifesto* is organized into four sections, which are summarized as follows.

Bourgeoisie and Proletarians

Marx presented his theoretical and political position early in the text when he emphasized, "The history of all hitherto existing society is the history of class struggles." He continued by observing that in every era

---

[16]See Richard Appelbaum, "Marx's Theory of the Falling Rate of Profit: Towards a Dialectical Analysis of Structural Change," *American Sociological Review* 43 (February 1978):73–92.

[17]Marx and Engels, *Communist Manifesto,* 87.

oppressor and oppressed stood in constant opposition to one another [and] carried on an uninterrupted, now hidden, now open fight, a fight that each time ended either in a revolutionary reconstitution of society at large or in the common ruin of the contending classes.[18]

Put differently, Marx believed that in every social order those who own the means of production always oppress those who do not. Thus, in his view, bourgeois society merely substituted a new form of oppression and, hence, struggle in place of the old feudal form. Marx argued, however, that bourgeois society was distinctive in that it had simplified class antagonisms, because the "society as a whole is splitting up more and more into two great hostile camps, into two great classes directly facing each other: Bourgeoisie and Proletariat."[19] Because one class owns the means of production and the other does not, the two have absolutely opposing interests: the bourgeoisie in maintaining the status quo and the proletariat in a complete reorganization of society so that production can benefit the collectivity as a whole. This situation reflected a long historical process. As in *The German Ideology,* the analysis in the *Manifesto* is an example of Marx's dialectical materialism.

Historically, Marx argued, capitalism emerged inexorably from feudalism. "From the serfs of the Middle Ages sprang the chartered burghers of the earliest towns. From these burgesses the first elements of the bourgeoisie [capitalists] were developed."[20] Such changes were not historical accidents, Marx said, but the inevitable result of people acting in their own interests. The rise of trade and exchange, stimulated by the European discovery of the Americas, constituted new and powerful productive forces, which faced a feudal nobility that had exhausted itself by constant warfare. Further, as they were increasingly exposed to other cultures, the members of the nobility wanted new amenities, and so they enclosed the land to raise cash crops, using new methods of production. It should be recalled that production and consumption reciprocally affect each other—they are part of a social system—and they are tied to the nature of the class structure. As this historical process occurred, the serfs were forced off the land and into the cities, where they had to find work.

During this same period, a merchant class arose. At first the nascent capitalists existed to serve the needs of the nobility by facilitating trade and exchange. Over time, however, capital became the dominant productive force. This process occurred as new sources of energy (such as steam) were discovered, as machines were invented and used to speed up the production process, and as the former serfs were pressed into service in the new industries as wage laborers. The result, Marx noted, was that in place of feudal retainers and patriarchal ties, there was "left no other nexus between man and man than naked self-interest, than callous 'cash payment.'"[21]

---

[18]Ibid., 88.

[19]Ibid., 89.

[20]Ibid., 90.

[21]Ibid., 91.

The *Manifesto* summarizes the situation in the following way:[22]

> The feudal system of industry, under which industrial production was monopolized by closed guilds, now no longer sufficed for the growing wants of the new markets. The manufacturing system took its place; the guild masters were pushed on one side by the manufacturing middle class; division of labor between the different corporate guilds vanished in the face of division of labor in each single workshop.
>
> Meantime, the markets kept ever growing, the demand ever rising. Even manufacture no longer sufficed. Thereupon steam and machinery revolutionized industrial production. The place of manufacture was taken by the giant, modern industry, the place of the industrial middle class by industrial millionaires, the leaders of whole industrial armies, the modern bourgeois.
>
> We see then: The means of production and of exchange, on whose foundation the bourgeoisie built itself up, were generated in feudal society. At a certain stage in the development of these means of production and of exchange, the conditions under which feudal society produced and exchanged, the feudal organization of agriculture and manufacturing industry, in one word, feudal relations of property, became no longer compatible with the already developed productive forces; they became so many fetters. They had to be burst asunder, they were burst asunder.

Thus, the rise of capitalism meant that the forces of production were revolutionized, and therefore, the class structure changed as well. Marx said that although these developments had been the result of freely acting people pursuing their self-interests, they had also been predictable—indeed, inevitable—historical events. Furthermore, because of the rise of capitalism, the class structure became simplified. Now there existed a new oppressed class, the proletarians, who had to sell their labor to survive. Because these people could no longer produce goods at home for their own consumption, they constituted a vast exploited and alienated workforce that was constantly increasing in size. Opposed to the proletarians was a new oppressor class, the bourgeoisie (or capitalists), as a few former artisans and petty burghers became entrepreneurs and eventually grew wealthy. These people owned the new productive forces on which the proletarians depended.

Marx then described the truly revolutionary nature of the capitalist mode of production. As a result of the Industrial Revolution, the bourgeoisie "has accomplished wonders far surpassing Egyptian pyramids, Roman aqueducts, and gothic cathedrals; it has conducted expeditions that put into the shade all former Exoduses of nations and crusades."[23] For the bourgeoisie to exist, Marx predicted, it must constantly develop new instruments of production and thereby create new needs that manufactured products can fill. As this process occurs, the bourgeoisie also seizes political power in each country, so that "the executive of the modern

---

[22]Ibid., 90, 94.

[23]Ibid., 92.

state is but a committee for managing the common affairs of the whole bourgeoisie."[24]

Having described the great historical changes accompanying the rise of capitalism, Marx then made two of his most famous predictions concerning the ultimate demise of the capitalist system. First, capitalism is inherently unstable. Periods of economic growth and high employment are followed by economic decline and unemployment. For Marx, these cycles—what today we call the "business cycle"—are endemic to capitalism. Capitalists and proletarians cannot escape them because eventually too many goods are produced relative to the demand for them, causing production to be cut back and thereby forcing capitalists to lay off labor. Once this process begins, it accelerates as those who have been laid off can no longer afford to purchase goods, pushing capitalists to terminate the employment of even more workers, in an escalating cycle that can lead to an economic depression. Capitalists try to avoid this cycle in many ways. For example, they may destroy older products and sell only new ones, they may try to eliminate their competitors and thus exploit their markets more efficiently, and they may seek new markets. Try as they might, however, they cannot escape the inherent tendency of capitalist economies to experience recessions and depressions. As proletarians' lives are made more miserable by these circumstances, they begin to sense that their interests do not reside with capitalists, leading Marx to make his second great prediction.

Marx's second prediction was that "the modern working class, the proletarians" would become increasingly impoverished and alienated under capitalism. Because they could no longer be self-supporting, the proletarians had become "a class of laborers who live only so long as they find work, and who find work only so long as their labor increases capital."[25] Thus, in a context characterized by the extensive use of machinery owned by others, proletarians have no control over their daily lives or the products of their activities. Each person becomes, in effect, a necessary but low-priced appendage to a machine. In this situation, Marx said, even women and children are thrown into the maelstrom. Thus, under capitalism, human beings are simply instruments of labor whose only worth is the cost of keeping them minimally fed, clothed, and housed. Confronted with their own misery, Marx predicted, proletarians will ultimately become class conscious and overthrow the entire system, especially as they live through cycles of recession and depression where their lives are made increasingly miserable.

The rise of the proletariat as a class proceeds with great difficulty, however, primarily because individual proletarians are forced to compete among themselves. For example, some are allowed to work in the capitalists' factories, and others are not. Within the factories, a few are allowed to work at somewhat better-paying or easier jobs, but most labor at lower-paying and more difficult tasks. After work, proletarians with too little money still must compete with one another for the inadequate food, clothing, and shelter that are available to people in their distressed situation. Under these competitive conditions, it is difficult to create class consciousness. Marx showed, however, that as the bourgeoisie introduce improvements in education,

---

[24]Ibid., 91.

[25]Ibid., 96.

force the proletarians to become better educated (in order to work the machines), and drag them into the political arena, proletarians' ability to recognize the source of their exploitation increases. But this process is slow and difficult; when workers did revolt, they usually directed their attacks against the instruments of production rather than the capitalists. When they did organize, the proletarians were often co-opted into serving the interests of the bourgeoisie.[26]

With the development of large-scale industry, the proletariat constantly increases in size. Like many other observers of nineteenth-century society, Marx predicted that the number of working-class people would continually increase as elements of the lower middle class—artisans, shopkeepers, and peasants—were gradually absorbed into it. Furthermore, he believed that even those in professions such as medicine, law, science, and art would increasingly become wage laborers. Modern industry thus sweeps aside all the skills of the past, creating but two great classes.

The revolutionary development of the proletariat would, Marx argued, be aided by the fact that it was becoming increasingly urban; hence its members were better able to communicate with one another. Further, they were becoming better educated and politically sophisticated, partly because the bourgeoisie constantly dragged them into the political arena. Although the proletarians' efforts at organizing against the bourgeoisie were often hindered, Marx believed that they are destined to destroy capitalism because the factors mentioned here would stimulate the development of their class consciousness.

Proletarians and Communists

As Marx expressed it, the major goal of the communists could be simply stated as the abolition of private property. After all, as he noted, under capitalism nine-tenths of the population has no property anyway. As might be imagined, the bourgeoisie were especially critical of this position. But Marx felt that just as the French Revolution had abolished feudal forms of private property in favor of bourgeois forms, so the communist revolution would abolish bourgeois control over capital, without substituting a new form of private ownership. Marx emphasized, however, that the abolition of the personal property of the petty artisan or the small peasant was not at issue. Rather the communists wished to abolish bourgeois "capital, i.e., that kind of property which exploits wage labor and which cannot increase except upon condition of begetting a new supply of wage labor for fresh exploitation."[27]

To change this situation, the proletarians periodically organized and rebelled during the nineteenth century. Indeed, shortly after publication of the *Manifesto,* revolts occurred throughout Europe. Even though such efforts were always smashed, Marx believed that the proletariat was destined to rise again, "stronger, firmer, mightier," ready for the final battle.

---

[26]See Karl Marx, "The Civil War in France," in Karl Marx and Friedrich Engels, *Selected Works* (Moscow, Russia: Progress, 1969), 178–244. Marx shows here how the proletarians actively participated in subjecting other classes to the rule of the bourgeoisie.

[27]Marx and Engels, *Communist Manifesto,* 104.

Marx viewed this process as an inevitable evolutionary development. In the *Manifesto,* Marx emphasized that "the theoretical conclusions of the Communists . . . express, in general terms, actual relations springing from an existing class struggle, from an historical movement going on under our very eyes."[28] According to Marx, just like the feudal nobility before it, "the Bourgeoisie [has] forged the weapons that bring death to itself." This process occurred because the productive forces of capitalism make it possible for all people to satisfy their needs and realize their human potential. For this possibility to occur, Marx contended, productive forces must be freed from private ownership and allowed to operate for the common good. Furthermore, the bourgeoisie has also "called into existence the men who are to wield those weapons—the modern working class—the proletarians." Marx believed that the working classes in all societies would, because of their exploitation and alienation, eventually bring about a worldwide communist revolution.

Although Marx did not say much about the future, he knew that the transition to communism would be difficult, probably violent. This is because the communists aimed at destroying the core of the capitalist system: private ownership of the means of production. Marx believed that to achieve this goal, the means of production had to be "a collective product" controlled by the "united action of all members of the society." Such cooperative arrangements are not possible in bourgeois society, with its emphasis on "free" competition and its apotheosis of private property. Collective control of the society, Marx thought, is only possible under communism, where capital can be used as a means to widen, enrich, and promote the existence of the laborer. This drastic change required a revolution.

The first step in a working-class revolution, Marx argued, would be for the proletariat to seize control of the state. After attaining political supremacy, the working class would then wrest "all capital from the bourgeoisie," "centralize all instruments of production in the hands of the state," and "increase the total of productive forces as rapidly as possible."[29] Furthermore, the following measures would also be taken in most countries:

1. Abolition of private ownership of land

2. A heavy progressive income tax

3. Abolition of all rights of inheritance

4. Confiscation of the property of emigrants and rebels

5. Centralization of credit and banking in the hands of the state

6. Centralization of communication and transportation in the hands of the state

7. State ownership of factories and all other instruments of production

8. Equal liability of all to labor

---

[28]Ibid., 103–104.

[29]Ibid., 111.

9. Combination of agricultural and manufacturing industries to abolish the distinction between town and country

10. Free public education for all children and abolition of child labor

Marx understood perfectly that these measures could only be implemented arbitrarily, and he forecast a period of temporary communist despotism in which the Communist party acted in the interests of the proletariat as a whole. In an essay written many years after the *Manifesto*, Marx labeled this transition period the "revolutionary dictatorship of the proletariat."[30] Ultimately, however, his apocalyptic vision of the transition to communism was one in which people would become free, self-governing, and cooperative instead of alienated and competitive. They would no longer be mutilated by a division of labor over which they had no control. "The public power will lose its political character," Marx wrote. "In place of the old bourgeois society with its classes and class antagonisms, we shall have an association in which the free development of each is the condition for the free development of all."[31] It is a splendid vision; unfortunately, it is not that of the sorcerer but of the sorcerer's apprentice.

Socialist and Communist Literature

In the third section of the *Manifesto*, Marx attacked the political literature of the day. He recognized that in all periods of turmoil and change, some inevitably desire to return to times past or to invent fantastic utopias as the way to solve humankind's ills. He believed that such dreams were, at best, a waste of time and, at worst, a vicious plot on the part of reactionaries. Thus, this section of the *Manifesto* is a brief critique of socialist literature as it then existed. He classified this literature as (a) reactionary socialism (including here feudal socialism, petit bourgeois socialism, and German "true" socialism); (b) conservative, or bourgeois, socialism; and (c) critical-utopian socialism.

Reactionary Socialism. Because the bourgeoisie had supplanted the feudal nobility as the ruling class in society, the remaining representatives of the aristocracy attempted revenge by trying to persuade the proletarians that life had been better under their rule. Marx characterized this literature as "half lamentation, half lampoon; half echo of the past, half menace of the future" and said that their efforts were misbegotten primarily because the mode of exploitation was different in an industrial context and a return to the past was not possible.

Petit bourgeois socialism is also ahistorical and reactionary. Although its adherents have dissected capitalist society with great acuity, they also have little to offer but a ridiculous return to the past: a situation in which corporate guilds exist in manufacturing and patriarchal relations dominate agriculture. Because they manage to be both reactionary and utopian, which is difficult, this form of socialism

---

[30]Karl Marx, "Critique of the Gotha Program," in Marx and Engels, *Selected Works,* 9–11.

[31]Marx and Engels, *Communist Manifesto,* 112.

always ends "in a miserable fit of the blues." Marx had previously criticized German, or "true," socialism in *The German Ideology*. In the *Manifesto* he merely emphasized again (with typically acerbic prose) that the Germans had written "philosophical nonsense" about the "interest of human nature, of Man in General, who belongs to no class, has no reality, who exists only in the misty realm of philosophical fantasy."[32]

Conservative or Bourgeois Socialism. In Marx's estimation, bourgeois socialists wanted to ameliorate the miserable conditions characteristic of proletarian life without abolishing the system itself. Today, he might call such persons liberals. In any case, Marx believed that this goal was impossible to achieve, for what other conservative socialists did not understand was that the bourgeoisie could not exist without the proletariat and all the abuses inflicted on it.

Critical-Utopian Socialism. Utopian socialists had many critical insights into the nature of society, but Marx believed that their efforts were historically premature because the full development of the proletariat had not yet occurred, and so they were unable to see the material conditions necessary for its emancipation. As a result, they tried to construct a new society independently of the flux of history. For the utopian socialists, the proletarians were merely the most suffering section of society rather than a revolutionary class destined to abolish the existence of all classes.

Communist and Other Opposition Parties

In the final section of the *Manifesto,* Marx described the relationship between the Communist party, representing the most advanced segment of the working class, and other opposition parties of the time. Basically, in every nation the communists were supportive of all efforts to oppose the existing order of things, for Marx believed that the process of opposition would eventually "instill into the working class the clearest possible recognition of the hostile antagonism between the bourgeoisie and the proletariat."[33] In this regard, communists would always emphasize the practical and theoretical importance of private property as the means of exploitation in capitalist society.

Marx, the revolutionary, concluded the *Manifesto* with a final thundering assault on the bourgeoisie:

> The communists disdain to conceal their views and aims. They openly declare that their ends can be attained only by the forcible overthrow of all existing social conditions. Let the ruling classes tremble at a Communist revolution. The proletarians have nothing to lose but their chains. They have a world to win. WORKING MEN OF ALL COUNTRIES, UNITE![34]

---

[32]Ibid., 117.

[33]Ibid., 125.

[34]Ibid., 125.

Marx's View of Capitalism in Historical Context

Reading *The Communist Manifesto* makes it clear that Marx saw human societies as having developed through a series of historical stages, each characterized by its unique class divisions and exploitations. His vision is summarized in Table 4.1.[35]

Marx believed that humans originally lived in hunting-and-gathering societies in which everyone worked at the same tasks to subsist. Private property did not exist, nor did a division of labor. Hence, there were no classes and no exploitation based on class. These societies, in short, were communist, with all members contributing according to their abilities and taking according to their needs. But this primitive communism collapsed, in his rendering of history, as social organization changed.

The first system of exploitation was slavery, in which ownership of other human beings determined rank and position. In slave societies, the interests of owners and slaves were obviously opposed. Slaves had an interest in minimizing daily work demands, improving their living conditions, providing mechanisms by which they could work their way out of bondage, and preventing the inheritability of slave status (so their children would be born free). Slave owners had an interest in maximizing daily work (productivity), minimizing expenditures for food and other maintenance costs, making it difficult for slaves to escape bondage, and ensuring the inheritability of slave status. These conflicts of interest grew more difficult to control as the number of slaves increased and owners competed with one another in ways that increased the plight of the slaves—for example, by demanding more work while reducing food rations. The resulting conflict, in Marx's interpretation, led to a revolution in which slaves rose and abolished the mechanism of their exploitation: the system of slavery.

Slavery was followed by feudalism, in which landless serfs and landowners represented the two great classes. Again, they had opposing interests. Those who owned the land wanted to increase productivity and, over time, to generate more cash income. Serfs were obliged to work the land under the presumption that they would have a share in a portion of its bounty. Their interest was to retain as much control

Table 4.1 Marx's View of the Stages of History

Stage	Oppressing Class	Oppressed Class
Primitive communism	No classes	
Slavery	Slave owners	Slaves
Feudalism	Landowners	Serfs
Capitalism	Bourgeoisie	Proletariat
Socialism	State managers	Workers
Communism	No classes	

[35]Marx, "Preface," in *A Contribution to the Critique of Political Economy*, 22.

over their crops as possible. In countries such as England, feudalism declined because landowners cleared the countryside of peasants to make room for products that would generate cash. For example, sheep were raised not for meat but as a source of raw material for the nascent wool industry. Sheep generated more profit, enabling landowners to purchase valued goods and amenities.

As described in the *Manifesto,* the feudal epoch gave way to capitalism. The name signifies that capital rather than land became the source of exploitation. The two great classes, of course, are the proletariat and the bourgeoisie (capitalists). Capitalists hire proletarians only if they generate profit, which is why capitalists are often described as leeches in Marx's writings. He believed that capitalism would grow like a giant octopus, spreading its tentacles over the entire globe, until nearly all human activity became debased because it was a commodity subject to purchase.

Marx argued that as the contradictions inherent in capitalism grew, it would collapse and be replaced by socialism. He described this stage as a transitory "dictatorship of the proletariat" in which the Communist party would seize control of the state in the name of the working class and expropriate private property (capital). Eventually, he believed, communism would emerge, a classless society in which all would give according to their ability and take according to their needs. The circle would be complete.

This depiction of the stages of history is superficial and, indeed, quite wrong.[36] Remember, however, that Marx did not have access to the data available to modern historians. But Marx's vision does reveal his view of history as successive systems of exploitation in which change emerges from within a society as people with competing interests attempt to satisfy their expanding needs. Thus, it reflects the use of dialectical materialism as a historical method. Moreover, despite its empirical flaws, it is possible to construct a model of stratification and conflict that remains useful.

Marx's Model of Stratification and Class Conflict

Modern readers often have two contrasting reactions when studying *The Communist Manifesto,* neither of which is very clearly articulated. On the one hand, it is easy to see how aspects of Marx's analysis can be applied to societies today. After all, exploitation does occur, and people in different classes do have opposing interests. On the other hand, Marx's political orientation seems both naive and threatening. It appears naive because a truly cooperative industrial society is hard to imagine. It appears threatening because subsequent history shows that a totalitarian government (like that in the former Soviet Union) seems to follow from any application of his ideas. Both these aspects of Marx's thinking reflect his peculiar combination of revolution and theory, which constitutes the greatest weakness in his writings. Nonetheless, it is possible to extrapolate a useful model of social stratification and class conflict from *The Communist Manifesto.*

Before doing so, however, we must recognize that any discussion of Marx's legacy demands a political confession: we are not Marxists. Thus, in what follows,

[36]See Fernand Braudel, *Civilization and Capitalism, 15th–18th Centuries,* vol. 1 (New York: Harper & Row, 1981) and Immanuel Wallerstein, *The Modern World System,* vols. 1 and 2 (New York: Academic, 1980).

the analysis implies nothing about the inevitability of a communist revolution or the transformation of society. Rather, it implies a concern with those ideas in Marx's writings that can still serve sociological theory.

Figure 4.2 displays a model of stratification and class conflict taken from the *Manifesto*. It illustrates some key variables to look for in studying social stratification and conflict, and it implies a modern sociological orientation. Marx asserted that in a stable social structure, goods are produced to satisfy the material needs of people, a process necessitating a division of labor and justified in terms of dominant values. This situation is depicted in the first box in Figure 4.2.

Many past observers have construed Marx's emphasis on productive activity to be a form of economic determinism. But this is too narrow a reading. Marx's point is not that economic activity determines behavior in other areas but, rather, that all social action is conditioned by, and reciprocally related to, the type of productive activity that exists. For example, family life is likely to be different in a hunting-and-gathering society than in an industrial one, as are the forms of government, education, religious beliefs, law, cultural values, and so on. These variations occur, in part, because the way people obtain food, clothing, and shelter differs. Alternatively, in two societies at the same level of economic development, the organization of economic activity is likely to vary, because of differences in religious beliefs, law, family life, and so on.[37]

The recognition of such variation implies an essential sociological orientation: the range of options available to people is shaped by the nature of the society, its way of producing goods, its division of labor, and its cultural values. This orientation is fundamental to sociology today. Some writers like to begin with economic issues, others focus on some aspect of the division of labor (such as the family or criminal

Figure 4.2   Marx's Model of the Generation of Stratification, Class, Conflict, and Change

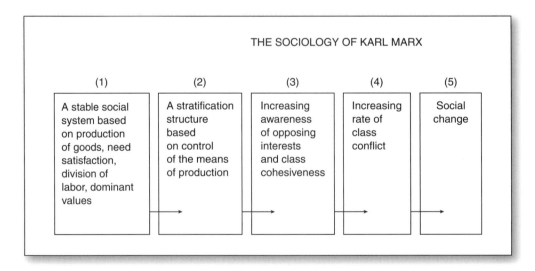

THE SOCIOLOGY OF KARL MARX

(1)	(2)	(3)	(4)	(5)
A stable social system based on production of goods, need satisfaction, division of labor, dominant values	A stratification structure based on control of the means of production	Increasing awareness of opposing interests and class cohesiveness	Increasing rate of class conflict	Social change

---

[37]All of these factors constitute what Marx called the forces of production. See Footnote 15.

justice), and still others start by looking at how values circumscribe behavior. In every case, however, sociologists emphasize that society is a social system with inter-related parts and that social facts circumscribe behavior.

Marx argued—and he is probably correct—that a structure of stratification emerges in all societies based, at least in part, on control of the means of production. This fact, which is depicted in the second box in Figure 4.2, means that the upper class also has the capacity to influence the distribution of resources because it dominates the state. Thus, those who benefit because they control the means of production have an interest in maintaining the status quo, in maintaining the cur-rent distribution of resources, and this interest is pervasive across all institutional arenas. For example, classes in the United States today have different sources of income, they have different political resources, they are treated differently in the criminal justice system, they provide for their children differently, they worship at different churches, and so forth.[38]

In assessing what modern sociologists can learn from Marx, the use of the word *control* rather than *ownership* in Box 2 in Figure 4.2 is an important change because control over the means of production can occur in ways that he did not realize. For example, in capitalist societies the basis of social stratification is private ownership of property, whereas in communist societies the basis of social stratification is the Communist party's control of property. In effect, the Communist party is a new kind of dominant class ushered in by the revolution.[39] In both cases, the group con-trolling the means of production exploits those who do not, while acting to justify its benefits by dominating the state and promulgating its values among the masses, values that legitimize its exploitation of them.

When he looked at social arrangements, Marx always asked a simple question, one that modern sociologists also ask: Who benefits? For example, the long empirical sec-tions of *Capital* (to be examined shortly) are designed to show how attempts at length-ening the working day and increasing productivity also increased the exploitation of the working class to benefit the capitalists. Marx also applied this question to nonobvious relationships. For example, his analysis of the "fetishism of commodities" in the early part of *Capital* shows how people's social relationships are altered by the reification (or worship) of machines and products that commonly occurs in capitalist societies, again to the benefit of capitalists. In effect, Marx teaches modern observers that an emphasis on who is benefiting from social arrangements and public policies can always improve analysis. For example, macroeconomic decisions that emphasize keeping inflation low and unemployment high benefit the middle class and rich in American society at the expense of working people. In every arena—at home, at work, in court, in church, in the doctor's office, and so forth—it is useful to ascertain who is benefiting from current social arrangements.

---

[38]See Leonard Beeghley, *The Structure of Stratification in the United States,* 4th ed. (Boston, MA: Allyn & Bacon, 2005).

[39]See Milovan Djilas, *The New Class* (New York: Praeger, 1965) and *Rise and Fall* (New York: Harcourt Brace Jovanovich, 1985). See also Michael Voslensky, *Nomenklatura: The Soviet Ruling Class* (Garden City, NY: Doubleday, 1986).

The second box in Figure 4.2 is important in another way as well. As emphasized in the *Manifesto,* Marx divided modern capitalist societies into two great classes: bourgeoisie and proletariat. Although he recognized that this basic distinction was too simplistic for detailed analyses, his purpose was to highlight the most fundamental division within these nations. Whenever he chose, Marx would depict the opposed interests and experiences of various segments of society, such as bankers, the "lower middle classes," or the *lumpenproletariat* (the very poor).

Boxes 3, 4, and 5 in Figure 4.2 outline the process of class conflict and social change. Under certain conditions, members of subordinate classes become aware that their interests oppose those of the dominant class. In such a context, Marx taught, class conflict ensues and social change occurs (see later analytical models for a more detailed analysis).

In Marx's work, of course, this process is linked to assumptions about the direction of history and the inevitability of a communist revolution. But this need not be the case. Members of a class can become aware of their true interests and be willing to act politically without seeking a revolutionary transformation of society. This process occurs because, although classes might be opposed to one another in any ongoing social structure, they are also tied to one another in a variety of ways. As Reinhard Bendix argues, citizenship, nationalism, religion, ethnicity, language, and many other factors bind aggregates of people together despite class divisions.[40] Furthermore, to the extent that a subordinate class participates effectively in a political system, as when it obtains some class-related goals, it then acquires an interest in maintaining that system and its place within it. In the United States, at least, most mass movements composed of politically disenfranchised people have sought to get into the system rather than overthrow it. The labor movement, various racial and ethnic movements, and the feminist movement are all examples of this tendency. Thus, although the middle class and the rich dominate the political process in the United States, subordinate classes also have resources that can influence public policy. This militates against a revolutionary transformation of U.S. society.

The emphasis on class conflict that pervades Marx's writings implies what sociologists today call a *structural* approach—that is, a focus on how rates of behavior among aggregates of people are influenced by their location in the society. Their differing locations dictate that classes have opposing interests. Moreover, Marx usually avoided looking at individual action because it is influenced by different variables. Rather, he wanted to know how the set of opportunities (or range of options) that people had influenced rates of behavior. For example, his analysis of the conditions under which proletarians transform themselves into a revolutionary class does not deal with the decision-making processes or cost-benefit calculations of individuals; rather, it shows that urbanity, education, political sophistication, and other factors are the social conditions that will produce class consciousness among the proletarians. Sociology at its best deals with structural variables. Although his work is misbegotten in many ways, Marx was a pioneer in this regard.

---

[40]Reinhard Bendix, "Inequality and Social Structure: A Comparison of Marx and Weber," *American Sociological Review* 39 (April 1974):149–161.

Capital

In *The German Ideology,* Marx attacked the Young Hegelians because they had avoided an empirical examination of social life. In *Capital,* he demonstrated the intent of this criticism by analyzing capitalist society. Using England (and copious amounts of British government data) as his primary example, he sought to show that the most important characteristic of the capitalist mode of production was the constant drive to accumulate capital using exploited and alienated labor. As a result of the need to accumulate capital, Marx argued, the processes of production are incessantly revolutionized, and over the long run, the instability and degradation of people characteristic of capitalist society will lead to its complete transformation. Thus, in contrast with the *Manifesto,* which is a call to arms, *Capital* is a scholarly attempt to show why such a transformation of capitalist society will inevitably occur. As such, *Capital* is much more than a narrow work of economics; it is an analysis of capitalist social structure and its inevitable transformation.

The Labor Theory of Value

Marx sketched the labor theory of value in the opening chapter of *Capital.* Although he approached this issue from what appears to be a strictly economic vantage point—the nature and value of commodities—his discussion turns out to have considerably broader implications. A *commodity* is "an object outside of us, a thing that by its properties satisfies human wants of some sort or another."[41] For his purposes, both the origin of people's wants and the manner in which commodities satisfy them are irrelevant. The more important problem is what makes a commodity valuable. The answer provides the key to Marx's analysis of capitalist society.

Two different sources of value are inherent to all commodities: (1) use value and (2) exchange value, and they denote the fact that commodities are produced to be consumed. For example, people use paper to write on, autos for transportation, and so forth. Clearly, some things that have value, such as air and water, are not produced but are there for the taking (at least they were in the nineteenth century). Marx, however, was primarily interested in manufactured items. Commodities having use value are qualitatively different from one another; for example, a coat cannot be compared with a table. The *exchange value* of commodities provides a basis for comparing the labor time required to produce them. For Marx, the value of commodities is determined by the labor time necessary to produce them. He phrased this *labor theory of value* in the following way:

> That which determines the magnitude of the value of any article is the amount of labour socially necessary, or the labour-time socially necessary for its production. Each individual commodity, in this connection, is to be considered as an average sample of its class. Commodities, therefore, in which equal quantities

---

[41]Karl Marx, *Capital: A Critical Analysis of Capitalist Production,* vol. 1 (New York: International, 1967). The original spelling is retained in all quotations.

of labour are embodied, or which can be produced in the same time, have the same value. The value of one commodity is to the value of any other, as the labour-time necessary for the production of the one is to that necessary for the production of the other. As values, all commodities are only definite masses of congealed labour-time.[42]

Marx supplemented the labor theory of value in five ways. First, different kinds of *useful labor* are not comparable. For example, the tasks involved in producing a coat are qualitatively different from those involved in producing linen. All that is comparable is the expenditure of human labor power in the form of brains, nerves, and muscles. Thus, the magnitude of exchange value is determined by the quantity of labor as indicated by its duration in hours, days, or weeks. Marx called this quantity *simple average labor.*

Second, although different skills exist among workers, Marx recognized that "skilled labour counts only as simple labour intensified, or rather, as multiplied simple labour."[43] Thus, to simplify the analysis, he assumed that all labor was unskilled. In practice, he asserted, people make a similar assumption in their everyday lives.

Third, the value of a commodity differs according to the technology available. With mechanization, the labor time necessary to produce a piece of cloth is greatly reduced (and so, by the way, is the value of the cloth—at least according to Marx). During the initial stages of his analysis, Marx wished to hold technology constant. Therefore, he asserted that the labor time socially necessary to produce an article under the normal conditions of production existing at the time determined the value of a commodity.

Fourth—and this point will become very important later on—under capitalism, labor itself is a commodity with exchange value, just like linen and coats. Thus, "the value of labor power is determined as in the case of every other commodity, by the labour time necessary for the production, and consequently, the reproduction, of this special article."[44]

Fifth, an important implication of the labor theory of value is the development of what Marx called the *fetishism of commodities,* whereby people come to believe that commodities possess human-like attributes and that exploitation as well as alienation arise from relations with machines, as a kind of commodity, rather than from those who own the machines. In capitalist society, the fetishism of commodities manifests itself in two different ways. (1) Machines (as a reified form of capital and a commodity) are seen as exploiting workers, which is something only other people can do. Thus, products that people designed and built and that can be used or discarded at will come to be seen not only as having human attributes but even as being independent participants in human social relationships. (2) When machines are seen to exploit workers, the social ties among people are hidden, so that their ability to understand or alter the way they live is impaired. In this context, Marx wrote, "There is a definite social

---

[42]Ibid., 39–40.

[43]Ibid., 44.

[44]Ibid., 170.

relation between men, that assumes, in their eyes, the fantastic form of a relation between things."[45]

In later chapters of *Capital,* Marx illustrated what he meant by the fetishism of commodities by showing that machines rather than laborers set the pace and style of work and by showing that machines rather than their owners "needed" the night work of laborers so they could be in continuous operation. Hidden behind machines stand their owners, the capitalists, who are the real villains in this exploitive and alienating relationship.

Capitalists have little interest in the use value of the commodities produced by human labor. Rather, it is their exchange value that interests them. Marx writes, "The restless never-ending process of profit-making alone is what [the capitalist] aims at."[46] His term for profit was *surplus value.*

Surplus Value

Because Marx believed that the source of all value was labor, he had to show how laborers create surplus value for capitalists. He did this by distinguishing between "labor" and "labor power." *Labor* is the work people actually do when they are employed by capitalists, whereas *labor power* is the capacity to work that the capitalist purchases from the worker. As Marx put it, "By labour-power or capacity for labour is to be understood the aggregate of those mental and physical capabilities existing in a human being, which he exercises whenever he produces a use-value of any description."[47] Labor power is a commodity just like any other, and it is all the workers have to sell. Marx noted that the laborer, "instead of being in the position to sell commodities in which his labour is incorporated, [is] obliged to offer for sale as a commodity that very labour-power, which exists only in his living self."[48] Furthermore, in a capitalist society, proletarians can sell their labor power only to capitalists, who own the means of production. The two meet, presumably on an equal basis, one to sell labor power and the other to buy it. In reality, Marx saw labor as always at a disadvantage in this exchange.

The value, or selling price, of labor power is "determined, as in the case of any other commodity, by the labour-time necessary for the production, and consequently also the reproduction, of this special article."[49] Thus, labor power is, at least for the capitalist, a mass of congealed labor time—as represented by the cost of food, clothing, shelter, and all the other things necessary to keep the workers returning to the marketplace with their peculiar commodity. Because workers must also reproduce new generations of workers, the cost of maintaining entire families must be included. Having discovered that labor power is the source of surplus value, Marx wanted to calculate its rate. To do so, he distinguished between absolute and relative surplus value.

---

[45]Ibid., 72.

[46]Ibid., 149.

[47]Ibid., 167.

[48]Ibid., 168–169.

[49]Ibid., 170.

Absolute surplus value occurs when capitalists lengthen the working day to increase laborers' productivity. This issue became a matter of conflict throughout the nineteenth century. Hence, Marx spent a considerable amount of space documenting the way in which the early capitalists had forced laborers to work as many hours as possible each day.[50] The data that he presented are significant for two reasons. First, despite their anecdotal quality (by today's standards), they are clearly correct: capitalists sought to extend the working day and keep the proletarians in an utterly depraved condition. For Marx, the effort to lengthen the number of hours that laborers worked was inherent to capitalism; and moreover, proletarians would always be helpless to resist. Second, these remarkable pages of *Capital* drew from historical and governmental data. Indeed, Marx took great satisfaction in using information the British government supplied to indict capitalism.

Relative surplus value occurs when capitalists increase laborers' productivity by enabling them to produce more in the same amount of time. This result can be achieved in two ways, he said. One is to alter the organization of work—for example, by placing workers together in factories. Another, more prevalent as capitalism advances, is to apply advanced technology to the productive process. By using machines, laborers can produce more goods (boots, pens, computers, or anything else) in less time. This means that capitalists can undersell their competitors and still make a profit. Because the reorganization of the workplace and the use of machines were methods of exploiting laborers, they were also the locus of much conflict during the nineteenth century. For such changes meant that proletarians had to work either harder or in a more dehumanizing environment. As in his analysis of absolute surplus value, Marx spent much time documenting capitalists' efforts to increase relative surplus value.[51] By using historical and governmental data, he again showed how productivity had increased steadily through greater exploitation of proletarians.

This analysis of the sources of surplus value provided Marx with a precise definition of exploitation. In his words, "The rate of surplus value is therefore an exact expression of the degree of exploitation of laborer-power by capital, or of the laborer by the capitalist."[52] In effect, surplus value is value created by workers but skimmed off by capitalists, just as beekeepers take a (large) fraction of the honey from the bees that make it.

More broadly, exploitation is not simply a form of economic injustice, although it originates the labor theory of value. The social classes that result from the acquisition of surplus value by one segment of society are also precisely defined. That class accruing surplus value, administering the government, passing laws, and regulating morals is the *bourgeoisie,* and that class being exploited is the *proletariat.*

By discovering the advantages of increasing productivity, Marx thought he had uncovered the hidden dynamic of capitalism that would lead inexorably to increasing exploitation of the proletarians, more frequent industrial crises, and, ultimately, the overthrow of the capitalist system itself. His rationale was that the capitalists'

---

[50]Ibid., 231–312.

[51]Ibid., 336–507.

[52]Ibid., 218.

increased profits were short-lived because other capitalists immediately copied any innovation. Thus, the extra surplus value generated by rising productivity disappeared "so soon as the new method of productivity has become general, and has consequently caused the difference between the individual value of the cheapened commodity and its social value to vanish."[53] The long-term result, Marx predicted, would be the sort of chaos originally described in *The Communist Manifesto.*

The Demise of Capitalism

Marx's description of surplus value was a systematic attempt at showing the dynamics of capitalist exploitation. His next task was to reveal the reasons why, despite its enormous productivity, capitalism contained the seeds of its own destruction. He proceeded in two steps.

The first deals with what he called *simple reproduction.* It occurs as workers continuously produce commodities that become translated into surplus value for capitalists and wages for themselves. Proletarians use their wages in ways that perpetuate the capitalist system. Because capitalists own the means of production and the commodities produced with them, proletarians must give their wages back to the capitalists as they purchase the necessities of life. The capitalists, of course, use that money to make still more money for themselves. In addition, after minimally satisfying their needs, workers return to the marketplace ready to sell their labor power and prepared once again to augment capital by creating surplus value. Over time, then, capitalist society is continuously renewed, because proletarians produce not only commodities, their own wages, and surplus value but also capitalist social relations: exploited and alienated workers on one side and capitalists on the other.

The second step focuses on what Marx called the *conversion of surplus value into capital.* Today, we refer to the reinvestment of capital. Thus, after consuming a small part of the surplus value they obtain from proletarians, capitalists reinvest the remainder to make even more money. As Marx observed, "The circle in which simple reproduction moves, alters its form and . . . changes into a spiral."[54] The result is a contradiction so great that the demise of capitalism and its transformation into "a higher form of society" become inevitable.

On this basis, Marx made three, now famous predictions. The first was that proletarians would be forever prevented from owning or controlling private property, even their own labor. Workers would always be at a disadvantage in labor markets, and as a result, they would sell their labor power and, thereby, give capitalists surplus value. Without this surplus value, the proletariat would never own or control private property. They would have just enough, perhaps, to survive and reproduce the next generation of exploited labor. Yet, paradoxically, laborers have not been defrauded—at least according to capitalist rules of the game—for as we saw earlier, capitalists merely pay laborers for the value of their commodity, labor power. Moreover,

---

[53]Ibid., 319.

[54]Ibid., 581.

because proletarians have only labor power to sell, they have little choice but to participate according to the capitalists' rules.

Marx's second prediction was that proletarians would become increasingly impoverished and that an industrial reserve army of poor people would be created. This outcome would increasingly occur as capitalists used ever more machines in the factories to make labor more productive and lower the price of goods; as a result, fewer laborers would be needed, and their labor power could be purchased at a lower price. Thus, Marx predicted not only that proletarians would continuously reproduce their relations with capitalists—that is, selling their labor and making profits for capitalists—but also that they would produce the means by which they were rendered a superfluous population, forced to work anywhere, anytime, for any wages. Under these extreme conditions, Marx believed, proletarians will become a self-conscious revolutionary class.

Marx's third prediction was that the *rate of profit* would fall and bring on industrial crises of ever greater severity. As capitalists compete with each other, the prices of commodities would have to fall to the point where it was not possible to make a profit. Even more efficient organization of work or the adoption of new technologies reducing costs for capitalists would not, in the end, keep profits from falling. As Marx emphasized, competitors would soon copy each new innovation, thereby eroding any pricing advantages. Yet the cutthroat competition would continue, forcing capitalists to lower prices relative to costs. Eventually, an insurmountable crisis would begin to emerge: capitalists would have increasing problems generating profits. And the fact that capitalists had laid off workers as they adopted new technologies would aggravate this situation, thus diminishing the ability of workers to buy commodities at any price. As an outcome, capitalism would fall. The contradictions built into its very nature, Marx felt, would increasingly disrupt the operation of the capitalist system, while at the same time making the proletariat more aware of their interests in overthrowing the bourgeoisie. Indeed, capitalism is locked into several self-destructive cycles, described in Table 4.2. Thus, according to Marx, the logic of capitalist development will produce the conditions necessary for its overthrow: an industrial base along with an impoverished and class-conscious proletariat. Ultimately, these dispossessed people will usher in a classless society in which production occurs for the common good.

Capitalism in Historical Context

Marx's analysis of capitalism presupposed that it was an ongoing social system. Thus, in the final pages of *Capital,* he once again sketched the origins of capitalism, which he now called the process of *primitive accumulation.* We should recall that capitalist social relations occur only under quite specific circumstances; that is, the owners of money (the means of production), who desire to increase their holdings, confront free laborers, who have no way of obtaining sustenance other than by selling their labor power. Thus, to understand the origins of capitalist social relations, Marx had to account for the rise of both the proletariat and the bourgeoisie. Typically, he opted for a structural explanation.

Table 4.2   Marx's Views on Why Capitalism Would Collapse

1. Capitalists must exploit labor—that is, extract surplus value from labor power—to make profits. This exploitation cannot be hidden from workers, especially as capitalists continuously increase the rate of exploitation.

2. Capitalists must compete with each other, forcing them to lower prices and to find new ways to reduce costs to maintain a profit. As they seek to find new ways to lower costs, capitalists gain only a short-term advantage until competitors copy these cost-cutting efforts; but this increases the longer-term likelihood that the proletariat will become aware of their interests.

    a. As capitalists build larger factories to take advantage of the cost benefits that come with "economies of scale," workers congregate so that they can better communicate their grievances with each other and form a more effective revolutionary force.
    b. As capitalists adopt new technologies to reduce their reliance on labor, unemployment increases, which makes labor more hostile to capitalists and also reduces the demand for the commodities produced by capitalists.
    c. As capitalists copy each other's innovations, a new round of price competition occurs, eventually creating a declining rate of profit, which begins to destroy capitalist enterprises.

3. Capitalism will always overproduce commodities relative to demand, causing recessions and depressions, which make workers even more aware of their misery and of who is to blame.

According to Marx, the modern proletariat arose because self-supporting peasants were driven from the land (and from the guilds) and transformed into rootless and dependent urban dwellers. This process began in England during the fifteenth and sixteenth centuries and then spread throughout Western Europe. Using England as his example, Marx argued that this process had begun with the clearing of the old estates by breaking up feudal retainers, robbing peasants of the use of common lands, and abolishing their rights of land tenure under circumstances he described as "reckless terrorism." In addition, Marx argued, one of the major effects of the Protestant Reformation was "the spoliation of the church's property" by its conversion into private property—illegally, of course. Finally, the widespread theft of state land and its conversion into privately owned property ensured that nowhere in England could peasants continue to live as they had during medieval times. In all these cases (although this analysis is clearly too simplistic), the methods used were far from idyllic, but they were effective, and they resulted in the rise of capitalist agriculture capable of supplying the needs of a "free" proletariat. Further, given that they had nowhere to go, thousands of displaced peasants became beggars, robbers, and vagabonds. Hence, throughout Western Europe, beginning in the sixteenth century, there was "bloody legislation against vagabondage," with severe sanctions against those who would not work for the nascent capitalists who were then emerging.

Marx believed that the emergence of the capitalist farmer and the industrial capitalist occurred concomitantly with the rise of the modern proletariat. Beginning in the fifteenth century, those who owned or controlled land typically had guarantees of long tenure, could employ the newly "freed" workers at very low wages, and benefited from a rise in the price of farm products. In addition, they were able to increase farm production, despite the smaller number of people working the land, through the use of improved methods and equipment, which increased cooperation among workers in the farming process and concentrated land ownership in fewer hands. Thus, primitive accumulation of capital could occur.

Marx believed that industrial capitalism had developed as the result of a variety of interrelated events. First, he emphasized, usury and commerce existed throughout antiquity—despite laws against such activity—and laid a basis for the primitive accumulation of capital to occur. Second, the exploration and exploitation of the New World brought great wealth into the hands of just a few people. In this regard, Marx pointed especially to the discovery of gold and silver, along with the existence of native populations that could be exploited. Finally, he noted the emergence of a system of public credit and its expansion into an international credit system. On this basis, he claimed, capitalism emerged in Western Europe.

Marx's Theoretical Legacy

Karl Marx considered himself a general theorist of history, portraying the evolution of society as a series of inevitable conflicts between superordinates and subordinates in the system of stratification. Although he sought to develop theoretical principles for *each* great epoch of human evolution—that is, primitive communism, slavery, feudalism, capitalism, and communism—a more general theory that transcends any historical period can be found in his work. To outline Marx's more general theory, I will first model the theory and then translate it into a series of highly theoretical principles. While Marx himself, and certainly most Marxist scholars today, would abhor this effort, I believe that Marx's ultimate contribution to sociology resides in this general theory. Moreover, by presenting Marx's theory in more formal terms, we can perhaps see where his predictions about the collapse of capitalism and the rise of communism go wrong. We might add that, at a time when the impact of Marxism as a political force is receding, the conversion of Marx's ideas to a more general theory provides one way to save the powerful theoretical legacy that Marx left to sociology.

Marx's Underlying Causal Model**

The General Model of History and Evolution. In Figure 4.3, we outline the general causal model that can be gleaned from Marx's discursive text. In presenting Marx's ideas in this form, I have made his concepts more abstract, converted them into variables, and outlined the direct and reverse causal connections among the forces denoted by the concepts listed in each box. I have had to make many inferences, but nonetheless, the model represents Marx's argument once it is taken out of historical context.

Starting at the far left of the model, Marx saw a series of fundamental relationships among human needs, production, and technology. Human needs ultimately drive

---

Note: **To protect my coauthor in this chapter from abuse for what may be perceived as too critical a stance, I accept responsibility for this last section.

Figure 4.3 Marx's View of Social Organization

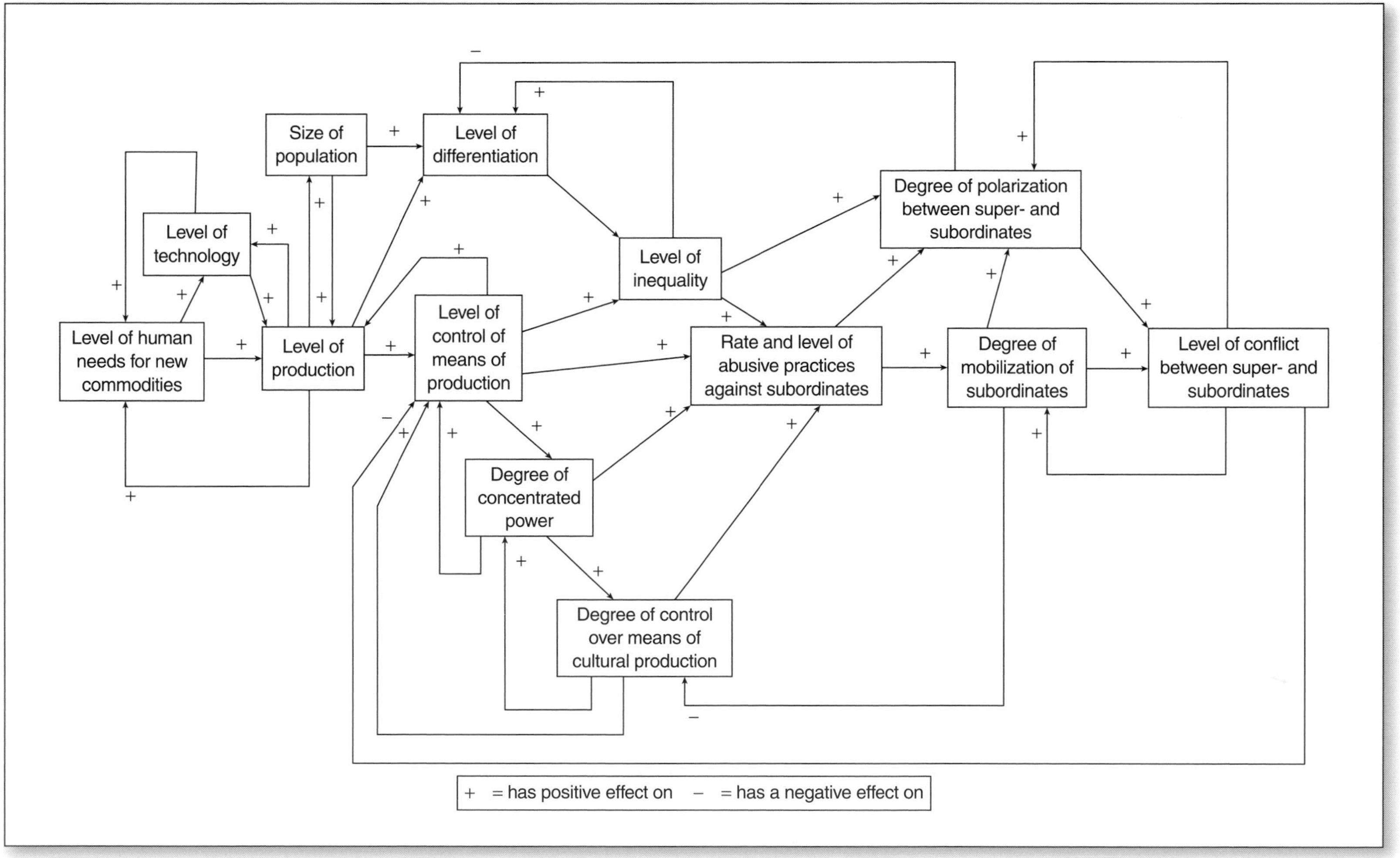

= has positive effect on   − = has a negative effect on

production and the invention of new technologies used in production. As Marx emphasized, the reverse causal processes are critical to understanding why societies have a history. As one level of needs is satisfied, new needs arise and push techno-logical innovation and production even further. These positive connections among needs, production, and technology are all represented by positive signs, which signal Marx's view that this escalating cycle is, ultimately, one of the key engines of history.

Marx also recognized, like Spencer and most nineteenth-century theorists, that increasing production allowed the population to grow and differentiate in an escalat-ing cycle. But this demographic process, found mostly in *The German Ideology,* is not the core of Marx's theory. Rather, Marx's theory of society centers on the relation-ships among control of the means of production, the instruments of power, and the production of culture. Those who own and control the means of production also are able to concentrate power among themselves and to use symbols, especially ideolo-gies, to legitimate their power and their ownership of productive forces. As the model indicates, the arrows among these variables are all positive, emphasizing that control of one of these critical forces allows control of the others. Those who own the means of production can also control the societal *superstructure,* as Marx called their ability to hold power and use culture to blind subordinates to their real interests.

This control of production (as well as power and symbols) increases the level of inequality in a society, as indicated by the positively signed arrow from production to inequality. Moreover, those who control production, power, and symbols are free to engage in practices that disrupt the routines and lives of subordinates, making them ever more miserable. At times, economic, political, and cultural elites are driven to do so by the nature of the means of production, as was the case with capitalists, locked in by cutthroat competition and a falling rate of profit. The end result is that these practices make subordinates more aware of their interests, leading them to mobilize ideologically, thereby attempting to break the control by economic and political elites of the production of cultural symbols (as denoted by the nega-tively signed reverse causal arrow from mobilization by subordinates to control of the means of cultural production). Because of abusive practices and mobilization, Marx saw society as polarizing into two potentially warring camps of superordinates and subordinates. As polarization occurred, it would, presumably, lower the level of differentiation, as indicated by the negatively signed arrow from polarization to dif-ferentiation. As mobilization proceeds, Marx felt that the growing tension between subordinates and superordinates would move beyond ideology to political organiza-tion. With political organization, subordinates would take control of the means of production from elites (as indicated by the reverse negative arrow from conflict to control of the means of production); as a result, the old elites' control of power and symbolic production would be broken.

Except for his communist utopia, in which the temporary "dictatorship of the proletariat" would somehow "wither away," a new elite group would own the means of production, setting into motion the dialectic once again. The model in Figure 4.3 cannot capture this argument; it only takes Marx's model for one historical epoch. The model challenges Marx's assumption that the very dynamics that had driven his-tory would be obviated with communism. Marx assumed that capitalist productivity allows for the support of all members of society to such a degree that private owner-ship of the means of production would no longer be necessary, and was indeed contradictory, to the social organization of production. With collective ownership of the means of production, somehow the superstructure—power and symbols—would not be used to forge a new basis of inequality.

When Marx's argument is modeled, however, there is no basis for this assumption; it is just a wish on his part. Even if the means of production is collectively owned or, more realistically, owned by the state, an entirely new basis for inequality is set into motion: control by the state of the means of economic and cultural production. The great contradiction in Marx's ideology, therefore, is that the state does not "wither away" but becomes a new basis for setting into motion the dynamics outlined in Figure 4.3. Indeed, when ideology is stripped away, we can see an abstract model of how societal organization systematically generates conflict. The key to this conflict is that elites engage in abusive practices that lead to mobilization of subordinates. This has never happened on a revolutionary scale in a capitalist society, and so we need to under-stand why Marx appears to have been so wrong on this issue.

Part of the answer resides in the assumption that control of production would be concentrated, which is generally true in capitalists economies but not to the degree that Marx prophesized (primarily because of stock markets, which diffuse ownership and often separate ownership from management). Thus, in practice, capitalism does not meet the key variable in Marx's model: increasing production does not always lead to high degrees of concentration of ownership. If this is so, then power and symbol production are not as concentrated as Marx would have predicted. Indeed, ironically, when the state controls the means of production (as was the case in the old Soviet Union and may be the case in the "new" Soviet Union), we see high degrees of concen-trated power in industrial systems, and as a result, the state also controls the means of cultural production. But translating Marx's idea into an abstract causal model shows that he was fundamentally correct: when control of the means of production is con-centrated, as is the case in feudalism and industrial communism, power is used to regulate cultural production, which, in turn, leads to high levels of inequality and abusive practices by elites.

Another part of the answer about why Marx's scheme goes wrong resides in his prediction that those who control the means of production will be driven to escalate their abusive practices because they have no choice or because they have the brute power to do so. Marx underestimated the extent to which those who do not own the means of production could mobilize power and symbols in nonrevolutionary ways, forcing centers of power and owners/managers of production to make concessions.

Still another part of the answer can be seen in the causal chain from production to differentiation to inequality to polarization. Marx clearly underestimated the extent to which increasing levels of production differentiate a population in general and the class structure in particular. Escalating production increases the number of classes rather than pushing people into two warring camps. Marx appears to have argued that the abusive practices of elites would polarize the population, thereby reducing differ-entiation and creating a simple two-class system; obviously, very high levels of produc-tion do just the opposite, differentiating the population to such a degree that class boundaries become more numerous but less distinct. And if such is the case, the polarizing dynamics so essential to Marx's theoretical predictions never emerge. As a result, revolutionary conflict does not occur, at least not the way Marx predicted. Indeed, it is in less productive economies, where elites do control the means of production and the societal superstructure, that one sees fewer classes, abusive practices, and potential polarization of the population.

Thus, the general model presented in Figure 4.3 exposes both the strengths and the weaknesses of Marx's thinking. The model is, in broad contours, correct on the key variables and the relationships among them, except that some of the signs are wrong. If I were to correct the model to reflect what has actually happened historically, we would need only to change some of the signs on a few key arrows. We would change the signs from differentiation to inequality to negative, or perhaps to a curvilinear relationship in which differentiation initially increases inequality but at high levels reduces inequality (the sign would thus be +/− rather than positive). We might also change the signs from production to control of the means of production from positive to more positively curvilinear; that is, increasing production does indeed lead to increased control of the means of production (and the societal superstructure as well), but at very high levels of production, this control is not so great, especially in capitalist systems where ownership is more diffused (although corporate power is still very strong, but hardly absolute). With these changes, the model holds up rather well. Marx had the basic elements right, but his vision was blinded by his ideology, which emerged in reaction to the abuses of early capitalism.

The Model of Conflict. In *The Communist Manifesto*, Marx and Engels outline a theory of conflict that I have only glossed over in Figure 4.3. Figure 4.4 presents this conflict model in a more robust form compared with Figure 4.2. Although this more robust model is powerful, it makes some fundamental mistakes in the signs on the causal arrows—much like the more general one. These mistakes account for why Marx's predictions about the revolutionary overthrow of capitalism go wrong. Before pointing out these mistakes, however, let me review the model as Marx might have drawn it.

The model begins on the left with Marx's view that control of production translates into control of the coercive/administrative apparatus of the state, which, in turn, gives economic elites power over symbolic resources. This concentrated control of production, power, and symbols increases the degree of inequality, as indicated by the positive arrows. Those who own and control the economy extract productive surplus for their privilege, thus increasing economic inequality, and they use their surplus to buy power and to manipulate the symbolic means of production. Thus, Marx argues, the overall level of inequality will increase under these conditions.

Whether they were driven to do so by the nature of production or by their desire to secure more valued resources, those who control the means of production are able to reorganize the productive processes to suit their needs and interests. Coupled with resentment by subordinates over inequalities, this reorganization sets into motion the dynamics that Marx felt leads subordinates to become aware of their interests in changing the system and, eventually, to their political and ideological mobilization to pursue revolutionary conflict.

Figure 4.4 Marx's Model of Conflict

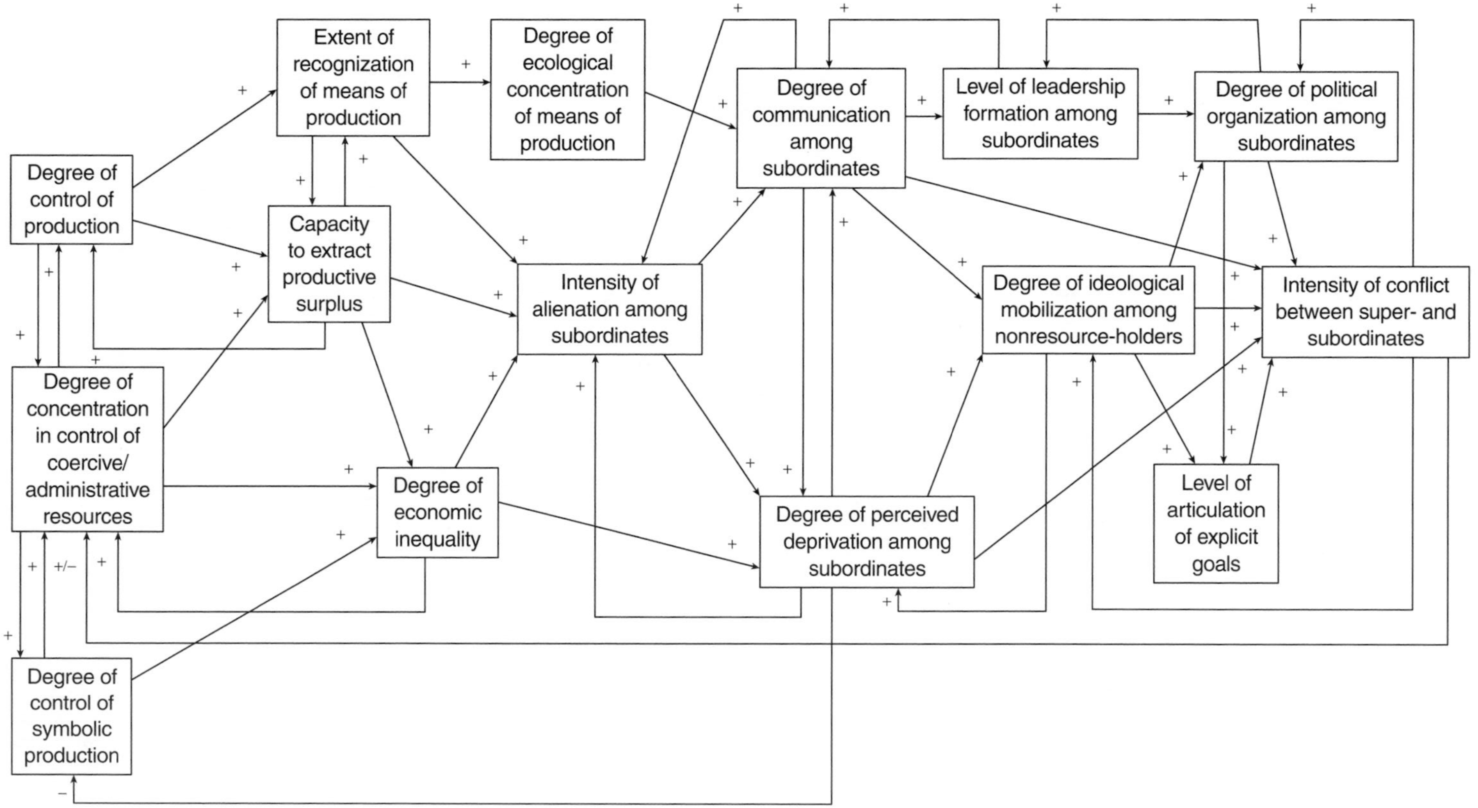

+ = has positive effect on   − = has a negative effect on   +/− = has an initially positive effect that turns negative

One causal path goes across the top of the figure. When reorganization by elites concentrates labor, the latter group can better communicate its grievances and nurture leaders who can articulate ideologies, with these together leading to political organization among non–resource holders or subordinates in the system of stratification. As subordinates become a class "for itself" because of political organization, they will pursue violent and intense conflict with superordinates. The positive signs on these causal paths emphasize that Marx saw these dynamics as inevitable.

Other causal paths similarly emphasize the inevitability of the causal forces unleashed. Inequality, per se, but more fundamentally the reorganization of the means of production so that workers have no say in what they produce, how they produce, and to whom they sell products increases alienation among subordinates. Marx argues that the intensity of alienation leads people to communicate their grievances, which, at the same time, raises their sense of deprivation. This sense of deprivation increases as communication of grievances occurs, and vice versa. As people communicate their grievances, and sense of deprivation, they become more ideologically mobilized, especially as leaders emerge to articulate and codify a revolutionary ideology. As is evident with all the positive signs connecting the causal paths, these forces are mutually reinforcing and escalating, thereby driving the process of conflict to more intense levels. As political leaders articulate ideologies and as political organization ensues, the goals of subordinates become more clearly articulated (as Marx tried to do in *The Communist Manifesto*). All together, ideology, clear articulation of goals, and political organization lead to intense and violent conflict against superordinates. A class moves from one "of itself" to one "for itself," where awareness of common interests, ideologies, goals, and organizations drives subordinates to pursue conflict. In Marx's version, all the direct causal arrows flowing from left to right are positive, making the revolutionary conflict inevitable. The only negative signs are on the reverse causal arrows, emphasizing how deprivations and conflict loosen elites' grip on symbolic, coercive, and administrative power.

Where did Marx go wrong in this model? The answer is that many of the relationships that he posited are not purely positive. Critical causal paths leading to conflict between superordinates and subordinates are, in fact, *curvilinear*. That is, the variables feeding into conflict (the last box on the right of the model) initially increase the potential for violent conflict, but as these variables reach high levels, they begin to lower the potential for violent conflict. Let me review these key causal connections that have led to this conclusion.

First, the relationship between political organization of subordinates and intensity of conflict is curvilinear. Initially, political organization increases violent conflict, but in high degrees, it reduces conflict. The union movement in America is a good example; violence was greatest in the early stages but declined as labor became ever more organized and instrumental. With organization, goals become more explicit, and leaders are more likely to bargain and compromise rather than risk the high costs of violent conflict. Second, ideology also has a curvilinear relationship to conflict. Initial ideological mobilization raises emotions but does not generally specify goals in detail, beyond general pronouncements; under these conditions of diffuse emotional arousal, violence is more likely. But as the ideology becomes ever more codified, goals and ends are more clearly articulated, and compromise is more likely, particularly when subordinates are well organized politically.

Thus, Marx had the variables right, but he made some key miscalculations on the signs for several of the critical forces feeding in the last variable in the model: the intensity and violence of conflict. If I were to redraw the model, it would look much the same except for the variables from degree of political organization to conflict, ideological mobilization to conflict, and level of articulation of goals to conflict; all of these would now be curvilinear, increasing the potential for violent conflict for a while and then decreasing this potential. Marx was living through the early stages of the conflict process, where increasing conflict between superordinates and subordinates was evident, but as the forces driving this conflict reached high levels—that is, high degrees of political organization, well-codified ideologies, and clearly articulated goals—the tendency for violence began to reduce. At least that is what the empirical record shows.

Marx's Theoretical Principles

Marx's ideas are rather easily converted into theoretical principles. In essence, such principles translate the causal models developed above into a series of abstract statements that, as I have suggested for the models, can be combined to produce a more powerful theory.

Principles of Social Organization. *The German Ideology, The Communist Manifesto,* and *Capital* all contain, to varying degrees, a set of fundamental ideas about the nature of social organization. Despite the varied contexts in which Marx presents these ideas, they imply a question that virtually all social theorists ask themselves: How is it that patterns of social organization emerge, persist, and change over time? Or, as Marx phrased it in *The German Ideology,* how is it possible for human societies to have a history? His answer to this question can be seen in a number of interrelated principles explained in the section to follow. Let us begin with five background propositions that summarize how Marx conceptualized the forces producing inequality:

1. Production increases the level of technology, and vice versa.

2. The level of differentiation in a society increases with productivity, and vice versa.

3. The more productivity and differentiation reciprocally affect each other, the greater the rate of population growth, and vice versa.

4. The larger a population and the greater its level of differentiation, the more concentrated is control of the means of production and, hence, the greater is the level of inequality.

5. The greater the control of the means of production and the more concentrated the power, the more economic and political elites can control the production and dissemination of symbols, especially ideologies justifying inequalities.

These principles emphasize Marx's conviction that the level of technology, productivity, social differentiation, population size, inequality, concentration of power, and use of ideologies to justify inequality are fundamentally related. We have phrased Marx's ideas more neutrally than he did so that the insights they offer into the nature of social organization can be divorced from his polemics.

Marx argued that members of social systems use technology to facilitate productivity and that increased productivity encourages social differentiation and population growth. As noted for his model, this portion of Marx's view of social organization does not go beyond Herbert Spencer's and others' analyses of these processes. The unique part of Marx's view is his analysis of how integration in differentiated systems is achieved. Marx argued that inequality, concentration of power, and manipulation of idea systems by those in power are the means by which differentiated social systems are maintained. As he also emphasized, however, this basis of organization contains the seeds for its transformation because inequality inexorably sets into motion forces for conflict and change. Marx's ultimate contribution to sociological theory thus resides in the principles generating conflict in systems of inequality.

Principles of Inequality and Change in Social Systems. Marx focused on how inequality generated in capitalist social systems leads to class conflict and the revolutionary transformation of society. Our goal, however, is to liberate Marxian principles from their historical embeddedness and to state them at a sufficiently high level of abstraction so they have relevance beyond the nineteenth century. For Marx, the key question is how a system of inequality in which those with power use beliefs and norms to perpetuate this situation inexorably generated the potential for conflict and change. He visualized the genesis of conflict and change by recognizing that those holding different shares of a system's resources have differing and conflicting interests. Those with resources have an interest in preserving their privileges, whereas those with few resources have an interest in taking them from the privileged. Power is the most critical resource because it can be used to secure other resources, and so unequal distribution of power signals the greatest conflict of interest. Marx's ideas can be expressed in the following proposition:

6. The greater is the level of inequality, the greater will be the conflict of interest between dominant and subordinate segments of a population, with this conflict of interest increasing as

    A. Those with power use their power to consolidate control over other material and symbolic resources
    B. Those with power limit upward mobility and access to resources by subordinates.

These propositions follow from Marx's observation that a conflict of interest is inherent in inequality and that those in advantageous positions will seek to increase their privileges at the expense of those in lower-ranked positions.

Marx's next theoretical task is thus quite straightforward: to document the conditions under which awareness of interests causes subordinates to question the legitimacy of inequality in resource distribution. These conditions are summarized in the following proposition:

7. The more subordinate segments become aware of their interests, the more they question the legitimacy of the unequal distribution of scarce resources, with awareness of subordinates' interests increasing as

   A. Social changes produced by dominant segments disrupt existing relations among subordinates

   B. Practices of dominant segments create alienation among subordinates

   C. Subordinates communicate their grievances to each other, which increase with

      1. The degree of spatial concentration among subordinates

      2. The level of education and rates of literacy among subordinates

   D. Subordinate segments develop unifying systems of ideologies that increase with

      1. The capacity of subordinates to recruit or generate ideological spokespersons

      2. The inability of dominant groups to regulate the socialization process and communication networks among subordinates.

Marx's great insight is that the concentration of power causes those with power to act in ways that increase subordinates' awareness of their interests. As those with power seek to consolidate their position, they often disrupt the routines of subordinates, while creating alienation. Or as those with power seek or organize subordinates to increase their productivity (and hence the resources of those with power), they create conditions favoring communication among subordinates and awareness of their common interests. Although Marx visualized these processes as occurring at the societal level, as the bourgeoisie used their power to exploit the proletariat in the interest of greater productivity and profit, his insights are, we believe, applicable to a broader range of social units and to any historical period. What principles 7-A, 7-B, 7-C, and 7-D underscore is the inherent tension built into the unequal distribution of resources, especially power, and the tendency of concentrated power to be used in ways that create sources of counterpower.

For those counter sources of power to become effective, however, Marx thought that awareness of common interests must be translated into organization among subordinates. In capitalist systems, he saw this process as one in which the proletariat went from a class "of itself" to one organized "for itself." Marx's insight applies, we would argue, to more than social classes in societal social systems. The process of organization among subordinates who are aware of their interests is both transhistorical and applicable to any social unit manifesting inequalities in power. The following proposition specifies some conditions that Marx believed important in translating an awareness of interests and a questioning of legitimacy into organization forms designed to pursue conflict:

8. The more subordinates are aware of their interests, the greater is their questioning of the legitimacy of the distribution of scarce resources; and the more they question legitimacy, the more likely are they to organize and initiate conflict against superordinates, especially as

    A. Deprivations of subordinates move from an absolute to a relative basis
    B. Superordinates fail to become aware of their common interests
    C. Subordinates develop leadership structures.

In these propositions, Marx summarized some of the conditions leading to those forms of organization among subordinates that will result in overt conflict. The first key question in addressing this issue is why an awareness of conflicting interests and a questioning of the legitimacy of the system would lead to organization and the initiation of conflict. Seemingly, awareness would have to be accompanied by intense emotions if people are to run the risks of opposing those holding power. Presumably, Marx's proposition on alienation would indicate one source of emotional arousal because, for Marx, alienation goes against human beings' basic needs. Further, ideological spokespersons could, as Marx's own career and works testify, arouse emotions through their prose and polemics. The key variable in the Marxian scheme is "relative deprivation." The emotions aroused by alienation and ideological spokespersons are necessary but insufficient conditions for taking the risks of organizing and initiating conflict against those with power. Only when these conditions are accompanied by rapidly escalating perceptions of deprivation by subordinates is the level of emotional arousal sufficient to prompt organization and open conflict with superordinates. Such organization, however, is not likely to be successful unless the dominant groups fail to organize around their interests and unless leaders can emerge among the subordinates to mobilize and channel the emotional energies.

Thus, although Marx assumed that conflict is inevitable, his theory of its origins was elaborate, setting down a series of necessary and sufficient conditions for the occurrence of conflict. Marx's great contribution to a theory of conflict resides in these propositions, for his subsequent propositions appear to be simple translations of his dialectical assumptions into statements of covariance, without the careful documentation of the necessary and sufficient conditions that would cause these conflict processes to occur.

Marx also sought to account for the degree of violence in the conflict between organized subordinates and superordinates. The key variable here is polarization, a concept denoting the increasing divisions within a system.

9. The greater is the unity among subordinates around common beliefs and the more developed is their political leadership structure, the greater is the polarization between superordinates and subordinates.

10. The more polarized superordinates and subordinates, the more violent their ensuing conflict becomes.

In contrast with his previous principles, propositions 9 and 10 do not specify the conditions under which polarization will occur, nor do they indicate when polarized groups will engage in violent conflict. Marx assumed that such would be the case as the dialectic mechanically unfolds. Presumably, highly organized subordinates in a state of emotional arousal will engage in violent conflict. As a cursory review of actual historical events underscores, such a state often results in just the opposite: less violent conflicts with a considerable degree of negotiation and compromise. This fact points to the Marxian scheme's failure to specify the conditions under which polarization first occurs and then leads to violent conflict. It is not just coincidental that, at this point in his scheme, Marx's predictions about class revolutions in capitalistic societies begin to go wrong. Thus, the Marxian legacy points rather dramatically to a needed area of theoretical and empirical research: Under what condition is conflict likely to be violent? More specifically, under what conditions is conflict involving highly organized and mobilized subordinates likely to be violent, and under what conditions are less combative forms of conflict likely to occur?

The final proposition in the Marxian inventory also appears to follow more from a philosophical commitment to the dialectic than from carefully reasoned conclusions:

11. The more violent is the conflict, the greater are the structural changes and the greater is the redistribution of scarce resources.

This proposition reveals Marx's faith in the success of revolutions as well as his assertion that successful revolutionaries would establish new sets of superordinate-subordinate relations of power. As such, the proposition is ideology rephrased in the language of theory, especially because no conditional statements are offered about just when violent conflict leads to change and redistribution and just when it does not. Had Marx not assumed that conflicts would become polarized and violent, he would have paid more attention to the degrees of violence and nonviolence in the conflict process, and this interest, in turn, would have alerted him to the variable outcomes of conflict for social systems.

Correcting Marx's Theory

As the causal models in Figures 4.3 and 4.4 suggest, Marx's theoretical principles need to be reformulated, in several subtle but important ways. First, the relationship among technology, productivity, and societal differentiation is positive, and it generates an ever more complex class system. Thus, in contrast to Marx's position, stratification does not inevitably polarize into two basic classes; rather, the greater the productivity, the more complex will the class system become.

Second, the relationship between ownership of the means of production, on the one hand, and concentration of power and symbolic production, on the other, is probably curvilinear. That is, as production increased through the agrarian era, the relationships posited by Marx hold essentially true, but as production reached very high levels under capitalism, (a) ownership became more dispersed, (b) ownership and management often became separated, and (c) economic elites' ability to control the societal superstructure declined. Today, in advanced capitalism, the less propertied classes can also exert both ideological and political pressure and, thereby, limit the activities of those managing the economy from becoming too abusive. This empirical fact, as it has become evident with advanced capitalism, changes the whole equation between ownership of the means of production, control of the societal superstructure, "immiseration" of the working class, polarization of society, and violent revolution. The relationships posited by Marx are more typical of agrarian-feudal societies of peasants and elites than of capitalistic societies, with their many diverse social classes. Ironically, the relationships among control of the economy, the state, and the ideological apparatus are even more typical of state ownership in communist societies than of capitalistic ones.

Third, the model of conflict needs to be adjusted to account for the curvilinear relationship between the intensity and violence of conflict, on one side, and the level of ideological mobilization, the clarity of goals and ends, and the degree of political organization, on the other. Initial ideological and political organization is more likely to generate violent or, at least, intense conflict than is the case when codification of ideologies, clear statements of goals, and well-structured political organizations have emerged. When Marx was writing, he was living through the early phases of mobilization by labor, but he did not live long enough to see that the intensity and violence in conflict declined as subordinates became well-organized and successful in conflicts with capitalists.

Finally, Marx did not see that the capitalists could be flexible because he assumed that they were caught in a downward spiral of intense competition leading to a declining rate of profit, which forced them to engage in the very activities that would facilitate mobilization of workers. He was essentially correct in much of his analysis, but he clearly miscalculated the extent to which (a) the proletariat could also exert both ideological and political pressure on the state to respond to their interests; (b) the state could manage the points of tension between capitalists and labor, while mitigating the business cycle; and (c) capitalists could avoid locking themselves into ruinous competition that forced them to be abusive and pushed the economy into ever deeper recessions.

Even with these miscalculations, Marx was correct in his assessment of the key forces organizing societies in general and producing conflicts between sub- and superordinates in particular. For this reason, we believe, Marx remains an important theorist today, especially as the more ideologically loaded portions of Marxism recede in relevance.

Conclusions

Karl Marx had a utopian vision of a classless society within which people acted cooperatively for the common good and, in the process, realized their human potential. Paradoxically, he believed that this goal could be achieved through centralization of political power in the hands of the state. This belief is why we described him previously as a sorcerer's apprentice. The image is that of a leader without wisdom who inadvertently releases the power of the netherworld on the earth. Put bluntly, Marx's vision of the transition from capitalism to communism invites the establishment of a regime in which the state has strict control over all aspects of an individual's life; it invites, in other words, modern totalitarianism.

To understand why Marx proceeded in this way, we need to appreciate the dilemma he faced. As a revolutionary, he sought to overthrow a brutal and exploitive society in favor of a humane and just community. It is worth remembering that Engels's description of the living conditions of the working class was horribly accurate, and many nineteenth-century observers saw the situation as becoming steadily worse. Thus, as Marx saw it, the problem was to get away from a competitive society to a communal one, which would free individuals to realize their potential as human beings.

So Marx made a series of proposals that are worth restating: abolition of private ownership of land; confiscation of the property of emigrants and rebels; centralization of credit, communications, and transportation; ownership of factories by the state, and several others. These measures imply a belief that unrestrained political power can be redemptive, that the way to freedom is through totalitarian control. As Marx put it, the transition to communism would require a temporary dictatorship of the proletariat. But experience has shown that this strategy can only mean total rule by the Communist party, which justifies its exploitation of the masses by invoking the common good. Now the political issue is not whether the ends justify the means. It is, rather, whether the means can produce the ends; that is, can power, unfettered by accountability, produce freedom for individuals? The answer is no. There is no evidence that totalitarianism can produce freedom. Despite its grandiose vision, Marx's writings had perverse political consequences.

Marx's predictions or prophecies go wrong not only because he failed to recognize that power, once given, does not "wither away," but also because he assumed that it would be the proletariat who would rise up and overthrow capitalism. Yet the great communist revolutions in Russia and China were really outcomes of longer-term civil wars, and the key actors were not the proletariat but peasants. The state did not wither away in either case, and ironically, only with the rise of capitalism in these countries, particularly China, can some hope for a less totalitarian regime be found. Clearly, Marx's grand predictions contain several significant miscalculations.

First, Marx saw the value of commodities as inhering in the labor power necessary to produce them (less other costs like machines and marketing). This assumption is perhaps his most fundamental mistake, and despite efforts by contemporary Marxists[55] to stay with this idea because it offers a measure of exploitation, it is fundamentally flawed. Value inheres in what one is willing to pay, or must pay under constrained conditions, for something in a market, and though Marxists would decry this as imposing capitalist categories, it is nonetheless true. People can still be exploited when they are paid little and forced to work under terrible

---

[55]See, for example, John A. Roemer, *A General Theory of Exploitation and Class* (Cambridge, MA: Harvard University Press, 1982) and Erik Olin Wright, *Class Counts* (Cambridge, UK: Cambridge University Press, 1997).

conditions, but we need not invoke the value theory of labor as our measure of the degree of exploitation. Rather, we invoke other values, such as fair wages, basic standards of living, and safe working conditions, to assess exploitation. The notion of exploitation is thus evaluative; it cannot be an objective construct, as Marx sought to make it. We can still see capitalist profits and wealth as coming from exploitation, if we choose, but the value theory of labor is an ideology disguised as science. Like Adam Smith, who had worked with the idea, we should abandon the notion of a labor theory of value because it is not useful.

Second, Marx miscalculated the extent to which capitalists and proletarians were inexorably on a collision course. The early capitalism that Marx observed did indeed seem to be locked into a self-destructive system, but Marx simply assumed that these crises of recession/depression and labor discontent were unresolvable within the framework of capitalism. Part of the reason for this miscalculation was that Marx overestimated the extent to which the state is simply a tool of the bourgeoisie, whereas in fact, capitalism is associated with the rise of political democracies, in which all citizens have some say, despite the fact that the rich certainly have more influence than the poor. Also, persistent crises forced the state to seek agreements between capitalists and labor over wages and working conditions. These crises have pulled the state into regulating markets and capitalists as recessions threatened political stability. Marx assumed that such flexibility by the state and capitalists could not exist. In fact, during the early days of capitalism, this flexibility was not so evident, but over time, masses of urban workers have been able to gain political power.

Third, Marx incorrectly assumed that workers were, and always would be, powerless in labor markets. Although this was certainly true in early capitalism as rural peasants migrated to cities (and indeed is still true for rural migrants to cities), workers were able to gain political power to force political interventions in labor markets. This gain in power was partly the result of the efforts of labor unions, which were far more successful than Marx could have envisioned at the time he was writing. Moreover, there is not always a perpetual availability of labor or a reserve labor force that can be drawn upon when existing workers demand higher wages. Labor shortages do emerge, and under these conditions, the proletariat is in a better bargaining position. Furthermore, as investments in technology and facilities mount, the costs of unused capital investments arising from prolonged labor disputes have often forced capitalists to bargain with workers rather than leave big machines idle.

Fourth, Marx did not anticipate the rise of the middle classes, another occurrence that has posed problems for Marxist theorists.[56] Indeed, he made the opposite prediction: most people would be pushed into the proletariat. History shows, however, that as the economy expands, especially as new technologies drive the expansion, the proportion of skilled, white-collar workers grows, and they eventually come to constitute the majority of workers. These more skilled workers are in a much better bargaining position over wages and working conditions than were the earlier industrial workers.

---

[56]Erik Olin Wright, *Classes* (London: Verso, 1985); Erik Olin Wright and Luca Perrone, "Marxist Class Categories and Income Inequality," *American Sociological Review* 42 (1977):32–55.

Fifth, Marx did not recognize the importance of government as a large employer. He tended to see government as the tool of the bourgeoisie, but as government intervenes in all spheres of society—from schools to economic regulation—a significant proportion of the labor force comes to work for government. As a result, it is difficult to typify the interests of government workers as part of conflicts between an exploited proletariat and capitalists.[57]

Sixth, late in his writings, Marx began to see some of the implications of joint stock companies, but he could not have predicted the revolution ushered in by the issuing of stocks in markets. Ownership was to become more diffused, with many workers having a stake in capitalism as they acquired stock. Moreover, not only was ownership diffused, but also it was separated from management such that owners would not directly manage companies and, hence, relations with labor. Under these conditions, management would increasingly be interested in rationalizing relations with labor to keep production going.

Thus, many specific forces in capitalism operated against Marx's predictions. Some of these forces he could not be expected to have anticipated, but he might have seen the effects of others if he had not been so committed ideologically to overthrowing capitalism. It is always hazardous to make predictions based on a historical trend, as Marx did, because specific historical events can change the trajectory of a prediction. Marx had confidence in his prophecies because his entire intellectual scheme forced these predictions, but he never questioned some of the assumptions on which this scheme was based; when some proved questionable, the entire system collapsed.

So we might ask: Why should sociologists still read Marx? After all, have not most of his predictions about revolution and the spread of communism failed to materialize? The communist revolution by the proletariat never really occurred. The class structure of the capitalist system did not polarize but, instead, became ever more complex. The state did not "wither away" in communist countries (indeed, it did so only when they turned capitalist). And the world has become more capitalist rather than communist. Some contemporary sociologists continue to hold out, arguing that as capitalism goes completely global, the contradictions in the system will finally emerge and usher in the communist revolution. Others have sustained an interest in exploitation and the value theory of labor, reworking these ideas to fit more contemporary conditions. Yet it must be said that much of the Marxian system of thinking, especially its more ideologically loaded portrayals of the future, has not held up—like most ideologically driven predictions.

Still, Marx anticipated and framed many of the issues that occupy discussion of the economy and society today. Marx saw, more than any other scholar of the last century, that the economy is the driving force of society, and he predicted that capitalism would spread or, in today's vocabulary, become a global force. He understood that economic power and political power are highly correlated and that those with power could disproportionately influence the formation of ideologies and the

---

[57]Erik Olin Wright, "Rethinking, Once Again, The Concept of Class," in *The Debate on Classes,* ed. Erik Olin Wright (London: Verso, 1989).

other elements of culture. He explained the incredible wealth-generating capacities of free markets, but this dynamism is tempered by the inequalities, exploitation, and alienation generated by such a system, as well as by the inherent tendency of the system to cycle in and out of ever deeper recessions and depressions. Moreover, he even anticipated the power of big capitalism to standardize activities, to impoverish small businesses and artisans, and to destroy old cultures in the relentless drive to make production more efficient and to penetrate all markets. Thus, Marx had a very good sense for many of the outcomes of capitalism, once unleashed. Why, then, did his more specific predictions about the revolution of the proletariat go wrong? The answer must reside in Marx's ideological fervor. Marx was blinded by his convictions and, hence, could not see that the state, bourgeoisie, and workers could change the capitalist system in ways that made it more benign.

Another way to make sure that Marx's ideas are still relevant is to make them more abstract and general, viewing them as unlocking some of the key dynamics of societies in all times and places. Rather than viewing it as describing the inevitable forces inherent in capitalism, Marx's theory of conflict should be generalized to conflict dynamics in all systems of inequality. And by making his ideas more abstract in this way, we can see where they went wrong and where his enduring legacy resides. And so we can look at Marx as a value-neutral scientist—obviously something that he would abhor, as would most contemporary Marxists[58]—and see the power of the theory, per se, disembodied from the call for revolutionary action.

---

[58]For a recent review of contemporary Marxist thinking, see Michael Burawoy and Erik Olin Wright, "Sociological Marxism" in *Handbook of Sociological Theory,* ed. J. H. Turner (New York: Kluwer Academic, 2002). For an effort to sustain Marx's utopian views, see Erik Olin Wright, *Envisioning Real Utopias* (London: Verso, 2010). See also Chapter 14 on conflict theory.

CHAPTER 5

Max Weber

Near the end of his career, Max Weber viewed the fledgling discipline of sociology in the following way:

> Sociology . . . is a science concerning itself with the interpretive understanding of social action and thereby with a causal explanation of its course and consequences. We shall speak of "action" insofar as the acting individual attaches a subjective meaning to his behavior—be it overt or covert, omission or acquiescence. Action is "social" insofar as its subjective meaning takes account of the behavior of others and is thereby oriented in its course.[1]

Weber believed that this definition would allow him to achieve two interrelated goals that, taken together, signify an altogether original approach to the study of social organization.[2] First, he wanted to understand the origin and unique characteristics of modern Western societies. Second, he wanted to construct a system of abstract concepts that would be useful in describing and, hence, understanding social action in such societies. Without a set of clear and precise concepts, Weber argued, systematic social scientific research is impossible. The result was a series of concepts designed to increase understanding of the modern world.

Note: * This chapter was coauthored with Leonard Beeghley.

[1] Max Weber, *Economy and Society*, trans. and ed. Guenther Roth and Claus Wittich (New York: Bedminster, 1968).

[2] Wolfgang Mommsen, *The Age of Bureaucracy: Perspectives on the Political Sociology of Max Weber* (New York: Harper Torchbooks, 1974), 2.

Weber's Methodology of the Social Sciences

In 1904, Weber posed a fundamental question: "In what sense are there 'objectively valid truths' in those disciplines concerned with social and cultural phenomena?"[3] All his subsequent writings can be seen as an answer to this simple query. Indeed, Weber's goal was to show that objective research was possible in those academic disciplines dealing with subjectively meaningful phenomena. The way he pursued this goal is presented here in two parts. First, his depiction of the problem of values in sociological research is shown. This was the central methodological issue for Weber; if sociology were to be a true science of society, he believed, it has to be objective. Second, he thought every science required a conceptual map, an inventory of the key concepts describing the phenomenon being studied, and he began to develop such a system of concepts, labeling them "ideal types."

The Problem of Values

During Weber's time, many observers did not think that an objective social science was plausible because it seemed impossible to separate values from the research process. So most scholars attempting to describe human behavior infused their analyses with political, religious, and other values. Karl Marx's writings constitute an extreme example of this tactic. Weber confronted the problem of values by observing that sociological inquiry should be objective or, to use his term, *value-free.* Having said that, he then suggested how values and economic interests were connected to social scientific analyses.

Value-Free Sociology

Weber's use of the term *value-free* is unfortunate, because it implies that social scientists should have no values at all, which is plainly an impossibility. What he meant is that researchers' personal values and economic interests should not affect the process of social scientific analysis. He believed that if such factors influenced the research process, the structure of social action could not be depicted objectively. This fundamental concern with attaining objective and verifiable knowledge links all the sciences, natural and social.[4]

In Weber's view, sociology should not be a moral science. It is not possible to state scientifically which norms, values, or patterns of action are correct or the best, but rather, it is only possible to describe them objectively. Weber believed that such descriptions would represent a considerable achievement. After all, they did not then exist. Thus, unlike many others, Weber explicitly distinguished between "what ought to be," the sphere of values, and "what is," the sphere of science, arguing that sociology should focus only on the latter. This distinction implies what Weber

---

[3]Max Weber, "'Objectivity' in Social Science and Social Policy," in *The Methodology of the Social Sciences,* trans. Edward A. Shils and Henry A. Finch (New York: Free Press, 1949), 51.

[4]Ibid., 143.

considered the underlying value that ought to guide social scientific inquiry: the search for truth.[5]

Another implication of Weber's argument for a value-free sociology is that the new science reflects an ongoing historical process in which magic and other forms of inherited wisdom become less acceptable as means of explaining events. Weber referred to this change as the process of *rationalization,* and it is the dominant theme in his work. Unlike Marx, who used the dialectic as a leitmotif, Weber believed that social life is becoming increasingly "rationalized" in the sense that people lead relatively methodical lives: they rely on reason buttressed by objective evidence. The rationalization of the economy—for example, by means of improved accounting, the use of technology, and other methods—produced modern capitalism. The rationalization of government—by reliance on technical training and legal procedures, for example—resulted in the rise of the modern political state. The sciences, of course, are the archetypal methodical disciplines.[6] In a "rationalized discipline," values should not affect the research process. But they remain relevant.

The Connection Between Values and Science

Although Weber knew that the separation between values and science is difficult to maintain in practice, the distinction highlighted the relevance of values before and after the research process. The choice of topics comes before the research takes place. The only basis for making such a decision is scientists' religious beliefs, economic interests, and other values, which lead some of them to each topic. But having chosen a topic for study, according to Weber's dictum, scientists must follow an objective research process.

The situation is more complex when dealing with public policy issues. Given a specific political goal, Weber said sociologists could determine (a) the alternative strategies for achieving it, (b) the outcomes of using different strategies, and (c) the consequences of attaining the goal.[7] Once this is done, however, there is no scientific way of choosing public policies. Selecting one goal rather than another and one strategy rather than another ultimately depends on people's political values, their economic interests, and other non-objective factors.

Having said that the research process must be objective and the sphere of values and the sphere of science must be kept separate, Weber drew a unique conclusion. Unlike nearly all the other classical sociologists (except Marx), Weber rejected the search for general laws in favor of historical theories that provide an "interpretive understanding

---

[5]In general, sociologists have followed Weber's lead in making the distinction between "what is" and "what ought to be." Nonetheless, some critics of positivism argue that Weber's methodological goal of objective knowledge is not attainable, a position with which we disagree. For a discussion of these issues as they relate to Weber's work, see Alan Scott, "Value Freedom and Intellectual Autonomy," *History of the Human Sciences* 8 (1995):69–88.

[6]Weber used the concept of rationalization in a number of different ways, and hence, subsequent scholars differ in how to interpret it. See, for example, Randall Collins, *Max Weber: A Skeleton Key* (Beverly Hills, CA: Sage, 1986); Stephen Kalberg, "Max Weber's Types of Rationality: Cornerstones for the Analysis of Rationalization Processes in History," *American Journal of Sociology* 85 (1980):1145–1179; and John Patrick Diggins, *Max Weber: Politics and the Spirit of Tragedy* (New York: Basic Books, 1996).

[7]Weber, "'Objectivity,'" 53.

of social action and . . . a causal explanation of its course and consequences."[8] A search for universal laws necessarily excludes from consideration important and unique historical events. Weber summarized his position in the following way:[9]

> For the knowledge of historical phenomena in their concreteness, the most general laws, because they are most devoid of content are also the least valuable. The more comprehensive the validity—or scope—of a term, the more it leads us away from the richness of reality since in order to include the common elements of the largest possible number of phenomena, it must necessarily be as abstract as possible and hence devoid of content. In the [social] sciences, the knowledge of the universal or general is never valuable in itself.

In effect, then, Weber was most interested in focusing on the "big empirical questions," such as why capitalism had originated in the West rather than somewhere else, and he knew that emphasis on the development of general theories would not allow for examination of such issues. Ideal types were his method for dealing with these issues.

Ideal Types

To study social phenomena, Weber argued that it is necessary to have a description of the key elements of phenomena. The goal is to describe forms of action and patterns of social organization, while seeking to identify the historical causes of these forms and patterns. The use of what he termed *ideal types* is central to this approach.[10] An *ideal type* or *pure type* summarizes the basic properties of a social phenomenon, which, in turn, can help the search for its historical causes. Weber developed two different kinds of ideal types: historical and general.[11] Following is a summary of each.

Historical Ideal Types. Historical events can be described by analytically accentuating their key components. For example, in Weber's famous analysis of "the spirit of capitalism," he drew up a list of the features of this belief system. Once the essence or pure form of this belief system is highlighted, it then becomes possible to seek the causes for the emergence of this distinctive historical event; and in Weber's analysis, the emergence of Protestantism appears to have been the key historical cause of the spirit of capitalism, as we will examine later. Thus, a historical ideal type accentuates the key properties of

---

[8]Weber, *Economy and Society,* 4.

[9]Weber, "'Objectivity,'" 80.

[10]See Theodore Abel, "The Operation Called Verstehen," *American Journal of Sociology* 54 (1948):211–218; Peter A. Munch, "Empirical Science and Max Weber's *Verstehen Sociologie,*" *American Sociological Review* 22 (1957):26–32; Murray L. Wax, "On Misunderstanding Verstehen: A Reply to Abel," *Sociology and Social Research* 51 (1967):322–333; and Theodore Abel, "A Reply to Professor Wax," *Sociology and Social Research* 51 (1967):334–336. A good recent summary can be found in Diggins, *Max Weber,* 114–122. For a more general analysis of Weber's methodology, see Stephen Kalberg, *Max Weber's Historical-Comparative Sociology* (Chicago, IL: University of Chicago Press, 1994).

[11]See Thomas Burger, *Max Weber's Theory of Concept Formation: History, Laws, and Ideal Types* (Durham, NC: Duke University Press, 1976), 130–134.

specific events in history, but it does more: once the key components of a property of the social world are delineated, the search for causes is given focus and direction.

General Ideal Types. Although Weber did not believe that general laws of human organization could be produced in the social sciences, he still wanted to make generalizations about generic social phenomena. This desire led him to formulate ideal types of phenomena that are always present in human action. These ideal types do not describe historical events, but rather, they accentuate certain key properties of actors, actions, and social organizations in general. The most famous of these more abstract and general ideal types is Weber's conceptualization of the types of action.

According to Weber, people's actions can be classified in four analytically distinct ways.[12] The first type of action is the *instrumentally rational,* which occurs when means and ends are systematically related to each other based on knowledge. Weber knew that the knowledge that people possess might not be accurate. Thus, both the rain dance and the timing of a stock purchase are instrumentally rational acts, from the point of view of the dancers and the buyers, even though the means-ends link might be based on magical beliefs or rumors, respectively. Thus, instrumentally rational action occurs in all societies. Nonetheless, Weber said, the archetypal form of instrumentally rational action is based on objective, ideally scientific, knowledge. Action buttressed by objective knowledge is more likely to be effective. Its effectiveness is one reason why the spheres in which instrumentally rational action occurs have widened over time, and its pervasiveness in modern societies reflects the historical process of rationalization. The second type of action is *value-rational,* which is a behavior undertaken in light of one's basic values. Weber emphasized that "value rational action always involves 'commands' or 'demands' which, in the actor's opinion are binding."[13] Religious people avoiding alcohol use because of their faith, parents paying for their children's braces and college education, politicians passing laws, and soldiers obeying orders are acting as a result of their values. The essential characteristic of value-rational action is that it constitutes an end in itself. The third type of action is *traditional,* which is behavior "determined by ingrained habituation." Weber's point is that in a context where beliefs and values are second nature and patterns of action have been stable for many years, people usually respond to situations from habit. In a sense, they regulate their behavior by customs handed down across generations. In such societies, people resist altering long-established ways of living, which are often sanctified in religious terms. As a result, when confronted with new situations or choices, they often continue in the old ways. Traditional action typifies behavior in contexts where choices are (or are perceived to be) limited. Traditional action thus characterizes people in preindustrial societies. The fourth type of action is *affectual,* which is behavior determined by people's emotions in a given situation. A parent slapping a child and a football player punching an opponent are examples. This type of behavior occurs, of course, in all societies, although it constitutes a residual category that Weber acknowledged but did not explore in detail.

---

[12]Weber, *Economy and Society,* 24–26. Again, scholars have interpreted the types of social action in various ways. Compare, for example, Collins, *Max Weber,* 42–43 and Raymond Aron, *Main Currents in Sociological Thought, II* (Garden City, NY: Doubleday, 1970), 220–221.

[13]Weber, *Economy and Society,* 26.

These types of action classify behavior by visualizing its four "pure forms." Although Weber knew that actual situations would not perfectly reflect these concepts, they provide a common reference point for comparison. That is, a variety of empirical cases can be systematically compared with one another and with the ideal type, in this case the types of social action. This strategy is presented in Figure 5.1. Ideal types thus represent for Weber a quasi-experimental method. The "ideal" serves as the functional equivalent of the control group in an experiment. Variations or deviations from the ideal are seen as the result of causal forces (or a stimulus in a real laboratory experiment), and an attempt is then made to find these causes. In this sense, Weber could achieve two goals: (1) analytically accentuate the elements of social action and (2) discover the causes of various types of action.

Figure 5.1 The Ideal Type of Methodology

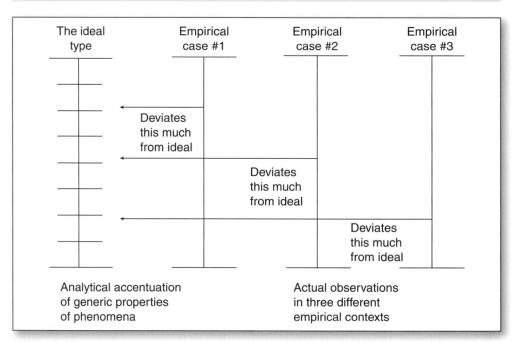

Weber's Image of Social Organization

Weber's analysis of social organization is detailed and complex, and indeed, it is often difficult to get a sense of how he visualized society as a whole. As noted earlier, Weber defined sociology as the study of *social action*, and as we have seen in the analysis of ideal types, he felt that there are four basic types of action: instrumental-rational, value-rational, traditional, and affectual.[14] Thus, human behavior is guided or, in Weber's terms, "oriented," by considerations of rationality, tradition, or affect. These types of action, however, need not be mutually exclusive; they can be combined,

---

[14]Ibid., 22–26.

although some orientations are more compatible with each other than others. For example, affectual and value-rational are more likely to be combined than, say, instrumental-rational and traditional. Still, even when combined, Weber implied that one type of action will generally dominate a social relationship.

As is typical of Weber, the nature of social relationships,[15] like the actions forming them, is portrayed as an ideal type. There are two basic kinds of social relationships arising out of social action: one is *communal* relationships, which are formed by individuals' feelings for each other, with such feelings based on affectual or traditional actions; the other is *associative* relationships, which are based on rationality, whether instrumental-rational or value-rational. Thus, in Weber's view, the two basic types of social relationships—communal and associational—are motivated by a split in the four types of action, with one of these splits revolving around the two types of rational action (value and instrumental) and the other around affectual and traditional orientations.

Social relationships, whether communal or associative, are generally connected to what Weber termed *legitimated orders*.[16] An "order" appears to be Weber's way of conceptualizing the larger structures that are built from social relationships. Action and social relationships almost always occur within the context of an existing legitimated order. Such orders "guarantee" that actions and social relationships will be conducted in accordance with "maxims" or rules, the violation of which will bring about negative sanctions on those failing to meet their obligations. Thus, the structure connecting the more micro processes of action and social relationships to more macro levels of reality is the legitimated order. Like so many concepts in Weber's work, there is a classification of orders into two basic types. One is organized around "subjective" guarantees that social relationships will proceed in accordance with the rules of the order, with this subjectivity arising from one of three routes: (1) affect, or "emotional surrender" to the order; (2) value-rationality, or a belief in the absolute validity of the order as the most efficient means to an end; and (3) religious beliefs that salvation depends on the order. The other type of order is organized by expectations among actors of certain "external effects" that are predictable outcomes to actions undertaken; thus, because actors calculate their actions in accordance with expected outcomes, Weber implied that this kind of order is organized by instrumental-rationality.

Weber then shifted to the basis of legitimation of orders—that is, routes by which actors ascribe rights to "the order" to control their conduct. Again, as is typical with Weber, there are several basic types of legitimation: (a) tradition, or the way things have always been; (b) affectual, or emotional attachments to the ways things are organized; (c) value-rational, or the "deduction" that the current order is the best possible way of organizing actions; and (d) legal, which is composed of binding agreements (entered into by considerations of instrumental-rationality) among actors or by an external authority that is considered to have the right to impose and enforce agreements.

In Figure 5.2, we have diagrammed what we think is Weber's intent, although we must confess that, despite all the definitions and categories, Weber's analytical

---

[15]Ibid., 26–28, 40–43.

[16]Ibid., 31–39.

Figure 5.2 Weber's Conception of Action, Relationships, and Orders

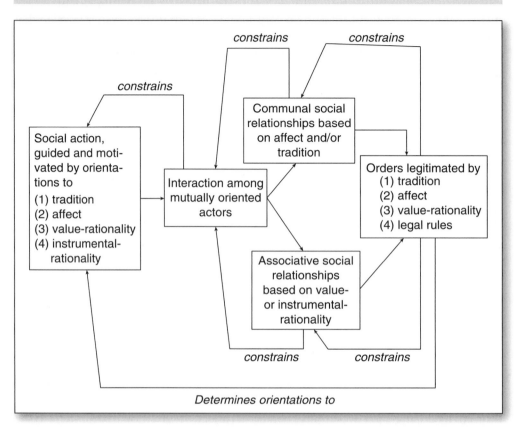

scheme is far from precise or clear. The subject matter of sociology is social action, whereby actors take cognizance of each other's behaviors. Actions are "oriented" to either affect, tradition, value-rationality, or instrumental-rationality; here, Weber implied that these orientations are cultural or part of the values, beliefs, and ideologies of a society, but they also become motivations that push actors to behave in certain ways. Various oriented and motivated social actions then lead to the formation of more stable social relationships, which can be either communal or associative, depending on the configuration of cultural orientations and motivations involved. Communal relations are guided by affectual and traditional orientations and motivations, whereas associational relations are composed from considerations of rationality, whether instrumental- or value-rationality. Social relationships are typically part of an order that structures action in accordance with rules. Such orders are organized by cultural orientations emphasizing affect, value-rationality, religion, and rationality; the order's basic legitimation can be traditional, affectual, value-rational, or legal.

At this point, Weber's view of social organization seems rather vague about how the model in Figure 5.2 leads us to the major topics of Weberian sociology. The definitional distinctions in the model were written rather late in Weber's career, after he had written much of his sociology; thus, the model does not provide clear guidelines back into the substantive topics addressed by Weber earlier in his career. Still, let us make an effort, if only to set the stage for our discussion in this chapter of Weber's sociology. Figure 5.3 begins where Figure 5.2 ends, with the formation of legitimated orders. Weber implies, but does not clearly state, that there are two basic types of orders: (1) *organizational orders*, composed of structures revealing a division of labor and pursuing particular goals, and (2) *stratification orders*, composed of categories of individuals in a system of inequality. These are not mutually exclusive because organizations can sustain a system of inequality, whereas an organization can exist as the result of a particular configuration of inequality in the distribution of resources. These come together under Weber's concept of *domination,* as we will see shortly. By this term, Weber meant that some segments of a society have the authority to tell others what to do, and as a result, those with authority can control the distribution of resources. Legitimated orders, therefore, generate systems of domination.

In Weberian sociology, then, a society cannot be understood without inquiry into its patterns of domination. Weber saw the long-term trends as revolving around a shift in the basis of domination in human societies. For Weber, history had been typified by periods of relative stability in patterns of domination revolving around traditional authority, punctuated by periodic emergence of charismatic leaders who had mobilized opposition movements and established new patterns of domination based on their charismatic authority that, over time, tended to turn into a new form of traditional authority. With the expansion of

Figure 5.3   Weber's Conception of Legitimated Orders and Domination

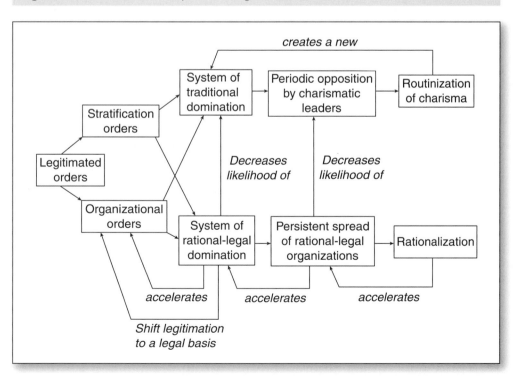

markets during capitalism, however, domination increasingly comes from *rational-legal authority* as personified by the law and bureaucratic organizations. These organizations were, in Weber's eyes, gaining control of all legitimated orders, replacing the affectual, traditional, and even value-rational legitimation of orders with the rule of law, while orienting action in all spheres of social life to instrumental-rationality. The social world was thus becoming "rationalized," as bureaucratic organizations in the state and economy became the basis for domination in society.

This was Weber's general view of the social world when he looked at historical trends and industrial capitalism as it was emerging in Germany around the turn into the twentieth century. He wanted to explain the shift in patterns of domination, and this led him to explore a variety of substantive topics—bureaucratic organizations, stratification, cities, law, religion, geopolitics, and markets—to see how these topics could help explain the shift in domination toward rational-legal authority. Unfortunately, there is no clear theory in all of these substantive concerns, only a set of topics organized around the theme of rationalization.

Weber's Analysis of Domination

Types of Domination

A society can be typified by its system of domination. In German, the term *herrschaft* connotes both domination and authority, and Weber probably meant this to be the case.[17] Any system of domination is ultimately built from what we termed *stratification orders* and *organizational orders*. All orders must be legitimated; so those who hold power seek to legitimate their power as "authority" in the eyes of those who are subject to this power.[18] Domination also requires organizational orders to administer and monitor conformity to directives given to subordinates. As was typical for Weber, he saw three basic types of domination—charismatic, traditional, and rational-legal—with each type relying on a different basis of legitimation and a different kind of administrative apparatus.[19]

Charismatic Domination. The first type of domination is called charismatic. The term *charisma* has a religious origin and literally means "gift of grace," implying that a person is endowed with divine powers.[20] In practice, Weber did not restrict his use of charisma to manifestations of divinity but, rather, employed the concept to refer to those extraordinary individuals who somehow identify themselves with the central facts or problems of people's lives and who, by the force of their personalities, communicate their inspiration to others and lead them in new directions. Thus,

---

[17]Considerable controversy exists over the proper translation of *herrschaft.*

[18]Weber, *Economy and Society,* 946.

[19]Ibid., 956–958.

[20]Ibid., 241.

people in other than religious roles can sometimes be considered charismatic: for example, politicians, soldiers, or artists.[21]

Weber believed that charismatic leadership emerges during times of crisis, when the dominant ways of confronting the problems faced by a society seem inappropriate, outmoded, or inadequate. In such a context, charismatic domination is revolutionary. People reject the past in favor of a new direction based on the master's inspiration. As Weber put it, every charismatic leader implicitly argues that "it is written . . . but I say unto you. . . ." Thus, charismatic domination is a vehicle for social change in both traditional and rational-legal contexts, which are the other two types of domination.

The legitimacy of charismatic domination lies both in the leader's demonstration of extraordinary insight and accomplishment and in the followers' acceptance of the master. It is irrelevant, from Weber's point of view, whether a charismatic leader turns out to be a charlatan or a hero; both Hitler and Gandhi were charismatic leaders. Rather, what is important is that the masses are inspired to freely follow the master. Weber believed that charisma constituted an unstable form of authority over extended periods because its legitimacy depended on the leader's claim to special insight and accomplishment. Thus, if success eludes the leader for long and crises are not resolved satisfactorily, the masses will probably reject the charismatic figure, and his or her authority will disappear.

In charismatic domination, the leader's administrative apparatus usually consists only of a band of faithful disciples who serve the master's immediate personal and political needs. Over the long run, however, every regime led by a charismatic leader faces the "problem of routinization," which involves both finding a successor to the leader and handling the day-to-day decisions that must be made.

Weber noted that the problem of succession could be resolved in a variety of ways: for example, by the masses searching for a new charismatic leader, by the leader's designation of a successor, or by the disciples' designation of a successor. But all these methods involve political instability. For this reason, either customs or legal procedures allowing the orderly transfer of power usually develop over time.

The problem of making day-to-day decisions (i.e., of governing) is usually resolved by either the development of a full-fledged administrative staff or the takeover of an already existing organization. In both cases, the typical result is the transformation of the relationship between the charismatic leader and his or her followers from one based on belief in the master's extraordinary qualities to one based on custom or law. "It is the fate of charisma," Weber wrote, "to recede before the powers of tradition or of rational association after it has entered the permanent structures of social action."[22] These new bases of legitimation represent the other two types of domination.

Traditional Domination. The second type of domination is based on tradition. In Weber's words, "Authority will be called traditional if legitimacy is claimed for it and

---

[21]See Reinhard Bendix, "Charismatic Leadership," in *Scholarship and Partnership: Essays on Max Weber,* ed. Reinhard Bendix & Guenther Roth (Berkeley: University of California Press, 1971), 170–187 and Edward A. Shils, "Charisma, Order, and Status," *American Sociological Review* 30 (1965):199–213.

[22]Weber, *Economy and Society,* 1148.

believed in by virtue of the sanctity of age-old rules and powers."[23] Put differently, traditional domination is justified by the belief that it is ancient and embodies an inherent (often religiously sanctified) state of affairs that cannot be challenged by reason. Weber distinguished between two forms of traditional authority. *Patriarchalism* is a type of traditional domination occurring in households and other small groups where the use of an organizational staff to enforce commands is not necessary. *Patrimonialism* is a form of traditional domination occurring in larger social structures that require an administrative apparatus to execute edicts.

In the patrimonial form of traditional domination, the administrative apparatus consists of a set of personal retainers exclusively loyal to the ruler. Weber observed that in addition to its grounding in custom, the officials' loyalties are based on either their dependence on the ruler for their positions and remuneration or their pledge of fealty to the leader, or both. As an ideal type, the essence of patrimonialism (traditional authority coupled with an administrative staff) is expressed by the following characteristics:

1. People obtain positions based on custom and loyalty to the leader.

2. Officials owe obedience to the leader issuing commands.

3. Personal and official affairs are combined.

4. Lines of authority are vague.

5. Task specialization is minimal.

In such a context, decisions are based on officials' views of what will benefit them and what the leader wants. Moreover, officials appropriate the means of production themselves or are granted them by the leader. Hence, where their jurisdiction begins and ends remains uncodified. A sheriff, for example, might both catch criminals and collect taxes (skimming off as much as possible). But how these tasks are accomplished will be idiosyncratic, subject to official whim rather than law. Thus, it should not be surprising that in *Economy and Society,* Weber described traditional domination as inhibiting the development of capitalism, primarily because rules are not logically established, officials have too wide a range for personal arbitrariness, and they are not technically trained.[24] Modern capitalism requires an emphasis on logic, procedure, and knowledge.

Rational-Legal Domination. The third type of domination is that based on law, what Weber called rational-legal authority. As he phrased it, "Legal domination [exists] by virtue of statute. . . . The basic conception is that any legal norm can be created or changed by a procedurally correct enactment.[25] Thus, the basis for legitimacy in a

---

[23]Ibid., 226.

[24]Ibid., 237–241.

[25]Quoted in Reinhard Bendix, *Max Weber: An Intellectual Portrait* (London: Heinemann, 1960), 418–419. For an analysis of Weber's views on rationality, see Stephen Kalberg, "Max Weber's Types of Rationality," *American Journal of Sociology* 85 (1980):1145–1179.

system of rational-legal domination lies in procedure. People believe that laws are legitimate when they are created and enforced in the proper manner. Similarly, people see leaders as having the right to act when they obtain positions in procedurally correct ways—for example, through election or appointment. In this context, then, Weber defined the modern state as based on the monopoly of physical coercion, a monopoly made legitimate by a system of laws binding both leaders and citizens. The rule of law, rather than of persons, reflects the process of rationalization. Nowhere is this more clearly observed than in a modern bureaucracy.

Weber called the administrative apparatus in a rational-legal system a *bureaucracy* and observed that it was oriented to the creation and enforcement of rules in the public interest. A bureaucracy is the archetypal example of instrumentally rational action. Although many people today condemn bureaucracies as inefficient, rigid, and incompetent, Weber argued that this mode of administration was the only means of attaining efficient, flexible, and competent regulation under a rule of law. In its logically pure form (as an ideal type), a bureaucratic administrative apparatus has different characteristics from those in traditional societies:[26]

1. People obtain positions based on knowledge and experience.

2. Obedience is owed to rules uniformly applicable to all.

3. Personal and official affairs are kept separate.

4. Lines of authority are explicit.

5. Task specialization is great.

According to Weber, bureaucratic administration in a rational-legal system is realized to the extent that staff members "succeed in eliminating from official business love, hatred, and all purely personal, irrational, and emotional elements."[27] But this is an ideal type. Weber knew that no actual bureaucracy operated in this way. People often obtain positions based on whom they know. Rules are often applied arbitrarily. Personal and official matters are often combined. Thus, the empirical task becomes assessing the degree to which a bureaucracy conforms to the ideal type (recall Figure 5.1). The issue is important because the bureaucratic ideal type reflects a fundamental value characteristic of modern societies: Political administration should be impersonal, objective, and based on knowledge, for only in this way can the rule of law be realized. Further, Weber emphasized that although this value seems commonplace today, it is historically new. It arose in the West and has become the dominant form of authority only in the last few 100 years. Finally, Weber's definition of bureaucracy points toward a fundamental arena of conflict in modern societies: Who is to make laws, and who is to administer them through their control of the bureaucracy?

---

[26]Weber, *Economy and Society,* 217–220. Our interpretation of the impact of bureaucracy is more benign than is Weber's. He saw bureaucracies as encasing people in an "iron cage" of reason and thereby stifling freedom; as such, bureaucracies are the archetype of the process of rationalization. This is why Diggins subtitled his book on Weber *Politics and the Spirit of Tragedy.*

[27]Weber, *Economy and Society,* 975.

Within the context of a rational-legal system of authority, political parties are the forms in which social strata struggle for power. As Weber puts it, "A political party . . . exists for the purpose of fighting for domination," to advance the economic interests or values of the group it represents, but it does so under the aegis of statutory regulation.[28] In general, the point of the struggle is to direct the bureaucracy via the creation of law, for in this way the goals of the various social strata are achieved. For example, the very rich, who own income-producing property in the United States, act to make sure that their economic interests are codified into law. Similarly, people in all social strata act to protect their interests and values, and the needs of those who do not participate are ignored.[29] The political process in Western societies, then, reflects basic cultural values: economic and social success are to be achieved through competition under the rule of law, and the process is rational in the sense of being pursued in a methodical manner.

Social Stratification: Class, Status Group, and Party

Weber tried to provide observers with a conceptual map outlining the parts of the stratification system. He believed that such an inventory of concepts would allow an objective description of stratification processes in modern capitalist societies. At the core of his scheme are three ideal types: class, status group, and party.

Class. For Weber, a *class* consists of those persons who have a similar ability to obtain positions in society, procure goods and services for themselves, and enjoy them via an appropriate lifestyle.[30] It should be recognized immediately that a class is defined, in part, by status considerations: the lifestyle of the stratum to which one belongs. In Weber's terminology, classes are statistical aggregates rather than groups. Behavior is class-oriented to the extent that the process by which people obtain positions, purchase goods and services, and enjoy them is characterized by an individualistic rather than a group perspective. For example, even though investors trying to make money on the stock market might have some common interests, share certain kinds of information with one another, and even join together to prevent outsiders from participating, each acts individually in seeking profits or in experiencing losses. Further, in the process of seeking profits, their behavior is typically characterized by an instrumentally rational orientation; that is, their action reflects a systematic calculation of means and ends based on knowledge (even if such knowledge is imperfect).

In Weber's analysis, classes are essentially economic phenomena that can exist only in a legally regulated money market where income and profit are the desired goals. In such a context, people's membership in a class can be determined objectively, based on their power to dispose of goods and services. For this reason Weber believed that one's "class situation is, in this sense, ultimately [a] market

---

[28]Ibid., 951.

[29]See Leonard Beeghley, "Social Structure and Voting in the United States: A Historical and International Analysis," *Perspectives on Social Problems* 3 (1992):265–287.

[30]Weber, *Economy and Society,* 302, 927.

situation."[31] The most important characteristic of a money market is that in its logically pure form, it is impersonal and democratic. Thus, all that should matter in the purchase of stock, groceries, housing, or any other commodity are factors such as one's cash and credit rating. Similarly, a person's class situation is also objectively determined, with the result that people can be ranked by their common economic characteristics and life chances.

In Weber's terminology, *rentiers* are those who live primarily off fixed incomes from investments or trust funds. For example, the large German landowners of his time were rentiers because these families had controlled much of the land for several generations and received their incomes from the peasants or tenant farmers who actually worked it. As a result of their possession of capital and values that they had acquired over time, the landowners chose to lead a less overtly acquisitive lifestyle. Weber called them rentiers because they did not work to increase their assets but simply lived off them, using their time for purposes other than earning a living. For example, they might hold public office or lead lives of idleness.

According to Weber, *entrepreneurs* are those, such as merchants, shipowners, and bankers, who own and operate businesses. Weber called them a commercial, or entrepreneurial, class because they actually work their property for the economic gain that it produces, with the result that in absolute terms the members of the entrepreneurial class often have more economic power, but less social honor (or prestige), than do rentiers.

This distinction between the uses to which income-producing property is put allowed Weber to differentiate between those who work as an avocation and those who work because they want to increase their assets; that is, this distinction reflects fundamental differences in values. In most societies, there exist privileged status groups, such as rentiers, the members of which "consider almost any kind of overt participation in economic acquisition as absolutely stigmatizing" despite its potential economic advantages. Usually, these families have possessed wealth for a long time, over several generations. Thus, even though economic-oriented (or class-oriented) action is individualistic and dominated by instrumentally rational action, value-rational behavior also occurs. Action at every stratum level varies along these two dimensions.

Weber asserted that the possession of capital by both rentiers and entrepreneurs provided them with great economic and political power and sharply distinguished them from those who did not own such property.[31] Both rentiers and entrepreneurs can monopolize the purchase of expensive consumer items. Both pursue monopolistic sales and pricing policies, whether legally or not. To some extent, both control opportunities for others to acquire wealth and property. Finally, both rentiers and entrepreneurs monopolize costly status privileges, such as education, that provide young people with future contacts and skills. In these terms, then, rentiers and entrepreneurs can be seen to have (roughly) similar levels of power; and because they are always a small proportion of the population, they often act together to protect their lifestyles. Even though they live rather differently, their source of income (ownership of

---

[31]Ibid., 303, 927.

capital) sets them apart from the other social classes. The distribution of property, in short, tends to prevent nonowners from competing for highly valued goods and perpetuates the structure of stratification from one generation to another.

In constructing his conceptual map of the class structure, Weber next considered those who do not own income-producing property. Despite not possessing the means of production, such people are not without economically and politically important resources in modern societies, and they can be meaningfully differentiated into a number of classes. The main criteria Weber used in making class distinctions among those without property are the worth of their services and the level of their skills; both factors are important indicators of people's ability to obtain positions, purchase goods, and enjoy them. In Weber's classificatory scheme, the "middle classes" comprised those individuals who today would be called white-collar workers because the skills that they sell do not involve manual labor: public officials, such as politicians and administrators; managers of businesses; members of the professions, such as doctors and lawyers; teachers and intellectuals; and specialists of various sorts, such as technicians, low-level white-collar employees, and civil servants. Because their skills are in relatively high demand in industrial societies, these people generally have more economic and political power than those who work with their hands.[32]

The less privileged, propertyless classes comprise people who today would be called blue-collar workers because their skills primarily involve manual labor. Without explanation, Weber said that such people could be divided into three levels: skilled, semiskilled, and unskilled workers. He did not elaborate much on the lifestyles of those without property.

By means of these ideal types, Weber described the parts of a modern class structure. The key factors distinguishing one class from another are (a) the uses to which property is put by those who own it and (b) the worth of the skills and services offered by those who do not own property. These factors combine in the marketplace to produce identifiable aggregates, or classes, the members of which have a similar ability to obtain positions, purchase goods, and enjoy them via an appropriate lifestyle

As described in Chapter 4, Marx posited that modern societies display a basic division between capitalists, those who own income-producing property, and proletarians, those who are forced to sell their labor power to survive. In his words, "Society as a whole is splitting up more and more into two great hostile camps, into two great classes facing each other: Bourgeoisie and Proletarian."[33]

Marx knew that this assertion was an exaggeration. He meant that historical evolution placed these two groups at the center of a class struggle, which would inevitably produce a communist society. But when examining actual historical events, Marx often looked at specific segments of society, such as bankers or the "lower middle class" or the *lumpenproletariat* (the very poor), analyzing their different

---

[32]Ibid., 304.

[33]Karl Marx and Friedrich Engels, *The Birth of the Communist Manifesto* (New York: International, 1975), 90.

experiences and interests with great insight.[34] Unlike Weber, however, Marx did not develop a systematic model (or map) of the class structure.

Table 5.1 shows that both Marx and Weber regarded the differences between those who own capital and those who do not as fundamental divisions in the class structure. The table also shows that Weber's map of the class structure is much more detailed than Marx's. Both those who own property and those who do not can be separated into classes (or strata) in a way that is useful to observers and subjectively meaningful to ordinary people. Thus, those capitalists who do not lead acquisitive lives are *rentiers*, and those who do are *entrepreneurs*. Sometimes the members of these two strata act together to preserve and protect their source of income, their property, but sometimes they do not, mainly because they have different values. Weber's distinction alerts observers to the need for specifying the conditions under which each type of capitalist—that is, rentiers or entrepreneurs— becomes prominent. Similarly, middle-class people see themselves as different from those who are skilled workers. As a result, they tend to live in different neighborhoods, make different friends, attend different schools, and participate in different leisure activities. Current research reveals that a semipermeable boundary separates middle-class people (white-collar workers) from working-class people (blue-collar workers) at all skill levels.

The final topic of importance in Weber's analysis of class is the possibility of group formation and unified political action by the propertyless classes. Like Marx, Weber said that this phenomenon was relatively rare in history because those who did not own property generally failed to recognize their common interests. As a result, action based on a similar class situation is often restricted to inchoate and relatively brief

Table 5.1   Marx's and Weber's Models of the Class Structure

Marx's Model	Weber's Model
1. Capitalists	1. Propertied
2. Proletarians	a. Rentiers
	b. Entrepreneurs
	2. Nonpropertied
	a. Middle classes
	b. Skilled workers
	c. Semiskilled workers
	d. Unskilled workers

---

[34]Karl Marx, *The Eighteenth Brumaire of Louis Bonaparte* (New York: International, 1963), "Critique of the Gotha Program," in *Selected Works*, vol. 3, ed. Karl Marx and Friedrich Engels (New York: International, 1969), 9–30.

mass reactions. Nonetheless, throughout history, perceived differences in life chances have periodically led to class struggles, although in most cases the point of the conflict focused on rather narrow economic issues, such as wages or prices, rather than on the nature of the political system that perpetuates their class situation.[35]

Although Weber alluded only briefly to the conditions under which the members of the propertyless classes might challenge the existing political order, he identified some of the same variables that Marx had:

1. Large numbers of people must perceive themselves to be in the same class situation.

2. They must be ecologically concentrated, as in urban areas.

3. Clearly understood goals must be articulated by an intelligentsia. Here, Weber suggested that people had to be shown that the causes and consequences of their class situation resulted from the structure of the political system itself.

4. The opponents must be clearly identified.

When these conditions are satisfied, Weber indicated, an organized class results. We turn now to another basis for action displayed by people in each stratum: the status group.

Status Groups. In Weber's work, a status group comprises those individuals who share "a specific, positive or negative, social estimation of honor."[36] Weber thus used the concepts of "status" and "status group" to distinguish the sphere of prestige evaluation (expressed by people's lifestyles) from that of monetary calculation (expressed by their economic behavior.). Although the two are interrelated, the distinction emphasizes that people's actions cannot be understood in economic terms alone. Rather, their values often channel action in specific directions.

The income from a person's job provides the ability to purchase goods and enjoy them; class membership is thus objectively determined by a simple monetary calculation. Status and honor are based on the judgments that people make about another's background, breeding, character, morals, and community standing; so a person's membership in a status group is always subjectively determined. Status-oriented behavior illustrates value-rational action—that is, action based on some value or values held for their own sake. Rather than acting on their economic interests, status-oriented people act as members of a group with whom they share a specific style of life and level of social honor. In Weber's words, "In contrast to classes, *Stände* (status groups) are normally groups. They are, however, of an amorphous kind."[37]

Status "always rests on distance and exclusiveness," in the sense that members of a status group actively express and protect their lifestyles in a number of specific

---

[35]Weber, *Economy and Society,* 305, 930–931.

[36]Ibid., 305–306, 932.

[37]Ibid., 932.

ways. (a) They extend hospitality only to social equals. Thus, they tend to invite into their homes, become friends with, eat with, and socialize with others who are like themselves in that they share similar lifestyles. (b) They restrict potential marriage partners to social equals (this practice is called connubium). Thus, they tend to live in the same areas as others who are like themselves and send their children to the same schools, with the result that their offspring generally marry others with similar values and ways of living. (c) They practice unique social conventions and activities. Thus, they tend to join organizations, such as churches and clubs, and spend their leisure time with others who share similar beliefs and lifestyles. (d) They try to monopolize "privileged modes of acquisition" of, for example, their property or occupations.[38]

This last tactic is important, for those in common status positions act politically to close off social and economic opportunities to outsiders to protect their capital or occupational investments. For example, because particular skills (say, in doctoring or carpentry) acquired over time necessarily limit the possibility of acquiring other skills, competing individuals "become interested in curbing competition" and preventing the free operation of the market. So they join together and, despite continued competition among themselves, attempt to close off opportunities for outsiders by influencing the creation and administration of law. Such attempts at occupational closure are ever recurring at all stratum levels, and they are "the source of property in land as well as of all guild [or union] monopolies."[39]

Party. As a theorist of power, Weber added another dimension to stratification: the party. For Weber, *party* denotes the "house of power," or the way in which power is organized and used to control members in a society; the distribution of power represents another dimension of stratification. In contrast to Marx, who tended to view power and status as mere reflections of who owned the means of production, Weber argued that class, status group, and party constitute separate bases of stratification, although they often highly correlate with each other; success in markets allows individuals to buy status group memberships and to exert a disproportionate influence on political decisions. Still, Weber saw stratification as multidimensional. People could hold different places along the three hierarchies marking a stratification system.

In fact, Weber's analysis of stratification emphasized that when there is a high correlation among class, status group, and party—that is, those high or low on one are also high and low on the other two—the potential for political conflict increases. Thus, when economic, political, and status group elites are pretty much the same individuals, those without power, money, or honor will become resentful. And if they have very little power, money, or honor and few chances to be upwardly mobile on any other or all of these three dimensions of stratification, they are even more likely to become angry and receptive to leaders who would advocate change in such a society. Thus, the more memberships in class, status group, and party correlate, the more those high in class, status group, and party horde resources and the more likely

---

[38]Ibid., 306, 935.

[39]Ibid., 342–343

tensions will surface in that society. These tensions over inequalities are often the fuel energizing social change.

Weber's Model of Social Change

Weber's analysis of systems of domination, especially his distinction between the three types of authority, implies a model of social change. Like Marx, Weber saw the source of change as endogenous (or internal) to the society. Figure 5.4 depicts Weber's vision of the internal system dynamics that change societies.

Weber saw the struggle for power as continuous in all societies. Those with power are organized and try to monopolize the means of coercion, while also seeking to legitimate their hold on power. Parties act strategically through the use of military force, co-optation, patronage, political alliances, and many other tactics to maintain power. At the same time, other segments of a society can seek to mobilize power and displace those who control government. Societies organized by patterns of traditional domination can remain relatively stable for many years, but eventually, tensions develop. These tensions can arise for many reasons, such as anger over unfair treatment, abuse of power, excessive taxation, lack of opportunities, inequalities in wealth and income, and just about any fault line in a stratified society. As these tensions mount, they increase the likelihood that charismatic leaders will emerge and

Figure 5.4 Weber's View of Chance and Social Change

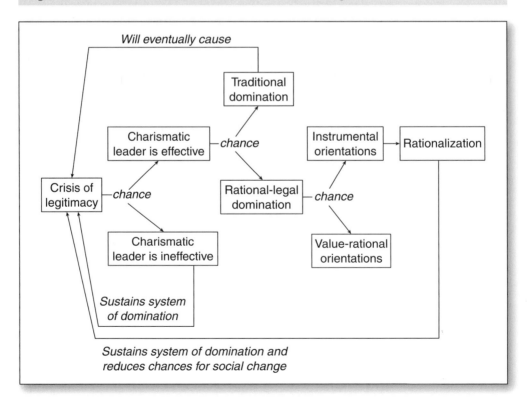

articulate the grievances of subordinates in the system of stratification. If the charismatic leaders are successful, they face the problem of how to "routinize" their charisma, thereby setting up yet another system of traditional domination or, potentially, a new system of rational-legal domination. If charisma is routinized via traditional authority, then a new system of stratification will emerge, revealing new sources of tension that will eventually lead to the emergence of new charismatic leaders to challenge the dominant party. If, however, a rational-legal system is put into place, it will have a greater capacity to resolve tensions.

Weber's Model of Stratification and Geopolitics

As a sociologist of power, seeking to explain how power is used in systems of domination, Weber was interested in the development of the state as an organizational order that could be used to administer power. Weber proposed a geopolitical theory of power, seeing both the legitimacy of political authority and the potential for the emergence of charismatic leaders as related to the relations of a society with other societies. In general, Weber argued that there is often a competition for prestige among states, with those that are successful in war and economic competition enjoying more prestige than do those that are not so successful.[40] Moreover, prestige in external relations with other states increases the legitimacy bestowed on political authority by the masses within the society. Thus, the administration of power, the degree of legitimacy given to those with power, and the potential for conflict are often tied to external, geopolitical events outside a society's borders.

Weber saw these dynamics as driven by several interrelated factors. The first was the size of the state, or the scale of the administrative structures used to exercise power. For the state to grow, production in the economy must be sufficient to create the surplus necessary to support specialized administrative personnel.

Another critical relation is between key economic actors and the state. When actors in the economy depend on the state for their right to engage in particular kinds of economic activity, as is the case with a chartered corporation or a company given a monopoly by the state, these economic actors will place pressure on the state to engage in external conflict if their interests are tied to success in the external system. For example, chartered corporations in America before the Revolutionary War gave economic actors in England a strong incentive to have the English government wage war or use coercion to protect their interests. When, however, the dependence of economic actors on the state is low but they still have interests in the external system, these economic actors are more likely, Weber believed, to exert pressures on the state to engage in co-optive strategies, such as trade agreements, rather than war. The success of the state in either war-making or deal-making in trade determines the prestige of a society and its ruling elites not only vis-à-vis other states but also in relation to the masses within the society. For example, Japan's prestige in the world economic system has been very high since World War II because of its success in achieving favorable trade relations with other countries; this prestige has, in turn, given the dominant political

---

[40]Ibid., 901–1372; see in particular, 901–920.

party prestige and legitimacy. Similarly, leaders in Japan enjoyed considerable prestige during the early phases of World War II, when they had military success, but this prestige declined with each setback in the Pacific and in Asia.

Another force entering this basic relationship between prestige in the world system and the legitimacy of its ruling elites is the level of inequality. Weber recognized that when high levels of inequality exist and when memberships in classes, parties, and status groups are highly correlated (i.e., members in upper classes are also members of ruling parties and high-prestige status groups, and vice versa), the potential for the emergence of charismatic leadership increases. Thus, a state that engages in diplomatic or military adventurism in relation with other states is more vulnerable if political power has been used in ways that increased the level of inequality within the society. Success in external relations will stave off the emergence of a charismatic leader, but if the state should lose prestige in external relations, then the conflict potential inhering in the stratification system increases dramatically, especially if charismatic leaders can emerge to take advantage of the state's loss of prestige.[41]

Thus, the dynamics of domination are very much tied to geopolitics, and in these, Weber can be considered an early world systems theorist. He saw clearly the connection between legitimation of a stratification order and the state, on one side, and the geopolitical position of a society in relation to its neighbors, on the other.

Weber on Capitalism and Rationalization

As we have emphasized, Weber was very much concerned with the process of rationalization. Why had rational-legal domination spread? Part of the answer can be found in Weber's famous analysis of religion, in which he argued that a change in religious beliefs (toward Protestantism) was the critical force in tipping Western European societies toward capitalism. We will examine this famous and controversial thesis in the next section, but before exploring this thesis, we address what Weber saw as a fundamental relationship between the use of money in free markets and the rationalization of orders in the political and economic arenas.[42] Weber recognized that market forces were an important precondition for the emergence of capitalism; moreover, once in place, they dramatically accelerated the process of rationalization.

For Weber, when money is introduced into exchanges, it becomes possible to engage in more precise and efficient calculations of value. That is, the worth of a good or commodity is more readily ascertained with money as a common measure of value. The use of money to mediate transactions and social relationships had slowly expanded in human history, primarily as the result of (a) the expansion of markets, where money would greatly facilitate transactions, and (b) the growth of the state, where liquid revenues could be taxed to expand state power. Money is a generalized medium that can be used to purchase any good or commodity, and so

---

[41]Theda Skocpol has pursued this Weberian argument in her *States and Social Revolutions* (New York: Cambridge University Press, 1979).

[42]Weber, *Economy and Society*, 63–212.

it greatly accelerated the ease of market transactions over the older patterns of barter (where one commodity is exchanged for another). As a result, it gave the state a means to purchase labor and other resources necessary to wield power. Moreover, Weber argued, rational-legal bureaucracy, whether the state's or that of economic actors, would not be possible without free labor willing to sell its services in a labor market for money. Thus, rationalization depended heavily on the emergence of free markets using money.

Money also facilitates the extension of credit because a debt can be expressed with one measure—the value of money—and the interest rate can similarly be calculated. With credit, economic activity can expand, as can the activities of the state, which, like any other actor, can enter credit markets. The use of credit further extends the calculability of utilities, and in so doing, money and credit rationalize market transactions. As this transition occurs, Weber believed, tradition, patronage, and other ways of regulating markets would decline. In their place come rational calculations of price, payments, debts, and interest. As older ways of organizing economic activity and exchange are pushed aside, productive units become more rational and begin to calculate their costs and profits against the yardstick of money, credit, interest notes, and market forces. Similarly, the relationship between labor and its employers shifts to one based on rational calculations rather than on patrimony or some other nonrational mechanism for organizing the workforce.

Once this level of rationalization has occurred, Weber felt, it will feed on itself, constantly expanding the rationality of the state. As the state becomes dependent on market-driven productivity to finance its operations, it will introduce legal rules, and enforce these rules, to ensure that contracts and agreements are honored. Thus, the rationality of the market becomes rational-legal domination by the state as increasingly rational actors use the law rather than tradition, affect, religion, and other nonrational bases of regulation to organize their affairs. Indeed, one of the most important bodies of law is the tax code, which specifies how, and how much, revenue the state can take from other actors to finance its operations. As the state depends more on this monetary source of revenue, coupled with its access to credit markets, it enacts more laws and expands its administrative structure to ensure a constant flow of revenue. As a result, the bureaucratized state becomes more instrumentally rational as it seeks ways to secure money (e.g., taxes, credit) to expand its functions and, hence, its capacity for domination.

Similarly, once money and credit fund economic actors and markets, markets and production expand, which further extends the use of money and credit. When the state begins to support markets through law, the use of money and credit in free markets can increase the scale of production and market distribution even more. Once a certain level of rationalization exists in the economy, organizations regulated by law and driven by instrumental-rationality (for profits) come to dominate.

Thus, Weber saw a dynamism in capitalism, much as Marx had, but with a very different prediction: the disenchantment of the social world by rational-legal domination in the economic and political arenas. Rather than sowing the seeds of its own destruction, as Marx had argued, Weber felt that rationalization had planted the seeds for its own perpetuation. The capacity to oppose this monolith would be lessened, and increasing aspects of social life would be calculable, rational, efficient, and dull. Weber thus came to a very different conclusion from Marx about the liberating potential of markets and capitalism. Humans would, in Weber's words, be locked in "the iron cage" of bureaucracy and rational-legal authority.

Weber also disagreed that this rational-legal juggernaut had been inevitable. He did not see history as marching inexorably anywhere, and certainly not to a liberating utopia. Rather, history was often random, moving in response to a chance confluence of events, and this had been the case for the rise of capitalism and the spread of rational-legal authority. Why had history made this turn toward increasing rationalization? For Weber, the answer resided in the emergence of Protestantism.

Weber had long been interested in religion, for its own sake, and particularly for an understanding of how it worked to legitimate orders and systems of domination, but he had also been interested in religion for another reason: to understand the rise of capitalism. Perhaps his most famous work, certainly outside of sociology, is *The Protestant Ethic and the Spirit of Capitalism.* In this essay, Weber argued that the key chance event turning the historical tide toward rational-legal forms of domination had been the rise of Protestantism in the West. This controversial work was only part of a more comprehensive study of religion, but even here, Weber was interested in explaining how religion in other, equally developed societies of the East had inhibited the rise of capitalism. Thus, one of the most important reasons why Weber studied religion was to discover the critical causal event that had unleashed capitalism and rationalization.

Weber's Study of Religion

The Protestant Ethic and the Spirit of Capitalism is Weber's most famous and probably most important study.[43] Published in two parts, in 1904 and 1905, it was one of his first works to be translated into English, and even more significantly, it was the first application of his mature methodological orientation. As a result, the *Protestant Ethic* is neither a historical analysis nor a politically committed interpretation of history. Rather, it is an exercise in historical hypothesis testing in which Weber constructed a logical experiment using ideal types as conceptual tools.

Although the *Protestant Ethic* is the most well-known of Weber's studies on the sociology of religion, it is nonetheless only a small portion of a much larger intellectual enterprise that Weber pursued intermittently for about fifteen years. In this grandiose "logical experiment," Weber tried not only to account for the confluence of events that were associated with the rise of modern capitalism in the West but also to explain why capitalism was not likely to have developed in any other section of the world—that is, "why did not the scientific, the artistic, the political, and the economic

---

[43]Max Weber, *The Protestant Ethic and the Spirit of Capitalism,* trans. Talcott Parsons (New York: Scribner's, 1958). For a more recent and better translation, see Stephen Kalberg, *The Protestant Ethic and the Spirit of Capitalism* (Los Angeles, CA: Roxbury, 2002); see especially the Introduction.

development [of China, India, and other areas] enter upon that path of rationalization which is peculiar to the occident?"[44] Thus, the *Protestant Ethic* is the first portion of a two-stage quasi-experiment. The second element in Weber's experiment is contained in a series of book-length studies on the religions of the East: *The Religion of China* (1913), *The Religion of India* (1916–1917), and *Ancient Judaism* (1917).[45]

The Quasi-Experimental Design

Before reviewing either the *Protestant Ethic* or Weber's other work on religion, we should make explicit the implicit research design of these works. In so doing, we will describe another sense in which Weber constructed "quasi-experimental designs" for understanding the causes of historical events. Weber's basic question is: Why did modern capitalism initially occur in the West and not in other parts of the world? To isolate the cause of this monumental historical change, Weber constructed the quasi-experimental design diagrammed in Figure 5.5.

In Figure 5.5, steps 1 through 5 approximate the stages of a laboratory situation as it must be adapted to historical analysis, which is why we label it a logical experiment. The West represents the experimental group in that something stimulated capitalism, whereas China and India represent the control groups because their economic systems did not change, even though they were as advanced as the West in technologies and other social forms. The stimulus that caused capitalism in the West was a set of religious beliefs associated with Protestantism (see step 3 of Figure 5.5). Weber wrote *The Protestant Ethic and the Spirit of Capitalism* for this reason.

The Protestant Ethic and the Spirit of Capitalism

Weber opened the *Protestant Ethic* with what was a commonplace observation at the end of the nineteenth century: occupational statistics in those nations of mixed religious composition seemed to show that those in higher socioeconomic positions were overwhelmingly Protestant. This relationship appeared especially true, Weber wrote, "wherever capitalism . . . has had a free hand."[46] Many observers in economics, literature, and history had commented on this phenomenon before Weber, and he

---

[44]Weber, "Author's Introduction," in *Protestant Ethic*, 25. It is important to recognize that Weber wrote this introduction in 1920 for the German edition of his *Collected Essays in the Sociology of Religion*. Thus, it is an overall view of Weber's work in the sociology of religion rather than an introduction to the *Protestant Ethic*. Scribner's 1976 edition of the book does not make this clear.

[45]Max Weber, *The Religion of China*, trans. Hans Gerth (New York: Free Press, 1951), *The Religion of India*, trans. Hans Gerth and Don Martindale (New York: Free Press, 1958), *Ancient Judaism*, trans. Hans Gerth and Don Martindale (New York: Free Press, 1952). In addition, Part 2 of *Economy and Society* contains a book-length study, "Religious Groups (The Sociology of Religion)," which is also available in paperback under the title *The Sociology of Religion*, trans. Ephraim Fishoff (Boston, MA: Beacon, 1963).

[46]Weber, *Protestant Ethic*, 25.

Figure 5.5 Weber's Quasi-Experimental Design in the Study of Religion

GROUP	STEP 1 Find "matched" societies in terms of their minimal conditions.	STEP 2 Do historical research on their properties before stimulus was introduced.	STEP 3 Examine the impact of the key stimulus, religious beliefs.	STEP 4 Use historical evidence to assess the impact of the stimulus.	STEP 5 View differences between Europe and China/India as caused by religious beliefs.
QUASI-EXPERIMENTAL GROUP	Western Europe	Descriptions of Europe (using historical ideal types)	Experiences stimulus with emergence of Protestantism	Modern capitalism	Western Europe is changed.
QUASI-CONTROL GROUP	China	Descriptions of China (using historical ideal types)	Experiences no stimulus	No capitalism	China is much the same as before.
QUASI-CONTROL GROUP	India	Descriptions of India (using historical ideal types)	Experiences no stimulus	No capitalism	India is much the same as before.

cited a number of them.[47] Hence, in the *Protestant Ethic,* Weber was not trying to prove that a relationship between Protestantism and economic success in capitalist societies existed because he took its existence as given. In his words, "It is not new that the existence of this relationship is maintained. . . . Our task here is to explain the relation."[48]

To show that Protestantism was related to the origin of the spirit of capitalism in the West, Weber began with a sketch of what he meant by the latter term. Like many of his key concepts, the spirit of capitalism is a historical ideal type in that it conceptually accentuates certain aspects of the real world as a tool for understanding historical processes.[49] Although he did not state what he meant very clearly, an omission that helped contribute to the tremendous controversy over the *Protestant Ethic*'s thesis, his concept of the spirit of capitalism appears to have the following components:[50]

1. Work is valued as an end in itself. Weber was fascinated by the fact that a person's "duty in a calling [or occupation] is what is most characteristic of the social ethic of capitalistic culture, and is in a sense the fundamental basis of it."

2. Trade and profit are taken not only as evidence of occupational success but also as indicators of personal virtue. In Weber's words, "The earning of money within the modern economic order is, so long as it is done legally, [seen as] the result and the expression of virtue and proficiency in a calling."

3. A methodically organized life governed by reason is valued not only as a means to a long-term goal, economic success, but also as an inherently proper and even righteous state of being.

4. Embodied in the righteous pursuit of economic success is a belief that immediate happiness and pleasure should be forgone in favor of future satisfaction. As Weber noted, "The *summum bonum* of this ethic, the earning of more and more money, combined with the strict avoidance of all spontaneous enjoyment of life, is above all completely devoid of an eudaemonistic, not to say hedonistic, admixture."

In sum, then, these values—the goodness of work, success as personal rectitude, the use of reason to guide one's life, and delayed gratification—reflect some of the most important cultural values in the West because they constitute perceptions of

---

[47] Ibid., 43–45, 191 (Note 23). See also Reinhard Bendix, "*The Protestant Ethic*—Revisited," in *Scholarship and Partisanship: Essays on Max Weber,* ed. Reinhard Bendix and Guenther Roth (Berkeley: University of California Press, 1971), 299–310.

[48] Ibid., 191.

[49] Weber hints at his ideal-type strategy but does not bother to explain it in the initial paragraphs of Chapter 2 of the *Protestant Ethic,* 47. He refers to the need to develop a "historical individual"—that is, "a complex of elements associated in historical reality which we unite into a conceptual whole from the standpoint of their cultural significance." This phrasing reveals the influence of Heinrich Rickert, as discussed in the last chapter.

[50] Weber, *Protestant Ethic,* 53–54.

appropriate behavior that are shared by all. Weber emphasized, however, that the widespread application of such values to everyday life was historically unique and of relatively recent origin. He believed that the greatest barrier to the rise of the spirit of capitalism in the West was the inertial force of traditional values. To varying degrees, European societies before the seventeenth century were dominated by "traditional modes of action." For example, religion rather than science was used as the primary means of verifying knowledge. Bureaucracies composed of technically trained experts were unknown. Patterns of commerce and most other forms of daily life were dominated by status rather than class considerations; that is, people's economic actions were dictated by their membership in religious groups rather than by market factors. Finally, legal adjudication did not involve the equal application of law to all individuals. In short, the choice between instrumentally rational action and value-rational action did not exist. Rather, customs dictated behavior.

In such a context, of course, some individuals tried to make money. As Weber remarks, "Capitalism existed in China, India, Babylon, in the classic world, and in the Middle Ages."[51] But it was traditional capitalism, in which the ideal was simply to acquire enough money without spending too much time doing it so one could live as one was "accustomed to live." Weber described the traditional enterprises of the nobility as "adventurer capitalism," referring to investment in long-distance trade (e.g., in spices or silk), from which one might obtain a windfall profit sufficient to last a lifetime, or the purchase of government offices (e.g., tax collector), from which one skimmed off a portion of the revenue. "Capitalistic acquisition as an adventure has been at home in all types of economic society which have known trade with the use of money."[52] Such activities, however, were not the center of these people's lives. The existence of individual adventurer capitalists, moreover, differs from a rationalized capitalist economy, based on the mass production of consumer goods, in which the entire population is oriented to making money.

In his *General Economic History,* written some years later, Weber identified the major structural changes that he believed, taken together, had caused the development of rationalized capitalist economies in Western Europe rather than elsewhere:

1. The process of industrialization through which muscle power was supplanted by new forms of energy
2. The rise of a free labor force, whose members had to work for wages or starve
3. The increasing use of systematic accounting methods
4. The rise of a free market unencumbered by religious restrictions
5. The gradual imposition and legitimation of a system of calculable law
6. The increasing commercialization of economic life through the use of stock certificates and other paper instruments
7. The rise of the spirit of capitalism

---

[51]Ibid., 52.

[52]Ibid., 57–58. See also Max Weber, "Anticritical Last Word on the Spirit of Capitalism," trans. Wallace A. Davis, *American Journal of Sociology* 83 (1978):1127.

Although all these historical developments were to varying degrees unique to the West, in the *General Economic History* Weber still regarded the last factor as the most decisive. Thus, in attempting to understand the origin of the economic differences between Protestants and Catholics, he was not trying to deny the fundamental significance of these structural changes but to show the significance of the culture of capitalism and its unintended relationship to Protestant ethical teachings.

Weber believed that the Puritans and the other Protestant sects destroyed the cultural values of traditional society, although this was not the intent of those who adopted the new faiths, nor could this effect have been predicted in advance. In the *Protestant Ethic,* Weber focused mainly on Calvinism, with much shorter discussions of Pietism, Methodism, and Baptism appended to the main analysis. His strategy was to describe Calvinist doctrines by quoting extensively from the writings of its various theologians, then to impute the psychological consequences those doctrines had on people who organized their lives in those terms, and finally to show how they resulted in specific (and historically new) secular values and ways of living. In Weber's words, he was interested in ascertaining "those psychological sanctions which, originating in religious belief and the practice of religion, gave a direction to practical conduct and held the individual to it."[53] In this way, he could give a powerful example of the manner in which cultural phenomena influence social action and, at the same time, rebut the "vulgar" Marxists, who thought economic factors were the sole causal agents in historical change.

Based on an analysis of Calvinist writings, such as the *Westminster Confession of 1647,* from which he quoted extensively, Weber interpreted Calvinist doctrine as having four consequences for those who accepted its tenets.

First, because the Calvinist doctrine of predestination led people to believe that God, for incomprehensible reasons, had divided the human population into two groups, the saved and the damned, a key problem for all individuals was to determine the group to which they belonged. Second, because people could not know with certainty whether they were saved, they inevitably felt a great inner loneliness and isolation. Third, since a change in one's relative state of grace was seen as impossible, people inevitably began to look for signs that they were among the elect. In general, Calvinists believed that two clues could be used as evidence: (1) faith, for all had an absolute duty to consider themselves chosen and to combat all doubts as temptations of the devil, and (2) intense worldly activity, for in this way the self-confidence necessary to alleviate religious doubts could be generated. Fourth, all believers were expected to lead methodical and ascetic lives unencumbered by irrational emotions, superstitions, or desires of the flesh. As Weber put it, the good Calvinist was expected to "Methodically supervise his own state of grace in his own conduct, and thus to penetrate it with asceticism," with the result that each person engaged in "A rational planning of the whole of one's life in accordance with God's will."[54] The significance of this last doctrine is that in Calvinist communities worldly

---

[53]Weber, *Protestant Ethic,* 97. See also Stephen Kalberg, "The Rationalization of Action in Max Weber's Sociology of Religion," *Sociological Theory* 8 (1990):58–84.

[54]Weber, *Protestant Ethic,* 153. As a Protestant, Weber may have overemphasized the distinction between Protestantism and Catholicism.

asceticism was not restricted to monks and other "religious virtuosi" (to use Weber's phrase) but was required of all as they conducted their everyday lives in their mundane occupations or callings.

To show the relationship between the worldly asceticism fostered by the Protestant sects and the rise of the spirit of capitalism, Weber chose to focus on Puritan ministers' guidelines for everyday behavior, as contained in their pastoral writings. The clergy's teachings, which were set forth in books such as Richard Baxter's *Christian Directory,* tended to reflect the major pastoral problems they encountered. As such, their writings provide an idealized version of everyday life in Puritan communities. Although it must be recognized that patterns of social action do not always conform to cultural ideals, such values do provide a general direction for people's behavior. Most people try, even if imperfectly, to adhere to those standards of appropriate behavior dominant in their communities, and the Puritans were no exception. Further, the use of these kinds of data suggests the broad way in which Weber interpreted the idea of "explanatory understanding" (*verstehen*): because people's own explanations of their actions often involve contradictory motives that are difficult to reconcile, he was perfectly willing to use an indirect means of ascertaining the subjective meaning of social action among the Puritans.

Based on Weber's analysis, it appears that the Puritan communities were dominated by three interrelated dictums, which, although a direct outgrowth of Puritan theology, eventuated over the long run in a secular culture of capitalism.

The first of these pronouncements is that God demands rational labor in a calling. As Weber noted, Puritan pastoral literature is characterized "By the continually repeated, often almost passionate preaching of hard, continuous bodily or mental labour."[55] From this point of view, there can be no relaxation, no relief from toil, for labor is an exercise in ascetic virtue and rational, methodical behavior in a calling is taken as a sign of grace. Hence, from the Puritan's standpoint, "waste of time is . . . the first and in principle the deadliest of sins," because "every hour lost is lost to labour for the glory of God." As Weber observed, this dictum not only provides an ethical justification for the modern division of labor (in which occupational tasks are divided up efficiently) but also reserves its highest accolades for those sober middle-class individuals who best exemplify the methodical nature of worldly asceticism. As an aside, it should be noted that members of this stratum became the primary carriers of Puritan religious beliefs precisely because they garnered immense economic, social, and political power as a result. In general, Weber emphasized that those who were able to define and sanctify standards of appropriate behavior also benefited materially.[56]

The second directive states that the enjoyment of those aspects of social life that do not have clear religious value is forbidden. Thus, from the point of view of the

---

[55]Ibid., 158.

[56]Ibid., 176. Although Weber's point was that religious values influenced behavior, he emphasized that values and lifestyles are interrelated. Religiosity permeated every aspect of daily life. See Robert Wuthnow, *Communities of Discourse: Ideology and Social Structure in the Reformation, the Enlightenment, and European Socialism* (Cambridge, MA: Harvard University Press, 1989).

Puritan ministers, secular literature, the theater, and nearly all other forms of leisure-time activity were irrelevant or even morally suspect. As a result, they tried to inculcate in their parishioners an extraordinarily serious approach to life, for people should direct their attention toward the practical problems dominating everyday life and subject them to rational solutions.

The third guideline specifies that people have a duty to use their possessions for socially beneficial purposes that redound to the glory of God. Thus, the pursuit of wealth for its own sake was regarded as sinful, for it could lead to enjoyment, idleness, and "temptations of the flesh." From this point of view, those who acquire wealth through God's grace and hard work are mere trustees who have an obligation to use it responsibly.

Even allowing for the usual amount of human imperfection, Weber argued, the accumulation of capital and the rise of the modern bourgeoisie were the inevitable result of whole communities sharing the values dictating hard work, limited enjoyment and consumption, and the practical use of money. Hence, modern capitalism emerged. Weber's causal argument is diagrammed in Figure 5.6. Over time, of course, Puritan ideals gave way under the secularizing influence of wealth because people began to enjoy their material possessions. Thus, although the religious roots of the spirit of capitalism died out, Puritanism bequeathed to modern people "an amazingly good, we may even say a pharisaically good, conscience in the acquisition of money."

The predominance of such a value in Western societies is historically unique. It led Weber to some rather pessimistic observations in the concluding paragraphs of the *Protestant Ethic.* He believed that the rise of modern capitalism reflected the process of rationalization we referred to earlier. People are now taught to lead methodical lives, using reason buttressed by knowledge to achieve their goals. As he

Figure 5.6 Weber's Causal Argument for the Emergence of Capitalism

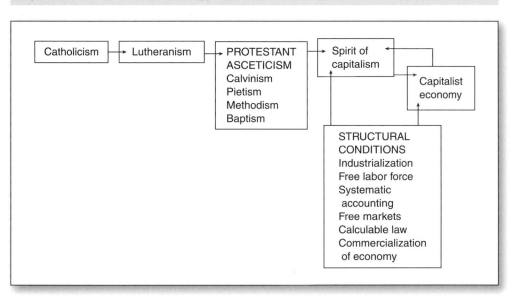

put it, "The idea of duty in one's calling prowls about in our lives like the ghost of dead religious beliefs," with the result that whereas "the Puritan wanted to work in a calling; we are forced to do so." In effect, the culture of capitalism, combined with capitalist social and economic institutions, places people in an iron cage from which there appears to be no escape and for which there is no longer a religious justification. This recognition leads to Weber's last, sad lament: "Specialists without spirit, sensualists without heart; this nullity imagines that it has attained a level of civilization never before achieved."[57]

Weber's Comparative Studies of Religion and Capitalism

During the years following publication of the *Protestant Ethic*, Weber continued his analysis of the relationship between religious belief and social structure to show why it was not very likely that capitalism as an economic system could have emerged anywhere else in the world.[58] Weber's most important works in this regard are *The Religion of China* and *The Religion of India*. They represent the extension of the "logical experiment" begun some years earlier.

Both of these extended essays are similar in format in that Weber began by assessing those characteristics of Chinese and Indian social structure that either inhibited or, under the right circumstances, could have contributed to the development of capitalism in that part of the world. For purposes of illustration, the examples used here come from *The Religion of China*. Thus, in China during the period when capitalism arose in the West, a number of structural factors existed that could have led to a similar development in the Orient. First, there was a great deal of internal commerce and trade with other nations. Second, because of the establishment and maintenance (for more than 1,200 years) of nationwide competitive examinations, there was an unusual degree of equality of opportunity in the process of status attainment. Third, the society was generally stable and peaceful, although Weber was clearly too accepting of the myth of the "unchanging China." Fourth, China had many large urban centers, and geographical mobility was a relatively common occurrence. Fifth, there were relatively few formal restrictions on economic activity. Finally, there were a number of technological developments in China that were more advanced than

---

[57]Weber, *Protestant Ethic*, 180–183.

[58]See Weber's "Anticritical Last Word," as well as the many explanatory footnotes in the *Protestant Ethic*. Most of these footnotes were added around 1920. The debate over Weber's "logical experiment" has continued as observers struggle to understand the origins of modernity. See Robert L. Green (ed.), *Protestantism and Capitalism: The Weber Thesis and Its Critics* (Lexington, MA: D. C. Heath, 1959); S. N. Eisenstadt (ed.), *The Protestant Ethic and Modernization* (New York: Basic Books, 1968); Gordon Marshall, *In Search of the Spirit of Capitalism: An Essay on Max Weber's Protestant Ethic Thesis* (New York: Columbia University Press, 1982); *Weber's Protestant Ethic: Origins, Evidence, Context,* ed. Hartmut Lehmann and Guenther Roth (New York: Cambridge University Press, 1993); Stephen Innes, *Creating the Commonwealth: The Economic Culture of Puritan New England* (New York: Norton, 1995); and Stanley Lieberson, "Einstein, Renoir, and Greeley: Some Thoughts about Evidence in Sociology," *American Sociological Review* 57 (1992):1–15.

those in Europe at the same time (the use of gunpowder, knowledge of astronomy, book printing, etc.). As Weber noted, all these structural factors could have aided in the development of a Chinese version of modern capitalism.

He emphasized, however, that the Chinese social structure also displayed a number of characteristics that had clearly inhibited the widespread development of any form of capitalism in that part of the world. First, although the Chinese possessed an abundance of precious metals, especially silver, an adequate monetary system had never developed. Second, because of the early unification and centralization of the Chinese empire, cities never became autonomous political units. As a result, the development of local capitalistic enterprises was inhibited. Third, Chinese society was characterized by the use of "substantive ethical law" rather than calculable legal procedure. As a result, legal judgments were made considering the particular characteristics of the participants and sacred tradition rather than by the equal imposition of common standards. Finally, the Chinese bureaucracy comprised classically learned persons rather than technically trained experts. Thus, the examinations regulating status attainment "tested whether the candidate's mind was thoroughly steeped in literature and whether or not he possessed the ways of thought suitable to a cultural man."[59] Hence, the idea of the trained expert was foreign to the Chinese experience.

In sum, according to Weber, all these characteristics of the Chinese social structure inhibited the development of an oriental form of modern capitalism. Nonetheless, the examples noted do suggest that such a development remained possible. Yet Weber argued that the rise of capitalism as an economic system was quite unlikely in either China or India, for he found no evidence of patterns of religious beliefs that could be compatible with the spirit of capitalism. Moreover, he believed that without the transformative power of religion, the rise of new cultural values was not likely. In China before this century, the religion of the dominant classes, the bureaucrats, was Confucianism. Weber characterized Confucianism by noting that it had no concept of sin but only of faults resulting from deficient education. Further, Confucianism had no metaphysics and thus no concern with the origin of the world or with the possibility of an afterlife, and hence, there was no tension between sacred and secular law. According to Weber, Confucianism was a rational religion concerned with events in this world, but with a peculiarly individualistic emphasis. Good Confucians were less interested in the state of society than with their own propriety, as indicated by their development as educated persons and by their pious relations with others (especially their parents). In Weber's words, the educated Chinese person "controls all his activities, physical gestures, and movements as well, with politeness and with grace in accordance with the status mores and the commands of 'propriety.'"[60] Rather than seeking salvation in the next world, the Confucian accepted this world as given and merely desired to behave prudently.

On this basis, Weber asserted that Confucianism was not very likely to result in an Asian form of the culture of capitalism. He made a similar argument about

---

[59]Weber, *Religion of China,* 156.

[60]Ibid., 156.

Hinduism four years later in *The Religion of India.* Thus, by means of these comparative studies, Weber tried to show logically not only why Protestantism was associated with the rise of the culture of capitalism in the West but also why other religions could not have stimulated similar developments in other parts of the world.[61]

Weber's Outline of the Social System

In all his work, Weber employed, at least implicitly, a vision of society as a social system that consists of three analytically separable dimensions: (1) culture, (2) social structure (patterns of social action), and (3) psychological orientations (see Figure 5.7). Cultural values and beliefs, patterned ways of acting in the world, and the psychological states are all reciprocally related.[62] *The Protestant Ethic and the Spirit of Capitalism* provides one illustration of this model. Weber also had to consider the extent to which both the social structure and people's psychological orientations were reciprocally related to the cultural values he was analyzing. Thus, he argued that the religious beliefs characteristic of the new faiths fundamentally influenced patterns of social action among people—not only among the Puritans but also among those who encountered the underlying beliefs of these faiths. Puritan values spread, in part, because people found them to be congenial to their own secular ambitions as they developed during a time of great change. Hence, as people adopted new beliefs and values, they altered their daily lives; conversely, as individuals began living in new ways (often because they were forced to), they changed their fundamental beliefs and values. Thus, historically new patterns of social action reinforced the new values that had arisen.

Weber, however, concentrated on the Puritans themselves, describing the psychological consequences that their beliefs must have had for their daily lives. Because of their uncertainty and isolation, people looked for signs of their salvation and found them in their ability to work hard and maintain their faith. Hence, the Puritans' psychological needs led them to historically new and unique patterns of social action characterized not only by hard work (medieval peasants certainly worked as hard) but also by a methodical pursuit of worldly goods.

Figure 5.7   Weber's Model of the Social System

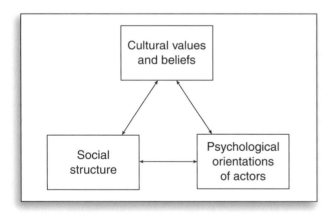

---

[61]Subsequent events, however, have shown that Confucianism is congenial to capitalism. See Peter M. Berger, *The Capitalist Revolution* (New York: Basic Books, 1986).

[62]The basis for our interpretation is Talcott Parsons, "Introduction," in Max Weber, *The Theory of Social and Economic Organization* (Glencoe, IL: Free Press, 1947), 3–86. Some scholars agree with Parsons's interpretation; see Mommsen, *The Age of Bureaucracy,* 1–21. Others disagree with it; see Bendix, *Max Weber: An Intellectual Portrait.*

The result was the secularization of Puritan religious values and their transformation into what he called the spirit of capitalism. Hence, it is possible to extrapolate from Weber's analysis a set of generic factors—culture, social structure, and psychological orientations—that are taken today as the fundamental features of social organization.

Weber's implicit model of the most general components of social organization has proved to be of tremendous significance in the development of sociology. For example, virtually all introductory sociology textbooks (which we will use here as a rough indicator of the state of the field) now contain a series of chapters, usually located at the beginning, titled something like "Culture," "Social Structure" or "Society," and "Personality and Socialization." The reason for this practice is that these topics provide an essential conceptual orientation to the discipline of sociology. Weber's model, then, serves as a heuristic device rather than as a dynamic analysis of the process of interaction. It can, however, lead to such an analysis—which is all Weber intended. Thus, the model is an essential first step in constructing a set of concepts that would be useful in describing and, hence, understanding modern societies.

Weber's Theoretical Legacy**

The first part of Weber's *Economy and Society* begins with an analysis of action, social relationships, and legitimated orders. Each of these phenomena is defined as an ideal type, revolving around the relative amounts of *rational*, *traditional*, and *affectual* orientations of actors. Weber gives the impression that he is building a theory from the micro level, moving through more meso structures like legitimated orders, and then on to macro-level societal processes like rationalization. These opening pages are misleading, however, because Weber does not develop a theory in this systematic way. Rather, most of his theorizing is at the meso and macro levels, emphasizing phenomena such as religious and legal systems, patterns of domination, organizational structures like bureaucracies and cities, and stratification systems revolving around classes, status groups, and parties. Weber continually refers to orientations of individuals, but he does not systematically analyze the relationships among culture, social structures, and individual actions. Probably the most systematic analysis among these various levels of reality can be found in *The Protestant Ethic and the Spirit of Capitalism*, but for most of Weberian sociology, we get only glimpses of a multidimensional approach. How, then, do we get a handle on Weber's sociology when our goal is to convert it into abstract models and general principles?

The answer to this question is that we must examine meso-level structures to get a picture of Weber's more macro views of society as a whole, but this strategy leaves the micro level of analysis of action and social relationships outside of the models

---

Note: **This section is written by me, and so my coauthor for other materials in this chapter, Leonard Beeghley, should not be held responsible for the implied criticisms and for what some will see as inappropriate formalization of Weber's ideas.

and principles. There is no easy way to include the micro portions of Weber's sociology because a systematic analysis of the connection between micro and meso levels of analysis is not undertaken, despite their discussion in the early pages of *Economy and Society*. In general, Weber simply stated that the structure of a given meso structure was sustained by a particular type of action, but assertions are not analyses. Thus, in our models of Weberian sociology, we will not explicitly incorporate the analysis of action, except to note where Weber sees certain cultural and structural forces as constraining the type of action orientations among actors, and vice versa.

Weber's Causal Models of Social Organization

Weber's Model of Rationalization. As emphasized earlier, Weber organized his work around the theme of rationalization. In Figure 5.8, I have abandoned much of Weber's vocabulary, which is too mired in ideal-type distinctions; instead, I offer my views on Weber's general image of the cultural and social forces causing rationalization. As these forces operate, Weber argued, actors are increasingly oriented to instrumental-rationality, whereas legitimated orders are structured by rational-legal rules. Thus, for each force listed in the model, there are organizational orders emerging that move away from tradition, affect, and even value-rationality toward instrumental-rationality, because these forces begin to play off each other and accelerate the dynamics involved, the iron cage of the rational-legal form of domination.

In the model in Figure 5.8, we can begin at the left with Weber's emphasis that certain material conditions are necessary for capitalism—the ultimate form of rational-legal authority—to emerge. One is inanimate sources of power, or some minimal level of industrial production; another is free markets for exchanging goods and services, including labor; and perhaps the most important is a system of ascetic cultural orientations, as personified by the "Protestant ethic." Added to these conditions is money, which makes utilities calculable and credit possible. With credit and money, the volume and velocity of market exchanges increase; and as more and more goods and services are bought and sold, the level of profit and wealth increases. The reverse causal loops are particularly important in Weber's argument because once ascetic values, markets, money, credit, and wealth are transformed, these very processes feed back on each other. As the scale of markets increases, so does production; as the use of money and credit expand, the volume and velocity of transactions increase, with the latter feeding back to increase the scale of markets. Once profits and wealth are created, these are reinvested in production, especially when ascetic cultural orientations dominate and encourage people to save. Both ascetic cultural orientations and market transactions operate to shift cultural values to emphasize instrumental-rationality over value-rationality, tradition, and affect, although this process takes time (as is illustrated by Weber in his view that the "spirit of capitalism" emerges out of the religious-inspired "Protestant ethic"). The important point is that all of the arrows in the model—direct, indirect, and reverse—are positive causal chains (except for the one heading to opposition movement), emphasizing that once a certain threshold of capitalism is initiated, economic growth and rationality continually accelerate and decrease the likelihood of revolt.

Figure 5.8 Weber's Model of Rationalization

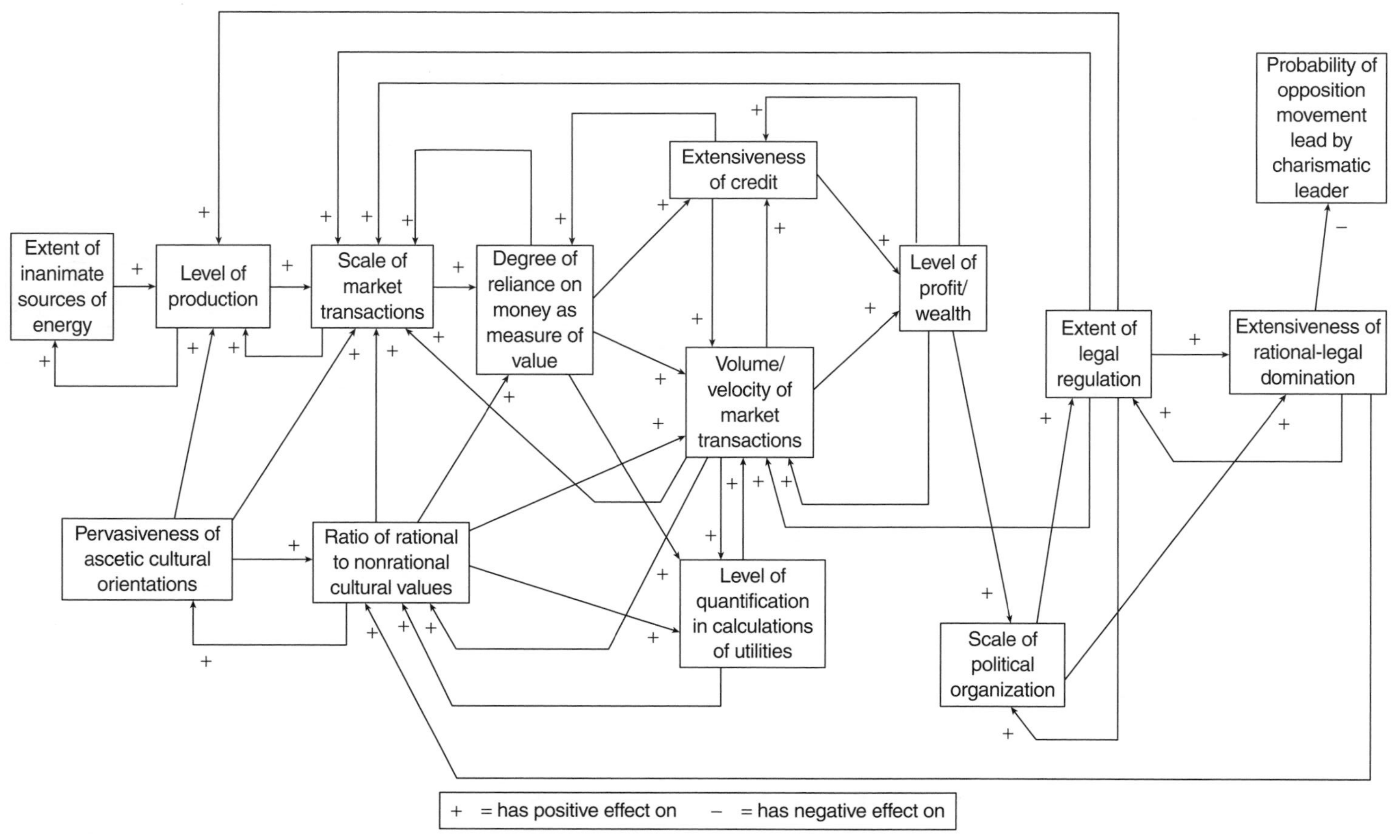

I have not yet mentioned the political and legal processes involved, but they are critical to rational-legal domination and, hence, the rationalization of society as a whole. Increased wealth allows for the expansion of the state, especially when wealth comes in the form of money, which can be used to buy labor (administrators, police, military) and to finance large-scale projects from war to domestic infrastructures (and, of course, elite privilege). Once the larger state becomes dependent on the flow of money, it begins to enact laws that allow it to regulate production and market activities (as indicated by the reverse causal arrows flowing out of legal regulation). Government increasingly has an interest in the productivity of the economy, and so it begins to shift the basis of regulation from tradition to law; as this occurs, the centers of power in a society begin to dominate through rational-legal means. Indeed, economic, political, and legal orders become heavily bureaucratized, and as this bureaucratic domination spreads, it reinforces cultural values emphasizing instrumental-rationality. In turn, these values encourage expansion of bureaucratization of production and market orders, as well as the state. In the end, these positively reinforcing cycles cause the spread of rational-legal domination, and in this form of domination, opposition movements are less likely to occur because the traditional forms of domination in which such movements had typically arisen have now been pushed aside by rational-legal orders. Indeed, the only negatively signed arrow in the model is from rational-legal domination to opposition movements led by a charismatic leader, a clear indicator of Weber's views about the iron cage imposed by instrumental-rationality.

The model in Figure 5.8 is rather complex, and it would be more so if we inserted a number of more micro- and meso-level factors, including (a) the action orientations among people (from traditional, affectual, and value-rational to instrumentally rational), (b) the shift in social relations from a communal to associative basis, (c) the movement in organizational forms from patrimonial to bureaucratic bases, and (d) the alteration of stratification systems from traditional status groups, parties, and classes to those increasingly shaped by market forces and the power of actors in the state. We can perhaps recapture some of this detail by examining key elements suggested by the model in more detail.

Weber's Model of Culture and Rationalization. The model in Figure 5.9 illustrates the relationship among ascetic cultural values emphasizing worldly activity and other key processes of rationalization. The first is the arrow from a chance event, as Weber thought the Protestant Reformation to be. Sometimes, by chance, charismatic leaders articulate a set of cultural values that, potentially, can initiate rationalization. As Weber would have emphasized, however, other material conditions need to be present, and these are outlined in the model. Ascetic values will direct action and social relationships in a rational direction, but it is also possible that rational activity at the micro level can, over time, generate a sufficient number of associative relations so that new, more ascetic value orientations gradually emerge in a society. These might or might not have a religious basis, but over time, they can evolve into purely secular values emphasizing instrumental-rationality. Once this causal sequence is initiated, ascetic and rational values become the "orientations" that motivate actors to behave rationally to form rational associative relations and to create legitimated orders based on law.

Figure 5.9 Weber's Model of Culture and Rationalization

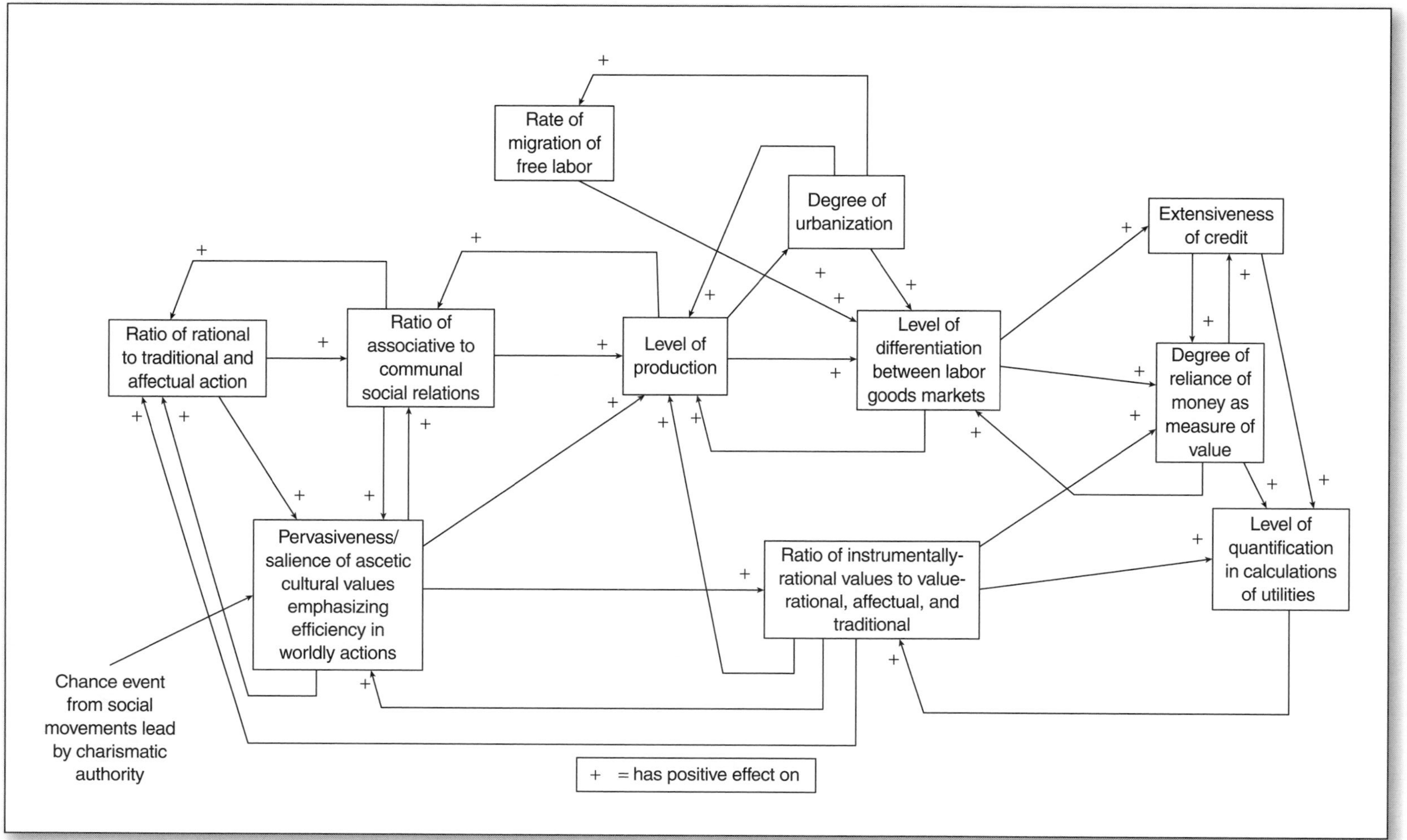

In the model, however, it is important to stress that for this set of causal chains to operate, other conditions (from Weber's model on the rise of capitalism) must be in place. Production must reach a certain threshold, with at least the beginnings of industrialism. Urban areas must grow to concentrate productive capital and labor. A distinct labor market must exist and should be differentiated from other markets. The use of money and credit will need to increase the extent to which people quantify the calculation of utilities, particularly through new kinds of accounting and bookkeeping systems. As the direct, indirect, and reverse causal arrows all indicate, these forces will increase the ratio of instrumentally rational values to those based on affect, value-rationality, and tradition. As this process occurs, a secular worldly asceticism will begin to provide the orientations that guide the motivations of individuals in all legitimated orders. As a result, people engage in associative social relations in organizational and stratification orders that push production, urbanization, market differentiation, use of money and credit, and quantification further along the road to rational-legal domination.

Weber's Model of Markets, Money, Power, and Law. In Figure 5.10, I outline in more detail Weber's underlying argument about the power of markets and the use of money to transform not only the economy but political and legal systems as well. For rational-legal domination to be complete, the centers of power and production must both be organized in bureaucratic organizational forms within institutional orders legitimated by law. Although cultural values are critical in this process, so are markets, money, and credit. Relations among this latter set of forces are arrayed in Figure 5.10.

When money is increasingly used in exchange relations, it has transforming effects, many of which are mediated by the extension of credit. With money, it becomes possible to offer credit, and the two together force a general increase in the quantitative calculation of utilities. Monies lent, monies paid back, and interest accrued must all be calculated when credit is extended; more generally, money orients people to the quantitative nature of exchange relations. All of these forces together will increase the velocity and volume of market activities. As such activities accelerate, they feed back and increase the pervasiveness of the very forces that expanded market activity in the first place—that is, use of money, credit, and quantitative calculations.

As markets grow, the ratio of rational, profit-oriented to nonrational forms of organizing production increases. For, once markets are up and running, using money, credit, and new ways of accounting, production becomes increasingly oriented to profits; and as profits become the motive for action, these new orientations of actors feed back and accelerate the processes that increase the ratio of profit-making to non–profit-making organizations.

The seat of power is never a passive bystander to these processes. With money and credit, government can tax and borrow, and in this way, the scale of political organization and authority can expand. Government can hire more people and do more things. No longer must political actors rely on traditional ways of financing their activities, such as patronage in exchange for soldiers or shares of crops; government can now use more direct mechanisms for securing the necessary resources once money is widely used and credit is readily available. This concern about direct

Figure 5.10 Weber's Model of Markets, Money, Power, and Law

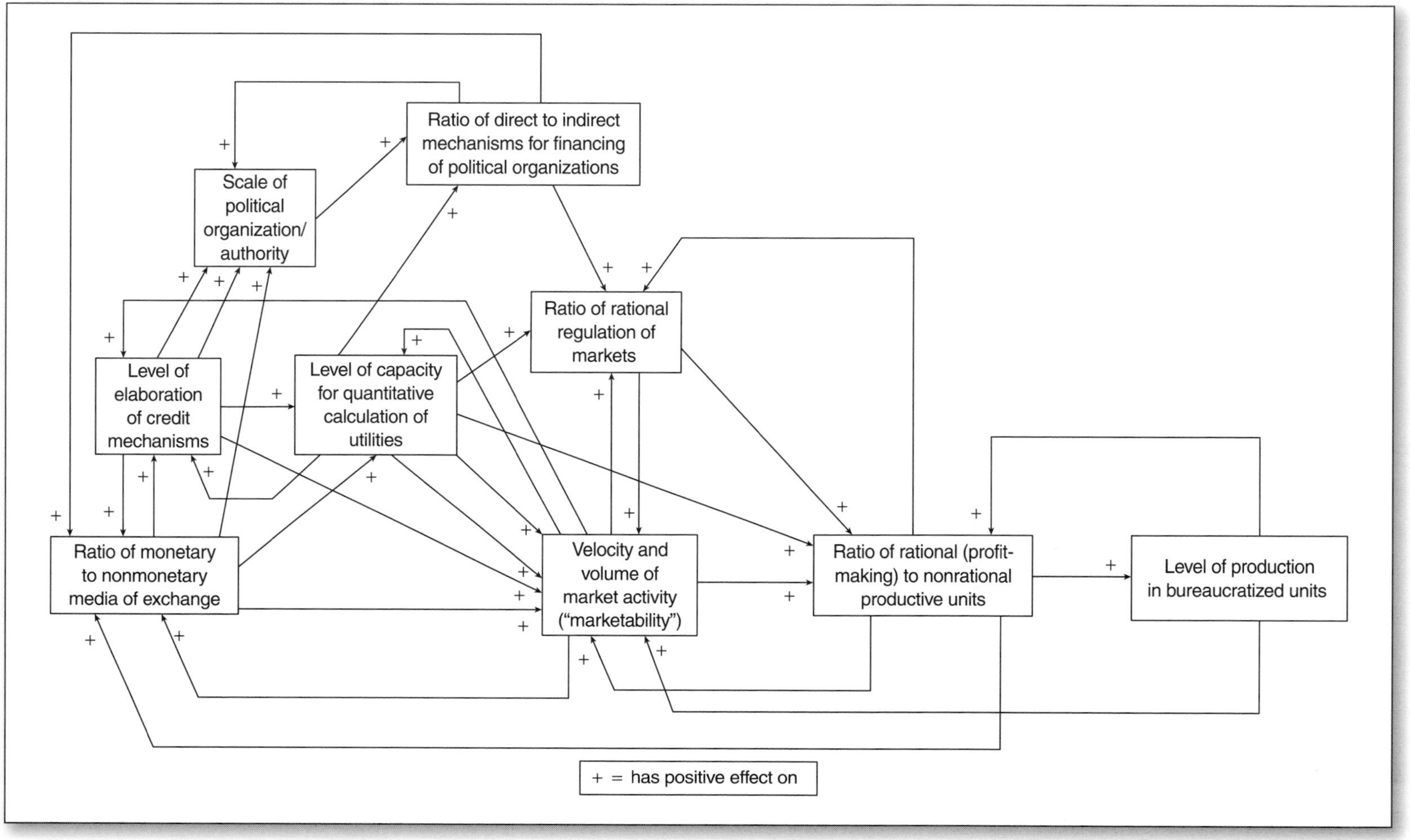

+ = has positive effect on

financing of its operations leads the center of power to begin the rational regulation of productive units and markets with laws. Once laws are used to regulate an ever-growing bureaucratic state and bureaucratized economic units, however, rational-legal domination accelerates.

Weber's Model of Stratification and Conflict. Although Weber saw the spread of rational-legal authority as decreasing the potential for conflict, he nonetheless posited a model of conflict that, in general terms, parallels Karl Marx's analysis. Unlike Marx, of course, Weber did not see inequality as inevitably leading to conflict; rather, chance has always played a part in determining if charismatic leaders can emerge to mobilize sentiments against elites. When we recast Weber's model in more abstract terms, we can see a more general theory on the conditions generating conflict between superordinates and subordinates in a system of inequality. Figure 5.11 summarizes the basic model in Weber's analysis.

For Weber, conflict emerges when the legitimacy of existing patterns of domination is questioned by subordinates. Thus, Weber saw the critical question as what conditions will increase the likelihood that this questioning of legitimacy will occur. One condition is the correlation among memberships in class, status groups, and parties. The more one's class position predicts status group membership, and vice versa, and the more one's status group membership and class position predict access to political power, and vice versa, the higher is the correlation among the three dimensions of inequality. The existence of this correlation increases the likelihood that charismatic leaders will emerge to question this situation. Another condition is the discontinuity among classes, status groups, and parties. To some extent, a high correlation will produce big gaps between classes, status groups, and access to power, but this force also operates on its own. If there are large differences between (a) the resources of those in high and low social classes, (b) the prestige and honor of those in high and low status groups, and (c) the respective power of those in different parties, then this kind of discontinuity increases the probability that charismatic leaders will emerge to challenge such high levels of inequality. A final condition, again often produced by discontinuity, revolves around rates of mobility across different classes, status groups, or parties. If little mobility is possible, and individuals are stuck in low positions along all three dimensions of stratification, then people will find charismatic leaders appealing.

When we look at Weber's model, it comes close to Karl Marx's notion of the polarization of society into two big classes, but Marx simply assumed that as class inequality increases, discontinuity and low mobility rates would follow. As a result, class conflict would be inevitable. In contrast, Weber emphasized that chance and context are important in determining if charismatic leaders will emerge and lead an opposition movement. Moreover, also in contrast to Marx, Weber saw high degrees of rationalization as lowering the probability of charismatic authority by (a) decreasing the correlation among class, status, and party and (b) decreasing the traditional and affectual orientations of actors. If, however, charismatic authority does emerge and is used to mobilize an opposition movement, the outcome of this movement is, once again, subject to chance and contextual events. If the movement is successful, then

Figure 5.11 Weber's Model of Stratification and Conflict

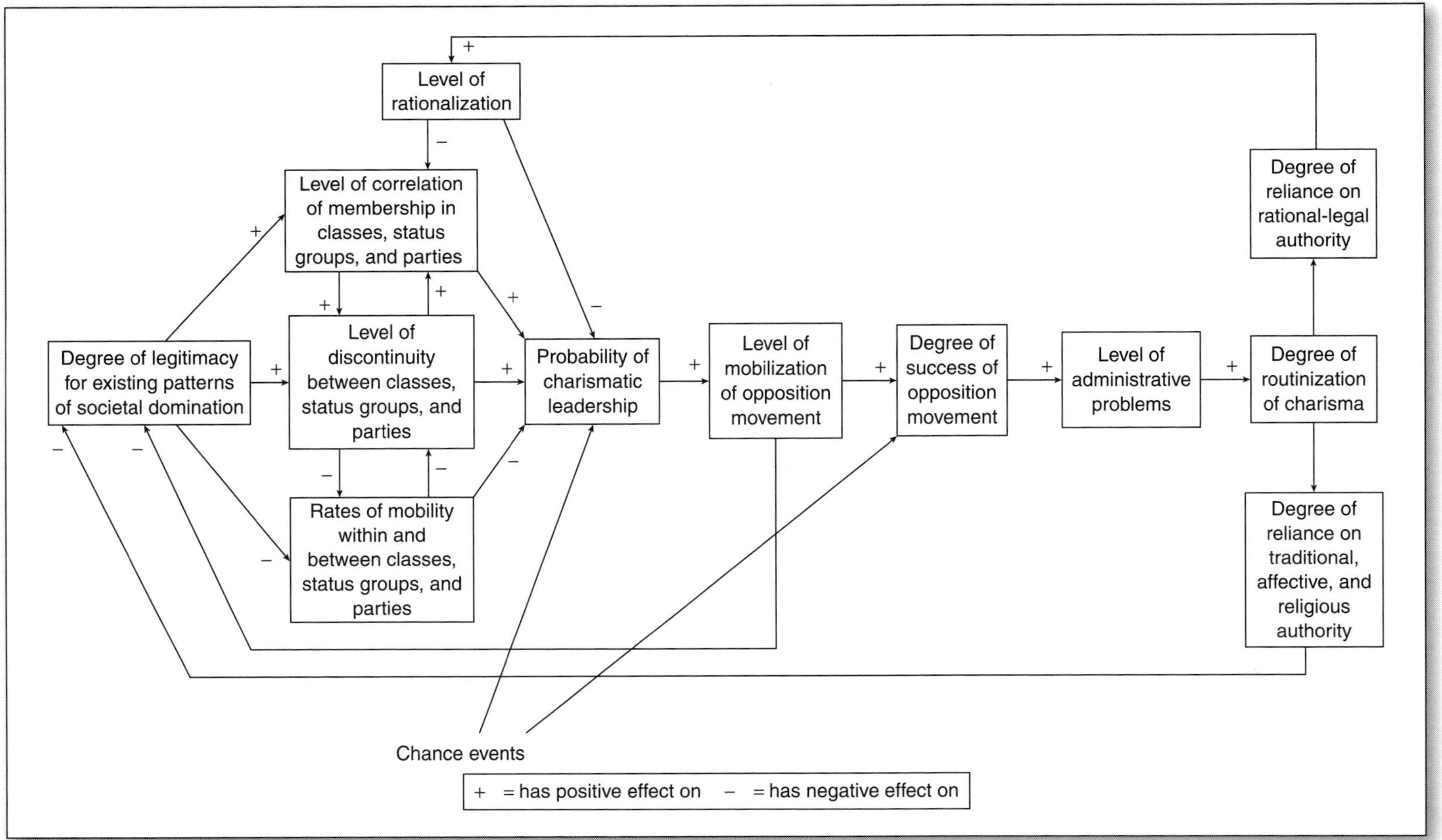

Degree of reliance on rational-legal authority

Degree of routinization of charisma

Degree of reliance on traditional, affective, and religious authority

Level of administrative problems

Degree of success of opposition movement

Level of mobilization of opposition movement

Probability of charismatic leadership

Level of rationalization

Level of correlation of membership in classes, status groups, and parties

Level of discontinuity between classes, status groups, and parties

Rates of mobility within and between classes, status groups, and parties

Degree of legitimacy for existing patterns of societal domination

Chance events

+ = has positive effect on   − = has negative effect on

problems revolving around the "routinization of charisma" emerge. As routinization occurs, the basis for creating a new system of domination is important in determining if this new system creates the conditions for future opposition movements. If routinization moves in the direction of rational-legal domination, then rationalization will decrease the rigidity of the stratification system and lower the potential for the reemergence of opposition movements led by charismatic leaders. In contrast, when routinization involves creating another traditional, religious, or affectual basis of legitimation, stratification is more likely to become rigid once again. This rigidity will increase the probability of a new opposition movement to the stratification system. Again, Weber believed that it is hard to predict which way routinization will go because chance confluences of events are always in play. Similarly, whether charismatic leaders can emerge and be successful is also subject to chance, although the probability of success decreases with rational-legal legitimation and increases with traditional, religious, and affectual legitimation.

Weber's Model of Geopolitics. Weber recognized that the internal stratification system and its potential for generating conflict are very much related to the level of prestige enjoyed by a society vis-à-vis its neighbors. In Figure 5.12, the causal model implied by Weber's analysis of geopolitics is delineated. Prestige in the external system is connected to the relations among (a) centers of power, (b) key actors in the economy, and (c) levels of inequality. When economic actors are dependent on the state, they push the state to use coercion in external relations with other societies when these economic actors' interests are tied to the local world system; conversely, when dependence on the state is low, economic actors seek to have the state engage in more co-optive strategies, such as encouraging dependence of other states on the goods provided by the productive sector or creating trade agreements that can facilitate the market relations with other societies.

When the state is successful in its external relations, the level of prestige of its government increases, even under conditions of high inequality in society, as the long reverse causal arrow from prestige in external relations to degree of legitimacy shows. Thus, the effect of inequalities in lowering legitimacy is, to a degree, mitigated by success in the external world system of societies. Although Weber says relatively little about war, he does imply that when a society engages in external conflict and is successful, then its territorial borders are extended, increasing minority groups and creating new classes, status groups, and parties. As these emerge, inequalities may increase as the new classes, status groups, and parties are pushed to the bottom of their respective hierarchies, thus increasing the likelihood of an opposition movement. Should a society lose a war, however, the resulting drop in prestige will erode legitimacy independently of inequalities; if high inequality and loss of war are combined, then the potential for opposition movements is dramatically increased.

Weber's Theoretical Principles

We immediately run into problems in trying to convert Weber's sociology into propositions, because of two factors: (a) the portrayal of phenomena in nominal

Figure 5.12 Weber's Model of Geopolitics

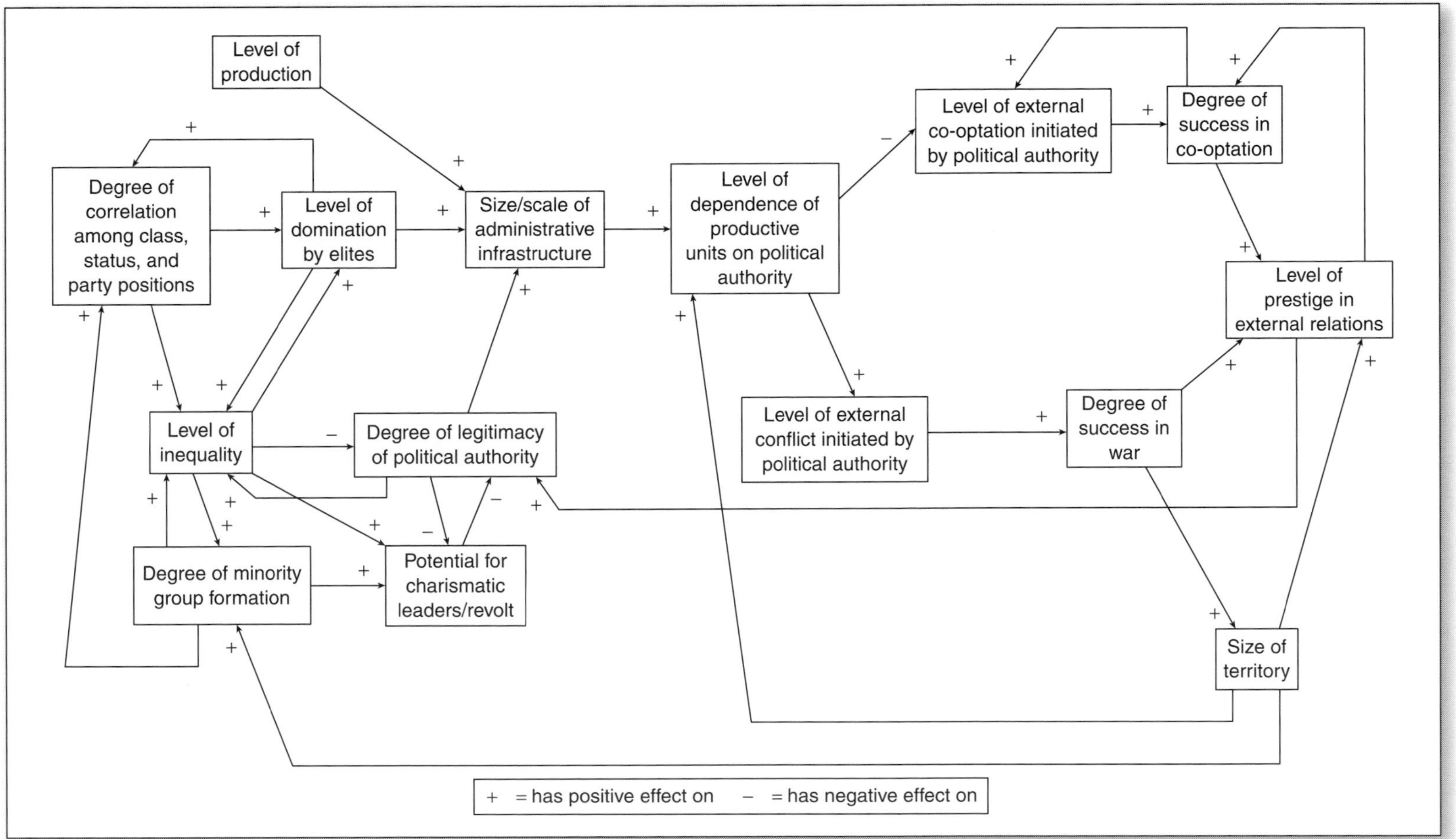

categories as ideal types rather than as variables and (b) the emphasis on chance events and historical context. Weber did not see phenomena as varying by degree but, rather, by type, and when this is the case, it is difficult to construct statements of the form "The degree of y varies with levels of x." Similarly, it is hard to make determinative statements when the social universe is seen as very much influenced by chance confluences of events. Nonetheless, it is worthwhile to see what we can do to convert Weber's sociology into a series of abstract theoretical principles.

Principles on the Process of Rationalization. The central theme in Weber's sociology is rationalization, especially its origins and its effects on patterns of domination in society. Thus, we can begin to articulate Weber's theory of society with some elementary principles on this master process:

1. The degree of rational-legal domination in a society increases as
   A. Free markets spread to distribute goods, services, and labor
   B. Money and credit become more widely available and reorient actors to calculations of utilities
   C. Ascetic cultural orientations become more prevalent and guide the actions of individuals and organizational systems
   D. The state has an interest in taxing, and using money and credit to finance its operations increases
   E. The state shifts the basis of its legitimation toward law.

Under these conditions, rationality will increasingly pervade action, social relationships, and legitimated orders, and organizational systems in the economy and state will increasingly become bureaucratic. Weber emphasized the importance of cultural orientations in this process of rationalization; it is useful to offer a supplemental proposition that clarifies the elements of 1-C:

2. The pervasiveness of ascetic cultural values emphasizing efficiency and rationality in worldly actions increases as
   A. The level of production increases, with production growing as
      1. The use of inanimate sources of energy (industrialization) spreads
      2. The size and prevalence of urban centers increase
      3. The movement of free labor into urban areas accelerates
      4. The prevalence of free markets using money and credit increases
   B. The volume and velocity of market exchanges increase, with the volume and velocity of markets increasing as
      1. The level of production increases
      2. The availability of money and credit increases
      3. The availability of money and markets increase quantitative calculation of utilities
   C. The ratio of associative to communal social relations in the society increases.

As is evident, these ascetic cultural values are very much tied to the market forces in a society, as is the overall process of rationalization. Thus, we should offer a supplemental principle to 1-A and 1-B:

3. The velocity and volume of market activity increase with the use of money and credit in exchange relations, with this use growing as

   A. The prevalence of ascetic cultural values to guide the actions of individuals and organizational systems increases
   B. The number of profit-oriented organizational systems increases
   C. The state's interests in taxing and using money for its ends increases
   D. The state's use of law to regulate exchange relations and to legitimate its actions increases.

The forces enumerated in these propositions are all interconnected. Weber thought the confluence of forces set off rationalization. Certain conditions had to prevail to start the process, but once it got going, the conditions would feed off one another, increasing the weights for each and pushing action, social relations, organizational systems, and stratification toward rational-legal forms.

Principles on De-legitimation and Conflict. Weber was always concerned with the way patterns of domination in society are legitimated. Because domination generates a stratification system composed of classes, status groups, and parties, this system of inequality is critical in sustaining legitimation. If those high along these three hierarchies of inequality are seen to have the right to be there, then not only is the stratification system legitimated but so is the overall system of domination. Inequality will generate the potential for opposition movements under conditions that increase the likelihood that charismatic leaders will emerge to articulate the grievances of subordinates and to lead them in opposition. These conditions are summarized in principle 4:

4. The more subordinates in a system of inequality withdraw legitimacy from superordinates, the higher the rate of conflict is with superordinates, with the withdrawal of legitimacy increasing as

   A. The correlation among memberships in class, status, and political hierarchies increases
   B. The discontinuity or degree of inequality along all hierarchies increases
   C. The chances for mobility of subordinates to higher positions in any or all hierarchies decline
   D. The opportunities for charismatic leaders who can articulate the grievances of subordinates and lead them in opposition to the current system of domination increase.

If charismatic leaders emerge and are successful in orchestrating an opposition movement, then, they would face the problem of how to routinize this charisma as the goal shifts from revolution to administration. This problem will become even more acute when a charismatic leader dies without a system for choosing a successor in place, but the problem always exists when opposition movements must transform themselves into systems of administration.

5. The more success charismatic leaders have in de-legitimating a system of domination and in overthrowing elites along each hierarchy of inequality, the more problematic is the establishment of a new system of domination through rules and organizational systems.

6. The stability of this new system in the aftermath of a charismatic revolt will increase to the extent that it is based on rational-legal domination, whereas the stability of the new system will decrease if it is based on traditional domination. The more a rational-legal system of authority is put into place, the more stable is this system and the less the conditions listed in proposition 4 are likely to prevail.

Principles on De-legitimation and Geopolitics. Systems of domination are very much connected to geopolitics. A society's prestige in the world system will determine, to some extent, the prestige and legitimacy of political leaders. Thus, the actions of these leaders vis-à-vis other societies in their region and beyond will be critical in determining whether or not they can sustain their power, and this is especially so when the conditions of inequality portrayed in proposition 4 prevail. We can translate Weber's argument into several interesting propositions:

7. The more those with power can sustain a sense of prestige and success in relations with external societies, the greater will be the capacity of leaders to be viewed as legitimate and the less the conditions listed in proposition 4 prevail.

A. The more productive sectors of a society depend on political authority for their viability, the more they encourage political authority to engage in military expansion to augment their interest; and the more successful these engagements, the more prestige and legitimacy are given to political authority.

B. The more productive sectors do not depend on the state for their viability, the more they encourage political authority to rely on co-optation rather than on military engagement; and the more successful these efforts at co-optation, the more prestige and legitimacy are given to political authority.

8. The less successful is political authority in external relations, the greater is its loss of prestige vis-à-vis other societies and the greater is its loss of prestige and legitimacy within a society.

9. The greater are the loss of prestige in external relations and of legitimacy in internal relations by centers of political authority, the more likely is an opposition movement, especially under the conditions of high inequality summarized in proposition 4.

In sum, then, we can convert many of Weber's critical arguments into theoretical principles, but these do not capture either the breadth or the depth of Weberian sociology. If Weber is to endure as a theorist, however, this kind of exercise is important because with each passing decade, the historical context of his sociology becomes ever more remote. Weber was a historical sociologist as much as a theorist, and although his descriptions of historical contexts may prove interesting to historians, his legacy is best kept alive by extracting the more general models and principles to be found in his work. If we refuse to perform exercises like the one in this chapter, Weber's sociology will become less relevant in the twenty-first century. The power of Weber's ideas resides, I believe, in the more general and abstract arguments that he made. In this chapter, we have tried to emphasize what we see as the most enduring of these arguments.

Conclusions

Weber did not believe that timeless, universal laws could ever be developed, because so much that had occurred in history was the result of chance events. Even without the ability to conduct inquiry in the same way as in the natural sciences, Weber still wanted to be scientific and objective. Moreover, he sought to do more than write historical descriptions; he also wanted to provide a methodology for more abstract and analytical statements. The result was a strange compromise: the study of historical causes through the vehicle of ideal types. For each cause and effect, Weber constructs an ideal type of its essential characteristics, and some of these are among sociology's more enduring descriptions of basic social forms. In this way, Weber could be more abstract and analytical than historians, but he would not posit laws of human organization. Too much of history, he believed, was the result of a random or chance confluence of events. Thus, we are given many, rather ponderous descriptions of the basic relationships among phenomena portrayed as ideal types, but in following Weber's methodology, we are kept from asking the most interesting question of any science: Are some of these relationships so generic and basic that they might constitute sociological laws?

Methodology aside, Weber's substantive works range widely. We have tried to give them more coherence than they actually reveal by emphasizing the theme of rationalization. Much like Herbert Spencer's work, which also is highly descriptive, Weber's presentation of details is often so convoluted that the main line of his argument becomes difficult to follow. We suspect that Weber came to the theme of rationalization rather late in his work, and he either tried to push and shove earlier works into this theme or, in many cases, did not bother to do so. Although the result was fascinating, though dense, essays on many diverse topics, these do not hang together as did those of Herbert Spencer, Karl Marx, and Émile Durkheim. As a consequence, it is hard to extract a general theory from Weber; rather, what emerge are rich descriptions, ideal types of empirical cases, and complex causal statements on many topics without a general model to guide us. Thus, we will simply have to live with the scattered character of Weberian sociology, taking from it what we find useful.[63]

---

[63]For a recent compilation of the breadth of Weber's scholarship, see Stephen Kalberg (ed.), *Max Weber: The Confrontation with Modernity* (Oxford, UK: Blackwell, 2005).

CHAPTER 6

Georg Simmel

U ntil late in his career, Georg Simmel was never able to hold a regular academic position. As a Jew, he was subject to discrimination, and despite efforts by Max Weber, most of his career was spent as a private scholar, lecturing to lay audiences for a fee. This marginal position between the lay and academic intellectual worlds may have prevented him from developing a coherent theoretical system. Instead, what emerged were flashes of insight into the basic dynamics of a wide variety of phenomena. Moreover, Simmel had a tendency to deal with the same topics repeatedly, each time revising and updating his thinking. If much of his work appears to be a series of lectures, that is just what it often was: lectures that prod and stimulate, often without detailed and scholarly annotation. Yet with each passing decade since the 1950s, the importance of Simmel's vision for sociology has been increasingly recognized. For despite the somewhat disjointed character of his life's work, his methodology for developing sociological theory and the substance of his insights into the form of modern society present a reasonably coherent program of sociological analysis.

Simmel's Methodological Approach to the Study of Society

In an essay titled "The Problem of Sociology," Simmel concluded as early as 1894 that an exploration of the basic and generic forms of interaction offered the only viable subject for the nascent discipline of sociology.[1] In Chapter 1 of *Sociology: Studies in the Forms of Sociation,* written in 1908, he reformulated and reaffirmed his thoughts on this issue.[2] In 1918, he revised his thinking again in

---

[1] The translation appeared the following year. See Georg Simmel, "The Problem of Sociology," *Annals of the American Academy of Political and Social Science* 6 (1895): 412–423.

[2] Georg Simmel, "The Problem of Sociology," in *Essays on Sociology, Philosophy and Aesthetics by Georg Simmel et al.,* ed. and trans. Kurt Wolff (New York: Harper & Row, 1959), 310–336. This is Chapter 1 of Simmel's *Sociology: Studies in the Forms of Sociation* (1908). This book, which is Simmel's major work, has not been translated into English, but portions appear in various edited collections. See Footnote 17.

one of his last works, *Fundamental Problems of Sociology.*[3] In what follows, we rely most heavily on this final brief sketch because it represents his most mature statement.

Simmel began the *Fundamental Problems of Sociology* by lamenting that "the first difficulty which arises if one wants to make a tenable statement about the science of sociology is that its claim to be a science is not undisputed." In Germany after the turn of the century, many scholars still denied that sociology constituted a legitimate science; and to retain their power within the university system, these critics wanted to stop sociology from becoming an academic field. Partly for these reasons, it was proposed that sociology should be merely a label to refer to all the social sciences dealing with specific content areas—such as economics, political science, and linguistics. This tactic was a ruse, of course, for Simmel (and many others) recognized that the existing disciplines had already divided up the study of human life and that nothing would be "gained by throwing their sum total into a pot and sticking a new label on it: 'sociology.'"[4] To combat this strategy and to justify the acceptance of sociology as an academic field of study, Simmel argued that it was necessary for the new discipline to develop a unique and "unambiguous content, dominated by one, methodologically certain, problem idea."[5] His discussion is organized around three questions: What is society? How should sociology study society? What are the problem areas of sociology?

What Is Society?

Simmel's answer to the first question is very simple: "Society" exists when "interaction among human beings" occurs with enough frequency and intensity so that people mutually affect one another and organize themselves into groups or other social units. Thus, he used the term *society* rather loosely to refer to any pattern of social organization in which he was interested. As he put it, society refers to relatively

> permanent interactions only. More specifically, the interactions we have in mind when we talk about 'society' are crystallized as definable, consistent structures such as the state and the family, the guild and the church, social classes and organizations based on common interests.[6]

---

[3]Georg Simmel, *Fundamental Problems of Sociology,* appears as Part 1 of *The Sociology of Georg Simmel,* trans. Kurt Wolff (New York: Free Press, 1950), 3–86.

[4]Ibid., 4.

[5]This remark is from the preface to Simmel's *Sociology: Studies in the Forms of Sociation;* it is quoted in Kurt Wolff's introduction to *The Sociology of Georg Simmel,* xxvi. For another review and analysis of Simmel's methodology, see Donald N. Levine, "Simmel and Parsons Reconsidered," *American Journal of Sociology* 96 (1991):1097–1116, "Simmel as a Resource for Sociological Metatheory," *Sociological Theory* 7 (1989):161–174, and "Sociology's Quest for the Classics: The Case of Simmel," in *The Future of Sociological Classics,* ed. Buford Rhea (London: Allen and Unwin, 1981), 60–80.

[6]Simmel, *Fundamental Problems,* 9.

The significance of defining society in this way lies in the recognition that patterns of social organization are constructed from basic processes of interaction. Hence, interaction, per se, becomes a significant area of study. Sociology, in his words, is founded on "the recognition that man in his whole nature and in all his manifestations is determined by the circumstances of living in interaction with other men."[7] Thus, as an academic discipline,

> sociology asks what happens to men and by what rules do they behave, not insofar as they unfold their understandable individual existences in their totalities, but insofar as they form groups and are determined by their group existence because of interaction.[8]

With this statement, Simmel gave sociology a unique and unambiguous subject matter: the basic forms of social interaction.

How Should Sociology Study Society?

Simmel's answer to the second question is again very simple: sociologists should begin their study of society by distinguishing between *form* and *content*. Subsequent scholars have often misunderstood his use of these particular terms, mainly because their Kantian origin has been ignored.[9] What must be remembered to understand these terms is that Simmel's writings are pervaded by analogies, with the distinction between form and content being drawn from an analogy to geometry. Geometry investigates the spatial forms of material objects; although these spatial forms might have material contents of various sorts, the process of abstraction in geometry involves ignoring their specific contents in favor of an emphasis on the common features, or forms, of the objects under examination. Simmel simply applied this geometric distinction between form and content to the study of society to suggest how sociology could investigate social processes independently of their content. The distinction between the forms and contents of interaction offers the only "possibility for a special science of society" because it is a means of focusing on the generic basic processes by which people establish social relations and social structures, while ignoring for analytical purposes the contents (goals and purposes) of social relations.

Thus, forms of interaction refer to the modes "of interaction among individuals through which, or in the shape of which, that content attains social reality."[10] Simmel

---

[7]Ibid., 12.

[8]Ibid., 11.

[9]The most well-known criticism of Simmel's presumably excessive "formalism" are by Theodore Abel, *Systematic Sociology in Germany* (New York: Octagon, 1965) and Pitirim Sorokin, *Contemporary Sociological Theories* (New York: Harper & Row, 1928). The best defenses of Simmel against this spurious charge are those by F. H. Tenbruck, "Formal Sociology," in *Essays on Sociology,* 61–69 and Levine, "Simmel and Parsons Reconsidered," as well as his *Simmel and Parsons: Two Approaches to the Study of Society* (New York: Arno, 1980).

[10]Simmel, "Problem of Sociology," 315.

argued that attention to social forms led sociology to goals that were fundamentally different from those of the other social scientific disciplines, especially in the Germany of his time. For example, sociology tries to discover the laws influencing small-group interaction rather than describing particular families or marriages; it attempts to uncover the principles of formal and impersonal interaction rather than examining specific bureaucratic organizations; it seeks to understand the nature and consequences of class struggle rather than portraying a particular strike or some specific conflict. Simmel believed that by focusing on the generic and basic properties of interaction, per se, sociology could discover the underlying processes of social reality.[11] Although social structures might reveal diverse contents, they can have similar forms:

> Social groups, which are the most diverse imaginable in purpose and general significance, may nevertheless show identical forms of behavior toward one another on the part of individual members. We find superiority and subordination, competition, division of labor, formation of parties, representation, inner solidarity coupled with exclusiveness toward the outside, and innumerable similar features in the state, in a religious community, in a band of conspirators, in an economic association, in an art school, in the family. However diverse the interests are that give rise to these sociations, the *forms* in which the interests are realized may yet be identical.[12]

On this basis, then, Simmel believed that it was possible to develop "timelessly valid laws" about social interaction. For example, the process of competition or other forms of conflict can be examined in many different social contexts at different times: within and among political parties, within and among different religious groups, within and among businesses, among artists, and even among family members. The result can be some theoretical insight into how the process of competition (as a form of conflict) affects the participants apart from their specific purposes or goals. Thus, even though the terminology has changed over the years, Simmel's distinction between form and content constitutes one of his most important contributions to the emergence of sociological theory. However, the next task he faced was identifying the most basic forms of interaction; in his words, sociology must delineate its specific problem areas. Sadly, his inability to complete this task represents the most significant flaw in his methodological work.

What Are the Problem Areas of Sociology?

Unlike his responses to the other two questions, Simmel's answer to the third query has not proved to be of enduring significance for the development of sociological theory. In his initial attempts at conceptualizing the basic social forms with which sociology ought to be concerned, he referred to "a difficulty in methodology."

---

[11]Simmel, *Fundamental Problems*, 18.

[12]Ibid., 22 (emphasis in original). See Levine, "Simmel and Parsons Reconsidered," for elaboration on this point of emphasis in Simmel's work.

For the present, he felt, the sociological viewpoint can be conveyed only by means of examples because only later will it be possible "to grasp it by methods that are fully conceptualized and are sure guides to research."[13]

Both the title and the organization of Simmel's *Fundamental Problems of Sociology* (1918) suggest that the major impetus for writing this last little book was his recognition that the "difficulty in methodology" remained unresolved. Unfortunately, this final effort at developing systematic procedures for identifying the generic properties of the social world studied by sociology was not very successful either. In this book, Simmel identified three areas that he said constituted the fundamental problems of sociology. First is the sociological study of historical life and development, which he called *general sociology.* Second is the sociological study of the forms of interaction independent of history, which he called *pure,* or *formal, sociology.* Third is the sociological study of the epistemological and metaphysical aspects of society, which he called *philosophical sociology.* In *Fundamental Problems,* which has only four chapters, Simmel devoted a separate chapter to each of these problem areas.

General Sociology. Simmel began by noting that "general sociology" was concerned with the study "of the whole of historical life insofar as it is formed societally"—that is, through interaction. The process of historical development can be interpreted in a number of ways, however, and Simmel believed that it was necessary to distinguish the sociological from the nonsociological approach. For example, he indicated that Émile Durkheim saw historical development "as a process proceeding from organic commonness to mechanical simultaneousness," whereas Auguste Comte saw it as occurring through three distinct stages: theological, metaphysical, and positive.[14] Although both claims are reasonable, Simmel observed, neither constitutes a justification for the existence of sociology. Rather, the historical development of those observable social structures studied by the existing disciplines (politics, economics, religion, law, language, etc.) must be subjected to a sociological analysis by distinguishing between social forms and social contents. For example, when the history of religious communities and that of labor unions are studied, it is possible to show that the members of both are characterized by patterns of self-sacrifice and devotion to ideals. These similarities can, in principle, be summarized by abstract laws.

What Simmel was apparently arguing, although this is not entirely clear, is that studies of the contents of interaction can yield valid theoretical insights only when attention is paid to the more generic properties of the social structures in which people participate. However, his chapter on general sociology, which deals with the problem of the development of individuality in society, proceeds in ways that are, at best, confusing.[15] Thus, the overall result is that readers are left wondering just what the subject of general sociology is and how it relates to the other problem areas.

---

[13]Simmel, "Problem of Sociology," 323–324.

[14]Simmel, *Fundamental Problems,* 19–20. In general, Simmel does not cite his sources. In these two pages, however, his references are relatively clear, even though neither Durkheim nor Comte is mentioned by name.

[15]Ibid., 26–39.

Pure, or Formal, Sociology. For Simmel, "pure, or formal, sociology" consists of investigating "the societal forms themselves." Thus, when "society is conceived as interaction among individuals, the description of this interaction is the task of the science of society in its strictest and most essential sense."[16] Simmel's problem was thus to isolate and identify fundamental forms of interaction. In his earlier work, he attempted to do this by focusing on a number of less observable but highly significant social forms, which can be divided (roughly) into two general categories, although he did not use these labels: (1) generic social processes, such as differentiation, conflict, and exchange, and (2) structured role relationships, such as the role of the stranger in society. Nearly all of his substantive work consists of studies of these less observable social forms. For example, a partial listing of the table of contents of *Sociology: Studies in the Forms of Sociation* reveals that the following topics are considered:[17]

1. The quantitative determinateness of the group

2. Superordination and subordination

3. Conflict

4. The secret and the secret society

5. Note on adornment

6. The intersection of social circles (the web of group affiliations)

7. The poor

8. The self-preservation of the group

9. Note on faithfulness and gratitude

10. Note on the stranger

11. The enlargement of the group and the development of the individual

12. Note on nobility

Yet Simmel's description of pure, or formal, sociology suffers from a fundamental defect: it does not remedy the "methodological difficulty" referred to.[18] In *Fundamental*

---

[16]Ibid., 22.

[17]Items 1, 2, 4, 5, and 9 are available in *The Sociology of Georg Simmel*. Items 3 and 6 are in *Conflict and the Web of Group Affiliations,* trans. Reinhard Bendix (New York: Free Press, 1955). Item 10 is in *Essays on Sociology.* Item 8 is in the *American Journal of Sociology* 3 (March 1900):577–603. Items 7, 11, and 12 are in *Georg Simmel on Individuality and Social Forms,* trans. Donald Levine (Chicago, IL: University of Chicago Press, 1971). The remaining chapters, about one-fourth of the book, are still untranslated. They deal with topics such as social psychology, hereditary office holding, the spatial organization of society, and the relationship between psychological and sociological phenomena.

[18]Simmel, *Fundamental Problems,* 40–57. For an effort to extract the basic forms from Simmel's work, see Levine, "Simmel and Parsons Reconsidered," 1107 and "Sociology's Quest for the Classics," 69–71.

Problems, Simmel failed to develop a precise method for either identifying the most basic forms of interaction or analyzing their systematic variation.

Philosophical Sociology. Simmel's "philosophical sociology" is an attempt to recognize the importance of philosophical issues in the development of sociology as an academic discipline. As he put it, the modern scientific attitude toward the nature of empirical facts suggests a "complex of questions concerning the fact 'society.'" These questions are philosophical, and they center on epistemology and metaphysics. The epistemological problem has to do with one of the main cognitive presuppositions underlying sociological research: Is society the purpose of human existence, or is it merely a means for individual ends?[19] Simmel's explanatory chapter on philosophical sociology deals with this question by studying the relationship between the individual and society in the eighteenth and nineteenth centuries.[20] As with the other chapters in *Fundamental Problems,* however, this material is so confusing that it is of little use. Apparently, Simmel wanted to argue that questions about the purpose of society or the reasons for individual existence could not be answered in scientific terms, but even this reasonable conclusion is uncertain.[21] Ultimately, then, his vision of philosophical sociology has simply been ignored, mainly because his analysis is both superficial and unclear.

In the end, Simmel had to confess that he had failed to lay a complete methodological foundation for the new discipline. This failure stems from his uncertainty about his ability to isolate truly basic or generic structures and processes. Thus, both *Sociology* and *Fundamental Problems* contain disclaimers suggesting that his analysis of specific topics—such as the significance of group affiliations, the functions of social conflict, and the process of social exchange—can only demonstrate the potential value of an analysis of social forms.[22] We now examine Simmel's three most important studies in formal, or pure, sociology.

The Web of Group Affiliations

"The Web of Group Affiliations" is a sociological analysis of how patterns of group participation are altered with social differentiation, as well as an analysis of the consequences of such alterations for people's everyday behavior. Simmel first dealt with this topic in his *Social Differentiation* (1890).[23] However, this early version is not very useful, and the text explicated here is taken from *Sociology: Studies in the Forms of*

---

[19]This same issue was dealt with 10 years earlier in Georg Simmel, "Note on the Problem: How Is Society Possible?" in *Essays on Sociology,* 337–356.

[20]Simmel, *Fundamental Problems,* 58–86.

[21]Ibid., 25.

[22]Ibid., 18.

[23]See Georg Simmel, "The Intersection of Social Spheres," in *Georg Simmel: Sociologist and European,* trans. Peter Lawrence (New York: Barnes & Noble, 1976), 95–110.

Sociation. Like all the classical sociologists, Simmel saw a general historical tendency toward increasing social differentiation in modern industrialized societies. Rather than tracing this development either chronologically or by increased functional specialization, he focused on the nature and significance of group memberships. In this way, he was able to identify a unique social form.

The Web of Group Affiliations as a Social Form

Social forms refer to the modes of interaction through which people attain their purposes or goals. In "The Web of Group Affiliations," Simmel was interested in the extent to which changes in the network of social structures making up society affect people. Indeed, he believed that the number of groups a person belongs to and the basis on which they are formed influence interaction apart from the interests that the groups are intended to satisfy.[24]

One of the most important variables influencing the number of groups to which people belong, as well as the basis of their attachment to groups, is the degree of *social differentiation,* or the number of different activities or structures organizing these activities. For example, in a hunting-and-gathering society, almost all tasks are done in and by the family (gathering and producing food, educating children, worshiping gods, making law, and the like). Thus, people have only a few roles in an undifferentiated society, and as a consequence, people are similar because they play the same roles in an undifferentiated structure. By contrast, in an industrial society, many important tasks are divided up. This increase in complexity, which sociologists call differentiation, affects interaction. People still produce goods, worship, educate, and adjudicate, but they do so differently. This disparity occurs because people increasingly choose which groups to belong to based on "similarity of talents, inclinations, activities," and other factors over which they have some control.[25] Thus, people play a far greater number and variety of roles and, in so doing, often interact with others different from themselves. The remainder of "The Web of Group Affiliations" explores the structural changes that result. In this way, Simmel demonstrated how a sociological analysis can reveal what happens to people "insofar as they form groups and are determined by their group existence because of interaction." He also demonstrated some implications of modernity.

Structural Changes Accompanying Social Differentiation

Simmel observed that the process of social differentiation produced two fundamental changes in patterns of interaction. First, the principle underlying group formation changed, in his words, from *organic* to *rational* criteria. As Simmel uses it, the term *organic* is a biological metaphor suggesting that a family or village is like a

---

[24]The remainder of this section draws on Leonard Beeghley, "Demystifying Theory: How the Theories of Georg Simmel (and Others) Help Us to Make Sense of Modern Life," in *The Blackwell Companion to Sociology,* ed., Jon Gubbay, Chris Middleton, and Chet Ballard (New York: Blackwell, 1997), chap. 34.

[25]Georg Simmel, "Web of Group Affiliations," in *Conflict and the Web of Group Affiliations* (New York: Free Press, 1955), 127.

living organism in which the parts are inherently connected.[26] Thus, when groups have an "organic" basis, people belong to them based on birth—into a family, a religion, a village—and they are so strongly identified with the group to which they belong that they are not seen as individuals in their own right. In Shakespeare's play, *Romeo and Juliet,* for example, Romeo did not have an identity apart from his family and village; they constituted who he was. This is why his banishment was so devastating. In contrast, the term *rational* suggests the use of reason and logic. Thus, as Simmel uses the term, when groups have a "rational" basis, people belong by choice. For example, Simmel noted that English trade unions had originally "tended toward local exclusiveness" and had been closed to workers who came from other cities or regions,[27] but over time workers ended their dependence on local relationships, choosing to build and join national unions to pursue their interests.[28]

Second, social differentiation also leads to an increase in the number of groups that people can join. When groups have an "organic" basis, people can only belong to a few primary groups (i.e., small, intimate, face-to-face groups): their family, their village, and not much more. In contrast, when groups have a "rational" basis, people can join a greater number and variety of them, based on skill, mutual interests, money, and other types of commonality. Simmel observed a trend in modern societies for people to join many groups and for such affiliations to be based on conscious reflection. This tendency applies even to intimate relationships, such as marriages. Many of these groups, however, are larger and more formal and are called *secondary groups.* Thus, people can also belong to occupational groups of various sorts, purely social groups, and a virtually unlimited number of special-interest groups. Further, individuals might also identify themselves as members of a social class and a military reserve unit. Finally, they might see themselves as citizens of cities, states, regions, and nations. Not surprisingly, Simmel concluded,

> This is a great variety of groups. Some of these groups are integrated. Others are, however, so arranged that one group appears as the original focus of an individual's affiliation, from which he then turns toward affiliation with other, quite different groups on the basis of his special qualities, which distinguish him from other members of his primary group.[29]

Put differently, group affiliations in differentiated societies are characterized by a superstructure of secondary groups that develops beyond primary group membership. From Simmel's point of view, the most important sociological characteristics of these groups—both primary and secondary—are that individuals choose to affiliate, everyone belongs to different groups, and people are often treated as

---

[26]The classical theorists were often searching for ways to communicate. Partly for this reason, they often used the same or similar concepts with quite different meanings. Thus, Simmel's notion of "organic" is the opposite of Durkheim's (considered in Chapter 13).

[27]Simmel, "Web of Group Affiliations," 129.

[28]Ibid., 137.

[29]Ibid., 137.

individuals with unique experiences. These attributes mean that in many important respects, every person differs from every other.

The Consequences of Differentiation

The implications of this change are profound. Simmel suggests, for example, that when groups are formed by choice and people belong to a large number of them, the possibility of role conflict arises because membership in diverse groups places competing demands on people. "As the individual leaves his established position within one primary group, he comes to stand at a point at which many groups 'intersect.'" As a result, "external and internal conflicts arise through the multiplicity of group affiliations, which threaten the individual with psychological tensions or even a schizophrenic break."[30] Thus, it is now common for people to have multiple obligations. Sometimes these duties lead to hard choices; this happens, for example, when obligations to one's employer compete with obligations to one's family. Usually, Simmel says, people try to balance their competing responsibilities by keeping them spatially and temporally separate. Nonetheless, the impact of conflicting expectations can lead to psychological stress and, hence, influence behavior.

Simmel's analysis also leads to insights about some of the positive consequences of modernity. For example, people now play many different roles: spouse, parent, son or daughter, athlete, employee, or political activist, among other roles. This list, which could be extended, gives each of them a distinct identity in relationship to other people. These others also have a unique set of characteristics (roles) that make them distinct. Thus, Simmel's theory implies that the changes produced by social differentiation lead to greater individuality (what he called a "core of inner unity"), which makes each person discrete. In Simmel's words, "The objective structure of society provides a framework within which an individual's noninterchangeable and singular characteristics may develop and find expression."[31] Such a result is impossible when everyone resembles everyone else. Ironically, then, modernity not only produces role conflict and psychological stress but also creates the conditions under which individuality emerges.

Such individuality emerges precisely because people in modern societies can, indeed must, make choices. Moreover, they must adjust their behavior to different people in different situations—an insight that carries many implications. For example, as people choose and become aware of their uniqueness, they enjoy greater personal freedom. As Simmel put it, although "the narrowly circumscribed and strict custom of earlier conditions was one in which the social group as a whole . . . regulated the conduct of the individual in the most varied ways," such regulation is not possible in differentiated societies because people belong to so many different groups.[32] It is not accidental, from this point of view, that the ideology of personal freedom as an inalienable right of every adult arose during the last two centuries. Its structural basis, Simmel said, lies in social differentiation.

---

[30]Ibid., 141.

[31]Ibid., 150; see also 139, 149, 151.

[32]Ibid., 165.

These insights lead to others. For example, when people play many roles and face conflicting expectations, they develop the capacity for empathy—the ability to identify with and understand another's situation or motives.[33] This capacity can sometimes reduce the level of conflict between people. Thus, the increasing complexity of modern societies provides a structural basis for an important personality characteristic. Note the two implications of this argument. First, role conflict now appears to be a positive feature of modern societies. Second, the distribution of psychological characteristics in a population (e.g., people's sense of individuality and empathy) does not happen by chance; they reflect the social structure. In addition, although role conflict burdens individuals, it also forces them to make choices and thereby encourages creativity.[34] After all, in a complex society, roles cannot be taken for granted; they must be negotiated; so people have to consider both their own and others' situations and be creative. Moreover, the aptitude for thinking imaginatively and originally extends to all arenas of life as people confront problems. The logic of this analysis suggests that modernity results from and, at the same time, produces a spiral effect such that as societies become more differentiated, more people become creative, and as more people become creative, societies become more complex (see Figure 6.1).

Figure 6.1 Simmel's Image of Group Affiliations

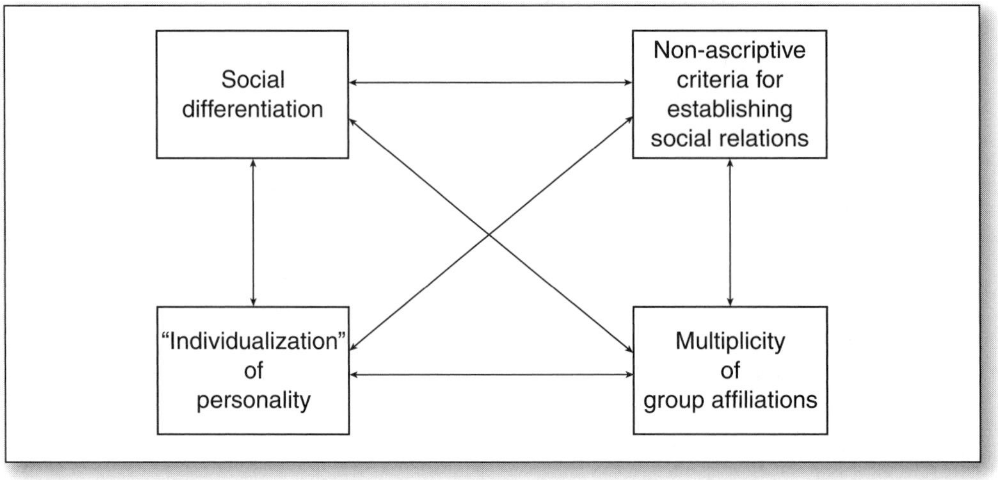

Conflict

Although his initial sketch of "The Sociology of Conflict" appeared in 1903, the basis for our commentary is a much revised version that was included as a chapter in *Sociology: Studies in the Forms of Sociation.*[35] Simmel began the latter essay by

---

[33]Robert K. Merton, *Social Theory and Social Structure* (New York: Free Press, 1968), 436.

[34]Rose Laub Coser, *In Defense of Modernity* (Stanford, CA: Stanford University Press, 1991).

[35]Georg Simmel, "The Sociology of Conflict," *American Journal of Sociology* 9 (1903–1904):490–525, 672–689, 798–811.

remarking that although the social "significance of conflict has in principle never been disputed," it has, most commonly, been seen as a purely destructive factor in people's relationships, one that should be prevented from occurring if possible. He believed that this orientation stemmed from an emphasis on exploring the contents of interaction; people observe the destructive consequences of conflict on other individuals (both physically and psychologically) and assume that it must have a similar effect on collectivities. In Simmel's view, this emphasis is shortsighted because it fails to recognize that conflict often serves as a means of maintaining or increasing integration within groups. In his words, "it is a way of achieving some kind of unity." For example, people's ability to express their hostilities toward one another can give them a sense of control over their destinies and thereby increase social solidarity within a group.

Conflict as a Social Form

Human beings, Simmel observed, have an "*a priori* fighting instinct"; that is, they have an easily aroused sense of hostility toward others. Although this fighting instinct is probably the ultimate cause of social conflict, he said, humans are distinguished from other species because, in general, conflicts are means to goals rather than merely instinctual reactions to external stimuli. This fundamental principle in Simmel's discussion means that conflict is a vehicle by which individuals achieve their purposes in innumerable social contexts, such as marriage, work, play, politics, and religion. As such, conflict reveals certain common properties in all contexts, and hence it can be viewed as a basic social form.

Moreover, conflict is nearly always combined with cooperation: people agree on norms that regulate when, where, and how to fight with one another, and this is true in marriage, business, games, war, and theological disputes. As Simmel wrote, "There probably exists no social unit in which convergent and divergent currents among its members are not inseparably interwoven. An absolutely centripetal and harmonious group . . . not only is empirically unreal, it could show no real life process."[36] The importance of this fusion of conflict and cooperation can be seen most clearly in those instances where a cooperative element appears to be lacking: for example, in interactions between muggers and their victims or when conflict is engendered exclusively by the lust to fight. Simmel believed that these examples are clearly limiting cases, however, for if "there is any consideration, any limit to violence, there already exists a socializing factor, even though only as the qualification of violence."[37] This is why he emphasized that social conflict is usually a means to a goal; its "superior purpose" implies that people can change or modify their tactics depending on the situation.

In his essay on conflict, Simmel sketched some of the alternative forms of conflict, the way in which they are combined with regulatory norms, and the significance that this form of interaction has for the groups to which people belong. He first

[36]Georg Simmel, "Conflict," in *Conflict and the Web of Group Affiliations,* 15. For an effort to extract the formal properties of conflict in Simmel's essay, see Levine, "Sociology's Quest for the Classics," 68.

[37]Simmel, "Conflict," 26.

examined how conflict within groups affects the reciprocal relations of the parties involved, then he turned to the consequences that conflict with an outgroup has for social relations within a group. The following sections deal with each of these topics.

Conflict Within Groups

Simmel's investigation of the sociological significance of conflict within groups revolves around three forms: (1) conflicts in which the opposing parties possess common personal qualities, (2) conflicts in which the opposing parties perceive each other as a threat to the existence of the group, and (3) conflicts in which the opposing parties recognize and accept each other as legitimate opponents.

Conflict Among Those With Common Personal Qualities[38]

Simmel noted that "people who have many common features often do one another worse or 'wronger' wrong than complete strangers do," mainly because they have so few differences that even the slightest conflict is magnified in its significance. As examples, he referred to conflict in "intimate relations," such as marriages, and to the relationship between renegades and their former colleagues. In both cases, the solidarity of the group is based on the parties possessing many common (or complementary) characteristics. As a result, people are involved with one another as whole persons, and even small antagonisms between them can be highly inflammatory, regardless of the content of the disagreements. Thus, when conflict does occur, the resulting battle is sometimes so intense that previous areas of agreement are forgotten. Most of the time, Simmel observed, the participants develop implicit or explicit norms that keep conflicts within manageable bounds. When emotions run high or when group members see the conflict as transcending their individual interests, however, the fight can become violent. At that point, he suggested, the very existence of those who differ might be taken as a threat to the group.

Conflict as a Threat to the Group[39]

Conflict sometimes occurs among opponents who have common membership in a group. Simmel argued that this type of conflict should be treated as a distinct form because when a group is divided into conflicting elements, the antagonistic parties "hate each other not only on the concrete ground which produced the conflict but also on the sociological ground of hatred for the enemy of the group itself." Such antagonism is especially intense and can easily become violent because each party identifies itself as representing the group and sees the other as a mortal enemy of the collective.

---

[38]Ibid., 43–48.

[39]Ibid., 48–50.

Conflict Among Recognized and Accepted Opponents

Simmel distinguished two forms of conflict among parties who recognize and accept each other as opponents. When conflict is "direct," the opposing parties act squarely against each other to obtain their goals.[40] When conflict is "indirect," the opponents interact only with a third party to obtain their goals. Simmel referred to this latter form of conflict as *competition*.[41] Yet both forms share certain distinguishing characteristics that differentiate them from the forms of conflict noted previously: the opponents are seen to have a right to strive for the same goal, conflict is pursued mercilessly yet nonviolently, personal antagonisms and feelings of hostility are often excluded from the conflict, and the opponents either develop agreements among themselves or accept the imposition of overriding norms that regulate the conflict.

The purest examples of direct conflict are antagonistic games and conflicts over causes. In the playing of games, "one *unites* [precisely] in order to fight, and one fights under the mutually recognized control of norms and rules."[42] Similarly, in the case of conflicts over causes, such as legal battles, the opponents' essential unity is again the underlying basis for interaction because, to fight in court, the opponents must always follow agreed-upon normative procedures. Thus, even as parties confront each other, they affirm their agreement on larger principles. The analysis of direct conflict within groups was, however, of less interest to Simmel, with the result that he did not devote much space to it. Rather, he emphasized the sociological importance of competition because this form of fighting most clearly illustrates how conflict can have positive social consequences. By proceeding indirectly, competition functions as a vital source of social solidarity within a group.

While recognizing the destructive and even shameful aspects of competition to which Marx and other observers had pointed, Simmel argued that even after all its negative aspects were taken into account, competition has positive consequences for the group because it forces people to establish ties with one another, thereby increasing social solidarity. Because competition between parties proceeds with the opponents trying to win over a third party, each of them is implicated in a web of affiliations that connects them with one another.[43]

With some exceptions, Simmel noted, the process of competition is restricted because unregulated conflict can too easily become violent and lead to the destruction of the group itself.[44] Hence, all collectivities that allow competition usually regulate it in some fashion, either through inter-individual restrictions, in which regulatory norms are simply agreed on by the participants, or through super-individual restrictions, in which laws and other normative principles are imposed on the

---

[40]Ibid., 34–43.

[41]Ibid., 57–86.

[42]Ibid., 35 (emphasis in original).

[43]Ibid., 62.

[44]Ibid., 68–70. Simmel recognized that within families and to some extent within religious groups the interests of the group often dictate that members refrain from competing with one another.

competitors.[45] Indeed, the existence of competition often stimulates normative regulation, thereby providing a basis for social integration.

Finally, Simmel recognized instances in which groups or societies try to eliminate competition in the name of a higher principle. For instance, in socialist or communist societies, competition is suspended in favor of an emphasis on organizing individual efforts in such a way as to (a) eliminate the wasted energy that accompanies conflict and (b) provide for the common good. Nonetheless, Simmel appears to have regarded a competitive environment as more useful than a noncompetitive one in modern, highly differentiated societies, not only in economic terms but also in most other arenas of social life. He believed that such an environment provides an outlet for people's "fighting instincts" that redounds to the common good and provides a stimulus for regulatory agreements that also contribute to the common good.

Conflict Between Groups

In the final section of his essay, Simmel examined the consequences that conflict between groups has "for the inner structure of each party itself."[46] Put differently, he was concerned with understanding the effect that conflict has on social relationships within each respective party to the conflict. To make his point, Simmel identified the following consequences of conflict between groups: (a) it increases the degree of centralization of authority within each group; (b) it increases the degree of social solidarity within each group and, at the same time, decreases the level of tolerance for deviance and dissent; and (c) it increases likelihood of coalitions among groups having similar opponents.

Conflict and Centralization of Power[47]

Just as fighters must psychologically "pull themselves together," Simmel observed, so must a group when it is engaged in conflict with another group. There is a "need for centralization, for the tight pulling together of all elements, which alone guarantees their use, without loss of energy and time, for whatever the requirements of the moment may be." This necessity is greatest during war, which "needs a centralistic intensification of the group form." In addition, Simmel noted, the development and maintenance of a centralized group is often "guaranteed best by despotism," and he argued that a centralized and despotic regime was more likely to wage war precisely because people's accumulated energies (or "hostile impulses") needed some means of expression. Finally, Simmel remarked that centralized groups generally preferred to engage in conflict with groups that were also centralized. For despite the conflict-producing consequences of fighting a tightly organized opponent, conflict with such an opponent can be more easily resolved, not only because the boundaries separating each side are clearly demarcated but also because each party "can supply a representative with whom one can negotiate with full certainty." For example, in conflicts between

---

[45]Ibid., 76.

[46]Ibid., 87.

[47]Ibid., 88–91.

workers and employers or between nations, Simmel argued, it is often "better" if each side is organized so that conflict resolution can proceed in a systematic manner.

Conflict, Solidarity, and Intolerance[48]

Simmel argued that conflict often increased social solidarity within each of the opposing groups. As he phrased it, a "tightening of the relations among [the party's] members and the intensification of its unity, in consciousness and in action, occur." This is especially true, he asserted, during wars or other violent conflicts. Moreover, increasing intolerance also accompanies rising solidarity, for whereas antagonistic members can often coexist during peacetime without harm to the group, this luxury is not possible during war. As a result, "groups in any sort of war situation are not tolerant" of deviance and dissent because they often see themselves as fighting for the existence of the group itself and demand total loyalty from members. Thus, in general, conflict between groups means that members must develop solidarity with one another, and those who cannot are often either expelled or punished. As a result of their intolerance toward deviance and dissent, Simmel remarked, groups in conflict often become smaller, as those who would compromise are silenced or cast out. This tendency can make an ongoing conflict more difficult to resolve, because "groups, and especially minorities, which live in conflict and persecution, often reject approaches or tolerance from the other side." The acceptance of such overtures would mean that "the closed nature of their opposition without which they cannot fight on would be blurred." Finally, Simmel suggested that the internal solidarity of many groups depends on their continued conflict with other parties and that their complete victory over an opponent could result in a lessening of internal social solidarity.

Conflict, Coalitions, and Group Formation[49]

Under certain conditions, Simmel wrote, conflict between groups can lead to the formation of coalitions and ultimately to new solidarities among groups where none had existed before. In his words,

> Each element in a plurality may have its own opponent, but because this opponent is the same for all elements, they all unite—and in this case, they may, prior to that, not have had anything to do with each other.

Sometimes such combinations are only for a single purpose, and the allies' solidarity declines immediately at the conclusion of the conflict. However, Simmel argued, when coalitions are engaged in wars or other violent conflicts and when their members become highly interdependent over a long period, more cohesive social relations are likely to ensue. This phenomenon is even more pronounced when a coalition is subjected to an ongoing or relatively permanent threat. As Simmel wrote,

---

[48]Ibid., 17–19, 91–98.

[49]Ibid., 98–107.

The synthetic strength of a common opposition may be determined, not [only] by the number of shared points of interest, but [also] by the duration and intensity of the unification. In this case, it is especially favorable to the unification if instead of an actual fight with an enemy, there is a permanent *threat* by him.

Like so much of Simmel's work, the essay on conflict does not embody a unified conceptual perspective; rather, we get a series of provocative insights. In addition, as always with discursive writings, problems arise in presenting his insights. Nonetheless, we can extrapolate a model of the process of differentiation in Figure 6.2. As societies differentiate (become more complex), the number of organized units and their potential for conflict increases. Increased numbers of units, per se, create pressures for regulation of social relations by mechanisms such as centralization of power, laws, courts, mediating agencies, and coalitions among varying social units. Conflict escalates these pressures while unifying or consolidating social units structurally (centralization of authority, normative clarity, increased sanctioning) and ideologically (increased salience of beliefs and values). If conflicts are sufficiently frequent, low in intensity, and regulated, they release tensions, thereby encouraging further differentiation and elaboration of regulative structures. Such structures also encourage further differentiation by providing the capacity to coordinate increased numbers of units, manage the tensions among them, and reduce their respective sense of threat when in potential conflict.

Figure 6.2   Simmel's Image of Social Conflict

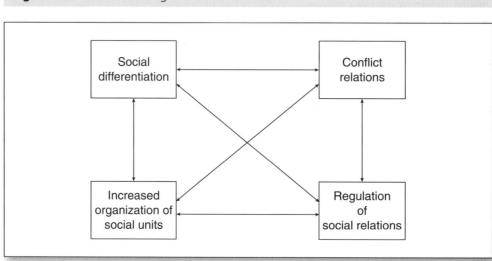

The Philosophy of Money

Simmel's *The Philosophy of Money* is a study of the social consequences of exchange relationships among human beings, with special emphasis on those forms of exchange in which money is used as an abstract measure of value. Like all his other work, *The Philosophy of Money* is an attempt at exposing how the forms of interaction affect the basic nature of social relations independently of their specific content. Although Simmel first considered this issue as early as 1889 in an untranslated article titled "The Psychology of Money," the final formulation of his ideas did not appear until the second edition of *The Philosophy of Money* was published in 1907.[50] Unlike the works reviewed earlier, *The Philosophy of Money* is both a sociological and a philosophical treatise,[51] forcing us to extract the more sociological ideas from a philosophical text.

Exchange as a Social Form

The Philosophy of Money represents Simmel's effort to isolate another basic social form. Not all interaction is exchange, but exchange is a universal form of interaction.[52] In analyzing social exchange, Simmel concentrated on "economic exchange" in general and on money exchanges in particular. Although not all economic exchanges involve the use of money, money has historically come into increasing use as a medium of exchange. This historical trend, Simmel emphasized, reflects the process of social differentiation. But it does much more: money is also a major cause and force behind this process. Thus, the sociological portions of *The Philosophy of Money* are devoted to analyzing the transforming effects on social life of the ever-increasing use of money in social relations.

In analyzing differentiation from an exchange perspective, Simmel developed a number of philosophical assumptions and linked these to a sociological analysis of the modern world. Much like his friend and intellectual defender, Max Weber, Simmel was interested in understanding not just the forms of modern life but also their historical origins.[53] But unlike Weber, Simmel did not engage in detailed historical analyses, nor was he interested in constructing elaborate taxonomies. Rather, his works always sought to link certain philosophical views about humans and the social universe to understanding the properties of a particular social form. Thus, before explicating Simmel's specific analysis of money and exchange, it is necessary to place his analysis in philosophical context.

---

[50]Georg Simmel, "Psychologie des Geldes," *Jahrbücher für Gesetzgebung, Verwaltung und Volkswirtschaft* 23 (1889):1251–1264, *The Philosophy of Money,* 2nd ed., trans. Tom Bottomore and David Frisby (Boston, MA: Routledge, 1990).

[51]It is often forgotten that Simmel was a philosopher as well as a sociologist. He wrote books and articles on the works of Kant, Goethe, Schopenhauer, and Nietzsche and considered more general philosophical issues and problems as well.

[52]Simmel, *The Philosophy of Money,* 82.

[53]Simmel was excluded from senior academic positions for much of his career, and his work was often attacked. Max Weber was one of his most consistent defenders and apparently helped him maintain at least a marginal intellectual standing in Germany. But Weber revealed some ambivalence toward Simmel; see Weber's "Georg Simmel as a Sociologist," with an introduction by Donald N. Levine, *Social Research* 39 (1972):154–165.

Simmel's Assumptions About Human Nature

In *The Philosophy of Money*, Simmel presented a vision of human nature that is implicit but less visible in his sociological works. He began by asserting that people are teleological beings; that is, they act on the environment in the pursuit of anticipated goals. In the essay on conflict, Simmel emphasized that this characteristic made human conflict different from that occurring among other animals. In *The Philosophy of Money*, Simmel took the position that although people's goals would vary in accordance with their biological impulses and social needs, all action reflected humans' ability to manipulate the environment in an attempt to realize goals. In so doing, individuals use a variety of "tools," but not just in the obvious material sense. Rather, people use subtler, more symbolic tools, such as language and money, to achieve their goals. In general, Simmel argued that the more tools people possessed, the greater would be their capacity to manipulate the environment and, hence, the more they could causally influence the flow of events. Moreover, the use of tools allows many events to be connected in chains that can form more extended social relations, as when money is used to buy a good. Money, for example, pays the salary of the seller, becomes profit for the manufacturer, and is transformed into wages for the worker, and so on, in a chain of social relations. Thus, Simmel thought that all action reveals the properties presented in Figure 6.3.

Money, Simmel asserted, is the ultimate social tool because it is generalized; that is, people can use it in many ways to manipulate the environment to obtain their goals. This means that money can potentially connect many events and persons who would not otherwise be related. In an indirect way, then, the use of money allows a vast increase in the number of groups to which individuals can belong; thus, it is a prime force behind social differentiation.

A related assumption is that humans have the capacity to divide their world into an internal, subjective state and an external, objective state. This division occurs only when impulses are not immediately satisfied—that is, when the environment presents barriers and obstacles. When such barriers exist, humans separate their

Figure 6.3 Simmel's Model of the Dynamics of Human Action

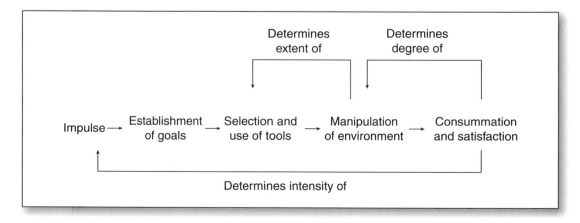

subjective experiences from the objects of the environment that are the source of need or impulse satisfaction. As Simmel emphasized,

> We desire objects only if they are not immediately given to us for our use and enjoyment; that is, to the extent that they resist our desire. The content of our desire becomes an object as soon as it is opposed to us, not only in the sense of being impervious to us, but also in terms of its distance as something not enjoyed.[54]

Value inheres in this subject/object division. In contrast with Marx, Simmel stressed that the value of an object existed not in the "labor power" required to produce it but in the extent to which it was both desired and unattainable; that is, value resides in the process of seeking objects that are scarce and distant. Value is thus tied to humans' basic capacity to distinguish a subjective from an objective world and in the relative difficulty in securing objects. Patterns of social organization, Simmel emphasized, perform much of this subject/object separation: they present barriers and obstacles, they create demands for some objects, and they determine how objects will circulate. The economic production of goods and their sale in a market is only a special case of the more general process of subject/object division among humans. Long before money, markets, and productive corporations existed, humans desired objects that were not easily obtainable. Thus, whether in the economic marketplace or the more general arena of life, value is a positive function of the extent to which an object of desire is difficult to obtain.[55]

Money, as Simmel showed, greatly increases the creation and acceleration of value because it provides a common yardstick for a quick calculation of values ("how much" a commodity or service is "worth"). Moreover, as a "tool," money greatly facilitates the acquisition of objects; as money circulates and is used at each juncture to calculate values, all objects in the environment come to be assessed by their monetary value. Unlike Marx, Simmel did not see this as a perverse process but as a natural reflection of humans' innate capacity and need to create values for the objects of their environment.

Another assumption about human nature is to be found in Simmel's discussion of "world view."[56] People naturally seek stability and order in their world, he argued. They seek to know the place of objects and of their relationship to these objects. For example, Simmel observed, humans develop totems and religious rituals to regularize their relations to the supernatural; similarly, the development of money as a standardized measurement of value is but another manifestation of this tendency of humans to seek order and stability in their view of the world. By developing money, they can readily compare objects by their respective value and can therefore develop a "sense of order" about their environment.

In sum, then, Simmel believed that the development of money is an expression and extension of basic human nature. Money is a kind of tool in teleological acts; it

---

[54]Simmel, *Philosophy of Money,* 66.

[55]Ibid., 80–98.

[56]Ibid., 102–110.

is a way to express the value inherent in humans' capacity for subject/object division; and it is a means of attaining stability and order in people's worldview. All these innate tendencies are the driving force behind much human action, and this is why exchange is such a basic form of social interaction. For exchange is nothing more than the sacrificing of one object of value for the attainment of another. Money greatly facilitates this process because it provides a common reference point for calculating the respective values of objects that are exchanged.

Money in Social Exchange

For Simmel, social exchange involves the following elements:

1. The desire for a valued object that one does not have

2. The possession of the valued object by an identifiable other

3. The offer of an object of value to secure from another the desired object

4. The acceptance of this offer by the possessor of the valued object[57]

Contained in this portrayal of social exchange are several additional points that Simmel emphasized. First, value is idiosyncratic and is ultimately tied to an individual's impulses and needs. Of course, what is defined as valuable is typically circumscribed by cultural and social patterns, but how valuable an object is will be a positive function of both the intensity of a person's needs and the scarcity of the object. Second, exchange mostly involves efforts to manipulate situations so that the intensity of the need for an object is concealed and the availability of the object is made to seem less than it actually is. Inherent in exchange, therefore, is a basic tension that can often erupt into other social forms, such as conflict. Third, to possess an object is to lessen its value and to increase the value of objects that one does not possess. Fourth, exchanges will occur only if both parties perceive that the object given is less valuable than the one received.[58] Fifth, collective units as well as individuals participate in exchange relations and, hence, are subject to the four processes listed. Sixth, the more liquid the resources of an actor are in an exchange—that is, the more resources that can be used in many types of exchanges—the greater that actor's options and power will be. If an actor is not bound to exchange with any other and can readily withdraw resources and exchange them with another, that actor has considerable power to manipulate any exchange.

Economic exchange involving money is only a special case of this more general social form. But it is a very special case. When money becomes the predominant

---

[57]Ibid., 85–88.

[58]Surprisingly, Simmel did not explore in any detail the consequences of unbalanced exchanges, in which people are forced to give up a more valuable object for a less valuable one. He simply assumed that at the time of exchange, both parties felt that an increase in value had occurred. Retrospectively, a redefinition might occur, but the exchange will not occur if at that moment people do not perceive that they are receiving more value than they are giving up.

means for establishing value in social relationships, the properties and dynamics of social relations are transformed. This process of displacing other criteria of value, such as logic, ethics, and aesthetics, with a monetary criterion is precisely the long-term historical trend in societies. This trend is, as we mentioned earlier, both a cause and an effect of money being the medium of exchange. Money emerged to facilitate exchanges and to realize even more completely humans' basic needs. Once established, however, the use of money has the power to transform the structure of social relations in society. In seeking to understand how money has this power to alter social relations, Simmel's *The Philosophy of Money* becomes distinctly sociological.

Money and Its Consequences for Social Relations

In much of Simmel's work, there is an implicit functionalism. He often asked, what are the consequences of a social form for the larger social whole, or what functions does it perform? This functionalism is most evident in Simmel's analysis of conflict, but it is also found in his analysis of money. He asked two related questions in tracing the consequences of money for social patterns: (1) What are the consequences of money for the structure of society as a whole? (2) What are the consequences of money for individuals?

In answering these two questions, Simmel added to his lifelong preoccupation with several issues. We mention these to place his specific analysis of the consequences of money for society and the individual into context. One prominent theme in all Simmel's work is the dialectic between individual attachments to and freedom from groups. On the one hand, he praised social relations that allow individuals freedom to choose their options, but on the other hand, he was somewhat dismayed at the alienation of individuals from the collective fiber of society (although not to the extent of other theorists during his time). This theme is tied to another prominent concern in his work: the growing rationalization of society, or, as he phrased it, the "objectification" of social life. As social relations lose their traditional and religious content, they become mediated by impersonal standards—law, intellect, logic, and money. The application of these standards increases individual freedom and social justice, but it also makes life less emotional and involving. It reduces relations to rational calculations, devoid of the emotional bonds that come with attachments to religious symbols and long-standing traditions. Simmel's analysis of the "functions" of money for individuals and the social whole must be viewed in the context of these two themes.

Money and the Social Whole

Much like Weber, but in a less systematic way, Simmel was concerned with the historical trend toward rationalization, or objectification, of social relations. In general, humans tend to symbolize their relations, both with one another and with the natural environment. In the past, this was done with religious totems and then with laws. More recently, Simmel believed, people expressed their relationships with physical entities and with one another in monetary terms, with the result that they have lost intimate and direct contact with others as well as with the objects in their environment. Thus, money represents the ultimate objective symbolization of social relations—unlike material entities, money has no intrinsic value. Money merely represents values, and it is used to express the value of one object in relation to another. Although initial forms of money, such as coins of valuable metals and stones that could be converted into jewelry, possessed intrinsic value, the evolutionary trend is toward the use of paper money and credit, which merely express values in exchanges. As paper money and credit dominate, social relations in society are profoundly altered, in at least the following ways:

1. The use of money enables actors to make quick calculations of respective values. People do not have to bargain and haggle over the standards to be used in establishing the respective values of objects—whether commodities or labor. As a result, the "velocity" of exchange dramatically increases. People move through social relations more quickly.[59]

2. Because money increases the rate of social interaction and exchange, it also increases value. Simmel felt that people did not engage in exchange unless they perceived that they would get more than they gave up. Hence, the greater the rate of exchange is, the greater people's accumulation of value will be—that is, the more they will perceive that their needs and desires can be realized.[60]

3. The use of money as a liquid and nonspecific resource allows for much greater continuity in social relations. It prevents gaps from developing in social relations, as is often the case when people have only hard goods, such as food products or jewelry, to exchange in social relations. Money gives people options to exchange almost anything because the respective values can be readily calculated. As a result, there is greater continuity in social relations because all individuals can potentially engage in exchanges.[61]

4. In a related vein, money also allows the creation of multiple social ties. With money, people join groups other than those established at birth and thereby interact with many more others than is possible with a more restrictive medium of exchange.[62]

5. Money also allows exchanges among human beings located at great distances. As long as interaction involves exchange of concrete objects, there are limits to how distant people can be from one another and how many actors can participate in a sequence of exchanges. With money, these limitations are removed. Nations can engage in exchanges; individuals who never see one another—such as a factory worker and consumers of goods produced in the

---

[59]Simmel, *Philosophy of Money,* 143, 488–512.

[60]Ibid., 292.

[61]Ibid., 124.

[62]Ibid., 307.

factory—can be indirectly connected in an exchange sequence (because some of the payment for a good or commodity will ultimately be translated into wages for the worker). Thus, money greatly extends the scope of social organization; money allows organization beyond face-to-face contact or beyond the simple barter of goods. With money, more and more people can become connected through direct and indirect linkages.[63]

6. Money also promotes social solidarity, in the sense that it represents a "trust"; that is, if people take money for goods or services, they believe that it can be used at a future date to buy other goods or services. This implicit trust in the capacity of money to meet future needs reinforces people's faith in and commitment to society.[64]

7. In a related argument, money increases the power of central authority, for the use of money requires that there be social stability and that a central authority guarantee the worth of money.[65] As exchange relations rely on government to maintain the stability of money, government acquires power. Moreover, money makes it much easier for a central government to tax people.[66] As long as only property could be taxed, there were limitations on the effectiveness of taxation by a remote central government because knowledge of property held would be incomplete and because property, such as land, is not easily converted into values that can be used to increase the power of central government. (How can, for example, property effectively buy labor services for the army or the administrative staff of a government?) As a liquid resource, however, tax money can be used to buy those services and goods necessary for effective central authority.

8. The creation of a tax on money also promotes a new basis of social solidarity. Because all social strata and other collectivities are subject to a monetary taxation system, they have at least one common goal: control and regulation of taxes imposed by the central government. This commonality laces diverse groupings together because of their common interest in the taxing powers of government.

9. The use of money often extends into virtually all spheres of interaction. As an efficient means for comparing values, money replaces other, less efficient ways to calculate value. As money begins to penetrate all social relations, resistance to its influence in areas of personal value increases. Efforts to maintain the "personal element" in transactions increase, and norms about when it is inappropriate to use money become established. For example, traditions of paying a bride price vanish, using money to buy influence is

---

[63]Ibid., 180–186.

[64]Ibid., 177–178.

[65]Ibid., 171–184.

[66]Ibid., 317.

considered much more offensive than personal persuasion, paying a price as punishment for certain crimes decreases, and so on.[67]

10. While these efforts are made to create spheres where the use of money is reduced, there is a general "quantification" and "objectification" of social relations.[68] Interactions become quantified as their value is expressed in terms of money. As a result, moral constraints on what is possible decrease because anything is possible if one just has the money. Money releases people from the constraints of tradition and moral authority; money creates a system in which it is difficult to restrain individual aspirations and desires. Deviance and "pathology" are, therefore, more likely in systems where money becomes the prevalent medium of interaction.[69]

Money and the Individual

For Simmel, the extensive use of money in social interaction has several consequences for individuals. Most of these reflect the inherent tension between individual freedom from constraint, on the one hand, and alienation and detachment from social groups, on the other hand. Money gives people new choices and options, but it also depersonalizes their social milieu. Simmel isolated the following consequences of money for individuals:

1. As a "tool," money is nonspecific and thus gives people an opportunity to pursue many diverse activities. Unlike less liquid forms of expressing value, money does not determine how it can be used. Hence, individuals in a society that uses money as its principal medium of exchange enjoy considerably more freedom of choice than is possible in a society that does not use money.[70]

2. In a similar vein, money gives people many options for self-expression. To the degree that individuals seek to express themselves through the objects of their possession, money allows unlimited means for self-expression. As a result, the use of money for self-expression leads to, and indeed encourages, diversity in a population that is no longer constrained in the pursuit of its needs (except, of course, by the amount of money its members have).[71]

---

[67]Ibid., 369–387.

[68]Ibid., 393.

[69]Ibid., 404. Many analysts of Simmel emphasize these pathologies, especially when factoring in his analysis in other works, such as those translated by Peter Etzkorn in *The Conflict in Modern Culture and Other Essays* (New York: Teacher's College Press, 1980) and famous essays such as "The Metropolis and Mental Life." See, for example, David Frisby, *Sociological Impressionism: A Reassessment of Simmel's Social Theory* (London: Heinemann, 1981) and *Georg Simmel* (Chichester, UK: Ellis Horwood, 1984). For a balanced assessment that corresponds to the one offered here, see Donald R. Levine, "Simmel as Educator: On Individuality and Modern Culture," *Theory, Culture, and Society* 8 (1991), 99–117.

[70]Simmel, *Philosophy of Money*, 307.

[71]Ibid., 326–327.

3. Yet money also creates a distance between one's sense of self and the objects of self-expression. With money, objects are easily acquired and discarded, and hence long-term attachments to objects do not develop.[72]

4. Money allows a person to enter many different types of social relations. One can, for example, buy such relationships by paying membership dues in organizations or by spending money on various activities that ensure contacts with particular types of people. Hence, money encourages a multiplicity of social relations and group memberships. At the same time, however, money discourages intimate attachments. Money increases the multiplicity of individuals' involvements, but it atomizes and compartmentalizes their activities and often keeps them from emotional involvement in each of their segregated activities. This trend is, Simmel felt, best personified by the division of labor that is made possible by money wages but that also compartmentalizes individuals, often alienating them from others and their work.[73]

5. Money also makes it less necessary to know people personally because their money "speaks" for them. In systems without money, social relations are mediated by intimate knowledge of others, and adjustments among people are made through the particular characteristics of each individual. As money begins to mediate interaction, the need to know another personally is correspondingly reduced.

Thus, in Simmel's analysis of consequences, money is a mixed blessing for both the individual and society. Money allows greater freedom and provides new and multiple ways of connecting individuals. Money also isolates, atomizes, and even alienates individuals from the persons and objects in their social milieu. As a result, money alters the nature of social relations among individuals in society, and therefore an analysis of its consequences is decidedly a sociological topic.

Embedded in this descriptive analysis of the consequences of money is a more general model of exchange, differentiation, and individualization of the person. Social differentiation increases the volume, rate, velocity, and potential scope of social ties among individuals and groups because there are more different kinds of units and, hence, more opportunities for multiple and varied social contacts. Increases in the number of social relations create pressures for the use of objective or rational symbolic media, such as money, to facilitate exchange transactions; reciprocally, the use of money allows an ever-increasing volume of social ties because money makes it easy to determine the value of each actor's resources and to conduct social transactions. Increases in social exchanges mediated by money feed back on differentiation, encouraging further differentiation, which in turn increases the volume, rate, velocity, and scope of the social ties mediated by money. Such processes cause ever more individualization of people—that is, increased involvement of only small parts of one's personality in groups, increased group affiliations,

---

[72]Ibid., 297.

[73]Ibid., 454.

and greater potential alienation from society. Yet these trends toward individualization are important contributors to the increased volume and rates of interaction, as well as the escalated use of money, on which social differentiation depends.

Simmel's Theoretical Legacy

If there is a central theme in Simmel's work, it is focused on the effects of the process of differentiation on forms of social relations, and vice versa. Like his fellow countryman, Max Weber, Simmel emphasized the growing reliance on rationality and calculation over ascription and tradition in establishing social relations in differentiated societies as the central dynamic of modernization. In particular, Simmel saw this shift in the nature of social relations as tied to the use of money in market exchanges. With differentiation, money, and markets, the number and diversity of social ties in a society increase, and this shift in patterns of group affiliations increases the level of individuality in society. People can now tailor their relations to their unique needs and tastes, and they can carry varying identities in different groups. This individualization gives individuals more freedom and choice, but there is a cost to pay in the increased potential for marginality, atomization, and alienation.

Like Karl Marx, Simmel examined conflict in complex differentiated societies. Unlike Marx, however, Simmel saw that conflict can potentially be an integrative force, especially if it occurs frequently at low levels of intensity and violence. Indeed, in complex societies, where diverse groups reveal different interests, conflict is inevitable, but if conflict can release tensions and be regulated by government and law, then it can help sustain society rather than rip it apart.

These are the general themes that run through Simmel's main core of work. There are many essays in Simmel's sociology, but those focusing on differentiation and the changing basis of integration in society for both individuals and groups mark Simmel's enduring theoretical legacy. Let us see if we can present these themes in a general model.

Simmel's Causal Models of Social Organization

Simmel's Model of Social Organization. In Figure 6.4, the key elements in Simmel's model of social organization are outlined. For Simmel, the major transformation of modern society is the increasing level of differentiation among individuals, their roles, and social relations as well as the groupings to which they belong. Thus, the model begins at the left with the level of social differentiation, and like Simmel's argument, it moves to the right, enumerating the outcomes of differentiation. As Simmel would have emphasized, these outcomes feed back as reverse causal effects (moving from right to left in the model), influencing the values for the forces that cause them. In Simmel's approach, all the direct, indirect, and reverse causal effects are positive, signaling his recognition that differentiation had unleashed powerful forces that dramatically change the form of social relations in society.

Figure 6.4 Simmel's Model of Social Organization

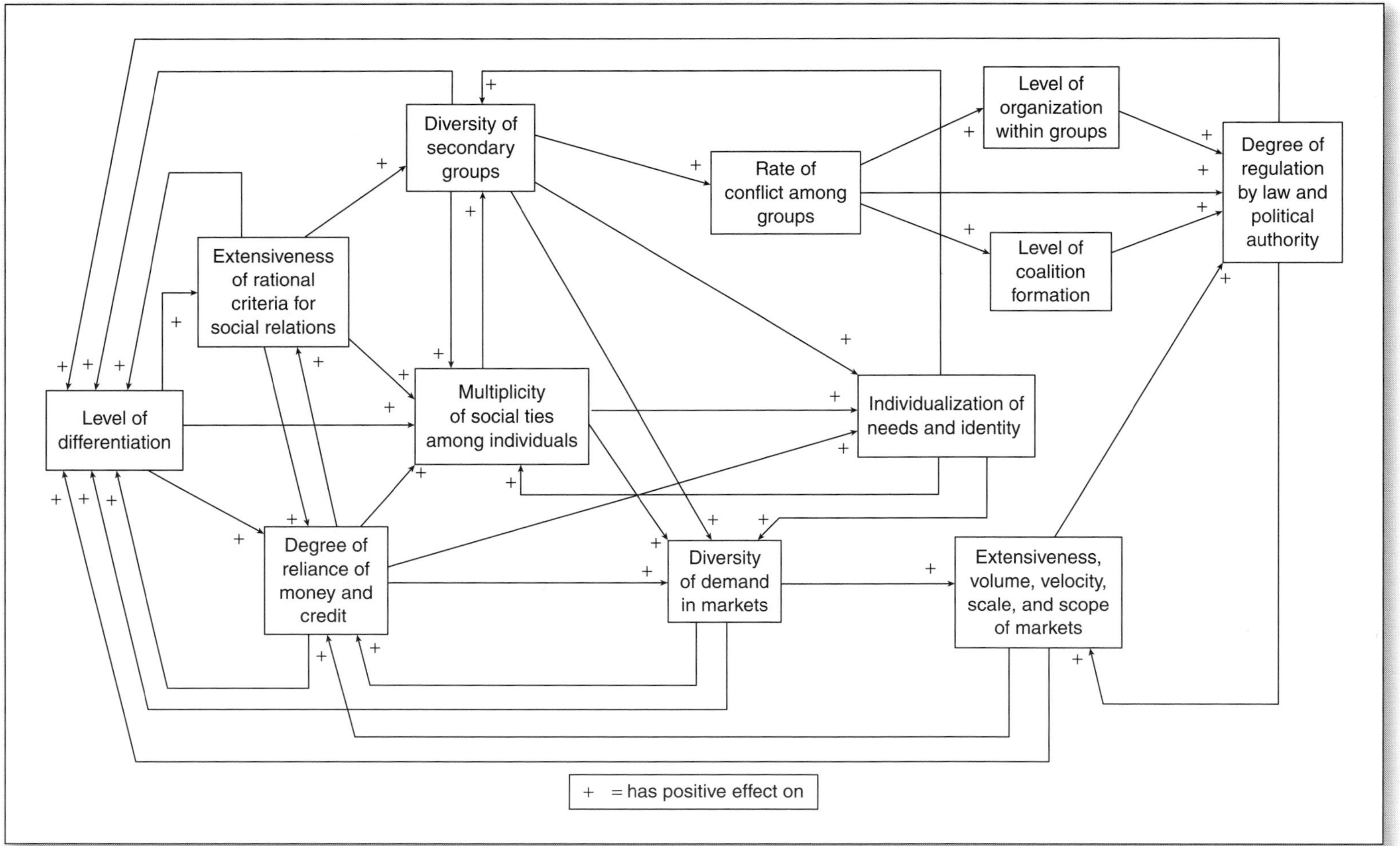

Degree of regulation by law and political authority

Level of organization within groups

Level of coalition formation

Individualization of needs and identity

Extensiveness, volume, velocity, scale, and scope of markets

Rate of conflict among groups

Diversity of demand in markets

Diversity of secondary groups

Multiplicity of social ties among individuals

Extensiveness of rational criteria for social relations

Degree of reliance of money and credit

Level of differentiation

+ = has positive effect on

Increased differentiation has several consequences, the most important of which is to *rationalize* social relations and give individuals the ability to choose group affiliations. This shift away from ascription as a basis for establishing social relations has the effect of increasing the multiplicity of social ties among individuals as well as the diversity of secondary groups to which individuals can belong. The introduction of money accelerates this shift in the basis for ties because it gives individuals a generalized marker of value to choose and buy affiliations. More generally, money alters people's worldviews and mindsets toward the calculation of utilities to be gained in social relations. The diversity of secondary groups, the multiplicity of ties, and the use of money as a marker of value all directly increase *individualization* of people. People can have different identities in various groups, and they have the ability to realize their idiosyncratic needs. The lower portions of the model denote some of the dynamics that accelerate individualization. When money circulates widely, diversity of demand increases because money can be used to buy whatever a person chooses; moreover, once individuals can express their tastes with money, this change encourages the further use of money and the rational calculation of utilities, both of which increase the level of differentiation. With diverse demand, markets can grow and differentiate, and as markets increase the volume and velocity of exchanges, reliance on money as the medium of exchange will become even greater. These self-reinforcing cycles give individuals further options to express their own needs, and as this process feeds back, it increases the level of differentiation and the rational bases for establishing social ties and group memberships, which in turn allow individuals to express distinctive but also multiple identities in differentiated groups.

Differentiation of secondary groups also increases rates of conflict. Differentiated groups have different interests and goals, and these interests can lead to competition, one form of conflict. Conflict will increase the degree of organization within units (e.g., authority systems, boundaries, normative clarity, and intolerance for deviance), and it often leads to the formation of coalitions among groups in larger networks and confederations. Most important, conflict will increase the extent to which law and government begin to regulate social relations, and if frequent and low-intensity conflicts can be consistently regulated, further differentiation is possible (as the long reverse causal chain across the top of the model underscores).

Political-legal regulation is also influenced by markets. Simmel argued that dynamic markets using money require political authority and laws to regulate exchanges; as markets become more extensive, they draw political authority into the economy. Reciprocally, with some degree of regulation, markets can expand further and set into motion the reverse causal paths back to differentiation. Thus, both conflict and markets will expand the use of power and law to regulate a society, and when this regulation can mitigate conflicts and facilitate exchanges, it creates the conditions for a new level of differentiation (and the outcomes of this differentiation that are enumerated in the model).

Thus, it is possible to pull a number of the prominent themes in Simmel's work into a general model. Perhaps more than any theorist of his time, Simmel recognized the power of reverse causal effects; that is, the outcomes of differentiation will accelerate each other as well as the general process of differentiation. The model in Figure 6.4 is, however, very general, and it only emphasizes the positive effects among forces.

Simmel understood that there are pathologies inhering in these forces, and we can see these better by breaking particular paths in Figure 6.4 into separate models.

Simmel's Model of Differentiation and Group Affiliations. Simmel argues that social differentiation increases the proliferation of non-ascriptive, or "rational," criteria for group membership. Such non-ascriptive, rational criteria allow individuals greater freedom and choice in establishing social relations. This increased choice stimulates the proliferation of secondary groups, and conversely, the existence of such groups encourages the use of rational or choice-based criteria. For Simmel, then, social differentiation dramatically changes the nature of the individual's relationship to groups, and in turn, these changes in social relations alter the nature of individuals. The basic model employed by Simmel is outlined in Figure 6.5.

As secondary groups proliferate and non-ascriptive criteria are used in establishing ties, individuals can have multiple group affiliations. Although primary group affiliations still exist, an increasing proportion of social relations occur within secondary groups created for particular goals and ends (what Simmel called "contents"). Members of these groups make explicit calculations about their needs and interests in joining. As the number of secondary groups increases and as the proportion of attachments to them increases, individualization of personality also becomes more frequent. By individualization, Simmel meant that people can have (a) multiple identities tied to their unique web of groups and (b) choice in their affiliations tailored to their particular needs. Without differentiation, this kind of individualization is not possible; rather, people remain embedded in a smaller number of more primary groups on the basis of ascription rather than choice.

However, there are potential problems for individuals that reverberate back and, potentially, influence the multiplicity of ties and social differentiation. One problem is role conflict stemming from too many obligations attached to too many roles in too many groups. Under these conditions, performing a role or maintaining a social relation makes it difficult to do the same in other roles and relations, thereby generating stress and anxiety in the individual. Under these conditions, individuals will, if they can, cut back on affiliations (as is underscored by the negatively signed arrow from anxiety, generated by role conflict, to multiplicity of group affiliations). Another problem is marginality, whereby the individual does not feel highly integrated into any one group. Rather, people stand between groups, being a part of many groups but also a stranger to each. This can lead individuals to cut back on secondary group memberships and seek more primary group affiliations.

Simmel argues that as non-ascriptive criteria are used in establishing social relations, *objectification* of the world ensues. This idea parallels Weber's notion of rationalization, but it focuses on the criteria that people use to affiliate with groups rather than on the structure of the groups themselves. Much as Weber did, Simmel saw this objectification as inevitable, once initiated. Simmel's assessment of rationalization is just the opposite of Weber's, however. Rationalization does not lead to an "iron cage" of rational-legal authority embodied in restrictive bureaucracies; on the contrary, there is now freedom of choice, which is not possible in more traditional patterns of group affiliation, and this freedom can enhance the quality of people's lives.

Figure 6.5 Simmel's Model of Differentiation and Group Affiliations

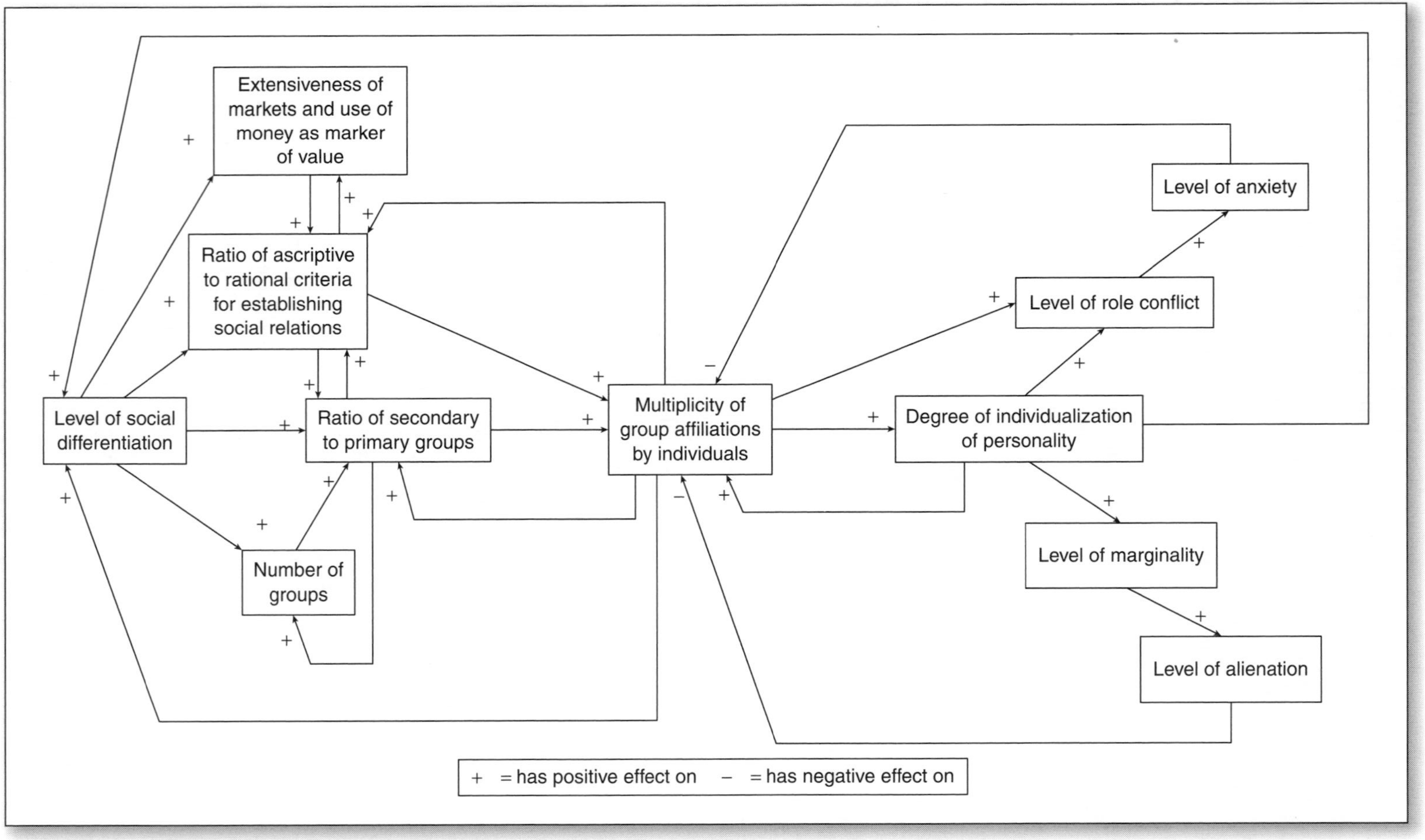

+ = has positive effect on   − = has negative effect on

Simmel's Model of Money, Markets, and Differentiation. Simmel's *The Philosophy of Money* contains a model of market dynamics, showing how these increase the level of differentiation in society. His model is very similar to the one developed by Weber, except that Simmel sees markets and the rationality that they encourage as more liberating than constraining. In Figure 6.6, I outline this model (its similarity to Weber's can be seen by comparing it with Figure 5.10). The model begins with the increasing penetration of money into social exchanges, although the long reverse causal arrow from differentiation on the far right emphasizes that differentiation is one of the causes behind the use of money in exchanges. With money, it becomes possible to calculate values rapidly. In turn, this ability to make rapid calculations increases the velocity of social exchanges. An increase in the velocity of exchanges has a positive effect on social differentiation because it becomes possible to specialize and still secure resources from other specialists by virtue of high-volume, high-velocity markets. Once markets using money come into existence, these processes all feed back and accelerate the use of money and the velocity of exchanges, as indicated by the positive signs on the arrows marking these reverse causal effects.

The row of causal effects running across the bottom of the figure recapitulates in the context of market dynamics Simmel's analysis of affiliations presented in the previous section. Money gives individuals freedom to choose, but it lowers the level of intimacy of relations. At the same time, money increases the potential for anxiety and alienation to the extent that it encourages a high ratio of secondary to primary group affiliations; and anxiety and alienation stemming from multiple group affiliations can work against further differentiation.

A countervailing force to these problems is the effect of markets in increasing the aggregate sense of value experienced by individuals. As Simmel noted, when people use money in markets, including markets for group memberships, they will do so because they perceive the bargain to be worthwhile. They engage in exchange because they think that they will receive increased value; and as many individuals do so, the aggregate sense of value in a society rises. When people sense that they are accumulating value (or rewards and utilities), this accumulated value can mitigate against anxiety or alienation (as indicated by the negatively signed arrow from value to the potential problems). Thus, Simmel was criticizing both Karl Marx and Max Weber in their respective views that money, rational calculation, and markets are dehumanizing: rather, Simmel argued that these forces allow individuals to enhance their sense of value or well-being.

Across the top of Figure 6.6 is Simmel's theory of how money influences the growth of the state. The use of money requires regulation, if only to coin the money and to sustain its value in markets. Moreover, money also represents a form of liquid revenue for the state, and as a result, the government soon learns how to tax the flows of money in order to expand government. But Simmel recognized something more: The value of money becomes a critical force in legitimating government. If the state can sustain the stability of currency (i.e., prevent inflation), then the value of money is preserved and people will have positive sentiments toward political authority.

Moreover, money increases the level of trust in a society, particularly when the value of money remains stable. This enhanced sense of trust further legitimizes

Figure 6.6 Simmel's Model of Markets, Money, and Differentiation

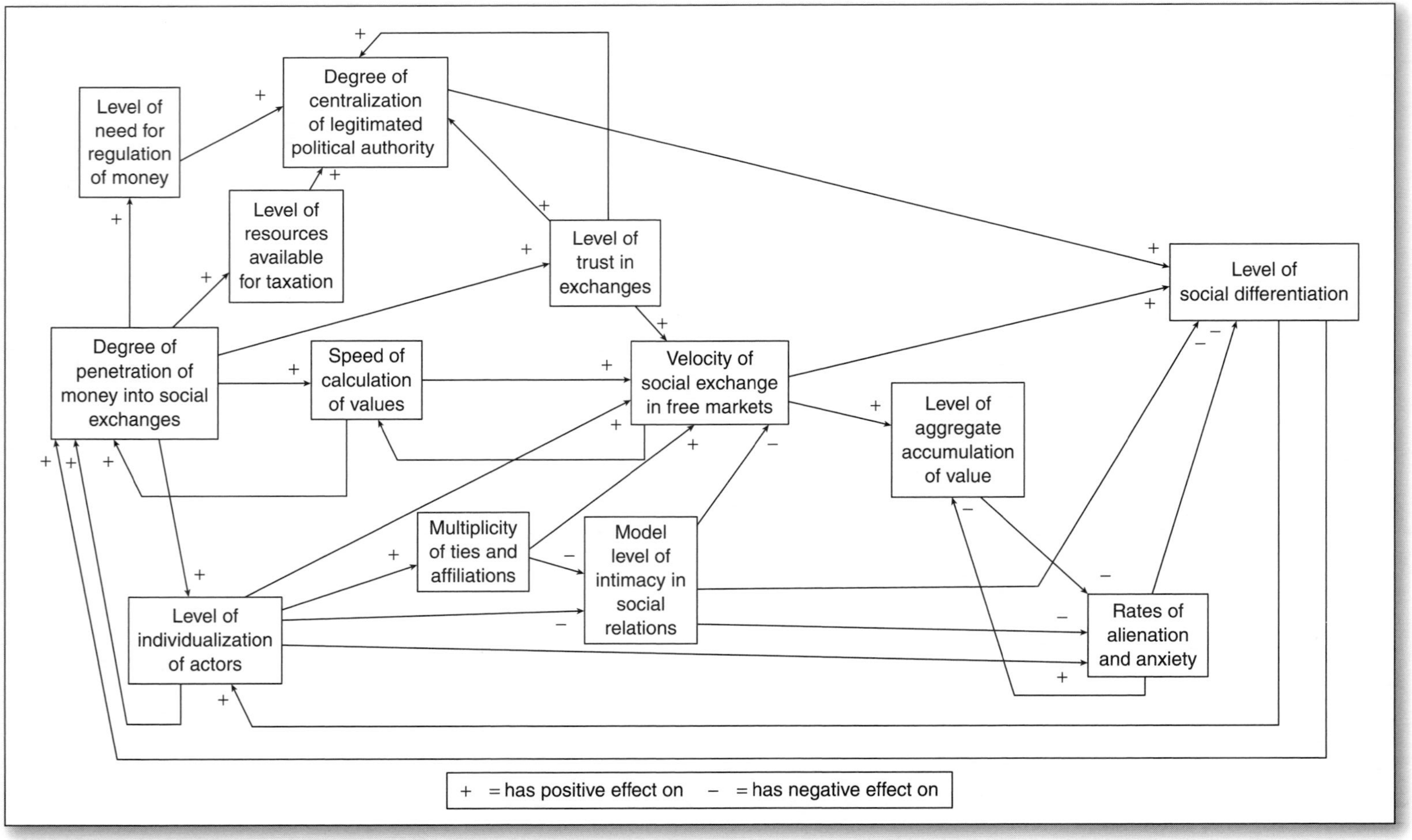

+ = has positive effect on   − = has negative effect on

the political system and the operation of markets, as denoted by the positive arrows leaving level of trust in exchanges. This trust is generated because money has no intrinsic value by itself, especially paper money. As a result, when money is accepted in exchange, there is an implied trust: The money has value in future purchases by those who take it. The more money is used and trusted, the greater will be the aggregate sense of trust in the society. This trust encourages individuals to use their money in markets, and because the state is involved in maintaining the value of money, this trust is reflected back on government in the form of enhanced legitimacy. Thus, for Simmel, the basis of trust shifts from ascription, tradition, and emotional attachments to a more diffuse sense that the means of exchange— money—carries and sustains value. Should money lose its value because of an increase in the rate of inflation, the process works in the opposite way: people withdraw legitimacy from government; they do not trust others using money; markets become stagnant or even revert back to older forms of exchange, such as barter (where goods are exchanged without the use of money); and as this occurs, the level of differentiation in a society is arrested or even reversed. Indeed, people may begin to use ascriptive criteria in forming fewer affiliations with more primary groups to re-create a sense of trust.

Simmel's Model of Social Differentiation, Conflict, and Societal Integration. Unlike his fellow Germans, Karl Marx and Max Weber, Simmel tended to focus on the positive outcomes, or functions, of conflict for societal integration. Integration can occur at two levels, within the parties to a conflict and across the broader society. Figure 6.7 outlines the model developed by Simmel on these two aspects of conflict and integration, although the forces denoted in the model give more attention to societal integration. Any conflict will increase the level of organization among the units engaged in conflict, but Simmel was most interested in frequent conflicts of low intensity because these kinds of conflicts offered the most potential for societal integration. Such conflicts are likely, Simmel argued, in differentiated systems, where they would not polarize all members into a few warring camps. Differentiated systems generate multiplicity of ties in secondary groups, and these groups are less likely to arouse the same emotions as more primary groups engaged in conflict. Moreover, given the many ties that exist among a large number of groups, conflicts would be more frequent, but this frequency would mitigate their intensity, as emphasized by the negatively signed causal arrow connecting frequency to intensity of conflict.

Frequent conflicts of lower intensity would allow for their regulation by political authority and law. Indeed, conflict would be the principle force behind the expansion of government, and once legitimated political authority is in a position to manage conflicts, it can work to reduce their intensity. Thus, as the negatively signed causal arrows from frequency of conflict and extensiveness of political regulation to level of accumulated hostility emphasize, frequent conflicts of low intensity regulated by political authority and law release tensions and, thereby, decrease the level of accumulated hostility among units.

Coalitions among groups are likely under all conditions of conflict, and such coalitions will increase the organization of social units and create larger confederations

Figure 6.7 Simmel's Model of Social Differentiation, Conflict, and Societal Integration

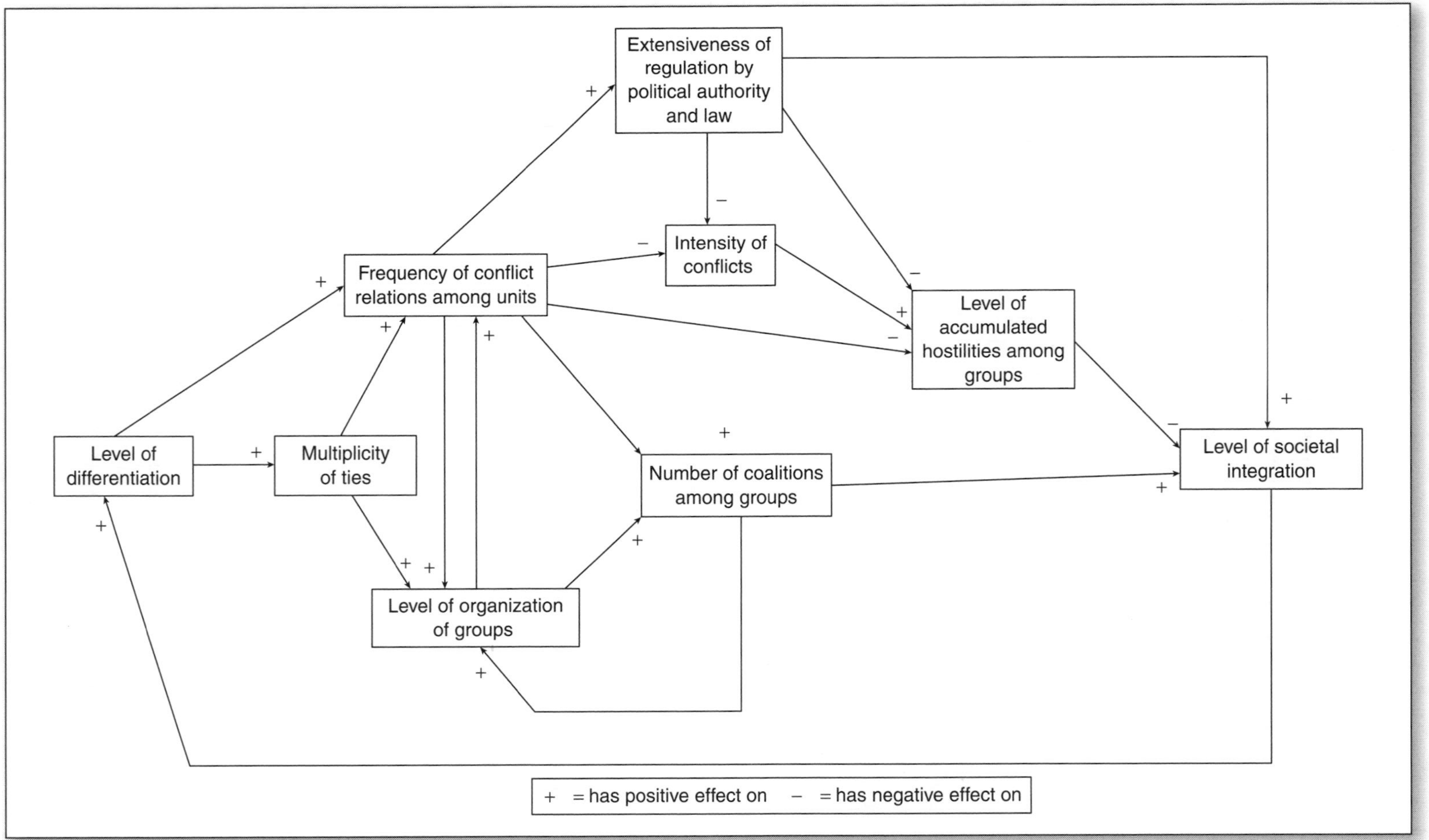

+ = has positive effect on   − = has negative effect on

of groups. But the relationship between coalitions and societal integration is more complex: A certain amount of confederation promotes integration among units, but when a society becomes confederated into just a few blocks standing in conflict, societal integration decreases. Thus, the relationship between coalitions and integration depends on the number of coalitions; the more the coalitions embracing a diversity of units, the more these confederations will work for integration depending on the number of coalitions, whereas the fewer are the coalitions and the more they embrace all units, the more potential for highly disruptive conflict that can destroy societal integration. This is why we have phrased the variable as number of coalitions, since this gives us a rough indicator of whether a society is composed of just a few confederated camps or many cross-cutting points of conflict that do not have the power to polarize a society.

In sum, then, these four models capture Simmel's general theory. I have pieced together somewhat disparate elements of Simmel's sociology, but this exercise demonstrates that Simmel did have an image of the key dynamics operating in differentiating social systems. Although he never presented a unified theory, the models reveal a certain coherence and consistency in the variables presented. Differentiation is the master force, both as an outcome and as a cause of other forces. Within differentiated systems, a variety of forces are unleashed—money, markets, expansion of political authority and law, conflicts, coalitions, individualization, alienation and anxiety, and trust—and each of these forces reverberates off the others, while increasing or decreasing the potential for further differentiation.

Simmel's Theoretical Principles

Simmel's Analysis of the Process of Differentiation. Although many would not see his work in quite this way, I believe that Simmel was a theorist of differentiation. Like so many in his time, he was fascinated by the dramatic changes that were occurring with "modernity," and as emphasized earlier, he was concerned with the consequences of differentiation for forms of social relations. Moreover, he believed that as the forms of social relations changed with differentiation, these new forms would encourage further differentiation, at least to the point where people felt too marginal and alienated or too conflicted and anxious. Simmel did not examine the causes of differentiation in detail because he tended to see the outcomes of differentiation as accelerating differentiation. Still, I should try to express Simmel's argument on the causes of differentiation before moving on to the consequences or outcomes of differentiation:

1. The level of differentiation will increase when non-ascriptive media of social exchange, like money, are available, with the availability of non-ascriptive criteria increasing as

   A. Free markets using money as their medium of exchange proliferate
   B. Secondary groups using non-ascriptive criteria for membership proliferate
   C. Individualization of preferences increases
   D. Centers of power increasingly rely on money to sustain their operations.

For Simmel, then, differentiation is the result of a breakdown of ascriptive criteria—such as tradition, community, family, and religion—as a basis for group membership and for determining individuals' preferences. When individuals are no longer controlled by ascription and, instead, can use non-ascriptive criteria like money or educational credentials for joining groups and for expressing preferences, the potential for greater diversity in ties and affiliations exists. This potential can be realized, however, only when markets operate as a mechanism for the distribution of goods, services, and even memberships. Markets rely on money, and together, money and markets allow people to calculate values (their preferences) and to make decisions based on these calculations. Yet markets alone cannot drive differentiation; secondary groups, as both a consequence and a cause of differentiation, must also become widespread. If individuals have few options beyond primary groups, where membership is often ascribed at birth, their affiliations will remain in these primary groups, thus shutting down demand for memberships in diverse secondary groups (and hence, for differentiation of groups). Not only must markets and secondary groups prevail, but also some degree of individualization of people's tastes and preferences must have already occurred to make them interested in using markets and money to express these preferences and in making calculations of their interests in joining new kinds of groups. Finally, centers of power must have an interest in using liquid resources like money for their ends, and they must come to have an interest in maintaining the stability or purchasing power of money to sustain legitimacy. Under these conditions, differentiation will increase, but the converse is also true; as differentiation increases, it will push for reliance on non-ascriptive media of exchange, for expansion of markets, for multiplication of secondary groups, for individualizing tastes and preferences expressed as demands in markets, for government regulation of relations among diverse groups, and for maintenance of the value of money.

Differentiation depends upon the use of generalized media of exchange, most particularly money; and for Simmel, the most interesting aspect of this relationship is how social relations are transformed as money becomes the dominant medium of exchange:

2. The greater is the use of money in exchanging relations, the greater will be
    A. The volume of exchange relations
    B. The rate of social exchange
    C. The scope of social exchange
    D. The accumulation of value in social exchange
    E. The accumulation of trust based on the value of money
    F. The calculation of utilities
    G. The multiplicity of social ties and exchanges
    H. The differentiation of power to regulate exchanges and the value of money
    I. The options for individuals
    J. The individualization of people.

These propositions read much like a "laundry list," but it is how Simmel argued. Simmel wanted to emphasize that the *form* or nature of social relations changes with differentiation, and he set out to "list the ways" this process occurred. He saw most of these outcomes as positive, but he also recognized the potential for pathological situations.

3. The greater the use of money in exchange relations, the greater is the multiplicity of ties and affiliations in secondary groups and, hence, the greater is the potential for

   A. Anxiety-generating role conflicts arising from too many diverse ties and group affiliations
   B. Alienation, stemming from weak attachments to groups and a sense of standing between, rather than within, groups.

Yet, unlike Weber and Marx, Simmel did not seem to see such outcomes as a chronic state of affairs. Role conflict and marginality are indeed potentials, and individuals frequently experience these states, but Simmel did not see them as overwhelming the mass of people in society or as posing threats to the stability and integration of society. Rather, he generally saw the outcomes of differentiation and use of money as positive because they gave individuals more freedom, increased options, and an enhanced sense of value. We can summarize Simmel's argument as follows:

4. The greater is the level of differentiation and the greater is the reliance on non-ascriptive media of exchange in a society, the more choice individuals have in their group affiliations and the greater will be the number of affiliations in diverse groups; the more choice individuals have in establishing their multiple group affiliations, the more they experience

   A. Enhanced value or utility because their affiliations better match their preferences
   B. Confirmation of identities from each group with which they choose to affiliate.

Simmel on Conflict. Differentiated social systems will reveal more secondary groups, thus increasing not only the diversity of groups but also the potential for conflicts of interest among various groups. Even in less differentiated societies, conflict is an ever present force in social relations; indeed, conflict will tend to be most violent in these less differentiated systems. Simmel's essay on conflict is much like all of his sociology in that it emphasizes the consequences of conflict rather than its causes. We can divide his theoretical principles accordingly: (a) those on the conditions affecting the violence of conflict, (b) those on the consequences of conflict for the overall social system within which the conflict occurs, and (c) those on the consequences of conflict for the units or parties involved.

Simmel's principle on the violence of conflict is incomplete, but it does contain some important insights:

5. The level of violence in conflict increases as the

   A. Parties to the conflict see it as transcending their individual interests and, hence, as a moral cause
   B. Parties to the conflict have a high degree of emotional involvement in the conflict, with such involvement increasing as the

1. Parties to the conflict perceive the conflict to be a moral cause
2. Parties to the conflict each reveal high solidarity
3. Parties to the conflict once had harmonious relations, and each perceives the breaking of this relation as a moral violation of trust and obligation.

6. The level of violence in conflict will decrease to the degree that parties to the conflict see it as a means to well-defined ends or goals.

What is perhaps the most interesting aspect of these propositions on the violence of conflict is the corrective they pose to Karl Marx' analysis. Simmel is saying that when conflicts are instrumental—that is, they are a means to explicit goals—they are less likely to be violent. His reasoning is that when clear goals exist, leaders are likely to negotiate and compromise rather than risk the high costs of violent conflict. Marx thought that the more clear-cut the goals of conflict are, the more violent it will be, or in his terms, when a class is transformed from a class "of itself" to one "for itself," a revolution is more likely. Marx would argue that revolution is a moral cause for workers with high solidarity who perceive that their superordinates have violated their obligations, thus leading to his prediction of a violent overthrow of the bourgeoisie. But Simmel counters that as the subordinates get increasingly organized and have a clearer understanding of their purposes and goals, the conflict will be seen in more instrumental than in emotional terms, thus leading to less violence. For Simmel, then, modern society was not polarizing into warring camps, but just the opposite was occurring: there was increasing differentiation of many diverse secondary groups, each with more clearly defined purposes and, hence, interests. Under these conditions, conflict would be more instrumental and, thereby, less violent. The less violent and the more frequent conflicts are, the more they have positive outcomes for the larger social whole in which they occur:

7. The less violent and more frequent the conflict among social units in a differentiated social system, the more likely is the conflict to

A. Allow units to release hostilities before they accumulate to extremely high levels
B. Encourage the creation of norms to regulate the conflict
C. Encourage the development of authority and judiciary systems to regulate the conflict.

Similarly, when analyzing the consequences of conflict for the respective parties involved, Simmel stressed its integrative impact, especially when the conflict is violent. Thus, for Simmel, although violent conflict can have disintegrative consequences for the social whole, it can also promote integration within the parties, as is evident in the following propositions:

8. The more violent are intergroup hostilities and the more frequent are the conflicts among groups, the less likely are groups' boundaries to disappear.

9. The more violent is the conflict, the more likely is centralization of power within the conflict groups.

10. The more violent is the conflict, the greater will be the internal solidarity of the conflict groups, especially as

   A. The size of the conflict groups decreases
   B. The conflict group represents a minority position
   C. The conflict group is engaged in self-defense.

11. The more violent and prolonged is the conflict between groups, the more likely is the formation of coalitions among previously unrelated groups in a system.

12. The more prolonged is the threat of violent conflict between groups, the more enduring are the coalitions of each of the conflict parties.

I have made Simmel's analysis of society more coherent than it really is. His work is a series of essays; in his books, he never pulled the contents of the essays together into a coherent theory. Simmel argued strongly for a "formal sociology" that would examine basic forms of social relations and extract the laws explaining the operation of these forms. As we have seen, he offered some interesting principles, but he did not develop a general theory of differentiation, group affiliations, or conflict. We get glimpses of insight but not a general theory.

Conclusions

In evaluating Simmel's work as a whole, his major theoretical contribution to sociology resides in his concern with the basic forms of interaction. By looking beyond differences in the "contents" of diverse social relations and by attempting to uncover their more generic forms, he was able to show that seemingly diverse situations reveal basic similarities. He implicitly argued that such similarities could be expressed as abstract models or laws, although one can criticize Simmel for not explicitly stating these laws.

Thus, although Simmel did not employ the vocabulary of abstract theory, his many essays on different topics reveal a commitment to formulating abstract statements about basic forms of human relationships. This orientation, however, is not always clear because Simmel tended to argue by example. His works tend to focus on a wide variety of empirical topics, and even when he explores a particular type of social relation, such as conflict and exchange, the discussion proceeds with many illustrations. He would, for instance, talk about conflicts among individuals and wars among nation-states in virtually the same passage. Such tendencies give his work an inductive and descriptive flair, but a more careful reading indicates that he clearly held a deductive view of theory in sociology.[74] For example, if conflict between such diverse entities as two individuals and two nations reveals certain common forms, diverse empirical situations can be understood by the same abstract law or principle.

---

[74]That is, explanation occurs by deduction to empirical cases from abstract laws, which are universal and context-free.

Many might criticize Simmel for his implicit functionalism. He tended to ask, what are the consequences of a phenomenon—for example, differentiation, conflict, exchange, money—for the social whole? Such questions are functional because they analyze social processes in terms of their outcomes. Simmel did not fall into the functionalist trap of seeing outcomes as the causes of these very outcomes, but his work does tend to emphasize the positive outcomes. True, he recognized the atomizing and alienating effects of differentiation of structure and objectification (rationalization) of social patterns, but in general, he tends to see conflict, money, and differentiation in terms of their positive outcomes. In some ways, this orientation is refreshing because most German theorists tended to see modernity as evil and as doing harmful things to people. In contrast, Simmel argued that the great events that were making society more complex, impersonal, and objectified could free individuals from constraints and give them options not available in simpler societies. Moreover, he saw the potential for low-intensity, frequent, and regulated conflicts in differentiated societies as potentially increasing their integration. In a sense, then, Simmel's work stands as a corrective to the rather dreary prognosis of Max Weber about rationalization or to the polemical views of Karl Marx on the evils of capitalism.

Simmel has enjoyed a great rebirth recently because he recognized historical trends that have been picked up by scholars within contemporary "postmodern" theory. Simmel saw that differentiation and the spread of exchanges using money created a new kind of person, one with potentially as many identities as affiliations in diverse groups. This theme has been used to condemn late capitalist society as destroying a unified self; Simmel recognized this potential, but unlike the postmodernists, he saw the liberating effects of being able to fashion one's own group affiliations and, hence, one's identity. Simmel, more than any other theorist of the classical founders, saw the transforming effects of money and markets on society. For postmodernists, everything is "commodified"—people, self, group culture, sacred symbols, and affiliations—and they see this power of money and markets as creating a world of unstable group structures whose culture is marketed and bought by people seeking to purchase an identity. Simmel saw this potential, but again, he came up on the more positive side, emphasizing that people are freed of the oppressive constraints associated with traditional, communal societies. Thus, because Simmel addressed the issues of interest to postmodernism, he has moved from a more minor place in sociology's pantheon to a plane just below that of Marx, Weber, and Durkheim.

CHAPTER 7

Émile Durkheim

Six decades after Auguste Comte proposed a field of inquiry called sociology, Émile Durkheim pulled together the long French lineage of social thought into a coherent theoretical approach. Throughout Durkheim's illustrious career, his theoretical work revolved around one fundamental question: What is the basis for integration and solidarity in human societies?[1] At first, he examined this question from a macro perspective, looking at society as a whole. Later, he shifted his attention to the micro bases of solidarity, examining ritual and the interaction of people in face-to-face contact. In all his works, he not only brought past theorizing together into a coherent scheme but also stimulated a number of twentieth-century intellectual movements that persist to this day.[2]

The Division of Labor in Society

Durkheim's first major work was the published version of his French doctoral thesis, *The Division of Labor in Society*.[3] The original subtitle of this thesis was *A Study of the Organization of Advanced Societies*.[4] On the surface, the book is about the causes,

---

[1]Commentators have disagreed about whether Durkheim's work changed fundamentally from a macro perspective to a micro one, or from structural to social psychological, between 1893 and 1916. For a relevant commentary on this issue and on Durkheim's approach in general see Anthony Giddens, *Capitalism and Modern Theory: An Analysis of the Writings of Marx, Durkheim, and Max Weber* (Cambridge, UK: Cambridge University Press, 1971); Anthony Giddens, ed. and trans., *Émile Durkheim: Selected Writings* (Cambridge, UK: Cambridge University Press, 1972); Talcott Parsons, *The Structure of Social Action* (New York: McGraw-Hill, 1937); Steven Lukes, *Émile Durkheim, His Life and Work: A Historical and Critical Study* (London: Allen Lane, 1973); and Robert Alun Jones, *Émile Durkheim* (Newbury Park, CA: Sage, 1985).

[2]For an extensive bibliography of Durkheim's published works, see Lukes, *Émile Durkheim*, 561–590. See also Robert A. Nisbet, *The Sociology of Émile Durkheim* (New York: Oxford University Press, 1974), 30–41, for an annotated bibliography of the most important works forming the core of Durkheim's theoretical system.

[3]Émile Durkheim, *The Division of Labor in Society* (New York: Free Press, 1947; originally published 1893).

[4]For a detailed discussion, see Lukes, *Émile Durkheim,* chap. 7.

characteristics, and functions of the division of labor in modern societies, but as we will explore, the book presents a more general theory of social organization, one that can still inform sociological theorists.[5] In this great work, Durkheim stressed a number of issues that will guide our review: (a) social solidarity,[6] (b) the collective conscience, (c) social morphology,[7] (d) mechanical and organic solidarity, (e) social change, (f) social functions, and (g) social pathology.

Social Solidarity

The Division of Labor is about the shifting basis of social solidarity as societies evolve from an undifferentiated and simple profile[8] to a complex and differentiated one.[9] Today, this topic would be termed *social integration* because the concern is with how the units of a social system are coordinated. Durkheim posited that the question of social solidarity, or integration, turns on several related issues: (a) How are individuals made to feel part of a larger social collective? (b) How are their desires and wants constrained in ways that allow them to participate in the collective? (c) How are the activities of individuals and other social units coordinated and adjusted to one another? These questions, we should emphasize, not only dominated *The Division of Labor* but also guided all of Durkheim's subsequent substantive works.

These questions take us into the basic problem of how patterns of social organization are created, maintained, and changed. It is little wonder, therefore, that Durkheim's analysis of social solidarity contains a more general theory of social organization; we should explore those concepts that he developed to explain social organization in general. One of the most important of these concepts is the *collective conscience.*

The Collective Conscience

Throughout his career, Durkheim was vitally concerned with "morality," or *moral facts.* Although he was often somewhat vague on what constituted a moral fact, we can interpret the concept of morality to embody what sociologists now call "culture." That is, Durkheim was concerned with the systems of symbols—particularly the norms, values, and beliefs—that humans create and use to organize their activities.

---

[5]Our view of Durkheim's *The Division of Labor in Society* underemphasizes the social evolutionism contained in this work because we think that too much concern is placed on the model of social change and not enough is placed on the implicit theory of social organization.

[6]Alternatively, social integration.

[7]Or the nature of social structure.

[8]Durkheim described such simple societies as based on mechanical solidarity. *Mechanical* was a term intended to connote an image of society as a body in which cohesion is achieved by each element revealing a similar cultural and structural form.

[9]Such societies were seen as based on organic solidarity. *Organic* was intended to be an analogy to an organism in which the elements are distinctive in form and operate independently, but for the welfare of the more inclusive social organism.

Durkheim had to assert the legitimacy of the scientific study of moral phenomena because other academic disciplines, such as law, ethics, religion, philosophy, and psychology, all laid claim to symbols as their subject matter. Thus, he insisted, "Moral facts are phenomena like others; they consist of rules of action recognizable by certain distinctive characteristics. It must, then, be possible to observe them, describe them, classify them, and look for laws explaining them."[10]

We should emphasize that Durkheim in his early work often used the concept of *moral facts* to denote structural patterns (groups, organizations, etc.) as well as systems of symbols (values, beliefs, laws, norms). In *The Division of Labor,* however, we can find clear indications that he wanted to separate analytically the purely structural from the symbolic aspects of social reality. This isolation of cultural or symbolic phenomena can best be seen in his formulation of another, somewhat ambiguous, concept that suffers in translation: the *collective conscience.* He later dropped extensive use of this term in favor of *collective representations,* which, unfortunately, adds little clarification. But we can begin to understand his meaning with the formal definition provided in *The Division of Labor:* "The totality of beliefs and sentiments common to average citizens of the same society forms a determinate system which has its own life; one may call it the *collective* or *common conscience.*"[11] He went on to indicate that although the terms *collective* and *common* were "not without ambiguity," they suggest that societies reveal a reality independent of "the particular conditions in which individuals are placed." Moreover, people are born into the collective conscience or the culture of a society, and this culture regulates their perceptions and behaviors. What Durkheim was denoting with the concept of collective conscience, then, is that aspects of culture—systems of values, beliefs, and norms—constrain the thoughts and actions of individuals.

In the course of his analysis of the collective conscience, Durkheim conceptualized its varying states as having four variables: (1) volume, (2) intensity, (3) determinateness, and (4) religious versus secular content.[12] *Volume* denotes the degree to which the values, beliefs, and rules of the collective conscience are shared by the members of a society; *intensity* indicates the extent to which the collective conscience has the power to guide a person's thoughts and actions; *determinateness* denotes the degree of clarity in the components of the collective conscience; and *content* pertains to the ratio of religious to purely secular symbolism in the collective conscience.

Social Morphology

Durkheim saw social structure (or as he termed it, *morphology*) as involving an assessment of the "nature," "number," "arrangement," and "interrelations" among

---

[10]Durkheim, *Division of Labor,* 32. This idea owes its inspiration to Comte. As Durkheim noted in his Latin thesis on Montesquieu, "No further progress could be made until it was recognized that the laws of societies are no different from those governing the rest of nature. . . . This was Auguste Comte's contribution." Émile Durkheim, *Montesquieu and Rousseau* (Ann Arbor: University of Michigan Press, 1960; originally published 1892), 63–64.

[11]Durkheim, *Division of Labor,* 79–80 (emphasis in original).

[12]Ibid., 152, for 1, 2, and 3 and throughout the book for 4. For interesting secondary discussions, see Lukes, *Émile Durkheim* and Giddens, *Selected Writings.*

parts, whether these parts are individuals or corporate units, such as groups and organizations. Their *nature* is usually assessed by variables such as size and functions (economic, political, familial, etc.). *Arrangement* concerns the distribution of parts in relationship to one another; *interrelations* deal with the modes of communication, movement, and mutual obligations among parts.

Although Durkheim's entire intellectual career involved an effort to demonstrate the impact of social structures on the collective conscience as well as on individual cognitions and behaviors, he never made explicit use of these variables—that is, nature, number, arrangement, and interrelations—for analyzing social structures. In his more methodological statements, he argued for the appropriateness of viewing social morphology by the nature, size, number, arrangement, and interrelations of specific parts. Yet his actual analysis of social structures in his major substantive works left these more formal properties of structure implicit.[13]

Mechanical and Organic Solidarity

With these views on the collective conscience and structural morphology, Durkheim developed a typology of societies based on their modes of integration or solidarity. One type is termed *mechanical* and the other, *organic*.[14] As we will show later, each of these types rests on different principles of social integration, involving different morphologies, different systems of symbols, and different relations between social and symbolic structures. Durkheim's distinction between mechanical and organic is both a descriptive typology of traditional and modern societies and a theoretical statement about the changing forms of social integration that emerge with increasing differentiation of social structure.

At a descriptive level, mechanical solidarity is based on a strong collective conscience regulating the thoughts and actions of individuals located within structural units that are alike. Of the four variables by which Durkheim conceptualized the collective conscience, the cultural system is high in volume, intensity, determinateness, and religious content. Legal codes, which in his view are the best empirical indicator of solidarity, are repressive, and sanctions are punitive. The reason for such repressiveness is that deviation from the dictates of the collective conscience is viewed as a crime against all members of the society and the gods. The morphology, or structure, of mechanical societies reveals independent kinship units that organize relatively small numbers of people who share strong commitments to their particular collective conscience. The interrelations among kin units are minimal, with each unit being like the others and autonomously meeting the needs of its members. Not surprisingly, then, individual freedom, choice, and autonomy are low in mechanical

---

[13]The concern for "social morphology" was, no doubt, an adaptation of Comte's idea of social statics, as these were influenced by the German organicist Albert Schäffle, with whom Durkheim had been highly impressed. See Lukes, *Émile Durkheim,* 86–95.

[14]Such typologizing was typical in the nineteenth century. Spencer distinguished societal types, but more influential was Tönnies's distinction between *Gemeinschaft* and *Gesellschaft.* Durkheim spent a year in Germany as a student in 1885–1886, and although Tönnies's famous work had not yet been published, his typology was well-known and influenced Durkheim's conceptualization of mechanical and organic solidarity.

societies. People are dominated by the collective conscience, and their actions are constrained by its dictates and by the constraints of cohesive kin units.

In contrast, organically structured societies are typified by large populations, distributed in specialized roles in many diverse structural units. Organic societies reveal high degrees of interdependence among individuals and corporate units, with exchange, legal contracts, and norms regulating these interrelations. The collective conscience becomes "enfeebled" and "more abstract," providing highly general and secular value premises for the exchanges, contracts, and norms regulating the interdependencies among specialized social units. This alteration is reflected in legal codes that become less punitive and more "restitutive," specifying nonpunitive ways to redress violations of normative arrangements and to reintegrate violators back into the network of interdependencies that typify organic societies. In such societies, individual freedom is great, and the secular and highly abstract collective conscience becomes dominated by values stressing respect for the personal dignity of the individual.

This descriptive contrast between mechanical and organic societies is summarized in Table 7.1.[15] At the more theoretical level, Durkheim's distinction between

Table 7.1   Descriptive Summary of Mechanical and Organic Societies

Morphological (Structural) Features	Mechanical Solidarity	Organic Solidarity
1. Size	Small	Large
2. Number of parts	Few	Many
3. Nature of parts	Kinship based	Diverse: dominated by economic and governmental content
4. Arrangement	Independent, autonomous	Interrelated, mutually interdependent
5. Nature of interrelations	Bound to the common conscience and punitive law	Bound together by exchange, contract, norms, and restitutive law
Collective Conscience (Culture)	Mechanical Solidarity	Organic Solidarity
1. Volume	High	Low
2. Intensity	High	Low
3. Determinateness	High	Low
4. Content	Religious, stressing commitment and conformity to the dictates of sacred powers	Secular, emphasizing individuality

---

[15]This table is similar to one developed by Lukes, *Émile Durkheim*, 151.

mechanical and organic solidarity posits a fundamental relationship in the social world among "structural differentiation," "value generalization," and "normative specification." Let us explore this relationship in more detail. As societies differentiate structurally, values become more abstract.[16] The collective conscience changes its nature as societies become more voluminous. Because these societies are spread over a vaster surface, the common conscience or culture rises above local diversities and consequently becomes more abstract. Only by becoming general can culture be common to distinctive environments.[17]

As basic values lose their capacity to regulate the specific actions of large numbers of differentiated units, normative regulations arise to compensate for the inability of general values to specify what people should do and how individuals as well as corporate units should interact:

> If society no longer imposes upon everybody certain uniform practices, it takes greater care to define and regulate the special relations between different social functions and this activity is not smaller because it is different.[18]

> It is certain that organized societies are not possible without a developed system of rules which predetermine the functions of each organ. Insofar as labor is divided, there arises a multitude of occupational moralities and laws.[19]

Thus, in his seemingly static comparison of mechanical and organic societies, Durkheim was actually proposing law-like relationships among the structural and symbolic elements of social systems.

Social Change

Durkheim's view of social change revolves around an analysis of the causes and consequences of increases in the division of labor:

> The division of labor varies in direct ratio with the volume and density of societies, and, if it progresses in a continuous manner in the course of social development, it is because societies become regularly denser and generally more voluminous.[20]

Some translation of terms is necessary if this "proposition," as Durkheim called it, is to be understood. *Volume* refers to population size and concentration, and *density* pertains to the increased interaction arising from escalated volume. Thus, the division of labor arises from increases in the concentration of populations

---

[16]Durkheim, *Division of Labor,* 171.

[17]Ibid., 287.

[18]Ibid., 205.

[19]Ibid., 302.

[20]Ibid., 262.

whose members increasingly come into contact. Durkheim also termed the increased rates of interaction among those thrust into contact *dynamic* and *moral density*. He then analyzed those factors that increase the material density of a population. Ecological boundaries (rivers, mountains, etc.), migration, urbanization, and population growth all directly increase volume and thus indirectly increase the likelihood of dynamic density (increased contact and interaction). Technological innovations, such as new modes of communication and transportation, directly increase the rates of contact and interaction among individuals. But all these direct and indirect influences are merely lists of empirical conditions influencing the primary explanatory variable, dynamic or moral density.

How, then, does dynamic density cause the division of labor? Dynamic density increases competition among individuals, who, if they are to survive the "struggle," must assume specialized roles and then establish exchange relations with each other. The division of labor is thus the mechanism by which competition is mitigated:

> Thus, Darwin says that in a small area, opened to immigration, and where, consequently, the conflict of individuals must be acute, there is always to be seen a very great diversity in the species inhabiting it. . . . Men submit to the same law. In the same city, different occupations can co-exist without being obliged mutually to destroy one another, for they pursue different objects.[21]

Figure 7.1 outlines these causal connections. To recapitulate, Durkheim saw migration, population growth, and ecological concentration as causing increased *material density,* which in turn caused increased *moral* or *dynamic density*—that is, escalated social contact and interaction. Such interaction could be further heightened by varied means of communication and transportation, as illustrated in the model in Figure 7.1. The increased rates of interaction characteristic of a larger population within a confined ecological space cause increased competition, or "struggle," among individuals. Such competition allows those who have the most resources and talents to maintain their present positions and assume high-rank positions, whereas the "less fit" seek alternative specialties to mitigate the competition. From this competition and differentiation comes the division of labor, which, when "normal," results in organic solidarity.

The major problem with the model is the implicit argument about "final causes": The function of the division of labor is to promote social solidarity. Durkheim implied that the need for social solidarity caused the struggle to be resolved by the division of labor; yet he never specified how the needs met by the division of labor (i.e., social solidarity) caused it to emerge. Still, the model in Figure 7.1 contains some suggestive ideas, particularly the notions that material density causes moral density, that moral density causes competition, that competition causes differentiation, and that differentiation causes new mechanisms of integration. On the other hand, without specifying the conditions under which these causal connections are generated, the model is vague.

---

[21]Ibid., 266–267.

Figure 7.1 Durkheim's Implicit Model of Social Statics

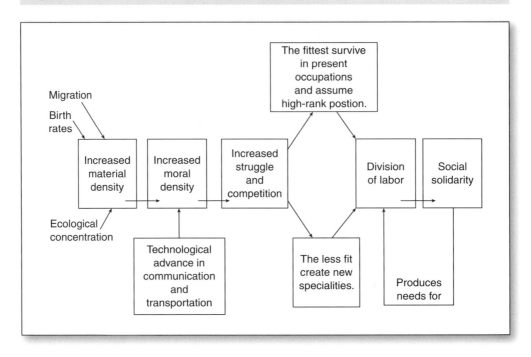

Social Functions

Herbert Spencer had clearly formulated the notions of structure and function, with functions assessed by the needs of the social organism being met by a structure. Durkheim appears to have borrowed these ideas, and indeed, opened *The Division of Labor* with an assessment of its functions.[22] The function of the division of labor is to promote social solidarity, or societal integration. Such functional analysis, Durkheim argued, must be kept separate from causal analysis.

Nonetheless, functional analysis was critical to Durkheim's desire to be the "physician" to society. By assessing what a structure "does for" a society of a particular type or at a specific stage of evolution, Durkheim felt that he was in a better position to determine what was "normal" and "abnormal" for that society—a point that Comte had first made in his advocacy of the experimental method as it could be used in sociology. The concept of function allowed Durkheim to judge whether a structure, such as the division of labor, was functioning normally for a particular type of society. Hence, to the degree that the division of labor fails to promote societal integration or social solidarity in a society, he viewed this society to be in a "pathological" state and in need of alterations to restore "normality" to the "body

---

[22]For a more detailed analysis of Durkheim's debt to Spencer and of his contribution to functionalism, see Jonathan H. Turner and Alexandra Maryanski, *Functionalism* (Menlo Park, CA: Benjamin/Cummings, 1979) and Jonathan H. Turner, "Durkheim's and Spencer's Principles of Social Organization," *Sociological Perspectives* 9 (1984):283–291.

social." These considerations led him to analyze "abnormal forms" of the division of labor at the close of this first major sociological work because the abnormality of structures can be determined only in reference to their "normal functions."

Pathology and Abnormal Forms

Durkheim opened his discussion of abnormal forms with the following statement:

> Up to now, we have studied the division of labor only as a normal phenomenon, but, like all social facts, and, more generally, all biological facts, it presents pathological forms which must be analyzed. Though normally the division of labor produces social solidarity, it sometimes happens that it has different, and even contrary results.[23]

Durkheim isolated three abnormal forms: (1) the anomic division of labor, (2) the forced division of labor, and (3) the inadequately coordinated division of labor. In discussing these abnormal forms, he drew considerable inspiration from his French predecessors, particularly Jean-Jacques Rousseau and Alexis de Tocqueville, while carrying on a silent dialogue with Karl Marx and other socialists. Thus, his analysis of abnormal forms represents his effort to address issues that had been discussed and contested by several previous generations of intellectuals. Indeed, individuals' isolation, their detachment from society, their sense of alienation, their exploitation by the powerful, and related issues had been hotly debated in both intellectual and lay circles. Yet, although Durkheim's selection of topics is not unique, his conclusions and their theoretical implications are highly original.

The Anomic Division of Labor. The concept of anomie was not well developed in *The Division of Labor*. Only later, in the 1897 work *Suicide*, did this concept become theoretically significant. Durkheim's discussion in *The Division of Labor* is explicitly directed at Comte, who had noted the essence of the basic dilemma confronting organic social systems:

> From the moral point of view, while each individual is thus made closely dependent on the mass, he is naturally drawn away from it by the nature of his special activity, constantly reminding him of his private interests, which he only very dimly perceives to be related to the public.[24]

For Durkheim, this dilemma was expressed as maintaining individuals' commitment to a common set of values and beliefs while allowing them to pursue their specialized interests. At this stage in his thinking, anomie represented insufficient normative regulation of individuals' activities, with the result that individuals do not feel attached to the collectivity.

---

[23]Durkheim, *Division of Labor,* 353.

[24]Quoted in Lukes, *Émile Durkheim,* 141.

Anomie is inevitable, Durkheim believed, when the transformation of society from a mechanical to an organic basis of social solidarity is rapid and causes the "generalization," or "enfeeblement," of values. With generalization, individuals' attachment to, and regulation by, values is lessened. The results of this anomic situation are diverse. One result is that individuals feel alienated because their only attachment is to the monotony and crushing schedule dictated by the machines of the industrial age. Another is the escalated frustrations and the sense of deprivation, manifested by the increased incidence of revolt, that come in a state of under-regulation.

Unlike Marx, however, Durkheim did not consider these consequences to be inevitable. He rejected the notion that there were inherent contradictions in capitalism, for "if, in certain cases, organic solidarity is not all it should be . . . [it is] because all the conditions for the existence of organic solidarity have not been realized."[25] Nor would he accept Comte's or Rousseau's solution to anomie: the establishment of a strong and somewhat dictatorial central organ, the state.

Yet in the first edition of *The Division of Labor,* Durkheim's own solution is vague; the solution to anomie involves reintegration of individuals into the collective life by virtue of their interdependence with other specialists and the common goals that all members of a society ultimately pursue.[26] In many ways this argument substitutes for Adam Smith's invisible hand the "invisible power of the collective," without specifying how this integration into the collective is to occur.

Durkheim recognized the inadequacy of this solution to the problem of anomie. Moreover, his more detailed analysis of anomie in *Suicide* (1897) must have further underscored the limitations of his analysis in *The Division of Labor.* Thus, the second edition of *The Division of Labor,* published in 1902, contained a long preface that sought to specify the mechanism by which anomie was to be curbed. This mechanism is the "occupational," or "corporate," group.[27]

Durkheim recognized that industrialism, urbanization, occupational specialization, and the growth of the bureaucratized state all lessened the functions of family, religion, region, and neighborhood as mechanisms promoting the integration of individuals into the societal collectivity. With the generalization and enfeeblement of the collective conscience, coupled with the potential isolation of individuals in an occupational specialty, Durkheim saw that new structures would have to evolve to avoid anomie. These structures promote social solidarity in several ways: (a) they organize occupational specialties into a collective; (b) they bridge the widening gap between the remote state and the specific needs and desires of the individual; and (c) they provide a functional alternative to the old loyalties generated by religion, regionalism, and kinship. These new intermediate structures are not only occupational but also political and moral groupings that lace together specialized occupations, counterbalance the power of the state, and provide specific interpretations for the more abstract values and beliefs of the collective conscience.

---

[25]Durkheim, *Division of Labor,* 364–365.

[26]Ibid., 373.

[27]Ibid., 1–31.

Durkheim had taken the idea of "occupational groups" from Tocqueville's analysis of intermediate organizations in nineteenth-century America. He extended the concept considerably, however, and in so doing, he posited a conception of how a society should be economically, politically, and morally organized.[28] Economically, occupational groups would bring together related occupational specialties into an organization that could set working hours and wage levels and that could bargain with the management of corporations and government.

Politically, the occupational group would become a kind of political party whose representatives would participate in government. Like most French scholars in the post-revolutionary era, Durkheim distrusted mass democracy, feeling that short-term individual passions and moods could render the state helpless in setting and reaching long-range goals. He also distrusted an all-powerful and bureaucratized state on the ground that its remote structure was too insensitive and cumbersome to deal with the specific needs and problems of diverse individuals. Moreover, Durkheim saw that unchecked state power inevitably led to abuses, an emphasis that comes close to Montesquieu's idea of a balance of powers in government—an idea adopted by the framers of the American constitution. Thus, the power of the state must be checked by intermediate groups, which channel public sentiment to the state and administer the policies of the state for a particular constituency.[29]

Morally, occupational groups are to provide many of the recreational, educational, and social functions formerly performed by the family, neighborhood, and church. By bringing together people who are likely to have common experiences because they belong to related occupations, occupational groups can provide a place where people feel integrated into the society and where the psychological tensions and monotony of their specialized jobs can be mitigated. Moreover, these groups can make the generalized values and beliefs of the entire society relevant to the life experiences of each individual. Through the vehicle of occupational groups, then, an entire society of specialists can be reattached to the collective conscience, thereby eliminating anomie.

Inequality and the Forced Division of Labor. Borrowing heavily from Rousseau, Claude-Henri de Saint-Simon, and Auguste Comte, but reacting to Karl Marx,[30] Durkheim saw inequalities based on ascription and inheritance of privilege as "abnormal." He advocated an inheritance tax that would eliminate the passing of wealth across generations, and indeed, he felt that in the normal course of things, this change would come about. Unlike Marx, however, Durkheim had no distaste for the accumulation of capital and privilege, as long as it was earned and not inherited.

---

[28]We are supplementing Durkheim's discussion of occupational groups with additional works; see Émile Durkheim, *Professional Ethics and Civil Morals* (Boston, MA: Routledge and Kegan Paul, 1957) and his *Socialism and Saint-Simon* (Yellow Springs, OH: Antioch, 1958).

[29]Durkheim, *Division of Labor,* 28.

[30]Durkheim rarely addressed Marx directly. Though he wanted to devote a special course to Marx's ideas in addition to his course on Saint-Simon and socialism, he never got around to doing so. Much as with Weber, however, one suspects that Durkheim's discussion of "abnormal forms" represented a silent dialogue with Marx.

What Durkheim desired was for the division of labor and inequalities in privilege to correspond to differences in people's ability. For him, it was abnormal in organic societies for wealth to be inherited and for this inherited privilege to be used by one class to oppress and exploit another. Such a situation represents a "forced division of labor," and in the context of analyzing this abnormality, Durkheim examined explicitly Marxian ideas: (a) the labor theory of value and exploitation and (b) the domination of one class by another. Let me examine each briefly:

1. Durkheim felt that the price one pays for a good or service should be proportional to the "useful labor which it contains."[31] To the degree that this is not so, he argued, an abnormal condition prevails. What is necessary, and inevitable in the long run, is for buyers and sellers to be "placed in conditions externally equal,"[32] in which the price charged for a good or service corresponds to the "socially useful labor" in it and where no seller or buyer enjoys an advantage or monopoly that would allow prices to exceed socially useful labor.

2. Durkheim recognized that as long as there is inherited privilege, especially wealth, one class can exploit and dominate another. He felt that the elimination of inheritance was inevitable because people could no longer be duped by a strong collective conscience into accepting privilege and exploitation (a position that parallels Marx's notion of *false consciousness*). For as religious and family bonds decrease in salience and as individuals are liberated from mechanical solidarity, people can free themselves from the beliefs that have often been used to legitimate exploitation.

Durkheim was certainly naive in his assumption that these aspects of the forced division of labor would, like Marx's state, "wither away." What he saw as normal was a situation that sounds reminiscent of Adam Smith's utilitarian vision of an "invisible hand of order."[33]

Lack of Coordination. Durkheim termed the lack of coordination *another abnormal form* and did not devote much space to its analysis.[34] At times, he noted, specialization of tasks is not accompanied by sufficient coordination, creating a situation where energy is wasted and individuals feel poorly integrated into the collective flow of life. In his view, specialization must be "continuous," with functions highly coordinated and individuals laced together through their mutual interdependence. Such a state, he argued, will be achieved as the natural and normal processes creating organic solidarity become dominant in modern society.

On this note, *The Division of Labor* ends. Durkheim's next major work, published two years after *The Division of Labor*, sought to make more explicit assumptions and

---

[31]Durkheim, *Division of Labor*, 382.

[32]Ibid., 383.

[33]Ibid., 377.

[34]Ibid., 389–395; see also Charles H. Powers, "Durkheim and Regulatory Authority," *Journal of the History of the Behavioral Sciences* 21 (1985):26–36.

methodological guidelines that were implicit in *The Division of Labor*. *The Rules of the Sociological Method* (1895) represents a methodological interlude that clarifies Durkheim's approach to sociological analysis.

The Rules of the Sociological Method

The Rules of the Sociological Method is both a philosophical treatise and a set of guidelines for conducting sociological inquiry.[35] Durkheim appears to have written the book for at least three reasons.[36] First, he sought intellectual justification for his approach to studying the social world, especially as evidenced in *The Division of Labor*. Second, he wanted to persuade a hostile academic community of the legitimacy of sociology as a distinctive science. Third, because he wanted to found a school of scholars, he needed a manifesto to attract and guide potential converts to the science of sociology. The chapter titles of *The Rules* best communicate Durkheim's intent: (1) "What Is a Social Fact?" (2) "Rules for the Observation of Social Facts," (3) "Rules for Distinguishing Between the Normal and the Pathological," (4) "Rules for the Classification of Social Types," (5) "Rules for the Explanation of Social Facts," and (6) "Rules Relative to Establishing Sociological Proofs." I examine each of these below.

What Is a Social Fact?

Durkheim was engaged in a battle to establish the legitimacy of sociology. In *The Division of Labor* he proclaimed "moral facts" to be sociology's subject, but in *The Rules* he changed his terminology to that employed earlier by Comte and argued that "social facts" were the distinctive subject of sociology. For Durkheim, a social fact "consists of ways of acting, thinking, and feeling, external to the individual, and endowed with power of coercion, by which they control him."[37]

In this definition, Durkheim lumped behaviors, thoughts, and emotions together as the subject of sociology. The morphological and symbolic structures in which individuals participate are thus to be the focus of sociology, but social facts are, by virtue of transcending any individual, "external" and "constraining." They are external in two senses:

1. Individuals are born into an established set of structures and an existing system of values, beliefs, and norms. Hence, these structural and symbolic "facts" are initially external to individuals, and as people learn to play roles in social structures, to abide by norms, and to accept basic values, they feel and sense "something" outside of them.

---

[35]Émile Durkheim, *The Rules of the Sociological Method* (New York: Free Press, 1938; originally published 1895).

[36]Lukes, *Émile Durkheim*, chap. 10.

[37]Durkheim, *The Rules*, 3.

2. Even when humans actively and collaboratively create social structures, values, beliefs, and norms, these social facts become an emergent reality that is external to their creators.

This externality is accompanied by a sense of constraint and coercion. The structures, norms, values, and beliefs of the social world compel certain actions, thoughts, and dispositions. They impose limits, and when deviations occur, sanctions are applied to the deviants. Moreover, social facts are "internalized" in that people want and desire to be a part of social structures and to accept the norms, values, and beliefs of the collective. In the 1895 edition of *The Rules,* this point had been under-emphasized, but in the second edition Durkheim noted,

> Institutions may impose themselves upon us, but we cling to them; they compel us, and we love them.[38]

> [Social facts] dominate us and impose beliefs and practices upon us. But they rule us from within, for they are in every case an integral part of ourself.[39]

Durkheim thus asserted that when individuals come into collaboration, a new reality consisting of social and symbolic structures emerges. This emergent reality cannot be reduced to individual psychology, because it is external to, and constraining on, any individual. And yet, like all social facts, it is registered on the individual and often "rules the individual from within." Having established that sociology has a distinct subject matter—social facts—Durkheim devoted the rest of the book to explicating rules for studying and explaining social facts.

Rules for the Observation of Social Facts

Durkheim offered several guidelines for observing social facts: (a) personal biases and preconceptions must be eliminated; (b) the phenomenon under study must be clearly defined; (c) an empirical indicator of the phenomenon under study must be found, as was the case for "law" in *The Division of Labor;* and (d) social facts must be considered "things." Social facts are things in two different, although related, ways. First, when a phenomenon is viewed as a thing, it is possible to assume "a particular mental attitude" toward it. We can search for the properties and characteristics of a thing, and we can draw verifiable conclusions about its nature. Such a position was highly controversial in Durkheim's time because moral phenomena—values, ideas, morals—were not often considered proper topics of scientific inquiry, and when they were, they were seen as a subarea in the study of individual psychology. Second, Durkheim asserted, phenomena such as morality, values, beliefs, and dogmas constitute a distinctive metaphysical

---

[38]Ibid., Footnote 5, 3.

[39]Ibid., 7.

reality, not reducible to individual psychology. Hence, they can be approached with the same scientific methods as any material phenomenon in the universe.[40]

Rules for Distinguishing Between the Normal and the Pathological

Throughout his career, Durkheim never wavered from Comte's position that science is to be used to serve human ends: "Why strive for knowledge of reality if this knowledge cannot serve us in life? To this we can reply that, by revealing the causes of phenomena, science furnishes the means of producing them."[41] To use scientific knowledge to implement social conditions requires knowledge of what is normal and pathological. Otherwise, one would not know what social facts to create and implement, or one might actually create a pathological condition. To determine normality, the best procedure, Durkheim argued, is to discover what is most frequent and typical of societies of a given type or at a given stage of evolution. That which deviates significantly from this average is pathological.

Such a position allowed Durkheim to make some startling conclusions for his time. In regard to deviance, for example, a particular rate of crime and some other form of deviance could be normal for certain types of societies. Abnormality is present only when rates of deviance exceed what is typical of a certain societal type.

Rules for the Classification of Social Types

Durkheim's evolutionary perspective, coupled with his strategy for diagnosing normality and pathology in social systems, made inevitable a concern with social classification. Although specific systems reveal considerable variability, it is possible to group them into general types on the basis of (a) the "nature" and "number" of their parts and (b) the "mode of combination" of parts.

In this way, Durkheim believed, societies that reveal superficial differences can be seen as belonging to a particular class or type. Moreover, by ignoring the distracting complexities of a society's "content" and "uniqueness," it is possible to establish the stage of evolutionary development of a society.

Rules for the Explanation of Social Facts

Durkheim emphasized again a point he had made in *The Division of Labor*: "When the explanation of social phenomena is undertaken, we must seek separately the efficient cause which produces it and the function it fulfills."[42] Causal

---

[40]Many commentators, such as Giddens, *Capitalism and Modern Theory*, and Lukes, *Émile Durkheim*, emphasize that Durkheim was not making a metaphysical statement. We think that he was making both a metaphysical and a methodological statement.

[41]Durkheim, *The Rules*, 48.

[42]Ibid., 95.

analysis involves searching for antecedent conditions that produce a given effect. Functional analysis is concerned with determining the consequences of a social fact (regardless of its cause) for the social whole or larger context in which it is located. Complete sociological explanation involves both causal and functional explanations, as Durkheim had sought to illustrate in *The Division of Labor*.

Rules for Establishing Sociological Proofs

Durkheim advocated two basic procedures for establishing "sociological proofs"—proofs being documentation that causal and, by implication, functional explanations are correct. One procedure involves comparing two or more societies of a given type (as determined by the rules for classification) to see if one fact, present in one but not the other(s), leads to differences in these otherwise similar societies.

The second procedure is the method of concomitant variation. If two social facts are correlated and one is assumed to cause the other and if all alternative facts that might also be considered causative cannot eliminate the correlation, it can be asserted that a causal explanation has been "proved." If an established correlation, and presumed causal relation, can be explained away by the operation of another social fact, the established explanation has been disproved and the new social fact can, until similarly disproved, be considered "proved." The logic of Durkheim's method of concomitant variation, then, was similar in intent to modern multivariate analyses: to assert a relation among variables, controlling for the impact of other variables.[43]

The Rules marks a turning point in Durkheim's intellectual career. It was written after his thesis on the division of labor, while he was pondering the question of suicide in his lectures. Yet it was written before his first public course on religion.[44] He had clearly established his guiding theoretical interests: the nature of social organization and its relationship to values, beliefs, and other symbolic systems. He had developed a clear methodology: asking causal and functional questions within a broad comparative, historical, and evolutionary framework. He had begun to win respect in intellectual and academic circles for the fact that social organization represents an emergent reality, sui generis, and is the proper subject matter for a discipline called sociology.

Durkheim's next work appears to have been an effort to demonstrate the utility of his methodological and ontological advocacy. For he sought to understand sociologically a phenomenon that, at the time, was considered uniquely psychological: suicide. In this work, he attempted to demonstrate the power of sociological investigation for seemingly psychological phenomena, employing social facts as explanatory variables. Far more important than the specifics of suicide, I believe, is his extension of concepts introduced in *The Division of Labor*.

---

[43]Durkheim made other assertions: a social fact can only have one cause, and this cause must be another social fact (rather than an individual or psychological fact).

[44]Lukes, *Émile Durkheim*, 227.

Suicide

In *Suicide*, Durkheim appears to follow self-consciously the "rules" of his sociological method.[45] He was interested in studying only a social fact, and hence he did not study individual suicides but, rather, the general pervasiveness of suicide in a population—that is, a society's aggregate tendency toward suicide. In this way, suicide could be considered a social rather than an individual fact, and it could be approached as a "thing." Suicide is clearly defined as "all causes of death resulting directly or indirectly from a positive or negative act of the victim himself which he knows will produce this result."[46] The statistical rate of suicide is then used as the indicator of this social fact.[47] Suicide is classified into four types: egoistic, altruistic, anomic, and fatalistic. The cause of these types is specified by the degree and nature of individual integration into the social collective. A variant of modern correlational techniques is employed to demonstrate, or "prove," that other hypothesized causes of suicide are spurious and that integration into social and symbolic structures is the key explanatory variable.

The statistical manipulations in *Suicide* are important because they represent the first systematic effort to apply correlational and contingency techniques to causal explanation. Our concern, however, is with the theoretical implications of this work, and hence the following summary will focus on theoretical rather than statistical issues.

Types of Suicide

As noted, Durkheim isolated four types of suicide by varying causes. I should emphasize that despite his statistical footwork, isolating types by causes and then explaining these types by the causes used to classify them is a dubious, if not spurious, way to go about understanding the social world. These flaws aside, Durkheim's analysis clarifies notions of social integration that are somewhat vague in *The Division of Labor*. Basically, Durkheim argued that suicides could be classified by the nature of an individual's integration into the social fabric. There are, in Durkheim's eye, two types of integration:

1. *Attachment* to social groups and their goals: Such attachment involves the maintenance of interpersonal ties and the perception that one is a part of a larger collectivity.

2. *Regulation* by the collective conscience (values, beliefs, and general norms) of social groupings: Such regulation limits individual aspirations and needs, keeping them in check.

---

[45]Émile Durkheim, *Suicide: A Study in Sociology* (New York: Free Press, 1951; originally published 1897).

[46]Ibid., 44.

[47]Ibid., 48. It should be emphasized that suicide had been subject to extensive statistical analysis during Durkheim's time, and thus he was able to borrow the data compiled by others.

In distinguishing these two bases of integration, Durkheim explicitly recognized the different "functions" of the structural and cultural elements of the social world. Interpersonal ties that bind individuals to the collective keep them from becoming too "egoistic"—a concept borrowed from Tocqueville and widely discussed in Durkheim's time. Unless individuals can be attached to a larger collective and its goals, they become egoistic, or self-centered, in ways that are highly destructive to their psychological well-being. In contrast, the regulation of individuals' aspirations, which are potentially infinite, prevents anomie. Without cultural constraints, individual aspirations, as Rousseau[48] and Tocqueville had emphasized, escalate and create perpetual misery for individuals who pursue goals that constantly recede as they are approached. These two varying bases of individual integration into society, then, form the basis for Durkheim's classification of four types of suicide—egoistic, altruistic, anomic, and fatalistic.

Egoistic Suicide. When a person's ties to groups and collectivities are weakened, there is the potential for excessive individualism and, hence, egoistic suicide. Durkheim stated this relation as a clear proposition: "Suicide varies inversely with the degree of integration of social groups of which the individual forms a part."[49] And as a result,

> The more weakened the groups to which he belongs, the less he depends on them, the more he consequently depends only on himself and recognizes no other rules of conduct than what are founded on private interest. If we agree to call this state egoism, in which the individual ego asserts itself to excess in the face of the social ego and at its expense, we may call egoistic the special type of suicide springing from excessive individualism.[50]

Altruistic Suicide. If the degree of individual integration into the group is visualized as a variable continuum, ranging from egoism on the one pole to a complete fusion of the individual with the collective at the other pole, the essence of Durkheim's next form of suicide can be captured. Altruistic suicide is the result of individuals being so attached to the group that they commit suicide for the good of the group. In such a situation, individuals count for little; the group is paramount, with individuals subordinating their interests to those of the group. Durkheim distinguished three types of altruistic suicide:

1. *Obligatory altruistic suicide,* in which individuals are obliged, under certain circumstances, to commit suicide

2. *Optional altruistic suicide,* in which individuals are not obligated to commit suicide, but it is the custom for them to do so under certain conditions

---

[48]This view of humans, I should note, is very similar to that of Marx.

[49]Durkheim, *Suicide,* 209.

[50]Ibid., 209.

3. *Acute altruistic suicide,* in which individuals kill themselves "purely for the joy of sacrifice, because, even with no particular reason, renunciation in itself is considered praiseworthy"[51]

In sum, then, egoistic and altruistic suicides result from either over- or under-integration into the collective. Altruistic suicide tends to occur in traditional systems—what Durkheim termed *mechanical* in *The Division of Labor*—and egoistic suicide is more frequent in modern, organic systems that reveal high degrees of individual autonomy. At the more abstract level, Durkheim posited a critical dimension of individual and societal integration: the maintenance of interpersonal bonds within coherent group structures.

Anomic Suicide. In *The Division of Labor,* Durkheim's conceptualization of anomie was somewhat vague. In many ways, he incorporated both anomie (deregulation by symbols) and egoism (detachment from structural relations in groups) into the original definition of anomie. In *Suicide,* Durkheim clarified this ambiguity: anomic suicide came to be viewed narrowly as the result of deregulation of individuals' desires and passions. Although both egoistic and anomic suicide "spring from society's insufficient presence in individuals,"[52] the nature of the disjuncture or deficiency between the individual and society differs.[53]

Fatalistic Suicide. Durkheim discussed fatalistic suicide in a short footnote. Just as altruism is the polar opposite of egoism, so fatalism is the opposite of anomie. Fatalistic suicide is the result of "excessive regulation, that of persons with futures pitilessly blocked and passions violently choked by oppressive discipline."[54] Thus, when individuals are overregulated by norms, beliefs, and values in their social relations, and when they have no individual freedom, discretion, or autonomy in their social relations, they are potential victims of fatalistic suicide.

Suicide and Social Integration

These four types of suicide reveal a great deal about Durkheim's conception of humans and the social order. The study of suicide allows us a glimpse at how he conceived of human nature. Reading between the lines in *Suicide,* the following features are posited:

1. Humans can potentially reveal unlimited desires and passions, which must be regulated and held in check.

2. Total regulation of passions and desires creates a situation where life loses all meaning.

---

[51]Ibid., 223.

[52]Ibid., 258.

[53]Ibid., 258.

[54]Ibid., 276, in footnote.

3. Humans need interpersonal attachments and a sense that these attachments connect them to collective purposes.

4. Excessive attachment can undermine personal autonomy to the point where life loses meaning for the individual.[55]

These implicit notions of human nature, it should be emphasized, involve a vision of the "normal" way in which individuals are integrated into the structural and cultural structures of society. Indeed, Durkheim was unable even to address the question of human nature without also talking about the social order. Durkheim believed that the social order is maintained only to the degree that individuals are attached to, and regulated by, patterns of collective organization. This belief led him later in his career to explore in more detail an essentially social psychological question: In what ways do individuals become attached to society and become willing to be regulated by its symbolic elements?

Suicide and Deviance

Durkheim made an effort to see if other forms of deviance, such as homicide and crime, were related to suicide rates, but the details of his correlations are not as important as the implications of his analysis for a general theory of deviance. As he had in *The Division of Labor,* he recognized that a society of a certain type would reveal a "typical," or "average," level of deviance, whether of suicide or some other form. However, when rates of suicide, or deviance in general, exceed certain average levels for a societal type, a "pathological" condition might exist.

Durkheim's great contribution is his recognition that deviance is caused by the same forces that maintain conformity in social systems. Moreover, he specified the two key variables in understanding both conformity and deviance: (1) the degree of group attachment and (2) the degree of value and normative regulation. Thus, excessive or insufficient attachment and regulation will cause varying forms of deviance in a social system. Moreover, the more a system reveals moderate degrees of regulation and attachment, the less likely are pathological rates of deviance and the greater is the social integration of individuals into the system.

Thus, Durkheim's analysis in *Suicide* is much more than a statistical analysis of a narrowly defined topic. It is also a venture into understanding how social organization is possible. This becomes particularly evident near the end of the book, where Durkheim proposes his solution to the high rates of suicide and other forms of deviance that typify modern or "organically" structured societies.

Suicide and the Social Organization of Organic Societies[56]

At the end of *Suicide,* Durkheim abandoned his cross-sectional statistical analysis and returned to the evolutionary perspective contained in *The Division*

---

[55]See also Lukes, *Émile Durkheim,* chap. 9, for a somewhat different discussion.

[56]Durkheim dropped the term *organic societies,* but we have retained it here to emphasize the continuity between *Suicide* and *The Division of Labor.*

of Labor. During social change, as societies move from one basis of social solidarity, deregulation (anomie) and detachment (egoism) of the individual from society can occur, especially if this transition is rapid. Deregulation and detachment create not only high rates of deviance but also problems in maintaining the social order. If these problems are to be avoided and if social "normality" is to be restored, new structures that provide attachment and regulation of individuals to society must be created.

In a series of enlightening pages, Durkheim analyzed the inability of traditional social structures to provide this new basis of social integration. The family is an insufficiently encompassing social structure, religious structures are similarly too limited in their scope and too oriented to the sacred, and government is too bureaucratized and hence remote from the individual. For Durkheim, the implications are that modern social structures require intermediate groups to replace the declining influence of family and religion, to mediate between the individual and the state, and to check the growing power of the state. He saw the occupational group as the only potential structural unit that could regulate and attach individuals to society.

Thus, in *Suicide,* the ideas that were later placed in the 1902 preface to the second edition of *The Division of Labor* found their first forceful expression. The analysis in suicide allowed Durkheim to explore further the concept of social integration, and for this reason *Suicide* represents both an application of the method advocated in *The Rules* and a clarification of substantive ideas contained in *The Division of Labor.* It also represents an effort to incorporate social psychology[57] into structural sociology.

The Elementary Forms of the Religious Life

Although Durkheim turned to the study of religion in his last major work, it had been an important interest for a long time. Indeed, his family background ensured that religion would be a central concern, and from 1895 on, he had taught courses on religion.[58] Regardless of any personal reasons for his interest, I suspect that Durkheim pursued the study of religion through most of his career because it allowed him to gain insight into the basic theoretical problem that guided all of his work: the nature of symbols and their reciprocal effects on patterns of social organization. In *The Division of Labor,* he had argued that in mechanical societies the collective conscience or culture is predominately religious in content and that it functions to integrate the individual into the collective. He had recognized that in organic systems the collective conscience becomes "enfeebled" and that religion as a pervasive influence recedes. The potential pathologies that can occur with the transition from mechanical to organic solidarity—particularly anomie—became increasingly evident to Durkheim. Indeed, the naive optimism that these pathologies would "spontaneously" wither away became increasingly untenable, and as is

---

[57]Durkheim would, of course, not admit to this label.

[58]Émile Durkheim, *The Elementary Forms of the Religious Life* (New York: Free Press, 1947; originally published 1912).

evident in *Suicide*, he began to ponder how to create a social system in which individuals are both regulated by a general set of values and attached to concrete groups. As he came to view the matter, these concerns revolve around the more general problem of "morality."

Durkheim never wrote what was to be the culmination of his life's work: a book on morality. In many ways, however, his study of religion represents the beginning of his formal work on morality. Although he had lectured on morality in his courses on education[59] and had written several articles on morality,[60] he saw in religion a chance to study how interaction among individuals leads to the creation of symbolic systems that (a) lace together individual actions into collective units, (b) regulate and control individual desires, and (c) attach individuals to both the cultural (symbolic) and the structural (morphological) facets of the social world. Given the rise of anomie and egoism in modern societies, he thought that an understanding of religious morality in primitive social systems would help explain how such morality could be created in modern, differentiated systems. Thus, we could re-title *The Elementary Forms of the Religious Life*, "The Fundamental Forms of Moral Integration" and be close to his purpose in examining religion in aboriginal societies, particularly the Arunta aborigines of Australia.[61]

In the course of writing what was his longest work, however, Durkheim introduced many other intellectual issues that had occupied his attention over the years. Thus, *Elementary Forms* is more than a study of social integration; it is also an excursion into human evolution, the sociology of knowledge, functional and causal analyses, the origin and basis of thought and mental categories, the process of internalization of beliefs and values, and many other issues. Between the long descriptive passages on life among the Australian tribes, myriad ideas burst forth and give evidence of the wide-ranging concerns of Durkheim's intellect.

Elementary Forms is thus a long, complex, and—compared with earlier works—less coherently organized book. This requires that our analysis be divided into a number of separate topics. After a brief overview of the argument in *Elementary Forms*, I will examine in more detail some of its implications.

---

[59]The work on "moral education" will be examined later in this chapter in a discussion of Durkheim's more general concern with "morality."

[60]See, for example, Émile Durkheim, "The Determination of Moral Facts," in *Sociology and Philosophy*, trans. D. F. Poccock (New York: Free Press, 1974; originally published 1906).

[61]Baldwin Spencer and F. J. Gillian, in *The Native Tribes of Central Australia* (New York: Macmillan, 1899), present the first collection of "accounts" of these aboriginal peoples, which was in itself fascinating to the urbane Europeans. Sigmund Freud, in *Totem and Taboo* (New York: Penguin Books, 1938; originally published 1913), and two anthropologists, Bronislaw Malinowski, in *The Family among the Australian Aborigines* (New York: Schocken, 1963, originally published 1913), and A. R. Radcliffe-Brown, in "Three Tribes of Western Australia," *Journal of Royal Anthropological Institute of Great Britain and Ireland* 43 (1913), were all preparing works on the aborigines of Australia at the same time when Durkheim was writing *The Elementary Forms of the Religious Life*.

An Overview of Durkheim's Argument

By studying the elementary forms of religion among the most primitive[62] peoples, it should be possible, Durkheim felt, to understand the essence of religious phenomena without the distracting complexities and sociocultural overlays of modern social systems.[63] As dictated in *The Rules,* a clear definition of the phenomenon under study was first necessary. Thus, Durkheim defined religion as "a unified system of beliefs and practices relative to sacred things, that is to say, things set apart and forbidden—beliefs and practices which unite into one single moral community called a Church, all those who adhere to them."[64]

Durkheim believed that religiosity had emerged among humans when they occasionally assembled in a larger mass. From the mutual stimulation and "effervescence" that comes from animated interaction, people came to perceive a force, or "mana," that seemed superior to them. The mutual stimulation of primitive peoples thus made them "feel" an "external" and "constraining" force above and beyond them.[65] This force seemed to be imbued with special significance and with a sense that it was not a part of this world. It was, then, the first notion of a "sacred" realm distinct from the routine or "secular" world of daily activities. The distinction between sacred and secular was thus one of the first sets of mental categories possessed by humans in their evolutionary development.

As humans came to form more permanent groupings, or clans, the force that emerged from their interaction needed to be more concretely represented.[66] Such representation came with "totems," which are animals and plants that symbolize the force of mana. In this way, the sacred forces could be given concrete representation, and groups of people organized into "cults" could develop "ritual" activities directed toward the totem and indirectly toward the sacred force that they collectively sensed.

Thus, the basic elements of religion are (a) the emergence of beliefs in the sacred, (b) the organization of people into cults, and (c) the enactment of rituals, or rites, toward totems that represent the forces of the sacred realm. What the aboriginals did

---

[62]Obviously Durkheim was wrong on this account, but this was one of his assumptions.

[63]This strategy was the exact opposite of that employed by Max Weber, who examined the most complex systems of religion with his ideal-type methodology.

[64]Durkheim, *Elementary Forms,* 47. His earlier definition of religious phenomena emphasized the sacred—beliefs and ritual—but did not stress the morphological units of community and church. For example, an early definition read, "Religious phenomena consist of obligatory beliefs united with divine practices which relate to the objects given in the beliefs" (quoted in Lukes, *Émile Durkheim,* 241). His exposure to the compilation in Spencer and Gillian, *Native Tribes,* apparently alerted him to these morphological features.

[65]Durkheim clearly borrowed the ideas of crowd behavior developed by Gustave LeBon and Gabriel Tarde, even though the latter was his lifelong intellectual enemy.

[66]Durkheim, in both *The Division of Labor* and *The Rules,* had stressed that the segmental clan was the most elementary society. He termed the presocietal "mass" from which the clan emerges the *horde.*

not recognize, Durkheim argued, is that in worshipping totems, they were worshipping society. Totemic cults are nothing but the material symbolization of a force created by their interaction and collective organization into clans.

As people first became organized into clans and associated totemic cults and as they perceived a sacred realm that influenced events in the secular world, their first categories of thought were also formed. Notions of causality, Durkheim argued, could emerge only after people perceived that sacred forces determined events in the secular world. Notions of time and space could exist only after the organization of clans and their totemic cults. According to Durkheim, the basic categories of human thought—cause, time, space, and so on—emerged after people developed religion. Thus, in an ultimate sense, science and all forms of thought have emerged from religion—an argument, we might note, reminiscent of Comte's law of the three stages. Before religion, humans experienced only physical sensations[67] from their physical environment, but with religion, their mental life became structured by categories. In Durkheim's view, mental categories are the cornerstone of all thought, including scientific thought and reasoning. Looking back on *Elementary Forms* a year after its publication, Durkheim was still moved to conclude,

> The most essential notions of the human mind, notions of time, of space, of genus and species, of force and causality, of personality, those in a word, which the philosophers have labeled categories and which dominate the whole logical thought, have been elaborated in the very womb of religion. It is from religion that science has taken them.[68]

For Durkheim, the cause of religion is the interaction among people created by their organization into the simplest form of society, the clan. The functions of religion are (a) to regulate human needs and actions through beliefs about the sacred and (b) to attach people, through ritual activities (rites) in cults, to the collective. Because they are internalized, religious beliefs generate needs for people to belong to cults and participate in rituals. As people participate in rituals, they reaffirm these internalized beliefs and, hence, reinforce their regulation by, and attachment to, the dictates of the clan. Moreover, the molding of such basic mental categories as cause, time, and space by religious beliefs and cults functions to give people a common view of the world, thus facilitating their interaction and organization.

This argument is represented in Figure 7.2, which delineates Durkheim's model of the origins of the functions of religion. Regarding origins, he had an image of

---

[67]As will be recalled, Durkheim took this idea from Rousseau and his description of the "natural state of man."

[68]Quoted in Lukes, *Émile Durkheim*, 445 (taken from *L'Année Sociologique,* 1913). This line of thought is simply Comte's idea of the movement of thought from the theological through the metaphysical to the positivistic.

Figure 7.2 Durkheim's Model of Religious Evolution

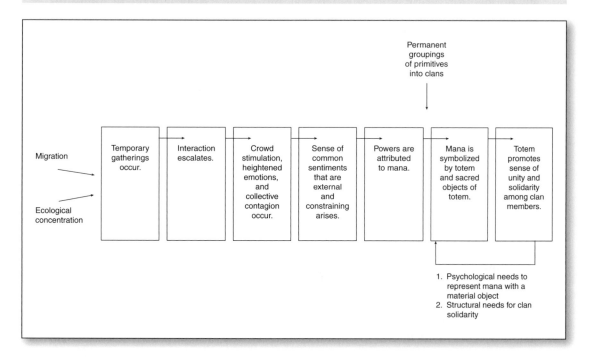

aboriginal peoples periodically migrating and concentrating themselves in temporary gatherings. Once they have gathered, increased interaction escalates collective emotions, which produce a sense that there is something external and constraining to each individual. This sense of constraint is given more articulate expression as a sacred force, or mana. This causal sequence occurs, Durkheim maintained, each time aboriginals gathered in their periodic festivals. Once they form more permanent groupings, called clans, the force of mana is given more concrete expression as a sacred totem. The creation of beliefs about and rituals toward the totem function to promote clan solidarity.

This model is substantively inaccurate, as are all of Durkheim's intellectual expeditions into the origins of society. For example, the clan was not the first kinship structure, and many hunter-gatherers like the aborigines do not worship totems. These errors can be attributed to Durkheim's reliance on Australian aborigine kinship and religious organization, which in many ways deviate from modal patterns among hunting-and-gathering peoples. Apart from these factual errors, the same problems evident in the model of the division of labor resurface. First, the conditions under which any causal connection holds true are not specified. Second, the functions of religious totems (for social solidarity) are also what appear to promote their very creation. In addition, a psychological need—the "primitive need" to make concrete and symbolize "mana"—is invoked to explain why totems emerge.

Because of these problems, it must be concluded that the model does not present any useful information in its causal format. But as a description of the relationships among rates of interaction, structural arrangements, emotional arousal, and symbolic representation, Durkheim's statements are suggestive and emphasize that (a) highly concentrated interactions increase collective sentiments, which mobilize actors' actions; (b) small social structures tend to develop symbols to represent their collective sentiments; and (c) these structures evidence high rates of ritual activity to reinforce their members' commitment.

Some Further Implications of *Elementary Forms*

Practical Concerns. Durkheim's analysis of pathologies in *Suicide*, along with other essays, forced the recognition that a more active program for avoiding egoism and anomie might be necessary to create a normal "organic" society. Religion, he thought, offers a key to understanding how this can be done. Early in his career, however, he rejected the idea that religion could ever again assume major integrative functions. The modern world is too secular and individualistic for the subordination of individuals to gods. He also rejected, to a much lesser degree, Saint-Simon's and Comte's desire to create a secular religion of humanity based on science and reason. Although Durkheim saw a need to maintain the functions and basic elements of religion, he had difficulty accepting Comte's ideal of positivism, which, as Robert Nisbet noted, was "Catholicism Minus Christianity." For Comte, the Grand Being was society, the church was the hierarchy of the sciences, and the rites were the sacred canons of the positive method.[69] Durkheim also rejected Max Weber's pessimistic view of a secular, rational world filled with disenchantment and lacking in commitments to a higher purpose.

The "solution" implied in *Elementary Forms* and advocated elsewhere in various essays is for the re-creation in secular form of the basic elements of religion: feelings of sacredness, beliefs and values about the sacred, common rituals directed toward the sacred, and cult structures in which these rituals and beliefs are reaffirmed. Because society is the source and object of religious activity anyway, the goal must be to make explicit this need to "worship" society. Occupational groups and the state would become the church and cults, nationalistic beliefs would become quasi-sacred and would provide the underlying symbols, and activities in occupational groups, when seen as furthering the collective goals of the nation, would assume the functions of religious ritual in (a) mobilizing individual commitment, (b) reaffirming beliefs and values, and (c) integrating individuals into the collective.

Theoretical Concerns. Contained in these practical concerns are several important theoretical issues. First, integration of social structures presupposes a system of

---

[69]Nisbet, *The Sociology of Émile Durkheim,* 159.

values and beliefs that reflects and symbolizes the structure of the collective. Second, these values and beliefs require rituals directed at reaffirming them as well as those social structures they represent or symbolize. Third, large collectivities, such as a nation, require subgroups in which values and beliefs can be affirmed by ritual activities among a more immediate community of individuals. Fourth, to the degree that values and beliefs do not correspond to actual structural arrangements and to the extent that substructures for the performance of actions that reaffirm these values and beliefs are not present, a societal social system will experience integrative problems.

We can see, then, that Durkheim's practical concerns follow from certain theoretical principles he had tentatively put forth in *The Division of Labor.* The study of religion seemingly provided him with a new source of data to affirm the utility of his first insights into the social order. There are, however, some noticeable shifts in emphasis, the most important of which is the recognition that the "collective conscience" cannot be totally "enfeebled"; it must be general but also strong and relevant to the specific organizations that make up a society. Despite these refinements, *Elementary Forms* affirms the conclusion contained in the preface to the second edition of *The Division of Labor.*

The most interesting aspect of the analysis is perhaps the social psychological emphasis of *Elementary Forms.* While Durkheim, in courses and essays, had begun to feel comfortable with inquiry into the social psychological dynamics of social and symbolic structures, these concerns are brought together in his last major book.

Social Psychological Concerns. *Elementary Forms* contains the explicit recognition that morality—that is, values, beliefs, and norms—can integrate the social order only if morality becomes part of an individual's psychological structure. Statements in *Elementary Forms* mitigate the rather hard line taken in the first edition of *The Rules,* where social facts are seen as external and constraining things. With the second edition of *The Rules,* Durkheim felt more secure in verbalizing the obvious internalization of values, beliefs, and other symbolic components of society into the human psyche. In *Elementary Forms,* he revealed even fewer reservations:

> For the collective force is not entirely outside of us; it does not act upon us wholly from without; but rather, since society cannot exist except in and through individual consciousnesses, this force must also penetrate us and organize itself within us, it thus becomes an integral part of our being.[70]

Durkheim hastened to add in a footnote, however, that although society was an "integral part of our being," it could not ever be seen as reducible to individuals.

---

[70]Durkheim, *Elementary Forms,* 209.

Another social psychological concern in *Elementary Forms* is the issue of human thought processes. For Durkheim, thought occurs in categories that structure experience for individuals:

> At the roots of all our judgments there are a certain number of essential ideas which dominate all our intellectual life; they are what philosophers since Aristotle have called the categories of the understanding: ideas of space, class, number, cause, substance, personality, etc. They correspond to the most universal properties of things. They are like the solid frame which encloses all thought.[71]

Durkheim sought in *Elementary Forms* to reject the philosophical positions of David Hume and Immanuel Kant. Hume, the staunch empiricist, argued that thought was simply the transfer of experiences to the mind and that categories of thought were merely the codification of repetitive experiences. In contrast with Hume, Kant argued that categories and mind were inseparable; the essence of mind is categorization. Categories are innate and not structured from experience. Durkheim rejected both of these positions; in their place, he wanted to insert the notion that categories of thought—indeed, all thinking and reflective mental activity—were imposed on individuals by the structure and morality of society. Indeed this imposition of society becomes a critical condition not just for the creation of the mind and thought but also for the preservation of society.[72] Thus, Durkheim believed that the basic categories of thought—such as cause, time, and space—were social products in that the structure of society determines them in the same way that values and beliefs also structure human "will," or motivations. For example, the idea of a sacred force, or mana, beyond individuals that could influence events in the mundane world became, in the course of human evolution, related to ideas of causality. Similarly, the idea of time emerged among humans as they developed calendrical rituals and related them to solar and lunar rhythms. The conception of space was shaped by the structure of villages, so that if the aboriginal village is organized in a circle, the world will be seen as circular and concentric in nature. These provocative insights were at times taken to excessive extremes in other essays, especially in one written with his nephew and student, Marcel Mauss, on "primitive classification."[73] Here, mental categories are seen to be exact representations of social structural divisions and arrangements. Moreover, Durkheim and Mauss appear to have selectively reported data from aboriginal societies to support their excessive claims.[74]

---

[71]Ibid., 9.

[72]Ibid., 17–18.

[73]Émile Durkheim and Marcel Mauss, *Primitive Classification,* trans. Rodney Needham (Chicago, IL: University of Chicago Press, 1963; originally published 1903).

[74]See the introduction to the translation for documentation of this fact.

Durkheim is often viewed as the "father of structuralism," a school of thought in the twentieth century that embraced social science, linguistics, and literature. In Durkheim's *Elementary Forms* and other works of this period can be found an implicit model that appears to have inspired this structuralist reasoning. Figure 7.3 outlines the contours of this model. In Durkheim's view, the morphology of a society (the number, nature, size, and arrangement of parts—see Table 7.1) determines the structure of the collective conscience or culture (the volume, density, intensity, and content of values, beliefs, and norms). Reciprocally, the collective conscience reinforces social morphology. Both morphology and the collective conscience circumscribe each individual's cognitive structure by determining the nature of basic categories of thought with respect to time, space, and causality. In turn, these categories mediate between morphology and the collective conscience, on the one hand, and the nature of rituals that individuals emit in face-to-face interaction, on the other. The reverse causal loops in the model are crucial to Durkheim's argument: The enactment of rituals reinforces not only cognitive categories but also the structure and idea systems of society. In this way the macrostructural features of society—morphology and idea systems—are conceptually tied to the microstructural dimensions of reality—that is, the internal psychological structure of thought and the face-to-face interactions among individuals in concrete settings.

Figure 7.3   Durkheim's Structuralism

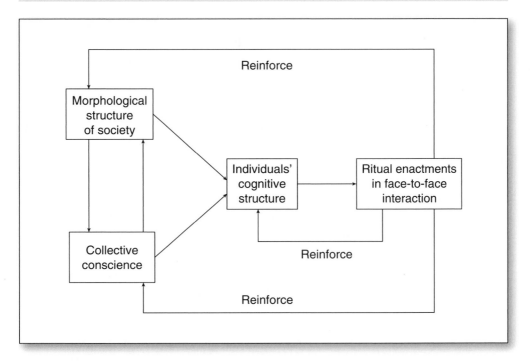

A Science of "Morality"

As early as *The Division of Labor*, Durkheim defined sociology as the science of "moral facts," and he always wanted to write a book on morality. In light of this unfulfilled goal, perhaps we should close our analysis by extracting from his various works what would have been the core ideas of this uncompleted work.[75]

What Is Morality?

In only two places did Durkheim provide a detailed discussion of morality.[76] For him, morality consists of (a) rules, (b) attachment to groups, and (c) voluntary constraint.

Rules. Morality is ultimately a system of rules that guides the actions of people. For rules to be moral, they must reveal two additional elements:

1. *Authority:* Moral rules are invested with authority; that is, people feel that they ought to obey them and they want to abide by them. Moral rules are a "system of commandments."

2. *Desirability:* Moral rules also specify the "desirable" ends toward which a collectivity of people should direct its energies. They are more than rules of convenience; they carry conceptions of the good and desirable and must therefore be distinguished from strictly utilitarian norms.

Attachment to Groups. Moral rules attach people to groups. They are the product of interactions in groups, and as they emerge, they bind people to groups and make individuals feel a part of a network of relations that transcend their individual being. Durkheim termed these two facets of morality *the spirit of discipline.* Morality provides a spirit of self-control and a commitment to the collective. In terms of the concepts developed in *Suicide,* morality reduces anomie and egoism to the degree that it regulates desires and attaches people to the collective. True morality in a modern society must do something else, however: it must allow people to recognize that the constraints and restraints imposed on them are in the "natural order of things."

Voluntary Constraint. Modern morality must allow people to recognize that unlimited desires (anomie) and excessive individualism (egoism) are pathological states. Durkheim felt that these states violate the nature of human society and can

---

[75]See, in particular, Émile Durkheim, *Moral Education: A Study in the Theory and Application of the Sociology of Education,* trans. E. K. Wilson and H. Schnurer (New York: Free Press, 1961; originally published 1922). This is a compilation of lectures given in 1902–1903; the course was repeated in 1906–1907.

[76]One is Durkheim, *Moral Education;* the other is an article, published in 1906, on "The Determination of Moral Facts." Reprinted in Émile Durkheim, *Sociology and Philosophy* (New York: Free Press, 1974), from papers originally collected and translated 1924.

be corrected only by morality. In simple societies, morality seems to operate auto-matically, but "the more societies become complex, the more difficult [it becomes] for morality to operate as a purely automatic mechanism."[77] Thus, morality must be constantly implemented and altered to changing conditions. Individuals must also come to see that such alteration is necessary and essential because to fail to establish a morality and to allow people to feel free of its power is to invite the agonies of anomie and egoism.

For Durkheim, as for other French philosophers such as Rousseau, morality must be seen as a natural constraint in the same way that the physical world constrains individuals' options and actions. So it is with morality; humans can no more rid themselves of its constraint than they can eliminate the physical and biological world on which their lives depend. The only recourse is to use science, just as we use the physical and biological sciences, to understand how morality works.[78]

Thus, Durkheim never abandoned his original notion, first given forceful expres-sion in *The Division of Labor*, that sociology is the science of moral facts. His concep-tion of morality had become considerably more refined, however, in three senses:

1. Morality is a certain type of rule that must be distinguished from both the mor-phological aspects of society and other, non-moral types of normative rules.

2. Morality is therefore a system of rules that reflects certain underlying value premises about the desirable.

3. Morality is not only external and constraining, it is also internal. It calls people to obey from within. For although morality "surpasses us it is within us, since it can only exist by and through us."[79]

By the end of Durkheim's career, the study of morality involved a clear separation between two types of norms and rules: those vested with value premises and those that simply mediate and regularize interactions. Moreover, an understanding of these types of rules could come only by visualizing their relationship to the morphological or structural aspects of society—nature, size, number, and relations of parts—and to the process by which internalization of symbols or culture occurs. Durkheim had thus begun to develop a clear conception of the complex relations among normative systems, social structures, and personality processes of individuals.

What would Durkheim have said in his last work—the book on morality—if he had lived to write it? *Moral Education,* when viewed in the context of his other pub-lished books, can perhaps provide some hints about the direction of his thought. For *Moral Education* offers a view of how a new secular morality can be instilled.

For a new secular morality to be effective, the source of all morality must be recog-nized: society. This means that moral rules must be linked to the goals of the broader society, but they must be made specific through the participation of individuals in

---

[77]Durkheim, *Moral Education,* 52.

[78]Ibid., 119–120.

[79]Durkheim, *Determination of Moral Facts,* 55.

occupational groups. The commitment to the common morality must be learned in schools, where the teacher operates as the functional equivalent of the priest. The teacher gives young students an understanding of and a reverence for the nature of the society and inculcates the need to have a morality that regulates passions and provides attachments to groupings organized to pursue societal goals. Such educational socialization must ensure that the common morality is a part of students' motivational needs (their "will," in Durkheim's language), their cognitive orientations ("categories of mind"), and their self-control processes ("self-mastery").

A modern society that cannot meet these general conditions, Durkheim would have argued in this unwritten work, is a society that will be rife with pathologies revolving around (a) the failure to limit individual passions, desires, and aspirations and (b) the failure to attach individuals to groups with higher purposes and common goals.

Durkheim must have felt that the implicit theory of social organization contained in this argument had allowed him to realize Comte's dream of a science that could create "the good society." Although Durkheim was cautious in implementing his proposals, they were often simplistic, if not somewhat reactionary. At the same time, one can find the germ of a theory of human organization in his work.

Durkheim's Theoretical Legacy

Émile Durkheim's sociology is, ultimately, a search for the conditions generating social integration or solidarity during the course of societal differentiation. As societies move from simple (what he called "mechanical") to more complex ("organic") forms, the basis of societal integration changes. Durkheim's goal was to discover the causes of differentiation and the mechanisms for reintegrating society around more diverse cultural and structural systems.

The problem with Durkheim's analysis is that it mixes causal, functional, and ideological statements. The causal arguments are relatively easy to isolate, but the functional statements are problematic, as are all functional arguments. For Durkheim, there is one functional requisite—the need for integration—and all social and cultural processes in society should be examined with reference to how they meet this master need. As we emphasized in the conclusion to the last chapter, it is difficult to sort out causality in functional arguments because the need for integration appears to be causing the very cultural and structural forms meeting this need. Causality seems backward, but as with Herbert Spencer, we can obviate this backward causality by positing a "selectionist" argument, emphasizing that differentiation sets into motion selection pressures for actors to find new ways of integrating in the social system. If such efforts are successful, then integration is achieved and the society is viable; if they are not, the society disintegrates. Unlike Spencer, however, Durkheim never holds out the option of disintegration. He believed that pathologies like anomie, poor coordination, forced division of labor, and the like are temporary aberrations that will be eliminated as the new, organic basis of solidarity falls into place. Here, Durkheim turns into a moral preacher who has faith that integration will naturally emerge as differentiation proceeds; what he wanted to transpire is conflated with statements about what would inevitably happen. Thus, Durkheim tended to assume that the new structural and cultural forms emerging with differentiation would automatically reintegrate society, perhaps after a brief period when pathological forms are evident. Even if we assume that Durkheim implicitly made a selectionist argument that pathological conditions alerted actors to problems and set them to find solutions to anomie, forced divisions of labor, and poorly coordinated structures, the causal argument is difficult to disentangle from the moral functionalism that pervades Durkheimian sociology. Yet despite these problems, we can pull from Durkheim's sociology causal models and abstract principles of social organization in differentiated social systems.

Durkheim's Underlying Causal Model

In Figure 7.4, a complex causal model of Durkheim's analysis of differentiation and integration is delineated. In this model, I summarize the arguments in *The Division of Labor* in society with elements of those in *Suicide* and *The Elementary Forms of the Religious Life* as these pertain to the bases for integrating complex societies. Moving across the top of the model from left to right is the argument presented in *The Division of Labor*. At the right side of the model are the ideas from *Suicide* and the preface to the second edition of *The Division of Labor*, as these bear on the bases for integrating differentiated social systems. On the bottom and middle portions of the model are the key micro-level ideas from *The Elementary Forms of the Religious Life* that are easily plugged into Durkheim's more macro analysis of differentiation.

Ecological concentration is a key force in Durkheim's theory because it sets into motion (a) the competition that leads to the division of labor and (b) the copresence of individuals that leads to those micro-interpersonal rituals generating the (religious) morality of the group. The power of ecological concentration is highlighted by the positive arrows from this force to competition for resources at the top and to copresence at the bottom. At the far left are listed the causal relations among those forces—population size, migration, and growth, as well as communication and transportation technologies—that reduce the space between individuals and thereby increase the rates of interaction and competition. Pursuing the argument in *The Division of Labor* first, competition for resources initiates Darwinian selection among individuals and collective actors for resources. Durkheim very explicitly draws an analogy from Darwin's explanation for speciation, seeing the ecological concentration of individuals and collective units as putting pressure on resources, forcing actors to compete, with this competition leading to specialization of activities (as opposed to speciation). This competition, Durkheim assumed, need not lead to the actual "extinction" or "death" of actors; rather, those less successful in one niche would simply move to another resource niche and differentiate themselves from those against whom they could not successfully compete. From such competition, then, came increased specialization and, hence, a more complex division of labor, or, as we have phrased the matter in the model, a higher degree of differentiation.

Figure 7.4 Durkheim's Causal Model of Differentiation and Integration

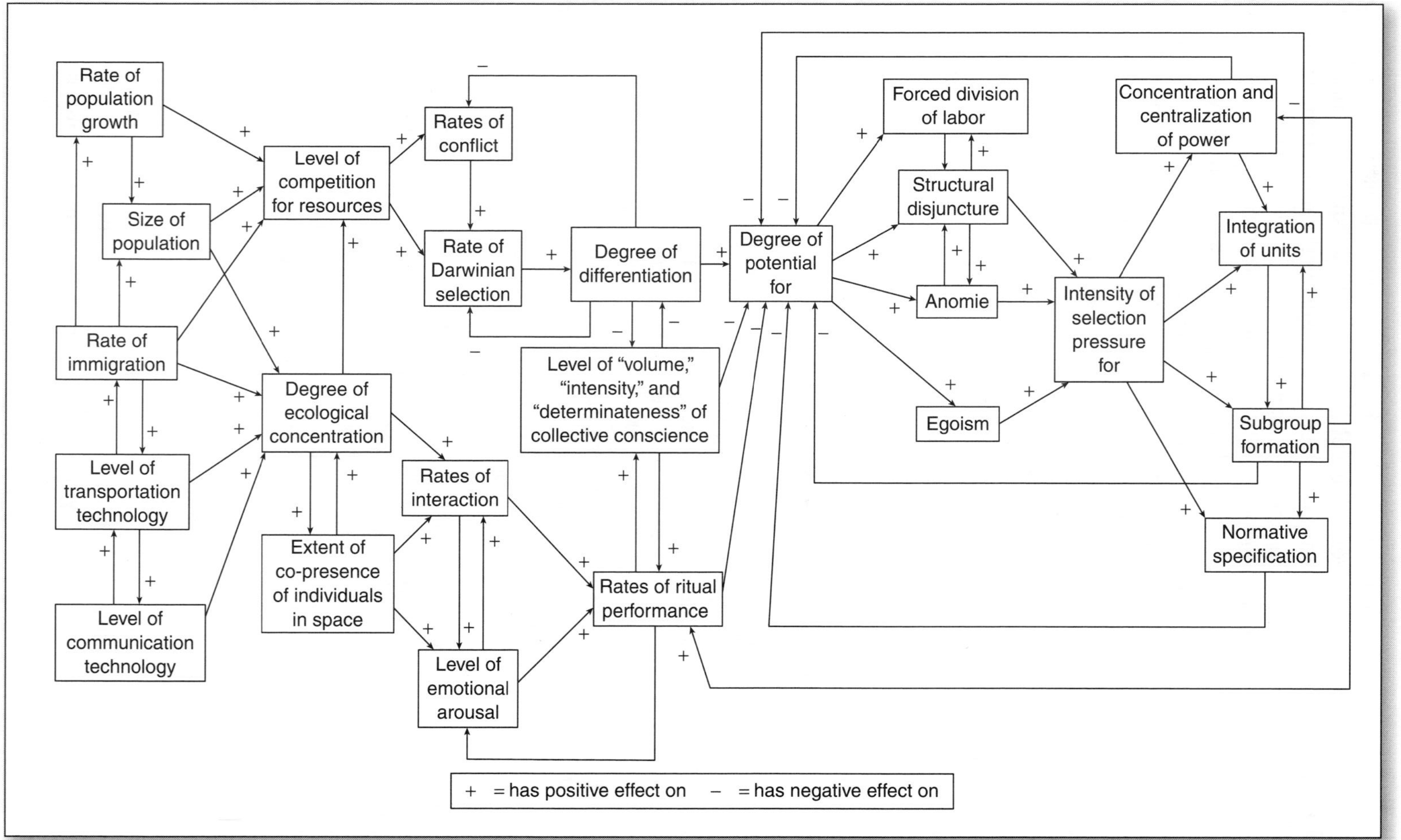

+ = has positive effect on   – = has negative effect on

In turn, increasing differentiation would reduce the conflict and struggle emerging from competition for resources, as denoted by the negative reverse causal arrow connecting differentiation to conflict/struggle as well as Darwinian selection. The negative arrow from differentiation to the volume, intensity, and determinateness of the collective conscious recapitulates Durkheim's view that the power of the collective conscious to regulate diversely situated actors must decline. That is, differentiated actors having somewhat diverse experiences could no longer share the exact same values and beliefs ("volume") as in mechanical societies; they could no longer be subject to precise regulation by the collective conscious ("intensity"); and they could not experience the collective conscious with the same degree of clarity ("determinateness"). Moreover, the secular to religious "content" of the collective conscious would increase with differentiation.

Differentiation, coupled with more abstract tenets in values and beliefs, increases the potential for the pathologies that emerge before the new basis of organic solidarity is in place. The forced division of labor, where resources are not distributed in line with people's talents, may increase. Coordination of structures through mutual interdependence and through regulation by laws and other norms may prove difficult. A generalized and, in Durkheim's words, "enfeebled" collective conscience may open the door to anomie or the lack of regulation of people's desires and passions and of their relations to each other and the units organizing their activities. Egoism may become rampant as differentiated structures force individuals to stand between structures rather than embed in them. Durkheim often assumes that these pathological conditions will simply go away, but we have converted his argument, much like I did for Spencer, into a selectionist statement. These pathologies will alert people and collective actors to problems, forcing actors to try to find ways to deal with these problems or face disintegration. Thus, the pathological forms of the division of labor can be conceptualized as the axes along which selection pressures are activated, pushing actors to find solutions. The more prevalent anomie, disjuncture among social units, forced division of labor, and egoism, the more intense are the selection pressures. The positive signs going out of selection pressures signal Durkheim's faith that solutions to these pathological forms in the division of labor would be found.

The solutions represent Durkheim's views on the bases for integrating complex societies. There is little to say about the forced division of labor because Durkheim simply assumed that it would disappear—a naive conviction. Therefore, we cannot draw a chain of causal events leading to the demise of this pathology. For the other pathologies, however, we can construct a causal argument from Durkheim's writings.

Structural disjunctions increase selection pressures for interdependence of units and for normative specification of the relations between units so that their relations are better coordinated. Moreover, if units could be collated into larger subgroups or federations, or what Durkheim termed "occupational groups" in the preface to the second edition of *The Division of Labor,* smaller structural units would be better coordinated as their interests converge (as indicated by the positively signed arrow from subgroup formation to integration of units). Finally, as the positive arrow underscores, the centralization of power also would facilitate the mutual interdependence because these centers provide the mechanism (regulation of money, systems of courts, and lawmaking legislative bodies) for creating and sustaining relations of mutual interdependence, although Durkheim does not offer much detail on these processes. In Durkheim's sociology, power and confederation of units into larger subgroups or "occupational groups" are important integrating forces. Although Durkheim did not develop this idea very far, he also argued that centralization of political authority (in the state) was necessary to enact and enforce many of the norms (as laws) essential to coordinating diverse social units and, hence, was critical to avoiding structural disjuncture and poor coordination of diverse units. Durkheim distrusted centralized power, and so he sought a source of counterpower in occupation groups or, in terms of the model in Figure 7.4, subgroups among members whose interests and experiences converge. With common experiences and interests, members of these subgroups could form political parties that would push for the common interests of broad sectors in the division of labor and pose a basis of counterpower to the centralized state. The negatively signed arrow from subgroup formation to the centralization and concentration of power emphasizes this counterbalancing effect of occupational groups mobilized as political parties.

Anomie is, of course, the most famous pathology in Durkheim's sociology, and he denoted several aspects of "regulation" with this term. One is the lack of regulation in the sense of coordinating activities within and between structural units. This was the meaning to be gleaned from *The Division of Labor*. Another meaning comes from *Suicide*: the lack of regulation of people's desires, needs, wants, and passions to the point of increasing rates of aberrant or deviant behavior, beyond what is "normal" for a society. The first meaning of anomie is managed by the same forces that reduce structural disjuncture—power, interdependence, normative specification, and confederation of individuals and groups into larger subgroups. The second meaning emphasizes the effects of developing norms—what is termed "normative specification" in the model—to fill in the gap between the generalized and enfeebled collective conscience for the whole society and the desires and passions of individuals. Durkheim felt that such norms would emerge and regulate people's actions and passions so that anomie would decline. This process is more likely to take place when normative specification occurs within group structures, thus providing a kind of group-based collective conscience that would translate the highly generalized tenets of the society-wide collective conscience into specific instructions and mandates that would provide regulation.

Another potential pathology in highly differentiated societies is "egoism," a force discussed by Durkheim in *Suicide* but one that can also be applied to his analysis of social differentiation. As Durkheim argued, egoism comes when individuals do not feel attached to groups or cultural symbols, and Durkheim's analysis of "occupational groups" in the preface to the second edition of *The Division of Labor* provides his answer to this problem of egoism. Individuals and collective actors located at similar places in the division of labor will have common interests and experiences, thereby leading them to develop common norms that attach them to the more general collective conscious and lower their sense of isolation or egoism. The negative arrow from subgroups and normative specification back to the box denoting the degree of potential for egoism underscores Durkheim's view that the expansion of normatively regulated subgroups would reduce rates of egoism and the deviant behaviors associated with the lack of integration of people into groups. Durkheim also felt that egoism can generate self-interest that is at odds with collective interest, and so he implicitly argued that as normatively regulated subgroups eliminate egoism, they would transform self-interest into group or collective interests more amenable to societal integration and political democracy.

Durkheim's discussion in *The Elementary Forms* can supplement the macro-level analysis thus far. Copresence of actors increases rates of interaction and emotional arousal, leading to the performance of rituals directed at the perceived power, or mana, of the collective conscience or culture. This is indicated by the positively signed arrows in the lower middle of the model in Figure 7.4. As rituals are performed, individuals "worship" the group or subgroups to which they belong, and consequently, the group becomes more salient and powerful in regulating individuals' actions. This relationship of micro-level rituals on subgroup formation is emphasized by the negative effects of rates of ritual performances strengthening the collective conscience by generating more consensus ("volume"), regulatory power ("intensity"), and clarity ("determinateness") in cultural values (as indicated by the vertical positive arrows to and from ritual performance to these variable dimensions of the collective conscious). Thus, Durkheim's "discovery" of the basis of solidarity in elementary religious forms allowed him to find the mechanisms by which normative specificity and subgroup formation would overcome the problems, of anomie and egoism, respectively. Moreover, once subgroups with more specific norms exist, the positive reverse causal arrow from subgroup formation to ritual performance underscores Durkheim's argument that these rituals would sustain group boundaries and a more powerful set of cultural symbols for regulating activities in these subgroups.

Durkheim underemphasized power and its effects on integrating complex social systems, and he did not address the modes of interdependence among differentiated actors in any detail. The usefulness of Durkheim's analysis, then, resides more in the dynamics occurring in values and beliefs as they are generalized and then made more specific in normatively regulated subgroups. Durkheim did not, therefore, provide a very complete model of integration in complex social systems, especially when his ideas are placed into a robust causal model. Yet, despite these shortcomings, Durkheim did present to sociology some powerful theoretical principles that state a number of fundamental relationships among forces in the social universe.

Durkheim's Theoretical Principles

Principles of Social Differentiation. For Durkheim, the level of social differentiation among members of a population and among the social units organizing their activities is related to the level of competition for resources. This competition for resources is, in turn, the result of increased "moral density" in which the rates of interaction among members of a population are high. This ecological view of the causes of differentiation was borrowed from Charles Darwin's analysis of speciation of life forms, although Durkheim clearly borrowed heavily from Herbert Spencer's analysis of differentiation. The basic relationship among density, rates of interaction, competition, and differentiation can be stated as a single principle:

1. The greater is the level of competition for resources among members of a population, the higher are rates of interaction and levels of differentiation.

2. The level of competition and rates of interaction increase as
   A. The concentration of the population in space increases, with this concentration rising with
      1. The absolute size of the population
      2. The existence of ecological barriers
      3. The existence of political, social, and cultural barriers
   B. Transportation and communication technologies and infrastructures reduce the social space among individuals.

Durkheim saw the concentration of the population as a physical fact created both by ecological barriers (mountains, bodies of water, etc.) and by large numbers of individuals, who inevitably must be more concentrated than small numbers, although the absolute size of the territory would determine to some extent how concentrated a large population would be. Political, cultural, and social barriers also influence the concentration of the population. When political organization is strong, geopolitical boundaries are likely to be sustained, and people will generally stay within them. Similarly, when cultural symbols and social structures are powerful and constraining, they will tend to hold members in the space. Density is also, Durkheim recognized, related to the level of development in transportation and communication technologies. Even when people, structural units, and cultural symbols are more dispersed, the ability to move in space and to communicate efficiently will increase the rates of interaction and moral density. Indeed, although Durkheim could not have anticipated the world system of the twenty-first century, where time and space are compressed and where cultural symbols circulate in fast-moving communication channels, he understood the basic relationship between transportation/communication technologies and moral density. Thus, forces that increase moral density will escalate the competition for resources, and this competition will increase the level of differentiation as actors seek viable resource niches in which to sustain themselves.

Principles of System Integration. For Durkheim, integration or, as he phrased it, social solidarity can be defined only by references to what he saw as "abnormal." Anomie, egoism, poor coordination, and the forced division of labor all represented to Durkheim instances of malintegration. Thus, "normal" integration would represent the converse of these conditions, allowing us to formulate the following definition: integration occurs when individual passions are regulated by cultural symbols, when individuals are attached to the social collective, when actions are regulated and coordinated by norms, and where inequalities correspond to the distribution of talents and, hence, are considered legitimate.

Differentiating systems face a dilemma: compartmentalization of actors into specialized roles also partitions them from each other, driving them apart and decreasing their common sentiments. In *The Division of Labor*, Durkheim recognized that differentiation is accompanied by the growing abstractness and generalization of cultural symbols, especially at the level of values and beliefs. Or, in terms of the specific variables he used to describe the collective conscience, there is less consensus ("volume"), less regulatory power ("intensity"), less clarity ("determinateness"), and less religious content in values and beliefs. Increasing generality of the collective conscience is essential if actors in specialized and secularized roles hold common values and beliefs. If values and beliefs are too specific, too rigid, too intense, and too sacred, they cannot be relevant to the diversity of actors' secular experiences and orientations in differentiated roles, nor can they allow the flexibility that comes with the division of labor in society. Hence, moral imperatives become more abstract and general. Durkheim thus saw a fundamental relationship between system differentiation and the generalization of cultural values and beliefs, as is summarized here:

3. The more differentiated a social system is, the more generalized are its values, beliefs, and other moral symbol systems.

The term *generalized* in this principle is used to summarize Durkheim's view of the collective conscience becoming less determinate, voluminous, and intense. In the dual processes of (1) generalization of evaluational symbols and (2) high levels of specialization in the division of labor, what force is to provide unity? In answering this question. Durkheim often asserted what he thought should occur. Yet, even with his moralistic bias, he saw certain fundamental integrative tendencies in differentiated systems. These can be summarized by a series of additional principles:

4. The greater is the level of structural differentiation and the more abstract and general are values and beliefs, the more norms emerge to specify evaluational premises and to regulate relations within and between social units.

Durkheim recognized that social integration in organic societies depends on the development among social units of functional interrelations regulated by "contract" and on the regularization of behaviors within social units through concrete norms. In reacting to Spencer and the utilitarians, Durkheim emphasized that there is always a "moral component" or "noncontractual" basis of contract and that norms are more than utilitarian and instrumental "conveniences." They are tied, or at least he hoped that they were, to general values and beliefs, giving actors a common set of premises and assumptions. Principle 5 extracts the essence of Durkheim's argument from its moralistic trappings and states that there is a fundamental relationship in the social world among structural differentiation, value generalization, and normative specification.

5. The greater is the level of structural differentiation and the more abstract and general are the values and beliefs, the more subgroups form around similar or related role activities sharing common interests.

Durkheim's discussion of occupational groups was, in many ways, an expression of his hopes and desires. At a more abstract level, however, he appears to have captured the essence of an important structural principle: as roles become differentiated and specialized and as common value premises generalize, clusters and networks of positions—or, in the terms of principle 4, subgroups—form among those engaged in similar activities. Such subgroup formation reinforces the process of normative specification delineated in principle 3.

In Durkheim's later work *The Elementary Forms of the Religious Life*, he emphasized the power of rituals directed toward symbols of groups as a key integrative mechanism. If we transpose this more micro view onto an analysis of the bases of integration in differentiated systems, then the following principle is suggested:

6. The greater is the level of structural differentiation and the more abstract and general are the values and beliefs, the more normative specification and subgroup formation depend on the enactment of rituals to sustain commitments to norms and subgroups.

From Rousseau, Durkheim appears to have absorbed the idea that the "state" could personify the "collective conscience" and coordinate activities in pursuit of collective goals and purposes. If we seek a more abstract principle to translate Durkheim's somewhat moralistic vision, it can be seen that in any system experiencing differentiation and value generalization, there are increased probabilities for not only normative specification (principle 4) and subgroup formation (principle 5) but also centralization of authority.

7. The greater is the level of structural differentiation and the more abstract and general are the values and beliefs, the more centers of power will coordinate diverse activities.

Durkheim also distrusted centralized authority that went unchecked by counter-authority, but if we are to be true to Durkheim's argument, this process must be stated as a general principle. Durkheim felt that subgroups in a differentiating system with centralized authority tend to become sources of power that check and balance the power of the central authority. Thus, we can formulate the following principle:

8. The more centralized is authority in a differentiated social system revealing subgroups, the more subgroups become centers of counter-authority, mitigating the power of centralized authority.

For Durkheim, as systems differentiate and "naturally" tend to form subgroups around specialized roles and functions as well as common interests (principle 5), these groups will resist the arbitrary use of power by the centralized authority, thereby creating a "balance of powers" in a system.

9. The greater is the level of structural differentiation and the more abstract and general are values and beliefs, the more the distribution of scarce resources will correspond to the unequal distribution of talents.

This is a highly questionable Durkheimian principle. What defines talent? Is it innate intelligence, training, or cunning? Why would those who have resources at one point in time not pass them on to designated others, creating an ascriptive system in which talent and rewards become poorly correlated. Despite these problems with the principle, however, resources in highly differentiated systems have a slight tendency to be distributed in accordance with the ability of actors to contribute to the system. This is not a strong tendency, however, and ascriptive processes weaken it. Thus, principle 10, more than principles 1 through 9, reflects Durkheim's hope for the future rather than a clear assessment of structural tendencies.

10. The greater is the level of structural differentiation and the more abstract and general are values and beliefs, the more sanctions against deviance will be restitutive rather than punitive.

Durkheim incorrectly overestimated the degree of punishment in mechanical (simple) social systems, and he underestimated the punitive sanctions in organic (complex) systems. Yet he might have been correct in his view that the ratio of restitutive to punitive sanctions increases with differentiation and value generalization. Because differentiated systems have less immediate value premises to offend and because they require coordination of parts, Durkheim might be correct in his view that there is a fundamental relationship in social systems among differentiation, value generalization, and restitutive sanctions.

Principles 3 through 10 summarize Durkheim's vision of the basis of integration in differentiating systems. These principles were developed by Durkheim for understanding whole societies, but I suspect that they apply to any differentiating social system, whether a group, organization, or community. Although these principles are not without ambiguities, we believe that they can still inform modern sociological theorizing and provide a promising place from which to begin further work.

Principles of Deviance. Durkheim's analysis of suicide is much more than a discussion of suicide rates; it is also an exploration into the structural and cultural sources of deviance in general. The basic issue in Durkheim's discussion of suicide is this question: What is the nature of individual integration into social systems? His answer is that there are two bases of individual integration: (1) regulation of individual desires and passions by values, beliefs, and norms and (2) attachment of individuals to collective units of organization. Regulation and attachment must be balanced so that there is not too much or too little of either. If the balance is disturbed, then suicide-prone individuals are likely to commit suicide, thereby raising the rate of suicide in society.

If we abstract away from suicide, which is only one type of deviance, we have a perspective for visualizing its general characteristics. Because anomie, or deregulation, and egoism, or detachment, are Durkheim's primary concern in relation to deviance in general, Durkheim saw deviance as intimately connected to the principles of differentiation already presented. He viewed increases in the rates of deviance as "normal" in differentiating systems, but under certain conditions, the rates increase to a point where a pathological condition prevails. If we ignore this distinction between normal and abnormal rates (for no objective criterion exists for determining what is normal and what is abnormal in social systems) and focus on his statements about the conditions increasing rates of deviance in general, then the following two principles are evident in Durkheim's work:

11. The greater is the level of structural differentiation and the more abstract and general are values and beliefs, without a corresponding degree of normative specification, the greater is the level of anomie and, hence, the higher are rates of deviance.

12. The greater is the level of structural differentiation and the more abstract and general are values and beliefs, without a corresponding increase in subgroup formation, the greater is the level of egoism and, hence, the higher are rates of deviance.

These two principles summarize Durkheim's view that deregulation of individual passions (anomie) and detachment of people from collective goals and purposes of groups (egoism) are related to basic processes of social differentiation. When the inevitable process of value generalization in differentiating systems is not accompanied by the processes denoted in principle 4 (normative specification), principle 5 (subgroup formation), and principle 6 (rituals), then anomie and egoism are likely. With either or both of these states, rates of deviance are likely to increase. Thus, Durkheim was arguing that a fundamental relationship exists in social systems among structural differentiation, value/belief generalization, normative specification, and subgroup formation, on the one hand, and rates of deviance, on the other. Such an insight was truly revolutionary for Durkheim's time, and it can still inform contemporary theorizing on deviation in social systems.

Principles of System Malintegration. Durkheim's view of social pathology represented a moral view of the world. Pathologies were simply defined as those processes that deviated from Durkheim's conception of "normal" for a given type of society. A scientific theory of the social should try to keep such moralistic evaluations out of the analysis. Yet much of Durkheim's view of the world concerns malintegration in social systems, and despite the moral connotation of his analysis, he presented a number of principles that might be useful to modern theory.

In many respects, Durkheim's statements on malintegration are the converse of Principles 3 through 10 on the conditions of integration, or they are extensions of those on deviance. In this view, malintegration of a social system can occur when

(a) anomie (deregulation) and egoism (detachment) are great, (b) coordination of functions is low, and (c) inequalities in the distribution of resources create tensions between those with and without resources.

13. The greater is the level of structural differentiation and the more abstract and general are values and beliefs, and the less is the degree of normative specification, the greater is the level of anomie and, hence, the less is the level of integration of individuals into society.

14. The greater is the level of structural differentiation and the more abstract and general are values and beliefs, and the less is the formation of subgroups, the greater is the level of egoism and, hence, the less is the level of integration of individuals into society.

15. The greater is the level of structural differentiation and the more abstract and general are values and beliefs, and the less is the degree of normative specification of relations among social units, the less is the coordination of units and, hence, the less integrated is a society.

16. The greater is the level of structural differentiation and the more abstract and general are values and beliefs, and the less centralized are systems of authority, then the less coordinated are social units and, hence, the less integrated is a society.

17. The greater is the level of structural differentiation, the more abstract and general are values and beliefs, and the more centralized are systems of authority, and the less effective is the countervailing power of subgroups, then the greater are the tensions between those with and those without power and, hence, the less integrated is a society.

18. The greater is the level of structural differentiation and the more abstract and general are values and beliefs, and the less is the correlation between distribution of scarce resources and talents, then the greater are tensions between those with and without resources and, hence, the less integrated is a society.

Principles 13 and 14 concern individual integration into the system; principles 15 and 16 deal with coordination among system units, whether individuals or corporate units; and principles 17 and 18 deal with the malintegrative impact of tensions between those with and those without scarce resources, including power. These last two principles are as close to Marx as Durkheim comes, for despite his acceptance of Rousseau's abhorrence of inherited inequalities, Durkheim was always more concerned with the dual issues of individual integration into the social system and coordination among differentiated system parts than he was with social inequality.

Yet principles 13 through 18 provide interesting theoretical leads about those forces that are involved in either the change or the breakdown of social systems. Of particular importance is the fact that these principles employ the same variables that are contained in the principles explaining social order and integration. Thus, the same variables explain order, disorder, and change in social systems. Principles 1 through 17 provide clear evidence that Durkheim took the task of sociological theorizing seriously.

Durkheim's sociology is consistently re-read because of the power in several of his theoretical principles. His ideas on population size, ecological concentration, and differentiation are not original; these ideas were developed in much more detail twenty years earlier by Herbert Spencer. The usefulness of Durkheim's theory thus resides in his analysis of the pathologies of highly differentiated structures and the mechanisms by which these pathologies are overcome. Again, the moralistic and functional statements are often difficult to disentangle, but we can at least see the strong points in his argument. First, Durkheim recognized that there is a fundamental relationship between differentiation and generalization of cultural symbols, especially values and beliefs. Second, as this generalization occurs, disintegrative pressures, or what he termed "pathological forms" of the division of labor, increase. These pressures mount along two interrelated fronts: (1) coordinating activities through power, mutual interdependence, norms, and confederations of differentiated units into subgroups and (2) specifying generalized evaluative symbols in the society-wide culture, with the more specific norms attached to subgroupings of individuals with common interests. Third, Durkheim understood the fundamental micro foundations of these more macro processes: rates of interaction and ritual performances directed toward the collective conscience. From these rituals, norms are generated, and commitments to these norms and the groups in which they are embedded are sustained.

Conclusions

Émile Durkheim is, along with Karl Marx and Max Weber, one of the "holy trinity" of sociology's early masters. He enjoys this high place in sociology's pantheon because he addressed issues that have long fascinated sociologists. Although he borrowed a great deal from Herbert Spencer in his early work, he nonetheless presented what is now termed an *ecological model,* emphasizing population growth, competition for resources, and differentiation—a model that is widely used in sociology today. More fundamentally, he isolated in *The Division of Labor in Society* some of the key mechanisms by which complex systems sustain integration: structural interdependence, abstract and general values and beliefs, more specific beliefs and norms to regulate relations within and between differentiated groups and organizations, and networks of subgroups forming larger coalitions and confederations with common interests. Moreover, his analysis of the pathologies that arise from the failure to achieve integration, such as anomie, produced some of sociology's most enduring ideas about integration and malintegration of societies.

Durkheim's later work, where questions of how individuals become integrated into society became increasingly important, has also had an enormous impact on sociology. The analysis in *Suicide,* emphasizing the individual's integration into social structures and culture, has been widely used in sociological studies of deviance, crime, and other social "pathologies." Perhaps more significant is Durkheim's recognition in his last major work, *The Elementary Forms of the Religious Life,* that rituals directed at symbolic representations of groups constitute the basis of integration at the micro level of social organization.

Finally, in his insistence on analyzing one set of social facts by another, Durkheim made a very strong case for sociology as a distinctive kind of enterprise. He was trying to make a place for sociology in the academic and broader intellectual worlds, and he argued for sociology in a way reminiscent of Comte's advocacy. Perhaps he argued too much, but he did gain an academic beachhead for sociology in France during the last decade of the nineteenth century.

Still, there are problems in Durkheim's approach. Functional reasoning almost always gets a theorist into trouble, and Durkheim is no exception. He often argued that, in seemingly mysterious ways, the need for social integration brought about the cultural and structural arrangements that would meet this need for integration. Arguing for a separate causal analysis (as distinct from a functional analysis) did not obviate this problem of seeing outcomes as the cause of these very outcomes. Such reasoning usually becomes rather circular, explaining very little.

Durkheim was at his best when making causal arguments, but even here, there are problems. First, he never gave Spencer much credit for presenting the key ideas on the causes on the division of labor some 20 years before his *The Division of Labor.* Second, he never really indicated the causal sequences by which new forms of integration are to be achieved with differentiation; he simply assumes that these forms will emerge, without specifying causality. As with Spencer, we can invoke a selection argument; that is, problems of integration generate selection pressures for new types of cultural symbols and social structures, but this too is vague.

More substantively, Durkheim ignored the importance of power and stratification in society. He assumed that the "forced division of labor" would simply go away, and he never addressed adequately the conflict potential in systems of stratification, assuming that this too would go away as new bases of integration were achieved. Like Marx before him, but in the opposite direction, Durkheim's ideological commitments to finding a new basis of integration led him to mistake what he wanted to occur for what would actually transpire in differentiated societies. Complex societies always reveal points of tension and conflict, but through Durkheim's rose-colored glasses, we would hardly know that this was the case.

Another substantive problem is Durkheim's overemphasis on cultural forces to the detriment of recognizing the importance of power and mutual interdependence as mechanisms of integration. Durkheim addressed these topics, to be sure, but one really does not get a sense of how power integrates complex societies or how markets and other mediators of interdependence operate. Rather, values, beliefs, and norms seem to do most of the integrative work, and although this point of emphasis has added a great deal to sociology's understanding of cultural processes, the more structural dimensions of integration are underemphasized—a rather remarkable conclusion given Durkheim's emphasis on studying "social facts."

Yet some of the most important models and principles in sociology today owe their origins to Durkheim's analysis. For all their problems, then, Durkheim's collective works continue to inspire sociology in the twenty-first century.

CHAPTER 8

George Herbert Mead

George Herbert Mead was a philosopher at the University of Chicago, but his most important ideas are sociological in nature. Indeed, Mead's famous course on social psychology, provided the theoretical framework for understanding micro-level processes of social interaction. The students taking this course were well aware of the importance of these lectures, and so after Mead's death in 1931, these lectures were assembled and published under the title of *Mind, Self, and Society*.[1] In fact, because Mead did not publish a great deal in his lifetime, his major works are to be found in the published lecture notes of his students, not only in social psychology but also from Mead's other, more philosophical courses. Mead's great breakthrough was to synthesize and integrate the works of other theorists in sociology and psychology into a unified theoretical framework for understanding the dynamics of action and interaction within ongoing organized social contexts. This synthesis is at the core of all interactionist theorizing. Let me begin a review of Mead's ideas by placing them within the broader philosophical context that guided his analysis in *Mind, Self, and Society*.

Mead's Broader Philosophy

Much of Mead's sociology is only a part of his broader philosophical view. This view was never fully articulated, nor was it well integrated, but two posthumous works, *Movements of Thought in the Nineteenth Century* and *The Philosophy of the Present*, provide a glimpse of his broader vision.

Many fascinating themes are contained in these works, but one of the most persistent is that all human activity represents an adjustment and adaptation to the social

---

[1]The philosophical tone of Mead's posthumously published lectures is revealed in the titles of the four books: *The Philosophy of the Present* (La Salle, IL: Open Court, 1959; originally published 1932), *Mind, Self, and Society* (Chicago, IL: University of Chicago Press, 1934), *Movements of Thought in the Nineteenth Century* (Chicago, IL: University of Chicago Press, 1936), and *The Philosophy of the Act* (Chicago, IL: University of Chicago Press, 1938). *Mind, Self, and Society*, 390–392, contains a bibliography of Mead's published work.

environment. In *Movements of Thought,* Mead traced the development of social thought from its early, pre-scientific phase to the contemporary, scientific stage. In a way reminiscent of Auguste Comte's law of the three stages (see Chapter 2), Mead saw the great ideas of history as moving toward an increasingly rational or scientific profile because, with the emergence of scientific thought, a better level of adaptation and adjustment to the world could be achieved.

The Philosophy of the Present contains a somewhat disjointed series of essays that represent a more philosophical treatment of the ideas contained in Mead's social psychology, particularly in *Mind, Self, and Society.* Here again, he emphasized that what was uniquely human is nothing but a series of particular behavioral capacities that have evolved from adaptations to the ongoing life process. Much of the discussion addresses purely philosophical topics about the ontological status of consciousnesses in the past, present, and future. But between the lines, he stressed that the capacities of humans for thought and self-reflection do not necessitate a dualism between mind and body because all the unique mental abilities of humans are behaviors directed toward facilitating their adjustment to the environment as it is encountered in the present.

Mind, Self, and Society

As noted above, Mead's *Mind, Self, and Society* consists of a compilation of verbatim transcripts from his famous course on social psychology at the University of Chicago. Although the notes come from the 1927 and 1930 versions of the course, the basic ideas on social interaction, personality, and social organization had been developed a decade earlier.

At the time Mead was addressing his students, he criticized behaviorists like J. B. Watson, who had once been his student, because they had abandoned the study of consciousness, which from a strict behaviorist perspective is not directly observable. Behaviorists like Watson and the late B. F. Skinner had simply abandoned any serious effort to understand consciousness, personality, and other variables in the "black box" of human cognition. Mead felt that such a "solution" to studying psychological processes was unacceptable.[2] He also felt that the opposite philosophical tendency to view "mind," "spirit," "will," and other psychological states as spiritual entities was untenable. What is required, he argued, is for mind and self, as the two most distinctive aspects of human personality, and for "society," as maintained by mind and self, to be viewed as part of *ongoing social processes.*

Mead's View of the "Life Process"

The Darwinian theory of evolution provided Mead with a view of life as a process of adaptation to environmental conditions. The attributes of a species, therefore, are the result of selection for those characteristics allowing for adaptation to

---

[2]As he observed with respect to Watson's efforts to deal with subjective experience, "John B. Watson's attitude was that of the Queen in *Alice in Wonderland*—Off with their heads!—there were no such things." Mead, *Mind, Self, and Society,* 2–3.

the conditions in which a species finds itself. This theory provided Mead with a general metaphor for analyzing human behavior and society. Pragmatism, as a philosophical doctrine developed in great detail by John Dewey, represents one way of translating the Darwinian metaphor into principles for understanding human behavior: humans are "pragmatic" creatures who use their faculties for achieving "adjustment" to the world; conversely, much of what is unique to any individual arises from making adjustments to the social world.

John Dewey's pragmatism, termed *instrumentalism,* stressed the importance of critical and rational thought in making life adjustments, and it gave Mead a view of thinking as the basic adjustment by which humans survive. Behaviorism, as a prominent psychological school of thought, converges with this element in pragmatism because it emphasizes that all animals tend to retain those responses to environmental stimuli that are rewarded or reinforced. Although behaviorists like Watson regarded the processes of thinking as too "psychical," the stress on the retention of reinforced behaviors was consistent with Darwinian notions of adaptation and survival as well as with pragmatist ideas of response and adjustment.

Mead even saw utilitarianism—especially that of thinkers such as Jeremy Bentham, who emphasized the pleasure and pain principles—as compatible with the theories of evolution, behaviorism, and pragmatism. The utilitarian emphasis on "utility," "pleasure," and "pain" was certainly compatible with behaviorist notions of reinforcement; the utilitarian concern with rational thought and the weighing of alternatives was compatible with Dewey's instrumentalism and its concept of critical thinking; and the utilitarian view that order emerges from competition among free individuals seemed to parallel Darwinian notions of struggle as the underlying principle of the biotic order.

Thus, the unique attributes of humans, such as their capacity to use language, their ability to view themselves as objects, and their facility to reason, must all be viewed as emerging from the life processes of adaptation and adjustment. Mind and self cannot be ignored, as behaviorists often sought to do, nor can they be seen as a kind of mystical and spiritual force that elevates humans out of the basic life processes influencing all species. Humans as a species evolved like other life forms, and, hence, their most distinctive attributes—mind, self, and society—must be viewed as emerging from the basic process of adaptation. Further, each individual member of the human species is like the individuals of other species: what they are is the result of the common biological heritage of their species as well as their adjustment to the particulars of a given environment.

Mead's Social Behaviorism

Mead did not define his work as *social* behaviorism, but subsequent commentators have used this term to distinguish his work from Watsonian behaviorism. In contrast with Watson, who simply denied the distinctiveness of subjective consciousness, Mead felt that it was possible to use broad behavioristic principles to understand "subjective behavior":

Watson apparently assumes that to deny the existence of mind or consciousness as a psychical stuff, substance, or entity is to deny its existence altogether, and that a naturalistic or behavioristic account of it as such is out of the question.

But, on the contrary, we may deny its existence as a psychical entity without denying its existence in some other sense at all; and if we then conceive of it functionally, and as a natural rather than a transcendental phenomenon, it becomes possible to deal with it in behavioristic terms.[3]

If subjective experiences in humans are viewed as behaviors, it is possible to understand them in behavioristic terms. The unique mental capacities of humans are a model of behavior that arises from the same reinforcement processes that explain directly observable behaviors. Of particular importance for understanding the attributes of humans, then, is the reinforcement that comes from adaptation and adjustment to environmental conditions. At some point in the distant past, the unique mental capacities of humans, and the creation of a society dependent upon these capacities, emerged by the process of natural selection under natural environmental conditions. Once the unique patterns of human organization are created, however, the "environment" for any individual is social; that is, it is an environment of other people to whom an individual must adapt and adjust.

Thus, social behaviorism stresses the processes by which individuals acquire a certain behavioral repertoire by virtue of their adjustments to ongoing patterns of social organization. Analysis must begin with the observable fact that organized activity occurs, and it must then attempt to understand the particular actions of individuals as they adjust to cooperative activity:

> We are not, in social psychology, building up the behavior of the social group in terms of the behavior of separate individuals composing it; rather, we are starting out with a given social whole of complex group activity, into which we analyze (as elements) the behavior of each of the separate individuals composing it. We attempt, that is, to explain the conduct of the individual in terms of the organized conduct of the social group, rather than to account for the organized conduct of the social group in terms of the conduct of the separate individuals belonging to it.[4]

The behavior of individuals—not just their observable actions but also their internal behaviors of thinking, assessing, and evaluating—must be analyzed within a social context. For what is distinctively human emerges from adjustment to ongoing social activity, or "society." Thus, Mead's social behaviorism must be distinguished from the behavioristic approach of Watson[5] in two ways. First, the existence of inner subjective experiences is not denied or viewed as methodologically irrelevant;[6] rather, these experiences are viewed as behavior. Second, the behaviors of humans, including those distinctly human behaviors that Mead called *mind* and *self*, arise from adaptation and adjustment to ongoing and organized social activity. Reinforcement is thus equated with the degree of adjustment and adaptation to society.

---

[3]Ibid., 10.

[4]Ibid., 7.

[5]And, of course, the more recent version of B. F. Skinner and others of this stripe.

[6]That is, because they cannot be directly observed, they cannot be studied.

Mead's Behavioristic View of Mind

For Mead, "mind" is a type of behavioral response that emerges from interaction with others in a social context. Without interaction, mind cannot exist:

> We must regard mind, then, arising and developing within the social process, within the empirical matrix of social interactions. We must, that is, get an inner individual experience from the standpoint of social acts which include the experiences of separate individuals in a social context wherein those individuals interact. The processes of experience which the human brain makes possible are made possible only for a group of interacting individuals: only for individual organisms which are members of a society; not for the organism in isolation from other individual organisms.[7]

Gestures and Mind. The social process in which mind emerges is one of communication with gestures. Mead gave the German psychologist Wilhelm Wundt credit for understanding the central significance of the gesture for communication and interaction. In contrast with Charles Darwin, who had viewed gestures as expressions of emotions, Wundt recognized gestures as that part of the ongoing behavior of one organism that stimulates the behavior of another organism.[8] Mead took this basic idea and extended it in ways that became the basis not only for the emergence of mind and self but also for the creation, maintenance, and change of society. Curiously, Mead also did not adopt Darwin's idea that gestures signal emotional states and that such states are also part of interaction and the maintenance of society. Indeed, Mead's lack of attention to emotions is the one glaring weakness in his theoretical scheme, and I suspect that this is what held back the sociology of emotions, which only began to emerge in the 1970s.

Mead formulated the concept of the "conversation of gestures" to describe the simplest form of interaction. One organism emits gestures that stimulate a response from a second organism. In turn, the second organism emits gestures that stimulate an "adjusted response" from the first organism. Then if interaction continues, the adjusted response of the first organism involves emitting gestures that result in yet another adjustment of behavior by the second organism, and so on, as long as the two organisms continue to interact. Mead frequently termed this conversation of gestures the *triadic matrix,* because it involves three interrelated elements:

1. Gestural emission by one organism as it acts on its environment

2. A response by another organism that becomes a gestural stimulus to the acting organism

3. An adjusted response by the acting organism that takes into account the gestural stimuli of the responding organism

---

[7]Mead, *Mind, Self, and Society,* 133.

[8]As Mead observed, "The term gesture may be identified with these beginnings of social acts which are stimuli for the response of other forms." *Mind, Self, and Society,* 43.

This triadic matrix constitutes the simplest form of communication and interaction among organisms. This form of interaction, Mead felt, typifies "lower animals" and human infants. For example, if one dog growls, indicating to another dog that it is about to attack, the other will react, perhaps by running away, requiring the growling dog to adjust its response by chasing the fleeing dog or turning elsewhere to vent its aggressive impulses. Or, to take another example, a hungry infant cries, which in turn arouses a response in its mother (e.g., the mother feeds the infant), which in turn results in an adjusted response by the infant.

Much of the significance of Mead's discussion of the triadic matrix is that the mentalistic concept of "meaning" is lodged in the interaction process rather than in the "ideas" or other mentalistic notions that might reside outside interaction. If a gesture "indicates to another organism the subsequent behavior of a given organism, then it has meaning."[9] Thus, if a dog growls and another dog uses this gesture to predict an attack, this gesture of growling has meaning. Meaning is thus given a behavioristic definition: it is a kind of behavior—a gesture—of one organism that signals to another, subsequent behavior of this organism. Meaning, therefore, need not involve complex cognitive activity. A dog that runs away from another growling dog, Mead would assert, is reacting without "ideas" or "elaborate deliberation"; yet the growl has meaning for the dog because it uses the growl as an early indicator of what will follow. Thus, *meaning* is

> not to be conceived, fundamentally, as a state of consciousness, or as a set of organized relations existing or subsisting mentally outside the field of experience into which they enter; on the contrary, it should be conceived objectively, as having its existence entirely within this field itself.[10]

The significance of the conversation of gestures for ongoing activity resides in the triadic matrix and associated meanings, allowing organisms to adjust their responses to one another. Thus, as organisms use one another's gestures as a means for adjusting their respective responses, they become increasingly capable of organized and concerted conduct. Yet such gestural conversations limit the capacity of organisms to organize themselves and to cooperate. Among humans, Mead asserted, a qualitatively different form of communication evolved. This is communication involving *significant symbols* that mean the same thing to all parties. He felt that the development of the capacity to use significant symbols distinguished humans from other species. *Mind* arises in a maturing human infant as the capacity to use significant symbols increases. In turn, as we will show, the existence of mind ensures the development of self and the perpetuation of society.

Significant Symbols and Mind. In "lower organisms," Mead felt, a gesture does not evoke the same response in the organism emitting the gesture and the one interpreting the gesture. As he observed, the roar of a lion does not mean the same thing to

---

[9]Ibid., 76.

[10]Ibid., 78.

the lion and to its potential victim. When organisms become capable of using gestures that evoke the same response in each other, then they are employing what he termed *significant,* or *conventional,* gestures. As he illustrated, if a person shouts "Fire!" in a movie theater, this gesture evokes the same response tendency (escape, fleeing, etc.) in the person emitting the gesture and in those receiving it. Such gestures, he felt, are unique to humans and make possible their capacities for mind, self, and society.[11]

Significant symbols are, as Mead emphasized, the basis for language. Of particular significance are vocal significant symbols because sounds can be readily heard by both sender and receiver, thus evoking a similar behavioral tendency. Other nonvocal gestures, however, are also significant in that they can come to mobilize similar tendencies to act. A frown, glare, clenched fist, rigid stance, and the like can all become significant because they serve as a stimulus to similar responses by senders and receivers. Thus, humans' capacity for language—that is, communication by significant symbols—allows the emergence of their unique capacities for mind and self. An infant of the species cannot have a mind until it acquires the rudimentary capacity for language.

In what ways, then, does language make mind possible? Mead borrowed Dewey's vision of "reflective" and "critical" thinking as well as the utilitarian's vision of "rational choice" in formulating his conceptualization of mind. For Mead, mind involves the behavioral capacities to

1. denote objects in the environment with significant symbols,

2. use these symbols as a stimulus to one's own response,

3. read and interpret the gestures of others and use these as a stimulus for one's response,

4. suspend temporarily or inhibit overt behavioral responses to one's own gestural denotations or those of others, and

5. engage in "imaginative rehearsal" of alternative lines of conduct, visualize their consequences, and select the response that will facilitate adjustment to the environment.

Mind is thus a behavior, not a substance or entity. It is a behavior that involves using significant symbols to stimulate responses but, at the same time, to inhibit or delay overt behavior so that potential responses can be covertly rehearsed and assessed. Mind is thus an "internal conversation of gestures" using significant symbols, because an individual with mind talks to himself or herself. The individual uses significant symbols to stimulate a line of response; the individual visualizes the consequences of this response; if necessary, the individual inhibits the response and uses another set of symbols to stimulate alternative responses; and the individual persists until he or she is satisfied with the response and then overtly pursues a given line of conduct.

---

[11]However, the evidence is now clear that other higher primates can use such "significant gestures."

This capacity for mind, Mead stressed, is not inborn; it depends on interaction with others and the acquisition of the ability to interpret and use their significant symbols (as well as biological maturation). As Mead noted, feral children, who are raised without significant symbols, do not seem "human" because they have not had to adjust to an environment mediated by significant symbols and, hence, have not acquired the behavioral capacities for mind.

Role-taking and Mind. Mind emerges in an individual because human infants, if they are to survive, must adjust and adapt to a social environment—that is, to a world of organized social activity. At first, an infant is like a "lower animal" in that it responds reflexively to the gestures of others and emits gestures that do not evoke similar responses in it and those in the environment. Such a level of adjustment, Mead implied, is neither efficient nor adaptive. A baby's cry does not indicate what it wants, whether food, water, warmth, or whatever, and by not reading accurately the vocal and other gestures emitted by others in their environment, the young can frequently create adjustment problems for themselves. Thus, in a metaphor that is both Darwinian and behavioristic, there is "selective pressure" for acquiring the ability to use and interpret significant gestures. Hence, those gestures that bring reinforcement—that is, adjustment to the environment—are likely to be retained in the response repertoire of the infant.

A critical process in using and interpreting significant gestures is what Mead termed "taking the role of the other," or *role-taking.* An ability to use significant symbols means that the gestures emitted by others in the environment allow a person to read or interpret the dispositions of these others. For example, an infant who has acquired the rudimentary ability to interpret significant symbols can use its mother's tone of voice, facial expressions, and words to imagine her feelings and potential actions—that is, to "take on" her role or perspective. Role-taking is critical to the emergence of mind, for unless the gestures of others, and the disposition to act that these gestures reveal, can become a part of the stimuli used to covertly rehearse alternative lines of conduct, overt behavior will often produce maladjustment to the environment. For without the ability to assume the perspective of others with whom one must deal, it is difficult to adjust to and coordinate responses with these others.

The Genesis of Mind. Mead saw mind as developing in a sequence of phases, as represented in Figure 8.1. Because an infant depends on others and, in turn, these others depend on society for their survival, mind develops from the forced dependency of an infant on society. Because society is held together by actors who use language and who can role-take, the infant must seek to meet its needs in a world mediated by symbols. Through conscious coaching by others and through simple trial and error, the infant comes to use significant symbols to denote objects relevant to satisfying its needs (such as food, mother, etc.). To consummate other impulses, the infant eventually must acquire greater capacities to use and understand language; once an infant can use language, it can begin to read the gestures of others and call out in itself the dispositions of others. Once a young child is able to role-take, it can soon begin to

Figure 8.1 Mead's Model of the Genesis of Mind

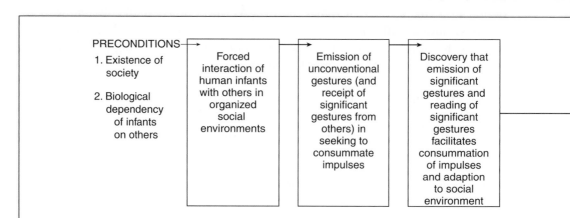

consciously think, reflect, and rehearse responses. In other words, it reveals the rudimentary behavioral abilities that Mead termed as *mind*.[12]

The causal arrows in Figure 8.1 actually represent a series of preconditions for the next stage of development. The model is "value-added" in that certain conditions must be met before subsequent events can occur. Underlying these conditions is Mead's implicit vision of "social selection," which represents his reconciliation of learning-theory principles with pragmatism and Darwinism. The abilities for language, role-taking, and mind are selected as the infant seeks to consummate impulses in society. If the infant is to adjust and adapt to society, it must acquire the ability for minded behavior. Thus, as the infant lives in a social environment, it must successively develop those behavioral capacities—first significant symbols, then role-taking, and eventually mind—that facilitate, to ever-increasing degrees, its adjustment to the social environment.

The model presented in Figure 8.1 underscores Mead's view that there is nothing mysterious or mystical about the human mind. It is a behavior acquired like other behavioral tendencies as a human organism attempts to adapt to its surroundings. Mind is a behavioral capacity acquired in stages, with each stage setting the conditions for the next. As mind emerges, so does self-awareness. In many respects, the emergence of mind is a precondition for the genesis of self. Yet the rudiments of self begin with an organism's ability to role-take, for the organism can then derive self-images or see itself as an object.

---

[12]For other published statements by Mead on the nature and operation of mind, see "Image and Sensation," *Journal of Philosophy* 1 (1904):604–607, "Social Consciousness and the Consciousness of Meaning," *Psychological Bulletin* 7 (1910):397–405, "The Mechanisms of Social Consciousness," *Journal of Philosophy* 9 (1912):401–406, "Scientific Method and Individual Thinker," in *Creative Intelligence* (New York: Holt, Rinehart and Winston, 1917), 176–227, and "A Behavioristic Account of the Significant Symbols," *Journal of Philosophy* 19 (1922):157–163.

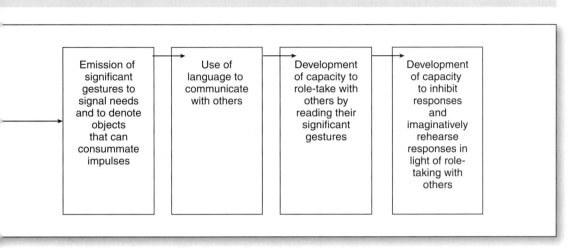

Mead's Behavioristic View of Self

The Social Nature of Self. As a "social behaviorist," Mead emphasized that the capacity to view oneself as an object in the field of experience is a type of learned behavior. This behavior is learned through interaction with others:

> The self is something which has a development; it is not initially there, at birth, but arises in the process of social experience and activity, that is, develops in the given individual as a result of his relations to that process as a whole and to other individuals within that process.[13]

Self emerges from the capacity to use language and to take the role of the other. Borrowing the essentials of Charles Horton Cooley's "looking-glass self,"[14] Mead viewed the social self as emerging from a process in which individuals read the gestures of others, or "take their attitudes," and derive an image, or picture, of themselves as a certain type of object in a situation. This image of oneself then acts as a behavioral stimulus, calling out certain responses in the individual. In turn, these responses of an individual cause further reactions by others, resulting in the emission of gestures that make possible role-taking by an individual, who then derives new self-images and new behavioral stimuli. Thus, like mind, self arises from the triadic matrix of people interacting and adjusting

---

[13]Mead, *Mind, Self, and Society,* 135.

[14]Mead did reject many of the specifics in Cooley's argument about "the looking-glass self." See, for example, *Mind, Self, and Society,* 173, "Cooley's Contribution to American Social Thought," *American Journal of Sociology* 35 (1929–1930):385–407, and "Smashing the Looking Glass," *Survey* 35 (1915–1916):349–361.

their responses to one another. The individual does not experience self directly, only through reading the gestures of others:

> The individual experiences himself, not directly, but only indirectly, from the particular standpoints of other individual members of the same social group, or from the generalized standpoint of the social group as a whole to which he belongs . . . and he becomes an object to himself only by taking the attitudes of other individuals toward himself within a social environment or context of experience and behavior in which both he and they are involved.[15]

The Structure of Self. Mead appeared to use the notion of "self" in two different ways. One usage involves viewing self as a "transitory image" of oneself as an object in a particular situation. Thus, as people interact, they role-take and derive self-images of themselves in that situation. Second, in contrast with this conceptualization, Mead also viewed self as a structure, or configuration of typical habitual meanings toward self, that people carry to all situations. For "after a self has arisen, it in a certain sense provides for itself its social experiences."[16]

These views are not, of course, contradictory. The process of deriving self-images in situations leads, over time, to the crystallization of a more permanent, trans-situational set of attitudes toward oneself as a certain type of object. Humans begin to interpret selectively the gestures of others in light of their attitudes toward themselves, and thus, their behaviors take on a consistency. For if the view of oneself as a certain type of object is relatively stable and if we use self like all other environmental objects as a stimulus for behavior, overt behavior will reveal a degree of consistency across social situations.

Mead sometimes termed this development of stable attitudes toward oneself as an object the *complete,* or *unified,* self. Yet he recognized that this complete self was not a rigid structure and that it was not imperviously and inflexibly imposed on diverse interactions. Rather, in different social contexts, various aspects of the complete self are more evident. Depending on one's audience, then, different "elementary selves" will be salient:

> The unity and structure of the complete self reflects the unity and structure of the social process as a whole; and each of the elementary selves of which it is composed reflects the unity and structure of one of the various aspects of that process in which the individual is implicated. In other words, the various elementary selves that constitute, or are organized into, a complete self are the various aspects of the structure of that complete self answering to the various aspects of the structure of the social process as a whole; the structure of the complete self is thus a reflection of the complete social process.[17]

---

[15]Mead, *Mind, Self, and Society,* 138.

[16]Ibid., 140.

[17]Ibid., 144.

In this passage, a further insight into the structure of self is evident: although elementary selves are unified by a complete self, people who experience a highly contradictory social environment with *dis*unity in the social process will also experience difficulty in developing a complete self, or a relatively stable and consistent set of attitudes toward themselves as a certain type of object. To some extent, then, people present different aspects of their more complete and unified selves to different audiences, but when these audiences demand radically contradictory actions, the development of a unified self-conception becomes problematic.

In sum, then, Mead's conceptualization is behavioristic in that he viewed seeing oneself as an object as a behavior unique to humans. Moreover, like other objects in one's environment, the self is a stimulus to behavior. Thus, as people develop a consistent view of themselves as a type of object—that is, as their self reveals a structure—their responses to this stable stimulus take on a consistency. Mead's conceptualization of the structure of self involves the recognition that the stability of self is largely a consequence of the unity and stability in the social processes from which the self arises.

Phases of the Self. Mead wanted to avoid connoting that the structure of self limited a person's repertoire of potential responses. Although a unified self-conception lends considerable stability and predictability to overt behaviors, there is always an element of spontaneity and unpredictability to action. This is inherent in the "phases of self," which Mead conceptualized in terms of the *I* and *me.*

The image that a person derives from his or her behavior in a situation is what Mead termed the "me." As such, the "me" represents the attitudes of others and the broader community as these influence an individual's retrospective interpretation of his or her behavior. For example, if we talk too loudly in a crowd of strangers, we see the startled looks of others and will become cognizant of general norms about voice levels and inflections when among strangers. These "me" images are received by reading the gestures of specific others in a situation and by role-taking, or assuming the attitude of the broader community. In contrast with the "me" is the "I," which is the actual emission of behavior. If a person speaks too loudly, this is "I," and when another person reacts to his or her loudness, the "me" phase of action is initiated. Mead emphasized that the "I" can only be known in experience because we must wait for "me" images to know just what the "I" did. People cannot know until after they have acted ("I") just how the expectations of others ("me") are actually carried out.

Mead's conceptualization of the "I" and "me" allowed him to conceptualize the self as a constant process of behavior and self-image. People act; they view themselves as objects; they assess the consequences of their actions; they interpret others' reactions to their actions; and they resolve how to act next. Then, they act again, calling forth new self-images of their actions. This conceptualization of the "I" and "me" phases of self enabled Mead to accomplish several conceptual tasks. First, he left room for spontaneity in human action; if the "I" can be known only in experience, or through the "me," one's actions are never completely circumscribed, nor are actions wholly predictable. Second, as we will explore in more detail later, it gave

Mead a way of visualizing the process of self-control. Humans are, in his view, cybernetic organisms who respond, receive feedback and make adjustment, and then respond again. In this way, he emphasized that self, like mind, is a process of adaptation; it is a behavior in which an organism successively responds to itself as an object as it adjusts to its environment. Third, the "I" and "me" phases of self gave Mead a way to conceptualize variations in the extent to which the expectations of others and the broader community constrain action. The *relative values* of the "I" and "me," as he phrased the matter,[18] are a positive function of people's status in a particular situation. The more involved they are in a group, the greater the values of "me" images and the greater the control of "I" impulses. Conversely, the less the involvement of a person in a situation, the less salient are "me" images and, hence, the greater is the variation in that person's overt behavior.

The Genesis of Self. Mead devoted considerable attention to the emergence of self and self-conceptions in humans. This attention allowed him to emphasize again that the self is a social product and emerges from the efforts of the human organism to adjust and adapt to its environment. Self arises from the same processes that lead to the development of "mind," while depending on the behavioral capacities of mind.

For self to develop, a human infant must acquire the capacity to use significant symbols. Without this ability, it is not possible to role-take with others and thereby develop an image of oneself by interpreting the gestures of others. Self also depends on mind because people must be able to designate themselves linguistically as an object in their field of experience and to organize responses toward themselves as an object. Thus, the use of significant symbols, the ability to role-take, and the behavioral capacities of mind are all preconditions for the development of self, particularly a more stable self-conception, or "unified" self.

Mead visualized self as developing in three stages, each marked by an increased capacity to role-take with a wider audience of others. The first stage is *play,* which is marked by a very limited capacity to role-take. A child can assume the perspective of only one or two others at a time, and play frequently involves little more than discourse and interaction with "imaginary companions" to whom the child talks in enacting a particular role. Thus, a child who plays "mother" can also, at the same time, assume the role of "baby," and the child might move back and forth between the roles of mother and infant. The play stage is thus typified by the ability to assume the perspective of only a few others at a time.

With biological maturation and with practice at assuming the perspectives of others, a child eventually acquires the capacity to take the role of multiple others engaged in ongoing and organized activity. The second stage is what Mead termed the *game,* in which individuals can role-take with multiple others at the same time. Perhaps the most prototypical form of such role-taking is to be a participant in a game, such as baseball, where the child must assume the role of other players, anticipate how they will act, and coordinate responses with other people's likely courses of actions. Thus, children begin to see themselves as objects in an organized field, and they begin to control and regulate other people's responses to themselves

---

[18]Ibid., 199.

and to others in order to facilitate the coordination of activity. During this stage in the development of self, the number and variety of such game situations expand:

> There are all sorts of social organizations, some of which are fairly lasting, some temporary, into which the child is entering, and he is playing a sort of social game in them. It is a period in which he likes "to belong," and he gets into organizations which come into existence and pass out of existence. He becomes something which can function in the organized whole, and thus tends to determine himself in his relationship with the group to which he belongs.[19]

In both the play and game situations, individuals view themselves in relation to specific others. By role-taking with specific others lodged in particular roles, individuals derive images of themselves from the viewpoint of these others. Yet the self, Mead contended, is incomplete until a third stage is realized: role-taking with *the generalized other*. He saw the generalized other as a "community of attitudes" among members of an ongoing social collective. When individuals can view themselves in relation to this community of attitudes and then adjust their conduct in accordance with the expectations of these attitudes, they have reached the third stage in the development of self. They can now role-take with the generalized other. For Mead, the play and game represent the initial stages in the development of self, but in the final stage, individuals can generalize the varied attitudes of others and see themselves and regulate their actions from a broader perspective.

Without this capacity to view oneself as an object in relation to the generalized other, behavior could only be situation-specific. Unless people can see themselves as objects implicated in a broader social process, their actions cannot reveal continuity across situations. Moreover, humans could not create larger societies, composed of multiple groupings, without the members of the society viewing themselves, and controlling their responses, in accordance with the expectations of the generalized other.[20]

Mead recognized that in complex social systems there could be multiple generalized others. Individuals can view themselves and control their behaviors from a variety of broader perspectives. Moreover, a generalized other can represent the embodiment of the collective attitudes of concrete and functioning groups, or it can be more abstract, pertaining to broad social classes and categories:

> In the most highly developed, organized, and complicated human social communities..., [the] various socially functional classes or subgroups of individuals to which any given individual belongs ... are of two kinds. Some of them are concrete social classes or subgroups, such as political parties, clubs, corporations, which are

---

[19]Ibid., 160.

[20]The similarity between Durkheim's notion of the collective conscience and Mead's conception of the generalized other should be immediately apparent. But in contrast with Durkheim, Mead provided the mechanism—role-taking and self-related behaviors—by which individuals become capable of viewing and controlling their actions in the perspective of the collectivity. For more details along this line, see Jonathan H. Turner, "A Note on G. H. Mead's Behavioristic Theory of Social Structure," *Journal for the Theory of Social Behavior* 12 (July 1982):213–222 and *A Theory of Social Interaction* (Stanford, CA: Stanford University Press, 1988), chap. 10.

all actually functional social units, in terms of which their individual members are directly related to one another. The others are abstract social classes or subgroups, such as the class of debtors and the class of creditors, in terms of which their individual members are related to one another only more or less indirectly, and which only more or less indirectly function as social units, but which afford or represent unlimited possibilities for the widening and ramifying and enriching of the social relations among all the individual members of the given society as an organized and unified whole.[21]

The capacity to take the role of multiple and diverse generalized others—from the perspective of a small group to that of an entire society—enables individuals to engage in the processes of self-evaluation, self-criticisms, and self-control from the perspective of what Mead termed *society*. Thus, by virtue of self-images derived from role-taking with specific others in concrete groups as well as from role-taking with generalized others personifying varying communities of attitudes, people come to see themselves as a particular type of object, with certain strengths, weaknesses, and other attributes.

Moreover, people become capable of regulating their responses to sustain this vision of themselves as a certain type of object. As people come to see themselves, and consistently respond to themselves, through their particular configuration of specific and generalized attitudes of others, they come to possess what Mead termed a *complete* and *unified* self.

Figure 8.2 attempts to summarize the dynamic processes involved in creating a self. Mead used the concept of "self" in several interrelated ways. Thus, for purposes of interpreting the model portrayed in Figure 8.2, let us recapitulate his various notions about self. First, he saw the development of self as a process of role-taking with increasingly varied and generalized others. This facet of self is represented across the top of Figure 8.2, because increasing acuity at role-taking influences the other aspects of self (this is emphasized by the vertical arrows connecting the boxes at each stage in the emergence of self). Second, as shown in the middle row of Figure 8.2, Mead visualized self as a process of self-control. As he emphasized in his notion of the "I" and "me" phases of self and in his view of "mind," this facet of self involves the growing ability to read the gestures of others, to inhibit inappropriate responses in relation to these others, and to adjust responses in a way that will facilitate interaction. In its more advanced stages, self-control also includes the capacity to assume the "general" perspective, or "community of attitudes," of specific groups and, eventually, of the broader community. The process of self-control thus represents the extensions of the capacities for mind, and for this reason, the precondition for self—that is, the "incipient capacities for mind" at the left of the model—is seen to tie almost directly into the self-control aspect of self. Third, as shown along the bottom row in Figure 8.2, Mead also saw self as involving the emergence of a self-conception, or a stable disposition to act toward oneself as a certain type of object. Such a stable self-conception evolves out of the accumulation of self-images and self-evaluations with reference to specific and then increasingly generalized others.

---

[21]Mead, *Mind, Self, and Society,* 157.

Figure 8.2 Mead's Model of the Genesis of Self

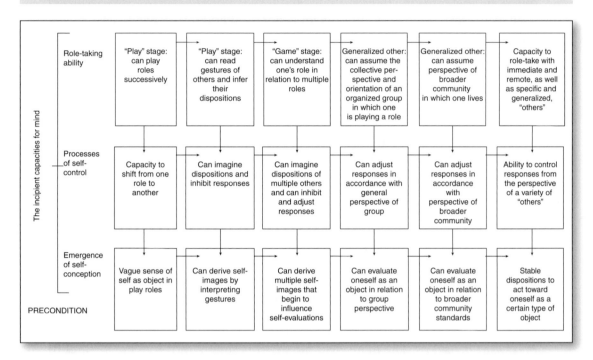

Thus, in reading Mead's model, the arrows that move from left to right denote the development of each aspect of self. The arrows that move down the columns stress his emphasis on the role-taking process and on how developments in the ability to role-take influence the etiology of self-control processes and self-conceptions. Of course, we might also draw arrows back up the columns because to some extent, self-control processes and self-conceptions influence role-taking abilities. But I feel that the arrows as currently drawn best capture Mead's vision of causal processes in the initial emergence of those multiple behavioral capacities that he subsumed under the label *self*. These capacities are, in turn, vital to the production and reproduction of society.

Mead's Conception of Society

The Behavioral Basis of Society. Mead labeled as *mind* those behavioral capacities in organisms that allow the use of symbols to denote objects and to role-take, to use objects as stimuli for various behaviors, to inhibit responses, to imaginatively rehearse alternative responses, and to select a line of conduct. Thus, mind allows cooperation among individuals as they attempt to select behaviors that will facilitate cooperation. *Self* is the term Mead used to describe the behavioral capacity to see oneself as an object in the environment and to use a stable conception of oneself as a certain type of object as a major stimulus for organizing behavior. The capacity for mind and self arises from, and continues to depend on, the process of role-taking because one's view of oneself as an object and one's capacity to select among alternative behaviors are possible through reading the gestures of others and determining their attitudes and dispositions.

In many ways, mind is the capacity for denoting alternatives, whereas self involves the capacity for ordering choices in a consistent framework. An organism with only mind could visualize alternatives but could not readily select among them. The capacity for self allows the selection of behaviors among alternatives. In doing so, self provides a source of stability and consistency in a person's behavior, while integrating that behavior into the social fabric or society.

Mead saw several ways in which self provides for the integration of behavior into society. First, the capacity to see oneself as an object in a field of objects allows individuals to see themselves in relation to other individuals. They can see their place in the field of perception and, hence, adjust their responses (through the capacity for mind) to coordinate their activities.

Second, the emergence of a unified and complete self, or stable self-conception, means that individuals consistently place into their perceptual field a view of themselves as a certain *type* of object. This ability makes behaviors of individuals more consistent and predictable because people generally seek to affirm their conceptions of themselves. People's behavior across widely divergent situations thus reveals consistency because they interject, to some degree, a stable self-conception of themselves as a certain type of individual who is deserving of certain responses from others. This object, as much as any of the objects peculiar to a situation, serves as a stimulus in organizing behaviors. The more rigid the self-conception, the more the gestures of others are selectively interpreted and used to organize responses consistent with one's self-conception. The consequence for society of these self-related processes is that as people's actions take on consistency from situation to situation or from time to time in the same situation, their behaviors become predictable, thereby making it easier for individuals to adjust to and cooperate with one another.

Third, the process of role-taking allows individuals to see themselves not only in relation to specific others in particular situations but also in relation to varieties of generalized others. Thus, if a person's actions are assessed by reference to the same generalized others, behaviors will take on consistency from situation to situation and across time. Moreover, to the degree that all participants to an interaction role-take with the same generalized other, they will approach and perceive situations within "common meanings" and they will be prepared to act in terms of the same perspective. By viewing themselves as objects relative to the same set of expectations, people approach situations with common understandings that will facilitate their adjustment to one another.

A fourth—and related—point is that the capacity to role-take with varieties of generalized others allows individuals to elaborate patterns of social organization. Individuals are now liberated from the need for face-to-face interaction as the basis for coordinating their activities. Once they can role-take with varieties of generalized others, some of whom are abstract conceptions, they can guide their conduct from a common perspective without directly role-taking with one another. Thus, the capacity to view oneself as an object and to adjust responses in relation to the perspective of an abstract generalized other greatly extends the potential scope of patterns of social organization.

Fifth, in addition to providing behavioral consistency and individual integration into extended networks of interaction, self also serves as a vehicle of social change. The phases of self—the "I" and "me," as Mead termed them—ensure that individual behaviors will, to some degree, alter the flow of the social process. Even if "me" images reflect perfectly the expectations in a situation, and even if one's view of oneself as a certain type of object is totally congruent with these expectations, actual behavior—that is, the "I"—can deviate from what is anticipated in "me" images. This deviation, however small or great, forces others in the situation to adjust their behaviors, providing new "me" images to guide subsequent behaviors ("I")—and so on, in the course of interaction that moves in and out of the "I" and "me" phases. Of course, when expectations are not clear and when one's self-conception is at odds with the expectations of others, "I" behaviors are likely to be less predictable, requiring greater adjustments by others. Or when the capacity to develop "me" images dictates changes in a situation for an individual—and this is often the case among individuals whose self-conception or generalized others are at odds—even greater behavioral variance and social change can be expected as the "I" phase of action occurs. Thus, the inherent phases of self—the "I" and "me"—make inevitable change in patterns of interaction. Sometimes these changes are small and imperceptible, and only after the long accumulation of small adjustments is the change noticeable.[22] At other times, the change is great, as when a person in political power initiates a new course of activity. In either case, as Mead went to great lengths to emphasize, self not only provides a source of continuity and integration for human behavior, but it also is a source of change in society.[23]

What emerges from Mead's view of society is not a vision of social structure and the emergent properties of these structures. Rather, he reaffirmed that patterns of social organization, whatever their form and profile, are mediated by human behavioral capacities for language, role-taking, mind, and self. Apart from a general view stressed by all thinkers of his time, that societies are becoming more differentiated and complex, he offered only a few clues about the properties of social structures in human societies. Mead's analysis of society, therefore, is actually a series of statements on the underlying behavioral processes that make coordination among individuals possible.

The Process of Society. For Mead, the term *society* is simply a way of denoting that interactive processes can reveal stability and that humans act within a framework imposed by stabilized social relations. The key to understanding society lies in the use of language and the practice of role-taking by individuals with mind and self. By means of the capacity to use and read significant gestures, individuals can role-take and use their mind and self to articulate their actions to specific others in a situation and to a variety of generalized others. Because generalized others embody the broader groups—organizations,

---

[22]Ibid., 180, 202, and 216, for the relevant statements.

[23]For Mead's explicitly published works on self, see "The Social Self," *Journal of Philosophy* 10 (1913):374–380, "The Genesis of the Self and Social Control," *International Journal of Ethics* 35 (1924–1925):251–277, and "Cooley's Contribution."

institutions, and communities—that mark the structure of society, they provide a common frame of reference for individuals to use in adjusting their conduct.

Society is thus maintained by virtue of humans' ability to role-take and to assume the perspective of generalized others. Mead implicitly argued that society as presented to any given individual represents a series of perspectives, or "attitudes," which the individual assumes in regulating behavior. Some attitudes are those of others in one's immediate field; other perspectives are those of less immediate groups; still other attitudes come from more remote social collectives; additional perspectives come from the abstract categories used as a frame of reference; and ultimately, the entire population using a common set of symbols and meanings constitutes the most remote generalized other. Thus, at any given time an individual is role-taking with some combination of specific and generalized others. The attitudes embodied by these others are then used in the processes of mind and self to construct lines of conduct.

Mead believed, then, that the structure and dynamics of society concern those variables that influence the number, salience, scope, and proximity of generalized others. Thus, by implication, Mead argued that to the degree individuals could accurately take the role of one another and assume the perspective of common generalized other(s), patterns of interaction would be stable and cooperative. Conversely, to the degree that role-taking is inaccurate and occurs relative to divergent generalized other(s), interaction will be disrupted and will perhaps be conflictual.[24]

From this perspective, the theoretical key to explaining patterns of social organization involves isolating those variables that influence (a) the accuracy of role-taking and (b) the convergence of generalized others. What might some of these variables be? Mead did not discuss them in detail because he was not interested in building formal sociological theory. Rather, his concerns were more philosophical, and hence he stressed recognizing the general nature of the processes underlying the maintenance of the social order. In a number of places, however, he offered some clues about what variables influence the capacity of actors to role-take with the same generalized other.

One barrier to role-taking with the same generalized other is social differentiation.[25] In complex societies, people play different roles, and often, the immediate generalized others for these roles will vary. This is, of course, a somewhat different way of stating Auguste Comte's and Émile Durkheim's concerns about the malintegrative effects of differentiation. Mead recognized that when individuals' immediate generalized others vary, it is possible to have a more general or abstract generalized other with which they can mutually role-take. As a result, despite their differences, people can role-take with a common perspective and use it to guide their conduct. Durkheim's similar conceptualization emphasized the "enfeeblement" or abstractness of the collective conscience (or culture) and the resulting anomie and egoism.

Mead's view, however, offers the recognition that although the community of attitudes of two individuals' immediate groups might diverge somewhat, they

---

[24]Mead, *Mind, Self, and Society,* 321–322.

[25]Ibid., 321–322.

can at the same time assume the perspective of a more remote, or abstract, generalized other and use this community of attitudes as a common perspective for guiding their conduct. Unlike Durkheim, who saw structural units like "occupational groups" as necessary mediators between the "collective conscience" and the individual, Mead's formulation of mind and self implicitly argues that through the capacity to role-take with multiple and remote others, diversely located individuals can become integrated into a common social fabric. Thus, structural differentiation will tend, Mead appears to have argued, to force role-taking with more remote and abstract generalized others. Thus, the dimensions of a society can be greatly extended because people's interactions are mediated and regulated by reference to a common community of attitudes rather than by face-to-face interaction.

Also related to differentiation—indeed, it is a type of differentiation—is stratification.[26] Class barriers increase the likelihood that individuals in different classes will not share the same community of attitudes. To the degree that a system of hierarchical differentiation is to be integrated, role-taking with a more distant generalized other will supplement the community of attitudes peculiar to a particular social class.

Another aspect of differentiation is population.[27] As populations increase in size, it becomes increasingly likely that any two individuals will role-take with somewhat different perspectives in their interaction with specific others in their immediate groups. If a large population is to remain integrated, Mead argued, individuals will supplement their immediate communities of attitudes by role-taking with more abstract generalized others. Hence, as the size of interaction networks increases, these networks will be integrated by role-taking with an increasingly abstract perspective or community of attitudes.

In sum, then, Mead's view of society is dominated by a concern with the social psychological mechanisms by which social structures are integrated. For Mead, *society* is just a term for the processes of role-taking with varieties of specific and generalized others and the consequent coordination of action made possible by the behavioral capacities of mind and self. By emphasizing the processes underlying social structures, Mead presented a highly dynamic view of society. Not only is society created by role-taking, it can be changed by these same processes. Thus, as diverse individuals come into contact, role-take, and adjust their responses, they create a community of attitudes, which they then use to regulate their subsequent actions. As more actors are implicated, or as their roles become more differentiated, they generate additional perspectives to guide their actions. Similarly, because actors possess unique self-conceptions and because they role-take with potentially diverse perspectives, they often must restructure existing patterns as they come to adjust to one another.

Thus, we get little feeling in Mead's work for the majesty of social structure. His conceptualization can perhaps be seen as a demystification of society because society

---

[26]Ibid., 327.

[27]Ibid., 326.

is nothing more than a process of role-taking by individuals who possess mind and self and who seek to make adjustments to one another. We should note, however, that Mead did offer some partial views of social morphology—that is, of the structural forms created by role-taking. We now briefly examine these more morphological or structural conceptualizations of society.

The Morphology of Society. Mead frequently used terms that carry structural connotations, with notions of *group, community, institution,* and *society* being the most common. To some degree, he used these terms interchangeably to denote regularity in the patterns of interaction among individuals. Yet at times he appears to have had an image of the basic structural units that compose a total society.

Mead used the term *society* in two senses: (1) society simply refers to ongoing, organized activity and (2) society pertains to geopolitical units, such as nation-states. The former usage is the most frequent, and thus, I will retain the view that *society* is the term for ongoing and organized activity among pluralities of actors, whether this activity is that of a small group or of a total society.

Mead's use of *community* was ambiguous, and he often appeared to equate it with society. His most general usage referred to a plurality of actors who share a common set of significant symbols, who perceive that they constitute a distinguishable entity, and who share a common generalized other, or community of attitudes. As such, a community can be quite small or large, depending on whether people perceive that they constitute an entity or not. Mead typically employed the concept of community to denote large pluralities of actors, and thus other structural units were seen to operate within communities.

Within every community, there are certain general ways in which people are supposed to act. These are what Mead defined as *institutions:*

> There are, then, whole series of such common responses in the community in which we live, and such responses are what we term "institutions." The institution represents a common response on the part of all members of the community to a particular situation.[28]

Institutions, Mead argued, are related, and thus, when people act in one institutional context, they implicitly invoke responses to others. As Mead emphasized,

> Institutions . . . present in a certain sense the life-habits of the community as such; and when an individual acts toward others in, say, economic terms, he is calling out not simply a single response but a whole group of related responses.[29]

Institutions represent only general lines of response to varying life situations, whether economic, political, familial, religious, or educational. People take the role of the generalized other for each institution, and because institutions are interrelated, they tend to call out appropriate responses for other institutions. In this way,

---

[28]Ibid., 261.

[29]Ibid., 264.

people can move readily from situation to situation within a broader community, calling out appropriate responses and inhibiting inappropriate ones. One moves smoothly, for example, from economic to familial situations because responses for both are evoked in the individual during role-taking with one or the other.

Mead recognized that institutions, and the attendant generalized other, provide only a broad framework guiding people's actions. People belong to a wide variety of smaller units that Mead tended to call *groups*. Economic activity, for example, is conducted by different individuals in varying economic groups. Familial actions occur within family groups, and so on for all institutional activity. Groups reveal their own generalized others, which are both unique and yet consistent within the community of attitudes of social institutions or of the broader community. Groups can vary enormously in size, differentiation, longevity, and restrictiveness, but Mead's general point is that the activity of individuals involves simultaneous role-taking with the generalized other in groups, clusters of interrelated institutions, and broad-community perspectives.

The Culture of Society. Mead never used the concept of *culture* in the modern sense of the term. Yet his view of social organization as mediated by generalized others is consistent with the view that culture is a system of symbols by which human thought, perception, and action are mobilized and regulated. As with social structure or morphology, however, Mead was not interested in analyzing in detail the varieties of symbol systems humans create and use to organize their affairs. Rather, he was primarily concerned with the more general insight that humans use significant symbols, or language, to create communities of attitudes. And by virtue of their capacity for role-taking, humans regulate their conduct not only in relation to the attitudes of specific others but also relative to generalized others who embody these communities of attitudes.

The concept of the *generalized other* is Mead's term for what would now be seen as those symbol systems of a broader cultural system that regulate perception, thought, and action. His generalized other is thus composed of norms, values, beliefs, and other regulatory systems of symbols. He never made careful distinctions, for example, among values, beliefs, and norms, for he was interested only in isolating the basic processes of society: individuals with mind and self role-take with varieties of generalized others to regulate their conduct and, thus, to coordinate their actions.

Mead's conception of society, therefore, emphasizes the basic nature of the processes underlying ongoing social activity. He was not concerned to any great degree with the details of social structure or the components of culture. His great insight was that regardless of the specific structure of society, the processes by which society is created, maintained, and changed are the same. Social organization is the result of the behavioral capacities for mind and self as these allow actors to role-take with varieties of others and, thus, to regulate and coordinate their actions. This insight into the fundamental relationship between the individual and society marks Mead's great contribution in *Mind, Self, and Society*.[30]

---

[30]See, in particular, Weber's and Durkheim's analyses to appreciate how crudely the interactive basis of social structure had been conceptualized before Mead's synthesis.

The Philosophy of the Act

Mead left numerous unpublished papers, many of which were published posthumously in *The Philosophy of the Act*.[31] Much of this work is not of great interest to sociologists; in the first essay, on which the editors imposed the unfortunate title "Stages of the Act," Mead offered new insights that cannot be found in his other essays or his lectures. In this piece, he presented a theory of human motivation that should be viewed as supplemental to his conceptualization of mind, self, and society.

Mead did not present his argument as the concept of *motivation,* but his intent was to understand why and how human action is initiated and given direction. For Mead, the most basic unit of behavior is "the act," and much of *The Philosophy of the Act* concerns understanding the nature of this fundamental unit. The behavior of an individual is ultimately nothing more than a series of acts, sometimes enacted singularly but more often emitted simultaneously. Thus, if we are to gain insight into the nature of human behavior, we must comprehend the constituent components of behavior—that is, "acts."

In his analysis of the act, Mead retained his basic assumptions. Acts are part of a larger life process of organisms adjusting to the environmental conditions in which they find themselves. Moreover, human acts are unique because of people's capacities for mind and self. Thus, Mead's theory of motivation revolves around understanding how the behavior of organisms with mind and self operating within society is initiated and directed. He visualized the act as composed of four "stages," although he emphasized that humans could simultaneously be involved in different stages of different acts. He also recognized that acts vary in length, degree of overlap, consistency, intensity, and other variable states, but in his analysis of the stages of the act, he was more interested in isolating the basic nature of the act than in developing propositions about its variable properties.

Mead saw acts as consisting of four stages: (1) impulse, (2) perception, (3) manipulation, and (4) consummation.[32] These are not entirely discrete, for they often blend into one another, but they constitute distinctive phases involving somewhat different behavioral capacities. Our discussion will focus on each stage separately, but I must emphasize that Mead did not view the stages of a given act as separable or as isolated from the stages of other acts.

Impulse

For Mead, an *impulse* represents a state of disequilibrium, or tension, between an organism and its environment. Although he was not concerned with the

---

[31]Mead, *Philosophy of the Act.*

[32]For an excellent secondary discussion of Mead's stages of the act, see Tamotsu Shibutani, "A Cybernetic Approach to Motivation," in *Modern Systems Research for the Behavioral Scientist,* ed. Walter Buckley (Hawthorne, NY: Aldine, 1968) and *Society and Personality: An Interactionist Approach to Social Psychology* (Englewood Cliffs, NJ: Prentice-Hall, 1961), 63–93.

varying states of impulses—that is, their direction, type, and intensity—he did offer two implicit propositions:

1. The greater the degree of disequilibrium between an organism and its environment, the stronger is the impulse and the more likely is behavior to reflect this.

2. The longer an impulse persists, the more it will direct behavior until it is consummated.

The source of disequilibrium for an organism can vary. Some impulses come from organic needs that are unfulfilled, whereas others come from interpersonal maladjustments.[33] Still other impulses stem from self-inflicted reflections, and many are a combination of organic, interpersonal, and intrapsychic sources of tension. The key point is that impulses initiate efforts at their consummation, while giving the behavior of an organism a general direction. Mead was quick to point out, however, that a state of disequilibrium could be eliminated in many different ways and that the conditions of the environment determined the specific direction of behavior. For Mead, humans are not pushed and pulled around by impulses. On the contrary, an impulse is defined as the degree of harmony with the environment, and the manner in which an organism is prepared to adjust to its environment influences the precise ways an impulse is consummated.

For example, even seemingly organic drives such as hunger and thirst are seen as arising from behavioral adaptations to the environment. Hunger is often defined by cultural standards for when meals are to be eaten, and it arises when the organism has not secured food from the environment. The individual's social world greatly constrains the way in which this disequilibrium will be eliminated. As environmental forces impinge on actors with mind and self, they will shape the types of foods considered edible, the way they are eaten, and when they can be eaten. Thus, for Mead, an impulse initiates behavior and gives it only a general direction. The next stage of the act—perception—will determine what aspects of the environment are relevant for eliminating the impulse.

Perception

What humans see in their environment, Mead argued, is highly selective. One basis for selective perception is the impulse: people become attuned to those objects in their environment perceived to be relevant to the elimination of an impulse. Even here, past socialization, self-conceptions, and expectations from specific and generalized others all constrain what objects are seen as relevant to eliminating a given impulse. For example, a hungry person in India will not see a cow as a relevant object of food but rather will become sensitized to other potential food objects.

---

[33]For Mead's conceptualization of biologic needs, see the supplementary essays in *Mind, Self, and Society,* particularly Essay 2.

The process of *perception* thus sensitizes an individual to certain objects in the environment. These objects become stimuli for repertoires of behavioral responses. Thus, as individuals become sensitized to certain objects, they are prepared to behave in certain ways toward those objects. Mead believed, then, that perception is simply the arousal of potential responses to stimuli; that is, as the organism becomes aware of relevant objects, it also is prepared to act in certain ways. Humans thus approach objects with a series of hypotheses, or notions, about how certain responses toward objects can eliminate their state of disequilibrium.

Manipulation

The testing of these hypotheses—that is, the emission of behaviors toward objects—is termed *manipulation.* Because humans have mind and self, they can engage in covert as well as overt manipulation. A human can often covertly imagine the consequences of action toward objects for eliminating an impulse. Hence, humans frequently manipulate their world mentally, and only after imagining the consequences of various actions do they emit an overt line of behavior. At other times, humans manipulate their environment without deliberate or delayed thinking; they simply emit a behavior perceived as likely to eliminate an impulse.

What determines whether manipulation will be covert before it is overt? The key condition is what Mead saw as *blockage,* a condition where the consummation of an impulse is inhibited or delayed. Blockage produces imagery and initiates the process of thinking. For example, breaking a pencil while writing (creating an impulse or disequilibrium with the environment) leads to efforts at manipulation. One actor may immediately perceive a pile of sharpened pencils next to the writing pad, pick up a new pencil, and continue writing without a moment's reflection. Another writer, who had not prepared a stack of pencils, might initially become attuned to the drawer of the desk, open it, and generally start searching "blindly" for a pencil. At some point, frequently after a person has "wandered around unconsciously" for a while, the blockage of the impulse begins to generate conscious imagery, and a person's manipulations become covert. Images of where one last left a pencil are now consciously evoked, or the probable location of a pencil sharpener is anticipated. Thus, when the impulse, perception, and overt manipulation stages of the act do not lead to consummation, thinking occurs, and manipulation becomes covert, using the behavioral capacities of mind and self.

Thinking can also be initiated earlier in the act. For example, if perception does not yield a field of relevant objects, blockage occurs at this stage, with the result that by virtue of the capacities for mind, an actor immediately begins covert thinking. Thus, because thinking is a behavioral adaptation of an organism experiencing disequilibrium with its environment and unable to perceive objects or manipulate behaviors in ways leading to consummation of an impulse.

In the process of thinking, then, an actor comes to perceive relevant objects; the actor might even role-take with the object if it is another individual or a group; a self-image may be derived, and one may see self as yet another object; and then various lines of conduct are imaginatively rehearsed until a proper line of conduct is selected and emitted. Of course, if the selected behavior does not eliminate the impulse, the process starts over and continues until the organism's behavior allows it to achieve a state of equilibrium with its environment.

The stage of manipulation is thus "cybernetic" in that it involves behavior, feedback, readjustment of behavior, feedback, readjustment, and so on until an impulse is eliminated.[34] Mead's vision of thinking as "imaginative rehearsal" and his conceptualization of the "I" and "me" fit into this more general cybernetic view of the act. Thinking involves imagining a behavior and then giving oneself the feedback about the probable consequences of the behavior. The "I" and "me" phases of self involve deriving "me" images (feedback) from behaviors ("I") and then using these images to adjust subsequent behaviors. Unlike many theorists of motivation, Mead saw acts as constructed from a succession of manipulations that yield feedback, which, in turn, is used to make subsequent manipulations. Thus, motivation is a process of constant adjustment and readjustment of behaviors to restore equilibrium with the environment.

Although Mead did not develop any formal propositions on the manipulatory stage of the act, he implicitly assumed that the more often an impulse is blocked, the more it grows in intensity and the more it consumes the process of thinking and the phases of self. Thus, individuals who have not eliminated a strong impulse through successful manipulation will have a considerable amount of their thinking and self-reflection consumed by imagery pertaining to objects and behaviors that might eliminate the impulse. For example, people who cannot satiate their hunger or sexual appetites or who cannot achieve the recognition they feel they deserve are likely to devote a considerable, and ever-increasing, amount of their time in covert and overt manipulations in an effort to control their impulses.

Consummation

The *consummation* stage of the act simply denotes the act's completion through the elimination of the disequilibrium between an organism and its environment. As a behaviorist, Mead emphasized that successful consummation of acts by the emission of behaviors in relation to certain objects leads to the development of stable behavior patterns. Thus, general classes, or types, of impulses will tend to elicit particular responses from an individual if these responses have been successful in the past in restoring equilibrium. Individuals will tend to perceive the same or similar objects as relevant to the elimination of the impulse, and they will tend to use these objects as stimuli for eliciting certain behaviors. In this way, people develop stable behavioral tendencies to act on their environment.

Figure 8.3 represents Mead's conceptualization of these phases of the act. For any person, of course, multiple impulses are operating, each at various stages of consummation and at potential points of blockage. For humans, perception involves seeing not only physical objects but also oneself, others, and various generalized others as part of the environment. Manipulation for humans with the capacities for mind and self involves both overt behavior and covert deliberations

---

[34]See Shibutani, "Cybernetic Approach," for a more detailed discussion.

where individuals weigh alternatives and assess their consequences with reference to their self-conception, to the expectations of specific others, and to various generalized others. Consummation for humans, who must live and survive in social groups, almost always revolves around adaptation to and cooperation with others in ongoing collective enterprises. As the feedback arrows denoting blockage emphasize, the point of blockage influences the salience of any phase in the flow of an act. Moreover, this process of blockage determines the strength of the causal arrows connecting stages in the act. Intense impulses are typically those that have been blocked, thereby causing heightened perception. In turn, heightened perception generates greater overt and covert manipulation; if blockage occurs, perception is further heightened, as are impulses. If manipulation is unsuccessful, escalated covert manipulation ensues, thereby heightening perception and the impulse (via the feedback arrows at the top of Figure 8.3).

This model of the act allows for an understanding of how individuals can be "driven" to seemingly irrational or excessively emotional behavior, and it can provide insight into the dynamics of compulsive behavior. These behaviors would result from the blockage of powerful impulses that persist and escalate in intensity, thereby distorting an individual's perceptions, covert thinking, and overt behavior. For example, individuals who were rejected by significant others in their early years might have a powerful series of unconsummated impulses that distort their perceptions and manipulations to abnormal extremes. Given that the unstable or abnormal self-conceptions of such individuals can distort the process of perception, as well as covert and overt manipulation, they might never be able to perceive that they have consummated their impulses in interpersonal relations.

Unlike Freud or other clinicians and psychologists of his time, Mead was not interested in types of abnormal behavior. He was more concerned with constructing a model that would denote the fundamental properties of human action, whether

Figure 8.3   Mead's Model of the Act

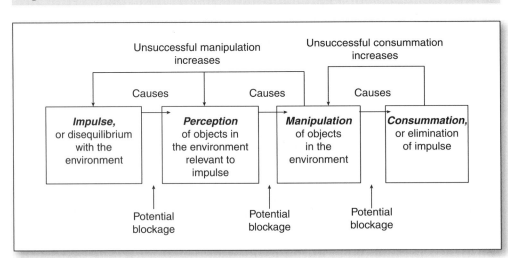

normal or abnormal. His critics often portray Mead's social behaviorism as overly rational, but this view does not consider his model of the act. This model contains the elements for emotional as well as rational action, and although he was not interested in assessing the consequences of various weights among the arrows in Figure 8.3, the model provides a valuable tool for those who are concerned with how various types of impulses, when coupled with different patterns of impulse blockage, will produce varying forms of covert and overt behavior.

Mead's view of motivation is distinctly sociological, emphasizing the relationship of individuals to one another and to the social as well as physical environments. What drives actors and shapes the course of their behaviors is the relationship of the organism to its environment. For human actors, who by virtue of mind and self are able to live and participate in society, this environment is decidedly social. Therefore, humans initiate and direct their actions in an effort to achieve integration into the ongoing social process. Mead's *social* behaviorism marked a synthesis of utilitarian, pragmatist, behaviorist, and even Darwinian notions. Mead's basic premise is this: behaviors that facilitate the adjustment and adaptation of organisms to their environment will be retained.

Mead's Theoretical Legacy

As I have emphasized, George Herbert Mead unlocked the basic mechanisms of human action and interaction. These mechanisms were viewed by Mead as the basic behavioral capacities necessary for participation in ongoing patterns of social organization; and these capacities are acquired by virtue of humans' fundamental need to adapt to the ongoing patterns of social organization in which they are born and in which they live out their lives. By virtue of these capacities for reading and using conventional gestures, role-taking, minded deliberations, and awareness of self as an object in relation to generalized others, people are able to cooperate and, thereby, sustain society. The basic process of interaction, then, involves individuals (a) mutually role-taking as they read the conventional gestures emitted by others, (b) deriving "me" images of themselves as an object while determining the likely course of action of others, (c) deriving additional "me" images from the point of view of various generalized others attached to the structure of the situation, (d) deliberating about the best course of action in light of these "me" images, and (e) finally behaving toward others (the "I" phase of interaction). As soon as this "I" phase is complete, Mead argues, the entire process is repeated.

Mead added to this model of interaction an analysis of the "phases of the act," which has not, in my view, been given sufficient consideration in sociological discussions of Mead's work (see Figure 8.3). In Mead's scheme, humans always have a configuration of "impulses" or needs at various states of consummation. Each of these impulses represents a point of *disequilibrium* with the environment. Some are long-term and chronic, others are in the process of being consummated, and still others are presently guiding perception and thought. The point that Mead emphasized is that interaction is motivated, but this process is complicated by the simultaneous operation of configurations of impulses at various phases of the act. As impulses or states of disequilibrium with the environment are activated, "perception" of the relevant objects that can consummate these impulses ensues. This perception is highly selective, oriented to those objects that can allow consummation of any impulse. The next phase of the act is "manipulation," in which individuals overtly behave in their environment or covertly engage in minded deliberations about how best to consummate the impulse. The final stage involves the consummation of the impulse or the failure to do so. When impulses go unconsummated, they increase in intensity and begin to distort the perception and manipulation phases of the act.

Acts and interaction all occur in cultural and social contexts, but these sociocultural contexts are rather under-theorized by Mead. He conceptualized culture in terms of generalized others, which can be temporary and immediate to a particular episode of interaction or attached to various levels of social structure, from the group through community and organizations to a whole society. The phrase "community of attitudes," used to describe the generalized other, is rather vague, but it connotes the perspective of collectives as represented by values, beliefs, norms, and perhaps cognitive processes such as categories of thought and perception. Social structure, or society, is even more imprecisely analyzed. At the level of acts and interaction, social structure is the pattern of activity in which individuals are cooperating, but beyond this more micro view, social structure at the macro level is not theorized beyond statements that *institutions* exist and constrain micro patterns of ongoing cooperative activity. In many ways, Mead is more a cultural theorist because the generalized other appears to be the way social structure influences acts and interactions. For each level of social structure—from groups to the society as a whole—there is a generalized other, individuals role-take with these generalized others, and thus, social structure influences acts and interactions through individuals' efforts at role-taking with generalized others.

Mead's Causal Model of Social Processes

With these considerations in mind, a model of the social process contained in Mead's sociology can be constructed. As shown in Figure 8.4, the model tries to reconcile Mead's analysis of the phases of the act with the analysis of interaction. As the left portion of the model emphasizes, behavior is initiated by impulses; and the more intense are the impulses, the more active are both overt and covert behaviors. Most impulses come from levels of adjustment and adaptation to social environments. Hence, when individuals feel out of synchronization with ongoing patterns of social organization, or sense that such might be the case, they become motivated to find a way to cooperate. Their perceptions of relevant objects are heightened and selective, and as the model emphasizes, two of the most important objects to be perceived are *self* and *generalized others*. Perceptions can lead to immediate behavioral responses, what is termed the "level of overt manipulation" in the model, but if impulses are powerful or have failed to be consummated in the past, then covert deliberations occur, and these are labeled "minded deliberations"

Figure 8.4   Mead's Model of Social Processes

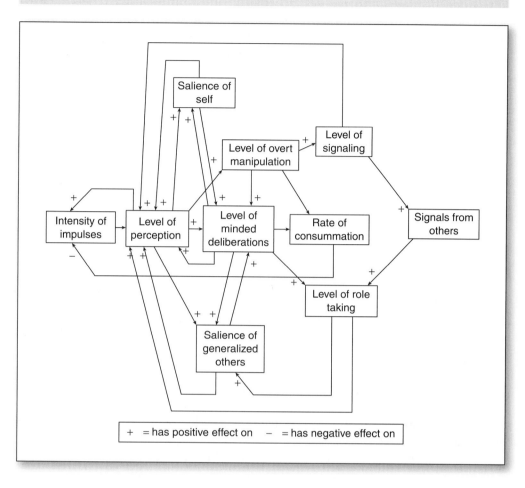

in the model. The more mind processes are activated, the more salient will self and generalized others become and the more they will influence the overt emission of gestures or signals to others.

Another important object in individuals' perceptions and manipulation are other people, whose dispositions to act are discovered through role-taking of their conventional gestures. The more active is role-taking, the more others become objects in the perceptual and manipulative phases of the act. Again, the more mind intervenes in the deliberation about what the gestures of others mean, the more overt behavior will reflect an effort to reconcile conceptions of self and dictates of generalized others with expectations and courses of actions of others in the situation. Mead also suggested that individuals can role-take with others not present in the situation, using these others' expectations and "actions" as a frame of reference in minded deliberations and overt behaviors.

Human interaction constantly activates these processes. Even before an interaction occurs, these processes can be in full operation. During the course of one episode of interaction, many iterations of these processes ensue as impulses, perceptions, minded deliberations involving self, generalized others, and specific others are constantly readjusted. As anyone who has thought about an interaction that has been completed knows, these processes can operate long after the face-to-face part of the interaction has ended, because often people play out alternative scenarios of how they could or should have acted. Mead's great contribution to general social theory is this model of action and interaction.

Most of Mead's work, however, examines how the capacities for using conventional gestures, for role-taking, for mind, and for self are acquired through learning. I have already reviewed these processes in detail in Figures 8.1, 8.2, and 8.3. Keeping in mind the models in Figures 8.1, 8.2, and 8.3, along with the general model in Figure 8.4, we can now examine the elementary principles that describe how humans acquire the behavioral capacities that allow them to engage in interactions sustaining the viability of society.

Mead's Theoretical Principles

Although Mead never stated his ideas as theoretical principles, it is clear that he thought in terms of the basic and fundamental relationships among phenomena. Mead is read, and then re-read today, because he articulated some universal features of interaction processes, and we can do justice to his genius by reviewing the principles that can be readily extracted from his lectures on social psychology and philosophy in general.

Mead sought to show how human action, interaction, and organization are qualitatively unique and yet are extensions of behavioral processes evident in other species of animals. Mead initially postulated principles of action and interaction in general and then attempted to show how the emergence of the behavioral capacities for *mind* and *self* make human action and interaction unique and how this uniqueness arises from, and at the same time allows for, the creation, maintenance, and change of society. Thus, I will first examine Mead's general principles of action and interaction and then explore his general principles of human action, interaction, and social organization.

Principles of Animal Action. In *The Philosophy of the Act*, Mead presented several general principles of action—that is, of what is involved in initiating and giving direction to behavior in all animals. As we saw, his ideas are expressed as "stages" and can be modeled. These ideas can also be expressed as a series of basic principles of action:

1. The greater is the degree of maladjustment of an organism to its environment, the stronger are the organism's impulses.

2. The greater is the intensity of an organism's impulse, the greater is the organism's perceptual awareness of objects that can potentially consummate the impulse and the more the organism manipulates objects in the environment.

A. The more maladjustment stems from unconsummated organic needs, the more intense is the impulse.

B. The longer an impulse has gone unconsummated, the more intense is the impulse.

3. The more impulses have been consummated by the perception and manipulation of certain classes of objects in the environment, the more perceptual and behavioral responses will be directed at these and similar classes of objects when similar impulses arise.

These three principles summarize Mead's social behaviorism. Action emerges from the adjustment and adaptation problems encountered by an organism. Behavior is directed at restoring equilibrium between the organism and the environment. The essence of behavior involves perception and manipulation of objects. Successful perception and manipulations are retained in an organism's behavioral repertoire. As Mead argued, human action emerged from this behavioral base, but the capacities for mind, self, and society require, as I will document shortly, additional theoretical principles if the distinctive qualities of human action are to be understood. To appreciate fully these additional principles, however, we need first to summarize Mead's general principles of interaction among animals without mind, self, and society.

Principles of Animal Interaction. Mead's view of interaction can be modeled as a causal sequence of events over time, or it can be expressed by the following two principles:

4. The more organisms seek to manipulate objects in their environment in an effort to consummate impulses, the greater is the visibility of the gestures marking their course of action.

5. The greater are the number and visibility of the gestures emitted by acting organisms, the more these organisms adjust their responses to each other.

These two principles underscore Mead's view that the essence of interaction involves (a) an organism emitting gestures as acts on the world; (b) another organism responding to these gestures and, hence, emitting its own gestures as it seeks to consummate its impulses; and (c) readjustments of the responses by each organism to the gestures emitted. Mead termed the process the triadic matrix, and it can occur without cognitive manipulations and without the development of common meanings. Indeed, as Mead argued, only among humans with mind and self, living in society, does this fundamental interactive process involve cognitive manipulations, normative regulations, and shared meanings. Mead may have underestimated the cognitive capacities of higher mammals, such as the great apes, which are genetically close to humans, but there is little doubt that humans have behavioral capacities for minded and self-conscious behaviors far in excess of even these close primate relatives.

Principles of Human Action, Interaction, and Organization. Critical to understanding Mead's view of human action, interaction, and organization is the recognition that humans develop mind and self from their participation in society. We first review Mead's formulation of principles on the development of mind and self, then we can see how these two behavioral capacities alter the principles of human action, interaction, and organization.

Principles on the Emergence of Mind. Any particular individual is born into a society of actors with mind and self. Mind, self, and human society were thus seen by Mead as intimately connected because mind and self are learned as a result of having to participate in society, while society is reproduced by virtue of mind and self. We must jump into this cycle of interconnections at some point, so we begin by isolating Mead's view of socialization and the emergence of mind. This view assumes the prior existence of society and adult actors with mind and self; young infants who do not possess these behavioral capacities must adapt and adjust into this social milieu. In attempting to understand how infants adjust to adult actors and to society, Mead offered a series of important principles describing the fundamental properties of the socialization process:

6. The more an infant must adapt to an environment composed of organized collectivities of actors, the more is its exposure to significant gestures.

7. The more an infant seeks to consummate its impulses in an organized social collectivity, the greater is the selective value for consummating impulses of learning how to read and use significant gestures.

8. The more an infant can use and read significant gestures, the greater is its ability to role-take with others in its environment and, hence, the greater is its capacity to communicate its needs and to anticipate the responses of others on whom it depends for the consummation of impulses.

9. The greater is the capacity of an infant to role-take and use significant gestures, the greater is its capacity to communicate with itself.

10. The greater is the capacity of an infant to communicate with itself, the greater is its ability to covertly designate objects in its environment, inhibit inappropriate responses, and select a response that will consummate its impulses and thereby facilitate its adjustment.

11. The more an infant reveals such minded behavior, the greater is its ability to control its responses and, hence, to cooperate with others in ongoing and organized collectivities.

These principles should be read in two ways. First, each principle by itself expresses a fundamental relationship in the nature of human development. For example, principle 6 states that human infants are, by virtue of being born into society, inevitably exposed to a collage of significant gestures; or principle 7 states that because infants must consummate impulses in a world of significant gestures, they will learn to read and use these gestures as a means of increasing their adjustment. Thus, each principle states that one variable condition, stated in the first clause of the principle, will lead to the development of another capacity, which is stated in the second clause of the principle, in the maturing human infant. Second, this sequence of six principles should be viewed as marking "stages" in the genesis of a critical behavioral capacity, mind.

Principles on the Emergence of Self. Any particular individual is born into a society of actors with mind and self. Mind, self, and human society were thus seen by Mead as intimately connected because mind and self are learned as a result of having to participate in society, while society is reproduced by virtue of mind and self. We must jump into this cycle of interconnections at some point, so we begin by isolating Mead's view of socialization and the emergence of mind. This view assumes the prior existence of society and adult actors with mind and self; young infants who do not possess these behavioral capacities must adapt and adjust into this social milieu. In attempting to understand how infants adjust to adult actors and to society, Mead offered a series of important principles describing the fundamental properties of the socialization process:

12. The more a young actor engages in minded behavior, the more this actor can read significant gestures, role-take, and communicate with itself.

13. The more a young actor reads significant gestures, role-takes, and communicates with itself, the more it can see itself as an object in any given situation.

14. The more diverse the specific others with whom a young actor can role-take, the more the actor sees itself as an object in relation to the dispositions of multiple others.

15. The more generalized is the perspective of others with whom a young infant can role-take, the more the infant sees itself as an object in relation to general values, beliefs, and norms of increasingly larger collectivities.

16. The greater the stability of a young actor's images of itself as an object has been in relation to both specific others and generalized perspectives, the more reflexive is the actor's role-taking and the more consistent are its behavioral responses.

    A. The more first self-images derived from role-taking with others have been consistent and noncontradictory, the more reflexive is role-taking and the more consistent are behaviors.

    B. The more self-images derived from role-taking with generalized perspectives are consistent and noncontradictory, the more reflexive is role-taking and the more consistent are behaviors.

17. The more a young actor reveals stability in its responses to itself as an object and the more this actor sees itself as an object in relation to specific others as well as generalized perspectives, the greater is its capacity to control responses and, hence, to cooperate with others in ongoing and organized collectivities.

These principles document Mead's view of certain fundamental relationships among role-taking acuity, images of the self as an object, and capacities for social control. These principles also summarize Mead's conceptualization of the sequence of events involved in generating a "unified" self in which an individual adjusts responses in relation to (a) a stable self-conception, (b) specific expectations of others, and (c) general values, beliefs, and norms.

As the consecutive number of the principles underscores, the development of mind and self is a continuous process. Once the behavioral abilities for mind and self in individual human organisms are evident, action and interaction as well as patterns of social organization among humans become qualitatively different from those of nonhuman animals—perhaps a bit of an overstatement but one that is defensible. Yet Mead emphasized that there is nothing mysterious or mystical about this qualitative difference. Indeed, even though human action, interaction, and organization are distinct by virtue of the capacity for mind, self, and symbolically mediated organization into society, this distinctiveness has been built on a base common to all acting organisms.

Principles of Human Action and Interaction. The emergence of mind and self somewhat complicate Mead's view of the act as involving impulse, perception, and manipulation, as well as his notion of the triadic matrix as a simple process of actors emitting and reading gestures as they adjust their responses to each other. Indeed, the complications introduced into the processes of action and interaction make up an entirely new way to organize a species into society—at least in Mead's eye. Concerning action, Mead noted one additional principle to account for the distinctive features of human acts:

18. The greater the intensity of impulses of humans with mind and self, (a) the more heightened is perceptual awareness of objects that can potentially consummate the impulse to be selective, (b) the more likely is manipulation to be covert, and (c) the more likely are both perception and manipulation to be circumscribed by self-conceptions, expectations of specific others, and generalized perspectives of organized collectivities.

When action as described in principle 18 occurs in a social context with others, it then becomes overt interaction. Even isolated acts, where others are not physically present, involve interaction with symbolically invoked others and generalized perspectives. The capacities for mind and self, Mead argued, ensure that humans will invoke the dispositions of others and broader communities of attitudes to guide behavior during the course of their acts even if specific others are not physically present and even if others do not directly react to their behaviors. When others are present, the use of significant symbols and role-taking becomes more direct and immediate, requiring several supplementary principles on interaction:

19. The more humans with mind and self seek to consummate impulses in the presence of others, the more they emit significant gestures and read the significant gestures of others and, hence, the greater is their role-taking activity.

20. The more humans role-take with each other, the more their interaction is guided by the specific disposition of others present in a situation, by images of the self as a certain type of object, and by generalized perspectives of organized collectivities.

When stated as principles, the key relationships among impulses, significant gestures, role-taking, self-conceptions, expectations of others, and generalized perspectives are highlighted. For Mead, impulses drive action, but most action occurs in a context of others and, hence, becomes interaction. Interaction among humans depends on role-taking, which, in turn, produces self-images, awareness of the dispositions of others, and cognizance of generalized perspectives. Such is the nature of human action and interaction among organisms with mind and self, who must consummate their impulses within the framework imposed by ongoing patterns of social organization. Thus, principles 18, 19, and 20 can be interpreted as Mead's "laws" of action and interaction among humans. By comparing these laws with his general principles of action and interaction among nonhuman organisms (principles 1 through 5), we can see that these principles on humans represent extensions of those on nonhumans.

I have now summarized Mead's principles on the emergence of mind and self as well as those on action and interaction. These principles place into theoretical context Mead's vision of how society is created, maintained, and changed. As a philosopher and social psychologist, rather than as a structural sociologist, Mead had a distinctively social psychological view of social organization. This vision supplements and complements the structural perspective developed in Europe by figures such as Herbert Spencer, Karl Marx, Max Weber, and Émile Durkheim. Although each of these scholars sought to uncover some of the social psychological dynamics of macro-social structures, none was able to achieve the insights that Mead developed on the fundamental social psychological properties underlying the patterns of social organization.

Principles of Human Social Organization. Because interaction among humans is possible by virtue of role-taking abilities and because society involves stabilized patterns of interaction, society for Mead is ultimately a process of (a) role-taking with various others and (b) using the dispositions and perspectives of these others for self-evaluation and self-control. The nature and scope of society, Mead implicitly argued, are a dual function of the number of specific others and the abstractness of the generalized others with whom individuals can role-take. In many ways, Mead viewed society as a "capacity" for various types of role-taking. If actors can role-take with only one other at a time, then the scale of society is limited, but once they can role-take with multiple others and then with generalized others, the scale of society is greatly extended. These fundamental relationships are summarized in Mead's two basic principles on the dynamics underlying society:

21. The more actors role-take with pluralities of others and use the dispositions of multiple others as a source of self-evaluation and self-control, the greater is their capacity to create and maintain patterns of social organization.

22. The more actors role-take with the generalized perspective of organized collectivities and use this perspective as a source of self-evaluation and self-control, the greater is their capacity to create and maintain patterns of social organization.

If actors cannot meet the conditions specified in these two "laws" of social organization, then instability and change in patterns of interaction are likely to occur. Actors who cannot role-take with multiple others at a time and use the dispositions of these others to see themselves as objects and to control their responses will not be able to coordinate their responses as well as actors who can perform such role-taking. Actors who cannot role-take with the general norms, beliefs, values, and other symbol systems of organized groups and use these to view themselves and to regulate their actions will not be able to extend patterns of social organization beyond immediate face-to-face contact. Only when actors can role-take with a broader community of attitudes and use a common set of expectations to guide their conduct do extended patterns of social organization become possible.

In addition to these two basic principles, Mead elaborated several propositions on role-taking with generalized others. Because the scope of society is ultimately a positive function of role-taking abilities with generalized others, Mead apparently felt it necessary to specify some of the variables influencing the relations among role-taking, generalized others, and the nature of society. Three variables are most prominent in Mead's scheme: (1) the degree to which actors can hold a common generalized other, (2) the degree of consistency among multiple generalized others, and (3) the degree of integration among different types and layers of generalized others. Mead implicitly incorporated these variables into additional principles of social organization:

23. The more actors role-take with a common generalized perspective and use this common perspective as a source of self-evaluation and self-control, the greater is their capacity to create and maintain cohesive patterns of social organization.
    A. The more similar are the positions of actors, the more they will role-take with a common generalized perspective.
    B. The smaller is the population of actors, the more they will role-take with a common generalized perspective.

In this principle, the ability to role-take with a common perspective (norms, values, beliefs, and other symbolic components) is linked to the degree of cohesiveness in patterns of social organization. Thus, Mead argued, a common collective perspective maintains unified and cohesive patterns of organization. On this score, Mead came close to Durkheim's emphasis on the need for a "common" or "collective" conscience. In contrast with Durkheim, however, Mead was able to tie this point to the theory of human action and interaction, and hence, he was in a position to specify the mechanisms by which individual conduct is regulated by a generalized other or, in Durkheim's terms, "collective conscience."

Much like Durkheim, Mead also recognized that the size of a population and its differentiation into roles influence the degree of commonality of the generalized other. Naturally, the converse of principle 23 could signal difficulties in achieving unified and cohesive patterns of social organization. If the members of a population cannot role-take with a common generalized other, then cohesive social organization will be more problematic. If a population is large or highly differentiated, role-taking with a common generalized other will be more difficult.

Like Durkheim, Mead recognized that a common generalized other becomes increasingly tenuous with the growing size and differentiation of a population. For large, differentiated populations, there are multiple generalized others because people participate in many different organized collectivities. These considerations led Mead to view consistency of generalized others as related to how extensive differentiation of social structure could become:

24. The more actors role-take with multiple but consistent generalized perspectives and use these perspectives as a source of self-evaluation and self-control, the greater is their capacity to differentiate roles and extend the scope of social organization.

In this principle, Mead argued that if the basic profile of norms, values, and beliefs of different groupings in which individuals participate are not contradictory, then differentiation does not lead to conflict and degeneration of social organization. On the contrary, multiple and consistent generalized others allow functional differentiation of roles and groups, which, in turn, expands the scope (size, territory, and other such variables) of society. Of course, if various generalized others are contradictory, then conflictual relations are likely, thereby limiting the extent of social organization.

Mead's analysis also resembled Durkheim's, who recognized that the symbolic components of culture exist at different levels of generality. Some are highly abstract and cut across diverse groupings, whereas others are tied to specific groups and organizations. Mead distinguished between "abstract" generalized others and concrete "organized" others to denote this facet of symbolic organization. Like Durkheim, Mead saw that the scope of social organization is limited by how well "abstract others" (e.g., values and beliefs) are integrated with more concrete "organized others" (e.g., the particular norms and doctrines of concrete groups, social classes, organizations, and regions). Large-scale social organization, Mead felt, depends on common and highly abstract values and beliefs that are integrated with the specific perspectives of differentiated collectivities. The concept of integration, Mead appeared to argue, involves more than consistency and lack of contradiction; it denotes that the generalized others of particular organized collectivities represent concrete applications of the abstract generalized other. The abstract generalized other sets the parameters for less abstract perspectives, thereby ensuring not just consistency between the two but also integration where the tenets of the specific follow from the abstract.

Mead's argument came close to that of Durkheim in this recognition. We can visualize this similarity in the following principle:

25. The more actors role-take with the specific perspectives of particular collectivities that follow from more general perspectives and the more these integrated perspectives are a source of self-evaluation and self-control, the greater is the capacity to extend the scope of social organization.

As with principles 1 through 24, the converse of this 25th principle can point to some of the conditions producing conflict and change. To the degree that abstract and specific perspectives are not integrated, actors will potentially have different interpretations of situations; and to the degree that they come into contact, the probability of conflict will increase.

Principles 21 to 25 summarize Mead's vision of the basic properties of social organization. For society to exist at all, actors must be able to role-take with multiple others and with generalized others (principles 21 and 22). For a highly cohesive organization to exist and persist, actors must be able to role-take a common generalized other (principle 23). For somewhat less cohesive but more differentiated and extensive patterns of social organization to be viable, actors must be able to role-take with multiple, but nevertheless noncontradictory, generalized others (principle 24). For large-scale and highly extensive patterns of organization, actors must role-take with well-integrated abstract and specific generalized others (principle 25).

In sum, we see that Mead's ideas can be converted into workable models and propositions. The propositions take time to delineate because they address the emergence of those behavioral capacities—use of significant gestures, role-taking, mind, and self—that make it possible for individuals to cooperate and, hence, for society to persist. Mead was a philosopher, but he gave sociology some of its most important ideas about the nature of human social interaction and about how micro-level processes arise from, and at the same time perpetuate, the macro-social order.

Conclusions

Before Mead, the process of interaction was not well understood. Various thinkers had captured a portion of the process, but Mead synthesized various lines of thinking into a coherent conceptual framework. The strength of Mead's analysis resides in his understanding of the relationship among ongoing patterns of social organization, or society, and the behavioral capacities that arise from human needs to adapt to these patterns and that, as a result, sustain society. Activities using conventional gestures, role-taking, mind, and self are, in Mead's eyes, behaviors rather than entities or things, and they are learned like all behaviors because they provide reinforcement to individuals or, alternatively in pragmatist terminology, because they allow for adaptation to society. Thus, for Mead, society always stands above the individual in the sense that it exists before a person is born and, consequently, is the environment to which individuals must adjust and adapt. Yet without learning conventional gestures and role-taking and without acquiring the ability to engage in minded deliberations or self-reflection and appraisal from the perspective of society and its various generalized others, society would not be possible.

It is difficult to criticize the thinker who, in essence, unlocked the mysteries of micro-social processes, but I can offer several criticisms. One is that Mead never developed a very clear conception of society or culture. He saw "institutions" as ongoing patterns of cooperative behavior, and he viewed culture in terms of various generalized others. Yet this is a rather minimal conception of the macrostructures that are sustained by microprocesses; so, even though Mead saw society as standing above the individual, his theory is really about how people acquire the behavioral capacities to adjust to society and culture. We are not, however, given a theory of society or culture.

One result of this failure is that many contemporary theorists assume that a separate theory, or set of theories, about the dynamics of society and culture is not necessary. Instead, all we need is a theory of interpersonal behavior to explain institutional and cultural systems. Such theories become, however, little more than pronouncements that, for example, assert that "society is symbolic interaction,"[35] which says very little and explains virtually nothing about society beyond the interpersonal processes necessary to sustain it. Thus, Mead's sociology is decidedly micro, which is fine as long as we realize this limitation; many contemporary sociologists unfortunately forget this fact.

We can even criticize Mead on the more micro level of analysis. Probably his greatest failing is the lack of a theory of emotions. One of the most critical aspects of interaction is its emotional content, and when individuals role-take, engage in minded deliberations, or make self-appraisals, they are being emotional. Mead even had a Freudian-looking theory of "the act" that could easily have been used to address the emotions involved as impulses go unconsummated or as they are consummated. But we are never given a word. Moreover, Mead had used Darwinian metaphors in all his work, and he was certainly aware of Darwin's book[36] on expressions and emotions in animals, and yet he did not pick up this lead. Thus, because Mead was considered the key figure in micro-sociology for most of the century, his lapse became the discipline's gap in knowledge. For not until the late 1970s did the sociology of emotions emerge as a field of inquiry in interactionist theorizing.[37] The only explanation for this late interest is the slavish conformity to Mead's lead, which, profound as it was, did not tell a complete story of micro-social processes.

---

[35]Herbert Blumer, *Symbolic Interactionism: Perspective and Method* (Englewood Cliffs, NJ: Prentice-Hall, 1969).

[36]Charles Darwin, *The Expressions of Emotions in Man and Animals* (London: Wats, 1982).

[37]For a review, see Jonathan H. Turner and Jan E. Stets, *The Sociology of Emotions* (Cambridge, UK: Cambridge University Press, 2005).

CHAPTER 9

The Classical Roots of Contemporary Theorizing

I have not reviewed all the theorists in the classical era of sociology, only those theorists who have had the greatest influence on contemporary theorizing. Some figures, such as Vilfredo Pareto, Charles Horton Cooley, Robert Park, Karl Mannheim, Alfred Schutz, and others, did highly important work that falls within the 1935 cutoff point, which I have set for the end of the classical period. Some of these, such as Cooley, Park, and Schutz, will be examined as key figures in the lead-up to contemporary perspectives in Part II, but others must be seen as of secondary importance when viewing the long-term development of sociology. It could be argued, of course, that I have included figures such as Auguste Comte and Herbert Spencer, who are virtually ignored today, but as will become clear, they still exert far more influence on the direction of sociology than others whom I have not included in Part I.

In addition to these less significant theorists in the classical period, there are key figures who are caught in the theoretical void that existed between the late 1920s and 1950s. Figures such as Pitirim Sorokin, for example, were giants of their times and developed interesting theories that garnered a great deal of attention, but in the end, their influence has not endured because it would be hard to identify a modern theoretical perspective that owes its inspiration to their works. True, a number of figures in ecological theorizing, for instance, were very active between the classical and modern periods; and they certainly developed the foundation for modern ecological theorizing. I will also mention these figures in the lead-up to modern ecological work and summarize the nature of the foundation that they laid down. Yet, as single figures, do they stand out as "giants" of sociology's past, reviewed in Part I? In my view, they did not do *enough* important theorizing to warrant separate treatment. The same can be said of many others, such as Herbert Blumer for symbolic interactionist theory, Alfred Schutz for phenomenologically oriented interactions theory, Jacob Moreno and S. F. Nadel for network analysis, Ralph Linton for status theory, and early critical theorists such as Antonio Gramsci, Gyorgy Lukacs, Louis Althusser, and others. These and other theorists did most of their work between the classical and modern eras, but unlike some who I only mention, I see these figures as making a contribution to the contemporary era, and so they will receive more treatment in Part II, in tracing the lead-up to a particular contemporary approach. But they do not stand out as giants who founded sociology and developed the theoretical ideas that changed the discipline, as had been the case for all of those examined in Chapters 2 through 8. I have, of course, made choices based on my judgment of who is most important; others might well disagree, and if so, they can make the case for these other important figures in sociology.

There are other historical figures, who, by our contemporary lenses, are made to seem more important than they really were in the development of sociological theory. For example, Harriet Martineau, Jane Adams, W. E. B. DuBois, and others are often included in textbooks today as "forgotten" theorists. Clearly, there is a "political correctness" in their inclusion in reviews of theory today; understandably, we may want to make early theorizing in sociology more diverse by gender and ethnicity than it was. As all would acknowledge, I think, there was underrepresentation of women and minorities in theorizing because of one simple force: discrimination in the educational, occupational, and academic systems. People of color and women were simply excluded from most academic tracks and, hence, did not even have the opportunity to become important theoretical figures. Some were not sociologists, for instance, Harriet Martineau, who was instead a very prominent journalist who, as an aside, translated Comte's great work into English; others, like Jane Adams, were trained sociologically and interacted with sociologists, but her real work was amelioration, not theorizing, and indeed, for her efforts she won the Nobel Peace Prize, which, to me, is a far greater honor than being shoved into classical theory texts; still others, like W. E. B. Dubois, were very solid and important sociological voices, but they were not major theorists who charted or changed the direction of theorizing. The impulse to resurrect individuals to atone for the discrimination of the past is certainly understandable, but we should not rewrite the history of sociology by making particular categories of individuals in sociology's past into seminally important theorists when, in fact, they were not. Similarly, a long list of important white, male sociological figures have slipped into obscurity because, as important as they were in the field of sociology for a time, they did *not* make enduring *theoretical* contributions. For example, in early American sociology alone, Albion Small, William Graham Sumner, Lester Frank Ward, Franklin Giddings, Howard Becker, Harry E. Barnes, Charles Ellwood, Ellsworth Faris, and others were very prominent sociologists who did some theoretical work, but they are not mentioned in history of theory texts today because their works do not stand out as transformational or foundational. Europe reveals an equally long list of figures—virtually all male—who were important for a time but were not enduring theorists. The same may well turn out to be true of the scholars whom I will examine in Part II; only another fifty years will tell us who stood the test of time and who did not. But, at least this time around, the scholars who endure and who disappear will be more diverse than a century ago.

In this chapter, however, my goal is not to enter the quagmire of contemporary academic politics but to make a simple point: contemporary theorizing in sociology still derives much inspiration from the early theorists examined in Part I. Present-day theorizing has, like everything else in sociology, become more specialized. Many current theories examine only a small range of phenomena, and thus there are many more theories than I can briefly review in this chapter or even in the very long chapters to follow. But, even with high degrees of specialization, there are still more general theoretical approaches or perspectives, almost all of which have been built upon the insights of these early masters and carried forward mostly by more specialized scholars. Within these perspectives, there is a number of variants whose adherents argue with each other or, sometimes, even pretend that a rival camp simply does not exist.

Intellectual life is always competitive, and scholars compete for limited attention space,[1] with the result that they work to differentiate their theories from the competition—even if these theories overlap and are, to any outsider looking in, theories of a certain type or genre. But, even with these tendencies for grabbing attention space by overspecialization, at least ten approaches can be isolated—which are a few too many for the current intellectual space in sociology. And such is, particularly, the case for the sub-variants of theorizing within one of these ten broad theoretical perspectives; there are perhaps as many as twenty or twenty-five approaches within the ten broad ones that I will outline shortly, while in most academic fields, there is room for perhaps six or seven prominent perspectives. As a consequence, just a few theories are dominant at any given time, while the rest must compete with each other to find a way into the sociological imagination.

Contemporary Traditions and Perspectives Inspired by the Classical Theorists

1. Functional Theorizing

Functional theorizing was sociology's first theoretical perspective. Auguste Comte was followed by Herbert Spencer and, then, by Émile Durkheim, who incorporated elements from both Comte and Spencer in his mode of functional analysis. The basic essence of functional analysis can be summarized by the points listed below:

1. Social systems are composed of interrelated parts.

2. These systems reveal both internal and external problems of adaptation to their environments that must be resolved if the system is to endure.

3. These problems of survival and adaptation can be visualized as system "needs" or "requisites" that must be met.

4. Understanding of social systems as a whole and their constituent parts is only possible by analyzing the need(s) or requisite(s) of the system that any given part meets.

---

[1]Randall Collins, *The Sociology of Philosophies: A Global Theory of Intellectual Change* (Cambridge, MA: Harvard University Press, 1998).

Differences among functional theories revolve around the number of functional requisites that are posited. Some theorists, like Durkheim,[2] posited only one master need: *social integration,* or the need for coordination and control of system parts. Thus, societies should be examined with respect to how each of their parts—whether structural, cultural, or interactional—contributes to the integration of the social whole. Other early functionalists, like Spencer,[3] delineated several functional requisites: *production,* or the securing of resources and their conversion into usable commodities; *reproduction* of societal members and social structures; *distribution* of resources, information, and people around a society and its social structures; and *regulation,* or coordination and control through the consolidation and use of power.

With Spencer's death in the first decade of the twentieth century, and then Durkheim's in the second decade, functional theorizing disappeared from sociology. The approach was kept alive by anthropologists, such as A. R. Radcliffe-Brown[4] and Bronislaw Malinowski,[5] because functionalism allowed them and other anthropologists to theorize about why a particular cultural form—such as, a belief, a ritual, or a social structure—existed in preliterate societies. They could ask the basic question of all functional theory: What does a part in any social system do to sustain the system in its environment? About the time when the problems[6] in this mode of analysis caused a sharp decline in anthropological functionalism, it came roaring back into sociology during the 1950s and continued to be sociology's dominant theoretical approach until the mid-1970s, when it then began once again to decline and almost disappeared by the end of the twentieth century.

Hard-core functional theories from the middle decades of the twentieth century all continued to emphasize the requisites of a social system. For Talcott Parsons,[7] there were four requisites, roughly paralleling those of Spencer and the anthropologist Bronislaw Malinowski. These include the needs for *adaptation* (production), *goal attainment* (regulation through power), *integration* (coordination), and *latency*

---

[2]For a review of Durkheim's functionalism, see Collins, *The Sociology of Philosophies,* 287–289, 295–297.

[3]For a review of Spencer's functional theorizing, see Collins, *The Sociology of Philosophies,* 59–60, 65.

[4]R. Radcliffe-Brown, *Structure and Function in Primitive Society* (Glencoe, IL: Free Press, 1952).

[5]Bronislaw Malinowski, *A Scientific Theory of Culture* (Chapel Hill: University of North Carolina Press, 1944). For a review of the history of functional theorizing in sociology and anthropology, see Jonathan H. Turner and Alexandra Maryanski, *Functionalism* (Menlo Park, CA: Benjamin/Cummings, 1979).

[6]Many of the problems of functionalism concerned its apparent conservative assumptions that any part exists because it meets functional needs. Thus, functionalism justified the status quo even if it was oppressive and unjust. Another problem was the tautological nature, or circular reasoning, in functional explanations. For example, how do I know that a part has functions for a social system? Answer: Because the system is functioning and surviving.

[7]Talcott Parsons, *The Social System* (Glencoe, IL: The Free Press, 1951); Talcott Parsons, Robert F. Bales, and Edward A. Shils, *Working Papers in the Theory of Action* (Glencoe, IL: The Free Press, 1953). For a more contemporary theorist who carries forth Parsons' functionalism, see Richard Munch's *Theory of Action: Towards Going Beyond Parsons* (London: Routledge, 1988).

(tension management and reproduction). In contrast, the German functionalist Niklas Luhmann[8] posited one master requisite—*complexity reduction*—along several dimensions of human existence—temporal, material, and symbolic. Thus, social structures and culture are viewed as arising in order to reduce the potential complex of the *temporal* dimension (which can extend back in all of history or forward toward infinity), *material* dimension (which can include all possible social relations in infinite space), and *symbolic* dimension (which includes all possible symbol systems). Social systems thus develop mechanisms—structural and cultural—to reduce this potential complexity, and so social systems are to be understood by how these mechanisms reducing complexity have evolved and how they now operate.

Other sociologists sympathetic to functional analysis but suspicious of the notion of universal requisites and needs took somewhat different tacks. Jeffrey Alexander and Paul Colomy[9] emphasize structural differentiation and integration by culture as key dynamics of societies, without invoking the notion of requisites. I, myself,[10] have converted requisites to a conception of fundamental *forces* that vary in intensity and that increase selection pressures on actors to create sociocultural formations to reduce the intensity of these pressures. Thus, even by other names, functional theory still persists in contemporary sociology, and the reason why it persists is that it has always asked an interesting question: What adaptive problems must all societies, and systems within societies, resolve if they are to sustain themselves in their respective environments? An answer to this question gets at what is essential to human existence in societies, and therefore, it remains at the center of sociological theory, even as functional theory has declined in influence. Functionalism, per se, has virtually disappeared, but its ghost in the form of newer approaches that capture the essence of functionalism persists, as we will come to see in Chapter 10.

2. Evolutionary Theorizing

Stage Theories. Among the classical theorists, theories about the stages of societal evolution from simple to more complex forms were common. Among functionalist theorists today, all theories still emphasize the increasing differentiation of social structures and culture in societies. Most of these early theorists had some notion of stages in this movement toward higher levels of differentiation. Some,

---

[8]Niklas Luhmann, *Systems Theory* (Stanford, CA: Stanford University Press, 1995), *The Differentiation of Society*, trans. S. Holmes and C. Larmore (New York: Columbia University Press, 1982).

[9]Jeffrey C. Alexander (ed.), *Neofunctionalism* (Beverly Hills, CA: Sage, 1985); Jeffrey C. Alexander and Paul Colomy, "Neofunctionalism Today: Restructuring a Theoretical Tradition" in *Frontiers of Social Theory*, ed. George Ritzer (New York: Columbia University Press, 1990); Paul Colomy (ed.), *Neofunctionalist Sociology: Contemporary Statements* (London: Edward Elgar, 1990).

[10]Jonathan H. Turner, *Macrodynamics: Toward a Theory on the Organization of Human Populations* (New Brunswick: Rutgers University Press, 1995), *Theoretical Principles of Sociology*, vol. 1: *Macrodynamics* (New York: Springer, 2010).

like Durkheim,[11] posited two basic stages from "mechanical" to "organic" solidarity; others, like Spencer,[12] outlined in rather great detail different stages of simple (nomadic hunting and gathering without a head), simple with head (settled hunting and gathering as well as horticultural societies), double compound (agrarian), and triple compound (industrial), while at the same time trying to explain the dynamics that cause this movement from simple to highly compounded or differentiated societies. Other theorists, like Max Weber, focused on the overarching evolutionary process of rationalization (although he would not have used the term *evolutionary*); Karl Marx posited five stages of history, from primitive communism (hunting and gathering) through slavery (roughly horticulture and early agrarianism), feudalism (agrarian), and industrial capitalism to the end of evolutionary history, communism; Georg Simmel and George Herbert Mead, like most functionalists, tended to view evolution as a master process of differentiation. Despite their many differences, all stage theories of evolution include the following assumptions:

1. Societies evolve from simple to ever more complex forms.

2. This evolution always involves several discrete stages.

3. There are always forces or mechanisms driving this movement of societies from simple to complex formations.

4. These forces can be constant or can vary, depending on the stage of development of a society.

5. Depending on the evolutionary theory, these mechanisms of change tend to revolve around (a) functional requisites pushing actors to develop structures to meet these requisites, (b) technology and production, (c) power and inequality, (d) geopolitics, (e) market dynamics, (f) energy capture, (g) population growth, and other forces or mechanisms that push societies along evolutionary stages.

Like functionalism, this line of theorizing disappeared by the third decade of the twentieth century, just as the classical period of sociological theorizing was closing. In the 1960s, however, after a half-century in hiding, stage modeling made a dramatic comeback and has been part of the theoretical landscape in sociology ever since. There is, however, no clear consensus about which mechanisms or which combination of mechanisms listed under (5) above is the key to explaining evolution. But what is particularly important is that the comeback occurred not just in

---

[11]For Durkheim's simple two-stage model, see Collins, *The Sociology of Philosophies,* 283–293.

[12]For Spencer's more elaborate stage model, one that is still contemporary, see p. 48;[13] for Max Weber's more implicit stage model, see pp. 152–160;[14] for Marx's stage model and theory, see pp. 101–116;[15] for Simmel's models of stages of differentiation, see pp. 192–199;[16] for Mead's very implicit assumptions about differentiation as the master trend in societies, see pp. 287–290.

functional theories, where stage models had always been present throughout the nineteenth century, but also in other theoretical approaches.[13] For example, ecological, conflict, world-systems, cultural, postmodern, and even critical theories have all introduced elements of stage modeling back into contemporary theory. Like the earlier theories, a series of stages of societal development are posited, and then driving forces—listed under (5) above—are posited. These new theories also introduce, as did Spencer's analysis of power, the more cyclical dynamics of societal oscillations within each stage.

Biological Theories. Social scientists in general, but relatively few sociologists, have sought to bring biological ideas and some elements of the general theory of biological evolution into sociological theorizing. Charles Darwin's *On the Origin of Species* was not published until 1859, right in the middle of sociology's emergence, but by then evolutionary thinking had been in the air for some decades. Some of this early evolutionary thinking was stage modeling, as discussed above, but there were other ideas that were closer to Darwin's theory of evolution by natural selection, which was later (in the early twentieth century) expanded to include the mechanisms creating the variation on which selection works.

Comte had realized, long before Darwin, that biology would be the dominant science of the nineteenth century, and this is why he postulated his hierarchy of the sciences as involving sociology emerging from biology and, surprisingly, becoming the "queen" of all the sciences. Spencer always had a vision of evolution as an outcome of competition, before Darwin published his great work, with the more fit organism or superorganism (society) prevailing and passing on its forms. George Herbert Mead, as a pragmatist philosopher, and social behaviorists similarly held the view that behaviors or societal forms that facilitate adaptation are retained in the behavioral repertoire and structural forms of the social universe. Durkheim explicitly borrowed Darwin's views on density increasing competition in his ecological analysis of societal evolution (see the section on ecological theories).

---

[13]Prominent stage model theorists include Gerhard Lenski, *Power and Privilege* (New York: McGraw-Hill, 1964, reissued by the University of North Carolina Press); Talcott Parsons, *Societies: Evolutionary and Comparative Perspectives* (Englewood Cliffs, NJ: Prentice-Hall, 1966) and *The System of Modern Societies* (Englewood Cliffs, NJ: Prentice-Hall, 1971); Patrick Nolan and Gerhard Lenski, *Human Societies* (Boulder, CO: Paradigm, 2009); and Jonathan H. Turner, *Human Institutions: A Theory of Societal Evolution* (Boulder, CO: Rowan and Littlefield, 2003). Theorists working in other traditions include the following: for conflict theory, Christopher Chase-Dunn and Thomas D. Hall, *Rise and Demise: Comparing World Systems* (Boulder, CO: Westview Press); for ecological theorizing, Amos Hawley, *Human Ecology: A Theoretical Essay* (Chicago, IL: University of Chicago Press, 1986); for evolutionary biology/conflict theory, Stephen K. Sanderson, *Social Transformations: A General Theory of Historical Development* (Oxford, UK: Rowan and Littlefield, 1999); for ecology, W. G. Runciman, *A Theory of Cultural and Social Selection* (Cambridge, UK: Cambridge University Press, 2009); for conflict theory, Immanuel M. Wallerstein, *The Modern World System* (New York: Academic Press, 1974); and for critical theory, Jürgen Habermas, *Communication and the Evolution of Society*, trans. T. McCarthy (London: Heinemann, 1979). Thus, as is evident, elements of stage modeling of evolution are still evident in sociology, just as they were in the first 100 years of sociological theory.

Thus, evolutionary thinking in sociology is closer to that in biology, even before the modern synthesis in biological evolution was reached near the end of sociology's classical period in 1830. This connection between sociology and biology was lost in the middle decades of the twentieth century, but it returned in the later decades and now constitutes a controversial approach, but one that is not likely to disappear as it did by this time in the last century. These theories all share certain assumptions as listed below:

1. Humans are animals and thus evolved like any other life-form under the basic forces (outlined in the modern synthesis) of evolutionary theory.

2. The traits that humans possess, including biologically based propensities for certain types of behaviors, are the outcome of natural selection as it worked on variations in human phenotypes (and the underlying genotypes) to promote fitness in particular environments.

3. Of particular importance are selection pressures that worked on the neuro-anatomy of humans' ancestors because thinking, emotions, decisions, behavior, and social organization are the outcome of processes operating in the brain as they direct and guide behaviors that build up the sociocultural formations that make up societies.

4. It is important to understand how selection worked on particular parts of humans' and their ancestors' brains to produce generalized human propensities to behave and, hence, organize in particular ways.

5. Patterns of human social organization are not the direct causal outcomes of humans' biologically based behavioral propensities, but these propensities exert some pressure on humans to interact and organize in certain general ways, although these can be significantly modified by nonbiological forces.

6. There are numerous ways to gain information about how natural selection worked on hominid and then human anatomy and neuroanatomy, including (a) cross-species comparisons of different life-forms that organize themselves into macro societies (e.g., insects and humans); (b) comparison of human anatomy, behaviors, and social structures with those of their closest primate relatives, the great apes; (c) analyzing the changing ecology of Africa to understand the selection pressures from the environment that were working on the anatomy of our ancestral line; and (d) extending the biological ideas in evolutionary theory to see if biological concepts and theories can explain the evolution of superorganisms or the sociocultural formations organizing humans into large-scale societies.

There are several, related approaches in biological theories that share these assumptions and that have made inroads into present-day sociological theorizing.

One is *sociobiology*,[14] where the argument is made that natural selection has generated particular behavioral propensities, all addressing the issue of fitness or the capacity of organisms to keep their genes in the gene pool. The structures of organisms and superorganisms (societies) are viewed as "survival machines" that enable genes of organisms to remain in the gene pool. And thus, by viewing how natural selection created these survival machines, it becomes possible to understand the sociocultural world as evolving in response to blind natural selection, which increases the fitness of organisms and superorganisms and the societies in which they and their genes live.

Related to sociobiology is *evolutionary psychology*,[15] which argues in much the same vein as sociobiology but adds the important caveat that natural selection worked mostly on the brain and wired in the brain certain behavioral capacities and propensities that make societies possible. By examining the ecology in which the human line evolved and the selection pressures from this environment on our ancestral line's neuroanatomy, it becomes possible today to discover the modules of the brain that give humans their unique behavioral characteristics, which, in turn, can help explain the sociocultural universe studied by sociologists.

Another approach goes back to the issues of human nature by performing a comparative analysis of humans with their closest primate relatives, chimpanzees and other great apes. In this approach, contemporary apes—the closest living relatives to humans—are considered to be a "distant mirror" in which to see humans' remote ancestors reflected. By studying the behavioral and organizational propensities of primates, it will be possible to understand human nature and how this biological nature still exerts some influence on human behavior and societal evolution.[16]

Still, many sociologists remain fearful about bringing biological ideas into sociology, especially since sociocultural evolution is not the same as biological evolution.

---

[14]Sociobiology was born in the study of insects, with Edward G. Wilson's large work *Sociobiology: The New Synthesis* (Cambridge, MA: Harvard University Press, 1978) taking dead aim at sociology, although the key ideas in this work were developed by a creative set of early thinkers in sociobiology. For sociologists who adhere to all or at least some of the assumptions of sociobiology, see Pierre van den Berghe, *Age and Sex in Human Societies: A Biosocial Perspective* (Belmont, CA: Wadsworth, 1973) and *The Ethnic Phenomenon* (New York: Elsevier, 1981); Joseph Lopreato, *Human Nature and Biosocial Evolution* (London: Allen and Unwin, 1984); Joseph Lopreato and Timothy Crippen, *Crisis in Sociology: The Need for Darwin* (Piscataway, NJ: Transaction Publishers, 1999); and Sanderson, *Social Transformations*.

[15]For foundational statements of evolutionary psychology, see Leda Cosmides and John Tooby, "Evolutionary Psychology and the Generation of Culture, Part II: Case Study: A Computational Theory of Social Exchange," *Ethology and Sociobiology* 10 (1989):51–97. For sociologists who employ this perspective, see Timothy Crippen, "Toward a Neo-Darwinian Sociology," *Sociological Perspectives* 37 (1994):309–335; Satoshi Kanazawa and Mary C. Still, "Why Men Commit Crimes," *Sociological Theory* 18 (2000):434–448; Richard Machalek and Michael W. Martin, "Sociology and the Second Darwinian Revolution," *Sociological Theory* 22 (2004):455–476; and Christine Horne, "Values and Evolutionary Psychology," *Sociological Theory* (2004):477–503.

[16]For examples of this approach to "human nature," see Alexandra Maryanski and Jonathan H. Turner, *The Social Cage: Human Nature and the Evolution of Society* (Stanford, CA: Stanford University Press, 1992) and Jonathan H. Turner and Alexandra Maryanski, *On the Origin of Societies by Natural Selection* (Boulder, CO: Paradigm Press, 2008).

One of their fears is that societal complexity will be subordinated to simple and simplistic explanations that ignore the larger repertoire of theories that have been developed within sociology proper to explain the social world. These fears have some merit because, thus far, the theories introduced by sociobiology and evolutionary psychology tend to be too simple and almost always ignore the emergent properties of the social world that are built from human behaviors and, more important, interpersonal behaviors. Yet at times, the fears of sociologists are somewhat irrational and prejudicial against any effort to understand human societies by the biological characteristics of humans. In Chapter 12, I will review in detail this wide range of evolutionary approaches.

3. General Systems Theorizing

This approach is probably the least prominent at present, although it still enjoys some currency outside sociology. The basic idea is that much of the physical, biological, and sociocultural world is organized as systems of relationships among the constituent parts and that these systems evidence some common properties. Spencer was probably the first general systems theorist in sociology because he argued that key domains of the universe—physical, biological, psychological, sociological, and even ethical—were subject to the forces of evolution, revolving around the movement of matter from simple to more complex forms by virtue of forces pushing on matter and the retained motion of matter. This was a metaphor taken from the physics of Spencer's time, and he employed these general principles, or what he termed *cardinal principles*, in the analysis of all the domains of his conception of the universe.

Another line of general systems theorizing was initiated by Spencer and Comte. Both Comte and Spencer posited an organismic analogy indicating that social systems can be viewed as a type of organism, revealing many similar properties to organisms. Indeed, Spencer even sometimes defined sociology as the study of superorganisms—that is, organization of life-forms. Spencer developed his famous organismic analogy, outlining the similarities and differences between organisms and social systems.[17] This kind of analogy was to morph into what became known as "living systems" theorizing, where correspondences of parts and their operation were analyzed for all living (biotic) systems,[18] even as some concepts were drawn from information systems models. I will examine living systems theory in more detail in Chapter 11.

Functional theorizing often has elements of this general systems approach, as is the case with Parsons's theorizing. Parsons posited that the organismic, biophysical, and teleic universes, as seen from the perspective of the four systems of action (behavioral, personality, social, and cultural), all reveal systemic processes as a result of having to meet the four functional needs for adaptation, goal attainment, integration, and latency.[19]

---

[17]For Spencer's organismic analogy, see pp. 41–43.

[18]See Chapter 11; see James G. Miller, *Living Systems* (New York: McGraw-Hill, 1978).

[19]For Parsons's general systems approach, see pp. 354–357.

The thrust of early general systems theorizing in the modern era, after 1950, was to recognize that systems have common properties and that theories to explain their dynamics might be adopted by different disciplines. It is difficult to describe how exciting this idea was to people in the social sciences; theoretical models could be borrowed from physics and biology to explain social processes that were somewhat isomorphic with those operating in the biophysical sciences. A *General Systems Yearbook* was published, mostly under the direction of physicists, in an effort to demonstrate the merits of this kind of general systems approach.

Functional theorists were the most intrigued by this approach, but many other social scientists were also fascinated. Indeed, groups of symbolic interactionists also proposed general systems approaches,[20] and from the 1960s through the 1970s, these works were read with considerable excitement. Indeed, the identity models that will be examined in Chapter 16 were built upon cybernetic ideas that first emerged in early work on computers but were soon extended to ecosystems and social systems. In fact, lay phrases such as "giving someone feedback" came early in efforts to translate cybernetic processes into ideas that could fit the social sciences.

Another approach that adopts at least some of the ideas of general systems theory is ecological theorizing, to be examined next. Here, biological systems and social systems are seen as systems in which biological and social units seek to adapt under selective pressures. Similarly, the effort to bring Darwinian theorizing into the social sciences represents yet another general systems approach, although its advocates do not phrase their work in general systems vocabularies, or perhaps even know about general systems theorizing. In Chapter 11, I will review the basic ideas of general systems theory, but for the present, let me summarize the key features of this argument—an argument that was evident in Spencer and other functional theorists:

1. Domains of the social, biotic, and physical universes all evidence system properties, revolving around

    A. Differentiation among system parts

    B. Integration of parts through a variety of mechanisms, including

        1. Structural interdependencies of parts
        2. Commonality of parts and their underlying properties, forms, and dynamics

---

[20]For example, see Walter Buckley, *Sociology and Modern Systems Theory* (Englewood Cliffs, NJ: Prentice-Hall, 1967); this work by a symbolic interactionist was widely read and cited. See also William T. Powers, *Behavior: The Control of Perception* (Chicago, IL: Aldine, 1973), which influenced later identity theorists such as Peter J. Burke, whose work is examined in Chapter 16. For some more general analyses of general systems concepts by sociologists, see Kenneth E. Bailey, *Social Entropy Theory* (Albany, NY: SUNY Press, 1989) and "Systems Theory," in *Handbook of Theoretical Sociology*, ed. Jonathan H. Turner (New York: Kluwer Academic, 2001). Richard Adams, *The Eighth Day: Social Evolution and Self-Organization of Energy* (Austin: University of Texas Press, 1988). See also Luhmann, *Systems Theory*.

3. Differentiation of hierarchies of control among parts
4. Cycles of reproduction of parts and their relations
5. Flows of processes that link parts to each other and more inclusive systems of integration.

2. To some degree, systems in different domains of the universe are isomorphic and evidence properties and dynamics that are similar in their basic operation.

3. The dynamics of these properties operate in similar ways, which means that models and theories that explain them in one domain of the universe (say, biology) may be useful in explaining them in another domain (say, sociology).

4. These models may have to be modified in particular ways to account for differences in the properties of systems, but the general models and the underlying principles explaining them may remain the same if summarized at a sufficiently high level of abstraction.

5. Even if there are some properties and dynamics in different systems in diverse domains of the universe that are not isomorphic, some are; and the more these isomorphic properties can be understood and isolated, the greater will be the unity of science and its understanding of all domains of the universe.

6. Even the process of sorting out where systems are isomorphic and where they are not will dramatically increase the potential for theoretical accumulation, especially in the social sciences, which lag behind the biological and physical sciences in their respective knowledge of how their domains of the universe operate.

General systems theorizing declined because it soon became evident that in order to see isomorphism among systems, it becomes necessary to couch concepts, describing them at such a high level of abstraction that many of the key properties and dynamics of systems for theorists in particular domains became too vague. For example, if cultural moral codes and norms in social systems are in some way isomorphic with genetic codes in organismic systems, the point of isomorphism is in the capacity of information to regulate production, growth, and control of parts of organismic and social systems. That said, what does it add to couch sociological concepts of values, norms, ideologies, and other cultural systems into the language of genetics? Are the mechanisms by which they operate the same? Are new insights gained by either geneticists or sociologists in making the claim that these are isomorphic? Answers to such questions were not so self-evident; and in the end, specific disciplines preferred to use their own vocabulary and concepts to describe and explain the operation of those systems operating within the purview of a discipline. And yet there remained some fascination among what was now a much smaller cohort of theorists to explore these isomorphisms and to see if, indeed, the universes studied by different disciplines are understandable with similar models.

4. Ecological Theorizing

Almost hidden in the functional theories of Spencer and Durkheim are two ecological theories that converge with the biological theory of evolution as it developed in the second half of the nineteenth century and early part of the twentieth century. These ecological theories might be seen as a subtype of evolutionary theory because they were part of Spencer's and Durkheim's stage theories, while hinting at notions of selection contained in more biological theories. Yet as they developed during the 1920s and 1930s and, then, during the last third of the twentieth century, ecological theory became a highly distinctive theoretical perspective that had long shed its functional roots. These ecological theories still contain elements of biological theory—for example, resource niches, density, selection, and evolution—but these theoretical ideas are adapted to understanding distinctly sociological phenomena.

Spencer's most famous phrase—"survival of the fittest"—was probably his biggest mistake, but this phrase—hitting on the essence of natural selection—was uttered some nine years before the publication of Charles Darwin's *On the Origin of Species* in 1859, and it was used by Spencer to explain the evolution of societal complexity in terms of intersocietal warfare. For Spencer, warfare among societies had been a powerful evolutionary force because the larger, more complex society would typically win a war; and as the victorious society would incorporate the conquered population, the level of differentiation and complexity of the consolidated society would increase, and over the long run, the size and complexity of societies in general would successively increase as a consequence of war. Unfortunately, however, Spencer also used this phrase to emphasize competition among individuals and collective units *within* a society, with the "more fit" selecting out the "less fit" as a natural part of the social order. This idea meant, literally, the dying off of individual and collective actors through the competition for resources (without societal intervention), and Spencer felt that this process was inevitable in the organization of human beings. But at times in his more philosophical works, he went further: selection operated to increase the fitness of those individuals who "won out" in the competition. Later, this idea was used to justify arguments in favor of what became known as *Social Darwinism* ("Social Spencerianism" would probably have been a more accurate description), where programs of eugenics were proposed, where the genetically unfit would be allowed to die or, worse, be killed off, in order to sustain the fitness of humans. Spencer never went this far in advocating eugenics, but his reputation never recovered from the association of his ideas with that discredited school of thought.

Durkheim[21] had a more benign view of competition and selection. For him, as populations grow, their material density and, hence, their moral density increase, thus raising the level of competition and selection for resources among individuals and collective actors in a given resource niche. For Durkheim, however, people did not die; they simply went to a new niche or created a new type of niche in

---

[21]Durkheim's model of ecological processes is outlined on p. 214.

which to secure resources, thereby increasing the differentiation of human societies. This rather idealized view was probably as extreme as Spencer's overly harsh view of competition.

Human ecology, as it came to be known, first emerged from scholars at the University of Chicago in the early twentieth century and later migrated to the human ecology program at the University of North Carolina at Chapel Hill. At Chicago, the ecologists downsized Spencer's and Durkheim's ideas about competition and selection to a more meso-level analysis of particular types of structures within communities. This Chicago School, as it came to be known, began to develop models of *urban ecology*,[22] in which the zones and sectors of urban areas were seen as the outcome of competition among actors with different levels of resources to purchase or rent urban space. This competition was seen to be institutionalized by real estate markets, which sorted people and corporate actors by their ability to "pay" for space. The result is that urban areas become differentiated by functions— for example, business, industry, schools, government, and the like. Similarly, residential neighborhoods become differentiated by class, ethnicity, and immigration status were sorted by competition for space in cutthroat real estate markets. They also noted, of course, that other forces such as prejudice and discrimination intersected with the housing market and unfairly confined some individuals to less desirable neighborhoods.

In the last third of the twentieth century, a new form of ecological analysis emerged: *organizational ecology*.[23] Organizational ecology emphasized that populations of organizations seek resources in niches; and as the density of organizations in a niche increases, so does the competition and selection among them. As density and competition increase, some organizations die out, while others survive. Thus, there are patterns to organizational founding and rates of demise. When niche density is low, organizational foundings will increase; and as they prove successful, their structures and cultures are copied by other organizations entering the niche. But as density increases, there comes a point when too many organizations now exist relative to the resources available in the niche, with the result that many begin to fail. As more organizations fail, the niche eventually becomes less dense, allowing existing organizations to sustain themselves; and often deaths overshoot the carrying capacity of the niche with the result that there is once again a more modest increase in organizational founding, but never to the extent that was the case when the initial founders opened up the niche.

Organizational ecology more explicitly adopted ideas from evolutionary biology and ecology, but the mentor (Amos Hawley) of the original organizational ecology

---

[22]The Chicago School was famous for using the city of Chicago as a laboratory for empirical work, but members of this school also tried to understand the dynamics of cities, per se, in terms of their ecology; for early urban ecological works, see Chauncey Harris and Edward Ullman, "The Nature of Cities," *The Annals of the American Academy of Political and Social Sciences* 242 (1945):7–14; Richard M. Hurd, *Principles of City Growth* (New York: Record and Guide, 1903); and Hawley, *Human Ecology* (New York: Ronald Press, 1950) and *Urban Society: An Ecological Approach* (New York: Ronald Press, 1981).

[23]Michael T. Hannan and John L. Freeman, "The Population Ecology of Organizations," *American Sociological Review* (1977):929–964.

theorists was from the Chicago School, where the Spencerian and Durkheimian roots of ecological theorizing were still recognized. Interestingly, late in his career, Hawley[24] began to take ecological ideas back up to the macro level, producing a theory more like the original theories of Spencer and Durkheim. Not surprisingly, the theory emphasized the ecological dynamics generating increased differentiation within societies, but with many new conceptual twists. Other theorists have also retained the macro-level emphasis and, like Spencer and Durkheim, blended functional and ecological ideas to produce new kinds of evolutionary and ecological theory.

The key ideas of sociological ecological theorizing have spread to many other theoretical perspectives and research traditions. These ecological theories all emphasize a set of important points as follows:

1. The social world, like the biotic world, can be viewed as composed of resource niches that are essential to the survival of social units in societies.

2. Different types of units seek resources from different niches.

3. The number of different types of social units making up a society is related to the number of diverse niches and the resources in these niches that can be used to sustain these units and their members.

4. The rate of founding of new types of organizational units is (a) positively related to the level of resources in a niche and (b) inversely related to the density of units in a resource niche.

5. The intensity of competition for resources in any given niche is a function of the density of corporate units seeking resources in a niche.

6. The death rate of corporate units in a niche and/or the rate of movement of corporate units out of a niche are both a function of (a) the density of social units and (b) the level of competition among the social units in a niche.

7. The level and patterns of social differentiation in a society are the outcome of processes of competition among social units in diverse resource niches.

These ideas can be applied to many different levels of social organization. Like Spencer and Durkheim, along with others in contemporary theory, they can be applied to societies or even intersocietal systems. They can be used to analyze urban dynamics within and between communities, or organizational processes within and between societies. It is unlikely that ecological theories can explain all social dynamics, but like Spencer and Durkheim, contemporary theory in sociology now appreciates that there are always ecological dimensions to almost every dimension of the social universe because, in the end, social structures and their cultures can only survive by securing resources from their environments.

---

[24]Hawley, *Human Ecology*.

5. Conflict Theorizing

All conflict theories emphasize that inequalities in the distribution of resources create tensions in societies and, eventually, cause conflict among subpopulations. Those who control resources seek to continue to do so, while those who do not have resources attempt to increase their share of resources. Thus, all conflict theories begin with a view of societies and even intersocietal systems as stratified, with some sectors and classes receiving more resources than other sectors and classes. Inherent in this inequality is one of the driving forces of all patterns of social organization. Marx[25] and Weber[26] are given the most credit for emphasizing this fundamental property of social systems, but Spencer[27] also made significant contributions that have been lost and then rediscovered in the latter half of the twentieth century. Simmel[28] also analyzed conflict, but from a different perspective, emphasizing the integrative functions of conflict as much as their disintegrative consequences for societies.

While sociologists have always studied stratification, conflict theorizing remained recessive in American sociology (unlike European sociology), especially its Marxist variants, until the 1960s. Because of Marx's association with communism, conflict theory became conflated with the politics of the Cold War and, hence, was discouraged in academia, even within sociology. Only with the discrediting of McCarthyism in the 1950s were European conflict theories embraced once again in the United States. Yet it was not the power of conflict theory, per se, that led to its renaissance in sociology but, rather, its use as a means of discrediting functional theorizing. Functionalism became the dominant theoretical perspective in American sociology in the 1950s and, to a lesser extent, world sociology, but it had never lacked for critics. At mid-century, European critics had begun to portray functionalism as a conservative, if not utopian, theory that served to legitimate the status quo (see Footnote 6)—a reasonable point of discussion that became rather overblown in the turbulent 1960s. Functionalism was seen to have failed to analyze inequality, conflict, and change; and thus, conflict theory was a mode of theorizing that could challenge the intellectual hegemony of functionalism.

Conflict theory was successful in toppling functionalism and, indeed, virtually eliminating it from sociology, although functionalism has never died but simply reconstituted itself in a different form (see above section on functionalism). With the spread of conflict dynamics all over the real world during the 1960s, the rise of conflict theory was perhaps inevitable, even without the added bonus of its attack on functionalism. And for a time, almost all theoretical approaches began emphasizing power, inequality, and conflict dynamics, while often ignoring the integrative processes that functional theory had, perhaps, overemphasized. Thus, a rather

---

[25]For Marx's analysis of inequality, stratification, and conflict, see pp. 88–93.

[26]For Weber's analysis of conflict, see pp. 130–138.

[27]For Spencer's analysis of power and conflict, see pp. 49–52.

[28]For Simmel's analysis of conflict, see pp. 199–200.

one-sided functionalism was replaced by an equally one-sided conflict theory, but only for a time. Just as functionalism disappeared only to rise again in a different guise, so was conflict theory simply reabsorbed across many perspectives, and in the present day, it is difficult to identify "conflict theory" as a distinctive theoretical approach. Just as few walk nowadays around calling themselves functionalists, not many proclaim themselves to be conflict theorists, as they did in the 1960s and 1970s. Indeed, both forms of theorizing persist, but in more muted and less polarizing forms, which is probably a useful turn of events. Still, the result of the intellectual clash between functionalism and conflict theory produced a number of distinctive types of theorizing. All emphasize most of the following points:

1. All social systems reveal inequalities in the distribution of valued resources.

2. These inequalities generate conflicts of interests between those subpopulations with varying levels of resources.

3. These inequalities also generate negative emotions and grievances among those who receive the lowest levels of resources.

4. Mobilization for conflict is likely to occur when individuals perceive that the distribution of resources is unfair and unjust.

5. Mobilization for conflict among subordinates revolves around (a) the development of ideologies and beliefs about inequalities, (b) the emergence of leaders to articulate grievances, and (c) the mobilization of resource materials to forge organizations dedicated to conflict.

6. Conflicts will generally cause some reorganization of a social system, typically creating new patterns of inequality that will serve as the target of the next round of conflict and change.

There has been a number of prominent approaches to conflict dynamics that begin with the above assumptions. Each approach takes a somewhat different tack in conceptualizing the operation of the processes listed above.

Neo-Marxist Analytical Theories. The thrust of Marx's analysis persists until the present day,[29] with many theorists employing Marxist assumptions and vocabulary and, yet at the same time, trying to account for why Marx's prediction about the imminent revolution by the proletariat never occurred in a capitalist society. Moreover, these approaches have also tried to explain why the polarization of classes into two camps—the bourgeoisie and the proletariat—never materialized. Instead, more like Weber's[30] prediction, the number of classes has proliferated with capitalism,

---

[29]For representative neo-Marxian theorists, see Michael Burawoy and Erik Olin Wright, "Sociological Marxism," In *Handbook of Sociological Theory*, ed. Jonathan H. Turner (New York: Springer, 2001); Michael Burawoy, *The Politics of Production* (London: New Left Books); and Erik Olin Wright, *Classes* (London: Verso, 1985) and *Class Counts* (Cambridge, UK: Cambridge University Press, 1997).

[30]For Weber's conception of classes in emerging capitalist societies, see p. 130–131.

especially the middle classes, with the boundaries among these middle classes being somewhat amorphous. They have also sought to account for the fact that ownership and management of capitalist organizations of production is often divided. Moreover, the creation of joint stock companies has diffused the ownership of companies to the point where it is hard to know just who the bourgeoisie are. Other issues that neo-Marxist theories have confronted include the rise of financial services industries and the employment of significant portions of labor by government, which is not a profit-making organization and, hence, not driven by capitalist needs for wealth and capital accumulation. Yet, even as they take account of changes in capitalism since Marx's time, neo-Marxist theories still want to sustain the emancipatory thrust of Marx's analysis, the value theory of labor as the metric by which the rate and level of exploitation of workers are measured and the belief that socialism still remains a viable alternative to capitalism.

Neo-Weberian Analytical Theories. These theories can be analytical, and they emphasize the degree of correlation among the dimensions of stratification outlined by Weber[31]—material wealth (class), power (party), and prestige (status groups)—as these cause conflict. These theories often emphasize the culture of diverse classes, the organizations that sustain inequalities while consolidating and using power to maintain the stratification system. They emphasize that conflict is often local, rather than society-wide, and they do not have the same emancipation and political agenda of neo-Marxist theories revolving around the emancipation of the lower classes.

Probably the most frequent adoption of Weber's ideas is in historical-comparative sociological analysis,[32] where considerable emphasis has been placed on revolutions and other transforming conflict processes—a subject more in line with Marx but with a mode of analysis that is entirely different and, in the end, more Weberian. A good deal of this historical-comparative analysis focuses on the powers of the state. Here, the processes that weaken state power, especially fiscal crises but also political delegitimization, are explored, emphasizing that conflict can be initiated by either elites or the masses, and sometimes both, and leads to state breakdown as the state's power is weakened.

These theories usually examine a series of internal dynamics of various historical societies. These dynamics can include some combination of population growth, price inflation, fiscal crises, demands for state patronage by elites, excessive consumption by elites, downward mobility by elites and upward mobility by the bourgeoisie, rural revolts, and migrations of younger-age cohorts, who are more likely to be

---

[31]For Weber's analysis of *class, party,* and *status groups,* see pp. 130–136.

[32]For representative and widely available neo-Weberian analyses, see Randall Collins, *Conflict Sociology* (San Diego, CA: Academic Press, 1975) and *Weberian Sociological Theory* (Cambridge, UK: Cambridge University Press, 1986). And for classic Weberian conflict analyses within comparative-historical sociology, see Barrington Moore, *Social Origins of Dictatorship and Democracy* (Boston, MA: Beacon Press, 1966); Charles Tilly, *From Mobilization to Revolution* (Reading, MA: Addison-Wesley, 1978) and *European Revolutions, 1492-1992* (Oxford, UK: Blackwell, 1993); Theda Skocpol, *States and Social Revolutions* (New York: Cambridge University Press, 1979); and Jack Goldstone, *Revolution and Rebellion in the Early Modern World* (Berkeley: University of California Press, 1991).

restive in urban areas. These events are seen to erode the state's power by sapping its financial strength and causing fiscal crises, which, in turn, leads to the state's delegitimization. At the same time, these internal events are often accelerated by other societal factors, such as market failures and inefficient tax collection, as well as by intersocietal pressures stemming from the failure of chartered corporations in economic competition with other societies, wars that deplete even further the resources of the state and hasten fiscal crises, and, most important, losing a war in the geopolitical system. All of these events increase the likelihood of state breakdown, and reorganization of the society will occur.

These neo-Weberian theories remain true to the historical-comparative methods championed by Weber, the general variables that he saw as important in understanding conflict processes, and the emphasis on understanding how these variables play out under different historical conditions. At times, elements of Marxian analysis are combined with these Weberian elements, especially since revolutions (in more agrarian societies, some of which evidence elements of capitalism) are a common theme in neo-Weberian theorizing.[33]

Analytical Synthetic Conflict Theories. This group of conflict theories has taken the basic Marxian model of conflict and revised it in several ways.[34] First, the theory is made more abstract, abandoning all of the Marxian terminology, which constrains the theory to a particular historical time and place (i.e., industrial capitalism and mobilization by the proletariat against the bourgeoisie). For contemporary Marxist theories, however, such an exercise "takes the Marx out of Marx," but for analytical theorists, the goal is to make Marx's key ideas about the conditions of conflict mobilization relevant to contemporary societies. Instead, relations are simply conceptualized as those between superordinates and subordinates in a system of inequality within social systems. Second, in making the ideas of Marx's theory more abstract, it also becomes possible to extend Marx's ideas to *any* type of social system, not just a society. And third, all of these more analytical theories add the necessary correctives to Marx's theory, particularly those suggested by his fellow Germans, Weber and Simmel.

The end result is a general theory of conflict mobilization in all social systems revealing inequality in the distribution of resources. The theory then outlines the basic conditions (specified by Marx) that sharpen conflicts of interests, increase awareness of subordinates of their interest in changing the system of inequality, mobilize subordinates for conflict, and raise the intensity and violence of the conflict. The biggest correction in Marx's basic theory is that internal violence in a society does not come from highly organized conflict parties but, rather, from situations where the subordinates are just beginning to get organized around

---

[33]For a blend of Marxian and Weberian analysis, see Jeffrey Paige, *Agrarian Revolution: Social Movements and Export Agriculture in the Underdeveloped World* (New York: Free Press, 1975).

[34]For representative analytical conflict theories, see Ralf Dahrendorf, *Class and Class Conflict in Industrial Societies* (Stanford, CA: Stanford University Press, 1967) and "Toward a Theory of Social Conflict," *Journal of Conflict Resolution* (1958):170–183 and Jonathan H. Turner, "A Strategy for Reformulating Dialectical and Functional Conflict Theories," *Social Forces* (1975):433–444.

counter-ideologies, competing leaders, escalated negative emotions, and diverse structures channeling their anger. Under these conditions, conflict can become more violent. In contrast, when subordinates become well organized and instrumental (Marx's notion of a "class for itself"), they are more likely to negotiate and compromise because they are now clearly organized with explicit goals that can only be partially met through compromises.

Fourth, there is also a conscious effort to convert Marx's time-bound theory (about the historical epoch of capitalism) into formally stated principles or abstract laws of conflict. The principles are presumed to be relevant to all times and places and to all social systems revealing inequalities. A group, organization, community, or whole society can be seen as operating in terms of a common set of laws about conflict mobilization among subordinates in a system of inequality.

A related field of inquiry into the dynamics of social movements also borrows key ideas from Marx in trying to explain the origins and operation of social movements. These theories draw from many other theoretical traditions, such as the symbolic interactionism initiated by Mead, Weber's emphasis on charisma, and variants of economic theory emphasizing resource mobilization and calculations of risks and benefits to be gained from collective participation in social movement organizations.[35] The goal is to explain how shared grievances push individuals to become collectively organized to pursue conflict (of varying types and forms) against the system of authority within various institutional domains, such as polity, economy, and religion.

World-Systems Theorizing. This approach shifts the unit of analysis from societies to intersocietal systems.[36] Relations among societies are conceptualized as being stratified in the sense that some societies have more resources than others and are, thereby, able to exploit weaker societies. They often do so by imposing unbalanced systems of trade, in which raw resources are taken from dependent societies at low costs and used to generate increased wealth in the more dominant society when extracted resources are converted to finished goods and products. Distinctions between geopolitical and geoeconomic systems are often made, with the geopolitical system being built by patterns of warfare and conquest, with dominant societies winning wars and controlling the resources of conquered societies. Empire formation is typically the main topic of these geopolitical systems, and their analysis is often conducted under historical-comparative approaches drawing from Weber as much as Marx.

When analysis shifts to geoeconomic systems, however, Marxian ideas become more prominent. In many respects, these geoeconomic theories retain the emancipatory

---

[35]For examples, see David A. Snow and Sarah A. Soule, *A Primer on Social Movements* (New York: Norton, 2010).

[36]For well-known and accessible world-system theories, see Christopher Chase-Dunn, *Global Formation: Structures of the World Economy*, 2nd ed. (Lanham, MD: Rowan and Littlefield, 1998); Andrew Gunner Frank, *Crisis in the World Economy* (New York: Holmes and Meier, 1980) and *Reorient: Global Economy in the Asian Age* (Berkeley: University of California Press, 1998); and Immanuel Wallerstein, *The Modern World System,* vol. 1 (New York: Academic Press, 1974).

thrust of Marx by emphasizing that the "contradictions" of capitalism will work themselves out in a global economic system. Here, the difficulties of ever forming a strong, world-level government, like those operating in individual capitalist societies, opens the doors for economic actors to use their power and control of world markets to exploit less developed and less powerful societies in a manner predicted by Marx's analysis of capitalist societies. This world-level system of stratification of societies reveals many of the contradictions of capitalism emphasized by Marx and eventually pushes for the mobilization for conflict as workers resent their exploitation and as global market speculation leads to market collapse. Under these conditions, sectors with exploited societies will mobilize for conflict and seek to form less exploitive intersocietal relations within and between societies. Thus, a good portion of world-system theorists recognize that the contradictions of capitalism have not produced conditions for intrasocietal revolutions, especially in capitalist societies, but the spread of capitalism across the globe has finally, it is believed, generated the conditions in which these contradictions of capitalism will be exposed. The result will be conflict at many intra- and intersocietal levels, which, in the end, will create one world government dedicated to socialism—or so it is hoped by many world-system theorists.

Analytical Functional Conflict Theory. For a period in the second half of the twentieth century, especially while the intellectual battle between conflict and functional theories raged on, scholars such as Lewis Coser[37] put "a pox on both of these houses" of thought. The argument was derived primarily from Simmel's emphasis that conflict can have integrative consequences for societies and the parties to the conflict. Conflict theory, it was argued, overemphasized the disintegrative effects of conflict, while functional theory overemphasized the integrative consequences of all social processes to the exclusion of conflict. What was needed, then, is a theoretical perspective—*functional* conflict theory—that reduces the overemphasis on either disintegrative or integrative processes.

With this kind of rhetorical ploy, functional conflict theory, derived from Simmel's thinking and, to a lesser extent, Weber's sociology, produced a theory emphasizing the causes of conflict (inequality, deprivations, emotional arousal), the violence of the conflict, the duration of the conflict, the effects of conflict on the respective parties, and the consequences of conflict for the more inclusive structure (society) in which the conflict has occurred. Similar arguments were made about other social processes, such as deviance, that are typically seen as dysfunctional; instead, these processes can have positive consequences for both individuals and societies. This approach did not last long, but it represented an effort to bring the other two German conflict theories—those formulated by Weber and Simmel—into the modern canon.

Thus, the theories of Marx, Weber, and Simmel are well represented in the modern sociological canon. Most of the theories make these classical giants' work more

---

[37]See, for example, Lewis A. Coser, *The Functions of Social Conflict* (Glencoe, IL: Free Press, 1956), "Some Functions of Violence," *Annals of the American Academy of Political and Social Science* (1960):334, "Some Functions of Deviant Behavior and Normative Flexibility," *American Journal of Sociology* (1962):172–181, and *Continuities in the Study of Social Conflict* (New York: Free Press, 1967).

analytical and abstract, even when it still has an emancipatory thrust, as is the case with most Marxian theories. The range of these more analytical theories outlined in this section will be analyzed in detail in Chapter 14, while the more evaluative and ideological theories derived from Marx and Weber will be examined in Chapters 22, 23, and 24.

6. Interactionist Theorizing

George Herbert Mead's[38] synthesis of pragmatist theories into a general theory of interaction has continued to exert a strong influence on all of micro-sociology, although other early masters such as Charles Horton Cooley,[39] Émile Durkheim,[40] and Alfred Schutz[41] are also part of interactionist theorizing as it has developed over the last century. There are now distinctive traditions of interactionist theorizing, some retaining all of Mead and other approaches introducing new ideas into Mead's general approach. Yet all interactionist theories begin with at least these assumptions derived from Mead:

1. Individuals are born into ongoing social structures and will retain in their behavioral repertoire those behaviors that facilitate adjustment and adaptation to these ongoing patterns of cooperative interpersonal behaviors.

2. The behavioral capacities for cooperation with others emerge from a process of imitation, active coaching by caretakers, and biological maturation.

3. The first critical behavioral capacity is learning conventional or significant gestures that mean the same thing to the person emitting the gestures as to the person reading these gestures.

4. With the capacity to understand conventional gestures, individuals can role-take and place themselves into the role of others and thus anticipate their likely actions and, thereby, cooperate with them.

5. With role-taking comes the capacity for mind, or the ability to imaginatively rehearse (in the mind, as it were) the consequences of various alternative behaviors, to inhibit those that would be inappropriate, and finally to emit those that would facilitate cooperation.

---

[38]For the basic outline of Mead's synthesis, see his *Mind, Self, and Society* (Chicago, IL: University of Chicago Press, 1934), 340–363.

[39]Cooley had been a colleague of Mead at the University of Michigan, early in Mead's career; see Mead, *Mind, Self, and Society*, 323–335.

[40]Durkheim's analysis of religion, especially emotion-arousing rituals, was never a part of Mead's approach but became important to interactionist theorizing in general in the later decades of the twentieth century.

[41]Schutz's career extends beyond the time frame adopted in this book,1830–1930, and his work has not been highly influential in mainstream interactionism today or in general sociology. Yet it is important in some of its variants, and thus, we are including mention and later a more detailed summary of what we term *phenomenological interactionism*.

6. With role-taking, individuals can begin to see themselves as objects in all situations, and by reading the gestures of others, they can derive self images about how others think of them and adjust their conduct so as to gain a positive evaluation from others.

7. These self-images will, over time, crystallize into more permanent conceptions of self along many dimensions, including how self is viewed in particular roles, in particular types of situations and social structures, or in all situations (in recent years, these types of selves have been denoted by the concept of multiple *identities*).

8. Individuals can also role-take with generalized others—or communities of attitudes, or beliefs—and use these in minded deliberations over alternative lines of potential conduct that will verify self and facilitate cooperation.

9. Societies are built up by individuals exhibiting these behavioral capacities outlined above, but more important, it is these capacities that enable societies and the institutions within them to reproduce themselves.

10. At the same time, existing social structures and their cultures (Mead's generalized others) constrain the significant gestures that people employ, their role-taking, their minded deliberations, and their sense of self or selves (identities) invoked in interaction, with the result that the behavioral capacities of individuals become aligned with the constraints and demands of social structure and culture.

Symbolic Interactionism. After his death, lecture notes from several years of Mead's famous social psychology course at the University of Chicago were edited and collected and published posthumously in the book *Mind, Self, and Society*. Later, Herbert Blumer, who had actually taken over Mead's course in the semester when he died, began to use the label *symbolic interactionism* to describe Mead-inspired theories.[42] These theories emphasized that humans create symbols to denote aspects of the social world; to role-take with various others, including generalized others (culture); and to use what they learn in role-taking to select courses of action that will facilitate cooperation. Humans also see images of self in the gestures of others (Cooley's famous notion of the "looking-glass self") and on the basis of these images experience emotions about how others evaluate them. All of these processes enable individuals to construct societies from the behavioral capacities for mind and self.

Almost immediately, as it evolved into a coherent theoretical perspective in the mid-twentieth century, symbolic interactionism split into two general camps. One emphasized that symbolic interactionism can develop scientific theory to explain even the seemingly fluid social processes of interaction, while the other argued that this fluidity is not amenable to the formulation of scientific laws but, instead, to only a general sensitizing conceptual scheme for describing empirical events. Most of those who held to this latter epistemology employed qualitative research methods involving thick descriptions of interaction processes, explained with the vocabulary

---

[42]See Herbert Blumer, *Symbolic Interactionism* (Englewood Cliffs, NJ: Prentice-Hall, 1969).

in Mead's (and later symbolic interactionists') conceptualizations of how humans interact with each other. But those who advocated for scientific use of symbolic interactionist ideas adopted more quantitative methods in experimental research designs and began to emphasize identities as the key dynamic in human interaction and, ultimately, in the building up of social structure and culture.

Identity Theories. All symbolic interactionist theories emphasize self as the basic gyroscope of behavior and interaction, but the more scientifically oriented symbolic interactionists began to conceptualize self as a series of identities that individuals present in various situations and that they seek to have verified in the eyes of others.[43] Several levels of identity have been theorized:[44] *role identities* (for roles that people play), *group identities* (or social structures to which people belong or to which they identify if they do not actually belong), *social identities* (about the social categories, like gender and ethnicity, to which people belong), *moral identities* (tied to values and beliefs about what is right and proper), and *core identities* (about the person as an individual). These identities obviously vary by their scope. Role identities are tied to just one specific role, while group identities are built around distinct groups. In contrast, social, moral, and core identities can be invoked in virtually all situations and, thus, are very general and portable to any group or role that a person may play.

These identities also vary in their importance to individuals, and to some extent, they can be arranged as a hierarchy of "salience" or "prominence."[45] Those identities high in the hierarchy are more likely to be presented to others; but if a person cannot have an identity verified, this identity is likely to fall down the hierarchy, or the individual will seek out others who are willing to verify the identity. Identity theories also emphasize emotions—a topic that Mead virtually ignored—as will be examined below in theories of emotion. Chapter 16 will examine these identity theories and the emotional consequences of verifying or failing to verify identities.

Role Theories. At one time, theories of role dynamics were quite common in the social sciences, especially sociology and psychology. Within sociology, they had a symbolic interactionist bias, emphasizing the processes of role-taking (determining the behavior dispositions of others) and, in Ralph Turner's works,[46] role-making, as the complement of Mead's concept of role-taking (emitting gestures to

---

[43]For examples, see Peter J. Burke and Jan E. Stets, *Identity Theory* (Oxford, UK: Oxford University Press, 2009); George McCall and J. L. Simmons, *Identities and Interactions* (New York: Free Press, 1978); and Sheldon S. Stryker, *Symbolic Interactionism: A Social Structural Version* (Menlo Park, CA: Benjamin-Cummings, 1980).

[44]Jonathan H. Turner, *Theoretical Principles of Sociology*, vol. 2: *Microdynamics* (New York: Springer, 2012).

[45]See McCall and Simmons, *Identities and Interactions* and Stryker, *Symbolic Interactionism.*

[46]Ralph H. Turner, "Role Taking: Process vs. Conformity," *in Human Behavior and Social Processes*, ed. A. Rose (Boston, MA: Houghton Mifflin), "Role Theory" in *Handbook of Sociological Theory*, ed. Jonathan H. Turner (New York: Kluwer Academic/Plenum, 2001); Peter Callero, "From Role-Playing to Role-Using: Understanding Role as Resource," *Social Psychology Quarterly* 57 (1994):228–243.

signal the role that self is trying to play). There has also been a more phenomeno-logical element (see discussion below) in role theory, emphasizing that individuals assume in any interaction that others are trying to play an identifiable role; and so they are generally willing to postpone judgments about another's behavior until they discern the role that is being made or presented by this person. Individuals have in their stocks of knowledge, inventories of various types and variants of roles, and thus role-taking involves reading the role-making gestures of others and then scanning these cognitive inventories of roles to determine the role that a person is seeking to make.

Like any symbolic interactionist approach, there is always an emphasis on self in the role-taking and role-making processes. Individuals always try to present self to others, and one of the principle vehicles for doing so is through role-making. Individuals are thus very motivated to have their roles verified by others because a sense of self or, in more contemporary terms, an identity or a set of identities is almost always at stake in making roles. As will be evident below, role theories blend into dramaturgical theories because they emphasize that culture provides a script for how to play a role, but this role must be played on a stage in front of an audience that also has expectations for how roles should be played. Individuals are given a certain amount of dramatic license in playing roles because they also must verify an identity in each of their performances on stage.

Roles are also a point of connection between individuals, on the one hand, and social structure, on the other. Individuals seek to play roles that meet the cultural expectations and normative requirements attached to status positions in social structures. Roles are not, however, mere behaviors that meet the expectations attached to status locations in social structures; they are also used strategically to receive valued resources and to verify self. As a result, role enactments can change social structure and culture, especially if many individuals seek to do so.

The most recent work on roles has emphasized that roles can be used as resources that can be deployed in order to gain access to other valued resources, and thus the strategic dimension of roles has gained more emphasis in recent years. And thus, from Mead's early work and then from the efforts of theorists in the early and late twentieth century to develop a theory of roles, there exists a rather sophis-ticated set of theoretical generalizations about role dynamics. Yet over the last thirty years, theorizing has emphasized status processes over role dynamics, as is examined later under structuralist theorizing. Role theories will be examined in detail in Chapter 17.

Status Theories. The interstitial period between the classical and modern eras—say, 1925–1950—involved efforts at conceptual clarification. Role and status were two concepts that sociologists had begun to use extensively, and yet it was not so clear as to what each was and how each should be distinguished from the other. Role theo-rizing began as part of an effort at clarification; and the same was true of the notion of status. In both cases, a great deal was learned about the key properties and dynamics of status and roles, although even today the concept still retains some ambiguity. Role theorizing dominated over status theorizing for the first two decades of the modern era, but the reverse has been true since the mid-1970s.

Several properties of status have been emphasized in theory. One is the conception of status as a *location* within various types of social units. Another is the view of status as embodying sets of *expectation states* for the behaviors of individuals, and it is this conception of status that led to a highly productive theory research program among generations of theorists and researchers. The emphasis on status as a location in a system of status positions led to research and theorizing on the effects of the network of status positions on people's actions and on the normative expectations attached to status positions. The emphasis on status as markers of bundles of expectation states led to the analysis of how differences in authority and prestige attached to status pull expectation states for people's behaviors from beliefs, while also generating expectations for people on the basis of their competence in behaviors. There is nothing contradictory in these points of interest; they are, in fact, quite complementary. Yet they lead to different types of theorizing. With status as location, concern shifts to the dynamics of the networks of status, and how these network properties affect status dynamics. With expectation states as the emphasis, attention shifts to how they are generated in the first place, how they become stabilized or change, and how they lead to the formation of more general status beliefs that constrain the expectation states attached to status. Combined, status theorizing emphasizes the following key features and dynamics of status:[47]

1. Status is a marker of locations in a system of status positions, the most important properties of which are their number, density, and differences in authority and power.

2. Status connects persons with social structure and culture by virtue of establishing their location in a system of status positions and by making relevant certain cultural beliefs, norms, and expectations.

3. Cultural beliefs always contain status beliefs about the characteristics of individuals occupying a particular status position, and these status beliefs become expectation states for performance and evaluations of social worth of individuals in varying status positions.

4. Status defines persons in two basic ways, as

    A. Incumbents in status positions within social structures revealing divisions of labor, with the dynamics of status in such structures revolving around the expectation states tied to differences in power, authority, and prestige of status positions relative to one another and to the differential expectation states inhering in status

    B. Members of general social categories—male, female, young, old, ethnicity, class affiliation, and the like—and the status beliefs about individuals in these social categories, evaluations of the moral worth of memberships in differentially evaluated social categories, and expectation states for members in diverse categories.

---

[47]For reviews of status dynamics, see Chapter 17 and Jonathan H. Turner, *Face-to-Face: Toward a Theory of Interpersonal Processes* (Stanford, CA: Stanford University Press, 2002) and *Theoretical Principles of Sociology*, vol. 2: *Microdynamics* (New York: Springer, 2011).

5. Many of the dynamics of status revolve around the impact of status within divisions of labor (4-A above) and status as membership in a more general social category (4-B above, sometimes conceptualized as a "diffuse status characteristic" because categoric-unit memberships are carried to many diverse status locations in division of labor), thereby causing intersection of their status locations in a division of labor.

6. Individuals almost always take cognizance of the expectation states attached to their locational status and diffuse status characteristics and the expectation states of others by virtue of their status location and their diffuse status characteristics.

7. If expectation states are ambiguous or unknown, individuals will seek to discover them and/or to develop them on the basis of performances or, if available or known, the basis of existing cultural beliefs and norms.

8. Those with higher ranks, more prestige, and moral worth attached to their status (whether the type described in 4-A or 4-B above, or both) will be more assertive and controlling over those in lower-ranked, less prestigious, and less valued status locations or memberships in social categories.

In Chapter 17, I will review the theorizing for status dynamics that has been built up over the last fifty years, using the assumptions listed above.

Dramaturgical Theories. Like role theories, dramaturgical approaches often make an analogy to the theater. There is a cultural script of norms and beliefs (ideologies), there is a cast or team of actors playing roles outlined by the cultural script, there is a stage that makes available various props to be used in dramatic presentations of self and determines the ecology of performances, and there is an audience of others who evaluate actors' performances. Unlike most symbolic interactionist perspectives, however, the importance of self and identities is given less emphasis as the central dynamic around which interaction revolves. Instead, self is less enduring and transitory, becoming part of the performance on a stage. And like any part of a dramatic performance, it can be altered and discarded for another self if required by the cultural script. In fact, self is presented strategically in order to carry off a performance.

Apart from the metaphor to the theater, dramaturgical theories emphasize that interactions occur in encounters and, in turn, are typically lodged inside more inclusive social units.[48] Encounters can be focused, whereby individuals face each other and mutually respond to each other's talk and body language. Encounters are often unfocused, typically occurring in public spaces where persons monitor each other's movements but avoid face engagement and talk. Because encounters are embedded

---

[48]Erving Goffman, *The Presentation in Everyday Life* (Garden City, NY: Anchor Books, 1959), *Encounters: Two Studies in the Sociology of Interaction* (Indianapolis, IN: Bobbs-Merrill, 1961), *Interaction Ritual* (Garden City, NY: Anchor Books, 1967), *Behavior in Public Places* (New York: Free Press, 1963), *Relations in Public* (New York: Harper and Row, 1972).

in larger social structures, the script is often written by the culture of this structure, with each encounter representing an opportunity and obligation to present an appropriate self to others and to play roles, talk, and emote in accordance with the cultural script.

It is through encounters that social structures and their cultures are built up and reproduced over time, and once in place, these sociocultural formations constrain the dynamics of encounters by providing the stage and the script for dramatic performances. Interaction in focused encounters then proceeds by successfully categorizing the type of interactions along several dimensions, such as (a) the relative amounts of work—practical, social, or ceremonial content; (b) the appropriate level of intimacy or formality; (c) the social categories (gender, ethnicity, age) of self and others; (d) the appropriate forms of talk; (e) the rituals that are to be used to open, structure, and close the encounter; (f) the feelings that should be felt and displayed; (g) the particular roles that should be taken up; (h) the situational props that can be used; (i) the appropriate spacing among participants; and (j) the type of self that can or should be presented. In unfocused encounters, emphasis is more on (a) the appropriate spacing of individuals in an ecological setting, (b) the proper movements through space and use of available props, (c) the avoidance of face engagement and talk, and (d) the use of proper rituals when face engagement inadvertently occurs or when unintended violations of spacing occur.[49] In Chapter 18, I will examine the range of dramaturgical theories that have emerged over the last forty years.

Theories of Emotions. Because Mead did not analyze emotions, they were not part of most interactionist theories for two-thirds of the twentieth century. If Cooley[50] had been the dominant theorist in the symbolic interactionist tradition, the study of emotions such as *shame* and *pride* would have become part of theorizing, and the sociology of emotions would have emerged in the early decades of the twentieth century. Interactionist theories are not the only theories that include emotions, but it is within this theoretical tradition that theorizing on the dynamics of emotions emerged in the 1970s.

Dramaturgical theories were an early perspective in which emotions were analyzed. Scholars like Erving Goffman, the founder of this approach, emphasized that emotions such as embarrassment emerge when individuals breach the smooth flow of the encounter, forcing them to offer repair rituals to restore the micro order. Others, such as Arlie Hochschild,[51] combined dramaturgical and Marxist theorizing by emphasizing that there is an *emotion culture* in a society, composed of emotion ideologies (about the emotions that should be felt and expressed in various types of situations), feeling rules about the specific emotions that should be experienced by

---

[49]Jonathan H. Turner, *Human Emotions: A Sociological Theory* (London: Routledge, 2008).

[50]Charles Horton Cooley, *Human Nature and Social Order* (New York: Scribner, 1902).

[51]Arlie Hochschild, *The Managed Heart: The Commercialization of Human Feeling* (Berkeley: University of California Press, 1983).

individuals in different types of situations, and display rules about the specific emotions that should be displayed in various roles. Moreover, because modern, market-driven societies often require that individuals display emotions that they do not feel, a great many encounters—particularly those associated with work—involve a considerable amount of "emotion work" in which individuals try, at a minimum, to display the appropriate emotions and, if they can, to feel these emotions. Such emotion work is inherently alienating because individuals often feel the opposite of the emotions that must be displayed, thereby forcing them to engage in alienated labor, which only increases their emotional burden.

Symbolic interactionists also began to emphasize emotions in the 1970s, along several lines of inquiry.[52] One was the view that individuals seek to sustain consistency among their cognitions and emotions about self, situations, others, and behaviors; and when there is inconsistency among these elements of interaction situations, individuals will experience negative emotions and be motivated to bring conceptions of self, behaviors, situation, and others back into line. Another tack was to emphasize that individuals all seek to have their identities verified by others in situations. When an identity (or identities) is (are) accepted by others, persons will experience positive emotions, whereas when an identity is not verified by others in a situation, individuals will adopt various strategies to bring their identities, behavioral outputs, and perceptions of others' responses to these outputs back into line; if they cannot, they may have to change identities, change behaviors, or leave the situation where their identities cannot be verified. A third line of inquiry involved blending more psychoanalytic ideas with interactionist theories. The goal of the more pyschoanalytic variants of symbolic interactionisms is to emphasize that negative emotions in general, and negative emotions about self in particular, are highly painful and are often pushed below the consciousness. These repressed emotions, however, can be transmuted (e.g., repressed shame may come out as anger along with aggressive behavior) and almost always intensified; and the result is that the flow of interaction is always influenced by the emotions that break through the mechanisms of repression. And moreover, if sufficiently large numbers of individuals experience similar emotions and repress them, these emotions can have large effects on social structures and culture when they emerge collectively.

As will become evident in Part II, I will analyze the emotional dynamics operating in all interactionists theories, whether symbolic interactionist, identity, role, status, or dramaturgical theories. Rather than have a separate chapter on emotions, I have decided to analyze the more recent way in which the sociology of emotions has been incorporated into diverse interactionist theories.

Phenomenological Theories. The term *phenomenology* generally denotes the study of consciousness. In Germany, a philosophical school with this name emerged under

---

[52]For detailed summaries of these approaches, see Jonathan H. Turner and Jan E. Stets, *The Sociology of Emotions* (Cambridge, UK: Cambridge University Press, 2005) and Jan E. Stets and Jonathan H. Turner, *Handbook of the Sociology of Emotions* (New York: Springer, 2006).

the influence of Edmund Husserl.[53] Alfred Schutz[54] converted Husserl's ideas into a more sociological approach that continues to inspire sociology because it converges with Mead's sociology. Husserl's philosophical project emphasized that the external world "out there" is mediated through the senses as these register on people's consciousness. Prior to any question about the nature of this external world, then, is the question of how consciousness works since the world out there is filtered through consciousness. He began using the term *world of the natural attitude,* later shortened to *lifeworld,* to emphasize that humans take for granted much of the world around them. Moreover, this lifeworld *is* reality for humans; and the critical points for the more sociological application of his ideas are that (a) the lifeworld is taken for granted, and yet it structures people's thoughts and perceptions of what is real, and (b) the lifeworld promotes the presumption among humans that they share the same experiences of the world out there. This lifeworld is the essence of consciousness, but the substance of this consciousness is less important than the process of consciousness, per se. Husserl then set about a philosophical project of trying to discover the "pure mind," or the fundamental nature of consciousness, by divorcing the substance of consciousness from the processes of consciousness. The project inevitably stalled, but it was taken up by Alfred Schutz, who built a more sociologically informed phenomenological theory.

Phenomenological Interactionism. Schutz took the basic problematic of Husserl's phenomenology and first blended it with Weber's concerns with action and *verstehen* and later with elements of symbolic interactionist theory. Schutz's critique of Weber was the latter's failure to explain how individuals come to experience the world subjectively and how intersubjectivity emerges—that is, how people come to feel that they are experiencing the same world. His theory parallels Mead's analysis of role-taking and perhaps even the notion of a "generalized other," but early pragmatist philosophers like Mead did not have a great influence on Schutz's early formulation of phenomenological sociology. His basic argument is that humans operate under the presumption of a "reciprocity of perspectives" and the presumption of sharing a common world despite unique biographical experiences.

---

[53]Edmund Husserl, *Phenomenology and the Crisis of Western Philosophy* (New York: Harper and Row, 1965; originally published 1936) is the best statement of his philosophy, but the philosophy itself was developed many years earlier.

[54]Alfred Schutz, *The Phenomenology of the Social World* (Evanston, IL: Northwestern University Press, 1967; originally published 1932). Schutz was a young scholar when he wrote this work, but it came out two years before Mead's collated lectures in *Mind, Self, and Society.* One can see immediately the differences between Mead's pragmatist philosophical background and Schutz's phenomenological approach, but they are, in reality, addressing similar processes of interaction and society. Schutz was not included in the classical canon because he was never part of sociology until the mid- to late twentieth century, when interactionist approaches drawn from phenomenology began to appear. See also Alfred Schutz and Thomas Luckmann, *The Structure of the Lifeworld* (Evanston, IL: Northwestern University Press, 1973) and Thomas Luckmann (ed.), *Phenomenology and Sociology* (New York: Penguin Books, 1978). Schutz's collected papers are found in Alfred Schutz, *Collected Papers I, II, III* (The Hague, Netherlands: Marinus Nijhoff, 1962, 1963, and 1966).

This presumption allows individuals to engage in the process of "typification," where others and situations are portrayed as having certain basic qualities.

In this manner, people come to act *as if* they see the world in similar ways and to believe that they can treat others and the situation *as if* it had common properties understood by all. By making these presumptions, individuals can interact and engage in cooperative behaviors. Thus, it is not so critical that individuals actually achieve true intersubjectivity; it is only necessary that they *think that they have* achieved intersubjectivity. Schutz's work will be summarized in Chapter 19 as a phenomenological approach that set the stage for the emergence of modern ethnomethodology.

Ethnomethodology. It is this line of thinking that provided one of the key ideas for contemporary ethnomethodology. Founded by Harold Garfinkel[55] and carried forth by his students, this approach emphasized that individuals use a series of "folk methods"—hence the name *ethnomethodology*—to sustain the illusion that they experience a common world. Unlike Mead, where emphasis was on reading gestures to place oneself in the other's role so as to anticipate the latter's behaviors, individuals employ a series of interpersonal techniques or methods that allows them to perceive and believe that they share a common world, without actually questioning this presumption. The goal of ethnomethodology is to isolate these ethnomethods. One of the common research strategies became the "breaching experiment," in which the experimenter would deliberately break the presumption of intersubjectivity in order to see how others tried to use ethnomethods to reconstruct the presumption of intersubjectivity. Early research looked promising as a number of such methods were uncovered by carefully reviewing transcripts of the conversation of people in interaction; and while this approach continues, it has less theoretical impact than it did in the last third of the twentieth century.

Both phenomenological and ethnomethodological theorizing question many of the assumptions of other interaction theories that are derived from Mead and Cooley. For these theorists, much interaction revolves around the following:

1. Individuals presume that they share, for the purposes at hand, a common internal state or intersubjectivity with others in a situation.

2. Individuals seek to sustain this sense that they are experiencing the situation by not, if they can, questioning ambiguities that might unravel the perception of a shared reality.

3. In order to realize (2), persons may often have to utilize subtle interpersonal methods to not question intersubjectivity in order to avoid a breach in the interaction and, hence, people's sense that they share and experience the world in similar ways.

---

[55]Harold Garfinkel, *Studies in Ethnomethodology* (Englewood Cliffs, NJ: Prentice-Hall, 1967). For more readable summaries of this approach, see Warren Handel, *Ethnomethodology: How People Make Sense* (Englewood Cliffs, NJ: Prentice-Hall, 1982); George Psathas (ed.), *Everyday Language: Studies in Ethnomethodology* (New York: Irvington, 1979); and Roy Turner (ed.), *Ethnomethodology* (Baltimore, MD: Penguin Books, 1974).

4. When these interpersonal methods fail, the breached interaction will cause individuals to experience negative emotions and push them to attempt to reconstruct the shared sense of intersubjectivity and feeling that they are experiencing the world in the same way for the purposes of the present interaction.

7. Exchange Theorizing

Exchange theorizing does not have its roots in the classical tradition of sociology, except perhaps indirectly via Adam Smith in economics and behaviorism in psychology. Smith's[56] work had its greatest effect on the early masters of sociological theorizing through the question he posed in his *The Theory of Moral Sentiments*: if the social world is differentiating and becoming more complex, individuals are living out their lives and daily routines in somewhat different niches in society and, thus, are experiencing different social worlds. If such is the case, what "force" can integrate social relations among these individuals? The force emphasized in *The Theory of Moral Sentiments* is, as the title suggests, a common morality of beliefs and values, but Smith's other answer, in *The Wealth of Nations*, is that the pursuit of self-interest in markets miraculously reveals an "invisible hand of order" promoting social equilibrium, just as it does for prices in markets. Sociologists of the nineteenth century were highly skeptical of this second argument, as are many contemporary sociologists. The first argument in *Moral Sentiments*, however, was in essence what functional theorizing, especially in the French tradition of Comte and Durkheim, developed. But the notion of life as a kind of marketplace where social relations are, in essence, exchanges of resources can certainly be found in Smith, even if most classical theorists did not pursue this lead. Only Marx, who sought to improve upon Smith's analysis of market dynamics in capitalism, appears to have paid much attention to Smith. But the notion of individuals seeking utility, or reward value, was not pursued as a general model of social life until well into the twentieth century.[57]

The other indirect route to exchange theory comes from behaviorism, which owes its initial inspiration to Ivanovich Pavlov in Russia and Edward Thorndike in America. Here, organisms are seen as retaining those behavioral responses to stimuli that have brought rewards and abandoning those that fail to bring gratification or imposed punishment. Only Mead,[58] who considered himself to be a *social* behaviorist, pursued this idea among the pantheon of classical sociological theorists. Mead reacted against what became known as behaviorism in the early twentieth century because of its extreme assumptions—including speculation about behaviors and

---

[56]For a discussion of Adam Smith in this book, see Chapters 1 and 2.

[57]Vilfredo Pareto, an early economist who by the turn of the twentieth century became a general sociology theorist and whose ideas are still prominent in neoclassical economics, certainly understood the arguments of utilitarians like Adam Smith, but in many ways his sociology is a repudiation of the limitations of classical and, hence, neoclassical economics today.

[58]See pp. 256–264 for a review of the behaviorism that influenced Mead.

psychological processes that cannot be directly observed as the only subject matter of behaviorist theorizing; thus, the "black box" of nonobservables—human thought, emotions, and cognition—must be ignored in favor of theories that explain the effects of *observable* stimuli on *observable* behaviors. For Mead, however, many of the key behavioral capacities of humans—use of significant gestures, role-taking, minded deliberations, and conceptions of self—are not directly observable but are nonetheless critical to understanding human behavior and society. Hence, he added the adjective "social" to his form of behaviorism—hence social behaviorism—in order to distinguish it from the extreme assumptions of behaviorism in American psychology.

Yet, despite Mead's sympathy for a more social behaviorism, sociologists stayed away from extreme behaviorism in psychology, thereby thwarting for many decades the more sociological perspectives using this approach, coupled with sociologists' antipathy for overly economic and utilitarian views of rational and maximizing actors as the best model for understanding social action. Thus, it is not surprising that approaches drawing from behaviorism and utilitarianism did not develop in the first half of the twentieth century. In the 1950s, however, exchange theories began to appear in sociology, and as this theoretical perspective developed, each theory tended to begin with the assumptions of either utilitarianism or behaviorism. These two perspectives converge on a number of assumptions, the most important of which are as follows:

1. The actions of individuals and collective actors are driven by needs for rewards or utilities.

2. The more rewarding or the more utilities to be gained from a social relationship, the more likely are individuals and collective actors to pursue lines of conduct and action that secure these rewards.

3. Individuals assess the reward value of alternative lines of behavior and choose that which offers the most, if not maximal, reward.

4. The more valuable to persons are the rewards received, the more likely are these individuals to pursue conduct allowing them to receive these valuable rewards.

5. Individuals will implicitly or explicitly calculate the costs (alternative sources of rewards forgone or resources that must be given up) and the investments (accumulated costs) in pursuing a line of conduct, and they will always seek to make a "profit" in the resources received. A profit is the value of the resources received less the costs and investments to get them, and those lines of conduct that yield the most profit are the most likely to be pursued.

6. The more of a reward of a given type is received in the recent past, the more will an individual's preferences for this reward decline and the less valuable to an actor will this reward become. (In psychology this is the principle of "satiation," whereas in economics it is described as "marginal utility"; still, the dynamic is the same for both perspectives: the more of a reward that a person gets, the less valuable it becomes, or the less utility it has for actors).

7. Individuals and collective actors thus exchange resources, giving up some as costs, in order to receive resources from others; and most resources in human interaction are intrinsic (e.g., affection, approval, prestige and honor, liking, self-verification, etc.), although some are also extrinsic (e.g., money, power).

8. Individuals and collective actors assess the "fairness" and "justice" of the resources that they received relative to their costs and investments, and they can invoke a number of different comparison points or standards for making this justice calculation. (For instance, they may invoke general cultural norms specifying what is fair; they may compare their rewards with those actors incurring equivalent costs and investments; they may use a sense of the rewards that they could have received in an alternative exchange; or they may invoke as a comparison point the rewards that they expected to receive relative to the rewards that they actually received.)

9. When payoffs to a person or collective actor fall below any of the several comparison points that can be invoked to assess fairness, individuals (and individuals making decisions for collective actors) will experience negative emotions and seek to renegotiate the exchange; they may pursue any number of strategies in these renegotiations, including punishing (and thus incurring costs on) those who have failed to provide a fair and just reward or, alternatively, seeking new exchange partners who will provide a fairer level of reward.

For sociological exchange theories, all social relations are driven by the basic assumptions listed above. And all social structures and cultures are ultimately built from the actions of individual and collective actors behaving in ways outlined by these assumptions. Yet within exchange theories, despite the common set of assumptions, theories emphasize different aspects of the exchange process.

One exchange approach termed *rational choice theory* follows the utilitarian model, emphasizing that individuals seek to maximize their utilities and minimize their costs.[59] There are many different versions of rational choice theorizing, but they all emphasize that social relations and social structures are created when actors perceive that they can lower "negative externalities" (or costs) and thereby increase their profits in exchanges. For example, if individuals are engaged in concerted and coordinated action, one negative externality is that some do not contribute their fair share of effort to the outcome, but they still receive the same utilities as those who have, and as a result, actors will develop norms, monitoring and sanctioning procedures to ensure that individuals do not "free ride." Thus, social structures and culture are built up to decrease negative externalities and, thereby, to ensure that each actor is contributing his or her (or its) fair share of effort to coordinated tasks.

Other approaches emphasize *power dynamics*.[60] Actors who have highly valued resources that are scarce and in high demand always enjoy an advantage

---

[59]For prominent examples, see James Coleman, *Foundations of Social Theory* (Cambridge, MA: Harvard University Press, 1990) and Michael Hechter, *Principles of Group Solidarity* (Berkeley: University of California Press, 1987).

[60]Peter M. Blau, *Exchange and Power in Social Life* (New York: Wiley, 1964); Richard Emerson, "Power-Dependence Relations," *American Sociological Review* (1962):31–41.

over those who have needs for these resources. The result is that those who hold valued resources will begin to impose higher costs on those who seek these highly valued resources by demanding more resources from these dependent actors. In many ways, this is the power dynamic emphasized by Marx. In Marx's theory, capitalists are in a position to exploit labor because they have a resource that is difficult to attain (money), while workers have a resource that is in over-supply (labor or willingness to work). The capitalist can thus offer less money than the work is actually worth (by Marx's "labor theory of value") and, thereby, make a profit when the capitalist sells the goods that are produced by exploited workers. All exchange theories that examine power dynamics follow Marx in recognizing that when exploitation by powerful actors occurs, those at a disadvantage seek to reduce their exploitation by a variety of strategies, including leaving the exchange relationship, seeking alternative sources for a highly valued resource, learning to do without a resource, collectively mobilizing to make their resources more valuable to exploiters or by agreeing to hold resources back from exploiters, or mobilizing to pursue conflict that will impose high costs on exploiters. Thus, exchange theories that emphasize the power dynamic in exchanges converge with the conflict theories examined earlier.

Exchange dynamics have been added to other theoretical traditions. For instance, some symbolic interactionist[61] theories recognize that approval and verification of self are highly valued rewards and individuals always calculate implicitly whether or not others in situations are providing enough of this valued reward relative to the resources that must be given up to receive approval. Another example is the piggybacking of exchange ideas to network theories (summarized below), where relations among points in a network (actors) are viewed as resource flows governed by exchange assumptions.[62] If actors must give up too many resources in order to secure resources in a given network, they will engage in balancing actions that increase the sense of fairness in the network and, in the process, change the structure of the network itself and the flow of resources among actors. As noted above, conflict theory has always had an implicit exchange dynamic, and some more contemporary theories have made this exchange process more explicit. Theories in the sociology of emotions have adopted exchange ideas, especially the notion that when exchanges are seen as unfair, deprived parties will experience a variety of negative emotions and engage in behaviors to ensure that they receive some profit in their exchanges with others.[63] Thus, even though exchange theory was not prominent in the

---

[61]For example, McCall and Simmons, *Identities and Interactions.*

[62]For examples, see Emerson, "Power-Dependence Relations"; Karen S. Cook, Richard M. Emerson, Mary R. Gillmore, and Toshio Yamagishi, "The Distribution of Power in Exchange Networks: Theory and Experimental Results," *American Journal of Sociology* (1983):275–305; and David Willer and Pamela Emanuelson, "Elementary Theory," In *Contemporary Social Psychological Theories*, ed. Peter J. Burke (Stanford, CA: Stanford University Press, 2006).

[63]Edward J. Lawler, Shane Thye, and Jeongkoo Yoon, *Social Commitments in a Depersonalized World* (New York: Russell Sage, 2009).

early sociological canon, it can now be found virtually everywhere in current theorizing, either as an explicit exchange theory or as a new element in an older theoretical tradition. In Chapter 15, I will examine the wide variety of exchange theories that have been developed in sociology over the last fifty years.

8. Structuralist Theories

Since the study of social structures is one of the defining features of sociology, it should not be surprising that there are numerous theories on this topic. Indeed, almost all sociological theories emphasize social structure, to some degree, and thus it becomes a somewhat arbitrary exercise to isolate a few general types of theories that can be labeled "structuralist theories." Among the early masters, several distinctive modes of structural inquiry emerged and have been carried forward.

One of the most enduring structural approaches comes from functionalist theories, like those developed by Comte,[64] Spencer,[65] and Durkheim,[66] where structure is conceptualized in terms of patterns of differentiation among institutional domains and among the social units in these domains. Another, related approach was initiated by Weber,[67] who emphasized that structure is built up from patterns of action among actors that generate inequalities and stratification, systems of power and domination, social orders that link organizations together, and legitimization through cultural beliefs. When stated at this level of abstraction, Weber's ideas converge with those of Marx, who emphasized that social structure is built from inequalities in the distribution of resources. The dynamics of societies are thus played out as the contradictions within the system of inequality, legitimatized by culture, and enforced by polity emerge and set off the process of conflict. This vision of structure emphasizes that relations to the means of production are the core of social structures, with other structures like the state and cultural forces like ideologies being superstructures arising from the economic base of societies.

Durkheim's sociology inspired several views of structure.[68] One emphasized the number, nature, and relations of the parts making up a society, a line of thinking that converges with Simmel's[69] and, as we will see, modern-day network analysis. Another view of structure is the emphasis on how patterns of social structure shape individuals' mental categories about such fundamental dimensions of the world as time, causality, classifications, and space. People's

---

[64]See pp. 23–29 for Comte's conception of social structure.

[65]See pp. 43–53 for Spencer's evolutionary conception of social structure.

[66]See pp. 239–243 for Durkheim's conception of social structure, which while looking similar to Spencer's was to be used in many different ways in structural analysis inside and outside of sociology.

[67]Weber's conception of social structure is best captured in the diagrams on pp. 157, 159.

[68]See Footnote 66.

[69]See pp. 172–179 for Simmel's conception of social structure.

cognitive categories will, therefore, reflect the patterns of social structure as they organize routines over time and in space.[70]

This argument influenced the emergence of various versions of structuralism. One version flipped Durkheim's approach on its head, viewing patterns of structure as reflections of the "deeper structures" lodged in human neurology.[71] Another, less dramatic version is an emphasis on viewing existing structures and their cultures as deeper structural principles inhering in social relations. This approach converges with Marx's view of superstructures reflecting the operation of economic structures.

Simmel's[72] view of structure as forms of social relationships in which the properties of relationships are more significant than the nature of the units in these relationships represented a radical break with early sociological views of structure. This kind of thinking would inspire contemporary network theory, where the patterns of relations among nodes or units are more important than the nature of the units or nodes in these relationships.

Mead's more micro view of structure as institutionalized patterns of relationships that are produced and reproduced by the behavioral capacities of individuals represents a final view of social structure.[73] Here, the capacity to role-take with others and with generalized others, to evaluate self from the perspective of generalized others (or cultural beliefs), and to make minded deliberation in order to select lines of conduct facilitating cooperation all signal that micro-level processes must be a part of structural analysis. Other, more micro traditions, such as psychoanalytical theories and dramaturgical theories, have also been incorporated into this form of analysis initiated by Mead.

Structural analysis, however, has moved in many different directions. Still, they all share a small number of assumptions:

1. Structure represents a set of relations among social units that persists over time.

2. These relations among units can take many different forms, and it is the nature of connections among units that is essential to understanding the dynamics of social structure.

---

[70]The outline for this view of structure appeared in Émile Durkheim and Marcel Mauss, *Primitive Classification* (London: Cohen and West, 1963; originally published 1903).

[71]*Primitive Classification* is a work that had little direct influence in sociology, but it set off structuralisms as a broad intellectual movement in the twentieth century. Even Ferdinand de Saussure, *Course in General Linguistics* (New York: McGraw-Hill, 1966; originally published 1915) and Roman Jakobson—see his collected works in *Philosophical Studies*, in multiple volumes (The Hague, Netherlands: Mouton, 1971, but written decades before), the founders of structural linguistics and grandfathers of structuralism, considered themselves to be more Durkheimian. Yet Claude Lévi-Strauss hinted in *The Elementary Structures of Kinship* (Paris: University of France, 1949) at what was to come. Still, as he pursued a linguistic analysis borrowing from Durkheim, de Saussure, and Jakobson, he turned Durkheim and all earlier structural analysts "on their heads" in works such as *Myth and Meaning* (New York: Schocken, 1979) and *A World on the Wane* (London: Hutchinson, 1961), arguing that structures come from mental categories and principles of the brain rather than the reverse.

[72]Simmel's methodology arguing for a formal sociology, summarized on pp. 171–172, offers the best glimpse of this conception of social structure that was later adopted in network analysis.

[73]See Footnote 39 on Mead's views.

3. Sometimes the nature of the units is critical in understanding the relationships that make up social structures, but at other times the only critical information is knowledge about the dynamics of relations, per se, regardless of the units standing in these relationships.

4. Relations among units evolve from varying sources, including: (a) relations of power, (b)neurology of the human brain, (c) human behavioral propensities as they affect social interaction, (d) systems of cultural symbols, and (e) means of economic production.

This obvious lack of shared assumptions would indicate that structural theories are a rather eclectic mix of approaches, none of which has ever gained dominance. In many ways, the lack of consensus over how to analyze the central topic of sociology—social structure—indicates how much more theoretical work must be done in the discipline. Indeed, sociologists often talk as if the notion of structure is so obvious that it requires no conceptualization, but in fact, it is probably sociology's most used and yet least defined concept. And even when "structure" is the focus of theorizing, it is evident that these specific theories remain, for the most part, rather vague.

Structuralism. This approach has a number of variants, but the general goal is to discover the underlying structures that generate surface empirical regularities that can be observed and measured. It is assumed that social regularities in patterns of social relationships are generated by less visible, underlying structures and that, until the principles of these underlying structures are discovered, empirical social structures cannot be fully explained. Much of the imagery of this approach was adopted from structural linguistics, in which languages are compared and analyzed for their underlying forms in an effort to discover which languages are related to each other and from which older root languages related languages have evolved.[74] Structuralism became a broader intellectual movement outside of sociology, penetrating such fields as cultural anthropology, English, linguistics and languages, and sociology.[75] There emerged three variants: (1) those theories that searched for the underlying principles of social structures, (2) those that sought the underlying cultural principles directing both culture and empirical social structures, and (3) those that argued that social structures and their cultures are generated by the underlying neurology of the human brain. This approach will be examined in Chapter 20.

Network Theory. This approach to theorizing social structure has its origins outside sociology, but it was adopted by sociologists by the mid-twentieth century. By employing matrices that indicated who forms relations with whom in variously sized groups, the network patterns among those forming relationships could be drawn. Most of the early work was done in social psychological theory, derived from

---

[74]See references to Jakobson and de Saussure in Footnote 71.

[75]None of this theorizing took a firm hold and was dying out by the end of the 1970s, although much of the imagery remained. For an overview from various authors, see Ino Rossi (ed.), *Structural Sociology* (New York: Columbia University Press, 1984). For a more general review, see Miriam Glucksmann, *Structural Analysis in Contemporary Social Thought* (London: Routledge, 1974).

Gestalt psychology but adopting the mathematical conventions of digraph theory, where actors were points in a network connected by lines indicating the direction of positive or negative relations. With the use of computers, much more complicated matrices could be developed revealing relations among large numbers of individual or collective actors. Key properties of networks, such as their size (the number of nodes and relations), density (the extent to which all possible relations among nodes are present in the network), cliques (sub-densities of actors in the overall network), centrality (the extent to which resources flow through particular nodes in the network), bridges (nodes that connect to cliques or subnetworks), and brokerage nodes (which distribute resources across gaps between networks or subnetworks), were viewed to drive the dynamics of networks, and hence all social structures.[76] While network analysis holds great potential, most of the work has been on the methodology for describing networks through computer programs; comparatively little theorizing within network analysis proper has been developed, although a number of other theoretical perspectives in sociology, such as exchange theorizing, have incorporated network principles and provided some explanatory power to network sociology. In Chapter 20, I will review network theorizing.

Structuration Theory. Some structuralist theories emphasize that structure is a mix of discursive practices and actions that generate structural principles that are used to organize social actions and to regulate talk and thinking at the micro level of social organization. The actions of individuals guided by these structural principles are, on the one hand, constrained and thus more likely to reproduce structures. On the other hand, actors always have some capacity for agency to change, if only slightly, the structural principles that guide their actions. Some of these approaches blend into the cultural theories summarized below or the structuralist theories outlined above. In both cases, theorizing emphasizes that individuals create systems of cultural codes, often as the result of the underlying cognitive structures of the human brain, that drive the formations of social structures. Others are more purely Durkheimian and emphasize that the cultural codes of social groups have large effects on the basic cognitive capacities of humans and on how they think and act. These approaches are not, however, fully in the camp of structuralism examined above. They typically add more elements.

For example, Anthony Giddens's structuration theory,[77] which will be examined in Chapter 20, emphasizes that there are structural principles or general cultural conceptions of social organization that constrain the formation of structural sets, which are bundles of rules and resources that are used by individuals to form social

---

[76]For early network works in sociology and anthropology, see S. F. Nadel, *The Study of Social Structures* (London: Cohen and West, 1957) and J. Clyde Mitchell, "The Concept and Use of Social Networks," in *Network Analysis: Studies of Human Interaction*, ed. Jeremy Boissevain and James Clyde Mitchell (The Hague, Netherlands: Mouton, 1973); for more recent network theoretical works, see Ronald Burt, "Models of Network Structure," *Annual Review of Sociology* 6 (1980):79–141 and Stanley Wasserman and Katherine Faust, *Network Analysis: Models and Methods* (Cambridge, UK: Cambridge University Press, 1994).

[77]Anthony Giddens, *The Constitution of Society* (Berkeley: University of California Press, 1984).

relations. As these principles and sets are used by agents and reproduced over time, they create the structural properties or the institutional systems of a society. There are, of course, structural contradictions in these structural properties because structural principles and sets are rarely without inconsistencies and conflicts of meaning and intent. And so, as institutional systems evolve, they almost always carry contradictions that, over time, become the focus of conflict and mobilization for change, as Marx would have emphasized.

There is always a certain vagueness in these kinds of structuralist theories, but the goal is to recognize that social structures have a cultural basis, emphasizing that the structural principles that undergird everything are sets of ideas that channel the actions of agents as they mobilize resources to form the structural properties of a society. They are much like a blueprint, but a blueprint in the categories of the mind that have combined key ideas into structural principles and sets and that outline how elements of culture and social structure are to be put together. Yet they are not as explicit as a blueprint; they operate more covertly by constraining both perceptions and behaviors as actors build social structures or act within structures that have already been built.

9. Cultural Theorizing

As these structuralist theories were emerging, so was a movement toward a more explicit analysis of culture. Conflict theories had tended to see culture as a "superstructure," to use Marx's term, when it reemerged in American sociology in the 1960s. Yet Weber clearly argued that culture operates as an independent force in societies, as did Durkheim. Weber's analysis of religion in general and Protestantism in particular underscores the causal power of culture, while Durkheim's early emphasis on the collective conscience is, in essence, an analysis of the power of culture. Indeed, even within conflict theory, some of the newer theories are quite conscious of cultural forces. But the intellectual movement toward reintroducing cultural theorizing wanted more: the recognition that culture is a force *in its own right*. As an autonomous force, it must be analyzed in terms of its own distinctive properties and dynamics. Only after this kind of analysis should it be connected to other, more structural forces.

Cultural theorizing can be found in all of contemporary theory. For example, functional theories almost always emphasize the importance of cultural values and beliefs; and conflict theories stress the creation of ideologies in mobilizing individuals to pursue and legitimate conflict. Even early cultural theorists such as Robert Wuthnow[78] combined elements of structuralism, ideology from conflict theory, and even exchange theory in emphasizing how the moral order is created, sustained, changed, and institutionalized in social structures. Similarly, Pierre Bourdieu[79] began to conceptualize social relations as organized by the distribution of

---

[78]Robert Wuthnow, *Meaning and Moral Order: Explorations in Cultural Analysis* (Berkeley: University of California Press, 1987).

[79]Pierre Bourdieu, *Language and Symbolic Power* (Cambridge, MA: Harvard University Press, 1989), *Distinction: A Social Critique of the Judgment of Taste* (Cambridge, MA: Harvard University Press, 1984).

material, social, cultural, and symbolic capital, thereby blending elements of traditional sociology into a new view of structures. Social structures are built up by the distribution of various forms of capital that circulate in a society and generate a common worldview among individuals with varying shares and configurations of these four forms of capital. Cultural capital comprises habits, manners, linguistic styles, credentials, tastes, and lifestyles, while symbolic capital is the set of symbols (ideologies, beliefs, and values) used to legitimate holding other types of capital—social, material, and cultural. Social capital is access to networks of social relations, and material capital is money and other forms of material resources that can be spent to buy other forms of capital. Thus, actors with different shares and mixes of capital can operate within particular structural domains, and not others; and the dynamics of the social universe revolve around how actors use their capital to form social structures or to navigate through existing structures, either changing or reproducing these structures. These theories will be explored in Chapter 21.

As the movement to bring culture back into sociology as a distinctive topic of inquiry increased, much analysis was empirical and examined the symbols systems that individuals and groups developed. Yet there was a more explicit push for a "strong program" in cultural sociology spearheaded by Alexander and colleagues, an approach to be examined in Chapter 21.[80] Their argument is that cultural sociology as it reemerged in modern theory was more of a "weak program" that was always subordinate to the analysis of social structure, whereas what is needed is a strong program that engages in thick descriptions of symbolic meanings and the mechanisms by which these are constructed. Such an analysis views culture as a text with themes, plotlines, moral evaluations, and other properties that give it some autonomy from social structures. Only after the analysis of culture, per se, can this strong program begin to examine the relationships of culture to other forces, such as rituals, interactions, and social structures.

Thus far, there are only a few coherent theoretical approaches in this strong program, but there is now an expanding set of descriptive works analyzing the textual qualities of culture. As these are used to develop more general theoretical ideas or to assess the plausibility of existing theoretical ideas, the analysis of culture will achieve the same status as the analysis of social structure and interaction, and indeed, it will contribute significantly to these analyses—or so it is presumed. For example, Jeffrey Alexander[81] has launched a program of "cultural pragmatics" that blends Durkheim's and Goffman's dramaturgy[82] with one strand of new cultural theorizing that emphasizes rituals and performances. In Alexander's scheme, actors are seen as motivated by moral concerns, seeking to bring background collective representations and scripts to the forefront of action and interaction with audiences.

---

[80]For a review, see Jeffrey Alexander and Philip Smith, "The Strong Program in Cultural Theory," in *Handbook of Sociological Theory*, ed. Jonathan H. Turner (New York: Springer, 2001), 135–150.

[81]Jeffrey C. Alexander, "Cultural Pragmatics: Social Performances Between Ritual and Strategy," *Sociological Theory* (2004):512–574. See also his *Meaning and Social Life: A Cultural Sociology* (New York: Oxford University Press, 2003).

[82]See Footnote 48.

The background representations and scripts are decoded into texts that are, thereby, made available for performances; and the behaviors in a performance revolve around achieving emotional attachment of both performer and audience to these decoded texts. In their performances, actors have access to the "symbolic means of production," and thus stages and props, but their performances are constrained by the available texts, by their power to gain access to stages and props, and by the audiences that are available. In simple societies, much like Durkheim's conceptualization of "mechanical solidarity,"[83] the elements of performances—collective representations, texts, stages, audiences, power, and the means of symbolic production—are fused together and taken for granted, thereby creating an easy basis for social solidarity. With differentiation and complexity of society, however, these elements of performances are not fused, nor are they so easily lined up or *re*-fused to give a successful performance. Differentiation of societies thus "de-fuses" the key elements of performances, with the result that it becomes necessary to reassemble the elements through considerable dramatic effort. A performance thus revolves around "re-fusing" what has to be "de-fused" by differentiation. There are various mechanisms—although Alexander does not use this term—that re-fuse background collective representations with the performance and that make texts salient to the performance: cognitive simplification, moral antagonisms, and twistings and turnings in the plot and story line. Re-fusing the script, action, and performance spaces is achieved by walking and talking in space, with some discretion for how actors (and directors) are to do so. Re-fusing of social power involves efforts to find the appropriate means of symbolic reproduction, the best means of symbolic distribution, and the appropriate forms of debate, discourse, and criticism. Re-fusing actors and roles must seem to be natural as part of an ongoing interpersonal flow. And by re-fusing the audience with performance texts, actors must pull them in and make them part of the performance and its text, script, and background representations.

Thus, Alexander's cultural pragmatics brings Durkheim's analysis of collective conscience, ritual, and emotions into a new form of cultural theorizing. His efforts represent only one of many new lines of theorizing about culture, which in the last decade have been reinvigorated by emphasis on having a "strong program" of cultural analysis. Time will tell how far this new cultural thrust in sociology will go.

10. Critical Theorizing

Sociology emerged, as I pointed out in Chapter 1, to explain the transformations associated with modernity. There has always been a critical bent to this analysis of modernity and, later, to postmodernism. The early masters all addressed the issue of what modernity was doing to humans as new cultural and structural formations were emerging. Marx, of course, was the most critical, but there were more implicit critiques in Weber's analysis of rationalization, in Durkheim's concerns about anomie

---

[83]See p. 210 for the table outlining Durkheim's distinction between mechanical and organic solidarity.

and egoism, and in Spencer's concern with concentrated power and its use to wage unnecessary warfare. There was also quiet dialogue and disagreement about the effects of modernity. For example, Simmel acknowledged both Durkheim's concerns about egoism and Marx's about alienation, but in the end, he argued that modern, highly differentiated, market-driven societies were more emancipatory than pathological. They give individuals freedom and options and, hence, provide rewards and value. Durkheim was implicitly critical of Marx in arguing that the "forced division of labor" was only a passing pathology that would eventually go away as organic solidarity became fully established; Weber saw Marx's inevitable march to revolution and communism as most unlikely, given the power of rationalization in the modern world.

Since most of the major founders of sociology were European, one of the forms of critical theory that emerged in the twentieth century carries forward this European legacy and concern about the modern condition, as will be examined in Chapter 22. The other critical theoretical lineage is distinctly American and focuses on domestic social problems, mostly injustices to particular subpopulations in societies—for example, women, minorities, poor, lower classes, and so on. Both lines remain critical of modern societies, especially of capitalism, but the European critical approach is more detached, abstract, and intellectual, whereas the American approach retains its roots in twentieth-century social movements that were carried into academia and institutionalized as intellectual disciplines, whose members are often still engaged activists. These two lines of critical theorizing will be examined in Chapters 22 and 24. All forms of critical theorizing operate with several basic assumptions.

1. Modernity has transformed the nature of societies and, in so doing, led to harmful patterns of social organization.

2. These "harms" are a consequence of the dynamics inhering in both early (nineteenth century) and advanced (late twentieth and early twenty-first century) capitalism.

3. For all the wealth produced and the dynamism of capitalism, this form of economic and social organization

    A. Exploits labor markets controlled by capitalists
    B. Splits and partitions labor markets so that women and people of color are less likely to be able to be successful in labor markets by virtue of institutionalized discrimination and stigmatizing beliefs
    C. Commodifies virtually every dimension of the social universe, including people, culture, and material objects
    D. Generates fiscal and productive crises that disrupt secure relations in society
    E. Outsources production globally, thereby disrupting domestic labor markets and, hence, the lifeways and security of labor.

4. Because advanced capitalism commodifies virtually everything, it dislodges culture from its structural base and meanings at particular times and places

and, in so doing, erodes the capacity of culture to provide stable meanings. And this process accelerates when the means of reproduction of symbols increases relative to the means of production of material goods.

5. Early capitalism exploits labor as a commodity in labor markets, while alienating labor from the capacity to determine what is made, how it is made, and to whom the products of labor are distributed.

6. Advanced capitalism fragments self and identity, removing them from traditional sources of meaning in stable groupings and communities; and in so doing, it fragments self, makes individuals overly reflexive, and commodifies self by providing a seemingly endless supply of commodified cultural symbols for individuals to try on and discard as they search in vain for meanings.

European Critical Theory. Unlike the United States, which repressed Marxist theorizing during the peak of the Cold War (especially during McCarthyism), European scholars considered the implications of Marxist theory for the whole of the twentieth century. With the installation of communism in the emerging Soviet Union (and later in China), theorizing began to ask the following questions. Why had these "revolutions" not been more emancipatory? Why did they lead to concentrations of oppressive power? During the 1930s, as fascism spread across Europe, a group of thinkers at the University of Frankfurt in Germany formed what became known as the Frankfurt School, even though not everyone identified with the school was German. And as Hitler's hold over Germany increased, some of these scholars, many of whom were Jews, escaped to the United States and continued the work of the Frankfurt School in several elite American universities. The basic problematic, which persists in all forms of most critical theories today, was this: how to retain the emancipatory thrust of Marx's argument against the backdrop of Weberian rationalization, where the state, legal system, and most institutional domains continue to oppress and dominate sectors of the population through rational-legal authority and its institutionalization in bureaucracies. Their answer was that the conditions had not yet emerged for emancipation, and so, in the meantime, the members of the Frankfurt School and their sympathizers should stress the importance of continuing to expose patterns of oppression in a wide variety of contexts until conditions would be in place for social movements leading to the elimination of such oppression.[84] And, to very great extent, this kind of theorizing persists today in sociology, not only in Europe and the United States but also in many other parts of the world. It is a highly intellectualized critique, confined primarily to academics who theorize and conduct research that exposes abuses of power and law without leaving the safety of the ivory tower.

American-Style Critical Theory. The two great social movements in the second half of the twentieth century—the civil rights movement for minorities and the feminist

---

[84]The most visible modern-day European critical theorist in the Frankfurt tradition is Jürgen Habermas. See his *Knowledge and Human Interest*, trans. J. Shapiro (London: Heinemann, 1970; originally published 1968) and *Theory of Communicative Action*, 2 vols. (Boston, MA: Beacon Press, 1981, 1984).

movement for women—are the source of a critical approach that emphasizes the continued existence of racism and sexism and, more broadly, that criticizes the failure of a more "civil rights approach" to eliminate both subtle and obvious forms of discrimination. These approaches were institutionalized in academia not only in many sociology departments but also in various types of ethnic and women's studies departments/programs within academia. These American variants of critical theorizing will be reviewed in Chapter 24.

Much as critical theory in Europe seeks to expose persisting patterns of oppression, critical theories in the United States document continued discrimination and oppression at many levels of social organization. Micro interactions, cultural beliefs, the inadequacy of laws or failure to enforce them, subtle forms of discrimination in a wide variety of contexts, continued stereotyping of minorities and women, the failures in seeking to eliminate "difference," the need to create new forms of consciousness among those oppressed in both subtle and obvious ways, and many other points of argumentation have been developed in *feminist theorizing*[85] and what became known as *critical race theory.*[86] These approaches are explicitly activist, although many of the theorists within this tradition can be highly philosophical in their theorizing.

Critical race theory is an extension of early American sociologists' concern with amelioration, but there is a major difference: critical theorists are, first and foremost, critical of such ameliorative efforts to extend civil rights because they have led to continued discrimination in new, more subtle forms. While there can be Marxist ideals as well as elements of all who have theorized about stratification in these critical approaches, they have adopted many other methodological and theoretical (and philosophical) approaches to understanding the wide spectrum of ways and contexts in which racism continues to operate. Indeed, much of the analysis is highly micro, examining how racism (and sexism) operate at the interpersonal level; and so early phenomenology and symbolic interactions might be relevant, although critical theorists rarely explicitly rely on these early theoretical approaches of the classical period.

Thus, while feminist and critical race theories have their European counterparts, this kind of theorizing in the United States remains distinctive. The main reason for this distinctiveness, I believe, is that this critical tradition is based on brining the ideologies of social movements into academia. Such approaches are caught between converting ideological goals into topics of more detached academic inquiry while at the same time sustaining the emancipatory zeal of the early days of feminism and the peak of civil rights protest.

---

[85]For overviews, see Pamela Abbott and Clare Wallace, *An Introduction to Sociology: Feminist Perspectives* (London: Routledge, 1990); Elizabeth Hackett and Sally Anne Haslanger, *Theorizing Feminism: A Reader* (New York: Oxford University Press); bell hooks, *Feminist Theory from Margin to Center* (Boston, MA: South End Press, 1984); Patricia Madoo Lengermann and Jill Niebrugge, "Contemporary Feminism," in *Sociological Theory*, ed. George Ritzer, (McGraw-Hill, 1996); and Paula England (ed.), *Theory on Gender/Feminism on Theory* (Chicago, IL: Aldine, 1985).

[86]Kimberlie Crenshaw, Neil Gotanda, Garry Peller, and Kendall Thomas (eds.), *Critical Race Theory* (New York: The New Press, 1996); Richard Delgado, *Critical Race Theory: An Introduction* (New York: New York University Press, 2001), *Critical Race Theory* (Philadelphia, PA: Temple University Press, 1999).

Postmodern Theorizing. Yet another critical approach that has both European and American sources postulates a new "postmodern condition," in which the fundamental way in which individuals, social structures, and culture are linked has changed under the effects of information media and globalization of the economy by transportation/communications technologies and global markets. There are two clear branches of postmodern theory: one concerned with economic forces[87] and globalization and another, more purely cultural approach[88] that emphasizes the increasing importance of culture, detached from its structural roots. The economic approach owes some of its inspiration to Marx, while the cultural approach reveals glimpses of Weber, Durkheim, Simmel, and Mead. Still, despite the concerns of the classical theorists with the "pathologies" of modernity, it is argued that the transformations of societies into a postmodern condition make the analyses of the first masters less relevant. So what are these fundamental changes? They include (a) the compression of time and space by communication and transportation technologies; (b) the spread of markets that can commodify virtually everything, including the elements of culture; (c) the growing importance of culture, often detached from its structural sources by commodification in global markets; (d) the rapid circulation in markets of standardized goods with little intrinsic meaning embedded in culture; and (e) the over-reflexive self, which is constantly redefined by purchases of cultural and material commodities in markets.

What is evident is that the same themes of the early classical theorists reappear in postmodernism, despite postmodernists' claims that modernity and postmodernity represent distinct stages of societal evolution. Still, the questions remain as to whether or not postmodernists have moved very far beyond the classical theorists.[89] But they have made far more explicit the critique that modernity—markets, media, compression of space/time, over-reflexivity, the detachment of culture from its structural roots, and the circulation of culture as a commodity in global markets— has weakened the power of social structure and culture to provide anchorage for individuals, who now have shallow, unstable, and reflexive selves that are no longer attached and embedded in communities. These concerns hearken back to Marx's concern with alienation, Durkheim's with anomie and egoism, Simmel's marginality, and Weber's concerns about rationality and rational-legal domination, but with a somewhat different vocabulary. Still, is there anything dramatically new about an updated critique of presumed pathologies of the postmodern condition? Postmodern theorizing will be explored in Chapter 23.

---

[87]For more economically oriented postmodern theories, see Fredric Jameson, *The Postmodern Condition* (Minneapolis: University of Minnesota Press, 1984); David Harvey, *The Conditions of Postmodernity* (Oxford, UK: Blackwell, 1989); and Scott Lash and John Urry, *The End of Organized Capitalism* (Madison: University of Wisconsin Press, 1987).

[88]For more cultural postmodern theories, see Steven Seidman (ed.), *The Postmodern Turn: New Perspectives on Social Theory* (Cambridge, UK: Cambridge University Press, 1994); Jean Baudrillard, *Simulacra and Simulation* (Ann Arbor: University of Michigan Press); and Jean-François Lyotard, *The Postmodern Condition: A Report on Knowledge* (Minneapolis: University of Minnesota Press, 1978).

[89]For a critical review of the theoretical and empirical claims of postmodern theory, see Kenneth Allan and Jonathan H. Turner, "A Formalization of Postmodern Theory," *Sociological Perspectives* (2000):363–385.

Conclusions

As is evident, the early masters continue to inspire sociological theorizing in obvious and more subtle ways. Over the last eighty years, theoretical sociology has gone in many directions and has proliferated into many specialized approaches. Yet each of these specialized theories reveals the influence of the first masters, as we have tried to emphasize in the footnotes pointing to relevant portions of the text that can be consulted. The classical theorists from 1830 to 1935 thought "big" and broadly. It should not be surprising, therefore, that their works would have relevance for a wide range of more specialized theories, and since many of the masters addressed modernity critically, it is also not surprising that their ideas are woven through the various branches of critical theorizing that now pervade sociology. Thus, the classical tradition is alive and well, not just *as an academic pursuit in itself* but also as a source of continued inspiration to theorists writing today, almost a century after the early masters had all died. Part II will now review the basic theoretical perspectives and their many variants that have built upon the seminal insights of the early masters described in Part I.

PART II

The Modern Era
of Theorizing

CHAPTER 10

Functional Theorizing

F unctional theorizing is as old as the discipline of sociology. Auguste Comte employed the organismic analogy in his call for a new science, and in so doing, he began to analyze social structures for the functions that they fulfill for the "body social." Later, Herbert Spencer and then Émile Durkheim developed a more analytical approach, positing functional "needs" or "requisites" that are essential to sustaining a social system in its environment. Spencer argued that there were four such requisites—production, reproduction, distribution, and regulation—whereas Durkheim posited only one master requisite—the need for integration. I have outlined in detail Spencer's and Durkheim's arguments in Chapters 3 and 7, while delineating the key elements of all functional analysis in Chapter 9. In this chapter, I will emphasize functionalism in the middle to late twentieth century, documenting its rise to theoretical dominance and, then, its swift decline.

Functionalism may well have died with Spencer's and then Durkheim's death because functionalism had always been tied in the nineteenth century to stage model evolutionary theories that by the second decade of the twentieth century had fallen into disfavor (see Chapter 13). Indeed, the quintessential twentieth-century functionalist of all, Talcott Parsons, began his career with the question of why few read Spencer any more, attributing his downfall to his evolutionary analysis of societies from simple to more complex forms.[1] Yet, as we will see, clearly Parsons had read Spencer, because his own career mimics Spencer's in using a functional form of analysis to explain an ever wider range of phenomena. Still, the intriguing questions remain: Why did functionalism *not* die? How did it survive? Why did it reemerge in the 1950s in sociology? And why does it persist today in somewhat transmuted form? The answer to these questions begins with what was transpiring in anthropology.

---

[1]Talcott Parsons, *The Structure of Social Action* (New York: McGraw-Hill, 1937).

How Functionalism Survived

Functionalism as a well-articulated conceptual perspective was perpetuated in the first half of the twentieth century by the writings of two anthropologists, Bronislaw Malinowski[2] and A. R. Radcliffe-Brown.[3] Each of these thinkers was heavily influenced by the organicism of Durkheim, as well as by their own field studies among preliterate societies. Despite the similarities in their intellectual background, however, the conceptual perspectives developed by Malinowski and Radcliffe-Brown reveal many dissimilarities. Let me start with Radcliffe-Brown's approach.

The Functionalism of A. R. Radcliffe-Brown

Recognizing that "the concept of function applied to human societies is based on an analogy between social life and organic life" and that "the first systematic formulation of the concept as applying to the strictly scientific study of society was performed by Durkheim," Radcliffe-Brown (1881–1955) tried to indicate how some problems of organismic analogizing might be overcome. Radcliffe-Brown believed the most serious problem with functionalism was the tendency for analysis to appear teleological—that is, seeing phenomena as always meeting some goal or requisite in the more inclusive social system. The result was that the outcome of a phenomenon was also seen as the cause of this phenomenon—a logic that can be an illegitimate teleology. Noting that Durkheim's definition of function pertained to the way in which a part fulfills system needs, Radcliffe-Brown emphasized that, to avoid the teleological implications of such analysis, it would be necessary to "substitute for the term 'needs' the term 'necessary condition of existence.'" In doing so, he felt that no universal human or societal needs would be postulated; rather, the question of which conditions were necessary for survival would be an *empirical* one, an issue that would have to be discovered for each given social system. Furthermore, in recognizing the diversity of conditions necessary for the survival of different systems, analysis would avoid asserting that every item of a culture must have a function and that items in different cultures must have the same function.

Once the dangers of illegitimate teleology were recognized, functional or (to use his term) "structural" analysis could legitimately proceed from several assumptions:

---

[2]For basic references on Malinowski's functionalism, see his "Anthropology," *Encyclopedia Britannica*, supplementary vol. 1 (London: Encyclopedia Britannica, Inc., 1936), *A Scientific Theory of Culture* (Chapel Hill: University of North Carolina Press, 1944), and *Magic, Science, and Religion and Other Essays* (Glencoe, IL: Free Press, 1948). For basic references on A. R. Radcliffe-Brown's functionalism, see his "Structure and Function in Primitive Society," *American Anthropologist* 37 (July–September 1935):58–72, *Structure and Function in Primitive Society* (Glencoe, IL: Free Press, 1952), and *The Andaman Islanders* (Glencoe, IL: Free Press, 1948). See also Jonathan Turner and Alexandra Maryanski, *Functionalism* (Menlo Park, CA: Benjamin Cummings, 1979).

[3]Radcliffe-Brown, "Structure and Function in Primitive Society," *American Anthropologist* 37 (July–September 1935):68. This statement is, of course, incorrect because the organismic analogy was far more developed in Spencer's work.

(a) one necessary condition for survival of a society is minimal integration of its parts, (b) the term *function* refers to those processes that maintain this necessary integration or solidarity, (c) thus, in each society, structural features can be shown to contribute to the maintenance of necessary solidarity. In such an analytical approach, social structure and the conditions necessary for its survival are irreducible. In a vein similar to that of Durkheim, Radcliffe-Brown saw society as a reality in and of itself. For this reason, he usually visualized cultural items, such as kinship rules and religious rituals, as explicable through social structure—particularly social structure's need for solidarity and integration. For example, in analyzing a lineage system, Radcliffe-Brown would first assume that some minimal degree of solidarity exists in the system. Processes associated with lineage systems would then be assessed to determine their consequences for maintaining this solidarity. The conclusion was that lineage systems provided a systematic way of adjudicating conflict in societies where families owned land because such a system specified who had the right to land and through which side of the family it would always pass. The integration of the economic system—landed "estates" owned by families—is thus "explained."[4]

This form of analysis poses a number of problems that continue to haunt functional theorists. Although Radcliffe-Brown admitted that "functional unity [integration] of a social system is, of course, a hypothesis," he failed to specify the analytical criteria for assessing just how much or how little functional unity is necessary for testing this hypothesis. As subsequent commentators discovered, without some analytical criteria for determining what is and what is not minimal functional integration and societal survival, the hypothesis cannot be tested, even in principle. Thus, what it typically does is to assume that the existing system is minimally integrated and surviving because it exists and persists. Without carefully documenting how various cultural items promote instances of both integration and malintegration of the social whole, such a strategy can reduce the hypothesis of functional unity to a tautology. If one can find a system to study, then it must be minimally integrated because it exists; lineages are a part of this system; therefore, they must promote its integration. To discover the contrary would be difficult, because the system, by virtue of being a surviving system, is already composed of integrated parts, such as a lineage system. There is a non-sequitur in such reasoning, because it is quite possible to view a cultural item such as a lineage system as having both integrative and malintegrative (and other) consequences for the social whole. In his actual ethnographic descriptions, Radcliffe-Brown often slips inadvertently into a pattern of circular reasoning: the fact of a system's existence requires that its existing parts, such as a lineage system, be viewed as contributing to the system's existence. Assuming integration and then assessing the contribution of individual parts to the integrated whole lead to an additional analytical problem. Such a mode of analysis implies that the causes of a particular structure—for example, lineages—lie in the system's needs for integration, which is most likely an illegitimate teleology.

---

[4]Radcliffe-Brown, *Structure and Function in Primitive Society* (Glencoe, IL: Free Press, 1952), 31–50. For a secondary analysis of this example, see Arthur L. Stinchcombe, "Specious Generality and Functional Theory," *American Sociological Review* 26 (December 1961):929–930.

Radcliffe-Brown would, of course, have denied this conclusion. His awareness of the dangers of illegitimate teleology would have seemingly eliminated the implication that the needs of a system cause the emergence of its parts. His repeated assertions that the notion of function "does not require the dogmatic assertion that everything in the life of every community has a function" should have led to a rejection of tautological reasoning.[5] However, much like Durkheim, what Radcliffe-Brown asserted analytically was frequently not practiced in the concrete empirical analysis of societies. Such lapses were not intended but appeared to be difficult to avoid with functional needs, functional integration, and equilibrium as the operating assumptions.[6]

Thus, although Radcliffe-Brown displayed an admirable awareness of the dangers of organicism—especially of the problem of illegitimate teleology and the hypothetical nature of notions of solidarity—he all too often slipped into a pattern of questionable teleological reasoning. Forgetting that integration was only a working hypothesis, he opened his analysis to problems of tautology. Such problems were persistent in Durkheim's analysis, and despite his attempts to the contrary, their specter haunted even Radcliffe-Brown's insightful essays and ethnographies. These problems with functionalism persisted, and once functional theory became dominant once again, they soon became one of several bases of critique of functionalism, eventually bringing it down to its current obscurity.

The Functionalism of Bronislaw Malinowski

Functionalism might have ended with Radcliffe-Brown because it had very little to offer sociologists attempting to study complex rather than simple, preliterate societies. Both Durkheim and Radcliffe-Brown posited one basic societal need—integration—and then analyzed system parts to determine how they meet this need. For sociologists who are concerned with complex, differentiated societies, this is likely to become a rather mechanical task. Moreover, it does not allow analysis of those aspects of a system part that are not involved in meeting the need for integration.

Bronislaw Malinowski's (1884–1942) functionalism removed these restrictions. By reintroducing Spencer's more robust analytical approach, Malinowski offered a way for modern sociologists to employ functional analysis.[7] Malinowski's scheme reintroduced two important ideas from Spencer: (1) the notion of *system levels* and (2) the concept of different and *multiple system needs* at each level. In making these two additions, Malinowski made functional analysis more appealing to twentieth-century sociological theorists.

---

[5]See, for example, Radcliffe-Brown, *Structure and Function in Primitive Society.*

[6]A perceptive critic of an earlier edition of this manuscript provided an interesting way to visualize the problems of tautology:

When do you have a surviving social system?

When certain survival requisites are met.

How do you know when certain survival requisites are met?

When you have a surviving social system.

[7]Don Martindale, *The Nature and Types of Sociological Theory* (Boston, MA: Houghton Mifflin, 1960), 459.

Malinowski's scheme has three system levels: the biological, the social structural, and the symbolic.[8] At each level, we can discern basic needs or survival requisites that must be met if biological health, social structural integrity, and cultural unity are to exist. Moreover, these system levels constitute a hierarchy, with biological systems at the bottom, social structural arrangements next, and symbolic systems at the highest level—an idea that was not too far from what Talcott Parsons was to term the "cybernetic hierarchy of control." Malinowski stressed that the way in which needs are met at one system level sets constraints on how they are met at the next level in the hierarchy. Yet he did not advocate a reductionism of any sort; indeed, he thought that each system level reveals its own distinctive requisites and processes meeting these needs. In addition, he argued that the important system levels for sociological or anthropological analysis are the structural and the symbolic. And in his actual discussion, the social structural level receives the most attention. Table 10.1 lists the requisites or needs of the two most sociologically relevant system levels.

Table 10.1   Requisites of System Levels

Cultural (Symbolic) System Level
1. Requisites for systems of symbols that provide information necessary to adjust to the environment
2. Requisites for systems of symbols that provide a sense of control over people's destiny and over chance events
3. Requisites for systems of symbols that provide members of a society with a sense of a "communal rhythm" in their daily lives and activities
Structural (Instrumental) System Level
1. The requisite for production and distribution of consumer goods
2. The requisite for social control of behavior and its regulation
3. The requisite for education of people in traditions and skills
4. The requisite for organization and execution of authority relations

In analyzing the structural system level, Malinowski stressed that institutional analysis is necessary. For Malinowski, *institutions* are the general and relatively stable ways in which activities are organized to meet critical requisites. All institutions, he felt, have certain universal properties or "elements" that can be listed and then used as dimensions for comparing different institutions. These universal elements are

1. *Personnel:* Who and how many people will participate in the institution?

2. *Charter:* What is the purpose of the institution? What are its avowed goals?

3. *Norms:* What are the key norms that regulate and organize conduct?

---

[8] Bronislaw Malinowski, *A Scientific Theory of Culture and Other Essays* (London: Oxford University Press, 1964), 71–125; see also Turner and Maryanski, *Functionalism,* 44–57.

4. *Material apparatus:* What is the nature of the tools and facilities used to organize and regulate conduct in pursuit of goals?

5. *Activity:* How are tasks and activities divided? Who does what?

6. *Function:* What requisite does a pattern of institutional activity meet?

By describing each institution along these six dimensions, Malinowski believed that he had provided a common analytical yardstick for comparing patterns of social organization within and between societies. He even constructed a list of universal institutions as they resolve not just structural but also biological and symbolic requisites.

In sum, Malinowski's functional approach opened new possibilities for sociologists who had long forgotten Spencer's similar arguments. Malinowski suggested to sociologists that attention to system levels is critical in analyzing requisites; he argued that there are universal requisites for each system level; he forcefully emphasized that the structural level is the essence of sociological analysis; and much like Spencer before him and Talcott Parsons a decade later, Malinowski posited four universal functional needs at this level—economic adaptation, political authority, educational socialization, and social control—which were to be prominent in subsequent functional schemes and were highly reminiscent of Spencer's four requisites. Moreover, he provided a clear method for analyzing institutions as they operate to meet functional requisites. It is fair to say, therefore, that Malinowski drew the rough contours of modern sociological functionalism.

Talcott Parsons and the Modern Revival of Functionalism

Talcott Parsons was probably the most prominent theorist of his time, and it is unlikely that any one theoretical approach will so dominate sociological theory again as did Parsonsian functional theory, for a brief time, at the midpoint of the twentieth century. In the years between 1950 and the late 1970s, Parsonsian functionalism was clearly the focal point around which theoretical controversy raged. Even those who despised Parsons's functional approach could not ignore it. Even now, years after his death and more than four decades since its period of dominance, Parsonsian functionalism is still the subject of controversy.[9] To appreciate Parsons's achievement in bringing functionalism to the second half of the twentieth century, it is best to start at the beginning, in 1937, when he published his first major work, *The Structure of Social Action.*[10]

---

[9]Although few appear to agree with all aspects of Parsonsian theory, rarely has anyone quarreled with the assertion that he has been the dominant sociological figure of this century. For documentation of Parsons's influence, see Robert W. Friedrichs, *A Sociology of Sociology* (New York: Free Press, 1970) and Alvin W. Gouldner, *The Coming Crisis of Western Sociology* (New York: Basic Books, 1970).

[10] Talcott Parsons, *The Structure of Social Action*, the paperback edition (New York: Free Press, 1968) will be used in subsequent footnotes.

The Structure of Social Action

In *The Structure of Social Action,* Parsons began his analysis by paraphrasing the historian Crane Britten's famous quote "Who now reads Spencer?" Spencer, Parsons went on to emphasize, had died with the god of evolutionism, and in its place, he advocated using an "analytical realism" to build sociological theory. Theory must involve the development of concepts that abstract from empirical reality, in all its diversity and confusion, common analytical elements. In this way, concepts will isolate phenomena from their embeddedness in the complex relations that constitute social reality.

The unique feature of Parson's analytical realism is the insistence on how these abstract concepts are to be employed in sociological analysis. Parsons did not advocate the immediate incorporation of these concepts into theoretical statements but rather advocated their use to develop a "generalized system of concepts." This use of abstract concepts would involve their ordering into a coherent whole that would reflect the important features of the "real world." What is sought is an organization of concepts into analytical systems that grasp the salient and systemic features of the universe without being overwhelmed by empirical details. This emphasis on systems of categories represents Parsons's application of Max Weber's ideal-type strategy for analytically accentuating salient features of the world. Thus, much like Weber, Parsons believed that theory should initially resemble an elaborate classification and categorization of social phenomena that reflect significant features in the organization of these social phenomena. This strategy was evident in Parsons's first major work, where he developed the "voluntaristic theory of action."

Parsons believed that the voluntaristic theory of action represented a synthesis of the useful assumptions and concepts of utilitarianism, positivism, and idealism. In reviewing the thought of classical economists, Parsons noted the excessiveness of their utilitarianism: unregulated and atomistic actors in a free and competitive marketplace rationally attempting to choose those behaviors that will maximize their profits in their transactions with others. Parsons believed such a formulation of the social order presented several critical problems. Do humans always behave rationally? Are they indeed free and unregulated? How is order possible in an unregulated and competitive system? Yet Parsons saw as fruitful several features of utilitarian thought, especially the concern with actors as seeking goals and the emphasis on the choice-making capacities of human beings who weigh alternative lines of action. Stated in this minimal form, Parsons felt that the utilitarian heritage could indeed continue to inform sociological theorizing.

In a similar critical stance, Parsons rejected the extreme formulations of radical positivists, who tended to view the social world in terms of observable cause-and-effect relationships among physical phenomena. In so doing, he felt, they ignored the complex symbolic functioning of the human mind. Furthermore, Parsons saw the emphasis on observable cause-and-effect relationships as too easily encouraging a sequence of infinite reductionism: groups were reduced to the causal relationships of their individual members, individuals were reducible to the cause-and-effect relationships of their physiological processes, these were reducible to physicochemical relationships, and so on, down to the most basic cause-and-effect connections among particles of physical matter. Nevertheless, despite these extremes, radical positivism draws attention to the physical parameters of social life and to the deterministic impact of these parameters on much—but of course not all—social organization. Finally, in assessing idealism, Parsons saw the conceptions of "ideas" to circumscribe both individual and social processes as useful, although all too frequently these ideas are seen as detached from the ongoing social life they were supposed to regulate.

The depth of scholarship in Parsons's analysis of these traditions is impossible to communicate, but his rather detailed, and often ponderous, analysis in *The Structure of Social Action* indicates that "voluntaristic action" involves these basic elements: (a) actors, at this point in Parsons's thinking, are individual persons, (b) actors are viewed as goal-seeking, (c) actors also possess alternative means to achieve the goals, (d) actors are confronted with a variety of situational conditions, such as their own biological makeup and heredity as well as various external ecological constraints that influence the selection of goals and means, (e) actors are governed by values, norms, and other ideas such that these ideas influence what is considered a goal and what means are selected to achieve it, (f) action involves actors making subjective decisions about the means to achieve goals, all of which are constrained by ideas and situational conditions.

Figure 10.1 represents this conceptualization of voluntarism. The processes diagrammed are often termed the *unit act*, with social action involving a succession of such unit acts by one or more actors. In many ways, I suspect, Parsons saw himself as refining and extending Max Weber's ideal type of the four types of action (see pp. 121–122).

Once these basic tasks were completed, Parsons began to ask, how are unit acts connected to each other, and how can this connectedness be conceptually represented? Indeed, near the end of *The Structure of Social Action,* he recognized that "any atomistic system that deals only with properties identifiable in the unit act . . . will of

Figure 10.1   The Units of Voluntaristic Action

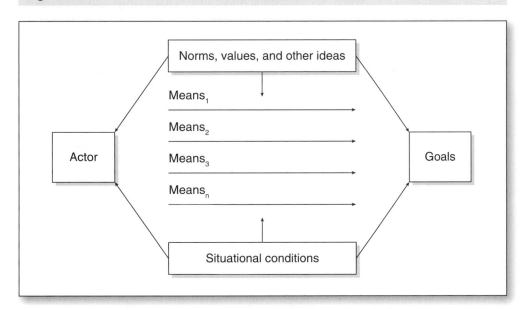

necessity fail to treat these latter elements adequately and be indeterminate as applied to complex systems."[11] However, only the barest hints of what was to come were evident in those closing pages.

The Social System

Figure 10.2 summarizes how Parsons made the conceptual transition from unit acts to social system. This transition occupies the early parts of Parsons's next significant work, *The Social System*.[12] Drawing inspiration from Weber's typological[13] approach to this same topic, Parsons viewed actors as "oriented" to situations in terms of motives (needs and readiness to mobilize energy) and values (conceptions about what is appropriate). There are three types of motives: (1) *cognitive* (need for information), (2) *cathectic* (need for emotional attachment), and (3) *evaluative* (need for assessment). Also, there are three corresponding types of values: (1) *cognitive* (evaluation by objective standards), (2) *appreciative* (evaluation by aesthetic standards), and (3) *moral* (evaluation by absolute rightness and wrongness). Parsons called these *modes of orientation*. Although this discussion is somewhat vague, the general idea seems to be that the relative salience of these motives and values for any actor creates a composite type of action, which can be one of three types: (1) *instrumental* (action oriented to realize explicit goals efficiently), (2) *expressive* (action directed at realizing emotional satisfaction), and (3) *moral* (action concerned with realizing standards of right and wrong). That is, depending on which modes of motivational and value orientation are strongest, an actor will act in one of these basic ways. For example, if cognitive motives are strong and cognitive values most salient, then action will be primarily instrumental, although the action will also have expressive and moral content. Thus, the various combinations and permutations of the modes of orientation—that is, motives and values—produce action geared in one of these general directions.

Unit acts, therefore, involve motivational and value orientations and have a general direction as a consequence of what combination of values and motives prevails for an actor. Thus far, Parsons had elaborated only on his conceptualization of the unit act. The critical next step, which was only hinted at in the closing pages of *The Structure of Social Action*, can be portrayed as follows: as variously oriented actors (in the configuration of motivational and value orientations) interact, they develop agreements and sustain patterns of interaction that become "institutionalized." Such institutionalized patterns can be, in Parsons's view, conceptualized as a social system. Such a system represents an emergent phenomenon that requires its own conceptual edifice. The normative organization of *status-roles* becomes Parsons's

---

[11]Ibid., 730, 748–749. For useful analyses of Parsons's work in relation to the issues he raised in *The Structure of Social Action*, see Leon Mayhew, "In Defense of Modernity: Talcott Parsons and the Utilitarian Tradition," *American Journal of Sociology* 89 (1984):1273–1306 and Jeffrey C. Alexander, "Formal and Substantive Voluntarism in the Work of Talcott Parsons: A Theoretical Reinterpretation," *American Sociological Review* 13 (1978):177–198.

[12]Talcott Parsons, *The Social System* (New York: Free Press, 1951).

[13]Max Weber, *Economy and Society*, vol. 1 (Totowa, NJ: Bedminster, 1968), 1–95.

Figure 10.2   Parsons's Conception of Action, Interaction, and Institutionalization

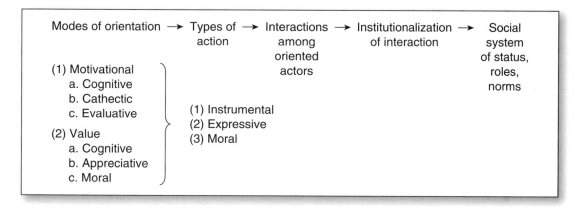

key to this conceptualization; that is, the subject matter of sociology is the organization of status, roles, and norms.

Yet Parsons recognized that the actors who are incumbent in status roles are motivational and value-oriented; thus, as with patterns of interaction, the task now becomes one of conceptualizing these dimensions of action in systemic terms. The result is the conceptualization of action as composed of three "interpenetrating action systems": the *cultural,* the *social,* and the *personality.* That is, the organization of unit acts into social systems requires a parallel conceptualization of motives and values that become the personality and cultural systems, respectively. The goal of action theory now becomes understanding how institutionalized patterns of interaction (the social system) are circumscribed by complexes of values, beliefs, norms, and other ideas (the cultural system).

Later, Parsons added the *organismic* (later called *behavioral*) system, but let me not get ahead of the story. At this stage of conceptualization, analyzing social systems involves developing a system of concepts that, first, captures the systemic features of society at all its diverse levels and, second, points to the modes of articulation among personality systems, social systems, and cultural patterns.

In his commitment to developing concepts that reflect the properties of all action systems, Parsons was led to a set of concepts denoting some of the variable properties of these systems. Termed *pattern variables,* they simultaneously allow the categorization of the modes of orientation in personality systems, the value patterns of culture, and the normative requirements in social systems. The variables are phrased as polar dichotomies that, depending on the system under analysis, allow a rough categorization of decisions by actors, the value orientations of culture, or the normative demands on status roles:

1. *Affectivity/affective* neutrality concerns the amount of emotion or affect that is appropriate in a given interaction situation. Should a great deal or little affect be expressed?

2. *Diffuseness/specificity* denotes the issue of how far-reaching obligations in an interaction situation are to be. Should the obligations be narrow and specific, or should they be extensive and diffuse?

3. *Universalism/particularism* points to the problem of whether evaluation of others in an interaction situation is to apply to all actors or whether all actors should be assessed by the same standards.

4. *Achievement/ascription* deals with the issue of how to assess an actor, whether by performance or by inborn qualities, such as sex, age, race, and family status. Should an actor treat another on the basis of achievements or ascriptive qualities that are unrelated to performance?

5. *Self-collectivity* denotes the extent to which action is to be oriented to self-interest and individual goals or to group interests and goals. Should actors consider their personal or self-related goals over those of the group or large collectivity in which they are involved?[14]

Some of these concepts, such as self-collectivity, were later dropped from the action scheme, but others, such as universalism-particularism, assumed greater importance. The intent of the pattern variables remained the same, however: to categorize dichotomies of decisions, normative demands, and value orientations. In *The Social System,* however, Parsons was inclined to view them as value orientations that circumscribe the norms of the social system and the decisions of the personality system. Thus, the structure of the personality and social systems reflects the dominant patterns of value orientations in culture. This implicit emphasis on the impact of cultural patterns in regulating and controlling other systems of action became ever-more explicit in his later work.

By 1951, Parsons had already woven a complex conceptual system that emphasizes the process of institutionalization of interaction into stabilized patterns called social systems, which are penetrated by personality and circumscribed by culture. The profile of institutionalized norms, of decisions by actors in roles, and of cultural value orientations can be typified by concepts—the pattern variables—that capture the variable properties in each of these action components.

Having built this analytical edifice, Parsons then returned to a question, first raised in *The Structure of Social Action,* that guided all his subsequent theoretical formulations: How do social systems survive? More specifically, why do institutionalized patterns of interaction persist? Such questions raise the issue of system imperatives or requisites. Parsons was asking how systems resolve their integrative problems. The answer is provided by the elaboration of additional concepts that point to how personality systems and culture are integrated into the social system, thereby providing assurance of some degree of normative coherence and a minimal amount of commitment by actors to conform to norms and play roles. Figure 10.3 delineates the key ideas in Parsons's reasoning.

Just how are personality systems integrated into the social system, thereby promoting equilibrium? At the most abstract level, Parsons conceptualized two

---

[14]These pattern variables were developed in collaboration with Edward Shils and were elaborated in *Toward a General Theory of Action* (New York: Harper and Row, 1951), 76–98, 183–189, 203–204. Again, Parsons's debt to Max Weber's concern with constructing ideal types can be seen in his presentation of the pattern variables.

mechanisms that integrate the personality into the social system: (1) mechanisms of socialization and (2) mechanisms of social control.

1. *Mechanisms of socialization* are the means through which cultural patterns—values, beliefs, language, and other symbols—are internalized into the personality system, thereby circumscribing its need structure. Through this process, actors are made willing to deposit motivational energy in roles (thereby willing to conform to norms) and are given the interpersonal and other skills necessary for playing roles. Another function of socialization mechanisms is to provide stable and secure interpersonal ties that alleviate much of the strain, anxiety, and tension associated with participation in social systems.

2. *Mechanisms of social control* involve those ways in which status-roles are organized in social systems to reduce strain and deviance. There are numerous specific control mechanisms, including (a) institutionalization, which makes role expectations clear and unambiguous while segregating in time and space contradictory expectations; (b) interpersonal sanctions and gestures, which actors subtly employ to mutually sanction conformity; (c) ritual activities, in which actors act out symbolically sources of strain that could prove disruptive, while they reinforce dominant cultural patterns; (d) safety valve structures, in which pervasive deviant propensities are segregated in time and space from normal institutional patterns; (e) reintegration structures, which are specifically charged with bringing deviant tendencies back into line; and, finally, (f) institutionalizing the capacity to use force and coercion in some sectors of a system.

These two mechanisms resolve one of the most persistent integrative problems facing social systems. The other major integrative problem facing social systems concerns how cultural patterns contribute to the maintenance of social order and equilibrium. Again, at the most abstract level, Parsons visualized two ways in which

Figure 10.3   Parsons's Early Conception of Integration Among Systems of Action

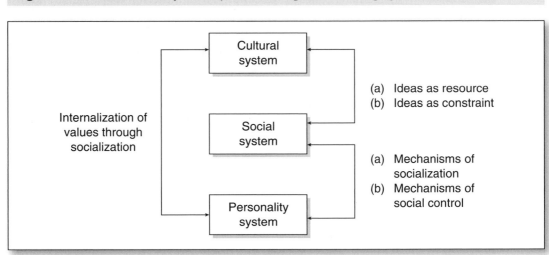

this occurs: (1) Some components of culture, such as language, are basic resources necessary for interaction to occur. Without symbolic resources, communication and, hence, interaction would not be possible. Thus, by providing common resources for all actors, interaction is made possible by culture. (2) A related but still separable influence of culture on interaction is exerted through the substance of ideas contained in cultural patterns (values, beliefs, ideology, and so forth). These ideas can provide actors with common viewpoints, personal ontologies, or, to borrow from W. I. Thomas, a common "definition of the situation." These common meanings allow interaction to proceed smoothly with minimal disruption.

Naturally, Parsons acknowledged that the mechanisms of socialization and social control are not always successful, hence allowing deviance and social change to occur. But clearly, the concepts developed in *The Social System* weight analysis in the direction of looking for processes that maintain the integration and, by implication, the equilibrium of social systems.

The Transition to Functional Requisites

In collaboration with Robert Bales and Edward Shils, Parsons published *Working Papers in the Theory of Action* shortly after *The Social System*. In *Working Papers,* conceptions of functional imperatives dominated the general theory of action,[15] and by 1956, with Parsons's and Neil Smelser's publication of *Economy and Society,* the functions of structures for meeting system requisites were well institutionalized into action theory.[16]

During this period, systems of action were conceptualized to have four survival problems, or requisites: adaptation, goal attainment, integration, and latency. *Adaptation* involves securing sufficient resources from the environment and then distributing these throughout the system. *Goal attainment* refers to establishing priorities among system goals and mobilizing system resources for their attainment. *Integration* denotes coordinating and maintaining viable interrelationships among system units. *Latency* embraces two related problems: pattern maintenance and tension management. Pattern maintenance pertains to how to ensure that actors in the social system display the appropriate characteristics (motives, needs, role-playing, etc.). Tension management concerns dealing with the internal tensions and strains of actors in the social system.

All these requisites were implicit in *The Social System,* but they tended to be viewed under the general problem of integration. In Parsons's discussion of integration within and between action systems, problems of securing facilities (adaptation), allocation and goal seeking (goal attainment), and socialization and social control (latency) were conspicuous. Thus, the development of the four functional requisites—abbreviated A, G, I, and L—was not so much a radical departure from earlier works as an elaboration of concepts implicit in *The Social System.*

---

[15]Talcott Parsons, Robert F. Bales, and Edward A. Shils, *Working Papers in the Theory of Action* (Glencoe, IL: Free Press, 1953).

[16]Talcott Parsons and Neil J. Smelser, *Economy and Society* (New York: Free Press, 1956). These requisites are the same as those enumerated by Malinowski. See Table 10.1.

With the introduction of A, G, I, and L, however, a subtle shift away from the analysis of structures to the analysis of functions occurs. Structures are now evaluated explicitly by their functional consequences of meeting the four requisites. Interrelationships among specific structures are now analyzed by how their interchanges affect the requisites that each must meet.

As Parsons's conceptual scheme became increasingly oriented to function, social systems are divided into sectors, each corresponding to a functional requisite—that is, A, G, I, or L. In turn, any subsystem can be divided into these four functional sectors. Then, each subsystem can be divided into four functional sectors, and so on. This process of "functional sectorization," to invent a word to describe it, is illustrated for the adaptive requisite in Figure 10.4.

Of critical analytical importance in this scheme are the interchanges among systems and subsystems. It is difficult to comprehend the functioning of a designated social system without examining the interchanges among its A, G, I, and L sectors, especially because these interchanges are affected by exchanges among constituent subsystems and other systems in the environment. In turn, the functioning of a designated subsystem cannot be understood without examining the

Figure 10.4 Parsons's Functional Imperativist View of Social Systems

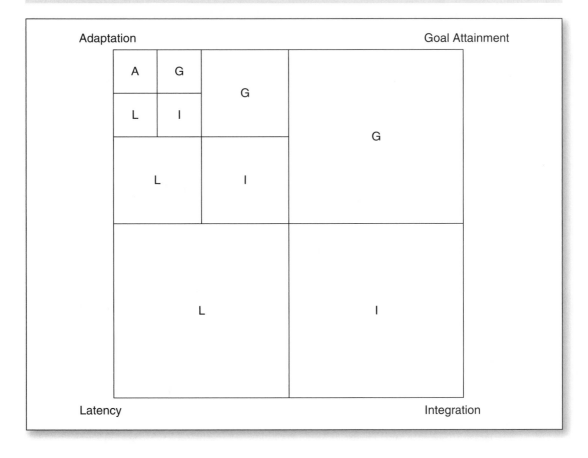

internal interchanges among its adaptive, goal attainment, integrative, and latency sectors, especially because these interchanges are influenced by exchanges with other subsystems and the more inclusive system of which it is a subsystem. Thus, at this juncture, as important interchanges among the functional sectors of systems and subsystems are outlined, the Parsonsian scheme begins to resemble an elaborate mapping operation.

The Informational Hierarchy of Control

Toward the end of the 1950s, Parsons turned his attention toward the interrelationships among (rather than within) what were then four distinct action systems: culture, social structure, personality, and organism. In many ways, this concern represented an odyssey back to the analysis of the basic components of the unit act outlined in *The Structure of Social Action*. But now each element of the unit act is a full-fledged action system, each confronting four functional problems to resolve: adaptation, goal attainment, integration, and latency. Furthermore, although individual decision-making is still a part of action as personalities adjust to the normative demands of status roles in the social system, the analytical emphasis has shifted to the input-output connections among the four action systems.

At this juncture, Parsons began to visualize an overall action system, with culture, social structure, personality, and organism composing its constituent subsystems.[17] Each of these subsystems is seen as fulfilling one of the four system requisites—A, G, I, and L—of the overall action system. The organism is considered to be the subsystem having the most consequences for resolving adaptive problems because it is ultimately through this system that environmental resources are made available to the other action subsystems. As the goal-seeking and decision-making system, personality is considered to have primary consequences for resolving goal attainment problems. As an organized network of status norms integrating the patterns of the cultural system and the needs of personality systems, the social system is viewed as the major integrative subsystem of the general action system. As the repository of the symbolic content of interaction, the cultural system is considered to have primary consequences for managing tensions of actors and ensuring that the proper symbolic resources are available to ensure the maintenance of institutional patterns (latency).

After viewing each action system as a subsystem of a more inclusive, overall system, Parsons explored the interrelations among the four subsystems. What emerged is a hierarchy of informational controls, with culture informationally circumscribing the social system, the structure of the social system informationally regulating the personality system, and personality informationally regulating the organismic system. For example, cultural value orientations would be seen as circumscribing or limiting the range of variation in the norms of the social system; in turn, these

---

[17]Talcott Parsons, "An Approach to Psychological Theory in Terms of the Theory of Action," in *Psychology: A Science,* ed. S. Koch, vol. 3 (New York: McGraw-Hill, 1958), 612–711. By 1961, these ideas were even more clearly formulated; see Talcott Parsons, "An Outline of the Social System," in *Theories of Society,* ed. T. Parsons, E. Shils, K. D. Naegele, and J. R. Pitts (New York: Free Press, 1961), 30–38. See also Jackson Toby, "Parsons' Theory of Social Evolution," *Contemporary Sociology* 1 (1972):395–401.

norms, as translated into expectations for actors playing roles, would be viewed as limiting the kinds of motives and decision-making processes in personality systems; these features of the personality system would then be seen as circumscribing bio-chemical processes in the organism.

Conversely, each system in the hierarchy is also viewed as providing the "energic conditions" necessary for action at the next higher system. That is, the organism provides the energy necessary for the personality system, the personality system provides the energic conditions for the social system, and the organization of personality systems into a social system provides the conditions necessary for a cultural system. Thus, the input-output relations among action systems are reciprocal, with systems exchanging information and energy. Systems high in information circumscribe the utilization of energy at the next lower system level, and each lower system provides the conditions and facilities necessary for action in the next higher system. This scheme has been termed a cybernetic hierarchy of control and is diagrammed in Figure 10.5.

Figure 10.5 Parsons's Cybernetic Hierarchy of Control

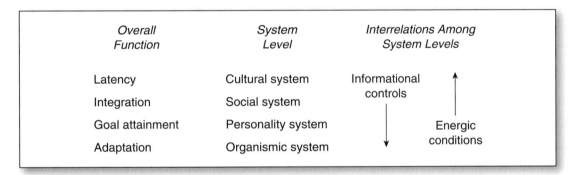

Generalized Media of Exchange

Until his death, Parsons maintained his interest in the intra- and intersystemic relationships of the four action systems. Although he never developed the concepts fully, he had begun to view these relationships as generalized symbolic media of exchange.[18] In any interchange, generalized media are employed—for example, money is used in the economy to facilitate the buying and selling of goods. What typifies these generalized media, such as money, is that they are really symbolic modes of communication. The money is not worth much by itself; its value is evident only for what it says symbolically in an exchange relationship.

---

[18]Parsons's writings on this topic are incomplete, but see "On the Concept of Political Power," *Proceedings of the American Philosophical Society* 107 (1963):232–262, "On the Concept of Influence," *Public Opinion Quarterly* 27 (Spring 1963):37–62, and "Some Problems of General Theory," in *Theoretical Sociology: Perspectives and Developments,* ed. J. C. McKinney and E. A. Tiryakian (New York: Appleton-Century-Crofts, 1970), 28–68. See also Talcott Parsons and Gerald M. Platt, *The American University* (Cambridge, MA: Harvard University Press, 1975).

Thus, what Parsons proposed is that the links among action components are ultimately informational. This means that transactions are mediated by symbols. Parsons's emphasis on information is consistent with a cybernetic hierarchy of control. Informational exchanges, or cybernetic controls, are seen as operating in at least three ways. First, the interchanges or exchanges among the four subsystems of the overall action system are carried out by different types of symbolic media: that is, *money, power, influence,* or *commitment*s. Second, the interchanges within any of the four action systems are also carried out by distinctive symbolic media. Finally, the system requisites of adaptation (A), goal attainment (G), integration (I), and latency (L) determine the type of generalized symbolic media used in an intra- or intersystemic exchange.

Within the social system, the adaptive sector uses *money* as the medium of exchange with the other three sectors; the goal attainment sector employs *power*— the capacity to induce conformity—as its principal medium of exchange; the integrative sector of a social system relies on *influence*—the capacity to persuade; and the latency sector uses commitments—especially the capacity to be *loyal.* The analysis of interchanges of specific structures within social systems should thus focus on the input-output exchanges using different symbolic media.

Among the subsystems of the overall action system, a similar analysis of the symbolic media used in exchanges should be undertaken, but Parsons never clearly described the nature of these media.[19] What he appeared to be approaching was a conceptual scheme for analyzing the basic types of symbolic media, or information, linking systems in the cybernetic hierarchy of control.[20]

The Analysis of Social Change

In the last decade of his career, Parsons became increasingly concerned with social change. Built into the cybernetic hierarchy of control is a conceptual scheme for classifying the locus of such social change. What Parsons visualized was that the information and energic interchanges among action systems provide the potential for change within or between the action systems. One source of change can be excesses in either information or energy in the exchange among action systems. In turn, these excesses alter the informational or energic outputs across systems and within any system. For example, excesses of motivation (energy) would have consequences for the enactment of roles and perhaps, ultimately, for the reorganization of these roles or the normative structure and, eventually, of cultural value orientations. Another source of change comes from an insufficient supply of either energy or information, again causing external and internal readjustments in the structure of action systems. For example, value (informational) conflict would cause normative conflict (or anomie), which in turn would have consequences for the personality

---

[19]For his first attempt at a statement, see Parsons, "Some Problems of General Theory," 61–68.

[20]For a more readable discussion of these generalized media, see T. S. Turner, "Parsons' Concept of Generalized Media of Social Interaction and Its Relevance for Social Anthropology," *Sociological Inquiry* 38 (Spring 1968):121–134.

and organismic systems. Thus, inherent in the cybernetic hierarchy of control are concepts that point to the sources of both stasis and change.

To augment this new macro emphasis on change, Parsons used the action scheme to analyze social evolution in historical societies. In this context, the first line of *The Structure of Social Action* is of interest: "Who now reads Spencer?" Parsons then answered the question by delineating some of the reasons why Spencer's evolutionary doctrine had been so thoroughly rejected by 1937. Yet, after some forty years, Parsons chose to reexamine the issue of societal evolution, which he had so easily dismissed in the beginning. And in so doing, he reintroduced Spencer's and Durkheim's evolutionary models back into functional theory.

In drawing heavily from Spencer's and Durkheim's insights into societal development, Parsons proposed that the processes of evolution display the following elements:

1. Increasing differentiation of system units into patterns of functional interdependence

2. Establishment of new principles and mechanisms of integration in differentiating systems

3. Increasing adaptive capacity of differentiated systems in their environments

From the perspective of action theory, then, evolution involves (a) increasing differentiation of the personality, social, cultural, and organismic systems from one another; (b) increasing differentiation within each of these four action subsystems; (c) escalating problems of integration and the emergence of new integrative structures; and (d) the upgrading of the survival capacity of each action subsystem, as well as the overall action system, within its environment.

Parsons then embarked on an ambitious effort in two short volumes to outline the pattern of evolution in historical systems through the primitive, intermediate, and modern stages.[21] In contrast with *The Social System,* where he stressed the problem of integration between social systems and personality, Parsons drew attention in his evolutionary model to the inter- and intra-differentiation of the cultural and social systems and to the resulting integrative problems. Each stage of evolution is seen as reflecting a new set of integrative problems between society and culture as each of these systems has become more differentiated internally as well as from the other. Thus, the concern with the issues of integration within and among action systems, so evident in earlier works, is not abandoned but is applied to the analysis of specific historical processes.

Even though Parsons was vague about the causes of evolutionary change, he saw evolution as guided by the cybernetic hierarchy of controls, especially the informational component. In his documenting of how integrative problems of the differentiating

---

[21]Talcott Parsons, *Societies: Evolutionary and Comparative Perspectives* and *The System of Modern Societies* (Englewood Cliffs, NJ: Prentice-Hall, 1966, 1971, respectively). The general stages of development were first outlined in Talcott Parsons, "Evolutionary Universals in Society," *American Sociological Review* 29 (1964):339–357.

social and cultural systems have been resolved in the evolution of historical systems, the informational hierarchy is regarded as crucial because the regulation of societal processes of differentiation must be accompanied by legitimization from cultural patterns (information). Without such informational control, movement to the next stage of development in an evolutionary sequence will be inhibited.

Thus, the analysis of social change is an attempt to use the analytical tools of the general theory of action to examine a specific process, the historical development of human societies. What is of interest in this effort is that Parsons developed many propositions about the sequences of change and the processes that will inhibit or accelerate the unfolding of these evolutionary sequences. It is of more than passing interest that tests of these propositions indicate that, on the whole, they have a great deal of empirical support.[22] [For a more detailed enumeration of the various stages of evolution in Parsons's theory, see the section in Chapter 13 on stage models of evolution, where Parsons's model is outlined on pp. 428–434.

The Human Condition

Again, in a way reminiscent of Spencer's grand theory, Parsons attempted to extend his analytical scheme to all aspects of the universe.[23] In this last conceptual addition, it is ironic that Parsons's work increasingly resembled Spencer's Synthetic Philosophy. Except for the opening line in *The Structure of Social Action*—"Who now reads Spencer?"—Parsons appeared to have ignored Spencer during his entire career. Indeed, he may not have realized how closely his analyses of societal evolution and his conceptualization of the "human condition" resembled Spencer's effort of 100 years earlier. At any rate, this last effort was more philosophy than sociology. Yet it represents the culmination of Parsons's thought.

Parsons began in 1937 with an analysis of the smallest and most elementary social unit, the act. He then developed a requisite functionalism that embraced four action systems: the social, cultural, personality, and what he called "the behavioral" in later years (he had earlier called this the *organismic*). Finally, in his desire to understand the basic parameters of the human condition, he viewed these four action systems as only one subsystem within the larger system of the universe. This vision is portrayed in Figure 10.6.

As can be seen in Figure 10.6, the universe is divided into four subsystems, each meeting one of the four requisites—that is, A, G, I, or L. The four action systems resolve integrative problems, the organic system handles goal attainment problems,

---

[22]For a fuller discussion, see Alvin L. Jacobson, "Talcott Parsons: A Theoretical and Empirical Analysis of Social Change and Conflict," in *Institutions and Social Exchange: The Sociologies of Talcott Parsons and George C. Homans,* ed. H. Turk and R. L. Simpson (Indianapolis, IN: Bobbs-Merrill, 1970). See also Gary L. Buck and Alvin L. Jacobson, "Social Evolution and Structural-Functional Analysis: An Empirical Test," *American Sociological Review* 33 (June 1968):343–355.

[23]Talcott Parsons, *Action Theory and the Human Condition* (New York: Free Press, 1978). See the last chapter in this book and my analysis in "Parsons on the Human Condition," *Contemporary Sociology* 9 (1980):380–383.

Figure 10.6   The Subsystems of the Human Condition

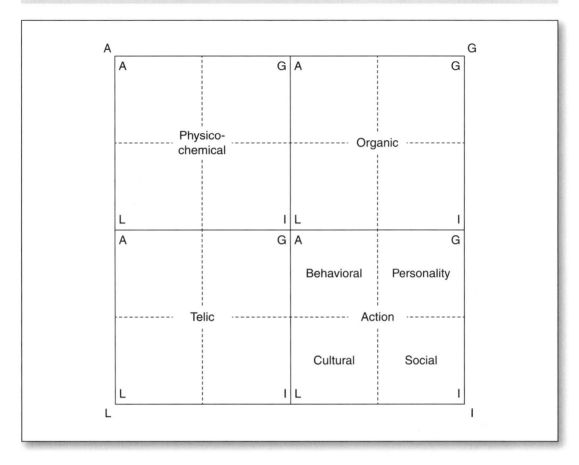

the physicochemical copes with adaptation problems, and the telic ("ultimate" problems of meaning and cognition) deals with latency problems.

Each subsystem employs its own media for intra- and inter-subsystem activity. For the action subsystem, the distinctive medium is symbolic meanings; for the telic, it is transcendental ordering; for the organic, it is health; and for the physicochemical, it is empirical ordering (law-like relations of matter, energy, etc.). There are double interchanges of these media among the four A, G, I, and L sectors, with "products" and "factors" being reciprocally exchanged. That is, each subsystem of the universe transmits a product to the others, while it also provides a factor necessary for the operation of other subsystems. This can be illustrated with the L (telic) and I (action) interchange. At the product level, the telic system provides "definitions of human responsibility" to the action subsystems and receives "sentiments of justification" from the action subsystem. At the factor level, the telic provides "categorical imperatives" and receives "acceptance of moral obligations." These double interchanges are, of course, carried out with the distinctive media of the I and A subsystems—that is, transcendental ordering and symbolic meaning, respectively.

The end result of this analysis was a grand metaphysical vision of the universe as it impinges on human existence. Parsons's analysis represents an effort to categorize the universe into systems, subsystems, system requisites, generalized media, and exchanges involving these media. As such, this analysis is no longer sociology but philosophy or, at best, a grand meta-theoretical vision. Parsons had indeed come a long way since the humble unit act made its entrance in 1937.

Niklas Luhmann's Systems Functionalism

The grand architecture of the Parsonsian functional scheme, as it evolved over a forty-year period at mid-century, inspired a great amount of criticism, both inside and outside the functionalist perspective. Within the functionalist camp, the Parsonsian conceptual edifice was heavily criticized for being too abstract and detached from empirical reality. Yet other functionalists were not so willing to abandon high-level abstractions. Rather, the alternative was to reduce the complexity and rigidity of the conceptual edifice, while maintaining a broad scheme at a high level of abstraction. Still, others continued to build on Parsons's approach, focusing on the same substantive questions as Parsons and sustaining a commitment to analyzing these problems within the four-functions paradigm.[24]

Niklas Luhmann took these criticisms about the analytical complexity of Parsons's four-functions approach seriously and dropped many particulars of this scheme itself but not the goal of producing abstract frameworks for analyzing social reality. Luhmann studied for a time with Parsons, but he eventually criticized Parsonsian action theory for being "overly concerned with its own architecture." Luhmann considered himself a systems theorist more than a functionalist (see Chapter 11 on systems theory), and in the last years of his life, the systems aspects of his scheme have been given increasing emphasis.[25] But he is still a functionalist because he tends to analyze system processes by how they meet one master functional requisite: reduction of environmental complexity.[26]

System and Environment

Luhmann employs a general systems approach to stress that human action becomes organized and structured into systems. When the actions of several people become interrelated, a social system can be said to exist. The basic mechanism by which actions become interrelated to create social systems is communication via

---

[24]For the best of these efforts, see Richard Münch's work: *Theory of Action: Towards a New Synthesis Going Beyond Parsons* (London: Routledge, 1988) and *Die Struktur der Modene* (Frankfurt, Germany: Suhrkamp, 1984).

[25]See, for example, Niklas Luhmann, *Systems Theory* (Stanford, CA: Stanford University Press, 1995).

[26]Luhmann has published extensively, but most of his work is in German. The best sample of his work in English is *Systems Theory and the Differentiation of Society,* trans. S. Holmes and C. Larmore (New York: Columbia University Press, 1982).

symbolic codes, such as words and other media. All social systems exist in multidimensional environments, posing the potentially endless complexity with which a system must deal. To exist in a complex environment, therefore, a social system must develop mechanisms for reducing complexity, lest the system simply merge with its environment. These mechanisms involve selecting ways and means for reducing complexity. Such selection creates a boundary between a system and its environment, thereby allowing the system to sustain patterns of interrelated actions.

The basic functional requisite in Luhmann's analysis is thus the need to reduce the complexity of the environment in relation to a system of interrelated actions. All social processes are analyzed with respect to their functions for reducing complexity in relation to an environment. Processes that function in this way are typically defined as mechanisms in a manner reminiscent of Talcott Parsons's early discussion in *The Social System*.[27] Indeed, the bulk of Luhmann's sociology revolves around discussions of such mechanisms—differentiation, ideology, law, symbolic media, and other critical elements of his scheme.

Dimensions of the Environment

There are three basic dimensions along which the complexity of the environment is reduced by these mechanisms: (1) a temporal dimension, (2) a material dimension, and (3) a symbolic dimension. More than most social theorists, Luhmann is concerned with time as a dimension of the social universe. Time always presents complexity for a system because it reaches into the past, because it embodies complex configurations of acts in the present, and because it involves the vast horizons of the future. Thus, a social system must develop mechanisms for reducing the complexity of time. The system must find a way to order this dimension by developing procedures to orient actions to the past, present, and future.[28]

Luhmann is also concerned with the material dimension of the environment—that is, with all the possible relations among actions in potentially limitless physical space. Luhmann always asks these questions: What mechanisms are developed to order interrelated actions in physical space? What is the structure and form of such ordering of relations?

Luhmann visualizes the third dimension of human systems as the symbolic. Of all the complex symbols and their combinations that humans can conceivably generate, what mechanisms select some symbols over others and organize them in some ways as opposed to the vast number of potential alternatives? What kinds of symbolic media are selected and used by a social system to organize social actions?

Thus, the mechanisms of a social system that reduce complexity and thereby maintain a boundary between the system and the environment function along three dimensions, the temporal, material, and symbolic. The nature of a social system—its size, form, and differentiations—will be reflected in the mechanisms that the system uses to reduce complexity along these dimensions.

---

[27]Talcott Parsons, *The Social System.*

[28]Luhmann, *The Differentiation*, chap. 12.

Types of Social Systems

A social system exists any time the actions of individuals are "meaningfully inter-related and interconnected," thereby setting them off from the temporal, material, and symbolic environment by virtue of the selection of functional mechanisms. From such processes come three basic types of social systems: (1) interaction systems, (2) organization systems, and (3) societal systems.[29]

Interaction Systems. An interaction system emerges when individuals are copresent and perceive each other. The very act of perception is a selection mechanism that sorts from a much more complex environment, creating a boundary and setting people off as a system. Such systems are elaborated by the use of language in face-to-face communication, thereby reducing complexity even further along the temporal, material, and symbolic dimensions. For example, Luhmann would ask these questions: How does the language and its organization into codes shape people's perceptions of time? Who is included in the conversation? And what codes and agreements guide conversation and other actions?

Interaction systems reveal certain inherent limitations and vulnerabilities, however. First, only one topic can be discussed at a time, lest the system collapse as everyone tries to talk at once (which, of course, frequently occurs). Second, the varying conversational resources of participants often lead to competition over who is to talk, creating inequalities and tensions that can potentially lead to conflict and system disintegration. Third, talk and conversation are time-consuming because they are sequential; as a result, an interaction system can never be very complex.

Thus, interaction systems are simple because they involve only those who can be copresent, perceived, and talked to; they are vulnerable to conflict and tension; and they consume a great deal of time. For a social system to be larger and more complex, additional organizing principles beyond perceptions of copresence and sequential talk are essential.

Organizational Systems. These systems coordinate the actions of individuals with respect to specific conditions, such as work on a specific task in exchange for a specific amount of money. Organizational systems typically have entry and exit rules (e.g., come to work for this period of time and leave with this much money), and their main function is to "stabilize highly 'artificial' modes of behavior over a long stretch of time." They resolve the basic problem of reconciling the motivations and dispositions of individuals and the need to get certain tasks done. An organization does not depend on the moral commitment of individuals, nor does it require normative consensus. Rather, the entrance and exit rules specify tasks in ways that allow individuals to do what is required without wholly identifying with the organization.

Organization systems are thus essential to a complex social order. They reduce environmental complexity by organizing people (a) in time by generating entrance and exit rules and by ordering activities in the present and future; (b) in space by

---

[29]Ibid., 71–89.

creating a division of labor, which authority coordinates; and (c) in symbolic terms by indicating what is appropriate, what rules apply, and what media, such as money or pay, are to guide action. In his delineation of organization systems, Luhmann stresses that complex social orders do not require consensus over the values, beliefs, or norms to be sustained; they can operate quite effectively without the motivational commitments of actors. Their very strength—flexibility and adaptability to changing environmental conditions—depends on the delimited and situational commitments of actors, along with neutral media of communication, such as money.[30]

Societal Systems. These systems cut across interaction and organization systems. A societal system is a "comprehensive system of all reciprocally accessible communication actions."[31] Historically, societal systems have been limited by geopolitical considerations, but today Luhmann sees a trend toward a one-world society. Luhmann's discussion on the societal system is rather vague, but the general idea can be inferred from his analysis of more specific topics: Societal systems use highly generalized communication codes, such as money and power, to reduce the complexity of the environment. In so doing, they set broad limits on how and where actions are to be interrelated into interaction and organization systems. These systems also organize how time is perceived and how actions are oriented to the past, present, and future.

System Differentiation, Integration, and Conflict

These three systems—interaction, organization, and societal—cannot be totally separated because "all social action obviously takes place in society and is ultimately possible only in the form of interaction."[32] Indeed, in very simple societies they are fused together, but as societies become larger and more complex, these systems become clearly differentiated from and irreducible to one another. Organizations become distinctive with respect to (a) their functional domains (government, law, education, economy, religion, and science), (b) their entrance and exit rules, and (c) their reliance on distinctive media of communication (money, truth, power, love, etc.). As a consequence, they cannot be reduced to a societal system. Interaction systems follow their own laws, for rarely do people strictly follow the guidelines of organizations and society in their conversations.

The differentiation of these systems poses several problems for the more inclusive system. First is the problem of what Luhmann calls "bottlenecks." Interaction systems are slow, sequentially organized patterns of talk, and they follow their own dynamics as people use their resources in conversations. As a result, interaction systems often prevent organizations from operating at high levels of efficiency. As people interact, they develop informal agreements and take their time, with the

---

[30]In making this assertion, Luhmann directly attacks Parsons. Luhmann, *The Differentiation,* chap. 3.

[31]Ibid., 73.

[32]Ibid., 79.

specific tasks of the organization going unperformed or underperformed. Similarly, as organization systems develop their own structure and programs, their interests often collide, and they become "bottlenecks" to action requirements at the societal level. Second is the problem of conflict in differentiated systems. Interactants may disagree on topics; they may become jealous or envious of those with conversational resources. And because interaction systems are small, they cannot become sufficiently complex "to consign marginals to their borders or to otherwise segregate them." At the organizational level, diverse organizations can pursue their interests in ways that are disruptive to both the organization and the more inclusive societal system.

Yet countervailing these disruptive tendencies are processes that maintain social integration. One critical set of processes is the "nesting" of system levels inside each other. Actions within an interactive system are often nested within an organization system, and organizational actions are conducted within a societal system. Hence the broader, more inclusive system can promote integration in two ways: (1) it provides the temporal, material, and social premises for the selection of actions and (2) it imposes an order or structure on the proximate environment around any of its subsystems. For example, an organizational system distributes people in space and in an authority hierarchy, it orients them to time, it specifies the relevant communication codes, and it orders the proximate environment (other people, groupings, offices, etc.) of any interaction system. Similarly, the functional division of a society into politics, education, law, economy, family, religion, and science determines the substance of an organization's action, while it orders the proximate environment of any particular organization. For example, societal differentiation of a distinctive economy delimits what any economic organization can do. Thus, a corporation in a capitalist economy will use money as its distinctive communications media; it will articulate with other organizations concerning market relations; it will organize its workers into bureaucratic organizations with distinctive entrance and exit rules ("work for money"); and it will be oriented to the future, with the past as only a collapsed framework to guide present activity in the pursuit of future outcomes (such as profits and promotions).

In addition to these nesting processes, integration is promoted by the deflection of people's activities across different organizations in diverse functional domains. When many organizations exist in a society, none consumes an individual's sense of identity and self because people's energies are dispersed across several organization systems. As a consequence of their piecemeal involvement, members are unlikely to be emotionally drawn into conflict among organization systems, and when individual members cannot be pulled emotionally into a conflict, its intensity and potential for social disruption are lessened. Moreover, because interaction systems are distinct from the more inclusive organization, any conflict between organizations is often seen by the rank and file as distant and remote to their interests and concerns; it is something "out there" in the environment of their interaction systems, and hence it is not very involving.

Yet another source of conflict mitigation are the entrance and exit rules of an organization. As these become elaborated into hierarchies, offices, established procedures, salary scales, and the like, these rules reduce the relevance of members' conflicts outside the organization—for example, their race and religion. Such outside conflicts are separated from those within the organization, and as a result, their salience in the broader societal system is reduced.

Finally, once differentiation of organizations is an established mechanism in a society, specific social control organizations—law, police, courts—can be easily created to mitigate and resolve conflicts. That is, the generation of distinct organizations that are functionally specific represents a new "social technology"; once this technology has been used in one context, it can be applied to additional contexts. Thus, the integrative problems created by the differentiation and proliferation of organizations create the very conditions that can resolve these problems—the capacity to create organizations to mediate among themselves.

And so, although differentiation of three system levels creates problems of integration and conditions conducive to conflict, it also produces countervailing forces for integration. In making this argument, Luhmann emphasizes that in complex systems order is not sustained by consensus on common values, beliefs, and norms. On the contrary, there is likely to be considerable disagreement about these, except perhaps at the most abstract level. This point of emphasis is an important contribution of Luhmann's sociology, for it distinguishes his theoretical approach from that of Talcott Parsons, who overstressed the need for value consensus in complex social systems. In addition, Luhmann stresses that individuals' moral and emotional attachment to the social fabric is not essential for social integration. To seek a romantic return to a cohesive community, as Émile Durkheim, Karl Marx, and others have, is impossible in most spheres of a complex society. And, rather than viewing this as a pathological state—as concepts like alienation, egoism, and anomie connote—the impersonality and neutrality of many encounters in complex systems can be seen as normal and analyzed less evaluatively. Moreover, people's lack of emotional embeddedness in complex systems gives them more freedom, more options, and more flexibility.[33] This also liberates them from the constraints of tradition, the restrictions of dependency on others, and the indignities of surveillance by the powerful that are so typical of less complex societies.

Communications Media, Reflexivity, and Self-Thematization

Luhmann's system theory stresses the relation of a system to its environment and the mechanisms used to reduce its complexity. All social systems are based on communication among actors as they align their respective modes of conduct. Because action systems are built from communication, Luhmann devotes considerable attention to communications theory, as he defines it. He stresses that human communications become reflexive and that this reflexiveness leads to *self-thematization*. Luhmann thus develops a communications theory revolving around communication codes and

---

[33]Here, Luhmann takes a page from Georg Simmel's *The Philosophy of Money*, trans. T. Bottomore and D. Frisby (Boston, MA: Routledge & Kegan Paul, 1978).

media as well as reflexiveness and self-thematization. Each of these elements in his theory will be explored briefly.

Communication and Codes. Luhmann waxes philosophically and metaphorically about these concepts, but in the end he concludes that communication occurs through symbols that signal actors' lines of behavior, and such symbols constitute a code with several properties.[34] First, the organization of symbols into a code guides the selection of alternatives that reduce the complexity of the environment. For example, when someone in an interaction system says that he or she wants to talk about a particular topic, these symbols operate as a code that reduces the complexity of the system in an environment (its members will now discuss this topic and ignore all the potential alternatives). Second, codes are binary and dialectical in that their symbols imply their opposite. For example, the linguistic code "Be a good boy" also implicitly signals its opposite—that is, what is not good and what is not male. As Luhmann notes, "Language makes negative copies available" by its very nature. Third, in implying their opposite, codes create the potential for the opposite action—for instance, "to be a bad boy." In human codes, then, the very process of selecting lines of action and reducing complexity with a code also expands potential options (to do just the opposite or some variant of the opposite). This makes the human system highly flexible because the communication codes used to organize the system and reduce complexity also contain implicit messages about alternatives.

Communications Media. Communication codes stabilize system responses to the environment (while implying alternative responses). Codes can organize communication into distinctive media that further order system responses. As a society differentiates into functional domains, distinctive media are used to organize the resources of the systems in each domain.[35] For example, the economy uses money as its medium of communication, which guides interactions within and among economic organizations. Thus, in an economy, relations among organizations are conducted in terms of money (buying and selling in markets), and intraorganizational relations among workers are guided by entrance and exit rules structured by money (pay for work at specified times and places). Similarly, power is the distinctive communications medium of the political domain, love is the medium of the family, truth is the medium of science, and so on for other functional domains.[36]

Several critical generalizations are implicit in Luhmann's analysis of communications media. First, the differentiation of social systems into functional domains cannot occur without the development of a distinctive medium of communication for that domain. Second, media reduce complexity because they limit the range of action in a system. (For example, love as a medium limits the kinds of relations that

---

[34]Luhmann, *The Differentiation,* 169.

[35]Obviously, Luhmann is borrowing Parsons's idea about generalized media. See Chapter 3.

[36]Much like Parsons, this analysis of communications media is never fully explicated or systematically discussed for all functional domains.

are possible in a family system.)[37] Third, even in reducing complexity, media imply their opposite and thus expand potential options, giving system flexibility (e.g., money for work implies its opposite, work without pay; the use of power implies its opposite, lack of compliance to political decisions).

Reflexivity and Self-Thematization. The use of media allows for reflexivity, or the capacity to examine the process of action as a part of the action itself. With communications media structuring action, we can use these media to think about or reflect on action. Social units can use money to make money; they employ power to decide how power is to be exercised; they can analyze love to decide what is true love; they can use truth to specify the procedures to get at truth; and so on. Luhmann sees this reflexivity as a mechanism that facilitates adaptation of a system to its environment. Reflexivity does so by ordering responses and reducing complexity, while providing actors in a system with the capacity to think about new options for action. For example, it becomes possible to mobilize power to think about new and more adaptive ways to exercise power in political decisions, as is the case when a society's political elite creates a constitutional system based on a separation of powers.

As communications media are used reflexively, they allow for what Luhmann terms *self-thematization*. Using media, a system can conceptualize itself and its relations with the environment as a "perspective" or "theme." Such self-thematization reduces complexity by providing guidelines about how to deal with the temporal, material, and symbolic dimensions of the environment. It becomes possible to have a guiding perspective about how to orient to time, to organize people in space, and to order symbols into codes. For example, money and its reflexive use for self-thematization in a capitalist economy create a concern with the future, an emphasis on rational organization of people, and a set of codes that emphasize impersonal exchanges of services and commodities. The consequence of these self-thematizations is that economic organizations reduce the complexity of their environments and, thereby, coordinate social action more effectively.

Luhmann's Basic Approach

In sum, Luhmann's general systems approach revolves around the system-versus-environment distinction. Systems need to reduce the complexity of their environments in their perceptions about time, their organization of actors in space, and their use of symbols. Processes that reduce complexity are conceptualized as functional mechanisms. There are three types of systems: interaction, organization, and societal. All system processes occur through communications that can develop into distinctive media and allow reflexivity and self-thematization in a system.

Luhmann's Conception of Evolution

Because Luhmann's substantive discussions are cast into an evolutionary framework, it is wise to begin by extracting from his diverse writings the key elements of this

---

[37]We will see shortly, however, that money is the sole exception here.

evolutionary approach. Like other evolutionary theorists, Luhmann views evolution as the process of increasing differentiation of a system in relation to its environment.[38] Such increased differentiation allows a system to develop more flexible relations to its environment and, as a result, to increase its level of adaptation. As systems differentiate, however, there is the problem of integrating diverse subsystems; as a consequence, new kinds of mechanisms emerge to sustain the integration of the overall system. But, unlike most evolutionary theorists, Luhmann uses this general image of evolution in a way that adds several new twists to previous evolutionary approaches.

The Underlying Mechanisms of Evolution. Luhmann is highly critical of the way traditional theory has analyzed the process of social differentiation.[39] First, traditional theories—from Marx and Durkheim to Parsons—all imply that there are limits to how divided a system can be, so they all postulate an end to the process, which, in Luhmann's view, is little more than an evaluative utopia. Second, traditional theories overstress the importance of value consensus as an integrating mechanism in differentiated systems. Third, these theories see many processes, such as crime, conflict, dissensus about values, and impersonality, as deviant or pathological; however, they are inevitable in differentiated systems. Fourth, previous theories have great difficulty handling the persistence of social stratification, viewing it as a source of evil or as a perpetual conflict-producing mechanism.

Luhmann's alternative to these evolutionary models is to use his systems theory to redirect the analysis of social differentiation. Like most functionalists, he analogizes to biology, but not to the physiology of an organism; rather, his analogies are to the processes delineated in the theory of evolution. Thus, he argues for an emphasis of those processes that produce (a) variation, (b) selection, and (c) stabilization of traits in societal systems.[40] The reasoning here is that sociocultural evolution is like other forms of biological evolution. Social systems have mechanisms that are the functional equivalents of those in biological evolution. These mechanisms generate variation in the structure of social systems, select those variations that facilitate adaptation of a system, and stabilize these adaptive structures.[41]

Luhmann argues that the "mechanism for variation" inheres in the process of communication and in the formation of codes and media. All symbols imply their opposite, so there is always the opportunity to act in new ways (a kind of "symbolic mutation"). The very nature of communication permits alternatives, and at times people act on these alternatives, thereby producing new variations. Indeed, compared with the process of biological mutation, the capacity of human systems for variation is much greater than in biological systems.

The "mechanism for selection" can be found in what Luhmann terms communicative success. The general idea behind this concept is that certain new forms of

---

[38]This is essentially Parsons's definition. It was Spencer's and Durkheim's as well (see Chapters 2 and 5).

[39]Luhmann, *The Differentiation,* 256–257.

[40]Luhmann's interpretation of the synthetic theory of evolution in biology is, at best, loose and inexact.

[41]Luhmann, *The Differentiation,* 265. Luhmann seems completely unaware that Herbert Spencer in his *The Principles of Sociology* (New York: D. Appleton, 1885; originally published 1874) performed a similar, and more detailed, analysis 100 years ago.

communication facilitate increased adjustment to an environment by reducing its complexity, while allowing more flexible responses to the environment. For example, the creation of money as a medium greatly facilitated adaptation of systems and subsystems to the environment, as did the development of centralized power to coordinate activity in systems. And because they facilitated survival and adaptation, they were retained in the structure of the social organism.

The "stabilization mechanism" resides in the very process of system formation. That is, new communication codes and media are used to order social actions among subsystems, and in so doing, they create structures, such as political systems and economic orders, that regularize for a time the use of the new communications media. For example, once money is used, it creates an economic order revolving around markets and exchange, which, in turn, feeds back and encourages the extension of money as a medium of communication. From this reciprocity ensues some degree of continuity and stability in the economic system.

Evolution and Social Differentiation. Luhmann believes that sociocultural evolution involves differentiation in seven senses:

1. Evolution is the increasing differentiation of interaction, organization, and societal systems from one another. That is, interaction systems increasingly become distinct from organization systems, which in turn are more clearly separated from societal systems. Although these system levels are nested in each other, they also have their unique dynamics.

2. Evolution involves the internal differentiation of these three types of systems. Diverse interaction systems multiply and become different from one another (e.g., compare conversations at work, at a party, at home, and at a funeral). Organization systems increase in number and specialize in different activities (compare economic with political organizations, or contrast different types of economic organizations, such as manufacturing and retail organizations). And the societal system becomes differentiated from the organization and interaction systems that it comprises. Moreover, there is an evolutionary trend, Luhmann claims, toward a one-world society.

3. Evolution involves the increasing differentiation of societal systems into functional domains, such as economy, polity, law, religion, family, science, and education. Organization subsystems within these domains are specialized to deal with a limited range of environmental contingencies, and in being specialized, subsystems can better deal with contingencies. The overall result for a societal system is increased adaptability and flexibility in its environment.

4. Functional differentiation is accompanied by (and is the result of) the increasing use of distinctive media of communication. For example, organization systems in the economy employ money, those in the polity or government exercise power, those in science depend on truth, and those in the family domain use love.

5. There is a clear differentiation during evolution among the persons, roles, programs, and values. Individuals are entities separated from the roles and

organizations in which they participate. One plays many roles, and each involves only a segment or part of a person's personality and sense of self; many roles are played with little or no investment of oneself in them. Moreover, most roles persist whether or not any one individual plays them, thereby emphasizing their separation from the person. Such roles are increasingly grouped together into an ever-increasing diversity of what Luhmann calls programs (work, family, play, politics, consumption, etc.), which typically exist inside different kinds of organization systems operating in a distinctive functional domain. In addition, these roles can be shuffled around into new programs, emphasizing the separation of roles and programs. Finally, societal values become increasingly abstract and general, with the result that they do not pertain to any one functional domain, program, role, or individual.[42] They exist as very general criteria that can be selectively invoked to help organize roles into programs or to mobilize individuals to play roles; however, their application to roles and programs is made possible by additional mechanisms such as ideologies, laws, technologies, and norms. For, by themselves, societal values are too general and abstract for individuals to use in concrete situations. Indeed, one of the most conspicuous features of highly differentiated systems is the evolution of mechanisms to attach abstract values to concrete roles and programs.

6. Evolution involves the movement through three distinctive forms of differentiation: (1) segmentation, (2) stratification, and (3) functional differentiation.[43] That is, the five processes outlined earlier have historically created, Luhmann believes, only three distinctive forms of differentiation. When the simplest societies initially differentiate, they do so *segmentally* in that they create like and equal subsystems that operate very much like the ones from which they emerged. For example, as it initially differentiates, a traditional society will create new lineages or new villages that duplicate previous lineages and villages. But segmentation limits a society's complexity and, hence, its capacity to adapt to its environment. And so alternative forms of differentiation are selected during sociocultural evolution. Further differentiation creates *stratified systems,* in which subsystems vary in their power, wealth, and other resources. These subsystems are ordered hierarchically, and this new form of structure allows for more complex relations with an environment but imposes limitations on how complex the system can become. As long as the hierarchical order must be maintained, the options of any subsystem are limited by its place in the hierarchy.[44] Thus, pressures build for a third form of differentiation, the *functional.* Here, communication processes are organized around the specific function to

---

[42]Luhmann is borrowing here from Émile Durkheim's analysis in *The Division of Labor in Society* (New York: Free Press, 1949; originally published 1893), as well as from Talcott Parsons's discussion of "value generalization." See Chapter 3.

[43]Luhmann, *The Differentiation,* 229–254.

[44]Ibid., 235.

be performed for the societal system. Such a system creates inequalities because some functions have more priority for the system (e.g., economics over religion). This inequality, however, is fundamentally different from that in hierarchically ordered or stratified systems. In a functionally differentiated society, the other subsystems are part of the environment of any given subsystem—for example, organizations in the polity, law, education, religions, science, and family domains are part of the environment of the economy. And although the economy might have functional priority in the society, it treats and responds to the other subsystems in its environment as equals. Thus, inequality in functionally differentiated societies does not create a rigid hierarchy of subsystems; as a consequence, it allows more autonomy of each subsystem, which in turn gives them more flexibility in dealing with their respective environments. The overall consequence of such subsystem autonomy is increased flexibility of the societal system to adjust and adapt to its environment.

7. Evolutionary differentiation increases the complexity of a system and its relationship with the environment. In so doing, it escalates the risks, as Luhmann terms the matter, of making incorrect and maladaptive decisions about how to relate to an environment. With increased complexity comes an expanded set of options for a system, but there is a corresponding chance that the selection of options will be dysfunctional for a system's relationship to an environment. For example, any organization in the economy must make decisions about its actions, but there are increased alternatives and escalated unknowns, resulting in expanded risks. In Luhmann's view, the ever-increasing risk level that accompanies evolutionary differentiation must be accompanied by mechanisms to reduce risk, or at least by the perception or sense that risk has been reduced. Thus, evolution always involves an increase in the number and complexity of risk-reducing mechanisms. Such mechanisms also decrease the complexity of a system's environment because they select some options over others. For example, a conservative political ideology is a risk-reducing mechanism because it selects some options from more general values and ignores others. In essence, an ideology assures decision makers that the risks are reduced by accepting the goals of the ideology.[45]

Before proceeding further, we should review these elements of Luhmann's view of evolution and how they change a society's and its constituent subsystems' relation to the temporal, material, and symbolic dimensions of the environment. Temporally, Luhmann argues that social evolution and differentiation lead to efforts at developing a chronological metric, or a standardized way to measure time (e.g., clocks). Equally fundamental is a shift in people's perspective from the past to the future. The past becomes highly generalized and lacks specific dictates of what should be done in the present and the future. For, as systems become more complex, the past cannot serve as a guide to the present or future because there are too many potential new contingencies and options. The present sees time as ever more scarce and in short

---

[45]Ibid., 151.

supply; thus, people become more oriented to the future and to the consequences of their present actions. Materially, social differentiation involves (a) the increasing separation of interaction, organization, and societal systems; (b) the compartmentalization of organization systems into functional domains; (c) the growing separation of person, role, program, and values; and (d) the movement toward functional differentiation and away from segmentation and stratification. And, symbolically, communication codes become more complex and organized as distinctive media for a particular functional domain. Moreover, they increasingly function as risk-reducing mechanisms for a universe filled with contingency and uncertainty.

Luhmann has approached the study of specific organizational systems from this overall view of sociocultural evolution and differentiation. As he has consistently argued, an analytical framework is only as good as the insights into empirical processes that it can generate. Luhmann's framework is much more complex than what he contends such a framework should be, and it is often more metaphorical than analytical. Yet it allows him to analyze political, legal, and economic processes in functionally differentiated societies in very intriguing ways.

The Functional Differentiation of Society

Politics as a Social System. As societies grow more complex, new structures emerge for reducing complexity. Old processes, such as appeals to traditional truths, mutual sympathy, exchange, and barter, become ever-more inadequate. A system that reaches this point of differentiation, Luhmann argues, must develop the "capacity to make binding decisions." Such capacity is generated from the problems of increased complexity, but this capacity also becomes an important condition for further differentiation.

To make binding decisions, the system must use a distinctive medium of communication: power.[46] Power is defined by Luhmann as "the possibility of having one's own decisions select alternatives or reduce complexity for others." Thus, whenever one social unit selects alternatives of action for other units, power is being employed as the medium of communication.

The use of power to make binding decisions functions to resolve conflicts, to mitigate tensions, and to coordinate activities in complex systems. Societies that can develop political systems capable of performing these functions can better deal with their environments. Several conditions, Luhmann believes, facilitate the development of this functional capacity. First, there must be time to make decisions; the less time an emerging political system is allowed, the more difficulty it will have in becoming autonomous. Second, the emerging political system must not confront a single power block in its environment, such as a powerful church. Rather, it requires an environment of multiple subsystems whose power is more equally balanced. So the more the power in the political subsystem's environment is concentrated, the more difficult is its emergence as an autonomous subsystem. Third, the political system must stabilize its relations with other subsystems in the environment in two distinctive ways: (1) at the level of diffuse legitimacy, so that its decisions are

---

[46]Ibid., 151.

accepted as its proper function, and (2) at the level of daily transactions among individuals and subsystems.[47] That is, the greater the problems of a political system are in gaining diffuse support for its right to make decisions for other subsystems and the less salient the decisions of the political system are for the day-to-day activities, transactions, and routines of system units, then the greater will be its problems in developing into an autonomous subsystem.

Thus, to the extent that a political system has time to develop procedures for making decisions, confront multiple sources of mitigated power, and achieve diffuse legitimacy as well as relevance for specific transactions, the more it can develop into an autonomous system and the greater will be a society's capacity to adjust to its environment. In so developing, the political system must achieve what Luhmann calls structural abstraction, or the capacity to (a) absorb multiple problems, dilemmas, and issues from a wide range of system units and (b) make binding decisions for each of these. Luhmann sees the political system as "absorbing" the problems of its environment and making them internal to the political system. Several variables, he argues, determine the extent to which the political system can perform this function: (a) the degree to which conflicts are defined as political (instead of moral, personal, etc.) and therefore in need of a binding decision, (b) the degree of administrative capacity of the political system to coordinate the activities of system units, and (c) the degree of structural differentiation within the political system itself.

This last variable is the most crucial in Luhmann's view. In response to environmental complexity and the need to absorb and deal with problems in this environment, the political system must differentiate along three lines: (1) the creation of a stable bureaucratic administration that executes decisions, (2) the evolution of a separate arena for politics and the emergence of political parties, and (3) the designation of the public as a relevant concern in making binding decisions. Such internal differentiation increases the capacity of the political system to absorb and deal with a wide variety of problems; as a consequence, it allows greater complexity in the societal system.

This increased complexity of the political and societal systems also increases the risks of making binding decisions that are maladaptive. As complexity increases, there are always unknown contingencies. Therefore, not only do political systems develop mechanisms such as internal differentiation for dealing with complexity, but they also develop mechanisms for reducing risk or the perception of risk. One mechanism is the growing reflexiveness of the political process—that is, its increased reflection on itself. Such reflection is built into the nature of party politics, where the manner and substance of political decisions are analyzed and debated. Another mechanism is what Luhmann calls the positivation of law, or the creation of a separate legal system that makes "laws about how to make laws" (more on this in the next section). Yet another mechanism is ideology or symbolic codes that select which values are relevant for a particular set of decisions. A related mechanism is the development of a political code that typifies and categorizes political decisions into a simple typology.[48] For example, the distinction between progressive and conservative

---

[47]Ibid., 143–144.

[48]Ibid., 168–189.

politics is, Luhmann argues, an important political code in differentiated societies. Such a code is obviously very general, but this is its virtue because it allows very diverse political acts and decisions to be categorized and interpreted with a simple dichotomy, thereby giving political action a sense of order and reducing perceptions of risk. Luhmann even indicates that it is a system's capacity to develop a political code, more than a consensus of values, that leads to social order. For in interpreting actions in terms of the code, a common perspective is maintained, but it is a perspective based on differences—progressive versus conservative—rather than on commonality and consensus. Thus, complex social orders are sustained by their very capacity to create generalized and binary categories for interpreting events rather than by value consensus.

Still another mechanism for reducing risks is arbitrary decision making by elites. However, although such a solution achieves order, it undermines the legitimacy of the political system in the long run because system units start to resent and to resist arbitrary decision making. And a final mechanism is invocation of a traditional moral code (e.g., fundamentalistic religious values) that, in Luhmann's terms, "remoralizes" the political process. But when such "remoralization" occurs, the political system must de-differentiate because strict adherence to a simple moral code precludes the capacity to deal with complexity (an example of this process would be Iran's return to a theocracy from its previously more complex political system).

In sum, then, it is fair to say that Luhmann uses his conceptual metaphor to analyze insightfully specific institutional processes, such as government. Yet he does not use his scheme in a rigorous deductive sense; much like Parsons before him, he employs the framework as a means for denoting and highlighting particular social phenomena. Although much of his analysis of political system differentiation is "old wine in new bottles," there is a shift in emphasis and, as a result, some intriguing but imprecise insights. In a similar vein, Luhmann analyzes the differentiation of the legal system and the economy.

The Autonomy of the Legal System. As discussed earlier, Luhmann visualizes social evolution as involving a separation of persons, roles, programs, and values. For him, differentiation of structure occurs at the level of roles and programs. Consequently, there is the problem of how to integrate values and persons into roles organized into programs within organization systems. The functional mechanism for mobilizing and coordinating individuals to play roles is law, whereas the mechanism for making values relevant to programs is ideology.[49] Thus, because law regulates and coordinates people's participation in roles and programs and because social differentiation must always occur at the level of roles, it becomes a critical subsystem if a society is to differentiate and evolve. That is, a society cannot become complex without the emergence of an autonomous legal system to specify the rights, duties, and obligations of people playing roles.[50]

---

[49]Ibid., 90–137.

[50]This is essentially the same conclusion Parsons reached in his description of evolution in *Societies: Evolutionary and Comparative Perspectives* and *The System of Modern Societies.*

A certain degree of political differentiation must precede legal differentiation because there must be a set of structures to make decisions and enforce them. But political processes often impede legal autonomy, as is the case when political elites have used the law for their own narrow purposes. For legal autonomy to emerge, therefore, political development is not enough. Two additional conditions are necessary: (1) "the invocation of sovereignty," or references by system units to legal codes that justify their communications and actions, and (2) "lawmaking sovereignty," or the capacity of organizations in the legal system to decide just what the law will be.

If these two conditions are met, then the legal system can become increasingly reflexive. It can become a topic unto itself, creating bodies of procedural and administrative law to regulate the enactment and enforcement of law. In turn, such procedural laws can themselves be the subject of scrutiny. Without this reflexive quality, the legal system cannot be sufficiently flexible to change in accordance with shifting events in its environment. Such flexibility is essential because only through the law can people's actions be tied to the roles that are being differentiated. For example, without what Luhmann calls the "positivization of law," or its capacity to change itself in response to altered circumstances, new laws and agencies (e.g., workers' compensation, binding arbitration of labor and management disputes, minimum wages, health and safety) could not be created to regulate people's involvement in roles (in this case, work roles in a differentiating economy).

Thus, positivization of the law is a critical condition for societal differentiation. It reduces complexity by specifying the relations of actors to roles and relegating cooperation among social system units. But it reduces complexity in a manner that presents options for change under new circumstances; thus, it becomes a condition for the further differentiation of other functional domains, such as the economic.

The Economy as a Social System. Luhmann defines the economy as "deferring a decision about the satisfaction of needs while providing a guarantee that they will be satisfied and so utilizing the time thus acquired."[51] The general idea seems to be that economic activity—the production and distribution of goods and services—functions to satisfy basic or primary needs for food, clothing, and shelter as well as derived or secondary needs for less basic goods and services. But this happens in a way not fully appreciated in economic analysis: economic activity restructures humans' orientation to time because economic action is oriented to the satisfaction of future needs. Present economic activity is typically directed at future consumption; so when a person works and a corporation acts in a market, they are doing so to guarantee that their future will be unproblematic.

Luhmann's definition of the economic subsystem is less critical than his analysis of the processes leading to the creation of an autonomous economic system in society. In traditional and undifferentiated societies, Luhmann argues, only small-scale solutions are possible with respect to doing something in the present to

---

[51]Luhmann, *The Differentiation*, 194.

satisfy future needs. One solution is the stockpiling of goods, with provision for the redistribution of stocks to societal members or trade with other societies.[52]

Another solution is mutual assistance agreements among individuals, kin groups, or villages. But such patterns of economic organization are very limited because they merge familial, political, religious, and community activity. Only with the differentiation of distinctly economic roles can more complexity and flexibility be structured into economic action. The first key differentiation along these lines is the development of markets with distinctive roles for buyers and sellers.

A market performs several crucial functions. First, it sets equivalences or the respective values of goods and services. Second, it neutralizes the relevance of other roles—for instance, the familial, religious, and political roles of parties in an exchange. Value is established by the qualities of respective goods, not by the positions or characteristics of the buyers and sellers.[53] Third, markets inevitably generate pressures for a new medium of communication that is not tied to other functional subsystems. This medium is money, and it allows quick assessments of equivalences and value in an agreed-on metric. In sum, then, markets create the conditions for the differentiation of distinctly economic roles, for their separation and insulation from other societal roles, and for the creation of a uniquely economic medium of communication.

Money is a very unusual medium, Luhmann believes, because it "transfers complexity." Unlike other media, money is distinctive because it does not reduce complexity in the environment. For example, the medium of power is used to make decisions that direct activity, thereby reducing the complexity of the environment. The medium of truth in science is designed to simplify the understanding of a complex universe. And the medium of love in the family circumscribes the actions and types of relations among kindred and, in so doing, reduces complexity. In contrast, money is a neutral vehicle that can always be used to buy and sell many different things. It does not limit; it opens up options and creates new opportunities. For example, to accept money for a good or for one's work does not reduce the seller's or worker's options. The money can be used in many different ways, thereby preserving and even increasing the complexity of the environment. Money thus sets the stage for—indeed it encourages—further internal differentiation in the economic subsystem of a society.

In addition to transferring complexity, Luhmann sees money as dramatically altering the time dimension of the environment. Money is a liquid resource that is always "usable in the future." When we have money, it can be used at some future date—whether the next minute or the following year. Money thus collapses time, because it is to be used in the future, hence making the past irrelevant; and the present is defined by what will be done with money in the future. However, this collapsing of time can come about only if (a) money does not inflate over time and (b) it is universally used as the medium of exchange (i.e., barter, mutual assistance, and other traditional forms of exchange do not still prevail).[54]

---

[52]Ibid., 197.

[53]Luhmann fails to cite the earlier work of Georg Simmel on these matters. See Simmel's *The Philosophy of Money.*

[54]Luhmann, *The Differentiation*, 207.

Like all media of communication, money is reflexive. It becomes a goal of reflection, debate, and action in itself. We can buy and sell money in markets; we can invest money to make more money; we can condemn money as the root of evil or praise it as a goal that is worth pursuing; we can hoard it in banks or spread it around in consumptive activity. This reflexive quality of money, coupled with its capacity to transfer complexity and reorient actors to time, is what allows money to become an ever more dominant medium of communication in complex societies. Indeed, the economy becomes the primary subsystem of complex societies because its medium encourages constant increases in complexity and growth in the economic system. As a consequence, the economy becomes a prominent subsystem in the environment of other functional subsystems—that is, science, polity, family, religion, and education. The economy becomes something that must always be dealt with by these other subsystems.

This growing complexity of the economic subsystem increases the risks in human conduct. The potential for making a mistake in providing for a person's future needs or a corporation's profits increases because the number of unknown contingencies dramatically multiplies. Such escalated risks generate pressures, Luhmann argues, for their reduction through the emergence of specific mechanisms. The most important of these mechanisms is the tri-part internal differentiation of the economy around (1) households, (2) firms, and (3) markets.[55] There is a "structural selection" for this division, Luhmann believes, because these are structurally and functionally different. Households are segmental systems (structurally the same) and the primary consumption units. Firms are structurally diverse and the primary productive units. And markets are not as much a unit as a set of processes for distributing goods and services. Luhmann is a bit vague on this point, but it seems that there is strength in this correspondence of basically different structures with major economic functions. Households are segmented structurally and functionally oriented to consumption; firms are highly differentiated structurally and functionally geared to production; and markets are processually differentiated by their function to distribute different types of goods and services. Such differentiation reduces complexity, but at the same time, it allows flexibility: households can change consumption patterns, firms can alter production, and markets can expand or contract. And because they are separated from one another, each has the capacity to change and redirect its actions independently of the others. This flexibility is what allows the economic system to become so prominent in modern industrial societies.

Yet, Luhmann warns, the very complexity of the economy and its importance for other subsystems create pressures for other risk-reducing mechanisms. One of these is intervention by government so that power is used to make binding decisions on production, consumption, and distribution as well as on the availability of money as a medium of communication. The extensive use of this mechanism, Luhmann believes, reduces risk and complexity in the economy at the expense of its capacity to meet needs in the future and to make flexible adjustments to the environment.

---

[55]Ibid., 216.

Conclusions

Talcott Parsons's and Niklas Luhmann's became the dominant function schemes in sociology; and while their influence had waned by the end of the twentieth century, their schemes still influenced sociological theorizing then as now, in the second decade of the twenty-first century. Parsons's scheme was more complex and, in the end, became an ever more complex category system by which empirical reality could be explained. In contrast, Luhmann's scheme was simpler, with only one functional requisite, the reduction of complexity—and then the analysis of the basic ways in which social systems differentiate and become integrated by reducing complexity associated with differentiation. And like the functionalists of the nineteenth century, they both offered an evolutionary analysis of the process of societal differentiation. Luhmann, in particular, considered himself to be a systems theorist, but so did Parsons when he began to adopt the terminology of cybernetic theorizing in his hierarchy of control; and in some ways, their self-identification with systems theorizing was accurate because systems theorizing also sought to understand the differentiation of systems and their integration through various functional mechanisms. Thus, we should pause in the next chapter to review what systems theory sought to do, and as we will see, the most prominent schemes in the social sciences appear to have drifted away from their origins into ever more functional-looking conceptualizations of living systems.

CHAPTER 11

General Systems Theorizing

Early Systems Approaches

One of the more cosmic goals of intellectual activity is to interpret all dimensions of the universe in terms of a common core of concepts. This has always been one of the appeals of religion, as well as of various philosophical systems. It is not surprising, therefore, that there would be efforts within science—the third of Auguste Comte's three modes of thought—to forge an intellectual scheme or "general system" of thought that could cut across the natural and social sciences. In a sense, Comte's famous "hierarchy of the sciences" represented an effort to articulate the relations of the sciences,[1] but the first sociological general systems theorist was Herbert Spencer.

As I noted in Chapter 3, Spencer saw himself as a philosopher who desired to demonstrate the unity of all realms of the universe with a common set of "first principles."[2] As with general systems theorists today, Spencer first turned to the physics of his time and culled from his understanding of this science a set of highly abstract laws, or principles, that could explain the physical, psychological,[3] organic,[4] superorganic (social),[5]

---

[1]For example, Auguste Comte, in *Positive Philosophy*, trans. H. Martineau (London: Bell and Sons, 1896; originally published between 1830 and 1842), saw mathematics as the language of science, and he believed that the cumulation of knowledge in each science in the hierarchy set the stage for the development of the next science in the hierarchy. Hence, sociology was seen to be possible only after the development of biology.

[2]Herbert Spencer, *First Principles* (New York: A. C. Burt, 1880; originally published 1862).

[3]Herbert Spencer, *The Principles of Psychology* (New York: D. Appleton, 1880; originally published 1855).

[4]Herbert Spencer, *The Principles of Biology* (New York: D. Appleton, 1897; originally published 1866).

[5]Herbert Spencer, *The Principles of Sociology* (New York: D. Appleton, 1898; originally published in serial form 1874–1896).

and even moral[6] dimensions of the universe. He conceptualized these laws under the rubrics of evolution and dissolution. In more modern terms, these processes are viewed in terms of *entropy* and *negative entropy*—that is, de-structuring to randomness (entropy) and structuring to complexity (negative entropy).

Spencer saw the matter of the universe as always in a process of aggregating to form more complex structures, fluctuating between phases of structuring and de-structuring in a precarious equilibrium, and disintegrating as elements begin to de-structure and lose their coherence. Thus, the systems of the universe were viewed by Spencer as composed of varying types of matter—physical, organic, psychical, moral—moving in space with "force" or energy and building up structure to the point where energy is dissipated and dissolution sets in. In the process of structuring, equilibrium is often achieved as forces of energy hold each other in balance, but eventually the equilibrium is disrupted, either by its own internal dissipation or by the introduction of new inputs of matter and energy from the environment.[7]

I need not dwell on the details of Spencer's analysis,[8] because many of the parallels that he drew among systems of the universe are dated. Yet, more than any other thinker of his time, he anticipated the intent of modern systems theory, as we will come to appreciate in this chapter. Although some versions of general systems theory are decidedly anti-functionalist,[9] many are clearly within the functionalist orientation because they sought to discover isomorphisms among realms of the universe in terms of structures being built up to meet the common functions of all systems. That is, what common activities must organic and societal systems perform in order to survive in an environment? Thus, modern systems theory created a new kind of organismic analogy, and as was the case for Spencer, this analogy usually brought along its inevitable sidekick: functionalism.

General Systems Theory

The development of general systems theory occurred with changes in the nature of scientific analysis. Rather than viewing the universe in simple cause-and-effect terms, theorists increasingly recognized that any cause-effect relationship occurs within a more *complex system of relationships*. At all levels of reality, from subatomic physics to the analysis of world systems on earth or the formation of galaxies in the universe, phenomena are analyzed not in isolation but in terms of their connections to a larger system. Moreover, such systems of interconnected events reveal emergent properties that make the whole greater than the sum of its parts. In the modern era, this philosophical position was given its most forceful expression by

---

[6]Herbert Spencer, *The Principles of Ethics* (New York: D. Appleton, 1892–1898).

[7]See pages 34–36 to 43–46.

[8]See Jonathan H. Turner, *Herbert Spencer: A Renewed Appreciation* (Newbury Park, CA: Sage, 1985), for a more detailed argument.

[9]For example, Walter Buckley, *Sociology and Modern Systems Theory* (Englewood Cliffs, NJ: Prentice-Hall, 1967).

Alfred North Whitehead[10] in the 1920s and culminated in sociology with functionalism, although as Chapter 12 will document, ecological theorizing also examines social and biological systems with many common concepts and principles, thereby making it another area where a general systems orientation dominates analysis.

Among modern scientists, Ludwig von Bertalanffy was probably the first to argue explicitly for a *general systems* approach.[11] But in the post–World War II period, this movement gained considerable impetus, with a number of important insights by Norbert Wiener[12] in cybernetics, Shannon and Weaver[13] in information theory, and Neumann and Morgenstern[14] in game theory. Coupled with the rediscovery of Walter Cannon's[15] concept of homeostasis and the rapid development of computer sciences and their engineering applications, a new conceptual base was established for the development of general systems theory.[16]

Of course, Comte's use of the organismic analogy, Spencer's analogies to the principles of physics[17] as well as his analysis of the social and biological spheres,[18] Vilfredo Pareto's equilibrium analysis,[19] and Émile Durkheim's forceful cry that society is a reality, sui generis,[20] all emphasized the importance of viewing sociocultural phenomena in systemic terms. But in the early 1950s, there was a genuine belief that systems in general, at all levels of reality, might reveal certain common properties and processes. If this were true, then the partitions among the sciences could be broken down.

Thus, in 1954, the Society for General Systems Research was organized to

(1) investigate the isomorphy of concepts, laws, and models in various fields, and to help in useful transfers from one field to another; (2) encourage the

---

[10]Alfred North Whitehead, *Science and the Modern World*, Lowell Lectures 1925 (New York: Macmillan, 1953).

[11]See his discussion in Ludwig von Bertalanffy, *General Systems Theory* (New York: Braziller, 1968), 28–29. Also, see early references to his work in the bibliography, 256–257.

[12]Norbert Wiener, *Human Use of Human Beings: Cybernetics and Society* (Garden City, NY: Doubleday, 1954; originally published 1949).

[13]Claude Shannon and Warren Weaver, *The Mathematical Theory of Communication* (Urbana: University of Illinois Press, 1949).

[14]John von Neumann and O. Morgenstern, *Theory of Games and Economic Behavior* (Princeton, NJ: Princeton University Press, 1947).

[15]Walter B. Cannon, *The Wisdom of the Body* (New York: Norton, 1932) and "Organization for Physiological Homeostasis," *Physiological Review* 9 (1929):397–402.

[16]A term that was first used by Bertalanffy, *General Systems Theory*.

[17]See Herbert Spencer, *First Principles*.

[18]See Herbert Spencer, *Principles of Biology* and *Principles of Sociology*.

[19]Vilfredo Pareto, *Manual on Political Economy* (New York: A. M. Kelly, 1971; originally published 1906 and 1909), *Treatise on General Sociology* (New York: Harcourt, Brace, 1935; originally published 1916), *The Rise and Fall of Elites* (Totowa, NJ: Bedminster Press, 1968; originally published 1901).

[20]See Émile Durkheim, *The Rules of the Sociological Method* (New York: Free Press, 1938; originally published 1895).

development of adequate theoretical models in fields which lack them; (3) minimize the duplication of theoretical effort in different fields; (4) promote the unity of science through improving communication among specialists.[21]

The impact of the Society and its advocacy have been far-reaching.[22] Indeed, Parsonian action theory[23] incorporated the metaphor of information theory and cybernetics in its "informal hierarchy of control," but such adoptions of systems-theoretic concepts tend to be metaphorical. Yet there are a few systems theorists who have sought to demonstrate in more precise terms the utility of systems concepts for understanding sociocultural phenomena.[24]

Basic Concepts of Systems Theory

Much as Herbert Spencer recognized in the nineteenth century, modern systems theorists stress that all systems reveal certain common properties. We can best visualize these common properties under the following headings: (a) energy, matter, and information, (b) entropy and negative entropy, (c) organization and system, (d) open and closed systems, (e) cybernetic systems, and (f) system levels.

Energy, Matter, and Information

Systems theory begins with the concepts of *energy, matter,* and *information.* Matter is anything that occupies physical space; energy and matter are, of course,

---

[21]Bertalanffy, *General Systems Theory,* 15.

[22]Its official publication is the annual *General Systems: Yearbook of the Society for General Systems* (more typically listed under General Systems Yearbook).

[23]See Chapter 10.

[24]In particular, see Alfred Kuhn, *The Logic of Social Systems* (San Francisco, CA: Jossey-Bass, 1974); Walter Buckley, *Sociology and Modern Systems Theory* and his edited volume, *Modern Systems Research for the Behavioral Scientist* (Chicago, IL: Aldine, 1968); James Grier Miller, *Living Systems* (New York: McGraw-Hill, 1978); Richard N. Adams, *The Eighth Day: Social Evolution and the Self-Organization of Energy* (Austin: University of Texas Press, 1988); Kenneth Boulding, *Ecodynamics: A New Theory of Societal Evolution* (Beverly Hills, CA: Sage, 1978); C. West Churchman, *The Systems Approach* (New York: Dell, 1968); Erich Jantsch (ed.), *The Evolutionary Vision: Toward a Unifying Paradigm of Physical, Biological, and Sociological Evolution* (Boulder, CO: Westview Press, 1981); and Kenneth E. Bailey, *Social Entropy Theory* (Albany: SUNY Press, 1989), "Beyond Functionalism: Toward a Nonequilibrium Analysis of Complex Social Systems," *British Journal of Sociology* 35 (1984):1–18, *Sociology and the New Systems Theory: Toward a Theoretical Synthesis* (Albany: SUNY Press, 1994), "The autopoiesis of Social Systems: Assessing Luhmann's Theory of Self-reference," *Systems Research and Behavioral Science* 14 (1997):83–100, "Structure, Structuralism, and Autopoiesis: The Emerging Significance of Recursive Theory," *Current Perspectives in Social Theory* 18 (1988):131–154, and "Systems Theory," in *Handbook of Sociological Theory,* ed. J. H. Turner (New York: Kluwer Academic/Plenum Publishers, 2001). See the bibliographies of these works for an overview of the diversity of work on general systems theory. As is also evident, the general systems and human ecology perspectives overlap (see Chapter 12), at least to some degree.

equivalent in the sense of Einstein's famous equation $E = mc^2$, but more practically, energy is the capacity to generate movement of matter and information. Information is oftentimes defined narrowly in terms of the number and pattern of binary bits involved in sending a signal, but at other times the meaning, or substantive content and significance, of signals is also seen as involved in a definition of information.

The great insight over the last seventy years is that information is a key element in most systems. Whether contained in the RNA and DNA molecules of a living cell, in the learned memory cells of a living organism, or in the cultural traditions of a society, the release of energy and the organization of matter are guided by informational controls. The analysis of information can become highly technical, but most systems theorists begin with the simple insight that much of the universe involves the organization of matter and energy by information.

Entropy and Negative Entropy

The second law of thermodynamics of classical physics states that matter and energy tend toward their least organized state. Thus, the organization of a solar system, an organic body, or a society is viewed as a temporary state of affairs, since in the long run these entities will lose their organization and degenerate. This process of organization and "de-organization" is termed *entropy;* systems theory studies *negative entropy* because it is concerned with how energy, matter, and information become organized into coherent systems, thereby holding in abeyance the second law of thermodynamics.

Organization and System

Organization refers to the ways in which identifiable units of energy, matter, and information are interrelated. When such interrelations reveal some degree of coherence, they constitute a system. The main focus of all systems theory thus becomes one of isolating different types of units, or subsystems, of a larger system and then specifying the nature of their relations to one another. For example, this analysis might examine the properties of a particular subsystem, such as its organization of matter and energy by information. Then it might focus on the inputs and outputs of energy/matter and information to and from this subsystem. Finally, it might explore the pattern of organization among this and various other subsystems whose inputs and outputs influence one another.

Open and Closed Systems

Closed systems do not engage in exchanges of energy, matter, or information with their surrounding environment. Their "boundary" is thus relatively impermeable. In contrast, open systems engage in exchanges across their boundaries with the surrounding environment. Open systems are most likely to be negatively entropic, since they take in energy, matter, and information; then they use them to build greater levels of organization. The study of an open system will therefore involve an analysis of the internal properties of the system (its subsystems and interrelations), the properties and processes of its boundary, the nature of the environment, and the exchanges of energy, matter, and information between the system and its environment.

Cybernetic Systems

Systems that act upon and receive inputs from the environment are often cybernetic. The term *cybernetic* denotes the process whereby a system is self-regulating in an environment. Originally, the concept of cybernetics referred to systems that (a) reveal "normal" internal states that are actively maintained, (b) exist in environments that exert pressures to alter these normal states, (c) have internal mechanisms or processes for correcting deviations from these normal states, and (d) evidence procedures for receiving information or feedback from the environment in order to check the state of the systems against the pressures of the environment.[25] Such feedback was typically viewed as "negative feedback" because the information is used to record movement of the system beyond its normal limits and to activate corrective processes. Walter Cannon's discussion of homeostasis of temperature levels in the human body represented an early analysis of such a cybernetic system (although he did not have available to him the term *cybernetic*).[26] A thermostatic system for controlling room temperature is another example of a mechanical cybernetic system. And Talcott Parsons's concern in *The Social System* (see the last chapter) with "mechanisms of social control" is another application of cybernetic ideas to sociocultural systems.[27]

Later, the concept of cybernetic systems was extended to include "positive feedback" or "deviation-amplifying" feedback.[28] Not all systems are programmed to maintain themselves within certain limits or parameters. Rather, they have goals that involve growth, expansion, and increased adaptation. Or they may not have any goals except perhaps undefined states of survival. Such systems receive feedback on their current actions in an environment and on the extent to which these actions help realize those goals that facilitate adaptation and survival. When this feedback is positive and indicates that current actions are facilitating survival or the realization of goals, then they will be continued and escalated. And if these renewed actions also have positive results, they will be further escalated. In this escalating and cyclical process, transformation in, rather than self-regulation of, systems is likely. In biological systems, the process of speciation by natural selection is one example of how positive feedback processes in ecological systems operate to generate a new species. Random mutations in organisms create attributes that facilitate survival in a given

---

[25]Wiener, *Human Use of Human Beings.*

[26]Cannon, *Wisdom of the Body.*

[27]See Chapter 3.

[28]Magoroh Maruyama, "The Second Cybernetics: Deviation Amplifying Mutual Causal Processes," *American Scientist* 51 (1963):164–179.

environment; subsequent mutations of this type further facilitate survival, and so on, until a new species can be distinguished from its ancestors. In contrast, an imperialistic society that successfully conquers its neighbors can use this positive feedback to seek further conquests of more distant neighbors, thereby transforming itself as it conquers more and more societies.

Most organic and social systems are cybernetic in that they engage, often simultaneously, in processes of self-regulation and deviation amplification. They use negative feedback to engage in self-regulation and positive feedback to increase their level of organization or their capacity to realize goals and adapt to a particular environment.

System Levels

Although general systems theory seeks to develop a common set of concepts and principles for understanding all systemic phenomena, there is a clear recognition that there are different types of systems. Such types are typically viewed as emergent levels of organization, with each emergent level revealing at least some distinctive properties that mark it off from lower- and higher-level systems. For example, organic systems are built from inorganic systems and are not understandable in terms of the properties of these inorganic systems alone. Similarly, among organic systems there are distinctive and emergent levels. For instance, James G. Miller argues that there are seven emergent levels among "living systems": the cell, organ, organism, group, organization, society, and supranational.[29] Similarly, Kenneth Boulding isolates the following levels in the "hierarchy of systems": (a) "static structures," such as crystals, molecules, and so forth; (b) "clock works," like machines, solar systems, and so forth; (c) "control mechanisms," such as thermostats and homeostatic mechanisms in organisms; (d) "open systems," like cells and organisms in general; (e) "lower organisms"; (f) "animals"; (g) "humans" and their capacities for self and thinking; (h) "sociocultural" systems; and (i) "symbolic systems," such as language, logic, mathematics, and so forth.[30] Thus, systems theory seeks, on the one hand, to use similar concepts to understand all systemic phenomena, but on the other hand, it attempts to isolate generic types of systems and to develop concepts and propositions that apply to distinctive system levels.

These, then, are the guiding ideas behind general systems theories. There are a number of such theories, with the result that it is difficult to select any one for more detailed coverage. In a sense, I have selected the most comprehensive approach—that of James G. Miller[31]—in order to illustrate this perspective; yet I should caution that it is not the most sophisticated or sociological of the current general systems theories.[32]

---

[29]Miller, *Living Systems.*

[30]Kenneth Boulding, *The Image* (Ann Arbor: University of Michigan Press, 1956).

[31]Miller, *Living Systems.*

[32]For example, I see Boulding's *Ecodynamics*, Adams's *The Eighth Day*, and Bailey's *Social Entropy Theory* as propounding better theories.

Nonetheless, Miller's approach represents an excellent illustration of both the problems and the prospects of general systems ideas as they are applied to socio-cultural systems.

Living Systems: James G. Miller's Analysis

The most ambitious general systems approach since Spencer's is that developed by James Grier Miller some decades ago. His efforts culminated in *Living Systems*, an encyclopedic work of over 1,000 pages. This effort is reminiscent of Spencer's Synthetic Philosophy, which sought to isolate common concepts and propositions for various systems levels. But in contrast to Spencer, who was also willing to address inorganic systems, Miller confines his analyses to what he perceives as the seven generic levels of "living systems." To qualify as a living system, phenomena must evidence the following characteristics:[33]

1. They must be open systems.

2. They must maintain a state of negative entropy in their environment.

3. They must reveal a minimum level of differentiation into integrated subparts.

4. They must evidence informational control through genetic material composed of DNA or reveal a charter.

5. They must reveal the chemical compounds of all organic life.

6. They must evidence a decider subsystem that regulates and controls their subsystems and relations with the environment.

As noted above, there are seven distinctive system levels of life that reveal these characteristics: (1) supranationals or systems of societies, (2) societies, (3) organizations, (4) groups, (5) organisms, (6) organs, and (7) cells. These seven levels constitute a hierarchy in that each is composed of all those below it in the hierarchy. For example, organs are composed of cells, organisms are constructed from cells and organs, groups are composed of cells, organs, and organisms, and so on to the most inclusive system level, a system of societies. Moreover, each system level will evidence greater numbers of subsystems and more complex arrangements of these subsystems. Miller outlines nineteen such subsystems, which are defined in Table 11.1.[34] As is evident, these subsystems are concerned with how either energy/matter or information is processed. The basic idea is that subsystems perform unique "functions" in regulating such critical matters as inputs, internal coordination, outputs, boundaries, and reproduction of new units. Thus, Miller's goal is to create a common category system for analyzing critical processes in the seven levels of living systems.[35] Near the

---

[33]Miller, *Living Systems.* I have collapsed some of Miller's categories, but the criteria are the same.

[34]Ibid., 3.

[35]In many ways, Miller and Talcott Parsons both use a biological model, or classificatory view of theory. Miller's system has more categories, but the intent is the same as in Parsons's scheme.

Table 11.1 Functional Subsystems of All Living Systems

Subsystems Which Process Both Energy/Matter and Information	
1. *Reproducer:* the subsystem which is capable of giving rise to other systems similar to the one it is in.	
2. *Boundary:* the subsystem at the perimeter of a system that holds together the components which make up the system, protects them from environmental stresses, and excludes or permits entry to various sorts of energy/matter and information.	
Subsystems Which Process Energy/Matter	*Subsystems Which Process Information*
3. *Ingestor:* the subsystem which brings energy/matter across the system boundary from the environment.	11. *Input transducer:* the sensory subsystem which brings markers bearing information into the system, changing them to other energy/matter forms suitable for transmission within it.
	12. *Internal transducer:* the sensory subsystem which receives, from subsystems or components within the system, markers bearing information about significant alterations in those subsystems or components, changing them to other energy/matter forms of a sort which can be transmitted within it.
4. *Distributor:* the subsystem which carries inputs from outside the system or outputs from its subsystems around the system to each component.	13. *Channel and net:* the subsystem composed of a single route in physical space, or multiple interconnected routes, by which markers bearing information are transmitted to all parts of the system.
5. *Converter:* the subsystem which changes certain inputs to the system into forms more useful for the special processes of that particular system.	14. *Decoder:* the subsystem which alters the code of information input to it through the input transducer or internal transducer into a *private* code that can be used internally by the system.
6. *Producer:* the materials being synthesized for growth, damage repair, replacement of components of the system, the energy for outputs of products or information.	15. *Associator:* the subsystem which carries out the first stage of the learning process, forming enduring associations among items of information in the system.
7. *Energy/matter storage:* the subsystem which retains in the system, for different periods of time, deposits of various sorts of energy/matter.	16. *Memory:* the subsystem which carries out the second stage of the learning process, storing various sorts of information in the system for different periods of time.
	17. *Decider:* the executive subsystem which receives information inputs from ail other subsystems and transmits to them information outputs that control the entire system.

(Continued)

Table 11.1 (Continued)

Subsystems Which Process Energy/Matter	Subsystems Which Process Information
	18. *Encoder:* the subsystem which alters the code of information input to it from other information processing subsystems, from a *private* code used internally by the system into a *public* code which can be interpreted by other systems in its environment.
8. *Extruder:* the subsystem which transmits energy/matter out of the system in the forms of products or wastes.	19. *Output transducer:* the subsystem which puts out markers bearing information from the system, changing markers within the system into other energy/matter forms which can be transmitted over channels in the system's environment.
9. *Motor:* the subsystem which moves the system or parts of it in relation to part or all of its environment or moves components of its environment in relation to each other.	
10. *Supporter:* the subsystem which maintains the proper spatiai relationship among components of the system, so that they can interact without weighting each other down or crowding each other.	

end of his book, this intent is made explicit in a large table in which examples of the nineteen subsystems are offered for each of the seven system levels. This table is reproduced in Table 11.2.[36]

Miller views Table 11.1 as the equivalent of the periodic table in chemistry in that it orders the crucial "elements" of living systems, primarily in terms of the functions of each subsystem for the large systemic whole. The scholarship and breadth of Miller's analysis of each cell in Table 11.2 are difficult to communicate in a short summary of his work. But more significant than these classificatory efforts, however, are his attempts at developing some propositions about critical processes occurring at various system levels.[37] These propositions are phrased as "hypotheses," primarily because they are inducted from systematic reviews of the research literature for each system level. As a result, the propositions are somewhat disjointed. To communicate Miller's intent, I have rephrased a number of the most central hypotheses and presented them in Table 11.3.

The propositions in Table 11.3 represent hypotheses that seem to apply to several types of living systems. One can see how they might be relevant to various types of

---

[36]Miller, *Living Systems*, 1028–1029.

[37]Ibid., 89–119.

Table 11.2 Examples of Functional Subsystems in Living Systems

Subsystem \ Level	Cell	Organ	Organism	Group	Organization	Society	Supranational System
Reproducer	Chromosome	*None: downwardly dispersed to cell level*	Genitalia	Mating dyad	Group that produces a charter for an organization	Constitutional convention	Supranational system which creates another supranational system
Boundary	Cell membrane	Capsule of viscus	Skin	Sargeant at arms	Guard of an organization's property	Organization of border guards	Supranational organization of border guards
Ingestor	Gap in cell membrane	Input artery of organ	Mouth	Refreshment chairman	Receiving department	Import company	Supranational system officials who operate international ports
Distributor	Endoplasmic reticulum	Blood vessels of organ	Vascular system	Mother who passes out food to family	Driver	Transportation company	United Nations Childrens Fund (UNICEF), which distributes food to needy children
Converter	Enzyme in mitochondrion	Parenchymal cell	Upper gastro-intestinal tract	Butcher	Oil refinery operating group	Oil refinery	European Atomic Energy Community (Euratom), concerned with conversion of atomic energy
Producer	Enzyme in mitochondrion	Parenchymal cell	*Unkown*	Cook	Factory production unit	Factory	World Health Organization (WHO)

(Continued)

Table 11.2 (Continued)

Subsystem \ Level	Cell	Organ	Organism	Group	Organization	Society	Supranational System
Energy/matter storage	Adenosine triphosphate (ATP)	Intercellular fluid	Fatty tissues	Family member who stores food	Stock-room operating group	Warehouse company	International Red Cross, which stores materials for disaster relief
Extruder	Gap in cell membrane	Output vein of organ	Urethra	Cleaning woman	Delivery department	Export company	Component of the International Atomic Energy Agency (IAEA) concerned with waste extrusion
Motor	Microtubule	Muscle tissue of legs organ	Muscle of legs	None: Laterally dispersed to all members of group who move jointly	Crew of machine that moves organization personnel	Trucking company	Transport component of the North Atlantic Treaty Organization (NATO)
Supporter	Microtubule	Stroma	Skeleton	Person who physically supports others in group	Group that operates organization's building	National officials who operate public buildings and land	Supranational officials who operate United Nations buildings and land
Input transducer	Specialized receptor site of cell membrane	Receptor cell of sense organ	Exteroceptive sense organ	Lookout	Telephone operator group	Foreign news service	News service that brings information into supranational system
Internal transducer	Repressor molecule	Specialized cell of sinoatrial node of heart	Receptor cell that responds to changes in blood states	Group member who reports group states to decider	Inspection unit	Public opinion polling agency	Supranational inspection organization

Level / Subsystem	Cell	Organ	Organism	Group	Organization	Society	Supranational System
Channel and net	Cell membrane	Nerve net of organ	Components of neural network	Group member who communicates by signals through the air to other members	Private telephone exchange	National telephone network	Universal Postal Union (UPU)
Decoder	Molecular binding site	Receptor of second-echelon cell of sense organ	Cells in sensory nuclei	Interpreter	Foreign-language translation group	Language-translation unit	Supranational language-translation unit
Associator	*Unknown*	*Unknown*	*Unknown*	*None: laterally dispersed to members who associate for group*	*None: downwardly dispersed to individual persons, organism level*	Teaching institution	Supranational university
Memory	*Unknown*	*Unknown*	*Unknown*	Adult in a family	Filling departments	Library	United Nations library
Decider	Regulator gene	Sympathetic fiber of sinoatrial node of heart	Part of cerebral cortex	Head of a family	Executive office	Government	Council of Ministers of the European Communities
Encoder	Component producing hormone	Presynaptic region of output neuron of organ	Temporo-parietal area of dominant hemisphere of human brain	Person who composes a group statement	Speech-writing department	Press secretary	United Nations Office of Public Information
Output transducer	Presynaptic membrane	Presynaptic region of output neuron of organ	Larynx	Spokesman	Public relations department	Office of national spokesman	Official spokesman of the Warsaw Treaty Organization

Table 11.3 Some Basic Laws of Living Systems

1. The larger is a living system, the more likely are (pp. 108–109):[a]
 	
  A. Patterns of structural differentiation among components
  B. Decentralized centers of decision making
  C. Interdependence of subsystems
  D. Elaborate adjustment processes
  E. Differences in input/output sensitivity of components
  F. Elaborate and varied outputs.

2. The greater is the level of structural differentiation of components in a living system, the greater are
 	
  A. The number of echelons or ranks among subsystems (p. 92)
  B. The segregation of functions (p. 109)
  C. The ratio of information transmitted within rather than across boundaries (pp. 93, 103).

3. The greater is the ratio of information to energy/matter processed across system boundaries as negative and positive feedback, the more likely a living system is to survive in its environment (p. 94).

4. The more hierarchically differentiated a living system into echelons, the more likely is
 	
  A. The presence of discordant information among differentiated subsystems (p. 109)
  B. The utilization by decider subsystems (high-ranking) of information from memory banks from lower-ranking echelons (pp. 99–100).

5. The greater is the number of channels for processing information in a structurally differentiated living system, the less likely are
 	
  A. Errors in transmission and reception of information (p. 96)
  B. Strains and tensions among subsystems (pp. 97, 107).

6. The greater is the level of stress experienced by a living system from its environment, the greater is (pp. 106–107)
 	
  A. The number of components devoted to its alleviation
  B. The less manifest previous tensions among internal system components
  C. The deviation of processes within the system, and each of its subsystems, from previously normal states
  D. The difficulty of returning the system and subsystem processes to previously normal states after alleviation of the strain.

7. The greater is the level of segregation of subsystems in a living system, the greater is their level of conflict and the greater is the total information and/or energy/matter mobilized in each subsystem for resolving the conflict and the less the information or energy/matter available for achieving overall system goals (p. 107).

Note: The above propositions have been rephrased and regrouped for more efficient presentation.

a. Page numbers in parentheses refer to pages in *Living Systems,* where the hypotheses were initially presented.

social forms, although it is not clear that they improve upon existing sociological formulations. For example, proposition 1 restates Spencer's and Durkheim's old "size, differentiation, and integration" propositions as these have been extended to several of the social sciences literatures, particularly organizations theory[38] and human ecology.[39] Moreover, in looking at other propositions, it is not clear that translating sociological terms into "energy" and "matter" adds very much to the analysis; indeed, in an effort to achieve isomorphism with other living systems, these translations make sociology even more vague than it already is.

Yet there is still something fascinating in the ability to view all living systems in terms of certain common functions. And, of course, this has always been the appeal of functionalism: to see events as embedded in, and a part of, systemic wholes that must meet certain requisites in order to survive in an environment. What, then, can we conclude about general systems theory?

Conclusions

Some general systems approaches, as I mentioned earlier, are not functional. But most of these are not very systemic either. What they usually involve is a modeling of variables with causal arrows and feedback loops in order to show the configurations of effects among various forces. For example, many of the models that I have drawn thus far as well as those to be drawn in subsequent chapters would follow a general systems approach in these loose terms. But general systems theory is more than just abstract modeling of complex causal effects—direct, indirect, and feedback—among variables. It is also a search for isomorphisms across different units and their ordering into systemic wholes. Miller and others[40] who take this next step usually begin to talk in terms of energy, matter, information, and related ideas as ways of bridging diverse, and perhaps very different, phenomena. My sense is that translating sociological concepts into another language in order to create conceptual

---

[38]See, for example, Peter Blau, "A Formal Theory of Differentiation in Organizations," *American Sociological Review* 35 (1970):201–218; Jerald Hage, Michael Aiken, and Cora Bagley Marrett, "Organizational Structure and Communications," *American Sociological Review* 36 (1971):860–871; Gerry E. Hendershot and Thomas F. James, "Size and Growth as Determinants of Administrative-Production Ratios in Organizations," *American Sociological Review* 37 (1972):149–153; Thomas F. James, "System Size and Structural Differentiation in Formal Organizations," *Sociological Quarterly* 16 (1975):124–130; Theodore R. Anderson and Seymour Warkov, "Organizational Size and Functional Complexity," *American Sociological Review* 26 (1961):23–28; and Marshall M. Meyer, "Size and Structure of Organizations," *American Sociological Review* 37 (1972):434–441.

[39]For example, see Amos H. Hawley, *Human Ecology* (Chicago, IL: University of Chicago Press, 1986); Brian J. Berry and John D. Kasarda, *Contemporary Urban Ecology* (New York: Macmillan, 1977); Amos H. Hawley (ed.), *Societal Growth: Processes and Implications* (New York: Free Press, 1979); and John D. Kasarda, "The Structural Implications of Social System Size," *American Sociological Review* 39 (1974):19–28. See the next chapter.

[40]For excellent examples, see Tom R. Burns and Helena Flam, *The Shaping of Social Organization* (Newbury Park, CA: Sage, 1987); Kenneth D. Bailey, "Equilibrium, Entropy, and Homeostasis: A Multidisciplinary Legacy," *Systems Research* 1 (1, 1984):25–43 and *Social Entropy Theory* (Albany: SUNY Press, 1989); Kenneth F. Berrier, *General and Social Systems* (New Brunswick, NJ: Rutgers University Press, 1968); Roger E. Cavallo, "Systems Research Movement," *General Systems Bulletin, Special Issue*, 9 (3, 1979); and Carl Slawski, "Evaluating Theories Comparatively," *Zeitschrift fur Soziologie* 3 (4, 1974):397–408.

unity across the sciences makes these concepts less precise. For example, notions of "information" do not communicate the properties denoted by more traditional concepts like norms, values, beliefs, ideology, and so on.

This general systems strategy may also make the mistake of earlier thinkers, such as Spencer, in assuming more unity in the universe than actually exists. Moreover, even if there are isomorphisms, these similarities are phrased so generally that, in generating explanations of particular social events, they will yield only vague insights. That is, such general points of isomorphism across system levels will not help very much in explaining the particular phenomena of most interest to sociologists (or, for that matter, to biologists, psychologists, or economists).[41]

Although there have been several efforts to apply general systems concepts to sociological phenomena, these all suffer from the problems of importing precise mathematical formulations that are not isomorphic with social events. For example, efforts to adopt decision theory, game theory, information theory, analysis of servomechanisms, and similar bodies of precise concepts have never proved very useful. And they probably never will, since they do not fit well with the way complex sociocultural systems actually operate. Still, there are processes in the social world that can, perhaps, adopt models from the natural sciences. For example, models in fluid dynamics can be adopted for use in studying social processes, but it is still unclear if this adoption of more precise models from physics leads to more insight in sociological analysis.

As a consequence of these shortcomings, the initial euphoria created by the founding of the Society for General Systems Research has not been sustained. Indeed, to the extent that a cross-disciplinary perspective has been maintained in sociology, it has been allied with narrower and less cosmic approaches, such as network analysis (see Chapter 20) and human ecology (see Chapter 13), or it is attached to older theoretical perspectives, such as exchange theory, that seek only to cut across the social sciences.

---

[41]Alfred Kuhn, "Differences vs. Similarities in Living Systems," *Contemporary Sociology* 8 (September 1979):691–696.

CHAPTER 12

Ecological Theorizing

Ecological theorizing has a clear lineage from Herbert Spencer to Émile Durkheim to the early twentieth-century Chicago School of Sociology, where it spread to such early centers of ecological theorizing such as the University of North Carolina at Chapel Hill. During this time frame, human ecology became a more general interdisciplinary field of research, but ecological theorizing within sociology proper followed a particular trajectory. First, from 1930 through the early 1970s, theorizing was downsized from the macro level of Spencer and Durkheim to the meso level of social organization, with an emphasis on the ecology of urban areas, where competition for space in cities was emphasized. Then, in the later 1970s, ecological theorizing in sociology was extended to the study of complex organizations, in which "populations of organizations" seeking resources in a particular niche became the unit of analysis. Finally, in the 1980s, ecological theorizing was taken back up to the macro-societal level by the key figures who connected the Chicago School to North Carolina. At the same time, many other types of macro theories, from world-systems analysis (see Chapter14) to stage model theories of evolution (see the next chapter), also began adding more ecological elements to their theories. Thus, even though the number of free-standing ecological theories remains comparatively small, the perspective has diffused into many other theoretical traditions.

In this chapter, I will begin by outlining the continuation of urban ecology to the present, then review the rise of organizational ecology, and finally trace the movement of these meso-level theories on urban and organizational dynamics back to the macro level, where ecological theorizing in sociology began in the works of Spencer and Durkheim.

Theorizing on Urban Ecology

Even after the decline of ecological work at the University of Chicago, urban ecology remains a viable and vibrant meso-level theoretical approach. Recast as the study of spatial processes, theorists have sought to explain such variables as the size of settlements, the concentration of populations within these settlements, the rate and form of geographical expansion of settlements, and the nature of connections among settlements. Much of what is termed "urban sociology" examines specific cases empirically, just as the original Chicago School once used the city of Chicago for its laboratory. But at a more purely theoretical level, an effort has been made to conceptualize urban processes generically as fundamental processes influencing patterns of organizing a population in space. This latter theoretical thrust can properly be seen as ecological, and the kinds of models developed by these spatial theorists owe a great deal to early Chicago School ecologists.

This debt can be best appreciated by examining Figure 12.1, which presents a composite and abstracted model of various approaches in urban ecology.[1] This model does not represent any one theorist's ideas but, rather, communicates the general thrust of various approaches combined.[2] As can be seen on the left of the model, technology and demographics influence two important variables, evident in Spencer's and Durkheim's respective theories. These two variables are (1) the level of development in communication and transportation technologies and (2) the level of production of goods and services. Population size and technology both determine the level of production directly, and as can be seen by the arrows flowing into production, other forces made possible by expanded production feedback and increase production even more. Similarly, transportation and communication technologies set into motion many urban processes, and these also feedback, especially via production, to increase the level of these technologies and, in turn, the store of a population's technology in general.

Both technology and production increase the scale of the material infrastructure of a population—that is, its roads and streets, canals, ports, railroads, airports, subways, buildings, and all other physical structures built in space. The scale of this infrastructure gets an extra boost as the distributive capacities of a population increase—that is, the capacity to move information, materials, goods, and services about space. As can be seen along the bottom of the model in Figure 12.1, the volume and velocity of markets is important in this process; among populations with well-developed market systems, distributive activities increase. They do so because markets create new kinds of administrative and authority systems—banks, governmental agencies, insurance, sales, advertising, services, wholesale and retail outlets, and all the organizational structures required to sustain high-volume markets.

---

[1]For a more detailed analysis, see Jonathan H. Turner, "The Assembling of Human Populations: Toward a Synthesis of Ecological and Geopolitical Theories," *Advances in Human Ecology* 3 (1994):65–91 and *Macrodynamics: Toward Theory on the Organization of Human Populations* (New Brunswick, NJ: Rutgers University Press for Rose Book Series, 1995), chap. 6.

[2]In particular, the model summarizes ideas from Parker W. Frisbie, "Theory and Research in Urban Ecology," in *Sociological Theory and Research: A Critical Approach*, ed. H. M. Blalock (New York: Free Press, 1980); Parker W. Frisbie and John D. Kasarda, "Spatial Processes," in *Handbook of Sociology*, ed. N. J. Smelser (Newbury Park, CA: Sage, 1988); Mark Gottdiener, *The Social Production of Urban Space* (Austin: University of Texas Press, 1985); Amos H. Hawley, *Urban Society: An Ecological Approach* (New York: Ronald, 1981); and John D. Kasarda, "The Theory of Ecological Expansion: An Empirical Test," *Social Forces* 51 (1972):165–175.

Figure 12.1 The Abstracted Urban Ecology Model

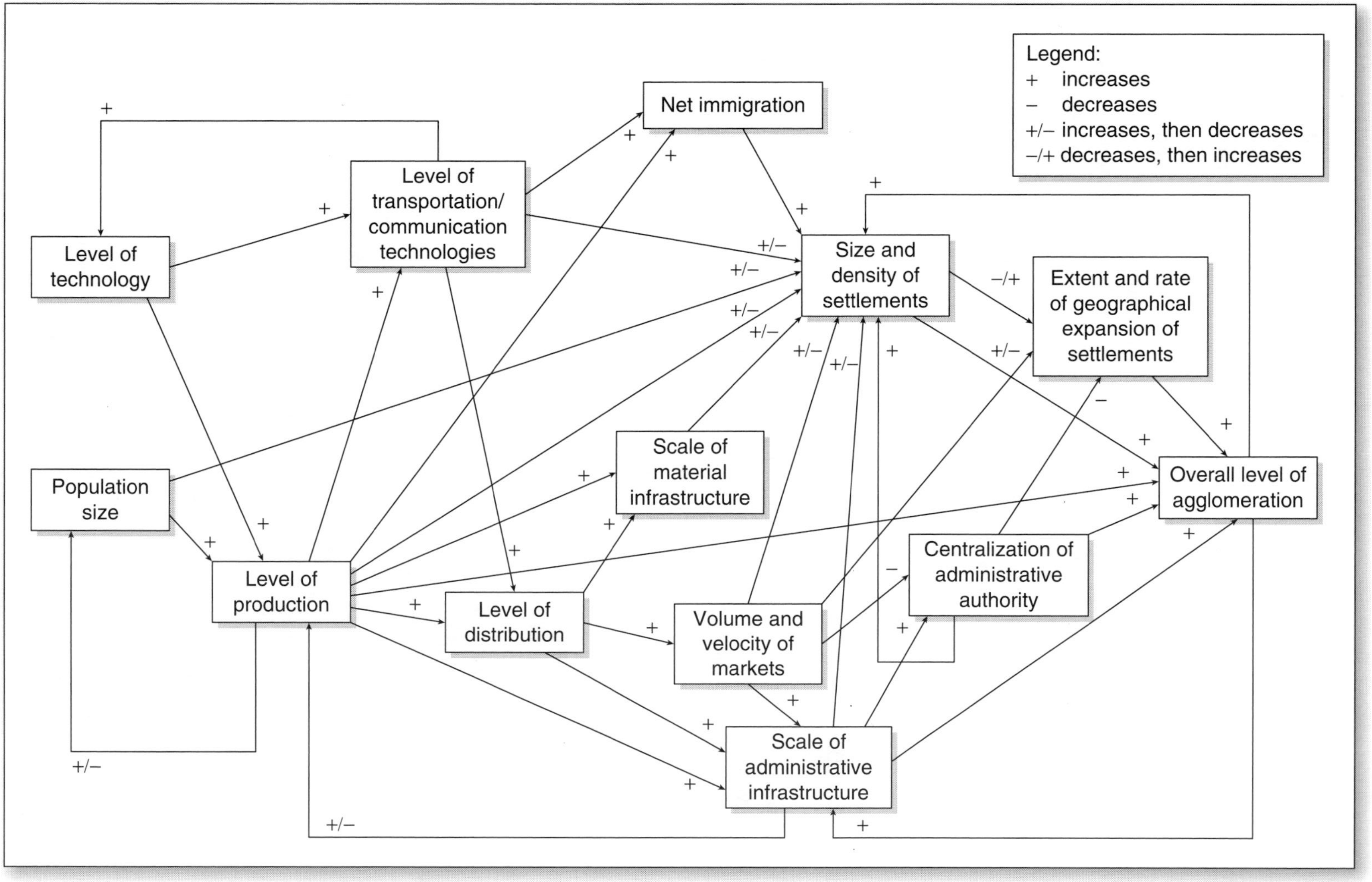

Legend:
+ increases
− decreases
+/− increases, then decreases
−/+ decreases, then increases

397

These are labeled "scale of administrative infrastructure" and "centralization of administrative authority" in the model, respectively, and they have important effects not only in increasing the level of distribution but also on settlement patterns.

These latter effects are most noticeable on the size and density of settlement patterns. Administrative infrastructures and authority systems directly influence the size and density of settlements by concentrating activities and, thereby, pulling a population to urban areas. These administrative variables also operate indirectly on density by increasing distribution and production, which, in turn, expand transportation and communication technologies and the scale of the material infrastructure, which have their own effects on increases in the size and density of settlements.

Immigration patterns are influenced not only by transportation and technology but also by the level of production. When these are high, existing dense settlements become magnets for new immigrants, especially settlements with dynamic market systems and administrative structures that offer opportunities to secure a living and other resources. Immigration, in turn, increases the size and density of settlements, particularly when previous waves of similar immigrants have already settled and can provide friends, relatives, and others of similar origins a place to live and, perhaps, job opportunities.

As the size and density of settlements increase, these forces concentrate populations in ways that discourage geographical expansion of the urban area. But eventually, the population in urban cores must begin to move outward. Such movement is facilitated by markets, especially real estate markets but also markets that can distribute goods and services in new locations. Centralized authority, such as governmental functions, can for a time discourage movement too far from this center of administrative control, but in the end, the growing size and density of the population, coupled with real estate and other markets, enable and, at times, force some of the population to extend the boundaries of the settlement or to create new settlements.

The term on the far right of the model in Figure 12.1—*agglomeration*—is meant to connote what is evident all over the world today: outward movement of settlements, even when this movement involves creating separate settlements, eventually leads to relatively contiguous systems of dense settlements—often termed urban or suburban "sprawl." That is, as movement out from the original urban core occurs, new settlements typically remain within physical proximity of this core; as these new areas attract migrants from the older core or new immigrants from other urban areas, these areas also become large and even more densely settled. Eventually, they begin to bump into each other, creating high levels of agglomeration or the proximity of contiguous and relatively dense settlements spread across a comparatively large geographical space. Such agglomeration increases the scale of the administrative infrastructure, which, in turn, increases governmental functions and its administrative structure across the urban space. Via the reverse causal arrows in the model, agglomeration increases, indirectly, the level of distribution of goods, services, materials, and information around the agglomerated urban space, which, in turn, affects the level of production and transportation, and communication technologies.

Much urban sociology describes specific empirical cases within these general ecological dynamics. Yet from these more specific empirical studies that began with the Chicago School have emerged interesting generalizations that can supplement the processes outlined in the model presented in Figure 12.1. One older principle is that the density of settlements in an urban area declines exponentially (i.e., at an accelerating rate) as the distance from the center of an urban area increases.[3] This idea follows from early Chicago School observations that high demand for space in the core of urban areas will raise market prices and force out those who cannot afford to live or do business in the core; these actors must now assume the additional mobility costs of settling in lower-cost, outlying areas.[4] Yet, as more recent studies indicate,[5] the recent technological and organizational changes, especially those associated with information technologies, have tended to qualify this generalization about the connection between the central urban core and outlying areas.

In fact, there is a movement of material and administrative infrastructure from the core to less densely settled outlying regions, creating a more polycentric system across agglomerated settlement patterns. Thus, the densities of settlements in outlying areas can increase as the distance from the old settlement core increases, but eventually, the principle that settlement density decreases with distance from urban core or cores in a polycentric system will become operative.

A related principle is that the relative size of settlements or cities decreases as movement from the urban core or cores increases.[6] That is, as movement from the large cities occurs, the size and density of settlements will decrease in a pattern: large urban cores will be surrounded by midsized cities, which, in turn, will be connected to smaller settlements.

Another related principle is that the flow of resources across settlements will reflect the degree to which they constitute an integrated system, especially in their markets and the hierarchies of their governmental structures.[7] When settlements are connected by markets and governmental agencies, the flow of resources—information, goods, and services—will be more rapid and efficient.

These and other principles specify in more detail what is subsumed in the model in Figure 12.1 under the label of agglomeration. These kinds of principles, in essence, indicate the ways in which settlements become connected to each other and

---

[3]C. Clark, "Urban Population Densities," *Journal of the Royal Statistical Society*, Series A, 114 (1951):490–496.

[4]B. J. L. Berry and John D. Kasarda, *Contemporary Urban Ecology* (New York: Macmillan, 1977).

[5]Frisbie and Kasarda, "Spatial Processes."

[6]This idea was originally formulated by George Zipf, *Human Behavior and the Principle of Least Effort* (Reading, MA: Addison-Wesley, 1949), and expanded on in other studies: Hawley, *Urban Society*; E. G. Stephan, "Variation in County Size: A Theory of Segmental Growth," *American Sociological Review* 36 (1979):451–461; and "Derivation of Some Socio-Demographic Regularities from the Theory of Time Minimization," *Social Forces* 57 (1979):812–823.

[7]Frisbie and Kasarda, "Spatial Processes." See also Jonathan H. Turner, *Theoretical Principles of Sociology*, vol. 1: *Macrodynamics* (New York: Springer, 2010).

form ever larger settlement patterns in physical space. Many of these generalizations are time-bound and relevant to particular empirical cases, but they do point to several more generic and fundamental forces that organize a population in physical space. Thus, the general intent of the early Chicago School of urban ecology has been retained in more recent work: to see the patterns of settlement of populations in physical space and, then, to develop more abstract generalizations describing these patterns.

Theories of Organizational Ecology

One creative extension of theory during the last thirty-five years has been the analysis of organizational dynamics from an ecological perspective. In these theories, populations of organizations of a given type are viewed as competing for resources, with selection favoring those most fit in a given resource niche. Thus, the rise and fall in the numbers and proportions of various kinds of organizational forms in a society can be seen as a kind of Darwinian struggle in which organizations compete with each other in resource niches, dying out if they are unsuccessful or, if they can, moving to find a new resource niche in which they can survive. The first well-developed theory about the ecology of complex organizations was presented by Michael Hannan and John Freeman in the late 1970s;[8] later, others have extended their approach, typically by analyzing empirically specific populations of organizations. We will first examine Hannan and Freeman's general theory, then review a creative addition to theorizing on organizational ecology by Miller McPherson and various collaborators.

Michael T. Hannan and John Freeman's Ecological Theory

Hannan and Freeman had an important insight:[9] populations of organizations of various kinds can be viewed as competing for resources. For example, automobile companies, clothing outlets, newspapers, governmental agencies, service clubs, and just about any organized corporate unit depend on particular kinds and levels of resources from their respective environments. Thus, a population of organizations, such as automobile companies, can be seen as competing in the same resource niche; for automobile companies, the resource environment consists of those who can afford to buy cars. This basic situation is analogous to evolutionary processes in that organizations must compete with each other to secure resources, particularly as the number of organizations occupying a given niche increases; from such competition comes selection of those organizational forms that are most fit. With this basic insight, Hannan and Freeman extended the

---

[8]Michael T. Hannan and John Freeman, "The Population Ecology of Organizations," *American Journal of Sociology* 82 (1977):929–964.

[9]Ibid.

Figure 12.2 Hannan and Freeman's Ecological Model

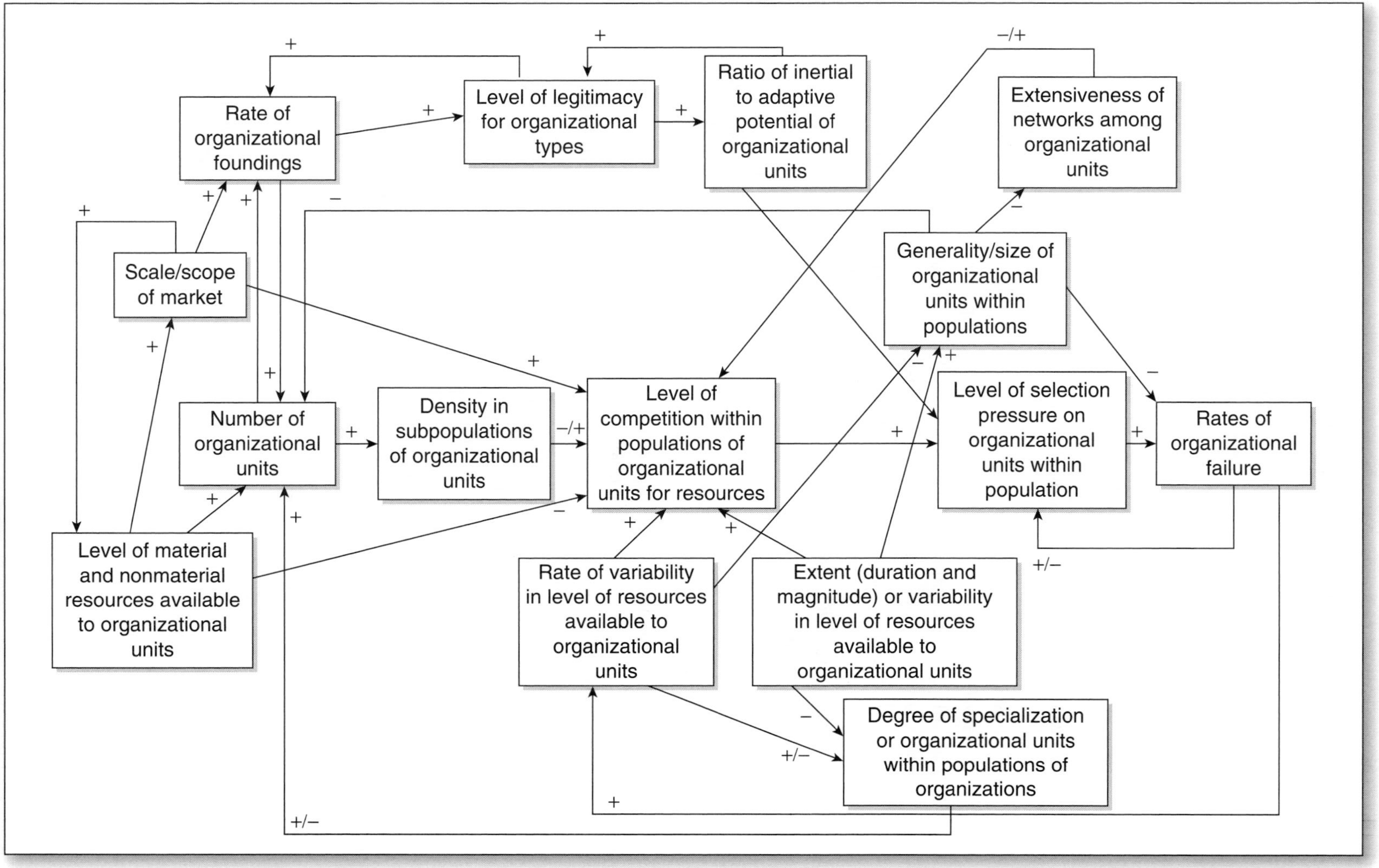

analogy, and Figure 12.2 attempts to summarize all the key variables in their theory as it has developed during the last twenty years.[10]

Hannan and Freeman's basic question focused on why organizations of a given type die out and others increase in frequency.[11] The key dynamic is shown at the center of the model in Figure 12.2: competition within a population of organizations for resources. High levels of competition increase the selection pressures on organizations; those that can secure resources in this competition survive, and those that cannot will fail or move to another resource niche. The theory then examines the forces that increase competition and selection. One critical set of organizational forces is presented in the middle of the model, moving from left to right: the number of organizations of a given type increases the density of organizations in a niche, thereby increasing competition, selection, and rates of organizational failure.

Another force increasing competition is open and free markets. Such markets institutionalize competition, forcing ever-more organizations to compete with each other for customers, members, or any other resources. Thus, as the scale and scope of markets increase, the level of competition increases, especially when niche density is high. If monopolies can emerge or government regulates markets extensively, however, the level of competition is reduced, thereby lowering selection pressures and rates of organizational failure.

Still another set of variables moves across the top of the model, from left to right. When an organization of a given type first emerges in a niche, it must legitimate itself by surviving, and once it enjoys success, then the rate of organizational foundings, or the creation of new organizations of this type, will increase. These new foundings escalate niche density, competition, and selection, but they also do something else: they make organizations of a given type legitimate, which only encourages more foundings. With legitimization also comes what is phrased in the model as the ratio of inertial to adaptive tendencies in organizations. When organizations have structured themselves successfully in a particular manner and thereby achieved legitimacy, they can also develop structural rigidities or inertial tendencies. They become conservative, locked into the old ways of performing activity. These inertial tendencies give selection processes something to work on. As density in a resource niche increases or the level of resources declines, then those organizations that are too rigid or inertial are likely

---

[10]For an analysis of the more macrostructural implications of the variables delineated in Figure 7.2, see Turner, *Macrodynamics*, chap. 7 and "The Ecology of Macrostructure."

[11]For representative works by Hannan and Freeman, see "Structural Inertia and Organizational Change," *American Sociological Review* 49 (1984):149–164, "The Ecology of Organizational Founding: American Labor Unions 1836–1985," *American Journal of Sociology* 92 (1987):910–943, "The Ecology of Organizational Mortality: American Labor Unions," *American Journal of Sociology* 94 (1988):25–52, and *Organizational Ecology* (Cambridge, MA: Harvard University Press, 1989). See also M. T. Hannan, "Ecologies of Organizations: Diversity and Identity," *Journal of Economic Perspectives* 19 (2005):51–70; M. T. Hannan, L. Pólos, and G. R. Carroll, *Logics of Organization Theory: Audiences, Codes, and Ecologies* (Princeton, NJ: Princeton University Press, 2007); and M. T. Hannan and G. R. Carroll, *Dynamics of Organizational Populations: Density, Legitimation, and Competition* (New York: Oxford University Press, 1992).

to be selected out of the population of organizations, whereas those that reveal flexibility or new and creative ways of organizing themselves in the pursuit of resources will be more likely to survive.

A third set of variables moves across the bottom portion of the model in Figure 12.2. The resources available to organizations will vary in several respects. One source of variation in resources is the rate of variability, or how often resources increase and decline. Are resources constantly shifting, or is the fluctuation gradual and slow? Another source of variation in the available resources is the magnitude and duration of variability, or the degree and length of fluctuation between high and low periods of resource availability. When there is rapid fluctuation in resources, specialized types of organizations are likely to emerge and be able to outcompete larger and more generalized organizational structures, which, because of their inertial tendencies, cannot move fast enough to respond to rapid shifts in the resources available. When the magnitude of shifts is great and prolonged, however, the specialization of organizations is discouraged because larger and more generalized organizations can ride out the dramatic drop in the level of resources available more effectively than can smaller and highly specialized organizations; these larger organizations have other resource niches that they can pursue, and they typically have bigger resource reserves, whereas the more specialized organizations are likely to have too few reserves to survive large drops in the resources available.

As can be seen from the arrows in the model going into the competition variable, environmental change, whether a rapid or severe drop in resources, or both, will increase the struggle among organizations. As Darwin noted, when the environment changes, the resource niches of species are disrupted, escalating competition and natural selection. When change occurs over longer periods and is of high magnitudes, selection favors larger, more generalized organizations, which draw from more than one niche and can ride out fluctuations of high magnitude in any one niche. As organizations become large and general, they often create extensive networks of ties and agreements to reduce competition that could potentially select them out. Examples of these networks can include cartels, trade agreements, interlocking boards of directors in private corporations, liaisons with government, joint production agreements, price fixing among oligopolies, and many other mechanisms by which organizations seek to reduce competition. These networks in effect decrease the density among organizations and hence their competition, which, in turn, reduces their rates of organizational failure.

Hannan and Freeman's theory has thus taken Spencer's and Durkheim's down to a more meso level of analysis, but more directly, the theory adapts Darwinian ideas to the analysis of organizations. Thus, Hannan and Freeman inject a new meso-level phenomenon into ecological analysis: the dynamics within populations of complex organizations. Their approach has stimulated an entirely new branch of research and theory in sociology, and this branch has dominated ecological theorizing during the last three decades, although new, more macro approaches to ecology have also begun to rival the preeminence of theory and research on the ecology of organizations.

J. Miller McPherson's Ecological Theory

J. Miller McPherson and various collaborators have developed a variant on Hannan and Freeman's model of organizational ecology.[12] McPherson's empirical work has been primarily on voluntary associations and organizations, and this emphasis has led to several additional insights into the dynamics of organizational ecology. McPherson begins with an idea that he adapted from Peter M. Blau's theory of macrostructure: the environment of organizations consists of members of a population who reveal a diversity of characteristics, such as age, sex, ethnicity, income, education, recreational interests, and so on. These characteristics distinguish individuals from each other and, often, become important markers of categorization (as is the case with sex and ethnicity) and inequality (as with income and years of education). These characteristics are also potential resource niches for organizations seeking members and clients. Thus, McPherson conceptualizes the diversity of characteristics among members of a population as *Blau space,* in deference to the theorist whose work gave him this idea. *Blau space* is the environment of organizations, and the greater the diversity of characteristics that differentiate members of a population, the greater is the number of resource niches in Blau-space available for organizations to recruit members and clients.

Figure 12.3 summarizes the model developed by McPherson in more general terms, giving us a way to visualize the causal relations among the variables in the theory. The size of the population is, as Spencer and Durkheim both recognized, an important determinant of the level of diversity of characteristics of individuals in Blau-space, as is indicated on the left of the model. The larger the population is, the more likely the characteristics of its members will be differentiated. Moreover, population size, per se, generates resources in the niches of Blau-space; that is, the more people there are, the more resources are available for organizational systems.

Population size also reduces the density of networks among members of a population; the more people there are to organize, the less likely individuals are to be connected to each other directly or indirectly (as summarized in Chapter 20 on networks, *network density* is a concept denoting the degree of connectedness among actors). With low density, or low rates of connectedness among members of a population, these members are more likely to develop distinctive characteristics

---

[12]See J. Miller McPherson, "A Dynamic Model of Voluntary Affiliation," *Social Forces* 59 (1981):705–728, "An Ecology of Affiliation," *American Sociological Review* 48 (1983):519–532, "The Size of Voluntary Organizations," *Social Forces* 61 (1983):1044–1064, "A Theory of Voluntary Organization," in *Community Organizations,* ed. C. Milofsky (New York: Oxford University Press, 1988), 42–76, and "Evolution in Communities of Voluntary Organization," in *Organizational Evolution,* ed. J. Singh (Newbury Park, CA: Sage, 1990); J. M. McPherson, P. A. Popielarz, and S. Drobnic, "Social Networks and Organizational Dynamics," *American Sociological Review* 57 (1992):153–170; J. M. McPherson and J. Ranger-Moore, "Evolution on a Dancing Landscape: Organizations and Networks in Dynamic Blau-Space," *Social Forces* 70 (1991):19–42; J. M. McPherson and T. Rotolo, "Testing a Dynamic Model of Social Composition: Diversity and Change in Voluntary Groups," *American Sociological Review* 61 (1996):179–202; and J. M. McPherson, "A Blau Space Primer: Prolegomenon to an Ecology of Affiliation," *Industrial and Corporate Change* 13 (2004):263–280 and "Ecological Theory," *Handbook of Social Theory,* ed. G. Ritzer (Newbury Park, CA: Sage, 2003).

Figure 12.3 McPherson's Ecological Model

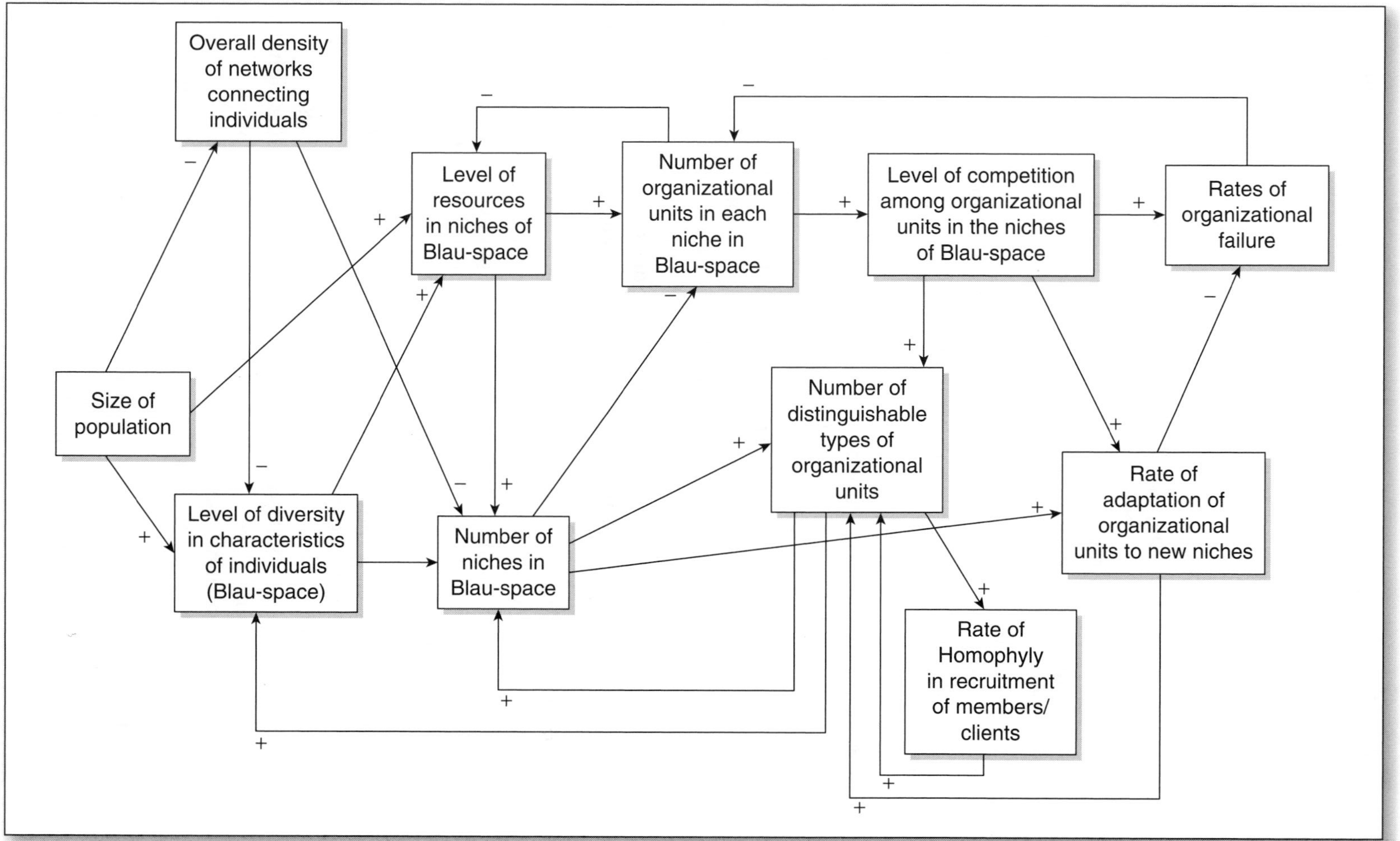

because they do not have direct contact and the informal social control and conformity that such contacts generate. Thus, low network density among members of a large population increases the niches in Blau-space available that organizations can exploit.

As the number of niches in Blau-space increases, the number of organizational units in each niche will also tend to increase, and as their numbers grow, the level of competition among organizational units in a niche will begin to escalate. In turn, as niches become densely populated with organizational units, rates of organizational failure will increase, thereby lowering the number of units competing for resources in a particular niche in Blau-space.

Competition among organizations will increase the number of distinguishable organizational units for two reasons: first, each organization seeks to distinguish itself from competitors, thereby increasing the diversity of organizations in a niche. Second, as organizational units distinguish themselves, they create more niches in Blau-space because the members of organizations can reveal somewhat different characteristics. Indeed, as the model portrays, there is a mutually reinforcing cycle between the number of niches and the number of distinguishable types of organizations in Blau-space. Competition only accelerates these forces.

Organizations in Blau-space also become distinctive because they tend to recruit members with similar characteristics, or what is termed rate of homophyly in the model. Thus, for example, service organizations such as the Lions, Kiwanis, Optimists, American Legion, and the like will seek members whose characteristics converge; as these organizations do so, they sustain their distinctiveness and, hence, the diversity of characteristics among members in a population and the corresponding niches in Blau-space. Competition for members or clients, however, places selection pressure on organizations, forcing them to adapt and change if they find themselves less able to compete in a niche. For example, in recent decades in America, service organizations have had great difficulty sustaining their memberships because the number of individuals in this niche has declined as the demographics and structure of the society have changed. Such competition has led to a decline in membership and some organizational failures, but it has also done something else: some organizations have been forced to seek new niches in Blau-space. For example, a service organization might shift from a middle-income and high-education pool of members to lower-income and less educated members because the competition is less intense. Rates of adaptation to new niches are influenced not only by the level of competition but also by the number of niches in Blau-space. If there are many niches, then an organization that is having trouble recruiting members and clients has options that would not be available if there were only a few niches in Blau-space. Adaptation to new niches is particularly likely when there are adjacent niches that do not require a complete restructuring of the organization. For example, when the polio vaccine was created, the March of Dimes lost its resource base because its cause for recruiting donations was obviated; to survive, the March of Dimes moved to a new but adjacent charity niche that still involved the basic structure of soliciting charitable contributions.

As is evident, the key idea of McPherson's model is much the same as in other organizational ecological models:[13] competition and selection among organizations, because these lead to organizational failure or movement of organizations to new niches. McPherson's most important addition is expansion of what constitutes the resource environment of organizations. Hannan and Freeman's model connoted a more money- and market-driven image of the resource environment, whereas McPherson's model expands the notion of what constitutes resources. Virtually any set of characteristics that distinguishes people in a population can become a resource niche for organizations that seek members, clients, or customers. The more varied the Blau-space is, the more diversity of organizational forms the environment can support and the more likely are less successful organizations in one niche to move to new, adjacent niches in efforts to survive.

Amos H. Hawley's Return to Macro-Level Ecological Theory

As noted earlier, the macro-level ideas of Herbert Spencer and Émile Durkheim about the ecology of human social organization were downsized in the first half of the twentieth century to the meso-level analysis of urban social processes. Amos Hawley, who was a direct descendant of the Chicago School tradition, continued this emphasis on the differentiation of urban space in his early work in the late 1940s and early 1950s,[14] and yet he felt he was becoming "increasingly disenchanted with the then received conception of human ecology. The prevailing preoccupation with spatial distributions, which had attracted me at first, seem to me a theoretical cul-de-sac."[15] By the 1980s, he had pushed ecological analysis back to the macro or societal level.[16]

---

[13]For some general overviews of research and theory on organizational ecology, see Glenn R. Carroll (ed.), *Ecological Models of Organizations* (Cambridge, MA: Ballinger, 1988) and "Organizational Ecology," *Annual Review of Sociology* 10 (1984):71–93 and Jitendra V. Singh and Charles J. Lumsden, "Theory and Research in Organizational Ecology," *Annual Review of Sociology* 16 (1990):161–195.

[14]Amos H. Hawley, *Human Ecology: A Theory of Community Structure* (New York: Ronald, 1950).

[15]Amos H. Hawley, "The Logic of Macrosociology," *Annual Review of Sociology* 18 (1992):1–14.

[16]The following list of titles from Hawley's work reviews this progression of thinking that culminated in the last reference at the end of this note: "Human Ecology," in *International Encyclopedia of the Social Sciences*, ed. D. C. Sills (New York: Crowell, Collier, and Macmillan, 1968), *Urban Society: An Ecological Approach* (New York: Ronald, 1971 and 1981), "Human Ecology: Persistence and Change," *American Behavioral Scientist* 24 (3, January 1981):423–444, "Human Ecological and Marxian Theories," *American Journal of Sociology* 89 (1984):904–917, "Ecology and Population," *Science* 179 (March 1973):1196–1201, "Cumulative Change in Theory and History," *American Sociological Review* 43 (1978):787–797, "Spatial Aspects of Populations: An Overview," in *Social Demography*, ed. K. W. Taueber, L. L. Bumpass, and J. A. Sweet (New York: Academic, 1978), "Sociological Human Ecology: Past, Present, and Future," in *Sociological Human Ecology*, ed. M. Micklin and H. M. Choldin (Boulder, CO: Westview, 1980), and, most significantly, *Human Ecology: A Theoretical Essay* (Chicago, IL: University of Chicago Press, 1986).

Production, Transportation, and Communication

Hawley's theory of ecological processes begins with three basic assumptions:

1. Adaptation to environment proceeds through the formation of a system of interdependencies among the members of a population.

2. System development continues, other things being equal, to the maximum complexity afforded by the existing facilities for transportation and communication.

3. System development is resumed with the introduction of new information that increases the capacity for movement of materials, people, and messages, and continues until that capacity is fully used.

Hawley terms these assumptions the *adaptive, growth,* and *evolution* "propositions," respectively. These assumptions resurrect in altered form the ideas developed by Herbert Spencer and Émile Durkheim. To survive and adapt to an environment, human populations become differentiated and integrated by a system of mutual interdependencies. The size of a population and the complexity of social organization for that population are limited by its knowledge base, particularly with respect to transportation and communication technologies. Populations cannot increase in size, or elaborate the complexity of their patterns of organization, without expansion of knowledge about (a) communication and (b) movement of people and materials.[17] Hawley conceptualized the combined effects of transportation and communication technologies as *mobility costs.*

Linked to transportation and communication technologies is another variable, *productivity.* Curiously, in his most recent theoretical essay, this variable is somewhat subordinate, whereas it is highlighted in earlier statements. There is no great contradiction or dramatic change in conceptualization in this more recent statement, and so we can merely reintroduce the productivity variable in more explicit terms. Basically, a reciprocal set of relations exists between production of materials, information, and services, on one side, and the capacity of a system to move these products to other system units, on the other. The development of new transportation and communication technologies encourages expanded production, whereas the expansion of production burdens existing capacities for mobility and thereby stimulates a search for new technologies. There is also a more indirect linkage among productivity, growth, and evolution, because productivity "constitutes the principal limiting condition on the extent to which a system can be elaborated, on the size of the population that can be sustained in the system, and on the area or space that the system can occupy."[18] Thus, to support a larger, more differentiated population in a more extended territory requires the capacity to (a) produce more goods and services and (b) distribute these goods and services through transportation and communication technologies. If productivity cannot be increased or if the

---

[17]Hawley, *Human Ecology: A Theoretical Essay.*

[18]Hawley, "Human Ecology."

mobility costs of transportation and communication cannot be reduced, then there is an upper limit on the size, scale, and complexity of the system.

The Environment

An ecosystem is "an arrangement of mutual dependencies in a population by which the whole operates as a unit and maintains a viable environmental relationship."[19] The environment is the source of energy and materials for productivity, but the environment reveals more than a biophysical dimension. There is also an "ecumenic" dimension composed of the "ecosystems or cultures possessed by peoples in adjacent areas and beyond."[20] Moreover, in Hawley's view, ecological analysis "posits an external origin of change" because "a thing cannot cause itself"[21]; and thus, in examining a population as a whole in its physical, social, or biological environment, Hawley's approach emphasizes that change comes more from these environmental systems than from processes internal to the organization of a population.

Functions and Key Functions

In Hawley's approach, the arrangement of mutual dependencies of a population in an environment is conceptualized as classes or types of *units* that form *relations* with one another with respect to functions.[22] *Functions* are defined as "repetitive activity that is reciprocated by another or other repetitive activities." Of particular importance are *key functions*, which are repetitive activities "directly engaged with the environment." As such, key functions transmit environmental inputs (materials and information) to other "contingent functions" (or repetitive activities joining units in a relation).[23] Hawley visualizes that a relatively small number of key functions exist, and "to the extent that the principle of key functions does not obtain, the system will be tenuous and incoherent."[24] A system is thus composed of functional units, a few of which have direct relations with the environment and perform key functions. Most other units, therefore, must "secure access to the environment indirectly through the agency of the key function."[25]

For example, production is a key function, and in earlier essays Hawley seemed to see productivity as the primary key function. Yet there are obviously other key functions—political, military, and perhaps ideological—that also influence the flow of resources to and from the environment. As a result, other functional units gain

---

[19]Hawley, *Human Ecology: A Theoretical Essay.*

[20]Ibid., 13.

[21]Hawley, "Human Ecological and Marxian Theories."

[22]Hawley, "Human Ecology" and *Human Ecology: A Theoretical Essay,* 32.

[23]Hawley, *Human Ecology: A Theoretical Essay,* 34.

[24]Hawley, "Human Ecology," 332.

[25]Ibid.

access to the environment only through their interconnections with those units engaged in these various key functions. Thus, the relations of units that form the structure of a population are conceptualized as functions and key functions, or classes of reciprocated repetitive activities that join units together. This is, of course, another way of denoting specialization and differentiation of various types in clusters of activity. Just why Hawley proposes this particular terminology is unclear, but in doing so, Hawley transforms the ecology perspective into a more functional form of analysis.

Indeed, slipping into Hawley's analysis is a stronger version of the term function. In part, this stronger notion of function is implied by the concept of "key function." A key function regulates inputs of energy, materials, and information into the system, and it is not hard to see how the next step on the road to functionalism is made: certain key functions are necessary for adaptation and survival. Hawley himself takes this step when he notes,

> We might suppose, for purposes of illustration, that every instance of collective life is sustained by a mix of activities that produce sustenance and related materials, distribute the production among the participants, maintain the number of units required to produce and distribute the products, and exercise the controls needed to assure an uninterrupted performance of all tasks with a minimum of friction.[26]

Indeed, these requisites look very much like those proposed by Herbert Spencer—production, regulation, distribution, and sustenance.

Whatever the merits or defects in such functionalism, Hawley translated his ideas into a series of "hypotheses." Table 12.1 restates in somewhat modified form some of the most critical propositions that can be pulled from his analysis thus far.[27] These propositions represent abstract "laws" from which Hawley's many hypotheses can be derived. The basic ideas in the propositions of Table 12.1 are these: key functions, or those that mediate exchanges with the environment, disproportionately influence other functions and hold power over these other functions (e.g., units involved in key economic or political functions in a society usually hold more power and influence than others because they are engaged in interchanges with the physical and social environment); the more proximate a function is to a key function, the greater this influence is; conversely, the more remote a function is from a key function, the less influence this function has on the key function. Differentiation of key functions decreases other functions' direct access to the environment because such access is now mediated by units involved in key functions (e.g., most people do not grow their own food or provide their own military defense in highly differentiated societies). As mobility costs for personnel and materials needed for functions increase, the functions' number and relations stabilize; under these conditions, a normative order can develop to regulate the internal relations of functions, as well as their interrelations.

---

[26]Hawley, *Human Ecology: A Theoretical Essay*, 32.

[27]Ibid., 43–44.

Table 12.1   General Propositions on Functions in Ecosystems

1. The more a function (recurrent and reciprocated activity) mediates critical environmental relationships (key function), the more it determines the conditions under which all other functions are performed.
2. The more proximate is a function to a key function, the more the latter constrains the other, and vice versa.
3. The more a function is a key function, the greater is the power of those actors and units involved in this function, and vice versa.
4. The more differentiated are functions, the greater is the proportion of all functions indirectly related to the environment.
5. The greater the number of units using the products of a function and the less the costs of the skills used in the function, the greater is the number of units in the population engaged in this function.
6. The greater the mobility costs (for communication and transportation) associated with a function, the more stable are the number of, and the interrelations among, units implicated in this function.
7. The more stable the number of, and interrelations among, units implicated in functions, the more a normative order corresponds to the functional order.

Equilibrium and Change

An ecosystem is thus a population organized to adapt to an environment, with change in this system being defined by Hawley as "a shift in the number and kinds of functions or as a rearrangement of functions in different combinations."[28] In contrast with change, growth is "the maturation of a system through the maximization of the potential for complexity and integration implicit in the technology for movement and communication possessed at a given point in time,"[29] whereas evolution is "the occurrence of new structural elements from environmental inputs that lead to synthesis of new with old information and a consequent increase in the scope of the accessible environment."[30] This series of definitions presents a picture of ecosystem dynamics as revolving around (a) the internal rearrangement of functions, (b) the increase of complexity to the maximum allowed by an existent level of communication and transportation technologies, and (c) the receipt of environmental inputs, especially new information that expands transportation and communication (or capacity for mobility) and that, as a consequence, increases the scale and complexity of the ecosystem (to the limits imposed by the new technologies).

---

[28]Ibid., 46.

[29]Ibid., 52.

[30]Ibid.

There is an image, then, of a system in equilibrium that is then placed into disequilibrium by new knowledge about production as it influences mobility (of people, materials, and information). Somewhat less clear is where this new information comes from. Must it be totally exogenous (from other societies, migrants, changes in the biophysical forces that generate new knowledge)? Or can the system itself generate the new information through a particular array of functions? It would appear that both can be the source of change, yet the imagery of Hawley's model[31] connotes a system that must be disrupted from the outside if it is to evolve and develop new levels of structural complexity. Internal dialectical processes, or self-transforming processes that increase technology, seem to be underemphasized as crucial ecosystem dynamics. Table 12.2 summarizes the more abstract "laws" that can be culled from Hawley's hypotheses on these dynamics.[32]

Table 12.2   General Propositions on Change, Growth, and Evolution in Ecosystems

1. The greater the exposure of an ecosystem to the ecumenic environment (other societies or cultures of other societies), the greater is the probability of new information and knowledge penetrating the system and, hence, the greater is the probability of change, growth, and evolution.
2. The more new information increases the mobility of people, materials, and information, as well as production, the more likely that change will be cumulative, or evolutionary, to the limits of complexity allowed by the new information as it is translated into technologies for production, transportation, and communication.
3. The more new information improves various mobility and productive processes at differential rates, the more the lower rate of technology will impose limits on the faster-changing technology.
4. The more a system approaches the scale and complexity allowed by technologies, the slower the rate of change, growth, and evolution is and the more likely the system is to achieve a state of closure (equilibrium) in its ecumenic environment.

These propositions reinforce the emphasis in human ecology that the source of change is exogenous, residing particularly in the "ecumenic" environment. From this environment, new knowledge will come and then become "synthesized" with the existing knowledge base. Such synthesized knowledge will then change production, transportation, and communication in ways that allow the system to increase its complexity, size, and territory. Yet new knowledge can introduce change only to a point. If some technologies lag behind others, the rate of change

---

[31]Ibid., 59. Hawley "boxes" lists of variables and then draws arrows among the boxes, but not among the variables within each box. Hence, detailed causal arguments need to be inferred.

[32]Ibid., 85–87.

will be pulled down by the lower technology. And eventually the maximal size, scale, and complexity of the system will be reached, unless new technologies are inserted into the system from the environment. Thus, systems that have grown to the maximum size, scope, and complexity allowed by production, transportation, and communication technologies will achieve equilibrium. New knowledge from the environment can disrupt the equilibrium when such knowledge is used to achieve increases in productivity and mobility. But each technology has limits on how much growth and evolution it can facilitate; when this limit is reached, the system will tend to re-equilibrate.

The concept of equilibrium is most problematic, although Hawley employs it only as a heuristic device. Hawley means the notion of equilibrium to connote "the balance of nature, denoting a tendency toward stabilization of the relative numbers of diverse organisms within the web of life and their several claims on the environment."[33] Yet Hawley recognizes that "equilibrium . . . is a logical construct"[34] and connotes that ecological systems tend toward stability, although Hawley also employs terms like *partial equilibrium* to connote only a tendency toward some degree of instability.

Growth and Evolution

The most interesting portions of ecological theory are those dealing with growth and evolution—that is, increasing size, scale, scope, and complexity of the systematic whole in its environment. This analysis builds on the propositions in Tables 12.1 and 12.2, but it extends them in creative ways and, as a result, goes considerably beyond the early formulations of Spencer and Durkheim.

In Figure 12.4, Hawley's model is redrawn in a way that makes the causal dynamics more explicit. Starting on the far left of the model, Hawley believes that an expanded knowledge base must come from the ecumenical environment. As the model stresses, new knowledge causes growth and change when it increases the level of communication and transportation technologies, either directly or indirectly, through increasing production (which then causes expansion of these technologies). A critical variable in Hawley's scheme is mobility costs; for any given technology, a cost (time, energy, money, materials) is associated with the movement of information, materials, and people. As these costs reach their maximum—that is, the system cannot "pay" for them without degenerating—they impose a limit on the scale of the system: the size of its population, the extent of its territory, the level of its productivity, and the level of complexity. Conversely, as the feedback arrows in the model indicate, the size of the territory and the population will, as they expand and grow, begin to impose higher mobility costs. Eventually, these costs will increase to a point at which the population cannot grow or expand its territory—unless new communication and transportation technologies that reduce costs are discovered.

Much as Spencer and Durkheim argued, population and territorial size, because they are influenced by mobility costs, cause specialization of functions—what is

---

[33]Hawley, "Human Ecology," 329.

[34]Ibid., 334.

Figure 12.4 Elaboration of Hawley's Model

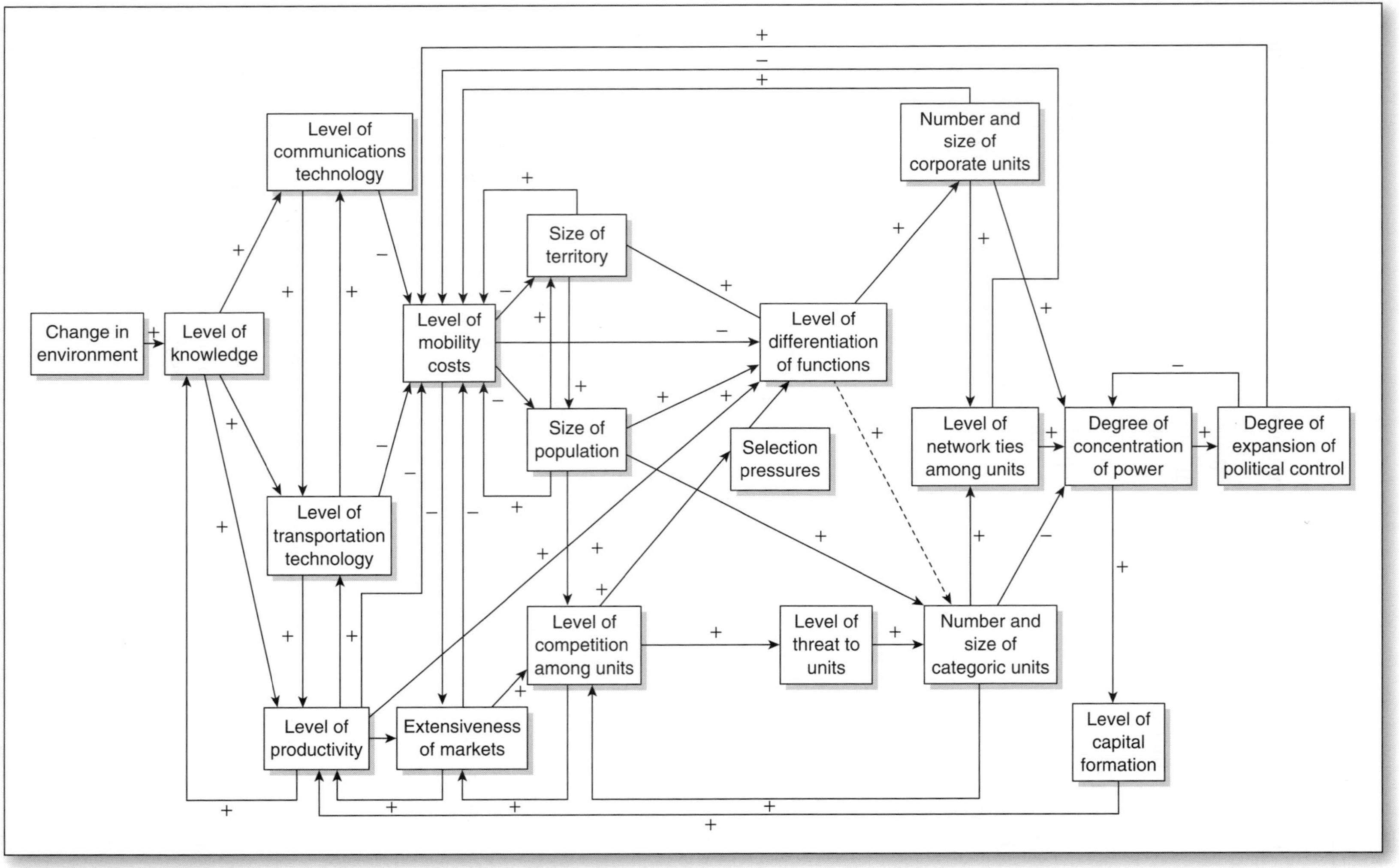

termed differentiation in the model. As Hawley notes, however, the relationship between population size and differentiation is not unambiguous, but it does create "conditions that foster, if not necessitate, increases in the sizes of subsystems" and the number of such subsystems serving various functions. Thus, for Hawley, "the greater the size, the greater the probable support for units with degrees of specialization." And as he adds, "Other pertinent conditions are the rate or volume of intersystem communications, scope of a market, and amount of stability in intersystem relations."[35]

These causal connections are not clearly delineated by Hawley, so the model involves making many causal inferences. The causal paths moving from level of productivity through extensiveness of markets and level of competition to selection pressures and differentiation of functions represent the old Spencerian and Durkheimian argument: expansion of markets increases the level of competitiveness among units and, at the same time, increases the capacity to distribute goods and services because these are constrained by mobility costs (note the arrows connecting markets and mobility costs); competition under conditions of increased production and population size allows—indeed encourages—specialization as actors seek their most viable niche. Similarly, the causal arrows moving from communication and transportation technologies through mobility costs, size of territory, and size of population to level of differentiation of functions restate Spencer's, but more particularly Durkheim's, argument in a more sophisticated form: changes in communication and transportation technologies reduce mobility costs and allow population growth and territorial expansion; all these forces together create selective pressures to adjust and adapt varying attributes and competencies, especially under conditions of intense competition for resources.

Hawley believed that differentiation of subunits engaged in various functions occurs along two axes: (1) corporate and (2) categoric.[36] *Corporate units* are constructed from "symbiotic relations" of mutual dependence among differentiated actors, whereas *categoric units* are composed of "commensalistic" relations among actors who reveal common interests and who pool their activities to adapt more effectively to their environments. Table 12.3 delineates these types of units along an

Table 12.3 A Typology of System Units

Unifying Principle	Relational Structure	
	Corporate Units	Categoric Units
Familial	Household units	Clan, tribe, kin
Territorial	Village, city, ecumene	Polity, neighborhood, ethnic enclave, ghetto
Associational	Industry, retail store	Caste, class, guild, union, school, government, professional organization

---

[35]Hawley, *Human Ecology: A Theoretical Essay,* 80–81.

[36]Ibid., 68–73 and "Human Ecology," 331–332.

additional dimension—their "unifying principle."[37] Thus, as differentiation increases, an ecosystem will represent a complex configuration of corporate and categoric units along various "unifying principles": familial, territorial, and associational. It is not clear if Hawley meant this typology to be exhaustive or merely illustrative. Nonetheless, the typology is provocative.

The dynamics of these two types of units are very different. Corporate units form around functions, or sets of related activities, and are engaged in interchanges with other corporate units. As a consequence of this contact, corporate units tend to resemble one another, especially those that engage in frequent interchanges or are closely linked to corporate units engaged in key functions (interchanges with the environment). Moreover, as they engage in interchanges, corporate units tend toward closure of structure and establishment of clear boundaries. The size and number of such corporate units depend, of course, on the size of the population, the inter- and intra-unit mobility costs associated with communication and transportation technologies, the capacity for production and distribution in markets (as constrained by mobility costs), and the level of competition among units.

In contrast, categoric units involve interdependencies that develop "on the basis of similarities among the members of a population";[38] their number and size are related to the size of the population and territory as well as to the level of threat imposed by their environment. As Hawley noted, the nature of the threat can vary—a "task too large for the individual to accomplish in a limited time, such as the harvesting of a crop," "losing land to an invader," the "possible destruction of a road or other amenity," "a technological shift that might render an occupation obsolete," and so on. If a threat is persistent, the actors in a categoric unit will form a more "lasting association," and if similar units are in competition (say, rival labor unions or ideologically similar political parties), the costs and destructiveness of such competition will eventually lead to their consolidation into a larger categoric unit. Moreover, those categoric units that persist will develop a corporate core to sustain the flow and coordination of resources necessary to deal with the persisting or recurring threat. Categoric units can also get much larger than corporate units because their membership criteria—mere possession of certain characteristics (ethnic, religious, occupational, ideological)—are much more lax than those of corporate units, which recruit members to perform certain specialized and interdependent activities or functions. Of course, the size and number of categoric units are still circumscribed by the size and complexity of the ecosystem and, to a lesser extent than with corporate units, by the mobility costs associated with communication and transportation technologies.

As indicated in the right portion of Figure 12.4, differentiation of categoric units leads corporate units to consolidate into networks, which create larger subsystems. This regularization of ties among units engaged in similar and symbiotic activities or functions reduces mobility costs. And reduced mobility costs facilitate the growth of the ecosystem (note the feedback arrow to mobility costs).

---

[37]Hawley, *Human Ecology: A Theoretical Essay,* 74.

[38]Ibid., 70.

Differentiation of units and their consolidation into larger networks also have consequences for the concentration of power. Categoric-unit formation and the consolidation of such units into larger networks and subsystems tend to reduce concentrations of power. The reason for this reduction of power is that various confederations of categoric units will pose a check on one another. In contrast, corporate units are more likely to cause the concentration of power. This concentration is directly related to the capacity of some units to perform key functions and thereby dictate the conditions under which interrelated functions must operate. This control is facilitated by consolidation of networks into subsystems because such networks connect outlying and remote corporate units, via configurations of successive network ties, to those engaged in key functions. Such connections among corporate units, as they facilitate the concentration of power, enable political control to expand to the far reaches of the ecosystem; political and territorial boundaries tend to become coterminous in ecosystems. Yet centralization of power and extension of control can increase mobility costs as rules and regulations associated with efforts at control escalate, setting limits on how complex the ecosystem can become, without a change in communication and transportation technologies (hence the long feedback arrow at the top of Figure 12.4).

We can add a variable to the model that is implicit but crucial: capital formation. Hawley does not address this issue extensively, so we are clearly adding it to his model. Nonetheless, it is important to recognize that concentration of power also consolidates the flow of resources, facilitating capital formation. If not squandered on maintenance of control, defense, or offensive efforts at military expansion, this capital can be used to expand productivity and, indirectly, to change the knowledge and technological base of the system (note the long feedback arrows at the bottom of Figure 12.4).

As with Tables 12.1 and 12.2, Table 12.4 extracts the most crucial hypothesis from Hawley's many hypotheses. As territory and population size increase, because of new knowledge about production, transportation, and communication, it is possible and perhaps necessary to differentiate units around specific functions. This is particularly true for corporate units, which represent clusters of interdependencies revolving around a particular function. Categoric units form in response to threats, which ultimately stem from the competition that results from increases in population size, productivity, and markets. As the number of differentiated units in a system increases, the number of relations increases at an exponential rate, increasing mobility costs. Corporate and categoric units both tend to consolidate into larger networks, forming subsystems and reducing mobility costs. But the effects of corporate and categoric unit differentiation and consolidation on the concentration of power vary. Corporate units consolidate, centralize, and extend power and regulation, whereas categoric units form power blocks that diffuse power in a system of checks and balances.

As with the other propositions, the many specific hypotheses in Hawley's scheme can be deduced from these and from the scenario delineated.[39] Thus, the propositions

---

[39]Ibid., 106–108, 123–124.

Table 12.4 Basic Propositions on Patterns of Ecosystem Differentiation

1. The greater is the size of a population and its territory and the greater is the selection pressure stemming from competition among members of this population, the greater will be the differentiation of functions and the number as well as size of corporate units, to the maximum allowed by mobility costs.

2. The greater is the size of a population and the greater are the threats posed by competition and environmental change, the greater will be the number of categoric units, to the maximum allowed by mobility costs.

3. The greater are the number and size of both categoric and corporate units, the more will increases in number of relations occur at a geometric rate and the greater will be the amount of time and energy allocated to mobility.

4. The greater is the number of relations among units and the higher are the costs of mobility, the more likely are differentiated units to establish networks and combine into more inclusive subsystems, thereby reducing mobility costs.

5. The more concentrated is power, the more prominent will be networks and subsystems and the more extensive will be political regulation of units in the ecosystem.

in Tables 12.1, 12.2, and 12.4 do not do full justice to the depth and extent of Hawley's scheme. They are intended as more abstract statements rather than as the many "hypotheses" that punctuate Hawley's theory.

In sum, then, Hawley's ecological theory retains some important ideas of early sociology. One of these ideas is the obvious but often ignored view that "society" represents the adaptation of the human species to its environment. Another related idea is that it is not possible to understand human social organization without reference to the interchanges between the environment and the internal social structure. Yet another crucial idea is that the basic dynamics of a society revolve around (a) the aggregation of actors in physical space, competition, and differentiation and (b) integration through subsystem formation and centralization of power. Still another useful point is the emphasis on population size, territory, productivity, communication and transportation technologies, and competition as important causes of those macrostructural processes—differentiation, conflict, class formation, consolidation of power, and the like—that have long interested sociologists. Finally, a significant, though problematic, idea is that the altered flow of resources— energy, information, materials—into the system is the ultimate source of the growth and evolution of a social system.

Conclusions

Ecological models in sociological theory have all represented an analogy to the forces of evolution, particularly *natural selection* through competition among social units and individuals for resources in a given niche. Whether operating at the macro or meso level, these theories seek to demonstrate that certain parallel processes operate in populations of collective actors within societies and populations of species in the biotic world. Ecological theorizing in sociology originally emerged in functionalist theorizing about the stages of societal evolution, and as I have noted, functionalism initially disappeared because of its use of stage models of societal evolution from simple to complex forms. Functionalism reemerged in the 1950s, only to begin to decline in the 1970s and 1980s, but this time, theorizing about the stages and phases of evolution reemerged in the 1960s in sociology and, unlike functionalism, has remained a key form of evolutionary theorizing in the present day. It is these stage models of evolution that will be examined in the next chapter, but such models can also be seen in a number of diverse theoretical traditions, such as Marxist-inspired world-systems (Chapter 14), analysis and critical theory (Chapter 22), as well as in functional theories that still persist (Chapter 10).

Yet evolutionary theorizing has moved far beyond stage models. More purely Darwinian-inspired ideas have generated a whole new, more biological way of viewing social processes. And while these kinds of theories are still controversial in sociology, they are prominent in the social sciences and, hence, are not likely to disappear. The basic thrust of these models is to bring biological ideas into sociology in order to explain how particular types of behavior predispositions to act in certain ways evolved as a consequence of selection on the ancestors of *Homo sapiens* and on humans themselves. Thus, any analysis of evolutionary theorizing in sociology—as I seek to do in the next chapter—must move beyond stage models and ecological models and include a variety of more explicitly biological models.

CHAPTER 13

Evolutionary Theorizing

As we saw in the last chapter, the most prominent form of biologically inspired theorizing in sociology has been ecological, where competition and selection processes are seen as the force behind social differentiation of whole societies, spatial arrangements in urban areas, and distributions among populations of complex organizations. Alongside ecological approaches, developmental theories of societal evolution from simple to ever more complex forms have also persisted, arising with Herbert Spencer's and Émile Durkheim's functional theorizing and moving forward within a number of theoretical traditions in the second half of the twentieth century. As I emphasized, stage models of societal evolution developed hand in hand with functional theory and were rejected in the first decades of the twentieth century, taking functional theory with them (only to be kept alive in anthropology for the first half of the twentieth century).

Some early stage models of evolution were considered too ethnocentric, if not racist, in that they tended to see the end stage of evolution as something like Western European societies, with the implication that other societies were more "primitive" than the European ideal. There was some merit to this criticism, but it was overdrawn; and so while stage models went out of fashion in sociology for four decades, they came back in the 1960s in a more sophisticated form. And since the 1960s, viewing evolution as movement from simple to more complex sociocultural forms has spread outside of functionalism proper.

At about the same time, in the 1960s, more biologically inspired theories of evolution began to emerge within the social sciences. Some of these were ecological, but most came from outside the social sciences, at least initially. These theories used the Modern Synthesis of evolutionary theory to explain what appear to be universal human behavioral propensities as hardwired bioprogrammers into human neuroanatomy, and the underlying genotype of this anatomy. And they argued that patterns of social organization could be explained by understanding the evolution of these behavioral propensities—a line of argument that was extremely threatening to sociologists.

Over the last decades, these two, somewhat independent forms of evolutionary theorizing have converged, at least to some degree, but they still represent very distinctive forms of theorizing. In this chapter, I will begin with sociological theories of societal evolution that emphasize the stages and phases of sociocultural evolution, typically from simple to ever more complex forms. Then, I will turn to Darwinian-inspired approaches that are much more willing to bring biological ideas into the social sciences.

Stage Model of Societal Evolution

In the mid-1960s, evolutionary theorizing about stages of societal evolution reemerged. I have already outlined in broad contours in Chapter 10 the model in Talcott Parsons's theory[1] and, of course, the models of Herbert Spencer and Émile Durkheim in Chapters 3 and 7, respectively. Preceding Parsons's effort at developing a new stage model theory of societal evolution within his functional scheme was Gerhard Lenski's work on societal evolution and stratification.[2] By outlining a stage theory of societal evolution and, at the same time, concentrating on power, inequality, and potential conflict, Lenski's model was more in tune with the times—the conflict-ridden 1960s. Conflict theorizing was reemerging in the United States in the post-McCarthy era, when Marx could once again be examined in public places, and Lenski's model was received much better than Parsons's because it did not carry functionalist trappings and, instead, focused on power, inequality, and conflict. Subsequently, in association with Jean Lenski and, later, Patrick Nolan,[3] this early approach was broadened to a full macro-level theory of social organization; and more recently, Lenski himself reconfigured his theory to emphasize the ecological dynamics woven into the stage model of societal-level evolution.[4]

I will begin with Lenski's and his associates' analysis of societal evolution; then I will examine Parsons's stage model of evolution. I will complete the review of stage model theorizing with some of my own ideas from recent works. The second half of the chapter will move fully into evolutionary theories that incorporate biological reasoning into theory; some of these retain elements of stage modeling and ecological theorizing, but all of them emphasize that evolution worked on human neuroanatomy to create behavioral propensities that have large effects on the nature and dynamics of sociocultural formations.

---

[1]Talcott Parsons, *Societies: Evolutionary and Comparative Perspectives* (Englewood Cliffs, NJ: Prentice-Hall, 1966) and *The System of Modern Societies* (Englewood Cliffs, NJ: Prentice-Hall, 1971).

[2]Gerhard Lenski, *Power and Privilege: A Theory of Social Stratification* (New York: McGraw-Hill, 1966; repr., Chapel Hill: The University of North Carolina Press, 1984).

[3]Gerhard Lenski, Patrick Nolan, and Jean Lenski, *Human Societies: An Introduction to Macrosociology*, 7th ed. (New York: McGraw-Hill, 1995). For the most recent edition, see Patrick Nolan and Gerhard Lenski, *Human Societies*, 11th ed. (Boulder, CO: Paradigm Press, 2009).

[4]Gerhard Lenski, *Ecological-Evolutionary Theory: Principles and Applications* (Boulder, CO: Paradigm Press, 2005).

Gerhard Lenski's Theorizing on Societal Evolution

The Early Theory. The basic argument developed in *Power and Privilege: A Theory of Stratification* is that the *level of technology* determines, along with other factors, the *level of production* in a society. The higher is the level of technology in a society, the greater will be the level of economic production; and the higher is the level of production, the greater will be the amount of *economic surplus* in a society. And as the level of economic surplus increases, the more it can be usurped by those consolidating power, thereby increasing inequality and the privilege of those with this power. This basic set of dynamics is outlined in Figure 13.1.

The fundamental relationship among technology, production, economic surplus, and inequality in a society is mediated by a number of factors. One factor is the set of environmental or ecological conditions, such as the resources in the available geographical space, as well as the presence of other societies and the potential threats that they might pose. Another key factor is demographic, revolving around the size of a population and the profile of characteristics (e.g., age, ethnicity, class locations, religious affiliation, etc.). Still another set of factors is the nature of social organization generated, in particularly the form of polity and its degree of consolidation of power, but also other institutional systems such as structure of kinship, religion, law, education, and science. Yet another factor is the geopolitical situation of a society revolving around competition for resources and warfare with other societies. Still another factor is the value and ideological cultural systems that emerge and constrain patterns of social organization and action.

These additional factors are all labeled in Figure 13.1, but as the bold-faced arrows try to make clear, the primary factors in Lenski's model revolve around technology, production, surplus, consolidation of power, inequality, and system of stratification. What made this analysis appealing in the 1960s is that Lenski used a stage model of evolution to explain variations in the primary influences affecting the forces generating stratification. Thus, the lower is the level of technology, the lower will be the level of production in a society, and hence, the less will be the size of the productive surplus, if any, generated. And, without surplus, there is nothing to usurp by those consolidating power and, as a consequence, degree of stratification in a society will be low. The history of human societies, then, has revolved around a series of basic stages during which the level of technology, production, and surplus have all increased. The stages proposed by Lenski are very similar to those developed by Spencer (see Figure 3.2 on p. 48): hunting-and-gathering without a head; hunting-and-gathering with a head (and hence, the beginnings of polity); simple and advanced horticultural (gardening without animal power); simple and advanced agrarian (farming using animal power); industrial (relying on inanimate sources of power). Within each of these stages there are variations in the degree of development, but each stage defines the basic mode of technology that is used to gather resources and produce material products. There are also fishing variants for nomadic hunting-and-gathering, as well as herding variants for horticultural and agrarian societies. Moreover, there is a marine variant for agrarian societies.

Figure 13.1 Lenski's Basic Model of Stratification

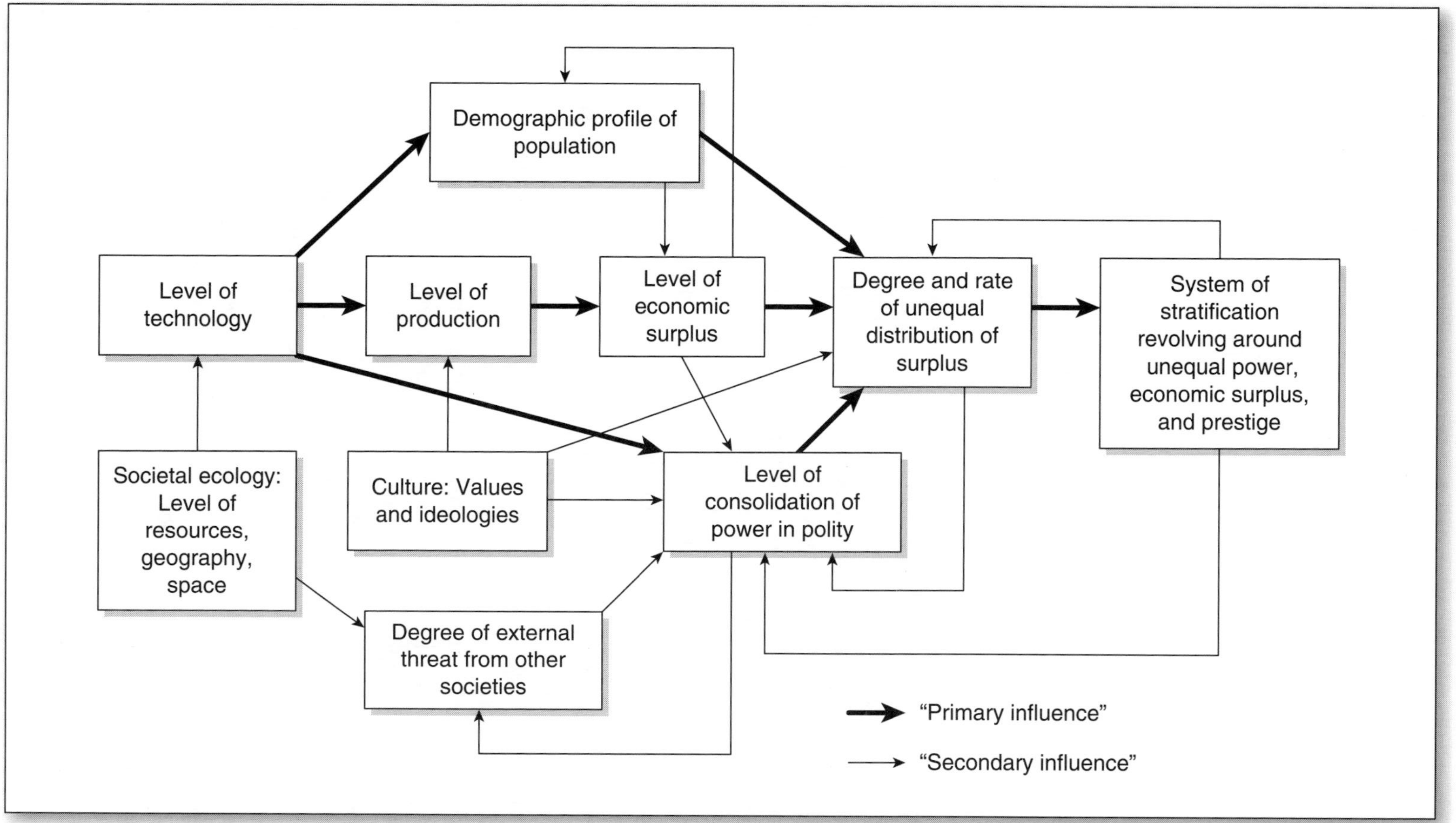

Lenski's analysis attempts to explain two facets of societal evolution. One is the same goal of earlier functional stage models: the growing complexity of societies by virtue increases the level of technology and production that, in turn, affect the number of people who can be supported in a society and, hence, a society's size. But this relationship is mediated by the consolidation of power in polity or government and, in turn, the degree to which power is used to usurp productive surplus to sustain elite privilege. So, Lenski like all functional theorists before him sought to isolate the driving forces of evolutionary history—in his case, technology, production, and economic surplus (whereas functionalists like Spencer and Durkheim tended to emphasize increases in population size and rates of growth as what kick starts the development of technologies and productive capacities). These demographic forces are also part of Lenski's model, as laid out in Figure 13.1, but they are given somewhat less significance than in early functional models outlining the stages of societal evolution.

The second facet of Lenski's effort is to explain the evolution and operation of stratification systems in human societies, with stratification hypothesized to increase with the level of technology, production, and surplus. In a very real sense, data assembled on societies at different stages of development are intended to assess the theory of inequality and stratification—thus, making this kind of evolutionary theorizing more in tune with the conflict theories that were emerging at the same time.

The hypothesized relationship among technology, production, surplus, and inequality is portrayed by the straight line in Figure 13.2, but the actual findings across stages of societal development were found more like those portrayed in the more curvilinear shape in Figure 13.2. The hypothesized relationship held up until the industrial stage. From hunting-and-gathering forward, stratification increases as technology and production generate ever more surplus that historically has led to the consolidation of power in polity and the usurpation of surplus—thereby, increasing the level of inequality in the stratification system. Going against this long-term evolutionary/historical trend, however, is a significant, though still rather modest decrease in inequality in industrial societies. This reversal requires an explanation, and hence, Lenski introduces what he terms secondary variables— (a) democratization of power, (b) reliance on education and its extensions to the masses as an important criterion for resource distribution, and (c) changes in societal ideologies toward advocating more equality or at least equality of opportunity. These variables become more highly valenced in industrial societies, and the result is a reversal of the long-term historical trend toward ever more inequality and stratification in human societies.

The influence of Lenski's analysis cannot be underestimated. He made stage modeling of evolutionary sequences respectable outside functional analysis because he emphasized the forces—power, inequality, and stratification—that are at the core of conflict theory, which was challenging functional theory in general and Parsons's version of functional and evolutionary theory in particular. And over the last five decades Lenski himself has continued to refine the model of societal evolution but, equally if not more important, a large number of theorists began to follow the path opened up by Lenski's *Power and Privilege.*

Figure 13.2 Hypothesized and Actual Trend in Inequality during Societal Evolution

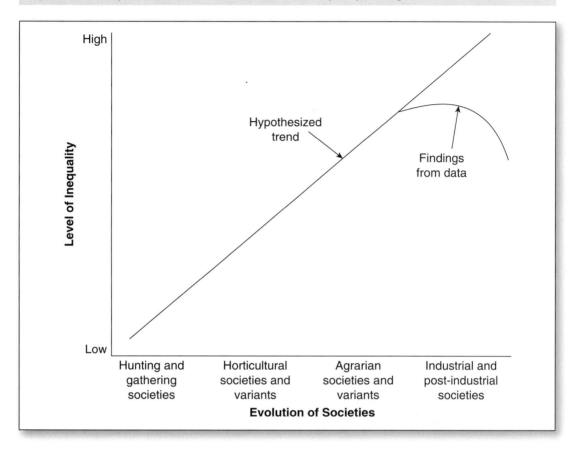

Gerhard Lenski, Patrick Nolan, and Jean Lenski's Evolutionary Theory

As Lenski continued to theorize on evolution, he increasingly added more biological and ecological forces to his analysis. Working with his wife before her early death and later with Patrick Nolan, Lenski began to include in his theory of societal development more Darwinian theoretic ideas as well as ideas that form the Modern Synthesis in biology—perhaps a good indicator of how much biological theorizing was beginning to influence the social sciences in the 1970s and 1980s.

Both biological and social evolution are, first, "based on records of experience that are preserved and transmitted from generation to generation in the form of coded systems of information" and, second, on "processes that involve random variation and selection" of those traits that promote adaptation to the environment.[5] Yet there are some important differences between biological and social evolution.

---

[5]Lenski, Nolan, and Lenski, *Human Societies,* 75.

One is that in organic evolution the genes are the preservers of the informational codes, whereas in social evolution cultural "symbol systems are the functional equivalents of the genetic alphabet."[6] Another difference revolves around the way that information is transmitted. In biological evolution, genetic information can be transmitted only through the reproduction of new organisms; moreover, diverse species cannot interbreed, so the transmission of information is limited to one species. In contrast, cultural information is more readily and broadly transmitted, moving from one type of society to another. The end result is that in biological evolution, speciation leads to ever new patterns of differentiation and diversification, whereas in social evolution the movement of information across societal types "is likely to eventuate in ever fewer and less dissimilar societies than exist today."[7] A related difference is that in biological evolution, both simple and complex species can continue to exist in their respective resource niches, whereas in social evolution simpler societal types tend to be extinguished by more complex types. Still another difference is that acquired traits can be transmitted through socialization, whereas in biological evolution such Lamarckian processes do not occur. An outcome of this difference is that genetic change in biological evolution is comparatively slow (because selection processes have to sort out genes across many generations), whereas cultural evolution can be very rapid (because new traits can be created, learned, transmitted, and diffused within one generation).

These similarities and differences lead to the recognition that (a) human societies are part of the natural world and subject to selection forces from both their biophysical and sociocultural environments, (b) humans like any other animal are influenced by their genetic heritage, and (c) only humans are the creators of their cultural heritage or the informational codes that guide behavior and social organization. A given society,[8] then, has social structural and cultural (symbolic) characteristics that, for analytical purposes, can be divided into (1) its population size and characteristics, (2) its culture or systems of symbols, particularly technologies, (3) its material products generated by the application of its technology to productive processes, (4) its organizational forms that structure activities, and (5) its institutional systems that combine (1) through (4) into systems addressing the basic problems of survival and adaptation for individuals and the society as a whole. These five components of a society influence, while being influenced by other forces: (a) a society's biophysical environment; (b) the social environment of other societies and their respective cultures; (c) the genetic heritage of humans as a species, namely an evolved ape; and (d) the prior social and cultural characteristics of a society as these continue to influence its internal operation and its adaptation to the external environment.

In this more recent analysis, Lenski's earlier emphasis on technologies as the driving force of social evolution is retained, but the argument is recast into an evolutionary

---

[6]Ibid., 75–76.

[7]Adapted from ibid., 21, 23–55; see also Gerhard Lenski, "Societal Taxonomies: Mapping the Social Universe." *Annual Review of Sociology* 20 (1994):33. See also Lenski, *Ecological-Evolutionary Theory*, 118.

[8]Lenski, "Societal Taxonomies," 23.

framework inspired by Darwin and the Modern Synthesis. As Lenski remarks, "It seems no exaggeration to say that advances in subsistence technology are functionally equivalent to adaptive changes in a population's gene pool; new energy resources and new materials enable populations to do things that they could not do before."[9]

Social evolution is a cumulative process in the sense that new technologies proving more adaptive alter the pattern of social organization, generally toward larger and more complex forms of organization. Two basic forces drive change in human societies:[10] (1) innovation where new information and social structural patterns are created, whether by chance or conscious intent and (2) extinction where old cultural and structural patterns are abandoned. Innovations in sociocultural evolution cause more rapid change than forces in biological evolution, because (a) humans have conscious capacities to develop new informational codes; (b) humans have "needs and desires" that are potentially "limitless" and, under certain conditions, drive them to make new discoveries as old needs are satisfied and new ones emerge; (c) humans can adopt the information of other societies through diffusion; (d) humans can force another society to adopt their informational codes through conquest and repression of older cultural and structural patterns, especially when larger and more complex societies conquer or co-opt smaller and less complex ones; (e) humans can institutionalize innovation in such structural forms as science, thereby creating a set of cultural codes and social structures specifically geared to constant innovation; and (f) humans can create complex interconnections among systems of information that force changes in other elements as changes in another occur.

Yet Lenski, Nolan, and Lenski stress that there are also forces operating to sustain continuity in the cultural systems that guide the organization of a population.[11] One force for continuity is *socialization*, in which older patterns are transmitted to each new generation. Another force is *ideology*, which preserves cultural systems and guides the transmission of culture from one generation to another. Still another force is the *systemic nature* of human sociocultural systems, which resist change in one element because so many other elements will be forced to change (although, as noted earlier, once change in one element does occur, it has a cascading effect and actually accelerates change). Another force is *vested interests*, especially of the powerful in stratified societies who have the power to suppress innovations when changes threaten status quo interests. Yet another force is *inertia*, where past practices appear to promote adaptation and sufficient satisfaction for individuals to resist adopting new practices whose impact cannot be fully known.

Yet despite these forces promoting continuity, the long-term historical record confirms that societal evolution has involved change, fueled by technological innovations, toward larger and more complex societies. Societies vary, of course, in their rates of innovation; these rates vary because of several important forces. First, the amount of information already possessed by a society greatly influences its capacity to create and adopt more information. Second, the size of a population is another

---

[9]Lenski, Nolan, and Lenski, *Human Societies,* 57–58.

[10]Ibid.

[11]Ibid., 84.

important factor because larger populations have more individuals who hold ideas and who can potentially generate new ideas. Third, the stability and nature of a society's environment, both social and biophysical, is another force of change; the more the environment changes, the more likely a society is to be innovative or adopt the innovations of another. Fourth, the nature of the innovations, per se, is a very significant factor; some innovations are fundamental and pave the way for additional innovations (for example, the discovery of metallurgy or new sources of energy stimulated even more innovations). And fifth, the ideology of a society greatly circumscribes the creation or adoption of innovations; powerful and conservative ideologies make it difficult for individuals to be innovative, while discouraging the diffusion of innovations from other societies.

Over the long course of societal development, however, productive technologies are the most important driving force of evolution. In the end, technological innovations can overcome the forces promoting continuity, even the ideologies and the vested interests of the powerful. The reason for this significance of technology is that those societies that can better gather, produce, and distribute resources will generate an economic surplus that can support a larger population and its differentiation into new organizational forms and institutional systems. Eventually, their technologies diffuse to other societies, and particularly so when larger, more complex societies conquer, co-opt, or out-compete smaller and less complex societies. Thus, a kind of "group selection" operates in the history of human societies, as more powerful societies (with better technologies, productive capacities, and organizational forms) impose their cultural systems and structural patterns on others through conquest, provide models and incentives for less developed societies to adopt their cultural and structural systems, or take the resources on which less developed societies depend for their survival.[12] These last points echo Spencer's argument that "survival of the fittest" operates at the group level where the better organized society will prevail in war and in economic competition over the less organized. Indeed, selection processes have favored an emerging world system of societies (see Niklas Luhmann's evolutionary argument in Chapter 10 and world-systems' analysis in Chapter 14).

Talcott Parsons's Stage Model of Evolution

Partly in response to intense criticism that functional analysis cannot explain change in social systems, Parsons developed an evolutionary model of societal change. Such a model did not silence the critics because the dynamics of power, stratification, and conflict were not sufficiently prominent in this theory; and this is the very kind of analysis that conflict theorists claimed functionalism cannot explain. Despite these criticisms, Parsons's theory helped bring stage model evolutionary theorizing back into sociology after nearly a fifty-year absence, and so it is worth examining this theory here.

---

[12]Ibid., 54. This is an idea that was originally proposed by Herbert Spencer, who emphasized that societies evolved from competition and war between societies, with the more complex, productive, and powerful society winning out in a struggle for the "survival of the fittest."

I will focus mostly on the first of the two slim volumes where this theory was outlined, *Societies: Evolutionary and Comparative Perspectives*,[13] and then just briefly summarize the key ideas in the second volume, *The System of Modern Societies*.[14] Parsons's theory begins with his general conception of the four action systems.

The Four Action Systems. As I reviewed in Chapter 10, Parsons began to conceptualize the social universe as composed of four action systems (see pp. 352–354): *cultural, social, personality,* and *organismic* (later termed *behavioral*). Each of these systems corresponded to one of the four functional requisites of action in general, with organismic meeting needs for *adaptation,* personality needs for *goal attainment,* social needs for *integration* of all action systems, and cultural needs for *latency* (tension management and pattern maintenance). Like all functional theories, such as those developed by Herbert Spencer and Émile Durkheim, Parsons argued that long-term societal evolution has been a process of differentiation; and in his eyes, this differentiation revolved around, first of all, differentiation *among* these action systems and, then, differentiation *within* these systems, particularly the cultural, social, and personality. That is, personality, social, and cultural systems began to differentiate from the organismic system and then from each other; and subsequent evolution revolved around increasing differentiation of social, cultural, and personality systems, particularly social systems. In many ways, Parsons was positing a kind of "mechanical solidarity" in Durkheim's terms because, in simple societies, the personality, social, and cultural systems are not differentiated from each other and are regulated by common cultural systems (see pp. 210–211). At the same time, Parsons was also drawing from Spencer, who saw the evolution of biological, social, psychological, and ethnical systems as evolving according to his law of evolution from homogeneous masses to ever more heterogeneity (see pp. 47–48).

Parsons also argued that this kind of differentiation generated, again à la Durkheim, integrative problems, but as these were resolved by new forms of culture and new units in the social system, societies became more adaptive. There was, then, a kind of *adaptive upgrading,* in Parsons's terms, to evolution because more complex systems have multiple ways to adapt and adjust to environmental contingencies.

Stages of Societal Evolution. Parsons's model is outlined in Figure13.3. He posited, as had Spencer, two types of "primitive societies" (low and advanced), two types of intermediate societies (archaic and advanced), and, finally, a transition to modern societies. Parsons's model corresponds roughly to Lenski's conception of the hunting-and-gathering (nomadic and settled), horticultural, agrarian, and industrial/postindustrial stages.

One key dynamic in the transition from one type of societal formation to another revolves around development of an earlier stage of evolution to a critical threshold point of differentiation in particular social structures and cultural forms; and once this threshold was reached, it then becomes possible for further evolution

---

[13]Talcott Parsons, *Societies* and *The System of Modern Societies.*

[14]Ibid.

Figure 13.3 Parsons's Image of Societal Evolution Up to Modernity

Primitive Societies		Intermediate Societies		Transition to Modern Societies
Low	*Advanced*	*Archaic*	*Advanced*	
Cultural System Differentiation:	**Cultural System Differentiation:**	**Cultural System Differentiation:**	**Cultural System Differentiation:**	**Key Cultural System Changes:**
symbolic communication religious beliefs about: magic supernatural forces powers of ancestors hunting-gathering technologies conceptions of territories normative regulation of: marriage economic roles kin roles relations between age/sex categories	Religio eliefs begin to legitimate: power and polity property inequality and stratification control of territories Normative systems elaborate and regulate: systems of lineages more complex divisions of labor emerging administrative structures of polity settlements and communities Expanded technologies	Written language system that: expands symbol systems, including: technological, religious, political, historical, norms and emerging laws allows for increased differentiation between and within social and cultural systems allows for increased structural differentiation in social system	Expansion of writing, leading to: coherent set of quasi-codified religious beliefs accumulation of knowledge and technology histories and stable traditions written contracts in expanded economy and emerging markets more codified sets of more universalistic laws in emerging	Universalistic and contract law Beliefs about capitalism New technologies using inanimate and fossil fuel sources of energy Ideologies emphasizing rights of persons and political democracy Sense of societal community, unified by common cultural and sustained by commitments to this culture
Social System Differentiation:	**Social System Differentiation:**	**Social System Differentiation:**	**Social System Differentiation:**	**Key Social System Changes:**
Kinship units (nuclear) Band Economic and kin divisions of labor	Settlements and communities Lineages and linkages among nuclear kin units Hierarchies of power in emerging polity Emerging stratification system Expanded economic and kin divisions of labor Emerging religious structures	Larger, more permanent settlements Centralized polity and expanded administrative functions Control of larger territories by polity and organized coercion Expanded religious structures	Increased differentiation among polity, kinship, religion Initial differentiation of legal system Expansion of markets and market relations among social structures Increasing use of money and credit markets Full institutionalization of contracts	**Emergence** of democractic polity Expansion of positivistic and universalistic legal legal system Expansion of free, profit oriented markets using money and credit Ascendance of polity over religion as agent of social control Legitimation of polity by law and more secular legal codes Expansion of educational system and access to citizenry to this system Institutionalization of science and innovation

Evolution = Increasing differentiation among and within cultural, social, and personality systems or differentiation among and within the four action systems. For example, in Parsons's view, industrial societies could not evolve, nor could truly advanced agrarian societies, without the evolution of a system of laws that contained elements of universalism (or equal application of laws to all types of actors). Thus, until this system of law evolved in the Roman civil codes, societies could not reach the necessary threshold to evolve more complexity.

Key Elements in Stages of Evolution. For Parsons, each stage of evolution involves the emergence of several key elements that, when all are present, allow a society to reach the threshold for evolution to the next stage. Let me briefly highlight these elements for the stages delineated in Figure 13.3.

Low Primitive Stage. The basic components of the simplest society are a means of *symbolic communication*, *kinship*, *religion*, and *technology*. For Parsons, symbolic communication revolves around "constitutive symbolism," which can denote and represent others, territories, oneself, lineages, and other properties of the social world. This kind of symbolism, in turn, enables members of a population to develop rules and regulations guiding interaction, in two senses: first, rules and regulations allow interactions to occur and, second, they regulate and control the interaction. In turn, such regulated interactions facilitate the formation of key institutional activities, such as marriage and kinship, economic activity, and religious practices; and, in turn, these activities increase the degree of differentiation among social structures and the stocks of symbols in culture, while enabling individuals to develop more unique personalities.

In low, primitive societies, kinship is the principle unit of social organization in the social system. Such kinship systems reveal incest rules and marriage rules, with (nuclear) kin units of mother, father, and children revealing very little differentiation from each other. The only differentiation in these low, primitive societies is between age and sex categories.

Advanced Primitive Societies. With the level of development outlined above, it becomes possible for a more complex primitive system to evolve. The social system begins to differentiate into clans within the larger kinship system; and these begin to appropriate territories and to create notions of property; and as property is acquired, inequalities and stratification begin to evolve. Stratification, however, generates integrative problems that require legitimization; and religion becomes the principle integrative mechanism, with religious beliefs emphasizing the right of those with resources to horde wealth. As religion provides this "integrative function," it becomes more complex and differentiated structurally (with distinctive religious personnel) and culturally (with legitimating beliefs about supernatural forces granting power and privilege).

Inequalities in property and the maintenance of these inequalities also stimulate the evolution of polity, or the consolidation and centralization of power around the chiefs of the wealthiest (in terms of property) lineages in clans. While still at a rudimentary level, kin-based incumbents in the emerging polity govern territories, carry out the chief's work, and form a military system to sustain order or to conquer more territory. Thus, as societies move from settled hunter-gatherers to horticulture, they reveal more cultural and social structural complexity.

At the cultural level, they have more complex communication codes, technologies, religious beliefs, and legitimating ideologies; at the structural level, they evidence more complex and differentiated systems of kinship (lineages and clans), stratification, religion, and polity (forming an incipient bureaucracy for administration and warfare). With this cultural and structural base, societies can evolve into a more intermediate stage of societal development, composed of two sub-stages, the archaic and the advanced.

The Archaic Stage. The key invention marking this stage is the invention of writing, which enables the cultural system to expand and differentiate. Symbolism is now freed from human memory and from face-to-face interaction. Indeed, symbolism is no longer tied to time and space; and this feature of communication allows for the efficient accumulation of knowledge, the recording of history, the preservation of customs and traditions, and the development of systematic and more complex systems of religious beliefs. It now becomes ever more possible for generations to build up knowledge and for innovations to accumulate; and as this accumulation occurs, culture becomes increasingly autonomous and differentiated from all other action systems.

Literacy is, of course, not universal in archaic societies; rather it is confined to a relatively few positions, primarily in religious and political structures. Yet as literacy comes to dominate religion and the administrative structures of the developing polity, these become further differentiated from kinship and, hence, more autonomous as institutional domains. Moreover, particularly in the administrative system of polity, differentiation will increase, enabling it to expand its influence and control, with the king legitimated—and considered almost "sacred"—by the legitimating power of religious beliefs.

Yet even as polity and its administrative structure expand and differentiate, it is not a full civil bureaucracy because recruitment and promotion in the system are still highly ascriptive, tied to kin units and religious affiliation (and perhaps other criteria such as ethnicity). Still, the growth and differentiation of this administrative structure increases the capacity of government to mobilize and coordinate activities, especially with respect to war-making, public works, taxation, and redistribution of resources. In expanding its activities, polity dramatically increases the adaptive capacity of a society to its environment and, in so doing, sets the stage for a more advanced intermediate stage.

Advanced Intermediate Societies. In more advanced intermediate societies, increased differentiation among polity, religion, and kinship occurs, and polity continues to differentiate internally as ever more power is concentrated and resources are extracted through taxation to support the elaboration of the administrative structure. In turn, stratification increases, and the class system differentiates to some degree. These large changes in societies come with the increasing secular content of law, thereby differentiating it from religion even further.

But, more important, a more universalistic legal system begins to emerge, which in turn gives the economy a more autonomous base, while insulating it from the continued ascription evident in polity and religion. Law and universalism in economic affairs encourage the development of money as the dominant medium of exchange, the expansion of markets that begin to differentiate to meet ever more diverse demand, the increased velocity of trade and commerce within and, increasingly, between societies, and the institutionalization in law of binding contracts on economic actors. These kinds of transformations are only possible when the economy is isolated from the ascription still prevalent in polity, religion, and kinship. But once law becomes more universalistic in the economic sphere and encourages the development of markets using money and credit, as well as contracts, the level of differentiation within a society will increase. Indeed, markets, money, contracts, and universalistic law are differentiating machines; and this differentiation increases the differentiation among the psychological action system (in terms of individuals' demands and preferences in markets), the cultural system composed of laws and other symbol systems that can be codified and written down, and social systems of more complex relations among diverse actors, not only in the economy but also in other institutional domains.

The Transition to the Modern System of Societies. Modernity grows out of this cultural, structural, and psychological base of advanced agrarian societies. Economies operating in profit-seeking markets create incentives for increased production, which eventually results in the development of industrial technologies harnessed to capitalism and the cultural ideology of capitalism. Universalistic laws and contracts in the economy provide a template for the same types of transactions within and among other institutional domains, eventually paving the way for movements toward political democracy and the decline of ascription in many institutional domains. The consolidation of power in polity and the expansion of culture eventually lead to what Parsons somewhat vaguely defined as "the societal community," or a sense of a population that they represent a culturally unified territorial unit regulated by polity; and once this sense of what today might be termed "nationalism" emerges, this sociocultural base coupled with common currencies, more dynamic markets, and universalistic laws increase the likelihood of political democracy, which Parsons saw as the last element of societal evolution.

Without going into more detail, we can see the thrust of Parsons's analysis. It is very functional in that it emphasizes differentiation among and within action systems, particularly personality, culture, and social action systems (each of which meets a fundamental functional need or requisite). And it seeks to outline the sequence of key transformations that pushed society along a number of stages during the course of societal evolution toward the current, postindustrial form. For Parsons, certain events had to occur before other elements in societies could evolve, and thus, each stage of evolution has been preceded by transformations that reach a critical threshold point that allows for, and indeed often pushes for, new kinds of social and cultural systems. Thus, Parsons's theory, unlike many other stage models, does not see a master force driving evolution; rather, there is a general increase in complexity or differentiation among and within the four action systems, but at different stages of societal development—somewhat different sociocultural forces and formations were necessary for movement to the next stage in societal evolution.

Jonathan Turner's Evolutionary Analysis of Macrostructures

In my efforts to develop general theory on all fundamental social processes, I find myself using a stage model of evolution when examining the macro level of social reality.[15] My goal has not been to theorize about the prime movers of the stages of evolution, or even the stages themselves, in the same manner that Lenski and Parsons have. Rather, my goal has been to develop abstract principles that explain the dynamics of the macro realm in all times and places—hence, at any stage of societal evolution. This is what is often seen as "grand theorizing," and such theorizing is considered passé in many contemporary circles, but if sociology does not develop general theories, it cannot explain the whole social universe. For many, the goal of theory is to chop and dice up the social universe into small bits and pieces, with the goal being to develop very narrow theories on each of these bits and pieces. Such work is often important, but at some point, theories must be consolidated; the conceptual Humpty Dumpty needs to be put back together.

Problems in Theoretical Sociology. At the macro level of social organization, contemporary sociology has very active theorizing in world systems, or the analysis of intersocietal systems, which often posits stages and phases of development in intersocietal networks (see Chapter 14). The macrodynamics of institutions, however, has been relegated to the analysis of the organizational basis of institutions, but the notion of institutions themselves is left under-theorized, or not even clearly defined, for that matter.[16] Theorizing on the dynamics of stratification in general has virtually disappeared, and in the United States the analysis of stratification has been chopped up into ideologically driven critical theories about class, race, and gender (see Chapter 24), with stratification as a whole system being rather neglected. Even conflict processes generated by stratification have declined from their peak in the 1960s and 1970s, when theories building on Marx, Weber, and Simmel were once commonplace. There are no theories of

---

[15]Jonathan H. Turner, *Theoretical Principles of Sociology*, 3 vols., vol. 1: *Macrodynamics*, vol. 2: *Microdynamics*, and vol. 3: *Mesodynamics* (New York: Springer, 2010–2011). Volume 1 on macrodynamics is the relevant volume for this section. See also the earlier *Macrodynamics: Toward a Theory on the Organization of Human Populations* (New Brunswick, NJ: Rutgers University Press, 1995).

[16]Seth Abrutyn and Jonathan H. Turner. "The Old Institutionalism Meets the New Institutionalism." *Sociological Perspectives*, 54 (2011):283–306.

societies as a distinctive macro-level unit, as was once a goal in sociology. When we retain a vision of societies as having evolved over a long period of time into ever more complex forms—as was once a vision shared by all sociologists before the twentieth century—the partitioning of even macro-sociology, to say nothing of meso- and micro-sociology, into many diverse and highly specialized theoretical research programs becomes glaringly apparent. This is why I set out two decades ago on my own theoretical crusade to bring grand theory back into sociology, ever since its last remnants were destroyed by critics of functional theory.

Saving the Useful Part of Functionalism. It is not necessary to bring functionalism back, however. If we seek out the fundamental properties and forces that have driven the macro realm of reality from the beginnings of human societies and, presumably, into all future societies, we need data on all types of societies that have ever existed. The goal is not to theorize about industrialism, agrarianism, horticulture, or any past or future stage of evolution but, instead, to theorize about *the common dynamics of all societies,* from their very beginning to the present day. This is what I have tried to do in my three-volume *Theoretical Principles of Sociology,*[17] and somewhat to my surprise (before I thought about it), I found myself using the data that I had assembled on diverse societies from hunting-and-gathering to all subsequent stages of evolutionary development to assess the plausibility of the models and propositions that I was developing. The more the dynamic forces outlined in these models and propositions seemed to operate in diverse societal and intersocietal formations that have been developed by humans, the more confident I became that, perhaps, I had formulated some of sociology's basic laws about the macro-level universe. Many of these laws represented only refinement of those implicitly articulated by the early masters of sociology examined in Chapters 2 through 8, but others incorporate the data and conceptual work from highly specialized fields that have emerged over the last fifty years.

The critical point here is that using evolutionary models, and the data on which they are based, in developing general theory at the macro level is essential for assessing the plausibility of theories. And, I suspect, this is one of the reasons why stage models of societal evolution made a comeback during the mid-twentieth century; they were needed in macro-level theorizing because they provide a wide array of data on diverse types of societal formations over the long-term evolutionary history.

Selection as a Driving Force of Evolution. I visualize the macrodynamic universe as driven by five fundamental forces—population, production, regulation, distribution, and reproduction.[18] These are not functionally requisite but, instead, properties and contingencies of the social universe—definitions are provided in Table 13.1. They vary in their valences, and if these valences increase, then they generate *selection pressures* on human populations. These can be Darwinian or *Durkheimian*

---

[17]Turner, *Theoretical Principles of Sociology,* vol. 1: *Macrodynamics.*

[18]Ibid., 116–125, 184–186, 223, 225, 275.

Table 13.1   Macrodynamic Forces

1. *Population:* The absolute number, rate of growth, composition, and distribution of members of a society
2. *Production:* The gathering of resources from the environment, the conversion of these resources into commodities, the creation of services to facilitate gathering and conversion
3. *Distribution:* The infrastructures for moving resources, information, and people about a territory as well as the exchange systems for distributing commodities and services among members of a society and, potentially, members of other societies
4. *Regulation:* The consolidation and centralization of power around four bases of power (coercion, administration, material incentives, and symbolic) and the creation of cultural systems to coordinate and control actors within institutional domains and stratification systems
5. *Reproduction:* The procreation of new members of a population and the transmission of culture to these members as well as the creation and maintenance of structural formations sustaining life and social order

(competition among social units in resource niches) or what I call *Spencerian*, or pressures on actors to develop responses and solutions to selection pressures in the absence of any existing structures that can successfully respond to these pressures. For example, if populations grow, then this growth generates pressures of its own, but it does more: it raises the valences of the other forces. New kinds of social structures and new systems of culture will have to be developed to meet pressures for more production, distribution, regulation, and reproduction. If new adaptive responses cannot occur, then the population and the society (and the constituent sociocultural formations organizing its activities) will disintegrate. Thus, much selection in sociocultural systems is not Darwinian but, rather, Spencerian. In Spencerian selection, selection occurs under low density of structures, or the nonexistence of any structures capable of solving new selection pressures from the five forces of the macrodynamic realm.

These selection pressures will often, but not always, cause the emergence of entrepreneurs who seek to mobilize cultural and organizational resources to meet the new challenges posed by selection pressures. There is no guarantee that entrepreneurs will emerge or, if they emerge, will be successful in creating new kinds of corporate units (units with divisions of labor to achieve goals) that can deal with the problems posed by Spencerian selection pressures. The theory thus begins with an analysis of the conditions that increase the valences of macrodynamic forces, the conditions that increase the likelihood (or vice versa) that entrepreneurs will emerge, and the conditions under which they are more likely to be successful in consolidating resources and forming new kinds of corporate units and new systems of cultural symbols. The basic contours of these forces of the macro level of social organization and the selection pressures that they generate are outlined in Figure 13.4.

Figure 13.4   Turner's Analysis of Macrodynamic Forces and the Evolution of Sociocultural Formations

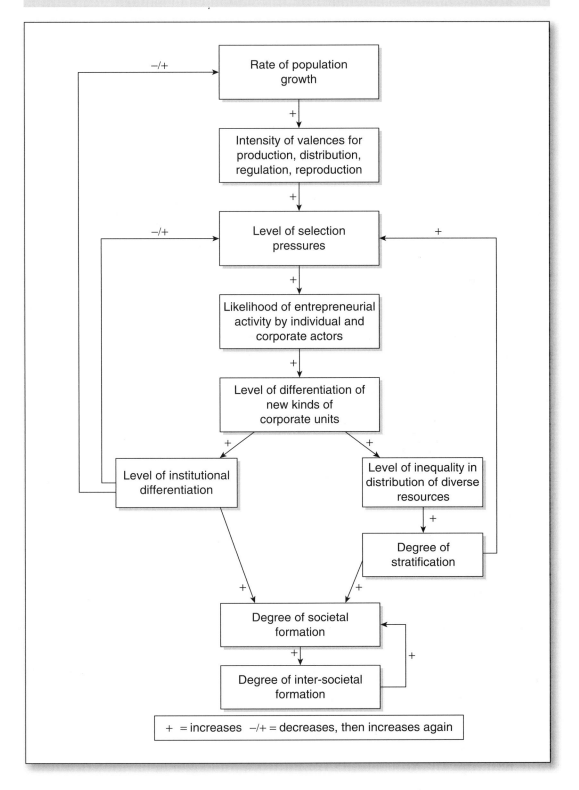

Building a Simple Analytical Scheme. Figure 13.5 outlines the basic properties of the social universe, when stripped to the barest number. This scheme is not a theory; rather, it simply denotes the basic types of sociocultural formations at the three basic levels of social organization. At the meso level, the dynamics of *corporate* and *categoric* units need to be explained as responses to forces driving actors at the macro and micro levels of social organization. At the macro level, the dynamics of institutional domains, stratification systems, societies, and intersocietal systems need to be explained if sociology is to have a viable theory of societal evolution. And at the micro level, the forces and dynamics driving encounters, and the relations among these, need to be explained. Complexity in the theory does not inhere in the typology in Figure 13.5 but in the propositions that describe the dynamics of the elements portrayed in the diagram.

Figure 13.5 A Simple Conceptual Scheme

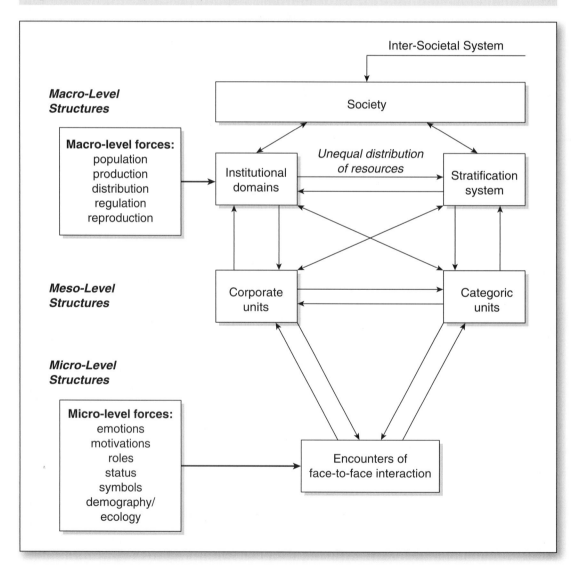

Theory will thus be a series of sociological laws on macro and micro forces, on the selection pressures that they generate, and on the emerging dynamics of encounters, corporate and categoric units, institutional domains, stratification systems, societies, and intersocietal systems. The result is a theory that articulates a series of sociological laws (and analytical models) that can be tested; a theory that covers all of the basic structures that organize the micro, meso, and macro realms of the social universe; a theory that makes linkages among these levels; a theory that is evolutionary without being locked into stages, but only changes over time; a theory that still captures what made the notion of requisites so appealing; and, most significantly, a theory that is explanatory (via propositions and analytical models) rather than classificatory. For more details, see my three-volume *Theoretical Principles of Sociology*.[19] Functionalism can, in a manner, be saved from itself, but it no longer looks like most functionalist schemes that build up a complex analytical scheme (Parsons) or a suggestive but vaguely discursive one (Luhmann).

As Parsons and Lenski both have emphasized, evolution is the building up of macro-level social structures from corporate and categoric units and the development of cultures attached to these units and the larger structures—for example, institutional domains (economy, polity, kinship, religion, etc.), stratification systems, societies, and intersocietal systems—that are constructed from meso-level corporate and categoric units. And like all functionalists, from Durkheim to the present, it is necessary to understand how differentiation of structure and culture becomes integrated during the course of societal evolution. This integration represents a selection pressure for regulation on actors, and unless they can build up new integrative formations and new systems of culture, evolution will—as Parsons emphasized—stall and perhaps cause societal disintegration to a simpler form. One critical idea to be taken from functional sociology is the notion of generalized symbolic media (see Chapter 10) because, ultimately, these media are used to build up culture that can integrate more complex and differentiated social systems.

Generalized Symbolic Media and Cultural Integration. As entrepreneurs mobilize resources, they organize people into new kinds of divisions of labor within corporate units capable of responding to selection pressures. If these units prove successful, they will be copied by other actors—thereby setting off their reproduction. At the same time, entrepreneurs use symbolic resources to regulate activities and justify and legitimate their actions and the new sociocultural formations that these actions create. Functional theorists, like Talcott Parsons and Niklas Luhmann, conceptualized these symbol systems as *generalized symbolic media* that are articulated and exchanged among actors. Depending on the symbolic media developed, these media become part of the culture of emerging institutional domains. For example, as Simmel first emphasized (see Chapter 6), *money* is a symbol of value (rarely does the money itself—that is the paper on which value is expressed by numbers—have inherent value); similarly, *power* as a symbolic medium is a highly valued resource, as are other symbolic media such a *love, health, knowledge, learning, competition*, and *aesthetics*. These are symbols that are a part of discourse among individuals and collective units

---

[19]Ibid., See Footnote 15.

engaged in particular kinds of activities that will eventually form a new, or change an old, institutional domain. But the media are more than symbolic; they are also *valued resources* that become unequally distributed and, hence, form the basis of a stratification system.

As these symbolic media are used, they also carry evaluations of what is good/bad and appropriate/inappropriate. They become evaluative and, if in wide circulation, are codified into *institutional ideologies* about what should, and should not, occur within particular institutional domains. For instance, the ideology of polity is built from the symbolic medium of *power;* the ideology of production, especially in a capitalist system, is built from the symbolic medium of *money;* the ideology of medicine is built from the symbolic medium of *health;* the system of law is constructed from symbols about *influence and justice;* the medium of kinship revolves around the medium of *love/loyalty;* the medium of religion is *sacredness/piety;* the medium of education is *learning;* and so on for all institutional domains.

As these symbolic media are used in the formation of new corporate units to address selection pressures, they become part of the culture of these organizational units, while framing and forming the basis of the *ideology* of the emerging institutional domain—e.g., economy, kinship, religion, polity, science, medicine, education, etc. Thus, the evolution of institutional domains, whether entirely new domains or significant transformations of existing domains, is built from congeries of corporate units that are integrated by structural and cultural mechanisms codified into *ideologies* that specify what should occur within a domain.

Thus, a large part of the theory that I develop consists of propositions about how the structure and culture of domains evolves by virtue of linking corporate units and culturally legitimating these linkages with ideologies. Moreover, generalized symbolic media are also the terms of discourse among people in a domain—e.g., capitalists talk about *money* incessantly, politicians about *power,* educators about *learning,* scientists about *new knowledge,* and members of churches about *sacredness and piety*. From this discourse, the culture of the corporate units within a domain is built from its symbolic medium as it is translated into normative expectations in the division of labor of a corporate unit. And, moreover, the symbolic medium is inherently rewarding and, thus, becomes the valued resource distributed by the corporate units in each, differentiated institutional domain—that is, economy, polity, kinship, religion, law, education, sport, art, etc.

Symbolic media circulate among corporate units within and between institutional domains; and thus, many domains have multiple media circulating. For example, polity franchises to actors in the domain of education certain limited *rights to power* as authority to organize and run an educational system; the polity does the same for religion; most corporate units in most domains in modern societies pay their incumbents with money, and so money also circulates. But some domains are more insulated, as is the case where kinship revolves around the medium of *love/loyalty*, and while some *money* (from the economic domain) and *authority* (from polity) circulate, their influence is less than in other domains because "love" should not be "tainted" by money (which is one of the basic tenets of the ideology of kinship in many societies). This circulation of media is often viewed critically, as is the case when academics bemoan the "corporatization" of university (i.e., bemoan the influence of money). But when media circulate, this can operate as a means of integrating highly differentiated societies because, as media circulate, so do the ideologies of a domain that have been built from these media. The result is that dominant institutional domains—say, economy, polity, education, science, and, in some societies, religion—will have their media circulate to most other domains, and as the ideologies of these domains are piggybacked on the symbolic medium, they will often be consolidated into *meta-ideologies*, which are mergers of several ideologies. These meta-ideologies also provide a basis for cultural integration across differentiated institutional domains. I do not have the space to outline the propositions that describe the conditions under which media circulate, become dominant, and become codified into meta-ideologies, but these events can be theorized in ways that are testable—often with the data from the diverse types of societies portrayed in stage model evolutionary schemes.

Symbolic Media and Stratification. Since symbolic media are also valued resources, they are distributed unequally in corporate units—usually as an outcome of an incumbent's place in the division of labor of a corporate unit. Thus, symbolic media are not only the symbolic building blocks of ideologies and norms, but they are *also the valued resources that are distributed unequally*. As such, they generate stratification systems. Historically, sociologists have focused on *money* and *power* (both of which are symbolic media) as the most important resources distributed unequally in a stratification system. Some schemes like Lenski's theory of stratification also note that *prestige,* as a generalized marker of social worth, is also part of the unequal distribution of a stratification system. But, in my view, *all* symbolic media are valued resources. And hence, the unequal distribution of resources involves *many more* resources than is typically conceptualized in sociological accounts of stratification. Not just *money* and *power* from economy and polity, respectively, but *love/loyalty* (family), *learning* (education), *knowledge* (science), *sacredness/piety* (religion), *aesthetics* (art), and all other symbolic media are distributed unequally by corporate units in various institutional domains. And, the more of these symbolic media that are held by people and their families, the more they can also enjoy more generalized reinforcements, such as *prestige* and *positive emotions*.[20]

What is important here is that some of these symbolic media are more equally distributed than other media. If emphasis is only on money and power, then inequality will be seen as greater in a society, whereas if other symbolic media as valued resources are also part of the assessment of the level of inequality, then individuals may not feel so deprived compared with their rich and powerful counterparts in other classes. Thus, inequalities in the distribution of money and power are, to some extent, countered by more equality in the distribution of, say, *love/loyalty, sacredness/piety, learning,* and perhaps *health*. And this more equal distribution can reduce the sense of deprivation that individuals in the class system feel, and in fact,

---

[20]Jonathan H. Turner, "The Stratification of Emotions: Some Preliminary Generalizations," *Sociological Inquiry*, 80 (2010):168–199.

it can make the boundaries of the class system, except at the very top (rich and powerful) and very bottom (impoverished and powerless), rather mushy. As is evident in the "middle classes" of a postindustrial society, their boundaries are porous because members have some money, plus somewhat varying shares of other generalized symbolic media. As a result, class homogeneity will decline, and if it declines, so does the clear, linear rank-ordering of moral worth since members have many additional symbolic media and the ideologies built from these media to measure favorably their moral worth, even if they do not have power or money.

Thus, part of a theory of macrodynamics requires propositions specifying the conditions under which symbolic media circulate to varying degrees; and these propositions then become part of a general theory of stratification. The tensions among classes and the potential for conflict generated by inequalities in the stratification system will be increased or mitigated depending on *which* and *how many* symbolic media are distributed unequally in a society. Again, to test out propositions derived from this analysis often requires, as Lenski first realized, analysis of stratification in the types of societies that can be found in stage models of evolution.[21]

Evolution, Differentiation, and Structural Integration. Analysis of institutional domains and stratification systems as part of the macro-level social universe inevitably takes us back to the question of integration so central to early functional analysis—as I emphasized earlier. As I outlined above, generalized symbolic media, as they circulate across institutional domains and as they are codified into ideologies and meta-ideologies, represent one powerful source of cultural integration, as Durkheim emphasized (even though he did not conceptualize this cultural integration in terms of generalized symbolic media). There is also, as all functionalists emphasized and, in reality, all sociologists as well, a structural basis of integration in societies. Differentiation of any sort, as stage model theorists and all functionalists have stressed, generates selection pressures for what I term regulation, and such regulation is created, if possible, by actors responding to these pressures as they generate symbolic media as terms of discourse and then ideology formation and as they attempt to forge new kinds of structural arrangements. Since I have already addressed the cultural basis of integration, let me now turn to the structural bases of macro-level integration.

I make no assumptions about whether particular structural mechanisms of integration are good or bad; rather, a theory predicts when various types of mechanisms of integration are likely to be activated, and with what effect on what structures of the macro realm of social reality. As I approached the issue of integration, it became immediately apparent that a wide range of societies was needed to assess propositions, and so, once again, stage models of societal evolution provided useful data. There is a variety of structural mechanisms of integration of corporate units within and between institutional domains; and in my theory, I emphasize[22]

---

[21]Lenski, *Power and Privilege.*

[22]For a tabular presentation of structural modes of integration, as they emerge in response to selection pressures for integration, during various stages of societal evolution, see Turner, *Theoretical Principles,* vol. 1, 224–227; also 231–234, for a tabular summary of the modes of cultural integration for societies at different stages of evolution.

(1) *segmentation* (reproduction of structurally and culturally equivalent corporate units); (2) *structural differentiation* (production of different units to manage complex selection pressures); (3) *structural interdependences* among differentiated units through (a) *structural inclusion* or embedding of smaller in larger corporate units, (b) *structural overlaps* among corporate units, and (c) *structural mobility* of incumbents across differentiated corporate units; (4) *structural domination* of corporate units by those with more power; and (5) *structural segregation* in time and space of corporate units with incompatible goals.

We can illustrate how useful stage models can be in assessing the conditions under which one or the other of these mechanisms dominate. Segmentation is the primary mode of integration among hunter-gathers, as both Spencer and Durkheim recognized; structural interdependences must increase as differentiation of corporate units and the institutional domains in which they are located occurs. Yet, historically, the consolidation of power and domination have also been responses to selection pressures generated by differentiation and problems of regulation (coordination and control). Indeed, structural interdependences only increased dramatically in societal evolution when markets and other distributive mechanisms expanded. Thus, by looking at data from hunter-gatherers, horticulturalists (and variants of these), agrarian societies (and their maritime and herding variants), and industrial and postindustrial formations, I could see the conditions under which one or the other of these various mechanisms dominates institutional integration and, hence, societal integration as well.

Similarly, mechanisms of cultural integration among texts, technologies, traditions, values, ideologies, and norms could only be assessed by looking at societies at different stages of evolution. For example, hunter-gatherers have only two basic units—bands and families—which means that they have differentiated only one institutional domain, kinship, although elements of religion are evident, as is an incipient polity among settled hunter-gatherers. Thus, cultural integration had to be built around *love/loyalty* in nomadic hunter-gatherers, since no other symbolic media had yet evolved. Indeed, the evolution of societies is, as the first functionalist emphasized, the successive differentiation of new institutional domains (built from new types of corporate units), and thus the only way to see the shift in modes of cultural integration is by examining how cultural systems change with (a) institutional differentiation and (b) emergence and then elaboration of the stratification system, which is also integrated by meta-ideologies built up from the ideologies of dominant institutional domains.

In turning to stratification system integration, it increasingly became evident to me that very low and high degrees of stratification were well integrated. (Again, forms of integration are not evaluated; they are either effective or ineffective in sustaining a population in its environment.) Systems of high stratification are sustained by domination at every level of society and at every linkage among corporate and categoric units. Low levels of stratification occur in societies where power is not consolidated because there is, as Lenski emphasized, a lack of economic surplus to distribute unequally. It is in societies in between these extremes that diverse patterns of structural and cultural integration can be found. For example, simple horticulturalists use *structural embedding* or *inclusion* of nuclear kinship units in lineages, which are in turn embedded subclans inside clans that are often moieties; and this system of structural embedding as a mechanism of integration is legitimated by cultural mechanisms, such as ideologies built from the symbolic medium of *love/loyalty* in kinship. Other mechanisms of integration are also part of this system. For example, even though kin units are differentiated, they tend to be reproduced across territories, and so there is a *segmentation* and structural equivalence processes in play; that is, nuclear units, lineages composed of nuclear units, and clans built from lineages are much the same in different villages and even in different horticultural societies. There is also a pattern of *domination* evident in these systems, a pattern that is also the same across territories of horticulturalists, with kin leaders of one clan often assuming dominance over those of others as a kind of "paramount chief." Once *power* as a symbolic medium is introduced into the hierarchy of kin units, the ideology built from *love/loyalty* is supplemented by the ideology built of *power* as a symbolic medium, making authority an important cultural means of legitimating structures, where domination is fast becoming a structural mode of societal integration.

Compared with the agrarian system, where kinship breaks down and polity is separated from kinship, but also where religion becomes a dominant institution, the basis of structural and cultural integration shifts to a new profile. Then, when markets as modes of *structural interdependence* evolve, the ideology built around *money* becomes more salient in the structural relations of corporate units not only in economy but in other domains as well, and this ideology will be incorporated into the meta-ideology of dominant domains (typically polity and religion), legitimating new configurations of structural interdependencies and domination as the primary structural mechanisms of integration. These patterns of cultural and structural integration will also be affected by the changes in the stratification system, and its modes of cultural and structural integration. All of these highly dynamic processes can be theorized and assessed against the data that are available in diverse types of societies in stage models of societal evolution.

I have only touched the surface of the theory, which is expressed in 23 abstract propositions in Volume 1 of *Theoretical Principles of Sociology.*[23] Thus, by keeping the analytical scheme simple, as outlined in Figure 13.5 on p. 438, by isolating only those properties of the macro-level social universe that are generic and universal (a relatively small number when this criterion is applied), and by putting the complexity of the social universe in the principles (rather than the analytical scheme, as Parsons did), a theory inspired by what was interesting in functionalism can be developed that is explanatory in the scientific sense of explanation. Moreover, as the functionalists recognized, such a "grand" theory can only be assessed by data from a wide variety of societal formations; and the accumulated knowledge derived from stage models describing diverse societal types can be used to assess the plausibility of each theoretical principle. Moreover, by stating the theory as principles and by outlining the key causal relations in analytical models, the grand theory can be decomposed to specific topics of interest to specialists. For example, I have not addressed here for lack of space how different configurations of stratification increase or decrease the potential for conflict in society, but the models developed and propositions listed for these dynamics can be easily extracted and imported into

---

[23]See Turner, *Theoretical Principles of Sociology,* vol. 1: *Macrodynamics,* 153–214. See also *Societal Stratification: A Theoretical Analysis* (New York: Columbia University Press, 1984).

more specialized literatures on conflict and social movements. In fact, the models and principles that I eventually developed in *Theoretical Principles of Sociology* are very much like those developed by analytical theorists, as outlined in Chapter 14. But, unlike conflict theorists, I began with a broader view of stratification across the full range of societal types that humans have created over the last 200,000 years. The result is principles that can apply to all societal types and formations.

The Utility of Stage Models of Societal Evolution

Viewing societies as evolving through distinct stages does not mean that every society must go through these stages. Conquest, diffusion, borrowing of technologies, markets, and many forces can transform societies dramatically, allowing them to jump over various stages. The real utility of stage models of societal evolution is twofold. First, these models give us a sense of the history of human societies, from their beginnings as small bands of hunter-gatherers to the large-scale macro societies of the industrial and postindustrial world. Second, by emphasizing the characteristics of different societies at varying stages of development, we assemble a large database for developing and assessing macro theories of human social organization.

This second point is the most important. To theorize at the macro level of social organization, we need more than just industrial societies; instead, we need *all types* of societies as a data source for assessing the plausibility of models and theories about societal dynamics. Otherwise, we would have theories of distinctive stages rather than societies and their dynamics more generally. For scientific theory seeks to isolate the key properties and dynamics of the social universe that are *always* operative when humans form societies; and so, to assess whether or not a theory or model meets this criterion of universality, we need to be sure that it is assessed against the full range of sociocultural formations that humans have created over the last 200,000 years.

Once the ethnocentrism of some early theories of stages in societal development was abandoned, the revival of this form of theorizing could now provide a more robust database for assessing new theories that seek to explain macrodynamic processes in societies. Moreover, evolutionary theories will, in the end, emphasize the dynamic forces that drive the formation, change, collapse, and re-formation of societies; and thus, new evolutionary theories will not have any of the connotations of being static and conservative that haunted functional analysis. They will be about the forces that drive societies across history and, hence, at any point in the past or future as societies and intersocietal systems continue to evolve.

Darwinian-Inspired Evolutionary Theories[*]

Darwinian theorizing on the dynamics of natural selection as a force of evolution influenced Émile Durkheim's analysis in *The Division of Labor in Society* and, later, the early Chicago School of urban ecology. This influence on urban and, later, organizational ecology has continued to the present day. As human ecology developed in

---

[*]This portion of the chapter was coauthored with Alexandra Maryanski.

sociology, the Modern Synthesis of evolutionary theorizing combined Darwin's emphasis on natural selection with newer understandings of other forces of evolution—namely, *mutation, gene flow,* and *genetic drift.* And closer to the present, many elements from the Modern Synthesis began to enter social science theorizing in general and, with some reluctance, sociology as well. The diversity of theories using Darwinian-inspired ideas as they were blended into the Modern Synthesis has grown considerably within sociology over the last two decades, but not without a great deal of criticism. In this section, then, we will review several of these approaches, which have grown up alongside the revival of stage models of societal evolution and theories of human ecology.

Sociobiological Theorizing

In the rise of sociobiology in the second half of the twentieth century, none of the founders of this approach were sociologists, and indeed, the reaction to pronouncements by sociobiologists that their approach could explain the social world studied by sociologists was almost universally rejected—"almost" but not completely. Some saw merit in this approach and began to apply the tenets—somewhat modified—of what I tend to call "hardcore" sociobiology.

Pierre van den Berghe's Approach. Pierre van den Berghe has consistently been among the most prolific advocates of a biological perspective on human affairs. Van den Berghe believes, it "is high time that we seriously look at ourselves as merely one biological species among many." Until this shift away from what he calls "species-wide anthropocentrism" is accomplished, sociology will remain stagnant, for there can be no doubt that biological forces shape and constrain patterns of human organization.[24] In his early advocacy, van den Berghe proposed a "biological" approach that corresponded to the instinct approach of some early sociologists and several contemporary thinkers, whereas in his later works, van den Berghe fully embraced the sociobiology and, since then, has consistently used sociobiological theory to interpret a variety of social behaviors among humans. Van den Berghe began his turn to sociobiology by posing the question "Why are humans 'social' in the first place?" His answer is that the banding together of animals in cooperative groups increases their reproductive fitness by (a) protecting them against predators and (b) providing them advantages in locating, gathering, and exploiting resources. Such fitness allows the alleles of those who are social to stay in the gene pool.

Three sociobiological mechanisms produce the sociality that promotes reproductive fitness:[25] (1) *kin selection* (or what is also termed as "inclusive fitness"),

---

[24]Pierre van den Berghe, *Age and Sex in Human Societies: A Biosocial Perspective* (Belmont, CA: Wadsworth, 1973), 2. See also van den Berghe, *Man in Society: A Biosocial View* (New York: Elsevier, 1975), "Territorial Behavior in a Natural Human Group," *Social Science Information* 16 (1977):421–430, "Bringing Beasts Back In: Toward a Biosocial Theory of Aggression," *American Sociological Review* 39 (1974):777–788, "Why Most Sociologists Don't (And Won't) Think Evolutionarily," *Sociological Forum* 5 (1990):173–185, and "Genes, Mind, and Culture," *Behavioral and Brain Sciences* 14 (1991):317–318.

[25]van den Berghe, "Bridging the Paradigms," *Society* 15 (1977–1978):42–49, *The Ethnic Phenomenon* (New York: Elsevier, 1981), and *Human Family Systems* (Prospect Heights, IL: Waveland, 1990), 14ff.

(2) *reciprocity* (or what is also labeled "reciprocal altruism"), and (3) *coercion.* Because each of these mechanisms promotes the reproductive fitness of individuals, they lie at the base of sociocultural phenomena. Let me examine each mechanism separately and then see how van den Berghe generates theoretical explanations with them.

Kin Selection. In van den Berghe's view, kin selection (i.e., a propensity to favor kin) is the oldest mechanism behind sociality. He sees this mechanism, as with all modern human sociobiological arguments, as operating at the genetic level, for

> the gene is the ultimate unit of natural selection, [although] each gene's reproduction can be modified by cultural forces and, overall, is dependent on what Robert Dawkins terms its "survival machine," the organism in which genes happen to be located at any given time.[26]

This "survivor machine" carrying genetic material in its genotype need not be consciously aware of how natural selection in the distant past has created "replicators" or genes in its body that seek to survive and to be immortal. But selection clearly favored those replicators that could pass themselves on to new and better survival machines. One early survivor machine was the body of individual organisms, and later types of survival machines were the cooperative arrangements among bodies sharing alleles in their genotypes. In van den Berghe's words,

> Since organisms are survival machines for genes, by definition those genes that program organisms for successful reproduction will spread. To maximize their reproduction, genes program organisms to do two things: successfully compete against . . . organisms that carry alternative alleles . . . and successfully cooperate with (and thereby contribute to the reproduction of) organisms that share the same alleles of the genes.[27]

So, in van den Berghe's terms, individuals are nepotistic and favor kin over nonkin, and close kin over distant kin, for the simple reason that close kin will share genetic material (in their genotypes):

> Each individual reproduces its genes directly through its own reproduction and indirectly through the reproduction of its relatives, to the extent that it shares genes with them. In simple terms, each organism may be said to have a 100 percent genetic interest in itself, a 50 percent interest in its parents, offspring, and full-siblings, a 25 percent interest in half-siblings, grandparents, grandchildren, uncles, aunts, nephews, and nieces, a 121⁄2 percent interest in first cousins, half-nephews, great-grandchildren, and so on.[28]

[26]van den Berghe, "Bridging the Paradigms," 46; and *Human Family Systems,* 15.

[27]van den Berghe, *The Ethnic Phenomenon,* 7. See also Pierre van den Berghe and Joseph Whitmeyer, "Social Class and Reproductive Success," *International Journal of Contemporary Sociology* 27 (1990):29–48.

[28]van den Berghe, "Bridging the Paradigms," 46–47; and *Human Family Systems,* 19–20.

The degree of "altruism" for kin or "nepotism" will vary with the amount of genetic material shared with a relative and with the ability of that relative to reproduce this genetic material. For van den Berghe, then, "blood is thicker than water" for a simple reason: reproductive fitness, or the capacity to help those "machines" carrying one's genetic material to survive and reproduce.

Van den Berghe is careful, however, to emphasize that these biologically based propensities for nepotism, or kin selection, are elaborated and modified by both environmental and cultural variations. Yet clearly a biological factor operates in the overwhelming tendency of humans to be nepotistic. One cannot, van den Berghe insists, visualize such nepotism as a purely cultural process.

Reciprocity. When individuals exchange assistance, they create a bond of reciprocity. Such reciprocity increases the "fitness" of genes carried by the organisms (as well as the organization of organisms in sociocultural survivor machines); that is, if organisms help each other or can be relied upon to reciprocate for past assistance, the survival of genetic material is increased for both organisms. Such exchange, or what sociobiologists sometimes term "reciprocal altruism,"[29] greatly extends cooperation beyond nepotism, or "inclusive fitness" and "kin selection" in sociobiological jargon. Thus, reciprocal exchange is not a purely social product; it is a behavioral tendency programmed by genes. Such programming occurred in the distant past as natural selection favored those genes that could create new kinds of survivor machines, such as non-kin groups and organizations, beyond an individual's physical body and social groupings of close kin. Those genes that could lodge themselves in non-kin groupings organized around bonds of exchange and reciprocity were more likely to survive; today, the descendants of these genes provide a biological push for creating and sustaining such bonds of reciprocity.

At this point, van den Berghe reveals the affinity of such arguments with utilitarianism by introducing the problem of "free riding", or, as he terms it, "freeloading." That is, what guarantee does an individual (and its genotype) have that others will indeed reciprocate for favors and assistance that has been given to these others? Here, van den Berghe appears to argue that this problem of free riding created selection pressures for greater intelligence so that our protohuman ancestors could remember and monitor whether or not others reciprocated past favors. But, ironically, intelligence also generated greater capacities for sophisticated deceit, cheating, and free riding, which in turn escalated selection pressures for the extended intelligence to "catch" and "detect" such concealed acts of non-reciprocation.

There is, then, a kind of selection cycle operating: reciprocity increases fitness, but it also leads to cheating and free riding. Hence, once reciprocity is a mechanism of cooperation, it can generate its own selection pressures for greater intelligence to monitor free riding, but ironically, increased intelligence enables individuals to engage in more subtle and sophisticated deceptions to hide their free riding; to combat this tendency, there is increased pressure for greater intelligence, and so on. At some point, culture and structure supplant this cycle by creating organizational mechanisms and

---

[29]See Robert L. Trivers, "The Evolution of Reciprocal Altruism," *Quarterly Review of Biology* 46 (1971):35–57.

cultural ideas to limit free riding (see the section on "rational choice" theories in Chapter 15 for a discussion of what these sociocultural mechanisms might be).

Van den Berghe does not pursue this discussion, however, except to point out that this cycle eventually produces "self-deceit." Van den Berghe believes that the best way to deceive is to believe one's own lies and deceptions, and in this way, one can sincerely make and believe verbal pronouncements that contradict, at least in some ways, one's actual behavior. Religion and ideology, van den Berghe posits, are "the ultimate forms of self-deceit," because religion "denies mortality" and ideology facilitates "the transmission of credible, self-serving lies."[30] This conceptual leap from free riding to religion and ideology is, to say the least, rather vague, but it does provide a sense of what sociobiology tries to do: connect what might be considered purely "cultural" processes (i.e., religion and ideology) to a fundamental biological process—in this case, reproductive fitness through reciprocity.

Coercion. There are limits to social organization for reciprocal exchanges, van den Berghe argues, because each party has to perceive that it receives benefits in the relationship.[31] Such perceptions of benefit can, of course, be manipulated by ideologies and other forms of deceit that hide the asymmetry of the relationship, but there are probably limits to the manipulation of perceptions. Power is an alternative mechanism to both kin selection and reciprocal exchanges because its mobilization allows some organisms to dominate others in their access to resources that promote fitness. Coercion thus enables some to increase their fitness at a cost to others. Although this mechanism is hardly unique to our species, humans "hold pride of place in their ability to use to good effect conscious, collective, organized, premeditated coercion in order to establish, maintain, and perpetuate systems of intra-species parasitism."[32] Coercion allows the elaboration of the size and scale of human organization (states, classes, armies, courts, etc.), but it is nonetheless tied to human biology as this was molded by selection. That is, genes that could use coercion to create larger and more elaborate social structures as their survival machines were more likely to survive and reproduce. In sum, then, sociality or cooperation and organization are the result of natural selection because they preserved genes that could produce better survival machines through nepotism (kin selection and inclusive fitness), reciprocity (or reciprocal altruism), and coercion (or territorial and hierarchical patterns of dominance). The linkages between biology, on the one side, and culture and society, on the other, are complex and often indirect, even after we recognize that these linkages occur along the three basic dimensions or axes of nepotism, reciprocity, and coercion. For there have certainly been complex interactions between ecological and genetic factors to produce patterns of human (and many other animal) organization; once initiated, selection processes producing greater intelligence allow culture, as "an impressive bag of tricks," to operate as a force of human evolution.

---

[30]van den Berghe, *The Ethnic Phenomenon,* 9 and "Bridging the Paradigms," 48.

[31]van den Berghe, "Bridging the Paradigms," 42–49.

[32]van den Berghe, *The Ethnic Phenomenon,* 10; van den Berghe and Whitmeyer, "Social Class and Reproductive Success," 31–32.

Conceptualizing Cultural Processes. From van den Berghe's vantage point, culture is created and transmitted in humans through mechanisms that are fundamentally different from those involved in genetic natural selection. Actually, van den Berghe portrays cultural evolution in Lamarckian rather than Darwinian terms: "Acquired cultural characteristics, unlike . . . genetic evolution, can be transmitted, modified, transformed, or eliminated through social learning." In recent years, van den Berghe has come to see culture in some ways as "an emergent phenomenon" that provides humans with another method of adaptation. For van den Berghe, the issue is not the genes versus culture but their interface, for both are intimately intertwined. Although culture is an outgrowth of biological evolution, it now has an autonomy, he says, that provides humans with the ability to modify their own genotypes, making the intricate feedbacks between nature and nurture more complex than ever.[33] So culture is not a separate entity; it is yet one more product and process of biological evolution driven by natural selection as it produced genes trying to maximize their fitness by nesting themselves in better and better survival machines.

Explanations of Social Phenomena with Sociobiology. At various times, van den Berghe has used the concepts of sociobiology to explain such empirical phenomena as kinship systems, incest taboos, ethnicity, skin color, sexual selection, and social classes. Probably his two most detailed empirical analyses are on (1) kinship systems and (2) ethnicity. Each of these will be briefly summarized.

Kinship. In one of his early sociobiological articles, van den Berghe and David Barash endeavored to explain various features of kinship systems by the behavioral strategies males and females pursue to maximize their fitness (i.e., keep their alleles in the gene pool). Because the details of their suggestive arguments can be complex, just one example of the kinds of arguments that they make will be summarized.[34]

The widespread preference in human societies for *polygyny* (males with the option for multiple wives), *hypergamy* (females marrying males of higher-ranking kin groups), and double standards of sexual morality (males being given more latitude than females) can be explained in terms of reproductive fitness strategies. Women have comparatively fewer eggs to offer in their lifetime, have intervals when they are infertile (e.g., during lactation), and, even in the most liberal or egalitarian societies, have to spend more time than men raising children. Hence, a female will seek a reproductive strategy that will ensure the survival of her less abundant genetical material, and the most maximizing strategy is to marry a male with the resources and capacity to ensure the survival of her offspring (and, thereby, one-half of her genotype). Thus, a woman will seek to "marry up" (hypergamy) in the sense of securing a man who has more resources than her kinship group.

On the male side, men produce an uninterrupted and large supply of sperm and have fewer child care responsibilities, and so they can afford to be more promiscuous

---

[33]van den Berghe, *The Ethnic Phenomenon,* 6 and *Human Family Systems,* 220.

[34]Pierre van den Berghe and David Barash, "Inclusive Fitness and Family Structure," *American Anthropologist* 79 (1977):809–823.

with little cost (and they will derive some benefit from the fitness that comes with spreading their genes around). Although men have an interest in ensuring that as many women as possible bear children with one-half of their genes, a male cannot know that a female is bearing his child if she is promiscuous, and so men also have an interest in restricting female sexual activity through monogamy to ensure that their genes are indeed contained in the genotype of the children born to their wives (creating limits for female sexuality outside marriage). Thus, what are commonly viewed as purely cultural phenomena—the preference for polygyny in human societies (or monogamy with male promiscuity), hypergamy ("marrying up"), and sexual double standards (favoring male promiscuity)—can be explained as the result of varying fitness strategies for males and females, which have become programmed into their respective genotypes.

Ethnicity. Turning to another empirical example, van den Berghe has sought to apply sociobiology to what has always been his main area of research, ethnicity.[35] Again, kin selection is his starting point, but he extends this idea beyond family relatives helping one another (to maximize their fitness) to a larger subpopulation. Historically, larger kin groups (composed of lineages) constituted a breeding population of close and distant kin who would sustain trust and solidarity with one another while mistrusting other breeding populations. Van den Berghe coined the term *ethny* for "ethnic group" and views an ethny as an extended nepotism of these more primordial breeding populations. An *ethny* is a cluster of kinship circles that is created by endogamy (intermarriage of its members) and territoriality (physical proximity of its members and relative isolation from nonmembers). An ethny represents a reproductive strategy for maximizing fitness beyond the narrower confines of kinship, because, by forming an ethny—even a very large one of millions of people—individuals can create extended bonds with those who can help preserve their fitness, whether by actually sharing genes or, more typically, by reciprocal acts of altruism to fellow "ethnys." An ethny is, therefore, a manifestation of more basic "urges" for helping "those like oneself." Whereas ethnys become genetically diluted as their size increases and become subject to social and cultural definitions, the very tendency to form and sustain ethnys is the result of natural selection as it produced nepotism. Van den Berghe's argument is, of course, much more complicated and sophisticated, but we can get at least a general sense for how a supposedly emergent phenomenon—ethnic groups—is explained by reduction to a theoretical perspective built on the principles of genetic evolution.

In summary, the sociobiology models developed by van den Berghe emphasize the interactive effects among genes, culture, and environment. Individuals are viewed as "selfish maximizers" who seek to maximize their own inclusive fitness. To accomplish this goal, different reproductive strategies are employed, with variations in reproductive strategies among human societies mostly the result of different cultural adaptations to particular environmental conditions. In recent years, however, van den Berghe and collaborators have highlighted the power of culture in overriding the reproductive

---

[35]van den Berghe, *The Ethnic Phenomenon*; see also van den Berghe, "Heritable Phenotypes and Ethnicity," *Behavioral and Brain Sciences* 12 (1989):544–545.

consequences of human actions, thereby subverting the genes' game of reproducing themselves. Van den Berghe[36] now says that this subversion of the genes is especially evident in industrial societies, where many individuals "are no longer maximizing fitness" because the contraceptive technology and the comforts and security of material affluence have separated the hedonistic rewards of the "good life" from reproductive efforts. Thus, in modern societies, van den Berghe suggests, a more complex model is necessary to assess the quality versus quantity of offspring and the balance between human needs for luxury goods and reproductive investment.

Joseph Lopreato's Approach

In the early, "hardcore" days of sociobiology, scholars followed the evolutionary logic that, in the past, natural selection favors those behavioral adaptations that increased the fitness of individuals in a given environment. All nonadaptive behaviors are weeded out, whereas adaptive behaviors are preserved and transmitted for the ultimate function of maximizing fitness. The research objective, then, is to discover how particular social behaviors are adaptive and, hence, how they promote fitness.[37] In the words of R. D. Alexander, who underscored the importance of viewing humans as organisms whose behaviors evolved to maximize reproductive fitness, "all organisms should have logically evolved to avoid every instance of beneficence or altruism unlikely to bring returns greater than the expenditure it entails."[38] Hence, through the application of such concepts as "kin selection" and "reciprocal altruism," even acts of cooperation or kindness were viewed as "selfish genes."

Joseph Lopreato[39] believes the "maximization principle" is still the fountainhead of sociobiology, but if we want to keep "with the logic of natural selection," its strict application is unwarranted. For this reason, Lopreato has undertaken the task of overhauling the maximization principle.

In revamping the maximization principle, Lopreato begins by rejecting the assumption that all adaptations are either related to reproduction or organized around the ultimate goal of reproductive success. Instead, he proposes that for all organisms there is only a tendency for individuals to behave in a way that maximizes their reproductive success.[40] This "could hardly be otherwise," he maintains, because many individual behaviors are clearly neutral or outright maladaptive, and there are good evolutionary reasons for this variability. As he points out, genotypic variation in every generation must exist for selection to act on. This pool of variability must

---

[36]van den Berghe, "Once More with Feeling: Genes, Mind and Culture," *Behavioral and Brain Sciences* 14 (1991):317–318; van den Berghe and Whitmeyer, "Social Class and Reproductive Success," 41–44.

[37]J. Maynard-Smith, "The Theory of Games and the Evolution of Animal Conflicts," *Journal of Theoretical Biology* 47 (1974):209–221; see Alexandra Maryanski, "The Pursuit of Human Nature in Sociobiology and Evolutionary Sociology," *Sociological Perspectives* 37 (Fall 1994):115–127.

[38]R. D. Alexander, "The Search for a General Theory of Behavior," *Behavior Science* 20 (1975):77–100.

[39]Joseph Lopreato, "The Maximization Principle: A Cause in Search of Conditions," in *Sociobiology and the Social Sciences*, ed. Robert and Nancy Bell (Lubbock: Texas Tech University Press, 1989):119–130.

[40]Ibid., 121.

include both neutral traits and maladaptive traits to provide a deviation of fitness from the maximization principle. This variability is retained when genes are recombined into new genotypes, virtually guaranteeing a differential in the adaptive quality of organisms. Over time, this differential will, in turn, produce "a more or less adaptive fit between variations and environmental pressures."[41]

The second step taken by Lopreato is acknowledging that cultural evolution has placed heavy constraints on the maximization principle. In particular, the trappings of human culture have greatly augmented the basic mammalian "pleasure principle," which is now skewed in humans toward creature comforts rather than the maximization of reproductive success. This requires a readjustment of the maximization principle: "Organisms are predisposed to behave so as to maximize their inclusive fitness, but this predisposition is conditioned by the quest for creature comforts."[42]

The third step taken by Lopreato is suggesting that complex causal agents in both evolutionary and cultural phenomena have generated a widespread predisposition for "self-deception," or the ability to engage in one form of behavior in the belief that it is actually another form of behavior.[43] Once self-deceptive behaviors evolved, Lopreato says, the necessary conditions were created for true ascetic altruism to evolve, where individuals in varying degrees evidence a type of "Mother Theresa complex" or desire for self-sacrifice, which can, in some instances, redirect the sex drive away from physical satisfaction to "spiritual satisfaction" through altruistic good works. Lopreato submits that, ironically, self-deceptive behaviors must have evolved through natural selection, making it possible to have "true altruism in the absence of altruistic genes."[44] For this reason, he recommends a third modification of the maximization principle: "Organisms are predisposed to behave so as to maximize their inclusive fitness, but this predisposition is conditioned by the quest for creature comforts and by self-deception."[45]

A fourth constraint on the maximization principle is sociopolitical revolution, which Lopreato defines as "forcible action in a dominance order by individuals who desire to replace those who have organizational . . . control of their group's resources."[46] Lopreato suggests that the "ultimate cause of revolution is the quest for fitness maximization," because in traditional societies, highly ranked individuals with resources are more likely to have access to multiple females through polygyny, thereby increasing their reproductive success. However, to the degree that resource accumulation becomes an end in itself in modern industrial societies, resource acquisition and maximization of fitness become detached. Here, culture once again disrupts the maximization as behaviors directed at resource acquisition become separated from considerations of genetic fitness. For this reason, Lopreato adds a

---

[41]Ibid., 120–121.

[42]Ibid., 125.

[43]Ibid., 126.

[44]Ibid., 127.

[45]Ibid., 127.

[46]Ibid., 127.

final variable in his restatement of the maximization principle: "Organisms are predisposed to behave so as to maximize their inclusive fitness, but this predisposition is conditioned by the quest for creature comforts, by self-deception, and by autonomization of phenotype from genotype."[47]

Lopreato has used his theoretical model to enhance traditional sociological explanations of social phenomena. In a paper with Arlen Carey,[48] for example, Lopreato examines the relationship between fertility and mortality in human societies. Essentially, Carey and Lopreato argue that variations in human fertility have typically been explained by such fertility-reducing mechanisms as abortion, use of contraceptives, sterility, age at marriage, economic value of children, social status of women, and the like. Yet, despite these obvious and important influences on fertility, these explanations cannot provide by themselves an adequate account of one fact: until recently, rates of reproduction have changed very little in humans' evolutionary history, with human females on average producing only two viable adult offspring. Why should this have historically been the case?

In considering this demographic puzzle, Carey and Lopreato submit that population dynamics do not fluctuate randomly but fertility rates roughly correspond with mortality rates, with these two rates tending to behave like systems in equilibrium. In traditional societies, there is a quasi-equilibrium between high mortality rates and high fertility rates. In addition, as Charles Darwin first realized (drawing his inspiration from Thomas Malthus), it is characteristic of most species, notwithstanding the tendency of populations to outpace their resources, to evidence a countertendency toward population stability, suggesting that "the fertility of individuals displays a vigorous tendency to track mortality—a tendency . . . toward a coupled-replacement reproductive strategy."[49] Carey and Lopreato ask this: In humans, what factors might be responsible for maintaining this "fertility-mortality quasi-equilibrium?"

Carey and Lopreato submit that although all humans are motivated in principle to maximize their reproductive success, they are constrained first by limited resources and the human need for "creature comforts." Instead, what the "demographic quasi-equilibrium" pattern suggests is a stabilizing reproductive strategy with natural selection tending to favor fertilities that meet and only slightly exceed the corresponding mortalities.[50]

A second mechanism used to regulate the fertility-mortality relationship in human populations, they maintain, is collectively called "life history characteristics."[51] Basically, life history theory holds that natural selection guides the life characteristic of a species to optimize and regulate fertility.[52] Evolutionary ecologists have documented

---

[47]Ibid., 129.

[48]Arlen Carey and Joseph Lopreato, "The Evolutionary Demography of the Fertility-Mortality Quasi-Equilibrium," *Population and Development Review* 21 (1995):613–630.

[49]Ibid., 616.

[50]Ibid., 617.

[51]Ibid., 617–619.

[52]Ibid., 619.

life history characteristics in other species, which include distinct reproductive periods, inter-birth intervals, litter size, parental investment, age-specific probabilities of survival, and size and maturity of newborns. Hence, animal populations with low rates of mortality will also have lower fertility rates, which are conditioned by smaller litters, delayed births, and bigger offspring because they represent a great investment of parental resources. Carey and Lopreato argue that the fertility-mortality relationship in humans also corresponds to life history characteristics. Members of the human species have a relatively high probability of survival through the reproductive period, which is matched historically by a low fertility rate. To regulate this process, puberty begins late in humankind, conception is relatively difficult, fetuses take nine months to develop, single births are the norm, newborns are large, and births are difficult. Carey and Lopreato suggest that "these life history characteristics contribute to a relatively low level of fertility that is associated with a relatively low probability of mortality."[53] Although these facts are well-known to demographers, they are rarely viewed as phenomena forged by natural selection.

Still, Carey and Lopreato do not consider these factors sufficient to explain the relationship between fertility and mortality. Instead, they seek a third explanation for the regulation of human fertility, suggesting that psychological attributes "most closely associated with survival and reproduction may be expected to be especially prone to fitness maximization tendencies."[54] In short, there are perhaps psychologically regulated reproductive behaviors toward an optimal level of reproductive behavior that is activated by environmental cues. These cues are used to gauge the relative probabilities of survival of the young.[55] Thus, in a society where infant and child mortality is high, a higher fertility rate would prevail.

Identifying some psychological mechanisms that help regulate human fertility rates is now possible. Belsky, Steinberg, and Draper[56] suggest, for example, that reproductive strategies for individuals in a given population are largely decided during the first five to seven years of life. The crucial determining factor here is resource availability. The amount of resources then influences family life and child rearing, and these shape both the psychological and the behavioral development of a child.[57] In turn, these affect the age of puberty and the lifelong reproductive strategy. For instance, Chisholm[58] maintains that this developmental process offers the proximate mechanisms by which individuals internalize the mortality characteristics of their population.

---

[53]Ibid., 620.

[54]Ibid.

[55]Ibid.

[56]Jay Belsky, Laurence Steinberg, and Patricia Draper, "Childhood Experience, Interpersonal Development, and Reproductive Strategy: An Evolutionary Theory of Socialization," *Child Development* 62 (1991):647–670.

[57]Ibid.

[58]James Chisholm, "Death, Hope, and Life: Life History Theory and the Development of Reproductive Strategies," *Current Anthropology* 34 (1993):1–12.

In concluding, they offer these propositions: (a) the greater the perceived probability of offspring survival is within a population, the more intense the two-child psychology is and (b) the greater the tendency toward creature comforts is among members of a society, the more widespread is the two-child psychology. Thus, Carey and Lopreato believe that human neurobiology has reproductively based predispositions, which are activated by the environment, charting the best reproductive strategy. As they note, "The evolution of the relationship between human fertility and human mortality has forged a tendency toward a reproductive psychology that revolves closely around a near-average two-child family."[59] This can be called the "two-child psychology" tendency. It charts that in human history an average of two offspring (or a little more) is typically the best strategy given the costs of motherhood in comfort, health, and overall quality of life. In supporting their thesis, they use historical data that suggest population growth was minimal—at least, until recently.

Evolutionary Psychology

Sociobiology was the beachhead to an invasion of the social sciences by biology, but over recent decades, evolutionary psychology has gained considerably more influence in the social sciences than sociobiology, especially in sociology. Evolutionary psychology accepts most of the tenets of sociobiology, such as behaviors evolved to maximize the fitness of humans, but inserts the operation of the human brain explicitly into the theory. Natural selection, as it worked on hominin and human phenotypes and the underlying genotypes, has rewired the brain by creating a series of specialized "brain modules" during the Pleistocene—the more immediate epoch of evolution of late hominins and early humans. These modules are responsible for many key behaviors that, in the past, solved recurrent problems in human's ancestral environments.

Evolutionary psychology operates under a number of key assumptions, as follows:

1. The brain is an information-processing device that has evolved like any other trait in organisms.

2. The brain and the adaptive mechanisms that it reveals evolved by natural selection.

3. The various neural mechanisms of the brain are specialized for solving the problems generated by selection pressures in humans' and hominins' evolutionary past.

4. The human mind, then, is a "Stone Age" mind because its specialized mechanisms for processing information, perception, and universal behaviors evolved during the Pleistocene.

5. Most contents and processes of the brain are unconscious, and mental problems that appear easy to solve are actually difficult problems that are solved unconsciously by a complicated set and modules of neurons that have evolved

[59]Carey and Lopreato, "The Evolutionary Demography," 621; Joseph Lopreato and Mei-Yu Yu, "Human Fertility and Fitness Optimization," *Ethnology and Sociobiology* 9 (1988):269–289.

to solve adaptive problems during the course of the evolution of late hominins and early humans.

6. The psychology of humans, then, consists of many specialized mechanisms wired into distinctive modules of neurons that are sensitive to different classes of information and external inputs and that combine to produce human behavior—and, by implication, patterns of interaction and even social structures and their cultures.

For example, an evolutionary psychologist might argue that human speech is an evolved psychological mechanism that evolved by selecting on the association cortices—such as the inferior parietal lobe that enables humans and higher primates the capacity for language facility—followed by selection on relatively discrete areas of the brain (Broca's area) and the surrounding tissues for speech production and Wernicke's area for speech comprehension and uploading of meanings into the brain's information processes. Moreover, there are modules along the fissure separating the parietal lobe that regulate touch muscle movements and the frontal cortex that gives humans (but not the great apes) the ability to produce articulated words in speech. Such speech capacities evolved to solve problems of communication and social bonding among humans; this line of argument might not be controversial because the modules can be found in the brain. Similarly, the evolution of humans' emotional capacities occurs in modules in subcortical areas of the brain. Some subcortical areas, like those generating *anger* and *fear*, which date back to the evolution of reptiles, are generated in a discrete module labeled the *amygdala;* but other emotions are not so easily isolated in discrete modules, but evolutionary psychologists still predict that the modules will be found with more research.

Other topics are potentially more controversial. Evolutionary psychologists suggest that, for instance, there are incest avoidance mechanisms (which is probably true, but where is the module for this?), as well as mechanisms for cheater detection, sex-specific preferences, reciprocity, kin selection, altruism, reciprocal altruism, inclusive fitness, alliance tracking, and other universal human behaviors. For evolutionary psychologists, the more universal is a behavior, the more likely is this behavior regulated by neurological mechanisms situated in modules of the human brain. These modules evolved because they enhanced the fitness of hominins and then humans during the Pleistocene.

These basic features of evolutionary psychology have been adopted by a small but growing number of sociologists and used to explain human behaviors, often reported in the sociological literature as rates of particular kinds of behaviors. For example, there is a universal behavioral propensity for crime rate, and especially violent crime rate, for crimes committed by males, increasing during male puberty and then declining dramatically with age. Sociobiologists[60] sought to explain this universal pattern, and evolutionary psychologists[61] have added characterizations of the

---

[60]Martin Daily and Margo Wilson, *Homicide* (New York: De Gruyter, 1988).

[61]Satoshi Kanazawa and Mary C. Still, Why Men Commit Crimes (and Why They Desist)," *Sociological Perspectives* 18 (2000):434–447.

mechanisms by which this behavior is produced. Such explanations become "just so" stories outlining what occurred in the distant past to produce brain modules (rarely specified) that produce particular patterns of behavior, like rates of crime and violent crime among adolescent males. For example, part of the "just so" story begins with men's need and desire to gain access to women (so as to pass on their genes), and young men are particularly driven to do so. They are thus more likely to take risks and incur costs in competition with other males to gain access to females. To ensure that such would be the case, natural selection created a module (not clearly specified except for the mention of those parts of the brain responsible for the production of the hormone testosterone). This module evolved long before individuals had much property and before a criminal justice system existed, but men still seek resources and status to impress females with their qualities and, thereby, maximize their reproductive success. In modern societies, young males have fewer resources than older males, with the result that they seek resources through crime. The story is much more nuanced than this, and it even adds interesting details. Smaller men, contrary to what we might think, will tend to be more aggressive and violent because they have to compensate for the lack of size and thus must gain status and resources to attract females—hence, they are more likely to commit violent crimes to do so.

Other arguments can be developed along these lines. As I outlined in the discussion of Pierre van den Berghe's approach, sociobiologists have argued that males and females develop somewhat different "strategies" to maximize their reproductive fitness. Women produce relatively few eggs in their lifetime and must make heavy investments in offspring (since they, rather than men, must bear and breast-feed them), whereas males generate daily millions of sperm. Thus, women have a vested interest in ensuring that they hook up with males who can provide resources to their offspring, whereas males maximize their reproductive fitness by being promiscuous. Thus, males tend to be more promiscuous than women because of biologically driven strategies for maximizing fitness. Evolutionary psychology adds to this scenario the notion that males possess evolved mechanisms in their brains that drive them to limit their female partners' access to other males. For example, males will generally become more *reflexively jealous* (from an emotional module) with infidelity by females and more likely to push for restrictive norms on female sexuality in order to ensure that the female's offspring carry their genes rather than those of another male. These norms can change, however, when women have resources independently of their male sexual partners, because, now, they do not need the resources provided by males and thus are likely to resist male control and demand more permissive sexual norms.[62] There are, again, more nuanced versions of this story, but the plotline of the "just so" story is clear.

One problematic issue with these "explanations" by "just so" stories is that they are almost always ad hoc. One could construct a "just so" story for empirical regularities in behavior that are just the opposite of those described above. The assumptions of evolutionary psychology, as it has incorporated the arguments of sociobiologists, are so general that it is easy to develop a story—or an explanation—for almost any behavioral regularity. All that is necessary is to hypothesize a module in the brain that evolved to produce a behavior that is asserted in the "just so" story to enhance

---

[62]Christine Horne, "Values and Evolutionary Psychology," *Sociological Perspectives* 22 (2004):477–493.

fitness. But these stories are not only ad hoc, they are generally post hoc, although some have sought to be more predictive.[63] Yet evolutionary psychologists seem undaunted by these criticisms and, in fact, are highly confident that their approach can explain more than the standard social science practices, which tend to assume that biology has very little influence on human behavior, interaction, and patterns of social organization.[64] In fact, Rosemary Hopcroft has produced an introduction to sociology demonstrating what she sees as the power of evolutionary psychology to explain standard sociology literatures.[65]

Cross-Species Comparisons

Other sociologists have developed theoretical approaches that compare humans with other species. Here, the goal is to highlight particular questions in the social sciences and to seek answers by comparing humans and their patterns of social organization with other species. These cross-species comparisons may, or may not, also include ideas from sociobiology or evolutionary psychology, but these are not so much emphasized. The basic idea is to provide answers to questions by comparing human behavior propensities and patterns of social organization with those of other species, sometimes species that are closely related to humans biologically and at other times species that are very distant from humans.

Richard Machalek's Approach. Richard Machalek has applied modern evolutionary theory to traditional sociological problems.[66] Machalek would like to see a truly comparative sociology or one that crosses species lines. His approach is to search for the foundations and development of "sociality" wherever it is found, in both human and nonhuman species. By identifying the elementary forms of social life among human and nonhuman organisms, information can be gleaned about how the organizational features among species are assembled. In this effort to create a comparative sociology, Machalek outlines a four-step protocol for conducting a sociological analysis of generic social forms, "with a priority on sociality, not the organism":[67]

1. Identify and describe a social form that is distributed across two or more species lines.

2. Identify the "design problems" that might constrain the evolution of this social form. In other words, what prerequisites are necessary for a particular social form to come into existence?

---

[63]Rosemary L. Hopcroft, "Status Characteristics Among Older Individuals: The Diminished Significance of Gender," *Sociological Quarterly* 47 (2006):361–374.

[64]For example, see essays in Jerome H. Barkow, Leda Cosmides, and John Tooby (eds.), *The Adapted Mind: Evolutionary Psychology and the Generation of Culture* (New York: Oxford University Press, 1992).

[65]Rosemary L. Hopcroff, *Sociology: A Biosocial Introduction* (Boulder, CO: Paradigm Press, 2010).

[66]Richard Machalek, "Why Are Large Societies Rare?" *Advances in Human Ecology* 1 (1992):33–64.

[67]Richard Machalek, "Crossing Species Boundaries: Comparing Basic Properties of Human and Nonhuman Societies" (unpublished manuscript).

3. Identify the processes that generate a social form.

4. Identify those benefits and beneficiaries of a social form that will help explain the persistence and proliferation of certain social forms over other forms.

In applying this protocol, Machalek focused on the evolution of macro societies, a social form that first appeared in human social evolution about 5,000 years ago. He asked this: What makes human macro societies possible? Machalek suggests that we cannot just look at agrarian and industrial societies to answer this question but, rather, we must subordinate the study of human macro-level societies to the study of macro societies as a general social form. If we take a cross-species comparative approach, it is evident that "macro sociality" is rare and exists in only two taxonomic orders: insects and human primates.

Machalek describes a macro society as a society with hundreds of millions of members with distinct social classes and a complex division of labor. Among social insects this social form is very old, but in humans it is very recent, beginning about 5,000 years ago with the emergence of agrarian societies. Obviously, humans and insects are remote species, separated by at least 600 million years of divergent evolution; hence, they cannot be compared by individual biological characteristics. Indeed, humans and insects are separated by major anatomical differences that include "six orders of magnitude in brain size"; so intelligence did not play a role in the evolution of insect macro societies. Instead, insect and human macro-societal social forms must be compared strictly for their "social structural design" features in what appears to be a case of convergent evolution.

In considering the fundamental similarities between the organization of human and insect macro societies, Machalek maintains that "whatever the species, all social organisms confront the same basic problems of organizational design and regulation if they are to succeed in evolving a macro society."[68] When looked at this way, the existence of this social form in two such distinctive and biologically remote taxa allows us to address questions such as this: What constraints must be surmounted before a species can create and/or sustain themselves in a macro society?

Machalek suggests that macro societies are rare because the evolution of this social form requires successful solutions to a series of difficult and complex problems. He suggests that only insects and humans have managed to push aside or overcome (a) organismic constraints, (b) ecological constraints, (c) cost-benefit constraints, and (d) sociological constraints. Each of these will be briefly examined.

Organismic Constraints. In detailing the organismic constraints that must be overcome before complex cooperative behavior can evolve, Machalek highlights the morphology of a species as an important factor that can either promote or inhibit the ability of a species to evolve a macro society. For example, aquatic social species such as whales, which are extremely intelligent and which clearly enjoy a "social life," are hopelessly constrained by their enormous "body plans," a constraint that makes it difficult for them to engage in "diverse forms of productive behavior."[69] And when

---

[68]Machalek, "Why Are Large Societies Rare?" 35.

[69]Ibid., 42.

a body plan constrains the variety of cooperative behaviors possible, it "also constrains the evolution of a complex and extensive division of labor."[70]

Ecological Constraints. In addition to organismic constraints, the ecological niche of a species sets limits on both the population size and the complexity of a society. An ecosystem's physical properties can vary in the number of predators, competition for resources like food and shelter, diversity of other species, and mortality rates because of disease. All these can become factors in limiting population size for a given species. Social insects are more likely to find a habitat with ample resources to support their macro societies because they are very small creatures.

Cost-Benefit Constraints. In addition to organismic and ecological constraints, the evolution of a macro society will depend on economic factors or various "costs and benefits" that accompany any macro society. Although the evolution of a macro society would seem to be beneficial to any social species, a society with complex and extensive cooperation has both costs and benefits. Using the logic of cost-benefit analysis, a particular evolved trait can be analyzed for the ratio of its costs to benefits. Among social insects like ants, costs (which include problems such as social parasitism, where alien species expropriate labor or food from unsuspecting ants) do not exceed benefits. This is because social insects greatly benefit from a complex division of labor that allows them to compensate for the small size of each individual "and thus increase their ergonomic efficiency and effectiveness."[71]

Sociological Constraints. Of all the constraints, this is the most important. Even if all the other constraints are overcome, the evolution of a macro society requires a unique form of social interaction that is rare in nature and beyond the capacity of most organisms. Essentially, an organism must overcome three large sociological problems to evolve a macro society:[72]

1. Individuals must be able to engage in impersonal cooperation.

2. The labor of members must be divided among distinct social categories.

3. The division of labor among members must be integrated and coordinated.

In considering these critical "design problems" that must be surmounted before a macro society can evolve, we should ask why it is that only the social insects and humans have been able to generate a rare and complex form of sociality. If we turn to other social species for clues, we find that the fundamental mechanism underlying social organization in most animals is kinship or genetic relatedness. Machalek argues that kinship bonds effectively restrict the number of individuals within a particular cooperative group, making it very difficult for most species to evolve a macro society. Machalek notes that the general principle that links

---

[70]Ibid.

[71]Ibid., 44.

[72]Ibid., 45.

kinship to social behavior among animals can be stated as follows: "The greater the degree of genetic relatedness among individuals, the higher the probability that they will interact cooperatively."[73] In other words, natural selection has seemingly favored social species with the basic capacity to distinguish individual kin from non-kin, thereby making kinship networks possible. Thus, kinship connections based on individual recognition of relatives are the basis for social cooperation in most social species.

In social insects, however, kin are distinguished from non-kin largely through remote chemical communication, for there is no evidence that "blood relatives" recognize each other as individuals. Thus, in ant societies, members interact with five or six types of ants—not millions of individual ants. Ants treat each other as members of distinct categories or castes. In turn, social categories or castes are occupationally specialized, allowing task specialization (i.e., foraging, brood tending, nest repair, defense, etc.) and leading to a complex division of labor. Caste types are recognized by olfactory cues, the dominant mechanism behind the organization of ants. Machalek notes that humans often link a complex division of labor to human intelligence, culture, and technological development, but this social form among insects clearly exists outside the range of human intelligence.

In contrast, despite selection for language and culture, human societies were small and based on face-to-face, individualized kinship relations for most of human evolutionary history. Yet in agrarian times, full-blown hierarchical stratification evolved, leading to this question: How were humans able to escape the constraining influences of personalized kinship relations and their highly evolved capacity for individual recognition? Following Machalek,

> Humans have evolved macro societies because they are empowered by culture to form highly cooperative patterns of behavior with "anonymous others." Thus, for the social insects, a state of permanent personal anonymity enables them to form large, complex societies comprising purely impersonal cooperation among members of different castes. Humans, on the other hand, are capable of forming cooperative social systems based either upon personal relationship or impersonal status-role attributes.[74]

Thus, chemical communication allows insects to convert individuals into social types, whereas humans employ "cognitive culture" and socially constructed typifications. This capacity allows humans to interact cooperatively not as individuals but as personal strangers, dividing individuals into types of social categories. Machalek believes "it is impersonal cooperation that lies at the very foundation of macrosociality."[75] Social insects and humans have thus "used different but functionally

---

[73]Ibid., 46.

[74]Ibid., 47.

[75]Ibid., 48.

analogous strategies to achieve the capacity for close cooperation among anonymous others, thereby facilitating the evolution of macrosociety."[76] In addition, this impersonality specifies and limits the rights and obligations between (or among) parties to an interaction, for—as Machalek notes—status-role constructs "are the evolutionary convergent human analogue to the chemical and tactile typification processes among social insects upon which caste systems are built."[77] Essentially, status role constructs allow humans to ignore the unique and distinctive qualities of persons, thereby increasing the economy of a cooperative interaction. Unlike social insects, however, humans can also move between personal and impersonal attributes in organizing their social lives.

In sum, then, only insects and humans were able to evolve a system of macro sociality, primarily because of the design problems in creating macro societies. Machalek emphasizes that sociologists have long struggled to understand the elementary forms of social behavior, but this quest has been limited because of a general reluctance by sociologists to expand their perspective to include inquiry into nonhuman social species. It is important, Machalek argues, to see how particular social traits are spread across species. The ability to research questions such as the emergence of a complex division of labor and why it is found in only a few societies can help us discover how it evolved in human societies. In addition, if we compare sociality forms across species by consequences, "we can enhance our understanding of the adaptive value of sociality as a response to ecological challenges."[78] Finally, beginning with the social form and then selecting for observation those species in which that form appears would also allow us to better understand the emergent properties of social systems, the adaptive value and processes that generate particular social forms, and the essential design features that might represent a solution to common problems facing diverse species.

Alexandra Maryanski's Approach. In recent years, Alexandra Maryanski, in conjunction with me—her sometime collaborator—has approached the question of human nature by examining the social network ties of humans' closest living relatives, the apes.[79] As is well-known, humans share well over 98.5 percent of their genetic material with chimpanzees (Pan); indeed, chimpanzees might be closer to humans than they are to gorillas (Gorilla). And both chimpanzees and gorillas are

---

[76]Ibid., 50.

[77]Ibid.

[78]Ibid., 61.

[79]Alexandra Maryanski, "The Last Ancestor: An Ecological Network Model on the Origins of Human Sociality," in *Advances in Human Ecology*, vol. 1, ed. L. Freese (Greenwich, England: Emerald Group, 1992), 1–32; Alexandra Maryanski and Jonathan Turner, *The Social Cage* (Stanford, CA: Stanford University Press, 1992); A. Maryanski, "African Ape Social Structure: Is There Strength in Weak Ties?" *Social Networks* 9 (1987):191–215. For the most recent statement of this argument, see Jonathan H. Turner and Alexandra Maryanski, *On the Origins of Societies by Natural Selection* (Boulder, CO: Paradigm Press, 2008).

African apes that are certainly closer to humans than they are to orangutans (Pongo) or gibbons (Hylobates), the other two genera constituting Asian apes. In fact, humans and chimpanzees came from the same ancestral primate, which lived only about five million years ago, according to the latest fossil and molecular data.[80]

Long-term field studies have documented that primates are highly intelligent, are slow to mature, undergo a long period of socialization, and live a long time. The majority of primates are organized into year-round societies that require the integration of a wide variety of age and sex classes, not just adult males and females. In addition, primates have clear-cut social bonding patterns that vary widely among the 187 species of primates.

Using a historical comparative technique, which is termed *cladistic analysis* in biology,[81] Maryanski began by examining the social relational data on present-day great-ape genera—that is, chimpanzees, gorillas, gibbons, and orangutans. Following this procedure, Maryanski first identified a limited group of entities—in this case, one crucial property of ape social structure, the strength of social bonds between (and among) age and sex classes in all ape genera—to see if there were structural regularities in the patterning of relations. If phyletically close species living in different environments reveal characteristic traits in common, then it can be assumed that their Last Common Ancestor (LCA) also had similar relational features. For this exercise, Maryanski undertook a comprehensive review of bonding propensities for apes living under natural field conditions, in an effort to profile their social network structures, with the goal of uncovering a blueprint of the LCA population to present-day apes and humans.

To assess the validity of these relational patterns, she followed the normal procedures of cladistic analysis by including an "out-group lineage"—a sample of Old World monkey social networks—for comparison with the networks of apes.[82] She also subjected her data set to two fundamental assumptions associated with this comparative technique: (1) the *Relatedness Hypothesis*, which indirectly assesses

---

[80]See Charles G. Sibley, John A. Comstock, and Jon E. Ahlquist, "DNA Hybridization Evidence of Hominoid Phylogeny: A Reanalysis of the Data," *Journal of Molecular Evolution* 30 (1990):202–236; M. Goodman, D. A. Tagle, D. H. A. Fitch, W. Bailey, J. Czelusnak, B. F. Koop, P. Benson, and J. L. Slightom, "Primate Evolution at the DNA Level and a Classification of Hominids," *Journal of Molecular Evolution* 30 (1990):260–266. See also Jonathan H. Turner and Alexandra Maryanski, *Incest: Origins of the Taboo* (Boulder, CO: Paradigm Press, 2005) and *On the Origins of Societies*.

[81]This technique is a standard tool for reconstruction in fields such as comparative biology, historical linguistics, and textual criticism. Essentially, the basic procedure is to identify a set of characters believed to be the end points or descendants of an evolutionary or developmental process, with the idea that an "original" or common ancestor can be reconstructed through the detection of shared diagnostic characters.

[82]For discussions of this methodology, see R. Jeffers and I. Lehiste, *Principles and Methods for Historical Linguistics* (Cambridge: MIT Press, 1979); M. Hass, "Historical Linguistics and the Genetic Relationship of Languages," *Current Trends in Linguistics* 3 (1966):113–153; and N. Platnick and H. D. Cameron, "Cladistic Methods in Textual, Linguistic, and Phylogenetic Analysis," *Systematic Zoology* 26 (1977):380–385.

whether or not the shared patterns of social relations are caused by chance, and (2) the *Regularity Hypothesis* which indirectly assesses whether the modifications from the ancestral to descendant forms evidence a systematic bias and are not randomly acquired. Both hypotheses provided strong empirical support for her reconstruction of the ancestral patterns of organization for hominoids (i.e., apes and humans).

Her analysis led to a striking conclusion: like the contemporary apes that are phyletically closest to humans, the Last Common Ancestral population evidenced a fluid organizational structure consisting of a relatively low level of sociality and a lack of intergenerational continuity in groups over time.

The proximal reasons for this structure are a combination of several forces that are still found in all living ape social networks: (a) a systematic bias toward female (and usually male) transfer from the natal unit at puberty, which is the opposite trend from monkeys, where only males transfer and females stay to form intergenerational matrilines; (b) a promiscuous mating pattern that makes paternity difficult to determine (the gibbon being the exception); and (c) an abundance of weak social ties and few strong ties among most adults. In addition, the modifications from the LCA social structure suggest that after the descendants separated from the ancestral population, the future trend in hominoid evolution (i.e., apes and humans) involved selection pressures for heightened sociality, seemingly to increase hominoid survival and reproductive success. Indeed, it is an established fact in the fossil record that about 18 million years ago, a huge number of the many species of apes underwent a dramatic decline and extinction, just when species of monkeys suddenly proliferated and, according to the fossil record, moved into the former ape niches, perhaps because monkeys developed a competitive dietary edge over apes. Whatever the explanation, the fossil record confirms that, when ape niches were being usurped by monkeys, apes began to undergo anatomical modifications in order to sustain themselves in the marginal niches in the arboreal habitat. These niches were at the less verdant tops of the trees, where branches are less substantial and food and space are less available. These adaptations revolved around a peculiar locomotion pattern that involves hand-over-hand movement in the trees through space, along with other novel skeletal features that characterize the anatomy of both apes and humans today.[83] Today, monkeys remain the dominant primates, and apes are a distinct tiny minority; moreover, the few remaining nonhuman hominoids—that is, the chimpanzee, gorilla, orangutan, and gibbon—are now considered "evolutionary failures" and "evolutionary leftovers" because of their small numbers and specialized and restricted niches.

The significance of this finding is important for thinking about human nature. If humans' closest relatives reveal a tendency for relatively weak social ties, then

---

[83]For discussions, see P. Andrews, "Species Diversity and Diet in Monkeys and Apes During the Miocene," in *Aspects of Human Evolution*, ed. C. B. Stringer (London: Taylor and Francis, 1981), 25–61; J. Temerin and J. Cant, "The Evolutionary Divergence of Old World Monkeys and Apes," *American Naturalist* 122 (1983):335–351; and R. Ciochon and R. Corruccini (eds.), *New Interpretations of Ape and Human Ancestry* (New York: Plenum Press, 1983).

humans are also likely to have this social tendency as part of their genetic coding. What, however, is meant by weak and fluid ties?[84] Maryanski confirmed in her review of the data that monkeys have many strong ties, especially among females, who live in high-density matri-focal networks. In monkey societies, males disperse at puberty to other groups, whereas females remain behind, forming as many as four generations of strongly tied matrilines (composed of grandmothers, mothers, sisters, aunts, cousins, and daughters). These extended female bonds provide intergenerational continuity and are the backbone of most monkey societies. In contrast, females in ape societies evidence the rare pattern of dispersal where, at puberty, females leave their natal community forever. In addition, males in ape societies (with the exception of the chimpanzee) also depart from their natal communities, migrating to a new community. Thus, with both sexes dispersing at puberty, most kinship ties are broken, intergenerational continuity is lost, and the result is a relatively fluid social structure with adult individuals moving about as a shifting collection of individuals within a larger regional population.

In Asia, adult orangutans are nearly solitary, rarely interacting with others. A mother with her dependent young are the only stable social unit. In Africa, chimpanzees and gorillas are more socially inclined, with gorillas living together peacefully in small groups, but individuals are so self-contained that it is uncommon to observe any overt social interactions between adults. Among our closest relatives, the common chimpanzees, adult females are also self-contained, spending most of their days traveling about alone with their dependent offspring. Adult chimpanzee males, in contrast, are relatively more social and are likely to have a few individual "friendships" with other males because, unlike females in the regional population, they have grown up in this larger regional community. A mother and son also form strong ties. But, except for the mother and her young offspring, there are no stable groupings in chimpanzee societies. Thus, chimpanzee males are still highly individualistic and self-reliant, preferring to move about independently in space within a large and fluid regional population.

Thus, if humans' closest African ape relatives evidence behavioral propensities for individualism, autonomy, mobility, and weak social ties, Maryanski argues that these genetically coded propensities are probably part of human nature as well. Indeed, if we examine the societal type within which humans as a species evolved—that is,

---

[84]To array social tie patterns, affective ties were assessed on the basis of mutually reinforcing and friendly interactions. Degrees of attachment were described along a simple scale of tie strength: null ties, weak ties, moderate ties, strong ties. Individuals without ties (e.g., father-daughter where paternity cannot be known) or who rarely, if ever, interact have null ties; those who interact in a positive manner on an occasional basis have weak ties; those who affiliate closely for a time but without endurance over time (at least for adults) have moderate ties; and those who exhibit extensive nonsexual physical contact with much observable affect (e.g., reciprocal grooming), have very high interactional rates, and show mutual support with stable and long-term relations over time have strong ties. Scaling tie strength for primates is a straightforward procedure because age and sex classes have clear-cut social tendencies that have been documented by field researchers during the last fifty years. See also Maryanski, "The Last Ancestor" and Maryanski and Turner, *The Social Cage*, for detailed discussions about how the network analysis of primate social ties was conducted. For general references on network analysis, see Chapter 28 on social network analysis in this book.

hunting-and-gathering—it is clear that it approximates the pattern among the great apes, especially African apes: there is considerable mobility within a larger home range of bands; there is a high degree of individualism and personal autonomy; and, except for married couples, relatively loose and fluid social ties are evident. At a biological level then, Maryanski argues, humans might not have the powerful biological urges for great sociality and collectivist-style social bonding that sociologists, and indeed social philosophy in general, frequently impute to our nature.[85]

In collaborative work with me, Maryanski has described the implications in a review of the stages of societal development. Hunting-and-gathering is the stage of evolution in which human's basic "human" biological coding evolved. In these societies of small societies, wandering bands within a territory evidence rather loose and fluid social ties among their members, high individual autonomy, self-reliance, and mobility from band to band.[86] Yet as human populations grew in size and were forced to adopt first horticulture and then agriculture to sustain themselves, they settled down to cultivate land, and in the process, they "caged" themselves in sociocultural forms that violated basic needs for freedom, some degree of individual autonomy, and fluid ties within a larger community of local groups.

Thus, sociocultural evolution began to override the basic nature of humans. Maryanski and I conclude that market-driven systems of the present industrial and postindustrial era are, despite their many obvious problems, closer than horticulture and agrarianism to the original societal type in which humans evolved biologically, at least in this sense: they offer more choices; they allow and indeed encourage individualism; they are structured in ways that make most social ties fluid and transitory; and they limit strong ties beyond family for many. Maryanski and I note that, for many sociologists of the past and today, the very features of human behavior required by market-driven societies are viewed as pathologies that violate humans' basic nature. For us, however, societal evolution has, since the hunting-and-gathering era, just begun once again to create conditions more compatible with humans' basic hominoid nature as an evolved ape.

Although many of these conclusions are obviously somewhat speculative, the point of Maryanski's analysis is clear: if we use evolutionary approaches from biology, such as cladistic analysis and cross-species comparison with humans' close biological relatives, we can make informed inferences about human nature. Then, we can use these inferences to determine whether sociocultural evolution has been compatible or incompatible with humans' primate legacy. From this analysis, it is possible to examine basic institutional systems, such as kinship, polity, religion, and

---

[85]See, for example, M. G. Bicchieri, *Hunters and Gatherers Today* (New York: Holt, Rinehart and Winston, 1972), for a study of eleven food-collecting societies. See also Margaret Power, *The Egalitarians—Human and Chimpanzee: An Anthropological View of Social Organization* (Cambridge, UK: Cambridge University Press, 1991), xviii, 290 and Robert C. Bailey and Robert Aunger, "Humans as Primates: The Social Relationships of Efe Pygmy Men in Comparative Perspective," *International Journal of Primatology*, 11(2, 1990):127–145, which details some of the similarities between chimpanzee and human hunter-gatherer societies.

[86]Maryanski and Turner, *The Social Cage*, chap. 4, 69–90. See also Jonathan H. Turner and Alexandra Maryanski, *The Evolution of Societies by Natural Selection* (Boulder, CO: Paradigm Press, 2008).

economy to determine how and why they evolved in the first societal type—that is, hunting-and-gathering—and how they have interacted with humans' basic nature as an evolved ape during the various stages of societal development.

Making Evolutionary Theorizing More Darwinian, Biological

As is evident, Darwinian-inspired theoretical approaches are highly diverse. Sociobiology and evolutionary psychology are closely linked, but outside this theoretical line, Darwinian approaches are diverse. Perhaps the most promising are those approaches that are comparative, examining humans and their societies with an eye to where they converge and diverge from other species of social life forms. Machalek's comparative approach looks for the design problems that natural selection had to overcome to produce macro societies; and in isolating these problems, he hits upon the key social forces involved in organizing large-scale macro societies in general. In many ways, his analysis confirms the insights of the first functional sociologists, who all recognized that evolution generates macro societies through differentiation and new modes of integration—whether this society be composed of insects or humans. Indeed, Herbert Spencer's emphasis on *superorganic systems* as the subject matter argues for a sociology that studies all animals and life forms that live in societies composed of organisms.

Maryanski's approach takes theorizing back to an issue that has always been prominent in theorizing: human nature. But her approach liberates analysis from speculation about the needs and drives of humans because it uses cladistic analysis to look back in time to the features of the LCA of apes and humans. In so doing, inferences about human nature are tied to data from the networks of primates to reconstruct the nature of sociality among those species of hominins from which all humans have descended. The picture that emerges of humans' distant ancestors—individualistic, mobile, promiscuous, and weak-tie animals that do not form permanent groupings—is very different from the popular image among both sociologists and the lay public of humans as group-oriented and collectivistic. No doubt, evolution has made humans more social than the LCA of apes and humans, and more social than apes as well. But natural selection does not typically wipe away older traits; rather, it adds new traits onto existing ones, with the result that humans are individualistic and weak-tie animals on whom natural selection has laid down a patina of sociality. There is, in many ways, a conflict in humans' neuroanatomy between individualism and collectivism that has large consequences on how humans behave, interact, and organize.

The fact that these Darwinian-inspired approaches address traditional sociological questions argues for their persistence in sociology, even as they come under criticism by those who do not think biological dynamics are necessary in developing sociological theories. Still, even in the face of persistent criticism, this line of evolutionary sociology is not likely to go away. It is not, as some have claimed, a "fad" but a pervasive effort to develop a more interdisciplinary sociology—one that recognizes that humans are animals and, hence, have evolved like all other animals, thereby making biological forces relevant in sociological theorizing.

Conclusions

For many sociologists, the revival of evolutionary theorizing in their stage models of societal evolution or in their adoption of key ideas from the Modern Synthesis in evolutionary theory has not been a good thing. These critics had hoped that evolutionary theorizing—whatever its guise—would simply stay dead, but this is only wishful thinking. As I tried to point out, not only is some notion of stages useful as a history of how human societies have evolved over the last 200,000 years, but the data assembled in tracing the stages of this history are critical to assessing the plausibility of all macro-level theorizing. It is also wishful thinking that the more Darwinian-inspired ideas could stay out of the social sciences because both biologists and then psychologists, and even economists, have brought them back into the social sciences. These are all much more prestigeful fields than sociology, and if they bring the ideas back, then sociologists had better be prepared to deal with them. Rather than reject biologically oriented theorizing, sociologists should bend it to their purposes. Rather than be threatened by the revival of biology in sociology, as so many are, sociologists should view it as an opportunity to do some new and interesting theorizing and research that does not make the mistakes so evident in sociobiology and evolutionary psychology.[87] Sociologists thus need to demonstrate where biological theorizing can be useful and supplement traditional sociological explanation and where biological reasoning is not useful. In this way, sociology will not make the same mistake it did at the beginning of the twentieth century by throwing "the baby out with the bathwater."

---

[87]See Jonathan H. Turner and Alexandra Maryanski, "The Limitations of Evolutionary Theory From Biology in Explaining Socio-Cultural Evolution," *Sociologica* 3 (2008): 1–38. This article indicates where we think biology can be used and where it is less useful in the study of human behavior, interaction, and organization.

CHAPTER 14

Conflict Theorizing

For the first half of the twentieth century, conflict theorizing remained somewhat dormant. There were, of course, analyses of conflict for specific empirical phenomena, such as ethnic strife, class tensions, intersocietal war, colonialism, and other dissociative processes. But the conflict ideas contained in the German masters had not been fully incorporated into the mainstream of sociological theory, especially in America. Marxist scholarship was particularly recessive, being repressed in America by the anticommunism of the Cold War era.

With the 1960s, however, came a broad social and intellectual movement that confronted the then current institutional practices in Western societies; in this new environment, conflict sociology was reborn, soon becoming an important part of the theoretical canon.

Early Analytical Conflict Theories: Lewis A. Coser and Ralf Dahrendorf

The early conflict theories were *analytical* because they are committed to the goals of science and thus sought to develop concepts and propositions that are highly abstract and, it was hoped, relevant for all times and places. Conflict was seen as a fundamental process in the social universe, with the goal of theorizing to specify the conditions and forces that generate conflict of varying degrees of intensity and violence with what effects on societies and social structures more generally. These early theories were, to varying degrees, also critical of Marxian theorizing because Marxist theorists had ignored the work of the other two great German theorists, Max Weber (Chapter 5) and Georg Simmel (Chapter 6). The two most important of these early analytical theorists were Ralf Dahrendorf and Lewis Coser, both of whom as German scholars were sympathetic to Weber and Simmel. Dahrendorf sought to develop a more value-neutral and abstract dialectical theory, while Coser's efforts followed Simmel in seeking to analyze the functions of conflict. Let me examine Dahrendorf's first.

Ralf Dahrendorf's Dialectical Conflict Theory

Making Marx's Theory More Abstract. In the late 1950s, Ralf Dahrendorf likened functional theories to a utopia.[1] Since theory had been so one-sided in studying the functions of structures, an equally one-sided conflict approach might be needed, at least for a time, to generate a more balanced theory of human social organization.[2] The model that emerged from this theoretical calling is a *dialectical conflict perspective,* which still represents one of the best efforts to incorporate the insights of Marx and (to a lesser extent) Weber and Simmel into a coherent and nonevaluative set of theoretical propositions. Dahrendorf believed that the process of institutionalization involves the creation of *imperatively coordinated associations* (ICAs) that, in terms of criteria not specified, represent a distinguishable organization of roles. This organization is characterized by power relationships, with some clusters of roles having power to extract conformity from others. Dahrendorf was somewhat vague on this point, but it appears that any social unit—from a small group or formal organization to a community or an entire society—could be considered an ICA for analytical purposes if an organization of roles displaying power differentials exists. Furthermore, although power denotes the coercion of some by others, these power relations in ICAs tend to become legitimated and can therefore be viewed as authority relations in which some positions have the "accepted" or "normative right" to dominate others. Dahrendorf thus conceived of the social order as maintained by processes creating authority relations in the various types of ICAs existing throughout all layers of social systems.[3]

At the same time, however, power and authority are the scarce resources over which subgroups within a designated ICA compete and fight. They are thus the major sources of conflict and change in these institutionalized patterns. This conflict is ultimately a reflection of where clusters of roles in an ICA stand in relation to authority, because the "objective interests" inherent in any role are a direct function of whether or not that role possesses authority and power over other roles. However, even though roles in ICAs possess varying degrees of authority, any particular ICA can be typified as just two basic types of roles, ruling and ruled. The ruling cluster of roles has an interest in preserving the status quo, and the ruled cluster has an interest in redistributing power, or authority. Under certain

---

[1]Ralf Dahrendorf, "Out of Utopia: Toward a Reorientation in Sociological Analysis," *American Journal of Sociology* 64 (1958):115–127.

[2]As Dahrendorf emphasizes in "Out of Utopia," "I do not intend to fall victim to the mistake of many structural-functional theorists and advance for the conflict model a claim to comprehensive and exclusive applicability . . . it may well be that in a philosophical sense, society has two faces of equal reality; one of stability, harmony, and consensus and one of change, conflict and constraint." Such disclaimers are, in reality, justifications for arguing for the primacy of conflict in society. By claiming that functionalists are one-sided, it becomes fair game to be equally one-sided to "balance" past one-sidedness.

[3]Ralf Dahrendorf, "Toward a Theory of Social Conflict," *Journal of Conflict Resolution* 2 (1958):170–183, *Class and Class Conflict in Industrial Society* (Stanford, CA: Stanford University Press, 1959), 168–169, *Gesellschaft un Freiheit* (Munich, Germany: R. Piper, 1961), *Essays in the Theory of Society* (Stanford, CA: Stanford University Press, 1967).

specified conditions, awareness of these contradictory interests increases, with the result that ICAs polarize into two conflict groups, each now aware of its objective interests, which then engage in a contest for authority. The resolution of this contest or conflict involves the redistribution of authority in the ICA, thus making conflict the source of change in social systems. In turn, the redistribution of authority represents the institutionalization of a new cluster of ruling and ruled roles that, under certain conditions, polarize into two interest groups that initiate another contest for authority. Social reality is thus typified by this unending cycle of conflict over authority within the various types of ICAs that constitute the social world.

Much like Marx, this image of institutionalization as a cyclical or dialectic process led Dahrendorf into the analysis of only certain key causal relations: (a) conflict is assumed to be an inexorable process arising from opposing forces within social and structural arrangements; (b) such conflict is accelerated or retarded by a series of intervening structural conditions or variables; and (c) conflict resolution at one point in time creates a structural situation that, under specifiable conditions, inevitably leads to further conflict among opposed forces. Moreover, Dahrendorf's and Marx's models reveal similar causal chains of events leading to conflict and the reorganization of social structure. Relations of domination and subjugation create an "objective" opposition of interests. Awareness or consciousness by the subjugated of this inherent opposition of interests occurs under certain specifiable conditions. Under other conditions this newfound awareness leads to the political organization and, then, to polarization of subjugated groups, which join in conflict with the dominant group. The outcome of the conflict will usher in a new pattern of social organization; this new pattern of social organization will have within it relations of domination and subjugation that set off another sequence of events leading to conflict and then change in patterns of social organization.

The intervening conditions affecting these processes are outlined by both Marx and Dahrendorf only with respect to the formation of awareness of opposed interests by the subjugated, the politicization and polarization of the subjugated into a conflict group, and the outcome of the conflict. The intervening conditions under which institutionalized patterns generate dominant and subjugated groups in the first place and the conditions under which these can be typified as having opposed interests remain unspecified by Dahrendorf, whereas for Marx they were to be understood as inhering in the dynamics of capitalism (see Chapter 4).

Developing Explanatory Propositions. Dahrendorf outlined three types of intervening empirical conditions that generate conflict. One set of conditions are those of *organization,* and they facilitate the transformation of latent quasi groups into manifest conflict groups; another set are those that determine the *form and intensity of conflict;* and the final set of conditions are those affecting the amount, speed, and depth of the changes in social structure that ensue from conflict. More formally, the variables in the theoretical scheme are (a) the degree of conflict group formation, (b) the degree of intensity of the conflict, (c) the degree of violence of the conflict,

(d) the magnitude of change in social structure arising from the conflict, and (e) the rate of such change. As is evident in Table 14.1, Dahrendorf's propositions appear to be an elaboration of those developed by Marx (compare Table 14.1 with propositions 6 through 11 on pp. 108–111 summarizing Marx's theory in a more abstract manner that is close to Darhendorf's effort).[4]

Table 14.1 Dahrendorf's Abstract Propositions

---

1. Conflict is likely to occur as members of quasi groups in ICAs can become aware of their objective interests and form a conflict group, which, in turn, is related to

   A. The "technical" conditions of organization, which, in turn, depend on

      1. The formation of a leadership cadre among quasi groups
      2. The codification of an idea system, or charter

   B. The "political" conditions of organization, which are dependent on dominant groups permitting organization of opposed interests

   C. The "social" conditions of organization, which, in turn, are related to

      1. Opportunities for members of quasi groups to communicate
      2. Opportunities for recruiting members.

2. The less the technical, political, and social conditions of organization are met, the more intense the conflict will be.

3. The more the distribution of authority and other rewards are associated with each other (superimposed), the more intense will be the conflict.

4. The less the mobility between superordinate and subordinate groups, the more intense will be the conflict.

5. The less the technical, political, and social conditions of organization are met, the more violent will be the conflict.

6. The more the deprivation of the subjugated in the distribution of rewards shifts from an absolute to a relative basis, the more violent will be the conflict.

7. The less the ability of conflict groups to develop regulatory agreements, the more violent will be the conflict.

8. The more intense the conflict, the more will be the degree of structural change and reorganization.

9. The more violent the conflict, the greater will be the rate of structural change.

---

[4]The propositions listed in the table differ from those in a list provided by Dahrendorf, *Class and Class Conflict*, 239–240, in two respects: (1) they are phrased consistently as statements of covariance and (2) they are phrased somewhat more abstractly without reference to "class," which in this particular work was Dahrendorf's primary concern.

Like Marx, Dahrendorf saw conflict as related to subordinates' growing awareness of their interests and formation into conflict groups (proposition 1). Such awareness and group formation are a positive function of the degree to which (a) the technical conditions (leadership and unifying ideology), (b) the political conditions (capacity to organize), and (c) the social conditions (ability to communicate) are met. These ideas clearly come from Marx's discussion. However, as shown in proposition 2, Dahrendorf borrows from Simmel and contradicts Marx, emphasizing that if groups are not well organized—that is, if the technical, political, and social conditions are not met—then conflict is likely to be emotionally involving. Then, Dahrendorf borrowed from Weber (proposition 3) by stressing that the superimposition of rewards—that is, the degree of correlation among those who enjoy privilege (power, wealth, and prestige)—also increases the emotional involvement of subordinates who pursue conflict. Proposition 4 shows that Dahrendorf also takes as much from Weber as from Marx: Dahrendorf believed that the lack of mobility into positions of authority escalates the emotional involvement of subordinates. Proposition 5 is clearly from Simmel and contradicts Marx in that the violence of conflict is related to the lack of organization and absence of clear articulation of interests. But in proposition 6, Dahrendorf returns to Marx's emphasis that sudden escalation in people's perception of deprivation—that is, relative deprivation—increases the likelihood of violent conflict. In proposition 7, however, Dahrendorf returns to Simmel and argues that violence is very much related to the capacity of a system to develop regulatory procedures for dealing with grievances and releasing tensions. And in propositions 8 and 9, Dahrendorf moves again to Marx's emphasis on how conflict produces varying rates and degrees of structural change in a social system.

Lewis Coser's Functional Conflict Theory

Lewis Coser was one of the first modern conflict theorists, and he published a major work on conflict before Ralf Dahrendorf. Yet because this work had a functional flavor and had borrowed from Simmel more than from Marx, it was not initially seen as a devastating critique of functionalism in quite the same way as Dahrendorf's early polemic. Still, in his more functional version of conflict theory, Coser launched what became the standard polemic against functionalism: conflict is not given sufficient attention, and related phenomena such as deviance and dissent are too easily viewed as "pathological" for the equilibrium of the social system.[5] Yet, although Coser consistently maintained that functional theorizing "has too often neglected the dimensions of power and interest," he did not follow either Marx's or Dahrendorf's emphasis on the disruptive consequences of violent conflict. Rather, Coser sought to correct Dahrendorf's analytical excesses by emphasizing the integrative and "adaptability" functions of conflict for social

---

[5]Lewis A. Coser, *The Functions of Social Conflict* (London: Free Press, 1956).

systems.[6] Thus, Coser justified his efforts by criticizing functionalism[7] for ignoring conflict and by criticizing conflict theory for underemphasizing the functions of conflict. In so doing, he turned to Georg Simmel's view of conflict as promoting social integration of the social systems, or at least of some of its critical parts.

Coser's analysis then proceeded as follows. Imbalances in the integration of system parts lead to the outbreak of varying types of conflict among these parts, which in turn causes temporary reintegration of the system, which leads to increased flexibility in the system's structure, increased capability to resolve future imbalances through conflict, and increased capacity to adapt to changing conditions. Coser executed this approach by developing, at least implicitly in his discursive argument, a variety of propositions that I have extracted and formalized in the tables below.

The Causes of Conflict. Much like Weber, Coser emphasized that the withdrawal of legitimacy from an existing system of inequality is a critical precondition for conflict. In contrast, dialectical theorists such as Dahrendorf tended to view the causes of conflict as residing in "contradictions" or "conflicts of interest." In such dialectical theories, as subordinates become aware of their interests, they pursue conflict; hence, the major theoretical task is to specify the conditions raising the levels of awareness. But Coser argued that conflicts of interest are likely to be exposed only after the deprived withdraw legitimacy. Coser emphasized that the social order is maintained by some degree of consensus over existing sociocultural arrangements and that "disorder" through conflict occurs only when certain conditions decrease this consensus.

Two such conditions are specified in propositions 1-A and 1-B of Table 14.2, both of which owe their inspiration more to Weber than to Marx. When channels for expressing grievances do not exist and when the deprived's desire for membership in higher ranks is thwarted, the withdrawal of legitimacy becomes more likely.

As proposition 2 in Table 14.2 indicates, the withdrawal of legitimacy, in itself, is not likely to result in conflict. People must first become emotionally aroused. The theoretical task then becomes one of specifying the conditions that translate the

---

[6]A listing of some of Coser's prominent works, to be used in subsequent analysis, reveals the functional flavor of his conflict perspective: *Functions of Social Conflict,* "Some Social Functions of Violence," *Annals of the American Academy of Political and Social Science* 364 (1960):81–102, "Some Functions of Deviant Behavior and Normative Flexibility," *American Journal of Sociology* 68 (1962):172–181, and "The Functions of Dissent," in *The Dynamics of Dissent,* ed. Jules H. Masserman (New York: Grune and Stratton, 1968), 158–170. Other prominent works with less revealing titles but critical substance include "Social Conflict and the Theory of Social Change," *British Journal of Sociology* 8 (1957):197–207 and "Violence and the Social Structure," in *Science and Psychoanalysis,* ed. Jules H. Masserman, vol. 7 (New York: Grune and Stratton, 1963), 30–42. These and other essays are collected in Lewis A. Coser, *Continuities in the Study of Social Conflict* (New York: Free Press, 1967). One should also consult his *Masters of Sociological Thought* (New York: Harcourt Brace Jovanovich, 1977; repr. Lake Zurich, IL: Waveland Press, 2003).

[7]Lewis Coser, "Durkheim's Conservatism and Its Implications for His Sociological Theory," in *Émile Durkheim, 1858–1917: A Collection of Essays,* ed. K. H. Wolff (Columbus: Ohio State University Press, 1960); also reprinted in Coser's *Continuities in the Study of Social Conflict.*

Table 14.2 Coser's Propositions on the Causes of Conflict

1. Subordinate members in a system of inequality are more likely to initiate conflict as they question the legitimacy of the existing distribution of scarce resources, which, in turn, is caused by

   A. Few channels for redressing grievances
   B. Low rates of mobility to more privileged positions.

2. Subordinates are most likely to initiate conflict with superordinates as their sense of relative deprivation and, hence, injustice increases, which, in turn, is related to

   A. The extent to which socialization experiences of subordinates do not generate internal ego constraints
   B. The failure of superordinates to apply external constraints on subordinates.

withdrawal of legitimacy into emotional arousal, instead of some other emotional state such as apathy and resignation. Here, Coser drew inspiration from Marx's notion of relative deprivation. For, as Marx observed and as a number of empirical studies have documented, absolute deprivation does not always foster revolt.[8] When people's expectations for a better future suddenly begin to exceed the perceived avenues for realizing these expectations, only then do they become sufficiently aroused to pursue conflict. The level of arousal will, in turn, be influenced by their commitment to the existing system, by the degree to which they have developed strong internal constraints, and by the nature and amount of social control in a system. Such propositions, for example, lead to predictions that revolt by the masses is less likely in systems with absolute dictators who ruthlessly repress the masses than in systems where some freedoms have been granted and where the deprived have been led to believe that things will be getting better. Under these conditions the withdrawal of legitimacy can be accompanied by released passions and emotions.

The Violence of Conflict. Coser's most important propositions on the level of violence in a conflict are presented in Table 14.3.[9] As most functional theorists emphasized, Coser's proposition 1 in Table 14.3 is directed at specifying the conditions under which conflict will be less violent. In contrast, dialectical theorists, such as Marx, often aimed at just the opposite: specifying the conditions under which conflict will be more violent. Yet the inverse of Coser's first proposition can indicate a condition under which conflict will be violent. The key concept in this proposition

---

[8]The propositions in Table 14.2 are extracted from Coser, *The Functions of Social Conflict*, 8–385, "Social Conflict and the Theory of Social Change," 197–207, and "Violence and the Social Structure"; James Davies, "Toward a Theory of Revolution," *American Journal of Sociology* 27 (1962):5–19; and Ted Robert Gurr, *Why Men Rebel* (Princeton, NJ: Princeton University Press, 1970) and "Sources of Rebellion in Western Societies: Some Quantitative Evidence," *Annals* 38 (1973):495–501.

[9]These propositions are taken from Coser's *Functions of Social Conflict*, 45–50. Again, they have been made more formal than Coser's more discursive text.

Table 14.3   Coser's Propositions on the Violence of Conflict

1. When groups engage in conflict over realistic issues (obtainable goals), they are more likely to seek compromises over the means to realize their interests and, hence, the less violent will the conflict be.

2. When groups engage in conflict over nonrealistic issues, the greater is the level of emotional arousal and involvement in the conflict and, hence, the more violent will the conflict be, especially when
 	
  A. Conflict occurs over core values
  B. Conflict endures over time.

3. When functional interdependence among social units is low, the less available are the institutional means for absorbing conflicts and tensions and, hence, the more violent will the conflict be.

is "realistic issues." Coser reasoned that realistic conflict involves the pursuit of specific aims against real sources of hostility, with some estimation of the costs to be incurred in such pursuit.

As noted in Chapter 6, Simmel recognized that when clear goals are sought, compromise and conciliation are likely alternatives to violence. Coser restated this proposition (shown in proposition 2 in Table 14.3) on conflict over "nonrealistic issues," such as ultimate values, beliefs, ideology, and vaguely defined class interests. When the goal is nonrealistic, the conflict will be violent. Such nonrealism is particularly likely when conflict is about core values, which emotionally mobilize participants and make them unwilling to compromise (proposition 2-A). Moreover, if conflict endures for a long period of time, it becomes increasingly nonrealistic as parties become emotionally involved, as ideologies become codified, and as "the enemy" is portrayed in increasingly negative terms (proposition 2-B). Proposition 3 shows a more structural variable to the analysis of conflict violence. In systems in which there are high degrees of functional interdependence among actors—that is, where there are mutual exchanges and cooperation—conflict is less likely to be violent.

The Duration of Conflict. As shown in the propositions of Table 14.4, Coser underscored that conflicts with a broad range of goals or with vague ones will be prolonged.[10] When goals are limited and articulated, it is possible to know when they have been attained. With perception of attainment, the conflict can be terminated. Conversely, with a wide variety or long list of goals, a sense of attainment is less likely to occur, thus prolonging the conflict. Coser also emphasized that knowledge of what would symbolically constitute victory and defeat will influence the length of the conflict. If the parties do not have the ability to recognize defeat or victory, conflict is likely to be prolonged to a point where one party destroys the other. Leadership has

---

[10]These propositions come from Coser's "The Termination of Conflict," in *Continuities*, 37–52 and *Functions of Social Conflict*, 20, 48–55, 59, 128–133.

Table 14.4   Coser's Propositions on the Duration of Conflict

1. Conflict will be prolonged when

   A. The goals of the opposing parties to a conflict are expansive
   B. The degree of consensus over the goals of conflict is low
   C. The parties in a conflict cannot easily interpret their adversary's symbolic points of victory and defeat.

2. Conflict will be shortened when

   A. Leaders of conflicting parties perceive that complete attainment of goals is possible only at very high costs, which, in turn, is related to

      1. The equality of power between the conflicting groups
      2. The clarity of indexes of defeat or victory in a conflict

   B. Leaders are able to persuade followers to terminate the conflict, which, in turn, is related to

      1. Centralization of power in the conflicting parties
      2. Integration within the conflicting parties.

important effects on conflict processes; the more leaders can perceive that complete attainment of goals is not possible and the greater their ability to convince followers to terminate conflict, the less prolonged will the conflict be.

The Functions of Conflict. For Coser, conflict is functional when it promotes integration based on solidarity, clear authority, functional interdependence, and normative control. In Coser's terms, it is more adaptive. Other conflict theorists might argue that conflict in such a system is dysfunctional because integration and adaptability in this specific context may be highly exploitive. Nonetheless, Coser divided his analysis of the functions of conflict along lines similar to those by Simmel: the functions of conflict for the respective parties to the conflict and the systemic whole in which the conflict occurs.

In the propositions listed in Table 14.5, the intensity of conflict—that is, people's involvement in and commitment to pursue the conflict—and its level of violence increase the demarcation of boundaries (proposition 1-A), centralization of authority (proposition 1-B), structural and ideological solidarity (proposition 1-C), and suppression of dissent and deviance (proposition 1-D) within each of the conflict parties.[11] Conflict intensity is presumably functional because it increases integration, although centralization of power as well as the suppression of deviance and dissent create malintegrative pressures in the long run (see proposition 2). Thus, there appears to be an inherent dialectic in conflict group unification—one that creates pressures toward disunification. Unfortunately, Coser did not specify the conditions under which these malintegrative pressures are likely to surface.

---

[11] These propositions are taken from Coser's *Functions of Social Conflict*, 37–38, 45, 69–72, 92–95.

In focusing on positive functions—that is, forces promoting integration—the analysis ignored a promising area of inquiry. This bias becomes even more evident when Coser shifts attention to the functions of conflict for the systemic whole within which the conflict occurs. These propositions are listed in Table 14.6.[12]

Table 14.5 Coser's Propositions on the Functions of Conflict for the Respective Parties

1. The more violent or intense is the conflict, the more the conflict will generate

   A. Clear-cut boundaries for each conflict party
   B. Centralized decision-making structures for each conflict party, especially when these parties are structurally differentiated
   C. Structural and ideological solidarity among members of each conflict party, especially when the conflict is perceived to affect the welfare of all segments of the conflict parties
   D. Suppression of dissent and deviance within each conflict party as well as forced conformity to norms and values.

2. The more the conflict between parties leads centers of power to force conformity within conflict groups, the greater is the accumulation of hostilities and the more likely is internal group conflict to surface in the long run.

Table 14.6 Coser's Propositions on the Functions of Conflict for the Social Whole

1. The more differentiated and functionally interdependent the units in a system, the more likely is conflict to be frequent but of low degrees of intensity and violence.

2. The lower the intensity and violence of conflicts, the more likely are conflicts to

   A. Increase the level of innovation and creativity of system units
   B. Release hostilities before they polarize system units
   C. Promote normative regulation of conflict relations
   D. Increase awareness of realistic issues
   E. Increase the number of associative coalitions among social units.

3. The more conflict promotes 2-A through 2-E, the greater will be the level of internal social integration of the system as a whole and the greater will be its capacity to adapt to its external environment.

Coser's propositions are not presented in their full complexity in Table 14.6, but the essentials of his analysis are clear. In proposition 1, complex systems that have

---

[12] Ibid., 45–48, "Social Conflict and the Theory of Social Change," "Some Social Functions of Violence," "The Functions of Dissent."

a large number of interdependencies and exchanges are more likely to have frequent conflicts that are less emotionally involving and violent than conflicts in those systems that are less complex and in which tensions accumulate. The nature of interdependence, Coser argued, causes conflicts to erupt frequently, but because they emerge periodically, emotions do not build to the point where violence is inevitable. Conversely, systems in which there are low degrees of functional interdependence will often polarize into hostile camps; when conflict does erupt, it will be intense and violent. In proposition 2, frequent conflicts of low intensity and violence are seen to have certain positive functions. First, such frequent and low-intensity conflicts will force those in conflict to reassess and reorganize their actions (proposition 2-A). Second, these conflicts will release tensions and hostilities before they build up to a point where adversaries become polarized around nonrealistic issues (proposition 2-B). Third, frequent conflicts of low intensity and violence encourage the development of normative procedures—laws, courts, mediating agencies, and the like—to regulate tensions (proposition 2-C). Fourth, these kinds of conflicts also increase a sense of realism over what the conflict is about. That is, frequent conflicts in which intensity and violence are kept under control allow the conflicting parties to articulate their interests and goals, thereby allowing them to bargain and compromise (proposition 2-D). Fifth, conflicts promote coalitions among units that are threatened by the action of one party or another. If conflicts are frequent and of low intensity and violence, such coalitions come and go, thereby promoting flexible alliances (proposition 2-E). If conflicts are infrequent and emotions accumulate, however, coalitions often polarize the threatened parties into ever more hostile camps, with the result that when conflict does occur, it is violent. And proposition 3 simply states Coser's functional conclusion that when conflicts are frequent and when violence and intensity are reduced, conflict will promote flexible coordination within the system and increased capacity to adjust and adapt to environmental circumstances. This increase in flexibility and adaptation is possible because of the processes listed in propositions 2-A through 2-E.

Later Analytical Theorizing: Randall Collins

During the last forty years, Randall Collins has consistently employed a conflict approach, emphasizing that inequalities inevitably set into motion conflict processes, some of which are relatively mild and routinized, but many of which can become more violent. As with any theorist committed to science, Collins sees the goal of a sociological theory of conflict as using a few key ideas to generate explanations of the full range of social processes in human interaction and organization. At the core of all of Collins's theorizing is an emphasis on micro-level social processes from which all other meso- and macro-level sociocultural formations are built, sustained, and changed. Micro-social processes are conceptualized in a number of ways, but through all of his work runs the notion of *interaction rituals;* so we should begin with this topic.

Interaction Rituals

In his *Conflict Sociology: Toward an Explanatory Science,*[13] Randall Collins is one of the most forceful advocates of a sociology grounded in conceptualizations of face-to-face interaction. Collins's early analytical theorizing draws upon a variety of theories. One source of theoretical inspiration is Max Weber's analysis; other elements of his theory come from Émile Durkheim's analysis of rituals (Chapter 5); still additional elements come from Erving Goffman's dramaturgical theory of ritual performances (see Chapter 18). And over time, the theory has come to emphasize the effects of emotions, as they are aroused in interaction rituals, on conflict processes. As noted above, Collins's argument is that macro-level phenomena are, ultimately, created and sustained by micro encounters among individuals.[14] In essence, large and long-term social structures are built from interaction rituals that have been strung together over time. If a true understanding of social reality is to be achieved by sociological theorizing, then face-to-face interaction must be theorized and examined empirically, even if this examination only involves sampling of interaction rituals within a macrostructure.[15]

The Early Conceptualization of Interaction Rituals

Interaction rituals occur when individuals are physically copresent, when these individuals reveal a common focus of attention, when they develop a common emotional mood, when they represent their common focus and mood with symbols (words, objects, phrases, speech styles, etc.), and when they develop a sense of moral righteousness about these symbols. The dynamics of these rituals revolve around several elements. First, individuals bring to a face-to-face encounter *cultural capital,* or resources that they command in the broader society (e.g., power and authority, knowledge, education, network ties and alliances, experiences) or that they accumulated in past interactions of a particular type (e.g., memories, information, knowledge, or other resources that they can use again when an interaction is reconstituted). Second, individuals bring a level of *emotional energy* to the interaction, which, in turn, is related to (a) the level of cultural capital they possess, (b) the power and prestige or status that they enjoy in the interaction situation, and (c) their memories about the levels of positive emotions or enhanced cultural capital experienced the previous time the interaction occurred. Third, individuals *monitor situations* along several lines: (a) the respective resources of other actors relative to self; (b) the number of others present in a situation; (c) the number of alternative options to the present interaction that are available to self and others; (d) the amount of work-practical, ceremonial, and

---

[13]Randall Collins, *Conflict Sociology: Toward an Explanatory Science* (New York: Academic Press, 1975).

[14]Randall Collins, "On the Micro-Foundation of Macro-Sociology," *American Journal of Sociology* 86 (1981):984–1014.

[15]Randall Collins, "Micro-Translation as a Theory of Building Strategy," in *Advances in Social Theory and Methodology: Toward an Integration of Micro- and Macro-Sociology,* ed. K. Knorr-Cetina and A. V. Cicourel (London: Routledge, 1981), 84–96.

social content of the interaction; and, most important, (e) the payoffs in the amount of positive emotional energy and augmentation of cultural capital likely to be gained from a person's assessment of the inequalities in resources, the alternatives that might be pursued, the number of others presently monitoring the situation, the nature of the situation (as social, work-practical, or ceremonial), and the experiences (emotional energy and cultural capital received) in previous interactions of this nature.

These properties of interaction rituals were first outlined in the mid-1970s in Collins's *Conflict Sociology*,[16] which was Weberian in several senses. First, interaction rituals are Collins's more robust portrayal of what Weber had viewed as "action," and like Weber, Collins moves rapidly from the analysis of micro-social processes to meso-level social forces, such as stratification and organizations, and then to truly macro-level processes operating at the societal and intersocietal levels. Yet in developing this early view of interaction rituals, there is a heavy dose of Émile Durkheim's theory of rituals developed in his *The Elementary Forms of the Religious Life*[17] and, closer to the present, Erving Goffman's theorizing on encounters of face-to-face interaction. Indeed, as we see in Chapter 18 on Goffman's work, Collins's initial conceptualization of interaction rituals is virtually identical to Goffmans' definition of "the encounter,"[18] but with a large difference: Collins theorizes the meso and macro levels of social organization, something that Goffman never did. Second, and this is what made Collins's early conflict theory Weberian, the dynamics of interaction rituals became ever more recessive as analysis became more macro—just as notions of individual action were soon abandoned as Weber theorized about meso- and macro-social processes.

In *Conflict Sociology*, Collins proposed the following steps for building social theory. First, examine typical real-life situations in which people encounter one another. Second, focus on the material arrangements that affect interaction—the physical layout of situations, the means and modes of communication, the available tools, weapons, and goods. Third, assess the relative resources that people bring to, use in, or extract from encounters. Fourth, entertain the general hypotheses that those with resources press their advantage, that those without resources seek the best deal they can get under the circumstances, and that stability and change are to be explained through the lineups and shifts in the distribution of resources. Fifth, assume that cultural symbols—ideas, beliefs, norms, values, and the like—are used to represent the interests of those parties who have the resources to make their views prevail. Sixth, look for the general and generic features of particular cases so that more abstract propositions can be extracted from the empirical particulars of a situation.

Collins is particularly concerned with the distribution of individuals in physical space, with their respective capital or resources for use in exchanges, and with inequalities in resources. The respective resources of individuals—especially power,

---

[16]See Collins, *Conflict Sociology*, 153, where the elements of what later became known as *interaction rituals* are listed.

[17]Émile Durkheim, *The Elementary Forms of the Religious Life* (New York: Free Press, 1947; originally published 1912).

[18]Erving Goffman, *Encounters* (Indianapolis, IN: Bobbs-Merrill, 1961) and *Interaction Ritual* (Garden City, NY: Anchor Books, 1967).

material, and symbolic resources—are critical to what transpires in interaction rituals. *Power resources* enable individuals to coerce or to have others do so on their behalf; *material resources* are wealth and the control of money, as well as property or the capacity to control the physical setting and people's place in it; and *symbolic resources* are the respective levels of linguistic and conversational resources as well as the capacity to use cultural ideas, such as ideologies, values, and beliefs, for one's purposes.

A central consideration in all Collins's propositions in his early work is *social density,* or the number of people copresent in a situation where an encounter takes place. Social density is, of course, part of the macrostructure because it is typically the result of past chains of interaction. But it can also be a "material resource" that some individuals can use to their advantage. Thus, the interaction in an encounter will be most affected by the participants' relative resources and the density or number of individuals copresent. These variables influence the two underlying microdynamics in Collins's scheme: talk and ritual.

Talk and Ritual

Collins sees talk as the emission of verbal and nonverbal gestures that carry meaning and that are used to communicate with others and to sustain (or create) a common sense of reality.[19] Talk is one of the key symbolic resources of individuals in encounters, and much of what transpires among interacting individuals is talk and the use of this cultural capital to develop their respective lines of conduct. As can be seen in proposition 1 in Table 14.7, the likelihood that people will talk is related to their sheer copresence: if others are near, a person is likely to strike up a conversation.

Table 14.7 Key Propositions on the Conditions

Producing Talk and Conversation
1. The likelihood of talk and conversational exchanges among individuals is a positive and additive function of (a) the degree of their physical copresence, (b) the emotional gratifications retained from their previous conversational exchanges, (c) the perceived attractiveness of their respective resources, and (d) their level of previous ritual activity.
2. The greater the degree of equality and similarity that exists in the resources of individuals, the more likely conversational exchanges are to be (a) personal, (b) flexible, and (c) long-term.
3. The greater the level of inequality that exists in the resources of individuals, the more likely conversational exchanges are to be (a) impersonal, (b) highly routinized, and (c) short-term.
4. The greater the amount of talk among individuals, especially among equals, the more likely are (a) strong, positive emotions; (b) sentiments of liking; (c) common agreements, moods, outlooks, and beliefs; and (d) strong social attachments sustained by rituals.

---

[19]Collins, *Conflict Sociology,* 156–157.

More important sociologically are conversations that are part of a "chain" of previous encounters. If people felt good about a past conversation, they will usually make efforts to have another; if they perceive each other's resources, especially symbolic or cultural but also material ones, as desirable, then they will seek to talk again. And if they have developed ritualized interaction that affirms their common group membership, they will be likely to enact those rituals again. As proposition 2 indicates, conversations among equals who share common levels of resources will be more personal, flexible, and long-term because people feel comfortable with such conversations.

As a result, the encounter raises their levels of emotional energy and increases their cultural capital. That is, they are eager to talk again and to pick up where they left off. However, the nature of talk in an encounter changes dramatically when there is inequality in the resources of the participants. As shown in proposition 3, subordinates will try to avoid wasting or losing emotional energy and spending their cultural capital by keeping the interaction brief, formal, and highly ritualized with trite and inexpensive words. Yet as proposition 4 indicates, even under conditions of inequality, and even more when equality exists, people who interact and talk in repeated encounters will tend, over time, to develop positive sentiments and have positive emotional feelings. Moreover, they will also converge in their definitions of situations and develop common moods, outlooks, beliefs, and ideas. And, finally, they will be likely to develop strong attachments and a sense of group solidarity, which is sustained through rituals.

Thus, the essence of interaction is talk and ritual as mediated by an exchange dynamic; as chains of encounters are linked together over time, conversations take on a more personal and also a ritualized character that results from, and at the same time reinforces, the growing sense of group solidarity among individuals. Such is the case because the individuals have "invested" their cultural capital (conversational resources) and have derived positive feelings from being defined as group members. Collins's intent is thus clear: to view social structure as the linking together of encounters through talk in rituals arousing emotions. This basic view of the micro reality of social life pervades all Collins's sociological theory to this day, although he has further developed the conception of interaction rituals, the analysis of inequalities in social life.

Deference and Demeanor

Inequality and stratification are structures only in the sense of being temporal chains of interaction rituals and exchanges among varying numbers of people with different levels of resources. Thus, to understand these structures, we must examine what people actually do across time and in space. One thing that people do in interaction is exhibit deference and demeanor. Collins and coauthor Joan Annett define deference as the process of manipulating gestures to show respect to others; or if one is in a position to command respect, the process of gesture manipulation is to elicit respect from others.[20] The actual manipulation of gestures is termed demeanor. Deference and demeanor are, therefore, intimately connected to each other. They are also tied to talk and rituals, because talk involves the use of gestures and because

---

[20]Randall Collins and Joan Annett, "A Short History of Deference and Demeanor," in *Conflict Sociology*, 161–224.

deference and demeanor tend to become routinized. Hence, deference and demeanor can be visualized as one form of talk and ritual activity—a form that is most evident in those interactions that create and sustain inequalities among people.

As would be expected from the above summary, Collins visualizes in *Conflict Sociology* several variables as central to understanding deference and demeanor:

1. Inequality in resources, particularly wealth and power.

2. Social density variables revolving around the degree to which behaviors are under the "surveillance of others" in a situation.

3. Social diversity variables revolving around the degree to which communication networks are "cosmopolitan" (i.e., not restricted to only those who are copresent in a situation).

In Table 14.8, these variables are incorporated into a few abstract propositions that capture the essence of Collins's and Annett's numerous propositions and descriptions of the history of deference and demeanor.[21] In these propositions, Collins and Annett argue that rituals and talk revealing deference and demeanor are most pronounced between people of unequal status, especially when their actions are observable and when communication outside the situation is restricted. Such density and surveillance are, of course, properties of the meso and macro structure as they distribute varying numbers of people in space. As surveillance decreases, however, unequals avoid contact or perform deference and demeanor rituals in a perfunctory manner. For example, military protocol will be much more pronounced between an officer and enlisted personnel in public on a military base than in situations where surveillance is lacking (e.g., off the base). Moreover, Collins and Annett stress that inequalities and low mobility between unequal groups create pressures for intra-group deference and demeanor rituals, especially when communications outside the group are low (e.g., between new army recruits and their officers or between prison inmates and guards). But as communication outside the group increases or as surveillance by group members decreases, then deference and demeanor will decrease.

Table 14.8   Key Propositions on Deference and Demeanor

1. The visibility, explicitness, and predictability of deference and demeanor rituals and talk among individuals increase with

   A. Inequality in resources among individuals, especially with respect to

      1. Material wealth

      2. Power

(Continued)

---

[21]Ibid., 216–219.

Table 14.8 (Continued)

B. Surveillance by others of behaviors, and surveillance increases with
  1. Copresence of others
  2. Homogeneity in the outlook of others
 	
C. Restrictiveness of communication networks (low cosmopolitanism), and restrictiveness decreases with
  1. Complexity in communications technologies
  2. Mobility of individuals.

2. The greater the degree of inequality among individuals and the lower the level of surveillance, the more likely behaviors are to be directed toward
 	
  A. Avoidance of contact and emission of deference and demeanor by individuals
  B. Perfunctory performance of deference and demeanor by individuals when avoidance is not possible.

3. The greater the degree of inequality among individuals and the lower the level of cosmopolitanism among individuals, the more likely behaviors are to be directed toward simplified but highly visible deference and demeanor.
4. The greater the degree of inequality among individuals and the less the degree of mobility among groups with varying levels of resources, the more visible, explicit, and predictable are deference and demeanor rituals and talk within these groups.
5. The greater the equality among individuals, the greater is the degree of cosmopolitanism, and the less is the level of surveillance and the less compelling are deference and demeanor talk and rituals.

Class Cultures

These exchange processes revolving around talk, ritual, deference, and demeanor explain what are often seen as more macro processes in societies. One such process is variation in the class cultures, a point of emphasis that also reveals the Weberian thrust of Collins's early theory of conflict. That is, people in different social classes tend to exhibit diverging behaviors, outlooks, and interpersonal styles. These differences can be seen in two main variables:

1. The degree to which one possesses and uses the capacity to coerce, to materially bestow, and to symbolically manipulate others so that one can give orders in an encounter and have these orders followed

2. The degree to which communication is confined to others who are physically copresent in a situation or, conversely, the degree to which communication is diverse, involving the use of multiple modes of contact with many others in different situations

Using these two variables, as well as several less central variables, such as wealth and physical exertion on the job, Collins describes the class cultures of American society. More significantly for theory building, he also offers several abstract propositions that stipulate certain important relationships among power, order-giving, communication networks, and behavioral tendencies among individuals. These relationships are restated in somewhat altered form in Table 14.9.[22] With these principles, Collins explains variations in the behaviors, outlooks, and inter-personal styles of individuals in different occupations and status groups. For example, those occupations that require order-giving, that reveal high copresence of others, and that involve little physical exertion will generate behaviors that are distinctive and that circumscribe other activities, such as whom one marries, where one lives, what one values, and what activities one pursues in various spheres of life. Different weights to these variables would cause varying behavioral tendencies in individuals. Thus, from the processes delineated in the propositions of Table 14.9, understanding of variables such as class culture, ethnic cultures, lifestyles, and other concerns of investigators of stratification is achieved. But such understanding is anchored in the recognition that these class cultures are built and sustained by interaction chains in which deference and demeanor rituals have figured prominently. Thus, a class culture is not mere internalization of values and beliefs or simple socialization (although this is no doubt involved); rather, a class culture is the result of repeated encounters among unequals under varying conditions imposed by the meso and macro structures as they have been built from past chains of interaction.

Table 14.9   Key Propositions on Class Cultures

1. Giving orders to others in a situation increases with the capacity to mobilize and use coercive, material, and symbolic resources.
2. The behavioral attributes of self-assuredness, the initiation of talk, positive self-feelings, and identification with the goals of a situation are positively related to the capacity to give orders to others in that situation.
3. The behavioral attributes of toughness and courage increase as the degree of physical exertion and danger in that situation escalates.
4. The degree of behavioral conformity exhibited in a situation is positively related to the degree to which people can communicate only with others who are physically copresent in that situation and is negatively related to the degree to which people can communicate with a diversity of others who are not physically copresent.
5. The outlook and behavioral tendencies of an individual are an additive function of those spheres of life—work, politics, home, recreation, community—where varying degrees of giving or receiving orders, physical exertion, danger, and communication occur.

---

[22]Collins, *Conflict Sociology,* 49–88.

Organizational Processes

Like Weber before him, Collins also uses an extensive analysis of organizations and develops a rather long inventory of propositions on organizations' properties and dynamics.[23] These propositions overlap, to some degree, with those on stratification, because an organization is typically internally stratified with a comparatively clear hierarchy of authority. Table 14.10 lists three groups of propositions from Collins's analysis. These revolve around processes of organizational control, the administration of control, and the general organizational structure.

Table 14.10   Key Propositions on Organizations

Processes of Organizational Control
1. Control in patterns of organizations is a positive and additive function of the concentration among individuals of (a) coercive resources, (b) material resources, and (c) symbolic resources.
2. The form of control in organizations depends on the configuration of resources held by those individuals seeking to control others.
3. The more control is sought through the use of coercive resources, the more likely those subject to the application of these resources are to (a) seek escape; (b) fight back if escape is impossible; (c) comply if (a) and (b) are impossible and if material incentives exist; and (d) sluggishly comply if (a), (b), and (c) do not apply.
4. The more control is sought through the use of material resources, the more likely those subject to the manipulation of material incentives are to (a) develop acquisitive orientations and (b) develop a strategy of self-interested manipulation.
5. The more control is sought through the use of symbolic resources, the more likely those subject to the application of such resources are to (a) experience indoctrination into values and beliefs; (b) be members of homogeneous cohorts of recruits; (c) be subject to efforts to encourage intra-organizational contact; (d) be subject to efforts to discourage extra-organizational contact; (e) participate in ritual activities, especially those involving rites of passage; and (f) be rewarded for conformity with upward mobility.
Administration of Control
6. The more those in authority employ coercive and material incentives to control others, the greater is the reliance on surveillance as an administrative device to control.
7. The more those in authority use surveillance to control, the greater are (a) the level of alienation by those subject to surveillance, (b) the level of conformity in only higher visible behaviors, and (c) the ratio of supervisory to nonsupervisory individuals.
8. The more those in authority employ symbolic resources to control others, the greater is their reliance on systems of standardized rules to achieve control.
9. The greater is the reliance on systems of standardized rules, the greater are (a) the impersonality of interactions, (b) the standardization of behaviors, and (c) the dispersion of authority.

[23]Ibid., 286–347.

Organizational Structure
10. Centralization of authority is a positive and additive function of (a) the concentration of resources; (b) the capacity to mobilize the administration of control through surveillance, material incentives, and systems of rules; (c) the capacity to control the flow of information; (d) the capacity to control contingencies of the environment; and (e) the degree to which tasks need to be routinized.
11. The bureaucratization of authority and social relations is a positive and additive function of (a) record-keeping technologies, (b) non-kinship agents of socialization of potential incumbents, (c) money markets, (d) transportation facilities, (e) nonpersonal centers of power, and (f) diverse centers of power and authority.

In the propositions shown in Table 14.10, control within an organization increases with the concentration of coercive, material, and symbolic resources. The pattern of control varies, however, with the particular type of resource—whether coercive, material, or symbolic—that is controlled and with the configuration among these resources, as summarized in propositions 3, 4, and 5. Control within an organization must be administered, and the pattern of such administrative control varies with the nature of the resources used to gain control. Collins extends Weber's analysis of organizations, and propositions 6 through 9 summarize various patterns in the administration of control. In the end, Collins sees the profile of an organization's structure as reflecting the nature and concentration of resources, as well as how these are used to administer control. Propositions 10 and 11 review Collins's basic argument.

The State and the Economy

As did Max Weber, Collins eventually moves to the analysis of the state, which, though a type of complex organization, still controls and regulates the entire society. As the propositions in Table 14.11 summarize,[24] the size and scale of the state depend on the productive capacity of the economy; in the end, the state can only be supported by a large economic surplus. In turn, as summarized in proposition 2, the productive capacity of the economy is related to technologies, natural resources, the number of people who must be supported, and the efficiency with which the division of labor is organized. The particular form of state power varies enormously, but these forms vary under the impact of the basic forces summarized in proposition 3. The stability of the state is also a crucial variable, especially for a conflict theory. As proposition 4 summarizes, the state must be able to prevent mobilization by groups pursuing counterpower, and it must be able to resolve periodic crises. When it cannot, the state becomes unstable.

Like Weber before him, Collins recognizes that much of the state's viability depends on the relation of the state to the surrounding societies. No society exists in isolation. A state almost always finds itself in competition with other societies.

---

[24]Ibid., 348–413.

Table 14.11 Key Propositions on the State, Economy, and Ideology

1. The size and scale of political organization are a positive function of the productive capacity of the economy.

2. The productive capacity of the economy is a positive and additive function of (a) level of technology, (b) level of natural resources, (c) population size, and (d) efficiency in the organization of labor.

3. The form of political organization is related to the levels of and interactive effects among (a) the size of territories to be governed, (b) the absolute numbers of people to be governed, (c) the distribution and diversity of people in a territory, (d) the organization of coercive forces (armies), (e) the distribution (dispersion or concentration) of power and other resources among a population, and (f) the degree of symbolic unification within and among social units.

4. The stability of the state is a negative and additive function of

   A. The capacity for political mobilization by other groups, which is a positive function of

      1. The level of wealth

      2. The capacity for organization as a status group

   B. The incapacity of the state to resolve periodic crises.

And the ability of the state to prevail in this world of geopolitics often determines its form, viability, and stability.

Geopolitics

Borrowing from Weber but adding his own ideas, Collins argues that there are sociological reasons for the historical facts that only certain societies can form stable empires and that societies can extend their empires only to a maximal size of about three to four million square miles.[25] When a society has a resource (money, technology, population base) and marchland advantage (no enemies on most of its borders), it can win wars, but eventually it will (a) extend itself beyond its logistical capacities, (b) bump up against another empire, (c) lose its marchland advantage as it extends its borders and becomes ever more surrounded by enemies, and (d) lose its technological advantages as enemies adopt them.

The result of these forces is that empires begin to stall at a certain size as each of these points of resistance is activated. These processes indicate that internal nation-states will not build long-term or extensive empires because they are surrounded by enemies, increasingly so as they extend territory. Rather, marchland states, with oceans, mountains, or unthreatening neighbors at their back, can move out and conquer others, because they have to fight a war on only one front. But eventually,

---

[25]See Randall Collins, *Weberian Sociological Theory* (Cambridge, UK: Cambridge University Press, 1986), 167–212 and "Long-Term Social Change and the Territorial Power of States," in *Sociology Since Midcentury: Essays in Theory Cumulation* (New York: Academic Press, 1981).

they overextend, confront another marchland empire, lose their technological advantage, and acquire enemies on a greater proportion of their borders (thereby losing the marchland advantage and, in effect, becoming an internal state that must now fight on several borders). Sea and air powers can provide a kind of marchland advantage, but the logistical loads of distance from home bases and maintenance of sophisticated technologies make such empires vulnerable. Only when it encounters little resistance can an empire be maintained across oceans and at great distances by air; as resistance mounts, the empire collapses quickly as its supply lines are disrupted. Table 14.12 summarizes these ideas more formally.

Table 14.12   Key Propositions on Geopolitics

---

1. The possibility of winning a war between nation-states is a positive and additive function of

   A. The level of resource advantage of one nation-state over another, which is a positive function of

      1. The level of technology

      2. The level of productivity

      3. The size of the population

      4. The level of wealth formation

   B. The degree of "marchland advantage" of one nation-state over another, which is a positive and additive function of

      1. The extent to which the borders of a nation-state are peripheral to those of other nation-states

      2. The extent to which a nation-state has enemies on only one border

      3. The extent to which a nation-state has natural buffers (mountains, oceans, large lakes, etc.) on most of its borders.

2. The likelihood of an empire is a positive function of the extent to which a marchland state has resource advantages over neighbors and uses these advantages to wage war.

3. The size of an empire is a positive and additive function of the dominant nation-state's capacity to

   A. Avoid a showdown war with the empire of other marchland states
   B. Sustain a marchland advantage
   C. Maintain territories with standing armies
   D. Maintain logistical capacity for communications and transportation, which is a positive function of levels of communication, transportation, and military technologies and a negative and additive function of

      1. the size of a territory

      2. the distances of borders from the home base

   E. Diffusion of technologies to potential enemies.

4. The collapse of an empire is a positive and additive function of

   A. The initiation of war between two empires
   B. The overextension of an empire beyond its logistical capacity
   C. The adoption of its superior technologies by enemy nation-states.

From these propositions listed in Tables 14.7 to 14.12, it is easy to see Collins's approach to conflict processes as neo-Weberian. Like Weber, Collins begins with a conceptualization of micro processes—in Weber's case, types of meaningful action and, in Collins's theory, interaction rituals. Then, their analysis shifts to the meso level, examining the patterns of stratification and forms of complex organizations. Finally, both Weber and Collins move to the analysis of the state and geopolitics. In all these levels of analysis, their concern is with inequalities of resources and how these inequalities generate tension and potential conflict. Collins's *Conflict Sociology* is now in its fourth decade in print, and so, it should not be surprising that Collins has expanded on this propositional scheme. As he has done so, stating arguments formally has declined, but it is still clear that he is generating explanatory ideas, but now in a more discursive format, or what I term discursive scheme in Chapter 25.

It encounters the theory of gender stratification as it has been synthesized with other theories in its most recent treatment. Thus, Collins is much more than a strict adherent to the Weberian tradition; indeed, Weber is only a starting point from which Collins has theorized about many social processes.

Ritual and Emotions

Over the last decade, Collins has refined and extended his original conception of interaction rituals and, as I will summarize in the next section, used this new view of interaction rituals to develop an explanation of interpersonal violence. In Figure 14.1, I have taken the liberty of revising Collins's analytical scheme into a more robust analytical model, where causal relations among the forces driving interaction rituals are delineated in ways that are consistent with his discursive scheme outlined in his *Interaction Ritual Chains*.[26] Let me review the elements in this analytical model, moving from left to right as the interaction ritual unfolds and builds up emotional energy, which Collins sees as the driving force of interaction. The theory emphasizes longer-term emotional energy that builds up and is sustained across chains of interaction rituals or episodes of interaction. When positive emotional energy is built up across chains of interaction rituals, social solidarity is increased, leading to the production or reproduction of social structures, whereas when negative emotional energy is aroused, conflict becomes more likely, and solidarity declines.

The variables on the left of Figure 14.1 indicate some of the conditions that increase the likelihood that interaction rituals will take place. The more separated are persons by *ecological barriers* from others, the more individuals will feel *copresent;* and the more individuals are engaged in *common actions* or tasks, the more likely are these individuals to have a *mutual focus of attention* and the more likely are they to emit *stereotypical greeting rituals* to each other. These rituals—often as simple as "How are you?" or some such formality—generate mildly positive *transient emotions* that, in turn, begin to shape a *shared mood,* which, in turn, increases the common or mutual focus of attention. As the interaction proceeds, it tends to fall

---

[26]Randall Collins, *Interaction Ritual Chains* (Princeton, NJ: Princeton University Press, 2004).

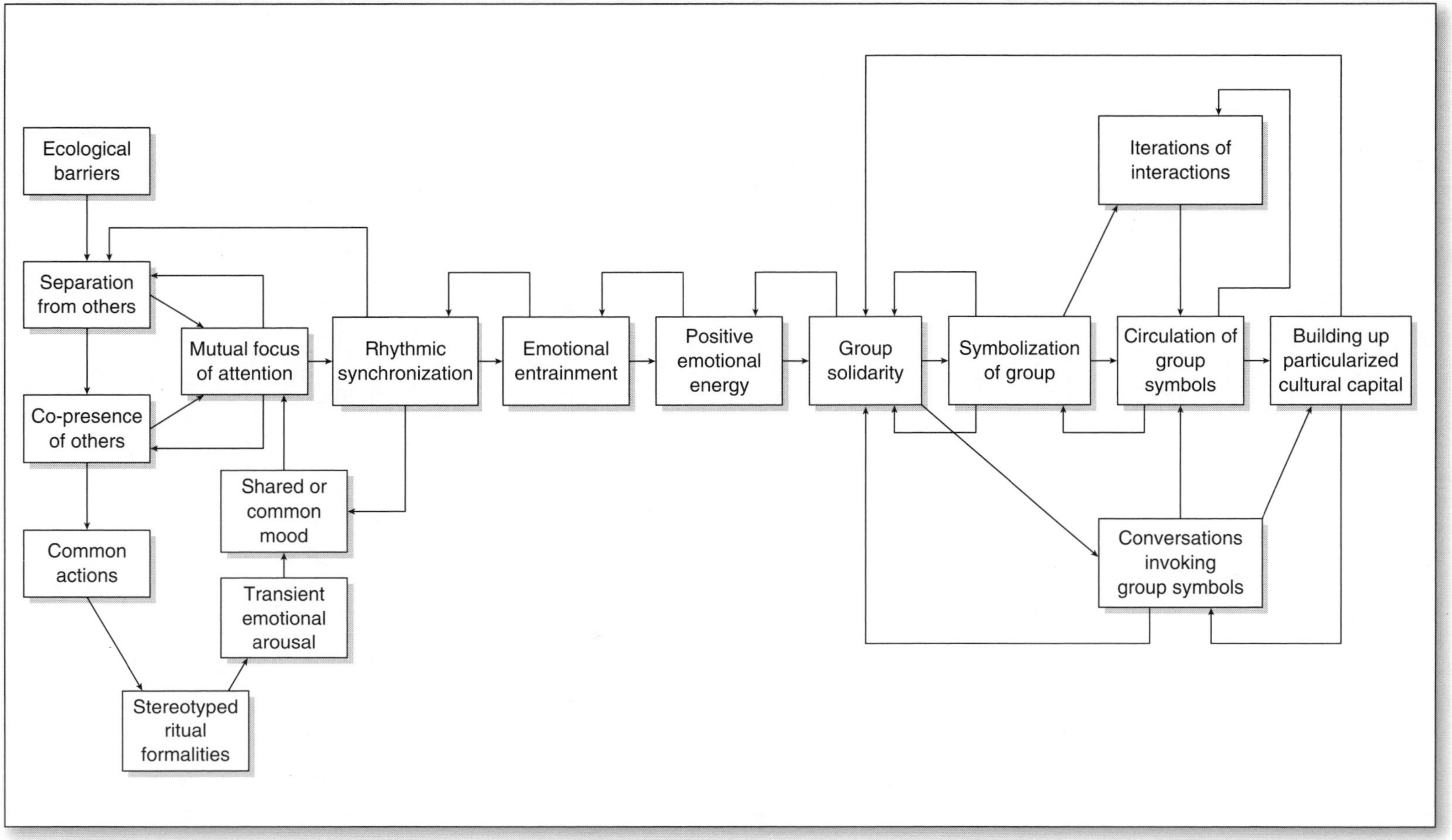

Figure 14.1 Collins's Elaborated Model of Interaction Rituals

into *rhythmic synchronization* of talk and body language. Individuals establish a rhythm to their verbal exchanges, as well as the movements of their bodies.

The more rhythmically "in sync" individuals become, the more likely are they to become emotionally entrained, with the result that the merely transient emotions initiated with stereotyped formalities are transformed into *collective effervescence* —an idea that comes from Émile Durkheim's analysis. This effervescence is evident in the continued synchronization of talk and bodies of individuals, and the more effervescence occurs, the greater will be individuals' sense of emotional entrainment, which, in turn, increases their level of positive emotional energy.

As positive emotions are aroused, the level of *group solidarity* among those copresent increases; and the greater is this sense of solidarity, and the more it is evoked in subsequent interaction rituals among the same individuals, the more likely are they to have needs to *symbolize the group* in some way—whether through words, physical objects, or particular behaviors. This process of symbolization—again, an idea borrowed from Émile Durkheim—emphasizes that solidarity and the positive emotions around it lead individuals to have needs to mark the group, much like a totem pole symbolized a community of preliterate peoples. Indeed, sometimes individuals erect physical objects to symbolize their solidarity, but they can also use phrases, songs, symbols on hats or uniforms, forms of dress, jokes, phrases, shared memories, and almost anything that marks a group. With symbols and continued interaction over time among individuals, the more these symbols are evoked, the more likely are they to sustain conversations at any given encounter and, equally important, the more likely are these symbols to motivate individuals to repeat the encounter over time, thus setting up chains of interaction rituals. As these chains of interaction continue, members develop *particularistic capital,* or experiences only shared among group members, and this capital can be used in subsequent interactions to reinforce group symbols and the sense of solidarity.

The reverse causal arrows flowing from right to left emphasize that interaction rituals are recursive in the sense that symbolization increases solidarity, as does particularized cultural capital; solidarity feeds back to increase positive emotional arousal; emotional arousal feeds back and increases the very sense of effervescence that generated the emotional arousal; effervescence feeds back on rhythmic synchronization, making people more animated and "in sync"; synchronization increases the shared mood and mutual focus of attention; and a heightened mutual focus of attention makes people feel a stronger sense of copresence and separation from others. And then these processes begin to feed forward, activating the cycle of the ritual once again.

As these cycles are iterated over time, they build up solidarity and group symbols; and in so doing, they build up social structures and their cultures or, if the structure already exists, they reproduce it or potentially change it. Collins has emphasized the relationship between emotions and interaction rituals, but he has generally emphasized only positive emotional energy. There is, of course, the converse process of arousing negative emotional energy. Such is likely to be the case when the ritual process breaks down or never really gets started. Or it is also possible when individuals are stuck in interactions where they gain no rewarding particularistic capital and consistently experience negative emotions at the hands of others. Under these conditions, people will leave an encounter or never repeat it again, but often people are stuck or perceive that they are stuck in a chain of interaction rituals that are painful—as an abusive marriage must be for the subordinate family member(s).[27]

Emotions and Micro-Level Violence

In his book, *Violence: A Micro-Sociological Theory,*[28] Collins employs his interaction ritual theory as a kind of interpretive framework in a more discursive manner to explain many manifestations of violence. He employs the theory of interaction rituals to draw attention to the sociology of violence, emphasizing that situations more than individuals are the appropriate units of analysis. Focus is on the dynamics of violent situations rather than on individuals. With this emphasis on situations, he sets out to explain many diverse kinds of situational violence. I will focus only on the theoretical argument, which is relatively brief, rather than on the many interesting empirical variations of situational violence.

Emotional Fields. Potentially violent situations are shaped by what Collins terms as an *emotional field,* which consists of fear and tension. *Fear* is almost always the dominant emotion of parties in a violent situation, with such fear being a physiological reaction. Tension comes from the fact that since most interactions most of the time generate some level of positive emotional arousal through the interaction ritual dynamics enumerated in Figure 14.1, a violent situation arousing fear stands in tension with what Collins considers is a hardwired propensity of humans to experience positive emotional energy in interaction rituals. Since this propensity stands in juxtaposition with fear about the possibility of violence, the emotional field will always evidence tension. For violence to occur, one side or potentially both must turn this tension into aggressive action and, in so doing, overcome fear.

The Power of Confrontational Tension and Fear. This "confrontational tension," as Collins terms it, signals that violence is not easy for people because it arouses intense fear and goes against the natural propensity of humans to fall into the phases of interaction rituals. Even when people are highly motivated to engage in violent conflict, they experience this confrontational tension, which makes it difficult to "pull the trigger" on violence. Indeed, most violent situations fail to become violent, or often protagonists dance around violence with posturing and threats but never actually engage in violent acts. And even if violent acts occur, they rarely are extended or even reciprocated by the other party. Collins documents that even in collective violence, such as in mobs, riots, and warfare, relatively few members of the groups

---

[27]See works by Erika Summers-Effler on negative emotional energy that seek to theorize this bias in Collins's theory. For example, see her "The Micro Potential for Social Change," *Sociological Theory* 20 (2002):41–60 and "Defensive Strategies: The Formation and Social Implications of Self-destructive Behavior," *Advances in Group Processes* 21 (2004):309–325.

[28]Randall Collins, *Violence: A Micro-Sociological Theory* (Princeton, NJ: Princeton University Press.)

supposedly engaged in violence actually commit violence. For example, only a relatively small proportion of soldiers actually aim their guns on the enemy, or in the case of riots, most people dance around or stand in the background rather than take part in actual violence against a target.

What, then, allows individuals to overcome the confrontational tension that holds them back from actual violence? Collins offers a number of conditions that can turn a violent situation into real, collective violence. One, and perhaps the most important, is that interaction rituals are used to mobilize actors to commit violence. That is, the stages of the ritual are unleashed so that individuals gain positive emotional entrainment, effervescence, positive emotional energy, solidarity, group symbols, and particularized culture by engaging in concerted violence against another group. It also helps if this group is geographically separated so that their cues cannot be observed, as would be the case with two groups of soldiers fighting each other from a distance. The military learned the power of interaction rituals redirected toward collective violence against enemies a long time ago. Soldiers are separated; they are required to engage in stereotyped formalities, to have a mutual focus of attention, to become rhythmically synchronized in their interactions during training, to become emotionally entrained and aroused, and to develop group solidarity that is symbolized by not only uniforms and badges/patches on these uniforms but also by symbols unique to a particular military group, such as flags and banners, which are reinforced by particularized cultural capital. Terrorist organizations also reveal these same qualities, using interaction rituals generating positive emotion for engaging in conflict to overcome the fear and confrontation tension of violent situations.

With this relatively simple conceptual framework, Collins is able to explore many facets of violence because situations all evidence fear among parties, which stands in tension with the pull of interaction rituals. The result is confrontational tension. The networks of the parties to a conflict and the solidarities that they have built up have large effects on whether or not individuals in a violent situation can overcome this confrontational tension. Thus, when violence is examined with a micro-level theory focusing on situations rather than on individuals or larger-scale meso- and macro-social structures, the dynamics of violence that emerge are very different from the images of violent individuals or organizations coordinating the violent acts of individuals—whether armies, terrorists, rioters, gang members, etc. Violence is not easy; it is often very short-lived and not even very violent; and when collectively organized, most participants do not really participate in the actual violence.

The Escalation and De-escalation of Conflict

Building on his analysis of the microdynamics of violence, Collins has recently developed a theory on the escalation (C-escalation) and de-escalation (D-escalation) of conflict, especially violent conflicts.[29] This theory builds upon both Georg Simmel's and Lewis Coser's theories, where conflict is seen to increase the solidarity of the

---

[29]Randall Collins, "C-Escalation and D-Escalation: A Theory of the Time-Dynamics of Conflict," *American Sociological Review* 77 (2012):1–20.

parties to the conflict, and vice versa, and where the duration of the conflict was a central consideration. See Figures 6.2 and 6.7 on pp. 182 and 200 as well as theoretical principles 5 through 12 on pp. 203–205 for Simmel's argument and Tables 14.1 to 14.6 in this chapter for Coser's theory. The theory also builds upon Émile Durkheim's analysis of how emotions aroused in micro situations lead to the solidarity symbolized by beliefs. In a series of what I term analytical causal models, Collins uses the theoretical framework outlined above to explain initial conflict escalation, or C-escalation, leading to increased violence, followed by two basic outcomes: (1) victory, defeat, or stalemate and (2) D-escalation of the conflict. Built into these models is a time dimension in which conflict and solidarity of the parties to the conflict rapidly escalate, rise to a peak, and then flatten out, only to begin to decline through one of the two routes listed above. The argument becomes quite complex, but let me try to highlight the key points of emphasis.

Conflict pushes adversaries to become better organized and to develop solidarity in order to meet their opposition; and this process works the other way around: group solidarity, particularly as it builds up symbols marking the group and portraying enemies in highly negative terms, increases the likelihood of conflict as the potential adversaries engage in dramaturgical (see Chapter 18) performances that heighten emotions, negatively portray enemies as evil, and lead each conflict party to perceive that they can win in the conflict. The basic dynamics of the interaction rituals portrayed earlier lead to polarization of the conflict parties, whereby enemies are insulted and portrayed negatively and one's fellow combatants are portrayed heroically. At the same time, fighters and potential fighters on both sides have to deal with confrontational tension and fear; and this fear often leads to incompetence and failure of self control such that atrocities occur. These become further fuel to the portrayal of enemies as evil and the ideological polarization of the conflict parties. The enemy is "evil, unprincipled, stupid, ugly, ridiculous, cowardly, and weak." As a result, both sides see the conflict as "winnable" and begin to pull in allies to support them and to force neutral parties out of the way; and as part of this pulling in of allies, conflict parties become more organized and mobilize material resources to pursue conflict. With emotions aroused, enemies demonized, allies in coalitions, polarization of ideologies, and mobilization of organizational and material resources, both sides become fully mobilized; and when skirmishes lead to atrocities because of the incompetence of those in real combat, where most do not fight and those who do must overcome their tensions and fears fueled by hormones, peptides, and neurotransmitters released in the brain, mistakes occur and lead individuals into a "forward panic," where they pile on a wounded or weak enemy that has been demonized. The resulting atrocities only escalate the polarization.

At this point, it may turn out that one party reveals more solidarity, organization, and resources; and if this party is successful in combat against another, the latter may lose resources, experience a loss of solidarity, and organizationally collapse, leading to victory for the former. As often occurs however, complete victory or defeat does not occur, leading to a stalemate, which, over time, will erode material and organizational resources, reduce solidarity, flatten emotions, and cause allies to leave. What often happens in such stalemates is that formerly excluded neutral parties may begin to try and broker a settlement and peace. A stalemate can lead to a victory, however, if these erosions of power occur more rapidly and extensively in one of the parties, which then becomes vulnerable to defeat by the more powerful party. The other route to D-escalation occurs as solidarity is disrupted or weakened, ideologies lose their polarizing power, confrontational tensions and fears cannot be circumvented, individuals begin to emotionally burn out, material resources are exhausted, logistics fail to deliver the needed supplies, organizational discipline begins to erode, allies become less supportive, and neutrals return and seek to broker a third-party settlement. And if both parties experience this D-escalation simultaneously, then the conflict may end. Moreover, internal conflicts within the conflict parties may arise between militant and less militant factions, and these internal conflicts further erode the capacity of each party to sustain goals or retain the necessary resources.

Collins does not outline this theory as a series of principles but, instead, uses analytical models delineating direct, indirect, and reversal causal chains and feedback and feed-forward processes. Depending upon a number of variables outlined in these models, D-escalation can take several routes. One route goes through a process in which group solidarity declines and individuals begin to pay attention to non–group members, even fraternize with the enemy, lose emotional energy or experience emotional burnout, and eventually disperse. Another route is, as noted above, for alliances to begin to erode or fail in the first place, allowing formerly excluded neutrals to come back and negotiate a settlement. Still another route is for more material resources to become exhausted and for logistical lines of supply to be interrupted, thereby causing defeat or leading parties to reach a settlement. Yet another route comes with confrontational tension and fear that cannot be overcome, not only leading to atrocities but also eroding solidarity. And a related route is emotional burnout not only from failures to circumvent confrontational tension and fear but also from trying to sustain emotional highs, solidarities, and polarized ideologies for too long. If one side moves along these routes before the other, then conflict can lead to victory of the latter; and if both sides go down these routes, even if in a slightly different configuration, then the conflict will D-escalate and even disappear. All of these routes and the forces outlined in Collins's models can explain not only the escalation but other outcomes as well: victory or defeat, or D-escalation. The theory is parsimonious because for both the escalation and the D-escalation phases as they unfold over time, the same dynamics are in play; it is the values of the variables as they interact with each other that determine all the phases of the conflict.

Neo-Marxian Class Analysis: Erik Olin Wright

In the late twentieth century, Marxist theory had to confront several problems. First, the predicted collapse of capitalism had not occurred, despite the Great Depression and periodic recessions throughout the century, continuing into the twenty-first century. Second, the projected polarization of capitalist societies into bourgeoisie and proletarians was countered by the growth of a large and varied middle class of managers, experts, small business operators, skilled manual workers, and others who do not seem highly disadvantaged and who do not see themselves as exploited. Third, capitalism had appeared to emerge as the clear victor in the contest between capitalism and communism, although state-managed societies operating under the ideological banner of communism were hardly what Marx had in mind. Nonetheless, the historical predictions of Marx and the trajectory of capitalism into socialism and communism had not occurred, and into the second decade of the new twenty-first century still have not done so.

Yet, despite these troubling issues, Marxism has remained a viable intellectual tradition, driven perhaps by an emancipatory zeal emphasizing the elimination of exploitation of the disadvantaged by the advantaged. Still, Marxist intellectual circles have been in crisis for more than a decade, as many former Marxists have moved to other forms of radical thinking or have become critical theorists and postmodernists—perspectives that are explored in Chapters 22 and 23. Although some still cling to the orthodox picture of Marx, most Marxists have changed Marx's core ideas to fit current historical realities.

Among these Marxists are several important scholars,[30] but in an effort to summarize the issues with which they have had to deal, we will focus on the work of Erik Olin Wright, who has, in his words, sought to do more than merely draw from the Marxian tradition but, instead, to contribute to "the reconstruction of Marxism." Wright has termed his and fellow travelers' approach as "analytical Marxism." But before discussing the basic concepts in Wright's scheme, let us set the stage with his more meta-theoretical assertions.

Analytical Marxism

The goal of analytical Marxism is to shed some of the baggage of orthodox Marxist analysis while retaining the core ideas that make Marx's theory unique.[31] Analytical Marxism retains the emancipatory thrust of Marx, stressing that the goal is to reduce, if not eliminate, inequalities and exploitation. Indeed, emphasis is on constructing scientific theory about how socialism can emerge from the dynamics inhering in capitalist exploitation. But this emancipatory thrust does not abandon a

---

[30]For example, see Perry Anderson, *Considerations on Western Marxism* (London: New Left Review, 1976); Michael Burawoy, *The Politics of Production* (London: Verso, 1985); Sam Bowles and Herbert Gintis, *Democracy and Capitalism* (New York: Basic Books, 1986); G. A. Cohen, *History of Labor and Freedom: Themes from Marx* (Oxford, UK: Clarendon, 1988) and *Karl Marx's Theory of History: A Defense* (Princeton, NJ: Princeton University Press, 1978); John Elster, *Making Sense of Marx* (Cambridge, UK: Cambridge University Press, 1978); Barry Hindess and Paul Q. Hirst, *Capital and Capitalism Today* (London: Routledge, 1977); Claus Offe, *Disorganized Capitalism: Contemporary Transformations of Work and Politics* (Cambridge, UK: Cambridge University Press, 1985); Adam Przeworski, *Capitalism and Social Democracy* (Cambridge, UK: Cambridge University Press, 1985); John A. Roemer, *A General Theory of Exploitation and Class* (Cambridge, MA: Harvard University Press, 1982) and *Analytical Foundations of Marxian Economic Theory* (Cambridge, UK: Cambridge University Press, 1981); and Michael Burawoy and Erik Olin Wright, "Sociological Marxism," in *Handbook of Sociological Theory,* ed. J. H. Turner (Kluwer Academic/Plenum Press, 2001), 459–486.

[31]Erik Olin Wright, "What Is Analytical Marxism?" *Socialist Review* 19 (1989):35–56.

commitment to the conventional norms of science, in which theoretical ideas are assessed against empirical observations. Moreover, the goal is to produce abstract formulations that specify the "mechanisms" generating empirical regularities in the world, and for the analytical Marxist, particular concern is with the mechanisms flowing from social class structures. As I will summarize later, Wright's most recent work has sought to outline in more detail these paths to emancipation.[32]

Social Class, Emancipation, and History

Marxist theory posits a historical trajectory: feudalism to capitalism, then capitalism to communism. In this historical trajectory, class inequalities will be eliminated, and communism will usher in a classless society. In this trajectory and outcome, class is the pivotal dynamic, mobilizing individuals to seek alternative social relations in which exploitation is eliminated. Wright believes that these three basic orienting assumptions—that is, historical trajectory, class emancipation, and class as the driving force of history—need to be mitigated somewhat.[33] Emphasis should be on how the dynamics of capitalism present possibilities for new, less exploitive social arrangements rather than on the inevitability of the forces driving human society toward communism. In this vein, emphasis on class emancipation should not blindly pursue the goal of a classless society but, rather, present a critique of existing social relations to reduce class inequalities and exploitation. Moreover, emphasis on class as the driving force of history must be tempered by a recognition that class is one of many forces shaping the organization of a society, both in the present and in the future.

Wright's theoretical work stresses this last consideration: What mechanisms revolving around social class generate what outcomes? As a Marxist, Wright views the class structure of a society as limiting the nature of class formation (the organization of individuals) and class struggle (the use of organization to transform class structures). He posits a simple model, as delineated in Figure 14.2.[34] In this model, class struggle transforms the nature of class formations and class structures, whereas class formations select or channel class struggle in certain directions depending on the nature of organization of class members. The key dynamic in Wright's program, however, is class structure; as the model outlines, class structure limits the nature of class formation and class struggle. The goal of a reconstituted Marxian analysis must, therefore, examine the properties of class structure in capitalist societies if class formations and emancipatory class struggles are to be understood.

Micro-Level Versus Macro-Level Class Analysis

In Wright's view, Marxian class analysis must confront two impulses. One is to retain Marx's vision of the class structure in society as ultimately polarizing into two conflictual classes—in the capitalist historical epoch, these are the bourgeoisie, who

---

[32]Erik Olin Wright, *Envisioning Real Utopias* (London: Verso, 2010).

[33]Erik Olin Wright, "Class Analysis, History and Emancipation," *New Left Review* 202 (1993):15–35.

[34]Ibid., 28.

Figure 14.2   Wright's General Model of Class Analysis

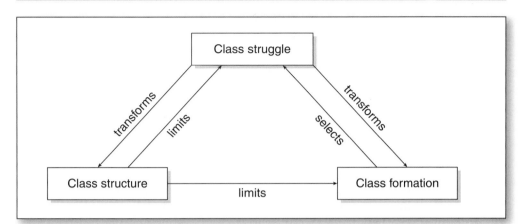

own the means of production, versus the proletariat, who are exploited. The other impulse is to explore "the complexity of the class structural concept itself in the hope that such complexity will more powerfully capture the explanatory mechanisms embedded in class relations."[35] Wright argues that this complexity is not as evident when analysis stays at the macro level, focusing on the global characteristics of capitalism as composed ultimately of owners and workers. However, when research moves to the micro level of the individual and seeks to understand the locations of individuals in the class system, a much more varied, complex, and contradictory picture emerges. If the causal effects of class relations are to be understood, then it is necessary to explore class processes at the micro level.

Wright's basic strategy has been to examine the jobs that people hold, because in their jobs, individuals connect to the system of production and the class relations that inhere in this system. For most of his work in the 1970s and 1980s,[36] Wright sought to construct a "relational map of locations of individuals" in the class system, but by the 1990s, he had recognized that "the simple linkage of individuals-in-jobs to classes" must be modified in several important ways: individuals can occupy more than one job; they can have indirect and mediated relations to a job (as is the case with children and others who do not directly participate in the system of formal employment); they can move about jobs and cross class locations during the course of a career; and they can have contradictory locations in the class system.[37] In essence, as we will see shortly, Wright's conceptual scheme has tried to deal with

[35]Erik Olin Wright, "Rethinking, Once Again, the Concept of Class Structure," in *The Debate on Classes,* ed. Erik Olin Wright (London: Verso, 1989), 269.

[36]See, in particular, Erik Olin Wright, *Class, Crisis, and the State* (London: Verso, 1978), *Class Structure and Income Distribution* (New York: Academic Press, 1979), and *Classes* (London: Verso, 1985) and Erik Olin Wright and Luca Perrone, "Marxist Class Categories and Income Inequality," *American Sociological Review* 42 (1977):32–55.

[37]Wright, "Rethinking, Once Again, the Concept of Class Structure."

these kinds of complexities that a micro-level analysis exposes; indeed, his concep-tualizations have changed during the course of the last twenty years as he has con-fronted both data[38] and conceptual criticisms.[39]

When class analysis turns micro, the vagueness of much macro-level Marxian theory is revealed. Wright argues that it is important in a reconstructed Marxian analysis to be specific about the mechanisms involved in generating class formation and class struggle effects. He illustrates the differences between a macro-level and micro-level view of class mechanisms by summarizing the three ways in traditional Marxism by which class structure is seen to exert effects on class formation and struggle:[40] (1) material interests, (2) lived experiences, and (3) collective capacities. Below, I examine each of these.

Material Interests. The first mechanism by which class structure exerts causal effects on class formation and struggle is through individuals' material interests. There are two basic types of material interests: (1) economic welfare, or "the total package of toil-leisure-incomes available to a person,"[41] with people having an interest in reducing their toil and in increasing their leisure and consumption, and (2) economic power, or the capacity to control how surplus products are distrib-uted, with surplus product being defined as "that part of the total social product that is left over after all the inputs into production (both labor power and physical capi-tal) have been reproduced."[42] Thus, the material interests of individuals are deter-mined by their economic welfare and economic power.

The concept of exploitation ties these two types of material interests together. Those with economic power can use this power to appropriate productive surplus from those without power. In so doing, they increase their economic welfare at the expense of those whose surplus product they take. In Marxian class analysis, then, the material interests of the classes are not just different; they are opposed in a kind of zero-sum game.

The material interests of individuals circumscribe their options. Depending on their respective material interests, people make different choices, employ diverse strategies, and make varying trade-offs. When individuals share material interests, their choices, strategies, and trade-offs should converge because they face similar dilemmas as they pursue economic welfare and economic power. In Marx's macro-level approach, social systems polarize around two classes with different material interests, fueled by exploitation. In a more micro-level approach to material inter-ests, a more complex and, at times, contradictory picture emerges of individuals

---

[38]See, for examples, Wright's own comparative survey research on class structures, which can be found in "The Comparative Project on Class Structures and Class Consciousness: An Overview," *Acta Socio-logica* 32 (1989):3–22, *Class Structure and Income Distribution*, and *Classes* and in Wright and Perrone, "Marxist Class Categories and Income Inequality."

[39]See the chapters in Wright, *The Debate on Classes.*

[40]Wright, "Rethinking, Once Again, the Concept of Class Structure."

[41]Ibid., 281.

[42]Ibid., 282.

with diverse perceptions about what they should do in pursuing their economic welfare and in seeking economic power. Moreover, the lived experiences of individuals as they make choices and pursue strategies can also diverge, or at a minimum, individuals do not perceive that they have common material interests (a problem that Marx dismissed, perhaps too quickly, as "false consciousness").

Lived Experiences. In Marxian theory, common material interests as dictated by class location lead to common experiences. Those who do not own capital are seen to have similar subjective understandings of the world because they are forced to sell their labor, because they are dominated and bossed around, and because they are unable to control the surplus products of their labor. When individuals are exploited this way, they are also alienated;[43] and together, these forces give alienated individuals a common experience that, Marx felt, would lead to their collective mobilization.[44] Yet a more micro-level approach reveals that individuals might not have similar experiences or, at the very least, they do not see their lived experiences as similar because they occupy somewhat different jobs that locate them at different points in the class system.

Collective Capacities. The third class force in traditional Marxian analysis flows from the first two: people with common material interests and lived experiences possess a capacity for collective action. Moreover, as Marx emphasized, capitalists are forced by their own material interests to create many of the conditions that facilitate collective mobilization, such as concentrating workers in factories and urban areas, making them appendages to machine technologies, disrupting their life routines through lay-offs, providing literacy and media access, and encouraging other forces that shape class formation and struggle. This kind of scenario has a certain plausibility when examined at the macro level, but on the individual level, the contradictory locations of individuals in jobs and their differentiation across an array of middle-class locations make collective mobilization more problematic. Individuals do not see that they have common material interests or that they share common lived experiences; so they do not naturally organize collectively. Even alliances and coalitions among individuals who see that they share some interests become problematic, although once formed these alliances have strength (because the costs of compromises have already been incurred).[45]

Thus, in Wright's micro approach, the three class forces in Marxian analysis do not reveal the same degree of coherence as when they are examined from a more macro level. Moreover, microanalysis shows that, in contrast with traditional Marxism, these forces are not necessarily correlated with each other. When analysis moves to the micro level, "there is no longer necessarily a simple coincidence of material

---

[43]Marx conceived of alienation as the result of workers' inability to determine what they produce, how they produce, and to whom the products of their labor are sold.

[44]See propositions in Table 3.1 for a list of these conditions.

[45]Wright, "Class Analysis, History and Emancipation."

interests, lived experience, and collective capacity."[46] People who might seem to have common material interests do not perceive this to be the case, nor do they reveal a driving need to mobilize collectively. In a micro approach to understanding class mechanisms, then, the complexity of the class system makes the traditional macro-level Marxian causal forces too global and rudimentary to account for the specifics of class formation and struggle.

The Problem of the Middle Classes

Wright's entry into Marxist analysis began with the question of how to account for the emergence and proliferation of jobs in the middle classes,[47] and although he has sought to move in different directions, this question is still at the core of his theoretical formulations. In his effort to build a "map of the class structure," Wright recognizes that the array of middle-class positions posed the biggest challenge to traditional Marxian class analysis. If class structures are to be seen as relevant to the class formation and to the struggle by classes for social emancipation, then a more fine-grained analysis of this structure is necessary. Wright's analytical project has thus involved an effort to isolate the mechanisms being generated by this more complex class system. Through his empirical and theoretical work during the last two decades, he has proposed several ways to conceptualize class structures and the mechanisms for class formation and struggle that inhere in these structures. Some of these have been rejected, others retained, and most modified and integrated in new ways by Wright. In contrast with orthodox Marxism, Wright has been willing to change his mind and to develop, elaborate, and qualify ideas in his effort to isolate the causal mechanisms of class structures in advanced capitalist societies. He has, in essence, proposed several models of class structures, the basic elements of which are briefly summarized here.

Contradictory Class Locations. Wright's first attempt at conceptualizing the middle classes in Marxian terms led him to develop the idea of contradictory class locations.[48] Individuals can occupy a class location that is contradictory because it puts people into different classes, presumably giving them contradictory material interests and diverse lived experiences and collective capacities. These locations are contradictory because, for example, many managers, semiautonomous wage earners, professionals and experts, and small-scale employers can reveal varying amounts and combinations of (a) owning the means of production, (b) purchasing the labor of others, (c) controlling and managing the labor of others, and (d) selling their labor. To illustrate, a manager sells labor to the owner of a business, but at the same time, this manager will be involved in hiring and controlling the labor of others. Similarly, a skilled consultant sells labor but might own the facilities by which this labor is organized. Such variations can put individuals in contradictory class

---

[46]Wright, "Rethinking, Once Again, the Concept of Class Structure."

[47]Wright and Perrone, "Marxist Class Categories"; Wright, *Classes* and *Class, Crisis, and the State.*

[48]Wright, *Class, Crisis, and the State* and *Class Structure and Income Distribution.*

locations in the sense that they are neither owners of the means of production nor helpless sellers of their labor; they have an element of both, and hence, they have contradictory material interests and, no doubt, lived experiences and collective capacities. They might not see themselves as exploiters or as the exploited; indeed, they can be both in varying proportions.

This approach made Wright a prominent Marxist theorist, but it also brought criticism that, in turn, led Wright to pursue an alternative conceptualization. One problem was that domination (telling others what to do) and exploitation (extracting surplus product) were somewhat decoupled. For example, managers could give orders, but they did not directly enjoy the economic welfare of appropriated surplus (this went to the owners of the means of production). Another problem revolved around employment in the state or government. Are those employed by the state also workers in the economy? If not, then their status is unclear: They are paid labor, but their products are not directly appropriated by capitalists. They are managers and hence can direct not only each other but perhaps workers and even owners in the economy. These conceptual problems, coupled with the difficulties that Wright encountered in measuring the contradictory locations of individuals, led him to propose a new conceptualization of the middle classes.[49]

Multiple Exploitation. Adopting ideas from John Roemer,[50] Wright's second solution to the problem of the middle classes was to posit an exploitation nexus that varies by the kinds of assets that individuals possess and their degree of ownership or control of these assets. The four assets are (1) labor power assets, (2) capital assets, (3) organization assets, and (4) skill or credential assets. Each of these leads to a particular type of exploitation: individuals who only have labor assets are likely to be exploited because they depend on those who have the economic power to appropriate the surplus value of their labor; capital assets can be used to invest in equipment and labor as a means of extracting the surplus product generated by technology and labor; organization assets can be used to manage and control others in ways that extract surplus products; and skills or educational credentials can be employed to extract extra resources beyond the resources it took to acquire and maintain them.

This approach allowed Wright to address the issue of the middle class by re-coupling the concepts of exploitation (of surplus) and domination (through control or order-giving). In essence, what had been domination was translated into a new type of exploitation by those with organization assets, highly valued skills, and educational credentials. At the same time, the exploitation envisioned by Marx— extraction by capitalists of surplus value from workers—could remain close to Marx's original formulation. A particular society could then be typified by the combinations and configurations of these various types of exploitation.

Wright preferred this conceptualization of the middle classes to the contradictory class location formulation because it allowed him to put exploitation back as the central mechanism by which economic welfare and economic power are connected,

---

[49]Wright, *Classes.*

[50]Roemer, *A General Theory of Exploitation and Class.*

thereby making his scheme more consistent with Marx's original formulation.[51] Moreover, it allowed him to conceptualize managers in state bureaucracies, professionals, and other skilled workers with some degree of autonomy through Marxian-inspired class dynamics: they too are exploiters, just like capitalists, but they use different assets to extract surplus value and product from others.

This approach also came under heavy criticism, leading Wright to back down from some of the assertions in this model.[52] First, those with skills and credentials are not so much exploiters of the less skilled as advantaged workers who can prevent capitalists from exploiting them as much as their less skilled counterparts are exploited (because capitalists value and need their skills and credentials). Second, managers inside government as well as in the private capitalist sector can move up the organizational hierarchy and use their higher salaries to buy into the capitalist sector (via purchase of stocks, bonds, etc.), thereby confusing their material interests. Third, the location of individuals in the state bureaucracy would determine the mix of assets; for example, those higher in the state might possess more capital assets or at least a mix of organization and capital assets, whereas those lower in the hierarchy would possess only organization assets, and those lower still would possess only labor assets to be exploited. In addition to the above, the problems of measuring these various types of assets and documenting empirically how they led to different forms of exploitation caused Wright to shift his scheme yet again.[53]

The Emerging Scheme. As Wright has dealt with the conceptual and empirical problems of measuring class locations at the micro level, he has responded to criticisms by elaborating new concepts or, perhaps more accurately, reformulating older ideas in a new guise. These new conceptualizations still revolve primarily around the problem of the middle classes, but they reveal a more eclectic character.[54]

One idea is the notion of multiple locations. Like most traditional Marxists, Wright had originally assumed that individuals had one class location, even if this location was contradictory and placed a person into classes with different material interests. But people often have more than one job and, hence, can actually have several class locations. For example, a person can have a salaried day job and then operate a small business at night or on weekends, thereby making this individual both a proletarian and a capitalist.

Another idea deals with mediated locations. Individuals are often connected to a class via networks to others who hold a job or own capital. Children, wives, and husbands can all have a mediated relation to a class location of a parent or spouse, and these mediated relations can become complicated. For example, if a female manager is married to a carpenter, each has a mediated relation to the other's class

---

[51]Wright, "Rethinking, Once Again, the Concept of Class Structure."

[52]Wright, "Class Analysis, History and Emancipation."

[53]Erik Olin Wright, *Class Counts* (Cambridge, UK: Cambridge University Press, 1997).

[54]For brief reviews of the ideas presented here, see Wright, "Rethinking, Once Again, the Concept of Class" and "Class Analysis, History and Emancipation."

location, and their children, if they have any, will bear mediated relations to both classes. Wright proposes the notion of an overall class interest in these situations, which is a "weighted combination of these direct and mediated locations," that may or may not be contradictory.

Still another idea in Wright's evolving scheme is a concern with temporal locations. Careers might not significantly change a person's class location, but often careers do involve movement across class locations, as when individuals move up government and corporate hierarchies, when a small business gets large, when workers begin to form companies, and when students move from school to job and then into a career track. People's class locations can thus change over time, giving them different material interests, lived experiences, and collective capacities.

Yet another idea is a conceptualization of distinct strata within classes. The argument is that within basic classes, such as owners and workers, there are distinctive strata whose members might have somewhat different material interests and most likely have very different lived experiences and collective capacities. These strata can take a number of forms. For example, professionals and experts with skills and credentials can be seen as able to collect rents on their skills and credentials, which make them distinct strata within the working class (they are still part of the working class because they must sell their labor power). Temporal mobility in a career can often increase these rents; if the rents are sufficiently high, they can be invested as capital, thereby giving a person a position within a stratum of the capitalist class as well as in the working class. Similarly, managers or manual workers can translate their skills and career mobility into rents that can then become capital. All these workers are in contradictory locations because they are, on the one hand, workers who are paid a salary and, on the other hand, investors in businesses that hire workers. Thus, the basic classes envisioned by Marx—workers and owners of the means of production—can be reconceptualized by distinct strata within these broad classes, with the incumbents in various strata potentially having a contradictory class location as both workers and capitalists.

The issue of state employment can be translated into a state mode of production. Rather than view high-level state workers as organization exploiters, it is better to visualize the state as producing goods and services of a particular kind and, hence, as revealing distinct classes (and perhaps strata within these classes). The dominant class would be those who direct the appropriation and allocation of surplus productivity that the state acquires to support itself (in forms such as taxes, fees, tariffs, etc.). The subordinate class would be those who actually perform the services and produce the goods provided by the state. Within the state mode of production could be various combinations of contradictory positions. For example, a state manager can control the actions of other workers but be controlled by elite decision makers in the dominant class of the state; a state manager who can command a high salary can invest this rent in the private sector, thereby placing this individual in both the economic and the state modes of production. Relations in the state mode of production can also be mediated, as when high-level members of the dominant class have relations with corporations doing business with government or being regulated by government. Moreover, the career path of many incumbents in both the economic and the government modes of production can involve movement back and forth between these modes, thereby shifting the class location of individuals.

A further set of ideas developed in Wright's evolving project moves beyond the problem of the middle classes. The existence of an unemployable and often welfare-dependent segment of a population has led Wright to introduce a distinction between "nonexploitive economic oppression" and "exploitive economic oppression." In exploitive economic oppression, one group's economic welfare is increased by virtue of the exploitation of another, whose welfare declines because the latter's surplus products are appropriated by the former. This situation is oppressive not just because of exploitation, per se, but because the exploiting group often uses morally sanctioned and legitimated coercion to get its way. Yet even under these oppressive conditions of exploitation, the exploited have some power because their exploiters depend on them; so the exploitation often involves implicit negotiation and consent. In nonexploitive economic oppression, there is no transfer of surplus productivity to the exploiter. Instead, the economic welfare of exploiters depends on the exclusion of the oppressed from access to valued resources being consumed by the oppressors. Under these conditions, Wright argues, genocide can occur because the goal of exploiters is to get rid of those who might seek access to resources that they have or covet. Yet even here, the nonexploited oppressed have a resource: the capacity to disrupt efforts at consumption by exploiters. Thus, the nonexploited oppressed can often force exploiters to provide some resources (as happens with those who pay for the welfare of those who are kept out of the economy).

Sustaining the Emancipatory Dream: Envisioning Real Utopias

Any theoretical approach that engages the substance of Marx's vision and seeks to explain why the predicted revolutions did not occur must, in the end, come back to this question. Much of Wright's theorizing has sought to explain, at one and the same time, why conditions in advanced capitalism made revolution in a Marxian sense difficult, while trying to use Marx's basic ideas to show how even advanced capitalism creates contradictions that, it is hoped, will lead to fundamental social change toward socialism. In his recent book, *Envisioning Real Utopias,*[55] Wright again outlines what is wrong with capitalism and explores alternatives guided by the "socialist compass" toward social empowerment of the people and construction of a new kind of state and economy.

Theoretically, perhaps the most interesting part of this effort comes in the book's last section, "Transformation." Here, Wright seeks to lay out various potential trajectories of change, guided by the socialist compass. In so doing, he specifies the conditions and circumstances under which such change is possible.

The Overall Model. In Figure 14.3, I have taken some liberties to lay out Wright's scenarios for how transformative change from capitalism to socialism can come about. Capitalism systematically generates harms, and "social structures and institutions that

---

[55]Wright, *Envisioning Real Utopias.*

systematically impose harms on people require vigorous mechanisms of active social reproduction in order to be sustained over time."[56] These harms come through oppression and exploitation; and as Figure 14.3 denotes under "mechanisms of social reproduction" (of harmful social relations), there are four basic mechanisms.

One is *coercion,* which involves "imposing various kinds of punishments for making . . . challenges"[57] to the system of oppression and exploitation. Coercion can

Figure 14.3   Wright's Envisioning of the Path to the Transformative Change

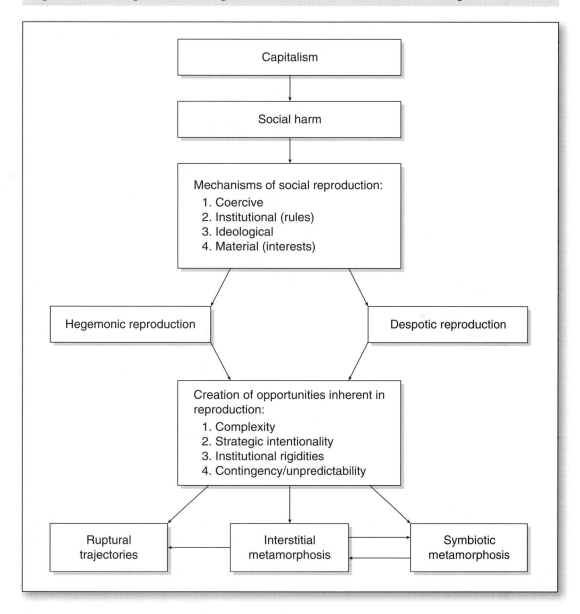

---

[56]Ibid., 276.

[57]Ibid., 279.

come from state and non-state actors that use actual coercion or the threat of coercion to keep people from mobilizing to change the system that is generating social harms. Another mechanism inheres in *institutional rules,* or "rules of the game" that make courses of action that challenge the system difficult to pursue. A third mechanism is built into *ideology* and, more broadly, culture, which are very much responsible for reproduction. The means of cultural production are dominated by those with power, who, through control of media and other domains where culture is produced, instill in individuals both consciously and unconsciously commitments to norms, beliefs, and ideologies that keep them mounting challenges to the system. And the fourth mechanism is *material interests* that people perceive they have in the capitalist system, with any proposal for transformation often being perceived to threaten these interests. This dependence on the system, even an exploitive system, will often make people fearful of change; and capitalism has a tendency to pull people into the very relations that exploit them and, yet, still sustain fears that another system will challenge their interests in this exploitive system.

The operation of various configurations of these four mechanisms generates two kinds of social reproduction: (1) despotic and (2) hegemonic. *Despotic reproduction* relies upon coercion and the institutional rules by which coercion is meted out, whereas *hegemonic reproduction* is less obvious and draws people into the system willingly because they see their material interests as inhering in the system. In addition to their indoctrination into beliefs, ideologies, and normative rules, people abide by the rules often because they believe in them and also because their interests are tied to the system that these rules legitimate.

Yet no system of exploitation and domination is so powerful that it does not reveal "limits," "gaps," and "contradictions" that are, in essence, inherent weaknesses of the system. These weaknesses generate not only recognition by at least some that the system is flawed and harmful but also that the system presents potential *opportunities for transformative change.* There are four principle sources of these opportunities. One is the *complexity* of the system. Complex systems have many gaps, cleavages, conflicts of interest, contradictions, needs for trade-offs, power use, and other forces that make people more aware of the broader system and, potentially, motivated to change it. A second source of opportunity is *strategic intentionality,* whereby efforts to deal with problems are fraught with potential problems such as struggles over designs of programs, inadequate or biased (by power) knowledge to deal with problems, arrogant and often stupid decisions by powerful actors, and unintended consequences of actions in complex systems. A third source of opportunity resides in *institutional rigidities* and path dependency, by which a social order is reproduced even as it generates tensions. Once institutional systems are in place and supported by powerful ideologies, they are difficult to change, even if they are creating discontent among sectors of a society that might increasingly see the system for what it is and be ready to engage in actions to change it. The last source of opportunity for transformation is the fact of *contingency and unpredictability.* Economic and political processes are not always predictable, even with powerful reproductive forces in play. One change can suddenly cascade across a system in an unpredictable manner, thereby opening people's eyes to problems and potentially motivating them to protest against the system.

Up to this point, Wright summarizes in a more abstract way the basic thrust of Marx's argument that there are contradictions in systems of inequality and the use of exploitive power; and coupled with actions of the powerful, who are locked into the system, they end up creating conditions that make the system vulnerable. It is at this point in his vision of realistic utopias that Wright cautions about the difficulty in making exact predictions about change trajectories, as the lesson of Marx's failed prophecy underscores. Yet Wright quickly adds that "many of the predictions of historical materialism have in fact been borne out by the actual history of capitalism."[58] For example, the globalization of capitalism; the growth and domination of corporations; the process of commodification of just about everything, including human relations; and other processes have come to pass. Yet there is always the problem of predicting which of many potential trajectories will emerge at any given time. His solution is to delineate a number of different trajectories, which he groups under three general labels: (1) ruptural, (2) interstitial metamorphosis, and (3) symbiotic metamorphosis. His analysis is complex and nuanced, and so I can only outline these in general terms.

Alternative Trajectories of Transformation. For each of these three potential trajectories, there are an associated logic of transformation, set of key actors for the transformation, strategic logic for dealing with the state, strategic logic for dealing with the capitalist class, and metaphors of what would constitute a success. Wright anticipates his more detailed discussion with a table somewhat like Table 14.13.

Table 14.13 Wright "Models" of Transformative Trajectories

	Reptural	*Interstitial Metamorphosis*	*Symbiotic Metamorphosis*
Politics and logic of transformation:	Revolution toward Socialism/communism	Anarchists/anarchism	Social democratic
Key actor in transformation:	Classes organized as political parties/actors	Social movements	Coalitions of social forces with labor
Strategic logic in dealing with state:	Attack the state	Propose and build alternative formations outside of state	Use the state by brining the struggle to terrain of state
Strategic logic in dealing with capitalist class:	Confront the bourgeoisie	Ignore the bourgeoise	Collaborate with bourgeoise
Metaphors of success:	War, conflict, and victories and defeats	Ecological competition among alternative social formations	Evolutionary aspirations for transformations

Source: Erik Olin Wright, Envisioning Realistic Utopias, p. 304

---

[58]Ibid., 301.

Ruptural Transformations. Wright recognizes that political democracy and capitalism coevolve; and while the harms of capitalism and the imperfections of democracy in capitalist systems generate grievances, the chances of ruptural changes are lower in capitalist systems where some degree of democracy exists. The receptiveness of the population to socialist goals depends upon the degree to which the material interests of the population can be tied to socialism, while at the same time diminishing the "pushback" of capitalists and their control of the means of ideological production. Moreover, there would need to be coalitions among middle- and working-class members of a society, an occurrence that appears unlikely in current capitalist societies. Wright thus appears to imply that this route to socialism is indeed a less realistic utopia.

Interstitial Transformation or Metamorphosis. These are transformations that begin in the holes, spaces, and cracks in the institutional structure of a capitalist society. Such *interstitial activities* are evident in almost all capitalist societies, with many having the goal of building "alternative institutions and emancipatory ideals and that are created primarily through direct action of one sort or another rather than through the state."[59] According to Wright these interstitial strategies have two routes to socialism—one by altering conditions that make a ruptural strategy feasible and the other by expanding the scope of interstitial action to the point that capitalism no longer imposes so many restraints. Wright ponders a number of trajectories but, in the end, concludes that "it is difficult to see how they could ever by themselves erode the basic structural power of capital sufficiently to dissolve the capitalist limits on emancipatory social change."[60] Thus, neither the expansion of interstitial activities and structural formations nor the ruptural strategy appears to offer feasible strategies for transformations. What, then, of the third transformative trajectory, symbiotic metamorphosis?

Symbiotic Metamorphosis. In this approach, the bottom-up actions of forces of change seek to empower people while, at the same time, resolving the problems that capitalists have faced. Change is evolutionary and involves a class compromise that balances the interests of labor and the general citizenry with the goals of capitalists. Several key spheres of activity are critical for this class compromise. First is the sphere of exchange and the dynamics of markets, where the population meets the capitalists. There must be real compromises in this sphere between the interests of nonelite and noncapitalist classes and those of capitalists. Second is the sphere of production, in which the relations between labor in firms and capital must be more balanced, with conflicts between the two involving negotiations among actors who are "more equal." And third is the sphere of politics, where compromises in the formation and implementation of state policies are made to meet the interests of the state as well as members of nonelite classes. Wright conducts a thought experiment in which the relative power of capital to realize its interests and that of classes to develop associational power are assessed. When capital's power is high, the

---

[59]Ibid., 324.

[60]Ibid., 355.

associational interests of labor are high, and vice versa. At either extreme, Wright argues, are zones of "unattainability," and thus, it is the middle ground, where both parties can realize some of their interests, that is the most viable. The United States is, Wright argues, on one side of this zone, favoring capital or class associational interests, while a society like Sweden is on the other side of this zone. Thus, the implication is that the United States needs to move toward the Swedish side, where the interests of capital and nonelite classes are more equally balanced so that each side is able to meet many of its goals.

Assessing Wright's Neo-Marxist Approach

Wright appears to have moved from trying to explain why the predictions by Marx about class formation and revolution did not ever come true in a capitalist system to developing scenarios whereby many of the emancipatory goals of Marx can be realized in societies that are still capitalist but more democratic, where class interests are equally weighted against those of capitalists. In this way, the constraints of modern capitalism imposed on class associational power are reduced, and the capacity of nonelite actors to realize their interests is increased. Rather than envisioning "real utopias" (plural), Wright appears to come down to one: a version of democratic socialism that currently exists in parts of the capitalist world. The other trajectories to socialism are, in essence, considered unrealistic, whereas the symbiotic metamorphosis is considered the most realistic. Along the way to this conclusion, Wright appears to argue that the globalization of capitalism has set up conditions whereby those capitalist societies that favor capital over class associational power, such as the United States, can be transformed. Thus, in the end, Wright has done what many Marxist scholars have done over the last few decades: considered the dynamics of the world system and its effects on class relations in capitalist societies.

Neo-Marxian World-Systems Analysis: Immanuel Wallerstein

In the 1970s, Marx-inspired theory began to shift the unit of analysis from nation-states to relations among societies. Capitalism was viewed as a dynamic engine of transformation that would create a world-level economy. This world-capitalist economy, in turn, would reveal many of the same contradictions that Marx had predicted for capitalism within a particular society. The study of empires and imperialism had, of course, long been a major topic in a variety of disciplines—history, political science, economics, and sociology. Some of the flavor of what world-system analysts would argue was captured early by the British economist J. A. Hobson;[61] in his view, capitalist nations need to conquer and exploit other nations to stave off

---

[61]John Atkinson Hobson, *Capitalism and Imperialism in South Africa* (London: Contemporary Review, 1900), *The Conditions of Industrial Peace* (New York: Macmillan, 1927), *Confessions of an Economic Heretic* (London: G. Allen and Unwin, 1938), *The Economics of Distribution* (London: Macmillan, 1900).

many of the problems predicted by Marx. But Immanuel Wallerstein[62] codified Marxist ideas into a coherent conceptual scheme for the analysis of the world system. His work, in turn, has stimulated much further theoretical and empirical effort.

World Empires and World Economy

Immanuel Wallerstein begins his historical analysis on the emergence of a capitalist world system by distinguishing between two basic forms of interconnection among societies: (1) world empires and (2) world economy. A world empire is created by military conquest or threats of such conquest and then by extraction of resources, usually in the form of tribute, from those populations that have been defeated or threatened. Often these conquered societies can retain considerable autonomy as long as they pay the tribute demanded by their conquerors. Whether through direct appropriation, taxation, or tribute, dominant nations can accumulate wealth and use their wealth to finance the privileges of elites and the military activities of the polity. Military empires are thus built around a strong state that administers the flow of taxes, franchises, and tributary wealth, while financing and coordinating the military for war-making and conquest. Wallerstein argues that this was, historically, the dominant form of societal interconnection among societies before the 1400s, when the capitalist revolution had begun, although many debate this point and emphasize that trade-based and empire-based systems of domination had existed long before modern European capitalism.[63] Moreover, many argue that imperial and trade forms of world-system domination had come and gone in various cycles many times in history,[64] long before the modern world system began to develop in the 1400s. Nonetheless, the important point is that one form of connection among nations is through state-based imperialism. Indeed, this form has persisted for most of the twentieth century, as the Soviet Union before its breakup can attest.

Wallerstein, as well as other historical sociologists, emphasize that the structural dilemma for imperial forms of governance is sustaining the resource levels necessary

---

[62]Immanuel Wallerstein, *The Modern World System,* 3 vols. (New York: Academic Press, 1974, 1980, 1989). Earlier work by scholars such as Andre Gunder Frank on "dependency theory" anticipated much of what Wallerstein was to argue: underdeveloped societies, especially those in Latin America, could not go through the stages to modernization because they were economically dependent on advanced economies, and this dependency and the corresponding exploitation by advanced industrial powers kept them from becoming fully industrialized and modern. See, for example, Frank's *Capitalism and Underdevelopment in Latin America* (New York: Monthly Review Press, 1967). See also his later work *Dependent Accumulation* (New York: Monthly Review Press, 1979). Also, historians such as Fernand Braudel had conducted analyses of world-system processes; for his overview, see *Civilization and Capitalism,* 3 vols. (New York: Harper and Row, 1964).

[63]For a review, see Christopher Chase-Dunn and Peter Grimes, "World-Systems Analysis," *Annual Review of Sociology* 21 (1995):387–417. See also Albert J. Bergesen (ed.), *Studies of the Modern World System* (New York: Academic Press, 1980).

[64]See Christopher Chase-Dunn and T. D. Hall's edited collection of essays on *Core/Periphery Relations in Precapitalist Worlds* (Boulder, CO: Westview, 1991) as well as their coauthored *Rise and Demise: Comparing World Systems* (Boulder, CO: Westview Press, 1997). See also Andre Gunder Frank and B. K. Gills (eds.), *The World System: Five Hundred Years or Five Thousand?* (London: Routledge, 1993).

to support the privileges of elites as well as a large military and administrative bureaucracy to control resentful peasants or other nonelites, especially those in conquered populations. Corruption and graft only aggravate these problems, but in the end, the state leaders face fiscal crises and must confront a variety of enemies within and outside their homeland borders. Eventually, the empire collapses, often because two imperial empires come to a showdown conflict, as Collins emphasized in his analysis of geopolitics (see Table 14.12 on p. 491).

In contrast with an empire, a world economy reveals a different structure, consisting of (a) multiple states at its core, some of which have approximately equal military power; (b) competition among these core states in both the military and the economic arena, with the latter being dominated by markets; and (c) peripheral states, whose cheap labor and raw resources are extracted through trade, but trade that is vastly unequal because of the military power and economic advantages of the core states in market transactions.

Core, Periphery, and Semi-periphery

Wallerstein's distinction among the core and periphery at the world-system level parallels in a rough way Marx's notion of capitalists and proletarians at the societal level. *Core* nations correspond to the capitalist class at the societal level and, like the capitalist class, extract surplus value through exploitation. The core areas of the world system are the great military powers of their time. Since military power ultimately rests on the economy's ability to support the use of coercive force, these military powers are also leading economic powers. There are external areas to the core, and these become the *periphery* when a core state decides to colonize them or engage in exploitive trade. The periphery consists of less developed countries whose resources are needed and, with threats of potential or actual military intervention, are taken in exploitive market transactions. Wallerstein also distinguishes what is termed the *semi-periphery,* which comprises (a) minor nations in the core area and (b) leading states in the periphery. These semi-peripheral states have a higher degree of economic development and military strength than the periphery, but not as much as the core states; they are often used as intermediaries in trade between the core and the periphery.[65]

The semi-periphery can also be the origin of mobility among states, and at times, areas of the periphery can become semi-peripheral and perhaps even part of the core area (as in the history of the United States and Japan). Similarly, much of Southeast Asia is moving today from either the semi-periphery (e.g., China) or even the periphery (e.g., India) to the core. Japan is clearly at the core in the current world system, whereas India and other parts of Asia are still somewhat semi-peripheral but clearly capable of moving to a new core over the next few decades.

The basic connection that drives the world economy, however, is the relationship between the core and the periphery. The core has a large consumer market for both

---

[65]For a somewhat different analysis, see Christopher Chase-Dunn, *Global Formation* (Cambridge, UK: Blackwell, 1989) and "World Systems Theorizing" in *Handbook of Sociological Theory.* See also Volker Bornschier and Christopher Chase-Dunn, *Transnational Corporations and Underdevelopment* (New York: Praeger, 1985).

basic and luxury goods; a well-paid labor force (at least relative to the labor force in the periphery); a comparatively low rate of taxation, enabling the accumulation of private wealth; a high level of technology (both economic and military), coupled with market-driven needs to sustain technological innovation; and a set of large-scale firms that engage in trade with peripheral states. The periphery has resources that consumers in the core states desire, and because states in the periphery are at a trading disadvantage (because of their lack of military strength and lack of technology and capital to develop their own resources), each exchange between the core and the periphery in a market transfers wealth to the core. This exploitation by the core perpetuates the problems of development in the periphery, because peripheral states do not receive sufficient money from the core to finance infrastructural development (roads, transportation, and communication) or to afford educational and other welfare state needs.[66] Moreover, because of the lack of economic development and the high degree of economic uncertainty in peripheral nations, individual citizens view children as their only potential source of economic security in the future, thereby having more babies and causing population growth, which places an even greater burden on the state. As a consequence, peripheral states not only remain poor and underdeveloped, they are typically becoming over-populated and politically unstable, a situation that only sustains their problems of development and their dependence on core states for trade.

The Dynamics of the World Economy

A world economy reveals its own dynamics, some of which are much the same as in empires, but others are unique to capitalism. What the core states have all had in common with older forms of empire building is the constant wars with each other, especially over conquest and control of the periphery. Moreover, they encounter many of the same fiscal problems of empires in trying to sustain wealth, profits, and well-being at home along with a large military and administrative system to wage war and to control their own citizens and dissidents in their conquered or dominated territories. Indeed, core states are often just ahead of problems as they colonize ever more territories to sustain the costs of their prosperity while financing the administrative and coercive basis of control at home and abroad. When these competing powers begin to fight closer to home, they often ruin their respective economies through the costs of financing war and then maintaining control. Such wars make core states vulnerable enough for new powers to move into the core and supplant them (as has occurred, e.g., with Spain and Portugal).

Another dynamic, Wallerstein argues, is the cyclical tendencies of the world economy. Wallerstein emphasizes what are termed *Kondratieff waves,* which are long-term oscillations[67] in the world system, lasting approximately 150 years. At the beginning

---

[66]This was the essential point of dependency theorists. See also Chase-Dunn and Grimes, "World Systems Analysis," for a brief overview of wave analysis. For a short but very clear summary of Wallerstein's argument, see Randall Collins, *Theoretical Sociology* (New York: Harcourt Brace Jovanovich, 1988), 96–97.

[67]See Chase-Dunn and Grimes, "World Systems Analysis," for a brief review of empirical and conceptual work on these cycles.

of a Kondratieff wave, the demand within core states for goods is high, which increases production and the need for ever more raw materials. This need for raw materials leads to the expansion of the core states into external areas, making the latter peripheral suppliers of resources to the core. The next step in the Kondratieff wave occurs when the supplies of raw materials and the production of goods exceed the demand for them, leading core states to reduce geographical expansion and, equally important, businesses to reduce production, thereby setting off the down cycle emphasized by Marx: lowered domestic demand; decreased production; intense competition for market share, driving profits down; increased unemployment as production declines and, consequently, even less demand for goods; further reductions in production; business failures; and growth of monopolies and oligopolies.

This concentration of capital, however, sets the stage for the next point in the wave: high unemployment generates class conflict as workers demand better working conditions and wages; such demands eventually lead to higher wages for workers as the state responds to political pressures and large corporations give in. Concentrated capital meantime seeks new technologies and ever more efficient means of production to lower costs. With more wages, economic demand increases, and with new technologies and capital investment, a new period of higher profits and relative prosperity ensues, leading to increased demand for raw materials from peripheral states. But eventually, this new round of prosperity falls victim to the forces predicted by Marx: market saturation through over-production of goods relative to demand, intense competition over price, increased unemployment, decreased demand, further decreases in production, increases in business failures, and financial crisis bring to a close this long, 150-year wave.

Other Cyclical Dynamics in the World Economy

Within these long waves are shorter cycles that have been extensively studied by not only conventional economists but world-system analysts as well.[68] These operate much as Marx had predicted, but without the great revolution at their end. The classic business cycle, sometimes termed *Juglar cycles,* appears to last from five to seven years. Production expands to increased market demand, unemployment declines, demand in markets increases further because workers have income, production expands more, and then oversupply of goods in relation to demand starts a recession. Some have argued that part of this cycle reflects the replacement costs of new machinery, which tends to wear out about every eight years, forcing new capital investments that can drive market demand, but once this demand is met, it can also set into motion the decline of demand for capital goods. Such capital demand is especially important in high-technology core nations, where much employment revolves around making equipment and providing services for other businesses. Capital demand can become as significant as, or more so than, household consumer demand for goods and services.[69]

---

[68]Ibid., 404.

[69]Ibid., 404–405.

Another cycle is what is termed the *Kuznet cycle;* these operate over a twenty-five-year period in core and semi-peripheral states.[70] Just why these cycles occur is not known, although there are several hypotheses. One is related to generational turnover, in which about every twenty years, the demand for basic household purchases, such as houses and other buildings, declines—and, hence, decreases production and employment—until the next generation has sufficient money to drive up demand for these goods, thereby setting off another wave of prosperity.

Hegemonic Sequences

As Wallerstein argued,[71] and as others have developed further, there are oscillations in the degree of centralization among the core nations of the world system. Before capitalism,[72] these oscillations revolved around the rise and fall of empires through war, conquest, tribute, and collapse. With the advent of capitalism, however, the nature of the oscillation changes. Hegemonic core states seek to control trade, particularly trade across oceans, and thereby connect core and periphery in an exploitive trade arrangement. The dominant state or states can prevent military empires from encroaching on this trade and can force empires to act as capitalists in the system of world trade (as with the former Soviet Union and China today).

Thus, the cycle of centralization revolves around the rise and fall of hegemonic core states that have been able to dictate the terms of trade in the world system. Shifts in this domination by a core state can come with wars, but unlike precapitalist empire building, the domination that ensues is oriented toward dictating the terms of trade as much as toward outright conquest of territory or extraction of tribute in response to military threats. The rise of a new hegemonic state gives the state greater access to the resources of other peripheral and semi-peripheral states, while enabling it to dominate other core states (as has been the case, e.g., with the United States in the post–World War II period, at least to this point).

In addition to war, hegemonic states often rise because of new economic or military technology that gives them advantages. Under these conditions, states can charge "rents" for their innovations or use them to control trade and, in the case of military technology, to make threats that improve the terms of trade. As these innovations are copied, however, the advantages can be lost or neutralized, setting the stage for another potential hegemonic state to emerge because of new technologies and other productive or military advantages.

The End of Capitalism

Wallerstein and many other world-systems analysts still accept Marx's vision that capitalism will collapse, but for world-systems theory, capitalism must first

---

[70]Wallerstein, *The Modern World System.*

[71]See Chase-Dunn and Grimes, "World Systems Analysis," 411–414, for a useful review.

[72]For an example of a test of the world-system model, see Ronan Van Rossem, "The World System Paradigm as General Theory of Development: A Cross-national Test," *American Sociological Review* 61 (1996):508–527.

penetrate the entire world for its contradictions to emerge. As long as peripheral states exist to be exploited by the core, capitalism can sustain itself by relying on the resources and the cheap labor of less developed countries. But once capitalism comes to exist everywhere, there is no longer an escape from the processes outlined by Marx. The problems endemic to capitalism—saturation of markets, decreased demand, lowered production, and further decreases in demand—will lead to the collapse of capitalist modes of production, a period of conflict between the old-line capitalists (along with their allies in the state) and the broader population, which seeks a better way to distribute resources fairly. In the wake of these crises will come world-level socialism, and perhaps even world government. Although the details of this ultimate scenario vary among analysts, the emancipatory thrust of Marx's predictions remains. Whether these predictions are any more accurate than Marx's remains to be seen, but regardless of their accuracy, world-systems theory has provided important insights into the basic dynamics of human organization.

Conclusion

As is evident from this sampling of conflict theories, Marx, Weber, and Simmel live on in these theories. The early analytical theorists, like Dahrendorf and Coser, brought the criticisms that Weber and Simmel had of Marx, while making the conflict more abstract and not tied to the dynamics of capitalism, per se, or even societies, and also any organized social unit.[73] More recent analytical theorists like Collins[74] have incorporated many more of the early theorists of the classical period, such as Durkheim, while blending conflict dynamics with more contemporary approaches, such as dramaturgy (see Chapter 18), exchange dynamics (Chapter18), and other present-day theories. These new theories no longer are dominated by the problematic set forth by Marx but, instead, are interested in explaining the nature of conflict in general at all levels of social organization.

Marx's ideas, however, remain very much alive in contemporary neo-Marxian schemes, especially in the work of analytical Marxists, who have sought to grapple with the shortcomings in Marx's theory. Their work has not fully resolved the problems in Marx's analysis; rather, it remains an intellectual project still in progress.

One strategy for overcoming the failure of Marx's predictions has been to shift the level of analysis from class antagonisms within societies to systems of societies. Here, the dynamics of capitalism play themselves out at a global level, where many of the "contradictions" that Marx saw in capitalism are clearly evident and less easily controlled than they were within nation-states. Thus, in most world-systems theorists, there is the hope that these contradictions would produce a global revolution that will reduce the inequalities within and between societies.

---

[73]For an effort at analytical conflict theorizing that seeks to synthesize Dahrendorf's and Coser's respective theories, see also Jonathan H. Turner, "A Strategy for Reformulating the Dialectical and Functional Theories of Conflict," *Social Forces* 53 (1975):433–444.

[74]For my efforts to produce an integrative theory of conflict dynamics that draws from many sources outside of conflict theory proper, see Jonathan H. Turner, *Theoretical Principles of Sociology,* vols. 1 and 3 (New York: Springer, 2010 and 2012, respectively).

CHAPTER 15

Exchange Theorizing

C lassical theorists in sociology were generally suspicious of utilitarian theorizing, with its emphasis on rational decision making among actors in free markets. Even Herbert Spencer, who was perhaps less critical than most, recognized that culture, power, social structure, and other sociocultural forces constrain rationality and bias decision making. And for most of the twentieth century, as neoclassical economics grew, especially in the United States, sociologists remained distrustful of what would become known as exchange theorizing. In fact, Talcott Parsons's early work on the structure of social action was, in part, an effort to broaden beyond utilitarianism the forces influencing human action.

But in the 1950s, exchange-theoretic ideas began to emerge in sociology. Some of these theories were based upon neoclassical economic arguments about rationality, while others were founded on psychological behaviorism. In the end, sociologists' use of neoclassical economics and behaviorism produced a convergence between these psychological and economic theoretical perspectives; and as the restrictive assumptions of these approaches were expanded, exchange theory in the second half of the twentieth century grew dramatically and, today, is one of the dominant theoretical approaches in the discipline.

In this chapter, I will first examine the three early strands of theorizing on exchange processes and, then, explore what I think are the two most important contemporary exchange theories in sociology. Exchange theorizing initially gained a foothold in sociology through the works of George C. Homans, Peter M. Blau, James S. Coleman, and Richard D. Emerson. Today, it appears that the approaches of Coleman and Emerson have had the greatest staying power and have been significantly improved by such scholars as Michael Hechter and Edward J. Lawler. Let me begin, therefore, with the foundational figures in exchange theory in the modern era.

Early Exchange Theories

George C. Homans's Behavioristic Approach

George C. Homans made a theoretical conversion to exchange theory in the late 1950s, borrowing ideas from his behaviorist colleague at Harvard, B. F. Skinner, who was the most prominent behaviorist in the world at the time. Like most behaviorists, Skinner had emphasized that theory can only be about what is observable, and hence, it is necessary to stay out of the "black box" of human thoughts and emotions, which cannot be directly observed. Yet, like any sociologist, Homans recognized that he would have to enter the black box of human cognition, perhaps through the back door, but nonetheless he would have to conceptualize what people feel and think. In so doing, he drew concepts from utilitarian tradition in economics and dressed them up in behaviorist conceptual clothing. In developing his behavioristic exchange theory, Homans also developed a view of theorizing using the vocabulary of axiomatic theory, without, however, its logical rigor or substance. But the basic idea was that the axioms from which all sociological laws can ultimately be deduced are psychological in nature (see Chapter 25, where the nature of axiomatic theory is summarized), and not only psychological but also behaviorist laws at that (with elements of utilitarian economics slipping in). To say the least, this advocacy created a rather heated debate because sociologists are highly defensive when it comes to reducing sociology to some other field, and psychology and economics no less! In making this argument for theoretical deduction and reduction, Homans also insisted that sociology must begin with behavior and interaction, seeing theories of macrostructures as ultimately explained by the actions of people seeking rewards and weighing their rewards against cost. This too threatened many sociologists.

Borrowing From B. F. Skinner. Given Homans's commitment to axiomatic theorizing and his concern with face-to-face interaction among individuals, it was perhaps inevitable that Homans would look toward Skinner and, indirectly, to the early founders of behaviorism—I. P. Pavlov, Edward Lee Thorndike, and J. B. Watson. But Homans borrowed directly from Skinner's reformulations of early behaviorist principles.[1] Stripped of its subtlety, Skinnerian behaviorism states as its basic principle that if an animal has a need, it will perform activities that in the past have satisfied this need. A first corollary to this principle is that organisms will attempt to avoid unpleasant experiences but will endure limited amounts of such experiences as a cost in emitting the behaviors that satisfy an overriding need. A second corollary is that organisms will continue emitting certain behaviors only as long as they continue to produce desired and expected effects. A third corollary of Skinnerian psychology

---

[1]George C. Homans, *Social Behavior: Its Elementary Forms* (New York: Harcourt Brace Jovanovich, 1961; 2nd ed. 1972).

emphasizes that as needs are satisfied by a particular behavior, animals are less likely to emit that behavior. A fourth corollary states that if in the recent past a behavior has brought rewards and if these rewards suddenly stop, the organism will appear angry and gradually cease emitting the behavior that formerly satisfied its needs. A final corollary holds that if an event has consistently occurred at the same time as a behavior that was rewarded or punished, the event becomes a stimulus and is likely to produce the behavior or its avoidance.

These principles were derived from behavioral psychologists' highly controlled observations of animals, whose needs could be inferred from deprivations imposed by the investigators. Although human needs are much more difficult to ascertain than those of laboratory pigeons and mice and despite the fact that humans interact in groupings that defy experimental controls, Homans believed that the principles of operant psychology could be applied to the explanation of human behavior in both simple and complex groupings.

One of the most important adjustments of Skinnerian principles to fit the facts of human social organization involved the recognition that needs are satisfied by other people and that people reward and punish one another. In contrast with Skinner's animals, which only indirectly interact with Skinner through the apparatus of the laboratory and which have little ability to reward Skinner (except perhaps to confirm his principles), humans constantly give and take, or exchange, rewards and punishments.

The conceptualization of human behavior as exchange of rewards (and punishments) among interacting individuals led Homans to incorporate, in altered form, the first principle of elementary economics: humans rationally calculate the long-range consequences of their actions in a marketplace and attempt to maximize their material profits in their transactions. However, this basic economic assumption must be altered in four ways: (1) People do not always attempt to maximize profits; they seek only to make some profit in exchange relations. (2) Humans do not usually make either long-run or rational calculations in exchanges; for, in everyday life, "the Theory of Games is good advice for human behavior but a poor description of it." (3) The things exchanged involve not only money but also other commodities, including approval, esteem, compliance, love, affection, and other less materialistic goods. (4) The marketplace is not a separate domain in human exchanges, for all interaction involves individuals exchanging rewards (and punishments) and seeking profits.

The Basic Exchange Principles. In propositions 1 through 3 of Table 15.1, Homans's reinterpretation of the principles of Skinnerian psychology are stated in their last form before Homans's death. Those actions that have brought people rewards are likely to be emitted again (principle 1); the more similar a situation is to the one that brought rewards, the more likely are people to emit behaviors to secure these rewards (principle 2); and people pursue those behaviors that bring them the most valuable rewards (principle 3).

Principle 4 indicates the condition under which the first three propositions fall into temporary abeyance. In accordance with the reinforcement principle of satiation or the economic law of marginal utility, humans eventually define activities that have been consistently rewarded as less valuable and begin to emit other activities in

Table 15.1 Homans's Exchange Propositions

1. *Success Proposition:* For all actions taken by persons, the more often a particular action of a person is rewarded, the more likely the person is to perform that action.
2. *Stimulus Proposition:* If in the past the occurrence of a particular stimulus or set of stimuli has been the occasion on which a person's action has been rewarded, then the more similar the present stimuli are to the past ones, the more likely the person is to perform the action or some similar action now.
3. *Value Proposition:* The more valuable to a person the result of his or her action is, the more likely he or she is to perform the action.
4. *Deprivation/Satiation Proposition:* The more often in the recent past a person has received a particular reward, the less valuable any further unit of that reward becomes for that person.
5. *Aggression/Approval Propositions:*   A. When a person's action does not receive the reward expected or receives punishment that was not expected, he or she will be angry and become more likely to perform aggressive behavior. The results of such behavior become more valuable to that person.   B. When a person's action receives the reward expected, especially greater reward than expected, or does not receive the punishment expected, he or she will be pleased and become more likely to perform approving behavior. The results of such behavior become more valuable to that person.
6. *Rationality Proposition:* In choosing between alternative actions, a person will choose the one for which, as perceived by him or her at the time, the value of the result, multiplied by the probability of getting that result, is greater.

search of different rewards (again, however, in accordance with the principles enumerated in propositions 1 through 3).

Principle 5 introduces a more complicated set of conditions that qualify propositions 1 through 4. From Skinner's observation that pigeons reveal "anger" and "frustration" when they do not receive an expected reward, Homans reasoned that humans will probably reveal the same behavior. This principle is close to Skinner's principle, but with the obvious addition of elements from the black box of human cognition—expectations for rewards, emotions like anger and satisfaction, and states of approval. Interestingly, this aggression/approval proposition was a reformulaton in Skinnerian vocabulary (but not substance) of an earlier principle in the first edition of *Social Behavior: Its Elementary Forms*, where Homans postulated a "law of distributive justice," which emphasized that individuals calculate the extent to which their rewards less costs and investments (accumulated costs) are seen as "fair" and "just"; and when these justice calculations lead persons to see that their rewards are not proportional to their costs and investments, compared with others, they become *angry*; conversely, when they see rewards as fair, they experience *satisfaction*. Ironically, it is this first formulation on what Homans termed *distributive justice* that was to have more influence on sociological exchange theories, perhaps because there has been a long tradition within philosophy and jurisprudence about justice. In either case, Homans has entered the black box because his actors now think and feel, whereas Skinner would never have entertained such notions in his insistence that only observable stimuli and overt behavior can be measured and, hence, only stimulus-response can be theorized.

In addition to principles 1 through 5, Homans introduces a "rationality proposition," which summarizes the stimulus, success, and value propositions. I have placed this proposition in Table 15.1 because it is so prominent in Homans's actual construction of illustrative deductive explanations. To translate the somewhat awkward vocabulary of principle 6 as Homans wrote it, people make calculations about various alternative lines of action. They perceive or calculate the value of the rewards that might be yielded by various actions. But they also temper this calculation through perceptions of how probable the receipt of rewards will be. Low probability of receiving highly valued rewards would lower their reward potential. Conversely, high probability of receiving a lower-valued reward increases the overall reward potential. This relationship can be stated by the following formula:

$$\text{Action} = \text{Value} \times \text{Probability}$$

People are, Homans asserted, rational in the sense that they are likely to emit that behavior, or action, among alternatives for which value on the right side of the equation is largest. For example, if Action_1 is highly valued (say, at a level of 10) but the probability of getting that value by emitting Action_1 is low (0.20, or 20%) and if Action_2 is less valued (say, 5) but the probability of receiving the value is greater (0.50) than for Action_1, then the actor will emit Action_2 (because $10 \times 0.20 = 2$ will yield less reward than $5 \times 0.50 = 2.5$).

Homans believed that these basic principles or laws explain, in the sense of deductive explanation, patterns of human organization. Indeed, he often saw these principles as "axioms." As is obvious, they are psychological in nature. What is more, these psychological axioms constitute from Homans's viewpoint the only general sociological propositions, because "there are no general sociological propositions that hold good of all societies or social groups as such." Yet Homans did not say that there cannot be sociological laws. On the contrary, these laws are the very propositions that are to be deduced from the psychological axioms. Thus, sociological propositions will be conspicuous in the deductive system emanating from the psychological principles. The basic form of deductive systems[2] that Homans sought, but never really developed, can be illustrated in Figure 15.1.

---

[2]Homans championed this conception of theory in a large number of works; see, for example, Homans, *Social Behavior, The Nature of Social Science* (New York: Harcourt, Brace, and World, 1967), "Fundamental Social Processes," in *Sociology*, ed. N. J. Smelser (New York: Wiley, 1967), 27–78, "Contemporary Theory in Sociology," in *Handbook of Modern Sociology*, ed. R. E. L. Faris (Skokie, IL: Rand McNally, 1964), 251–277, and "Bringing Men Back In," *American Sociological Review* 29 (December 1964):809–818. For an early statement of his position, see George C. Homans, "Social Behavior as Exchange," *American Journal of Sociology* 63 (August 1958):597–606 and "Discovery and the Discovered in Social Theory," *Humboldt Journal of Social Relations* 7 (Fall–Winter 1979–1980):89–102.

Figure 15.1   Form of Homans's Deductive Explanations

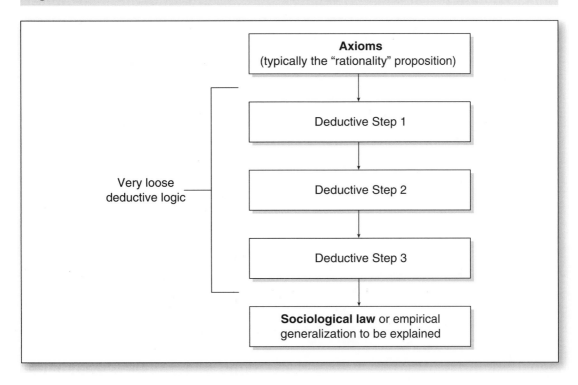

Homans argued that the goal of science is always to be reductive, wherever possible. Thus, if sociological principles can be deduced from psychological ones, this is nothing more than one of the goals of science. Moreover, reduction should not stop there; the principles of psychology or behavior should, to some degree, be deducible from biology, and so on through chemistry and physics. Homans would often deride sociologists for their over concern with reduction, arguing in essence that if they had some laws, they would worry less about whether or not they are reducible to the principles of behavior. Yet, for all of his bravado on these points, Homans never pursued the most obvious issue: develop principles of sociology. He had, in some ways, the cart before the horse because if the goal is to use psychological axioms about behavior to explain sociological principles about interaction and social organization, it is necessary to have some sociological principles. Of course, there were laws in sociology, but he never used these in "demonstrations" of his deductive logic, which in the end would argue that people do things because they are rewarding; and thus, any law of sociology can be "deduced" from one or more of his axioms[3] presented in Table 15.1. This epistemological argument never went very far, but the substance of Homans's behavioristic exchange theory did.

---

[3]Axiomatic theory for sociology is unrealistic; and Homans's "deductions" were so loose and descriptive as to fall far short of any resemblance to a real axiomatic explanation. See Chapter 24 for a discussion of theoretical formats.

Figure 15.2 Homans's Image of Social Organization

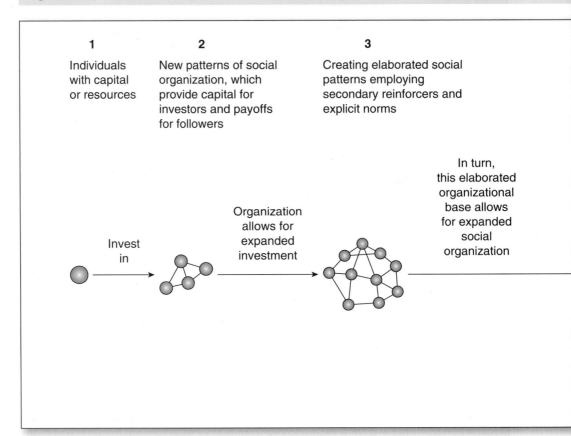

1

Individuals
with capital
or resources

2

New patterns of social
organization, which
provide capital for
investors and payoffs
for followers

3

Creating elaborated social
patterns employing
secondary reinforcers and
explicit norms

In turn,
this elaborated
organizational
base allows
for expanded
social
organization

Invest
in

Organization
allows for
expanded
investment

From Behavior to Macrostructure. Homans provided many illustrations of how behavioristic principles can explain research findings in social psychology, but there was little rigor in them. They were simply statements stacked on top of each other, typically with the rationality proposition at the top. The logic of deduction was simply words rather than any formal or precise calculus of deduction. Yet one of the most interesting chapters in *Social Behavior*[4] comes at the end of the book, where he offered a view of how exchange processes can explain population-level and societal-level social phenomena. Phrased as a "last orgy" in his explication, Homans addressed the issue of how societies and civilizations are, ultimately, built from the face-to-face exchanges of people in groups. His scenario is diagrammed in Figure 15.2 and, more discursively, went something like this: At points in history, some people have the "capital" to reinforce or provide rewards for others, whether it comes from their possessing a surplus of food, money, a moral code, or valued leadership qualities. With such capital, "institutional elaboration" can occur because some can invest their capital by trying to induce others (through rewards or threats of punishment) to engage in novel activities.

---

[4]Homans, *Social Behavior*, chap. 16.

4

Involving differentiation
of social structures in
terms of power and
enforcement capacities

5

This can provide the basis
for even more complex
social patterns, but they may
fail to meet the primary
needs of some individuals

This differentiation
allows for more
complex social
patterns

More elaborate
social structures

Opposition structures by those
whose primary needs are
not met—these becoming
susceptible to stage (1) in
the exchange process

These new activities can involve an "intermeshing of the behavior of a large number of persons in a more complicated or roundabout way than has hitherto been the custom." Whether this investment involves conquering territory and organizing a kingdom or creating a new form of business organization, those actors making the investment must have the resources to provide for people's subsistence needs and to give people the sense that they are deriving some profit in following those actors making investments in new forms of social organization. At some point in this process, such organizations can become more efficient and hence rewarding to all when the rewards are clearly specified as generalized reinforcers, such as money, and when the activities expended to get their rewards are more clearly specified, such as when explicit norms and rules emerge. In turn, this increased efficiency allows greater organization of activities. This new efficiency increases the likelihood that generalized reinforcers and explicit norms will be used to regulate exchange relations and hence increase the profits to those involved. Eventually, the exchange networks involving generalized reinforcers and an increasingly complex body of rules require differentiation of subunits—such as a legal and banking system—that can maintain the stability of the generalized reinforcers and the integrity of the norms.

From this kind of exchange process, then, social organization—whether at a societal, group, organizational, or institutional level—is constructed. The emergence of most patterns of organization is frequently buried in the recesses of history, but such emergence is typified by these accelerating processes: (a) People with capital (reward capacity) invest in creating more complex social relations that increase their rewards and allow those whose activities are organized to realize a profit. (b) With increased rewards, these people can invest in more complex patterns of organization. (c) Increasingly complex patterns of organization require, first of all, the use of generalized reinforcers and then the codification of norms to regulate activity. (d) With this organizational base, it then becomes possible to elaborate further the pattern of organization, creating the necessity for differentiation of subunits that ensure the stability of the generalized reinforcers and the integrity of norms. (e) With this differentiation, it is possible to expand even further the networks of interaction, because there are standardized means for rewarding activities and codifying new norms as well as for enforcing the old rules.

However, these complex patterns of social organization employing formal rules and secondary or generalized reinforcers can never cease to meet the more primary needs of individuals. Institutions first emerged to meet these needs, and no matter how complex institutional arrangements become and how many norms and formal rules are elaborated, these extended interaction networks must ultimately reinforce humans' more primary needs. When these arrangements cease meeting the primary needs from which they ultimately sprang, an institution is vulnerable and apt to collapse if alternative actions, which can provide primary rewards, present themselves as a possibility. In this situation, low- or high-status persons—those who have little to lose by nonconformity to existing prescriptions—will break from established ways to present to others a more rewarding alternative. Institutions might continue to extract conformity for a period, but they will cease to do so when they lose the capacity to provide primary rewards.

Thus, complex institutional arrangements must ultimately be satisfying to individuals, not simply because of the weight of culture or norms but because they are constructed to serve people:

> Institutions do not keep going just because they are enshrined in norms, and it seems extraordinary that anyone should ever talk as if they did. They keep going because they have payoffs, ultimately payoffs for individuals. Nor is society a perpetual motion machine, supplying its own fuel. It cannot keep itself going by planting in the young a desire for these goods and only those goods that it happens to be able to provide. It must provide goods that men (and presumably women) find rewarding not simply because they are sharers in a particular culture but because they are men.[5]

That institutions of society must also meet primary needs sets the stage for a continual conflict between institutional elaboration and the primary needs of humans. As one form of institutional elaboration meets one set of needs, it can

---

[5]Ibid., 366.

deprive people of other important rewards—opening the way for deviation and innovation by those presenting the alternative rewards that have been suppressed by dominant institutional arrangements. In turn, the new institutional elaborations that can ensue from innovators who have the capital to reward others will suppress other needs, which, through processes similar to their inception, will set off another process of institutional elaboration.

In sum, this sketch of how social organization is linked to elementary processes of exchange represents an interesting perspective for analyzing how patterns of social organization are built, maintained, altered, and broken down. Moreover, the broad contours of this kind of argument were repeated by other exchange theorists as they applied the principles of behaviorism or classical economics to explanations of larger-scale patterns of human organization. Yet little of Homans's explicit imagery was retained in later theories, although the effort to move from micro principles about behavior of individuals to macro-level patterns of organization remained a critical concern in exchange theories.

Peter M. Blau's Dialectical Theory of Exchange

A few years after George C. Homans's behavioristic approach appeared, another leading sociological theorist—Peter M. Blau—explored exchange theory.[6] Though he accepted the behavioristic underpinnings of exchange as a basic social process, Blau recognized that sociological theory had to move beyond simplistic behavioristic conceptualizations of human behavior. Similarly, crude views of humans as wholly rational had to be modified to fit the realities of human behavior. In the end, he developed a dialectical approach, emphasizing that within the strains toward integration arising from exchange are forces of opposition and potential conflict. Moreover, his analysis has a Simmelian thrust because, much like Georg Simmel, Blau tried to discover the form of exchange processes at both micro and macro levels, and in so doing, he sought to highlight what was common to exchanges among individuals as well as among collective units of organization.

The Basic Exchange Principles. Although Blau never listed his principles in a formal inventory, general principles are nonetheless easy to extract from his discursive discussion. In Table 15.2, the basic principles are summarized. Proposition 1, which can be termed the *rationality principle*, states that the frequency of rewards and the value of these rewards increases the likelihood that actions to secure these rewards will be emitted by persons and collective actors. Propositions 2-A and 2-B, on *reciprocity,* borrow from Bronislaw Malinowski's and

---

[6]Peter M. Blau's major exchange work is *Exchange and Power in Social Life* (New York: Wiley, 1964). This formal and expanded statement on his exchange perspective was anticipated in earlier works. For example, see Peter M. Blau, "A Theory of Social Integration," *American Journal of Sociology* 65 (May 1960):545–556, "Interaction: Social Exchange," in *International Encyclopedia of the Social Sciences*, vol. 7 (New York: Macmillan, 1968), 452–458, and *The Dynamics of Bureaucracy*, 1st and 2nd eds. (Chicago, IL: University of Chicago Press, 1955, 1963).

Table 15.2 Blau's Implicit Exchange Principles

1. *Rationality Principle:* The more profit people expect from one another in emitting a particular activity, the more likely they are to emit that activity.

2. *Reciprocity Principles:*
  A. The more people have exchanged rewards with one another, the more likely are reciprocal obligations to emerge and guide subsequent exchanges among these people
  B. The more the reciprocal obligations of an exchange relationship are violated, the more disposed deprived parties are to sanction negatively those violating the norm of reciprocity.

3. *Justice Principles:*
  A. The more exchange relations have been established, the more likely they are to be governed by norms of "fair exchange"
  B. The less norms of fairness are realized in an exchange, the more disposed deprived parties are to sanction negatively those violating the norms.

4. *Marginal Utility Principle:* The more expected rewards have been forthcoming from the emission of a particular activity, the less valuable the activity is and the less likely its emission is.
5. *Imbalance Principle:* The more stabilized and balanced some exchange relations are among social units, the more likely are other exchange relations to become imbalanced and unstable.

Claude Lévi-Strauss's initial discussion as reinterpreted by Alvin Gouldner.[7] Blau postulated that "the need to reciprocate for benefits received in order to continue receiving them serves as a 'starting mechanism' of social interaction."[8] Equally important, once exchanges have occurred, a "fundamental and ubiquitous norm of reciprocity" emerges to regulate subsequent exchanges. Thus, inherent in the exchange process, per se, is a principle of reciprocity. Over time, and as the conditions of principle 1 are met, a social "norm of reciprocity," whose violation brings about social disapproval and other negative sanctions, emerges in exchange relations.

Blau recognized that people establish expectations about what level of reward particular exchange relations should yield and that these expectations are normatively regulated. These norms are termed *norms of fair exchange* because they determine what the proportion of rewards to costs should be in a given exchange relation. Blau also asserted that aggression is forthcoming when these norms of fair exchange are violated. These ideas are incorporated into Principles 3-A and 3-B and are termed the *justice principles*.[9] Following economists' analyses of transactions in the

---

[7]Alvin W. Gouldner, "The Norm of Reciprocity," *American Sociological Review* 25 (April 1960):161–178.

[8]Blau, *Exchange and Power*, 92.

[9]See Peter M. Blau, "Justice in Social Exchange," in *Institutions and Social Exchange: The Sociologies of Talcott Parsons and George C. Homans*, ed. H. Turk and R. L. Simpson (Indianapolis, IL: Bobbs-Merrill, 1971), 56–68. See also Blau, *Exchange and Power*, 156–157.

marketplace, Blau introduced a principle on "marginal utility" (proposition 4). The more a person has received a reward, the more satiated he or she is with that reward and the less valuable are further increments of the reward.[10] Proposition 5, on imbalance, completes the listing of Blau's abstract laws. For Blau, as for all exchange theorists, established exchange relations are seen to involve costs or alternative rewards foregone. Most actors must engage in more than one exchange relation, and so the balance and stabilization of one exchange relation is likely to create imbalance and strain in other necessary exchange relations. Blau believed that social life is thus filled with dilemmas in which people must successively trade off stability and balance in one exchange relation for strain in others as they attempt to cope with the variety of relations that they must maintain.

Elementary Systems of Exchange. Blau initiated his discussion of elementary exchange processes with the assumption that people enter into social exchange because they perceive the possibility of deriving rewards (principle 1). Blau labeled this perception *social attraction* and postulated that unless relationships involve such attraction, they are not relationships of exchange. In entering an exchange relationship, each actor assumes the perspective of another and thereby derives some perception of the other's needs. Actors then manipulate their presentation of self to convince one another that they have the valued qualities that others should desire. In adjusting role behaviors in an effort to impress others with the resources that they have to offer, people operate under the principle of reciprocity, for, by indicating that one possesses valued qualities, each person is attempting to establish a claim on others for the receipt of rewards from them. All exchange operates under the presumption that people who bestow rewards will receive rewards in turn as payment for value received.

Individuals attempt to impress one another through competition, in which they reveal the rewards that they have to offer in an effort to force others, in accordance with the norm of reciprocity, to reciprocate with an even more valuable reward. Social life is thus rife with people's competitive efforts to impress one another and thereby extract valuable rewards. But as interaction proceeds, it inevitably becomes evident to the parties in an exchange that some people have more valued resources to offer than others, putting them in a unique position to extract rewards from all others who value the resources that they have to offer.

At this point in exchange relations, groups of individuals become differentiated by the resources that their members possess and the kinds of reciprocal demands that they can make on others. Blau then asked an analytical question: What generic types or classes of rewards can those with resources extract in return for bestowing their valued resources on others? Blau conceptualized four general classes of such rewards: *money, social approval, esteem or respect,* and *compliance.*

Blau first ranked these generalized reinforcers by their value in exchange relations among individuals. In most social relations, money is an inappropriate reward and hence is the least valuable. Social approval is an appropriate reward, but for most humans it is not very valuable, thus forcing those who derive valued services to offer

---

[10]Blau, *Exchange and Power*, 90.

with great frequency more valuable rewards like esteem or respect to those providing valued services. In many situations, the services offered can command no more than respect and esteem from others. At times, however, the services offered are sufficiently valuable for those receiving them to offer, in accordance with the principles of reciprocity and justice, the most valuable class of rewards—compliance with one's requests.

When people can extract compliance in an exchange relationship, they have *power*. They have the capacity to withhold rewarding services and thereby punish or inflict heavy costs on those who might not comply. To conceptualize the degree of power possessed by individuals, Blau formulated four general propositions that determine the capacity of powerful individuals to extract compliance. These are listed and reformulated in Table 15.3.[11]

These four propositions list the conditions leading to differentiation of members in social groups by their power. To the extent that group members cannot supply some services in return, seek alternative rewards, potentially use physical force, or do without certain valuable services, individuals who provide valuable services will be able to extract esteem and approval from the group members; and if the group members value these resources highly, those who provide them can use power and command compliance. Naturally, as Blau emphasized, most social groups reveal complex patterns of differentiation of power, prestige, and approval, but of particular interest to him are the dynamics involved in generating power, authority, and opposition. Blau believed that power differentials in groups create two contradictory forces: (a) strains toward integration and (b) strains toward opposition and conflict.

Strains Toward Integration. Differences in power inevitably create the potential for conflict. However, such potential is frequently suspended by a series of forces promoting the conversion of power into authority, in which subordinates accept as legitimate the leaders' demands for compliance. Principles 2 and 3 in Table 15.4 denote two processes fostering such group integration: exchange relations always operate under the presumption of reciprocity and justice, forcing those deriving valued services to provide other rewards in payment. In providing these rewards,

Table 15.3 Conditions for Gaining Power in Social Exchanges

1. The fewer services people can supply in return for the receipt of particularly valued services, the more those providing these particularly valued services can extract compliance.
2. The fewer alternative sources of rewards people have, the more those providing valuable services can extract compliance.
3. The less those receiving valuable services from particular individuals can employ physical force and coercion, the more those providing the services can extract compliance.
4. The less those receiving valuable services can do without them, the more those providing the services can extract compliance.

[11]Ibid.

Table 15.4 Blau's Propositions on Exchange Conflict

1. The probability of opposition to those with power increases when exchange relations between superordinates and subordinates become imbalanced, with imbalance increasing when   A. Norms of reciprocity are violated by the superordinates   B. Norms of fair exchange are violated by the superordinates.
2. The probability of opposition increases as the sense of deprivation among subordinates escalates, with this sense of deprivation increasing when subordinates can experience collectively their sense of deprivation. Such collective experience increases when   A. Subordinates are ecologically and spatially concentrated   B. Subordinates can communicate with one another.
3. The more subordinates can collectively experience deprivations in exchange relations with superordinates, the more likely are they to codify ideologically their deprivations and the more likely are they to oppose those with power.
4. The more deprivations of subordinates are ideologically codified, the greater is their sense of solidarity and the more likely are they to oppose those with power.
5. The greater the sense of solidarity is among subordinates, the more they can define their opposition as a noble and worthy cause and the more likely they are to oppose those with power.
6. The greater is the sense of ideological solidarity, the more likely are subordinates to view opposition as an end in itself and the more likely are they to oppose those with power.

subordinates are guided by norms of fair exchange, in which the costs that they incur in offering compliance are to be proportional to the value of the services that they receive from leaders. Thus, to the extent that actors engage in exchanges with leaders and to the degree that the services provided by leaders are highly valued, subordination must be accepted as legitimate in accordance with the norms of reciprocity and fairness that emerge in all exchanges.

Under these conditions, groups elaborate additional norms specifying just how exchanges with leaders are to be conducted to regularize the requirements for reciprocity and to maintain fair rates of exchange. Leaders who conform to these emergent norms can usually assure themselves that their leadership will be considered legitimate. Blau emphasized that if leaders abide by the norms regulating exchange of their services for compliance, norms carrying negative sanctions typically emerge among subordinates, stressing the need for compliance to leaders' requests. Through this process, subordinates exercise considerable social control over one another's actions and thereby promote the integration of superordinate and subordinate segments of groupings.

Authority, therefore, "rests on the common norms in a collectivity of subordinates that constrain its individual members to conform to the orders of a superior."[12] In many patterns of social organization, these norms simply emerge from the

---

[12]Ibid., 208.

competitive exchanges among collective groups of actors. Frequently, however, for such "normative agreements" to be struck, the participants in an exchange must be socialized into a common set of values that define not only what constitutes fair exchange in a given situation but also the way such exchange should be institutionalized into norms for both leaders and subordinates. Although it is quite possible for actors to arrive at a normative consensus in the course of the exchange process itself, an initial set of common values facilitates the legitimization of power. Actors can now enter into exchanges with a common definition of the situation, which can provide a general framework for the normative regulation of emerging power differentials. Without common values, the competition for power is likely to be severe. In the absence of guidelines about reciprocity and fair exchange, considerable strain and tension will persist as definitions of these are worked out. For Blau, then, legitimization "entails not merely tolerant approval but active confirmation and promotion of social patterns by common values, either preexisting ones or those that emerge in a collectivity in the course of social interaction."[13]

With the legitimization of power through the normative regulation of interaction, as confirmed by common values, the structure of collective organization is altered. One of the most evident changes is the decline in interpersonal competition, for now actors' presentations of self can shift from a concern about impressing others with their valuable qualities to an emphasis on confirming their status as loyal group members. Subordinates accept their status and manipulate their role behaviors to ensure that they receive social approval from their peers as a reward for conformity to group norms. Leaders can typically assume a lower profile because they no longer need to demonstrate their superior qualities in each and every encounter with subordinates—especially because norms now define when and how they should extract conformity and esteem for providing their valued services. Thus, with the legitimization of power as authority, the interactive processes (involving the way group members define the situation and present themselves to others) undergo a dramatic change, reducing the degree of competition and thereby fostering group integration.

With these events, the amount of direct interaction between leaders and subordinates usually declines, because power and ranking no longer must be constantly negotiated. This decline in direct interaction marks the formation of distinct subgroupings as members interact with those of their own social rank, avoiding the costs of interacting with either their inferiors or their superiors. In interacting primarily among themselves, subordinates avoid the high costs of interacting with leaders, and although social approval from their peers is not a particularly valuable reward, it can be extracted with comparatively few costs, thus allowing a sufficient profit. Conversely, leaders can avoid the high costs (of time and energy) of constantly competing and negotiating with inferiors regarding when and how compliance and esteem are to be bestowed on them. Instead, by having relatively limited and well-defined contact with subordinates, they can derive the high rewards that come from compliance and esteem without incurring excessive costs in interacting with subordinates—thereby allowing for a profit.

---

[13]Ibid., 221.

Strains Toward Opposition. Thus far, Blau's exchange perspective is decidedly functional. Social exchange processes—attraction, competition, differentiation, and integration—are analyzed by how they contribute to creating a legitimated set of normatively regulated relations. Yet Blau was keenly aware that social organization is always rife with conflict and opposition, creating an inevitable dialectic between integration and opposition in social structures.

Blau's exchange principles, summarized in Table 15.4, allow the conceptualization of these strains for opposition and conflict. As principle 2-B, on reciprocity, documents, the failure to receive expected rewards in return for various activities leads actors to attempt to apply negative sanctions that, when ineffective, can drive people to violent retaliation against those who have denied them an expected reward. Such retaliation is intensified by the dynamics summarized in principle 3-B on justice and fair exchange, because when those in power violate such norms, they inflict excessive costs on subordinates, creating a situation that leads, at a minimum, to attempts to sanction negatively and, at most, to retaliation. Finally, principle 5, on the inevitable imbalances emerging from multiple exchange relations, emphasizes that to balance relations in one exchange context by meeting reciprocal obligations and conforming to norms of fairness is to put other relations into imbalance. Thus, the imbalances potentially encourage a cyclical process in which actors seek to balance previously unbalanced relations and thereby throw into imbalance currently balanced exchanges. In turn, exchange relations that are thrown into imbalance violate the norms of reciprocity and fair exchange, thus causing attempts at negative sanctioning and, under some conditions, retaliation.

Blau hypothesizes that the more imbalanced exchange relations are experienced collectively, the greater is the sense of deprivation and the greater is the potential for opposition. Although he did not explicitly state the case, Blau appears to argue that increasing ideological codification of deprivations, the formation of group solidarity, and the emergence of conflict as a way of life—that is, members' emotional involvement in and commitment to opposition to those with power—will increase the intensity of the opposition. These propositions offered a suggestive lead for conceptualizing inherent processes of opposition in exchange relations.[14]

Macrostructural Exchange Systems. Although the general processes of attraction, competition, differentiation, integration, and opposition are evident in the exchanges among units forming macrostructures, Blau saw several fundamental differences between these exchanges and those among microstructures.

1. In complex exchanges among macrostructures, the significance of "shared values" increases, for through such values indirect exchanges among macrostructures are mediated.

2. Exchange networks among macrostructures are typically institutionalized. Although spontaneous exchange is a ubiquitous feature of social life, there are

---

[14]Peter M. Blau, "Dialectical Sociology: Comments," *Sociological Inquiry* 42 (Spring 1972):185; Michael A. Weinstein and Deena Weinstein, "Blau's Dialectical Sociology," *Sociological Inquiry* 42 (Spring 1972):173–182.

usually well-established historical arrangements that circumscribe the basic exchange processes of attraction, competition, differentiation, integration, and even opposition among collective units.

3. Macrostructures are themselves the product of more elementary exchange processes, so the analysis of macrostructures requires the analysis of more than one level of social organization.[15]

Mediating Values. Blau believed that the "interpersonal attraction" of elementary exchange among individuals is replaced by shared values at the macro level. These values can be conceptualized as "media of social transactions" in that they provide a common set of standards for conducting the complex chains of indirect exchanges among social structures and their individual members. Such values are viewed by Blau as providing effective mediation of complex exchanges because the individual members of social structures have usually been socialized into a set of common values, leading them to accept these values as appropriate. Furthermore, when coupled with codification into laws and enforcement procedures by those groups and organizations with power, shared values provide a means for mediating the complex and indirect exchanges among the macrostructures of large-scale systems. In mediating indirect exchanges among groups and organizations, shared values provide standards for the calculation of (a) expected rewards, (b) reciprocity, and (c) fair exchange.

Thus, because individuals are not the units of complex exchanges, Blau emphasizes that for complex patterns of social organization to emerge and persist, a "functional equivalent" of direct interpersonal attraction must exist. Values assume this function and ensure that exchange can proceed in accordance with the principles presented in Table 15.2. And even when complex exchanges do involve people, their interactions are frequently so protracted and indirect that one individual's rewards are contingent on others who are far removed, requiring that common values guide and regulate the exchanges.

Institutionalization. Whereas values facilitate processes of indirect exchange among diverse types of social units, institutionalization denotes those processes that regularize and stabilize complex exchange processes.[16] As people and various forms of collective organization become dependent on particular networks of indirect exchange for expected rewards, pressures for formalizing exchange networks through explicit norms increase. This formalization and regularization of complex exchange systems can be effective under three minimal conditions: (1) the formalized exchange networks must have profitable payoffs for most parties to the exchange; (2) most individuals organized into collective units must have internalized through prior socialization the mediating values used to build the exchange networks; and (3) those units with power in the exchange system must receive a level of rewards that moves them to seek actively the formalization of rules governing exchange relations.

---

[15]Blau, "Contrasting Theoretical Perspectives," in *The Micro-Macro Link*, ed. J. C. Alexander, B. Gisen, R. Münch, and N. J. Smelser (Berkeley: University of California Press, 1987), 253–311.

[16]Blau, *Exchange and Power*, 273–280.

Institutions are historical products whose norms and underlying mediating values are handed down from one generation to another, thereby limiting and circumscribing the kinds of indirect exchange networks that can emerge. Institutions exert a kind of external constraint on individuals and various types of collective units, bending exchange processes to fit their prescriptions and proscriptions. Institutions thus represent sets of relatively stable and general norms regularizing different patterns of indirect and complex exchange relations among diverse social units.

Blau stresses that all institutionalized exchange systems reveal a counterinstitutional component "consisting of those basic values and ideals that have not been realized and have not found expression in explicit institutional forms, and which are the ultimate source of social change."[17] To the extent that these values remain unrealized in institutionalized exchange relations, individuals who have internalized them will derive little payoff from existing institutional arrangements and will therefore feel deprived, seeking alternatives to dominant institutions. These unrealized values, even when codified into an opposition ideology advocating open revolution, usually contain at least some of the ideals and ultimate objectives legitimated by the prevailing culture. This indicates that institutional arrangements "contain the seeds of their potential destruction" by failing to meet all the expectations of reward raised by institutionalized values.

Blau never enumerates the conditions for mobilization of individuals into conflict groups, but his scheme explicitly denoted the source of conflict and change: counterinstitutional values whose failure of realization by dominant institutional arrangements creates deprivations that can lead to conflict and change in social systems. Such tendencies for complex exchange systems to generate opposition can be explained by the basic principles of exchange. When certain mediating values are not institutionalized in a social system, exchange relations will not be viewed as reciprocated by those who have internalized these values.

Thus, in accordance with Blau's principles on reciprocity (see Table 15.2), these segments of a collectivity are more likely to feel deprived and to seek ways of retaliating against the dominant institutional arrangements, which, from the perspective dictated by their values, have failed to reciprocate. For those who have internalized values that are not institutionalized, it is also likely that perceptions of fair exchange have been violated, leading them, in accordance with the principles of justice, to attempt to sanction negatively those arrangements that violate alternative norms of fair exchange. Finally, in institutionalized exchange networks, the balancing of exchange relations with some segments of a collectivity inevitably creates imbalances in relations with other segments (the imbalance principle in Table 15.2), thereby violating norms of reciprocity and fairness and setting into motion forces of opposition.

Unlike direct interpersonal exchanges, however, opposition in complex exchange systems is between large collective units of organization, which, in their internal dynamics, reveal their own propensities for integration and opposition. This requires that the analysis of integration and opposition in complex exchange

---

[17]Ibid., 279.

networks be attuned to various levels of social organization. Such analysis needs to show, in particular, how exchange processes among the units comprising macrostructures, whether for integration or for opposition, are partly influenced by the exchange processes occurring among their constituent substructures.

Levels of Social Organization. For Blau, the "dynamics of macrostructures rest on the manifold interdependences between the social forces within and among their substructures."[18] Blau simplifies the complex analytical tasks of examining the dynamics of substructures by positing that organized collectivities, especially formal organizations, are the most important substructures in the analysis of macrostructures. Thus, the theoretical analysis of complex exchange systems among macrostructures requires that primary attention be drawn to the relations of attraction, competition, differentiation, integration, and opposition among various types of complex organizations. In emphasizing the pivotal significance of complex organizations, Blau posited a particular image of society that should guide the ultimate construction of sociological theory.

Organizations in a society must typically derive rewards from one another, thus creating a situation in which they are both attracted to and in competition with one another. Hierarchical differentiation between successful and less successful organizations operating in the same sphere emerges from this competition. Such differentiation usually creates strains toward specialization in different fields among less successful organizations as they seek new sources of resources. To provide effective means for integration, separate political organizations must also emerge to regulate their exchanges. These political organizations possess power and are viewed as legitimate only as long as they are considered by individuals and organizations to follow the dictates of shared cultural values. Typically, political organizations are charged with several objectives: (a) regulating complex networks of indirect exchange by the enactment of laws; (b) controlling through law competition among dominant organizations, thereby assuring the latter of scarce resources; and (c) protecting existing exchange networks among organizations, especially those with power, from encroachment on these rewards by organizations opposing the current distribution of resources.

Blau believed that differentiation and specialization occur among macrostructures because of the competition among organizations in a society. Although mediating values allow differentiation and specialization among organizations to occur, it is also necessary for separate political organizations to exist and regularize, through laws and the use of force, existent patterns of exchange among other organizations. Such political organizations will be viewed as legitimate as long as they normatively regulate exchanges that reflect the tenets of mediating values and protect the payoffs for most organizations, especially the most powerful. The existence of political authority inevitably encourages opposition movements, however, for now opposition groups have a clear target—the political organizations—against which to address their grievances. As long as political authority remains

---

[18]Ibid., 284.

Figure 15.3 Blau's Image of Social Organization

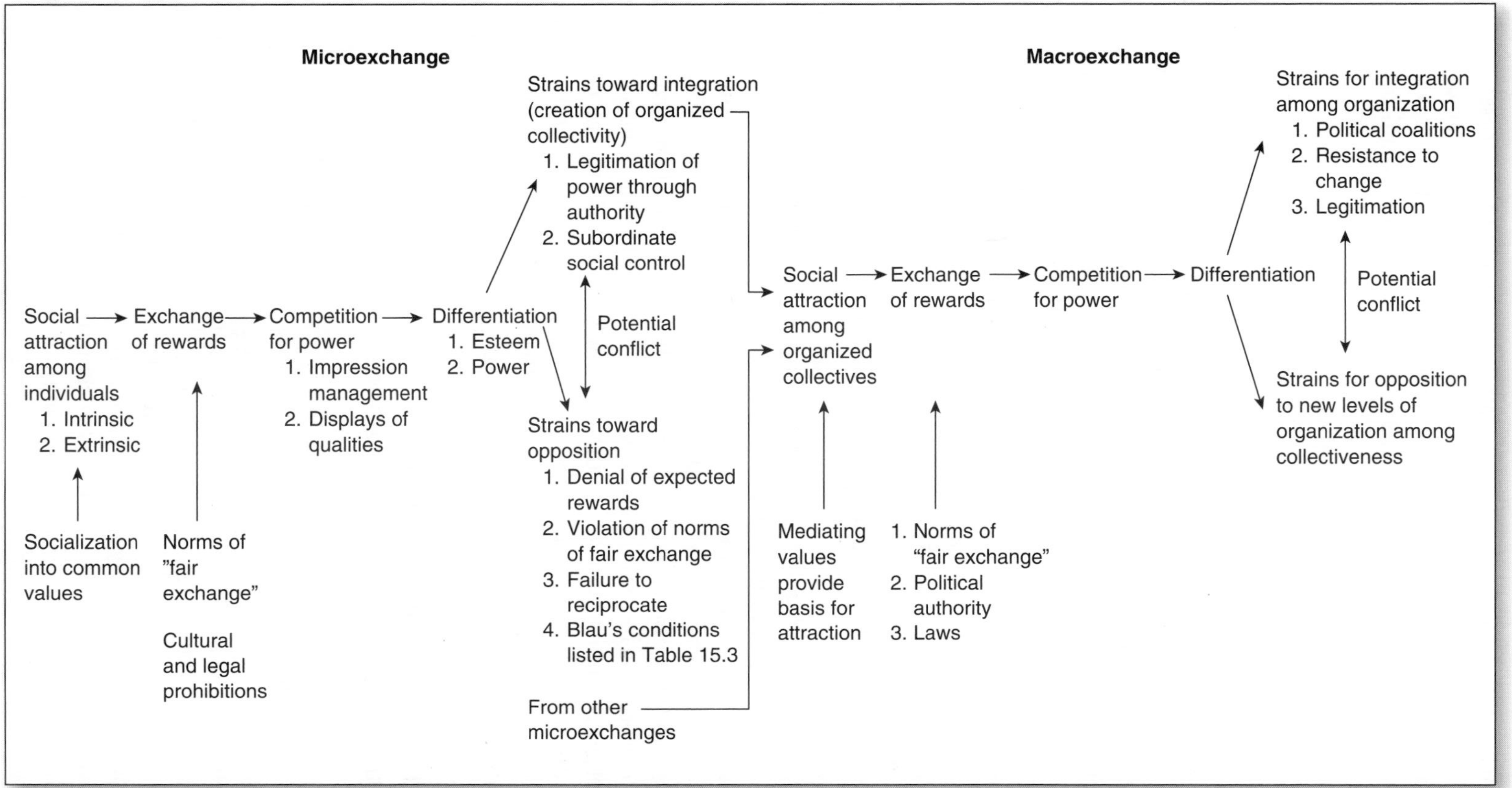

diffuse, opposition organizations can only compete unsuccessfully against various dominant organizations. With the legitimization of clear-cut political organizations charged with preserving current patterns of organization, opposition movements can concentrate their energies against one organization, the political system.

In addition to providing deprived groups with a target for their aggressions, political organizations inevitably must aggravate the deprivations of various segments of a population because political control involves exerting constraints and distributing resources unequally. Those segments of the population that must bear the brunt of such constraints and unequal distribution usually experience great deprivation of the principles of reciprocity and fair exchange, which, under various conditions, creates a movement against the existing political authorities. To the extent that this organized opposition forces redistribution of rewards, other segments of the population are likely to feel constrained and deprived, leading them to organize into an opposition movement. The organization of political authority ensures that, in accordance with the principle of imbalance, attempts to balance one set of exchange relations among organizations throw into imbalance other exchange relations, causing the formation of opposition organizations. Thus, built into the structure of political authority in a society are inherent forces of opposition that give society a dialectical and dynamic character.

Blau's Image of Social Organization. Figure 15.3 summarizes Blau's view of social organization at the micro level and the macro organizational level. Clearly, the same processes operate at both levels of exchange: (a) social attraction, (b) exchange of rewards, (c) competition for power, (d) differentiation, (e) strains toward integration, and (f) strains toward opposition. Thus, the Simmelian thrust of Blau's effort is clear because he sees the basic *form of exchange* as much the same, regardless of whether the units involved in the exchange are individuals or collective units of organization. There are, of course, some differences between exchange among individuals and organizational units, and these are noted across the bottom of the figure.

Richard M. Emerson's Power Dependence Theory of Exchange

In the early 1960s, Richard M. Emerson followed Georg Simmel's lead in seeking a formal sociology of basic exchange processes—much as Blau had sought to do in seeing micro and macro exchange processes as revealing the same basic form. In essence, Emerson asked this: Could exchange among individual and collective actors be understood by the same basic principles? Emerson provided a creative answer to this question by synthesizing behaviorist psychology and sociological network analysis. The psychology gave him the driving force behind exchanges, whereas the network sociology allowed him to conceptualize the form of social relations among both individual and collective actors in the same terms. What emerged was exchange network analysis that, after Emerson's early death, was carried forward by colleagues and students. Emerson[19] borrowed the basic ideas of behaviorist psychology, but unlike many working in this tradition, he became more concerned with the forms of relationships among the actors rather than the properties and characteristics of the actors themselves. This simple shift in emphasis profoundly affected how he built his exchange theory. The most significant departure from earlier exchange theories was that concern with why actors entered an exchange relationship in the first place given their values and preferences[20] was replaced by an emphasis on the existing exchange relationship and what is likely to transpire in this relationship in the future. Emerson believed that if an exchange relationship exists, it means that actors are willing to exchange valued resources, and the goal of theory is not so much to understand how this relationship originally came about but, instead, what will happen to it over time. Thus, the existing exchange relationship between actors becomes the unit of sociological analysis, not the actors themselves. In Emerson's view, then, social structure is composed of exchanges among actors seeking to enhance the value of their resources. And so behaviorism, which posited a dynamic but atomized actor, was blended with network sociology, which conceptualized structure without dynamic actors.

The Core Ideas. The key dynamics in Emerson's theory are, (a) *power*, (b) *power use*, and (c) *balancing*. Actors have *power* to the extent that others depend on them for resources; hence, the power of actor A over actor B is determined by the dependence of B on A for a resource that B values, and vice versa. *Dependence*, which is the ultimate source of power in Emerson's scheme, is determined by the degree to which (a) resources sought from other actors are highly valued and (b) alternatives for these resources are few or too costly to pursue. Under these conditions, where B values A's resources and where no attractive alternatives are available, B's dependence on A is high; hence, the power of A over B is high. Conversely, where B has resources that A values and where alternatives for A are limited, B has power over A. Thus, both actors can reveal a high degree of mutual dependence, giving each *absolute power* over the other and, thereby, increasing

---

[19]Emerson's perspective is best stated in his "Exchange Theory, Part I: A Psychological Basis for Social Exchange" and "Exchange Theory, Part II: Exchange Relations and Network Structures," in *Sociological Theories in Progress*, ed. J. Berger, M. Zelditch, and B. Anderson (New York: Houghton Mifflin, 1972), 38–87. Earlier empirical work that provided the initial impetus to, or empirical support of, this theoretical perspective includes his "Power-Dependence Relations," *American Sociological Review* 17 (February 1962):31–41 and "Power-Dependence Relations: Two Experiments," *Sociometry* 27 (September 1964):282–298 and John F. Stolte and Richard M. Emerson, "Structural Inequality: Position and Power in Network Structures," in *Behavioral Theory in Sociology*, ed. R. Hamblin (New Brunswick, NJ: Transaction Books, 1977). Other, more conceptual works include his "Operant Psychology and Exchange Theory," in *Behavioral Sociology*, ed. R. Burgess and D. Bushell (New York: Columbia University Press, 1969) and "Social Exchange Theory," in *Annual Review of Sociology*, ed. A. Inkeles and N. Smelser, vol. 2 (1976):335–362.

[20]Curiously, Emerson returned to this question in his last article. See Richard M. Emerson, "Toward a Theory of Value in Social Exchange," in *Social Exchange Theory*, ed. Karen S. Cook (Newbury Park, CA: Sage, 1987), 11–46. See, in the same volume, Jonathan H. Turner's critique of this shift in Emerson's thought: "Social Exchange Theory: Future Directions," 223–239.

structural cohesion because of the high amounts of *total* or *average power* in the exchange relationship.

When one actor has more power than an exchange partner, however, this actor will engage in *power use* and exploit its exchange partner's dependence to secure additional resources or to reduce the costs it must incur in getting resources from this dependent partner. If A has power over B because of B's dependency on A, then A has the *power advantage* and will use it.

Such relations are *power imbalanced,* and Emerson felt that imbalance and power use would activate what he termed *balancing operations.* In a situation where A has a power advantage over B, B has four options: (1) actor B can value less the resources provided by A, (2) B can find alternative sources for the resources provided by A, (3) B can increase the value of the resources it provides A, and (4) B can find ways to reduce A's alternatives for the resources that B provides. All these balancing mechanisms are designed to reduce dependency on A or, alternatively, to increase A's dependency on B in ways that balance the exchange relationship and give it a certain equilibrium.

Exchange in networks can be of two general types: (1) those where actors negotiate and bargain over the distribution of resources and (2) those where actors do not negotiate but, instead, sequentially provide resources with the expectation that these rewards will be reciprocated. This distinction between what can be termed *negotiated exchanges* and *reciprocal exchanges* is important because it reflects different types of exchanges in the real world. When actors negotiate, they try to influence each other before the resources are divided, as when labor and management negotiate a contract or when individuals argue about whether to go to the movies or to the beach. The dynamics of negotiated exchange are distinctive because they typically take longer to execute, because they generally involve considerably more explicit awareness and calculation of costs and benefits, and because they are often part of conflicts among parties who seek a compromise acceptable to all. In contrast, reciprocal exchanges involve the giving of resources unilaterally by one party to another with, of course, some expectation that valued resources will be given back, as occurs when a person initiates affection with the intent that the other will respond with the same emotion. Reciprocal exchanges are thus constructed in sequences of contingent rewarding, whereas negotiated exchanges unfold in a series of offers and counteroffers before resources are distributed.

These seminal ideas form the core of Emerson's theoretical scheme. Before his untimely death, Emerson had been collaborating with Karen Cook and their mutual students to test the implications of these ideas for different types of networks. The basic goal was to determine how the structure of the network—that is, the pattern of connections among actors—influences, and is influenced by, the distribution of power, power use, and balancing.[21]

Social Structure, Networks, and Exchange. Emerson's portrayal of social networks will be simplified; for our purposes here, the full details of his network terminology

---

[21]Karen S. Cook, Richard M. Emerson, Mary R. Gilmore, and Toshio Yamagishi, "The Distribution of Power in Exchange Networks," *American Journal of Sociology* 87 (1983):275–305.

need not be addressed. Although Emerson followed the conventions of graph theory and developed a number of definitions, only two definitions are critical:

Actors: Points A, B, C, . . ., *n* in a network of relations. Different letters represent actors with different resources to exchange. The same letters—that is, A_1, A_2, A_3, and so forth—represent different actors exchanging similar resources.

Exchange relations: A–B, A–B–C, A_1–A_2, and other patterns of ties that can connect different actors to each other, forming a network of relations.

The next conceptual task was to visualize the forms of networks that could be represented with these two definitions. For each basic form, new corollaries and theorems were added as Emerson documented the way in which the basic processes of dependence, power, and balance operate. His discussion was only preliminary, but it illustrated his perspective's potential. Several basic social forms are given special treatment: (a) unilateral monopoly, (b) division of labor, (c) social circles, and (d) stratification.

Unilateral Monopoly. In the network illustrated in Figure 15.4, actor A is a source of valuable resources for actors B_1, B_2, and B_3. Actors B_1, B_2, and B_3 provide rewards for A, but because A has multiple sources for rewards and the Bs have only A as a source for their rewards, the situation is a unilateral monopoly. Such a structure often typifies interpersonal as well as intercorporate units. For example, A could be a female date for three different men, B_1, B_2, and B_3. Or A could be a corporation that is the sole supplier of raw resources for three other manufacturing corporations, B_1, B_2, and B_3. Or A could be a governmental body, and the Bs could be dependent agencies. An important feature of the unilateral monopoly is that, by Emerson's definitions, it is imbalanced, and thus its structure is subject to change.

Emerson developed additional corollaries and theorems to account for the various ways this unilateral monopoly can change and become balanced. For instance, if no A_2, A_3, . . . , A_n exist and the Bs cannot communicate with each other, the following proposition would apply (termed by Emerson *Exploitation Type I*):

> *The more an exchange relation between A and multiple Bs approximates a unilateral monopoly, the more additional resources each B will introduce into the exchange relation, with A's resource utilization remaining constant or decreasing.*

Emerson saw this adaptation as short-lived, because the network will become even more unbalanced. Assuming that the Bs can survive as an entity without resources from A, then a new proposition applies (termed by Emerson *Exploitation Type II*):

> *The more an exchange relation between A and multiple Bs approximates a unilateral monopoly, the less valuable to Bs are the resources provided by A across continuing transactions.*

Figure 15.4 A Unilateral Monopoly

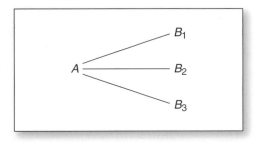

This proposition thus predicts that balancing operation 1—a decrease in the value of the reward for those at a power disadvantage—will balance a unilateral monopoly where no alternative sources of rewards exist and where Bs cannot effectively communicate. Other balancing operations are possible if other conditions exist. If Bs can communicate, they might form a coalition (balancing operation 4) and require A to balance exchanges with a united coalition of Bs. If one B can provide a resource not possessed by the other Bs, then a division of labor among Bs (operations 3 and 4) would emerge. Or if another source of resources, A_2, can be found (operation 2), then the power advantage of A_1 is decreased. Each of these possible changes will occur under varying conditions, but these propositions provide a reason for the initiation of changes—a reason derived from the basic principles of operant psychology (the details of these derivations are not discussed here).

Division of Labor. The emergence of a division of labor is one of many ways to balance exchange relations in a unilateral monopoly. If each of the Bs can provide different resources for A, then they are likely to use these in the exchange with A and to specialize in providing A with these resources. This decreases the power of A and establishes a new type of network. For example, in Figure 15.5, the unilateral monopoly at the left is transformed to the division of labor form at the right, with B_1 becoming a new type of actor, C, with its own resources; with B_2 also specializing and becoming a new actor, D; and with B_3 doing the same and becoming actor E.

Emerson developed an additional proposition to describe this kind of change, in which each B has its own unique resources: the more resources are distributed *nonuni*formly across Bs in a unilateral monopoly with A, the more likely is each B to specialize and establish a separate exchange relation with A. Several points should be emphasized. First, the units in this transformation can be individual or collective actors. Second, the change in the structure or form of the network is described as a proposition systematically derived from operant principles, corollaries, and other theorems. The proposition could thus apply to a wide variety of micro contexts and macro contexts. For example, it could apply to workers in an office who specialize and provide A with resources not available from others. This proposition could also apply to a division in a corporation

Figure 15.5 Transformation of Unilateral Monopoly to a Division of Labor

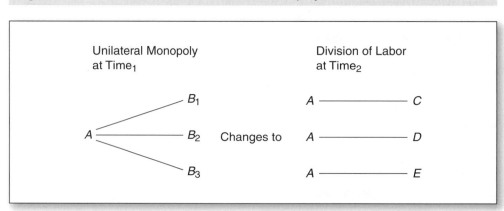

that seeks to balance its relations with the central authority by reorganizing itself in ways that distinguish it, and the services it can provide, from other divisions. Or this proposition could apply to relations between a colonial power (A) and its colonized nations (B_1, B_2, B_3), which specialize (become C, D, and E) in their predominant economic activities to establish a less dependent relationship with A.

Social Circles. Emerson emphasized that some exchanges are inter-category and others intra-category. An inter-category exchange is one in which one type of resource is exchanged for another type—money for goods, advice for esteem, tobacco for steel knives, and so on. The networks discussed thus far have involved inter-category exchanges between actors with different resources (A, B, C, D, E). An intra-category exchange is one in which the same resources are being exchanged—affection for affection, advice for advice, goods for goods, and so on. As indicated earlier, such exchanges are symbolized in Emerson's graph approach by using the same letter—A_1, A_2, A_3, and so forth—to represent actors with similar resources. Emerson then developed another proposition to describe what will occur in these intra-category exchanges:

> *The more an exchange approximates an intra-category exchange, the more likely are exchange relations to become closed.*

Emerson defined "closed" either as a circle of relations, as diagrammed in Figure 15.6, or as a balanced network in which all actors exchange with one another. Emerson offered the example of tennis networks to illustrate the balancing process. If two tennis players of equal ability, A_1 and A_2, play together regularly, it is a balanced intra-category exchange—tennis for tennis. However, if A_3 enters and plays with A_2, then A_2 now enjoys a power advantage, as diagrammed in Figure 15.7.

This is now a unilateral monopoly, but unlike those discussed earlier, it is an intra-category monopoly. A_1 and A_3 are dependent on A_2 for tennis. This relation is unbalanced and sets into motion processes of balance. A_4 might be recruited, creating either the circle or the balanced network diagrammed in Figure 15.6. Once this kind of closed and balanced network is achieved, it resists entry by others, A_5, A_6, A_7, . . ., A_n, because as each additional actor enters, the network becomes unbalanced.

Figure 15.6 Closure of Intra-category Exchanges

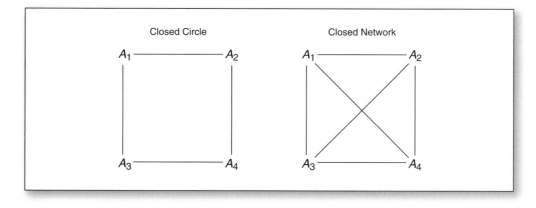

Figure 15.7 Imbalanced Intra-category Exchange

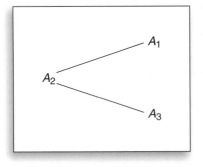

Such a network, of course, is not confined to individuals; it can apply to nations forming a military alliance or common market, to cartels of corporations, and to other collective units.

Stratified Networks. The discussion about how intra-category exchanges often achieve balance through closure can help us understand the processes of stratification. If, for example, tennis players A_1, A_2, A_3, and A_4 are unequal in ability, with A_1 and A_2 having more ability than A_3 and A_4, an initial circle might form among A_1, A_2, A_3, and A_4, but over time, A_1 and A_2 will find more gratification in playing each other, and A_3 and A_4 might have to incur too many costs in initiating invitations to A_1 and A_2. An A_1 and A_3 tennis match is unbalanced; A_3 will have to provide additional resources—the tennis balls, praise, esteem, self-deprecation. The result will be for two classes to develop:

Upper social class A_1–A_2

Lower social class A_3–A_4

Moreover, A_1 and A_2 might enter into new exchanges with A_5 and A_6 at their ability level, forming a new social circle or network. Similarly, A_3 and A_4 might form new tennis relations with A_7 and A_8, creating social circles and networks with players at their ability level. The result is stratification that reveals the pattern in Figure 15.8. Emerson's discussion of stratification processes was tentative, but he developed a proposition to describe these stratifying tendencies:

The more resources are equally valued and the more resources are unequally distributed across a number of actors, the more likely is the network to stratify by resource magnitudes and the more likely are actors with a given level of resources to form closed exchange networks.

Figure 15.8 Stratification and Closure in Exchanges

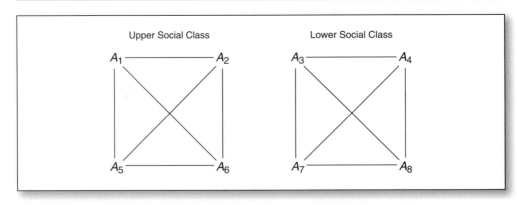

Again, this theorem can apply to corporate units as well as to individuals. Nations become stratified and form social circles, as is the case with the distinctions between developed and underdeveloped nations and the alliances among countries within these two classes. Or this theorem can apply to traditional sociological definitions of class, because closed networks tend to form among members within, rather than across, social classes.

Centrality in Networks and the Distribution of Power. In Figure 15.9, actor A_1 is in a position of centrality in relation to actors A_2, A_3, and A_4. Centrality can be measured and conceptualized in several ways, but the basic theoretical idea is relatively straightforward: some positions in a network mediate the flow of resources by virtue of being in the middle of ties to other points. Thus, in Figure 15.9, actor A_1 mediates the flow of resources among actors A_2, A_3, and A_4; hence, in this network, A_1 is in a position of high centrality. Similarly, further out on the network, actors A_2, A_3, and A_4 are also central between the peripheral actors at the ends of the network (A_1 through A_{13}) and the most central actor, A_1. For example, A_2 is central with respect to A_1, on the one side, and A_5, A_6, and A_7, on the other. The same is true for the other peripheral As connected to A_3 and A_4. Emerson and his coauthors then hypothesize thus:

In networks revealing centrality, power will decentralize toward those actors who possess the highest degree of direct access to resources.

Figure 15.9   Power and Centrality in Exchange Networks

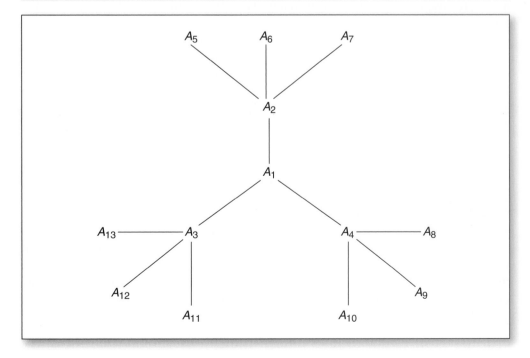

In the network in Figure 15.9, resources are flowing from actors A_5 through A_{13} to A_4, A_3, and A_2, and then on to A_1. Power dependence theory predicts that this network will have a tendency to collapse around those actors who can control direct access to resources—in this case, actors A_2, A_3, and A_4. Why should this be so?

The answer resides in the power advantage A_2, A_3, and A_4 have over the respective As from whom they are getting resources. A_5 through A_{13} have no other source for resources than A_2, A_3, and A_4, whereas each of these more central As has alternative sources for resources. Thus, those actors at the edges of the network depend on A_2, A_3, and A_4; indeed, each of these three As enjoys a unilateral monopoly. They have, therefore, the most direct access to resources, and they enjoy a power advantage because they can play the dependent As (i.e., A_5 through A_{13}) off against each other. A_1 ultimately depends on A_2, A_3, and A_4; hence, if the latter are willing to trade with A_1, then A_1 must have resources that they value. If not, the network will collapse into its three unilateral monopolies revolving around A_2, A_3, and A_4. For this network to remain stable, therefore, A_1 actually has to possess another resource that A_2, A_3, and A_4 value highly and that they cannot get readily elsewhere (hence, in the conventions of network diagrams, A_1 actually becomes B or some other letter, indicating that it is providing different resources to As).

Let me put some empirical content into these network dynamics. Let me make the most central figure, A_1, represent the king in a feudal system and A_2, A_3, and A_4, the lords of the king's realm. These lords provide resources to the king through their unilateral monopoly over peasants on their estates, and so they pass on to the king some portion of the resources ultimately generated by peasants. What, then, does the king give back in exchange for this flow of resources? The answer is almost always problematic for kings, and this is why feudal systems tend to collapse, because the lords of the realm are closer to the material resources that sustain the king. Typically, the king provides the coordination of armies and other necessary activities among the lords (who are often feuding among themselves) for defense of the realm. This capacity to organize a kingdom is the resource that the king gives back to lords.

Many network structures approximate this one. The important point is that they are inherently unstable because those who enjoy the unilateral monopolies eventually become resentful that they have to pass on resources to a more central actor, and if they begin to perceive that this actor does not provide enough in return, they break off the exchange and thereby change the distribution of power in the network. More recent work in networks, even in networks where actors are less likely to break off the exchange, also found that the locus of power shifted toward the sources of supply of resources that were most highly valued.

In sum, Richard Emerson infused exchange theory with a means to analyze social structures by conceptualizing exchange processes as occurring in networks. The same dynamics—power, dependence, and balancing operations—drive the formation of these networks, whether the actors in them be individual people or collective actors like groups, organizations, and nation-states. While most of the empirical work in this exchange tradition has been done in experimental laboratories, the fact that the dynamics are the same for individuals and corporate actors means that tests of the theory can be applied to macro-level social processes—just as Georg Simmel argued in his "formal sociology."

James S. Coleman's Early Advocacy and Mature Theory

James S. Coleman was an early advocate of what today is known as *rational choice* theorizing in sociology. This approach relies heavily on classical and neoclassical economics. Let me begin with Adam Smith and the classical model. As is well-known, Adam Smith formulated the basic laws of supply and demand for free markets, and as a result, he is often viewed as the founder of *utilitarian economics.* In Smith's formulation, actors are conceptualized as rational and as seeking to maximize their utilities, or benefits.[22] Yet his utilitarian ideas also led Smith to formulate the basic question guiding much of sociological theory in the nineteenth century: What forces are to hold society together in a world where market-driven production and consumption lead individuals into ever more specialized social niches where they pursue their self-interests rather than collective interests? What, then, was to keep specialization from splitting society apart? Adam Smith had two answers: (1) the laws of supply and demand in markets would operate as a kind of "invisible hand of order" in matching people's needs to production and in controlling fraud, abuse, and exploitation and (2) differentiated societies would develop sentiments (i.e., values, beliefs, ideologies, norms) appropriate to the new social order being created by markets.[23]

Through the midpoint of the twentieth century, sociologists were, as I emphasized earlier, highly suspicious of the first answer, wondering how social order could emerge from rational actors pursuing their own self-interests in markets operating by profit and greed. The second answer—an emphasis on moral codes—was more appealing but was basically unknown to most sociologists, who had long forgotten that Adam Smith had recognized the importance of cultural codes as an essential force of social organization. As a result, for more than half of the twentieth century, sociologists were critical of the utilitarians' views.

James Coleman was one of the first sociologists to see the power in Smith's ideas for a new kind of theorizing in sociology. Carrying forth Smith's arguments and then borrowing liberally from contemporary neoclassical theorizing, Coleman brought utilitarian economics back into sociology after a half-century.[24]

Yet Coleman's early work[25] only gave glimpses of how it would be possible to develop both the approaches first advocated by Adam Smith—that is, an emphasis on rationality and how it could explain the emergence of norms and other cultural constraints on human rationality. Thus, we must turn to his later theory to appreciate fully Coleman's contribution to a more general theory, where many of the elements of this theory can be found in his early work but not systematically pulled

---

[22]Adam Smith, *An Inquiry into the Nature and Causes of the Wealth of Nations* (Indianapolis, IN: Liberty Fund, 1981; originally published 1775–1776).

[23]Adam Smith, *The Theory of Moral Sentiments* (Indianapolis, IL: Liberty Fund, 1974; originally published 1759 and later revised in light of the questions raised in *The Wealth of Nations*).

[24]This approach has different names in other disciplines, but the core ideas come from neoclassical and game theory in economics and political science and, to an extent, in sociology and anthropology.

[25]See, for examples of his earlier essay, James S. Coleman, *Individual Interests and Collective Action: Selected Essays* (Cambridge, UK: Cambridge University Press, 1986).

together as they were in the early 1990s.[26] This more synthetic theory was published not long before Coleman's early death.

Coleman believed that actors have *resources* and *interest* in the resources of others; hence, interaction and ultimately social organization revolve around transactions between those who have and those who seek resources. These transactions can occur between individuals directly; they can also occur indirectly through intermediaries or chains of resource transfer; and they can occur in markets where resources are aggregated and bought and sold according to the laws of supply and demand.

Transferring Rights to Act. Coleman conceived of resources as *rights to act*. These rights can be given away in exchange for other rights to act. Thus, for example, authority relations consist of two types: (1) *conjoint authority,* where actors unilaterally give control of their rights to act to another because the vesting of others with authority is seen as in the best interests of all actors, and (2) *disjoint authority,* where actors give their rights away for extrinsic compensation, such as money. The same is true for norms that, in Coleman's view, represent the transfer of rights of control to a system of rules that are sanctioned by others. Thus, social structures and cultural norms are ultimately built by virtue of individuals giving up their rights to control resources in exchange for expected benefits.

For Coleman, then, the key theoretical questions in understanding social solidarity are as follows: (a) What conditions within a larger collectivity of individuals create a demand for rational actors to give their rights of control over resources to normative rules and the sanctions associated with these rules? (b) What conditions make for realization of effective control by norms and sanctions?

The Demand for Norms and Sanctions. These two questions—(1) the demand for norms and (2) their realization through effective sanctioning—are at the core of Coleman's theory. This theory goes in many directions, but I will confine our analysis to Coleman's discussion of the conditions producing group solidarity, since this is the most sociological part of his theory. Thus, given the two questions guiding his approach, Coleman asked, "What basic conditions increase the demand for social norms, and what makes them effective?" In his answer, Coleman demonstrated how a view of actors as rational, self-interested, calculating, and resource maximizing can explain emergent phenomena such as norms and group solidarity.

What conditions, then, increase the demand for norms? One is that actors are experiencing *negative externalities*, or harmful consequences in a particular context. Another is that actors cannot successfully bargain "tit for tat" or make offers or threats back and forth to reach agreements that reduce the negative externalities. Another condition is that there are too many actors involved for successful tit-for-tat bargaining, making bargaining cumbersome, difficult, and time-consuming. And the most important condition is *free-riding*, where some actors do not contribute to

---

[26]James S. Coleman, *Foundations of Social Theory* (Cambridge, MA: Belknap, 1990).

the production of a joint good and tit-for-tat bargaining cannot resolve the problem. Such free-riding, Coleman argued, is most likely in those groupings using disjoint authority or *extrinsic compensation* for productive activity. But ultimately in Coleman's model, negative externalities give actors an interest in elaborating social structure and cultural systems. They begin to see that by giving up some of their rights of control over their resources and behaviors, they can reduce negative externalities and, thereby, increase their utilities. Free-riding can become a negative externality, to the degree that it imposes costs and harm on others.

As we will see, free-riding becomes an important dynamic in Coleman's model of solidarity. But there can be other sources of negative externalities—threats, conflict, abusive use of authority, or any source of punishment or costly action by others. Generally, actors will first engage in tit-for-tat bargaining to resolve a problem creating negative externalities. For example, a threat might be met by a counterthreat, followed by an agreement to let the matter pass. But as the size of the group increases, this kind of bargaining becomes less viable: pair-wise bargaining among larger sets of actors to reduce negative externalities becomes difficult because of the time and energy consumed; bargaining can create new negative externalities for actors who must constantly negotiate and for those who are left out of bargains.

Coleman argues that the creation of markets represents one solution to problems of pair-wise, tit-for-tat bargaining among larger numbers of actors. As the volume of resources to be exchanged increases and the number of buyers and sellers expands, markets determine the price or the resources that one must give up to get another valued resource, with price being determined by the relative supply and demand for resources, Yet markets generate their own negative externalities associated with cheating, failure to meet obligations, unavailability of credit, and many other problems, and like all negative externalities, they can create a demand for norms to regulate transactions.

Thus, wherever norms (and other features of social systems like authority) emerge, they do so because actors have an interest in giving up certain rights to eliminate negative externalities and, thereby, to increase their utilities. Systems of norms, trust, and authority all represent ways to organize actors when tit-for-tat bargaining is difficult or unsuccessful, when the number of people involved grows beyond the capacity to bargain face-to-face, and when markets are no longer "frictionless" and begin to create their own negative externalities.

Under these conditions, actors will then bestow some of their rights to control resources to create proscriptive norms, or rules that prohibit certain types of behavior, and they will impose negative sanctions on those who violate these proscriptions or prohibitions. Such proscriptions and negative sanctions represent a solution by rational actors to the *first-order free-riding problem*, where actors are not contributing to the production of a jointly produced good. But this solution to free-riding creates a *second-order free-rider problem*: monitoring and sanctioning others are costly in time and energy, to say nothing of the emotional stress and other negatives involved; hence, rational individuals are likely to engage in free-riding on the monitoring and administration of sanctions. The solution to first-order free-riding can, therefore, generate a new set of negative externalities associated with the costs and problems of sanctioning conformity to prohibitions.

The solution to this second-order free-rider problem is to *create prescriptive norms*, or norms that indicate what is supposed to be done (as opposed to what cannot be done, or is prohibited), coupled with positive sanctioning for conformity. Such positive sanctions can become, in themselves, a joint good and a source of positive externalities; indeed, receipt of positive sanctions (approval, support, congratulatory statements, esteem, etc.) increases the utilities that rational actors experience. And so as the costs or negative externalities of the first-order free-rider problem create a demand for prescriptive norms and positive sanctions, actors can enjoy enhanced benefits and reduced costs when they give up their control of some resources and behavioral alternatives to normative prescriptions. Actors thus develop an interest in prescriptive normative control, and it becomes rational for them to do so.

The problem with systems of prescriptive norms and positive sanctions is that they are only viable in relatively small groupings and dense networks where monitoring and sanctioning can be part of the normal interaction among actors as they pursue a common goal or produce a joint good. Otherwise, the admission of positive sanctions becomes costly, as does the monitoring of conformity. High degrees of solidarity are thus only possible, Coleman argues, when relatively small numbers of actors give up control over their resources to prescriptive norms and rely heavily on positive sanctions, which, themselves, become positive externalities that increase the utilities for actors. Yet in the end, as groups get larger, *proscriptive norms* may also need to be introduced as mechanisms of social control. Thus, it is rational for actors to create norms that constrain their options; and the key condition for setting off this chain of events is the need and desire by rational actors to reduce negative externalities since these incur costs and thereby inhibit the maximization of utilities among rational actors.

Exchange Theorizing Today in Sociology

Exchange theorizing is now a dominant theoretical perspective in sociology; all theories build upon the ideas of Homans, Blau, Emerson, and Coleman. One of the two most enduring exchange approaches in sociology is the rational choice tradition, initiated by Coleman and carried forth by a number of scholars,[27] the most important of whom is probably Michael Hechter, even though he is not presently actively engaged in rational choice theorizing. There is a large set of rational choice theorists using many techniques, such as game theorizing, but the most coherent and general approaches are the later theory developed by Coleman and Michael Hechter's theory of group solidarity.

The second contemporary approach comes from Edward J. Lawler and his collaborators; and this approach draws upon the work of Richard Emerson. To be

---

[27]The journal *Rationality and Society* is a very good source for others employing utilitarian assumptions within sociology.

sure, Emerson's approach has produced a large number of interesting theories,[28] but over the last decade, I think that the approach by Edward J. Lawler and associates has become the most creative and general. Beginning with the assumptions of Emerson's power-dependence approach, Lawler and colleagues have developed a more general theory of emotions and a theory of commitment to larger-scale social structures.

Thus, in this section, I will focus first on the theory of rational choice developed by Hechter, which can be compared with that offered in Coleman's more mature theory. Then, I will outline Lawler's theory in detail, while at the same time recognizing that others have also developed important extensions and elaborations of Emerson's ideas. [29]

Michael Hechter's Theory of Group Solidarity

Michael Hechter's theory of group solidarity seeks to explain how rational, resource-maximizing actors create and remain committed to the normative structure

---

[28]Cook, Emerson, Gilmore, and Yamagishi, "The Distribution of Power in Exchange Networks" and "Network Connections and the Distribution of Power in Exchange Networks," *American Journal of Sociology* 93 (1988):833–851. See also Kazuo Yamaguchi, "Power in Networks of Substitutable and Complementary Exchange Relations: A Rational-Choice Model and An Analysis of Power Centralization," *American Sociological Review* 61 (1996):308–332; Karen Hegtvedt, "Distributive Justice, Equity, and Equality," *Annual Review of Sociology* 9 (1983):217–241; Karen Hegtvedt, Elaine Thompson, and Karen S. Cook, "Power and Equity: What Counts in Attributions for Exchange Outcomes," *Social Psychology Quarterly* 56 (1993):100–119; Hegtvedt and Cook, "The Role of Justice in Conflict Situations"; and Cook and Hegtvedt, "Distributive Justice, Equity, and Equality" for a review of the justice and injustice literature. See also Karen Hegtvedt and Barry Markovsky, "Justice and Injustice," in *Sociological Perspectives on Social Psychology*, ed. K. S. Cook, G. A. Fine, and J. S. House (Boston, MA: Allyn & Bacon, 1995); Toshio Yamagishi and Karen S. Cook, "Generalized Exchange and Social Dilemmas," *Social Psychology Quarterly* 56 (1993):235–249; and Toshio Yamagishi, "The Provision of a Sanctioning System in the United States and Japan," *Social Psychology Quarterly* 51 (1988):267–270, "Seriousness of Social Dilemmas and the Provision of a Sanctioning System," *Social Psychology Quarterly* 51 (1988):32–42, and "Unintended Consequences of Some Solutions to the Social Dilemmas Problem," *Sociological Theory and Method* 4 (1989):21–47.

[29]For one of the most important extensions, see: Linda D. Molm, *Coercive Power in Social Exchange* (Cambridge, UK: University of Cambridge Press, 1997), "Risk and Power Use: Constraints on the Use of Coercion in Exchange," *American Sociological Review* 62 (1997):113–133, "Punishment and Coercion in Social Exchange," *Advances in Group Processes* 13 (1996):151–190, and "Is Punishment Effective?: Coercive Strategies in Social Exchange," *Social Psychology Quarterly* 57 (1994):79–94. For more general reviews of her work within the general context of exchange network theory, see Linda D. Molm and Karen S. Cook, "Social Exchange and Exchange Networks," in *Sociological Perspectives on Social Psychology*, ed. K. S. Cook, G. A. Fine, and J. S. House (Boston, MA: Allyn and Bacon, 1995); Linda D. Molm, "The Structure and Use of Power: A Comparison of Reward and Punishment Power," *Social Psychology Quarterly* 51 (1988):108–122, "An Experimental Analysis of Imbalance in Punishment Power," *Social Forces* 68 (1989):178–203, "Punishment Power: A Balancing Process in Power-Dependence Relations," *American Journal of Sociology* 94 (1989):1392–1428, "Structure, Action, and Outcomes: The Dynamics of Power in Social Exchange," *American Sociological Review* 55 (1990):427–447, and "Dependence and Risk: Transforming the Structure of Social Exchange," *Social Psychology Quarterly* 57 (1994):163–176.

of groups.[30] Table 15.5 summarizes his utilitarian assumptions, but the basic ideas are straightforward: individuals reveal preferences or hierarchies of utility (value); they seek to maximize these preferences; and under certain conditions, it is rational for them to construct cultural and social systems to maximize utilities. Most theories of culture and social structure, Hechter argues, simply assume the existence of emergent sociocultural phenomena but do not explain *how* and *why* they would ever emerge in the first place. Rational choice theory can, he believes, offer this explanation for why actors construct and then abide by the normative obligations of groups. And if such a fundamental process as group solidarity can be explained by rational choice assumptions, virtually all emergent social phenomena can be similarly understood.

The Basic Problem of Order in Rational Choice Theorizing

Individuals depend upon others in a group context for those resources, or goods, that will maximize their utilities, or rewards. These individuals cannot produce the good for themselves and, hence, must rely on others to produce it for them or join others in its joint production. For example, if companionship and affection are high preferences, this good can be attained only in interaction with others, usually in groups; if money is a preference, then this good can usually be attained in modern settings through work in an organizational context. Thus, the goods that meet individual preferences can often be secured only in a group. Groups are thus conceptualized in rational choice theory as existing to provide or produce goods for their members.

Table 15.5 Assumptions of Rational Choice Theory

1. Humans are purposive and goal oriented.
2. Humans have sets of hierarchically ordered preferences or utilities.
3. In choosing lines of behavior, humans make rational calculations about 　A. The utility of alternative lines of conduct with reference to the preference hierarchy 　B. The costs of each alternative in terms of utilities foregone 　C. The best way to maximize utility.
4. Emergent social phenomena—social structures, collective decisions, and collective behavior—are ultimately the result of rational choices made by utility-maximizing individuals.
5. Emergent social phenomena that arise from rational choices constitute a set of parameters for subsequent rational choices of individuals in the sense that they determine 　A. The distribution of resources among individuals 　B. The distribution of opportunities for various lines of behavior 　C. The distribution and nature of norms and obligations in a situation.

---

[30]Michael Hechter, *Principles of Group Solidarity* (Berkeley: University of California Press, 1987), "Rational Choice Foundations of Social Order," in *Theory Building in Sociology*, ed. J. H. Turner (Newbury Park, CA: Sage, 1988).

Those goods that are produced by the activities of group members can be viewed as *joint goods*, because they are produced jointly in the coordinated activities of group members. Such joint goods vary along a critical dimension: their degree of "publicness." A *public good* is available not only to the members of a group but to others outside the group as well. Furthermore, once the good is produced, its use by one person does not diminish its supply for another. For instance, radio waves, navigational aids, and roads are public goods because they can be used by those who did not produce them and because their use by one person does not (at least to a point) preclude use by another. In contrast to public goods are *private goods*, which are produced for consumption by their producers. Moreover, consumption by one person decreases the capacity of others to consume the good. Private goods are thus kept out of the reach of others to ensure that only a person, or persons, in the group producing them can consume them.

The basic problem of order for rational choice theorists revolves around the question of public goods. This problem is described as the *free-rider* dilemma.[31] People are supposed to produce public goods jointly. Yet it is "rational" to consume public goods without paying the costs of contributing to their production. To avoid the costs of contributing to production is *free-riding*. If everybody free-rides, then the joint good will never be produced. How, then, is this dilemma avoided?

An answer to this question has been controversial in the larger literature in economics, but the basic thrust of the argument is that if a good is highly public, people can be coerced (e.g., through taxes) to contribute to its production (say, national defense) or they can be induced to contribute by being rewarded (salaries, praise) for their contribution. Another way to prevent free-riding is to exclude those who do not contribute to production from consumption, thereby decreasing the degree of "publicness" of the good. This exclusion can result in a group that "throws out" non-contributing members or does not allow them to join in the first place. A final way to control free-riders is to impose user fees or prices for goods that are consumed.

Thus, for rational choice theory, the basis of social order revolves around creating group structures to produce goods that are consumed in ways that limit free-riding—that is, consumption without contributing in some way, directly or indirectly, to the production of the good. The sociologically central problem of social solidarity thus becomes one of understanding how rational egoists go about (a) establishing groups that create normative obligations on their members to contribute and, then, (b) enforcing their conformity—thereby diminishing the problem of free-riding. Solidarity is thus seen as a problem of *social control*.

The Basis of Social Control. In rational choice theory, groups exist to provide joint goods. The more an individual depends on a group for resources or goods that rank high in his or her preference hierarchy, the greater is the potential power of the group over that individual. When people depend on a group for a valued good, it is rational for them to create rules and obligations that will ensure access to this joint

---

[31]Mancur Olson, *The Logic of Collective Action* (Cambridge, MA: Harvard University Press, 1965). Coleman also drew from this source in emphasizing the free-rider problem, as it produces negative externalities that, in turn, prompt individuals to develop normative agreements that constrain action.

good. Such is particularly likely to be the case when (a) the valued joint goods are not readily available elsewhere, (b) individuals lack information about alternatives, (c) the costs of exiting the group are high, (d) moving or transfer costs to new groups are high, and (e) personal ties, as unredeemable sunk investments, are strong.

Dependence is thus the incentive behind efforts to create normative obligations in order to ensure that actors get their share of a joint good. Groups thus have power over individuals who are dependent on the resources generated by the group; as a result of this power, the *extensiveness of normative* obligations in a group is related to the degree of *dependence*. Hence, dependence creates incentives not just for norms but for extensive norms that guide and regulate to a high degree.

Yet Hechter is quick to emphasize that "the extensiveness of a group alone . . . has no necessary implications for group solidarity."[32] What is crucial is that group members comply with these norms. Compliance is related to a group's *control capacity*, which in turn is a function of (a) monitoring and (b) sanctioning. *Monitoring* is the process of detecting nonconformity to group norms and obligations, whereas *sanctioning* is the use of rewards and punishments to induce conformity. When the monitoring capacity of a group is low, then it becomes difficult to ensure compliance to norms because conformity is a cost that rational individuals will avoid, if they can. And without monitoring, sanctioning (imposing costs) cannot effectively serve as an inducement to conformity.

Hechter believes, then, that solidarity is the product of dependence, monitoring, and sanctioning. But solidarity is also related to the nature of the group, which led Hechter to distinguish types of groups by the nature of joint goods produced.

Types of Groups. Hechter views *control capacity*—that is, monitoring and sanctioning—as operating differently in two basic types of groups. If a grouping produces a joint good for a market and does not itself consume the good, then control capacity can be potentially reduced because the profits from the sale of the good can be used to "buy" conformity of those producing the good for consumption by others. Conformity can be bought, for example, because members are compensated for their labor; and if they are highly dependent on a group for this compensation, then it is rational to conform to norms. But because the same compensation can be achieved in other groups, it is less likely that dependence on the group will be high, which thereby reduces the extensiveness of norms. The result is that the level of monitoring and the use of sanctions must be high in such groups, for it would be rational for the individual to free-ride and take compensation without a corresponding effort to produce the marketable good. Yet if monitoring and sanctioning are too intrusive and impose costs on individuals, then it is rational to leave the group and seek compensation elsewhere. Moreover, as we will see, extensive monitoring and sanctioning are costly and cut into profits—hence limiting the social control capacity of the group. The control capacity of these *compensatory groups*, as Hechter calls them, is thus problematic and ensures that solidarity will be considerably lower than in obligatory groups.

---

[32]Hechter, *Principles of Group Solidarity*, 49.

Obligatory groups produce a joint good for their members' *own* consumption. Under these conditions, it is rational to create obligations for contributions from members; if dependence on the joint good is high, then there is considerable incentive for conformity because there is no easy alternative to the joint good (unlike the case in groups in which a generalized medium like money is employed as compensation). Moreover, monitoring and sanctioning can usually be more efficient because monitoring typically occurs as a by-product of joint production of a good that the members consume and because the ultimate sanction—expulsion from the group—is very costly to members who value this good. As Hechter notes,

> Due to greater dependence, obligatory groups have lower sanctioning and monitoring costs. Since every group has one relatively costless sanction at its disposal—the threat of expulsion—then the greater the dependence of group members, the more weight this sanctioning causes. [Moreover,] . . . monitoring and sanctioning are to some extent substitutable. If the value of the joint good is relatively large, the threat of expulsion can partly compensate for inadequate monitoring. The more one has to lose by noncompliance, the less likely one is to risk it.[33]

There is an implicit variable in Hechter's analysis: *group size.* In general terms, compensatory groups organize larger numbers of individuals to produce marketable goods, whereas obligatory groups are smaller and provide goods for their members that cannot be obtained (or only at great cost) in a market. Thus, not only will dependence be higher in obligatory groups, but monitoring and sanctioning also will be considerably easier, thereby increasing solidarity, which Hechter defines as the extent to which members' private resources are contributed to a collective end. High contributions of private resources can occur only with extensive norms and high conformity—two conditions unlikely to prevail in compensatory groups. In Hechter's terms, then, high solidarity can be achieved only in obligatory groups, in which (a) dependence on a jointly produced and consumed good is high, (b) monitoring is comparatively easy because of small size and because members can observe one another's production and consumption of the good, and (c) sanctioning is built into the very nature of the good (i.e., receiving a good is a positive sanction, whereas expulsion or not receiving the good is a very costly negative sanction). Under these conditions, people will commit their private resources—time, energy, and self—to the production of the joint good and, in the process, promote high solidarity.

For Hechter, then, high degrees of solidarity are possible only in obligatory groups, in which dependence, monitoring, and sanctioning are high. Figure 15.10 represents his argument, modified in several respects. First, group size is added as a crucial variable. As obligatory groups get large, their monitoring and sanctioning capacity decreases. Second, on the far left is added a variable that is perhaps more typical of many human groupings: the ratio of consumption to compensation. That is, many groupings involve a mixture of extrinsic compensation for the production of goods consumed by others and internal consumption of goods produced and consumed by

---

[33]Ibid., 126.

Figure 15.10 Lawler and Yoon's Model of Commitment

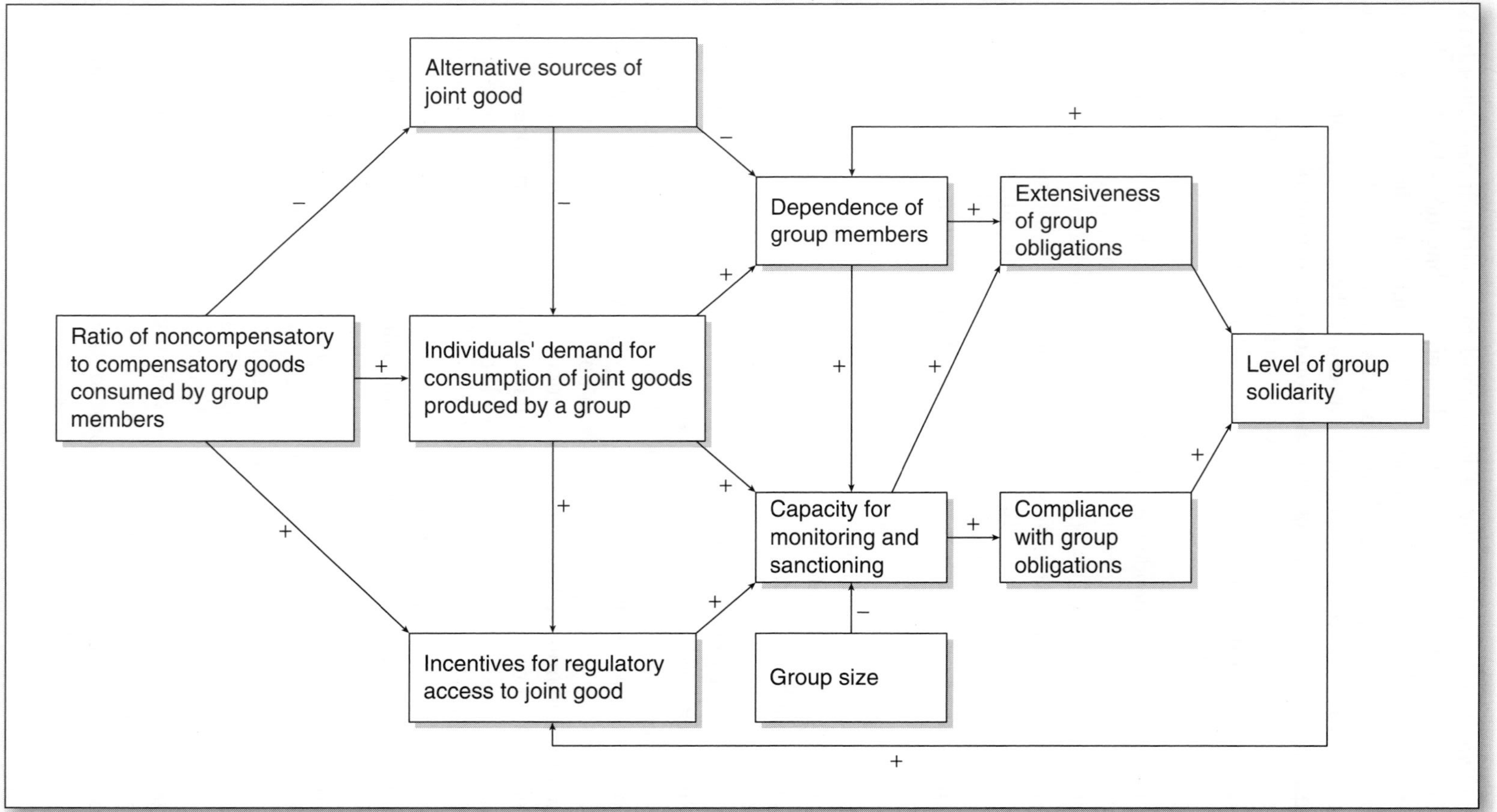

group members. For example, groups composed of members working for a salary in an organization often develop solidarity because they also produce joint goods—friendship, approval, assistance, and the like. Indeed, at times, solidarity develops around obligations that run counter to the official work norms of the organization.

The Determinants of Group Solidarity

We need to conceptualize groups not so much as two polar types but as mixtures of (a) external compensation for goods jointly produced by and consumed by others and (b) internal consumption of goods jointly produced and consumed by members. The greater the proportion of compensation is to internal consumption, the less likely are the processes depicted in Figure 15.10 to operate; conversely, the less the ratio of compensation to internal consumption is, the more likely these processes are to be activated in ways that produce solidarity. This proposition does not violate the intent of Hechter's typology, because he argues that the control capacity of compensatory groups increases if such groups also produce a joint good for their members' own consumption.

A larger-scale social system, such as an organization, community, or society, is a configuration of obligatory and compensatory groups. Solidarity will be confined mostly to obligatory groups, whereas the problems of free-riding will be most evident in compensatory groups, unless these compensatory groups also develop joint goods that are highly valued and consumed by group members. Hechter thus turns back to the basic distinctions that dominated early sociological theory—*gemeinschaft* versus *gesellschaft*, "primary" versus "secondary" groups, "mechanical" versus "organic" solidarity, "traditional" versus "rational" authority, "folk" versus "urban"—and has sought to explain these distinctions as the production of joint goods and the nature of the control process, which stems from whether a joint good is consumed by members or produced for a market in exchange for extrinsic compensation. Hechter believes the nature of the joint good determines the level of dependence of individuals on the group and the control capacity of the group. High dependence and control are most likely when joint goods are consumed, and hence solidarity is high under these conditions. A society with only compensatory groups will, therefore, reveal low solidarity. What is distinctive about Hechter's conceptualization is that it is tied to a utilitarian theory in which both high and low levels of solidarity follow from the rational choices of individuals.

Patterns of Control in Groups. In a vein similar to classical sociological theory, Hechter examines the process of formalization.[34] As groups get larger, informal controls become inadequate, even in obligatory groups. Of course, if compensatory groups proliferate or grow in size, the process of creating formal controls escalates to an even greater degree. There is, however, a basic dilemma in this process: formal monitoring and sanctioning are costly because they involve creating special agents, offices, procedures, and roles, thereby cutting into the production of goods. Obligatory

---

[34]Ibid., 59–77, 104–124.

groups can put off the process of formal controls because of high dependence and control that comes from joint consumption of a good that is valued, but when obligatory groups get too large, more formal controls become necessary. Compensatory groups can try to keep formal controls to a minimum, especially if they can create consumption of joint goods that reinforces the production norms for those goods that will be externally consumed. If they get too large, however, then they must also increase formal monitoring and sanctioning. In all these cases, it is rational for actors in groups to resist imposing formal controls because they are costly and cut into profits or joint consumption. But if free-riding becomes too widespread and cuts into production, then it is rational to begin to impose formal controls.

To some extent the implementation of formal controls can be delayed, or mitigated, by several forces. One is common socialization, and groups often seek members who share similar outlooks and commitments to reduce the risks of free-riding and to cut the costs of monitoring. Another is selection for altruism, especially in obligatory groups, in which unselfish members are recruited. Yet there are clearly limits to how effective these forces can be in maintaining social control, especially in compensatory groups but also in obligatory groups as they get larger.

The result of this basic dilemma between the costs of free-riding, on the one side, and formalization of control, on the other, is for groups to seek "economizing" measures for monitoring and sanctioning.[35] These are particularly visible in compensatory groups, in which formal social control is more essential for production, but elements of these "economizing tactics" can be seen also in obligatory groups as they get larger or as they produce a joint good that creates problems of free-riding.

Hechter lists a number of monitoring economies. One way to decrease monitoring costs is to increase the visibility of individuals in the group through a variety of techniques: designing the architecture of the group so that people are physically visible to one another, requiring members to engage in public rituals to reaffirm their commitment to the group, encouraging group decision making so that individuals' preferences are exposed to others, and administering positive public sanctions for behavior that exemplifies group norms. Another set of techniques for reducing monitoring costs involves having members share the monitoring burden, as is the case when (a) rewards are given to groups rather than individuals (under the assumption that if your rewards depend on others, you will monitor their activity), (b) privacy is limited, (c) informants are rewarded, and (d) gossips are encouraged. A final economizing technique, which follows from socialization processes, is to minimize errors of interpretation of behavior through recruitment and training of members into a homogeneous culture.

With respect to sanctions, one technique for economizing on sanctions is symbolic sanctioning through the creation of a prestige hierarchy, and the differential rewarding of prestige to group members who personify group norms. Another technique is public sanctioning of deviance from group norms. A final sanctioning technique is to increase the exit costs of group members through geographical isolation from other groups, imposition of nonrefundable investments on entry to the group, and limitation of extra-group affiliations.

---

[35]Ibid., 126–146.

Yet there are limits to these monitoring and sanctioning economies, especially in compensatory groups. The result is that, at some point, a group must create formal agents and offices to monitor and control. Thus, a formal organization always employs some of the economizing processes listed and also creates agents charged with monitoring and control—for example, comptrollers, supervisors, personnel officers, quality control agents, and the like. Such monitoring and sanctioning are extremely costly, and so it is not surprising that organizations try to economize here as well.

In addition to the more general techniques previously listed, a variety of mechanisms for reducing agency costs or increasing productive efficiency, and hence profitability, can be employed. For example, inside and outside contractors are often used to perform work (incurring their own monitoring and sanctioning costs) at a set price for an organization. Standardization of tools, work flow, and other features of work is another way to reduce the need for monitoring. Assessment of only outputs (and ignoring how these are generated) is yet another technique for economizing on at least some phases of monitoring. Setting production goals for each stage in production is still another technique. And, perhaps most effective, the creation of an obligatory group within the larger compensatory organization is the most powerful economizing technique, as long as the norms of the obligatory group correspond to those of the more inclusive compensatory organization (sometimes, however, just the opposite is the case, which thereby increases monitoring costs to even higher levels).

The Theory Summarized. In Table 15.6, Hechter's theory is stated in more formal and abstract terms than in Hechter's work. When stated in this way, the theory can be applied to a wide range of empirical processes—social class formation, ethnic solidarity, complex organization, communities, and other social units. The propositions in Table 15.6 must be seen as building on the assumptions delineated in Table 15.5. When this is done, it is clear that Hechter has tried to explain, as he phrases the matter, "the micro foundations of the macro social order."

Macrostructural Implications. Hechter sees the basic ideas of rational choice theory as useful in understanding the more macrostructural processes among large populations of individuals. For example, the basic theory as outlined in Figure 15.10 and Tables 15.5 and 15.6 can be used to explain processes within nation-states. A state or a government imposes relatively extensive obligations on its citizens—pay your taxes, be loyal, be willing to die in war, and so on. The reason for this capacity is that citizens are often highly dependent on government for public goods and cannot leave the society easily (because they like where they live, cannot incur the exit and transfer costs, enjoy many benefits from the joint goods produced by the citizenry, etc.). Compliance with the demands of the state involves more than dependence and extensive obligations. Compliance also hinges on the state's control capacity to monitor and sanction. But how is it possible for the state to monitor and sanction all its citizens, who are organized into diverse configurations of obligatory and compensatory groups?

The answer to this question, Hechter argues, lies in economies of control. Such economies can be generated within and between groups. The key process is to get

Table 15.6 Hechter's Implicit Principles of Social Structure

1. The more members of a group jointly produce goods for consumption outside the group, the more their productive efforts will depend on increases in the ratio of extrinsic compensation to intrinsic compensation.
2. The more members of a group jointly produce goods for their own consumption, the more their efforts will depend on the development of normative obligations.

3. The power of the group to constrain the decisions and behaviors of its members is positively related to the dependence of these members on the group for a good or compensation, with dependence increasing when
  A. More attractive alternative sources for a good or compensation are not available
  B. Information about alternative sources for a good or compensation is not readily available
  C. The costs of exiting the group are high
  D. The moving or transfer costs to another group are high
  E. The intensity of personal ties among group members is high.

4. The more a group produces a joint good for its own consumption and develops normative obligations to regulate productive activity, the more likely are conditions 3-A, 3-B, 3-C, 3-D, and 3-E to be met; conversely, the more a group produces a joint good for the consumption of others outside the group, the less likely these conditions are to be met.
5. The more a group produces a joint good for its own consumption and develops extensive normative obligations to regulate productive activity, the more likely is social control through monitoring and sanctioning to be informal and implicit and, hence, less costly.
6. The more a group produces a good for external consumption and must rely on a high ratio of extrinsic over intrinsic compensation for members, the more likely is social control through monitoring and sanctioning to be formal and explicit and, hence, more costly.
7. The larger is the size of a group, the more likely is social control to be formal and explicit and the greater will be its cost.
8. The greater is the cost of social control through monitoring and sanctioning, the more likely are economizing procedures to be employed in a group.

the citizens themselves monitoring and sanctioning one another within groups, then to link these groups together in ways that maximize dependence and control capacity.

Edward J. Lawler's Power Dependence Theory of Emotions and Commitment

Edward J. Lawler and his collaborators have developed another line of power dependence theory (from Richard Emerson's assumptions) that, in just the last few years, has taken Emerson's theory into the sociology of emotions and, more generally, to the process of commitment to macrostructures in societies. In my view, it is now the most important of the several extensions of Emerson's ideas.[36]

Commitment in Exchange Networks. In conjunction with Jeongkoo Yoon, Edward J. Lawler has sought to understand how affective commitments develop in exchange relations.[37] In their model, structural power increases exchange frequency, which then reduces uncertainty about payoffs. In turn, the reduction of uncertainty increases actors' commitment to the exchange relationship because predictability ensures expected levels of payoffs from the exchange. Lawler and Yoon, however, theorize that this presumed relationship between frequency, uncertainty reduction, and commitment is really a proxy for the underlying emotional dynamics. In their view, once these emotional forces can be isolated in experiments, the uncertainty reduction argument would be obviated by a theory of emotional attachment. Although the uncertainty reduction processes remain an independent force in producing commitments, the experiments of Lawler and Yoon confirm most of their hypotheses.

The model tested by Lawler and Yoon is presented in Figure 15.11, and then we tease out the details of the argument. On the left side of the model are the structural conditions that follow from Emerson's original formulation of power dependence. *Total power* is the degree of actors' mutual dependence on each other for resources. The greater this mutual dependence is, the higher is the total power in the relationship. Another concept that follows from Emerson's formulation is *relative power*, which is the level of inequality in the dependence of actors on each other for resources (i.e., the relative power of actor A is the ratio of A's power over B as a proportion of both A's and B's power; the greater is A's proportion, the more is A's relative power and the greater is the inequality in the relationship). As shown in Figure 15.11, Lawler and Yoon only express relative power as "equal power," but the argument is really about structural situations where there is high total power and low relative power or equality. The greater is the mutual dependence of actors on the resources that they provide for each other (high total power) and the more equal are their respective dependencies for these resources (equal power or low relative power), the more *structural cohesion* is built into their power relations. As

[36]For an effort to synthesize Coleman's and Hechter's respective theories, see Jonathan H. Turner, "The Production and Reproduction of Social Solidarity: A Synthesis of Two Rational Choice Theories," *Journal for the Theory of Social Behavior* 22 (1993):311–328.

[37]Edward J. Lawler and Jeongkoo Yoon, "Commitment in Exchange Relations: A Test of a Theory of Relational Cohesion," *American Sociological Review* 61 (1996):89–108; Edward Lawler, Jeongkoo Yoon, Mouraine R. Baker, and Michael D. Large, "Mutual Dependence and Gift Giving in Exchange Relations," *Advances in Group Processes* 12 (1995):271–298; Edward J. Lawler and Jeongkoo Yoon, "Power and the Emergence of Commitment Behavior in Negotiated Exchange," *American Sociological Review* 58 (1993):465–481. For earlier works on commitment dynamics within power dependence theorizing, see Karen S. Cook and Richard M. Emerson, "Power, Equity, and Commitment in Exchange Networks," *American Sociological Review* 43 (1978):721–739; Karen S. Cook and Richard M. Emerson, "Exchange Networks and the Analysis of Complex Organizations," *Research on the Sociology of Organizations* 3 (1984):1–30; and Peter Kollock, "The Emergence of Exchange Structures: An Experimental Study of Uncertainty, Commitment, and Trust," *American Journal of Sociology* 100 (1994):315–345.

a consequence, the more frequent are exchanges and agreements in these exchanges. Thus, the effects of structural cohesion (or high total power and low relative power) on emotions and commitments operate through exchange frequency.

Emotions for Lawler and Yoon are relatively short-term positive or negative evaluative states; Lawler and Yoon emphasize mild positive emotions and their effects on commitment. Two particular types of mild emotions are emphasized: (1) interest and excitement, which revolve around anticipation of payoffs that give value, and (2) pleasure and satisfaction, which orient actors to past and present payoffs yielding value. As the model outlines, exchange frequency under conditions of high total power and equality of power increases agreements in these exchanges, which then activate these two types of mild emotions, interest and excitement and pleasure and satisfaction.

As these emotions are activated, they increase relational cohesion. Relational cohesion is simply a combined function of the frequency of agreements in bargaining over resources and the positive emotions that are thereby aroused. Hence, the more frequent the interactions and the more positive emotions generated from such interactions, the greater is the level of *relational cohesion*. Relational cohesion, in turn, produces commitment behaviors that in the experimental settings developed by Lawler and Yoon were divided into three types: (1) staying in the exchange relation even when attractive alternatives for resources were available, (2) giving token gifts to exchange partners unilaterally and without expectation of reciprocation, and (3) contributing to joint ventures with exchange partners, even under conditions of risk and uncertainty.

The results of the series of experiments supported the argument presented in Figure 15.11, but they did not obviate the effects of exchange frequency on uncertainty reduction in generating commitment behaviors. Thus, commitment is related to the effects of exchange frequency on uncertainty reduction and arousal of mild positive emotions, although there is good reason to believe that the two are related: uncertainty reduction probably generates positive emotions, and vice versa. In explaining their model and research findings, Lawler and Yoon introduce concepts and causal relationships not specified in the model in Figure 15.11.

Figure 15.11   Lawler and Yoon's Model of Commitment

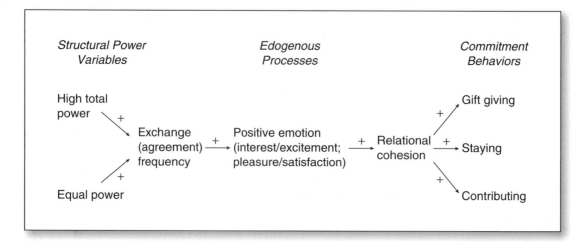

One key concept is objectification of the relationship, or the perception by individuals that the exchange relationship, per se, is an object and source of the positive emotions experienced. Such objectification becomes a "force" furthering commitment behaviors, as people stay in the relationship because the relationship, per se, gives value, as individuals give token gifts to symbolize their relationship, and as they undertake joint ventures in the name of the relationship.

Once the discursive discussion around the model is finished, the model in Figure 15.11 becomes more complicated. These additional complications are presented in Figure 15.12, where (a) the direct, indirect, and reverse causal forces operating in Lawler and Yoon's theorizing are delineated and (b) the uncertainty reduction argument from earlier theorizing by Emerson and (c) the discussion of objectification are added. The basic arguments remain the same, even in this more robust form. High total power increases exchange frequency, whereas high relative power or inequality works against high rates of exchange agreement (as would be expected by virtue of the earlier discussion of Lawler's and various collaborators' analysis of bargaining). Thus, high mutual dependence and equality will increase exchange frequency, which then reduces uncertainty about payoffs and arouses mild positive emotions that, by themselves but also in combination, increase the level of objectification of the relationship as a gratifying entity, per se, beyond the specific bargains and payoffs in any particular round of exchange.

Together, objectification and relational cohesion increase attachments and commitments to the exchange relationship, which, in turn, increase the level of bonding and group formation. Some of these causal paths are inferred from and some represent extensions of Lawler and Yoon's theory; what is true of the direct causal paths is even more true of the reverse causal chains that flow from right to left in the model. These paths represent elaborations and extensions of the theory, but they do so in ways consistent with the theory.

As group bonds are formed from commitment behaviors, these feed back and increase the level of objectification, which, in turn, adds an extra dose of positive emotion. Similarly, bonding, commitments, and relational cohesion all feed back, increasing positive emotions that lower uncertainty. Together, these feed back to increase the frequency of exchange agreements. As uncertainty is reduced and relational cohesion increased, this escalated cohesion increases mutual dependence for valued resources, which sets the commitment process in motion once again. Obviously, these positive direct, indirect, and reverse causal effects cannot go on forever, making people committed, "emotional junkies," but the model emphasizes how structural conditions of high total and low relative power initiate a series of recursive processes that feed off each other and generate commitments to relationships.

In many ways, this theory on emotions converges with Émile Durkheim's analysis of emotions in *The Elementary Forms*, where proximity of individuals generates an increased sense of effervescence, which, in turn, exerts a feeling of external power that needs to be symbolized; and once symbolized in totems or other means of objectification, rituals enacted toward these symbols arouse emotions and a sense of commitment toward the larger social group. Moreover, the theory also converges with Randall Collins's analysis of interaction rituals; and indeed, comparing Figure 14.1 on p. 493 with Figure 15.12 immediately reveals the convergence. Thus, we can see

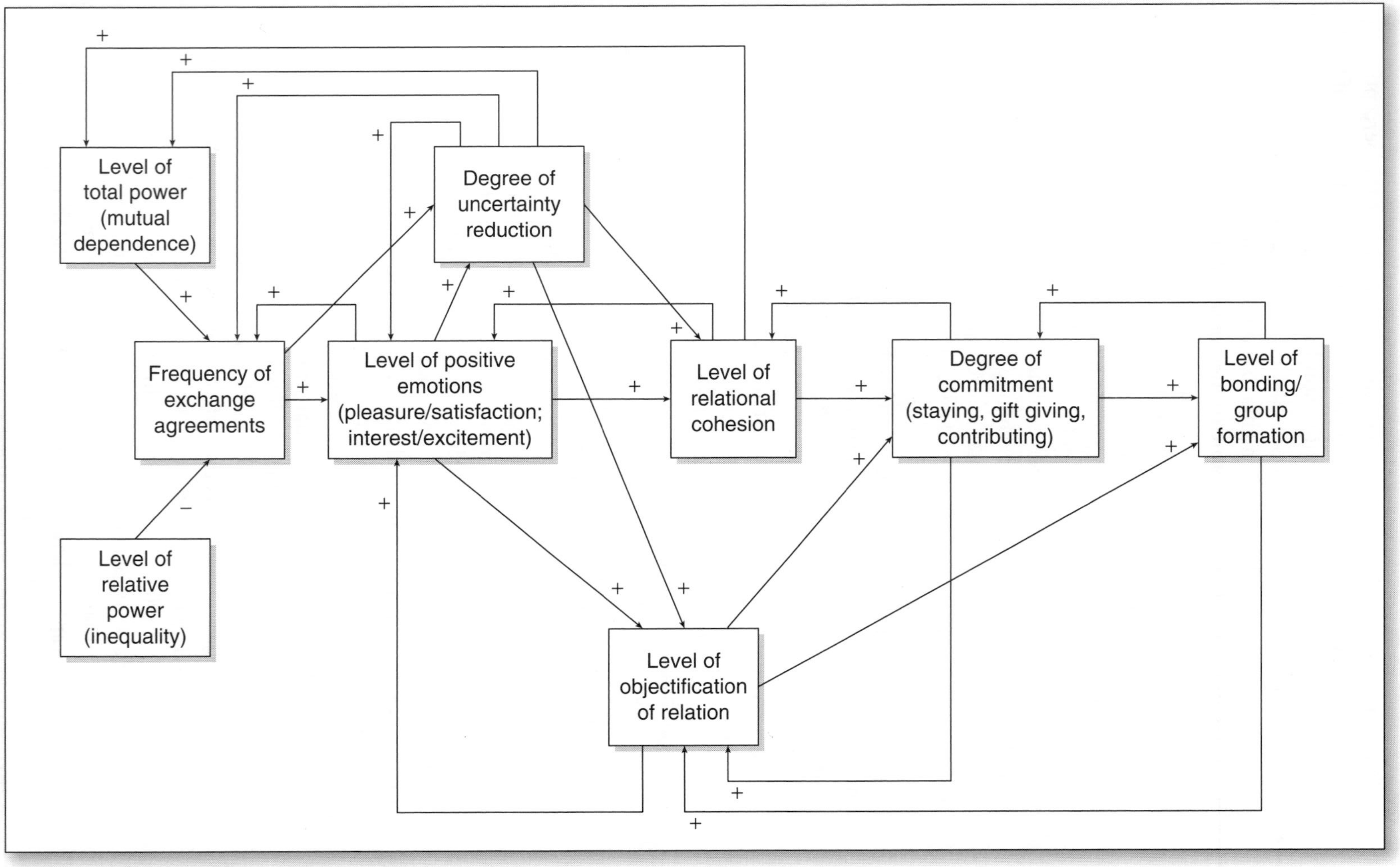

Figure 15.12 An Extension of Lawler's Model of Relational Cohesion and Commitment

convergence among three theoretical traditions—the functionalism of Émile Durkheim, the conflict emphasis in Randall Collins's theory, and now the exchange network approach of Edward Lawler and collaborators.

Refining the Theory of Emotions. Lawler has expanded his early theory of emotions and commitment, described earlier, into a more robust theory of affect.[38] He distinguishes between (a) *emotions* that are diffuse and global feelings arrayed along a positive–negative continuum and (b) *sentiments* directed at specific social objects, particularly task activities, self, others, and groups. In introducing this distinction, Lawler argues that as individuals experience positive or negative emotions in exchange relations, they try to understand the sources and causes of their more global emotions, and from these more cognitive deliberations, they develop sentiments directed toward various social objects. And once these sentiments emerge, they feed back and affect the valences or types of negative and positive emotions experienced by persons. Table 15.7 summarizes this argument.

If the global emotion is attributed (as a sentiment) to the task at hand during an exchange, persons feel *pleasantness* or *unpleasantness*. If they make the attribution to self as being responsible for the emotions, individuals will experience *pride* when the experience is positive and *shame* when it is negative. If other persons are viewed as causing the emotional experience, individuals will experience, depending upon the positive or negative feelings, either *gratitude* or *anger* toward those others. And if the social unit in which the exchanges have occurred is viewed as the source of the emotion, people will have a sense of *affective attachment* or *affective detachment*.

In general, individuals will see themselves as responsible for positive outcomes in an exchange, while making an external attribution by blaming others or social units

Table 15.7 Emotions Related to Social Objects

Valence of Emotion	Emotion	Social Object
Positive	Pleasantness	Task
Negative	Unpleasantness	
Positive	Pride	Self
Negative	Shame	
Positive	Gratitude	Other
Negative	Anger	
Positive	Affective attachment	Social unit
Negative	Affective detachment	

Source: E. J. Lawler, "An Affect Theory of Social Exchange," *American Sociological Review* 107 (2001):321–352. Adapted by permission.

---

[38]Edward J. Lawler, "An Affect Theory of Social Exchange," *American Journal of Sociology* 107 (2001):321–352.

for failures in exchanges. Given this *distal bias* for attributions about the causes of negative feelings and the *proximal bias* toward self or immediate others for positive feelings, the interesting question is "How do people break the hold of the proximal bias and make attributions to relationships and social units for positive experiences?" Lawler's answer is complex, but it revolves around two key factors: (1) the *separability* or *inseparability* of joint exchanges and (2) the type of exchange. Each of these factors is discussed below.

1. When a person's contribution to a joint task cannot easily be isolated from the contributions of others, this is a situation of *inseparability.* Under this condition of non-separability of contributions from positive outcomes, individuals have difficulty taking all of the credit for exchanges that lead to successful completion of the task, nor can they easily blame others for failures. The result is a sense of *socially mediated self-efficacy,* where a person's sense of efficacy is tied to the actions of others. Perceptions of efficacy, in general, generate positive emotions, like *joy, pride, elation,* whereas the absence of a sense of efficacy produces negative emotions, such as *sadness, depression,* and *shame.* Lawler concludes that the "greater the non-separability of individuals' impact on task success or failure, the greater the perception of shared responsibility" and "the greater the perception of shared responsibility for success/failure at a joint task, the more inclined actors are to attribute the resulting global and specific emotions to social units (i.e., relations, networks, or groups)."[39]

2. Exchange relations can, Lawler concludes, be one of four basic types: (1) productive, (2) negotiated, (3) reciprocal, and (4) generalized. *Productive exchanges* revolve around the coordination of activities with others and the exchanging of resources with these others to produce a *joint good* or outcome. *Negotiated exchanges* involve direct bargaining over payoffs between two or more actors and arriving at an agreement on the terms of exchange. *Reciprocal exchanges* are sequential, with one person giving off resources to another without explicit assurances that this other will reciprocate in the future. *Generalized exchanges,* as discussed earlier, involve giving resources to one member of a network (who, in turn, gives them to other members, and so on), while receiving resources from others with whom one has not engaged in direct exchange.

Lawler further typifies in several additional ways. One is *productive, direct* exchanges (which includes both negotiated and reciprocal exchange, defined above). Another is *indirect* (which includes all generalized exchange as defined above). Moreover, borrowing a key distinction made by Emerson, Lawler typifies exchange dynamics by emphasizing that exchange networks can be *positively connected,* whereby exchange between actors A and B increases the probability of exchange with other actors, say, C and D. Alternatively, exchange can occur in *negatively connected* networks, whereby exchange between actors A and B decreases the likelihood of exchange with other actors because A and B sustain an exclusive tie to each other.

---

[39]Ibid., 334.

With these distinctions, Lawler develops additional propositions on how the arousal of global emotions leads to varying degrees and types of *attributions* to different social objects. Productive exchanges will reveal high non-separability because activities are coordinated to realize a joint outcome, leading individuals to have perceptions of shared responsibility and causing them to experience high levels of positive or negative affect depending on how successful the activities prove to be in producing a joint good valued by all. Negotiated exchanges, revolving around bargaining, will reveal (a) a medium level of non-separability because individuals can see their own success or failure in the negotiations, (b) a high level of perception of shared responsibility (over the outcome of the negotiations), and (c) a medium to high emotional response to success or failure of the negotiations. Reciprocal exchanges, with unilateral giving of resources with no agreed-upon obligation to return the favor, will evidence (a) a low non-separability because of the clear separation in time of the giving and receiving, (b) a low sense of shared responsibility, and (c) low arousal of global emotions.

In Lawler's view, then, productive exchange relations produce stronger global emotions (whether positive or negative) than either direct (negotiated or reciprocal) or indirect (generalized) exchanges because of the high level of non-separability of each actor's contribution and the strong sense of shared responsibility. Direct exchange will generate stronger global emotions and stronger perceptions of shared responsibility than indirect (generalized) exchange. The stronger emotions for direct exchanges over indirect, generalized exchanges arise because the outcome depends upon each actor's active contribution to the negotiated agreement (disagreement) or the reciprocation (nonreciprocation) of a gift offered by another, but these positive or negative emotions will not be as intense as they are in productive exchanges, where actors are closely coordinated and where their contributions are not easily separated. Indirect exchanges will generate the lowest-intensity global emotions because actors are separated and have a low sense of shared responsibility for outcomes.

These dynamics also explain the nature of attributions that transform a global sense of positive or negative arousal into specific sentiments directed at objects. Lawler asks, "What forces increase the likelihood that actors will make attributions to relationships, networks, and groups rather than to self and others?"

His answer is that relational and group attributions are most likely in productive exchanges because of the joint, non-separable nature of each actor's contributions and the sense of shared responsibility for success or failure in coordinated activities in producing a valuable outcome. Negotiated exchanges can produce relational and group attributions because of the medium level of non-separability, coupled with a high sense of shared responsibility for outcomes, but not to the extent of productive exchanges.

Reciprocal exchanges are less likely than either negotiated or productive exchanges to cause relational and group attributions because of the high separability of activities in time (between giving and its reciprocation) and only a medium to high level of shared responsibility. And generalized exchanges are the least likely to cause group-level attributions because of the separability of each actor's behavior and low perceptions of shared responsibility.

When individuals who are engaged in productive exchanges make attributions to the larger structure (e.g., a relationship, network, or group), they subordinate self-serving tendencies to take credit for success (self-attributions) and to blame others for failure (other-attributions).

The nature of networks, whether positive or negative, also influences attributions and attachments. In *positively connected networks*, where exchange of one dyad is likely to cause exchange with others in the network, the *density* (connectedness of all persons or nodes in the network to each other) will increase over time as the positive emotions from exchange in one dyad are extended to others. When people feel good about one exchange, they typically enter another, bringing to the new exchange positive emotions that increase the likelihood of successful exchange and the positive global emotions that ensue from such success. As these dynamics radiate out across the network, the network will become denser, with all individuals exchanging with each other.

Under these conditions, the network may begin to approximate a productive exchange if individuals begin to coordinate their actions, leading to network or group-level attributions that enhance positive global emotions and social solidarity. However, if dyadic exchanges activate negative emotions and if this outcome is repeated over time, group formation will be arrested and will generate networks with sparse ties. In *negatively connected networks*, where successful exchanges strengthen dyadic ties at the expense of ties to other actors, global emotions and specific sentiments will remain in the local exchange, thereby lowering the chances that the overall density of ties in the network will increase.

The *stability of social units* within which exchanges occur is also important in generating group-level attributions and attachments. If positive global emotions emerge from successful exchanges in the group and if the group is seen by individuals as a stable source of these emotions as a result of group-level attributions, individuals' sense of efficacy increases, and they will attribute this sense to the stable structure of the group, thereby increasing their attachments to the group (what Lawler termed *affective attachment;* Table 15.7). Conversely, when individuals see the stable structure of the group as causing negative emotional arousal, they are likely to believe that this structure will continue to arouse such emotions, leading them to feel *affective detachment* and alienation from the group.

A final consideration in Lawler's theory is the fact that social relations of exchange are *nested* in larger, more inclusive social structures. As a consequence, there is always a tension between making attributions for positive or negative global emotions to either the local exchange relationship or the larger, more inclusive social unit within which exchange relations are lodged. One implicit proposition not explicitly included in the current theory is that individuals will tend to give credit to the most immediate and proximate unit—the exchange relationship—for positive global emotions, while blaming the larger, more inclusive social unit for negative emotional arousal.

More generally, Lawler argues that since the local relationship with specific others is the locus for the exchange of resources, while being the place where the situation is defined and emotions aroused, there is a bias for attributions beyond self and other to target the relationship rather than the more distant group within which the relationship is established and maintained. Accordingly, structures of direct exchange—that is, negotiated and reciprocal exchanges—will produce relational attributions rather than group attributions for emotions. In contrast, productive and indirect (generalized exchanges) are more likely to produce group-level attributions for emotions because the focus moves out beyond any particular dyadic relationship.

A General Theory of Commitments to Macrostructures. With this expanded version of the earlier theory of commitment in exchange relations, Lawler teamed again with Yoon and Shane Thye to extend the theory to a more general analysis of how individuals become committed to macrostructures that are far removed from their daily exchanges.[40] As Lawler's and Yoon's original theory of commitment emphasized, person-to-person ties are created by repeated interactions with others, and these ties are infused with emotions. This arousal of emotions in micro exchanges is seen as potentially generating commitments not only to others but also to larger social structures under specific conditions, especially when (a) *joint tasks* must be coordinated and the respective contributions of each person are not easily separable; (b) *shared responsibility* for outcomes of task activities, whether successful or unsuccessful, is perceived by participants; (c) *efficacy* or control over individuals' activities and the outcomes of these activities is felt by persons; and (d) *distal attributions* are made for the experience of positive emotions. Many of these ideas appeared a decade ago, but they are now blended into a general theory of social commitments. The target of commitments depends upon the attributions that persons make for either positive or negative emotions. As summarized above, if individuals make self-attributions for positive or negative emotions, they experience *pride* or *shame,* respectively; if they make attributions to others for their emotions, they will experience *gratitude* toward these others when the emotions experienced are positive and *anger* when the emotions aroused are negative; and if they make attributions to social units for their emotional experiences, they experience *affective attachment* when the emotions have been positive and *affective detachment* (alienation) when they have been negative.

Thus, the key to more macro-level commitments occurs when individuals begin to make external attributions to social units for positive emotional experiences, but as I have emphasized, these more distal attributions must overcome the *proximal bias* of positive emotional arousal that tends to stay local, focusing on self and others as well as the micro encounter where these emotions are aroused. Commitments must also overcome the *distal bias* of negative emotions, which tends to target others or more remote social units rather than self. And so, as Lawler emphasized a decade ago, the key question is how to overcome these biases and make external attributions to distal structures for positive emotional experiences in local exchanges.

Here is where the other conditions listed above come into play: the greater is (a) the degree of *non-separability* of *joint tasks,* (b) the sense of *shared responsibility* for

---

[40]Edward J. Lawler, Shane R. Thye, and Jeongkoo Yoon, *Social Commitment in a Depersonalized World* (New York: Russell Sage Foundation, 2009).

outcomes of these joint activities, and (c) the sense of *efficacy* in activities, the more likely will individuals make more distal attributions and develop commitments to more remote social structures. Under these conditions, positive emotions circulate among individuals and, as Durkheim might have argued, there is an emotional effervescence that pushes attributions outward toward social structures, which are seen as the ultimate source of positive emotional experiences.

The conduits for these external attributions are often along the paths of successively embedded or nested structures—from person-to-person ties lodged in groups that are embedded in organizations, from organizations located in communities, from communities to regional governments, and from regions to societies. As long as individuals are experiencing positive emotions, shared responsibility, and efficacy from their iterated interactions/exchanges, positive emotions work their way to more distal objects, including whole societies. Thus, social structures that foster structural embeddedness will evidence more potential for creating distal commitments, whereas social structures that evidence high levels of inequality will lower commitments because they reduce the sense of jointness, shared responsibility, and efficacy so essential to moving emotion to distal social units.

Other mechanisms intervene in these processes. One is simple repetition of activities; these generate positive emotions that, in turn, create demands for norms that enshrine expectations for positive affect, channel activities to ensure that positive emotions will be experienced, and provide informal sanctions to those not sharing responsibilities in collective action. Repeated interactions arousing positive emotions also generate different forms of trust: *generalized* trust (about humans in general), *knowledge-based* trust at specific interactions in a social unit, and *relational* trust in the benefits of cooperation to generate predictability and reduce uncertainty in interactions.

Yet another mechanism of social order inheres in *identity dynamics*, and here Lawler brings his exchange approach into symbolic interactionist theory (see Chapter 16). To the extent that role, social, and group identities are verified in exchanges, they increase individuals' identification with the social units in which the exchanges occur. In fact, to the degree that identities of any sort are salient in an exchange, the arousal of positive emotions causes the verification of these identities. When identities are verified, it increases the sense of efficacy (of self), which enhances the arousal of positive emotions and increases the circulation of these emotions in local encounters (as would be predicted by the proximal bias). But as positive emotions circulate, a person's sense of self becomes attached to the structures in which identities are lodged; and the larger the social unit and/or social categories defining the sense of identity that is verified in exchanges, the more likely are the positive emotions experienced when these identities are verified to carry over to macro-level social units, thereby breaking the hold of the proximal bias. And as identities are aligned with ever more macro-social units, commitments to these units increase.

In sum, from the more modest beginnings in experimental laboratories, Lawler and his former students have provided a plausible answer to one of the big questions in theoretical sociology: How are the macro and micro levels of social reality to be linked? Lawler's, Thye's, and Yoon's answer is that commitment processes are built into the very nature of exchanges in groups. While some types of structures—impersonal markets, stratification of resources, and rigid/punitive organizational hierarchies—can work against the dynamics unleashed by frequency of interaction and exchange, other dynamics in exchanges operate to increase commitments to more remote social units. Frequency of interactions, shared responsibility, a sense of efficacy, verification of identities, and positive emotional arousal can all begin to break the hold of the proximal bias, causing attributions to become more distal. This distal movement is more likely when social units are embedded in each other, thereby providing conduits for attributions from micro- to macro-social structures. The result is that commitments to macro-level sociocultural formations increase.

Conclusions

Despite its late start in the 1950s, exchange theorizing has become one of the discipline's strongest subfields because so much of the research in this area has been driven by theories. The differences between the behaviorist and utilitarian origins of various approaches are not nearly as great as they once were, although some differences remain, especially among those fully committed to the rational choice approach to exchange theorizing. Early efforts to bridge the micro-macro gap revolved around images of how exchanges at the micro level build up social structures and their cultures, whereas more recent efforts approach the micro-macro issue by trying to link theoretically the dynamics of the micro realm to those of the macro. In Lawler's approach, the emphasis is on the arousal of emotions at the micro level and then the extension of these emotions into commitments to macro-structures and their cultures. In rational choice theories, the link is made by positing the conditions under which it is rational to develop structures and cultural systems that impose constraints on options and decision making. In both types of approach, there is still ample room for conceptualizing the linkages between micro and macro processes.

There are limits, however, to how far an exchange perspective can go without incorporating key dynamics from other theoretical perspectives. For example, Lawler greatly extended exchange theory by introducing ideas from symbolic interactionism, especially individuals' need to verify identities as an important emotion-arousing process that pervades all exchanges. Indeed, as we will see in the next chapter, some symbolic interactionist approaches have already met exchange theorizing half-way in positing exchange dynamics in the dynamics of identity formation and verification.

CHAPTER 16

Symbolic Interactionist Theorizing

S*ymbolic interactionism* is the term given to George Herbert Mead's foundational work by Herbert Blumer, who took over Mead's famous social psychology course at the University of Chicago after the latter's death in 1931. I am not sure if Mead would have approved this label, but it has stuck for many decades, and thus, the discipline is forced to use a label that does not, in my mind, fully communicate the thrust of interactionist theorizing. In particular, as it has evolved over the last eighty years, symbolic interactionism has tended to focus on the dynamics of self more than either symbols or interaction. People's behaviors in interaction with others in social settings are, to be sure, conducted in terms of symbolic meanings, but the interaction itself is governed by individuals' conceptions and evaluations of themselves. Self serves as a kind of gyroscope for keeping behaviors consistent and in line; and as has increasingly been emphasized in symbolic interactionist theory, individuals are motivated to verify their sense of self in the eyes of others and in the eyes of generalized others or the cultural frames of the situation.

The notion of *identity* became one prominent way to reconceptualize self over the last few decades.[1] In general terms, self is now viewed as a set or series of identities

---

[1]Apart from these figures, others seeking a theory of self and identity include Eugene Weinstein, Mary Glenn Wiley, and William DeVaughn, "Role and Interpersonal Style as Components of Interaction," *Social Forces* 45 (1966):210–216; Peter J. Burke and Judy C. Tully, "The Measurement of Role/Identity," *Social Forces* 55 (1977):881–897; Nelson N. Foote, "Identification as the Basis for a Theory of Motivation," *American Sociological Review* 16 (1951):14–21; Tamotsu Shibutani, *Society and Personality* (Englewood Cliffs, NJ: Prentice-Hall, 1961); Anselm Strauss, *Mirrors and Masks* (Glencoe, IL: Free Press, 1959); Gregory P. Stone, "Appearance and the Self," in *Behavior and Social Processes*, ed. Arnold M. Rose (Boston, MA: Houghton Mifflin, 1962). For a review of the history of identity and self theories, see Viktor Gecas and Peter J. Burke, "Self and Identity," in *Sociological Perspectives on Social Psychology*, ed. Karen S. Cook, Gary Alan Fine, and James S. House (Boston, MA: Allyn and Bacon, 1995), 41–67. For a very recent review of identity theories, see Peter J. Burke and Jan E. Stets, *Identity Theory* (New York: Oxford University Press, 2009).

that can be invoked individually or simultaneously in situations, but once salient, individuals' actions are directed at having others verify their identity or identities. At the same time, identities can act as filters of selective perception and interpretation as individuals mutually role-take with one another.

Thus, the effort to develop a more refined theory of self has been the major thrust of much interactionist theorizing. In this chapter, I will review several of these new theories of identity dynamics. Moreover, the most recent work on identity processes has converged with the sociology of emotions for the obvious reason that people put their identities on the line during an interaction; and depending upon whether they succeed or fail in verifying an identity or identities, the emotions that are aroused will shape the subsequent flow of the interaction and, over time, the structure of a person's identity system.

Sheldon Stryker's Identity Theory

Designations and Definitions

In Sheldon Stryker's view,[2] human social behavior is organized by symbolic designations of all aspects of the environment, both physical and social. Among the most important of these designations are the symbols, and their associated meanings, of the positions that people occupy in social structures. These positions carry with them shared expectations about how people are to enact roles and, in general, to comport themselves in relation to others. As individuals designate their own positions, they call forth in themselves expectations about how they are to behave, and as they designate the positions of others, they become cognizant of the expectations guiding the role behaviors of these others. They also become aware of broader frames of reference and definitions of the situation as these positional designations are made. And most important, individuals designate themselves as objects in relation to their location in structural positions and their perceptions of broader definitions of the situation.

Behavior is, however, not wholly determined or dictated by these designations and definitions. True, people are almost always aware of the expectations associated with positions, but as they present themselves to others, the form and content of the interaction can change. The amount of such change will vary with the type of larger

---

[2]Sheldon Stryker, *Symbolic Interactionism: A Structural Version* (Menlo Park, CA: Benjamin/Cummings, 1980), "Identity Salience and Role Performance: The Relevance of Symbolic Interaction Theory for Family Research," *Journal of Marriage and the Family* (1968):558–564, "Fundamental Principles of Social Interaction," in *Sociology,* 2nd ed., ed. Neil J. Smelser (New York: Wiley, 1973), 495–547. For a more recent version of the theory, see Sheldon Stryker and Richard T. Serpe, "Commitment, Identity Salience, and Role Behavior," in *Personality, Roles, and Social Behavior,* ed. William Ickes and Eric Knowles (New York: Springer-Verlag, 1982), 199–218; Richard T. Serpe and Sheldon Stryker, "The Construction of Self and the Reconstruction of Social Relationships," *Advances in Group Processes* 4 (1987):41–66; and Sheldon Stryker, "Exploring the Relevance of Social Cognition for the Relationship of Self and Society," in *The Self-Society Dynamic: Cognition, Emotion, and Action,* ed. Judith Howard and Peter L. Callero (Cambridge, UK: Cambridge University Press, 1991), 19–41.

social structure within which the interaction occurs; some structures are open and flexible, whereas others are more closed and rigid. Still, all structures impose limits and constraints on what individuals do when engaged in face-to-face interaction.

Identities and the Salience Hierarchy

Stryker reasoned that identities are "parts" of a larger sense of self, and as such, they are internalized self-designations that are associated with the positions that individuals occupy within various social contexts. Identity is thus a critical link between the individual and the social structure, because identities are designations that people make about themselves in relation to their location in social structures and the roles that they play by virtue of this location. Identities are organized into a *salience hierarchy*, and those identities high in the hierarchy are more likely to be evoked than those lower in this hierarchy. Not all situations will invoke multiple identities, but many do. The salience hierarchy determines those identities that are invoked by people as they orchestrate their roles and interpret the role behaviors of others. As a general rule, Stryker proposes that when an interaction situation is isolated from structural constraints, or these structural constraints are ambiguous, individuals will have more options in their choice of an identity, and hence, they will be more likely to evoke more than one identity. But as a situation becomes embedded within social structures, the salience hierarchy becomes a good predictor of what identities will be used in interaction with others.

Commitment and Self

Stryker introduced the idea of *commitment* as a means of conceptualizing the link between social structure and self. *Commitment* designates the degree to which a person's relationship to others depends on being a certain kind of individual with a particular identity. The greater this dependence is, the more a person will be committed to a particular identity and the higher this identity will be in the person's salience hierarchy. Having an identity that is based on the views of others, as well as on broader social definitions, will tend to produce behaviors that conform to these views and definitions.

When people reveal such commitment to an identity in a situation, their sense of self-esteem becomes dependent on the successful execution of their identity. Moreover, when an identity is established by reference to the norms, values, and other symbols of the broader society, esteem is even more dependent on successful implementation of the identity. In this way, cultural definitions and expectations, social structural location, identity, and esteem associated with that identity all become interwoven. And in this process, social structure constrains behavior and people's perceptions of themselves and others.

The Key Propositions

In the early version of the theory, Stryker developed a series of "hypotheses" about the conditions producing the salience of an identity, the effects of identities high in the salience hierarchy on role behaviors, the influence of commitment on esteem, and the nature of changes in identity. These are rephrased somewhat and summarized in Table 16.1. To state Stryker's argument more discursively, here is what he proposed: the more individuals reveal commitment to an identity, the higher this identity will be in the salience hierarchy. If this identity is positively evaluated in terms of the reactions of others and broader value standards, then this identity will move up a person's hierarchy. When the expectations of others are congruent and consistent, revealing few conflicts and disagreements, individuals will be even more committed to the identity presented to these others because they "speak with the same voice." And finally, when the network of these others on whom one depends for identity is large and extended, encompassing many others rather than just a few, the higher in the salience hierarchy will this identity become.

Once an identity is high in the salience hierarchy of an individual, role performances will become ever more consistent with the expectations attached to this

Table 16.1   A Revised Formulation of Stryker's Hypotheses on the Salience of Identity

1. The more individuals are committed to an identity, the higher will this identity be in their salience hierarchy.

2. The degree of commitment to an identity is a positive and additive function of
 	
    A. The extent to which this identity is positively valued by others and broader cultural definitions
    B. The more congruent the expectations of others on whom one depends for an identity
    C. The more extensive the network of individuals on whom one depends
    D. The larger the number of persons in a network on whom one depends for an identity.

The Consequences of High Salience

3. The higher in a person's salience hierarchy is an identity, the more likely will that individual
 	
    A. Emit role performances that are consistent with the role expectations associated with that identity
    B. Perceive a given situation as an opportunity to perform in that identity
    C. Seek out situations that provide opportunities to perform in that identity.

The Consequences of Commitment to Identity

4. The greater the commitment to an identity, the greater will be
 	
    A. The effect of role performances on self-esteem
    B. The likelihood that role performances will reflect institutionalized values and norms.

Changing Commitments to Identity
5. The more external events alter the structure of a situation, the more likely are individuals to adopt new or novel identities.
6. The more changes in identity reinforce and reflect the value commitments of the individual, the less the individual resists change in adopting a new identity.

identity. Moreover, when an identity is high in the salience hierarchy, individuals will tend to perceive situations as opportunities to play out this identity in roles, and they will actively seek out situations where they can use this identity. In this way, the congruence between those identities high in people's hierarchies and their expectations for identity verification from situations increases.

This congruence increases commitment because individuals come to see their identities as depending on the continued willingness of others to confirm their identities. As commitment increases, and as individuals become dependent on confirmation of their identities by others, their role performances have ever more consequences for their level of self-esteem. Moreover, as people become committed to identities and these identities move up in their salience hierarchy, they come to evaluate their role performances through broader cultural definitions and normative expectations; as people make such evaluations, they become even more committed to their identities.

External events can, however, erode commitments to an identity. When this occurs, people are more likely to adopt new identities, even novel identities. As individuals begin to seek new identities, change is likely to move in the direction of those identities that reflect their values. In this way, cultural values pull the formation of new identities in directions that will increase the congruence between cultural definitions and role performance as individuals develop new identity commitments and as their self-esteem becomes dependent on successful role performance of these identity commitments.

Identity and Emotions

Emotions are implicated in these processes in several ways.[3] First, those role enactments that generate positive affect and reinforcement from others in a situation strengthen a person's commitment to an identity, moving it higher in the salience hierarchy. As individuals receive this positive feedback from others, their self-esteem is enhanced, which further increases commitment to the identity, raising it in the salience hierarchy and increasing the chances that this identity will shape subsequent role performances.

Second, when the role performances of a person and others are judged to be inadequate in light of normative expectations, cultural values, definitions of the situation, or identities being asserted, negative emotional reactions mark this inadequacy. Conversely, when role performances are adequate or even more than adequate and exemplary, positive emotions signal this fact. Thus, emotions are *markers of adequacy* in role performances, telling individuals that their performances are acceptable or unacceptable. This marking function of emotions works in several ways. The individual reads the gestures of others to see if a role performance has

---

[3]Sheldon Stryker, "The Interplay of Affect and Identity: Exploring the Relationship of Social Structure, Social Interaction, Self, and Emotions" (paper presented at the American Sociological Association meetings, Chicago, IL, 1987); Sheldon Stryker and Richard Serpe, "Commitment, Identity Salience, and Role Behavior: Theory and a Research Example," in *Personality, Roles, and Social Behavior,* ed. W. Ickes and E. Knowles (New York: Springer-Verlag, 1982), 199–218.

been accepted, and if it has, then the person experiences positive emotions and will become further committed to the identity presented in the role performance. If, on the other hand, the reaction is less than positive, then the individual will experience negative emotions—such as *anger* at self, *shame*, and *guilt*—and mobilize to improve the role performance or, if this is not possible, to lower the commitment to the identity being asserted in this role, moving it lower in the salience hierarchy and, thereby, causing selection of a different identity that can be more adequately played out in the role. Not only do individuals get emotional about their own performances as they role-take with others and assess themselves in light of the responses of others, but they also inform others about the latter's role performances. Because role performances must be coordinated and meshed together to be effective, inadequate performance by others will disrupt one's own role performance, and if this occurs, a person will manifest some form of *anger* and negatively sanction others. Thus, emotions become ways for individuals to mutually signal and mark the adequacy of their respective role performances in ways that facilitate the coordination and integration of roles.

Finally, emotions are also a sign of *which* identities are high in a person's salience hierarchy. If emotional reactions are intense when a role performance fails or when it is successful, this intensity indicates that a person is committed to the identity being played in the role and that it is high in the salience hierarchy. Conversely, if the emotional reaction of the individual is of low intensity, then this might signal that the identity is lower in the salience hierarchy and relatively unimportant to the individual.

In identity theory, then, emotions motivate individuals to play roles in which they receive positive reinforcement, and emotions also inform individuals about the adequacy of their performances and their commitments to identities in the salience hierarchy. Emotions thus drive individuals to play roles in ways that are consistent with normative expectations, definitions of the situation, cultural values, and highly salient feelings about self.

George J. McCall's and J. L. Simmons's Theory of Identity

Role Identity and Role Support

In contrast with Stryker's more structural theory, where culture and social structure designate many of the identities held by individuals, George J. McCall and J. L. Simmons[4] emphasized that roles are typically improvised as individuals seek to realize their various plans and goals. A role identity is, therefore, "the character and the role that an individual devises for himself (herself as well) as an occupant of a particular social position."[5] Role identity constitutes an "imaginative view of oneself"

---

[4]George P. McCall and J. L. Simmons, *Identities and Interactions* (New York: Basic Books, 1960). A second edition of this book was published in 1978, although the theory remained virtually unchanged.

[5]Ibid., p. 67.

in a position, often a rather idealized view of oneself. Each role identity thus has a conventional portion linked to positions in social structure as well as an idiosyncratic portion constructed in people's imaginations.

Role identities become part of individuals' plans and goals because legitimating one's identity in the eyes of others is always a driving force of human behavior. Moreover, people evaluate themselves through the role performances intended to confirm a role identity. But, as McCall and Simmons emphasized, the most important audiences for a role performance are the individuals themselves, who assess their performances with respect to their own idealized view of their role identity. Still, people must also seek role support from relevant audiences outside their own minds for their role identities. This support involves more than audiences granting a person the right to occupy a position, and it includes more than approval from others for conduct by those in a position. For an individual to feel legitimated in a role, audiences must also approve of the more expressive content—the style, emotion, manner, and tone—of role performances designed to legitimate a role identity.

Because much of a role identity is rather idealized in the individual's mind and because a person must seek legitimization along several fronts, there is always discrepancy and disjuncture between the role identity and the role support received for that identity. People idealize too much, and they must seek support for performances that can be misinterpreted. As a result, there is almost always some *dissatisfaction* by individuals about how much their role identity has been legitimated by audiences. These points of disjuncture between identity and legitimating support motivate and drive individual behavior. Indeed, for McCall and Simmons, the most distinctive emotion among humans is the "drive to acquire support for (their) idealized conceptions of (themselves)."

The Mechanisms for Maintaining Role Support

To overcome the discrepancy between what people desire and get in role support for an identity, several mechanisms are employed. One is the accumulation of *short-term credit* from interactions where discrepancies have been minimal; these emotional credits can then carry individuals through episodes where the responses from others provide less than whole-hearted role support. A second mechanism is *selective perception of cues* from others, where individuals only see those responses confirming an identity. A third mechanism is *selective interpretation* of cues, whereby the individual sees the cues accurately but puts "a spin" or interpretation on them that supports a role identity. A fourth mechanism is *withdrawing from interactions* that do not support an identity and seeking alternative situations where more support can be garnered. A fifth mechanism is *switching to a new role identity* whose performance will bring more support from others. A sixth mechanism is *scapegoating* audiences, blaming them for causing the discrepancy between performance and support. A seventh mechanism is *disavowing unsuccessful performances* that individuals had hoped to legitimate. And a final defensive mechanism is deprecating and *rejecting the audience* that withholds support for a role identity. When these mechanisms fail, individuals experience misery and anguish, and through such experiences, people learn to be cautious in committing themselves so openly and fully to particular role performances in front of certain audiences.[6]

The Hierarchy of Prominence

The cohesiveness role identities of individuals vary, McCall and Simmons argued, in how the elements of an identity fit together and in the compatibility among various role identities. There is also a hierarchy of prominence among role identities; although this hierarchy can shift and change as circumstances dictate, it tends to exist at any given point in an interaction. This prominence reflects the idealized view of individuals, the extent to which these ideals have been supported by audiences, the degree to which individuals have committed themselves to these identities, the extrinsic and intrinsic rewards (to be discussed later) associated with an identity, and the amount of previous investment in time and energy that has been devoted to an identity.

From this perspective, interaction revolves around individuals asserting through role performances identities that are high in their prominence hierarchy and that they seek to legitimate, in their own eyes as well as in the eyes of others. At the same time, each individual is interpreting the gestures of others to determine just what identity is high in the prominence hierarchy of others and whether or not the role performances of others are worthy of role support and other rewards. To some degree, the external structure of the situation provides the necessary information about what positions people occupy and what expectations are placed on them by virtue of incumbency in these positions. Yet, for McCall and Simmons, most interactions are to some degree ambiguous and unstructured, allowing alternative role performances and varying interpretations of these performances.

Much of the ambiguity in interaction is eliminated through simple role-taking in a person's "inner forum" or cognitive repertoire of vocabularies, gestures, motives, and other information that marks various identities and role performances. Humans have, therefore, the capacity to construct interpretations in light of the vast amounts of information that they accumulate in their inner forum, or what Alfred Schutz called "stocks of knowledge at hand." This information might have to be assembled in somewhat "different proportions and balances" but humans' capacity for mind and thought enables them to do so with amazing speed and accuracy.

Individuals will often improvise a role, adjusting their identities and role performances in light of how they interpret the roles of others. As such improvisation occurs, various expressive strategies are employed; these strategies revolve around orchestrating gestures to present a certain image of self and to claim a particular identity that is high in the prominence hierarchy. Conversely, individuals read the dramaturgical presentations of others to "altercast" and determine the self that is being claimed by these others. In essence, then, interaction is the negotiation of identities whereby people make expressive and dramaturgical presentations over identities that are high in their respective prominence hierarchies and that can be supported, or that can go unsupported, on the basis of role performances.

---

[6]Ibid., p. 75.

The Underlying Exchange Dynamic

This process of negotiation among individuals is complex and subtle, involving an initial but very tentative agreement to accept each others' claims. In this way, people avoid interrupting the expressive strategies that are being used to impart their respective identities. As this process unfolds, however, it moves into a real exchange negotiation whereby individuals seek the rewards that come with legitimization of their role performances. At this point, McCall and Simmons merge their interactionist theory with exchange theory.

They begin by classifying three basic types of rewards: First, there are *extrinsic rewards*, such as money or other reinforcers that are visible to all. Second, there are *intrinsic rewards*, which provide less visible means of reinforcement for the individual—rewards such as satisfaction, pride, and comfort. And third, and most important, there is *support for an identity*, which McCall and Simmons believe is the most valuable of all rewards. Individuals are motivated to seek a profit—rewards less the costs of securing them—in all their interactions. Moreover, there are separate types of calculi for each of these three categories of reward, and there are rules of the marketplace: the rewards received by each party to an exchange should be roughly comparable in their type (whether extrinsic, intrinsic, or identity support), and rewards should be received in proportion to the investments individuals incur in receiving them (a principle of "distributive justice").

These negotiations are affected by what McCall and Simmons term *the salience of identities*, which are those identities that, for the immediate interaction at hand, are the most relevant in an individual's hierarchy of prominence. This salience of identities constitutes, in McCall and Simmons's words, a situated self that is most pertinent to the present interaction. This situational self determines a person's preferences about which role identities he or she will enact in a given situation, but the preferences of the situational self are fluid and changeable. In contrast, the ideal self is more stable than the situated self, while being the highest-order identity in the prominence hierarchy. A person's ideal self will thus influence which identities should be salient in an interaction and how they will be invoked to constitute a situated self. Besides the prominence hierarchy, other factors also influence the formation of a situated identity. The needs that an individual feels for support of an identity, the extrinsic and intrinsic rewards to be received by claiming a situated self, and the opportunity for profitable enactment of a role in relation to a situated self, all shape identity formation.

All these factors are, in McCall and Simmons's view, potential reinforcers or payoffs for roles emitted in claiming an identity. These payoffs vary in value, however. Support of the *ideal self* brings greater rewards than either extrinsic or intrinsic rewards. The patterns of payoffs for rewards can also vary. For extrinsic and intrinsic types of rewards, when payoffs match expectations and desires, needs for them decline somewhat (in accordance with satiation or the principle of marginal utility). If people receive either more or less than they expected or desired of these two types of rewards, then their immediate need for these rewards suddenly escalates. In contrast, the payoff schedule for role support for an identity reveals a more complicated pattern. Role support that is equal to what was desired or expected does not increase the desire for further role support of an identity. A moderate discrepancy between the support sought and received increases the desire for support of an identity. But extreme discrepancies operate differently, depending on the sign of the discrepancy: if people receive support that greatly exceeds their expectations, they immediately desire more role support, whereas if they receive significantly less role support than expected, their desire for this role support drops rapidly.

Because payoffs will almost always, or at least eventually, be less than expected, discrepancies will be chronic, even after individuals have employed all the defense mechanisms to reduce discrepancies that were discussed earlier. Hence, people are constantly driven to overcome this discrepancy, but this search to reduce discrepancy is complicated by the payoff schedule for role support. Moderate discrepancies drive people to seek more role support, whereas large ones reduce efforts to secure role support for an identity. And when people have received more support than they expected for an identity, they want even more of this reward, raising this identity in salience and, over time, increasing its prominence in the hierarchy.

Peter J. Burke's Identity Control Theory

Working squarely within the symbolic interactionist tradition, Peter Burke and various colleagues, particularly Jan E. Stets, have developed yet another variant of identity theory.[7] For Burke, individuals carry general views of themselves to all situations, or an *idealized self*, but it is the *working self* or *self-image* that guides moment-to-moment interaction.[8] The idealized self may, of course, influence just how individuals see themselves in a situation, but the key dynamics of self revolve around trying to verify this working self or self-image in situations as individuals play roles. At other times,[9] Burke has also conceptualized self as a rough hierarchy. At the more abstract level is a *principle self*, in which cultural standards contained in broader values and beliefs become part of how individuals see themselves, but this principle-level self influences behavior in situations through *a program-level identity* consisting of the goals that individuals seek to realize in a concrete situation. In general, the more a program-level identity is guided by a principle-level self and the more the goals of the program-level self are realized in a situation, the greater will be persons' sense of efficacy and the more positive are their sentiments toward themselves and

---

[7]Peter J. Burke, "The Self: Measurement Implications from a Symbolic Interactionist Perspective," *Social Psychology Quarterly* 43 (1980):18–20, "An Identity Model for Network Exchange," *American Sociological Review* 62 (1997):134–150, "Attitudes, Behavior, and the Self" in *The Self-Society Dynamic*, 189–208, "Identity Processes and Social Stress," *American Sociological Review* 56 (1991):836–849; P. J. Burke and D. C. Reitzes, "An Identity Theory Approach to Commitment," *Social Psychology Quarterly* 54 (1991):239–251; P. J. Burke and Jan E. Stets, "Trust and Commitment through Self Verification," *Social Psychology Quarterly* 62 (1999):347–366; Peter J. Burke and Jan E. Stets, *Identity Theory* (New York: Oxford University Press, 2009).

[8]Burke, "The Self: Measurement Implications."

[9]T. Tsushima and P. J. Burke, "Levels, Agency, and Control in Parent Identity," *Social Psychology Quarterly* 62 (1999):173–189.

the situation.[10] Yet, unlike other identity theories, Burke's approach does not place great emphasis on a salience or prominence hierarchy. Instead, the theory seeks to explain the internal dynamics of self as individuals play a role in an effort to verify the identity associated with this role.

Role Identities

For Burke, self is an occupant of a role in a situation. This situation is, in turn, typically embedded in a larger social structure and associated cultural meanings. Roles are thus the link between self, on the one side, and social structure and culture, on the other. By virtue of playing a role, individuals incorporate the meanings and expectations associated with this role into their identity in the situation. Individuals have diverse experiences, and any role has multiple meanings; so the identities associated with a role will vary from person to person. Burke's identity theory, however, is less concerned with the actual content of a role identity than with the dynamics of how this identity is sustained in interaction with others in a situation. This emphasis leads Burke to see identity as a cybernetic control system, as individuals seek to regulate their behaviors so that others will verify their identity in a role.

Identity as a Cybernetic Control System

In conceptualizing identity as a cybernetic control system, Burke sees the dynamics of this system as revolving around the following elements:[11]

1. An *identity standard* operating as a *comparator* or criterion for assessing whether or not an identity is verified and for directing initial behavior in a role

2. A set of inputs from others who are responding to the behaviors of a person playing a role and asserting an identity

3. A comparison of inputs with the comparator to determine if the responses of others are congruent with the identity standard guiding role behaviors

4. A set of behavioral outputs on the environment guided by the degree to which inputs match the identity standard contained in the comparator

These elements are delineated in Figure 16.1. Individuals have a set of meanings about their identity in a situation. This identity is translated into a standard that, in turn, becomes a comparator or basis for matching inputs to the standard to see if, indeed, the standard has been realized. As individuals play a role in a situation, they emit outputs of meaningful behavior on the environment, particularly to other individuals in the situation, who, in turn, respond to these behavioral outputs. As individuals emitting outputs role-take with others in a situation, they experience

---

[10]Ibid. See also Burke, "Identity Processes and Social Stress."

[11]Ibid.

Figure 16.1 The Cybernetic Control System in Burke's Theory

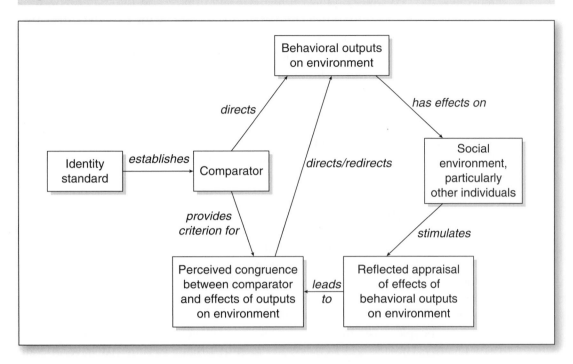

"reflected appraisals" that become inputs of self-meanings that are compared with the identity standard. Depending on whether or not the identity standard is met, the next round of behavioral outputs will vary. When the identity standard is realized, individuals will experience more positive emotions, and their subsequent behavioral outputs will revolve around commitments to others in the situation. When inputs from others signal that the identity standard is not realized, people will experience negative emotions, and the next round of behavioral outputs will seek to change the responses of others so that a role identity can be confirmed.

Thus, in Burke's theory, humans are motivated to have inputs match up with identity standards. Behavior is goal directed, in the sense that individuals try to elicit from others in a situation responses that match their identity standard. To achieve this result, individuals orchestrate their gestures and use other signs[12] in behavioral performances that, they hope, will allow them to receive inputs that match the identity standard.

In Burke's model, a separate control system is operative for each identity.[13] That is, if multiple identities are presented in a situation, each is guided by the dynamics outlined in Figure 16.1. For example, if a professor seeks to present an identity as

---

[12]Lee Freese and Peter J. Burke, "Persons, Identities, and Social Interaction," in *Advances in Group Processes,* ed. Barry Markovsky, K. Heimer, and Jody O'Brien (Greenwich, CT: JAI Press, 1994), 1–24.

[13]Peter J. Burke, "Relationships among Multiple Identities" (paper presented at The Future of Identity Theory and Research Conference in Bloomington, IN, 2001).

both an intellectual and a sexually attractive person, then two role identities—intellectual and sexy—are revealed in behavioral outputs, and two cybernetic control systems revolving around two comparators (dictated by the two identities), two sets of inputs, two comparisons, and two outputs are operative. However, higher-level identities—or what Burke sometimes terms *principle-level identities*—often provide more general frames of reference for lower-level or program identities, thereby simplifying the control process. For instance, if a college professor is in the classroom, the higher-level identity revolving around beliefs in the importance of intellectual activity, per se, may provide guidance for how the lower-level program identity of being sexually attractive is to be orchestrated in role behaviors. In this way, the two identities are not contradictory, and the control systems guiding efforts at confirmation will not work at cross-purposes.

Multiple Identities

In recent years, Burke, in collaboration with Jan Stets,[14] has identified three types of identities: (1) person identity, or an individual self-conception (or what some call core identity); (2) role identity, tied to particular roles; and (3) social identity, tied to a social group. Individuals can have all three of these identities in play during an interaction, but the dynamics of identity control operate in the manner described above. Also, people have different levels of identity, such as a principle identity or a moral identity. These too, as well as other identities that a person may have, operate in the same cybernetic manner outlined in Figure 16.1.

Since many potential identities can be in play at any given moment for a person, identity control dynamics can become complicated. Still, there is probably some limit on how many identities can be salient since humans have limited cognitive capacities to store the relevant information and bring it to bear in a particular situation.

Identity and Emotions

Burke and Jan Stets have explored in a number of research projects the effects of identity verification, or the failure to verify an identity, on people's emotional arousal.[15] When role identities are verified by the responses of others, people will experience positive emotions, and moreover, they will generally have enhanced self-esteem, which can insulate them from the negative efforts of periodic failures to confirm the identity. When a role identity is not verified, people will experience *distress*, *anxiety*, and other negative emotions, including lowered self-esteem.

Identity Verification. If a role identity is consistently confirmed in interaction with others, individuals will increasingly come to trust these others; they will develop commitments to these others; they will reveal emotional attachments to

---

[14]Burke and Stets, *Identity Theory*; see table on p. 129.

[15]Burke and Stets, "Trust and Commitment through Self Verification."

these others; and they will become more oriented to the group and social structure in which the role identity is confirmed. For example, a person whose identity standard demands that he or she be considered a "good student" will feel positive emotions toward others, such as professors and fellow students, when this identity is confirmed; if this verification consistently occurs in school situations, this person will trust these others, develop attachments to them, and become oriented to the intellectual culture of the university community.

As a role identity is verified across repeated encounters with others in a situation, not only does the individual trust these others and develop commitments and emotional attachments to them and the structure of the situation, but also the salience to the person of the role identity being presented increases. And the more salient an identity—that is, the more important it is to the individual and the more it guides behavioral outputs—the greater the motivation of the individual to ensure that inputs from the environment do indeed confirm this identity. Thus, a student who has enjoyed success in confirming the role identity of a good student will be increasingly motivated to verify this identity as it takes on greater salience.

Failure to Verify Identity. More interesting, perhaps, are situations where inputs from others' responses do not match the identity standard. Several conditions produce this outcome. One is where a person's outputs cannot change the situation, no matter how hard he or she tries; under these conditions, a person experiences a loss of efficacy and a greater sense of *alienation, disaffection,* and *estrangement*. For instance, a person who cannot match performance with a work identity and, yet, who cannot leave his or her job will experience this range of negative emotions. Another condition is interference from other identities possessed by a person, where confirmation of one role identity does not allow another to be confirmed. For instance, a person who has an identity as a "good student" and a "great athlete" will often discover in college that only one of these two identities can be consistently confirmed. Still another condition is an overcontrolled identity, in which the elements of a role identity are so rigidly woven together that a person sees a perceived slight to one of these elements as an attack on all elements. Such identities will be difficult to verify, even if most of the elements are accepted by others in the situation, because the individual is simply too rigid in his or her expectations of how others should respond. A final condition increasing the likelihood of failure to verify an identity is where an identity is only episodically played out in a role or only occasionally becomes salient, with the result that the individual is simply out of practice in emitting the behavioral outputs that allow others to verify the identity.[16]

Whatever the source of incongruence between the expectations dictated by an identity standard and the responses of others, the stage is set for distressful responses from individuals who experience this inconsistency. Several conditions

---

[16]Burke, "Identity and Social Stress," "Social Identities and Psychosocial Stress," in *Perspectives on Structure, Theory, Life-Course, and Methods*, ed. H. Kaplan (San Diego, CA: Academic Press, 1996); Burke and Stets, *Identity Theory*, 77–79.

increase the level of distress experienced. One is the importance of the others to a person who have failed to verify a role identity. The more significant to an individual are others whose responses fail to match identity standards, the more intense is the sense of *distress* and the more motivated is the individual to adjust behavioral outputs to secure the appropriate responses from these significant others. Another condition is the salience of the role identity itself. The more important to a person the verification of a role identity in a situation, the more distressed that person will become when this identity is not verified. Still another condition is that the more a role identity reflects a commitment to others and the group, the more intense is the sense of distress when others do not verify the identity, especially if this identity is built around principle-level elements or the cultural values and beliefs of the group. Another condition influencing the level of stress is the direction and degree of incongruity between the expectations set by a role identity and the non-confirming responses of others. When the responses of others fall below expectations, individuals will experience distress and be motivated to adjust behavioral outputs to secure verifying responses from others. More complicated is the individual's response when the expectations established by an identity standard are exceeded. Preliminary research indicates that the degree to which expectations are exceeded determines the responses of individuals.[17] The more expectations are exceeded, the more individuals are forced to adjust their identity standards and, as a result, the more they will experience distress, whereas if expectations are exceeded to a more moderate degree, the identity standards do not have to be radically adjusted and, hence, the person will experience positive emotions.

Failure to verify an identity repeatedly will, over time, cause less intense negative emotions because people begin to adjust their identity standards downward, lowering their expectations of how others will respond.[18] But when an identity standard is not initially verified, individuals will adjust their outputs in an effort to get the identity verified. Thus, for example, a student who has the identity of "good student" will study much harder if he or she does not meet expectations on an examination, although if this individual consistently fails to do well, the role identity and expectations associated with this identity will be adjusted downward, and the student's motivation to study harder will likely decline. Another option when an identity standard is not verified is for the individual to leave the situation, if possible, and thereby avoid the negative emotions that come from the incongruities between expectations and the responses of others.

---

[17]Jan E. Stets and Michael J. Carter, "A Theory of the Self for the Sociology of Morality," *American Sociological Review* 77 (2012):120–140, "The Moral Self: Applying Identity Theory," *Social Psychology Quarterly* 74 (2011):192–215; Jan E. Stets, "Applying Identity Theory to Moral Acts of Commission and Omission," *Advances in Group Processes* 28 (2011):97–124, "The Social Psychology of the Moral Identity," in *Handbook of the Sociology of Morality*, ed. Steven Hitlin and Stephen Vaisey (New York: Springer, 2010), 385–409; Jan E. Stets, Michael J. Carter, Michael M. Harrod, Christine Cerven, and Seth Abrutyn, "The Moral Identity, Moral Emotions, and the Normative Order," in *Social Structure and Emotion*, ed. Jody Clay-Warner and Dawn T. Robinson (San Diego, CA: Elsevier), 227–251.

[18]Ibid.

CHAPTER 16: Symbolic Interactionist Theorizing   **589**

In sum, Burke's identity theory generates a number of testable propositions, some of which are summarized in Table 16.2. These and other propositions are implied by the theory, but equally important, they also come from efforts to test the theory. Although some research has been performed on the other identity theories summarized in this chapter, Burke's theory is subject to ongoing research. The generalizations offered in this chapter have, to varying degrees, been confirmed by research. Moreover, in recent years, efforts have been made to reconcile Burke's identity theory with that offered by Stryker as well as by McCall and Simmons,[19] and so it is likely that in the future various theories of self can become more unified.

Table 16.2   Key Propositions of Burke's Identity Theory

1. The more salient an identity in a role, the more motivated are individuals to achieve a sense of congruence between the expectations established by the identity standard and the responses of others in a situation.
2. The more the responses of others match the expectations dictated by an identity standard, the more positive are the emotions experienced by individuals and the greater their self-esteem, and the more enhanced are positive emotions toward self, the more likely are individuals to   A. Develop a sense of trust with others who have verified their identity   B. Develop emotional attachments to these others   C. Develop commitments to these others   D. Become oriented to the standards of the group in which the situation is embedded.
3. The less the responses of others match an identity standard, the more likely are the emotions experienced by individuals to be negative, with the incongruence between the expectations set by an identity standard and the responses of others increasing with   A. Multiple and incompatible identity standards from two or more role identities   B. An overcontrolled self, in which the elements of the identity are tightly woven and create inflexible identity standards   C. Lack of practice in displaying an identity in a role   D. Consistent failure of efforts to change and/or leave the situation.
4. The intensity of negative emotions from a failure to verify an identity increases with   A. The salience of an identity in the situation   B. The significance of the others who have not verified the identity   C. The degree of incongruity, whether above or below the expectations associated with an identity standard.
5. The intensity of negative emotions from a failure to verify an identity will decrease over time as the identity standard is readjusted downward so as to lower expectations.

---

[19]Jan E. Stets and Peter J. Burke, "A Sociological Approach to Self and Identity Theory," in *Handbook of Self and Identity*, ed. Mark Leary and June Tangney (New York: Guilford Press, 2003), 128–152; Sheldon Stryker and Peter J. Burke, "The Past, Present, and Future of Identity Theory," *Social Psychology Quarterly* 63 (2000):284–297.

Psychoanalytically Oriented Symbolic Interactionist Theories: Thomas Scheff and Jonathan Turner

One of the great shortcomings of George Herbert Mead's synthesis of theories in *Mind, Self, and Society*[20] is that emotions are not examined. The potential to address emotions surrounding self and identity was there in the sources of Mead's synthesis; indeed, Charles Horton Cooley[21] emphasized that people have feelings about themselves as they read the gestures of others in role-taking. Cooley's famous phrase "the looking-glass self" emphasizes that the gestures of others are "a looking glass," or mirror, in which humans see themselves reflected; and on the basis of this reflection, they evaluate themselves and thus develop emotional feelings about themselves as objects in a situation. Moreover, identities are not purely cognitive constructions; they are emotionally charged cognitions, and when self goes unverified, individuals experience negative emotions. For Cooley, people are in a constant state of low-level pride and shame, depending on what they "see" in the looking glass. When the gestures of others signal that a person has behaved properly, this person will experience mild levels of *pride*. But when the gestures of others signal that a person has acted inappropriately, the negative feelings about self will revolve around various levels of *shame*.

Symbolic interactionists who have followed Cooley as much as Mead have generally been sympathetic to psychoanalytic theorizing because, as Sigmund Freud[22] emphasized, negative emotions like *shame* and *guilt* are painful and individuals will often invoke defense mechanisms to protect self. They will repress negative emotions, removing them from consciousness, but these repressed emotions do not disappear in the subconscious; they actively affect how people respond in situations, and moreover, repressed emotions eventually come out in transmuted forms of affect that drive the behaviors of persons in situations.

Several theories examined thus far recognize that emotions are a critical dynamic in identity processes; and McCall and Simmons even go so far as to suggest that individuals invoke "defensive strategies" to protect identities and to avoid experiencing emotional pain. But none of the theories examined above go as far as those willing to incorporate psychoanalytic ideas into symbolic interactionist theorizing. Thomas Scheff has for many decades been the most persistent advocate of incorporating at least elements of psychoanalytical theory into symbolic interactionism. I myself (at one time an undergraduate student in Scheff's classes) have been willing to go much further and bring a full package of psychoanalytic concepts into symbolic interactionist theorizing. Let me first outline Scheff's theory.

---

[20]George Herbert Mead, *Mind, Self, and Society* (Chicago, IL: University of Chicago Press, 1932).

[21]Charles Horton Cooley, *Human Nature and the Social Order* (New York: Schocken Books, 1964; originally published 1902).

[22]Sigmund Freud, *The Interpretation of Dreams* (London: Hogarth Press, 1900).

Thomas Scheff's Theory of Pride and Shame

Thomas Scheff[23] adopts Cooley's view that humans are in a constant state of self-feeling, particularly with respect to *pride* and *shame*. This state of self-feeling is an outcome of the fact that people are also in a constant state of self-evaluation, even when they are alone and think back on situations; and as they evaluate themselves in situations, they will experience either *pride* or *shame*. Pride is a positive emotion that verifies self and thus generates a sense of well-being; moreover, pride generally makes individuals more attuned to others and more willing to offer supportive responses to these others. Thus, pride is a key mechanism by which strong social bonds and social solidarity are generated in face-to-face encounters and, ultimately, in societies. In contrast, shame is a negative emotion and, if unrecognized by a person, leads to a loss of attunement with others and, if widespread among many others, in a society as a whole.

Thus, *pride* and *shame* not only have consequences for individuals' self-feelings, they also affect attunement in social relations and, potentially, the viability of larger-scale social structures, including the society as a whole. Pride and shame, Scheff argues, are emotions that are essential to the social order; yet they are virtually invisible, for several reasons. One is that they are generally experienced at relatively low levels of intensity. Another is that they can be repressed to a certain degree—because a person does not want to reveal "too much" pride to others (lest they see it as vanity) or too much shame to others and to oneself. Scheff borrows from the psychoanalyst Helen Lewis[24] to emphasize that shame is often unacknowledged, denied, or repressed. When such is the case, a shame-anger cycle can be initiated in which *shame* is transmuted to *anger*, with each outburst of anger causing more *shame*, which is denied in ways escalating the intensity of the next outburst of *anger*.

From Lewis, Scheff takes the notion that one path to denying shame is through the experience of *overt, undifferentiated shame*, in which the person has painful feelings that come with shame but hides from the real source of these feelings: shame. The shame is disguised by words and gestures signaling other than shame. People can blush, slow their speech, lower the auditory levels of their voices, and utter words such as "foolish," "silly," "stupid," and other such labels that denote negative feelings but hide the fact that these feelings have arisen because of shame.

Another path to denying the shame is to *bypass the shame*. When this defense mechanism is employed, individuals engage in hyperactive behavior such as rapid

---

[23]For examples of Scheff's work, see "Shame and Conformity: The Deference-Emotion System," *American Sociological Review* 53 (1988):395–406, "Socialization of Emotion: Pride and Shame as Causal Agents," in *Research Agendas in the Sociology of Emotions*, ed. T. Kemper (Albany: SUNY Press, 1990), 281–304, "Shame and the Social Bond: A Sociological Theory," *Sociological Theory* 18 (2000):84–99, "Shame and Community: Social Components in Depression," *Psychiatry* 64 (2001):212–224, and "Shame and Self in Society," *Symbolic Interaction* 26 (2002):239–262.

[24]Helen Lewis, *Shame and Guilt in Neurosis* (New York: International Universities Press, 1971).

speech and demonstrative gesturing before the shame can be fully experienced for what it is. The result is that individuals avoid the pain of shame but at the high cost of having to live with unacknowledged shame, which, in turn, will often disrupt social relations.

Later, Scheff began to term these two paths to denial of shame *under-distancing* (overt, undifferentiated) and *over-distancing* (bypassed) shame. In both cases, the shame is repressed from conscious awareness, ultimately leading to anger and hostility, which, in turn, disrupts interpersonal attunement. Without attunement, it is difficult for individuals to develop mutual respect and solidarity. In Figure 16.2, I have drawn out Scheff's underlying model.

Across the top of the figure, the receipt of deference from others leads to positive self-evaluations and a sense of pride, which encourages interpersonal attunement, mutual respect, and social solidarity. It is the dynamics below this top row of processes that is the cause of problems for persons and, potentially, larger-scale social structures. When individuals perceive that others exhibit a lack of deference, they experience negative self-evaluations that cause shame. If, however, the shame can be "acknowledged" and seen for what it is, it can lead to efforts at *interpersonal attunement,* between a person and others, ultimately causing mutual respect and social solidarity. When the shame is denied by over- or under-distancing, then it initiates the anger-shame cycle, which ensures that individuals will lack proper deference to others and perceive a lack of deference from others. In turn, the negative evaluations will cause shame that, if acknowledged at this point, can perhaps lead to attunement and mutual respect, but if the anger-shame cycle becomes habitual, then the denial of shame only stokes the emotional hostility that sustains the cycle at the bottom of Figure 16.2.

Figure 16.3 outlines some of the more macrostructural implications of the anger-shame cycle outlined in Figure 16.2.[25] If social structures and the culture in the broader society systematically generate shame, as is often the case when relations are hierarchical, but at the same time impose prohibitions against acknowledging shame, societies can reveal the potential for collective violence. If enough persons in enough encounters over long periods of time are forced to endure shame but cannot acknowledge it and, instead, must repress it, the lack of interpersonal attunement and the *shame–anger–more shame–more hostility* cycle are sustained; individuals in this state can be mobilized for collective action, often of a highly violent nature. Thus, if the experience of shame is widespread and if cultural prohibitions inhibit individuals from acknowledging their shame, denial of this negative emotion can become an emotional powder keg in a society. Events at the micro-interpersonal level can, therefore, have far-reaching consequences for the stability of macrostructural formations and their cultures.

---

[25]For examples of work on conflict and violence from repressed shame, see Thomas J. Scheff and Suzanne M. Retzinger, *Emotions and Violence: Shame and Rage in Destructive Conflicts* (Lexington, MA: Lexington Books, 1991). For an example of work by a psychiatrist arguing much the same as Scheff, see Vamik Volkan, *Killing in the Name of Identity: A Study in Bloody Conflicts* (Charlottesville, VA: Pitchstone Press, 2006) and *Bloodlines: From Ethnic Pride to Ethnic Terrorism* (Charlottesville, VA: Pitchstone Press, 1999).

Figure 16.2 Scheff's Model of Emotions, Attunement, and Solidarity

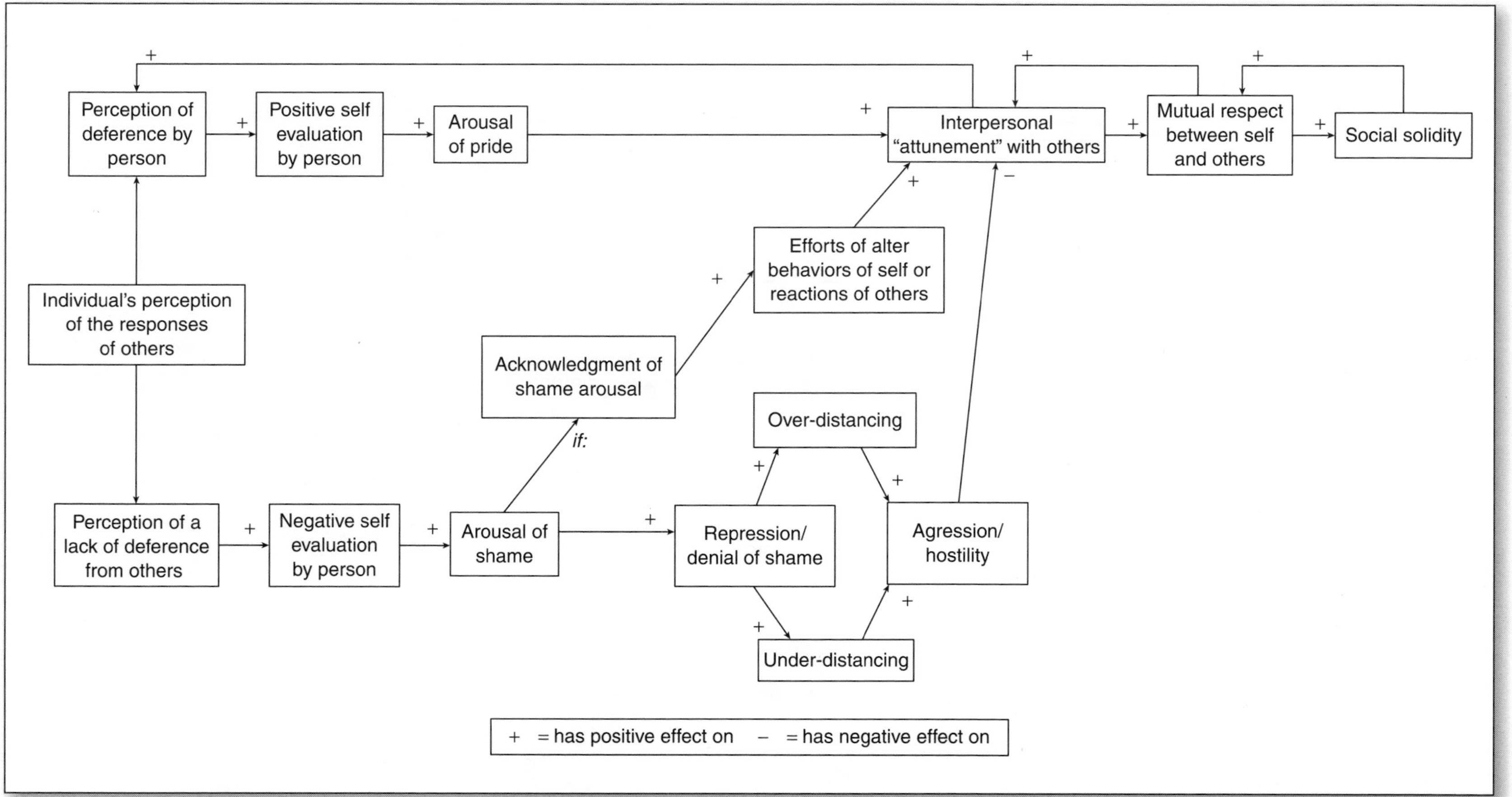

Figure 16.3 Scheff's Model of Emotions, Macrostructures, and Potential for Collective Violence

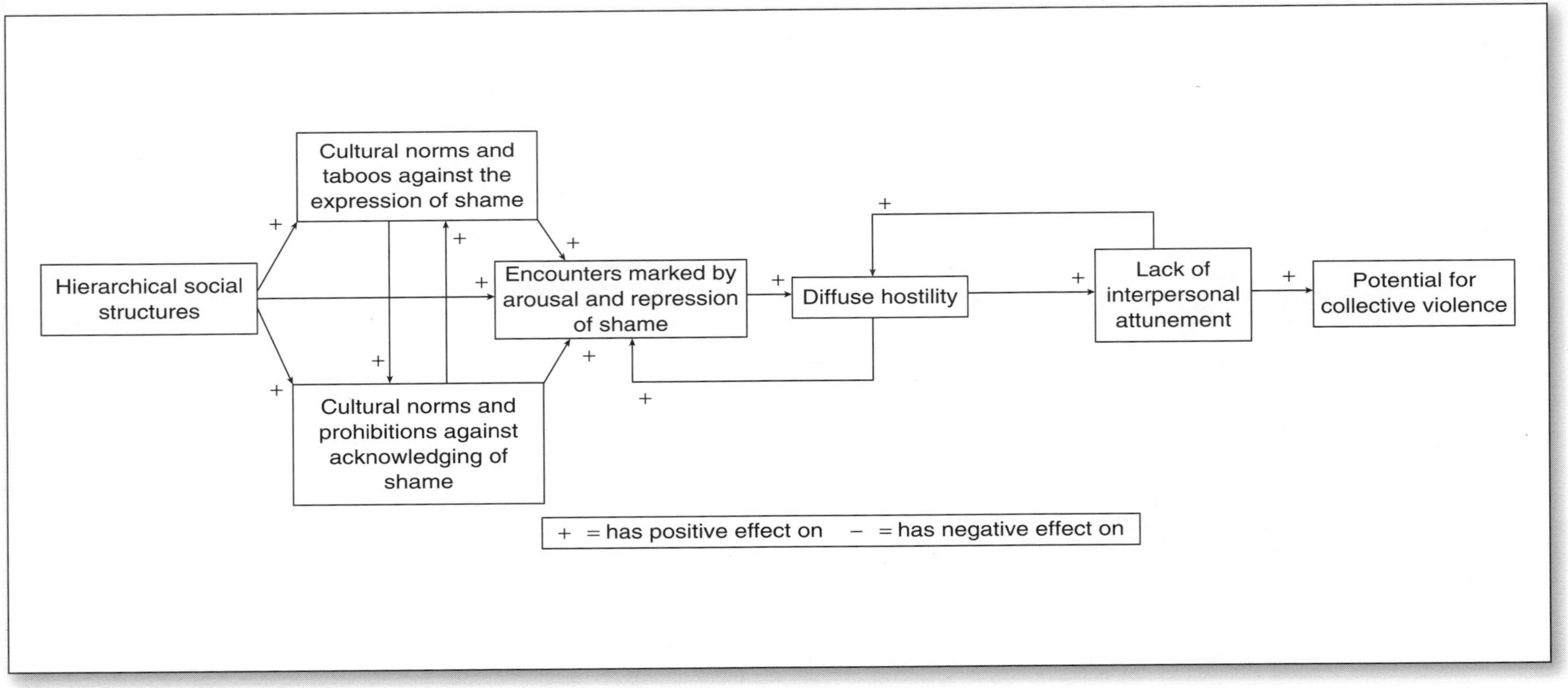

Jonathan Turner's Theory of Emotions and Transactional Needs

As part of my general theory of microdynamic processes,[26] I see *transactional needs* as a critical force in human interaction. Humans have certain fundamental need states that, to varying degrees, are always activated when individuals interact. These are transactional needs in two senses: first, some of these needs, and typically all of them, are activated during interaction, and second, success or failure in meeting these needs dramatically affects the flow of interaction. These needs are listed in Table 16.3, but I will only focus on the most important need in this hierarchy of need states: the need to verify the identities making up self. I have come to visualize self as composed of four fundamental *identities*, although people can probably have an identity about almost anything. For example, recently there has been great interest in people's moral identities[27] or the extent to which, and the arenas in which, people see themselves as "moral." Still, the most central identities are (a) *core identity*, or the fundamental cognitions and feelings that people have about themselves that are generally salient in almost all situations (some have termed this *person identity*); (b) *social identities*, or the cognitions and feelings that people have of themselves as members of social categories (e.g., gender, sexual preference, ethnicity, class, or any social category), that define people as distinctive, and that generally lead to differential evaluation of memberships in social categories; (c) *group identities*, or cognitions and feelings about self that stem from membership in, or identification with, corporate units revealing divisions of labor (groups, communities, and organizations being the most likely sources of a group identity); and (d) *role identities*, or the roles that people play in any social context, but particularly the roles associated with membership in the divisions of labor in corporate units and, at times, memberships in social categories, or what I term *categoric units*. [28]

---

[26]See, for examples, Jonathan H. Turner, *A Theory of Social Interaction* (Stanford, CA: Stanford University Press, 1988), *Face-to-Face: Toward a Sociological Theory of Interpersonal Behavior* (Stanford, CA: Stanford University Press, 2002), *Theoretical Principles of Sociology*, vol. 2: *Microdynamics* (New York: Springer, 2010), *Human Emotions: A Sociological Theory* (London: Routledge, 2008), "Toward a Theory of Embedded Encounters," *Advances in Group Processes* 17 (2000):285–322, "Emotions and Social Structure: Toward a General Theory," in *Emotions and Social Structure*, ed. D. Robinson and J. Clay-Warner (New York: Elsevier, 2008), 319–342, "Self, Emotions, and Extreme Violence: Extending Symbolic Interactionist Theorizing," *Symbolic Interaction* 30 (2008):501–530, "Toward a Theory of Interpersonal Processes," in *Sociological Social Psychology*, ed. J. Chin and J. Cardell (Boston, MA: Allyn and Bacon, 2008), 65–95, and "Identities, Emotions, and Interaction Processes," *Symbolic Interaction* 34 (2011):330–339 and Jonathan H. Turner and Jan E. Stets, "The Moral Emotions," in *Handbook of the Sociology of Emotions*, ed. Jan E. Stets and Jonathan H. Turner (New York: Springer, 2006), 544–568.

[27]See, for example, Jan E. Stets and Michael J. Carter, "A Theory of the Self for the Sociology of Morality," *American Sociological Review* 77 (2012):120–140; see also Steven Hitlin (ed.), *Handbook of the Sociology of Morality* (New York: Springer, 2010) and Steven Hitlin, *Moral Selves, Evil Selves: The Social Psychology of Conscience* (London: Palgrave/Macmillan, 2008).

[28]This label comes from Amos Hawley, *Human Ecology: A Theoretical Essay* (Chicago, IL: University of Chicago Press, 1986). I now use this term to denote a category of persons, seeing this category as constituting a social unit that defines individuals as distinctive, while carrying a level of evaluation of moral worth and a set of expectations for the behavior of persons who are members of such "categoric units."

Table 16.3 Transactional Needs

1. *Verification of identities:* Needs to verify one or more of the four basic identities that individuals present in all encounters:

   a. *Core identity:* The conceptions and emotions that individuals have about themselves as persons that they carry to most encounters

   b. *Social identity:* The conception that individuals have of themselves by virtue of their membership in categoric units, which, depending upon the situation, will vary in salience to self and others—when salient, individuals seek to have others verify this identity

   c. *Group identity:* The conception that individuals have about their incumbency in corporate units (groups, organizations, and communities) and/or their identification with the members, structure, and culture of a corporate unit—when individuals have a strong sense of identification with a corporate unit, they seek to have others verify this identity

   d. *Role identity:* The conception that individuals have about themselves as role players, particularly roles embedded in corporate units nested in institutional domains—the more a role identity is lodged in a domain, the more likely will individuals seek to have others verify this identity

2. *Making a profit of the exchange of resources*: Needs to feel that the receipt of resources by persons in encounters exceeds their costs and investments in securing these resources and that their shares of resources are "just" and "fair" compared with (a) the shares that others receive in the situation and (b) the reference points that are used to establish what is a just share

3. *Group inclusion*: Needs to feel that one is a part of the ongoing flow of interaction in an encounter—and the more focused is the encounter, the more powerful is this need

4. *Trust*: Needs to feel that others are predictable, sincere, respective of self, and capable of sustaining rhythmic synchronization through talk and body language

5. *Facticity*: Needs to feel that, for the purposes of the present interaction, individuals share a common inter-subjectivity, that the situation is indeed as it seems, and that the situation has an obdurate character

I am skeptical that there is a neat linear hierarchy of prominence or salience among identities, as is posited by most identity theories, but I would argue that some are more general than others; and the more general is the identity and the more it is relevant and salient in a wide variety of situations, the more individuals seek to have it verified by others. Figure 16.4 summarizes the relations among the four identities that I am emphasizing. The core identity is the most general, followed successively by the social identity, group identity, and role identity.

I also emphasize several properties of this "hierarchy" of identities. First, the lower an identity is in generality, the more likely are individuals to be consciously aware and able to articulate this identity. For example, most people can probably tick off the cognitions and feelings that they have of themselves in role and group

Figure 16.4   Types and Levels of Identity Formation

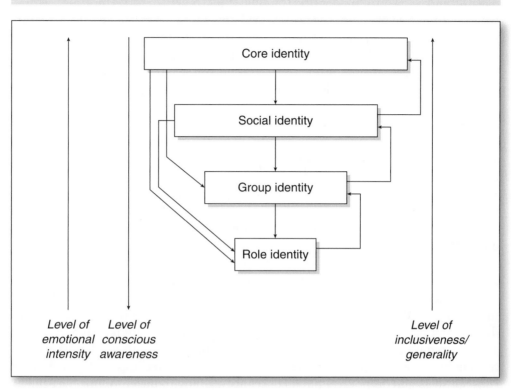

identities, whereas social and core identities are not only more complex, but they also have elements that are unconscious, even as they affect the behaviors of persons.

Second, the more general is an identity, as shown in Figure 16.4, the more intense are the emotions about this identity. Moreover, many of the emotions, particularly negative ones, may be repressed, but this does not prevent these repressed emotions from affecting behavior or individuals' emotional reactions when these identities are not verified by others.

Third, because they are more general, social and core identities are carried to virtually all social situations, whereas role and group identities are more likely to be salient when actually in a role or responding to a group. Yet I should not overgeneralize, because some roles can be highly salient—say, the role of mother—and invoked outside the family in a wide variety of situations, while group identities can often be carried about to many situations, as is the case with a die-hard fan of a sports team.

Fourth, identities are often embedded in each other, with lower-level or narrower identities being successively embedded in more general identities, with the result that, for example, failure to verify a role identity can arouse intense emotions because it is also part of a group, social, or core identity. For example, a person's role identity as mother may be a larger component of her core identity, with the result that a great deal is at stake when this mother seeks to have her mother identity verified through various roles. In fact, it may also be involved in social identity (as a female) and even group identity (family), thus making its verification critical, because if the role of mother is not verified, this mother's entire identity structure will be perceived as under attack and potentially collapsing.

The dynamics of identities reveal many of the cybernetic processes outlined in Burke's theory. People orchestrate their behaviors in an effort to verify any or all of the four identities in a situation; if others signal their acceptance of an identity or identities, a person will experience positive emotions, from *satisfaction* at the lower-intensity end to *joy* and *pride* at the higher-intensity end of positive emotions. In contrast, if an identity is not verified, individuals will experience negative emotions, such as *anger, fear, embarrassment, shame, guilt,* and many others. When people become aware of their negative emotions, these emotions signal to them that, à la Stryker's argument, something has gone wrong in the presentation of self, and that, following Burke's theory, motivates individuals to reappraise their behavior and modify their actions so as to secure verification of the identity. But these dynamics only unfold if a person becomes fully aware that an identity has not been verified.

As McCall and Simmons suggest, people often invoke a variety of "defensive strategies" to protect self from this fate. People often engage in selective perception and/or interpretation of the responses of others; they often disavow the audience that has rejected their claims to verification; and they often leave situations where they cannot have identities confirmed by others. Yet I do not think that McCall and Simmons go far enough; people often repress the negative emotions that have come from failure to verify an identity. They simply push these feelings below the level of consciousness and do not feel them consciously, although the emotions may still be evident to others or become transmuted to a new, often more volatile emotion that others must endure. Thus, true defense mechanisms break the cybernetic cycle outlined by Burke and implied in other identity theories. The break prevents individuals from experiencing accurate reflected appraisals of their identity standard, behaviors, and others' responses to behaviors.

In Table 16.4, I enumerate various types of *defense mechanisms*, seeing *repression* as the master mechanism that removes emotions from consciousness; then, additional types of defense mechanisms may be subsequently activated: *displacement* (venting emotions directed at self on others), *projection* (imputing the repressed emotion[s] to other[s]), *sublimation* (converting negative emotions into positive emotional energy), *reaction formation* (converting intense negative emotions into positive emotions directed at the others who caused the negative emotion), and *attribution* (imputing the source cause of emotional reactions). The first five defense mechanisms are those often posited by those working in the psychoanalytic tradition, while the last—*attribution*—comes from cognitive psychology (earlier from Gestalt psychology).

Attribution is generally not considered a defense mechanism, but I think that it may be the most sociologically important mechanism. People make attributions for their experiences, and they generally make self-attributions (i.e., see themselves as responsible) when experiencing positive emotions, whereas with negative emotions, they may blame others, categories of others, or social structures in an effort to protect self from having negative self-feelings.

Table 16.4 Repression, Defense, Transmutation, and Targeting Emotions

Repressed Emotions	Defense Mechanism	Transmutation to	Target
Anger, sadness, fear, shame, guilt, and alienation	Displacement	Anger	Others, corporate units and categoric units
Anger, sadness, fear, shame, guilt, and alienation	Projection	Little, but some anger	Imputation of anger, sadness, fear, shame, or guilt to dispositional states of others
Anger, sadness, fear, shame, guilt, and alienation	Reaction formation	Positive emotions	Others, corporate units, categoric units
Anger, sadness, fear, shame, guilt, and alienation	Sublimation	Positive emotions	Tasks in corporate units
Anger, sadness, fear, shame, guilt, and alienation	Attribution	Anger	Others, corporate units, or categoric units

This *proximal bias* for positive emotions to be attributed to self or others in the immediate situation and the *distal bias* for negative emotions to target more remote objects as responsible for these negative feelings have important implications for people's commitment to others and to social structures. People feel positive emotions about themselves and, perhaps, immediate others when experiencing the positive emotions that come with identity verification. They feel that they have been positively sanctioned and have met situational expectations, and in so doing, they feel good about themselves because their identity or identities have been verified. In contrast, when people have not met expectations, have been negatively sanctioned, and hence have failed to confirm an identity in a situation, the negative emotions aroused, such as *shame*, are too painful and are repressed; then, more remote social units, such as members of a social category or the social structures of a corporate unit, are blamed for their feelings. In this way, despite feeling negative emotions, individuals can protect self by seeing objects outside of self as causally responsible for their negative feelings. These negative emotions generate prejudices against members of social categories (e.g., by gender, ethnicity, religious affiliation) and alienation and/or loss of commitment to social structures. In contrast, positive emotions increase commitments to others and situations.

Yet, if emotions have these proximal and distal biases, how are more remote objects, such as social structures, to be the targets of commitments by individuals when self-verification, meeting expectations, and receiving positive sanctions from others activate the proximal bias—thereby remaining local, tied to encounters at the micro level of social organizations? What would allow for positive emotions to break the centripetal force of the proximal bias built into attribution processes? My answer is that when people *consistently experience* positive emotions in particular types of situations, they begin to make attributions to the larger social structures in which these situations are embedded. As they do so, they develop positive feelings about, and commitments to, these structures because they see these structures as causally responsible for the verification of self and the positive feelings that arise from identity verification.

In this manner, consistent self-verification will ultimately lead to commitments to those social structures in which encounters have aroused the positive emotions that come with self-verification. And the more identities that are verified, the greater will these commitments ultimately be. Indeed, if a group identity with particular types of corporate units or even a whole society did not already exist, it is likely to form when individuals validate other identities within a particular type of social structure. And to the extent that other identities are tied to roles in divisions of labor and are verified in encounters within this division of labor, identity dynamics become the underlying force behind commitments to this social structure and perhaps the larger institutional domain in which this structure is lodged. For example, a good student who has consistently been rewarded and had the role identity of student verified will, over time, develop commitments to successive schools and, eventually, the entire institutional domain of education.

In this way, forces such as transactional needs for verification of self can have large effects on more macro-level social structures, and vice versa. Macrostructures that set people up for success in verifying role identities and any other identities tied to these roles in groups and organizations will reap what they sow: commitments from individuals. And these commitments may eventually move to the institutional domains or the whole society in which these groups and organizations are embedded.[29]

Conclusions

Over the last eighty years, Mead's seminal ideas about the dynamics of self have been significantly extended and refined theoretically and assessed by careful empirical research. Theories now emphasize that individuals carry multiple identities, although there is some disagreement as to whether or not, or perhaps the degree to which, they constitute a linear hierarchy of prominence or salience. What is clear is that there are cybernetic/Gestalt dynamics operating for self. Persons seek to have their identities verified by others by assessing others' reactions to their behavioral outputs to see if these outputs are consistent with an identity and acceptable to others.

Yet some argue that this cybernetic process can be distorted by the repression of the negative emotions that are aroused when such an important dimension of human behavior—verification of identities—becomes problematic. But all identity theories agree that the failure to verify an identity generates negative emotions that motivate

---

[29]I have developed many formal propositions on these identity dynamics and their effects on macrostructures. See, for examples, my *Face-to-Face* and *Theoretical Principles of Sociology*.

individuals to bring perceptions of self in line with others' responses to self, even if these responses and the emotions felt must be repressed to gain congruence among people's identities, behavioral outputs, identity standards, and reflected appraisals of others' reactions to behavioral outputs. For most identity theories, there is a clear cognitive bias, emphasizing that people generally bring their behavioral outputs, their identities, and the reactions of others to presentations of identities into congruence; only the more psychoanalytically oriented identity theories would also suggest that congruence can be achieved by the activation of defense mechanisms. For all symbolic interactionists, needs for verification of identities are the driving force of interaction, and the flow of interaction revolves around the extent to which people's identities are mutually verified. And when they are, individuals feel positive emotions and may, if these emotions persist, begin to make commitments to the larger social structures in which interactions occur.

Identity verification dynamics, then, are one key to understanding the connection between micro interactions and macro-social structures. Emotions are the key link, and the most powerful emotions come from identity dynamics; so larger-scale social structures depend upon the consistent arousal of the positive emotions that come with identity verification in face-to-face interactions. Thus, identity theories go a long way toward closing what is often considered the "gap" between the micro level of interaction among people and the macro level of social structure of a society.

CHAPTER 17

Role and Status Theorizing

Although George Herbert Mead's great synthesis provided the initial conceptual breakthrough on micro-level theorizing about interaction processes, this synthesis did not satisfactorily resolve the problem of how participation in the structure of society shapes individual conduct, and vice versa. And, as is evident from the analysis of symbolic interactionists theory in the last chapter, contemporary approaches have focused on identity dynamics more than the linkage among behavior and social structure, although symbolic interactionist approaches emphasizing emotional dynamics have begun to make micro-macro theoretical connections.

Early on, many sociologists realized the shortcomings of Mead's theory, where society or social structure is only vaguely conceptualized, and began to develop concepts that could better connect individuals, behaviors, and social structure. Their efforts led them to invoke existing words in the lay vocabulary—*roles* and *status*—to conceptualize individuals' connections to social structures and the culture of these structures.

Early Efforts to Conceptualize Roles and Status

In an effort to resolve this vagueness, sociological inquiry began to focus on the concept of "role." Individuals were seen as playing roles associated with positions in larger networks of positions. With this vision, efforts to understand more about social structures and how individuals are implicated in them intensified during the 1920s and 1930s. This line of inquiry eventually became known as "role theory," which I will examine first in this chapter.

Robert Park's Role Theory

Robert Park, who came to the University of Chicago near the end of Mead's career, was one of the first to extend Mead's ideas through an emphasis on roles. As

Park observed, "Everybody is always and everywhere, more or less consciously, playing a role."[1] But Park stressed that roles are linked to structural positions in society and that self is intimately linked to playing roles within the confines of the positions of social structure:

> The conceptions which men form of themselves seem to depend upon their vocations, and in general upon the role they seek to play in communities and social groups in which they live, as well as upon the recognition and status which society accords them in these roles. It is status, i.e., recognition by the community, that confers upon the individual the character of a person, since a person is an individual who has status, not necessarily legal, but social.[2]

Park's analysis stressed that self emerges from the multiple roles that people play.[3] In turn, roles are connected to positions in social structures. This kind of analysis shifts attention to the nature of society and how its structure influences the processes outlined in Mead's synthesis.

Jacob Moreno's Role Theory

Inspired in part by Mead's concept of role-taking and by his own earlier studies in Europe, Jacob Moreno, who immigrated to the United States, was one of the first to develop the concept of *role-playing*. In *Who Shall Survive?* and in many publications in the journals that he founded in America, Moreno began to view social organization as a network of roles that constrain and channel behavior.[4] In his early works, Moreno distinguished different types of roles: (a) "psychosomatic roles," in which behavior is related to basic biological needs, as conditioned by culture, and in which role enactment is typically unconscious; (b) "psychodramatic roles," in which individuals behave in accordance with the specific expectations of a particular social context; and (c) "social roles," in which individuals conform to the more general expectations of various conventional social categories (e.g., worker, Christian, mother, and father).

Despite the suggestiveness of these distinctions, their importance comes not so much from their substantive content as from their intent: to conceptualize social structures as organized networks of expectations that require varying types of role

---

[1]Robert E. Park, "Behind Our Masks," *Survey Graphic* 56 (May 1926):135. For a convenient summary of the thrust of early research efforts in role theory, see Ralph H. Turner, "Social Roles: Sociological Aspects," in *International Encyclopedia of the Social Sciences*, ed. David L. Sills (New York: Macmillan, 1968) as well as his "Role Theory," in *Handbook of Sociological Theory*, ed. Jonathan H. Turner (Kluwer Academic/Plenum Press, 2001), 223–254.

[2]Robert E. Park, *Society* (New York: Free Press, 1955), 285–286.

[3]Indeed, Park studied briefly with Simmel in Berlin and apparently acquired insight into Simmel's study of the individual and the web of group affiliations (see later discussion).

[4]Jacob Moreno, *Who Shall Survive* (Washington, DC: Nervous and Mental Disease Publishing, 1934); rev. ed. (New York: Beacon House, 1953).

enactments by individuals. In this way, analysis can move beyond the vague Meadian conceptualization of society as coordinated activity regulated by the generalized other to a conceptualization of social organization as various types of interrelated role enactments regulated by varying types of expectations.

Ralph Linton on Status and Roles

Shortly after Moreno's publication of *Who Shall Survive?*, the anthropologist Ralph Linton further conceptualized the nature of social organization, and the individual's embeddedness in it, by distinguishing among the concepts of *role*, *status*, and *individuals:*

> A status, as distinct from the individual who may occupy it, is simply a collection of rights and duties. . . . A role represents the dynamic aspect of status. The individual is socially assigned to a status and occupies it with relation to other statuses. When he puts the rights and duties which constitute the status into effect, he is performing a role.[5]

This passage contains several important conceptual distinctions. Social structure reveals several distinct elements: (a) a network of status positions, (b) a corresponding system of expectations attached to these positions, and (c) a set of individual behaviors that are enacted to meet the expectations of particular networks of interrelated positions. In retrospect, these distinctions might appear self-evident and trivial, but they made possible the subsequent elaboration of many interactionist concepts, as follows:

1. Linton's distinctions allow us to conceptualize society as clear-cut variables: the nature and kinds of interrelations among status positions and the types of expectations attending these positions.

2. The variables Mead denoted by the concepts of *mind* and *self* can be analytically distinguished from both social structure (status positions and expectations) and behavior (role enactments).

3. By conceptually separating the processes of role-taking and imaginative rehearsal from both social structure and behavior (see Chapter 8 on G. H. Mead), the points of articulation between society and the individual can be more clearly marked, because role-taking denotes the process of interpreting the expectations attached to networks of statuses and role denotes the enactment of these expectations as mediated by self.

Thus, by offering more conceptual insight into the nature of social organization, Park, Moreno, and Linton provided a needed supplement to Mead's suggestive concepts that provided the theoretical base for symbolic interactionism. Now, it would be possible to understand more precisely the interrelations among individuals with

---

[5]Ralph Linton, *The Study of Man* (New York: Appleton-Century-Crofts, 1936), 28.

the behavior capacities for role-taking, minded deliberations, and self-appraisals, on the one side, and social structure and culture, on the other.

Role Theorizing

By the middle of the last century, the idea that individuals are connected to larger social structures by virtue of incumbency in status positions and role behaviors pervaded sociological theory. Role was the key concept that linked individuals and social structure, and as a result of this emphasis, role theorizing became prominent. Yet much of this role theorizing was, in reality, descriptions of expectations and behaviors in various empirical settings or, at best, more theoretical conceptualizations of a narrow range of role processes. Still, there were several efforts to build a general theory of role dynamics, the most important of which was the theoretical approach developed by Ralph H. Turner. Then, after a burst of role theorizing, conceptualizations about roles seemed to disappear in the last two decades of the twentieth century. At about the same time that role theorizing declined, theorizing on status processes increased. It may be that understanding of roles had become so complete that theorizing on this fundamental property of the social universe was felt to be no longer necessary. Still some more modest efforts to add to the existing body of theorizing have emerged in recent years; and thus, theorizing on roles continues on a more modest scale, while theorizing on status processes remains the more dominant approach. Let me begin with a discussion of role theorizing, emphasizing Ralph H. Turner's approach,[6] and then later in the chapter, I will examine with David Wagner status theorizing in sociology.

Ralph H. Turner's Role Theory

Over the course of several decades, Ralph H. Turner mounted a consistent line of criticism against what he characterized as structural role theory.[7] This criticism incorporated several lines of attack: (a) Earlier role theory had presented an overly structured vision of the social world, with its emphasis on norms, status positions, and the enactment of normative expectations. (b) Role theory had tended to concentrate an inordinate amount of research and theory-building effort on "abnormal" social processes, such as role conflict and role strain, thereby ignoring the normal processes of human interaction. (c) Role theory is not theory but, rather, a series of disjointed and unconnected propositions and empirical generalizations. (d) Role theory did not recognize Mead's concept of role-taking as its central dynamic. As a corrective to these problems, Turner offered in the decades around

---

[6]I should emphasize that, despite our similar names, Ralph H. Turner is not related to Jonathan H. Turner.

[7]See, for example, Ralph H. Turner, "Role-Taking: Processes versus Conformity," in *Human Behavior and Social Processes*, ed. A. Rose (Boston, MA: Houghton Mifflin, 1962), 20–40 and Jonathan H. Turner, "Role," in *Blackwell Encyclopedia of 20th Century Social Thought*, ed. William Outhwaite and Tom Bottomore (Oxford, UK: Blackwell, 1996).

the mid-century a conceptualization of roles that emphasized the process of interaction over the dictates of social structures and cultural scripts.[8]

The Process of Role-making. Turner used Mead's concept of role-taking to describe the nature of social action. Turner assumed that "it is the tendency to shape the phenomenal world into roles which is the key to the role-taking as the core process in interaction."[9] Turner stressed that actors emit gestures or cues—words, bodily countenance, voice inflections, dress, facial expressions, and other gestures—as they interact to "put themselves in the other's role" and, thereby, adjust their lines of conduct in ways that can facilitate cooperation. In emphasizing this point, Turner was simply following Mead's definition of taking the role of the other, or role-taking.

Turner then extended Mead's concept. He first argued that cultural definitions of roles are often vague and even contradictory. At best, they provide a general framework within which actors must construct a line of conduct. Thus, actors make their roles and communicate to others what role they are playing. Turner then argued that humans *act as* if all others in their environment are playing identifiable roles.[10] Humans assume others to be playing a role, and this assumption is what gives interaction a common basis. Operating with this folk assumption, people then read gestures and cues in an effort to determine what role others are playing.[11] This effort is facilitated by others creating and asserting their roles, with the result that they actively emit cues about what roles they are attempting to play.

For Turner, then, role-taking was also role-making. Humans make roles in three senses: (1) people are often faced with only a loose cultural framework in which they must make a role to play; (2) they assume others are playing a role and thus make an effort to discover the underlying role behind a person's acts; and (3) they seek to make a role for themselves in all social situations by emitting cues to others that give them a claim on a particular role. Interaction is, therefore, a joint and reciprocal process of role-taking and role-making.

The Folk Norm of Consistency. As people interact with one another, Turner argued, they assess behavior less for its conformity to imputed norms or positions in a social structure and more for the consistency of the behavior. Humans seek to group one another's behavior into coherent wholes or gestalts; and by doing so, they can make sense of one another's actions, anticipate one another's behavior, and adjust to one another's responses. If another's responses are inconsistent and not seen as part of an

---

[8]Ralph H. Turner, "Unanswered Questions in the Convergence between Structuralist and Interactionist Role Theories," in *Micro-Sociological Theory: Perspectives on Sociological Theory*, ed. S. N. Eisenstadt and H. J. Helle (London: Sage, 1985). In particular, this article addresses Warren Handel, "Normative Expectations and the Emergence of Meaning as Solutions to Problems: Convergence of Structural and Interactionist Views," *American Journal of Sociology* 84 (1979):855–881.

[9]Turner, "Role-Taking."

[10]Ibid.; Turner, "Social Roles: Sociological Aspects."

[11]Ralph H. Turner, "The Normative Coherence of Folk Concepts," *Research Studies of the State College of Washington* 25 (1957):127–136.

underlying role, then interaction will prove difficult. Thus, there is an implicit "norm of consistency" in people's interactions with one another. Humans attempt to assess the consistency of others' actions to discern the underlying role that is being played.

The Tentative Nature of Interaction. Turner echoed Herbert Blumer's position when he stated that "interaction is always a tentative process, a process of continuously testing the conception one has of the role of the other."[12] Humans are constantly interpreting additional cues emitted by others and using these new cues to see if they are consistent with those previously emitted and with the imputed roles of others. If they are consistent, then the actor will continue to adjust responses in accordance with the imputed role of the other. But as soon as inconsistent cues are emitted, the identification of the other's role will undergo revision. Thus, the imputation of a particular role to another person will persist only as long as it provides a stable framework for interaction. The tentative nature of the role-making process points to another facet of roles: the process of role verification.

Role Verification. Actors seek to verify that the behaviors emitted by people in a situation do indeed constitute a role. Turner argued that such efforts at verification or validation are achieved by applying external and internal criteria. The most often used internal criterion is the degree to which an actor perceives a role to facilitate interaction. External criteria can vary, but in general they involve assessment of a role by important others, relevant groups, or commonly agreed-on standards. When an imputed role is validated or verified in this way, then it can serve as a stable basis for continued interaction among actors.

Self-Conceptions and Roles. All humans reveal self-conceptions of themselves as certain kinds of objects. Humans develop self-attitudes and feelings from their interactions with others, but as Turner and all role theorists emphasized, actors attempt to present themselves in ways that will reinforce their self-conceptions.[13] Because others will always seek to determine an individual's role, it becomes necessary for the individual to inform others, through cues and gestures, about the degree to which self is anchored in a role. Thus, actors will signal one another about their self-identity and the extent to which their role is consistent with their self-conception. For example, roles not consistent with a person's self-conception will likely be played with considerable distance and disdain, whereas those that an individual considers central to self-definitions will be played much differently.[14]

---

[12]Turner, "Role-Taking," 23.

[13]Ralph H. Turner, "The Role and the Person," *American Journal of Sociology* 84 (1978):1–23.

[14]Turner, "Social Roles: Sociological Aspects." Turner has extensively analyzed this process of self-anchorage in roles. See, for example, Ralph H. Turner, "The Real Self: From Institution to Impulse," *American Journal of Sociology* 81 (1970):989–1016; Ralph H. Turner and Victoria Billings, "Social Context of Self-Feeling," in *The Self-Society Interface: Cognition, Emotion, and Action*, ed. J. Howard and P. Callero (Cambridge, UK: Cambridge University Press, 1990), 103–122; and Ralph H. Turner and Steven Gordon, "The Boundaries of the Self: The Relationship of Authenticity to Inauthenticity in the Self-Conception," in *Self-Concept: Advances in Theory and Research*, ed. M. D. Lynch, A. A. Norem-Hebeisen, and Kenneth Gergen (Cambridge, MA: Ballinger, 1981), 39–57.

In sum, Turner's approach maintains much of the dramaturgical metaphor of early role theory, but with an emphasis on the behavioral aspect of roles, because actors impute roles to one another through behavioral cues. The notion in early analysis that roles are conceptions of expected behaviors is preserved, for assigning a role to a person invokes an expectation that a certain type and range of responses will ensue. The view that roles are the norms attendant on status positions is given less emphasis than in early theories but not ignored, because norms and positions can be the basis for assigning and verifying roles.[15] And the conception in the dramaturgical metaphor of roles as parts that people learn to play is preserved, for people can denote one another's roles by virtue of their prior socialization into a common role repertoire.

Building a Role Theory. Although Turner accepted a process orientation, he was committed to developing interactionism into "something akin to axiomatic theory."[16] He had recognized that role theory was segmented into a series of narrow propositions and hypotheses and that role theorists had been reluctant "to find unifying themes to link various role processes."

Turner's strategy was to use propositions from the numerous research studies to build more formal and abstract theoretical statements. His goal was to maintain a productive dialogue between specific empirical propositions and more abstract theoretical statements. Turner advocated the use of what he termed main tendency propositions to link concepts to empirical regularities and to consolidate the thrust of these regularities.[17] What Turner sought was a series of statements that highlight what tends to occur in the normal operation of systems of interaction. To this end, Turner provided a long list of main tendency propositions on (a) roles as they emerge, (b) roles as an interactive framework, (c) roles in relation to actors, (d) roles in organizational settings, (e) roles in societal settings, and (f) roles and the person. The most important of these propositions will be examined here.[18]

Emergence and Character of Roles. Turner begins by outlining certain empirical tendencies on the initial emergence of roles and then the properties of roles once they have emerged. Five of these generalizations about the emergence and character of roles are summarized below:

1. In any interactive situation, behavior, sentiments, and motives tend to be differentiated into units that can be termed roles; once differentiated, elements of behavior, sentiment, and motives that appear in the same situation tend to be assigned to existing roles. (Tendencies for *role differentiation and accretion*)

---

[15]Ralph H. Turner, "Rule Learning as Role Learning," *International Journal of Critical Sociology* 1 (1974):10–28.

[16]Ralph H. Turner, "Strategy for Developing an Integrated Role Theory," *Humboldt Journal of Social Relations* 7 (1980):123–139, "Role Theory as Theory" (unpublished manuscript).

[17]Turner, "Strategy for Developing," 123–124.

[18]Turner, "Social Roles: Sociological Aspects."

2. In any interactive situation, the meaning of individual actions for ego (the actor) and for any alter (others) is assigned on the basis of the imputed role. (Tendencies for *meaningfulness*)

3. In connection with every role, there is a tendency for certain attributes of actors, aspects of behavior, and features of situations to become salient cues for the identification of roles. (Tendencies for *role cues*)

4. Every role tends to acquire an evaluation for rank and social desirability. (Tendencies for *evaluation*)

5. The character of a role—that is, its definition—will tend to change if there are persistent changes in either the behaviors of those presumed to be playing the role or the contexts in which the role is played. (Tendencies for *behavioral correspondence*)

In these five propositions, individuals are seen as viewing the world in terms of roles, as employing a "folk norm" to discover the consistency of behaviors and to assign behavioral elements to an imputed role (role differentiation and accretion), as using roles to interpret and define situations (meaningfulness tendency), as searching roles for signals about the attributes of actors as well as the nature of the situation (role cues), and as evaluating roles for their power, prestige, and esteem, while assessing them for their degree of social desirability and worth (tendency for evaluation). When role behaviors or situations are permanently altered, the definition of the role will also undergo change (behavioral correspondence).

Role as an Interactive Framework. Next, Turner argues that interactions are only viable when individuals can identify each other's roles. Moreover, roles tend to be complements of other roles—as is the case with wife/husband, parent/child, boss/employee roles—and thus operate to regularize interaction among complementary roles. Finally, roles that prove useful and that allow stable and fruitful interaction are translated into expectations that future transactions will and should occur as in the past. Below are additional generalizations on these dynamics.

6. The establishment and persistence of interaction tend to depend on the emergence and identification of ego and alter roles. (Tendency for *interaction in roles*)

7. Each role tends to form as a comprehensive way of coping with one or more relevant alter roles. (Tendency for *role complementarity*)

8. There is a tendency for stabilized roles to be assigned the character of legitimate expectations and to be seen as the appropriate way to behave in a situation. (Tendency for *legitimate expectations*)

Role in Relation to Actor. Once actors identify roles and assign one another to them, Turner argues, the roles persist, and new actors will tend to be assigned to those roles that already exist in a situation. Humans also tend to adopt roles for the duration of an interaction, while having knowledge of the roles that others are playing. In addition, individuals carry with them general conceptions of what a role entails and what constitutes adequate performance. Finally, the adequacy of a person's role performance greatly influences the extent to which the role, along with the rights, privileges, and complementary behaviors that it deserves, will be acknowledged. These processes are summarized in the generalizations below:

9. Once stabilized, the role structure tends to persist, regardless of changes in actors. (Tendency for *role persistence*)

10. There is a tendency to identify a given individual with a given role and a complementary tendency for an individual to adopt a given role for the duration of the interaction. (Tendency for *role allocation*)

11. To the extent that ego's role is an adaptation to alter's role, it incorporates some conception of alter's role. (Tendency for *role-taking*)

12. Role behavior tends to be judged as adequate or inadequate by comparison with a conception of the role in question. (Tendency to assess *role adequacy*)

13. The degree of an actor's adequacy in role performance determines the extent to which others will respond to and reciprocate the actor's role performance. (Tendency for *role reciprocity*)

Role in Organizational Settings. Roles are often played out in organizations revealing divisions of labor to achieve particular goals. By emphasizing that roles are often embedded in organizations, Turner incorporated Ralph Linton's and other early theorists' insight that status and role can be highly related. When so coupled, the goals and authority systems of the organization constrain all role dynamics, although Turner also emphasizes that not all roles are part of networks of status positions in social structures, but Turner never abandoned Mead's and Blumer's emphasis that much interaction occurs in contexts where roles are not immersed within networks of clearly defined status positions. The following generalizations summarize Turner's views on the relation of roles to organizational settings.

14. To the extent that roles are incorporated into an organizational setting, organizational goals tend to become crucial criteria for role differentiation, evaluation, complementarity, legitimacy or expectation, consensus, allocation, and judgments of adequacy. (Tendency for *organizational goal dominance*)

15. To the extent that roles are incorporated into an organizational setting, the right to define the legitimate character of roles, to set the evaluations on roles, to allocate roles, and to judge role adequacy tends to be lodged in particular roles. (Tendency for *legitimate role definers*)

16. To the extent that roles are incorporated into an organizational setting, differentiation tends to link roles to statuses in the organization. (Tendency for *status*)

17. To the extent that roles are incorporated into an organizational setting, each role tends to develop as a pattern of adaptation to multiple alter roles. (Tendency for *role sets*)

18. To the extent that roles are incorporated into an organizational setting, the persistence of roles is intensified through tradition and formalization. (Tendency for *formalization*)

Role in Societal Setting. Many roles are identified, assumed, and imputed in relation to a broader societal context. In the tendencies listed previously, Turner first argued that people tend to group behaviors in different social contexts into as few unifying roles as is possible or practical. Thus, people will identify a role as a way of making sense of disparate behaviors in different contexts. At the societal level, values are the equivalent of goals in organizational settings for identifying, differentiating, allocating, evaluating, and legitimating roles. As people assume multiple roles in societal settings, however, they tend to assume roles that are consistent with one another. These dynamics are summarized in the following propositions in Turner's scheme.

19. Similar roles in different contexts tend to become merged, so they are identified as a single role recurring in different relationships. (Tendency for *economy of roles*)

20. To the extent that roles refer to more general social contexts and situations, differentiation tends to link roles to social values. (Tendency for *value anchorage*)

21. The individual in society tends to be assigned to and to assume roles consistent with one another. (Tendency for *allocation consistency*)

Role and the Person. The "person" is a concept employed by Turner to denote "the distinctive repertoire of roles" that an individual enacts, an idea borrowed from Georg Simmel, who argued that individuals are the sum total of their configurations of roles played in societies. Individuals always seek to resolve tensions among roles and to avoid contradictions between their self-conceptions and roles, because to have contradictions decreases the chances that self will be verified.

22. Actors tend to act to alleviate role strain arising from role contradiction, role conflict, and role inadequacy and to heighten the gratifications of high role adequacy. (Tendency to resolve *role strain*)

23. Individuals in society tend to adopt a repertoire of role relationships as a framework for their own behavior and as a perspective for interpretation of the behavior of others. (Tendency to be *socialized into the common culture*)

24. Individuals tend to form self-conceptions by selectively identifying certain roles from their repertoires as more characteristically "themselves" than other roles. (Tendency to *anchor self-conception*)

25. The self-conception tends to stress those roles that supply the basis for effective adaptation to relevant alters. (*Adaptation of self-conception* tendency)

26. To the extent that roles must be played in situations that contradict the self-conception, those roles will be assigned role distance, and mechanisms for demonstrating lack of personal involvement will be employed. (Tendency for *role distance*)

In developing these "tendency propositions" summarizing what occurs empirically when roles are played, Turner recognizes that these and other tendency propositions do not specify the conditions under which the tendency actually would occur. The propositions are thus only descriptive; they do not say why such tendencies should occur. Yet Turner believed that to be true theory, role analysis must specify some of these basic conditions causing these tendencies in roles to occur. Without this extra step, there is no theory because the propositions outlined above are in need of a theoretical explanation of why these are the prevailing tendencies in role behaviors. So Turner has sought to add more explanatory content—that is, to indicate when and why the tendencies exist.

Generating Explanatory Laws. Turner's initial efforts were more explanatory in specifying the conditions under which particular tendencies become evident. For example, the tendencies for individuals to identify with a role and for others around the individual to make such an identification are likely to emerge when[19] (a) allocation of roles is less flexible, (b) roles are highly differentiated, (c) roles are implicated in conflictual relationships, (d) performance of roles is judged as competent, (e) roles are considered difficult, (f) roles are either of high or of low rank, (g) power is vested in a role, and so on.[20] These kinds of propositions were very suggestive, but Turner began to feel that they were somewhat ad hoc. Hence, he was led to ask, "Are there some underlying processes that can explain the tendencies and the conditions under which they become manifest?" This question inspired him, along with various collaborators, to develop what he felt were true "explanatory propositions" that would stand at the top of a deductive system explaining the tendencies and the conditions under which they are activated.

These explanatory propositions bring Turner's work from the mid-century into the more contemporary theoretical time frame. But for ease of exposition, it is best to deal with these explanatory "laws" here. In their most recent reworking, Turner and Paul Colomy[21] posit three underlying processes that can explain the other propositions in Turner's developing theory: (1) functionality, (2) representation, and (3) tenability. We will briefly examine each of these. I should emphasize that Turner later narrows the explanatory focus of functionality, representation, and tenability to account primarily for role differentiation.[22]

Functionality. When activities are organized to meet explicit goals in an efficient and effective manner, then considerations of functionality are dominant. Such

---

[19]Turner, "Role and the Person," 1–23.

[20]In his most recent effort, "Strategy for Developing an Integrated Role Theory," Turner focused on "role allocation" and "role differentiation" because he views these as the two most critical tendencies. The example of "the person and role" results in the same explanatory principles. Thus, this illustration provides additional examples of Turner's strategy.

[21]Ralph H. Turner and Paul Colomy, "Role Differentiation: Orienting Principles," *Advances in Group Processes* 5 (1987):1–47.

[22]Ralph H. Turner, "Role Theory," in *Handbook of Sociological Theory*, ed. J. H. Turner (Kluwer Academic/Plenum Press, 2001), 233–254.

considerations are most likely when the organization of individuals (into a division of labor composed of status positions) to achieve goals can potentially involve conflicts of interest among the participants and when these participants must be recruited from diverse pools of individuals who differ in their abilities. Under these conditions, the differentiation and accretion of roles are organized in highly instrumental ways so that goals can be achieved with a minimum of conflict and friction.

Tenability. When roles form and differentiate in ways that allow individuals to gain personal rewards and gratifications, considerations of tenability are evident. Thus, as individuals calculate their costs and rewards, and indeed are encouraged by the organization of roles to do so, tenability dominates functionality.

Representation. When the accretion and differentiation of roles involve the embodiment of cultural values, considerations of representation are evident. Moreover, the salience of representation of roles increases when roles are implicated in group conflict and when incumbents in roles are recruited from homogeneous pools of individuals. When representation dominates the organization of roles, tenability will become more important than functionality.

The propositions developed for functionality, tenability, and representation are too complex for this brief discussion, but the general intent is clear. These propositions serve as the higher-order "laws" in a propositional scheme that is explanatory because they "explain" the tendency propositions by specifying the conditions under which they hold true. Although this strategy is suggestive, Turner has never fully implemented it by subsuming all the tendency propositions under these three laws in an explanatory proposition scheme. Yet, unlike much role theorizing from the mid-century, Turner's approach recognized that generalizations about roles from empirical observations need to be organized in ways facilitating their explanation by more abstract principles.[23] For Turner, the relative amounts of functionality, tenability, and representation would provide the needed explanatory push. This strategy has not, I believe, been entirely successful; and this may be because the explanatory propositions do not adequately take account of the

---

[23]For representative examples of the variety of empirical research conducted by Turner, see Ralph H. Turner, "The Navy Disbursing Officer as a Bureaucrat," *American Sociological Review* 12 (1947):342–348, "Moral Judgment: A Study in Roles," *American Sociological Review* 17 (1952):70–77, "Occupational Patterns of Inequality," *American Journal of Sociology* 50 (1954):437–447, "The Changing Ideology of Success: A Study of Aspirations of High School Men in Los Angeles," *Transactions of the Third World Congress of Sociology* 5 (1956):35–44, "An Experiment in Modification of the Role Conceptions," *Yearbook of the American Philosophical Society* (1959):329–332, "Some Family Determinants of Ambition," *Sociology and Social Research* 46 (1962):397–411, *The Social Context of Ambition* (San Francisco, CA: Chandler & Sharp, 1964), and "The True Self Method for Studying Self-Conception," *Symbolic Interaction* 4 (1981):1–20; Ralph H. Turner and Samuel J. Surace, "Zoot-Suiters and Mexicans: Symbols in Crowd Behavior," *American Journal of Sociology* 62 (1956):14–20; and Ralph H. Turner and Norma Shosid, "Ambiguity and Interchangeability in Role Attribution," *American Sociological Review* 41 (1976):993–1006.

close connection between status and role. Moreover, the failure of role theory to be fully explanatory may also explain why theorizing turned increasingly to status dynamics in the latter decades of the twentieth century and up to the present. Thus, a theory of roles may require first a theory of status dynamics, as is explored shortly.

Jonathan Turner's Supplementary Analysis of Role Dynamics

The Centrality of Roles. For some years, I have been trying to extend Ralph Turner's views on the dynamics of roles within the context of micro-level interaction processes more generally. Increasingly, as the behavioral component of microdynamics, roles are at the center of what occurs as people interact face-to-face. In a very real sense, role behaviors are the vehicle by which all other microprocesses operate (see Table 17.1). For example, status dynamics (see the major section of this chapter below) revolving around one's location in a social structure are partially determined by how one plays a role; the same is true for what aspects of culture are made relevant to a situation. Thus, it is from roles that we assess such critical matters as what stocks of knowledge are important in a situation, what motives are driving people in an interaction, what the use of situational ecology and physical props mean in a situation to a person and others, what identity is salient and how it is to be verified, what the emotional dispositions of others are, and virtually all other micro-social processes. True, we often know much about a situation and others in that situation by familiarity with social structures, but humans will need to fine-tune this knowledge of social structures through the visible role behaviors of each person in a situation. Thus, Mead was certainly correct in stating that role-taking or reading the gestures of others is critical to being able to cooperate with others, and Ralph Turner has provided an important reciprocal of role-taking in his concept of role-making. Role-taking is possible only through the role-making efforts of others. These role-making processes can be consciously orchestrated and manipulated or unconsciously presented to others as they role-take.

Expanding the Notions of Role-taking and Role-making. In my general theory of microdynamic processes,[24] I have emphasized that certain forces drive interaction processes, including (a) roles, (b) emotions, (c) status, (d) motives and need states, (e) culture, (f) situational ecology, and (g) situational demography. In Table 17.1, I define each of these fundamental microdynamic forces. Mead and Ralph Turner's dual ideas of role-taking and role-making have led me recently to reconceptualize

---

[24]Jonathan H. Turner, *Theoretical Principles of Sociology*, vol. 2: *Microdynamics* (New York: Springer, 2010). See also Jonathan H. Turner, *Face-to-Face: Toward a Sociological Theory of Interpersonal Behavior* (Stanford, CA: Stanford University Press, 2002), "Extending the Symbolic Interactionist Theory of Interaction Processes: A Conceptual Outline," *Symbolic Interaction* 34 (3, 2010):330–339, as well as "Neurology and Interpersonal Behavior: The Basic Challenge for Neurosociology," in *Handbook of Neurosociology*, ed. D. Franks and J. Turner (New York: Springer, forthcoming).

Table 17.1   Broad Definitions of Microdynamic Forces

Ecological forces: Boundaries, configurations of the physical space, and the props in space as these constrain the behaviors of individuals in focused and unfocused encounters

Demographic forces: Number of individuals copresent, their density, their movements, and their characteristics as these constrain the behaviors of individuals in focused and unfocused encounters

Status forces: Positional locations and their organization within corporate units revealing divisions of labor and memberships in categoric units defined by parameters as they constrain the behaviors of individuals in focused and unfocused encounters

Roles forces: Moment-by-moment configurations of gestures mutually emitted and interpreted by persons to communicate their respective dispositions and likely courses of action as these constrain behaviors in focused and unfocused encounters

Cultural forces: Systems of symbols organized into texts, values, beliefs and ideologies, and norms as they generate expectations and thereby constrain the behaviors of individuals in focused and unfocused encounters

Motivational forces: Universal need states as these constrain the behaviors of individuals in focused and unfocused encounters. The most important need states are (a) verifying identities, (b) realizing profits in exchanges of resources with others, and (c) achieving a sense of inclusion in the ongoing flow of interaction.

Emotional forces: Types and valences of affect aroused, experienced, and expressed that constrain the behaviors of individuals in focused and unfocused encounters

the processes by which people execute the microdynamic processes delineated in Table 17.1. Just as people role-make and role-take, so do they *emotion-take* and *emotion-make*, *status-take* and *status-make*, *motive-take* and *motive-make*, *culture-take* and *culture-make*, *ecology-take* and *ecology-make*, and *demography-take* and *demography-make*. Much of this "taking and making" on dynamics other than roles occurs through role-taking and role-making—by observing the role behaviors of others in order to determine the emotions, status, motive states, relevant culture, and meanings of ecology and demography that apply to an interaction. Reciprocally, by orchestrating both consciously and unconsciously behaviors that signal to others a person's emotional state, status claims, need states and motives, cultural preferences, and interpretations of situational ecology and demography, individuals can greatly facilitate the role-taking of others as they seek to cooperate with them. Let me now elaborate briefly on these dual dynamics of *making* and *taking* that not only operate and rely upon role-taking and role-making but also operate in the same way as these for other micro-level processes.

Activating Microdynamic Forces in Interaction. Ralph Turner's conception of roles implicitly includes the idea that individuals have a certain amount of knowledgeability about roles. If they did not, they probably could not role-take effectively. For Turner, this stock of knowledge at hand about what elements of behaviors go together to make up a coherent role is governed as a "folk norm of consistency." My conceptualization of roles, however, conceptualizes this knowledgeability somewhat differently.

Stocks of Knowledge at Hand. I do not see these dynamics as normative but as hard-wired cognitive capacities and propensities to order perceptions into coherent and understandable patterns. As people role-take and thus read the gestures of others, they scan their stocks of knowledge, to borrow Alfred Schutz's term (see Chapter 19), to discern the role being played by others; and then, on the basis of this scanning, they will try to play a role that is complementary, unless they deliberately wish to initiate conflict (which people often do). This search for patterns is directed by a hardwired bias in humans for consistency and congruence among cognitions, not only for those coming from observations but also for those cognitions stored in the human prefrontal cortex.

As part of the structure and operation of the human brain, then, humans always seek consistency and patterns among elements of cognitions, whether these are about roles, status, culture, motive states, or situational ecology or demography. Gestalt psychology made this point many decades ago, and once again, I do not think that is a "norm" of consistency but simply the way the brain works. Human brains seek to understand meanings of the outside world, and one way to establish meanings is to understand what elements of situations fit into a pattern of gestures marking roles that can then be interpreted. During interactions, people wait for the consistency in patterns to emerge, but if a situation remains chaotic to a person, then it will be highly stressful and force this person to continue scanning stocks of knowledge for a consistent pattern of information. If this pattern is not found in stocks of knowledge, individuals will generally leave such situations and avoid them in the future.

What is true of roles is also the case for other microdynamic processes. Humans have stored in their stocks of knowledge vast inventories of information about emotions, status, motive states, culture, ecology, and demography, which they draw upon to understand the dispositions and behaviors of others. People are naturally scanning their stocks of knowledge for the salient expectations from cultural norms, for status cues, for beliefs, and values, for motives of others, for the attributions others are making, for the meanings of situational ecology and the use of spaces and props in situations, and for the meanings of the various categories of others and their movements and distribution in space. As individuals role-take, then, they access their stocks of knowledge not only for information about roles but also for information about emotions, status, culture, motives, situational ecology, situational demography, and the attributions people are making. At the same time, in their role-making efforts, persons are also signaling their intentions and preferences to others about their emotions, their status, their motives, and their interpretations of the relevant culture, the meanings of situational ecology, and their views on the significance—if any—of situational demography.

Drawing Upon Stocks of Knowledge. Often people already know much of this information by virtue of previous experiences or general knowledge about particular types of situations. For example, before you enter a classroom, you already know about the roles, status, emotions, culture, motives, ecology, and demography of such a situation, with the result that it is not necessary to so actively role-take with specific others in the situation. If we wanted to extend Mead's knowledge of the generalized other, we could view this as role-taking with a generalized other or a set of prescriptions and proscriptions about classrooms, but I prefer Schutz's terms about stocks of knowledgeability that we have acquired over our lifetimes about emotions, status, roles, culture, motives, ecology, and demography of interpersonal situations. We scan this knowledge and then go on "automatic pilot" when, for example, entering a classroom.

Still, despite generalized knowledge about classrooms, we may have to actively role-take and -make, emotion-take and -make, status-take and -make, culture-take and -make, motive-take and -make, ecology-take and -make, or demography-take and -make. For example, if the classroom is much smaller than expected, if the teacher is older or younger, if others are of diverse social categories (say, ethnicity and gender) or of the same category (e.g., all female and young), if there are no chairs lined in a row but chairs around a large table, if the class is important to your sense of identity as a student, if you recognize that the rules of a "seminar class" are different from those of a lecture class, and so on, then you will have to re-scan your stocks of knowledge and begin to more actively read the gestures of others to recalibrate your sense of the situation and the actions of others. So even when situations are familiar and relatively structured, people often must actively role-take and scan their stocks of knowledge for additional information about appropriate roles and also about culture, emotions, status, and the meanings of situational ecology and demography.

As a general rule, the more embedded is a situation within a group, organization, or community, the more likely are people to understand the relevant roles, appropriate emotions, distribution of status, salient elements of culture, and meanings of situational ecology and demography. As a result, they will have an easy time scanning the relevant stocks of knowledge and will not have to be so active in role-taking when interacting with others, *unless* something is new or different about the situation that goes against the stocks of knowledge that have been accessed during the initial scans. If something is new and unexpected, then a person will need to reinterpret the gestures of others and the situation in general with respect to roles, status, motives, culture, ecology, and demography. This person will have to work harder at finding the relevant stocks of knowledge in order to cooperate with others.

Conclusion. The key point in presenting some of my own work with the pioneering work of Ralph Turner is to demonstrate that, despite the decline of theorizing about roles, there is still very much theorizing to be done. Roles are central to, and intertwined with, all other microdynamic processes; and the key to a more general theory of not only role dynamics but all other forces driving interpersonal behavior is to unpack the notions of role-taking and role-making, and to see them as the essentially dynamic forces revolving around all other micro forces driving interaction (my views about these forces are delineated in Table 17.1).

There are, then, many potential leads to expanding the theory of roles, once we link roles to all else that occurs when humans interact. Thus, Ralph H. Turner's theorizing takes us much of the way in developing a more robust theory of role processes; my approach, I hope, opens up further avenues for building on Ralph Turner's theorizing.

Status Theorizing[25]

Early twentieth-century sociology and anthropology developed the concept of *status* to denote the location of persons in social structures and cultural fields. Each status position was seen as part of a structure composed of interrelated positions regulated by cultural norms, ideologies, and beliefs. Yet there still remains considerable ambiguity over just what status denotes. One view is that, as I have mentioned above, status is a location in a network of positions within varying types of social units. Another view is that status is the prestige that persons are able to garner in a situation. Still another is that status is the power and authority that individuals can have vis-à-vis other status locations. Yet another conception is that status is the location of expectations attached to positions that govern how individuals should behave in a particular position and vis-à-vis other status positions. A related position is that status and the expectations associated with status direct the role behaviors of individuals. Another view is that status—conceptualized as *diffuse status characteristics*—is a marker of membership of persons in social categories (e.g., gender, ethnicity, class, religious affiliation). In turn, there are expectation states for, and evaluations of, members in such categories.

All of these visions of status are not contradictory; each highlights a particular property of status. In recent decades, as theorizing about roles has declined, theorizing about status has increased. Most of this theorizing comes from those emphasizing the *differential expectation states* that emerge when (a) individuals occupy different positions in divisions of labor of collectively organized social units, or what I have termed as *corporate units;* (b) individuals behave in ways that allow them to claim prestige and power/authority over others in a situation; and (c) individuals are members of differentially evaluated social categories. Our review of status theories will emphasize these dimensions of status.

---

[25]This section of status dynamics is coauthored with David G. Wagner, whose contribution is significantly greater than mine.

The Phenomenology of Status

As was emphasized in the last section,[26] individuals engage in a process of *status-making* and *status-taking*. They seek to assert and claim, if they can, a status relative to others (status-making) and, reciprocally, interpret the gestures of others and situational cues to determine the status of others. Often, social structures determine people's respective status locations, but even under this condition, people seek to present status cues to others about matters that they can control, such as their competence, which, in turn, entitles them to deference and prestige from others. Status can also be constrained by the social categories in which people are placed—categories such as gender, race, ethnicity, class, or any social difference that marks individuals as distinctive and as subject to a certain level of evaluation. As noted above, these have been termed *diffuse status characteristics* by those theorizing within the expectation states tradition (to be discussed shortly); and these diffuse status characteristics establish expectations for how people should behave and, at the same time, may impose standards of evaluation for the social and moral worth of persons. These evaluative standards, or what are sometimes termed *referential structures* in expectation states theorizing, are beliefs about the qualities and characteristics of members of social categories.

Much like roles, individuals acquire a considerable amount of knowledgeability about the various dimensions of status. And when interacting with others in a situation, they scan these stocks of knowledge in order to determine the expectations for, and evaluations of, individuals' locations in divisions of labor, their performances relative to the performances of others, and their membership in differentially evaluated social categories. People thus carry in their brains inventories of conceptions about status as locations in a social structure, behavioral performances marking competence or its converse, or memberships in a social category. Copresence will typically activate a scanning for the status of self and others in a situation, and with interaction comes even more pressure on individuals for individuals to determine each other's status so as to know the expectations for, and evaluations of, self and others.

Moreover, individuals carry in their stocks of knowledge information about the roles that can be played by virtue of status locations and diffuse status characteristics, what identities can be presented to others, what emotions can and should be displayed, what resources can be used and secured in exchanges with others, what elements of culture (norms, beliefs, ideologies, and values) can be invoked to regulate and evaluate each other, what situational props can be used and by whom with what status, and many other features that drive encounters.

Thus, people carry a great deal of information about status, and they actively pull from their stocks of knowledge the relevant information in status-taking and

---

[26]Turner, *Face-To-Face, Theoretical Principles of Sociology,* vol. 2, "Identities, Emotions, and Interaction Processes," "Toward a Theory of Interpersonal Processes," in *Sociological Social Psychology,* ed. J. Chin and J. Cardell (Boston, MA: Allyn and Bacon, 2008), 65–95, "Emotions and Social Structure: Toward a General Theory," in *Emotions and Social Structure,* ed. D. Robinson and J. Clay-Warner (New York: Elsevier, 2008), 319–342.

status-making with others. And as they play roles, people continue to status-take and status-make to verify that self and others are living up to the expectations attached to their respective status.

Clarity of Status in Situations

Individuals are selectively attentive to status cues when they interact with others, and especially so when status is ambiguous.[27] A key variable in status-taking and -making, then, is the clarity of status. The more the status of self and others is easily understood, the more likely is the interaction to proceed smoothly because all persons understand the expectations for, and the respective evaluations of, self and all other persons in the situation. For example, if we know that a person is a professor and others are students, expectations are relatively clear and unambiguous; and as a result, the interaction can proceed. In contrast, if students encounter professors, and vice versa, in a store in a shopping mall, there is some ambiguity as to which dimensions of status apply. Are professors fellow shoppers, or do the respective status locations at the college or university trump all status considerations? The answer to such questions might well depend on more fine-grained status distinctions, such as whether or not the students are graduate students and the professor is an assistant professor. Here a diffuse status characteristic—respective age—intersects with status as a location in the division of labor of the university and, in all likelihood, reduces status distance and activates expectation states for individuals behaving in the status of shoppers.

In general, the more embedded a status is in a social structure and the more a status is embedded in what Jonathan Turner calls a categoric unit (conceived as diffuse status characteristics by expectation states theorizing), the greater will be the clarity of status and the less individuals will need to status-take in that situation. And status-taking will be made even easier if diffuse status characteristics are highly visible, such as is the case with gender and ethnicity when accompanied by distinctive phenotypical traits like skin color or an eye fold. This clarity increases when there is correlation or consolidation of differentially evaluated diffuse status characteristics with inequality in the power and prestige of locations in the division of labor of corporate units. That is, high-, middle-, and low-ranking status positions are filled by individuals with diffuse status characteristics that match the hierarchy of positional locations in the social structure. If, on the other hand, the two types of status intersect, in that high- and low-evaluation individuals (by virtue of their diffuse status characteristics) are distributed across high and low positions in the division of labor, then status-taking and status-making as well as role-taking and role-making become more complicated for all because clarity has been reduced. The consequence is that individuals will need to exert more effort at status-taking and status-making.

Thus, clarity will increase when positions in divisions of labor are more hierarchical, when memberships in categoric units are more discrete (one is either a member or not, as would be the case with gender), and when differential evaluations of

---

[27]Turner, *Face-To-Face*, 192–205.

diffuse status characteristics are correlated with location in a hierarchy of positions. Much of this clarity in status also makes what I termed *culture-taking* and *culture-making* easier. Individuals know which norms, beliefs, and ideologies to invoke in setting up expectations for how individuals should behave; and the greater the differential evaluation in what are sometimes termed *status beliefs* and the greater is the clarity of these beliefs, the easier will status-taking and -making become. And if these beliefs are tied to societal-level values and institutional-level ideologies (about good/bad, right/wrong, appropriate/inappropriate), the clarity and degree of differential evaluation in status beliefs will be that much more evident to individuals.

Expectation States and Status

One of the most carefully and explicitly developed theoretical research programs in sociology that emerged in the second half of the twentieth century is a related set of theories known as expectation states theory. Although this program was originally the pursuit of Joseph Berger and his colleagues, students, and associates, expectation states theory has in recent years attracted the attention of many other investigators as well.[28]

Expectation states approaches are interactionist theories in several senses. First, behavior is assumed to be situationally constrained, with actors learning how to behave from social and cultural frames of reference available in the situation. Second, these frames of reference exert their influence through the perceptions of individuals, and what people believe or expect to be true about the situation can dictate perceptions of reality; indeed, expectations are the reality for persons in most situations. Finally, these beliefs and expectations emerge and are maintained by the process of interaction itself.

---

[28]Many others have been integral to the development of theories in the expectation states program, particularly Morris Zelditch Jr. and Bernard P. Cohen. Nevertheless, Berger has been the intellectual force at the center of the program since its inception. Many of those who have since made separate contributions to the program first made contributions in collaboration with Berger. For examples of overviews of the progress, see Joseph Berger, Thomas L. Conner, and M. Hamit Fisek (eds.), *Expectation States Theory: A Theoretical Research Program* (Cambridge, MA: Winthrop, 1974; repr., Lanham, MD: University Press of America, 1982); Joseph Berger, David G. Wagner, and Morris Zelditch Jr., "Theory Growth, Social Processes, and Metatheory," in *Theory Building in Sociology*, ed. J. H. Turner (Newbury Park, CA: Sage, 1989), 19–43; Joseph Berger and Morris Zelditch Jr. (eds.), *Status Rewards and Influence* (San Francisco, CA: Jossey-Bass, 1985); Joseph Berger, Bernard P. Cohen, and Morris Zelditch Jr., "Status Characteristics and Expectation States," in *Sociological Theories in Progress*, ed. J. Berger, M. Zelditch Jr., and B. Anderson (Boston, MA: Houghton Mifflin, 1966), 29–46; David G. Wagner and Joseph Berger, "Status Characteristics Theory: The Growth of a Program," in *Theoretical Research Programs: Studies in the Growth of Theory*, ed. J. Berger and M. Zelditch Jr. (Palo Alto, CA: Stanford University Press, 1993), 23–63 and "Expectation States Theory: An Evolving Research Program," in *New Directions in Contemporary Sociological Theory*, ed. J. Berger and M. Zelditch Jr. (New York: Rowman and Littlefield, 2002), 41–76; Shelley J. Correll and Cecilia L. Ridgeway, "Expectation States Theory," in *The Handbook of Social Psychology*, ed. John Delamater (New York: Kluwer-Plenum, 2003), 29–51; and Joseph Berger and Murray Webster Jr., "Expectations, Status, and Behavior," in *Contemporary Social Psychological Theories*, ed. Peter J. Burke (Palo Alto, CA: Stanford University Press, 2006), 268–300.

The Core Ideas of Expectation States Theorizing. The most central concept to the theory is, perhaps obviously, the notion of an *expectation state.* Expectation states represent stabilized anticipations of the future behavior of one actor relative to that of another. Thus, a person is expected to perform more capably or less capably relative to another individual or other individuals. Furthermore, expectations are always both task-specific and person-specific in the sense that person A may be expected to perform more capably than person B with respect to one task (say, repairing an automobile engine) and less capably than B on a second task (say, playing a Beethoven quartet). Similarly, A may be expected to perform more capably than B but less capably than C on the same task.

Because the self constitutes a social object, actors can also have expectations for themselves relative to specific others, although what actors are able to report about self-expectations is just as prone to error and misinterpretation as what they can report about expectations for others. Nevertheless, individuals behave *as if* they have adopted a specific set of expectations.

Expectation states are generated from a variety of sources, such as evaluation of task performances during the course of an interaction, locations in divisions of labor, memberships in social categories, reflection on the appraisals of significant others, allocation of material or symbolic rewards, activation of differences in people's power and prestige, and assessment of justice and equity. These and other sources provide information from the broader social environment, and when individuals interact on a task, this information becomes salient in the immediate, local situation. Expectation states then emerge and organize information into a coherent picture, or definition, of the situation. This picture enables individuals to select behaviors that are appropriate to the situation and to avoid those that are not. Because these behaviors are generally consistent with definitions of the situation, they tend to reinforce established expectations, and typically, it requires the introduction of new information or a change in the local situation to break this self-perpetuating cycle. These core ideas can be summarized as follows:

1. Given certain conditions, individuals organize salient information from the social environment into expectations for behavior in the immediate situation of interaction. (*The salience of social information for expectation formation*)

2. Individuals behave in accordance with their expectations regarding the immediate situation of interaction. (*The behavioral implications of expectations*)

3. Individuals' behavior in the immediate situation of interaction tends to reinforce established expectations. (*The reinforcement of expectations*)

Conditions sufficient to activate the information-organizing process are not always present, however. Consequently, behavior can be relatively stable over extended periods of time, changing only when the new conditions arise. Indeed, from the perspective of expectation states theory, individuals do not continuously reorganize or renegotiate their definitions of the situation; rather, they generally behave in accordance with their existing definitions, reorganizing or renegotiating only when necessary.

Application of Core Ideas in Expectation States Theorizing. Expectation states theorizing has gone in many directions, and so we cannot summarize all of the applications. We will focus primarily on those that affect the dynamics of status as a process locating individuals within social structures.

Power and Prestige. The expectation states program began with Joseph Berger's interest in accounting for the behaviors of individuals in undifferentiated groups. In particular, he sought to understand the emergence and maintenance of power and prestige differences in the behavior of two actors in these initially undifferentiated groups. Berger's behavior expectation theory was initially designed to explain why inequalities in power and prestige evolve so very quickly in groups, even when members are initially similar in status. These inequalities include differences in opportunities to contribute to consideration of the group's task or problem (e.g., asking a question), actual attempts to provide solutions to these tasks and problems (e.g., answering a question), evaluations of the contributions (e.g., criticism of a proposed answer), and acceptance or rejection of influence (e.g., deferring to another actor with whom one has disagreed). Moreover, these inequalities were highly correlated, forming a single hierarchy of observable power and prestige differences among members of the group. Once such a hierarchy emerged, it tended to be stable—even over different group discussions on different days.

Behavior expectation theories were developed initially to explain these phenomena as a consequence of an underlying structure of expectations for future task performance that seemed to emerge from the interactions among group members. Once these expectations exist, they determine the course of future interaction in the group, thereby reinforcing the existing structure of expectations. Thus, the inequalities are highly correlated because they are generated by the same underlying expectations. Further, unless other structural factors intervene (e.g., new group members and new information are introduced or the task focus of the group changes), the structure of expectations and the observable power and prestige hierarchy will remain stable. By adopting the principles described earlier, this process can be summarized as follows:

1. Actors behave toward others in a manner consistent with their expectations. An actor who is considered more capable than others is offered more opportunities to interact, makes more contributions to the interaction, more often has those contributions evaluated positively, and has more influence when disagreements occur. (*The behavioral consequences of expectations*)

2. Expectations tend to remain the same as long as the actors involved in the situation and the tasks that they are performing remain the same. (*The persistence of expectations*)

Although these expectation state processes occur under a wide variety of conditions, they are most evident in situations where actors who are initially similar in status work together collectively on a task that they value. Thus, we might observe expectation processes in jury deliberations, business conferences, family vacation planning, or a group of teenagers planning a trip to the movies. They might also be evident in the interaction among members of a basketball team but might be less likely to occur in the interaction between members of opposing teams because they are not working toward a common goal.[29]

Other work in behavior expectation theory has focused on the process by which expectations emerge from an interaction.[30] This work suggests that resolving disagreements forces actors to evaluate their own and others' performances and to accept or reject influence from others on the basis of these evaluations. Any time a decision must be made, there is some likelihood that individuals will develop an expectation state for each other, that is—in a very real sense—an anticipation of the quality of an actor's future contributions. This expectation state will be consistent with the preponderance of evaluations for the contributions of each individual in the group. More generally, we can summarize the process in these terms:

3. The more consistent the evaluations of an actor's past interaction are, the more likely the actor and others are to expect a level of capability from the actor in the future that realizes past evaluations. (*The emergence of expectations*)

Later work has developed and extended these arguments. For example, inequalities with respect to any aspect of the group's interaction, not just the evaluation of an individual's performance, might generate expectations and spread to other aspects of the interaction.[31] Power and prestige hierarchies can emerge from interaction involving any number of actors as well as from different types of actors.[32] Finally, objective evaluations from external sources of information that contradict established expectations can help overcome existing expectations. Such changes depend on the number and extremity of the contradicting evaluations.[33]

Status Characteristics. As noted earlier, actors are similar or differ with respect to status distinctions, such as ethnicity, age, race, or gender, that might be significant in a society at large. Status characteristics theory describes how actors organize information about

---

[29]Berger first developed this argument in his doctoral dissertation, Joseph Berger, "Relations Between Performance, Rewards, and Action-Opportunities in Small Groups" (unpublished doctoral dissertation, Harvard University, 1958). See also Joseph Berger and Thomas L. Conner, "Performance Expectations and Behavior in Small Groups," *Acta Sociologica* 12 (1969):186–198.

[30]See, for example, Joseph Berger, Thomas L. Conner, and W. McKeown, "Evaluations and the Formation and Maintenance of Performance Expectations," *Human Relations* 22 (1969):481–502 and Thomas J. Fararo (ed.), "An Expectation States Process Model," in *Mathematical Sociology* (New York: Wiley, 1973), 229–237.

[31]Joseph Berger and Thomas L. Conner, "Performance Expectations and Behavior in Small Groups: A Revised Formulation," in *Expectation States Theory: A Theoretical Research Program*, ed. Berger, Conner, and Fisek (Cambridge, MA: Winthrop, 1974; repr., Lanham, MD: University Press of America, 1982), 85–109; see also M. Hamit Fisek, "A Model for the Evolution of Status Structures," 55–83, in the same volume.

[32]Thomas J. Fararo and John Skvoretz, "E-State Structuralism: A Theoretical Method," *American Sociological Review* 51 (1986):591–602.

[33]See, for example, Martha Foschi and R. Foschi, "A Bayesian Model for Performance Expectations: Extension and Simulation," *Social Psychology Quarterly* 42 (1979):232–241.

the initial status differences that they use to generate expectations for performance. As with behavior expectation theory, these expectations then govern the interaction, ensuring that power and prestige are distributed in accord with expectations.

Research has shown that external status distinctions become the basis for internal ones; status inequalities that are significant in the larger society become important in the task situation of a small group. These distinctions present even as the group is being formed, govern the distribution of power and prestige, and, furthermore, occur whether or not the status distinction is associated with the group's task.[34]

Status distinctions are, as emphasized earlier, characterized as *diffuse status characteristics*, with a characteristic being diffuse for a particular individual in the situation if (a) the characteristic has two or more states that the individual evaluates differently, (b) the individual associates a general expectation with each status state, and (c) the individual associates a distinct set of expectations for specific abilities or traits with each state.[35] Gender, race, ethnicity, educational attainment, occupation, and physical attractiveness are each examples of these kinds of diffuse status characteristics, because they generally meet the three features listed above. The properties that define a characteristic are based on attributions made by the individual representing beliefs in cultural systems to which the individual is exposed. Thus,

1. If actors have differentiated diffuse status or if a status they share is culturally associated with a task that the actors perform, then the actors will attribute generalized expectations and specific abilities to themselves and each other consistent with their status. (*The salience of status information*)

A second principle concerns establishing the relevance of salient status; hence, the "burden of proof" principle emphasizes that status information will be assumed to be task-relevant *unless* there is specific information to the contrary.

2. Actors assume that salient status information applies to every new task and every new situation unless they have a specific knowledge or belief that demonstrates its inapplicability. (*The relevance of status information*)

3. An actor with a status advantage is expected to perform more capably than an actor with a status disadvantage. (*The assignment of expectations*)

Finally, in line with this basic expectation assumption, people behave in accordance with their expectations. Opportunities to initiate action, actual performance outputs, communicated evaluations of performance, and influence will all reflect the difference in self-expectations and expectations for others. Thus, the presence of a single diffuse status characteristic that discriminates between actors is sufficient to

---

[34]For a summary of some of this research, see Bernard P. Cohen, Joseph Berger, and Morris Zelditch Jr., "Status Conceptions and Interaction: A Case Study of the Problem of Developing Cumulative Knowledge," in *Experimental Social Psychology*, ed. C. G. McClintock (New York: Holt, Rinehart, and Winston, 1972), 449–483.

[35]See Berger, Cohen, and Zelditch Jr., "Status Characteristics and Expectation States"; the paper was updated with a report on empirical results in *American Sociological Review* 37 (1972):241–255.

generate differentiated power and prestige behavior, provided that the status differences are not dissociated from the task.

Multiple-Characteristic Status Situations. One important dilemma for individuals in interaction, and hence for a theory of expectation states, occurs where multiple status characteristics are present.[36] In essence, theorists and researchers asked, "What are the implications for expectations and behavior when individuals can be distinguished by more than one status characteristic, especially when the implications of these statuses are inconsistent?"[37]

What appears to occur is that individuals add up two subsets of information. One combines all the positive information relevant to a person in a situation, and the other has all the negative information. Then, the positive and negative subsets are subtracted from each other, leaving a net evaluation of expectations that is either positive or negative depending upon which subset was greater. Once this composite of information is established, additional information will have less impact on the already established evaluation and expectation states derived from this evaluation. The following principles summarize this process:

1. Actors combine information from multiple salient status differences to form aggregated expectations for self and others. (*The combining principle*)

2. Actors combine positive status information into one (positively valued) set and negative information into a second (negatively valued) set. Expectations are aggregated by summing the values of these two sets. (*The principle of organized subsets*)

3. Each additional piece of status information added to a set increases the value of that set at a decreasing rate. (*The attenuation principle*)

Finally, the basic expectation assumption is modified to accommodate the multiple bases for the formation of expectations.

4. Once expectation states form from multiple bases, this combination of expectation states determines each actor's power and prestige relative to other actors. (*The behavioral implications of combined expectations*)

The Evolution of Expectation States. While expectation states may be established by clearly defined positions in social structures and by pervasive status beliefs, status may not be clear or specified. The result is that expectations will evolve in situations because individuals are disposed to look for status information and to use this information to establish expectations for self and

---

[36]See Joseph Berger and M. Hamit Fisek, "A Generalization of the Theory of Status Characteristics and Expectation States," in *Expectation States Theory*, 163–205 and Joseph Berger, M. Hamit Fisek, Robert Z. Norman, and Morris Zelditch Jr., *Status Characteristics and Social Interaction* (New York: Elsevier, 1977).

[37]The effects of another kind of status difference, referred to as a specific status characteristic, are also considered. Specific status differences apply only to a specific task or kind of task (e.g., involving mathematical or artistic ability).

others.[38] Once expectation states form, they will exert a disproportionate influence on the expectations for individuals during subsequent interactions, as long as no new status information is introduced into the situation. The results of these processes are as follows:

1. The expectations and behavior of actors will tend to become stable across consecutive interaction situations as long as no new information is introduced into the situation. (*Stability of status positions*)

2. Given the external evaluations of an actor's performance in a previous situation, (a) differential evaluations that are consistent with the actors' power and prestige positions in the group increase the inequality; (b) differential evaluations that are inconsistent with the actors' power and prestige positions in the group decrease the inequality (and can even invert it); and (c) if the evaluations of both actors are similar, then any expectation advantage held by one of the actors will be reduced. (*Assignment of success or failure*)

3. If actors have diffuse status characteristics from outside the group and specific status positions within the local situation that are inconsistent with each other, then their expectations and behavior will stabilize across consecutive interaction situations at a value between what would result from either the diffuse or the specific statuses alone, again as long as no new information is introduced into the situation. (*The effects of interventions*)

Status Cues, Expectations, and Behavior. Individuals use a variety of social cues (such as patterns of speech, posture, direct references to background or experience, styles of dress) to help form expectations. And when status is ambiguous, unspecified, or unknown, individuals will rely even more on these cues, typically associated with the role-making and status-making behaviors of individuals.

In expectation states theory, indicative cues are distinguished from expressive cues, and task cues are separated from categorical cues. Indicative cues (e.g., "I'm a doctor.") directly label the actor's status state, whereas expressive cues (e.g., a man's style of dress) provide information from which status states can be inferred. The task/categorical distinction is independent of the indicative/expressive distinction. Task cues (e.g., fluency of speech) provide information about the actor's capacities on an immediate task, whereas categorical cues (e.g., language syntax) provide information about the expectation states of status characteristics that actors possess. Using these distinctions, status cues theory[39] yields the following propositions:

1. If no prior status differences exist in the situation, then differences in task cues will help generate expectation states, which in turn determine the distribution of power and prestige behavior in the situation. (*Task cues in the absence of status differences*)

---

[38]Joseph Berger, M. Hamit Fisek, and Robert Z. Norman, "The Evolution of Status Expectations: A Theoretical Extension," *in Sociological Theories in Progress: New Formulations*, ed. J. Berger, M. Zelditch Jr., and B. Anderson (Newbury Park, CA: Sage, 1989), 100–130.

[39]Joseph Berger, Murray A. Webster Jr., Cecilia Ridgeway, and Susan J. Rosenholtz, "Status Cues, Expectations, and Behavior," *Advances in Group Processes* 3 (1986):1–22.

2. If status differences exist from the outset in a situation, then the differentiation in task cues will produce congruent differences in expectations, which in turn determine congruent differences in the rates of task cue behaviors. Consequently, rates of task cue behaviors will be consistent with the initial status differences. (*Status governance of task cues*)

3. If for some reason, the differentiation in task cues is inconsistent with differentiation in categorical cues, then information from both sets combines to determine the actors' expectations and behavior. (*Combining inconsistent task and categorical cues*)

Task cues provide information about capacities on an immediate task, whereas categorical cues provide information about diffuse status characteristics that might become relevant to the task. Hence, the strength of relevance of task cues is greater than that of categorical cues, signaling that, when inconsistent, the effect of task cues will be greater than the effect of categorical cues. We should add, however, that most experimental studies of expectation states theory are oriented to the completion of tasks in artificial and temporary groups; when groups are more stable, these dynamics, especially those outlined in proposition 3 above, may change. In longer-term interactions, the effect of initially salient diffuse status characteristics may become diluted as individuals get to know each other and much of the additional status information becomes salient. However, this effect will be minimized if diffuse status characteristics are correlated with inequalities in positional status in divisions of labor (e.g., all bosses are men and all secretaries are women; under these conditions, both expectations for, and evaluations of, positional and diffuse status characteristics will be reinforced). In contrast, if diffuse status characteristics and inequalities in status and prestige are not correlated, then the expectations for tasks in the differentiated positional status will remain, while the salience of diffuse status characteristics may be diluted. Thus, it could be hypothesized that[40]

4. The relative salience and power of expectation states for positional status and diffuse status characteristics increase for both to the extent that they are correlated with each other (e.g., high-rank positions are held by individuals possessing highly evaluated diffuse status characteristics, and vice versa).

5. The relative salience and power of expectation states for positional status and diffuse status characteristics will be diluted for diffuse characteristics over time with high rates of interaction and more dramatically so and more rapidly when there is no correlation between incumbency in ranked positions and differentially evaluated members possessing diffuse status characteristics; and as a result, task expectations and evaluations associated with status will be more salient than diffuse status characteristics.

---

[40]Unlike most generalizations, these propositions are not documented with research findings; they are hypotheses derived from theories outside the experimental tradition of expectation states research and theory. See Turner, *Face-to-Face* and *Theoretical Principles of Sociology*.

Legitimation of Power and Prestige Hierarchies. Another theory in the expectation states program is concerned with the process of the legitimization of power and prestige orders, and with inequalities in status more generally. Legitimization processes are especially important for leaders with traditionally low diffuse status characteristics (e.g., women or minorities) as they seek to engage successfully in the directive behaviors ordinarily expected of a leader. Legitimation is also likely to influence the effectiveness of controlling behaviors, such as dominating and propitiating behaviors. For without being seen as having the right to engage in leadership activities, the power and prestige order will be disrupted.

Part of any person's social framework is consensual beliefs, operating as referential structures to connect status positions with the diffuse statuses, task capacities, and task achievements.[41] This information becomes activated in the local situation and helps generate expectations regarding status in the group. As actors behave in accordance with these expectations, they validate the expectations and establish their legitimacy.

1. When referential beliefs from the larger society are activated in the immediate interaction situation, actors create expectations about who will occupy high- and low-valued status positions in the situation. (*Referential beliefs and valued status positions*)

2. Given expectations regarding the possession of high- and low-valued status positions in a situation, actors are likely to display differences in respect, esteem, and generalized deference behavior to others that are consistent with these expectations. (*Valued status positions and behavior*)

3. When behaviors consistent with expected status positions are validated by others and when they coincide with actual differences in power and prestige behaviors, the power and prestige hierarchy is likely to become legitimated. (*Behavioral validation and legitimacy*)

An actor's behavior is validated by another if this other engages in supportive behavior or if this other's behavior does not contradict the behavior of the actor seeking validation and, hence, legitimacy. Legitimization requires actors to make assumptions about "what ought to be" in the immediate situation. Expectations become normative, with the presumption that there will be collective support for these norms. A person of high status has a right to expect a higher degree of esteem, respect, and generalized deference than does a person of low status. At the same time, others have the right to expect more valued contributions from this high-status person than from low-status actors. In addition, actors of high status develop

---

[41]See Cecilia L. Ridgeway and Joseph Berger, "Expectations, Legitimacy, and Dominance in Task Groups," *American Sociological Review* 51 (1986):603–617 and "The Legitimation of Power and Prestige Orders in Task Groups," in *Status Generalization: New Theory and Research*, ed. M. A. Webster and M. Foschi (Stanford, CA: Stanford University Press, 1988), 207–231 and Cecilia L. Ridgeway, "Gender Differences in Task Groups: A Status and Legitimacy Account," in *Status Generalization: New Theory and Research*, 188–206.

the right to exercise, if necessary, controlling behaviors—dominating and propitiating behaviors—over the actions of others.

Formation of Reward Expectations. Referential structures can be activated in a particular task situation, and when activated, each provides a standard for the formation of individuals' expectations for reward in a situation.[42] Several propositions have been derived from expectation states theories on the operation of standards as determined by the activation of referential structures. The first of these concerns how information from multiple standards is treated in generating reward expectations.

1. If multiple referential structures establishing standards for allocation of rewards are activated in the immediate situation of interaction, actors combine the information from all activated structures in generating expectations for reward. (*Combining referential structures*)

The second and third theorems consider how increases in the consistency or inconsistency of status characteristics affect the degree of inequality in reward expectations.

2. Increases in the amount of consistent status information salient for an actor in the immediate interaction situation increase the inequality in reward expectations. (*Status consistency and inequality in reward expectations*)

3. Increases in the amount of inconsistent status information salient for an actor in the immediate interaction situation, however, decrease the inequality in reward expectations. (*Status inconsistency and equality in reward expectations*)

The fourth proposition focuses on the interdependence of task and reward expectations:

4. Changes in an actor's task expectations (accomplished by adding or eliminating relevant status distinctions) produce correlated changes in the actor's reward expectations; in turn, changes in an actor's reward expectations (accomplished by adding or deleting standards of allocation) produce correlated changes in task expectations. (*The interdependence of expectations*)

One consequence of the interdependence of task and reward expectations is that referential standards can produce differences in the *significance* of status characteristics. Differences in the relative importance of status characteristics often depend on whether or not these characteristics are the basis on which rewards and privileges are expected to be distributed. Statuses that differ in this respect should also differ in their significance

---

[42]Joseph Berger, M. Hamit Fisek, Robert Z. Norman, and David G. Wagner, "The Formation of Reward Expectations in Status Situations," in *Status, Rewards, and Influence: How Expectations Organize Interaction*, ed. Joseph Berger and Morris Zelditch Jr. (San Francisco, CA: Jossey-Bass, 1985), 215–261.

or importance (or "weight") in the interaction. The fifth theorem establishes the differential significance of status characteristics:

5. Status characteristics have a greater effect on the actor's task expectations if they are the basis for referential standards of allocation than if they are not. (*The social significance of status differences*)

Distributive Justice. Individuals may make an assessment about whether or not their rewards, however calculated and expected, are fair and just. Expectation states theorizing offers an alternative to exchange theories on how justice is determined by individuals.[43] How do individuals respond when they perceive an injustice in the distribution of rewards? The status value theory of distributive justice considers these questions. Exchange theories develop what is, in essence, an equity theory,[44] emphasizing that evaluations of justice and injustice are based on comparisons of one actor's ratio of the rewards received to the actual investments made to receive these rewards with the ratio of rewards to costs/investments of at least one other actor in the immediate situation. If the rewards are in excess of costs and investments and the same as for those who are also incurring similar costs and investments, then the payoff for activities is considered fair and just.

In contrast, the status value theory of distributive justice argues that theories emphasizing comparisons of rewards to investments are inadequate. As an alternative explanation, the value of objects to individuals is based on the status that they represent rather than only their consummatory value (less costs and investments), as is the case in equity theories. For example, the value of the key to the executive washroom is viewed by the status, honor, esteem, and importance that it conveys to the person who possesses the valued good (rather than by the consummatory value that comes with convenience and privacy).

Justice issues, therefore, involve questions of status consistency and inconsistency between expectations and allocations of rewards. As long as actors receive the status value that they expect, the situation is seen as just. If actors receive a status value different from what they expect, however, then the situation is seen as unjust. Thus, one's sense of justice is not so much a matter of the ratio of rewards received to investments made, compared with the ratio for others in that situation, as an assessment of rewards in relation to what was expected by virtue of status.

These expectations for reward depend on referential structures, and the activation of referential structures enables actors to relate their general cultural framework to their immediate situation. When a particular referential structure is activated, individuals expect to receive rewards commensurate with their relevant status. Basically, "what is" in general cultural definitions becomes "what is expected to be" in the immediate situation. Thus, a man who believes that men are generally better paid

---

[43]See Joseph Berger, Morris Zelditch Jr., Bo Anderson, and Bernard P. Cohen, "Structural Aspects of Distributive Justice: A Status Value Formulation," in *Sociological Theories in Progress*, vol. 2., ed. J. Berger, M. Zelditch Jr., and B. Anderson (Boston, MA: Houghton Mifflin, 1972), 119–146.

[44]See J. S. Adams, "Inequity in Social Exchange," *Advances in Experimental Social Psychology*, 2 (1965):267–299.

than women will expect a higher level of reward when he is interacting with a woman—provided, of course, that gender is a relevant and salient status characteristic to the actors and a relevant referential structure has been activated. To summarize more formally,

1. If an actor activates referential structures, and thereby culturally associates different levels of reward with different status positions, then he or she is likely to develop expectations for the allocation of rewards in the immediate interaction situation that are consistent with this cultural association. (*The activation of referential structures*)

2. If an actor receives the level of reward that is consistent with expectations created by the cultural association of referential structures to status characteristics, then the actor will regard the situation as just. (*The effect of expectations on assessments of justice*)

3. If an actor receives a level of reward inconsistent with expectations generated by the cultural association of referential structures with status characteristics, the actor will regard the situation as unjust. (*The effect of expectations on assessments of injustice*)

A "reverse process" can also operate in the sense that an allocation of differentially evaluated rewards can generate performance expectations consistent with this allocation. This process is most likely to occur when a referential structure is activated and when the relevant status distinction is based primarily on performance. To state this more formally,

4. If an actor is allocated a differentiated level of reward, differentiated performance expectations consistent with the allocated level of reward are likely to develop. (*The effect of differential rewards on expectations*)

Sources of Self-Evaluation. Source theory considers how expectations can emerge through the reflected appraisals of significant others. Source theory uses ideas regarding unit evaluations and expectations developed in behavior expectation theory, as well as ideas from status characteristics theory. As with status characteristics theory in general, the original version of source theory dealt only with the simplest situation, involving a single evaluator. How do the appraisals of those with the right to evaluate affect the expectations and behavior of others in a situation? Under some circumstances, an evaluator can become a source of evaluations for the actor—that is, an evaluator whose assessments matter to the actor or, in other words, a "significant other." The likelihood of a particular evaluator becoming a source is directly related to an individual's expectations for this evaluator:

1. The higher is an actor's expectations for an evaluator, the greater is the likelihood that this evaluator will become a source of evaluations for the actor. (*The effect of external evaluations on expectations*)

When this occurs, the actor's expectations and behavior are determined by the evaluations of the source:

2. Given a source as evaluator, an actor's evaluations, expectations, and behavior will be shaped and directed by this source's evaluations. (*The effects of sources of evaluation*)

An actor's expectations for an evaluator are likely to be affected by any status characteristics that the evaluator possesses. An extension of the original source theory by Murray Webster showed that status is directly related to the likelihood of becoming a source:

3. A high-status evaluator is more likely to become a source for an actor than is a low-status evaluator. (*The effect of evaluator status on evaluation importance*)[45]

If there are multiple evaluators and their evaluations conflict, actors apparently use source information in much the same way as they use status information. They process and combine all the salient cues to form composite expectations:

4. Actors combine the unit evaluations of multiple conflicting sources to form self-expectations. (*Combining source evaluations*)[46]

Stability and Change in Status Beliefs. Expectation states for status will tend to endure unless new information is added that forces people to revise expectations. Indeed, as we will see later, negative emotions are aroused when individuals go against expectations, leading to sanctions by others on those who would violate the status order.[47] Once expectation states have emerged, they are difficult to change; and this stability in expectation states is particularly problematic for members of less valued social categories by virtue of the expectations on, and evaluations of, their diffuse status characteristics. The reason for this difficulty is that status beliefs are more than situations; rather, they tend to be part of the more general beliefs that people in a society carry. For example, prejudices against particular categories of persons are universal in societies, and these become a backup for local status beliefs that are used to establish expectations for individuals in encounters and groupings that carry a heavy evaluative element. When there is general consensus over status

---

[45]Murray A. Webster Jr., "Sources of Evaluations and Expectations for Performance," *Sociometry* 32 (1969):243–258.

[46]See especially Murray A. Webster Jr. and B. Sobieszek, *Sources of Self Evaluation* (New York: Wiley, 1974). For further extensions of this idea, see J. C. Moore, "Role Enactment and Self-Identity: An Expectation States Approach," in *Status, Rewards, and Influence*, 262–316.

[47]Cecilia L. Ridgeway, "Affect," in *Group Processes: Sociological Analyses*, ed. M. Foschi and E. J. Lawler (Chicago, IL: NelsonHall), 205–230 and "Status and Emotions from an Expectation States Theory," in *Handbook of the Sociology of Emotion*, ed. J. E. Stets and J. H. Turner (New York: Springer, 2006).

beliefs about members possessing diffuse status characteristics,[48] they are very difficult to eliminate, but there are certain conditions when this is possible. The key is persistent and consistent challenges to status beliefs. These challenges can come from broader social movements—for example, the civil rights movement, women's movement—that mount a persistent attack on prejudicial beliefs and the attendant status beliefs about members of particular social categories. In conjunction with such movements, but potentially as a separate force, individuals can persistently challenge status beliefs in face-to-face situations. Such challenges are particularly effective if members of more valued social categories lead the way. Over time, and with persistent questioning of implicit status beliefs, change in general status beliefs in a society can occur. For example, in the United States these dynamics have dramatically altered status beliefs about formerly devalued categories of persons: minorities (African Americans, Latinos, Asians), women, and gays/lesbians. Thus,

1. The more local status beliefs are drawn from broader status beliefs in a society and the greater is the consensus over these beliefs, the more resistant to change are beliefs about members of social categories possessing devalued diffuse status characteristics.

2. The more persistent and widespread are challenges to these beliefs at the local level, especially by higher-status members of groups, and the more these efforts are backed up by a social movement and counter-ideology against these believers, the more likely will status beliefs about diffuse status characteristics change toward a more favorable evaluation.

3. The more these status beliefs change, the less salient will older status beliefs be and, hence, the more likely are members of formerly devalued social categories to hold a higher status in groupings and in the division of labor in larger social units.

Status beliefs about individuals in positions carrying different amounts of power and prestige are also subject to these dynamics, but there are additional processes whereby status beliefs about particular individuals in specific situations can be

---

[48]Cecilia L. Ridgeway, "Conformity, Group-Oriented Motivation, and Status Attainment in Small Groups," *Social Psychology Quarterly* 41 (1978):175–188, "Status in Groups: The Importance of Emotion," *American Sociological Review* 47 (1982):76–88. See also C. L. Ridgeway, K. Backor, Y. E. Li, J. E. Tinkler, and K. G. Erickson, "How Easily Does a Social Difference Become a Status Distinction: Gender Matters," *American Sociological Review* 74 (2009):44–62; C. L. Ridgeway and J. Berger, "Expectations, Legitimacy, and Dominance in Task Groups," *American Sociological Review* 51 (1986):603–617 and "The Legitimation of Power and Prestige Orders in Task Groups" in *Status Generalization: New Theory and Research* (Stanford, CA: Stanford University Press, 1988); C. L. Ridgeway, E. Boyle, K. Kulpers, and D. Robinson, "How Do Status Beliefs Develop? The Role of Resources and Interaction," *American Sociological Review* 63 (1998):331–350; C. L. Ridgeway and S. J. Correll, "Unpacking the Gender System: A Theoretical Perspective on Cultural Beliefs and Social Relations," *Gender and Society* 18 (2004):510–531; C. L. Ridgeway and K. G. Erickson, "Creating and Spreading Status Beliefs," *American Journal of Sociology* 106 (2000):579–615; C. L. Ridgeway and C. Johnson, "What Is the Relationship between Socioemotional Behavior and Status in Task Groups?" *American Journal of Sociology* 95 (1990):1189–1212; and C. L. Ridgeway and H. A. Walker, "Status Structure" in *Sociological Perspectives on Social Psychology*, ed. K. S. Cook, G. A. Fine, and J. S. House (Boston, MA: Allyn and Bacon, 1995), 282–310.

altered.[49] Whether status beliefs evolve from individuals' performances or are imposed by an existing structure, those in lower-status positions will generally have a difficult time breaking the expectations attached to their status location, as earlier propositions summarizing research have documented. And, as we will see below in the analysis of emotions, efforts of lower-status people to change their status and/or challenge high-status individuals will generally invite negative sanctions from the higher-status persons who are challenged but also negative sanctions from their fellow lower-status individuals. Disruption of the status order represents a failure, per se, to abide by the expectations, which, in turn, arouses negative emotions. People generally seek to avoid negative emotions, and thus, they will sanction negatively those who violate the status order and the expectation states on which it is based. How, then, in local situations where expectations are established are lower-status persons to display their competence without threatening the status order and inviting negative sanctions? The key appears to be to consistently demonstrate competence in activities without directly challenging the legitimated status order. Strategically, this often means using rather indirect methods—asking polite questions, offering tentative suggestions, and other nonconfrontational techniques—that still evidence the trappings of subordination while demonstrating competence. Over time, under these conditions, an individual's status and associated expectation states can rise through a more evolutionary than revolutionary process. Thus,

4. Direct challenges by lower-status individuals to the legitimated status order will invite negative emotional reactions from both higher- and lower-status individuals. They do so because of the power of legitimated expectations attached to lower and higher status.

5. The status order can change when lower-status individuals use indirect interpersonal techniques to demonstrate their higher levels of competence; and by using indirect challenges without making direct ones, they can over time cause a revaluation of their competence and, thus, a revision of the expectation states attached to them and their rights to claim greater prestige and, potentially, greater power.

Status and Emotions

When expectations are realized in a situation, individuals will generally experience positive emotions, whereas when they are not, they will feel negative emotions. There are several general theories[50] outside the status-theorizing tradition that make this fundamental point about any set of expectations, but here we focus on theories

---

[49]Cecilia L. Ridgeway, "Where Do Status Beliefs Come From?" in *Status, Network, and Structure,* ed. J. Szmatka and J. Berger (Stanford, CA: Stanford University Press, 1998), "The Formation of Status Beliefs: Improving Status Construction Theory," *Advances in Group Processes* 17 (2000):77–102, "Inequality, Status, and the Construction of Status Beliefs," in *Handbook of Sociological Theory,* ed. Jonathan H. Turner (New York: Kluwer/Plenum Press, 2001), 323–342.

[50]Jonathan H. Turner, *Human Emotions: A Sociological Theory* (London: Routledge, 2008).

that are within the status-theorizing tradition. Many of these come from the expectation states theory-research program, and so we will begin with these.

Expectation States Theories of Affect. As is evident from the above review of theory-research traditions in expectation states theorizing, the central idea in these theories is that members of groups are assigned a status by virtue of their performances and/or an existing status structure within some unit organization. Incumbency in status or possession of diffuse status characteristics establishes expectations for people's competence and for their role behaviors. Such assignment to a status and its corresponding expectations can thus be based on diffuse characteristics, such as age, ethnicity, education, gender, wealth, and other traits that individuals bring to the group from the outside, as well as on internal organizational forces establishing lines of authority, rank, and division of labor. In more recent years, one of the many creative branches in this general theoretical program has been the analysis of emotions. Let us review them, but without the formalizations since most of these theories have not been formalized.

Cecilia Ridgeway's Theory. Like most research and theory within the expectation states tradition, Ridgeway's[51] and Johnson's[52] work focuses mostly on task-oriented groups, where individuals are temporarily assembled to realize a clearly stated goal or purpose. As Ridgeway and Johnson argue, even the most transitory task-oriented group develops an affect structure as members agree and disagree on how best to accomplish the group's goals. Moreover, disagreements can also involve status challenges as lower-status members seek to raise their position and refuse to defer to the arguments of higher-status members.

In all groups, Ridgeway has argued, a broader societal culture penetrates group structures as a set of norms or blueprint rules that indicate how people are supposed to behave in particular types of groups, whether task-oriented work groups or more informal and intimate groups. Following Hochschild's point of emphasis, these blueprint rules include (a) "feeling rules" about what kinds of emotions are to be experienced in a situation and (b) "display rules" about what emotions can be expressed publicly and how they are to be expressed. An affect-arousing event will, therefore, activate these feeling and display rules; yet status expectation processes are still important in organizing the way affect is mobilized and managed.

Disagreements represent one class of affect-arousing events, and when such disagreements occur among group members, status in the group determines whether individuals will blame themselves or others for the disagreement. If a person holds an equal or higher status compared with the other(s) with whom a disagreement exists, then this person will be likely to attribute the disagreement to the other(s), and this person will feel and express *annoyance* (a mild form of anger). On the other hand, if an individual is of lower status than the person(s) with whom there is a

---

[51]Ridgeway, "Status in Groups," "Affect," in *Group Processes.*

[52]Ridgeway and Johnson, "What Is the Relationship Between Socioemotional Behavior and Status in Task Groups?"

disagreement, then this individual will tend to blame self and will experience depression. For this reason, Ridgeway and Johnson note that superiors are far more likely to express anger and annoyance with subordinates than the reverse: The superior is expected to be more competent, and when authority is challenged, anger ensues because expectation states are being violated by inferiors, whereas when subordinates disagree with superordinates, expectation states force them to attribute the blame to themselves (because they are presumed to be less knowledgeable and competent). And because no reward is to be gained from continuing to blame oneself, individuals tend not to pursue the disagreement. Instead, the lower-status person withdraws, often to the point of experiencing *depression.*

These disagreement-anger episodes can disrupt the solidarity of the group, however, even as the status order is reconfirmed. Anger and annoyance do not promote positive sentiments of liking and mutual trust. *Depression* in subordinates leads them to withdraw commitment from the group, thereby eroding solidarity further. In contrast, agreement among people of different status has the opposite effect: it promotes solidarity. If those who agree are of lower status, then the higher-status persons feel *satisfaction* (a moderate form of *happiness*) about the fact that the subordinates agree with them. If those who agree are of equal or higher status, then these individuals are likely to feel a more intense form of happiness, such as *gratitude,* that comes when superordinates agree with them. When people experience these positive emotions, Ridgeway and Johnson argue, they become motivated to reward those who agree with them; as they do so, all parties develop positive sentiments and become more likely to agree in the future. From this cycle of positive reinforcement comes enhanced group solidarity.

These status processes also help explain why groups typically reveal more positive than negative affect. As noted earlier, disagreements emanating from lower-status persons are sanctioned because they violate the expectations associated with lower- and higher-status group members, and hence, lower-status individuals soon stop punishing themselves and keep quiet. If disagreement can be avoided and agreement can be reached, then the positive emotions of *satisfaction, happiness,* and *gratitude* initiate cycles of positive reinforcement that evolve into solidarity, which further orients group members to express agreement and to reward each other with positive sentiments.

As noted earlier, an interesting dynamic is initiated when a lower-status person is highly assertive and refuses to back down. Expectation states lead others to sanction the lower-status person negatively as being too pushy and self-interested—what is termed the "backlash effect" against those who violate the status order. Thus, lower-status individuals will almost always have difficulty in groups where they seek to raise their status by displaying competence in an assertive manner; assertions of such competence will be defined as violating the status order and the expectations associated with this order. One strategy for overcoming this backlash effect is to couch assertions of competence in friendly and unthreatening ways, perhaps as suggestions rather than as challenges. In this manner, lower-status group members can, over time, slowly raise their status and change the expectations associated with them.

Another interesting facet of this theory is the argument that the degree of congruence between the status structure and the distribution of affect shapes rates of participation in making decisions. When high-status members are liked more than low-status members, their power to influence decisions is enhanced. Lower-status members not only see the higher-status members as more competent, they also like them. Because of this congruence in status and sentiment, lower-status individuals are more likely to accept the decisions of the higher-status members. Congruence of affect and status thus amplifies the influence of status in task groups; and research by Janet R. Johnston demonstrates that such is also the case in more long-term and intimate groups. Johnston's findings have, in turn, stimulated Joseph Berger's long-standing research program exploring expectation processes in more intimate and longer-term groups.

Joseph Berger's Affect Expectations Theory. Joseph Berger argues that as emotional reactions emerge and are repeated over time within groups, these reactions generate *affect expectation states* that shape and guide the flow of interaction.[53] Such affect expectation states unfold in a series of stages: (a) affect is aroused during the interaction; (b) an exchange of affect occurs and begins to set up expectations for what will happen in the current interaction; (c) these affect states also begin to generate an emotional orientation toward others in the situation that involves more stable sentiments—whether positive or negative—which will shape the course of subsequent interactions; and, eventually, (d) assignment of personality characteristics consistent with the affect that is exchanged and the emotional orientations of individuals will occur, further circumscribing current and future interactions.

Through this approximate sequence, the affect structure of a group stabilizes the interaction, giving it consistency over time. Moreover, people develop situational identities as they exchange affect and impute personalities to each other. Once these identities are formed, they become expectations for what will occur in the situation, thereby further stabilizing the interaction. Individuals thus become driven and constrained to act in certain ways through the exchange of affect and the development of affect expectations. Yet this kind of affective structure does not completely determine or circumscribe what occurs in the group. For if expressive exchanges consistently do not confirm the affect expectations that have developed, then the affective orientations of individuals, the imputation of personality traits, and perhaps the situational identities of individuals will all change, and new affect expectations will begin to emerge.

Robert Shelly's Theory of Status and Sentiments. Robert Shelly argues that emotions and sentiments can be seen as different.[54] Sentiments are milder, low-intensity

---

[53]Joseph Berger, "Directions in Expectation States Research," in *Status Generalization: New Theory and Research*, ed. M. Webster and M. Foschi (Stanford, CA: Stanford University Press, 1988), 450–474.

[54]Robert K. Shelly, "How Sentiments Organize Interaction," *Advances in Group Processes* 16 (1993):113–132, "How Performance Expectations Arise from Sentiments," *Social Psychology Quarterly*, 64 (2001):72–87, "Emotions, Sentiments, and Performance Expectations," *Advances in Group Processes* 21 (2004):146–165. See also R. K. Shelly, I. M. Handley, J. Baer, and S. Watson, "Group and Affect: Sentiments, Emotions, and Performance Expectations," *Current Research in Social Psychology*, 6 (2001):1–12 and R. K. Shelly and M. Webster Jr., "Compatible Social Processes: Some New Theoretical Principles and a Test," *Sociological Perspectives*, 40 (1997):1317–1334.

emotions that vary along a continuum of liking and disliking others in a situation. In Shelly's theory, sentiments arise from people's reactions to performances and behaviors, and they set up expectation states for future interactions in a situation. These sentiment-based expectation states exert, he believes, an independent effect on behaviors distinct from that exerted by expectations associated with status. However, if status is highly salient in a situation because performances among individuals have already created a status order or because it is built into the social structure of a larger social unit, then status will trump expectation states arising from sentiments. Thus, the effect of sentiments will exert less influence on expectation states than will status, as long as status considerations—and the expectations that come with differential levels of power and prestige that accompany status—influence people's behaviors, their evaluations of these behaviors, and the formation of expectation states for future interaction.

Shelly posits two potential models of these processes. One is the constituent model, outlined in Figure 17.1a, in which status and sentiment each exerts an independent influence on the formation of expectation states. The other is the translation model, delineated in Figure 17.1b, where sentiments are part of the expectations that form around status. That is, as individuals interact, they come to reveal positive or negative sentiments about one another, which arise as they interact, and these sentiments affect how persons will interact with others in varying status positions. They also become incorporated into the expectation states—as expectations of how much they will like or dislike others—that individuals have for these others as they exercise the rights and obligations in their performances by virtue of having a particular status—whether status in a situation that has evolved, status in a division of labor that is imposed, or status that comes with memberships in categoric units or with diffuse status characteristics.

It is, of course, possible that both processes operate. When, for instance, status becomes salient, the expectation states from sentiments get blended with those for status. For example, a person may come to possess mild negative sentiments toward a boss in a high-status (authority) position; and these are blended with expectation states for this high-status person as, say, "a competent but irritating jerk whose directive I must follow." If this same person's status is not salient, then the negative sentiments would dominate in the absence of status cues.

Lovaglia and Houser's Status-Compatible Theory. Michael Lovaglia, at times in collaboration with Jeffrey Houser, developed a theory that examines the degree to which the emotions that arise among lower- and higher-status persons in groups increase or decrease the social distance between these persons.[55] Expectation states theories all argue that higher-status individuals will be given more opportunities to perform, will receive higher evaluations, and will have more influence over decisions

---

[55]Michael J. Lovaglia and Jeffrey A. Houser, "Emotional Reactions and Status in Groups," *American Sociological Review*, 61 (1996):867–883; Michael J. Lovaglia, "Status, Emotion, and Structural Power," in *Status, Network, and Structure*, ed. J. Szmatka and J. Skvoretz (Stanford, CA: Stanford University Press, 1997), 159–178. See also J. H. Houser and M. J. Lovaglia, "Status, Emotion, and the Development of Solidarity in Stratified Task Groups," *Advances in Group Processes* 19 (2002):109–137.

Figure 17.1 Shelly's Two Models

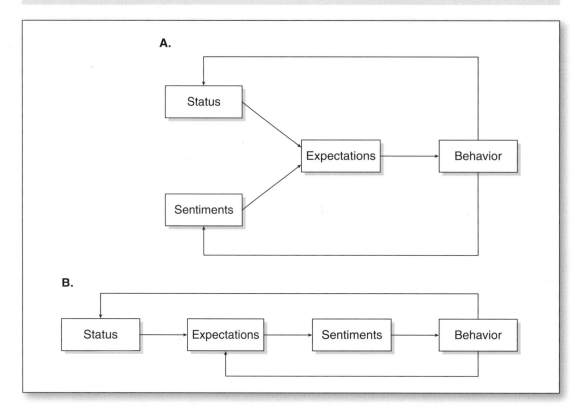

than lower-status individuals. The result is that higher-status persons will experience more positive emotions like *pleasure* and *happiness* while lower-status persons will experience more negative emotions such as *anger* and *frustration*. The more the emotions of individuals are compatible with their status—positive emotions for higher-status individuals and negative emotions for lower-status persons—the more likely is the degree of the social distance between higher- and lower-status members to *decrease*.

We will not provide a complete description of the dynamics involved, but basically, the process works as follows: when high-status persons feel positive emotions, they are likely to treat lower-status individuals better, giving them more chances to contribute, praising them positively, and in general evaluating their performances more positively. The result is that social distance between the two ranks decreases. Compared with higher-status individuals, lower-status persons experience more negative emotions in general and more specifically, they often hold negative feelings about higher-status persons; as a result of these negative emotions, the social distance between the two ranks will decrease because these individuals may give higher-status persons fewer opportunities to talk, evaluate them negatively, and not easily defer to the higher-status person's wishes and directions.

Thus, one generalization is that when individuals feel emotions appropriate for their status—positive for higher-status persons, negative for lower-status individuals—and act on these feelings, social status differences are, ironically, reduced. In being pleasant to lower-status persons, the higher-status person reduces social distance, whereas in their negativity and failure to honor the status order, lower-status members can reduce the status distance with higher-status persons.

There are more complicated dynamics in this process that revolve around *attributions*. For example, higher-status persons who feel that they do not deserve their rank (they were just lucky) will experience status-incompatible emotions, such as *anxiety, fear,* and perhaps even *guilt*. These emotions reduce the distance between higher- and lower-ranking persons. If lower-ranking persons make a negative self-attribution that they do not have the ability to be anything else, they will see their lower rank as proper, will accept the status differences, and will thereby increase the social distance with higher-ranking individuals. There are a number of other potential scenarios that lead to increased and decreased solidarity in a group by virtue of the level of status differences and people's emotional reactions to their particular status.

Theodore Kemper's Status-Power Theory. Theodore Kemper was one of the pioneers in the sociology of emotions. Originally, he termed his approach "a social interactional theory of emotions,"[56] and more recently, he has teamed with Randall Collins to develop the theory further.[57] The basic idea of the theory is quite simple: individuals' relative power and status in social relationships, and changes in their power and status, have important effects on their emotional states. Power is the ability to compel others to follow one's wishes and dictates, whereas status is the giving and receiving of unforced deference, compliance, respect, and honor. All social relationships reveal power and status dimensions. According to Kemper and Collins, these dimensions are fundamental to understanding interaction and emotions. From his review of the literature on emotions,[58] Kemper concluded that there are four basic and primary emotions: *fear, anger, happiness/satisfaction,* and *sadness/depression*. These primary emotions can, however, be elaborated into more complex combinations and variants, creating such complex and important emotions as *guilt, shame, pride, jealousy, love,* and other variants and combinations of the four primary emotions. Indeed, Kemper has argued that these primary emotions have a neurophysiological basis, having been selected in humans' evolutionary history because they promoted survival. Kemper thus attempts to explain how power and status generate the four basic emotions and important variants.

The theory distinguishes among (a) *structural emotions,* which are those affective states aroused by the relative power and status of individuals within social structures; (b) *situational emotions,* which arise by virtue of changes in power and status during

---

[56]Theodore D. Kemper, *A Social Interactional Theory of Emotions* (New York: Wiley, 1979), "Predicting Emotions from Social Relations," *Social Psychology Quarterly* 54 (1991):330–342. See also Kemper's recently published *Status, Power, and Ritual: A Relational Reading of Durkheim, Goffman, and Collins* (Surrey, UK: Ashgate, 2011).

[57]Theodore D. Kemper and Randall Collins, "Dimensions of Microinteractionism," *American Journal of Sociology* 96 (1990):32–68.

[58]Theodore D. Kemper, "How Many Emotions Are There? Wedding the Social and the Autonomic Component," *American Journal of Sociology* 93 (1987):263–289.

the process of interaction; and (c) *anticipatory emotions*, which revolve around individuals' expectations of power and status in social relations. The dynamics of emotion thus inhere in the status and power that individuals actually hold, the status and power gained or lost during interaction, and the power and status expected in an interaction. The basic propositions of the theory are extracted and summarized in Table 17.2. What follows is a more discursive review of the argument made.

Table 17.2   Kemper's Status-Power Theory of Emotions

Power and Status
1. The more a person experiences an increase in power in social relations, the greater will be this person's sense of security and confidence; conversely, the more a person experiences a loss of power in social relations, the greater will be this person's sense of anxiety and fear, leading to a loss of confidence.
2. The more a person anticipates a gain in power in social relations but does not receive this gain, the greater will be this person's sense of anxiety and, potentially, sense of fear; conversely, the more a person anticipates a loss of power in social relations but does not receive this loss, the greater will be this person's sense of satisfaction and, potentially, sense of confidence.
Status and Emotions
3. The more a person experiences an increase in status in social relations, the greater will be this person's sense of satisfaction and well-being, the greater will be this person's sense of liking for those who gave status, and the more likely will the givers and receivers of status form bonds of solidarity.
4. The more a person experiences a loss of status in social relations as a result of his or her own actions, the greater will be this person's sense of shame and embarrassment and, if the loss is sufficiently great, sense of depression as well.
5. The more a person experiences a loss of status in social relations as a result of another's actions, the greater will be the person's sense of anger and the more likely will this person be ready to fight, transforming this person's conduct to a power mode of behavior.

6. A person's reaction to no change in status in social relations will
 	
  A. Lead to satisfaction, if this person anticipated no change
  B. Lead to shame and perhaps depression, if this person anticipated an increase in status and perceives that the failure to realize this anticipated increase was caused by his or her own actions
  C. Lead to anger and aggression, if this person anticipated an increase in status and perceives that the failure to realize this anticipated increase was caused by the actions of others
  D. Lead to satisfaction and well-being, if this person receives more status than anticipated.

7. The more a person gives status, the greater will be the sense of satisfaction, if this status is given freely, and the more the receiver of status will express appreciation and gratitude, which, in turn, increases the sense of satisfaction for the giver of status.
8. The more a person withholds status when the giving of status is due, the greater will be the sense of guilt and shame.

When people have power and increase their power within social relationships, they experience a sense of satisfaction, security, and confidence. If individuals do not have power and, more important, lose power, they will experience *anxiety* and *fear*, leading them to lose confidence. Thus, to have power or to gain it gives people the confidence to secure and use more power, whereas to not possess power or to lose it does just the opposite and takes away the confidence so necessary to garnering and sustaining power.

Just what people expect before they interact and what they actually get are very important in the production of emotions. When individuals expect or anticipate a gain in power but do not receive this gain, their *anxiety* and *fear* will escalate, and they begin to lose confidence in themselves. Conversely, when individuals have anticipated a loss of power but do not lose power, they experience satisfaction, and they might begin to gain confidence.

For status, a more extensive set of arguments is presented. Much like power, when people experience a gain in status, they will also experience satisfaction. Moreover, they will come to like those who have given them status, and if the relationship persists, they will form stronger bonds with these supportive others. If individuals experience a loss of status in social relations, they will experience *shame* and *embarrassment*, especially if they believe that this loss of status is the result of their own actions and, hence, their own fault. If this loss is sufficiently great, they will experience not only shame but also depression. However, if they perceive that this loss of status is caused by the unfair and inappropriate actions of others, they will experience anger and become aggressive toward these others. As their *anger* rises, they move into a power mode of interaction, seeking to compel others to acknowledge their status.

The attribution of status loss to oneself or to others is, however, complicated by what people have anticipated before the interaction. If they have anticipated no gain or loss in status and experience neither, then they feel *satisfied* (a mild version of happiness). If they have anticipated an increase in status but did not get it and if they perceive that this failure to receive status has been the result of their own actions, then they will experience *shame* and, perhaps, *depression*. If the failure to receive the expected status is seen as the result of others' inappropriate actions, then individuals will mobilize *anger* and become *aggressive*. And if individuals get more status than they anticipated, they will become satisfied.

The giving of status to others also generates emotions. When a person freely bestows status on another, the giver of status experiences satisfaction and the recipient of the status will express appreciation and gratitude, which will feed back and increase the giver's sense of satisfaction. When a person withholds status that another deserves, this individual will feel *guilt* and *shame* for not doing what is appropriate and persons who did not receive what they deserved (and expected) will experience *anger* if they correctly perceive that the other has wronged them.

In sum, then, the arousal of emotion is ultimately tied to the relative power and status of individuals in social relationships, to shifts in status and power, and to both anticipation and attribution of who is responsible for these shifts. In the end, for

Kemper, emotion is driven by those conditions (a) that give people the power to tell others what to do, or that take this power away, and (b) that bestow prestige, deference, and voluntary compliance, or that take this status away.

Conclusions

Theorizing on roles and status has continued into the twenty-first century because it is one important way for understanding the relationships among persons, behaviors, social structure, and culture. Sociologists between the classical and modern eras began to conceptualize roles and status, and during the modern era of theorizing, rather robust and useful theories have been developed about the dynamics of roles and status. Role theorizing has declined, but as I sought to demonstrate, there are many important micro-level dynamics that can be conceptualized through roles because, in the end, roles are behaviors, and microdynamics are played out in these behaviors as they are constrained and directed by role dynamics. Similarly, despite the large amount of research and theorizing on status dynamics, much of this work has, surprisingly, disembodied status from social structures and culture. It is true that status beliefs are often examined and are a part of a society's culture; and it is equally true that status is seen as a position within the social structure. Yet the dynamics of roles and status often are not connected conceptually to the broader dynamics of social structures and cultures at the meso and macro levels of social organizations. And so there is a need for theorizing to move beyond micro-level interpersonal dynamics and connect the robust theories of roles and status to meso-level and macro-level dynamics.

CHAPTER 18

Dramaturgical Theorizing

Erving Goffman on Dramaturgy

The Interaction Order

Erving Goffman was, perhaps, the most creative theorist of interaction processes in the second half of the twentieth century. In one of his last statements before his death in 1982, he defined the analysis of face-to-face interaction as the *interaction order,*[1] but unlike many micro-level theorists and researchers, Goffman did not proclaim that the interaction order is all that is real. Rather, he simply argued that this interaction order constitutes a distinctive realm of reality that reveals its own unique dynamics. For, "to speak of the relative autonomous forms of life in the interaction order . . . is not to put forward these forms as somehow prior, fundamental, or constitutive of the shape of macroscopic phenomena."[2] Goffman recognized that, at best, there is a "loose coupling" of the micro and macro realms. Macro phenomena, such as commodities markets, urban land-use values, economic growth, and society-wide stratification, cannot be explained by micro-level analysis.[3] Of course, one can supplement macro-level explanations by recording how individuals interact in various types of settings and encounters, but these analyses will not supplant macro-level explanations. Conversely, what transpires in the interaction order cannot be explained solely by macro processes. Rather, macro-level phenomena are always transformed in ways unique to the individuals involved in interaction.

To be sure, macro phenomena constrain and circumscribe interaction and, at times, guide the general form of the interaction, but the inherent dynamics of the

---

[1]Erving Goffman, "The Interaction Order," *American Sociological Review* (February 1983):1–17. See also Anne W. Rawls, "The Interaction Order Sui Generis: Goffman's Contribution to Social Theory," *Sociological Theory* 5 (2, 1987):136–149 and Stephan Fuchs, "The Constitution of Emergent Interaction Orders, a Comment on Rawls," *Sociological Theory* 5 (1, 1988):122–124.

[2]Goffman, "The Interaction Order," 9.

[3]Ibid.

interaction itself preclude a one-to-one relation to these structural parameters. Indeed, the form of interaction can often be at odds with macrostructures, operating smoothly in ways that contradict these structures without dramatically changing them. Thus, the crude notion that interaction is constrained by macrostructures in ways that "reproduce" social structure does not recognize the autonomy of the interaction order. For, interaction

> is not an expression of structural arrangements in any simple sense; at best it is an expression advanced in regard to these arrangements. Social structures don't "determine" culturally standard displays (of interaction rituals), they merely help select from the available repertoire of them.[4]

Thus, there is a "loose coupling" of "interactional practices and social structures, a collapsing of strata and structures into broader categories, the categories themselves not corresponding one-to-one to anything in the structural world."[5] There is, then, "a set of transformation rules, or a membrane selecting how various externally relevant social distinctions will be managed within the interaction."[6]

These "transformations" are, however, far from insignificant phenomena. Much of what gives the social world a sense of "being real" arises from the practices of individuals as they deal with one another in various situations. "We owe our unshaking sense of realities,"[7] to the rules of interpersonal contact. Moreover, although a single gathering and episode of interaction might not have great social significance, "through these comings together much of our social life is organized."[8] The interaction order is thus a central topic of sociological theory.

Goffman's approach to this domain is unique.[9] Although we must "keep faith with the spirit of natural science, and lurch along, seriously kidding ourselves that our rut has a forward direction,"[10] we must not become overenamored with the mature sciences. Social life is "ours to study naturalistically," but our study should not be rigid.[11] Instead, ad hoc observation, cultivation of anecdotes, creative thinking, illustrations from literature, examination of books of etiquette, personal experiences, and many

---

[4]Ibid., 11 (emphasis in original).

[5]Ibid.

[6]Ibid.

[7]Erving Goffman, *Encounters: Two Studies in the Sociology of Interaction* (Indianapolis, IN: Bobbs-Merrill, 1961), 81.

[8]Erving Goffman, *Behavior in Public Places: Notes on the Social Organization of Gatherings* (New York: Free Press, 1963), 234.

[9]For a useful set of essays on Goffman's analysis, see Paul Drew and Anthony Wootton (ed.), *Erving Goffman: Exploring the Interaction Order* (Cambridge, UK: Polity, 1988); see also the proceedings of a recent symposium on Goffman, published in *Sociological Perspectives,* 39 (3, 1996): and Thomas Scheff, *Goffman Unbound* (Boulder, CO: Paradigm Press, 2006).

[10]Goffman, "The Interaction Order," 2.

[11]Ibid., 17.

other sources of unsystematic data should guide inquiry into the micro order. Indeed, "human life is only a small irregular scab on the face of nature, not particularly amenable to deep systematic analysis."[12] Yet human life can be studied in the spirit of scientific inquiry.

The Dramaturgical Metaphor

In his first and last major works—*The Presentation of Self in Everyday Life* and *Frame Analysis,* respectively—Goffman analogized to the stage and theater. Hence, the designation of his work as "dramaturgical" has become commonplace.[13] This designation is, however, somewhat misleading because it creates the impression that there is a script, a stage, an audience, props, and actors playing roles. Such imagery is in tune with role theory (discussed in Chapter 18); and while Goffman did not reject this analogy, and indeed he frequently used it, the interaction order is "dramatic" in another sense: individuals are actors who "put on" a performance, often cynical and deceptive, for one another; and people actively manipulate the script, stage, props, and roles for their own purposes and self-interest. This more cynical view of Goffman's dramaturgy is perhaps closer to the mark,[14] but it too is somewhat misleading. Commentators have often portrayed Goffman as presenting a kind of "con man"[15] view of human social interaction—a metaphor that captures some of the examples and topics of his approach but obscures the more fundamental processes found in Goffman's theorizing.

We can use the metaphor of dramaturgy in a less extreme sense. In Goffman's work there is concern with a cultural script, or a set of normative rules; there is a heavy emphasis on how individuals manage their impressions and play roles; there is a concern with stages and props (physical space and objects); there is an emphasis on staging, on the manipulation of gestures, on the meanings attached to spacing, and on the use of props and other physical aspects of a setting. Moreover, in contrast to the approaches of symbolic interactionists, where self and identities are the anchors for interaction, Goffman views self as situational, determined more by the cultural script, stage, strategic actors, and audience than by enduring and trans-situational configurations of self-attitudes, self-feelings, or identities. And finally, there is a particular emphasis on how performances create a theatrical ambiance—a mood, definition, and sense of reality.

This version of the dramatic metaphor provides only a broad orientation to Goffman's approach. We need to "fill in" this orientation with more details. To do so,

---

[12]Ibid.

[13]Erving Goffman, *The Presentation of Self in Everyday Life* (Garden City, NY: Anchor, 1959), *Frame Analysis: An Essay on the Organization of Experience* (Boston, MA: Northeastern University Press, 1986; originally published 1974 by Harper and Row).

[14]See, for example, Randall Collins, *Theoretical Sociology* (San Diego, CA: Harcourt Brace Jovanovich, 1988), 203–207, 291–298 and *Four Sociological Traditions* (New York: Oxford University Press, 1998).

[15]For example, see: R. P. Cuzzort and E. W. King, *Twentieth-Century Social Thought*, 4th ed. (Fort Worth, TX: Holt, Rinehart and Winston, 1989), chap. 12.

I will review Goffman's most important works and try to pull the diverse vocabularies and concepts together into a more unified theoretical perspective—dramaturgical in its general contours but more than just a clever metaphor.[16]

The Presentation of Self

The *Presentation of Self in Everyday Life*[17] was Goffman's first major work, and it was largely responsible for the designation of Goffman as a dramaturgical theorist. The basic argument is that individuals deliberately and inadvertently "give off" signs that provide others with information about how to respond. From such mutual use of "sign-vehicles," individuals develop a "definition of the situation," which is a "plan for cooperative activity" but which, at the same time, is "not so much a real agreement as to what exists but rather a real agreement as to whose claims concerning what issues will be temporarily honored."[18] In constructing this overall definition of a situation, individuals engage in performances in which each orchestrates gestures to "present oneself" in a particular manner as a person having identifiable characteristics and deserving treatment in a certain fashion. These performances revolve around several interrelated dynamics:

1. A performance involves the creation of a *front*. A front includes the physical "setting" and the use of the physical layout, its fixed equipment, like furniture, and other "stage props" to create a certain impression. A front also involves (a) "items of expressive equipment" (emotions, energy, and other capacities for expression); (b) "appearance," or those signs that tell others of an individual's social position and status as well as the "ritual state" of the individual with respect to social, work, or recreational activity;[19] and (c) "manner," or those signs that inform others about the role that an individual expects to play.[20] As a general rule, people expect consistency in these elements of their fronts—use of setting and its props, mobilization of expressive equipment, social status, expression of ritual readiness for various types of activity, and efforts to assume certain roles.[21] There are a relatively small number of fronts, and people know them all. Moreover, fronts tend to be established, institutionalized, and stereotypical for various kinds of settings, with the result that

---

[16]See Stephan Fuchs, "Second Thoughts on Emergent Interaction Orders," *Sociological Theory* 7 (1, 1989):121–123.

[17]Goffman, *The Presentation of Self in Everyday Life.*

[18]Ibid., 9–10.

[19]Randall Collins (see Chapter 12 in this work) took his idea of situations as work-practical, ceremonial, or social from this discussion. Also, Collins's notion of interaction rituals is much the same as Goffman's definition of encounters. See Collins's recent *Interaction Ritual Chains* (Princeton, NJ: Princeton University Press, 2004).

[20]Note the similarity of this idea to Ralph H. Turner's discussion (see Chapter 17) on role-making.

[21]Goffman, *The Presentation of Self,* 24–25.

"when an actor takes an established role, usually he (she) finds that a particular front has already been established for it."[22]

2. In addition to presenting a front, individuals use gestures in what Goffman termed *dramatic realization,* or the infusion into activity of signs that highlight commitment to a given definition of a situation. The more a situation creates problems in presenting a front, Goffman argued, the greater will be efforts at dramatic realization.[23]

3. Performances also involve *idealizations,* or efforts to present oneself in ways that "incorporate and exemplify the officially accredited values of society."[24] When individuals are mobile, moving into a new setting, dramatic efforts at idealization will be most pronounced. Idealization creates a problem for individuals; however, if the idealization is to be effective, individuals must suppress, conceal, and underplay those elements of themselves that might contradict more general values.

4. Such efforts at concealment are part of a more general process of *maintaining expressive control.* Because minor cues and signs are read by others and contribute to a definition of a situation, actors must regulate their muscular activity, their signals of involvement, their orchestration of front, and their ability to be fit for interaction. The most picayune discrepancy between behavior and the definition of a situation can unsettle the interaction, because "the impression of reality fostered by a performance is a delicate, fragile thing that can be shattered by very minor mishaps."[25]

5. Individuals can also engage in *misrepresentation.* The eagerness of one's audience to read gestures and determine one's front makes that audience vulnerable to manipulation and duping.[26]

6. Individuals often attempt to engage in *mystification,* or the maintenance of distance from others as a way to keep them in awe and in conformity to a definition of a situation. Such mystification is, however, limited primarily to those of higher rank and status.

7. Individuals seek to make their performances seem real and to avoid communicating a sense of contrivance. Thus, individuals must communicate that they are, or at least appear to others as, sincere, natural, and spontaneous.

---

[22]Ibid., 27.

[23]Ibid., 32.

[24]Ibid., 35. Note how this idea parallels the notion of "representational" aspect of roles developed by Ralph H. Turner and Paul Colomy (see Chapter 17).

[25]Ibid., 56.

[26]This is a consistent theme in Goffman's work that, perhaps, he overemphasized. See, for example, Erving Goffman, *Strategic Interaction* (Philadelphia: University of Pennsylvania Press, 1969).

These procedures for bringing off a successful performance and thereby creating an overall definition of a situation are the core of Goffmanian sociology. They become elaborated and extended in subsequent works, but Goffman never abandoned the idea that fundamental to the interaction order are the efforts of individuals to orchestrate their performances, even in deceptive and manipulative ways, so as to maintain a particular definition of the situation. These ideas are presented propositionally in Table 18.1.

Although the propositions in Table 18.1 constitute only an opening chapter in *The Presentation of Self*, they are by far the most enduring portions of this first major work. The rest of the book is concerned with performances sustained by more than one individual. Goffman introduced the concept of *team* to denote performances that are presented by individuals who must cooperate to effect a particular definition of the situation. Often, two teams must present performances to each other, but more typically one team constitutes a performer and the other an audience. Team performers generally move between a front region, or *frontstage*, where they coordinate their performances before an audience, and a back region, or *backstage*, where team members can relax. Goffman also introduced the

Table 18.1 Goffman's Propositions on Interaction and Performance

1. As individuals make visual and verbal contact, the more likely they are to use gestures to orchestrate a performance, with the success of this performance depending on
A. Presentation of a coherent front that, in turn, is a positive and additive function of
1. Control of physical space, props, and equipment in a setting
2. Control of expressive equipment in a setting
3. Control of signals marking propensity for types of ritual activity
4. Control of signals marking status outside and inside the interaction
5. Control of signals pertaining to identifiable roles.
B. Incorporation and exemplification of general cultural values
C. Imbuing a situation with a personal mystique
D. Signaling sincerity.
2. As individuals in a setting orchestrate their performances and, at the same time, accept one another's performances, they are likely to develop a common definition of the situation.
3. As a common definition of the situation emerges, the ease of the interaction increases.

notion of *outside*, or the residual region beyond the frontstage and backstage. Frontstage behavior is polite, maintaining a decorum appropriate to a team performance (e.g., selling cars, serving food, meeting students, etc.), whereas backstage behavior is more informal and geared toward maintaining the solidarity and morale of team performers. When outsiders or members of the audience intrude on performers in the backstage, a tension is created because team members are caught in their nonperforming roles.[27]

A basic problem of all team performances is maintaining a particular definition of the situation in front of the audience. This problem is accentuated when there are large rank or status differences among team members,[28] when the team has many members,[29] when the front- and backstages are not clearly partitioned, and when the team must hide information contrary to its image of itself. To counteract these kinds of problems, social control among the team's members is essential. When members are backstage, such control is achieved through morale-boosting activities, such as denigrating the audience, kidding one another, shifting to informal address, and engaging in stage talk (talk about performances on frontstage). When they are onstage, control is sustained by realigning actions revolving around subtle communications among team members that, hopefully, the audience will not understand.

Breaches of the performances occur when a team member acts in ways that challenge the definition of the situation created by the team's performances. Attempts to prevent such incidents involve further efforts at social control, especially a backstage emphasis on (a) playing one's part and not emitting unmeant gestures, (b) showing loyalty to the team and not the audience, and (c) exercising foresight and anticipating potential problems with the team or the audience. Team members are assisted in social control by members of the audience who (a) tend to stay away from the backstage, (b) act disinterested when exposed to backstage behavior, and (c) employ elaborate etiquette (exhibiting proper attention and interest, inhibiting their own potential performances, avoiding faux pas) to avoid a "scene" with the team.

What is true of teams and audiences is, Goffman implied, also true of individuals. Interaction involves a performance for others who constitute an audience. One seeks to sustain a performance when moving to the frontstage; and when moving backstage, actors seek to relax and interact with each other more informally and without the need to "put on" a performance. People try very hard to avoid mistakes and faux pas that could breach the definition of the situation, and they are assisted in this effort by others in their audience who exercise tact and etiquette to avoid a scene. Such are the themes of *The Presentation of Self,* and most of Goffman's work represented a conceptual elaboration of them. The notion of "teams" recedes, but a general model elaborating these themes into a theory of interaction among individuals emerges.

Focused Interaction in Encounters

Goffman generally employed the terms *unfocused* and *focused* to denote two basic types of interaction. *Unfocused interaction*

> consists of interpersonal communications that result solely by virtue of persons being in one another's presence, as when two strangers across the room from each

---

[27]Goffman, *The Presentation of Self,* 137–138.

[28]Ibid., 92.

[29]Ibid., 141.

other check up on each other's clothing, posture, and general manner, while each modifies his (her) own demeanor because he himself is under observation.[30]

As will be explored later, such unfocused interaction is, Goffman argued, an important part of the interaction order, for much of what people do is exchange glances and monitor each other in public places. *Focused interaction,* in contrast, "occurs when people effectively agree to sustain for a time a single focus of cognitive and visual attention, as in a conversation, a board game, or a joint task sustained by a close face-to-face circle of contributors."[31]

Encounters. Focused interaction occurs within what Goffman termed *encounters,* which constitute one of the core structural units of the interaction order. Goffman mentioned encounters in his first work, *The Presentation of Self in Everyday Life,* but their full dimensions are explored in his next book, *Encounters.*[32] There, an encounter is defined as focused interaction revealing the following characteristics:[33]

1. A single visual and cognitive focus of attention

2. A mutual and preferential openness to verbal communication

3. A heightened mutual relevance of acts

4. An eye-to-eye ecological huddle, maximizing mutual perception and monitoring

5. An emergent "we" feeling of solidarity and flow of feeling

6. A ritual and ceremonial punctuation of openings, closings, entrances, and exits

7. A set of procedures for corrective compensation for deviant acts

To sustain itself, an encounter develops a *membrane,* or penetrable barrier to the larger social world in which the interaction is located. Goffman typically conceptualized the immediate setting of an encounter as a gathering, or the assembling in space of copresent individuals; in turn, gatherings are lodged within a more inclusive unit, the social occasion, or the larger undertaking sustained by fixed equipment, a distinctive ethos and emotional structure, a program or agenda of actors or those setting the stage, rules of proper and improper conduct, and a preestablished sequencing of activities (beginning, phases, high point, and ending). Thus, encounters emerge from episodes of focused interaction within gatherings that are lodged in social occasions.[34]

---

[30]Goffman, *Encounters,* 7.

[31]Ibid.

[32]Ibid.

[33]Ibid., 18. Note the similarity of this definition to Randall Collins's portrayal of "interaction rituals" (see Chapter 12).

[34]Goffman, *Behavior in Public Places,* 18–20.

The membrane of an encounter, as well as its distinctive characteristics previously listed, are sustained by a set of rules. In *Encounters*, Goffman lists several; later, in what is probably his most significant work, *Interaction Ritual*, he lists several more.[35] Let me combine both discussions by listing the rules that guide focused interaction in encounters:

1. *Rules of irrelevance*, which "frame" a situation as excluding certain materials (attributes of participants, psychological states, cultural values, norms, etc.)[36]

2. *Rules of transformation*, which specify how materials moving through the membrane created by rules of irrelevance are to be altered to fit into the interaction

3. *Rules of realized resources*, which provide a general schemata and framework for expression and interpretation for activities among participants

4. *Rules of talk*, which are the procedures, conventions, and practices guiding the flow of verbalizations with respect to[37]

   a. Maintaining a single focus of attention
   b. Establishing "clearance cues" for determining when one speaker is done and another can begin
   c. Determining how long and how frequently any one person can hold the floor
   d. Regulating interruptions and lulls in the conversation
   e. Sanctioning participants whose attention wanders to matters outside the conversation
   f. Ensuring that nearby people do not interfere with the conversation
   g. Guiding the use of politeness and tact, even in the face of disagreements

5. *Rules of self-respect*, which encourage participants to honor with tact and etiquette their respective efforts to present themselves in a certain light

Interaction is thus guided by complex configurations of rules that individuals learn how to use and apply in different types of encounters, lodged in varying types of gatherings and social occasions. The "reality" of the world is, to a very great extent, sustained by people's ability to invoke and use these rules;[38] when these rules are operating effectively, individuals develop a "state of euphoria," or what Randall Collins has termed enhanced "emotional energy." However, encounters are vulnerable to "dysphoria," or tension when these rules do not exclude troublesome external materials or fail to regulate the flow of interaction. Such failures are seen by Goffman as incidents or breaches; when they can be effectively handled by tact and corrective procedures, they are then viewed as integrations because they are

---

[35]Goffman, *Encounters*, 20–33 and *Interaction Ritual: Essays on Face-to-Face Behavior* (Garden City, NY: Anchor, 1967), 33.

[36]The concept of frame, which Goffman said that he took from Gregory Bateson, became central in Goffman's later work. See the closing section in this chapter.

[37]These rules come from Goffman, *Interaction Ritual*, 33.

[38]Here, Goffman anticipates much of ethnomethodology, which is examined in Chapter 20.

blended into the ongoing encounter. The key mechanism for avoiding dysphoria and maintaining the integration of the encounter is the use of ritual.

Ritual. In *Interaction Ritual,*[39] Goffman's great contribution is the recognition that minor, seemingly trivial, and everyday rituals—such as "Hello, how are you?," "Good morning," "Please, after you," and so on—are crucial to the maintenance of social order. In his words, he "reformulated Émile Durkheim's social psychology in a modern dress"[40] by recognizing that when individuals gather and begin to interact, their behaviors are highly ritualized. That is, actors punctuate each phase of interpersonal contact with stereotypical sequences of behavior that invoke the rules of the encounter and, at the same time, become the medium or vehicle by which the rules are followed. Rituals are thus essential for (a) mobilizing individuals to participate in the interaction; (b) making them cognizant of the relevant rules of irrelevance, transformation, resource use, and talk; (c) guiding them during the course of the interaction; and (d) helping them correct for breaches and incidents.

Among the most significant are those rituals revolving around deference and demeanor. *Deference* pertains to interpersonal rituals that express individuals' respect for others, their willingness to interact, their affection and other emotions, and their engagement in the encounter. In Goffman's words, deference establishes the "marks of devotion" by which an actor "celebrates and confirms his [her] relationship to a recipient."[41] As a result, deference contains a "kind of promise, expressing in truncated form the actor's avowal and pledge to treat the recipient in a particular way in the on-coming activity."[42] Thus, seemingly innocuous gestures—"It's nice to see you again," "How are things?" "What are you doing?" "Good bye," "See you later," and many other stereotypical phrases as well as bodily movements—are rituals that present a demeanor invoking relevant rules and guiding the opening, sequencing, and closing of the interaction.

Deference rituals, Goffman argued, can be of two types: (1) *avoidance rituals* and (2) *presentational rituals.* Avoidance rituals are those that an individual uses to keep a distance from another and to avoid violating the "ideal sphere" that lies around the other. Such rituals are most typical among unequals. Presentational rituals "encompass acts through which the individual makes specific attestations to recipients concerning how he regards them and how he will treat them in the on-coming interaction."[43] Goffman saw interaction as constantly involving a dialectic between avoidance and presentational rituals as individuals respect each other and maintain a distance while trying to make contact and get things done.[44]

---

[39]Goffman, *Interaction Ritual.*

[40]Particularly, Durkheim's later work, as it culminated in *Elementary Forms of the Religious Life* (New York: Free Press, 1947; originally published 1912).

[41]Goffman, *Interaction Ritual,* 56–67.

[42]Ibid., 60.

[43]Ibid.

[44]Ibid., 75–76.

In contrast, *demeanor* is "that element of the individual's ceremonial behavior conveyed through deportment, dress, and bearing which serves to (inform) those in his immediate presence that he is a person of certain desirable or undesirable qualities."[45] Through demeanor rituals, individuals present images of themselves to others and, at the same time, communicate that they are reliable, trustworthy, and tactful.

Thus, through deference and demeanor rituals, individuals plug themselves into an encounter by invoking the relevant rules and demonstrating their capacity to follow them, while indicating their respect for others and presenting themselves as certain kinds of individuals. The enactment of such deference and demeanor rituals in concrete gatherings, especially encounters but also including unfocused situations, provides a basis for the integration of society. For

> throughout . . . ceremonial obligations and expectations, a constant flow of indulgences is spread through society, with others who are present constantly reminding the individual that he must keep himself together as a well demeaned person and affirm the sacred quality of these others.[46]

Roles. In presenting themselves to others, individuals also seek to play a particular role. Thus, as people present a front, invoke relevant rules, and emit rituals, they also try to orchestrate a role for themselves. For Goffman, then, a role is "a bundle of activities visibly performed before a set of others and visibly meshed into the activities these others perform."[47] In the terms of Ralph Turner's analysis (see Chapter 17), individuals attempt to "make a role" for themselves; if successful, this effort contributes to the overall definition of the situation.

In trying to establish a role, the individual "must see to it that the impressions of him that are conveyed in the situation are compatible with role-appropriate personal qualities effectively imputed to him."[48] Thus, individuals in a situation are expected to try to make roles for themselves that are consistent with their demeanor, their self as performed before others, and their front (stage props, expressive equipment, appearance). And if the inconsistency between the attempted role and these additional aspects of a performance becomes evident, then others in the situation are likely to sanction the individual through subtle cues and gestures. These others are driven to do so because discrepancy between another's role and other performance cues disrupts the definition of the situation and the underlying sense of reality that this definition promotes. Thus, role is contingent on the responses and reactions of others, and because their sense of reality partially depends on successful and appropriate role assumption, an individual will have difficulty changing a role in a situation once it is established.

---

[45] Ibid., 77.

[46] Ibid., 91.

[47] Goffman, *Encounters*, 96.

[48] Ibid., 87.

Often, however, people perceive a role to be incompatible with their image of themselves in a situation. Under these conditions, they will display what Goffman termed *role distance,* whereby a "separation" of the person from a role is communicated. Such distancing, Goffman argued,[49] allows the individual to (a) release the tension associated with a role considered to be "beneath his (her) dignity," (b) present additional aspects of self that extend beyond the role, and (c) remove the burden of "complete compliance to the role," thereby making minor transgressions less dramatic and troublesome for others.

Role distance is but an extreme response to the more general process of role embracement. For any role, individuals will reveal varying degrees of attachment and involvement in the role. One extreme is role distance, whereas the other extreme is what Goffman termed engrossment, or complete involvement in a role. In general, Goffman argued,[50] those roles in which individuals can direct what is going on are likely to involve high degrees of embracement, whereas those roles in which the individual is subordinate will be played with considerable role distance.

As is evident, then, the assumption of a role is connected to the self-image that actors project in their performance. Although the self that one reveals in a situation depends on the responses of others who can confirm or disconfirm that person's self in a situation, the organization of a performance onstage before others is still greatly circumscribed by self.

Self. Goffman's view of self is highly situational and contingent on the responses of others. Although one of the main activities of actors in a situation is to present themselves to others, Goffman was highly skeptical about a "core" or "trans-situational" self-conception that is part of an individual's "personality." In almost all his works, he took care to emphasize that individuals do not have an underlying "personality" or "identity" that is carried from situation to situation—as most symbolic interactionists would emphasize. For example, in his last major book, *Frame Analysis,*[51] he argued that people in interaction often presume that the presented self provides a glimpse at a more coherent and core self, but in reality this is simply a folk presumption because there is "no reason to think that all these gleanings about himself that an individual makes available, all these pointings from his current situation to the way he is in his other occasions, have anything very much in common."[52]

Yet even though there is no trans-situational or core self, people's efforts to present images of themselves in a particular situation and others' reactions to this presentation are central dynamics in all encounters. Individuals constantly emit demeanor cues that project images of themselves as certain kinds of persons, or, in the vocabulary of *The Presentation of Self,* they engage in *performances.* In *Interaction Ritual,* Goffman rephrased this argument somewhat, and in so doing, he refined

---

[49]Ibid., 113.

[50]Ibid., 107.

[51]Goffman, *Frame Analysis.*

[52]Ibid., 299.

his views on self. In encounters, an individual *acts out a line,* which is "a pattern of verbal and nonverbal acts by which he expresses his view of the situation and, through this, his evaluation of the participants, especially himself."[53] In developing a line, an individual presents a face, which is "the positive social value a person effectively claims for himself by the line others assume he has during a particular contact."[54] Individuals seek to *stay in face* or to maintain face by presenting an image of themselves through their line that is supported by the responses of others and, if possible, sustained by impersonal agencies in a situation. Conversely, a person is in wrong face or out of face when the line emitted is inappropriate and unaccepted by others. Thus, although a person's social face "can be his most personal possession and the center of his security and pleasure, it is only on loan to him from society; it will be withdrawn unless he conducts himself in a way that is worthy of it."[55]

As noted earlier, Goffman argued that a key norm in any encounter is "the rule of self respect," which requires individuals to maintain face and, through tact and etiquette, the face of others. Thus, by virtue of tact or the "language of hint . . . innuendo, ambiguities, well-placed phrases, carefully worked jokes, and so on,"[56] individuals sustain each other's face; in so doing, they confirm the definition of the situation and promote a sense of a common reality. For this reason, a given line and face in an encounter are difficult to change, once established, because to alter face (and the line by which it is presented) would require redefining the situation and re-creating a sense of reality. And because face is "on loan" to a person from the responses of others, the individual must incur high costs—such as embarrassment or a breach of the situation—to alter a line and a face.

Face engagements are usually initiated with eye contact, and once initiated, they involve ritual openings appropriate to the situation (as determined by the length of the last engagement, the amount of time since the previous engagement, the level of inequality, etc.). During the course of the face engagement, each individual uses tact to maintain, if possible, each other's face and to sanction, if necessary, each other into their appropriate line. In particular, participants seek to avoid "a scene" or breach in the situation; so they use tact and etiquette to save their own face and that of others. Moreover, as deemed appropriate for the type of encounter (as well as for the larger gathering and more inclusive social occasion), individuals will attempt to maintain what Goffman sometimes termed the territories of self, revolving around such matters as physical props, ecological space, personal preserve (territory around one's body), and conversational rights (to talk and be heard), which are necessary for people to execute their line and maintain face.[57] In general, the higher the rank of individuals, the greater their *territories of self* in an encounter.[58] To violate such

---

[53]Goffman, *Interaction Ritual,* 5.

[54]Ibid.

[55]Ibid., 10.

[56]Ibid., 30.

[57]Erving Goffman, *Relations in Public: Micro Studies of the Public Order* (New York: Harper Colophon, 1972; originally published 1971 by Basic Books), 38–41.

[58]Ibid., 40–41.

territories disrupts or breaches the situation, forcing remedial action by participants to restore their respective lines, face, definitions of the situation, and sense of reality.

Talk. Throughout his work, but especially in later books such as *Frame Analysis*[59] and in numerous essays (see those collected in *Forms of Talk*[60]), Goffman emphasized the significance of verbalizations for focusing people's attention. When "talk" is viewed interactionally, "it is an example of that arrangement by which individuals come together and sustain matters having a ratified, joint, current, and running claim upon attention, a claim which lodges them together in some sort of intersubjective, mental world."[61] Thus, in Goffman's view, "no resource is more effective as a basis for joint involvement than speaking," because it fetches "speaker and hearer into the same interpretation schema that applies to what is thus attended."[62]

Talk is thus a crucial mechanism for drawing individuals together, focusing their attention, and adjudicating an overall definition of the situation. Because talk is so central to focusing interaction, it is normatively regulated and ritualized. One significant norm is the prohibition against self-talk, because when people talk to themselves, it "warns others that they might be wrong in assuming a jointly maintained base of ready mutual intelligibility."[63] Moreover, other kinds of quasi talk are also regulated and ritualized. For example, response cues or "exclamatory interjections which are not full-fledged words"—"Oops," "Wow," "Oh," and "Yikes"—are regulated as to when they can be used and the way they are uttered.[64] Verbal fillers—"ah," "uh," "um," and the like—are also ritualized and are used to facilitate "conversational tracking." In essence, they indicate that "the speaker does not have, as of yet, the proper word but is working on the matter" and that he or she is still engaged in the conversation. Even seemingly emotional cues and tabooed expressions, such as all the "four-letter words," are not so much an expression of emotion as "self-other alignment" and assert that "our inner concerns should be theirs." Such outbursts are normative and ritualized because this "invitation into our interiors tends to be made only when it will be easy to other persons present to see where the voyage takes them."[65]

In creating a definition of the situation, Goffman argued, talk operates in extremely complex ways. When individuals talk, they create what Goffman termed *a footing*, or assumed foundation for the conversation and the interaction. Because verbal symbols are easily manipulated, people can readily change the footing or the basic premises underlying the conversation.[66] Such shifts in

---

[59]Goffman, *Frame Analysis*.

[60]Erving Goffman, *Forms of Talk* (Philadelphia: University of Pennsylvania Press, 1981).

[61]Ibid., 70–71.

[62]Ibid., 71.

[63]Ibid., 85.

[64]Ibid., 120.

[65]Ibid., 121.

[66]Goffman termed this reframing (see later section) when it involved a shift in frame. However, footing and re-footing can occur within an existing frame, so a person can change the footing of a conversation without breaking or changing a frame.

footing are, however, highly ritualized and usually reveal clear markers. For example, when a person says something like "Let's not talk about that," the footing of the conversation is shifted, but in a ritualized way; similarly, when someone utters a phrase like "That's great, but what about . . . ?" this person is also changing the footing through ritual.

Shifts in footing raise a question that increasingly dominated Goffman's later works: the issue of embedding. Goffman came to recognize that conversations are layered and, hence, embedded in different footings. There are often multiple footings for talk, as when someone "says one thing but means another" or when a person "hints" or "implies" something else. These "layerings" of conversations, which embed them in different contexts, are possible because speech is capable of generating subtle and complex meanings. For example, irony, sarcasm, puns, wit, double-entendres, inflections, shadings, and other manipulations of speech demonstrate the capacity of individuals to shift the footings and contextual embeddings of a conversation (e.g., think of a conversation in a work setting involving romantic flirtations; it will involve constant movement in footing and context). Yet, for encounters to proceed smoothly, these alterations in footing are, to some extent, normatively regulated and ritualized, enabling individuals to sustain a sense of common reality—an idea that ethnomethodology was to pursue (see the next chapter).

Talk is thus a critical dimension of focused interaction. Without it, the gestures and cues that people can emit are limited and lack the subtlety and complexity of language. And as Goffman began to explore this complexity in later works, earlier notions about "definitions of situations" seemed too crude because people could construct multiple, as well as subtly layered, definitions of any situation—an issue that we will explore near the end of this chapter. For our purposes here, the critical point is that talk focuses attention and pulls actors together, forcing their interaction

Table 18.2 Goffman's General Proposition on Focused Interaction

1. Encounters are created when
  A. Social occasions put individuals in physical proximity
  B. Gatherings allow face-to-face contact revolving around talk.

2. The viability of an encounter is a positive and multiplicative function of
  A. The availability of relevant normative rules to guide participants with respect to such issues as
    1. Irrelevance, or excluded matters
    2. Transformation, or how external matters are to be incorporated
    3. Resource use, or what local resources are to be drawn from
    4. Talk, or how verbalizations are to be ordered
    5. Self-respect, or the maintenance of lines and face.

(Continued)

Table 18.2 (Continued)

B. The availability of ritual practices that can be used to
  1. Regulate talk and conversation
  2. Express appropriate deference and demeanor
  3. Invoke and punctuate normative rules
  4. Repair breaches to the interaction.
C. The capacity of individuals to present acceptable performances with respect to
  1. Lines, or directions of conduct
  2. Roles, or specific clusters of rights and duties
  3. Faces, or specific presentations of personal characteristics
  4. Self, or particular images of oneself.

on a face-to-face basis. But, despite the complexity of how this focusing can be done, talk is still normatively and ritually regulated in ways that produce a sense of shared reality for individuals.[67]

Table 18.2 summarizes Goffman's analysis of focused encounters. Focused encounters occur when social occasions put people in face-to-face contact; and the viability of the encounter depends on rules, rituals, and the capacity of individuals to present acceptable performances. The statements under (1) and (2) reveal the basic argument in Goffman's approach.

Disruption and Repair in Focused Interaction. Goffman stressed that disruption in encounters is never a trivial matter:

> Social encounters differ a great deal in the importance that participants give to them but, whether crucial or picayune, all encounters represent occasions when the individual can become spontaneously involved in the proceedings and derive from this a firm sense of reality. And this feeling is not a trivial thing, regardless of the package in which it comes. When an incident occurs . . . then the reality is threatened. Unless the disturbance is checked, unless the interactants regain their proper involvement, the illusion of reality will be shattered.[68]

When a person emits gestures that contradict normative roles, present a contradictory front, fail to enact appropriate rituals, seek an inappropriate role, attempt a normatively or ritually incorrect line, or present a wrong face, there is potential for a scene. From the person's point of view, there is a possibility of embarrassment, to

---

[67]Again, this line of emphasis is what gives Goffman's work an ethnomethodological flair. See the next chapter.

[68]Goffman, *Interaction Ritual,* 135.

use Goffman's favorite phrase; once embarrassed, an individual's responses can further degenerate in an escalating cycle of ever greater levels of embarrassment. From the perspective of others, a scene disrupts the definition of the situation and threatens the sense of reality necessary for them to feel comfortable. Individuals implicitly assume that people are reliable and trustworthy, that they are what they appear to be, that they are competent, and that they can be relied on; thus, when a scene occurs, these implicit assumptions are challenged and threaten the organization of the encounter (and, potentially, the larger gathering and social occasion).

For this reason, an individual will seek to repair a scene caused by the use of inappropriate gestures, and others will use tact to assist the individual in such repair efforts. The sense of order of a situation is thus sustained by a variety of corrective responses by individuals and by the willingness of others to use tact in ignoring minor mistakes and, if this is not possible, to employ tact to facilitate an offending individual's corrective efforts. People "disattend" much potentially discrepant behavior, and when this is no longer an option, they are prepared to accept apologies, accounts, new information, excuses, and other ritually and normatively appropriate efforts at repair. Of course, this willingness to accept people as they are, to assume their competence, and to overlook minor interpersonal mistakes makes them vulnerable to manipulation and deceit.

Unfocused Encounters

Goffman was one of the few sociologists to recognize that behavior and interaction in public places or in unfocused settings are important features of the interaction order and, by extension, of social organization in general. Such simple acts as walking down the street, standing in line, sitting in a waiting room or on a park bench, standing in an elevator, going to and from a public restroom, and many other activities represent a significant realm of social organization. These unfocused situations in which people are copresent but not involved in prolonged talk and "face encounters" represent a crucial topic of sociological inquiry—a topic that is often seen as trivial but that embraces much of people's time and attention. In two works, *Relations in Public* and *Behavior in Public Places,* Goffman explored the dynamics of unfocused gatherings.[69]

Unfocused gatherings are like focused interactions in their general contours: they are normatively regulated; they call for performances by individuals; they include the presentation of a self; they involve the use of rituals; they have normatively and ritually appropriate procedures for repair; and they depend on a considerable amount of etiquette, tact, and inattention. Let us explore each of these features in somewhat greater detail.

Much like a focused interaction, unfocused gatherings involve normative rules concerning spacing, movement, positioning, listening, talking, and self-presentation. But, unlike focused interaction, norms do not have to sustain a well-defined membrane. There is no closure, intense focus of attention, or face-to-face obligations in

---

[69]Goffman, *Behavior in Public Places* and *Relations in Public.*

unfocused encounters. Rather, rules pertain to how individuals are to comport themselves *without* becoming the focus of attention and involved in a face encounter. Rules are thus about how to move, talk, sit, stand, present self, apologize, and perform other actions necessary to sustain public order without creating a situation requiring the additional interpersonal "work" of focused interaction.

When in public, individuals still engage in performances, but because the audience is not involved in a face engagement or prolonged tracks of talk, the presentation can be more muted and less animated. Goffman used a variety of terms to describe these presentations, two of the most frequent being *body idiom*[70] and *body gloss.*[71] Both terms denote the overall configuration of gestures, or demeanor, that an individual makes available and gleanable to others. (Conversely, others are constantly scanning to determine the content of others' body idiom and body gloss.) Such a demeanor denotes a person's direction, speed, resoluteness, purpose, and other aspects of a course of action. In *Relations in Public,* Goffman enumerated three types of body gloss:[72] (1) *orientation gloss,* or gestures giving evidence to others confirming that a person is engaged in a recognizable and appropriate activity in the present time and place; (2) *circumspection gloss,* or gestures indicating to others that a person is not going to encroach on or threaten the activity of others; and (3) *overplay gloss,* or gestures signaling that a person is not constrained or under duress and is, therefore, fully in charge and in control of his or her other movements and actions. Thus, the public performance of an individual in unfocused interaction revolves around providing information that one is of "sound character and reasonable competency."[73]

In public and during unfocused interactions, the territories of self become an important consideration. Goffman listed various kinds of territorial considerations that can become salient during unfocused interaction, including[74] (a) *fixed geographical spaces* attached to a particular person; (b) *egocentric preserves* of non-encroachment that surround individuals as they move in space; (c) *personal spaces* that others are not to violate under any circumstances; (d) *stalls,* or bounded places that an individual can temporarily claim; (e) *use spaces* that can be claimed as an individual engages in some instrumental activity; (f) *turns,* or the claimed order of doing or receiving something relative to others in a situation; (g) *possessional territory,* or objects identified with self and arrayed around an individual's body; (h) *informational preserve,* or the body of facts about a person that is controlled and regulated; and (i) *conversational preserve,* or the right to control who can summon and talk to an individual. Depending on the type of unfocused interaction, as well as on the number, age, sex, rank, position, and other characteristics of the participants, the territories of self will vary, but in all societies there

---

[70]Goffman, *Behavior in Public Places,* 35.

[71]Goffman, *Relations in Public,* 8.

[72]Ibid., 129–138.

[73]Ibid., 162.

[74]Ibid., chap. 2.

are clearly understood norms about which configuration of these territories is relevant and to what degree it can be invoked.

These territories of self are made visible through what Goffman termed *markers.* Markers are signals and objects that denote the type of territorial claim, its extent and boundary, and its duration. Violation of these markers involves an encroachment on a person's self and invites sanctioning, perhaps creating a breach or scene in the public order. Indeed, seemingly innocent acts—such as inadvertently taking someone's place, butting in line, cutting someone off, and the like—can become a violation or "befoulment" of another's self and, as a result, invite an extreme reaction. Thus, social organization in general depends on the capacity of individuals to read those markers that establish their territories of self in public situations.

Violations of norms and territories create breaches and potential scenes, even when individuals are not engaged in focused interaction. These are usually repaired through ritual activity, such as (a) *accounts* explaining why a transgression has occurred (ignorance, unusual circumstances, temporary incompetence, "unmindfulness," etc.), (b) *apologies* (some combination of expressed embarrassment or chagrin, clarification that the proper conduct is known and understood, disavowal and rejection of one's behavior, penance, volunteering of restitution, etc.), and (c) *requests,* or a preemptive asking for license to do something that might otherwise be considered a violation of a norm or a person's self.[75] The use of these ritualized forms of repair sustains the positioning, movement, and smooth flow of activity among people in unfocused situations; without these repair rituals, tempers would flare, and other disruptive acts would overwhelm the public order.

The significance of ritualized responses for repair only highlights the importance of ritual in general for unfocused interaction. As individuals move about, stand, sit, and engage in other acts in public, these activities are punctuated with rituals, especially as people come close to contact with each other. Nods, smiles, hand gestures, bodily movements, and, if necessary, brief episodes of talk (especially during repairs) are all highly ritualized, involving stereotyped sequences of behavior that reinforce norms and signal individuals' willingness to get along with and accommodate each other.

In addition to ritual, much unfocused interaction involves tact and inattention. By simply ignoring or quietly tolerating small breaches of norms, self, and ritual practices, people can gather and move about without undue tension and acrimony. In this way, unfocused interactions are made to seem uneventful, enabling individuals to cultivate a sense of obdurate reality in subtle glances, nods, momentary eye contact, shifting of direction, and other acts of public life where individuals are negotiating their way through public places.

In Table 18.3, the key propositions implied in Goffman's discussion are enumerated. The relationships among the variables listed in the propositions are multiplicative in that each one accelerates the effects of the other in maintaining order in public situations of unfocused gatherings. This interactive effect allows public order to be sustained without reliance on focused talk and conversation.

---

[75]Ibid., 109–120.

Table 18.3 Goffman's General Propositions on Unfocused Interaction

1. Order in unfocused interaction is a positive and multiplicative function of
   A. The clarity of normative rules regulating behavior in ways that limit face encounters and talk
   B. The capacity of individuals to provide demeanor cues with respect to
      1. Orientation, or the appropriateness of activities at the present time and place
      2. Circumspection, or the willingness to avoid encroachment on, and threat to, others
      3. Overplays, or the capacity to signal that one can control and regulate conduct without duress and constraint.
   C. The capacity of individuals to signal with clear markers those configurations of normatively appropriate territories of self with respect to
      1. Fixed geographical spaces that can be claimed
      2. Egocentric preserves of non-encroachment that can be claimed during movement in space
      3. Personal spaces that can be claimed
      4. Stalls of territory that can be temporarily used
      5. Use spaces that can be occupied for instrumental purposes
      6. Turns of performing or receiving goods that can be claimed
      7. Possessional territory and objects identified with, and arrayed around, self
      8. Informational preserves that can be used to regulate facts about individuals
      9. Conversational preserves that can be invoked to control talk.
   D. The availability of configurations of normatively appropriate repair rituals revolving around
      1. Accounts, or explanations for transgressions
      2. Apologies, or expressions of embarrassment, regret, and penance for mistakes
      3. Requests, or redemptive inquiries about making a potential transgression.
   E. The availability and clarity of rituals to reinforce norms and to order conduct by restricting face engagements among individuals
   F. The availability of ritualized procedures for ignoring minor transgressions of norms and territories of self (tact and etiquette).

Frames and the Organization of Experience

Goffman's last major work, *Frame Analysis: An Essay on the Organization of Experience*,[76] is hardly an "essay" but, rather, an 800-page treatise on phenomenology, or the subjective organization of experience in social situations. It is a dense and rambling work, but it nonetheless returns to a feature of interaction that guided Goffman's work from the very beginning: the construction of "definitions of situations." That is, how is it that people define the reality of situations?

---

[76]Goffman, *Frame Analysis.*

What Is a Frame? The concept of frame appeared in Goffman's first major work, *The Presentation of Self,* and periodically thereafter. Surprisingly, he never offered a precise definition of this term, but the basic idea is that people "interpret" events or "strips of activity" in situations with a "schemata" that cognitively encircles or frames what is occurring.[77] The frame is much like a picture frame in that it marks off the boundary of the pictured events, encapsulating and distinguishing them from the surrounding environment. Goffman's early discussion of the "rules of irrelevance" in encounters—that is, considerations, characteristics, aspects, and events in the external world to be excluded during a focused interaction—represented an earlier way of communicating the dynamics of framing. Thus, as people look at the world, they impose a frame that defines what is to be pictured on the inside and what is to be excluded by what Goffman termed the *rim of the frame* on the outside. Human experience is organized by frames, which provide an interpretive "framework" or "frame of reference" for designating events or "strips of activity."

Primary Frames. Goffman argued that, ultimately, interpretations of events are anchored in a primary framework, which is a frame that does not depend on some prior interpretation of events.[78] Primary frameworks are thus anchored in the real world, at least from the point of view of the individual's organization of experience. Goffman emphasized that people tend to distinguish between natural and social frameworks.[79] A *natural frame* is anchored in purely physical means for interpreting the world—body, ecology, terrain, objects, natural events, and the like. A *social frame* is lodged in the world, created by acts of intelligence and social life. These two kinds of primary frameworks can vary enormously in their organization; some are clearly organized as "entities, postulates, and roles," whereas most others "provide only a lore of understanding, an approach, a perspective."[80] All social frameworks involve rules about what is to be excluded beyond the rim of the frame, what is to be pictured inside the frame, and what is to be done when acting within the frame. Yet as humans perceive and act, they are likely to apply several frameworks, giving the organization of experience a complexity that Goffman only alluded to in his earlier works.

Although Goffman stressed that he was not analyzing social structure with the concept of frames, he was clearly developing a neo-Durkheimian argument, recasting Durkheim's social psychology—especially the notion of how the "collective conscience rules people from within"—into more complex and dynamic terms.[81] For, as he argued,[82] taken all together, the primary frameworks of a particular social group constitute a central element of its culture, especially insofar as understandings

---

[77]See Goffman, *Frame Analysis,* 10, for the vagueness of his portrayal.

[78]Ibid., 21.

[79]Ibid., 21–24.

[80]Ibid., 21.

[81]See Durkheim, *Elementary Forms of the Religious Life.*

[82]Goffman, *Frame Analysis,* 27.

emerge concerning principal classes of schemata, the relations of these classes to one another, and the sum total of forces and agents that these interpretive designs acknowledge to be loose in the world.

Yet, for the most part, Goffman concentrated on the dynamics of framing within the realms of personal experiences and the interaction order, leaving Durkheim's concerns about macro-cultural processes to others. Indeed, as was so often the case with Goffman, he became so intrigued with the interpersonal manipulation of frames for deceitful purposes and with the fluidity and complexity of framing in contingent situations that it is often difficult to discern whether or not the analysis is still sociological.

Keys and Keying. What makes framing a complex process, Goffman argued, is that frames can be transformed. One basic way to transform a primary frame is to engage in *keying,* which is "a set of conventions by which a given activity, one already meaningful in terms of some primary framework, is transformed into something patterned on this activity but seen by the participants to be something quite else."[83] For example, a theatrical production of a family setting is a keying of "real families," a hobby such as woodworking is a keying of a more primary set of occupational activities, a daydream about a love affair is a keying of real love, a sporting event is a keying of some more primary activity (running, fleeing, fighting, etc.), practicing and rehearsing are keyings of real performances, joking about someone's "love life" is a keying of love affairs, and so on. Primary frameworks are seen by people as "real," whereas keyings are seen as "less real"; and the more one rekeys a primary framework—say, performing a keying of a keying of a keying, and so on—the "less real" is the frame. The rim of the frame is still ultimately a primary framework, anchored in some natural or social reality, but humans have the capacity to continually rekey and layer or *laminate* their experiences. Thus, terms like *definition of the situation* do not adequately capture this layering of experience through keying, nor do such terms adequately denote the multiplicity of frameworks that people can invoke because of their capacities for shifting primary frameworks and rekeying existing ones.

Fabrications. The second type of frame transformation—in addition to keying—is *fabrication,* which is "the intentional effort of one or more individuals to manage activity so that a party of one or more others will be induced to have a false belief about what it is that is going on."[84] Unlike a key, a fabrication is not a copy (or a copy of a copy) of some primary framework but an effort to make others think that something else is going on. Hoaxes, con games, and strategic manipulations all involve fabrications—getting others to frame a situation in one way while others manipulate them as another, hidden, framework.

The Complexity of Experience. Thus, as people interact, they frame situations as primary frameworks, but they can also key these primary frames and fabricate new ones for purposes of deception and manipulation. From Goffman's viewpoint, an interaction can involve many keyings and rekeyings (i.e., layers and laminations of

---

[83]Ibid., 43–44.

[84]Ibid., 83.

interpretation), as well as fabrications. Once keying or fabrication occurs, further keying and fabrication actually are facilitated because they initiate an escalating movement away from a primary framework. Goffman never stated how much fabrication (and fabrication on fabrications) and keying (or keying on keyings) can occur in interaction, but he did see novels, dramatic theater, and cinema as providing the vehicles for the deepest layering of interaction (because each is an initial keying of some primary frame in the real world, which then opens the almost infinite possibilities for rekeying and fabrication).

Yet there are procedures in interaction—typically ritualized and normatively regulated—for bringing participants' experiences back to the original primary frame—that is, for wiping away layers of keyings and fabrications. For example, when people have become caught up in benign ridicule and joking about something, a person saying "Seriously now . . ." is trying to wipe the slate clean of keyings (and rekeyings) and come back to the primary frame on which the mocking and joking were based. Such rituals (with the normative obligation to "try to be serious for a moment") seek to re-anchor the interaction in "the real world."

In addition to keyings and deliberate fabrications, individuals can *mis-frame* events—whether from ignorance, ambiguity, error, or initial disputes over framing among participants. Such mis-framing can persist for a time, but eventually individuals seek to clear the frame by getting a correct reading of information so they can reframe the situation correctly. Such efforts to clear the frame become particularly difficult and problematic, however, when fabrication has been at least part of the reason for the mis-framing.[85]

Thus, framing is a very complex process—one that, Goffman contended, sociologists are willing to address seriously. The world that people experience is not unitary, and it is subject to considerable manipulation, whether for benign or deceptive purposes. And because of humans' capacity for symbol use (especially talk), the processes of reframing, keying, and fabrication can create highly layered and complex experiences. Yet during interaction, people seek to maintain a common frame (a need that, Goffman was all too willing to assert, makes them vulnerable to manipulation through fabrication). For without a common frame—even one that has been keyed or fabricated—the interaction cannot proceed smoothly. Unfortunately, Goffman concentrated on framing as "organizing experience," per se, rather than on framing as it organizes experience during focused and unfocused interaction. Hence, the analysis of framing is provocative and suggestive, but too often it wanders away from the sociologically relevant topic—"the interaction order."

In sum, then, Erving Goffman's works represent a truly seminal breakthrough in the analysis of social interaction. The emphasis on self-presentations, norms, rituals, and frames presented sociological theory at the mid-century with many important conceptual leads that have been adopted by diverse theoretical traditions. There are, however, some questionable points of emphasis that should, in closing, be mentioned. First, Goffman's somewhat cynical and manipulative view of humans and interaction—which have been consistently downplayed in this chapter—often takes analysis in directions that are not as fundamental to human organization as he

---

[85]See ibid., 449, for a list of the conditions that make individuals inadvertently vulnerable to mis-framing, and 463, for how mis-framing can be the result of deception and manipulation.

implied. Second, Goffman's rather extreme situational view of self as only a projected image, and perhaps a mirage, in each and every situation is probably overdrawn. The denial of a core self or permanent identity certainly runs against the mainstream of interactionist theorizing and, perhaps, reality itself. And, third, Goffman's work tended, at times, to wander into a rather extreme subjectivism and interpersonal nihilism where experience is too layered and fickle and where interaction is too fluid and changeable by the slightest shift in frame and ritual. Yet, even with these points of criticism, Goffman's sociology represents a monumental achievement—certainly equal to that of George Herbert Mead, Alfred Schutz, and Émile Durkheim. Indeed, looking back at the twentieth century, it is clear that Goffman's work is the most important micro theorizing of the last seven decades.

Extensions of Goffmanian Dramaturgy

Goffman was, rather surprisingly, one of the first contemporary sociologists to conceptualize emotions. Indeed, sociology in general tended to ignore the topic of emotions from Charles Horton Cooley's analysis of pride and shame in the first decade of the twentieth century to the late 1960s and 1970s—a significant gap in theorizing given the significance of emotions in human affairs. Yet Goffman never developed a robust theory of emotions but, instead, frequently mentioned the importance of *embarrassment,* or what we might see as a mild form of *shame.* When an individual cannot successfully present a self and when he or she fails to abide by the script by talking inappropriately, incorrectly using rituals, failing to stay within the frame, inappropriately categorizing a situation, misusing stage props, or expressing inappropriate emotions, the negative emotions aroused in the audience will lead to negative sanctioning of the person, who will, in turn, experience embarrassment. Often, the audience will not actually need to sanction those who have breached an encounter because individuals will typically recognize the breach and feel embarrassed. Under these conditions, a sequence of repair rituals ensues, revolving around sanctions, apologies, and re-presentation of a more appropriate face and line. People are motivated to do so because they implicitly recognize that the social fabric and moral order are at stake. Encounters depend upon the smooth flow of interaction that sustains the moral order. People in encounters are thus highly attuned to the cultural script and the mutual presentations of self in accordance with the script.

Even though Goffman himself did not develop a very robust conception of emotions, many of those who followed him did. The sociology of emotions did not exist in sociology during most of Goffman's career, but by the time he died in the 1980s, the study of emotions and, hence, theorizing about emotional dynamics had become more prevalent and, today, is one of the leading edges of micro theorizing in sociology.[86] Let me follow up on this observation by reviewing a sample of the sociologists who used the dramaturgical perspective pioneered by Goffman to develop new theories of emotional processes.

---

[86]See for reviews, Jonathan H. Turner and Jan E. Stets, *The Sociology of Emotions* (Cambridge, UK: Cambridge University Press, 2005) and Jan E. Stets and Jonathan H. Turner (ed.), *Handbook of the Sociology of Emotions* (New York: Springer, 2006).

Arlie Hochschild on Emotional Labor

Arlie Russell Hochschild[87] was one of the first sociologists to develop a view of emotions as managed performances by individuals within the constraints of situational norms and broader cultural ideas about what emotions can be felt and presented in front of others. For Hochschild, the *emotion culture*[88] consists of a series of ideas about how and what people are supposed to experience in various types of situations, and this culture is filled with emotional ideologies about the appropriate attitudes and feelings for specific spheres and activities. Emotional markers are events in the biographies of individuals that personify and symbolize more general emotional ideologies.

In any context, Hochschild emphasizes, there are norms of two basic types: (1) *feeling rules,* which indicate (a) the amount of appropriate emotion that can be felt in a situation, (b) the direction, whether positive or negative, of the emotion, and (c) the duration of the emotion and (2) *display rules,* which indicate the nature, intensity, and style of expressive behavior to be emitted. Thus, for any interaction, feeling and display rules circumscribe what can be done. These rules reflect ideologies of the broader emotion culture, the goals and purposes of groups in which interactions are lodged, and the distribution of power and other organizational features of the situation.

The existence of cultural ideologies and normative constraints on the selection and emission of emotions forces individuals to manage the feelings that they experience and present to others. At this point, Hochschild's analysis becomes dramaturgic, for, much like Goffman before her, she sees actors as having to manage a presentation of self in situations guided by a cultural script of norms and broader ideologies. There are various types of what Hochschild terms *emotion work,* or mechanisms for managing emotions and making the appropriate self-presentation: (a) *body work,* whereby individuals actually seek to change their bodily sensations in an effort to evoke the appropriate emotion (e.g., deep breathing to create calm); (b) *surface acting,* where individuals alter their external expressive gestures in ways that they hope will make them actually feel the appropriate emotion (e.g., emitting gestures expressing joy and sociality at a party in an attempt to feel happy); (c) *deep acting,* where individuals attempt to change their internal feelings, or at least some of these feelings, in the hope that the rest of the appropriate emotions will be activated and fall into place (e.g., evoking feelings of *sadness* in an effort to feel sad at a funeral); and (d) *cognitive work,* where the thoughts and ideas associated with particular emotions are evoked, in an attempt to activate the corresponding feelings.

---

[87] Arlie R. Hochschild, "Emotion Work, Feeling Rules, and Social Structure," *American Journal of Sociology* 85 (1979):551–575, *The Managed Heart: The Commercialization of Human Feeling* (Berkeley: University of California Press, 1983).

[88] Steven L. Gordon has provided a useful analysis of emotion culture, one that has been highly influential not only in Hochschild's work but in the work of other theorists and researchers as well. See "The Sociology of Emotion," in *Social Psychology: Sociological Perspectives*, ed. M. Rosenberg and R. H. Turner (New York: Basic Books, 1981), 562–592, "Institutional and Impulsive Orientations in Selectively Appropriating Emotions to the Self," in *The Sociology of Emotions: Original Essays and Research Papers*, ed. D. D. Franks and E. D. McCarthy (Greenwich, CT: JAI Press, 1989), 115–126, and "Social Structural Effects on Emotions," in *Research Agendas in the Sociology of Emotions*, ed. T. D. Kemper (Albany: State University of New York Press, 1990), 145–179.

As Hochschild stresses, individuals are often put in situations where a considerable amount of emotion work must be performed. For example, in her pioneering study of airline attendants,[89] the requirement that attendants always be friendly, pleasant, and helpful even as passengers were rude and unpleasant placed an enormous emotional burden on the attendants. They had to manage their emotions through emotion work and present themselves in ways consistent with highly restrictive feeling and display rules. Virtually all encounters require emotion work, although some, such as the one faced by airline attendants, are particularly taxing and require a considerable amount of emotion management in self-presentations.

In emphasizing emotion work, Hochschild not only incorporates elements of Erving Goffman's but also adds a critical edge that is more reminiscent of Karl Marx's views on alienation. For Hochschild, individuals often engage in strategic performances that are not gratifying. Cultural scripts thus impose requirements on how they feel. As a general rule, then, emotion work will be most evident when people confront emotion ideologies, emotion rules, and display rules that go against their actual feelings, and especially when they are required by these rules to express and display emotions that they do not feel. Complex social systems with hierarchies of authority or market systems forcing sellers of goods and providers of services to act in certain ways with customers who have more latitude in the expression of emotions are likely to generate situations where individuals must engage in emotion work. Since these types of systems are more typical of industrial and postindustrial societies, Hochschild sees modernity as dramatically increasing the amount of emotion work that people must perform. Such work is always costly because people must, to some degree, repress their "true emotions" as they try to present themselves in ways demanded by the cultural script.

Another extension of this line of reasoning is more in tune with Erving Goffman's repeated fascination with how individuals "con" one another. If the feeling and display rules are known by all participants in an encounter, an individual is in a position to manipulate gestures in order to convince others that he or she also feels the same emotions and has the same goals, when, in fact, he or she may have a devious purpose. A good "con man," for instance, can appear to be helpful to people experiencing difficulty by displaying gestures indicating that he feels their pain and that he is doing his best to help them out of a difficult situation, when, in reality, he is trying to cheat them. Yet most of the time in most situations, individuals make a good-faith effort to feel and express the appropriate emotions because the rules of culture have a moral quality that invites negative feelings and sanctions for their violation, even in seemingly trivial interactions. Thus, people implicitly understand that to violate feeling and display rules will inevitably disrupt the encounter and, potentially, the larger social occasion.

Morris Rosenberg on Reflexivity and Dramatic Presentations

Morris Rosenberg's basic argument is that reflexivity, or thinking about the effects of one's actions, changes the physiological nature of human emotions.[90]

---

[89]Hochschild, *The Managed Heart.*

[90]Morris Rosenberg, "Reflexivity and Emotions," *Social Psychology Quarterly* 53 (1990):3–12, "Self Processes and Emotional Experiences," in *The Self-Society Interface: Cognition, Emotion, and Action,* ed. J. A. Howard and P. L. Callero (New York: Cambridge University Press, 1991).

Through the reflexive process, a person's emotions are transformed into something different. The reflexive process operates through at least three different paths: (1) emotional identification, (2) emotional displays, and (3) emotional experiences. In *emotional identification,* reflexivity is cognitive, with individuals making interpretations, inferences, or attributions to understand their inner feelings. In *emotional displays,* reflexivity is reflected in individuals' regulation of emotional gestures to produce a certain effect on the audience, a point that has an affinity with Hochschild's surface acting. In *emotional experiences,* reflexivity appears in internal states of arousal, an idea similar to Hochschild's deep acting. Each of these is examined below.

Emotional Identification. People's internal states of arousal are ambiguous, with the result that they turn to information in the environment to help them make sense of what they are feeling. Alternatively, people may be feeling multiple emotions in a situation, as, for example, when one feels mournful and relieved at the death of a loved one. This ambiguity over emotional experience forces people to *think about* their feelings and, hence, become reflexive.

There are, Rosenberg argues, three cognitive factors influencing emotional identification: (1) causal assumptions, (2) social consensus, and (3) cultural scenarios. *Causal assumptions* emerge from the socialization process. Adults and peers teach culturally specified connections among stimuli/events and the outcomes generated. As these assumptions are learned and stored in memory, individuals develop what Rosenberg calls an *emotional logic.* People learn, for example, that when someone offers an insult, the sensation of heart pounding is to be labeled anger (rather than some other emotion like happiness). Thus, when actors are faced with ambiguous internal feelings, they turn to the emotional logic that they have learned in order to make sense of the ambiguity. *Social consensus* helps inform actors as to what they are inwardly feeling. By observing how others respond, and in particular if others are responding in the same way, individuals are given guidance about how to label their inner feelings. Finally, inner experiences become more identifiable by calling up in one's mind *cultural criteria* against which they can compare their current experiences. For example, if a person is trying to identify whether or not a feeling is love for another, this person ponders the current situation to determine if it reflects "love" as presented in cultural ideologies and lore.

Emotional Displays. Reflexivity also operates at the behavioral level, in which individuals either reveal or hide their emotions. The goal is to convince an audience that they are experiencing certain emotions. There are three "devices" or mechanisms that people use to manage emotional displays: (1) *verbal devices,* such as words, metaphors, or poetic imagery, that convey emotionality; (2) *facial expressions* and other *physical expressions* such as voice pitch, volume, and speed of speech (e.g., when one is upset, pitch and volume are higher and speech is faster); and (3) *physical objects* such as props or costumes (e.g., wearing black conveys sorrow) to signal one's emotions.

Persons engage in three types of emotional display: (1) emotions signaling conformity to norms, thereby giving actions a moral character and affirming that there is commitment to the cultural script; (2) emotions as a means toward obtaining a goal, thus communicating that actions are instrumental; and (3) emotions designed to reveal the experience of pleasure, thereby revealing a concern with positive emotional outcomes for both self and others.

Emotional Experiences. As Hochschild emphasizes, individuals often manipulate inner emotional experiences in order to feel differently. Through *body work,* such as, running, controlled breathing, relaxation techniques, and biochemical strategies (e.g., alcohol, drugs, or hypnosis), individuals attempt to change their feelings. Through *cognitive work,* individuals attempt to think differently in order to feel differently. These efforts to change emotional experiences can only work, however, if individuals can succeed in achieving *selective attention, perspectual selectivity,* and *selective interpretation.* In *selective attention,* individuals actively try to control what they think, either directly or indirectly. In direct selective attention, people seek to push particular emotions out of their minds and substitute new emotions in their place, whereas in indirect cognitive work, individuals will try to avoid situations activating emotions that they do not wish to experience. In *perspectival selectivity,* people seek to manage emotions by altering their perspective or frame of reference. For example, a person who is feeling impatient may alter the time perspective ("Everything will work out in time," "Time heals all wounds"); or an individual who is feeling depressed may think about others who are worse off, thereby making the current problem seem less significant. In *selective interpretation,* people seek to assign meanings to events that will generate positive emotional outcomes. One strategy is selective attribution, or the assignment of causality in a manner that benefits the self. For example, people have a tendency to take responsibility for successes while denying responsibility for failures. Another strategy of attribution is to attribute failure to a lack of effort rather than a lack of ability.

Peggy Thoits's Theory of Emotional Deviance

Peggy Thoits uses the dramaturgical perspective to develop a theory[91] of emotional deviance; and in so doing, she adds to Hochschild's theory. Her theory revolves around three basic issues: (1) the *sources* for which a discrepancy between one's feeling state and feeling rules is likely to emerge, (2) the various *emotion management strategies* or *coping styles* to resolve the discrepancy, and (3) the conditions under which *emotion management fails* and, thereby, causes motivational deviance. Each of these is discussed below.

The Sources of Discrepancy. Discrepancy between what is felt and what is expected by feeling rules causes individuals to feel *stress.* Stress increases under certain conditions: (a) multiple-role occupancy, (b) subcultural marginality, (c) normative and nonnormative role transitions, and (d) rigid rules governing

---

[91]Peggy A. Thoits, "Self-labeling Processes in Mental Illness: The Role of Emotional Deviance," *American Journal of Sociology* 91(1985):317–342, "Emotional Deviance: Research Agendas" in *Research Agendas in the Sociology of Emotions,* ed. T. D. Kemper (Albany, NY: State University of New York Press, 1990), 180–203.

roles and rituals. Both *multiple-role occupancy* and *subcultural marginality* involve instances where a person may be subjected to conflicting feeling rules because of participation in different roles or groups. In either case, persons must cope with potentially contradictory expectations (whether in multiple roles or in subcultural differences among subpopulations); the greater is the contradiction, the greater will be the level of stress experienced by individuals. Movement to a new role or *nonnormative role transition* often generates ambiguity over the appropriate behavior and feelings in the new role. Finally, *strict feeling rules* associated with roles and rituals in a situation ensure that even minor departures from feeling rules will be stressful.

Emotion Management Strategies. When feelings depart from the feeling rules, individuals seek to manage their emotions by bringing subjective emotional experiences in line with the normative requirements of the situation. Thoits identifies two primary modes that persons use to change their emotional experience: behavioral and cognitive. In *behavioral manipulations,* individuals alter their behaviors in the hope that their feelings will fall in line with the cultural script. In *cognitive manipulations,* individuals try to change the *meaning* of the situation (to them) in order to bring feelings in line with normative expectations for how one should feel in the situation.

Emotional Deviance. No matter how hard they try, behavioral and cognitive strategies to reduce the discrepancy between actual feelings and feeling rules simply do not work for some individuals. The result is, of course, stress. This stress may be seen by others as a sign of a psychological problem (in its mild form) or mental illness (in its more severe form). The level of stress experienced by individuals is related to (a) the degree of discrepancy in the situation and (b) the level of social support individuals feeling stressed can draw upon. If the negative feelings revolving around stress continue, however, others may withdraw their social support, thereby making the situation even more stressful. And if these others begin to label a person as "deviant," they may push the stressed individual further into a state of emotional deviance. And, ironically, when people cannot get support from others, they may turn to mental health professionals, who, in turn, will also implicitly label them as emotionally deviant.

Candace Clark's Theory on the Dramaturgy and Strategy of Sympathy

Candace Clark has extended the dramaturgical perspective with the detailed analysis of sympathy as both a dramatic and a strategic process[92]—two points of emphasis in Goffman's theory. Like all dramaturgical theories, Clark visualizes a

---

[92]Candace Clark, *Misery and Company: Sympathy in Everyday Life* (Chicago, IL: University of Chicago Press, 1997), "Sympathy Biography and Sympathy Margin," *American Journal of Sociology* 93 (1987):290–321, "Emotions and Micropolitics in Everyday Life: Some Patterns and Paradoxes," in *Research Agendas in the Sociology of Emotions,* ed. T. D. Kemper (Albany: State University of New York Press, 1990).

feeling culture consisting of beliefs, values, rules, logics, vocabularies, and other symbolic elements that frame and direct the process of sympathizing. Individuals are implicitly aware of these cultural elements, drawing upon them to make dramaturgical presentations and displays on a stage in front of an audience of others. Although there are cultural rules guiding behavior, many dimensions of culture do not constitute a clear script but, instead, operate more like the rules of grammar that allow actors to organize feeling elements, such as feeling ideologies, feeling rules, feeling logics, and feeling vocabularies, into a framework for emitting and responding to sympathy.

Each individual feels the weight of expectations from culture about how sympathizing is to occur, and each must engage in a performance using whatever techniques are appropriate to feeling and displaying the appropriate emotions. In particular, surface acting, deep acting, and the use of rituals to arouse and track emotions are often employed by actors who are seeking to present a self in accordance with a script assembled from relevant cultural elements.

Strategic Dimensions of Sympathy Giving. There is also a strategic dimension to sympathizing, a point of emphasis that follows Goffman's view of encounters as highly strategic. Individuals do not passively play roles directed by a cultural script; rather, they also engage in games of *microeconomics* and *micropolitics*. With respect to *microeconomics,* Clark argues that emotions are often exchanged in sympathy giving and taking, and even sympathy as an act of kindness and altruism is subject to these exchange dynamics. Feeling rules often require that recipients of sympathy give back to their sympathizers emotions like *gratitude, pleasure,* and *relief.* In regard to *micropolitics,* individuals always seek to enhance their place or standing vis-à-vis others, even when they remain unaware of their efforts to gain standing at the expense of others. Such contests over *place* vis-à-vis others introduce inequalities into encounters and, hence, the tensions that always arise from inequality. Sympathy, like any set of emotions, can be an important tool for individuals to enhance their place or standing in an encounter. By giving sympathy to someone, a person establishes that he or she is in a higher place, since the person receiving sympathy needs help. There is a kind of strategic dramaturgy involved. And Clark outlines several strategies for gaining a favorable place: display mock sympathy that draws attention to another's negative qualities; bestow an emotional gift in a way that underscores another's weakness, vulnerability, and problems; bestow sympathy on superordinates to reduce the distance between places marked by inequalities; remind others of an emotional debt by pointing out problems for which sympathy is given, thereby not only lowering the other's place but also establishing an obligation for the recipient of sympathy to reciprocate; and use sympathy in ways that make the others feel negative emotions such as *worry, humiliation, shame,* or *anger,* thereby lowering their place.

Integrative Effects of Sympathy. Even though there is a darker side to sympathy processes in games of microeconomics and micropolitics, sympathy at the level of the encounter has integrative effects on the larger social order. First, positive emotions are exchanged—that is, sympathy for other positive emotions like *gratitude,* thereby making both parties to the exchange feel better. Second, the plight of those in need of sympathy is acknowledged by those giving sympathy, thus reinforcing social bonds, per se, above and beyond whatever exchange will eventually occur. Third, sympathy operates as a "safety valve" in allowing those in difficulty a temporary release from normal cultural proscriptions and prescriptions while remobilizing their energies to meeting cultural expectations in the future. Fourth, sympathizing is also the enactment of a moral drama because it always involves invoking cultural guidelines about justice, fairness, and worthiness for those who receive the emotions marking sympathy. Fifth, even though games of micropolitics can make one party superior and another inferior (the receiver of sympathy), they do establish hierarchies that order social relations, although they also create the potential for negative emotional arousal and conflict.

Societal Changes and the Extension of Sympathy. Clark argues that the range of plights for which sympathy can be claimed is expanding. Part of the reason for this change is that high levels of structural differentiation, especially in market-driven systems emphasizing individualism, have isolated the person from traditional patterns of embeddedness in social structures. As a result, culture highlights the importance of the individual and the problems that individuals confront. Sympathy is now to be extended to "emotional problems" that individuals have, such as stress, identity crises, divorce, loneliness, criminal victimization, difficult relationships, dissatisfaction at work, home, and school, and many other plights of individuals in complex societies. This same differentiation has created new professions that operate as "sympathy entrepreneurs," highlighting certain plights and advocating their inclusion in the list of conditions invoking sympathetic responses. The expansion of medicine and psychotherapy has added a host of new ills, both physical and mental, that are to be objects of sympathy. The social sciences have added even more, including the plight of people suffering due to racism, sexism, patriarchy, discrimination, urban blight, lower-class position, poor job skills, difficult family life, and the like. Thus, modern societies, at least those in the West, have greatly expanded the list of conditions calling for sympathetic responses.

Given the wide array of plights that can be defined as deserving of sympathetic responses, there are implicit sorting mechanisms or cultural logics that enable actors to assemble from cultural elements definitions of who is worthy of sympathy. One cultural logic revolves around establishing responsibility for a person's plight. Americans, for example, implicitly array a person's plight, Clark argues, on a continuum ranging from blameless at one pole to blameworthy at the other. Those who are blameless are deserving of sympathy, whereas those who are blameworthy deserve less sympathy. "Bad luck" is one way in which blame is established; those who have had bad luck deserve sympathy, while those who have brought problems on themselves are not deserving of sympathy.

Clark adds a list of competing rules for "determining what plights were unlucky for members of a category" and, hence, deserving of sympathy. One rule is "the special deprivation principle," which highlights deprivations experienced by individuals that are out of the ordinary. Another is "the special burden principle," emphasizing that those who have particularly difficult tasks to perform are entitled to sympathy. Still another is "the balance of fortune principle," which highlights that those who lead fortunate and pampered lives (celebrities, rich people, and the powerful) deserve less sympathy than the ordinary person or the unfortunate individual. Still another rule is "the vulnerability principle," stressing that some categories of persons (e.g., children, the aged, and women) are more vulnerable to misfortune than others and are thereby deserving of sympathy. Another rule is "the potential principle," arguing that those whose futures have been cut short or delayed (e.g., children) are more deserving than those who have already had a chance to realize their potential (e.g., the elderly). Yet another rule is "the special responsibility principle," arguing that those who have special abilities and knowledge but do not use them well or wisely are less deserving of sympathy. And a final rule that is particularly important in establishing whether or not people are deserving of sympathy is "the social worth principle," emphasizing that people who are worthy by virtue of possessing status, power, wealth, cultural capital, and other resources are entitled to sympathy. There is, then, a cultural script for deciding who is deserving of how much sympathy in a society.

Clark notes that there are "off-the-shelf" ways in contemporary societies for expressing sympathy that involve a considerable reduction of the emotion work that a person giving sympathy must endure. These include greeting cards, offerings (e.g., flowers), prayers, tolerance of behaviors, time off from obligations, easing the pressure, listening, visitations, stereotyped rituals of touching and talk, composure work giving people time to put on a face, offers of help, and the like. But the use of standardized ways to offer sympathy still requires some emotion work as the sympathizer tries to decide upon the right combination of these off-the-shelf actions.

One of the most interesting concepts in Clark's conceptualization is the notion of *lines of sympathy credit* given to individuals. Each individual has, in essence, a *sympathy margin*, which is a line of emotional credit indicating how much sympathy is available to a person. These sympathy margins are, like all credit, subject to negotiation; and just how much of a margin an individual can claim depends upon the individual's moral worth, his or her past history of being a good individual who has been sympathetic to others, and the nature of his or her plight. Cultural rules dictate that family members get the largest sympathy margins, that people who have social value (in terms of wealth, education, authority, beauty, fame, and other forms of social capital) receive large margins, that those who have demonstrated kindness and goodness in their other roles be given large margins, and that the deserving poor (and others in plight) who are trying to help themselves receive large sympathy margins.

There is, however, a limit to sympathy margins. If a person has used all of his or her sympathy credits, no more credit will be offered. And in fact, others will often feel and express negative emotions to those who have sought to overextend their line of credit. Moreover, if individuals who have been given sympathy credits do not attempt to pay others back with the appropriate emotions, those who extended the sympathy credits will withdraw further credit and experience negative emotional arousal.

Sympathy Etiquette. The processes of claiming, accepting, and repaying credit are guided, Clark argues, by "sympathy etiquette"—an idea that pervades Goffman's analysis of encounters. Indeed, if the rules of sympathy etiquette have been breached in the past actions of a person, this individual will have his or her line of credit reduced. Thus, individuals calculate whether a person has a flawed-biography or problem credit rating when deciding how much sympathy to offer. There are several basic cultural rules, Clark's data indicate, that guide efforts by individuals to claim sympathy. These are phrased as prohibitions about claiming sympathy: do not make false claims; do not claim too much sympathy; do not take sympathy too readily; do not take it for granted; be sure to secure some sympathy to keep your emotional accounts open and emotional credit rating high; and respond with gratitude and appreciation to those who have given sympathy.

To these rules are corresponding rules for sympathizers: do not give sympathy that is not due; do not give too much sympathy out of proportion to the plight; and do not give sympathy that goes unacknowledged or underappreciated. People can underinvest or overinvest in sympathy. Overinvestors do not follow the rules above, whereas underinvestors do not keep their sympathy accounts open so that they can, if needed, make claims to sympathy in the future.

Randall Collins on Interaction Rituals

Randall Collins's conflict theory was examined in Chapter 14. At the core of this theory is the notion of interaction rituals,[93] the elements of which roughly correspond to Goffman's analysis of the encounter. For Collins, interaction rituals contain the following elements: (a) a physical assembly of copresent individuals; (b) mutual awareness of each other; (c) a common focus of attention; (d) a common emotional mood among copresent individuals; (e) rhythmic coordination and synchronization of conversation and nonverbal gestures; (f) emotional entrainment of participants; (g) a symbolic representation of this group focus and mood with objects, persons, gestures, words, and ideas among interacting individuals; (h) circulation of particularized cultural capital; and (i) a sense of moral righteousness about these symbols marking group membership. Figure 14.1 on p. 493 portrays the dynamics of such rituals.

In Collins's view, there is a kind of market for interaction rituals, which increases people's strategic actions in interaction rituals. Individuals weigh the costs in time, energy, cultural capital, and other resources that they must spend to participate in the various rituals available to them; then, they select those rituals that maximize emotional profits. In this sense, Collins proclaims emotional energy to be the common denominator of rational choice.[94] Thus, rather than representing an irrational force in human interaction, Collins sees the pursuit of emotions as highly rational: people seek out those interaction rituals in a marketplace of rituals that maximize

---

[93]Randall Collins, *Conflict Sociology: Toward an Explanatory Science* (New York: Academic Press, 1975), *Interaction Ritual Chains* (Princeton, NJ: Princeton University Press, 2004).

[94]Randall Collins, "Emotional Energy as the Common Denominator of Rational Action," *Rationality and Society* 5 (1993):203–230.

profits (costs less the positive emotional energy produced by the ritual). The search for emotional energy is, therefore, the criterion by which various alternative encounters are assessed for how much emotional profit they can generate.

Humans are, in a sense, "emotional junkies," but they are implicitly rational about it. They must constantly balance those encounters where interaction rituals produce high levels of positive emotional energy (such as lovemaking, family activities, religious participation, and gatherings of friends) with those, more practical, work activities that give them the material resources to participate in more emotionally arousing encounters. Indeed, those who opt out of these work-practical activities and seek only high-emotion encounters (such as dropouts in a drug culture) soon lose the material resources to enjoy emotion-arousing encounters. Moreover, within the context of work-practical activity, individuals typically seek out or create encounters that provide increases in emotional energy. For example, workers might create an informal subculture in which social encounters produce emotional energy that makes work more bearable, or as is often the case with professionals, they seek the rituals involved in acquiring power, authority, and status on the job as highly rewarding and as giving them an emotional charge (such is almost always the case, e.g., with "workaholics," who use the work setting as a place to charge up their levels of emotional energy).

Not only are there material costs as well as expenditures of cultural capital in interaction rituals, but emotional energy is, itself, a cost. People spend their emotional energy in interaction rituals, and they are willing to do so as long as they realize an emotional profit—that is, the emotional energy spent is repaid with even more positive emotions flowing from the common focus of attention, mood, arousal, rhythmic synchronization, and symbolization. When interaction rituals require too much emotional energy without sufficient emotional payoff, then individuals gravitate to other interaction rituals where their profits are higher.

What kinds of rituals provide the most positive emotional energy for the costs involved? For Collins, those encounters where individuals can have power (the capacity to tell others what to do) and status (the capacity to receive deference and honor) are the most likely to generate high emotional payoffs. Hence, those who possess the cultural capital to command respect and obedience are likely to receive the most positive emotional energy from interaction rituals.

Meso- and macro-level social orders are built up, sustained, and changed by interaction rituals, depending upon the degree to which they generate positive and negative emotional energy. When the elements in Collins's model portrayed on p. 493 are working successfully, people develop positive emotions, experience increases in their cultural capital, and develop commitments to groups. When these processes do not flow smoothly, or are breached, then the converse ensues—a line of argument consistent with Goffman's analysis of when encounters are breached.

Finally, interaction rituals impose barriers to violent conflict at the micro level[95] because individuals in a conflict situation have a legacy of the gravitational pull of interaction rituals, which are the opposite of violent conflict, and because potential

---

[95]Randall Collins, *Violence: A Micro-sociological Theory* (Princeton, NJ: Princeton University Press, 2008).

conflict activates fear. This combination keeps individuals from participating in conflict and generally limits the duration and intensity of interpersonal violence. Yet if interaction rituals can be chained together toward the pursuit of conflict, then violence is more likely to occur, but even then, fear and the pull of successful interaction rituals reduce the involvement of many who are organized for conflict.

If Goffman were developing the theory, he would make much the same argument, indicating that people derive positive emotions from encounters and are highly motivated to repair them when they are breached. Encounters thus sustain the social and moral orders of more meso- and macro-social organization, and they pull people away from interpersonal violence. Only when encounters are organized for violence that is perceived to sustain a moral order can they effectively be used for longer-term violence.

Conclusions

As is clear, then, Goffman's dramaturgical theory has been extended in interesting directions, especially in the sociology of emotions. In these theories of emotions, emphasis is on the discrepancy between the cultural script in situations and individuals' feelings and emotions. In complex and differentiated societies driven by market forces, many situations require people to express emotions that they do not feel. Or, as is the case with Clark's theory, the occasions and situations for expressing sympathy have expanded in modern societies. In both cases, there are both dramatic and strategic processes involved, as Goffman emphasized.

People seek to present self in ways that conform to the culture, particularly the feeling and display rules, and if they cannot feel what they are supposed to feel, they seek to alter their feelings and, failing this, at least express overtly the appropriate emotions. They must, therefore, engage in stress drama to sustain encounters. At the same time, actors always behave strategically; their dramatic presentations are often instrumental and revolve around securing resources in situations through strategic actions and dramatic presentations of self.

Until Goffman, sociological theorizing did not emphasize these dynamics, which is particularly surprising in light of the fact that humans in their daily lives talk about these matters all the time. Indeed, gossip is often about the dramatic, manipulative, and strategic actions of others. And so it was appropriate for Goffman to build a micro-sociology about the dynamics that occur in virtually all encounters, and since people respond emotionally in encounters and, once again, gossip about other people's emotional state, it was equally appropriate to take dramaturgy into the sociology of emotions.

CHAPTER 19

Phenomenological and Ethnomethodological Theorizing

G eorge Herbert Mead's analysis of interaction (see Chapter 8) emphasized the active processes involved in face-to-face encounters. Individuals were seen by Mead to read each other's gestures, to role-take with specific others and generalized others, to engage in minded deliberations about courses of action, and to seek to verify self. In the 1960s and for several decades thereafter, an alternative view of interaction emerged. This alternative emphasized, at its core, that individuals employ a series of "folk methods" to sustain the presumption that they share and experience a common reality, even if this is only an illusionary sense of commonality. Successful interaction, then, does not always involve active role-taking, but instead, it requires a willingness to "not question" the presumption that, for the purposes of an interaction in a given situation, individuals share a common reality. It is when this presumption of commonality breaks down that interactions become breached, forcing individuals to invoke implicit "folk methods" to reestablish the presumption that they are experiencing the same reality.

This theoretical perspective—labeled *ethnomethodology*—challenged much of conventional sociology, arguing that theorizing in the discipline did not understand the processes by which the presumption of a social order is created and sustained. Indeed, the discourse among sociologists could be seen as simply a set of "folk methods" employed by sociologists to convince each other that the social world is held together by such things as social structures, norms, values, beliefs, and other concepts used by sociologists to account for the social order. This last point went a bit far; and indeed, ethnomethodology made some rather extravagant claims, but it did discover a set of interpersonal practices that other interactionist perspectives had not adequately conceptualized. In more recent years, ethnomethodology has retreated into the analysis of conversations and, at present, does not enjoy the high visibility that it once had, when it was first introduced.

Phenomenology, or the study of how meanings are created through consciousness, has a long history in philosophy and, later, in the social sciences. Ethnomethodology was the most successful of the phenomenological approaches that emerged in sociology during the modern era, and so I will spend some time, at the outset, tracing the origins of phenomenological sociology in Europe and, then, turn to the explicit theoretical approaches among ethnomethodologists.

The Origins of European Phenomenology

Phenomenology began as the project of the German philosopher Edmund Husserl (1859–1938).[1] In his hands, this project showed few signs of being anything more than an orgy of subjectivism.[2] The German social thinker Alfred Schutz, however, took Husserl's concepts and transformed them into an interactionist analysis that has exerted considerable influence on modern-day interactionism. Schutz's migration to the United States in 1939 facilitated this translation, especially as he came into contact with American interactionism, but his most important ideas were formulated before he immigrated. His subsequent work in America involved an elaboration of the basic ideas originally developed in Europe.

Edmund Husserl's Project

Husserl's ideas have been selectively borrowed and used in ways that he would not have condoned to develop modern phenomenology and various forms of interactionist thought. In reviewing Husserl's contribution, therefore, it is best to focus more on what was borrowed than on the details of his complete philosophical scheme. With this goal in mind, several features of his work can be highlighted: (a) the basic philosophical dilemma, (b) the properties of consciousness, (c) the

---

[1]For some readable, general references on phenomenology, see George Psathas (ed.), *Phenomenological Sociology* (New York: Wiley, 1973); Richard M. Zaner, *The Way of Phenomenology: Criticism as a Philosophical Discipline* (New York: Pegasus, 1970); Peter L. Berger and Thomas Luckman, *The Social Construction of Reality* (Garden City, NY: Doubleday, 1966); Herbert Spiegelberg, *The Phenomenological Movement*, vols. 1 and 2, 2nd ed. (The Hague, Netherlands: Martinus Nijhoff, 1969); Hans P. Neisser, "The Phenomenological Approach in Social Science," *Philosophy and Phenomenological Research* 20 (1959):198–212; Stephen Strasser, *Phenomenology and the Human Sciences* (Pittsburgh, PA: Duquesne University Press, 1963); Maurice Natanson (ed.), *Phenomenology and the Social Sciences* (Evanston, IL: Northwestern University Press, 1973); and Quentin Lauer, *Phenomenology: Its Genesis and Prospect* (New York: Harper Torchbooks, 1965).

[2]Zygmunt Bauman, "On the Philosophical Status of Ethnomethodology," *Sociological Review* 21 (February 1973): 6.

critique of naturalistic empiricism, and (d) the philosophical alternative to social science.[3] These are briefly reviewed below:

1. The basic questions confronting all inquiry are the following: What is real? What actually exists in the world? How is it possible to know what exists? For the philosopher Husserl, these are central questions that required attention. Husserl reasoned that humans know about the world only through experience. All notions of an external world "out there" are mediated through the senses and can be known only through mental consciousness. The existence of other people, values, norms, and physical objects is always mediated by experiences as these register on people's conscious awareness. One does not directly have contact with reality; contact is always indirect and mediated through the processes of the human mind. Because the process of consciousness is so important and central to knowledge, philosophic inquiry must first attempt to understand how the process operates and how it influences human affairs. This concern with the process of consciousness—of how experience creates a sense of an external reality—became the central concern of phenomenology.

2. Husserl initially made reference to the "world of the natural attitude." Later, he used the phrase *lifeworld*. In either case, with these concepts, he emphasized that humans operate in a taken-for-granted world that permeates their mental life. It is the world that humans sense to exist. It is composed of the objects, people, places, ideas, and other things that people see and perceive as setting the parameters for their existence, for their activities, and for their pursuits.

This lifeworld or world of the natural attitude *is* reality for humans. Two features of Husserl's conception of natural attitude influenced modern interactionist thought. (1) The lifeworld is taken for granted. It is rarely the topic of reflective thought, and yet it structures and shapes the way people act and think. (2) Humans operate on the presumption that they experience the same world. Because people experience only their own consciousness, they have little capacity to determine directly if this presumption is correct. Yet people act as if they experience a common world.

---

[3]Husserl's basic ideas are contained in the following: *Phenomenology and the Crisis of Western Philosophy* (New York: Harper & Row, 1965; originally published 1936), *Ideas: General Introduction to Pure Phenomenology* (London: Collier-Macmillan, 1969; originally published 1913), and "Phenomenology," in *The Encyclopedia Britannica*, 14th ed., vol. 17, col. 699–702, 1929. For excellent secondary analyses, see Helmut R. Wagner, "The Scope of Phenomenological Sociology," in *Phenomenological Sociology: Issues and Applications*, ed. G. Psathas (New York: Wiley), 61–86 and "Husserl and Historicism," *Social Research* 39 (Winter 1972):696–719; Aron Gurwitsch, "The Common-Sense World as Social Reality," *Social Research* 29 (Spring 1962):50–72; Robert J. Antonio, "Phenomenological Sociology," in *Sociology: A Multiple Paradigm Science*, ed. G. Ritzer (Boston, MA: Allyn and Bacon, 1975), 109–112; and Robert Welsh Jordan, "Husserl's Phenomenology as an 'Historical Science,'" *Social Research* 35 (Summer 1968):245–259.

Human activity, then, is conducted in a lifeworld that is taken for granted and that is presumed to be experienced collectively. This brought Husserl back to his original problem: How do humans break out of their lifeworld and ascertain what is real? If people's lifeworld structures their consciousness and their actions, how is an objective science of human behavior and organization possible? These questions led Husserl to criticize what he termed naturalistic science.

3. Science assumes that a factual world exists, independent of and external to human senses and consciousness. Through the scientific method, this factual world can be directly known. With successive efforts at its measurement, increasing understanding of its properties can be ascertained. But Husserl challenged this vision of science: if one can know only through consciousness and if consciousness is structured by an implicit *lifeworld*, then how can objective measurement of some external and real world be possible? How can science measure objectively an external world when the only world that individuals experience is the lifeworld of their consciousness?

4. Husserl's solution to this problem is a philosophical one. He advocated what he termed the search for the essence of consciousness. To understand social events, the basic process through which these events are mediated—that is, consciousness—must be comprehended. The substantive content of consciousness, or the lifeworld, is not what is important; the abstract processes of consciousness, per se, are to be the topic of philosophic inquiry.

Husserl advocated what he termed the radical abstraction of the individual from interpersonal experience. Investigators must suspend their natural attitude and seek to understand the fundamental processes of consciousness, per se. One must discover, in Husserl's words, "Pure Mind." To do this, it is necessary to perform "epoch"—that is, to see if the substance of one's lifeworld can be suspended. Only when divorced from the substance of the lifeworld can the fundamental and abstract properties of consciousness be exposed and understood. With understanding of these properties, real insight into the nature of reality would be possible. If all that humans know is presented through consciousness, it is necessary to understand the nature of consciousness in abstraction from the specific substance or content of the lifeworld.

Husserl was not advocating Weber's method of *verstehen*, or sympathetic introspection into an investigator's own mind. Nor was Husserl suggesting the unstructured and intuitive search for people's definitions of situations. These methods would, he argued, only produce data on the substance of the *lifeworld* and would be no different from the structured measuring instruments of positivism. Rather, Husserl's goal was to create an abstract theory of consciousness that bracketed out, or suspended, any presumption of "an external social world out there." Not surprisingly, Husserl's philosophical doctrine failed. He never succeeded in developing an abstract theory of consciousness, radically abstracted from the lifeworld. But his ideas set into motion a new line of thought that became the basis for modern phenomenology and for its elaboration into ethnomethodology and other forms of theory.

Alfred Schutz's Phenomenological Interactionism

Alfred Schutz (1899–1959) migrated to the United States in 1939 from Austria, after spending a year in Paris. With his interaction in American intellectual circles and the translation of his early works into English, Schutz's contribution to sociological theorizing has become increasingly recognized.[4] This contribution resided in his ability to blend Husserl's radical phenomenology with Weber's action theory and American interactionism. This blend, in turn, stimulated the further development of phenomenology, the emergence of ethnomethodology, and the refinement of other interactionist theoretical perspectives.

Schutz's work began with a critique of his compatriot Weber, who employed the concept of social action in his many and varied inquiries.[5] Social action occurs when actors are consciously aware of each other and attribute meanings to their common situation. For Weber, then, a science of society must seek to understand social reality "at the level of meaning." Sociological inquiry must penetrate people's consciousness and discover how they view, define, and see the world. Weber advocated the method of *verstehen*, or sympathetic introspection. Investigators must become sufficiently involved in situations to be able to get inside the subjective world of actors. Causal and statistical analysis of complex social structures would be incomplete and inaccurate without such *verstehen* analysis.

Schutz's first major work addressed Weber's conception of action. Schutz's analysis is critical and detailed and need not be summarized here, except to note that the basic critique turns on Weber's failure to use his *verstehen* method and to explore why, and *through what processes*, actors come to share common meanings. In Schutz's view, Weber simply assumed that actors share subjective meanings, leading him to ask these questions: Why and how do actors come to acquire common subjective states in a situation? How do they create a common view of the world? This is the problem of "intersubjectivity," and it is central to Schutz's intellectual scheme.

Schutz departed immediately from Husserl's strategy of holding the individual in radical abstraction and of searching for the "Pure Mind," or the abstract laws of consciousness. He accepted Husserl's notion that humans hold a natural attitude and lifeworld that is taken for granted and that shapes who they are and what they will do. He also accepted Husserl's notion that people perceive that they share the same lifeworld and act *as if* they live in a common world of experiences and sensations. Moreover, Schutz acknowledged the power of Husserl's argument that social scientists cannot know about an external social world out there independently of their own lifeworld.[6]

---

[4]For the basic ideas of Alfred Schutz, see his *The Phenomenology of the Social World* (Evanston, IL: Northwestern University Press, 1967; originally published 1932), *Collected Papers I: The Problem of Social Reality* (The Hague, Netherlands: Martinus Nijhoff, 1964), *Collected Papers II: Studies in Social Theory*, ed. Arvid Broderson (The Hague, Netherlands: Martinus Nijhoff, 1970), and *Collected Papers III: Studies in Phenomenological Philosophy* (The Hague, Netherlands: Martinus Nijhoff, 1971). For excellent secondary analyses, see Maurice Natanson, "Alfred Schutz on Social Reality and Social Science," *Social Research* 35 (Summer 1968):217–244.

[5]Schutz, *The Phenomenology of the Social World*.

[6]Richard M. Zaner, "Theory of Intersubjectivity: Alfred Schutz," *Social Research* 28 (Spring 1961):76.

Having accepted these lines of thought from Husserl, however, Schutz advocated Weber's strategy of sympathetic introspection into people's consciousness. Only by observing people in interaction, rather than in radical abstraction, can the processes whereby actors come to share the same world be discovered. Social science cannot understand how and why actors create a common subjective world independently of watching them do so. This abandonment of Husserl's phenomenological project liberated phenomenology from philosophy and allowed sociologists to study empirically what Schutz considered the most important social reality: the creation and maintenance of *intersubjectivity*—that is, the sense among people in interaction of a common subjective world.[7] Unfortunately, Schutz died just as he was beginning a systematic synthesis of his ideas; as a result, only a somewhat fragmented but suggestive framework is evident in his collective work. But his early analysis of Weber, Husserl, and interactionism led Schutz to ask two basic questions: (a) How do actors create a common subjective world? (b) What implications does this creation have for how social order is maintained?

All humans, Schutz asserted, carry in their minds rules, social recipes, conceptions of appropriate conduct, and other information that allows them to act in their social world. Extending Husserl's concept of lifeworld, Schutz views the sum of these rules, recipes, conceptions, and information as the individual's "stock knowledge at hand." This stock knowledge gives people a frame of reference or orientation with which they can interpret events as they pragmatically act on the world around them. Several features of this stock of knowledge at hand are given particular emphasis by Schutz, as follows:

1. People's reality *is* their stocks of knowledge. For the members of a society, stocks knowledge constitute a "paramount reality"—a sense of an absolute reality that shapes and guides all social events. Actors use this stock knowledge and sense of reality as they pragmatically seek to deal with others in their environment.

2. The existence of stocks of knowledge bestows on events in the social world, as Schutz agreed with Husserl, a *taken-for-granted* character. Stocks of knowledge are rarely the object of conscious reflection but, rather, an implicit set of assumptions and procedures that are silently used by individuals as they interact.

3. Stocks of knowledge are learned. They are acquired through socialization within a common social and cultural world, but they become the reality for actors in this world.

4. People operate under a number of assumptions that allow them to create a sense of "reciprocity of perspectives." That is, others with whom an actor must deal are considered to share an actor's stocks of knowledge at hand. And although these others might have unique components in their stocks of knowledge because of their particular biographies, these can be ignored by actors.

---

[7]For references to interactionists, see Schutz, *Collected Papers.*

5. The existence of stocks of knowledge, their acquisition through socialization, and their capacity to promote reciprocity of perspectives all give actors in a situation a sense or presumption that the world is the same for all and that it reveals identical properties for all. What often holds society together is this presumption of a common world.

6. The presumption of a common world allows actors to engage in the *process of typification.* Action in most situations, except the most personal and intimate, can proceed through mutual typification as they use their stocks knowledge to categorize one another and to adjust their responses to these typifications. With typification, actors can effectively deal with their world; every nuance and characteristic of their situations do not have to be examined. Moreover, typification facilitates entrance into the social world; it simplifies adjustment because humans can treat each other as categories or as "typical" objects of a particular kind.

These points of emphasis in Schutz's thought represented a blending of ideas from European phenomenology and American interactionism. The emphasis on stocks of knowledge is clearly borrowed from Husserl, but it is highly compatible with Mead's notion of the generalized other. The concern with the taken-for-granted character of the world as it is shaped by stocks of knowledge is also borrowed from Husserl but is similar to early interactionists' discussions of habit and routine behaviors. The emphasis on the acquired nature of stocks of knowledge coincides with the early interactionists' discussions of the socialization process. The concern with the reciprocity of perspectives and with the process of typification owes much to Husserl and Weber but is compatible with Mead's notion of role-taking, by which actors read one another's role and perspective.

Still, the major departure from much of interactionist theory should also be emphasized: actors operate on an unverified presumption that they share a common world, and this sense of a common world and the practices that produce this sense are crucial in maintaining social order. In other words, social organization might be possible not so much by the substance and content of stocks of knowledge, by the reciprocity of perspectives, or by successful typification as by the often fragile and unverifiable *presumption* that actors share intersubjective states. Schutz did not carry this line of inquiry far, but he inspired new avenues of phenomenological inquiry that did.

Contemporary Ethnomethodological Theorizing

As ethnomethodological theorizing emerged in the 1960s, it drew more from the phenomenological tradition of Alfred Schutz than from the pragmatist tradition of George Herbert Mead and proposed an alternative approach to analyzing interaction: explore the methods used by people to construct *a sense of* ongoing reality. This emphasis became known as *ethnomethodology.* As this label underscores, ethnomethodology is the study of ("ology") the interpersonal "methods" that people ("ethno") use.[8] Like Edmund Husserl and Schutz, ethnomethodologists ask how people create and sustain for each other the *presumption* that the social world has a real character.

The Reflexive and Indexical Nature of Interaction

Schutz postulated one basic reality—*the paramount*—in which people's conduct of their everyday affairs occurs.[9] Most early ethnomethodologists, however, were less interested in whether or not there are one or multiple "realities," "lifeworlds," or "natural attitudes." Far more important in ethnomethodological analysis was the development of concepts and principles that could help explain how people construct, maintain, and change their lines of conduct as they seek to *sustain the presumption* that they share the same reality. At the core of ethnomethodological analysis are two basic assumptions about (1) the reflexive and (2) the indexical nature of all interaction.

Reflexive Action and Interaction. Much interaction sustains a particular vision of reality. For example, ritual activity directed toward the gods sustains the belief that the gods influence everyday affairs. Such ritual activity is an example of reflexive action; it maintains a certain vision of reality. Even when intense prayer and ritual activity do not bring forth the desired intervention from the gods, the devout, rather than reject beliefs, proclaim that they did not pray hard enough, that their cause was not just, or that the gods in their wisdom have a greater plan. Such behavior is *reflexive*. It upholds or reinforces a belief, even in the face of evidence that the belief might be incorrect.

Much human interaction is reflexive. Humans interpret cues, gestures, words, and other information from one another in a way that sustains a particular vision of reality. Even contradictory evidence is reflexively interpreted to maintain a body of

[8]For some readable summaries of ethnomethodology, see Hugh Mehan and Houston Wood, *The Reality of Ethnomethodology* (New York: Wiley, 1975); John Heritage, *Garfinkel and Ethnomethodology* (Cambridge, UK: Polity, 1984) and "Ethnomethodology," in *Social Theory Today*, ed. Anthony Giddens and Jonathan Turner (Cambridge, UK: Polity Press, 1987); Melvin Pollner, *Mundane Reasoning: Reality in Everyday Sociological Discourse* (Cambridge, UK: Cambridge University Press, 1987); and Wes Sharrock, "Fundamentals of Ethnomethodology" in *Handbook of Social Theory*, ed., George Ritzer and Barry Smart (Thousand Oaks, CA: Sage, 2001). See, in particular, Schutz, *Collected Papers I, Collected Papers II*, and *Collected Papers III*. For adaptations of these ideas to interactionism and ethnomethodology, see Alfred Schutz and Thomas Luckmann, *The Structure of the Lifeworld* (Evanston, IL: Northwestern University Press, 1973) and Thomas Luckmann (ed.), *Phenomenology and Sociology* (New York: Penguin, 1978). See also Robert C. Freeman, "Phenomenological Sociology and Ethnomethodology," in *Introduction to the Sociologies of Everyday Life*, ed. J. Douglas and Patricia Adler (Boston, MA: Allyn and Bacon, 1980).

[9]See, in particular, Schutz, *Collected Papers I, Collected Papers II,* and *Collected Papers III*. For adaptations of these ideas to interactionism and ethnomethodology, see Alfred Schutz and Thomas Luckmann, *The Structure of the Lifeworld* (Evanston, IL: Northwestern University Press, 1973) and Thomas Luckmann (ed.), *Phenomenology and Sociology* (New York: Penguin, 1978). See also Robert C. Freeman, "Phenomenological Sociology and Ethnomethodology," in *Introduction to the Sociologies of Everyday Life*, ed. J. Douglas and Patricia Adler (Boston, MA: Allyn and Bacon, 1980).

belief and knowledge. The concept of reflexivity thus focuses attention on how people in interaction go about maintaining the presumption that they are guided by a particular reality. Much of ethnomethodological inquiry has addressed this question of how reflexive interaction occurs. That is, what concepts and principles can be developed to explain the conditions under which different reflexive actions among interacting parties are likely to occur?

The Indexicality of Meaning. The gestures, cues, words, and other information sent and received by the interacting parties have meaning in a *particular context.* Without some knowledge of the context—the biographies of the interacting parties, their avowed purpose, their past interactive experiences, and so forth—it would be easy to misinterpret the symbolic communication among interacting individuals. To say that an expression is *indexical,* then, is to emphasize that the meaning of that expression is tied to a particular context.

This notion of indexicality drew attention to the problem of how actors in a context construct a vision of reality in that context. They develop expressions that invoke their common vision about what is real in their situation. The concept of *indexicality* thus directs investigators to actual interactive contexts to see how actors go about creating indexical expressions—words, facial and body gestures, and other cues—to sustain the presumption that a particular reality governs their affairs.

With these two key concepts, reflexivity and indexicality, the interactionists' concern with the process of symbolic communication was retained by ethnomethodology, and much of the phenomenological legacy of Schutz was rejuvenated. Concern was with how actors use gestures to construct a lifeworld, body of knowledge, or natural attitude about what is real. The emphasis was not on the content of the lifeworld but on the methods or techniques that actors use to create, maintain, or even alter a vision of reality.

Harold Garfinkel's Early Studies

Harold Garfinkel's *Studies in Ethnomethodology* firmly established ethnomethodology as a distinctive theoretical perspective.[10] Although the book was not a formal theoretical statement, the studies and the commentary in it established the domain of ethnomethodological inquiry; subsequent ethnomethodological research and theory began with Garfinkel's insights and took them in a variety of directions.

Garfinkel's work saw ethnomethodology as a field of inquiry that sought to understand the methods people employ to make sense of their world. He placed considerable emphasis on language as the vehicle by which this reality construction is done. Indeed, for Garfinkel, interacting individuals' efforts to account for their actions—that is, to represent them verbally to others—are the primary method by which a sense of the world is constructed. In Garfinkel's terms, *to do* interaction is *to tell* interaction, or—in other words—the primary folk technique used by actors is verbal description. In this way, people use their accounts to construct a sense of reality.

---

[10]Harold Garfinkel, *Studies in Ethnomethodology* (Englewood Cliffs, NJ: Prentice-Hall, 1967).

Garfinkel placed enormous emphasis on indexicality—that is, members' accounts are tied to particular contexts and situations. An utterance, Garfinkel noted, indexes much more than it actually says; it also evokes connotations that can be understood only in the context of a situation. Garfinkel's work was thus the first to stress the indexical nature of interpersonal cues and to emphasize that individuals seek accounts to create a sense of reality.

In addition to laying much of the groundwork for ethnomethodology, Garfinkel and his associates conducted several interesting empirical studies to validate their assumptions about what is real. One line of empirical inquiry became known as the *breaching experiment,* in which the normal course of interaction was deliberately interrupted. For example, Garfinkel reported a series of conversations in which student experimenters challenged every statement of selected subjects. The end result was a series of conversations revealing the following pattern:[11]

Subject:　　　　I had a flat tire.

Experimenter:　What do you mean, you had a flat tire?

Subject:　　　　(appears momentarily stunned and then replies in a hostile manner): What do you mean, "What do you mean?" A flat tire is a flat tire. That is what I meant. Nothing special. What a crazy question!

In this situation, the experimenter was apparently violating an implicit rule for this type of interaction (such as "accepting statements at face value") and thereby aroused not only the hostility of the subject but also a negative sanction, "What a crazy question!" Seemingly, in any interaction there are certain background features that everyone should understand and that should not be questioned so that all parties can "conduct their common conversational affairs without interference."[12] Such implicit methods appear to guide a considerable number of everyday affairs and are critical for the construction of at least the perception among interacting humans that an external social order exists. Through breaching, Garfinkel hoped to discover the implicit ethnomethods being used by forcing actors to engage *actively* in the process of reality reconstruction after the situation had been disrupted.

Other research strategies also yielded insights into the methods parties use in an interaction for constructing a sense of reality. For example, Garfinkel and his associates summarized the "decision rules" jurors employed in reaching a verdict.[13] By examining a group such as a jury, which must by the nature of its task develop an interpretation of what really happened, the ethnomethodologist sought to achieve some insight into the generic properties of the processes of constructing a *sense of social reality.* From the investigators' observations of jurors, it appeared that "a person is 95 percent juror before [coming] near the court," indicating that, through

---

[11]Ibid., 42.

[12]Ibid.

[13]Ibid., 104–115.

their participation in other social settings and through instructions from the court, they had accepted the "official" rules for reaching a verdict. However, these rules were altered somewhat as participants came together in an actual jury setting and began the "work of assembling the 'corpus' which serves as grounds for inferring the correctness of a verdict."[14] Because the inevitable ambiguities of the cases before them made it difficult for strict conformity to the official rules of jury deliberation, new decision rules were invoked to allow jurors to achieve a "correct" view of "what actually happened." But in their retrospective reporting to interviewers of how they reached the verdicts, jurors typically invoked the "official line" to justify the correctness of their decisions. When interviewers drew attention to discrepancies between the jurors' ideal accounts and their actual practices, jurors became anxious, an indication that somewhat different rules had been used to construct the corpus of what really happened.

In sum, these two examples of Garfinkel's research strategy illustrate the general intent of much of early ethnomethodological inquiry: to penetrate natural social settings or to create social settings in which the investigator could observe humans attempting to assert, create, maintain, or change the rules for constructing the appearance of consensus over the structure of the real world. By focusing on the process or methods for constructing a reality rather than on the substance or content of the reality itself, research from the ethnomethodological point of view could potentially provide a more interesting and relevant answer to the question of "how and why society is possible." Garfinkel's studies stimulated a variety of research and theoretical strategies.

Aaron V. Cicourel's Critique

Aaron V. Cicourel has been one of the most persistent critics of sociological research methodologies, particularly the notion that more quantitative methods somehow reduce bias.[15] But he also created a more substantive approach that had much in common with ethnomethodology. Cicourel even questions Garfinkel's assertion that interaction and verbal accounts are the same process.[16] Cicourel notes that humans see, sense, and feel much that they cannot communicate with words. Humans use "multiple modalities" for communicating in situations. Verbal accounts represent crude and incomplete translations of what is actually communicated in interaction. This recognition has led Cicourel to rename his brand of ethnomethodology: *cognitive sociology*.

The details of his analysis are less important than the general intent of his effort to transform sociological research and theory. Basically, he sought to uncover the

---

[14]Ibid., 110.

[15]Aaron V. Cicourel, *Method and Measurement in Sociology* (New York: Free Press, 1964) and "Cross Modal Communication," in *Linguistics and Language Science,* Monograph 25, ed. R. Shuy (Washington, DC: Georgetown University Press, 1973).

[16]Aaron V. Cicourel, *Cognitive Sociology* (London: Macmillan, 1973) and "Basic Normative Rules in the Negotiation of Status and Role," in *Recent Sociology No. 2: Patterns of Communicative Behavior,* ed. H. P. Dreitzel (New York: Macmillan, 1970).

universal "interpretive procedures" by which humans organize their cognitions and give meaning to situations.[17] Through these interpretive procedures, people develop a sense of social structure and can organize their actions. These interpretive procedures are universal and invariant in humans, and their discovery would allow understanding of how humans create a sense of social structure in the world around them.

When analysis is one of the methods that people use to construct a sense of reality, the task of the theorist is to isolate the general types of interpersonal techniques that people employ in interaction. Cicourel, for example, summarized several such techniques or methods isolated by ethnomethodologists: (a) searching for the normal form, (b) doing reciprocity of perspectives, and (c) using the et cetera principle.

Searching for the Normal Form. If interacting parties sense that ambiguity exists about what is real and that their interaction is strained, they will emit gestures to tell each other to return to what is "normal" in their contextual situation. Actors are presumed to hold a vision of a normal form for situations or to be motivated to create one; hence, much of their action is designed to reach this form.

Doing a Reciprocity of Perspectives. Borrowing from Schutz's formulation, ethnomethodologists emphasized that actors operate under the presumption that they would have the same experiences if they were to switch places. Furthermore, until they are so informed by specific gestures, actors can ignore differences in perspectives that might arise from their unique biographies. Thus, much interaction will be punctuated by gestures that seek to assure others that reciprocity of perspectives does indeed exist.

Using the Et Cetera Principle. In examining an actual interaction, much is left unsaid. Actors must constantly "fill in" or "wait for" information necessary to "make sense" of another's words or deeds. When actors do so, they are using the *et cetera principle*. They are agreeing not to disrupt the interaction by asking for the needed information; they are willing to wait or to fill in. For example, in the conversation reported by Garfinkel about the "flat tire," the experimenter who asked, "What do you mean, you had a flat tire?" was not observing the et cetera principle, and as a result, the subject became angry in an effort to sanction the experimenter to abide by the "folk rules." Or, to take another example, the common phrase "you know," which often appears after an utterance, is typically an assertion by one actor to another invoking the et cetera principle. The other is thus informed not to disrupt the interaction or the sense of reality in the situation with a counter-utterance, such as "No, I do not know."

These three general types of folk methods were examples of what ethnomethodologists sought to discover, although most researchers appear reluctant to make these explicit or to theorize beyond their empirical observations of how particular folk methods are used. For some ethnomethodologists, the ultimate goal of theory

---

[17]Cicourel, *Cognitive Sociology*, 85–88. It should be noted that these principles were implicit in Garfinkel's *Studies in Ethnomethodology*.

is to determine the conditions under which these and other interpersonal techniques would be used to construct, maintain, or change a sense of reality. Yet few such propositions are to be found in the ethnomethodological literature.

Harvey Sacks's Analysis of Conversational Turn Taking

Until his early death in 1976, Harvey Sacks exerted considerable influence within ethnomethodology.[18] Although his work was not well-known outside ethnomethodological circles, it represented an attempt to extend Garfinkel's concern with verbal accounts, while eliminating some of the problems posed by indexicality.

Sacks was one of the first ethnomethodologists to articulate the phenomenological critique of sociology and to use this critique to build what he thought was an alternative form of theorizing. The basic thrust of Sacks's critique can be stated as follows: sociologists assume that language is a resource used in generating concepts and theories of the social world. However, sociologists are confusing resource and topic. In using language, sociologists are creating a reality; their words are not a neutral vehicle but *the* topic of inquiry for true sociological analysis—a point of emphasis that is, today, the core topic of ethnomethodological inquiry.

If the pure properties of language can be understood, then it would be possible to have an objective social science without confusing resource with subject matter. Sacks's research tended to concentrate on the formal properties of language-in-use. Typically, Sacks took verbatim transcripts of actors in interaction and sought to understand the formal properties of the conversation while ignoring its substance. Such a tactic resolved the problem of indexicality because Sacks simply ignored the substance and context of conversation and focused on its form. For example, "sequences of talk" among actors might occupy his attention.

In analyzing conversational talk, Sacks and various collaborators would emphasize the fact that conversations involve turn taking. One party in a conversation talks, then another does. The ways in which turns are taken become a key dynamic in the conversation as, for instance, when individuals pause and offer clearance cues that the other can talk now, when they interrupt each other, when they talk over each other, when they pause but keep the conversational floor, and other methods that people use to structure the flow of everyday conversations. For Sacks, the formal properties of turn taking offered a new way to examine action and interaction.

Sacks thus began to take ethnomethodology into formal linguistics, a trend that has continued and now seems to dominate current ethnomethodology in an

---

[18]Harvey Sacks, "Sociological Description," *Berkeley Journal of Sociology* 8 (1963):1–17, "An Initial Investigation of the Usability of Conversational Data for Doing Sociology," in *Studies in Interaction,* ed. David Sudnow (New York: Free Press, 1972); see also Harvey Sacks, *Lectures on Conversation,* 2 vols. (New York: Blackwell, 1992). Sack's best-known study, for example, is the coauthored article with Emanuel Schegloff and Gail Jefferson, "A Simplest Systematics for the Analysis of Turn Taking in Conversation," *Language* 50 (1974):696–697. For a review of the current techniques of conversational analysis, see Alain Coulon, *Ethnomethodology* (London, UK: Sage, 1995) and Douglas W. Maynard and Marilyn R. Whalen, "Language, Action, and Social Interaction," in *Sociological Perspectives on Social Psychology,* ed. K. S. Cook, G. A. Fine, and J. S. House (Boston, MA: Allyn and Bacon, 1995).

approach that has been labeled *conversational analysis.* More important, Sacks sought to discover universal forms of interaction—that is, abstracted terms of talk—that might apply to all conversations. In this way, he began to search for the laws of reality construction among interacting individuals.

Zimmerman, Pollner, and Wieder's Situational Approach

Sacks and Cicourel focused on the universal properties of language use and cognitive perception/representation, respectively. This concern with invariance, or universal folk methods, became increasingly prominent in ethnomethodological inquiry. In several essays, for example, Don Zimmerman, D. Lawrence Wieder, and Melvin Pollner developed an approach that sought the universal procedures people employ to construct a sense of reality.[19] Their position is perhaps the most clearly stated of all ethnomethodologies, drawing inspiration from Garfinkel but extending his ideas. To summarize their argument,

1. In all interaction situations, humans attempt to construct the appearance of consensus over relevant features of the interaction setting.

2. These setting features can include attitudes, opinions, beliefs, and other cognitions about the nature of the social setting in which they interact.

3. Humans engage in a variety of explicit and implicit interpersonal practices and methods to construct, maintain, and perhaps alter *the appearance* of consensus over these setting features.

4. Such interpersonal practices and methods result in the assembling and disassembling of what can be termed an *occasional corpus*—that is, the *perception* by interacting humans that the current setting has an orderly and understandable structure.

5. This appearance of consensus is not only the result of agreement on the substance and content of the occasioned corpus but also a reflection of each participant's compliance with the rules and procedures for assemblage and disassemblage of this consensus. In communicating, in however subtle a manner, that parties accept the implicit rules for constructing an occasioned corpus, they go a long way in establishing consensus about what is in the interaction setting.

6. In each interaction situation, the rules for constructing the occasioned corpus will be unique in some respects and hence not completely generalizable to other settings—thus requiring that humans in each and every interaction situation use interpersonal methods in searching for agreement on the implicit rules for the assembly of an occasioned corpus.

---

[19]Don H. Zimmerman and Melvin Pollner, "The Everyday World as a Phenomenon," in *Understanding Everyday Life*, ed. J. D. Douglas (Chicago, IL: Aldine, 1970); Lawrence Wieder, *Language and Social Reality* (The Hague, Netherlands: Mouton, 1973).

7. Thus, by constructing, reaffirming, or altering the rules for constructing an occasioned corpus, members in a setting can offer one another the appearance of an orderly and connected world, which compels certain perceptions and actions on their part.

From these kinds of assumptions about human interaction, Zimmerman, Pollner, and Wieder's ethnomethodology took its subject matter. Rather than focusing on the actual content and substance of the occasioned corpus and on the ways members believe it to force certain perceptions and actions, attention was drawn primarily to the *methods humans use* to construct, maintain, and change the *appearance* of an orderly and connected social world. These methods are directly observable and constitute a major portion of people's actions in everyday life. In contrast, the actual substance and content of the occasioned corpus are not directly observable and can only be inferred. Furthermore, in concentrating on the *process* of creating, sustaining, and changing the occasioned corpus, we can ask as follows: Is not the process of creating the appearance of a stable social order for one another more critical to understanding how society is possible than the actual substance and content of the occasioned corpus? Is there anything more to society than members' presumptions that society is "out there," forcing them to do and see certain things? Hence, order is not the result of the particular structure of the corpus; rather, order resides in the human capacity *to continually assemble and disassemble the corpus* in each and every interaction situation. This perspective suggested to ethnomethodologists that theoretical attention should therefore be placed on the ongoing process of assembling and disassembling the appearance of social order and on the particular methods people employ in doing so.

Emanuel Schegloff's Conversation Analysis

Over the last several decades, Emanuel Schegloff has been one of the most important figures working within the conversation approach suggested by Garfinkel and firmly established by Sacks. Indeed, some of Sacks's most important early works were coauthored with Schegloff.[20] Like Garfinkel before him, Schegloff has mounted a critique of how sociologists conceptualize action and how actions generate intersubjectivity. Most sociologists visualize action without really looking at what individuals do in face-to-face interaction, while seeing intersubjectivity as achieved by socialization into a common culture. By analyzing the dynamics revolving around conversations as they unfold, it is possible to get a much more fine-grained view of action; equally significant, it is possible to understand the problem of order—of how society is held together—from the elementary and more fundamental processes by which it is constructed: talk and conversation among people in situations.

Conversation analysis is now a highly technical way of analyzing strips of conversations, typically recorded and then converted into a transcript. There is a system of notation for indicating pauses, points of emphasis, overlaps, and other features of

---

[20]For example, Sacks, Schegloff, and Jefferson, "A Simplest Systematics," 696–697 and Emanuel A. Schegloff, "Opening Up Closings," *Semiotic* 7 (1973):280–327.

conversations. What has typified Schegloff's work is a detailed analysis of conversations using this notation system, but for our purposes, the details of how the data are arrayed are less important than the actual methods employed by individuals in conversations. These patterns can contribute to a theory of action at its most fundamental level. Of the various discoveries in Schegloff's ongoing research, several sets of findings can be used to illustrate the potential of conversational analysis.

Confirming Allusions.[21] In conversations, individuals often allude to something. At times these allusions are explicit; at other times the allusion implies more than the explicit reference. Schegloff notes that in some conversations, another party in the conversation repeats the phrasing of words, indicating an allusion. For example, a phone conversation (made up for illustration) may proceed something like this:

Janice: How are you John?

John: Fine. How are you?

Janice: Doing ok, I guess.

John: Oh!

Janice: Went drinking.

John: Went drinking, eh?

The last two turns of the conversation involve Janice making an allusion to drinking (and to the fact that she is only "ok, I guess"), and then John repeats the phrase "Went drinking." He could have said "I see," or some other phrase, but rather, he repeats the phrase. This pattern is noticeable in many conversations, and Schegloff asks, "Is something special going on here? What are these repeats doing?" Schegloff's analysis and answer are complex, but the basic generalization is that when people confirm allusions they indicate that indeed they understand what is being indicated explicitly but, moreover, they understand the less explicit allusions accompanying those that are explicit. For instance, if Janice is depressed as a result of drinking, John's repetition of "went drinking" confirms the sense of what drinking does to Janice above and beyond making her tired. Confirmation of allusions thus becomes a mechanism for achieving intersubjectivity, and as such, this particular pattern in conversations can be seen as an ethnomethod used by individuals to create a sense of a shared reality.

Repair After Next Turn.[22] In conversations, minor and major misunderstandings occur all the time. When these occur, people's sense of intersubjectivity—that is, of sharing a common sense for what is occurring—breaks down, and if such

---

[21]Emanuel A. Schegloff, "Confirming Allusions: Toward an Empirical Account of Action," *American Journal of Sociology* 102 (1996):161–216.

[22]Emanuel A. Schegloff, "Repair After Next Turn: The Last Structurally Provided Defense of Intersubjectivity in Conversation," *American Journal of Sociology* 97 (1992):1295–1345.

misunderstandings cannot be "repaired" in the flow of the conversation, the interaction will remain breached. Schegloff initially observed in many conversations that there is what he termed "a third-position repair" revealing the following basic structure: person A makes a statement that he or she feels adequate (first position); person B hears this statement and emits a response appropriate to his or her understanding of what person A has said (the second position); but sensing that his or her original statement has not communicated the intended meaning, person A (in the third position) now seeks to make the repair and communicate the intended meaning; and then, person B typically begins the response to the repair with the word "Oh," indicating that the repair has been understood. For example, below is a simplified version of a more detailed and coded conversation reported by Schegloff:

Annie: Which ones are closed, and which ones are open?

Zebrach: Most of them. This, this, this. (pointing)

Annie: I don't mean the shelters. I mean the roads.

Zebrach: Oh! (and after a pause, he tells Annie about the roads)

This form of conversation can be found often, and it allows parties to effortlessly make repairs to conversations that are off track. The process can be more complicated in that several more sequences of conversation can occur before the party in the third position of the sequence realizes the misunderstanding, but it is still possible, when the third position is taken, to make the necessary corrections.

A "fourth-position repair" allows the person who has misunderstood to acknowledge the repair effort and thereafter put the conversation back on an intersubjective footing. For example, (a) person A makes a statement, (b) person B responds, (c) person A makes the repair after sensing that B did not get the intended meaning, and then (d) person B (now in the fourth position) acknowledges the repair effort, perhaps initially by the word, "Oh," followed by more talk that moves the conversation further along in the proper direction.

Overlaps in Conversations.[23] People often begin talk at the same time, and this can be problematic because it is in the nature of conversations for people to turn take, with one speaking, then another speaking, and so on. Some overlaps are nonproblematic because they do not deny the speaker holding the floor the right to talk. For example, another person might begin talking just as another is winding down; another speaker might add "continuers," such as "uh huh," to let the speaker know that his or her talk is understood; another may add a word that the speaker is searching for without grabbing the conversational floor; and others may add speech and other vocalizations in a kind of "chorus" to support the line of talk by a speaker. Moreover, overlaps are generally over very quickly, although at times they can persist.

---

[23]Emanuel A. Schegloff, "Overlapping Talk and the Organization of Turn-Taking for Conversation," *Language in Society* 29 (2000):1–63; see also his "Accounts of Conduct in Interaction Interruption, Overlap, and Turn-Taking," in *Handbook of Sociological Theory*, ed. J. H. Turner (New York: Kluwer Academic/Plenum Press, 2001).

Schegloff visualizes a number of procedures for dealing with overlaps, and their use constitutes a set of mechanisms or "folk methods" for managing overlaps in ways that allow the parties to sustain the conversation. One set of mechanisms revolves around shifts in the way talk is produced: getting louder, variations of pitch, talking faster, suddenly cutting off talk in progress with special markers (such as bringing teeth and lips together in a dramatic fashion). Another set of mechanisms revolves around the rhythm of the conversation, which can be conceptualized as successive "beats" of talk production. Overlaps proceed in such beats, with people—often all—stopping after the first beat of overlap or with one person continuing after a beat or two. Yet another is what Schegloff calls "pre-onset" strategies to keep others from starting to talk, such as speeding up the talk, and there are "post-onset" strategies, such as slowing down and deliberately over-pronouncing words.

Those working within the broad confines of ethnomethodology have studied these and other aspects of conversations. Such work is highly suggestive, but at present there is virtually no theoretical integration of the many observations of researchers. Thus, there is relatively little theorizing in conversational analysis; most work is highly descriptive, and yet many scholars like Schegloff clearly have theoretical intentions.

Conclusions

Ethnomethodology has uncovered a series of interpersonal processes that traditional symbolic interactionists, who tend to follow Mead more than Schutz, have failed to recognize. The implicit methods that people use to communicate a sense of social order are a very crucial dimension of social interaction and organization, and the theoretical goal of ethnomethodology is to specify the generic conditions under which various folk methods are used by individuals. But despite many interesting findings, this goal still seems far away—even after forty years of research.

In the end, ethnomethodology has become a rather isolated theoretical research program. Its practitioners increasingly focused on conversational analysis—a mode of inquiry initiated by Sacks and carried forward by a number of creative scholars. But their work has not had a great impact on mainstream sociological theory, inside or outside the interactionist tradition, although scholars as diverse as Jürgen Habermas (Chapter 23), Pierre Bourdieu (Chapter 21), Anthony Giddens (Chapter 20), and Randall Collins (Chapter 14) have all acknowledged a debt to ethnomethodology. There is, then, something important and fundamental about the assertions of ethnomethodologists.

Structural and Structuralist Theorizing

Perhaps it is a bit embarrassing, but sociologists have not agreed upon definitions of such basic topics as social structure and culture. Sociology defines itself as the study of social organization, and the dynamics of social structures and culture are certainly an important force in creating, sustaining, and changing patterns of social organization. And yet there is little consensus over what the nature and dynamics of structure and culture are. True, social structure can be viewed as patterns of social relations among individuals, but this is such a broad definition as to obfuscate as much as clarify. The same might be said of culture as systems of symbols that regulate social actions and interactions. The consequence of this ambiguity over sociology's basic subject matter is that theorizing on structure has been rather diverse. In this chapter, I will outline several distinctive approaches, but these represent only a sample of many different forms of theorizing on structure. In the next chapter, I will do the same for culture.

In the decades between the classical and contemporary periods of sociological theory, structural and cultural theorizing was greatly influenced by scholars in France, England, and the United States. The French tradition was decidedly cultural, as might be expected given the long lineage from Auguste Comte to Durkheim, but some rather interesting twists were added to conceptualizing structure as it became intertwined with a broader intellectual movement known as *structuralism* or *structuralist* theory. The British also borrowed from Durkheim, but less from his statements on culture and more from his analysis on the morphological properties of structures, although more contemporary British scholars like Anthony Giddens were to blend French structuralists ideas with many other approaches to produce a more synthetic theory. Finally, the American tradition began to develop tools for mapping networks, with social structure increasingly seen as patterns of connections among nodes in a network, with considerably less attention paid to the cultural dimensions of social structures. Let me begin with the French structuralist approach, then move to Giddens's more integrative theory, and conclude with network analysis. More purely cultural approaches to understanding interaction and structure will be examined in the next chapter.

The French Structural Tradition: Claude Lévi-Strauss

French sociology has always emphasized the cultural basis of social structures. While Durkheim did address the morphological properties of social structures—the size of the population, its density, and its basic modes of connectedness—there has always been a view that structures are directed and regulated by systems of culture—norms, law, beliefs, ideologies, values, and moral codes. We will see how these ideas have been played out in cultural theorizing in the next chapter, but as scholars began to address the question of social structure, the French lineage went in a number of interesting directions. One of the most influential was initiated by the French anthropologist Claude Lévi-Strauss.

In 1949, Lévi-Strauss launched an analysis of cross-cousin marriage in his classic work *The Elementary Structures of Kinship*, which follows Durkheim's and Marcel Mauss's view that structures created by exchange are not so much economic as cultural in that they symbolized patterns of relations among actors.[1] Lévi-Strauss emphasized that "it is the exchange which counts and not the things exchanged." For Lévi-Strauss, exchange must be viewed by its functions for integrating the larger social structure—an idea borrowed from Durkheim's student and nephew, Marcel Mauss. Lévi-Strauss then attacked utilitarians' assumption that the first principles of social behavior are economic. Such an assumption contradicts the view that social structure is an emergent phenomenon that operates according to its own irreducible laws and principles.

Lévi-Strauss also rejected psychological interpretations of exchange processes, especially the position advocated by behaviorists (see Chapter 15). In contrast with psychological behaviorists, who see little real difference in the laws of behavior between animals and humans, Lévi-Strauss emphasized that humans possess a cultural heritage of norms and values that separates their behavior and societal organization from that of animal species. Human action is thus qualitatively different from animal behavior. Nonhuman animals are not guided by values and rules that specify when, where, and how they are to carry out social transactions. Humans, however, carry with them into any exchange situation learned definitions of how they are to behave—thus ensuring that the principles of human exchange will be distinctive.

Furthermore, exchange is more than the result of psychological needs, even those that have been acquired through socialization. Exchange cannot be understood solely through individual motives, because exchange relations are a reflection of *patterns of social organization* that exist as an entity, sui generis. Exchange behavior is thus regulated from without by norms and values, resulting in processes that can be analyzed only by their consequences, or functions, for these norms and values.

---

[1]Claude Lévi-Strauss, *The Elementary Structures of Kinship* (Boston, MA: Beacon, 1969). This is a translation of Lévi-Strauss's 1967 revision of the original *Les structures élémentaires de la parenté* (Paris, France: Presses universitaires de France, 1949).

In arguing this view, Lévi-Strauss posited several fundamental exchange principles. First, all exchange relations involve costs for individuals, but in contrast with economic or psychological explanations of exchange, such costs are attributed to society—to those customs, rules, laws, and values that require behaviors incurring costs. Yet individuals do not assign the costs to themselves but to the "social order." Second, for all those scarce and valued resources in society—whether wives or symbolic resources like esteem and prestige—their distribution is regulated by norms and values. As long as resources are in abundant supply or are not highly valued in a society, their distribution goes unregulated, but once they become scarce and highly valued, their distribution is soon regulated. Third, all exchange relations are governed by a norm of reciprocity, requiring those receiving valued resources to bestow on their benefactors other valued resources. In Lévi-Strauss's conception of reciprocity are various patterns of reciprocation specified by norms and values. In some situations, norms dictate "mutual" and direct rewarding of one's benefactor, whereas in other situations the reciprocity can be "univocal," involving diverse patterns of indirect exchange in which actors do not reciprocate directly but only through various third (fourth, fifth, etc.) parties. Within these two general types of exchange reciprocity—mutual and univocal—numerous subtypes of exchange networks can be normatively regulated.

Lévi-Strauss believed that these three exchange principles offer a more useful set of concepts to describe cross-cousin marriage patterns, because these patterns can now be viewed by their functions for the larger social structure. Particular marriage patterns and other features of kinship organization no longer need be interpreted merely as direct exchanges among individuals but can be conceptualized as exchanges between individuals and society. In freeing exchange from the analysis of only direct and mutual exchanges, Lévi-Strauss offered a tentative theory of societal integration and solidarity. His explanation extended Durkheim's provocative analysis and indicated how various subtypes of direct and univocal exchange both reflect and reinforce different patterns of societal integration and organization. And so,

1. Various forms of social structure, rather than individual motives, are the critical variables in the analysis of exchange relations.

2. Exchange relations in social systems are frequently not restricted to direct interaction among individuals but are protracted into complex networks of indirect exchange. On the one hand, these exchange processes are caused by patterns of social integration and organization; on the other hand, they promote diverse forms of such organization.

Lévi-Strauss's work represents the culmination of a reaction to economic utilitarianism as it was originally incorporated into anthropology but rejected by most sociologists, especially those in the French tradition. Marcel Mauss had drawn explicit attention to the significance of social structure in regulating exchange processes and to the consequences of such processes for maintaining social structure. Finally, in this intellectual chain of events in anthropology, Lévi-Strauss began to indicate how different types of direct and indirect exchange are linked to different patterns of social and cultural structures.

In *The Elementary Structures of Kinship*, Lévi-Strauss only hinted at the more philosophical view of the world that his analysis of kinship implied.[2] Most of this book examined the varying levels of social solidarity that emerge from direct and indirect bridal exchanges among kin groups. Yet in many ways, *The Elementary Structures of Kinship* was a transitional work because, though it was influenced by Durkheim's and Mauss's work, it began to depart from the earlier foundations provided by these giants of French sociology.[3] Indeed, these departures from Durkheim and Mauss signaled that Lévi-Strauss was about to "turn Durkheim on his head" in much the same way that Marx was to revise Georg Wilhelm Friedrich Hegel. As Durkheim and Mauss argued in *Primitive Classification*, human cognitive categories reflect the structure of society.[4] In contrast, Lévi-Strauss came to the opposite conclusion: the structure of society is but a surface manifestation of fundamental mental processes hardwired in the human brain. Lévi-Strauss came to this position under the influence of structural linguistics, as initially chartered by Ferdinand de Saussure[5] and Roman Jakobson. De Saussure is typically considered the father both of structural linguistics[6] and of Lévi-Strauss's structuralism. Commentators have often viewed Lévi-Strauss's interest in linguistics as decisive in his reversal of the Durkheimian tradition. Yet the Swiss linguist de Saussure saw himself as a Durkheimian. De Saussure's posthumously published lectures, *Course in General Linguistics,* had a decidedly Durkheimian tone: he argued that the parts of language acquire their meaning only in relation to the structure of the whole; the units of language—whether sounds or morphemes—are only points in an overall structure that transcends the individual; language is "based entirely on the opposition of concrete units";[7] the underlying structure of language (*langue*) can be known and understood only by reference to surface phenomena, such as speech (*parole*); and the structure of language is "no longer looked upon as an organism that developed independently but as a product of the collective mind of linguistic groups."[8]

---

[2]Actually, an earlier work, "The Analysis of Structure in Linguistics and in Anthropology," *Word* 1 (1945):1–21, provided a better clue to the form of Lévi-Strauss's structuralism.

[3]Marcel Mauss, *The Gift: Forms and Functions of Exchange* (New York: Free Press, 1954; originally published 1924), is given particular credit. It must be remembered, of course, that Mauss was Durkheim's student and nephew.

[4]Émile Durkheim and Marcel Mauss, *Primitive Classification* (Chicago, IL: University of Chicago Press, 1963). Originally published 1903, this is a rather extreme and unsuccessful effort to show how mental categories directly reflect the spatial and structural organization of a population. It is a horribly flawed work, but it is the most extreme statement of Durkheim's sociologistic position.

[5]Ferdinand de Saussure, *Course in General Linguistics* (New York: McGraw-Hill, 1966); originally compiled posthumously by his students from their lecture notes in 1915.

[6]Ibid.

[7]Ibid., 107.

[8]Ibid., 108.

Thus, as a contemporary of Durkheim, de Saussure was far more committed to Durkheim's vision of reality than is typically acknowledged, but he made a critical breakthrough in linguistic analysis: speech is but a surface manifestation of more fundamental mental processes. Language is not speech or the written word; rather, it is a particular *way of thinking*, which, in true Durkheimian fashion, de Saussure viewed as a product of the general patterns of social and cultural organization among people.

Yet this distinction of speech as a mere surface manifestation of underlying mental processes was increasingly used as a metaphor for Lévi-Strauss's structuralism. Of course, this metaphor is as old as Plato's view that reality is a mere reflection of universal essences and as recent as Marx's dictum that cultural values and beliefs, as well as institutional arrangements, are reflections of an underlying substructure of economic relations.

Lévi-Strauss also borrowed from the early twentieth-century linguist Jakobson the notion that the mental thought underlying language occurs as binary contrasts, such as good/bad, male/female, yes/no, black/white, and human/nonhuman. Moreover, drawing from Jakobson and others, Lévi-Strauss viewed the underlying mental reality of binary opposites as organized, or mediated, by a series of "innate codes" or rules that could be used to generate many different social forms: language, art, music, social structure, myths, values, beliefs, and so on.[9]

As Lévi-Strauss received these very Durkheimian ideas, he appeared to focus primarily on the distinction between *langue* and *parole* and on the notion of language as constructed from oppositions, while ignoring de Saussure's emphasis on the social structural origins of langue. Yet why did Lévi-Strauss find linguistic analysis so appealing, and why did he ignore the Durkheimian thrust of de Saussure's work? Lévi-Strauss's own self-reflective answers are not particularly revealing. For example, he claimed that he was probably born a structuralist, recalling that even when he was a two-year-old and still unable to read, he sought to decipher signs with similar groupings of letters. Another childhood influence, he claimed, was geology, in which the task was to discover the underlying geological operations for the tremendous diversity of landscapes.[10] He also constructed many genealogies, and for a time, Lévi-Strauss declared that he was an "anti-Durkheimian" and would embrace Anglo-American methods as an alternative to the Durkheimian approach.[11] Still, he always kept a foot in the French tradition. For example, he dedicated his essay "French Sociology" to Mauss and emphasized,

> One could say that the entire purpose of the French school lies in an attempt to break up the categories of the layman, and to group the data into a deeper,

---

[9]Actually, Jakobson simply argued that children's phonological development occurs as a system in which contrasts are critical—for example, "papa versus mama" or the contrasts that children learn between vowels and consonants. Lévi-Strauss appears to have added the jargon of information theory and computer technology. See Roman Jakobson, *Selected Writings I: Phonological Studies* (The Hague, Netherlands: Mouton, 1962) and *Selected Writings II: Word and Language* (The Hague, Netherlands: Mouton, 1971). For more detail, see A. R. Maryanski and Jonathan H. Turner, "The Offspring of Functionalism: French and British Structuralism," *Sociological Theory* 9 (1991): 106–115.

[10]Claude Lévi-Strauss, *Myth and Meaning* (New York: Schocken, 1979).

[11]Claude Lévi-Strauss, *A World on the Wane* (London: Hutchinson, 1961).

sounder classification. As was emphasized by Durkheim, the true and only basis of sociology is social morphology, i.e., this part of sociology the task of which is to constitute and to classify social types.[12]

Lévi-Strauss's goal increasingly became one of reworking the French tradition for analyzing morphology or structure. His earlier work seemed to lie squarely in the Durkheimian tradition. In *The Elementary Structures of Kinship*[13] (certainly a very Durkheimian-sounding title), he focused on how kinship rules regulate marriage, which owes a great deal to Mauss's *The Gift*.[14] Lévi-Strauss concluded that exchange is a "common denominator of a large number of apparently heterogeneous social activities," and like Mauss before him, he posited a universal structural "principle of reciprocity." Moreover, drawing from and criticizing Durkheim's early analysis of incest,[15] whereby incest was seen as the product of rules of exogamy, Lévi-Strauss viewed rules regarding incest as ordering principles in their own right. The details here are not as important as the recognition that his work was basically Durkheimian, but there were hints of significant additions. In particular, Lévi-Strauss postulated an unconscious mind involving a blueprint or model for coding operations. For example, "reciprocity" is perhaps a universal unconscious code, lodged in the neuroanatomy of the brain and existing before the material and cultural structure of society.

Why, then, did Lévi-Strauss make this change in Durkheimian sociology? The simple answer might be that he wanted to say something new. If he merely borrowed Durkheim's idea of morphology, Mauss's and Hertz's concern with underlying structural principles, Mauss's principle of reciprocity, Durkheim's and Mauss's concern with categories of thought, mythology, and ritual, and de Saussure's as well as Jakobson's basic ideas in linguistics, what would be original about his work? His strategy was simply to turn the Durkheimian school upside down and to view *mental* morphology as the underlying cause of cultural and material morphology. He decided essentially to convert what Durkheim saw as "real," "a thing," and a "social fact" into an unreality. In doing so, he changed what Durkheim saw as unreal into the ultimate reality. Thus, structuralism was born as the result of Lévi-Strauss's search for something new to say in the long and distinguished French lineage. All elements of the French lineage remain, but they are reversed.

Thus, during the decades of the mid-century, Lévi-Strauss's structuralism became concerned with understanding cultural and social patterns as the universal mental processes that are rooted in the biochemistry of the human brain.[16] In this sense

---

[12]Claude Lévi-Strauss, "French Sociology," in *Twentieth Century Sociology,* ed. Georges Gurvitch and Wilbert E. Moore (New York: Books for Libraries, 1945).

[13]Lévi-Strauss, *The Elementary Structures of Kinship.*

[14]Mauss, *The Gift.*

[15]Émile Durkheim, "Incest: The Nature and Origin of the Taboo." *Anneé Sociologique* 1 (1898):1–70.

[16]See, for example, Claude Lévi-Strauss, "Social Structure," in *Anthropology Today*, ed. A. Kroeber (Chicago, IL: University of Chicago Press, 1953), 524–553, *Structural Anthropology* (Paris, France: Plon, 1958; trans. 1963 by Basic Books), and *Mythologiques: le cru et le cuit* (Paris, France: Plon, 1964).

Lévi-Strauss's structuralism is mentalistic and reductionistic. To summarize what became the basic argument,[17]

1. The empirically observable must be viewed as a system of relationships among components—whether these components be elements of myths and folk tales or positions in a kinship system.

2. It is appropriate to construct "statistical models" of these observable systems to summarize the empirically observable relationships among components.

3. Such models, however, are only a surface manifestation of more fundamental forms of reality. These forms are the result of using various codes or rules to organize different binary opposites, which can be conceptualized as "mechanical models" that are less directly observable.

4. The tendencies of statistical models will reflect, imperfectly, the properties of the mechanical model. But the latter is "more real."

5. The mechanical model is built from rules and binary oppositions that are innate to humans and rooted in the neurology of the brain.

Steps 1 and 2 are about as far as Lévi-Strauss had gone in the first publication of *The Elementary Structures of Kinship*. Subsequent work on kinship and on myths invoked at least the rhetoric of steps 3, 4, and 5. What made structuralism distinctive, therefore, was the commitment to the assumptions and strategy implied in these last steps. The major problem with this strategy is that it cannot be tested. If mechanical models are never perfectly reflected in the empirical world, how is it possible to confirm or disconfirm the application of rules to binary opposites? As Marshall Sahlins sarcastically remarked, "What is apparent is false and what is hidden from perception and contradicts it is true."[18] Yet, despite such criticisms, the imagery communicated by Lévi-Strauss, especially in steps 1 and 3, has influenced a great deal of structural theorizing. Although the extremes of Lévi-Strauss's approach have not been adopted by many, the idea of structure as involving "grammars" and "codes" that guide actors in their actions and in the production of social structures has remained appealing to cultural theorists.

The imagery created by Lévi-Strauss's theorizing has influenced both structural and cultural sociology in much the same way as did Durkheim's analysis of structure. The imagery from linguistics came to be emphasized more than the contention that social and cultural structures are driven by the hardwiring of the human brain.

---

[17]Miriam Glucksmann, *Structuralist Analysis in Contemporary Social Thought* (London: Routledge and Kegan Paul, 1974). A more sympathetic review of Lévi-Strauss, as well as a more general review of structuralist thought, can be found in Tom Bottomore and Robert Nisbet, "Structuralism," in their *A History of Sociological Analysis* (New York: Basic Books, 1978).

[18]Marshall D. Sahlins, "On the Delphic Writings of Claude Lévi-Strauss," *Scientific American* 214 (1966):134. For other relevant critiques, see Marvin Harris, *The Rise of Anthropological Theory* (New York: Crowell, 1968), 464–513 and Eugene A. Hammel, "The Myth of Structural Analysis: Lévi-Strauss and the Three Bears," Module in Anthropology No. 25 (Reading, MA: Addison-Wesley, 1972).

The result is that many "structural" or "structuralist" approaches emphasized that empirical patterns and regularities are driven by underlying structural principles, whether from the neurology of the human brain or, as was more common, from the systems of cultural symbols that have developed within a population. Structure was thus something "hiding" just beneath the surface of empirical regularities, and theorizing should seek to discover how the underlying structural principles operate to produce surface patterns and empirical regularities.

Unfortunately, the theories pushing this imagery never really went beyond what I have just said above. Few structural principles or mechanisms have been isolated, and most of structuralist sociology just continued to assert that their image of the social universe is correct. They added additional embellishments found in Lévi-Straus, and for that matter in many perspectives, that culture is organized as sets of binary oppositions that, somehow and in some way that was never really specified, generate social structures. Yet even though the imagery remained just that—imagery—more recent theorists of structure drew from this imagery as they tried to gain a better purchase in theorizing structure. Perhaps the best-known theorist who drew from, but was not a slave to, the imagery of structuralism is Anthony Giddens.

The British Structuralist Tradition: Anthony Giddens's Structuration Theory

Over the last forty years, Anthony Giddens has been one of the most prominent critics of the scientific pretensions of sociology. Yet, at the same time, he has developed a relatively formal abstract conceptual scheme for analyzing the social world. In his *The Constitution of Society*,[19] Giddens brought elements of his advocacy together into an important theoretical synthesis of diverse theoretical traditions—structuralism, Marxism, dramaturgy, psychoanalysis, and even elements of functionalism—an approach that he had earlier titled "structuration theory." This theory represents one of the more creative theoretical efforts of the second half of the twentieth century. Although Giddens has developed theoretical interests in modernity and, indeed, has become an important contributor to the debate about modernity and postmodernity,[20] his theoretical contribution still resides primarily in the more formal statement of structuration theory.

---

[19]Anthony Giddens, *The Constitution of Society: Outline of the Theory of Structuration* (Oxford, UK: Polity, 1984), *Central Problems in Social Theory* (London: Macmillan, 1979). The University of California Press also has editions of these two books. For an excellent overview, both sociologically and philosophically, of Giddens's theoretical project, see Ira Cohen, *Structuration Theory: Anthony Giddens and the Constitution of Social Life* (London: Macmillan, 1989). For a commentary and debate on Giddens's work, see J. Clark, C. Modgil, and S. Modgil (eds.), *Anthony Giddens: Consensus and Controversy* (London: Falmer, 1990). For a selection of readings, see *The Giddens Reader*, ed. Philip Cassell (Stanford, CA: Stanford University Press, 1993).

[20]See, for examples, Anthony Giddens, *The Consequences of Modernity* (Stanford, CA: Stanford University Press, 1990); Ulrich Beck, Anthony Giddens, and Scott Lash, *Reflexive Modernization* (Stanford, CA: Stanford University Press, 1994); and Anthony Giddens, *Modernity and Self-Identity* (Stanford, CA: Stanford University Press, 1991).

Giddens's Critique of Science in Sociology

Anthony Giddens reasoned that there can never be any universal and timeless sociological laws, like those in physics or the biological sciences. Humans have the capacity for agency, and hence, they can change the very nature of social organization—thereby obviating any laws that are proposed to be universal. At best, "the concepts of theory should for many research purposes be regarded as sensitizing devices, nothing more."[21] Giddens buttresses this conclusion with two points of argument.

First, Giddens asserts that social theorizing involves a "double hermeneutic." Stripped of its jargon, this means that the concepts and generalizations used by social scientists to understand social processes can be employed by lay persons as agents who can alter these social processes. We must recognize, Giddens contends, that ordinary actors are also "social theorists who alter their theories in the light of their experience and are receptive to incoming information."[22] Thus, social science theories are not often "news" to individuals; when they are, such theories can be used to transform the very order they describe. Within the capacity of humans to be reflexive—that is, to think about their situation—is the ability to change it.[23]

Second, social theory is by its nature social criticism. Social theory often contradicts "the reasons that people give for doing things" and is, therefore, a critique of these reasons and the social arrangements that people construct in the name of these reasons. Sociology does not, therefore, need to develop a separate body of critical theory, as others have argued; it is critical theory by its very nature and by virtue of the effects it can have on social processes.

The implications, Giddens believes, are profound. We need to stop imitating the natural sciences. We must cease evaluating our success as intellectuals by whether or not we have discovered "timeless laws." We must recognize that social theory does not exist "outside" our universe. We should accept that what sociologists and lay actors do is, in a fundamental sense, very much the same. And we must redirect our efforts to developing "sensitizing concepts" that allow us to understand the active processes of interaction among individuals as they produce and reproduce social structures while being guided by these structures.

Structuration

Because Giddens does not believe that abstract laws of social action, interaction, and organization exist, his "theory of structuration" is not a series of propositions. Instead, as Giddens's critique of science would suggest, his "theory" is a cluster of sensitizing concepts, linked together discursively. The key concept is structuration,

---

[21]Giddens, *The Constitution of Society*, 326.

[22]Ibid., 335.

[23]See, in particular, Anthony Giddens, *Profiles and Critiques in Social Theory* (London: Macmillan, 1982) and *New Rules of Sociological Method: A Positive Critique of Interpretative Sociologies*, 2nd ed. (Stanford, CA: Stanford University Press, 1993).

which is intended to communicate the duality of structure.[24] That is, social structure is used by active agents; in so using the properties of structure, they transform or reproduce this structure. Thus the process of structuration requires a conceptualization of the nature of structure, of the agents who use structure, and of the ways that these are mutually implicated in each other to produce varying patterns of human organization.

Reconceptualizing Structure and Social System. Giddens believes structure can be conceptualized as *rules* and *resources* that actors use in "interaction contexts" that extend across "space" and over "time." In so using these rules and resources, actors sustain or reproduce structures in space and time.

Rules. Giddens sees *rules* as "generalizable procedures" that actors understand and use in various circumstances. Giddens posits that a rule is a methodology or technique that actors know about, often only implicitly, and that provides a relevant formula for action.[25] From a sociological perspective, the most important rules are those that agents use in the reproduction of social relations over significant lengths of time and across space. These rules reveal certain characteristics: (1) they are frequently used in (a) conversations, (b) interaction rituals, and (c) the daily routines of individuals; (2) they are tacitly grasped and understood and are part of the "stocks knowledge" of competent actors; (3) they are informal, remaining unwritten and unarticulated; and (4) they are weakly sanctioned through interpersonal techniques.[26]

The thrust of Giddens's argument is that rules are part of actors' "knowledgeability." Some can be normative in that actors can articulate and explicitly make reference to them, but many other rules are more implicitly understood and used to guide the flow of interaction in ways that are not easily expressed or verbalized. Moreover, actors can transform rules into new combinations as they confront and deal with one another and the contextual particulars of their interaction.

Resources. As the other critical property of structure, *resources* are facilities that actors use to get things done. For, even if there are well-understood methodologies and formulas—that is, rules—to guide action, there must also be the capacity to perform tasks. Such capacity requires resources, or the material equipment and the organizational ability to act in situations. Giddens visualizes resources as what generate power.[27] Power is not a resource, as much social theory argues. Rather, the mobilization of other resources is what gives actors power to get things done. Thus, power is integral to the very existence of structure: as actors interact, they use resources, and they use these resources to mobilize power to shape the actions of others.

---

[24]See Giddens, *The Constitution of Society*, 207–213.

[25]Ibid., 20–21.

[26]Ibid., 22.

[27]Ibid., 14–16.

Giddens visualizes rules and resources as "transformational" and as "mediating."[28] What he means by these terms is that rules and resources can be transformed into many different patterns and profiles. Resources can be mobilized in various ways to perform activities and achieve ends through the exercise of different forms and degrees of power; rules can generate many diverse combinations of methodologies and formulas to guide how people communicate, interact, and adjust to one another. Rules and resources are mediating in that they are what tie social relations together. They are what actors use to create, sustain, or transform relations across time and in space. And because rules and resources are inherently transformational—that is, generative of diverse combinations—they can lace together many different patterns of social relations in time and space.

Giddens developed a typology of rules and resources that is rather vague and imprecise.[29] He sees the three concepts in this typology—domination, legitimation, and signification—as "theoretical primitives," which is, perhaps, an excuse for defining them imprecisely. The basic idea is that resources are the stuff of domination because they involve the mobilization of material and organizational facilities to do things. Some rules are transformed into instruments of legitimization because they make things seem correct and appropriate. Other rules are used to create signification, or meaningful symbolic systems, because they provide people with ways to see and interpret events. Actually, the scheme makes more sense if the concepts of domination, legitimation, and signification are given less emphasis and the elements of his discussion are selectively extracted to create the typology presented in Figure 20.1.

In the left column of Figure 20.1, structure is viewed by Giddens as composed of rules and resources. Rules are transformed into two basic types of mediating processes: (1) normative, or the creation of rights and obligations in a context, and (2) interpretative, or the generation of schemes and stocks of taken-for-granted knowledge in a context. Resources are transformed into two major types of facilities that can mediate social relations: (1) authoritative resources, or the organizational capacity to control and direct the patterns of interactions in a context, and (2) allocative resources, or the use of material features, artifacts, and goods to control and direct patterns of interaction in a context.

Giddens sees these types of rules and resources as mediating interaction via three modalities, as portrayed in column 2 of Figure 20.1: rights and obligations, facilities, and interpretative schemes. The figure deviates somewhat from Giddens's discussion, but the idea is the same: that rules and resources are attached to interaction (or the "social system" in Giddens's terms) via these three modalities. These modalities are then used to (a) generate the power that enables some actors to control others; (b) affirm the norms that, in turn, allow actors to be sanctioned for their conformity or nonconformity; and (c) create and use the interpretative schemes that make it possible for actors to communicate with one another.

---

[28]Here, Giddens seems to be taking what is useful from "structuralism" and reworking these ideas into a more sociological approach. Giddens remains, however, extremely critical of structuralism; see his "Structuralism, Post-Structuralism and the Production of Culture" in *Social Theory Today*, ed. A. Giddens and J. Turner (Cambridge, UK: Polity, 2000).

[29]Giddens, *The Constitution of Society*, 29 and *Central Problems in Social Theory*, 97–107.

Figure 20.1   Social Structure, Social System, and the Modalities of Connection

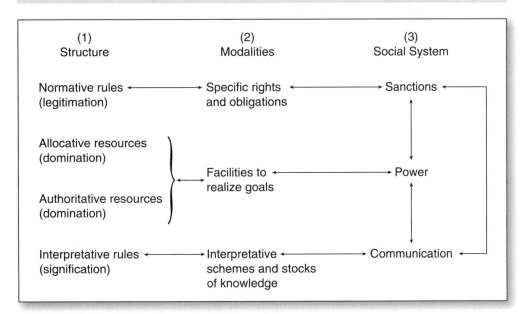

Giddens also stresses that rules and resources are interrelated, emphasizing that the modalities and their use in interaction are separated only analytically. In the actual flow of interaction in the real empirical world, they exist simultaneously, thereby making their separation merely an exercise of analytical decomposition. Thus, power, sanctions, and media of communication are interconnected, as are the rules and resources of social structure. In social systems, where people are copresent and interact, power is used to secure a particular set of rights and obligations as well as a system of communication; conversely, power can be exercised only through communication and sanctioning.

Giddens, then, sees social structure as something used by actors, not as some external reality that pushes and shoves actors around. Social structure is defined as the rules and resources that can be transformed as actors use them in concrete settings. But the following question arises: How is structure to be connected to what people actually do in interaction settings, or what Giddens terms "social systems"? The answer is the notion of modalities, whereby rules and resources are transformed into power, sanctions, and communication. Thus, structure is not a mysterious system of codes, as Lévi-Strauss and other structural idealists imply, nor is it a set of determinative parameters and external constraints on actors. In Giddens's conceptualization, social structure is transformative and flexible, it is "part of" actors in concrete situations, and it is used by them to create patterns of social relations across space and through time.

Moreover, this typology allows Giddens to emphasize that, as agents interact in social systems, they can reproduce rules and resources (via the modalities) or they can transform them. Thus, social interaction and social structure are reciprocally implicated. Structuration is, therefore, the dual processes in which rules and resources are used to organize interaction across time and in space and, by virtue of this use, to reproduce or transform these rules and resources.

Reconceptualizing Institutions. Giddens believes that institutions are systems of interaction in societies that endure over time and that distribute people in space. Giddens uses phrases like "deeply sedimented across time and in space in societies" to express the idea that when rules and resources are reproduced over long periods of time and in explicit regions of space, then institutions can be said to exist in a society. Giddens offers a typology of institutions showing the weights and combinations of rules and resources that are implicated in interaction.[30] If signification (interpretative rules) is primary, followed by domination (allocative and authoritative resources) and then legitimization (normative rules), respectively, a "symbolic order" exists. If authoritative domination, signification, and legitimization are successively combined, political institutionalization occurs. If allocative dominance, signification, and legitimization are ordered, economic institutionalization prevails. And if legitimation, domination and signification are rank-ordered, institutionalization of law occurs. Table 20.1 summarizes Giddens's argument.

In this conceptualization of institutions, Giddens seeks to avoid a mechanical view of institutionalization, in several senses. First, systems of interaction in empirical contexts are a mixture of institutional processes. Economic, political, legal, and symbolic orders are not easily separated; there is usually an element of each in any social system context. Second, institutions are tied to the rules and resources that agents employ and thereby reproduce; they are not external to individuals because they are formed by the use of varying rules and resources in actual social relations. Third, the most basic dimensions of all rules and resources—signification, domination,

Table 20.1   The Typology of Institutions

Type of Institution		Rank Order of Emphasis on Rules and Resources
1. Symbolic orders, or modes of discourse, and patterns of communication	are produced and reproduced by	the use of interpretative rules (signification) in conjuction with normative rules (legitimation) and allocative as well as authoritative resources (domination).
2. Political institutions	are produced and reproduced by	the use of authoritative resources (domination) in conjunction with interpretative rules (signification) and normative rules (legitimation).
3. Economic institutions	are produced and reproduced by	the use of allocative resources (domination) in conjunction with interpretative rules (signification) and normative rules (legitimation).
4. Legal institutions	are produced and reproduced by	the use of normative rules (legitimation) in conjunction with authoritative and allocative resources (domination) and interpretative rules (signification).

---

[30]Giddens, *Central Problems in Social Theory*, 107 and *The Constitution of Society*, 31.

and legitimization—are all involved in institutionalization; it is only their relative salience for actors that gives the stabilization of relations across time and in space its distinctive institutional character.

Structural Principles, Sets, and Properties. The extent and form of institutionalization in societies are related to what Giddens terms structural principles.[31] These are the most general principles that guide the organization of societal totalities. These are what "stretch systems across time and space," and they allow for "system integration," or the maintenance of reciprocal relations among units in a society. For Giddens, "structural principles can thus be understood as the principles of organization which allow recognizably consistent forms of time-space distanciation on the basis of definite mechanisms of societal integration."[32] The basic idea seems to be that rules and resources are used by active agents in accordance with fundamental principles of organization. Such principles guide just how rules and resources are transformed and employed to mediate social relations.

On the basis of their underlying structural principles, three basic types of societies have existed: (1) "tribal societies," which are organized by structural principles that emphasize kinship and tradition as the mediating force behind social relations across time and in space; (2) "class-divided societies," which are organized by an urban/rural differentiation, with urban areas revealing distinctive political institutions that can be separated from economic institutions, formal codes of law or legal institutions, and modes of symbolic coordination or ordering through written texts and testaments; and (3) "class societies," which involve structural principles that separate and yet interconnect all four institutional spheres, especially the economic and political.[33]

Structural principles are implicated in the production and reproduction of "structures" or "structural sets." These structural sets are rule and resource bundles, or combinations and configurations of rules and resources, which are used to produce and reproduce certain types and forms of social relations across time and space. Giddens offers the example of how the structural principles of class societies (differentiation and clear separation of economy and polity) guide the use of the following structural set: private *property–money–capital–labor–contract–profit*. The details of his analysis are less important than the general idea that the general structural principles of class societies are transformed into more specific sets of rules and resources that agents use to mediate social relations. This structural set is used in capitalist societies and, as a consequence, is reproduced. In turn, such reproduction of the structural set reaffirms the more abstract structural principles of class societies.

As these and other structural sets are used by agents and as they are thereby reproduced, societies develop "structural properties," which are "institutionalized features of social systems, stretching across time and space."[34] That is, social relations

---

[31]Giddens, *The Constitution of Society*, 179–193.

[32]Ibid., 181.

[33]For an extensive discussion of this typology, see Anthony Giddens, *A Contemporary Critique of Historical Materialism: Power, Property, and the State* (London: Macmillan, 1981).

[34]Giddens, *The Constitution of Society*, 185.

become patterned in certain typical ways. Thus, the structural set of *private property–money–capital–labor–contract–profit* can mediate only certain patterns of relations; that is, if this is the rule and resource bundle with which agents must work, then only certain forms of relations can be produced and reproduced in the economic sphere. Hence, the institutionalization of relations in time and space reveals a particular form or, in Giddens's terms, structural property.

Structural Contradictions. Giddens always emphasizes the inherent "transformative" potential of rules and resources. Structural principles, he argues, "operate in terms of one another but yet also contravene each other."[35] In other words, they reveal contradictions that can be either primary or secondary. A "primary contradiction" is one between structural principles that are formative and constitute a society, whereas a "secondary contradiction" is one that is "brought into being by primary contradictions."[36] For example, there is a contradiction between structural principles that mediate the institutionalization of private profits, on the one hand, and those that mediate socialized production, on the other. If workers pool their labor to produce goods and services, it is contradictory to allow only some to enjoy the profits of such socialized labor.

Contradictions are not, Giddens emphasizes, the same as conflicts. Contradiction is a "disjunction of structural principles of system organization," whereas conflict is the actual struggle between actors in "definite social practices."[37] Thus, the contradiction between private profits and socialized labor is not, in itself, a conflict. It can create situations of conflict, such as struggles between management and labor in a specific time and place, but such conflicts are not the same as contradiction.

For Giddens, then, the institutional patterns of a society represent the creation and use by agents of very generalized and abstract principles. These principles represent the development of particular rules and the mobilization of certain resources; such principles generate more concrete "bundles" or "sets" of rules and resources that agents actively use to produce and reproduce social relations in concrete settings; and many of these principles and sets contain contradictory elements that can encourage actual conflicts among actors. In this way, structure "constrains" but is not disembodied from agents. Rather, the "properties" of total societies are not external to individuals and collectivities but are persistently reproduced through the use of structural principles and sets by agents who act. Let us now turn to Giddens's discussion of these active agents.

Agents, Agency, and Action. As is evident, Giddens visualizes structure as a duality, as something that is part of the actions of agents. And so in Giddens's approach it is essential to understand the dynamics of human agency. He proposes a "stratification model," which is an effort to synthesize psychoanalytic theory, phenomenology,

---

[35]Ibid., 193.

[36]Ibid.

[37]Ibid., 198.

ethnomethodology, and elements of action theory. This model is depicted in Figure 20.2. For Giddens, "agency" denotes the events that an actor perpetrates rather than "intentions," "purposes," "ends," or other states. Agency is what an actor actually does in a situation that has visible consequences (not necessarily intended consequences). To understand the dynamics of agency requires analysis of each element in the model.

As drawn, the model in Figure 20.2 actually combines two overlapping models in Giddens's discussion, but his intent is reasonably clear: humans "reflexively monitor" their own conduct and that of others; in other words, they pay attention to, note, calculate, and assess the consequences of actions.[38] Monitoring is influenced by two levels of consciousness.[39] One is "discursive consciousness," which involves the capacity to give reasons for or rationalize what one does (and presumably to do the same for others' behavior). "Practical consciousness" are the stocks of knowledge that one implicitly uses to act in situations and to interpret the actions of others. This knowledgeability is constantly used, but rarely articulated, to interpret events—one's own and those of others. Almost all acts are indexical in that they must be interpreted by their context, and this implicit stock of knowledge provides these contextual interpretations and frameworks.

There are also unconscious dimensions to human agency. There are many pressures to act in certain ways, which an actor does not perceive. Indeed, Giddens argues that much motivation is unconscious. Moreover, motivation is often much more diffuse than action theories portray. That is, there is no one-to-one relation between an act and a motive. Actors might be able to rationalize through their capacity for discursive consciousness in ways that make this one-to-one relationship seem to be what directs action. But much of what propels action lies below consciousness and, at best, provides very general and diffuse pressures to act. Moreover, much action might not be motivated at all; an actor simply monitors and responds to the environment.

In trying to reintroduce the unconscious into social theory, Giddens adopts Erik Erikson's psychoanalytic ideas.[40] The basic "force" behind much action is an unconscious set of processes to gain a "sense of trust" in interaction with others. Giddens

Figure 20.2   The Dynamics of Agency

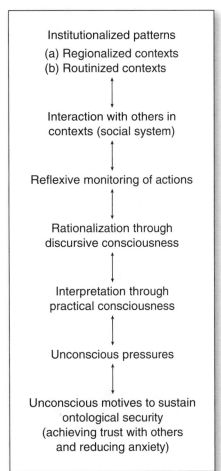

---

[38]Ibid., 5–7; see also *Central Problems in Social Theory*, 56–59.

[39]His debt to Alfred Schutz and phenomenology is evident here, but he has liberated it from its subjectivism. See Chapter 15 on the rise of interactionist theorizing.

[40]Giddens, *The Constitution of Society*, 45–59.

terms this set of processes the ontological security system of an agent. That is, one of the driving but highly diffuse forces behind action is the desire to sustain ontological security or the sense of trust that comes from being able to reduce anxiety in social relations. Actors need to have this sense of trust. How they go about reducing anxiety to secure this sense is often unconscious because the mechanisms involved are developed before linguistic skills emerge in the young and because psychodynamics, such as repression, might also keep these fundamental feelings and their resolution from becoming conscious. In general, Giddens argues that ontological security is maintained through the routinization of encounters with others, through the successful interpretation of acts as practical or stock knowledge, and through the capacity for rationalization that comes with discursive consciousness.

As the top portions of Figure 20.2 emphasize, institutionalized patterns have an effect on, while being a consequence of, the dynamics of agency. As we will see shortly, unconscious motives for ontological security require routinized interactions (predictable, stable over time) that are regionalized (ordered in space). Such regionalization and routinization are the products of past interactions of agents and are sustained or reproduced through the present (and future) actions of agents. To sustain routines and regions, actors must monitor their actions while drawing on their stock knowledge and discursive capacities. In this way, Giddens visualizes institutionalized patterns implicated in the very nature of agency. Institutions and agents cannot exist without each other, for institutions are reproduced practices by agents, whereas the conscious and unconscious dynamics of agency depend on the routines and regions provided by institutionalized patterns.

Routinization and Regionalization of Interaction. Both the ontological security of agents and the institutionalization of structures in time and space depend on routinized and regionalized interaction among actors. Routinization of interaction patterns is what gives them continuity across time, thereby reproducing structure (rules and resources) and institutions. At the same time, routinization gives predictability to actions and, in so doing, provides a sense of ontological security. Thus, routines become critical for the most basic aspects of structure and human agency. Similarly, regionalization orders action in space by positioning actors in places relative to one another and by circumscribing how they are to present themselves and act. As with routines, the regionalization of interaction is essential to the sustenance of broader structural patterns and ontological security of actors, because it orders people's interactions in space and time, which in turn reproduces structures and meets an agent's need for ontological security.

Routines. Giddens sees routines as the key link between the episodic character of interactions (they start, proceed, and end), on the one hand, and basic trust and security, on the other.[41] Moreover, "the routinization of encounters is of major significance in binding the fleeting encounter to social reproduction and thus to the seeming 'fixity' of

---

[41]Ibid., 60–109.

institutions."[42] In a very interesting discussion in which he borrows heavily from Erving Goffman (but with a phenomenological twist), Giddens proposed several procedures, or mechanisms, that humans use to sustain routines: (a) opening and closing rituals, (b) turn taking, (c) tact, (d) positioning, and (e) framing.[43] Each of these is discussed below:

1. Because interaction is serial—that is, it occurs sequentially—there must be symbolic markers of opening and closing. Such markers are essential to the maintenance of routines because they indicate when in the flow of time the elements of routine interaction are to begin and end. There are many such interpersonal markers—words, facial gestures, positions of bodies—and there are physical markers, such as rooms, buildings, roads, and equipment, that also signal when certain routinized interactions are to begin and end (note, e.g., the interpersonal and physical markers for a lecture, which is a highly routinized interaction that sustains the ontological security of agents and perpetuates institutional patterns).

2. Turn taking in a conversation is another process that sustains a routine. All competent actors contain in their practical consciousness, or implicit stock of knowledge, a sense of how conversations are to proceed sequentially. People rely on "folk methods" to construct sequences of talk; in so doing, they sustain a routine and, hence, their psychological sense of security and the larger institutional context (think, e.g., about a conversation that did not proceed smoothly in conversational turn taking; recall how disruptive this was for your sense of order and routine).

3. Tact is, in Giddens's view, "the main mechanism that sustains 'trust' or 'ontological security' over long time-space spans." By tact, Giddens means "a latent conceptual agreement among participants in interaction" about just how each party is to gesture and respond and about what is appropriate and inappropriate. People carry implicit stocks of knowledge that define for them what would be "tactful" and what would be "rude" and "intrusive." And they use this sense of tact to regulate their emission of gestures, their talking, and their relative positioning in situations "to remain tactful," thereby sustaining their sense of trust and the larger social order. (Imagine interactions in which tact is not exercised—how they disrupt our routines, our sense of comfort, and our perceptions of an orderly situation).

4. Giddens rejects the idea of "role" as very useful and substitutes the notion of "position." People bring to situations a position or "social identity that carries with it a certain range of prerogatives and obligations," and they emit gestures in a process of mutual positioning, such as locating their bodies in certain points, asserting their prerogatives, and signaling their obligations. In this way, interactions can be routinized, and people can sustain their sense of mutual trust as well as the larger social structures in which their interaction occurs (e.g., examine a

---

[42]Ibid., 72.

[43]This list has been created from what is a much more discursive text.

student–student or professor–student interaction for positioning, and determine how it sustains a sense of trust and the institutional structure.)

5. Much of the coherence of positioning activities is made possible by "frames," which provide formulas for interpreting a context. Interactions tend to be framed in the sense that there are rules that apply to them, but these are not purely normative in the sense of precise instructions for participants. Equally important, frames are more implicitly held, and they operate as markers that assert when certain behaviors and demeanors should be activated (e.g., compare your sense of how to comport yourself at a funeral, at a cocktail party, in class, and in other contexts that are "framed.")

In sum, social structure is extended across time by these techniques that produce and reproduce routines. In so stretching interaction across time in an orderly and predictable manner, people realize their need for a sense of trust in others. In this way, then, Giddens connects the most basic properties of structure (rules and resources) to the most fundamental features of human agents (unconscious motives).

Regionalization. Structuration theory is concerned with the reproduction of relations not only across time but also in space. With the concept of regionalization of interaction, Giddens addresses the intersection of space and time.[44] For interaction is not just serial, moving in time; it is also located in space. Again borrowing from Goffman and also from time and space geography, Giddens introduces the concept of "locale" to account for the physical space in which interaction occurs as well as the contextual knowledge about what is to occur in this space. In a locale, actors are not only establishing their presence in relation to one another, but they are also using their stocks of practical knowledge to interpret the context of the locale. Such interpretations provide them with the relevant frames, the appropriate procedures for tact, and the salient forms for sequencing gestures and talk.

Giddens classifies locales by their "modes." Locales vary in (a) their physical and symbolic boundaries, (b) their duration across time, (c) their span or extension in physical space, and (d) their character, or the ways they connect to other locales and to broader institutional patterns. Locales also vary in the degree to which they force people to sustain a high public presence (what Goffman termed frontstage) or allow retreats to back regions, where public presence is reduced (Goffman's backstage).[45] They also vary in how much disclosure of self (feelings, attitudes, and emotions) they require, some allowing "enclosure," or the withholding of self, and other locales requiring "disclosure" of at least some aspects of self.

Regionalization of interaction through the creation of locales facilitates the maintenance of routines. In turn, the maintenance of routines across time and space sustains institutional structures. Thus, it is through routinized and regionalized systems of interaction that the reflexive capacities of agents reproduce institutional patterns.

---

[44]Ibid., 110–144.

[45]See Erving Goffman, *The Presentation of Self in Everyday Life* (Garden City, NY: Doubleday, 1959); see also Chapter 19 on dramaturgical theorizing.

Figure 20.3 represents one way to summarize Giddens's conceptual scheme and the theoretical traditions from which he has drawn. In a rough sense, as one moves from left to right, the scheme gets increasingly micro, although Giddens would probably not visualize his theory in these macro versus micro terms. But the general message is clear: rules and resources are used to construct structures; these rules and resources are also a part of structural principles that include structural sets; these structural properties are involved in institutionalization of systems of interaction; such interaction systems are organized by the processes of regionalization and routinization; and all these processes are influenced by practical and discursive consciousness, which, in turn, are driven by unconscious motives, especially needs for ontological security.

Figure 20.3   Key Elements of "Structuration Theory"

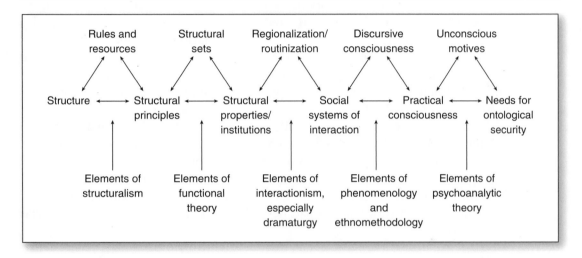

Giddens would not consider his "theory" anything more than a conceptual scheme for describing, analyzing, and interpreting empirical events. Moreover, he would not see this scheme as representing timeless social processes, although the reason his works are read and respected is because these do seem like basic and fundamental processes that transcend time, context, and place.

The British and American Tradition: Network Theorizing on Structure

S. F. Nadel and Network Analysis

S. F. Nadel's *The Theory of Social Structure*[46] was decisive for many anthropologists in separating "structure" and "function." In so doing, Nadel proposed a mode of analysis compatible with contemporary network analysis. Nadel began his

---

[46]S. F. Nadel, *The Theory of Social Structure* (London: Cohen and West, 1957).

argument with the assertion that conceptions of structure in the social sciences are too vague. Indeed, we should begin with a more precise, yet general, notion of all structure: "Structure indicates an ordered arrangement of parts which can be treated as transposable, being relations invariant, while the parts themselves are variable."[47] Thus, structure must concentrate on the properties of relations rather than actors, especially on those properties of relations that are invariant and always occur.

From this general conception of all structure, Nadel proposed that "we arrive at the structure of a society through abstracting from the concrete population and its behavior the pattern or network (or system) of relationships obtaining between actors in their capacity of playing roles relative to one another."[48] Within structures exist embedded "subgroups" characterized by certain types of relationships that hold people together. Thus, social structure is to be viewed as layers and clusters of networks—from the total network of a society to varying congeries of subnetworks. The key to discerning structure is to avoid what he termed "the distribution of relations on the grounds of their similarity and dissimilarity" and concentrate, instead, on the "interlocking of relationships whereby interactions implicit in one determine those occurring in others." That is, one should examine specific configurations of linkages among actors playing roles rather than the statistical distributions of actors in this or that type of role.

From these general ideas, several anthropologists, most notably J. Clyde Mitchell[49] and John A. Barnes,[50] welded the metaphorical imagery of work like Nadel's to the more specific techniques for conceptualizing the properties of networks. Coupled with path-breaking empirical studies,[51] the anthropological tradition began to merge with work in sociology and social psychology. This merger came about, however, only after network analysis had developed in the United States within social psychology.

American Social Psychology and Network Analysis

At about the same time that network analysis was emerging in England in anthropology, a parallel line of development was occurring in the United States, although some figures and ideas in this American program had roots in Europe. Most of this work came from social psychology, a discipline that at the time was unique to

---

[47]Ibid., 8.

[48]Ibid., 21.

[49]J. Clyde Mitchell, "The Concept and Use of Social Networks," in Jeremy F. Boissevain and J. Clyde Mitchell, eds., *Network Analysis: Studies in Human Interaction* (The Hague, Netherlands: Mouton, 1973).

[50]John A. Barnes, "Social Networks" Module in Anthropology No. 26 (Reading, MA: Addison-Wesley, 1974). See also his "Network and Political Processes" in J. F. Boissevain and J. C. Mitchell, eds., *Network Analysis: Studies in Human Interaction* (The Hague, Netherlands: Mouton, 1973).

[51]Perhaps the most significant was Elizabeth Bott, *Family and Social Network: Roles, Norms, and External Relationships in Ordinary Urban Families* (London: Tavistock, 1957, 1971).

America, where the possibilities of experiments in group settings were beginning to create considerable excitement. This experimental tradition is very much alive today, but my concern here is with how the general network approach emerged in America within social psychological research.

Jacob Moreno and Sociometric Techniques. A transplanted European, Jacob Moreno was an eclectic thinker; we have already encountered his ideas on role and role playing in Chapter 17, but perhaps his more enduring contribution to sociology was the development of sociograms.[52] Moreno was interested in the processes of attraction and repulsion among individuals in groups, so he sought a way to conceptualize and measure these processes. What Moreno and subsequent researchers did was to ask group members about their preferences for associating with others in the group. Typically, group members would be asked questions about whom they liked and with whom they would want to spend time or engage in activity. Often, subjects were asked to give their first, second, third, and so on, choices on these and related issues. The results could then be arrayed in a matrix (this was not always done) in which each person's rating of others in a group is recorded (see Figure 20.4 for a simplified example). The construction of such matrices became an important part of network analysis, but equally significant was the development of a sociogram in which group members were arrayed in a visual space, with their relative juxtaposition and connective lines representing the pattern of

Figure 20.4   An Example of an Early Matrix

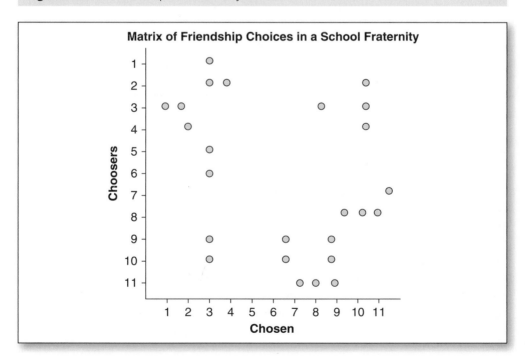

---

[52]Jacob L. Moreno, *Who Shall Survive?* (Washington, DC: Nervous and Mental Diseases Publishing, 1934; republished in revised form by Beacon House, New York, 1953).

choices (those closest and connected being attracted in the direction of the arrows and those distant and unconnected being less attracted to each other). Figure 20.5 illustrates the nature of Moreno's sociograms.

Figure 20.5 An Example of a Sociogram

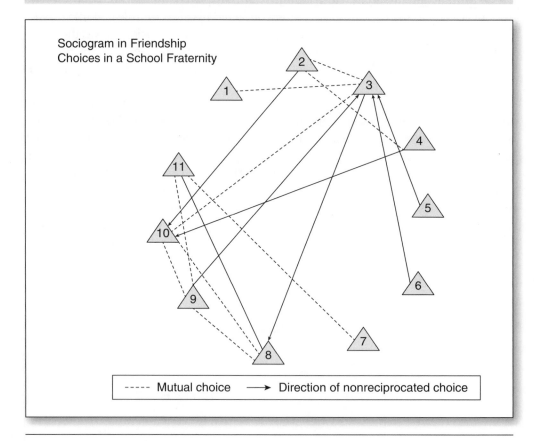

Sociogram in Friendship
Choices in a School Fraternity

----- Mutual choice   ⟶ Direction of nonreciprocated choice

Source: J. Moreno, *Who Shall Survive?* (New York: Beacon House, 1953), p. 171.

This visual representation of choices, as pulled from a matrix, captures the "structure" of preferences or, in Moreno's terms, the patterns of attraction and repulsion among individuals in groups. This visual array can be viewed as a network, because the "connections" among individuals are what is most significant. Moreover, in looking at the network, structural features emerge.

Moreno thus introduced some key conceptual ingredients of contemporary network analysis: the mapping of relations among actors in visual space to represent the structure of these relations. Yet alongside Moreno's sociograms, other research and theoretical traditions were developing and pointing toward the same kind of structural analysis.

Studies of Communications in Groups. Alex Bavelas[53] was one of the first to study how the structure of a network influences the flow of communication in experimental

[53]Alex Bavelas, "A Mathematical Model for Group Structures," *Applied Anthropology* 7 (3, 1948):16–30.

groups. Others such as Harold Leavitt[54] followed Bavelas's lead and also began to study how communication patterns influence the task performances of people in experimental groups. The network structure in these experiments usually involved artificially partitioning groups in such a way that messages could flow only in certain directions and through particular persons. Emerging from Bavelas's original study was the notion of *centrality*, which was evident when positions lie between other positions in a network. When communications had to flow through this central position, certain styles and levels of task performance prevailed, whereas other patterns of information flow produced different results. Figure 20.6 outlines some chains of communication flow that Bavelas originally isolated and that Leavitt later improved.

The results of these experiments are perhaps less important than the image of structure that is offered, although we should note in passing that occupying central positions, such as C in Figure 20.6, exerted the most influence on the emergence of leadership, task performance, and effective communication. These diagrams in

Figure 20.6   Types of Communication Structures in Experimental Groups

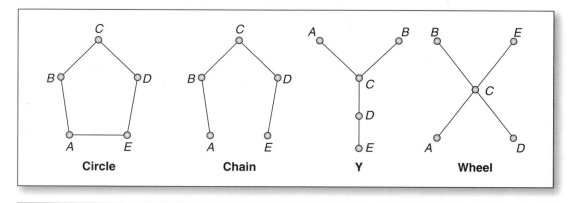

Source: Harold J. Leavitt, "Some Effects of Certain Communication Patterns on Group Performance," *The Journal of Abnormal and Social Psychology* 56 (1951): p. 40.

Figure 20.6 resemble the sociograms, but there are some important differences that became critical in modern network analysis. First, the network is conceptualized in communication studies as consisting of positions rather than of persons, with the result that the pattern of relations among positions is viewed as a basic or generic type of structure. Indeed, different people can occupy the positions, and the experimental results would be the same. Thus, there is a real sense that structure constitutes an emergent reality, above and beyond the individuals involved. Second, the idea that the links among positions involve flows of resources—in these studies,

---

[54]Harold J. Leavitt, "Some Effects of Certain Communication Patterns on Group Performance," *Journal of Abnormal and Social Psychology* 56 (1951):38–50; Harold J. Leavitt and Kenneth E. Knight, "Most 'Efficient' Solution to Communication Networks: Empirical versus Analytical Search," *Sociometry* 26 (1963):260–267.

information and messages—anticipates the thrust of much network analysis. Of course, we could also see Moreno's sociograms as involving flows of affect and preferences among people, but the idea is less explicit and less embedded in a conception of networks as relations among positions.

Thus, these early experimental studies on communication created a new conceptualization of networks as (a) composed of positions, (b) connected by relations, and (c) involving the flows of resources.

Early Gestalt and Balance Approaches: Heider, Newcomb, Cartwright, and Harary

Fritz Heider,[55] who is often considered the founder of Gestalt psychology, developed some of the initial concepts in various theories of "balance" and "equilibrium" in cognitive perceptions. In Heider's view, individuals seek to balance[56] their cognitive conceptions; in his famous P, O, X model, Heider argued that a person (P) will attempt to balance cognitions toward an object or entity (X) with those of another person (O). If a person (P) has positive sentiments toward an object (X) and another person (O) but O has negative sentiments toward X, then a state of *cognitive imbalance* exists. A person has two options if the imbalance is to be resolved: (1) to change sentiments toward X or (2) to alter sentiments toward O. By altering sentiments toward X to the negative, cognitive balance is achieved, because P and O now reveal a negative orientation toward X, thereby affirming their positive feelings toward each other. Or by altering sentiments directed toward O to the negative, cognitive balance is achieved because P has a positive attitude toward X and negative feelings for O, who has a negative orientation to X.

Figure 20.7   The Dynamics of Cognitive Balance

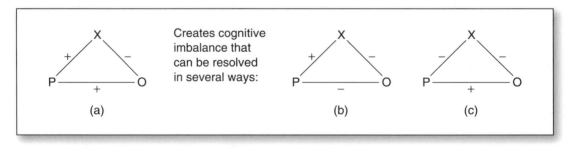

(a)

Creates cognitive imbalance that can be resolved in several ways:

(b)

(c)

Source: Adapted from Fritz Heider, *The Psychology of Interpersonal Relations* (New York, Wiley: 1958), with (+) and (–) used instead of Heider's notation.

---

[55]Fritz Heider, "Attitudes and Cognitive Organization," *Journal of Psychology* 2 (1946):107–112. For the best review of his thought as it accumulated over four decades, see his *The Psychology of Interpersonal Relations* (New York: Wiley, 1958).

[56]The process of "attribution" was, along with the notion of "balance," the cornerstones of Heider's Gestalt approach.

Although Heider did not explicitly do so, this conception of balance can be expressed in algebraic terms, as is done in Figure 20.7 by multiplying the cognitive links in Figure 20.7(a): $(+) \times (-) \times (+) = (-)$, or imbalance. This imbalance can be resolved by changing the sign of the links toward a $(-)$ or a $(+)$, as is done for Figures 20.7(b) and 20.7(c). By multiplying the signs for the lines in (b) or (c), a $(+)$ product is achieved, indicating that the relation is now in balance.

Theodore Newcomb[57] extrapolated Heider's logic to the analysis of interpersonal communication. Newcomb argued that this tendency to seek balance applies equally to interpersonal as well as to the intrapersonal situations represented by the P, O, X model, and he constructed an A, B, X model to emphasize this conclusion. A person (A) and another (B) who communicate and develop positive sentiments will, in an effort to maintain balance with each other, develop similar sentiments toward a third entity (X), which can be an object, an idea, or a third person. However, if A's orientation to X is very strong in either a positive or a negative sense and B's orientation is just the opposite, several options are available: (1) A can convince B to change its orientation toward X, and vice versa, or (2) A can change its orientation to B, and vice versa. Figure 20.8 represents this interpersonal situation for A, B, X in the same manner as Heider's P, O, X model in Figure 20.7.

Figure 20.8 The Dynamics of Interpersonal Balance

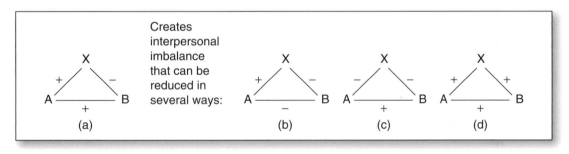

Source: Adapted from Theodore Newcomb, "An Approach to the Study of Communicative Arts," *Psychological Review* 60 (1953): pp. 393–404, with alterations to Newcomb's system of notation.

Situation 20.8(a) is in interpersonal imbalance, as can be determined by multiplying the signs $(+) \times (+) \times (-) = (-)$, or imbalance. Figures 20.8(b), 20.8(c), and 20.8(d) represent three options that restore balance to the relations among A, B, and X. (In Figures 20.8(a), 20.8(b), and 20.8(c), the product of multiplying the signs now equals a $(+)$, or balance.)

Heider's and Newcomb's approaches were to stimulate research that would more explicitly employ mathematics as a way to conceptualize the links in

[57]Theodore M. Newcomb, "An Approach to the Study of Communicative Acts," *Psychological Review* 60 (1953):393–404. See his earlier work where these ideas took form, *Personality and Social Change* (New York: Dryden, 1943).

interpersonal networks. The key breakthrough had come earlier[58] in the use of the mathematical theory of linear graphs. Somewhat later, in the mid-1950s, Dorin Cartwright and Frank Harary[59] similarly employed the logic of signed-digraph theory to examine balance in larger groups consisting of more than three persons. Figure 20.9 presents a model developed by Cartwright and Harary for a larger set of actors.

Figure 20.9 An S-Graph of Eight Points

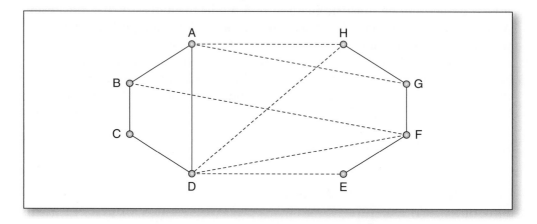

Source: D. Cartwright and F. Harary, "Structural Balance: A Generalization of Heider's Theory," *Psychological Review* 63, no. 5 (1956), p. 286.

The basic idea is much the same as in the P, O, X and A, B, X models, but now the nature of sentiments is specified by dotted (negative) and solid (positive) lines. By multiplying the signs—(+) = solid line; (−) = dotted line—across all the lines, points of imbalance and balance can be identified. For Cartwright and Harary, one way to

---

[58]For example, D. König, *Theorie der Endlichen und Undlichen Graphen* (Leipzig, Teubner, 1936 but reissued, New York: Chelsea, 1950), is, as best I can tell, the first work on graph theory. It appears that the first important application of this theory to the social sciences came with R. Duncan Luce and A. D. Perry, "A Method of Matrix Analysis of Group Structure," *Psychometrika* 14 (1949):94–116, followed by R. Duncan Luce, "Connectivity and Generalized Cliques in Sociometric Group Structure," *Psychometrika* 15 (1950):169–190. Frank Harary's Graph Theory (Reading, MA: Addison-Wesley, 1969) later became a standard reference, which had been preceded by Frank Harary and R. Z. Norman, *Graph Theory as a Mathematical Model in Social Science* (Ann Arbor, MI: University of Michigan Institute for Social Research, 1953) and Frank Harary, R. Z. Norman, and Dorin Cartwright, *Structural Models: An Introduction to the Theory of Directed Graphs* (New York: Wiley, 1965).

[59]Dorin Cartwright and Frank Harary, "Structural Balance: A Generalization of Heider's Theory," *Psychological Review* 63 (1956):277–293. For more recent work, see their "Balance and Clusterability: An Overview," in Holland and Leinhardt, (eds.), *Perspectives on Social Network Research* (New York: Academic, 1979).

assess balance is to multiply the various cycles on the graph—for example, ABCD, ABCDEFGH, HDFG, DFE, and so on. If multiplying the signs for each connection yields a positive outcome, then this structure is in balance. Another procedure is specified by a theorem: An S-graph is balanced if and only if all paths joining the same pair of points have the same sign.

The significance of introducing graph theory into balance models is that it facilitated the representation of social relations with mathematical conventions—something that Moreno, Heider, and Newcomb had failed to do. But the basic thrust of earlier analysis was retained: graph theory could represent directions of links between actors (this is done by simply placing arrows on the lines as they intersect with a point); graph theory could represent two different types of relations between points, to be specified by double lines and arrows; it could represent different positive or negative states (the sign being denoted by solid or dotted lines); it offered a better procedure for analyzing more complex social structures; and unlike the matrices behind Moreno's and others' sociograms, graph theory would make them more amenable to mathematical and statistical manipulation. Thus, although the conventions of graph theory have not remained exactly the same, especially as adopted for network use, the logic of the analysis that graph theory facilitated was essential for the development of the network approach beyond crude matrices and sociograms or simple triadic relations to more complex networks involving the flows of multiple resources in varying directions.

The Development of Network Analysis

During the last forty years, work within anthropology, social psychology, sociology, communications, psychology, geography, and political science has converged on the conceptualization of "structure" as "social networks." During this period, rather metaphorical and intuitive ideas about networks have been reconceptualized in various types of algebra, graph theory, and probability theory. This convergence has, in some ways, been a mixed blessing. On the one hand, grounding concepts in mathematics can give them greater precision and provide a common language for pulling together a common conceptual core from the overlapping metaphors of different disciplines. On the other hand, the extensive use of mathematics and computer algorithms far exceeds the technical skills of most social scientists. More important, the use and application of quantitative techniques, per se, have become a preoccupation among many who seem less and less interested in explaining how the actual social world operates. Nonetheless, despite these drawbacks, the potential for network analysis as a theoretical approach is great because it captures an important property of social structure—patterns of relations among social units, whether people, collectivities, locations, or status positions. As Georg Simmel emphasized, at the core of any conceptualization of social structure is the notion that structure consists of relations and links among entities. Network analysis forces us to conceptualize carefully the nature of the entities and relations as well as the properties and dynamics that inhere in these relations.[60]

Basic Theoretical Concepts in Network Analysis

Points and Nodes. The units of a network can be persons, positions, corporate or collective actors, or virtually any entity that can be connected to another entity. In general, these units are conceptualized as *points or nodes*, and they are typically symbolized by letters or numbers. In Figure 20.10, a very simple network is drawn, with each letter representing a point or node in the network. One goal of network analysis, then, is to array in visual space a pattern of connections among the units that are related to each other. In a mathematical sense, it makes little difference what the points and nodes are, and this has great virtue because it provides a common set of analytical tools for analyzing very diverse phenomena. Another goal of network analysis is to explain the dynamics of various patterns of ties among nodes, although this goal is often subordinated to developing computer algorithms for representing the connections among points and nodes in more complex networks than the one portrayed in Figure 20.10.

Figure 20.10   A Simple Network

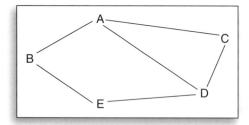

Links, Ties, and Connections. The letters in Figure 20.10 represent the nodes or points of a structure. The lines connecting the letters indicate that these points are attached to each other in a particular pattern. The concept of *tie* is the most frequent way to denote this property of a network, and so in Figure 20.10, there are ties between *A-B, A-C, A-D, B-E, C-D,* and *D-E.* We not only need to know that points in a network are connected, but we also must have some idea of what it is that connects these points. That is, what is the nature of the tie? What resources flow from node to node? From the point of view of graph theory, it does not make much difference, but when the substantive concerns of sociologists are considered, it is important to know the nature of the ties. As we saw in the early sociograms constructed by Jacob Moreno, the ties involved emotional states such as liking and friendship, and the nodes themselves were individual people. But the nature of the tie can be

---

[60]For some readable overviews on network analysis, see Barry Wellman, "Network Analysis: Some Basic Principles," *Sociological Theory* (1983):155–200; Jeremy F. Boissevain and J. Clyde Mitchell, (eds.), *Network Analysis* (The Hague, Netherlands: Mouton, 1973) and *Social Networks in Urban Situations* (Manchester: Manchester University Press, 1969); J. A. Barnes, "Social Networks" Module in Anthropology No. 26 (Reading, MA: Addison-Wesley, 1974); and Barry S. Wellman and S. D. Berkowitz, *Social Structures: A Network Approach* (Cambridge, UK: Cambridge University Press, 1988). Somewhat more technical summaries of recent network research can be found in Samuel Leinhardt, (ed.), *Social Networks: A Developing Paradigm* (New York: Academic, 1977); Paul Holland and Samuel Leinhardt, (eds.), *Perspectives in Social Network Research* (New York: Academic, 1979); Ronald S. Burt, "Models of Network Structure," *Annual Review of Sociology* 6 (1980):79–141; and Peter Marsden and Nan Lin, (eds.), *Social Structure and Network Analysis* (Newbury Park, CA: Sage, 1982). For advanced research on networks, consult recent issues of the journal *Social Networks*.

diverse: the flow of information, money, goods, services, influence, emotions, deference, prestige, and virtually any force or resource that binds actors to each other.

Often, as we saw in Chapter 15 on exchange network theory, the ties are conceptualized as resources. When points or nodes are represented by different letters, this denotes that actors are exchanging different resources, such as prestige for advice, money for services, deference for information, and so on. Conversely, if they were exchanging similar resources, the nodes would be represented by the same letter and subscripted numbers, such as A_1, A_2, and A_3. But this is only one convention; the nature of the tie can also be represented by different kinds of lines, such as dotted, dashed, or colored lines. In graph theory, the lines can also reveal direction, indicated by arrows. Moreover, if multiple resources are connecting positions in the graph, multiple lines (and, if necessary, arrows specifying direction) would be used. Thus, the graph represented in Figure 20.10 is obviously very simple, but it communicates the basic goal of network analysis: to represent in visual space the structure of connections among units.

One way to rise above the diversity of resources examined in network analysis is to visualize resource flows in networks for three generic types: materials, symbols, and emotions. That is, what connects persons, positions, and corporate actors in the social world is the flow of (a) symbols (information, ideas, values, norms, messages, etc.), (b) materials (physical things and perhaps symbols, such as money, that give access to physical things), and (c) emotions (approval, respect, liking, pleasure, etc.). In non-sociological uses of networks, the ties or links can be other types of phenomena, but when the ties are social, they exist along material, symbolic, and emotional dimensions.

The configuration of ties can also be represented as a matrix, and in most network studies, the matrix is created before the actual network diagram. Moreover, when large numbers of nodes are involved, the matrix is often a better way to grasp the complexity of connections than a diagram, which would become too cumbersome to be useful. Figure 20.11 presents the logic of a matrix, using the very simple network represented in Figure 20.11. The mathematics of such matrices can become very complicated, but the general point is clear: to cross-tabulate which nodes are connected to each other (as has been done inside the triangular area of the matrix in Figure 20.11). If possible, once the matrix is constructed, it can be used to generate a graph, something like the one in Figure 20.10. With the use of sophisticated computer algorithms in network analysis, the matrix is the essential step for subsequent analysis; an actual diagram might not be drawn because the mathematical manipulations are too complex. Yet most matrices will eventually be converted in network analysis into some form of visual representation in space—perhaps not a network digraph, but some other technique, such as three-dimensional bar graphs or clusters of points, will be used to express in visual space the relations among the units.

Patterns and Configurations of Ties

From a network perspective, social structure is conceptualized as the form of ties among positions or nodes. That is, what is the pattern or configuration among what resources flowing among what sets of nodes or points in a graph? To answer questions like this, network sociology addresses several properties of networks. The most

Figure 20.11   A Simple Matrix

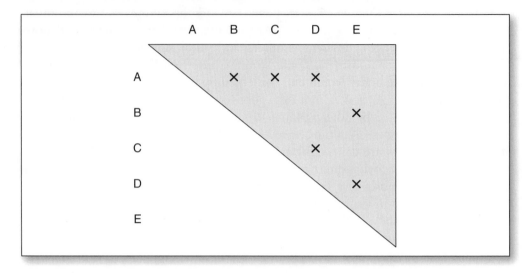

important of these are number of ties, directedness, reciprocity of ties, transitivity of ties, density of ties, strength of ties, bridges, brokerage, centrality, and equivalence.

Number of Ties. An important piece of information in performing network analysis is the total number of ties among all points and nodes. Naturally, the number of potential ties depends on the number of points in a graph and the number of resources involved in connecting the points. Yet, for any given number of points and resources, it is important to calculate both the actual and potential number of ties that are (and can be) generated. This information can then be used to calculate other dimensions of a network structure.

Directedness. It is important to know the direction in which resources flow through a network; so, as indicated earlier, arrows are often placed on the lines of a graph, making it a digraph. As a consequence, a better sense of the structure of the network emerges. For example, if the lines denote information, we would have a better understanding of how the ties in the network are constructed and maintained, because we could see the direction and sequence of the information flow.

Reciprocity of Ties. Another significant feature of networks is the reciprocity of ties among positions. That is, is the flow of resources one-way, or is it reciprocated for any two positions? If the flow of resources is reciprocated, then it is conventional to have double lines with arrows pointing in the direction of the resource flow. Moreover, if different resources flow back and forth, this too can be represented. Surprisingly, conventions about how to represent this multiplicity of resource flows are not fully developed. One way to denote the flow of different resources is to use varying-colored lines or numbered lines; another is to label the points with the same letter subscripted (i.e., $A_1, A_2, A_3, \ldots$) if similar resources flow and with varying letters (i.e., A, B, C, D) if the resources connecting the actors are different. But whatever the notation, the extent and nature of reciprocity in ties become an important property of a social network.

Transitivity of Ties. A critical dimension of networks is the level of transitivity among sets of positions. *Transitivity* refers to the degree to which there is a "transfer" of a relation among subsets of positions. For example, if nodes A_1 and A_2 are connected with positive affect and positions A_2 and A_3 are similarly connected, we can ask, will positions A_1 and A_3 also be tied together with positive affect? If the answer to this question is "yes," then the relations among A_1, A_2, and A_3 are transitive. Discovering patterns of transitivity in a network can be important because it helps explain other critical properties of a network, such as density and the formation of cliques.

Density of Ties. A significant property of a network is its degree of connectedness, or the extent to which nodes reveal the maximum possible number of ties. The more the actual number of ties among nodes approaches the total possible number among a set of nodes, the greater is the overall *density* of a network.[61] Figure 20.12 compares the same five-node network under conditions of high and low density of ties.

Figure 20.12   High- and Low-Density Networks

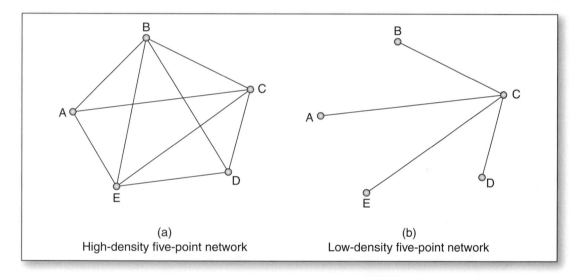

| (a) | (b) |
| High-density five-point network | Low-density five-point network |

Of even greater interest are sub-densities of ties within a larger network structure. Such sub-densities, which are sometimes referred to as *cliques*, reveal strong, reciprocated, and transitive ties among a particular subset of positions within the overall network.[62] For example, in Figure 20.13, there are three clusters of dense ties in the network, thus revealing three distinct cliques within the larger network.

Strength of Ties. Yet another crucial aspect of a network is the volume and level of resources that flow among positions. A weak tie is one where few or sporadic

---

[61]There are other ways to measure density; this definition is meant to be illustrative of the general idea.

[62]The terminology on sub-densities varies. "Clique" is still the most prominent term, but "alliances" has been offered as an alternative. Moreover, the old sociological standbys "group" and "subgroup" seem to have made a comeback in network analysis.

Figure 20.13   A Network with Three Distinct Cliques

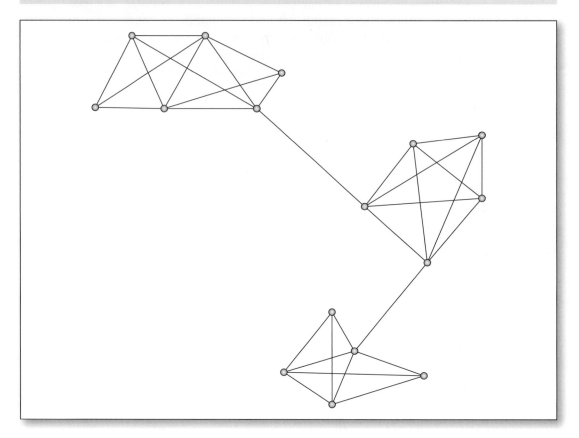

amounts of resources flow among positions, whereas a strong tie evidences a high level of resource flow. The overall structure of a network is significantly influenced by clusters and configurations of strong and weak ties. For example, if the ties in the cliques in Figure 20.13 are all strong, the network is composed of cohesive sub-groupings that have relatively sparse ties to one another. On the other hand, if the ties in these sub-densities are weak, then the subgroupings will involve less intense linkages,[63] with the result that the structure of the whole network will be very different from what would be the case if these ties were strong.

Bridges. When networks reveal sub-densities, it is always interesting to know which positions connect the sub-densities, or cliques, to one another. For example, in Figure 20.14, those ties connecting sub-densities are bridges and are crucial in maintaining the overall connectedness of the network. Indeed, if one removed one of these positions or severed the tie, the structure of the network would be very different—it would become three separate networks. These bridging ties are

---

[63]At one time, "intensity" appears to have been used in preference to "strength." See Mitchell, "The Concept and Use of Social Networks." It appears that Granovetter's classic article shifted usage in favor of "strength" and "weakness." See Note 5.

Figure 20.14 A Network With Brokerage Potential

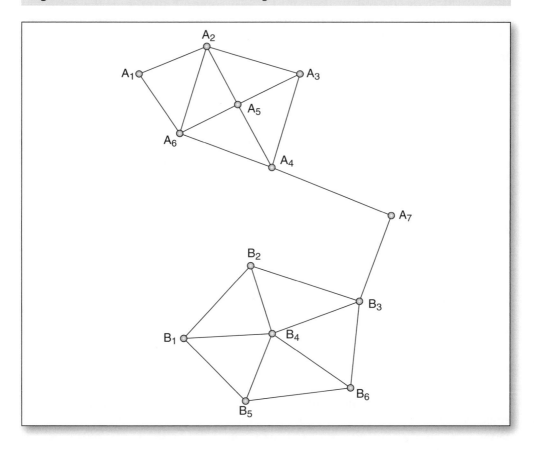

typically weak,[64] because each position in the bridge is more embedded in the flow of resources of a particular sub-density or clique. But, nonetheless, such ties are often crucial for the maintenance of a larger social structure; it is not surprising that the number and nature of bridges within a network structure are highlighted in network analysis.

Brokerage. At times, a particular position is outside subsets of positions but is crucial to the flow of resources to and from these subsets. This position is often in a brokerage situation because its activities determine the nature and level of resources that flow to and from subsets of positions.[65] In Figure 20.14, position A_7 is potentially a

---

[64]See Mark Granovetter, "The Strength of Weak Ties," *American Journal of Sociology* 78 (1973):1360–1380 and "The Strength of Weak Ties: A Network Theory Revisited," *Sociological Theory* (1983):201–233. The basic network "law" from Granovetter's original study can be expressed as follows: *The degree of integration of a network composed of highly dense subcliques is a positive function of the extensiveness of bridges, involving weak ties, among these subcliques.*

[65]Ronald S. Burt has, perhaps, done the most interesting work here. See, for example, his *Toward a Structural Theory of Action* (New York: Academic, 1982) and "A Structural Theory of Interlocking Corporate Directorships," *Social Networks* 1 (1978–1979):415–435.

broker for the flow of resources from subsets consisting of positions A_1, A_2, A_3, A_4, and A_5 to B_1, B_2, B_3, B_4, B_5, and B_6. Position A_7 can become a broker if (a) the distinctive resources that pass to, and from, these two subsets are needed or valued by at least one of these subsets and (b) direct ties, or bridges, between the two subsets do not exist. Indeed, a person or actor in a brokerage position often seeks to prevent the development of bridges (like those in Figure 20.14) and to manipulate the flow of resources such that at least one and if possible both subsets are highly dependent on its activities.

Centrality. An extremely important property of a network is *centrality*, as was noted for Bavelas's and Leavitt's studies of communication in experimental groups. There are several ways to calculate centrality:[66] (a) the number of other positions with which a particular position is connected, (b) the number of points between which a position falls, and (c) the closeness of a position to others in a network. Although these three measures might denote somewhat different points as central, the theoretical idea is fairly straightforward: some positions in a network mediate the flow of resources by virtue of their patterns of ties to other points. For example, in Figure 20.12, point C is central in a network consisting of positions A, B, C, D, and E; or, to take another example, points A_5 and B_4 in Figure 20.14 are more central than other positions because they are directly connected to all, or to most, positions and because a higher proportion of resources will tend to pass through these positions. A network can also reveal several nodes of centrality, as is evident in Figure 20.15. Moreover, patterns of centrality can shift over time. Thus, many of the dynamics of network structure revolve around the nature and pattern of centrality.

Equivalence. When positions stand in the same relation to another position, they are considered *equivalent*. When this idea was first introduced into network analysis, it was termed *structural equivalence* and restricted to situations in which a set of positions is connected to another position or set of positions in exactly the same way.[67] For example, positions C_2, C_3, and C_4 in Figure 20.15 are structurally equivalent because they reveal the same relation to position C_1. Figure 20.15 provides another illustration of structural equivalence, as well. A_2, A_3, and A_4 are structurally equivalent to A_1; similarly, D_2, D_3, and D_4 are equivalent to D_1, and A_1, C_1, and D_1 are structurally equivalent to B.

 This original formulation of equivalence was limited, however, in that positions could be equivalent only when *actually connected to the same position*. We might also want to consider all positions as equivalent when they are connected to different positions but in the same form, pattern, or manner. For instance, in

---

[66]The definitive works here are Linton C. Freeman, "Centrality in Social Networks: Conceptual Clarification," *Social Networks* 1 (1979):215–239 and Linton C. Freeman, Douglas Boeder, and Robert R. Mulholland, "Centrality in Social Networks: Experimental Results," *Social Networks* 2 (1979):119–141. See also Linton C. Freeman, "Centered Graphs and the Structure of Ego Networks," *Mathematical Social Sciences* 3 (1982):291–304 and Philip Bonacich, "Power and Centrality: A Family of Measures," *American Journal of Sociology* 92 (1987):1170–1182.

[67]François Lorrain and Harrison C. White, "Structural Equivalence of Individuals in Social Networks," *Journal of Mathematical Sociology* 1 (1971):49–80 and Harrison C. White, Scott A. Boorman, and Ronald L. Breiger, "Social Structure from Multiple Networks: I. Block Models of Roles and Positions," *American Journal of Sociology* 8 (1976):730–780.

Figure 20.15   Equivalence in Social Networks

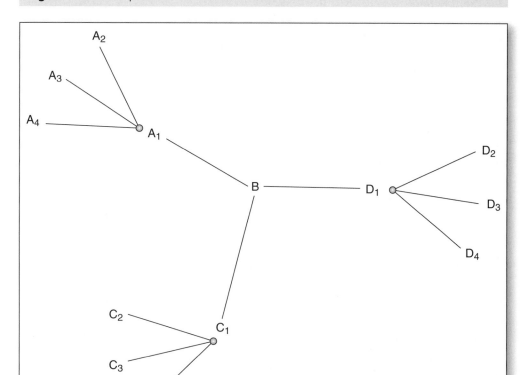

Figure 20.15, A_2, A_3, A_4, D_2, D_3, D_4, C_2, C_3, and C_4 can all be seen as equivalent because they bear the *same type* of relation to another position—that is, to A_1, D_1, and C_1, respectively. This way of conceptualizing equivalence is termed *regular equivalence*,[68] and in a sense, it subsumes the original notion of *structural equivalence*. That is, structural equivalence, wherein the equivalent *positions must actually be connected to the same position in the same way*, is a particular type of a more general equivalence phenomenon. These terms, *structural* and *regular,* are awkward, but they have become conventional in network analysis, so we are stuck with them. The critical idea is that the number and nature of equivalent positions in a network have important influences on the dynamics of the network.[69] The general

---

[68]Lee Douglas Sailer, "Structural Equivalence," *Social Networks* 1 (1978):73–90; John Paul Boyd, "Finding and Testing Regular Equivalence," *Social Networks* 24 (2002):315–331; John Paul Boyd and Kai J. Jonas, "Are Social Equivalences Ever Regular? Permutation and Exact Tests," 32 (2001):87–123; Katherine Faust, "Comparison of Methods for Positional Analysis: Structural Equivalence and General Equivalence, " *Social Networks* 10 (1988):313–341.

[69]In many ways Karl Marx's idea that those who stand in a common relationship to the means of production have common interests is an equivalence agreement. Thus, the idea of equivalence is not new to sociology—just the formalism used to express it is new.

hypothesis is that actors in structurally equivalent or regularly equivalent positions will behave or act in similar ways.

Can Network Analysis Make Conceptions of Structure More Precise?

The mathematics of network analysis can become quite complicated, as can the computer algorithms used to analyze data sets of the processes outlined above. This listing of concepts is somewhat metaphorical because it eliminates the formal and quantitative thrust of much network analysis. Indeed, much network analysis bypasses the conversion of matrices into graphs like those in the various figures presented and, instead, performs mathematical and statistical operations on just the matrices themselves. Yet if network analysis is to realize its full theoretical (as opposed to methodological) potential, it might be wise to use concepts, at least initially, in a more verbal and intuitive sense.

Few would disagree with the notion that social structure is composed of relations among positions. But is this all that social structure is? Can the concepts denoting nodes, ties, and patterns of ties (number, strength, reciprocity, transitivity, bridges, brokerage, centrality, and equivalence) capture all the critical properties of social structure?

The answer to these questions is probably "no." Social structure probably involves other crucial processes that are not captured by these concepts. Yet a major property of social structure *is* its network characteristics, as Georg Simmel was perhaps the first to really appreciate. For, whatever other dimensions social structure might reveal—cultural, behavioral, ecological, temporal, psychological, and so forth—its backbone is a system of interconnections among actors who occupy positions relative to one another and who exchange resources. And so network analysis has great potential for theories of social structure. Has this potential been realized? Probably not, for several reasons.

First, as just noted, network analysis is overly methodological and concerned with generating quantitative techniques for arraying data in matrices and then converting the matrices into descriptions of particular networks (whether as graphs or as equations). As long as this is the case, network sociology will remain primarily a tool for empirical description.

Second, there has been little effort to develop principles of network dynamics, per se. Few[70] seem to ask theoretical questions within the network tradition itself. For example, how does the degree of density, centrality, equivalence, bridging, and brokerage influence the nature of the network and the flow of relations among positions

---

[70]There are, of course, some notable exceptions to this statement. For an example, John Levi Martin, *Social Structures* (Princeton, NJ: Princeton University Press, 2009), "Structures of Power in Naturally Occurring Communities," *Social Networks* 20 (1998):197–225, "Formation and Stabilization of Vertical Hierarchies among Adolescents, *Social Psychology Quarterly* (2010); Ronald S. Burt, *Toward a Structural Theory of Action, and Structural Holes: The Social Structure of Competition* (Cambridge, MA: Harvard University Press, 1992); and Noah E. Friedkin, *A Structural Theory of Social Influence* (Cambridge, UK: Cambridge University Press, 1998).

in the network? There are many empirical descriptions of events that touch on this question but few actual theoretical laws or principles.[71]

Third, network sociology has yet to translate traditional theoretical concerns and concepts into network terminology in a way that highlights the superiority, or at least the viability, of using network theoretical constructs for mainstream theory in sociology. For example, power, hierarchy, differentiation, integration, stratification, conflict, and many other concerns of sociological theory have not been adequately reconceptualized in network terms, and hence, it is unlikely that sociological theory will adopt or incorporate a network approach until this translation of traditional questions occurs.

All these points, however, need to be qualified because numerous sociologists have actually sought to develop laws of network processes and to address traditional theoretical concerns with network concepts. Although these efforts are far from constituting a coherent theory of network dynamics, they do illustrate the potential utility of network sociology, as we saw, for example, in the review of network exchange theory in Chapter 15.

Conclusions

Theorizing on social structure is highly diverse, perhaps not so surprising given the lack of a clear definition of what the concept of "structure" denotes. As the theories reviewed here demonstrate, there is a cultural dimension of structure, consisting of rules, beliefs, ideologies, and value premises. There are also sets of principles or underlying logics that, in still unknown ways, generate structures; some of these may be cultural, while others are potentially lodged in human neurology. There is also a relational property of social structure consisting of positions and notes that are connected by the movement of resources among actors at particular nodes. What sociology has, then, is the contours of a more rigorous conceptualization of the properties of structure, although the dynamic aspects of structure can be found in the many theories that are outlined in the chapters of this book. These dynamics inhere in the forms of networks; in the levels of power, inequality, and conflict; in the nature of interaction and exchange; in the dramaturgical presentations; in the dynamics of roles and status locations; in the use of ethnomethods; and in my other topics of theoretical sociology. What has not been done, however, is an integration of these into a more general theory on the properties and dynamics of structures. Giddens's structuration theory is one example of an effort to achieve this necessary integration, and while it is provocative, it is also incomplete. Thus, the agenda for structural sociology is clear: define the properties and dimensions of structures and then use existing theories in various combinations to explain the operative dynamics that produce, reproduce, and change these properties and dimensions of structure.

---

[71]Mark Granovetter, "The Theory-Gap in Social Network Analysis" in *Perspectives on Social Network Research*, ed. P. Holland and S. Leinhardt (New York: Academic, 1979).

CHAPTER 21

Cultural Theorizing

F rench structuralism has exerted an enormous influence on modern social thought—from anthropology and sociology to literary criticism, with many other fields of inquiry in between. These many forms of structuralist analyses vary enormously, but they all have a common theme: there is a deep underlying structure to most surface phenomena, and this structure can be conceptualized as a series of generative rules that can create a wide variety of empirical phenomena. That is, empirically observable phenomena—from a literary text to a social structure— are constructed in conformity to an implicit logic and background assumptions. Some see this logic as lodged in the biology of the human brain, whereas others would view this underlying structure as a cultural product.

Purely structuralist analysis has had its greatest impact in linguistics and literary criticism, and for a time it enjoyed considerable popularity in anthropology and sociology.[1] Over the last two decades, however, rigid and orthodox structuralist approaches emphasizing searches for those deep and universal structures that order all phenomena have declined in sociology. In their place, several more eclectic perspectives have emerged. These theories borrow elements of structuralist analysis and blend them with other conceptual traditions, such as conflict theory, Durkheimian functionalism, dramaturgy, and phenomenology. There is still an emphasis on symbolic codes and the ways in which these are produced by the underlying generative rules, logics,

---

[1]For some general works reviewing structuralism, see Anthony Giddens, "Structuralism, Post-structuralism and the Production of Culture," in *Social Theory Today*, ed. A. Giddens and J. H. Turner (Cambridge, UK: Polity Press, 2000); S. Clarke, *The Foundations of Structuralism* (Sussex, UK: Harvester, 1981); J. Sturrock (ed.), *Structuralism and Science* (Oxford, UK: Oxford University Press, 1979); W. G. Runciman, "What Is Structuralism?" in *Sociology in Its Place* (Cambridge, UK: Cambridge University Press, 1970), 45–58; Ino Rossi, *From the Sociology of Symbols to the Sociology of Signs* (New York: Columbia University Press, 1983) and Ino Rossi (ed.), *Structural Sociology* (New York: Columbia University Press, 1982); Jacques Ehrmann, *Structuralism* (New York: Doubleday, 1970); Philip Pettit, *The Concept of Structuralism: A Critical Analysis* (Berkeley: University of California Press, 1977); Charles C. Lemert, "The Uses of French Structuralism in Sociology" and Michelle Lamont and Robert Wuthnow, "Recent Cultural Sociology in Europe and the United States," in *Frontiers of Social Theory*, ed. G. Ritzer (New York: Columbia University Press, 1990).

and assumptions, but such codes are causally influenced by material conditions and are subject to interpretation by lay agents. Thus, just as Claude Lévi-Strauss "turned Durkheim on his head" in seeing social structure as a reflection of mental structures, many recent efforts have put Émile Durkheim back on his feet, emphasizing the ritual basis for charging up cultural symbols, while augmenting the analysis of symbol systems with Marxian conflict analysis, dramaturgy, interactionism and phenomenology, and other traditions in theoretical sociology. The result has been a revival of "cultural sociology" in a less ponderous guise than Parsonian functionalism, although I have emphasized in my own work a cultural approach that borrows heavily from Parsons's and Luhmann's conceptualizations of generalized symbolic media of exchange. In these newer approaches, the structure of cultural codes is causally linked not only to the behavioral and interpersonal activities of individuals but also to the institutional parameters within which such activities are conducted.

Although several possible candidates can be seen as squarely in this more eclectic structuralist approach, I have selected for review here the French scholar Pierre Bourdieu and two American theorists, Robert Wuthnow and Jeffrey C. Alexander. Their work can provide a sample of what will be termed here cultural structuralism. Each draws from Durkheim, incorporates some of the insights of Lévi-Strauss, without viewing social structure as a mere surface manifestation of cultural codes, and connects the French tradition to theories emphasizing the causal priority of material social conditions and the interpersonal processes that create, reproduce, and change cultural systems. For my approach to cultural analysis, see my discussion of cultural integration in Chapter 13, on evolutionary theorizing.

Cultural Analysis: Robert Wuthnow

Even though there has been a revival of cultural analysis in sociology,[2] the nature of "culture" is still rather vaguely conceptualized, much as is the case for social structure. The result is that just about anything—physical objects, ideas, worldviews, subjective states, behaviors, rituals, thoughts, emotions, and so on—can be considered "cultural." One effort to narrow somewhat the domain of cultural analysis is the work of Robert Wuthnow. Although most of his research has focused on religion, he has sought a more general theoretical approach.[3]

This theoretical effort preaches against positivism, incorrectly portrayed as sheer empiricism, but it nonetheless synthesizes several theoretical traditions and, in so doing,

---

[2]For a review, see Robert Wuthnow and Marsha Witten, "New Directions in the Study of Culture," *Annual Review of Sociology* 14 (1988):149–167. See also Robert Wuthnow, James Davidson Hunter, Albert Bergesen, and Edith Kurzweil, *Cultural Analysis: The World of Peter L. Berger, Mary Douglas, Michel Foucault, and Jürgen Habermas* (London: Routledge and Kegan Paul, 1984).

[3]For examples of the work on religion, see Robert Wuthnow, *The Consciousness Reformation* (Berkeley: University of California Press, 1976) and *Experimentation in American Religion* (Berkeley: University of California Press, 1978); for a review of a more general theory, see Robert Wuthnow, *Meaning and Moral Order: Explorations in Cultural Analysis* (Berkeley: University of California Press, 1987). For a review of this work, see Jonathan H. Turner, "Cultural Analysis and Social Theory," *American Journal of Sociology* 94 (1988):637–644.

develops some general propositions on cultural processes.[4] Wuthnow's approach is, therefore, one of the more creative approaches to structuralism, primarily because it blends structuralist concerns about the relations among symbolic codes with other theoretical traditions. Among these other traditions are elements of dramaturgy, institutional analysis, and subjective approaches that owe some inspiration to phenomenology.

Cultural Structure, Ritual, and Institutional Context

In Wuthnow's view, it is wise to avoid "radical subjectivity," for the "problem of meaning may well be more of a curse than a blessing in cultural analysis."[5] It is best, he argues, to move away from an overemphasis on attitudes, beliefs, and meanings of individuals because these are difficult to measure. Instead, the structure of culture as revealed through observable communications and interactions is a more appropriate line of inquiry. In this way, one does "not become embroiled in the ultimate phenomenological quest to probe and describe subjective meanings in all their rich detail."[6] Rather, the structure of cultural codes as produced, reproduced, or changed by interaction and communication is examined. Once emphasis shifts away from meaning, per se, to the structure of culture in social contexts and socially produced texts, other theoretical approaches become useful.

Dramaturgy is one essential supplement because of its emphasis on ritual as a mechanism for expressing and dramatizing symbols—an emphasis that clearly owes its roots to Durkheimian theory. In a sense, individual interpersonal rituals as well as collective rituals express deeply held meanings, but at the same time they affirm particular cultural structures. In so doing, ritual performs such diverse functions as reinforcing collective values, dramatizing certain relations, denoting key positions, embellishing certain messages, and highlighting particular activities.[7]

Another important theoretical supplement is institutional analysis. Culture does not exist as an abstract structure in its own right. Nor is it simply dramatic and ritualized performances; it is also embedded in organized social structures. Culture is produced by actors and organizations that require resources—material, organizational, and political—if they are to develop systems of cultural codes, ritualize them, and transmit them to others. Once the institutional basis of cultural activity is recognized, then the significance of inequalities in resources, the use of power, and the outbreak of conflict become essential parts of cultural analysis.

In sum, then, Wuthnow blends a muted subjective approach with structuralism, dramaturgy, and institutional analysis. He tries to view the subjective as manifested in cultural products, dramatic performances, and institutional processes. In attempting this synthesis, Wuthnow defines his topic as *the moral order*.

---

[4]Wuthnow would, seemingly, not view these laws or principles as universal, but his articulation of such laws (often implicitly) is what makes the work theoretically interesting.

[5]Wuthnow, *Meaning and Moral Order*, 64.

[6]Ibid., 65.

[7]Ibid., 132.

The Moral Order

Wuthnow views the moral order as involving the (a) construction of systems of cultural codes, (b) emission of rituals, and (c) mobilization of resources to produce and sustain these cultural codes and rituals. Let me examine each of these in turn.

The Structure of Moral Codes. A moral code is viewed by Wuthnow "as a set of cultural elements that define the nature of commitment to a particular course of behavior." These sets of cultural elements have an "identifiable structure," involving not so much a "tightly organized or logically consistent system" as some basic "distinctions" that can be used "to make sense of areas in which problems in moral obligations may be likely to arise."[8] Wuthnow sees three such distinctions as crucial to structuring the moral order: (1) moral objects versus real programs, (2) core self versus enacted social roles, and (3) inevitable constraints versus intentional options. Below, I examine each of these.

1. The structure of a moral order distinguishes between (a) the *objects of commitment* and (b) the activities or *real programs* in which the committed engage. The objects of commitment can be varied—a person, a set of beliefs and values, a text, and so on—and the real programs can be almost any kind of activity. The critical point, Wuthnow argues, is that the objects of moral commitment and the behavior emitted to demonstrate this commitment are "connected" and yet "different." For example, one's object of commitment might be "making a better life for one's children," which is to be realized through "hard work" and other activities or real programs. For the structure of a moral order to be effective, it must implicitly distinguish and, at the same time, connect such objects and real programs.

2. The structure of moral codes must also, in Wuthnow's view, distinguish between (a) the person's "real self" or "true self" and (b) the various "roles" that he or she plays. Moral structures always link self-worth and behavior but, at the same time, allow them to be distinguished so that there is a "real me" who is morally worthy and who can be separated from the roles that can potentially compromise this sense of self-worth. For example, when someone reveals "role distance," an assertion is being made that a role is beneath one's dignity or self-worth.

3. Moral codes must also distinguish between (a) those forces that are out of people's control and (b) those that are within the realm of their will. That is, the inevitable must be distinguished from the intentional. In this way, cultural codes posit a moral evaluation of those behaviors that can be controlled through intent and will power, while excusing or suspending evaluation for what is out of a person's control. Without this distinction, it becomes impossible to know what kinds of behaviors of individuals are to be subject to moral evaluations.

---

[8]Ibid., 66.

Thus, the structure of a moral order revolves around three basic types of codes that denote and distinguish commitments with respect to (1) moral objects/real programs, (2) self/roles, and (3) inevitable constraint/intentional options. These three basic types of codes indicate what is desirable by separating and, yet at the same time, also linking objects, behavior, self, roles, constraints, and intentions. Without this denotation of, and a distinction along, these three axes, a moral order and the institutional system in which it is lodged will reveal crises and will begin to break down. If objects and programs are not denoted, distinguished, and yet linked, then cynicism becomes rampant; if self and roles are confused, then loss of self-worth spreads; and if constraints and control are blurred, then apathy or frustration increases. Thus for Wuthnow,

> Morality . . . deals primarily with moral commitment—commitment to an object, ranging from an abstract value to a specific person, that involves behavior, that contributes to self-worth, and that takes place within broad definitions of what is inevitable or intentional. Moral commitment, although in some sense deeply personal and subjective, also involves symbolic constructions—codes—that define these various relations.[9]

The Nature of Ritual. Wuthnow believes that ritual is "a symbolic-expressive aspect of behavior that communicates something about social relations, often in a relatively dramatic or formal manner."[10] A moral ritual "dramatizes collective values and demonstrates individuals' moral responsibility for such values."[11] In so doing, rituals operate to maintain the moral order—that is, the system of symbolic codes ordering moral objects/real programs, self/roles, and constraints/options. Such rituals can be embedded in normal interaction as well as in more elaborate collective ceremonies, and they can be privately or publicly performed.[12] But the key point is that ritual is a basic mechanism for sustaining the moral order.

However, as Wuthnow stresses, ritual is also used to cope with uncertainty in the social relations regulated by the codes of the moral order. Whether through increased options, uses of authority, ambiguity in expectations, lack of clarity in values, "equivocality" in key symbols, or unpredictability in key social relations, rituals are often invoked to deal with these varying bases of uncertainty. Uncertainty is thus one of the sources of escalated ritual activity. However, such uses of ritual are usually tied to efforts at mobilizing resources in institutional contexts to create a new moral order—a process that, as we will examine shortly, Wuthnow examines under the rubric of "ideology."

Institutional Context. For a moral order to exist, it must be produced and reproduced, and for new moral codes to emerge—that is, *ideologies*—they too must be

---

[9]Ibid., 70.

[10]Ibid., 109.

[11]Ibid., 140.

[12]Here, Wuthnow is drawing from the late Durkheimian tradition.

actively produced by actors using resources. Thus, systems of symbolic codes depend on material and organizational resources. If a moral order is to persist and if a new ideology is to become a part of the moral order, it must have a stable supply of resources for actors to use in sustaining the moral order or in propagating a new ideology. That is, actors must have the material goods necessary to sustain themselves and the organizations in which they participate; they must have organizational bases that depend not only on material goods, such as money, but also on organizational "know-how," communication networks, and leadership; and at times they must also have power. Thus, the moral order is anchored in institutional structures revolving around material goods, money, leadership, communication networks, and organizational capacities.

Ideology. One of the central and yet ambiguous concepts in Wuthnow's analysis is his portrayal of ideology, which he defines as "symbols that express or dramatize something about the moral order."[13] This definition is very close to the one used for ritual, and so, what Wuthnow had in mind is somewhat unclear.[14] The basic idea appears to be that an ideology is a subset of symbolic codes emphasizing a particular aspect of the more inclusive moral order. Ideologies are also the vehicles for change in the moral order because the moral order is altered through the development and subsequent institutionalization of new ideologies.

The production and institutionalization of these subsets of symbolic codes depend on the mobilization of resources (leaders, communication networks, organizations, and material goods) and the creation and emission of rituals. New ideologies must often compete with one another, and those ideologies with superior resource bases are more likely to survive and become a part of the moral order.

In sum, then, the moral order consists of a structure of codes, a system of rituals, and a configuration of resources that define the manner in which social relations should be constituted.[15] An important feature of the moral order is the production of ideologies, which are subsets of codes, ritual practices, and resource bases. With this conceptual baggage in hand, Wuthnow then turns to the analysis of dynamic processes in the moral order.

The Dynamics of the Moral Order

Wuthnow employs an ecological framework for the analysis of dynamics.[16] When a moral order (a) does not specify the ordering of moral objects/real programs, self/roles, and inevitable constraints/intentional controls, (b) cannot specify the appropriate communicative and ritual practices for its affirmation and dramatization and,

---

[13]Wuthnow, *Meaning and Moral Order*, 145.

[14]See Turner, "Cultural Analysis and Social Theory," 637–644, for a more detailed critique.

[15]Wuthnow, *Meaning and Moral Order*, 145.

[16]See Chapters 8 and 9 for other theories using such a framework. For the outline of this ecological framework, see Wuthnow, *Meaning and Moral Order*, especially chap. 5 and 6.

as a result of these conditions, (c) cannot reduce the risks associated with various activities, ambiguity in most situations will increase, and just how individuals will behave becomes increasingly unpredictable. As a consequence, the level of uncertainty among the members of a population increases. Under conditions of uncertainty, new ideologies are likely to be produced as a way of coping. Such ideological production is facilitated by (a) high degrees of heterogeneity in the types of social units—classes, groups, organizations, and so forth—in a social system; (b) high levels of diversity in resources and their distribution; (c) high rates of change (realignment of power, redistribution of resources, establishment of new structures, creation of new types of social relations); (d) inflexibility in cultural codes (created by tight connections among a few codes); and (e) reduced capacity of political authority to repress new cultural codes, rituals, and mobilizations of resources.

Wuthnow portrays these processes as an increase in "ideological variation" that results in "competition" among ideologies. Some ideologies are "more fit" to survive this competition and, as a consequence, are "selected." Such "fitness" and "selection" depends on an ideology's capacity to (1) define social relations in ways that reduce uncertainty (over moral objects, programs, self, roles, constraints, options, risks, ambiguities, and unpredictability), (2) reveal a flexible structure consisting of many elements weakly connected, (3) secure a resource base (particularly money, adherents, organizations, leadership, and communication channels), (4) specify ritual and communicative practices, (5) establish autonomous goals, and (6) achieve legitimacy in the eyes of political authority and in terms of existing values and procedural rules.

The more these six conditions can be met, the more likely is an ideology to survive in competition with other ideologies and the more likely it is to become institutionalized as part of the moral order. In particular, the institutionalization of an ideology depends on the establishment of rituals and modes of communication affirming the new moral codes within organizational arrangements that allows for *ritual dramatization* of new codes reducing uncertainty, secures a stable resource base, and eventually receives acceptance by political authority.

Wuthnow appears to argue that different types of ideological movements will emerge under varying configurations of conditions that produce variation, selection, and institutionalization.[17]

Although Wuthnow offers many illustrations of ideological movements, particularly of various kinds of religious movements as well as the emergence of science as an ideology, he does not systematically indicate how varying configurations of these general conditions produce basic types of ideological movements. Yet these variables all appear, in a rather ad hoc and discursive way, in his analysis of ideological movements. And so there is at least an implicit effort to test the theory. By way of summary, Table 21.1 formalizes Wuthnow's theory. Wuthnow would probably reject this formalization as being too "positivistic," but if his ideas are to be more explanatory and less discursive, I see formalization along these lines as desirable.

---

[17]Wuthnow offers examples in *Meaning and Moral Order*, chap. 5–9, but the variables are woven into discursive text and rearranged in an ad hoc manner.

Table 21.1   Wuthnow's Principles of Cultural Dynamics

1. The degree of stability in the moral order of a social system is a positive function of its legitimacy, with the latter being a positive and additive function of

   A. The extent to which the symbolic codes of the moral order facilitate the ordering of

      1. Moral objects and real programs
      2. Self and roles
      3. Inevitable constraints and intentional control

   B. The extent to which the symbolic codes of the moral order are dramatized by ritual activities
   C. The extent to which the symbolic codes of the moral order are affirmed by communicative acts.

2. The rate and degree of change in the moral order of a social system are a positive function of the degree of ideological variation, with the latter being a positive and additive function of

   A. The degree of uncertainty in the social relations of actors, which in turn is an additive function of the inability of

      1. Cultural codes to order moral objects/real projects, self/roles, and constraints/options
      2. Rituals to dramatize key cultural codes
      3. Communicative acts to affirm key cultural codes
      4. Cultural codes to specify the risks associated with various activities and relations
      5. Cultural codes to reduce the ambiguity of various activities and relations
      6. Cultural codes to reduce the unpredictability of various acts and relations

   B. The level of ideological production and variation, which in turn is a positive and additive function of

      1. The degree of heterogeneity among social units
      2. The diversity of resources and their distribution
      3. The rate and degree of change in institutional structures
      4. The degree of inflexibility in the sets of cultural codes, which is an inverse function of
         a. The number of symbolic codes
         b. The weakness of connections among symbolic codes
      5. the inability of political authority to repress ideological production.

3. The likelihood of survival and institutionization of new ideological variants is a positive and multiplicative function of

   A. The capacity of an ideological variant to secure a resource base, which in turn is a positive and additive function of the capacity to generate

      1. Material resources
      2. Communication networks
      3. Rituals
      4. Organizational footings
      5. Leadership

(Continued)

Table 21.1 (Continued)

B. The capacity of an ideological variant to establish goals and pursue them
C. The capacity of an ideological variant to maintain legitimacy with respect to

1. Existing values and procedural rules

2. Existing political authority

D. The capacity of an ideological variant to remain flexible, which in turn is a positive function of

1. The number of symbolic codes

2. The weakness of connections among symbolic codes.

Constructivist Structuralism: Pierre Bourdieu*

Pierre Bourdieu's sociology defies easy classification because it cuts across disciplinary boundaries—sociology, anthropology, education, cultural history, art, science, linguistics, and philosophy—and moves easily between empirical and conceptual inquiry.[18] Yet Bourdieu has characterized his work as constructivist structuralism or structuralist constructivism; in so doing, he distances himself somewhat from the Lévi-Straussian tradition:

> By structuralism or structuralist, I mean that there exists, within the social world itself and not only within symbolic systems (language, myth, etc.), objective structures independent of the consciousness and will of agents, which are capable of guiding and constraining their practices or their representations.[19]

Structures constrain and circumscribe volition; but at the same time, people use their capacities for thought, reflection, and action to construct social and cultural phenomena. They do so within the parameters of existing structures. These structures are not rigid constraints but, rather, materials for a wide variety of social and cultural constructions. Acknowledging his structuralist roots, Bourdieu analogizes to the relation of grammar and language in order to make this point: the grammar of a language only loosely constrains the production of actual speech; it can be seen as defining the possibilities for new kinds of speech acts. So it is with social and cultural structures: they exist independently of agents and

---

*This section is coauthored with Stephan Fuchs.

[18]Indeed, Bourdieu has been enormously prolific, having authored some twenty-five books and hundreds of articles in a variety of fields, including anthropology, education, cultural history, linguistics, philosophy, and sociology. His empirical work covers a wide spectrum of topics—art, academics, unemployment, peasants, classes, religion, sports, kinship, politics, law, and intellectuals. See Loïc J. D. Wacquant, "Towards a Reflexive Sociology: A Workshop with Pierre Bourdieu," *Sociological Theory* 7 (1, Spring 1989):26–63. This article also contains a selected bibliography on Bourdieu's own works as well as secondary analyses and comments on Bourdieu.

[19]Pierre Bourdieu, "Social Space and Symbolic Power," *Sociological Theory* 7 (1, Spring, 1989):14–25.

guide their conduct, and at the same time, they also create options, possibilities, and paths for creative actions and for the construction of new and unique cultural and social phenomena. This perspective is best appreciated by highlighting Bourdieu's criticisms of those theoretical approaches from which he selectively borrows ideas.

Criticisms of Existing Theories

The Critique of Structuralism. Bourdieu's critique of structuralism is similar to symbolic interactionists' attacks on Parsonian functionalism and its emphasis on norms. According to Bourdieu, structuralists ignore the indeterminacy of situations and the practical ingenuity of agents who are not mechanical rule-following and role-playing robots in standard contexts. Rather, agents use their "practical sense" (*sens pratique*) to adapt to situational contingencies within certain "structural limits" that follow from "objective constraints." Social practice is more than the mere execution of an underlying structural "grammar" of action, just as "speech" (*parole*) is more than "language" (*langue*). What is missing, says Bourdieu, are the variable uses and contexts of speech and action.[20] Structuralism dismisses action as mere execution of underlying principles (lodged in the human brain or culture), just as normativism forgets that following rules and playing roles require skillful adjustment and flexible improvisations by creative agents.

Most important, Bourdieu argues that structuralism hypostatizes the "objectifying glance" of the outside academic observer. The "Homo academicus" transfers a particular relation to the world, the distant and objectifying gaze of the professional academic, onto the very properties of that world.[21] As a result, the outside observer constructs the world as a mere "spectacle," which is subject to neutral observation. The distant and uninvolved observer's relation to the world is not only systematic but also a passive cognition, so the world itself is viewed as consisting of cognition rather than active practices. According to Bourdieu, structuralism and other approaches that "objectify" the world do not simply research the empirical world "out there"; rather, they construct it as an "objective fact" through the distancing perspective of the outside observer.

However, Bourdieu does not completely reject structuralism and other "objectifying" approaches that seek, in Durkheim's words, to discover external and constraining "social facts." As we will see, Bourdieu views social classes, and factions within such classes, as "social facts" whose structure can be objectively observed and viewed as external to, and constraining on, the thoughts and activities of individuals.[22] Moreover, Bourdieu at least borrows the metaphor, if not the essence, of structuralism in his efforts to discover the "generative principles" that people use to construct social

---

[20]Pierre Bourdieu, *Language and Symbolic Power* (Cambridge, MA: Harvard University Press, 1989).

[21]Pierre Bourdieu, *Homo Academicus* (Stanford, CA: Stanford University Press, 1988).

[22]Pierre Bourdieu, *Distinction: A Social Critique of the Judgement of Taste* (Cambridge, MA: Harvard University Press, 1984).

and cultural phenomena—systems of classification, ideologies, forms of legitimating social practices, and other elements of "constructivist structuralism."[23]

The Critique of Interactionism and Phenomenology. Bourdieu is also critical of interactionism, phenomenology, and other subjectivist approaches.[24] Bourdieu believes that there is more to social life than interaction and that there is more to interaction than the "definitions of situations" in symbolic interactionism or the "accounting practices" in ethnomethodology. The "actor" of symbolic interactionism and the "member" of ethnomethodology are abstractions that fail to realize that members are always incumbents in particular groups and classes. Interactions are always *interactions-in-contexts*, and the most important of these contexts is *class location*. Even such an elementary feature of interaction as the possibility that it might even occur among particular sets of individuals varies with class background. Interaction is thus embedded in structure, and the structure constrains what is possible.

Moreover, in addition to this rather widespread critique of interactionism as "astructural," Bourdieu argues that interactionism is too cognitive in its overemphasis on the accounting and sense-making activities of agents. As a result, it forgets that actors have objective class-based interests. And, once again, the biases of Homo academicus are evident. It is in the nature of academics to define, assess, reflect, ponder, and interpret the social world; as a result of this propensity, a purely academic relation to the world is imposed on real people in social contexts. For interactionists, then, people are merely disinterested lay academics who define, reflect, interpret, and account for actions and situations. But lay interpretations, and academic portrayals of these lay interpretations, cannot accurately describe social reality, for two reasons. First, as noted, these interpretations are constrained by existing structures, especially class and class factions. Second, these interpretations are themselves part of objective class struggles as individuals construct legitimating definitions for their conduct.[25]

Bourdieu then borrows from Karl Marx the notion that people are located in a class position, that this position gives them certain interests, and that their interpretative actions are often ideologies designed to legitimate these interests. People's "definitions of situations" are neither neutral nor innocent but are often ideological weapons that are very much a part of the objective class structures and the inherent conflicts of interests generated by such structures.[26]

The Critique of Utilitarianism. Rational economic theories also portray, and at the same time betray, Homo academicus's relation to the social world. Like academics in general, utilitarian economic theorists[27] see humans as rational, calculating, and

---

[23]See Wacquant, "Towards a Reflexive Sociology," 26–63 and Bourdieu, "Social Space and Symbolic Power," 14–25.

[24]See Wacquant, "Towards a Reflexive Sociology," 26–63.

[25]See Bourdieu, *Outline of a Theory of Practice* (Cambridge, UK: Cambridge University Press, 1977), 22ff and *Distinction*.

[26]Ibid.

[27]See the brief summary of utilitarianism in Chapter 15.

maximizing (*sujets ravauts*); and rational exchange theories thus mistake a model of the human actor for real individuals, thereby reifying their theoretical abstractions.

Yet Bourdieu does not replace the economic model of rational action with an interpretative model of symbolic action. He does not argue that rational action theory is wrong because it is too rationalistic or because it ignores the interpretative side of action. On the contrary, he holds that rational action theory does not realize that even symbolic action is rational and based on class interests. Thus, according to Bourdieu, the error of the economic model is not that it presents all action as rational and interested; rather, the big mistake is to restrict interests and rationality to the immediate material payoffs collected by reflective and profit-seeking individuals.[28]

Bourdieu reasons that all social practices are a part of and embedded in individuals' (self-) "interests," even if individual agents are unaware of their interests and even if the stakes of these practices are not material profits. Social practices are attuned to the conditions of particular arenas in which actions might yield profits without deliberate intention. For example, in science it is the most "disinterested" and "pure" research that yields the highest cultural profits—that is, academic recognition and reputation. In social fields other than economic exchange, it is the structural denial of any "interests" that often yields the highest gains. It is not that agents cynically deny being interested to increase their gains even more; rather, innocence ensures that honest disinterestedness nevertheless is the most profitable practice.

For example, gift exchange economies—the subject of Bourdieu's early anthropological research[29]—might illustrate this complex idea. Gift exchange economies are typically embedded in larger social relations and solidarities so that exchange is not purely instrumental and material but has a strong *moral* quality to it. Economic exchanges are expected to follow the social logic of solidarity and group memberships at least as much as they follow the economic logic of material gain. From the narrow economic perspective of rational action theory, the logic of solidarity would seem like an intrusion of "nonrational" forces, such as tradition or emotion, into an otherwise purely rational system of exchange. Yet the logic of solidarity points to those processes by which *symbolic* and *social capital* are accumulated—a "social fact" that is missed by the narrow economic determinism of rational action theory. But once the notion of "capital" is extended to include symbolic and social capital, apparently "irrational" practices can now be seen to follow their own (self-) interested logic, and contrary to initial impressions, these practices are not irrational at all. The denial of narrow economic interests in gift exchange economies conceals the fact that, as the social and economic capital is increased, the more will the purely instrumental aspects of exchange move into the background. For instance, birthday and Christmas presents are socially more effective when they appear less material and economic; those who brag about the high costs of their presents do not understand the nature of gift exchanges and, as a consequence, are considered rude, thereby losing symbolic and social capital.

---

[28]See Wacquant, "Towards a Reflexive Sociology," 43.

[29]Bourdieu, *Outline of a Theory of Practice,* 22ff.

Thus, in broadening economic exchange to include social and symbolic resources, as all sociological exchange theories eventually do,[30] Bourdieu introduces a central concept in his approach: capital.[31] Those in different classes reveal not only varying levels or amounts of capital but also divergent types and configurations of capital. Bourdieu's view of capital recognizes that the resources individuals possess can be material, symbolic, social, and cultural; moreover, these resources reflect class location and are used to further the interests of those in a particular class position.

Bourdieu's Cultural Conflict Theory

Although Bourdieu has explored many topics, the conceptual core of his sociology is a vision of social classes and the cultural forms associated with these classes.[32] In essence, Bourdieu combines a Marxian theory of objective class position in relation to the means of production with a Weberian analysis of status groups (lifestyles, tastes, and prestige) and politics (organized efforts to have one's class culture dominate). The key to this reconciliation of Karl Marx's and Max Weber's views of stratification is the expanded conceptualization of *capital* as more than economic and material resources, coupled with elements of French structuralism.

Classes and Capital. To understand Bourdieu's view of classes, it is first necessary to recognize a distinction among four types of capital:[33] (1) *economic capital,* or productive property (money and material objects that can be used to produce goods and services); (2) *social capital,* or positions and relations in groupings and social networks; (3) *cultural capital,* or informal interpersonal skills, habits, manners, linguistic styles, educational credentials, tastes, and lifestyles; and (4) *symbolic capital,* or the use of symbols to legitimate the possession of varying levels and configurations of the other three types of capital.

These forms of capital can be converted into one another, but only to a certain extent. The degree of convertibility of capital in various markets is itself at stake in social struggles. The overproduction of academic qualifications, for example, can decrease the convertibility of educational credentials into economic capital ("credential inflation"). As a

---

[30]See Chapter 15.

[31]Pierre Bourdieu, "The Forms of Capital," in *Handbook of Theory and Research in the Sociology of Education,* ed. J. G. Richardson (New York: Greenwood, 1986). See also Michele Lamont and Annette P. Larreau, "Cultural Capital: Allusions, Gaps, and Glissandos in Recent Theoretical Developments," *Sociological Theory* 6 (2, Fall 1988):153–168.

[32]Bourdieu, *Distinction* and *Outline of a Theory of Practice.*

[33]Bourdieu, "The Forms of Capital". For another cultural approach to analyzing classes, see Michelle Lamont, *Money, Morals, and Manners: The Culture of the French and American Upper-Middle Class* (Chicago, IL: University of Chicago Press, 1992), "Symbolic Boundaries and Status" in *Cultural Sociology,* ed. Lyn Spillman (Malden, MA/Oxford, UK: Blackwell, 2002), 98–119, and *The Dignity of Working Men: Morality and the Boundaries of Race, Class, and Immigration* (Cambridge, MA: Harvard University Press, 2002).

result, owners of credentials must struggle to get their cultural capital converted into economic gains, such as high-paying jobs. Likewise, the extent to which economic capital can be converted into social capital is at stake in struggles over control of the political apparatus, and the efforts of those with economic capital to "buy" cultural capital can often be limited by their perceived lack of "taste" (a type of cultural capital).

The distribution of these four types of capital determines the objective class structure of a social system. The overall class structure reflects the total amount of capital possessed by various groupings. Hence the dominant class will possess the most economic, social, cultural, and symbolic capital; the middle class will possess less of these forms of capital; and the lower classes will have the least amount of these capital resources.

The class structure is not, however, a simple lineal hierarchy. Within each class are *factions* that can be distinguished by (a) the composition or configuration of their capital and (b) the social origin and the amount of time that individuals in families have possessed a particular profile or configuration of capital resources.

Table 21.2 schematically represents Bourdieu's portrayal of the factions in the three classes. The top faction within a given class controls the greatest proportion of economic or productive capital typical of a class; the bottom faction possesses the greatest amount of cultural and symbolic capital for a class; and the middle faction possesses an intermediate amount of economic, cultural, and symbolic capital. The top faction is the dominant faction within a given class, and the bottom faction is the dominated faction for that class, with the middle faction being both superordinate over the dominated faction and subordinate to the top faction. As factions engage in struggles to control resources and legitimate themselves, they mobilize social capital to form groupings and networks of relations, but their capacity to form such networks is limited by their other forms of capital. Thus, the overall distribution of social capital (groups and organizational memberships, network ties, social relations, etc.) for classes and their factions will correspond to the overall distribution of other forms of capital. However, the particular forms of groupings, networks, and social ties will reflect the particular configuration of economic, cultural, and symbolic capital typically possessed by a particular faction within a given class.

Bourdieu borrows Marx's distinction between a class "for itself" (organized to pursue its interests) and one "in itself" (unorganized but having common interests and objective location in a class and class faction) and then argues that classes are not real groups but only "potentialities." As noted earlier, the objective distribution of resources for Bourdieu relates to actual groups as grammar relates to speech: it defines the possibilities for actors but requires actual people and concrete settings to become real. And it is the transformation of class and class faction interests into actual groupings that marks the dynamics of a society.

Such transformation involves the use of productive material, cultural, and symbolic capital to mobilize social capital (groups and networks); even more important, class conflict tends to revolve around the mobilization of symbols into ideologies that legitimate a particular composition of resources.[34] Much conflict in human societies,

---

[34]Pierre Bourdieu, "Social Space and the Genesis of Groups," *Theory and Society* 14 (November 1985):723–744.

therefore, revolves around efforts to manipulate symbols to make a particular pattern of social, cultural, and productive resources seem the most appropriate. For example, when intellectuals and artists decry the "crass commercialism," "acquisitiveness," and "greed" of big business, this activity involves the mobilization of symbols into an ideology that seeks to mitigate their domination by the owners of the means of production.

But class relations involve more than a simple pecking order. There are also homologies among similarly located factions within different classes. For example, the rich capitalists of the dominant class and the small-business owners of the

Table 21.2 Representation of Classes and Class Factions in Industrial Societies

Dominant Class: Richest in all forms of capital
Dominant faction: Richest in economic capital, which can be used to buy other types of capital. This faction is composed primarily of those who own the means of production—that is, the classical bourgeoisie.
Intermediate faction: Some economic capital, coupled with moderate levels of social, cultural, and symbolic capital. This faction is composed of high-credential professionals.
Dominated faction: Little economic capital but with high levels of cultural and symbolic capital. This faction is composed of intellectuals, artists, writers, and others who possess cultural resources valued in a society.
Middle Class: Moderate Levels of All Forms of Capital
Dominant faction: Highest in this class in economic capital but having considerably less economic capital than the dominant faction of the dominant class. This faction is composed of petite bourgeoisie (small-business owners).
Intermediate faction: Some economic, social, cultural, and symbolic capital but considerably less than the intermediate faction of the dominant class. This faction is composed of skilled clerical workers.
Dominated faction: Little or no economic capital and with comparatively high social, cultural, and symbolic capital. This class is composed of educational workers, such as schoolteachers, and other low-income and routinized professions that are involved in cultural production.
Lower Class: Low levels of all forms of capital
Dominant faction: Comparatively high economic capital for this general class. This faction is composed of skilled manual workers.
Intermediate faction: Lower amounts of economic and other types of capital. This faction is composed of semiskilled workers without credentials.
Dominated faction: Very low amounts of economic capital, with some symbolic capital in uneducated ideologues and intellectuals for the poor and working person.

Note: We have had to make inferences from Bourdieu's somewhat rambling text, but the table captures the imagery of Bourdieu's analysis. He probably would not like this layered (like a cake) imagery in the table, but the critical point is that individuals and families from factions of different classes often have more in common than individuals and families from different factions within a class. This makes stratification a much more complex phenomenon than is typically portrayed by sociologists.

middle class are equivalent in their control of productive resources and their dominant position relative to other factions in their respective classes.[35] Similarly, intellectuals, artists, and other cultural elites in the dominant class are equivalent to schoolteachers in the middle class because of their reliance on cultural capital and because of their subordinate position in relation to those who control the material resources of their respective classes.

These homologies in class factions across different classes make class conflict complex, because those in similar objective positions in different classes—say, intellectuals and schoolteachers—will mobilize symbolic resources into somewhat similar ideologies—in this example, emphasizing learning, knowledge for its own sake, and life of the mind and, at the same time, decrying crass materialism. Such ideologies legitimate their own class position and attack those who dominate them (by emphasizing the importance of those cultural resources that they have more of). At the same time, their homologous positions are separated by the different amounts of cultural capital owned: the intellectuals despise the strained efforts of schoolteachers to appear more sophisticated than they are, whereas the schoolteachers resent the decadent and irresponsible relativism of snobbish intellectuals. Thus, ideological conflict is complicated by the simultaneous convergence of factions within different classes and by the divergence of these factions, by virtue of their position, in different social classes.

Moreover, an additional complication stems from people sharing similar types and amounts of resources but having very different origins and social trajectories. Those who have recently moved to a class faction—say, the dominant productive elite or intermediate faction of the middle class—will have somewhat different styles and tastes than those who have been born into these classes, and these differences in social origin and mobility can create yet another source of ideological conflict. For example, the "old rich" will often comment on the "lack of class" and "ostentatiousness" of the "new rich"; or the "solid middle class" will be somewhat snobbish toward the "poor boy who made good" but who "still has a lot to learn" or who "still is a bit crude."

All those points of convergence and divergence within and between classes and class factions make the dynamics of stratification complex. Although there is always an "objective class location," as determined by the amount and composition of capital and by the social origins of capital holders, the development of organizations and ideologies is not a simple process. Bourdieu often ventures into a more structuralist mode when trying to sort out how various classes, class factions, and splits of individuals with different social origins within class factions generate categories of thought, systems of speech, signs of distinction, forms of mythology, modes of appreciation, tastes, and lifestyles.

The general argument is that objective location—(a) class, (b) faction within class, and (c) social origin—creates interests and structural constraints that, in turn,

---

[35]Bourdieu makes what in network analysis (see Chapter 20) is termed regular structural equivalence. That is, those incumbents in positions that stand in an equivalent (similar) relation to other positions will act in a convergent way and evidence common attributes.

allow different social constructions.[36] Such constructions might involve the use of "formal rules" (implicitly known by individuals with varying interests) to construct cultural codes that classify and organize "things," "signs," and "people" in the world. This kind of analysis by Bourdieu has not produced a fine-grained structuralist model of how individuals construct particular cultural codes, but it has provided an interesting analysis of "class cultures." Such class cultures are always the dependent variable for Bourdieu, with objective class location being the independent variable and with rather poorly conceptualized structuralist processes of generative rules and cultural codes being the "intervening variables." Yet the detailed description of these class cultures is perhaps Bourdieu's most unique contribution to sociology and is captured by his concept of *habitus.*

Class Cultures and Habitus. Those within a given class share certain modes of classification, appreciation, judgment, perception, and behavior. Bourdieu conceptualizes this mediating process between class and individual perceptions, choices, and behavior as habitus.[37] In a sense, *habitus* is the "collective unconscious" of those in similar positions because it provides cognitive and emotional guidelines that enable individuals to represent the world in common ways and to classify, choose, evaluate, and act in a particular manner.

The habitus creates syndromes of taste, speech, dress, manner, and other responses. For example, a preference for particular foods will tend to correspond to tastes in art, ways of dressing, styles of speech, manners of eating, and other cultural actions among those sharing a common class location. There is, then, a correlation between the class hierarchy and the cultural objects, preferences, and behaviors of those located at particular ranks in the hierarchy. For instance, Bourdieu devotes considerable attention to "taste," which is seen as one of the most visible manifestations of the habitus.

Bourdieu views taste in a holistic and anthropological sense to include appreciation of art, ways of dressing, and preferences for foods.[38] Although taste appears as an innocent, natural, and personal phenomenon, it covaries with objective class location: the upper class is to the working class what an art museum is to television; the old upper class is to the new upper class what polite and distant elegance is to noisy and conspicuous consumption; and the dominant is to the dominated faction of the upper class what opera is to avant-garde theater. Because tastes are organized in a cultural hierarchy that mirrors the social hierarchy of objective class location, conflicts between tastes are class conflicts.

---

[36]Bourdieu is not very clear about the issue of how the structural potentialities of a given objective class location become transformed into actual social groups capable of historical action. Like Lévi-Strauss (see Chapter 20), Bourdieu pursues the formal analogies between deep structures and actual practices, but he lacks a theory about how and when the transformations are going to be made, and made successfully.

[37]Bourdieu, *Distinction.*

[38]Ibid.

Bourdieu roughly distinguishes between two types of tastes, which correspond to high versus low overall capital or high versus low objective class position.[39] The "taste of liberty and luxury" is the taste of the upper class; as such, it is removed from direct economic necessity and material need. The taste of liberty is the philosophy of art for its own sake. Following Immanuel Kant, Bourdieu calls this aesthetic the "pure gaze." The pure gaze looks at the sheer form of art and places this form above function and content. The upper-class taste of luxury is not concerned with art illustrating or representing some external reality; art is removed from life, just as upper-class life is removed from harsh material necessity. Consequently, the taste of luxury purifies and sublimates the ordinary and profane into the aesthetic and beautiful. The pure gaze confers aesthetic meaning to ordinary and profane objects because the taste of liberty is at leisure to relieve objects from their pragmatic functions. Thus, as the distance from basic material necessities increases, the pure gaze or the taste of luxury transforms the ordinary into the aesthetic, the material into the symbolic, and the functional into the formal. And because the taste of liberty is that of the dominant class, it is also the dominant and legitimate taste in society.

In contrast, the working class cultivates a "popular" aesthetic. Their taste is the taste of necessity, for working-class life is constrained by harsh economic imperatives. The popular taste wants art to represent reality and despises formal and self-sufficient art as decadent and degenerate. The popular taste favors the simple and honest rather than the complex and sophisticated. It is downgraded by the "legitimate" taste of luxury as naive and complacent, and these conflicts over tastes are class conflicts over cultural and symbolic capital.

Preferences for certain works and styles of art, however, are only part of "tastes" as ordered by habitus. Aesthetic choices are correlated with choices made in other cultural fields. The taste of liberty and luxury, for example, corresponds to the polite, distant, and disciplined style of upper-class conversation. Just as art is expected to be removed from life, so are the bodies of interlocutors expected to be removed from one another, and so is the spirit expected to be removed from matter. Distance from economic necessity in the upper-class lifestyle not only corresponds to an aesthetic of pure form but also entails that all natural and physical desires are to be sublimated and dematerialized. Hence, upper-class eating is highly regulated and disciplined, and foods that are less filling are preferred over fatty dishes. Similarly, items of clothing are chosen for fashion and aesthetic harmony rather than for functional appropriateness. "Distance from necessity" is the motif underlying the upper-class lifestyle as a whole, not just aesthetic tastes as one area of practice.

Conversely, because they are immersed in physical reality and economic necessity, working-class people interact in more physical ways, touching one another's bodies, laughing heartily, and valuing straightforward outspokenness more than distant and "false" politeness. Similarly, the working-class taste favors foods that are more filling and less "refined" but more physically gratifying. The popular taste chooses clothes and furniture that are functional, and this is so not only because of the sheer

---

[39]Ibid. Actually, Bourdieu makes more fine-tuned distinctions, but we focus only on the main oppositions here.

economic constraints but also because of a true and profound dislike of that which is "formal" and "fancy."

In sum, then, Bourdieu has provided a conceptual model of class conflict that combines elements of Marxian, Weberian, and Durkheimian sociology. The structuralist aspects of Bourdieu's conceptualization of habitus as the mediating process between class position and individual behavior have been underemphasized in this review, but Bourdieu clearly places Durkheim "back on his feet" by emphasizing that class position determines habitus. But the useful elements of structuralism—systems of symbols as generative structures of codes—are retained and incorporated into a theory of class conflict as revolving around the mobilization of symbols into ideologies legitimating a class position and the associated lifestyle and habitus.

Cultural Pragmatics: Jeffrey C. Alexander

As theorizing about cultural dynamics has gained traction in sociology once again, some have advocated a "strong program" in cultural sociology. To many cultural sociologists, much analysis of culture is part of a "weak program" where culture is seen as something that emerges out of structural arrangements and that can only be theorized in reference to social structures. A strong program, in contrast, would make culture the principle topic rather than an adjunct or, in Marx's works, a "superstructure" to material social structural conditions. Moreover, this program would involve "thick descriptions" of symbolic meanings and the mechanisms by which such meanings are constructed. Culture would be seen as texts with themes, plotlines, moral evaluations, traditions, frameworks, and other properties that make culture an autonomous realm, separated from social structure.[40] Much of the work in such a strong program would be empirical, examining specific types of cultural formations and analyzing them in detail. And only after such a strong program has existed for a time could the relationship between culture and social structure be examined through processes such as rituals and interactions. To a degree, both Wuthnow's and Bourdieu's theories evidence some elements of a strong program, but I would imagine that they could be criticized for devoting too much effort at connecting cultural processes to social structural dynamics, thus giving short shrift to culture as a distinctive realm of social reality.

Jeffrey Alexander and his colleagues at Yale and other key centers of cultural theorizing have been part of the movement pushing for a strong program. Even though not all cultural sociologists go this far, most cultural sociologists have been

---

[40]See, for example, Jeffrey C. Alexander, Ron Eyerman, Bernard Giessen, and Neil J. Smelser, *Cultural Trauma and Collective Identity* (Berkeley: University of California Press, 2004); Jeffrey Alexander, Bernard Giessen, and Jason Mast, *Social Performance: Symbolic Action, Cultural Pragmatics, and Ritual* (Cambridge, UK: Cambridge University Press, 2006); Philip Smith and A. T. Riley, *Cultural Theory*, 2nd ed. (Oxford, UK: Blackwell); Jeffrey C. Alexander, *The Civil Sphere* (Oxford, UK: Oxford University Press, 2006) and *The Meaning of Social Life: A Cultural Sociology* (New York: Oxford University Press, 2005); and Jeffrey Alexander, Ronald Jacobs, and Philip Smith, *The Oxford Handbook of Cultural Sociology* (New York: Oxford University Press, 2012).

influenced by the call for the analysis of culture, per se, and by the need to engage in rich and thick empirical descriptions of cultural processes. Of course, description does not always lead to theorizing about why the culture described exists and operates the way it does. Thus, even a strong program must eventually begin to explain cultural dynamics rather than simply describing empirical manifestations of these dynamics. Alexander's work on "cultural pragmatics"[41] is a good illustration of moving beyond description to explain at least a limited range of cultural processes.

In pursuing the goal of developing theories about culture, Alexander blends a heavy dose of Émile Durkheim's analysis of ritual and emotion in *The Elementary Forms of the Religious Life* (see pp. 226–236 in Chapter 7) with Erving Goffman's dramaturgy (see Chapter 19). This mix makes sense because one of the most conspicuous strands of cultural theorizing revolves around rituals and performances that arouse emotions that bring background "collective representations," implicit "scripts," and "themes" to the foreground of interaction with audiences of others.

History of Ritualized Performances

Alexander draws from Durkheim's distinction between mechanical and organic solidarity to present, to say the least, a condensed history of ritualized performances. In simple, homogeneous societies, all the elements of performances are fused together and seamless, so that culture is always in the foreground, making individuals experience rituals as personal, immediate, and iconographic. The cultural script, texts, collective representations, stage, props, actors, audience, means for symbolic production, and social powers of individuals are, what he terms, *fused* together, allowing interaction to seem not only seamless but authentic as individuals engage in ritual performances to immediate audiences.

With the differentiation of societies, however, there comes (a) a separation of foreground texts and background symbolic representations, (b) an estrangement of the symbolic means of production from the mass of social actors, and (c) a disconnect between elites who carry out symbolic actions and their mass audiences. The result is that successful performances are no longer automatic but something that takes skill and effort to *re-fuse* the elements of background representations with *texts* that are used in the foreground, on a stage, through ritual performances in front of audiences. Rituals become the means by which the disparate elements of culture are *re*assembled through effort and performances.

At times in primary groups, re-fusion is not so necessary, even in complex societies; interaction rituals proceed smoothly and seamlessly as background comes to foreground in an emotionally gratifying way. Still, the dramatic increase in the number and scale of social spaces and the vast public sphere in modern, complex societies inevitably cause separation among the elements of performances. As a consequence, it is always problematic how to re-fuse them through ritual performances among people. The cultural world is fragmented and detached from many

---

[41]Jeffrey C. Alexander, "Cultural Pragmatics: Social Performances Between Ritual and Strategy," *Sociological Theory* 22 (2004):512–574.

performances, giving the modern world problems of cultural integration and meaning in social situations—very old themes that go back to the founding of sociology.

Alexander has, with a different vocabulary, rephrased the basic problem that Durkheim emphasized in his earlier work in *The Division of Labor in Society*. How can performances be made in ways that re-fuse what inevitably gets decomposed with structural and cultural differentiation in a society? For Alexander, a successful performance that re-fuses background to foreground "stands or falls" upon individual and collective actions to achieve what he terms (a) *cultural extension* of the background representations and its interpretation in a text to the audience and (2) *psychological* (and emotional) *identification* of the audience with performances and its interpretation of the background representations as text. Only in this way can the fragmentation of complex societies be overcome in performances. Alexander's theory is thus about the steps and strategies of actors in successfully re-fusing culture during their performances. I will come back to these shortly, but let me now backtrack to outline some of the basic assumptions that Alexander makes in developing his theory of cultural pragmatics.

Assumptions About Actors and Performances

Alexander assumes that actors are motivated by moral concerns and that they seek to bring both background representations and scripts of culture to the forefront of action and interaction with audiences. In realizing this fundamental goal, Alexander lists several key properties of re-fusing:

1. Actors convert background representation of culture and scripts into *texts* that decode and interpret these background elements of culture.

2. To bring off a successful performance, they must also achieve *cathexis*, or some kind of emotional attachment to the text as it has been decoded.

3. With interpretations of background representations and scripts that are emotionally valenced, individuals and potential collective actors are in a better position to engage in cultural extension of the text to the audience; and if successful, the audience will psychologically identify with the performance and the underlying text, script, and background representations.

4. In making a performance to an audience, actors always assess the means of symbolic reproduction, or the stage and props that are available for a performance.

5. The dramatic presentation of text thus involves physical and verbal gestures on a stage and the use of props.

6. Performances, like all actions, are constrained by power, which can delimit, limit, or facilitate access to text as well as the availability of stages, staging props, actors who can engage in performances, and audiences that these actors can reach in interpreting and decoding background cultural elements into a text.

As is evident, the dramatic metaphor is central to cultural pragmatics, which perhaps makes it a part of dramaturgy. Moreover, much like dramaturgy as summarized in Chapter 19, there is an emphasis on *strategic* elements in just how to go about (a) reaching, or achieving *cultural extension* to, an audience and (b) getting the members of the audience to *identify* with the performance and the cultural text.

Challenges and Strategies Employed in Performances

Re-fusing always poses challenges that, in turn, lead actors to adopt various strategies for achieving cultural extension and audience identification with a performance and its underlying text. First, in order to give a successful performance, an effective *script* must be created that compresses background cultural meanings and intensifies these meanings in ways that facilitate an effective performance. Alexander lists several techniques for doing so: (a) *cognitive simplification* of background representations so that audiences do not need to deal with too much complexity; (b) *time-space compression,* which collapse elements in time and space so that the elements are highlighted and less dependent upon contextual interpretations; (c) *moral agonism,* whereby representations are stated as dichotomies, such as good versus evil, conflicts against enemies, and challenges that must overcome obstacles; and (d) *twistings and turnings* in the plotline that keep audiences engaged.

Second, re-fusing involves a script, action, and performances as actors "walk and talk" in space. This process is more engaging when writers of scripts leave room for dramatic inventions and interpretations and when directors of staged actions allow for some dramatic license on the part of performers. When scripts, direction, and staging are too tightly orchestrated, performances come off as stiff, artificial, and less engaging than when actors are seen as authentically brining to an audience emotionally charged background elements of culture.

Third, re-fusing always involves the use of social power; and this power must be mobilized on at least three fronts: (1) the appropriation of relevant symbolic means of production, such as the right venues and stages where a performance can be most effective and can reach the right audience; (2) the appropriation of the means of symbolic distribution, in which the background representations can be secured and then, through performances, distributed to audiences; and (3) the appropriation of some control over the subsequent debate, discourse, and criticism of a performance.

Fourth, actors are always in a double re-fusing situation. They have to connect with the (a) text and, then, the (b) audience. The best way to bring off this "double re-fusion" is by giving a performance that seems natural and as part of the ongoing flow of the situation, whereas disjointed performances will only exacerbate the process of re-fusing. This problem is aggravated in complex societies as individuals play different roles in a highly diverse social context; under these conditions, it is often difficult to give a performance in all stages that is natural rather than somewhat disjointed. The result is that re-fusing will fail, or partially fail, thereby reducing the extension of culture and audience identification.

And fifth, there is the challenge of re-fusing the audience with the performance text because in complex societies audiences are frequently diverse, larger, and separated in time and space from actors, as is especially the case with performances that are given through various media. This reality of the stages and audiences in complex societies places enormous demands on actors, directors, and scriptwriters to pull off an effective performance. Some of the strategies listed above—cognitive simplification, time-space compression, moral agonism, and twists and turns—are one set of means for overcoming the problems of appealing to the larger, more diverse, and separated audiences. These strategies simplify, decontextualize (to a degree), moralize, and make engaging the text and performance in ways that extend the culture to the audience and emotionally pull them into the point of identifying with the performance and the text.

Why Pragmatics?

I have stated Alexander's argument abstractly, as he does, but without examples. I believe the point of the theory is to emphasize that fusing of background cultural elements with performances is a generic and universal process that has been made more difficult and challenging in complex, highly differentiated societies. Yet if the background culture of a society cannot be fused with actors' performances, the problems of integration in complex societies become that much greater. In simple, homogeneous societies of the past, performances were naturally fused, but with complexity re-fusing must occur. This re-fusing, I believe Alexander intends to argue, can occur at many different levels and among different types of actors. The process is perhaps easiest at the level of face-to-face interaction, but if those interacting are strangers to each other and from different backgrounds, then the interaction will often be awkward and stilted because the script, direction, staging, use of props, and acting in front of the audience are disjointed or unclear. At the other extreme are dramatic performances by (political, economic, and religious) actors to large audiences given through the mass media; and here too the same problems exist. The actors confront a large, diverse, and spatially disconnected audience, where the script, performance, text, and staging must somehow pull in diverse audiences who are asked to emotionally identify with the performance and the text being brought forward. Relatively few actors can pull this off in natural settings, although good actors in movies and the stage are often able to pull audiences into their performances; but these successful performances only highlight the difficulty of doing so in real-life situations. In between encounters of individuals and media presentations are performances at all the intervening levels of society—groups, organizations, civic meeting, lectures, rallies, protest events, revolutions, and other stages[42]—where actors confront audiences of varying sizes and backgrounds and where they must give a performance that extends culture and pulls the audience

---

[42]For example, the titles of the following books by Jeffrey Alexander reveal more macro-level effects of performance dynamics: *Performative Revolution in Egypt: An Essay on Cultural Power* (New York: Oxford University Press, 2011); *The Performance of Politics: Obama's Victory and the Democratic Struggle for Power* (New York: Oxford University Press, 2010); and *Performance of Power* (Cambridge, UK: Polity Press, 2011).

into the performance and the text, so that they identify emotionally with both. Again, only relatively few actors can bring these kinds of performances off and achieve full re-fusion; yet the viability of complex societies depends upon some degree of success in such performances.

Thus, ritual performances that connect audiences with texts that decode background cultural representations are the key dynamics, in Alexander's view, in all social situations. Yet many situations in complex societies are fragmented because they have been subject to de-fusion as a simple consequence of the scale and differentiation of society. In these de-fused situations, the importance of performance rituals becomes ever more evident because performances are not automatic, nor do they seamlessly unfold. Whether it be one person in an encounter writing the script, decoding background representations in a text, appropriating stages and props, and giving the performance or a large team of actors coordinating the writing, directing, staging, marketing, and securing actors and audiences, the dynamics are the same, and they are critical to the integration of societies.

Alexander seems to argue that only when a strong program exists in cultural sociology would this need to bring cultural representations from the background to the front stage, to borrow Goffman's term, be seen as critical. Without a prior understanding of the dynamics of culture, per se, the ritual performances needed to make it salient, relevant, and engrossing to audiences would not be appreciated and, hence, theorized.

Conclusions

With the conflict critique on functional theories in the 1960s and 1970s, especially the approach of Talcott Parsons, who did emphasize culture dynamics, sociological attention shifted to the material bases of society as they generated conflicts of interests that, under various conditions, would lead to varying types of conflict. Culture was not irrelevant in this conceptual shift, but it was relegated to the analysis of beliefs and ideologies as they aroused parties to conflict or legitimated oppressive social structures. Just as conflict theory reacted to functionalism, I suspect that the new cultural sociology emerged as a reaction to the simplification of cultural analysis, when it was seen as the sidekick of conflict dynamics, ultimately generated by the material conditions of societies.

There were intellectual traditions such as phenomenology and hermeneutics that remained viable during this period, but they did not explore culture in all its manifestations; these were specialized theories that were often more cognitive than cultural. It is obvious, but surprisingly underappreciated, that everything humans do when they act and organize is cultural. Ideas are expressed with language, not just words but the language of emotions; ideas take hold when they are used by interacting persons and collective actors to build up social structures, reproduce such structures, or tear them down, only to rebuild them in another form. But culture is more robust and dynamic—as new cultural theories appear to argue—because it is a domain of reality where symbols are organized and stored, and then brought into use in dramatic performances. They are not simply superstructures to material social structures but an autonomous set of dynamics that need to be theorized and, eventually, connected to the structural properties of social reality. The notion of *performances* seems to be one wedge for recognizing the autonomous dynamics of culture, per se, and the necessity of bringing culture to stages and props in social settings that are part of social structures. It is through its capacity to extend cultural representations to audiences and to get audiences to emotionally identify with these representations through scripts, direction, texts, staging, and acting that culture exerts its power over the actions of persons and corporate units as they build up, reproduce, dismantle, and build up anew social structures.

In somewhat different ways, Wuthnow, Bourdieu, and Alexander have sought to highlight the properties of culture and how culture is used in social settings. Each explicitly, or more implicitly in the case of Bourdieu, sees ritual and performances as critical in generating the emotions necessary to give culture its power to influence how people behave and how social structures are created, reproduced, or changed. Yet when theorized by these scholars and others, the conceptualization of culture becomes a bit vague—*moral order, habitus, cultural and symbolic capital, background representations, texts, scripts,* and the like. These are not precise conceptualizations. They are evocative, to be sure, but they are not denotative in any precise sense. From empirical descriptions of these in real empirical contexts, perhaps, it will be possible to isolate the properties and dynamics of each of these evocative terms, which I think would represent a much stronger program in cultural sociology.

CHAPTER 22

Postmodern Theorizing*

T he label "postmodern" encompasses many divergent points of view, but the term contains two common themes: (1) a critique of sociology as a science and (2) a substantive argument that there has been a decisive break with modernity in which cultural symbols, media-driven images, and other forces of symbolic signification have changed the nature of social organization and the relation of individuals to the social world. Postmodernism is critical because it doubts what it sees as the "pretentions" of scientific sociology and because it sees the new postmodern social universe as harmful to individuals and societies. Let us begin with the critique of science.

The Postmodern Critique of Science

The Age of Science, as it emerged from The Enlightenment, posited that it would be possible to use language to denote key properties of the universe and to communicate among scientists the nature and dynamics of these properties. Indeed, it was believed that as knowledge accumulated by testing general theories against empirical cases, ever-more formal languages, such as mathematics, could be used by theorists and ever-more precise measuring instruments could be developed by experimental researchers. In this manner, the accumulation of knowledge about the properties and dynamics of the universe would accelerate. For such accumulation to occur, the degree of correspondence between theories stated in languages and the actual nature of the universe would have to increase. No scientist assumed, of course, that there could ever be a perfect correspondence, but there was a faith that the use of more precise languages and measuring instruments calibrated for these languages could make representations of the universe increasingly accurate.

This faith in science was one of the cornerstones of "modernism," in at least this sense: Scientific knowledge could be used to forge a better society. As knowledge

---

*This chapter is coauthored with Kenneth Allan.

about the world accumulated, it could be used to increase productivity, democracy, and fairness in patterns of social organization. As with all critical approaches, postmodernism attacks modernity's faith in science. Postmodernism poses three interrelated problems associated with human knowledge.

First is the problem of representation. Postmodernists often question the view that science could be used to demystify the world by discovering and using the law-like principles governing its operation. Undergirding this modern belief was the notion that there is a single best mode—scientific theory and research findings—for expressing "truth" about the world. Postmodernists typically challenge this assumed correspondence between the signs of scientific language and obdurate reality. Does the language of science, or any language, provide a direct window through which we can view reality; that is, does language simply represent reality? Or is language a social construction that by its very existence distorts the picture of reality? To the degree that language is a social construction and, thus, related to social groups and their interests, the assumption of the direct representation of language is rendered problematic.

Second are the problems of power and vested interests. Though some postmodernists may concede that the physical world might operate by laws, the very process of discovering these laws creates culture that, in turn, is subject to interests, politics, and forms of domination. For example, law-like knowledge in subatomic physics has reflected political interests in war-making, or the laws of genetics can be seen to serve the interests of biotechnology firms. What is true of the laws of the physical and organic worlds is even more true of social laws whose very articulation reflects moral, political, economic, and other interests within the social sphere. From a postmodernist's view, "truth" in science, especially social science, is not a correspondence between theoretical statements and the actual social universe but a cultural production like any other sign system. Science cannot, therefore, enjoy a "privileged voice" because it is like all cultural texts.

Third is the problem of continuity. Postmodernists question the view that knowledge accumulates in ways that increase continuity among understandings about the world and that can be used to advance society. This faith in knowledge was a hallmark of modernity, but to postmodernists, who see discontinuities in knowledge as tied to shifts in the interests of dominant factions in society, such faith in the progressing continuity of knowledge and culture is not only misguided but empirically wrong. Postmodernists argue that because there is no truth that exists apart from the ideological interests of humans, discontinuity of knowledge is the norm, and a permanent pluralism of cultures is the only real truth that humans must continually face.

In the end, the postmodern philosophical attack on science denies privileged status to any knowledge system, including its own "because any place of arrival is but a temporary station. No place is privileged, no place better than another, as from no place the horizon is nearer than from any other."[1] Postmodernism emphasizes that, as a human creation, knowledge is relative to, and contingent on, the circumstances in which it was generated. Because knowledge is ultimately a system of signs, or a language of human expression, it is about itself as much as an external world "out there."

---

[1]Zygmunt Bauman, *Intimations of Postmodernity* (London: Routledge, 1992).

This critique has many of the same elements as those expressed by the first critical theorists examined in Chapter 22, but it adds new twists and takes new turns. We should, thereby, examine this shift in emphasis within the postmodern critique, but we should pursue the more general argument further by examining the key founding thinkers and contemporary figures in the postmodern intellectual movement.

Jean-François Lyotard

Jean-François Lyotard built much of his critique of science[2] on a notion borrowed from Ludwig Wittgenstein: language as a game.[3] Wittgenstein had posited an analogous relationship between the manner in which language functions and the way games are played. He argued that language, like a game, is an autonomous creation that requires no justification for its existence other than itself and is subject only to its own rules. With the term *language,* Wittgenstein was denoting not simply words and their syntactical arrangements but, rather, all that is wrapped up in the presentation, reception, and enactment of human expression. And this expression exists for no other reason than itself and is subject to no other rules than its own.

Lyotard, using Wittgenstein's analogy, proposes a comparison between the narrative form of knowledge, on the one side, and the denotative, scientific form of knowledge, on the other. Narrative is a form of expression that is close to the social world of real people; it is expressed within a social circle for the purpose of creating and sustaining this social circle. In this view of narratives, Lyotard means something akin to the oral histories of small familial-based groups, in which there are internal rules concerning who has the right to speak and who has the responsibility to listen. Verification of the knowledge created in such a narrative is reflexive because such verification of the narrative refers to its own rules of discourse.

In contrast, the denotative, scientific form of knowledge does not originate from social bonds, but rather, science proposes to simply represent what is in the physical universe, thereby subjugating the narrative form of knowledge. Lyotard argues that narrative and tradition are no longer needed in science because theory and research will reveal the true nature of the universe. Yet there is a problem with science: to be heard, science must appeal to a form of narrative knowledge—in this case a grand narrative. This grand narrative is based on The Enlightenment's promise of human emancipation and encompasses the vision of progress most clearly expressed by Georg Hegel. Lyotard maintains that postmodernism is defined by a diffuse sense of doubt concerning any such grand narrative and that this need to appeal to a narrative reveals science to be a language game like any other. Thus, science has no special authority or power to supervise other language games. According to Lyotard's vision, dissension must now be emphasized rather than consensus; heterogeneous claims to knowledge, in which one voice is not privileged over another, are the only true basis of knowledge.

---

[2]Jean-François Lyotard, *The Postmodern Condition* (Minneapolis: University of Minnesota Press, 1979, 1984).

[3]Ludwig Wittgenstein, *Philosophical Investigations* (New York: Macmillan, 1936–1949, 1973).

Richard Rorty

The philosopher Richard Rorty[4] pushes the philosophical critique of science further to the extreme—indeed, to the point of appearing to assert that there is no external, obdurate reality "out there." Science argues, of course, that there is a reality "out there," that languages can be used in increasingly precise ways to denote and understand its properties and dynamics, that language can be used to communicate the discoveries of science to fellow scientists and others as well, that truth is the degree of correspondence between theory and data, and that efforts to increase this correspondence make science self-correcting. Hence, science does use language in ways that make it a more "objective" representation of the external world, thereby ensuring that certain languages are more objective than others. But, Rorty asserts, the issue can never be which language is more objective or scientific because the use of language is always directed toward pragmatic ends. Underlying every claim that one language brings a better understanding of a phenomenon than another is the assumption that it is more useful for a particular purpose. As Rorty claims, "Vocabularies are useful or useless, good or bad, helpful or misleading, sensitive or coarse, and so on; but they are not 'more objective' or 'less objective' nor more or less 'scientific.'"[5]

In addition, even if there is a true reality and a true language with which to represent that reality, the moment humans use a language, it becomes evaluative. Thus, discovering the "true nature" of reality is not the goal of language use, scientific or otherwise, but rather, this use is directed at practical concerns, and such pragmatic concerns are always value based. Social scientists can tell stories that converge and reflect their common value concerns, thereby increasing their sense of solidarity and community as social scientists. Social scientists can also tell stories of power or of forces that divide them, thereby revealing the discordant features of any collective. But these stories are about this community of individuals more than about any "real world out there."

What, then, is left for social analysts? Rorty's answer is typical of many postmodernists: deconstruct texts produced by communities of individuals using language for some value-laden, practical purpose. Deconstruction refers to the process of taking apart the elements of a text, and in Rorty's view, such deconstruction can be (a) critical, exposing the interests and ideology contained in the text, or (b) affirming, revealing elements of a text to enlighten and inform.

As becomes evident, then, Lyotard and Rorty would take sociological theory in a very different direction. Emphasis would be on language and texts,[6] and scientific

---

[4]Richard Rorty, "Philosophy as a Kind of Writing: An Essay on Derrida," *New Literary History* 10 (1978):141–160, *Philosophy and the Mirror of Nature* (Princeton, NJ: Princeton University Press, 1979), "Method, Social Science, and Social Hope," in *The Postmodern Turn: New Perspectives on Social Theory,* ed. Steven Seidman (Cambridge, UK: Cambridge University Press, 1994).

[5]Rorty, "Method, Social Science, and Social Hope," 57.

[6]For the postmodernist, all cultural expressions are to be understood as language. But the use of linguistic systems as a basis for understanding all social phenomena is not new with postmodernism. For example, this linguistic equivalence model is central to the work of Claude Lévi-Strauss. But postmodernism has, building on the poststructuralist work of Jacques Derrida and Michel Foucault, explicitly made signs, sign systems, and texts human reality in toto.

explanations of an obdurate social reality would be seen as yet another form of text. This new direction—which represents a philosophical assault on scientific socio- logical theory—can be further appraised with illustrative examples of sociologists who have used the thrust of this philosophical critique in their more explicitly sociological works.

Illustrative Elaborations and Extensions Within Sociology

Richard Harvey Brown's "Society as Text." Richard Harvey Brown[7] specifically applies the philosophical critique of postmodernism to social science, positing that social and cultural realities, and social science itself, are linguistic construc- tions. Brown advocates an approach termed symbolic realism,[8] in which the universe is seen as existing for humans through communicative action. Moreover, each act of communication is based on previously constructed communicative actions—modes and forms of discourse, ideologies, worldviews, and other lin- guistic forms. Hence, the search for the first or ultimate reality is a fruitless endeavor. Indeed, the "worlds" that are accepted as "true" at any one point in human history are constituted through normative, practical, epistemological, political, aesthetic, and moral practices, which, in turn, are themselves symbolic constructions. Symbolic realism is thus a critical approach that seeks to uncover the ideologies surrounding the premises on which knowledge, senses of self, and portrayals of realities are constructed.

In this critical vein, Brown concludes that sociological theories themselves are "practices through which things take on meaning and value, and not merely as rep- resentations of a reality that is wholly exterior to them."[9] Theory in sociology ought to be critical and reflexive, with theorists recognizing that their own theories are themselves rhetorical constructions and, thus, texts constructed in time, place, and context as well as through linguistic conventions. This kind of approach to social theory as rhetoric sees its own discourse as not being about society—that is, as an effort to construct "true" representations on the nature of society—but, rather, as being simply part of what constitutes society, particularly its forms of textual dis- course and representation.[10]

---

[7]Richard Harvey Brown, *Society as Text: Essays on Rhetoric, Reason, and Reality* (Chicago, IL: The Uni- versity of Chicago Press, 1987), *Social Science as Civic Discourse: Essays on the Invention, Legitimation, and Uses of Social Theory* (Chicago, IL: The University of Chicago Press, 1989), "Rhetoric, Textuality, and the Postmodern Turn in Sociological Theory," *Sociological Theory* 8 (1990):188–197.

[8]Brown, *Social Science as Civic Discourse*, 49–54.

[9]Ibid., 188.

[10]In the postmodern literature, a distinction is often made between social and sociological theory. Social theory is generally understood to be a text that is self-consciously directed toward improving social conditions through entering the social discourse, whereas sociological theory is a denotative text that is abstracted from social concerns and involvement. In the view of postmodernism, social theory is preferred to sociological theory.

Charles C. Lemert's Emphasis on Rhetoric. For Charles Lemert,[11] all social theory is inherently discursive, stated in loose languages and constructed within particular social circles. What discursive theoretical texts explain—that is, "empirical reality"— is itself a discursive text, constructed like any text and subject to all the distorting properties of any text production. That theoretical texts depend on empirical texts, and vice versa, for their scientific value increases science's discursiveness. Each scientific portrayal of reality—whether from the "theory" or "research findings" side— is a text and, actually, a kind of "text on top of another text." This compounding of texts has implications for social scientific explanations: social science explanations are often less adequate to understanding reality than are ordinary discursive texts that are less convoluted and compounded.

This understanding of the primacy of language leads to the use of irony in social theory. But the social theorist's use of irony is more than a literary device; it is a position from which the theorist views reality and its relationship to language. The physical universe is known to humans only through representation, culture, or language. Thus, reality shifts in response to different modes of representation. For example, in the eyes of humanity, the earth has shifted from being the center of the universe to being simply one of many planets circling one of a multitude of stars. But this position of the theorist also views language as humanity's certainty: language is certain, and in that sense real, because the fundamental qualities and meanings of a linguistic system are known, valid, and replicable within itself. Because language is certain, theorists can make general statements concerning the properties of the physical universe, but the certitude of those statements rests in language and not in the physical reality or even the assumed relationship between culture and reality. The only position, then, for a social theorist is an ironic one: general theoretical statements can be made, but with a "tongue-in-cheek" attitude because the author of such statements is reflexively aware that the only certitude of the statements rests in the linguistic system and not in the physical or social reality.

Mark Gottdiener's and Steven Seidman's Critique. Steven Seidman[12] adopts Rorty's distinction between enriching and critical forms of text deconstruction. And, along with Mark Gottdiener,[13] and many others as well, Seidman questions any social theory that posits a foundationalism, or the view that knowledge accumulates such that one level of knowledge can serve as the base on which ever more knowledge is built. Foundationalism is, of course, at the very core of science, and so this critique is truly fundamental for the activities that intellectuals can pursue. For Seidman and

[11]Charles C. Lemert, "The Uses of French Structuralisms in Sociology," *Frontiers of Social Theory: The New Syntheses*, ed. George Ritzer (New York: Columbia University Press, 1990), 230–254, "General Social Theory, Irony, Postmodernism," *Postmodernism and Social Theory*, ed. Steven Seidman and David G. Wagner (Cambridge, MA: Blackwell, 1990), 17–46.

[12]Steven Seidman, "The End of Sociological Theory," in *The Postmodern Turn: New Perspectives on Social Theory*, ed. Steven Seidman (Cambridge, UK: Cambridge University Press, 1994), 84–96.

[13]Mark Gottdiener, "The Logocentrism of the Classics," *American Sociological Review* 55 (June 1990):460– 463, "Ideology, Foundationalism, and Sociological Theory," *Sociological Quarterly* 34 (1993):653–671.

Gottdiener, however, foundationalism is just another effort to impose a grand narrative as a privileged voice.

Gottdiener sees foundationalism in sociological theory as an ideology, based on a *logocentrism* where "the classics" in theory are seen as the base on which a theoretical position is built. Such logocentrism is nothing more than a political ploy by established theorists to maintain their privileged position. Thus, sociological theory is about language and power games among theorists seeking to construct a grand narrative that also sustains their privilege and authority within an intellectual community.[14]

If such is the case, Seidman argues, the hope of human emancipation through sociological theory must be replaced by "the more modest aspiration of a relentless defense of immediate, local pleasures and struggles for justice."[15] But Gottdiener sees this position as akin to Rorty's concern with the use of vocabularies to sustain communities of scholars. Because of the inherent and ultimate privileging of one morality over another in such communities—not all moralities, even local ones, are commensurable one with another—theory does not become sufficiently critical. Instead, Gottdiener advocates a continuous, critical, and reflexive cycle of evaluation relative to the relationship between power and knowledge for evaluating all theories—postmodern or otherwise—that seek some grand narrative or self-legitimating tradition.

In sum, these representative commentaries offer a sense of the postmodern critique of science. Yet postmodernism is much more than a philosophical critique. If this were all that postmodernists had to offer, there would be little point in examining these criticisms. Moreover, not all postmodernist theorists accept the philosophical critique just outlined, although most are highly suspicious of the "hard-science" view of sociological theory.[16] Indeed, most are committed to analysis of contemporary societies, especially the effects that dramatic changes in distribution, transportation, and information systems have had on the individual self and patterns of social organization. We can begin with "economic postmodernists," who generally employ extensions of Karl Marx's ideas and who, to varying degrees, still retain some of Marx's emancipatory zeal or, if not zeal, guarded hope that a better future may lie ahead.

Economic Postmodernism

Economic postmodernists are concerned with *capital*, especially its *overaccumulation* (i.e., overabundance) as well as its level of dispersion and rapid movement in the new world system of markets driven and connected by information technologies.

---

[14]Gottdiener, "Ideology, Foundationalism, and Sociological Theory," 667.

[15]Seidman, "The End of Sociological Theory," 120.

[16]For example, Lemert, *Sociology After the Crisis* (Boulder, CO: Westview, 1995), 78 makes a distinction between radical postmodernism and strategic postmodernism. Radical postmodernists disavow any possibility of truth or reality, whereas strategic postmodernists attempt to undercut the authority that modernist knowledge claims, while preserving the language and categories that modernist knowledge uses. Strategic postmodernists, according to Lemert, still maintain the modernist hope of emancipation.

Moreover, culture or systems of symbols are seen to emerge from economic processes, but they exert independent effects not only on the economy but also on every other facet of human endeavor. Indeed, for some economic postmodernists, advanced capitalism has evolved into a new stage of human history[17] that, like earlier modernity, is typified by a series of "problems," including the loss of a core or essential sense of self, the use of symbolic as much as material means to control individuals, the increased salience of cultural resources as both tools of repression and potential resistance, the emotional disengagement of individuals from culture, and the loss of national identities and a corresponding shift to local and personal identities. This list, and other "pathologies" of the postmodern era, sound much like those that concerned early sociologists when they worried about such matters as anomie and egoism (Émile Durkheim), alienation (Marx), the marginal and fractured self (Georg Simmel), ideological control and manipulation by the powerful (Marx and, later, Antonio Gramsci and Louis Althusser), political-ideological mobilization as resistance (Marx), overdifferentiation and fragmentation of the social structure (Adam Smith, Herbert Spencer, and Durkheim), rationalization and domination by overconcern with efficiency (Max Weber), and so on. Thus, economically oriented postmodernists evidence many of the same analytical tendencies as those who first sought to theorize about modernity.

Figure 22.1 juxtaposes the economic postmodernists' argument on the left with the cultural analysis on the right. It is presumed that the dynamics of advanced capitalism generate consequences that are emphasized by cultural postmodernists. The theorists examined here in this section emphasize the dynamics of capitalism, while those examined later under cultural postmodernisms examine the consequences of these economic dynamics.

Fredric Jameson

Among the central figures in economic postmodernism, Fredric Jameson is the most explicitly Marxist.[18] Although his theory is about the complex interplay among multinational capitalism, technological advance, and the mass media, "the truth of postmodernism . . . [is] the world space of multinational capital."[19] He posits that capitalism has gone through three distinct phases, with each phase linked to a particular kind of technology. Early-market capitalism was linked to steam-driven machinery; mid-monopoly capitalism was characterized by steam and combustion engines; and late-multinational capitalism is associated with nuclear power and electronic machines.

Late-multinational capitalism is the subject of postmodern theory. In particular, the nature of praxis, or the use of thought to organize action to change conditions and the use of experiences in action to reexamine thought, is transformed and

---

[17]See, for example, Stephen Crook, Jan Pakulski, and Malcolm Waters, *Postmodernization* (London: Sage, 1992).

[18]Fredric Jameson, *The Postmodern Condition* (Minneapolis: University of Minnesota Press, 1984).

[19]Ibid., 92.

Figure 22.1   The Effects of Advanced Capitalism in Creating the Postmodern Condition

Advanced Capitalism	Consequences of Advanced Capitalism
High volume and velocity global markets fueled by advertising	Increased significance of culture over material structures
Rapid movement of capital on a global scale, fueled by meta-markets selling forms of capital	Detachment of culture from the material structures in local times and places
Global movement of capital seeks to prevent over-accumulation of capital	Marketing of detached symbols and culture on a global scale
Increased commodification of objects, people, and, most important, cultural symbols	Destabilization of cultural symbols and their capacity to provide stable meanings
Transportation and communication technologies compress time and space on a global scale	Increased salience of the individual over groups and collectivities
Technologies of reproduction–imaging, technographics—over technologies of production	Increased reflexivity of self, instability, and fragmentation of self
	Decreased viability, stability, and coherence of self

Source: Kenneth Allan and Jonathan Turner, "A Formalization of Postmodern Theory," *Sociological Perspectives* (2000), pp. 363–85.

confounded by the changed nature of signification that comes when the machines of symbolic reproduction—cameras, computers, videos, movies, tape recorders, fax machines—remove the direct connection between human production and its symbolic representation. These machines generate sequences of signs on top of signs that alter the nature of praxis—that is, how can thought guide action on the world, and vice versa, when concepts in such thought are so detached from material conditions?

Drawing from Marx's philosophy of knowledge, Jameson still attempts to use the method of praxis to critique the social construction of reality in postmodernity. Marx argued that reality did not exist in concepts, ideas, or reflexive thought but in the material world of production. Indeed, he broke with the young Hegelians over this issue, seeing them as "blowing theoretical bubbles" about the reality of ideas. But like the earlier generation of critical theorists in the first decades of the twentieth century (see Chapter 22), those of the late twentieth century begin to sound even more Hegelian. According to Jameson, the creation of consciousness through production was unproblematically represented by the aesthetic of the machine in earlier phases of capitalism, but in multinational capitalism, electronic machines like movie cameras, videos, tape recorders, and computers do not have the same capacity for signification because they are machines of reproduction rather than of production.

Thus, the foundation of thought and knowledge in postmodernity is not simply false; as Marx's view of "false consciousness" emphasized, it is nonexistent. Because the machines of late capitalism reproduce knowledge rather than produce it, and because the reproduction itself is focused more on the medium than on the message, the signification chain from object to sign has broken down. Jameson characterizes this breakdown as the schizophrenia of culture. Based on de Saussure's notion that meaning is a function of the relationship between signifiers (see Chapter 20), the concept of a break in the signification chain indicates that each sign stands alone, or in a relatively loose association with fragmented groups of other signs, and that meaning is free-floating and untied to any clear material reality.

Moreover, in a postmodern world dominated by machines of reproduction, language loses the capacity to ground concepts to places, to moments of time, or to objects, in addition to losing its ability to organize symbols into coherent systems of concepts about place, time, and object. As language loses these capacities, time and space become disassociated. If a sign system becomes detached and free-floating and if it is fragmented and without order, the meaning of concepts in relation to time and space cannot be guaranteed. Indeed, meaning in any sense becomes problematic. The conceptual connection between the "here-and-now" and its relation to the previous "there-and-then" has broken down, and the individual experiences "a series of pure and unrelated presents in time."[20]

Jameson goes on to argue that culture in the postmodern condition has created a fragmented rather than alienated subject. Self is not so much alienated from the failure to control its own productive activities; rather, self is now a series of images in a material world dominated by the instruments of reproduction rather than production. In addition, the decentering of the postmodern self produces a kind of emotional flatness or depthlessness "since there is no longer any self to do the feeling . . . [and emotions] are now free-floating and impersonal."[21] Subjects are thus fragmented and dissolved, having no material basis for consciousness or narratives about their situation; under these conditions, individuals' capacity for praxis—using thought to act and action to generate thought—is diminished. Of course, this capacity for praxis is not so diminished that Jameson cannot develop a critical theory of the postmodern condition, although the action side of Marx's notion of praxis is as notably absent, if not impotent, as it was for the first generation of Frankfurt critical theorists.

David Harvey

In a manner like that of Jameson, David Harvey[22] posits that capitalism has brought about significant problems associated with humans' capacity to conceptualize

---

[20]Ibid., 72.

[21]Ibid., 64.

[22]David Harvey, *The Conditions of Postmodernity: An Inquiry into the Origins of Cultural Change* (Oxford, UK: Blackwell, 1989).

time and space. Yet for Harvey the cultural and perceptual problems associated with postmodernism are not new. Some of the same tendencies toward fragmentation and confusion in political, cultural, and philosophical movements occurred around the turn of the century. And, in Harvey's view, the cultural features of the postmodern world are no more permanent—as many postmodernists imply—than were those of the modernity that emerged in the nineteenth and early twentieth centuries.

Unlike Jameson, Harvey does not see the critical condition of postmodernity as the problem of praxis—of anchoring signs and symbols in a material reality that can be changed through thought and action—but, rather, as a condition of *over-accumulation,* or the modes by which too much capital is assembled and disseminated. All capitalist systems—as Marx recognized—have evidenced this problem of over-accumulation, because capitalism is a system designed to grow through exploitation of labor, technological innovation, and organizational retrenchment. At some point, there is overabundance: too many products to sell to nonexistent buyers, too much productive capacity that goes unused, or too much money to invest with insufficient prospects for profits.

This over-accumulation is met in a variety of ways, the most common being the business cycle, where workers are laid off, plants are closed, bankruptcies are increased, and money is devalued. Such cycles generally restore macro-level economic controls (usually by government) over money supply, interest rates, unemployment compensation, bankruptcy laws, tax policies, and the like. But Harvey emphasizes another response to over-accumulation: absorption of surplus capital through "temporal" and "spatial" displacement. Temporal displacement occurs when investors buy "futures" on commodities yet to be produced, when they purchase stock options in the hope of stock prices rising, when they invest in other financial instruments (mortgages, long-term bonds, government securities), or when they pursue any strategy for using time and the swings of all markets to displace capital and reduce over-accumulation. Spatial displacement involves moving capital away from areas of over-accumulation to new locations in need of investment capital. Harvey argues that displacement is most effective when both its temporal and its spatial aspects are combined, as when money raised in London is sent to Latin America to buy bonds (which will probably be resold again in the future) to finance infrastructural development.

The use of both spatial and temporal displacement to meet the issue of over-accumulation can contribute to the more general problem of time and space displacement. Time and space displacement occurs because of four factors: (1) advanced communication and transportation technologies, (2) increased rationalization of distribution processes, (3) meta- and world-level money markets that accelerate the circulation of money, and (4) decreased spatial concentration of capital in geographical locations (cities, nations, and regions). These changes create a perceived sense of time and space compression that must be matched by changes in beliefs, ideologies, perceptions, and other systems of symbols. As technologies combine to allow us to move people and objects more quickly through space—as with the advent of travel by rail, automobile, jet, rocket—space becomes compressed; that is, distance is reduced, and space is not as forbidding or meaningful as it was at one time. Ironically, as the speed of transportation, communication, market exchanges, commodity distribution, and capital circulation increases, the amount of available time decreases, because there are more things to do and more ways to do them. Thus, our sense of time and space compresses in response to increases in specific technologies and structural capacities. If these technological and structural changes occur gradually, then the culture that renders the resulting alterations in time and space understandable and meaningful will evolve along with the changes. But if the changes in structure and technology occur rapidly, as in postmodernity, then the modifications in symbolic categories will not keep pace, and people will be left with a sense of disorientation concerning two primary categories of human existence, time and space. The present response to over-accumulation, "flexible capitalism," helps create a sense of time and space compression as capital is rapidly moved and manipulated on a global scale in response to portfolio management techniques.

In addition, because the new mode of accumulation is designed to move capital spatially and temporally in a flexible and thus ever-changing manner, disorientation ensues as the mode of regulation struggles to keep up with the mode of accumulation. For example, if capital-sustaining jobs in one country can be immediately exported to another with lower-priced labor, beliefs among workers about loyalty to the company, conceptions about how to develop a career, commitments of companies to local communities, ideologies of government, import policies, beliefs about training and retraining, conceptions of labor markets, ideologies of corporate responsibility, laws about foreign investment, and many other cultural modes for regulating the flow of capital will all begin to change. Thus, in postmodernity, physical place has been replaced by a new social space driven by the new technologies of highly differentiated and dynamic markets, but cultural orientations have yet to catch up to this pattern of time and space compression.

As with most economic postmodernists, Harvey emphasizes that markets now distribute services as much as they deliver commodities or "hard goods," and many of the commodities and services that are distributed concern the formation of an image of self and identity. Cultural images are now market driven, emphasizing fashion and corporate logos as well as other markers of culture, lifestyle, group membership, taste, status, and virtually anything that individuals can see as relevant to their identity. As boredom, saturation, and imitation create demands for new images with which to define self, cultural images constantly shift—being limited only by the imagination of people, advertisers, and profit-seeking producers. As a result, the pace and volatility of products to be consumed accelerate, and producers for markets as well as agents in markets (such as advertisers, bankers, and investors) search for new images to market as commodities or services.

Given a culture that values instant gratification and easy disposability of commodities, people generally react with sensory block, denial, a blasé attitude, myopic specialization, increased nostalgia (for stable old ways), and an increased search for eternal but simplified truths and collective or personal identity. To the extent that these reactions are the mark of postmodernity, Harvey argues that they represent the lag between cultural responses to new patterns of capital displacement over time and place. Eventually, culture and people's perceptions will catch up to these new mechanisms for overcoming the latest incarnation of capital over-accumulation.

Scott Lash and John Urry

Like David Harvey, Scott Lash and John Urry argue that a postmodern disposition occurs with changes in advanced capitalism that shift time and space boundaries.[23] In their view, shifting conceptualizations of time and space are associated with changes in the distribution of capital. Moreover, like most postmodern theorists, they stress that postmodern culture is heavily influenced by the mass media and advertising. Yet, revealing their Marxian roots, they add that the postmodern disposition is particularly dependent on the fragmentation of class experience and the rise of the service class. With their emphasis on capital and the class structure, the focus of Lash and Urry's analysis is thus Marxian, but their method is Weberian: they disavow causal sequences, preferring to speak in terms of preconditions and ideal types. Thus, they see the postmodernism forms outlined by Lyotard, Jameson, and, as we will see, Baudrillard as an ideal type against which different systems of culture can be compared.

Like Harvey, Lash and Urry do not see postmodern culture as entirely new, but unlike Harvey, they are less sure that it is a temporary phase waiting for culture to catch up to changed material conditions. Lash and Urry believe that postmodern culture will always appeal to certain audiences with "postmodern dispositions." These dispositions emerge in response to three forces: first, the boundary between reality and image must become blurred as the media, and especially advertising, present ready-made rather than socially constructed cultural images. Second, the traditional working class must be fractured and fragmented; at the same time, a new service class oriented to the consumption of commodities for their symbolic power to produce, mark, and proclaim distinctions in group memberships, tastes, lifestyles, preferences, gender orientation, ethnicity, and many other distinctions must become prominent. And third, the construction of personal and subjective identities must increasingly be built from cultural symbols detached from physical space and location, such as neighborhood, town, or region; as this detachment occurs, images of self become ever more transitory. As these three forces intensify, a postmodern disposition becomes more likely, and these dispositions can come to support a broader postmodern culture where symbols marking difference, identity, and location are purchased by the expanding service class.

Although Lash and Urry are reluctant to speak of causation, it appears that at least four deciding factors bring about these postmodern conditions. The first factor involves the shift from Taylorist or regimented forms of production, such as the old factory assembly line, to more flexible forms of organizing and controlling labor, such as production teams, "flex-time" working hours, reduced hierarchies of authority, and deconcentration of work extending to computer terminals at home. Like Harvey, Lash and Urry believe that these shifts cause and reflect decreased spatial concentration of capital, and expanded communication and transportation technologies, spatial dispersion, deconcentration of capital, and rapid movement of

---

[23]Scott Lash and John Urry, *The End of Organized Capitalism* (Madison: University of Wisconsin Press, 1987), *Economies of Signs and Space* (Newbury Park, CA: Sage, 1994).

information, people, and resources are the principle dynamics of change. The second factor concerns large-scale economic changes—the globalization of a market economy, the expansion of industry and banking across national boundaries, and the spread of capitalism to less developed countries. The third factor is the increased distributive capacities that accelerate and extend the flow of commodities from the local and national to international markets. This increased scope and speed of circulation can empty many commodities of their ethnic, local, national, and other traditional anchors of symbolic and affective meaning. This rapid circulation of commodities increases the likelihood that many other commodities will be made and purchased for what they communicate aesthetically and cognitively about ever-shifting tastes, preferences, lifestyles, personal statements, and new boundaries of prestige and status group membership. And the fourth factor is really a set of forces that follows from the other factors: (a) the commodification of leisure as yet another purchased symbolic statement; (b) the breakdown of, and merger among, previously distinct and coherent cultural forms (revolving around music, art, literature, class, ethnic, or gender identity and other cultural distinctions in modernism); (c) the general collapse of social space, designated physical locations, and temporal frames within which activities are conducted and personal identifications are sustained; and (d) the undermining of politics as tied to traditional constituencies (a time dimension) located in physical places like neighborhoods and social spaces such as classes and ethnic groups.

Together these factors create a spatially fragmented division of labor, a less clear-cut working class, a larger service class, a shift to symbolic rather than material or coercive domination, the use of cultural more than material resources for resistance, and a level of cultural fragmentation and pluralism that erodes nationalism. But Lash and Urry argue, in contrast with Jameson, that this emptying out process is not as deregulated as it might appear. They posit that new forms of distribution, communication, and transportation all create networks in time, social spaces, and physical places. Economic governance occurs where the networks are dense, with communications having an increasingly important impact on the difference between core and peripheral sites. Core sites are heavily networked communication sites that function as a "wired village of noncontiguous communities."[24]

All these economic postmodernists clearly have roots in Marxian analysis, both the critical forms that emerged in the early decades of the century and the world-system forms of analysis that arose in the 1970s and continue to the present day. Early critical theorists had to come to terms with the Weberian specter of coercive and rational-legal authority as crushing emancipatory class activity, but this generation of postmodern critics has had to reconcile their rather muted emancipatory goals with the spread of world capitalism as the preferred economic system; the prosperity generated by capitalism; the breakdown of the proletariat as a coherent class (much less a vanguard of emancipation); the commodification of everything in fluid and dynamic markets; the production and consumption of symbols more than hard goods (as commodities are bought for their symbolic value);

---

[24]Lash and Urry, *Economies of Signs and Space*, 28.

the destruction of social, physical, and temporal boundaries as restrictions of space and time are changed by technologies; the purchase of personal and subjective identities by consumer-driven actors; and the importance of symbolic and cultural "superstructures" as driving forces in world markets glutted with mass media and advertising images. Given these forced adaptations of the Marxian perspective, it is not surprising that many postmodernists have shifted their focus from the economic base to culture.

Cultural Postmodernism

All postmodern theories emphasize the fragmenting character of culture and the blurring of differences marked by symbols. Individuals are seen as caught in these transformations, participating in, and defining self from, an increasing array of social categories, such as race, class, gender, ethnicity, or status, while being exposed to ever-increasing varieties of cultural images as potential markers of self. At the same time, individuals lose their sense of being located in stable places and time frames. Many of the forces examined by economic postmodernists can account for this fragmentation of culture, decline in the salience of markers of differences, and loss of identity in time, place, and social space, but cultural postmodernists place particular emphasis on mass media and advertising because these are driven by markets and information technologies.

Jean Baudrillard

The strongest postmodern statement concerning the effects of the media on culture comes from Jean Baudrillard,[25] who sees the task before the social sciences today as challenging the "meaning that comes from the media and its fascination."[26] In contrast with philosophical postmodernism, Baudrillard's theory is based on the assumption that there is a potential equivalence or correspondence between the sign and its object, and based on this proposition, Baudrillard posits four historical phases of the sign.

In the first phase, the sign represented a profound reality, with the correlation and correspondence between the sign and the obdurate reality it signified being very high. In the next two phases, signs dissimulated or hid reality in some way: in the second phase, signs masked or counterfeited reality, as when art elaborated or commented on life, whereas in the third phase, signs masked the absence of any profound reality, as when mass commodification produced a plethora of signs that have no real basis in group identity but have the appearance of originating in group interaction.

---

[25]Jean Baudrillard, *For a Critique of the Political Economy of the Sign* (St. Louis, MO: Telos, 1972, 1981), *The Mirror of Production* (St. Louis, MO: Telos, 1973, 1975), *Simulacra and Simulation* (Ann Arbor: University of Michigan Press, 1981, 1994), *Symbolic Exchange and Death* (Newbury Park, CA: Sage, 1993).

[26]Baudrillard, *Simulacra and Simulation,* 84.

The second phase roughly corresponds to the period of time from the Renaissance to the Industrial Revolution, whereas the third phase came with the Industrial Age as production and new market forces created commodities whose sign values marking tastes, style, status, and other symbolic representations of individuals began to rival the use value (for some practical purpose) or exchange value (for some other commodity or resource like money) of commodities. In Baudrillard's view, then, the evolution of signs has involved decreasing, if not obfuscating, their connection to real objects in the actual world.

The fourth stage in the evolution of the sign is the present postmodern era. In this age, the sign "has no relation to any reality whatsoever: It is its own pure simulacrum."[27] Signs are about themselves and, hence, are simulations or simulacrums of other signs, with little connection to the basic nature of the social or material world. Baudrillard's prime example of simulacrum is Disneyland. Disneyland presents itself as a representation of Americana, embodying the values and joys of American life. Disneyland is offered as imagery—a place to symbolically celebrate and enjoy all that is good in the real world. But Baudrillard argues that Disneyland is presented as imagery to hide the fact that it is American reality itself. Life in the surrounding "real" communities, for example, Los Angeles and Anaheim, consists simply of emulations of past realities. People no longer walk as a mode of transportation; rather, they jog or power walk. People no longer touch one another in daily interaction; rather, they go to contact-therapy groups. The essence of life in postmodernity is imagery; behavior is determined by image potential and is thus simply image. Baudrillard depicts Los Angeles as "no longer anything but an immense scenario and a perpetual pan shot."[28] Thus, when Disneyland is presented as a symbolic representation of life in America and when life there is itself an image or simulation of a past reality, then Disneyland becomes a simulation of a simulation, with no relationship to any reality whatsoever, and it hides the nonreality of daily life.

Baudrillard argues that the presentation of information by the media destroys information. This destruction occurs because there is a natural entropy within the information process; any information about a social event is a degraded form of that event and, hence, represents a dissolving of the social. The media is nothing more than a constant barrage of bits of image and sign that have been removed an infinite number of times from actual social events. Thus, the media does not present a surplus of information, but on the contrary, what is communicated represents total entropy of information and, hence, of the social world that is supposedly denoted by signs organized into information. The media also destroys information because it stages the presentation of information, presenting it in a prepackaged meaning form. As information is staged, the subject is told what constitutes his or her particular relationship to that information, thereby simulating for individuals their place and location in a universe of signs about signs.

Baudrillard argues that the break between reality and the sign was facilitated by advertising. Advertising eventually reduces objects from their use value to their sign

---

[27]Ibid., 6.

[28]Ibid., 13.

value; the symbols of advertisements become commodities in and of themselves, and image more than information about the commodity is communicated. Thus, advertisements typically juxtapose a commodity with a desirable image—for example, a watch showing one young male and two young females with their naked bodies overlapping one another—rather than providing information about the quality and durability of the commodity. So that what is being sold and purchased is the image rather than the commodity itself. But, further, advertising itself can become the commodity sought after by the consuming public rather than the image of the advertisement. In the postmodern era, the form of the advertisement rather than the advertisement itself becomes paramount. For example, a currently popular form of television commercial is what could be called the "MTV-style." Certain groups of people respond to these commercials not because of the product and not simply because of the images contained within the advertisements but because they respond to the overall form of the message (and not to its content at all). Thus, in postmodernity, the medium is the message, and what people are faced with, according to Baudrillard, is simulations of simulations and an utter absence of any reality.

Further Elaborations of Cultural Postmodernism

Kenneth Gergen. The self is best understood, in Kenneth Gergen's view,[29] as the process through which individuals categorize their own behaviors. This process depends on the linguistic system used in the physical and social spaces that locate the individual at a given time. Because conceptualizations of self are situational, the self generally tends to be experienced by individuals as fragmented and sometimes contradictory. Yet people are generally motivated to eliminate inconsistencies in conceptualizations, and though Gergen grants that other possible factors influence efforts to resolve inconsistencies, people in Western societies try to create a consistent self-identity because they are socialized to dislike cognitive dissonance in much the same way that they are taught to reason rationally. Gergen thus sees an intrinsic relationship between the individual's experience of a self and the culture within which that experience takes place, a cultural stand that he exploits in his understanding of the postmodern self.

Gergen argues that the culture of the self has gone through at least three distinct stages—the romantic, modern, and current postmodern phases. During the romantic period, the self as an autonomous individual and agent was stressed as individuals came out from the domination of various institutions, including the church and the manorial estate; during the modern period, the self was perceived as possessing essential or basic qualities, such as psychologically defined inherent personality traits. But the postmodern self consists only of images, revealing no inherent qualities, and, most significantly, has lost the ability as well as the desire to create self-consistency. Further, because knowledge and culture are fragmented in the postmodern era, the very concept of the individual self must be questioned and the

---

[29]Kenneth J. Gergen, *The Saturated Self* (New York: Basic Books, 1991), *The Concept of Self* (New York: Holt, Rinehart and Winston, 1971).

distinction between the subject and the object dropped. According to Gergen, then, the very category of the self has been erased as a result of postmodern culture.

Thus, like Baudrillard, Gergen sees the self in postmodern culture as becoming saturated with images that are incoherent, communicating unrelated elements in different languages. And corresponding to Baudrillard's death of the subject, Gergen posits that the category of the self has been eradicated because efforts to formulate consistent and coherent definitions of who people are have been overwhelmed by images on images, couched in diverse languages that cannot order self-reflection.

Norman Denzin and Douglas Kellner. In contrast with Baudrillard's claim that television is simply a flow of incessant disjointed and empty images, both Norman Denzin[30] and Douglas Kellner[31] argue that television and other media have formed people's ideas and actions in much the same way as traditional myth and ritual: These media integrate individuals into a social fabric of values, norms, and roles. In the postmodern culture and economy, media images themselves are the basis from which people get their identities—in particular, their identities of race, class, and gender.

In addition, Denzin and Kellner advocate a method of social activism: a critical reading of the texts from media presentations to discover the underlying ideologies, discourses, and meanings that the political economy produces. The purpose of these critical readings is to "give a voice to the voiceless, as it deconstructs those popular culture texts which reproduce stereotypes about the powerless."[32] Both theorists disavow any grand narrative, and like the more radical postmodernists, neither advocates a center point, ultimate hope, and grand or totalizing discourse. Yet, like critical theorists before them, they both hold out the hope of forming new solidarities and initiating emancipatory conflicts through the exposé of the political economy of signs.

But Denzin, unlike Kellner, takes issue with Baudrillard's and Jameson's views on self as an incoherent mirage of signs and symbols and as incapable of ordering images into some coherence. Denzin argues that the "lived experience" itself has become the final commodity in the circulation of capital and that the producers of postmodern culture selectively choose which lived experiences will be commodified and marketed to members of a society. Postmodern culture only commodifies those cultures that present a particular aesthetic picture of race, class, and gender relations, but because culture has become centrally important in postmodernity, this process of commodification has a positive value for giving individuals a sense of identity and for enabling them to act in the material world on the basis of this identity.

[30]Norman K. Denzin, "Postmodern Social Theory," *Sociological Theory* 4 (1986):194–204, *Images of Postmodern Society: Social Theory and Contemporary Cinema* (London: Sage, 1991), *Symbolic Interactionism and Cultural Studies* (Oxford, UK: Blackwell, 1992).

[31]Douglas Kellner, "Popular Culture and the Construction of Postmodern Identities," in *Modernity and Identity,* ed. Scott Lash and Jonathan Friedman (Oxford, UK: Blackwell, 1992), *Media Culture: Cultural Studies, Identity, and Politics Between the Modern and the Postmodern* (London: Routledge, 1995).

[32]Denzin, *Images of Postmodern Society,* 153.

Mark Gottdiener. Like Denzin and Kellner, Mark Gottdiener wants not only to maintain a critical postmodern stand but also to argue that an objective referent is behind the infinite regress of meaning. In contrast with Denzin and Kellner, Gottdiener sees the effects of media and markets as trivializing the culture of postmodernity.[33] According to Gottdiener, signs in technologically advanced societies can circulate between the levels of lived experience and the level where the sign is expropriated by some center of power, including producers and marketers of symbols.

Capitalizing on Baudrillard's notion of sign value, Gottdiener argues that there are three separate phases of interaction wherein a sign can be endowed with meaning. In the first stage, economically motivated producers create objects of exchange value for money and profit, an intent that is decidedly different from the goals of those who purchase the objects for their use value. In the second stage, these objects become involved in the everyday life of the social groups that use them. During this stage, users might "transfunctionalize" the object from its use value into a sign value to connect the object to their subgroup or culture (e.g., a type of denim jacket is personalized to represent a group, such as the Hell's Angels). The third stage occurs if and when the economic producers and retailers adopt these personalized and trans-functionalized objects and commodify them (e.g., the Hell's Angels' style of jacket can now be bought by any suburban teenager in a shopping mall). This third stage involves a "symbolic leveling" or "trivialization" of the signed object.[34]

Thomas Luckmann. Although Thomas Luckmann[35] recognizes the importance of the media and advertising in creating a postmodern culture, he focuses on the process of deinstitutionalization as it pushes people into the cultural markets found in the mass media. The basic function of any institution, Luckmann argues, is to provide a set of predetermined meanings for the perceived world and, simultaneously, to provide legitimation for these meanings. Religion, in particular, provides a shield of solidarity against any doubts, fears, and questions about ultimate meaning by giving and legitimating an ultimate meaning set. Yet modern structural differentiation and specialization have, Luckmann contends, made the ultimate meanings of religion structurally unstable because individuals must confront a diverse array of secular tasks and obligations that carry alternative meanings. This structural instability has, in turn, resulted in the privatization of religion. This privatization of religion is, however, more than a retreat from secular structural forces; it is also a response to forces of the sacralization of subjectivity found in mass culture.

Because of the effects of structural differentiation, markets, and mass culture, consciousness within individuals is one of the immediate sensations and emotions.

---

[33]Mark Gottdiener, "Hegemony and Mass Culture: A Semiotic Approach," *American Journal of Sociology* 90 (1985):979–1001, *Postmodern Semiotics: Material Culture and the Forms of Postmodern Life* (Oxford, UK: Blackwell, 1995).

[34]Gottdiener, "Hegemony and Mass Culture," 996.

[35]Thomas Luckmann, "The New and the Old in Religion," *Social Theory for a Changing Society*, ed. Pierre Bourdieu and James S. Coleman (Boulder, CO: Westview, 1991).

As a consequence, consciousness is unstable, making acceptance of general legitimating myths, symbols, and dogmas problematic—Lyotard's "incredulity toward grand narratives." Yet capitalist markets have turned this challenge into profitable business. The individual is now faced with a highly competitive market for the ultimate meanings created by mass media, churches and sects, residual nineteenth-century secular ideologies, and substitute religious communities. The products of this market form a more or less systematically arranged meaning set that refers to minimal and intermediate meanings but rarely to ultimate meanings. Under these conditions, a meaning set can be taken up by an individual for a long or short period of time and combined with elements from other meaning sets. Thus, just as early capitalism and the structural forces that it unleashed undermined the integrative power of religion, so advanced capitalism creates a new, more postmodern diversity of commodified meaning sets that can be mass produced and consumed by individuals in search of a cultural coherence that can stave off their anxieties and fears in a structurally differentiated and culturally fragmented social world.

Zygmunt Bauman. Like Luckmann, Zygmunt Bauman[36] examines the effects of deinstitutionalization on meanings about self in chaotic, often random, and highly differentiated systems. Within these kinds of systems, identity formation consists of self-constitution, with no reference point for evaluation or monitoring, no clear anchorage in place and time, and no lifelong and consistent project of self-formation. People thus experience a high degree of uncertainty about their identity, and as a consequence, Bauman argues, the only visible vehicle for identity formation is the body.

Thus, in postmodernity, body cultivation becomes an extremely important dynamic in the process of self-constitution. Because the body plays such an important role in constituting the postmodern-self, uncertainty is highest around bodily concerns, such as health, physique, aging, and skin blemishes; these issues become causes of increased reflexivity, evaluation, and, thus, uncertainty.

Bauman, like Luckmann, argues that the absence of any firm and objective evaluative guide tends to create a demand for a substitute. These substitutes are symbolically created as other people and groups are seen as "unguarded totemic poles which one can approach or abandon without applying for permission to enter or leave."[37] Individuals use these others as reference points and adopt the symbols of belonging to the other. The availability of the symbolic tokens depends on their visibility, which, in turn, depends on the use of the symbolic token to produce a satisfactory self-construction. In the end, the efficacy of these symbols rests on either expertise in some task or mass following.

Bauman also argues that accessibility of the tokens depends on an agent's resources and increasingly is understood as knowledge and information. So, for example, people might adopt the symbols associated with a specific professional athlete—wearing the same type of shoe or physically moving in the same defining

---

[36]Zygmunt Bauman, *Modernity and Ambivalence* (Ithaca, NY: Cornell University Press, 1991), *Intimations of Postmodernity* (London: Routledge, 1992).

[37]Bauman, *Intimations of Postmodernity,* 195.

manner—or individuals might assume all the outward symbols and cultural capital associated with a perceived group of computer wizards. The important issue for Bauman is that these symbols of group membership can be taken up or cast off without any commitment or punitive action because the individuals using the symbols have never been an interactive part of these groups' or celebrities' lives.

The need for these tokens results in "tribal politics," defined as self-constructing practices that are collectivized.[38] These tribes function as imagined communities and, unlike premodern communities, exist only in symbolic form through the shared commitments of their members.[39] For example, a girl in rural North Carolina might pierce various body parts, wear mismatched clothing three sizes too large, have the music of "Bio-Hazard" habitually running through her mind, and see herself as a member of the grunge or punk community but never once interact with group members. Or an individual might develop a concern for the use of animals in laboratory experiments, talk about it to others, wear proclamations on tee shirts and bumper stickers, and attend an occasional rally, and thus, he might perceive himself as a group member but not be part of any kind of social group or interaction network. These quasi groups function without the powers of inclusion and exclusion that earlier groups possessed; indeed, these "neo-tribes" are created only through the repetitive performance of symbolic rituals and exist only as long as the members perform the rituals.

Neo-tribes are thus formed through concepts rather than through face-to-face encounters in actual social groups. They exist as "imagined communities" through self-identification and persist solely because people use them as vehicles for self-definition and as "imaginary sediments." Because the persistence of these tribes depends on the affective allegiance of the members, self-identifying rituals become more extravagant and spectacular. Spectacular displays, such as body scarring or extreme or random violence, are necessary because in postmodernity the true scarce resource on which self and other is based is public attention.

Formalizing the Postmodernist Argument

One way to assess the plausibility of postmodernist theorizing is to formalize the argument, especially of cultural postmodernists, who posit a dramatically new form of social organization. The economic postmodernists' arguments are more plausible, but when formalized, the generalizations of cultural postmodernists (indeed, their own version of "grand narratives," which they so despise in others' work) can be assessed in terms of their plausibility. As long as their theory remains embedded in often rather vague text, it is difficult to assess it; once stated in clear language, we will leave it mostly to readers to determine which parts of the argument seem plausible.[40]

---

[38]Ibid., 198–199.

[39]See Benedict Anderson, *Imagined Communities* (London: Verso, 1983).

[40]The propositions in this section are drawn from Kenneth Allan and Jonathan H. Turner, "A Formalization of Postmodern Theory," *Sociological Perspectives* 43 (2000):363–385.

Below is listed a series of four long principles that summarize the basic argument of postmodernists. Principle 1 emphasizes the increasing importance of culture over social structures, the effects of educational credentialing, the growing detachment of culture from its material base with the emergence of postmodern capitalism. Principle 2 examines the destabilization of culture as it becomes uprooted from the local structures in which it originally evolved and is increasingly commodified to be bought and sold in high-volume global markets. Principle 3 examines the increasing importance of individuals vis-à-vis social structures, during which meanings are increasingly tied to self rather than to groups. Finally, principle 4 outlines the argument by cultural postmodernists about the declining viability of the subject or the person as coherent entity. While the formal language in which the postmodern arguments are phrased can be a bit off-putting, the argument is at least clear; and by reading the propositions quickly, it is possible to get a better sense for the grand narrative they have produced, despite their distaste for and constant critiques of such narratives by others. Also, it is easier to evaluate the truth or falsity of the claims being made; most of the claims, I would argue, are rather overdrawn. Moreover, they are not nearly as original as many postmodernists proclaim because similar arguments can be found in Marx, Simmel, Weber, and Durkheim. They all worried about the effects of modernity—differentiation and capitalism—on the stability and integration of social structures, about the attachment of culture to material structures, and about alienation, anomies, marginality, the blasé self, and the effects of loosened ties to culture and differentiated social structures. And so, in reading down the list of propositions, it is a good idea to keep in mind what the early masters of sociological theorizing had to say. Here are the principles:

1. The relative salience, significance, and influence of culture over material social conditions in a society increases with

   A. The level of commodification of objects, people, and symbols marking differences increases with growth in the volume, velocity, and extensiveness of market exchanges, with the pervasiveness and extensiveness of markets increasing with

      1. The multiplicative effects between production and ideology, on the one hand, and scientific inquiry and ideology, on the other, in driving constant expansion of production and technologies

      2. The extent to which production allows for satisfaction of basic needs so that discretionary purchases of symbols become possible

      3. The level of abstraction of money as an accepted and stable marker of relative values, which, in turn, increase with

         a. The rationalization of communication and transportation infrastructures that expand trade relying on stable currencies

         b. The extensiveness, volume, and velocity of markets, especially meta-markets exchanging the instruments of value and capital as commodities

    4. The level of advertising of goods and commodities available in markets, which, in turn, increases with

       a. The conditions listed under 1-A(3) above

       b. The conditions listed under 1-D below

B. The level of formal credentialing of individuals, which is a positive and additive function of the level of the division of labor and, more generally, differentiation in a society, which, in turn, are a positive and additive function of

    1. The degree to which flexible capitalism is institutionalized

    2. The level of competition among individuals for positions in productive organizations and for material and symbolic resources

    3. The level of manufacturing technology as it expands the range of skills needed in production

    4. The size of the infrastructure-producing technology, which, in turn, increases with

       a. The level of development of higher education and ideologies supporting such development

       b. The level of institutionalization of scientific activity and ideologies supporting the constant expansion of knowledge

       c. The degree to which capitalists' practices and ideology rely on marketing new knowledge

C. The level of development of imaging technologies, products, and infrastructures increasing the quantity and rate of circulation of visual images, which, in turn, increases with

    1. The level of development in communication and transportation infrastructures

    2. The level of development of markets and the conditions listed under 1-A above

    3. The degree to which the distribution of commodities, including images, is driven by advertising

D. The degree to which symbols and symbolic boundaries are detached from local times and places, which, in turn, increases with

    1. The degree to which development of information and communication technologies is sufficient to compress time and space, thereby accelerating the rate and extensiveness of distribution of culture and images of culture

    2. The development of markets and conditions listed under 1-A above

    3. The degree of deconcentration of economic capital and the rate of its movement across the globe in order to avoid overaccumulation, which, in turn, increases with

       a. The rate and level of local capital accumulation

       b. The conditions listed under 3-A and 3-B below

       c. The level of development of meta-markets and the rate of circulation of money as a commodity through these markets

    4. The number and diversity of potential cultural identities for individuals to adopt, which, in turn, increases with

        a. The extent to which grand cultural narratives have declined in their capacity to influence individuals' sense of self

        b. The degree and rate of social and cultural differentiation.

2. The degree of cultural destabilization and de-reification in a society, which, in turn, increases with

    A. The degree of deinstitutionalization to which (a) structural constraints on interaction are weakened, (b) legitimating cultural myths are challenged, and (c) cultural symbols are emotionally flat and unclear, with this deinstitutionalization increasing with

        1. The level of structural differentiation in a society

        2. The level of development of transportation and communication technologies and infrastructures

        3. The level of development of markets and the expansiveness and velocity of exchange within and between societies

        4. The degree and rate of commodification of people, things, and symbols in a society and between societies

        5. The level of uncertainty, doubt, and anxiety about the viability of institutional systems within a society

    B. The degree to which symbols and symbolic boundaries are detached from local times and places, which, in turn, increases with the conditions listed under 1-D above.

3. The degree to which self is tied to the individual over collective units of social organization and their shared culture, thereby increasing the salience of self over groups and their cultures, which, in turn, increases with

    A. The degree of cultural destabilization and de-reification in a society, which, in turn, increases with the conditions listed under 2-A above

    B. The multiplicative effects among

        1. Market velocity and scope

        2. Level of advertising of commodities in markets

        3. Level of commodification of people, objects, and cultural symbols

    C. The level of social and cultural differentiation and diversity

    D. The level of development in communication and transportation infrastructures.

4. The degree to which the individual subject is less viable as a coherent whole, with this sense of personhood declining with

    A. Sensory overload and the resulting inability to cope with overload, which increase with

        1. The level and rate of commodification in high-volume markets

        2. The level of credentialing requiring constant redefinition of individuals' qualifications

3. The number, diversity, and velocity of circulation of images, which, in turn, increases with

   a. The level of development of communication and transportation infrastructures

   b. The level of development and scope of markets

4. The level of cultural circumvention, in which cultural symbols are extracted from their local origins and circulated across cultural and structural boundaries as images that can potentially be codified, which increases with the conditions listed under 1-D

B. The level of emotional flatness of individuals and the resulting incapacity to invest emotionally in social structures and their cultures, which increases with

   1. The rate and degree of environmental changes to which individuals must adapt, which, in turn, increases with

      a. The rate of technological innovation creating new structures and cultural systems

      b. The degree and rate of social and cultural differentiation forcing constant adjustments to new social and cultural niches

      c. The velocity and scope of markets increasing commodification and circulation of cultural images and symbols

      d. The destablization and de-reification of culture, causing instability in cultural boundaries

C. The degree of reflexivity of individuals about self and identity, with this constant experimentation with definitions of self increasing with

   1. The degree of commodification of cultural images and affiliations with groups

   2. The scope and velocity of market exchanges for commodified images of, and options for, definitions of self

   3. The level of development of communication and transportation infrastructures

   4. The level of doubt and uncertainty about the stability and viability of places, locations, structures, cultural symbols, and affiliations for self-anchorage.

Conclusions

The more formal propositions only aggravate postmodernists' distrust of science, but if we cannot state their theoretical assertions formally and clearly, how then do we evaluate their truth or falsity? Of course, to even suggest that we can do so is, to most postmodernists, simply imposing a failed epistemology (of science) on postmodernist theory, which, in essence, means that it can never be evaluated. Yet postmodernism is based on a critique of science against which postmodernism itself cannot stand firmly. All culture and language is distanced from the physical world.

Such abstraction is a necessary condition of culture and language because, without some degree of removal from the physical world, there would only be the thing-in-itself and no human meaning as we understand it. Because language and meaning are not moored in the physical world but are, actually, representations of the world, they are inherently contingent and unstable and, thus, must be reified and stabilized in some way. In addition, because culture is by its very nature abstract and contingent, it is self-referential and is undergirded by incorrigible propositions or unchallenged beliefs about the world.[41] Reification of ideas into reality, stabilization, and the protection of incorrigible assumptions occur principally through (a) the structuring or institutionalization of collective activities and (b) the investment of emotions by individuals—both of which are tied to group processes and identity.

The function of all cultural knowledge, particularly language and theory, is to call attention to some elements in the world, both social and physical, while excluding others. The process of inclusion and exclusion is a fundamental way in which meaning is created. As Max Weber indicated, culture is the process of singling out from "the meaningless infinity of the world process" a finite portion that is, in turn, infused with meaning and significance. And the incorrigible propositions undergirding any knowledge system also function through inclusion and exclusion: a system cannot simultaneously be based on pragmatism and mysticism.

Thus, postmodernists are in a sense correct in their critique of science: science, like any knowledge system, is based on incorrigible assumptions, is an abstraction from physical reality, is in need of reification and stabilization through the processes of institutionalization and emotional investment, and is bent on systematically subjugating other knowledge systems to assert its own reality. But what postmodernists have missed—despite disclaimers about having no "privileged voice"—is that their own knowledge systems are subject to the same properties. In creating a system of knowledge, postmodernists must reify and stabilize their knowledge through the same processes of institutionalization, emotional investment, and exclusion—or be subject to the nihilism of endless regression.

Mark Gottdiener and the early critical theorists summarized in Chapter 23 are correct when they assert that knowledge, beliefs, and group interests are inseparable. What he and most other critical theorists fail to understand, however, is that their own knowledge systems function in the same way as science and are open to the same critique. The battle over the definition of science, knowledge, and theory is a cultural war for legitimization on which turns the allocation of institutional and material resources. Based on a generalized understanding of how culture functions within and between groups, the behavior of both postmodernists and social scientists is fairly predictable, especially because most of the protagonists are situated within academia.

Postmodernism is premised on a fundamental error that originated with structuralism (see Chapter 20). The structure of the sign system is posited to be the dynamic on which human action and interaction depend. This prejudicial favoring

---

[41]See H. Mehan and H. Wood, *Reality of Ethnomethodology* (New York: Wiley, 1975) and Niklas Luhmann, "Society, Meaning, Religion—Based on Self-Reference," *Sociological Analysis* 46 (1985):5–20.

of culture over other properties and processes in social life might be one defining characteristic of postmodernism. Even those who appear to want to consider other factors, such as Denzin, Kellner, and Gottdiener, end up simply analyzing cultural artifacts such as film or billboards and then imputing their findings to the social actors who might or might not interpret the artifact in the same manner or use the culture in the way the researcher supposes. This error has resulted in a general over-emphasis on culture, the signification system, and the problem of representation to the neglect of human agency and interaction. Even if culture is as fragmented and free-floating as postmodernists claim, it will have little effect on people until it becomes the focus of their interactions. And in micro-level interaction, there are processes that tend to mitigate the problems of free-floating signifiers and emotionally flat symbols, as the theories of interaction presented in Chapters 16, 17, and 18 indicate. People respond to the contingent nature of culture at the micro level by producing a Goffmanian type of interaction equilibrium and natural rituals to emotionally infuse symbols (see Chapter 18).

This fundamental error has also produced some questionable assertions by post-modernists concerning the self. For the category of the self to be obliterated or to be fragmented, as postmodernists claim, culture must be exclusively determinative, and it is not. The creation and organization of the self is informed and constrained by culture, but it is not a direct function of the sign system. From a sociological point of view, the self is a process that is the joint work of individuals and groups in relation to their social environment. The self is an internalized structure of meanings that has as its source the process of role-taking in real groups and with real people in a person's particular biographical history. Media images can inform the interaction through which the self is constituted, but the interaction itself determines how those images will be used and what meanings will be attached to them.

It appears that postmodernism is moving toward a more moderated position. Each of the founders of postmodern thought posited a radical break with modernity and a universal problem of meaning and signification, but most subsequent postmodern thinkers have made attempts at grounding their analyses in the material world. Thus, the intellectual crisis is not as deep as was first supposed. The economic postmodernists, in particular, are using more generalized principles and processes to explain social phenomena. If postmodernism is to have a substantial voice beyond a critical stand against social science, it must move toward these more moderated positions.

CHAPTER 23

European Critical Theorizing

Strains of Critical Theorizing in Europe

Virtually all early sociologists were influenced by a broad intellectual movement, often termed "The Enlightenment," which grew out of both the Renaissance and, later, the Age of Science in the seventeenth century.[1] As we have seen for the emergence of most theoretical perspectives in sociology, The Enlightenment still inspires thinkers, in at least two respects. First, the social universe has often been seen as "progressing," moving from one stage of development to another. To be sure, theorists have disagreed about the stages, and many have had doubts about the notion of "progress," but it would be hard to deny that sociologists see directional movement of society or world systems as a central theme. A second legacy from The Enlightenment has been the belief that science can be used to further social progress. As with the idea of progress, this faith in science has not been universal, but even those who have doubted that science is the key to social progress still tend to believe that scientific analysis of the human condition and its pathologies can be used for human betterment.

These two points of emphasis from The Enlightenment were part of a more general effort to come to terms with what is often termed "modernity," or the transformations associated with the rise of commerce and industrial capitalism from the debris of the old feudal order. Indeed, the central problem for all early sociologists was to understand the dramatic transformations of the social order being caused by the expansion of commerce and markets, the industrialization of production, the urbanization of labor, the decline of cohesive and local communities, the rise of the bureaucratic state, the decreasing salience of sacred symbols as a result of expanding

---

[1]Jonathan H. Turner, "Founders and Classics: A Canon in Motion" in *The Student Sociologist's Handbook*, ed. C. Middleton, J. Gubbay, and C. Ballard (Oxford, UK: Blackwell, 1997).

secular law and science, the conflicts among new social classes, and many other disruptive transformations. These were changes that early theorists sought to comprehend. Some were pessimistic and worried about what was occurring; others were optimistic about the new modern age; still others believed that things would get better after the current turmoil subsided. But no one who was considered a serious social thinker could ignore "modernity."

Critical theorizing in all its forms enters this old debate about modernity from a number of different directions. As the name implies, most theorists in this "critical" tradition view industrial capitalism in negative terms, and some have even posited a new stage of history, "postmodernity," which is similarly viewed in a negative light (see the last chapter). Almost all critical theorists disparage the optimism of The Enlightenment, seeing the use of science for constructing a better society as naive, as pursuit of an illusion, or even as harmful. For most, science is part of a broader culture of commerce and capitalism, which, to critical theorists, are the cause of the problems in the modern or postmodern era, not part of their solution. Yet ironically, these very same critics often appear to be figures of The Enlightenment because they address the very same problems of the earlier Enlightenment-inspired theorists, because they use analysis and reason to pronounce the problems of the modern or postmodern era, and because they often propose solutions to the ills of the current era, even as they drown their pronouncements in pessimism. True, most critical theorists maintain a hearty disdain for science and the implicit Enlightenment projects of the theories examined in earlier chapters, but they have not escaped the mood, tone, and problematic of The Enlightenment.

The Critical Thrust of Karl Marx's Analysis of Capitalism

In 1846, Karl Marx and Friedrich Engels completed *The German Ideology*, which was initially rejected by the publisher.[2] Much of this work is an attack on the "Young Hegelians," who were advocates of the German philosopher Georg Hegel, and is of little interest today. Yet this attack contained certain basic ideas that have served as the impetus behind "critical theory," or the view that social theory must be critical of oppressive arrangements and propose emancipatory alternatives. This theme exists, of course, in all of Marx's work,[3] but the key elements of contemporary critical theory are most evident in this first statement.

Marx criticized the Young Hegelians severely because he had once been one of them and was now making an irrevocable break. Marx saw the Hegelians as hopeless idealists, in the philosophical sense. That is, they saw the world as reflective of ideas, with the dynamics of social life revolving around consciousness and other cognitive processes by which "ideal essences" work their magic on humans. Marx

---

[2]Karl Marx and Friedrich Engels, *The German Ideology* (New York: International, 1947; written in 1846).

[3]Karl Marx, *Capital: A Critical Analysis of Capitalist Production*, vol. 1 (New York: International, 1967; originally published 1867); Karl Marx and Friedrich Engels, *The Communist Manifesto* (New York: International, 1971; originally published 1848).

saw this emphasis on the "reality of ideas" as nothing more than a conservative ideology that supports people's oppression by the material forces of their existence. His alternative was "to stand Hegel on his head," but in this early work there is still an emphasis on the relation between consciousness and self-reflection, on the one hand, and social reality, on the other. This dualism became central to contemporary critical theory.

Actually, Marx's "standing of Hegel on his head" has been reversed by some contemporary theorists, who, in essence, have put Hegel back on his feet. Indeed, for many who commented on the condition of modernity or postmodernity (see Chapter 22) in the first decade of the twenty-first century, the world has been transformed into a sea of symbols that have lost anchorage in material conditions and that have, as a result, changed the very nature of society from one driven by control of the means of material production to one dominated by signs and texts symbolizing little but themselves. For critical theorists schooled in the Marxian tradition, even those who call themselves postmodernists, such arguments go too far, but there can be little doubt that Marx's dismissal of Hegel and the Young Hegelians was not the final word on the place of ideas, symbols, and signs in societal evolution.

Marx was a modernist, not a postmodernist, and so he went in a different direction. For Marx, humans are unique by virtue of their conscious awareness of themselves and their situation; they are capable of self-reflection and, hence, assessment of their positions in society. Such consciousness arises from people's daily existence and is not a realm of ideas that is somehow independent of the material world, as much German philosophy argued or as later versions of postmodernism implied. For Marx, people produce their ideas and conceptions of the world because of the social structures in which they are born, raised, and live.

The essence of people's lives is the process of production. For Marx, human "life involves, before anything else, eating and drinking, a habitation, clothing, and many other material things."[4] To meet these contingencies of life, production is necessary, but as production satisfies one set of needs, new needs arise and encourage alterations in the ways productive activity is organized. The elaboration of productive activity creates a division of labor that, in the end, is alienating because it increasingly deprives humans of their capacity to control their productive activities. Moreover, as people work, they are exploited in ways that generate private property and capital for those who enslave them. Thus, as people work as alienated cogs in the division of labor, they produce that which enslaves them: private property and profits for those who control the modes and means of production. Marx provided a more detailed discussion of the evolution of productive forces to this capitalist stage, and like any Enlightenment thinker, he argued that this capitalist stage would lead to a new era of human organization.

Marx believed that humans' capacity to use language, to think, and to analyze their conditions would enable them to alter their environment. People do not merely have to react to their material conditions in some mechanical way; they can

---

[4]Marx and Engels, *The German Ideology*, 15.

also use their capacities for thought and reflection to construct new material conditions and corresponding social relations. Indeed, the course of history involved such processes as people actively restructured the material conditions of their existence. The goal of social theory, Marx implicitly argued, is to use humans' unique facility to expose those oppressive social relations and to propose alternatives. Marx's entire career was devoted to this goal, and this emancipatory aspect of Marx's thought forms the foundation for critical theory, even in some of its postmodern manifestations.

Marx used the somewhat ambiguous term *praxis* to describe this blending of theory and action. The basic notion is that action to change social conditions generates increased knowledge that can then be used to mount more effective change-producing action. Thus, the interplay between action and theoretical understanding can eventually lead individuals to a better social life. Although those with power can impose their ideologies on subordinates and, thereby, distort the latter's perceptions of their true interests, Marx had typical Enlightenment-inspired faith that subordinates possessed the capacity for praxis and that they would eventually use their capacities for agency to change the nature of modernity.

Today, contemporary critical theorists appear somewhat divided on the question of whether analysis of modernity and postmodernity can be used to improve the human condition. As we will see shortly, many confronted Max Weber's pessimism about the ever tightening "steel enclosure," or what Talcott Parsons posed as "the iron cage" of rational-legal authority and state domination. Others sustained the emancipatory faith of Marx's belief in praxis.

Still others emphasized an inherent force articulated in Marx's analysis of capitalism—the capacity of money-driven markets to "commodify" all things, symbols, and ideals—as a basis for a renewed pessimism about the human condition. To *commodify* means that symbols, signs, objects, cultures, relationships, and virtually anything can be turned into a marketable thing, to be bought and sold for a price stated in terms of money and subject to Adam Smith's laws of supply and demand. Hence, as capitalists seek profits, they not just buy and sell the material objects necessary for human survival, but they also produce and sell symbols and signs that, as commodities, lose their power to provide meaning to human life. Coupled with information technologies that Marx could never have visualized, as well as markets for services and cultural symbols that Marx did not fully anticipate, the social world is now dominated by the production and distribution of signs, symbols, texts, and other cultural commodities. This transformation has changed the very nature of humans' capacities to understand and respond to their conditions.

Weber's Pessimism and the Basic Problem for Early European Theory

Max Weber was concerned with the historical transition to modern capitalist societies, and his description and explanation of this transition represent a devastating critique of Marx's optimism about revolutionary movements toward a new utopian society. Weber's analysis is complex, and the historical detail that he presented to document his case is impressive, but his argument is captured by the concept of *rationalization*.[5] Weber argued that the rationality that defines modern societies is "means-ends rationality" and, hence, involves a search for the most efficient means to achieve a defined end. The process of rationalization, Weber felt, involves the ever-increasing penetration of means-ends rationality into more spheres of life, thereby destroying older traditions. As bureaucracies expand in the economic and governmental sphere, and as markets allow individuals to pursue their personal ends rationally, the traditional moral fabric is broken. Weber agreed with Georg Simmel that this rationalization of life brings individuals a new freedom from domination by religious dogmatism, community, class, and other traditional forces; but in their place it creates a new kind of domination by impersonal economic forces, such as markets and corporate bureaucracies, and by the vast administrative apparatus of the ever-expanding state. Human options were, in Weber's view, becoming ever more constrained by the "iron cage" of rational and legal authority. Unlike Marx, Weber did not see such a situation as rife with revolutionary potential; rather, he saw the social world as increasingly administered by impersonal bureaucratic forces.

This pessimistic view seemed, by the early 1930s, to be a far more reasonable assessment of modernity than was Marx's utopian dream. Indeed, the communist revolution in Russia had degenerated into Stalinism and bureaucratic totalitarianism by the Communist Party; in the West, particularly in the United States, workers seemed ever more willing to sell themselves in markets and work in large-scale organizations; and political fascism in Germany and Italy was creating large authoritarian bureaucracies. How, then, was the first generation of critical theorists to reconcile Weber's more accurate assessment of empirical trends with Marx's optimistic and emancipatory vision? This became the central question of early critical theory.

Simmel's Defense of Modernity and Implicit Attack on Marx

Many of Georg Simmel's ideas represent an important qualification to Marx's reasoning and, to a lesser extent, to Weber's as well. Marx's more emancipatory side saw capitalism as producing the conditions that would lead to a revolution, ushering in a new form of human organization in which individuals are freed from the capitalists' domination. Thus, as capitalism expands, the division of labor makes workers appendages to machines, concentrates workers in urban areas, quantifies social relations through money and markets, and forces workers to be mere role players (rather than fully involved participants) in social relations. In so doing, capitalism generates the personal alienation and resentments as well as the social structural conditions that will lead subordinates to become aware of their domination and to organize in an effort to change their plight.

---

[5]Max Weber, *Economy and Society*, trans. G. Roth (Berkeley: University of California Press, 1978).

Simmel challenged much of Marx's analysis in his *The Philosophy of Money*.[6] This critique revolves around one of the themes in Marx's writing: Capitalism quantifies social life with money and, in so doing, makes exchanges in markets paramount; the result is that human social relations are increasingly commodified. Such commodification is personified in the labor market, where workers sell themselves as a thing, and coupled with the growing division of labor, workers become mere cogs in an impersonal organizational machine. Such processes, Marx believed, would be so oppressive as to initiate revolutionary pressures for their elimination.

Simmel, however, looked at these forces much differently. Although a certain level of alienation from work and the commodification of relations through the use of money are inevitable with increasing differentiation and expansion of productive forces and markets, Simmel saw these forces of modernity as liberating individuals from the constraints of tradition. In Simmel's Enlightenment-oriented view, people have more options about how they spend their money and what they do; they can move about with more freedom and form new and varied social relations; they can live lifestyles that reflect their tastes and values; and in general, they are more liberated than their counterparts in less complex, traditional societies.

This critique of Marx was, however, rejected by the early critical theorists, who did not want to visualize modern societies as liberating. And yet these theorists were confronted with the failure of Marx's predictions about the communist revolution and the coming emancipation of society. And by the end of the twentieth century, they would also have to confront the triumph of world-level capitalism over socialism. In an attempt to reconstruct Marx's vision of humans' capacity to make history, they were forced to accept Weber's highly pessimistic view of the constraints of modern society and to reject Simmel's more optimistic diagnosis. But in so doing, they became trapped in a dilemma: if capitalism is not as self-transforming as Marx's revolutionary model indicates, if modern life is not so liberating as Simmel felt, and if Weber's analysis of increasing constraint in societies must therefore be accepted as true, then how is liberation to occur? What force will drive people's emancipation from domination? The early critical theorists would not accept Simmel's judgment—that is, that people are more *free* than in traditional societies—and so they conceptually retreated into a contemplative subjectivism. They viewed the liberating force as somehow springing from human nature and its capacity for conscious reflection—a kind of "watered down," even impotent, sense of praxis.

The Rise of the Frankfurt School of Critical Theory

The Frankfurt School and the Cultural Turn

The spirit of Georg Wilhelm Friedrich Hegel (1770–1831) could not be exorcised by much of twentieth-century critical theory. Key elements of the Marxian scheme—such as the dialectical view of history, the concept of alienation, or the

---

[6]Georg Simmel, *The Philosophy of Money*, trans. T. Bottomore and D. Frisbie (Boston, MA: Routledge and Kegan Paul, 1978; originally published 1907).

notion of praxis, for example—came from Hegel. Karl Marx converted these basic ideas to a materialism emphasizing that the alienation created by inequalities in the material relations of production generated an inherent dialectic of history led by humans who possessed the capacities for agency and praxis and who, thereby, would move human society to its final state of communism. In contrast with Hegel, Marx believed that ideas, politics, and other institutional systems were "superstructures" reflecting, and indeed being controlled by, a "substructure" lodged in the patterns of organization and ownership of economic production.

More than any Enlightenment-inspired sociologist of his time, Marx saw that the critique of existing relations of domination, the emergence of class conflict, the emancipation of humans, and the progress of society were all interwoven. The critique was to begin with attacks on the inequalities generated by the economic system and, then, on the political and ideological superstructures that legitimated the means and modes of production. Yet by the third decade of the twentieth century, even the Great Depression had not produced the predicted revolution by the proletariat, nor was it possible to see humans as progressing. Even when times were better after World War II, capitalism was not collapsing but, if anything, gaining converts. And China's "communist revolution" and subsequent "cultural revolution" had begun to look very much like the Stalin purges in Russia.

The collapse of communism in the 1990s forced further adjustments in critical theory.[7] Indeed, criticism moved from revolving around the "immiseration" of the population to censuring its tasteless overconsumption and its manipulation by the symbols of advertising. In the end, critical theory and postmodernism began to blend together as concerns with symbols, signs, culture, and ideology seemed to hold sway over older Marxian views about the economic substructure. Or, at the very least, critical theorists were working very hard to find problems in the cultural products of mature capitalist systems and the developing capitalist world order. Marx was perhaps turning over in his grave, but Hegelian themes were nonetheless reemerging.

I will pause, therefore, and offer a few representative samples of how the critical theorists working in the decades before the twentieth century's midpoint were trying to keep their Marxian faith given a reality that was no longer on its Marxian

---

[7]See, for examples, David Hoy and Thomas McCarthy, *Critical Theory* (Oxford, UK: Blackwell, 1994) and Stephen Regan (ed.), *The Year's Work in Critical and Cultural Theory* (Oxford, UK: Blackwell, 1995). Earlier reviews and analyses of critical theory and sociology include Paul Connerton (ed.), *Critical Sociology* (New York: Penguin Books, 1970); Raymond Geuss, *The Idea of a Critical Theory* (New York: Cambridge University Press, 1981); David Held, *Introduction to Critical Theory* (Berkeley: University of California Press, 1980); Trent Schroyer, *The Critique of Domination: The Origins and Development of Critical Theory* (New York: Braziller, 1973); Albrecht Wellmer, *Critical Theory of Society* (New York: Seabury, 1974); Ellsworth R. Fuhrman and William E. Snizek, "Some Observations on the Nature and Content of Critical Theory," *Humboldt Journal of Social Relations* 7 (Fall–Winter 1979–1980): 33–51; Zygmunt Bauman, *Towards a Critical Society* (Boston: Routledge and Kegan Paul, 1976); Robert J. Antonio, "The Origin, Development, and Contemporary Status of Critical Theory," *Sociological Quarterly* 24 (Summer 1983):325–351; and Jim Faught, "Objective Reason and the Justification of Norms," *California Sociologist* 4 (Winter 1981):33–53.

trajectory. In so doing, Marxian materialism and Hegelian idealism were put back together in an uneasy accommodation.

Thus, the first generation of critical theorists, who are frequently referred to as the Frankfurt School because of their location in Germany and their explicit inter-disciplinary effort to interpret the oppressive events of the twentieth century, confronted a real dilemma: how to reconcile Marx's emancipatory dream with the stark reality of modern society as conceptualized by Max Weber.[8] Indeed, when the Frankfurt Institute for Social Research was founded in 1923, there seemed little reason to be optimistic about developing a theoretically informed program for freeing people from unnecessary domination. The defeat of the left-wing working-class movements, the rise of fascism in the aftermath of World War I, and the degeneration of the Russian Revolution into Stalinism had, by the 1930s, made it clear that Marx's analysis needed drastic revision. Moreover, the expansion of the state, the spread of bureaucracy, and the emphasis on means-ends rationality through the application of science and technology all signaled that Weber's analysis had to be confronted.

The members of the Frankfurt School wanted to maintain Marx's views on praxis—that is, a blending of theory and action or the use of theory to stimulate action, and vice versa. And they wanted theory to expose oppression in society and to propose less constrictive options. Yet they were confronted with the spread of political and economic domination of the masses. Thus, modern critical theory in sociology was born in a time when there was little reason to be optimistic about realizing emancipatory goals.

Three members of the Frankfurt School are most central: György Lukács, Max Horkheimer, and Theodor Adorno.[9] Lukács's major work appeared in the 1920s,[10] whereas Horkheimer and Adorno[11] were active well into the 1960s. In many ways, Lukács was the key link in the transition from Marx and Weber to modern critical theory, because Horkheimer and Adorno were reacting to much of Lukács's analysis

---

[8]For descriptions of this activity, see Martin Jay, *The Dialectical Imagination* (Boston, MA: Little, Brown, 1973) and "The Frankfurt School's Critique of Marxist Humanism," *Social Research* 39 (1972): 285–305; Held, *Introduction to Critical Theory*, 29–110; Robert J. Antonio, "The Origin, Development, and Contemporary Status of Critical Theory," *Sociological Quarterly* 24 (Summer 1983):325–351; and Phil Slater, *Origin and Significance of the Frankfurt School* (London: Routledge and Kegan Paul, 1977).

[9]Other prominent members included Friedrich Pollock (economist), Erich Fromm (psychoanalyst, social psychologist), Franz Neumann (political scientist), Herbert Marcuse (philosopher), and Leo Loenthal (sociologist). During the Nazi years, the school relocated to the United States, and many of its members never returned to Germany.

[10]György Lukács, *History and Class Consciousness* (Cambridge: MIT Press, 1968; originally published 1922).

[11]Max Horkheimer, *Critical Theory: Selected Essays* (New York: Herder and Herder, 1972) is a translation of essays written in German in the 1930s and 1940s. *Eclipse of Reason* (New York: Oxford University Press, 1947; repr. New York: Seabury, 1974) was the only book by Horkheimer originally published in English. It takes a slightly different turn than earlier works, but it does present the ideas that emerged from his association with Theodor Adorno. See also Horkheimer, *Critique of Instrumental Reason* (New York: Seabury, 1974). See Held, *Introduction to Critical Theory*, 489–491, for a more complete listing of Horkheimer's works in German.

and approach. All these scholars are important because they directly influenced the intellectual development and subsequent work of Jürgen Habermas, the most prolific contemporary critical theorist, whose work is examined later in this next chapter.[12]

György Lukács. Lukács blended Marx and Weber together by seeing a convergence of Marx's ideas about the commodification of social relations through money and markets with Weber's thesis about the penetration of rationality into ever more spheres of modern life. Borrowing from Marx's analysis of the "fetishism of commodities," Lukács employed the concept of *reification* to denote the process by which social relationships become "objects" that can be manipulated, bought, and sold. Then, reinterpreting Weber's notion of "rationalization" to mean a growing emphasis on the process of "calculation" of exchange values, Lukács combined Weber's and Marx's ideas. As traditional societies change, he argued, there is less reliance on moral standards and processes of communication to achieve societal integration; instead, there is more use of money, markets, and rational calculations. As a result, relations are coordinated by exchange values and by people's perceptions of one another as "things."[13]

Lukács painted himself into a conceptual corner, however. If indeed such is the historical process, how is it to be stopped? Lukács's answer was to resurrect a contrite Hegel; that is, rather than look to contradictions in material conditions or economic and political forces, one must examine the dialectical forces inherent in human consciousness. There are limits, Lukács argued, to how much reification and rationalization people will endure. Human subjects have an inner quality that keeps rationalization from completely taking over.[14]

This emphasis on the process of consciousness is very much a part of critical theory that borrows much from the early Marx[15] and that, at the Frankfurt School, had a heavy dose of Freud and psychoanalytic theory. As a result, unlike its sources of inspiration, Marx and Weber, early critical theory was subjectivist and failed to analyze *intersubjectivity,* or the ways people interact through mutually shared conscious activity. Emphasizing the inherent resistance of subjects to their total reification, Lukács could only propose that the critical theorist's role is to expose reification at work by analyzing the historical processes that have dehumanized people. As a consequence, Lukács made critical theory highly contemplative, emphasizing that the solution to

---

[12]Theodor W. Adorno, *Negative Dialectics* (New York: Seabury, 1973; originally published 1966); Max Horkheimer, *Dialectic of Enlightenment* (New York: Herder and Herder, 1972; originally published 1947). See Held, *Introduction to Critical Theory,* 485–487, for a more complete listing of his works. See also Jürgen Habermas, "From Lukács to Adorno: Rationalization as Reification," in *The Theory of Communicative Action,* vol. 1 (Boston, MA: Beacon, 1984), 339–399, which contains Habermas's critique of Lukács, Horkheimer, and Adorno.

[13]Lukács, *History and Class Consciousness.*

[14]Ibid., 89–102. In a sense, Lukács becomes another "Young Hegelian" whom Marx would have criticized. Yet, in Marx's own analysis, he sees alienation, per se, as producing resistance by workers to further alienation by the forces of production. This is the image that Lukács seems to take from Marx.

[15]Marx and Engels, *The German Ideology.*

the problem of domination resides in making people more aware and conscious of their situation through a detailed, historical analysis of reification.

Max Horkheimer and Theodor Adorno. Both Horkheimer and Adorno were highly suspicious of Lukács's Hegelian solution to the dilemma of reification and rationalization. These processes do not imply their own critique, as Hegel would have suggested. Subjective consciousness and material reality cannot be separated. Consciousness does not automatically offer resistance to those material forces that commodify, reify, and rationalize. Critical theory must, therefore, actively (a) describe the historical forces that dominate human freedom and (b) expose the ideological justifications of these forces. This is to be achieved through interdisciplinary research among variously trained researchers and theorists, who confront one another's ideas and use this dialogue to analyze concrete social conditions and to propose courses of ameliorative action. This emphasis on praxis—the confrontation between theory and action in the world—involves developing ideas about the causes of oppression and the potential solutions to such oppression. As Horkheimer argued, "The value of theory is not decided alone by the formal criteria of truth . . . but by its connection with tasks, which in the particular historical moment are taken up by progressive social forces."[16] Such critical theory is, Horkheimer claimed, guided by a "particular practical interest" in the emancipation of people from class domination.[17] Thus, critical theory is tied, in a sense that Marx might have appreciated, to people's practical interests.

As Adorno and Horkheimer interacted and collaborated, their positions converged (although by the late 1950s Horkheimer had seemingly rejected much of his earlier work). Adorno was more philosophical and, yet, more research oriented than Horkheimer; Adorno's empirical work on "the authoritarian personality" had a major impact on research in sociology and psychology, but his theoretical impact came from his collaboration with Horkheimer and, in many ways, through Horkheimer's single-authored work.[18] Adorno was very pessimistic about the chances of critical theory making great changes, although his essays were designed to expose patterns of recognized and unrecognized domination of individuals by social and psychological forces. At best, his "negative dialectics" could allow humans to "tread water" until historical circumstances were more favorable to emancipatory movements. The goal of negative dialectics was to sustain a constant critique of ideas, conceptions, and conditions. This critique could not by itself change anything, for it operates only on the plane of ideas and concepts. But it can keep ideological dogmatisms from obscuring conditions that might eventually allow emancipatory action.

---

[16]Max Horkheimer, *Zum Rationalismusstreit in der gegenwartigen Philosophie*, vol. 1, ed. A. Schmidt (Frankfurt, Germany: Fischer Verlag, 1968; originally published 1935; repr. in *Kritische Theorie*), 146–147. This and Volume 2, by the way, represent a compilation of many of the essays Horkheimer wrote while at the Institute in Frankfurt.

[17]Habermas used this idea, but he extended it in several ways.

[18]Theodor W. Adorno, Else Frenkel-Brunswick, Daniel Levinson, and R. Nevitt Sanford, *The Authoritarian Personality* (New York: Harper and Row, 1950).

Both Horkheimer and Adorno emphasized that humans' "subjective side" is restricted by the spread of rationalization. In conceptualizing this process, they created a kind of dualism between the subjective world and the realm of material objects, seeing the latter as oppressing the former. From their viewpoint, critical theory must expose this dualism, and it must analyze how this "instrumental reason" (means-ends rationality) has invaded the human spirit. In this way, some resistance can be offered to these oppressive forces.

Within the Frankfurt School, then, the idealism of Lukács had been brought partially back into a more orthodox Marxian position, but not completely so. The damage had been done to pure Marxian materialism, and outside the narrow confines of Frankfurt, critical theory once again turned to idealism, even among those critical Marxists who had emigrated to America from Frankfurt during the rise of Nazism.[19]

Gramsci's Theory of Ideological Hegemony. Antonio Gramsci was an Italian Marxist who obviously cannot be considered part of the Frankfurt School. Yet he is a key figure in continuing what the Frankfurt School emphasized: criticism acknowledging that the capitalist systems of the twentieth century's midpoint were generating prosperity and that the working classes in these systems did not seem particularly disposed to revolution. Gramsci completed the turning of Marx's ideas back into a more Hegelian mode.[20] Marx believed that ideology and the "false consciousness" of workers were ideological obfuscations created and maintained by those who controlled the material (economic) "substructure." Marx had argued that those who control the means and modes of production also control the state, which, in turn, generates ideologies justifying this control and power (see Chapter 9 for more details about how this idea was carried forward in the twentieth century). In this way, the proletariat is kept, for a time until the full contradictions of capitalism are manifest, from becoming a class "for themselves," ready to pursue revolutionary conflict with their oppressors. Gramsci simply turned this argument around: the "superstructure" of state and ideology drives the organization of society and the consciousness of the population.

Gramsci believed that the ruling social class is *hegemonic*, controlling not only property and power but ideology as well. Indeed, the ruling class holds onto its power and wealth by virtue of its ability to use ideologies to manipulate workers and all others. The state is no longer a crude tool of coercion or an intrusive and insensitive bureaucratic authority; it has become the propagator of culture and the civic education of the population, creating and controlling key institutional systems in more indirect, unobtrusive, and seemingly inoffensive ways. Thus, the views of capitalists become the dominant views of all, with workers believing in the appropriateness of the market-driven systems of competition; the commodification of objects, signs, and symbols; the buying and selling of their labor; the use of law to

---

[19]See Footnote 8.

[20]Antonio Gramsci, *Selections from the Prison Notebooks* (New York: International, 1971; originally published 1928).

enforce contracts favoring the interests of the wealthy; the encouragement of private charities, the sponsorship of clubs and voluntary organizations; the state's conception of a "good citizen"; the civics curriculum of the schools; and virtually all spheres of institutional activity that are penetrated by the ideology of the state. Culture and ideology are, in Albert Bergesen's words,[21] "no longer the thing to be explained but . . . now a thing that does the explaining." A dominant material class rules, to be sure, but it does so by cultural symbols, and the real battle in capitalist societies is over whose symbols will prevail. Or, more accurately, can subordinates generate alternative ideologies to those controlled by the state?

This view of critical theory takes much of the mechanical menace out of Weber's "iron cage" metaphor, because the state's control is now "soft" and "internal." It has bars that bend flexibly around those whose perceptions of the world it seeks to control. The Marxian view of emancipation is still alive in Gramsci's theories, because the goal of "theory" is to expose the full extent to which ideology has been effectively used to manipulate subordinates. Moreover, the recognition that systems of symbols become the base of society is a theme that resonated well with later postmodernists and structuralists, who began to conceptualized modernity as the production of signs and symbols.

Althusser's Structuralism. Initially, Louis Althusser seems more strictly orthodox in his Marxism than Gramsci;[22] yet he was also a French scholar in a long line of structuralists whose emphasis is on the logic of the deeper, underlying structure of surface empirical reality.[23] Althusser remains close to Marx in this sense: the underlying structure and logic of the economy is ultimately determinative. But having said this, he then developed a theory of "The Ideological State Apparatus,"[24] which gave prominence to the state's use of ideology to sustain control within a society.

For Althusser, economic, political, and ideological systems reveal their own structures, hidden beneath the surface and operating by their own logics. The economic might be the dominant system, circumscribing the operation of political and ideological structures, but these latter have a certain autonomy. History is, in essence, a reshuffling of these deep structures, and the individual actor becomes merely a vessel through which the inherent properties of structures operate. Individual actions, perceptions, beliefs, emotions, convictions, and other states of consciousness are somehow "less real" than the underlying structure that cannot be directly observed. To analogize the structuralist theories from which Althusser drew inspiration, social control comes from individuals perceiving that they are but words in a grammatical system generated by an even more fundamental structure. Each actor is at a surface

---

[21]Albert Bergesen, "The Rise of Semiotic Marxism," *Sociological Perspectives* 36 (1993):5.

[22]Louis Althusser, *For Marx* (New York: Pantheon, 1965), *Lenin and Philosophy* (New York: Monthly Review Press, 1971); Louis Althusser and Etienne Balabar, *Reading Capital* (London: New Left, 1968).

[23]See Chapters 34, 35, and 37 for examples of this French lineage of structuralism.

[24]"Ideology and Ideological Status Apparatus," in Althusser, *Lenin and Philosophy*.

place in the economic and political structures of a society, and their perceptions of these places also put them within an ideological or cultural sphere. But these places and spheres are only one level of reality; people also see themselves as part of a deeper set of structures that, in essence, defines who and what they are. Under these conditions, ideology has even more power because it is doing much more than blinding the subjects to some other reality, such as their objective class interests. Ideology is also defining actors' places in a reality beyond their direct control and a reality operating by its own logic of structure.

Thus, unlike Marx or Gramsci, who believe ideology is a tool—an invidious and insidious one—used by those in power, Althusser sees the *Ideological State Apparatus* as more controlling because it is perceived not just as conventions, rules, mores, traditions, and beliefs but also as the essence of order and persons' place in this order. The subject is thus trapped in the deeper logics of economic, political, and ideological systems that erode human capacities for praxis and agency.

The Transformation of Marx's Project

In sum, by the middle of the twentieth century, when the contemporary period of sociological theory began, Marx's emancipatory project had been turned into something very different from what he had visualized. His and Engels's *The Communist Manifesto* was a call to arms, based on a view of the inherent contradictions in the nature of capitalist systems. Within 100 years of this call, critical theory had become decidedly more philosophical. Indeed, Marx's dismissal of the "Young Hegelians" in *The German Ideology* had apparently not worked; they were back in different forms and guises, but they increasingly dominated critical theorizing in the twentieth century. The "Young Hegelians," so viciously criticized by Marx and Engels, had considered themselves revolutionaries, but Marx saw them as more concerned with ideas about reality than with reality itself. They were accused of "blowing theoretical bubbles" about ideals and essences, and it could be imagined that he and Engels might make the very same criticisms of the critical theories that developed in the second half of the twentieth century, especially as these theories began to merge with postmodernism, as we saw in Chapter 22.

The Modern Frankfurt School: Jürgen Habermas

The German philosopher-sociologist Jürgen Habermas undoubtedly has been the most prolific descendant of the original Frankfurt School. As with the earlier generation of Frankfurt School social theorists, Habermas's work revolves around four important questions: (1) How can social theory develop ideas that keep Karl Marx's emancipatory project alive, and yet, at the same time, recognize the empirical inadequacy of his prognosis for advanced capitalist societies? (2) How can social theory confront Max Weber's historical analysis of rationalization in a way that avoids his pessimism and thereby keeps Marx's emancipatory goals at the center of theory? (3) How can social theory avoid the retreat into subjectivism of earlier critical theorists, such as György Lukács, Max Horkheimer, and Theodor Adorno, who increasingly focused on states of subjective consciousness within individuals and, as a consequence, lost Marx's insight that society is constructed from, and must therefore be emancipated by, the processes that sustain social relations among individuals? (4) How can social theory conceptualize and develop a theory that reconciles the forces of material production and political organization with the forces of intersubjectivity among reflective and conscious individuals in such a way that it avoids (a) Weber's pessimism about the domination of consciousness by rational economic and political forces,[25] (b) Marx's naive optimism about the inevitability of class consciousness and revolt, and (c) early critical theorists' retreat into the subjectivism of Hegel's dialectic, where oppression mysteriously mobilizes its negation through increases in subjective consciousnesses and resistance?

At different points in his career, Habermas has focused on one or another of these questions, but all four have always guided his approach, at least implicitly. Habermas has been accused of abandoning the critical thrust of his earlier works, but this conclusion is too harsh. For, in trying to answer the above questions, he has increasingly recognized that mere critique of oppression is not enough. Such critique becomes a "reified object itself." Although the early critical theorists knew this, they never developed conceptual schemes that accounted for the underlying dynamics of societies. For critique to be useful in liberating people from domination, it is necessary, Habermas seems to say, for the critique to discuss the fundamental processes integrating social systems. In this way, the critique has some possibility of suggesting ways to create new types of social relations. Without theoretical understanding about how society works, critique is only superficial debunking and becomes an exercise in futility. This willingness to theorize about the underlying dynamics of society, to avoid the retreat into subjectivism, to reject superficial criticism and instead to base critique on reasoned theoretical analysis, and to incorporate ideas from many diverse theoretical approaches makes Habermas's work theoretically significant.[26]

Habermas's Conception of "The Public Sphere"

In his first major publication, *Structural Transformation of the Public Sphere*, Habermas traced the evolution and dissolution of what he termed the *public sphere*.[27] This sphere is a realm of social life where people can discuss matters of general interest; where they can discuss and debate these issues without recourse to custom, dogma, and force; and where they can resolve differences of opinion by rational argument. To say the least, this conception of a public sphere is rather

---

[25]That is, the spread of means-ends rationality into ever more spheres of life.

[26]Jürgen Habermas, *The Theory of Communicative Action* (Boston, MA: Beacon, 1981, 1984). Some useful reviews and critiques of Habermas's work include John B. Thompson and David Held (eds.), *Habermas: Critical Debates* (London: Macmillan, 1982) and David Held, *An Introduction to Critical Theory* (London: Hutchinson, 1980), chap. 9–12.

[27]Jürgen Habermas, *Strukturwandel der Offentlichkeit* (Neuwied, Germany: Luchterhand, 1962).

romanticized, but the imagery of free and open discussion that is resolved by ratio-nal argumentation became a central theme in Habermas's subsequent approach. Increasingly throughout his career, Habermas came to see emancipation from domination as possible through "communicative action," which is a reincarnation of the public sphere in more conceptual clothing.

In this early work, however, Habermas appeared more interested in history and viewed the emergence of the public sphere as occurring in the eighteenth century, when various forums for public debate—clubs, cafés, journals, newspapers—proliferated. He concluded that these forums helped erode the basic structure of feudalism, which is legitimated by religion and custom rather than by agreements that have been reached through public debate and discourse. The public sphere was greatly expanded, Habermas argued, by the extension of market economies and the resulting liberation of the individual from the constraints of feudalism. Free citizens, property holders, traders, merchants, and members of other new sectors in society could now be actively concerned about the governance of society and could openly discuss and debate issues. But, in a vein similar to Weber's analysis of rationalization, Habermas argued that the public sphere was eroded by some of the very forces that stimulated its expansion. As market economies experience instability, the powers of the state are extended in an effort to stabilize the economy; with the expansion of bureaucracy to ever more contexts of social life, the public sphere is constricted. And, increasingly, the state seeks to redefine problems as technical and soluble by technolo-gies and administrative procedures rather than by public debate and argumentation.

The details of this argument are less important than the fact that this work estab-lished Habermas's credentials as a critical theorist. All the key elements of critical theory are there—the decline of freedom with the expansion of capitalism and the bureaucra-tized state, as well as the seeming power of the state to construct and control social life. The solution to these problems is to resurrect the public sphere, but how is this to be done given the growing power of the state? Thus, in this early work, Habermas had painted himself into the same conceptual corner as his teachers in the Frankfurt School. The next phase of his work extended this critique of capitalist society, but he also tried to redirect critical theory so that it did not have to retreat into the contemplative sub-jectivism of Lukács, Horkheimer, and Adorno. He began this project in the late 1960s with an analysis of knowledge systems and a critique of science.

The Critique of Science

In *The Logic of the Social Sciences*[28] and *Knowledge and Human Interest*,[29] Habermas analyzes systems of knowledge in an effort to elaborate a framework for critical theory. The ultimate goal of this analysis is to establish the fact that science is but

---

[28]Jürgen Habermas, *Zur Logik der Sozialwissenschaften* (Frankfurt, Germany: Suhrkamp, 1970).

[29]Jürgen Habermas, *Knowledge and Human Interest*, trans. J. Shapiro (London: Heinemann, 1970; origi-nally published 1968 in German). The basic ideas in *Zur Logik der Sozialwissenschaften* and *Knowledge and Human Interest* were stated in Habermas's inaugural lecture at the University of Frankfurt in 1965 and were first published in Jürgen Habermas, "Knowledge and Interest," *Inquiry* 9 (1966):285–300.

one type of knowledge and exists to meet only one set of human interests. To realize this goal, Habermas posits three basic types of knowledge that encompass the full range of human reason: (1) *empirical-analytic* knowledge, which is concerned with understanding the lawful properties of the material world; (2) *hermeneutic-historical* knowledge, which is devoted to the understanding of meanings, especially through the interpretations of historical texts; and (3) *critical* knowledge, which is devoted to uncovering conditions of constraint and domination.

These three types of knowledge reflect three basic types of human interests: (1) a technical interest in the reproduction of existence through control of the environment, (2) a practical interest in understanding the meaning of situations, and (3) an emancipatory interest in freedom for growth and improvement. Such interests reside not in individuals but in more general imperatives for reproduction, meaning, and freedom that presumably are built into the species as it has become organized into societies. These three interests create, therefore, three types of knowledge. The interest in material reproduction has produced science or empirical/analytic knowledge, the interest in understanding of meaning has led to the development of hermeneutic-historical knowledge, and the interest in freedom has required the development of critical theory.

These interests in technical control, practical understanding, and emancipation generate different types of knowledge through three types of media: (1) "work," for realizing interests in technical control through the development of empirical-analytic knowledge; (2) "language," for realizing practical interests in understanding through hermeneutic knowledge; and (3) "authority," for realizing interests in emancipation through the development of critical theory. There is a kind of functionalism in this analysis: needs for "material survival and social reproduction," for "continuity of society through interpretive understanding," and for "utopian fulfillment" create interests. Then, through the media of work, language, and authority, these needs produce three types of knowledge: scientific, hermeneutical, and critical.

This kind of typologizing is, of course, highly reminiscent of Weber and is the vehicle through which Habermas makes the central point: positivism and the search for natural laws constitute only one type of knowledge, although the historical trend has been for the empirical-analytic to dominate the other types of knowledge. Interests in technical control through work and the development of science have dominated interests in understanding and emancipation. And so, if social life seems meaningless and cold, it is because technical interests in producing science have dictated what kind of knowledge is permissible and legitimate. Thus, Weber's "rationalization thesis" is restated with the typological distinction among interest, knowledge, and media. Table 23.1 summarizes Habermas's argument.

This typology allowed Habermas to achieve several goals. First, he attacked the assumption that science is value-free because, like all knowledge, it is attached to a set of interests. Second, he revised the Weberian thesis of rationalization in such a way that it dictates a renewed emphasis on hermeneutics and criticism. These other two types of knowledge are being driven out by empirical-analytic knowledge, or science. Therefore, it is necessary to reemphasize these neglected types of

Table 23.1 Types of Knowledge, Interests, Media (and Functional Needs)

Functional Needs	Interests	Knowledge	Media
Material survival and social reproduction generate pressures for	technical control of the environment, which leads to the development of	empirical/analytic knowledge, which is achieved through	work
Continuity of social relations generates pressures for	practical understanding through interpretations of other's subjective states, which leads to the development of	hermeneutic and historical knowledge, which is achieved through	language
Desires for utopian fulfillment generate pressures for	emancipation from unnecessary domination, which leads to the development of	critical theory, which is achieved through	authority

knowledge. Third, by viewing positivism in the social sciences as a type of empirical-analytic knowledge, Habermas associated it with human interests in technical control. He, therefore, visualized social science as a tool of economic and political interests.

Science thus becomes an ideology; actually, Habermas sees it as the underlying cause of the *legitimation crises* of advanced capitalist societies (more on this shortly). In dismissing positivism in this way, he oriented his own project to hermeneutics, with a critical twist. That is, he visualized the major task of critical theory as the analysis of those processes by which people achieve interpretative understanding of one another in ways that give social life a sense of continuity and meaning. Increasingly, Habermas came to focus on the communicative processes among actors as the theoretical core for critical theorizing. Goals of emancipation cannot be realized without knowledge about how people interact and communicate. Such an emphasis represents a restatement in a new guise of Habermas's early analysis of the public sphere, but now the process of public discourse and debate is viewed as the essence of human interaction in general. Moreover, to understand interaction, it is necessary to analyze language and linguistic processes among individuals. Knowledge of these processes can, in turn, give critical theory a firm conceptual basis from which to launch a critique of society and to suggest paths for the emancipation of individuals. Yet, to justify this emphasis on hermeneutics and criticism, Habermas had to first analyze the crises of capitalist societies through the overextension of empirical-analytic systems of knowledge.

Legitimation Crisis in Societies

As Habermas had argued in his earlier work, there are several historical trends in modern societies: (a) the decline of the public sphere, (b) the increasing intervention of the state into the economy, and (c) the growing dominance of science in the service of the state's interests in technical control. These ideas are woven together in *Legitimation Crisis*.[30]

The basic argument in *Legitimation Crisis* is that as the state increasingly intervenes in the economy, it also seeks to translate political issues into "technical problems." Issues thus are not topics for public debate; rather, they represent technical problems that require the use of technologies by experts in bureaucratic organizations. As a result, there is a "depoliticization" of practical issues by redefining them as technical problems. To do this, the state propagates a "technocratic consciousness" that Habermas believed represents a new kind of ideology. Unlike previous ideologies, however, it does not promise a future utopia; but, like other ideologies, it is seductive in its ability to veil problems, to simplify perceived options, and to justify a particular way of organizing social life. At the core of this technocratic consciousness is an emphasis on "instrumental reason," or what Weber termed means-ends rationality. That is, criteria of the efficiency of means in realizing explicit goals increasingly guide evaluations of social action and people's approach to problems. This emphasis on instrumental reason displaces other types of action, such as behaviors oriented to mutual understanding. This displacement occurs in a series of stages: science is first used by the state to realize specific goals; then, the criterion of efficiency is used by the state to reconcile the competing goals of groupings; next, basic cultural values are themselves assessed and evaluated for their efficiency and rationality; finally, in Habermas's version of Brave New World, decisions are completely delegated to computers, which seek the most rational and efficient course of action.

This reliance on the ideology of technocratic consciousnesses creates, Habermas argues, new dilemmas of political legitimation. Habermas believes that capitalist societies can be divided into three basic subsystems: (1) the economic, (2) the politico-administrative, and (3) the cultural (what he later calls lifeworld). From this division of societies into these subsystems, Habermas then posits four points of crises: (1) an "economic crisis" occurs if the economic subsystem cannot generate sufficient productivity to meet people's needs; (2) a "rationality crisis" exists when the politico-administrative subsystem cannot generate a sufficient number of instrumental decisions; (3) a "motivation crisis" exists when actors cannot use cultural symbols to generate sufficient meaning to feel committed to participate fully in the society; and (4) a "legitimation crisis" arises when actors do not possess the "requisite number of generalized motivations" or diffuse commitments to the political subsystem's right to make decisions. Much of this analysis of crises is described in Marxian terms but emphasizes that economic and rationality crises are perhaps less important than either motivational or legitimation crises. For, as technocratic consciousness penetrates all spheres of social life and creates productive economies and an intrusive state, the crisis tendencies of late capitalism shift from the inability to produce sufficient economic goods or political decisions to the failure to generate (a) diffuse commitments to political processes and (b) adequate levels of meaning among individual actors.

---

[30]Jürgen Habermas, *Legitimation Crisis*, trans. T. McCarthy (London: Heinemann, 1976; originally published 1973 in German).

In *Legitimation Crisis* is an early form of what becomes an important distinction: "systemic" processes revolving around the economy and the politico-administrative apparatus of the state must be distinguished from "cultural" processes. This distinction will later be conceptualized as *system* and *lifeworld,* respectively, but the central point is this: in tune with his Frankfurt School roots, Habermas is shifting emphasis from Marx's analysis of the economic crisis of production to crises of meaning and commitment; if the problems or crises of capitalist societies are in these areas, then critical theory must focus on the communicative and interactive processes by which humans generate understandings and meanings among themselves. If instrumental reason, or means-ends rationality, is driving out action based on mutual understanding and commitment, then the goal of critical theory is to expose this trend and to suggest ways of overcoming it, especially because legitimation and motivational crises make people aware that something is missing from their lives, thereby making them receptive to more emancipatory alternatives. So the task of critical theory is to develop a theoretical perspective that allows the restructuring of meaning and commitment in social life. This goal will be realized, Habermas argues, by further understanding of how people communicate, interact, and develop symbolic meanings.

Early Analysis of Speech and Interaction

In 1970, Habermas wrote two articles that marked a return to the idea of the public sphere, but with a new, more theoretical thrust. They also signaled an increasing emphasis on the process of speech, communication, and interaction. In his "On Systematically Distorted Communication," Habermas outlined the nature of undistorted communication.[31] True to Habermas's Weberian origins, this outline is an ideal type. The goal is to determine the essentials and essence of undistorted communication so that those processes that distort communication, such as domination, can be better exposed. What, then, are the features of undistorted communication? Habermas lists five: (1) expressions, actions, and gestures are noncontradictory; (2) communication is public and conforms to cultural standards of what is appropriate; (3) actors can distinguish between the properties of language, per se, and the events and processes that are described by language; (4) communication leads to, and is the product of, intersubjectivity, or the capacity of actors to understand one another's subjective states and to develop a sense of shared collective meanings; and (5) conceptualizations of time and space are understood by actors to mean different things when externally observed and when subjectively experienced in the process of interaction. The details of his analysis on the distortion of communication are less essential than the assertions about what critical theory must conceptualize. For Habermas, the conceptualization of undistorted communication is used as a foil for mounting a critique against those social forces that make such idealized communication difficult to realize. Moreover, as his subsequent work testifies, Habermas emphasizes condition (4), or communication and intersubjectivity among actors.

---

[31]Jürgen Habermas, "On Systematically Distorted Communication," *Inquiry* 13 (1970):205–218.

This emphasis became evident in his other 1970 article, "Toward a Theory of Communicative Competence."[32] The details of this argument are not as critical as the overall intent, especially because his ideas undergo subsequent modification. Habermas argues that for actors to be competent, they must know more than the linguistic rules of how to construct sentences and to talk; they must also master "idealogue-constitutive universals," which are part of the "social linguistic structure of society." Behind this jargon is the idea that the meaning of language and speech is contextual and that actors use implicit stores or stocks of knowledge to interpret the meaning of utterances. Habermas then proposes yet another ideal type, "the ideal speech situation," in which actors possess all the relevant background knowledge and linguistic skills to communicate without distortion.

Thus, in the early 1970s, Habermas began to view the mission of critical theory as emphasizing the process of interaction as mediated by speech. But such speech acts draw on stores of knowledge—rules, norms, values, tacit understandings, memory traces, and the like—for their interpretation. These ideals of the speech process represent a restatement of the romanticized public sphere, where issues were openly debated, discussed, and rationally resolved. What Habermas has done, of course, is to restate this view of "what is good and desirable" in more theoretical and conceptual terms, although it could be argued that there is not much difference between the romanticized portrayal of the public sphere and the ideal-typical conceptualization of speech. But with this conceptualization, the goal of critical theory must be to expose those conditions that distort communication and that inhibit realization of the ideal speech situation. Habermas's utopia is thus a society where actors can communicate without distortion, achieve a sense of one another's subjective states, and openly reconcile their differences through argumentation that is free from external constraint and coercion. In other words, he wants to restore the public sphere but in a more encompassing way—that is, in people's day-to-day interactions.

Habermas moved in several different directions in trying to construct a rational approach for realizing this utopia. He borrows metaphorically from psychoanalytic theory as a way to uncover the distortions that inhibit open discourse,[33] but this psychoanalytic journey is far less important than his growing concentration on the process of communicative action and interaction as the basis for creating a society that reduces domination and constraint. Thus, by the mid-1970s, he labels his analysis universal pragmatics, whose centerpiece is the "theory of communicative action."[34] This theory will be discussed in more detail shortly, but let us briefly review its key elements. Communication involves more than words, grammar, and syntax; it also involves what Habermas terms *validity claims*. There are three types

---

[32]Jürgen Habermas, "Toward a Theory of Communicative Competence," *Inquiry* 13 (1970):360–375.

[33]Habermas sometimes calls this aspect of his program "depth hermeneutics." The idea is to create a methodology of inquiry for social systems that parallels the approach of psychoanalysis—that is, dialogue, removal of barriers to understanding, analysis of the underlying causal processes, and efforts to use this understanding to dissolve distortions in interaction.

[34]For an early statement, see Jürgen Habermas, "Some Distinctions in Universal Pragmatics: A Working Paper," *Theory and Society* 3 (1976):155–167.

808 PART II: THE MODERN ERA OF THEORIZING

of claims: (1) those asserting that a course of action as indicated through speech is the most effective and efficient means for attaining ends, (2) those claiming that an action is correct and proper in accordance with the relevant norms, and (3) those maintaining that the subjective experiences as expressed in a speech act are sincere and authentic. All speech acts implicitly make these three claims, although a speech act can emphasize one more than the other two. Those responding to communication can accept or challenge these validity claims; if challenged, then the actors contest, debate, criticize, and revise their communication. They use, of course, shared "stocks of knowledge" about norms, means-ends effectiveness, and sincerity to make their claims as well as to contest and revise them. This process (which restates the public sphere in yet one more guise) is often usurped when claims are settled by recourse to power and authority. But if claims are settled by the "giving of reasons for" and "reasons against" the claim in a mutual give-and-take among individuals, then Habermas sees it as "rational discourse." Thus, built into the very process of interaction is the potential for rational discourse that can be used to create a more just, open, and free society. Such discourse is not merely means-ends rationality, for it involves adjudication of two other validity claims: those concerned with normative appropriateness and those concerned with subjective sincerity. Actors thus implicitly assess and critique one another for effectiveness, normative appropriateness, and sincerity of their respective speech acts; so the goal of critical theory is to expose those societal conditions that keep such processes from occurring for all three types of validity claims.

In this way, Habermas moves critical theory from Lukács's, Horkheimer's, and Adorno's emphasis on subjective consciousness to a concern with intersubjective consciousness and the interactive processes by which intersubjectivity is created, maintained, and changed through the validity claims in each speech act. Moreover, rather than viewing the potential for liberating alternatives as residing in the subjective consciousness, Habermas could assert that emancipatory potential inheres in each and every communicative interaction. Because speech and communication are the basis of interaction and because society is ultimately sustained by interaction, the creation of less restrictive societies will come about by realizing the inherent dynamics of the communication process.

Habermas's Reconceptualization of Evolution

All critical theory is historical in the sense that it tries to analyze the long-term development of oppressive arrangements in society. Indeed, the central problem of critical theory is to reconcile Marx's and Weber's respective analyses of the development of advanced capitalism. It is not surprising, therefore, that Habermas produces a historical-evolutionary analysis, but in contrast with Weber, he sees emancipatory potential in evolutionary trends. Yet at the same time he wants to avoid the incorrect prognosis in Marx's analysis and to retain the emancipatory thrust of Marx's approach. Habermas's first major effort to effect this reconciliation appeared in his *The Reconstruction of Historical Materialism*,[35]

---

[35]Jürgen Habermas, *Zur Rekonstruktion des Historischen Materialismus* (Frankfurt, Germany: Suhrkamp, 1976).

parts of which have been translated and appear in *Communication and the Evolution of Society*.[36]

Habermas's approach to evolution pulls together many of the themes discussed earlier, so a brief review of his general argument can set the stage for an analysis of his most recent theoretical synthesis, *The Theory of Communicative Action*.[37] In many ways, Habermas reintroduces traditional functionalism into Marx's and Weber's evolutionary descriptions, but with both a phenomenological and a structuralist emphasis.

As have all functional theorists, he views evolution as the process of structural differentiation and the emergence of integrative problems. He also borrows from Herbert Spencer, Talcott Parsons, and Niklas Luhmann when he argues that the integration of complex systems leads to an adaptive upgrading, increasing the capacity of society to cope with the environment.[38] That is, complex systems that are integrated are better adapted to their environments than are less complex systems. The key issue, then, is this: What conditions increase or decrease integration? For without integration, differentiation produces severe problems.

Habermas's analysis of system integration argues that contained in the worldviews or stocks of knowledge of individual actors are learning capacities and stores of information that determine the overall learning level of a society. In turn, this learning level shapes the society's steering capacity to respond to environmental problems. At times, Habermas refers to these learning levels as organization principles. Thus, as systems confront problems of internal integration and external contingencies, the stocks of knowledge and worldviews of individual actors are translated into organization principles and steering capacities, which in turn set limits on just how a system can respond. For example, a society with only religious mythology will be less complex and less able to respond to environmental challenges than a more complex society with large stores of technology and stocks of normative procedures determining its organization principles. But societies can "learn"[39] that, when confronted with problems beyond the capacity of their current organization principles and steering mechanisms, they can draw upon the "cognitive potential" in the worldviews and stocks of knowledge of individuals who reorganize their actions. The result of this learning creates new levels of information that allow the development of new organization principles for securing integration despite increased societal differentiation and complexity.

The basis for societal integration lies in the processes by which actors communicate and develop mutual understandings and stores of knowledge. To the extent that

---

[36]Jürgen Habermas, *Communication and the Evolution of Society*, trans. T. McCarthy (London: Heinemann, 1979).

[37]For an earlier statement, see Jürgen Habermas, "Towards a Reconstruction of Historical Materialism," *Theory and Society* 2 (3 1975):84–98.

[38]He borrows from Niklas Luhmann here (see Chapter 10), although much of Habermas's approach is a reaction to Luhmann.

[39]Habermas analogizes here to Jean Piaget's and Lawrence Kohlberg's analysis of the cognitive development of children, seeing societies as able to "learn" as they become more structurally complex.

these interactive processes are arrested by the patterns of economic and political organization, the society's learning capacity is correspondingly diminished. One of the main integrative problems of capitalist societies is the integration of the material forces of production (economy as administered by the state), on one side, and the cultural stores of knowledge that are produced by communicative interaction, on the other. Societies that differentiate materially in the economic and political realms without achieving integration on a normative and cultural level (i.e., shared understandings) will remain unintegrated and experience crises.

Built into these dynamics, however, is their resolution. The processes of "communicative interaction" that produce and reproduce unifying cultural symbols must be given equal weight with the "labor" processes that generate material production and reproduction. At this point, Habermas developed his more synthetic approach in *The Theory of Communicative Action*.

The Theory of Communicative Action

The two-volume *The Theory of Communicative Action* pulls together into a reasonably coherent framework various strands of Habermas's thought.[40] Yet, true to his general style of scholarship, Habermas wandered over a rather large intellectual landscape. In Thomas McCarthy's words, Habermas develops his ideas through "a somewhat unusual combination of theoretical constructions with historical reconstructions of the ideas of 'classical' social theorists."[41] Such thinkers as Marx, Weber, Durkheim, Mead, Lukács, Horkheimer, Adorno, and Parsons are, for Habermas, "still very much alive" and are treated as "virtual dialogue partners."[42] As a consequence, the two volumes meander through selected portions of various thinkers' work, critiquing and yet using key ideas. After the dust settles, however, the end result is a very creative synthesis of ideas into a critical theory.

Habermas's basic premise is summarized near the end of Volume 1: If we assume that the human species maintains itself through the socially coordinated activities of its members and that this coordination is established through communication— and in certain spheres of life, through communication aimed at reaching agreement— then the reproduction of the species also requires satisfying the conditions of a rationality inherent in communicative action.[43]

In other words, intrinsic to the process of communicative action, where actors implicitly make, challenge, and accept one another's validity claims, is a rationality that can potentially serve as the basis for reconstructing the social order in less

---

[40]Habermas, *The Theory of Communicative Action*, 2 vols. The subtitle of Volume 1, *Reason and the Rationalization of Society*, gives some indication of its thrust. The translator, Thomas McCarthy, has done an excellent service in translating very difficult prose. Also, his "Translator's Introduction" to Volume 1, v–xxxvii, is the best summary of Habermas's recent theory that I have come across.

[41]McCarthy, "Translator's Introduction," p. vii.

[42]Ibid.

[43]Habermas, *The Theory of Communicative Action*, vol. 1, 397.

oppressive ways. The first volume of *The Theory of Communicative Action* thus focuses on action and rationality in an effort to reconceptualize both processes in a manner that shifts emphasis from the subjectivity and consciousness of the individual to the process of symbolic interaction. In a sense, Volume 1 is Habermas's microsociology, whereas Volume 2 is his macrosociology. In the second volume, Habermas introduces the concept of *system* and tries to connect it to microprocesses of action and interaction through reconceptualization of the phenomenological concept of *lifeworld.*

The Overall Project

Let me begin by briefly reviewing the overall argument and then return to Volumes 1 and 2 with a more detailed analysis. There are four types of action: (1) teleological, (2) normative, (3) dramaturgical, and (4) communicative. Only communicative action contains the elements whereby actors reach intersubjective understanding. Such communicative action—which is, actually, interaction— presupposes a set of background assumptions and stocks of knowledge, or, in Habermas's terms, a *lifeworld.* Also operating in any society are *system processes,* which revolve around the material maintenance of the species and its survival. The evolutionary trend is for system processes and lifeworld processes to become internally differentiated and differentiated from each other. The integration of a society depends on a balance between system and lifeworld processes. As modern societies have evolved, however, this balance has been upset as system processes revolving around the economy and the state (also law, family, and other reproductive structures) have "colonized" and dominated lifeworld processes concerned with mutually shared meanings, understandings, and intersubjectivity. As a result, modern society is poorly integrated.

These integrative problems in capitalist societies are manifested in crises concerning the "reproduction of the lifeworld"; that is, the acts of communicative interaction that reproduce this lifeworld are displaced by "delinguistified media," such as money and power, that are used in the reproduction of system processes (economy and government). The solution to these crises is a rebalancing of relations between lifeworld and system. This rebalancing is to come through the resurrection of the public sphere in the economic and political arenas and in the creation of more situations in which communicative action (interaction) can proceed uninhibited by the intrusion of systems media, such as power and money. The goal of critical theory, therefore, is to document those facets of society in which the lifeworld has been colonized and to suggest approaches whereby situations of communicative action (interaction) can be reestablished. Such is Habermas's general argument, and now we can fill in some of the details.

The Reconceptualization of Action and Rationality

In Volume 1 of *The Theory of Communicative Action,* Habermas undertakes a long and detailed analysis of Weber's conceptualization of action and rationalization. He wants to reconceptualize rationality and action in ways that allow him to view rational action as a potentially liberating rather than an imprisoning force.[44] In this way, he feels, he can avoid the pessimism of Weber and the retreat into subjectivity of Lukács, Adorno, and Horkheimer. There are, Habermas concludes, several basic types of action:[45]

1. *Teleological* action is behavior-oriented to calculating various means and selecting the most appropriate ones to realize explicit goals. Such action becomes strategic when other acting agents are involved in one's calculations. Habermas also calls this action "instrumental" because it is concerned with means to achieve ends. Most important, he emphasizes that this kind of action is too often considered to be "rational action" in previous conceptualizations of rationality. As he argues, this view of rationality is too narrow and forces critical theory into a conceptual trap: if teleological or means-ends rationality has taken over the modern world and has, as a consequence, oppressed people, then how can critical theory propose rational alternatives? Would not such a rational theory be yet one more oppressive application of means-and-ends rationality? The answers to these questions lie in recognizing that there are several types of action and that true rationality resides not in teleological action but in communicative action.

2. *Normatively regulated* action is behavior that is oriented to the common values of a group. Thus, normative action is directed toward complying with the normative expectations of collectively organized groupings of individuals.

3. *Dramaturgical action* is action that involves the conscious manipulation of oneself before an audience or public. It is egocentered in that it involves actors mutually manipulating their behaviors to present their own intentions, but it is also social in that such manipulation is done in the context of organized activity.

4. *Communicative action* is interaction among agents who use speech and nonverbal symbols as a way of understanding their mutual situation and their respective plans of action to agree on how to coordinate their behaviors.

These four types of action presuppose different kinds of "worlds." That is, each action is oriented to a somewhat different aspect of the universe, which can be divided into the (a) "objective or external world" of manipulable objects; (b) "social world" of norms, values, and other socially recognized expectations; and (c) "subjective world" of experiences. Teleological action is concerned primarily with the objective world, normatively regulated action with the social, and dramaturgical with the subjective and external. But only with communicative action do actors

---

[44]Recall that its subtitle is *Reason and the Rationalization of Society.*

[45]Habermas, *The Theory of Communicative Action*, 85–102.

"refer simultaneously to things in the objective, social, and subjective worlds in order to negotiate common definitions of the situation."[46]

Such communicative action is, therefore, potentially more rational than all of the others because it deals with all three worlds and because it proceeds as speech acts that assert three types of validity claims. Such speech acts assert that (1) statements are true in "propositional content," or in reference to the external and objective world; (2) statements are correct with respect to the existing normative context, or social world; and (3) statements are sincere and manifest the subjective world of the intention and experiences of the actor.[47] The process of communicative action in which these three types of validity claims are made, accepted, or challenged by others is inherently more rational than other types of action. If a validity claim is not accepted, then it is debated and discussed in an effort to reach understanding without recourse to force and authority.[48] The process of reaching an understanding through validity claims, their acceptance, or their discussion takes place against the background of a culturally ingrained pre-understanding. This background remains unproblematic as a whole; only that part of the stock of knowledge that participants make use of and thematize at a given time is put to the test. To the extent that definitions of situations are negotiated by the participants themselves, this thematic segment of the lifeworld is at their disposal with the negotiation of each new definition of the situation.[49]

Thus, in the process of making validity claims through speech acts, actors use existing definitions of situations or create new ones that establish order in their social relations. Such definitions become part of the stocks of knowledge in their lifeworlds, and they become the standards by which validity claims are made, accepted, and challenged. Thus, in reaching an understanding through communicative action, the lifeworld serves as a point of reference for the adjudication of validity claims, which encompass the full range of worlds—the objective, social, and subjective. And so, in Habermas's view, there is more rationality inherent in the very process of communicative interaction than in means-ends or teleological action.[50] As Habermas summarizes,

> We have . . . characterized the rational structure of the processes of reaching understanding in terms of (a) the three world-relations of actors and the corresponding concepts of the objective, social, and subjective worlds; (b) the validity claims of propositional truth, normative rightness, and sincerity or authenticity; (c) the concept of a rationally motivated agreement, that is, one based on the intersubjective recognition of criticizable validity claims; and

---

[46]Ibid., 95.

[47]Ibid., 99.

[48]Recall Habermas's earlier discussion of non-distorted communication and the ideal speech act. This is his most recent reconceptualization of these ideas.

[49]Ibid., 100 (emphasis in original).

[50]Ibid., 302.

(d) the concept of reaching understanding as the cooperative negotiation of common definitions of the situation.[51]

Thus, as people communicatively act (interact), they use and at the same time produce common definitions of the situation. Such definitions are part of the lifeworld of a society; if they have been produced and reproduced through the communicative action, then they are the basis for the rational and non-oppressive integration of a society. Let us now turn to Habermas's discussion of this lifeworld, which serves as the "court of appeals" in communicative action.

The Lifeworld and System Processes of Society

Habermas believes the lifeworld is a "culturally transmitted and linguistically organized stock of interpretative patterns." But what are these "interpretative patterns" about? What do they pertain to? His answer, as one expects from Habermas, is yet another typology. There are three different types of interpretative patterns in the lifeworld: There are interpretative patterns with respect to culture, or systems of symbols; there are those pertaining to society or social institutions; and there are those oriented to personality, or aspects of self and being. That is, (1) actors possess implicit and shared stocks of knowledge about cultural traditions, values, beliefs, linguistic structures, and their use in interaction; (2) actors also know how to organize social relations and what kinds and patterns of coordinated interaction are proper and appropriate; and (3) actors understand what people are like, how they should act, and what is normal or aberrant.

These three types of interpretative patterns correspond, Habermas asserts, to the following functional needs for reproducing the lifeworld (and, by implication, for integrating society): (1) reaching understanding through communicative action transmits, preserves, and renews cultural knowledge; (2) communicative action that coordinates interaction meets the need for social integration and group solidarity; and (3) communicative action that socializes agents meets the need for the formation of personal identities.[52]

Thus, the three components of the lifeworld—culture, society, and personality—meet the corresponding needs of society—cultural reproduction, social integration, and personality formation—through the three dimensions along which communicative action is conducted: reaching understanding, coordinating interaction, and affecting socialization. As Habermas summarizes in Volume 2,

> In coming to an understanding with one another about their situation, participants in communication stand in a cultural tradition which they use and at the same time renew; in coordinating their actions via intersubjective recognition of criticizable validity claims, they rely upon their membership in groupings

---

[51]Ibid., 137.

[52]We are now into ibid., vol. 2: *System and Lifeworld: A Critique of Functionalist Reason*, 205–240, which is a somewhat ironic title because of the heavily functional arguments. But, as noted earlier, Habermas's earlier work has always had an implicit functionalism.

and at the same time reenforce their integration; through participating in inter-action with competent persons, growing children internalize value orientations and acquire generalized capacities for action.[53]

These lifeworld processes are interrelated with system processes in a society. Action in economic, political, familial, and other institutional contexts draws on, and reproduces, the cultural, societal, and personality dimensions of the lifeworld. Yet evolutionary trends are for differentiation of the lifeworld into separate stocks of knowledge with respect to culture, society, and personality and for differentiation of system processes into distinctive and separate institutional clusters, such as economy, state, family, and law. Such differentiation creates problems of integration and balance between the lifeworld and the system.[54] And therein reside the dilem-mas and crises of modern societies.

Evolutionary Dynamics and Societal Crises

In a sense, Habermas blends traditional analysis by functionalists of societal and cultural differentiation with a Marxian dialectic whereby the seeds for eman-cipation are sown in the creation of an ever more rationalized and differentiated society. Borrowing from Durkheim's analysis of mechanical solidarity, Habermas argues that

the more cultural traditions pre-decide which validity claims, when, where, for what, from whom, and to whom must be accepted, the less the participants themselves have the possibility of making explicit and examining the potential groups in which their yes/no positions are based.[55]

But "as mechanical solidarity gives way to organic solidarity based upon func-tional interdependence," then "the more the worldview that furnishes the cultural stock of knowledge is decentered" and "the less the need for understanding is cov-ered in advance by an interpreted lifeworld immune from critique," and therefore, "the more this need has to be met by the interpretative accomplishments of the participants themselves." That is, if the lifeworld is to be sustained and reproduced, it becomes ever more necessary with growing societal complexity for social actions to be based on communicative processes. The result is that there is greater potential for rational communicative action because less and less of the social order is pre-ordained by a simple and undifferentiated lifeworld. But system processes have reduced this potential, and the task of critical theory is to document how system processes have colonized the lifeworld and thereby arrested this potentially supe-rior rationality inherent in the speech acts of communicative action.

---

[53]Ibid., 208.

[54]This is the old functionalist argument of "differentiation" producing "integrative problems," which is as old as Spencer and which is Parsons reincarnated with a phenomenological twist.

[55]All quotes here are from ibid., vol. 1, 70.

How have system processes restricted this potential contained in communicative action? As the sacred and traditional basis of the lifeworld organization has dissolved and been replaced by linguistic interaction around a lifeworld differentiated along cultural, social, and personality axes, there is a countertrend in the differentiation of system processes. System evolution involves the expansion of material production through the greater use of technologies, science, and "delinguistified steering mechanisms" such as money and power to carry out system processes.[56] These media do not rely on the validity claims of communicative action; when they become the media of interaction in ever more spheres of life—markets, bureaucracies, welfare state policies, legal systems, and even family relations—the processes of communicative action so essential for lifeworld reproduction are invaded and colonized. Thus, system processes use power and money as their media of integration, and in the process, they "decouple the lifeworld" from its functions for societal integration.[57] There is an irony here because differentiation of the lifeworld facilitated the differentiation of system processes and the use of money and power,[58] so "the rationalized lifeworld makes possible the rise of growth of subsystems which strike back at it in a destructive fashion."[59]

Through this ironical process, capitalism creates market dynamics using money, which in turn spawn a welfare state employing power in ways that reduce political and economic crises but that increase those crises revolving around lifeworld reproduction. For the new crises and conflicts "arise in areas of cultural reproduction, of social integration and of socialization."[60]

Conclusions: The Goal of Critical Theory

Habermas has now circled back to this initial concern, and those of early critical theorists. He has recast the Weberian thesis by asserting that true rationality inheres in communicative action, not teleological (and strategic or instrumental) action, as Weber claimed. And he has redefined the critical theorist's view on modern crises; they are not crises of rationalization but crises of colonization of those truly rational processes that inhere in the speech acts of communicative action, which reproduce the lifeworld so essential to societal integration. Thus, built into the integrating processes of differentiated societies (not the subjective processes of individuals, as the early critical theorists claimed) is the potential for a critical theory that seeks to

---

[56]Here, Habermas is borrowing from Simmel's analysis in *The Philosophy of Money* (see Chapter 21 of this work) and from Parsons's conceptualization of generalized media (see Chapter 3).

[57]Habermas, *The Theory of Communicative Action*, vol. 2, 256–276.

[58]Habermas appears in these arguments to borrow heavily from Parsons's analysis of evolution (see Chapter 4 of this work).

[59]Habermas, *The Theory of Communicative Action*, vol. 2, 227.

[60]Ibid., 576.

restore communicative rationality despite the impersonal steering mechanisms. If system differentiation occurs in delinguistified media, like money and power, and if these reduce the reliance on communicative action, then crises are inevitable. The resulting collective frustration over the lack of meaning in social life can be used by critical theorists to mobilize people to restore the proper balance between system and lifeworld processes. Thus, crises of material production will not be the impetus for change, as Marx contended. Rather, the crises of lifeworld reproduction will serve as the stimulus to societal reorganization. And returning to his first work, Habermas sees such reorganization as involving (a) the restoration of the public sphere in politics, where relinguistified debate and argumentation, rather than delinguistified power and authority, are used to make political decisions (thus reducing "legitimation crises") and (b) the extension of communicative action back into those spheres—family, work, and social relations—that have become increasingly dominated by delinguistified steering media (thereby eliminating "motivational crises").

The potential for this reorganization inheres in the nature of societal integration through the rationality inherent in the communicative actions that reproduce the lifeworld. The purpose of critical theory is to release this rational potential.

CHAPTER 24

American-Style Critical Theorizing

C ritical theories are driven by a moral vision of what "the good society" *should* be; and one of the reasons why students, in America at least, take sociology courses and become majors is that they share this vision. Sociology is about the social organization of people in all its manifestations; if the problems of society inhere in these dynamics of social organization, then sociology is the best discipline for understanding these problems and, more important, doing something about them. Many of the first generation of American sociologists, beginning in the late 1800s, founded sociology with this motivation—to make a better society—at the same time that they espoused the virtues of science. Auguste Comte in Europe gave sociology a name with the same goal because he felt that science was the path to human salvation. Most early American sociologists, in contrast, did not know much about science, despite their rhetorical support of it.

In American sociology today, critical theory is not only an artifact of this long history of activist motivations among sociologists but also the consequence of internalizing external social movements into departments and programs within academia. Thus, for example, the civil rights, feminist, and gay-lesbian social movements in the broader society have become part of the academic mission of universities that have hired within departments or created new departments and programs to include scholarship about the issues, history, and forces that pushed people to mobilize collectively in the name of justice and fairness for categories of persons who have been subjected to discrimination.

As a starting point for the founding of academic programs, then, it was inevitable that these critical theories would not only be critical of existing conditions in a society, they would be activist in their intentions to change these conditions. Sociology is an obvious place for activists fueled by beliefs about "what is wrong" and "what must exist in a just society"; and so it should not be surprising that even theorizing should be influenced by these beliefs and motivations.

There will always be tension between science as one kind of belief system and ideology as another kind of belief system (see Figure 1.1 on p. 8), and this tension reverberates throughout academia and the broader society as well. This is a tension that will simply have to be endured because it is endemic to sociology and, now, to academia more generally.

In this chapter, feminism will be given the most attention because it has evolved a powerful critique and a complex set of theoretical arguments that are only rivaled by Marxist-inspired class analysis and European critical theories. A much less coherent intellectual movement can be found in critical theories about race and ethnicity, but over the last few decades, these critical theories have gained some prominence, although there is still much less active theorizing in these areas than is the case with feminist theories. These two critical approaches to theory are uniquely American in tone and style and are, thus, worthy of attention in a book devoted to contemporary sociological theorizing.

The Feminist Critique of Sociological Theory: Gender, Politics, and Patriarchy*

Since the early 1970s, one of the most sustained challenges to "mainstream" socio-logical theory has come from critical feminist theorists. Appearing shortly after the beginning of the "second wave" of the women's movement in the mid- to late 1960s, the first feminist critiques focused on the underrepresentation of women and women's experiences within sociology, both as the subjects of research and the pro-ducers of theory. Concurrently, feminist theorists examined the construction of gender and sex roles in modern society to demonstrate the existence of a "female world" that sociology had hitherto ignored.[1] Subsequent critiques went further, as feminists used the concepts of gender and patriarchy to reveal masculine (or andro-centric) stances in social research methodologies and in sociological theory. These more radical critiques questioned the capacity of sociological research and theory, as a body of knowledge constructed from the experiences of men, to address the experiences of women.

Critical feminist theorists proposed alternative methodological approaches, includ-ing the construction of a "feminist standpoint" or women's sociology that would begin with the social universe of women and reflect women's perspectives on society.[2]

Note: *This section on feminism is primarily authored by Patricia R. Turner, with my contributions being relatively minor.

[1]Jessie Bernard, *The Female World* (New York: Free Press, 1981); Ann Oakley, *The Sociology of House-work* (New York: Pantheon, 1974).

[2]Dorothy Smith, "Women's Perspective as a Radical Critique of Sociology," *Sociological Inquiry* 44 (1974):7–15, "Sociological Theory: Methods of Writing Patriarchy," in *Feminism and Sociological The-ory*, ed. Ruth A. Wallace (Newbury Park, CA: Sage, 1989), 34–64, *The Everyday World as Problematic: A Feminist Sociology* (Boston, MA: Northeastern University Press, 1987). See also Nancy Hartsock, *Money, Sex, and Power* (New York: Longman, 1983).

In the past decades, several radical feminist theorists have also used the epistemological issues inherent in feminist methodologies to critique the "positivistic" foundations of sociological understanding and to lay the groundwork for a "feminist epistemology."[3]

The feminist critique, like much of sociological theory at present, does not form a coherent paradigm. There is little consensus among critical feminist theorists about what constitutes "the feminist critique" or about how sociological understandings should be restructured to obviate the criticisms of feminists. Nevertheless, several common threads distinguish the feminist position from other forms of critical theory. What the critical feminist theorists share with their more scientifically oriented colleagues is the conviction that gender represents a fundamental form of social division within society. They also share a commitment to analyzing the sources of oppression and inequality of women, the most important being the patriarchal structure of society and its institutions. Still, the feminist theorists examined in this chapter have focused on gender and forms of patriarchy to criticize social research practices and the production of sociological theory itself.[4] Indeed, they have questioned the legitimacy and objectivity of these "scientific" methods by exploring the ways in which they embody androcentric (male-oriented) modes of thought. Finally, these critical feminist theorists are often self-consciously aware of the political and practical implications of their attacks for feminist politics and the status of women. As Mary Jo Neitz stated, "The critical questions for feminist scholarship came out of the women's movement, not out of the disciplines."[5] Consequently, most critical feminist theorists want to preserve the emancipatory dimension of feminist theory—that is, its ability to serve, like Marxism, as "both a mode of understanding and a call to action."[6] This self-conscious conflation of theory, method, politics, and praxis, combined with a focus on gender and patriarchy as the primary sources of oppression and inequality, constitutes the common denominators distinguishing the feminist critique of sociological theory.

---

[3]For example, see Chris Weedon, *Feminist Practice and Poststructuralist Theory* (New York: Basil Blackwell, 1987); Judith Butler, "Contingent Foundations: Feminism and the Question of Post-Modernism," in *The Postmodern Turn: New Perspectives on Social Theory,* ed. Steven Seldman (Cambridge, UK: Cambridge University Press, 1994), 152–170; Susan Hekman, *Gender and Knowledge: Elements of a Postmodern Feminism* (Boston, MA: Northeastern University Press, 1990); Sondra Farganis, "Postmodernism and Feminism," in *Postmodernism and Social Inquiry,* ed. David R. Dickens and Andrea Fontana (New York: Guilford Press, 1994), 101–127; and Thomas Meisenhelder, "Habermas and Feminism: The Future of Critical Theory," in *Feminism and Sociological Theory,* ed. Ruth A. Wallace (Newbury Park, CA: Sage, 1989), 119–134.

[4]This has led some to question whether many feminist critiques should properly be called "theory." See Mary Jo Neitz, "Introduction to the Special Issue: Sociology and Feminist Scholarship," *The American Sociologist* 20 (1989):5.

[5]Ibid., 4.

[6]Sondra Farganis, "Social Theory and Feminist Theory: The Need for Dialogue," *Social Inquiry* 56 (1986):56.

Representation and the Construction of Gender

Early Challenges to Social Science. Early feminist critiques of sociological research and theory were concerned primarily with the issue of representation, especially with respect to the[7]

1. Omission and underrepresentation of women as research subjects

2. Concentration on masculine-dominated sectors of social life

3. Use of paradigms, concepts, methods, and theories that more faithfully portray men's than women's experiences

4. Use of men and male lifestyles as the norms against which social phenomena were interpreted

One of the most influential early works that addressed all of these issues is Ann Oakley's survey of housewives and their opinions of housework. Oakley argued that discrimination against women in society is mirrored by sexism in sociology, and she used the academic neglect of housework *as work* to address the broader issue of sexual bias within sociological research and theory in general.[8] Oakley stated that women's "invisibility" in sociology can be seen in all the major subject areas of sociology. In the subject area of deviance, for example, Oakley argued that until the mid-1970s very little data had been collected on women and that "theories of deviance may include some passing reference to women, but interpretations of female behavior are uncomfortably subsumed under the umbrella of explanation geared to the model of masculine behavior."[9] She also questioned whether or not standard definitions of deviance consider patterns of behavior that are gender-related or

---

[7]Kathryn Ward and Linda Grant, "The Feminist Critique and a Decade of Published Research in Sociology Journals," *The Sociological Quarterly* 26 (1985):140. On the issue of inadequate representation of women as the subjects of research, see Arlie Russell Hochschild, "A Review of Sex Role Research," *American Journal of Sociology* 78 (1973):1011–1029 and Cynthia Fuchs Epstein, "A Different Angle of Vision: Notes on the Selective Eye of Sociology," *Social Science Quarterly* 55 (1974):645–656. Critiques on the neglect of female-dominated social sectors include Ann Oakley, *Sociology of Housework* (New York: Pantheon, 1974) and Jessie Bernard, "My Four Revolutions: An Autobiographical History of the ASA," *American Journal of Sociology* 78 (1973):773–791. For early critiques of sociological methods and their failure to reflect women's experiences and perspectives, see Smith, "Women's Perspective as a Radical Critique of Sociology" and Arlie Russell Hochschild, "The Sociology of Feeling and Emotion: Selected Possibilities," in *Another Voice: Feminist Perspectives on Social Life and Social Science,* ed. Marcia Millman and Rosabeth Moss Kanter (New York: Octagon, 1976), 280–307. Finally, among the early feminist theorists to criticize the use of men and their lifestyles as "normative" were Joan Acker, "Women and Social Stratification: A Case of Intellectual Sexism," *American Journal of Sociology* 78 (1973):936–945 and Jessie Bernard, "Research on Sex Differences: An Overview of the State of the Art" in *Women, Wives, Mothers* (Chicago, IL: Aldine Publishing Company, 1975), 7–29.

[8]Oakley, *Sociology of Housework,* 2.

[9]Ibid., 5.

associated only with women.[10] With regard to social stratification theory, to take an example from another prominent subject area of sociology, Oakley posited that the following untested assumptions about class membership effectively render women invisible and irrelevant: (a) the family is the unit of stratification, (b) the social position of the family is determined by the status of the man in it, and (c) only in rare circumstances is a woman's social position not determined by the men to whom she is attached by marriage or family of origin.[11] Oakley argued that these assumptions often do not reflect social reality, because many people do not live in families, many families are headed by women, and many husbands and wives do not have identical social status rankings. The problematics of these assumptions would be revealed, according to Oakley, if the significance of gender as a criterion for social differentiation and stratification is recognized by sociologists. Without such recognition, women's roles and position in the social stratification system would continue to be hidden and misrepresented.[12]

Oakley attributed the inherent sexism in sociological theory and research to the male-oriented attitudes of its "founding fathers,"[13] the paucity of women social researchers and theorists, and the pervasiveness of ideologies advocating gender roles within contemporary societies. The ideology of gender, she argued, contains stereotypical assumptions about women's social status and behavior that are uncritically reproduced within sociology, and these stereotypes will only be overcome if women's experiences are made the focus of analysis and viewed from their perspective.[14]

Most of these early critiques of sociological research and theory share with Oakley two related assumptions about the primacy and construction of gender: first, gender is a fundamental determinant of social relations and behavior and, second, gender divisions in a society shape the experiences and perspectives of each sex, with the result that women's experiences are distinctly different from those of men. Some feminist scholars went further than Oakley and began to argue that society is gendered in ways that segregate men and women into distinct and often exclusionary homosocial worlds. Building on Georg Simmel's insight that "women possess a world

---

[10]Ibid., 8.

[11]Ibid., 8–9. In a similar critique of social stratification literature, Joan Acker adds two additional assumptions: "(1) women determine their own social status only when they are not attached to a man; and (2) women are unequal to men in many ways, are differentially evaluated on the basis of sex, but this is irrelevant to the structure of stratification systems." See Acker, "Women and Social Stratification: A Case of Intellectual Sexism," *American Journal of Sociology* 78 (1973):937.

[12]Oakley, *Sociology of Housework,* 12–13.

[13]Ibid., 21. Oakley argues that of the five "founding fathers" of sociology—Marx, Comte, Spencer, Durkheim, and Weber—only two, Marx and Weber, had "emancipated views" about women. Terry Kandal, in a more recent analysis of the "woman question" in classical sociological theory, offers a less condemnatory accounting, asserting that there were "complex and contradictory variations in the writings about women by different classical theorists"; see *The Woman Question in Classical Sociological Theory* (Miami: Florida International University Press, 1988), 245.

[14]Ibid., 21–28.

of their own which is not comparable with the world of men,"[15] Jessie Bernard argued in *The Female World* that society is divided into "single-sex" worlds. Sociology and other disciplines in the humanities and human sciences have dealt heretofore almost exclusively with the male world. Bernard sought to correct this imbalance by tracing the historical development of the female world and the uniquely female experiences and perspectives that have emerged from it. She has argued that the female world differs subjectively and objectively from that of men, and hence, the female world must be examined "as an entity in its own right, not as a byproduct of the male world."[16] The neglect of the female world and women's experiences by sociology and other disciplines, Bernard has asserted, deprives public debate of perspectives that might provide innovative solutions and approaches to contemporary problems.[17]

Other feminist theorists have used the concept of gendered social spheres to explore more specifically the stratification of sex roles and the social construction of gender. Jean Lipman-Blumen proposed a homosocial theory of sex roles to account for the traditional barriers that restrict women's entry into male spheres—such as politics, the military, and major league sports—and that often confine women to the domestic sphere.[18] She hypothesized that men are socialized to be attracted to, and to be interested in, other men. This attraction is reinforced and perpetuated by patriarchal social institutions that traditionally value men over women and give to men nearly exclusive control of resources.[19] With the important exceptions of reproductive and sexual needs, men look to men for support, whereas women are forced to transform themselves into sex objects to acquire resources and support from men. Lipman-Blumen argued that the preeminence of men in the exchange and protection of resources creates "dominance hierarchies" that persist even when technology eliminates the need for the differentiation and stratification of sex roles.[20]

In her highly influential book *The Reproduction of Mothering: Psychoanalysis and the Sociology of Gender,* Nancy Chadorow theorized that women's responsibility for childrearing (and the collateral absence of male domestic roles) has profound consequences for the construction of gender identity and the sexual division of labor. Chadorow posits that "all societies are constituted around a structural split, growing out of women's mothering, between the private, domestic world of women and the public, social world of men."[21] This structural split is created by a sexual division of labor that is itself reproduced each generation by gender personality differences between men and women. These behavioral differences or "intrapsychic structures"

---

[15]As quoted in the opening epigraphs in Jessie Bernard's *The Female World* (New York: Free Press, 1981).

[16]Ibid., 3.

[17]Ibid., 12–15.

[18]See, for example, Jean Lipman-Blumen, "Toward a Homosocial Theory of Sex Roles: An Explanation of the Sex Segregation of Social Institutions," *Signs* (1976):15–31.

[19]Ibid., 16.

[20]Ibid., 17.

[21]Nancy Chadorow, *The Reproduction of Mothering: Psychoanalysis and the Sociology of Gender* (Berkeley: University of California Press, 1978), 173–174.

are not biological; rather, they stem from the distinct social relationships girls and boys develop with their mothers. Girls learn to be women and to mother by identifying with their mothers, whereas boys must develop a masculine gender identification in opposition to their mothers and often in the absence of affective, ongoing relationships to a father figure. This results in different "relational capacities" and "senses of self" in men and women that prepare them "to assume the adult gender roles which situate women primarily within the sphere of reproduction in a sexually unequal society."[22]

A Sociology for Women: Feminist Methodologies, Epistemologies, and Standpoint Theories. Efforts in the late 1970s and 1980s to devise a sociology for women arose from a growing conviction among more radical critical feminist theorists that to simply refocus the discipline's theoretical and methodological lenses on gender and women's domains would do little to correct the androcentric (male) biases and patterns of patriarchal thought inhering in sociological work. Because of these biases, traditional forms of explanation within sociology were increasingly seen as fundamentally incapable of representing accurately a social world in which, many feminist critics began to assert, all social relations are gendered.[23] Recognizing the link between feminist thought and politics, John Shotter and Josephine Logan argued that only by finding a "new voice" can feminist scholars and the women's movement as a whole escape the "pervasiveness of patriarchy":

> The women's movement must of necessity develop itself within a patriarchal culture of such a depth and pervasiveness that, even in reacting to or resisting its oppressive nature, the women's movement continually "reinfects" or "contaminates" itself with it. All of us, women and men alike, are "soaked" in it. . . . Patriarchy is enshrined in our social practices, in our ways of positioning and relating ourselves to one another, and in the resources we use in making sense of one another. . . . We must find a different voice, a new place currently unrecognized, from which to speak about the nature of our lives together.[24]

This kind of more radical attack on the sociology of knowledge was fueled by the growing frustration among feminist critics in general about what they saw as continued resistance within sociology—and sociological theory in particular—to studying gender and to drawing out the conceptual and theoretical implications of this research. In their analysis of articles published in ten sociology journals between 1974 and 1983, Grant and Ward found that the number of theoretical papers, reviews, and critiques focusing on gender in mainstream journals was still relatively

---

[22]Ibid., 173.

[23]Joan Acker, "Making Gender Visible," in *Feminism and Sociological Theory,* ed. R. A. Wallace (Newbury Park, CA: Sage, 1989), 73.

[24]John Shotter and Josephine Logan, "The Pervasiveness of Patriarchy: On Finding a Different Voice," in *Feminist Thought and the Structure of Knowledge,* ed. Mary Gergen (New York: New York University Press, 1988), 69–86.

small compared with those dealing with other traditional topics—an indication, they felt, that journal editors continue to view gender as a peripheral in contemporary sociology.[25]

Other feminist critics have echoed Grant and Ward's concerns. Acker's review of stratification literature asserts that, apart from Rae Lesser Blumberg's landmark book,[26] stratification texts still do not "successfully integrate women into the analysis and generally evade the problem by including brief descriptions of sex-based inequality generally ungrounded in a conceptualization of societal-wide stratification."[27] Judith Stacey and Barrie Thorne conclude that although feminist scholars have made valuable contributions to numerous traditional branches of sociological research (e.g., organizations, occupations, criminology, deviance, and stratification) and have pioneered work in many others (e.g., sexual harassment and feminization of poverty), they had yet to effect significant conceptual transformations in the field.[28] Feminist scholars in sociology—unlike their counterparts in anthropology, history, and literary criticism—have not succeeded in influencing the discipline to the point where women are being put regularly at the center of analysis. Instead, Stacey and Thorne argue, "feminist sociology seems to have been both co-opted and ghettoized, while the discipline as a whole and its dominant paradigms have proceeded relatively unchanged."[29]

Feminist scholars propose a variety of explanations to account for the "ghettoization" of gender issues within sociological research and theory. In their study of women's involvement in theory production, Ward and Grant emphasize that the relative lack of theorizing on gender might be partly due to the scarcity and low profile of women theorists. Compared with their male colleagues, Ward and Grant found, women sociologists (a) affiliate with the ASA theory section less, (b) self-identify as theorists less, (c) write fewer textbooks and journal articles, (d) receive less visibility in textbooks and popular teaching materials, and (e) serve less frequently as editors or board members of theory journals.[30] As possible explanations for the "peculiar eclipsing" of women as theorists, Ward and Grant cite (a) the comparatively high status of theory production, which, in turn, can lead to higher barriers against the entry of women, and (b) the fragmentation of contemporary sociological theory into multiple and competing paradigms that can restrict the spread of feminist thought.

---

[25]Linda Grant and Kathryn Ward, "Is There an Association Between Gender and Methods in Sociological Research?" *American Sociological Review* 52 (1987):861.

[26]Rae Lesser Blumberg, *Stratification: Social, Economic, and Sexual Inequality* (Dubuque, IA: William C. Brown, 1978).

[27]Joan Acker, "Women and Stratification: A Review of Recent Literature," *Contemporary Sociology* 9 (1980):26.

[28]Judith Stacey and Barrie Thorne, "The Missing Feminist Revolution in Sociology," *Social Problems* 32 (1985):301–316.

[29]Ibid., 302.

[30]Kathryn Ward and Linda Grant, "On a Wavelength of Their Own? Women and Sociological Theory," *Current Perspectives in Social Theory* 11 (1991):134.

Ward and Grant also speculate that differences in how women sociologists approach their research subjects might decrease the likelihood of their work on gender being accepted for publication. They have found that there are "systematic links" between gender and methods within sociology, with women scholars publishing in major sociological journals employing qualitative methods more often than their male colleagues.[31] Many feminist theorists argue that qualitative methods (e.g., intensive interviews and participant observation) are more appropriate for exploring gender and women's issues, which tend to be more private, context-bound, and hence less easily quantifiable.[32] Yet Grant and Ward have failed to find a correlation between gender and methods in published research on gender among mainstream sociological journals. In gender articles, both sexes preferred quantitative methods, leading them to speculate that "qualitative papers on gender might have presented double nonconformity, reducing the likelihood of acceptance for publication."[33] Finally, Ward and Grant also refer to Judith A. Howard's contention that the influence of feminist perspectives is limited by

> the inability of extant social theories (including Marxism) to conceptualize gender as a major organizing principle of society and culture and by the predominance of positivist epistemological traditions that encourage emphasis on gender as a variable rather than a concept.[34]

Acker takes a different tack, suggesting that sociological theory "continues in a prefeminist mode" because of both institutional resistance within the discipline and the underdevelopment of feminist alternatives to mainstream theoretical concepts and methodologies.[35] Sociology, Acker argues, shares with other academic disciplines

> a particular connection to power in society as a whole or to the relations of ruling: The almost exclusively male domain of academic thought is associated with abstract, intellectual, textually mediated processes through which organizing,

---

[31]Grant and Ward, "Is There an Association Between Gender and Methods in Sociological Research?", 856–862.

[32]See Marlene Mackie, "Female Sociologists' Productivity, Collegial Relations, and Research Style Examined through Journal Publications," *Social and Social Research* 69 (1985):189–209; Ellen Carol Dubois (ed.), *Feminist Scholarship: Kindling in the Groves of Academe* (Urbana: University of Illinois Press, 1985); and Rhoda Unger, "Through the Looking Glass: No Wonderland Yet! The Reciprocal Relationship between Methodology and Models of Reality," *Psychology of Women Quarterly* 8 (1983):9–32.

[33]Grant and Ward, "Is There an Association Between Gender and Methods in Sociological Research?", 861.

[34]See J. A. Howard, "Dilemmas in Feminist Theorizing: Politics and the Academy," *Current Perspectives in Social Theory* 8 (1987):279–312.

[35]Joan Acker, "Making Gender Visible," 65–81.

managing and governing are carried out . . . The perspectives that develop their concepts and problematics from within what is relevant to the relations of ruling are successful.[36]

Acker questions whether critical feminist theories can ever effect a paradigm shift within sociological theory as long as societal institutions remain patriarchally structured and power relations continue to be dominated by men.[37] Yet Acker also holds feminist theory accountable for its relative lack of influence within mainstream sociological theory. Feminist scholars, she argues, "have not, as yet, been able to suggest new ways of looking at things that are obviously better than the old ways for comprehending a whole range of problems."[38] Acker outlines her vision of a feminist paradigm capable of competing with or supplanting established theoretical positions. Such a paradigm would[39]

1. provide a better understanding of class structure, the state, social revolution, and militarism, as well as a better understanding of the sex segregation of labor, male dominance in the family, and sexual violence;

2. place women and their lives in a central place in understanding social relations as a whole, while creating a more accurate and comprehensive account of industrial, capitalist society; and

3. contain a methodology that produces knowledge for rather than of women in all their diverse situations.

Implicit in Acker's proposal for a feminist paradigm is a radical critique of the very concepts, methodologies, and epistemological assumptions that form the foundation of sociological understandings of the social universe. As espoused by feminist theorists such as Dorothy Smith, Sandra Harding, and Evelyn Fox Keller, feminist theorists have failed thus far to transform the prevailing mainstream theoretical paradigms because the underlying epistemologies and methodologies give privilege to the male experience.[40]

Dorothy Smith, one of the first feminist critical theorists to call for a "woman-centered" sociology, asserts that sociological thought has been "based on and built up within the male social universe,"[41] and as a consequence, sociology contains unexamined androcentric (male) modes of thought that serve the interests of men

---

[36]Ibid., 68–69. As Acker readily acknowledges, her analysis of sociology's relationship to ruling power structures owes much to Dorothy Smith. See Smith, *The Everyday World as Problematic.*

[37]Acker, "Making Gender Visible," 78.

[38]Ibid., 72.

[39]Ibid., 67.

[40]Smith, *The Everyday World as Problematic.* See also Sandra Harding, *The Science Question in Feminism* (Ithaca, NY: Cornell University Press, 1986) and Evelyn Fox Keller, "Feminism and Science," *Signs* 7 (1982):589–602.

[41]Smith, "Women's Perspective," 7.

and that are by definition gender biased and exclusionary of women's perspectives.[42] She argues that as long as feminist scholars work within forms of thought made or controlled by men, women will be constrained to view themselves not as subjects but as the "other," and their experience will be marginalized accordingly.[43] It is not enough, she claims,

> to supplement an established sociology by addressing ourselves to what has been left out, overlooked, or by making sociological issues of the relevances of the world of women. That merely extends the authority of the existing socio-logical procedures and makes of a women's sociology an addendum.[44]

This radical feminist critique has taken three main forms. First, it criticizes the standard methodological practices and proposes to replace them with feminist methodologies. Second, it questions the epistemological assumptions of "positivistic" science because science, like the broader society, is gendered, and therefore, new epis-temologies need to be developed that eliminate gender bias while recognizing the primacy of gender and its implications for knowledge production. Finally, radical feminist theorists propose the construction of an independent feminist "standpoint" that can avoid both the androcentric biases inherent in social research practices and the "positivistic" epistemological foundations of mainstream sociological theory.[45]

One of the first detailed feminist critiques of contemporary social methodology was a volume of essays edited by the sociologists Marcia Millman and Rosabeth Moss Kanter.[46] Viewing the various critiques collectively, Millman and Moss identify six standard methodological practices that can lead to gender bias in social research. During the past twenty years, these practices have remained central to the feminist critique of social methodology:

1. The use of conventional field-defining models that overlook important areas of social inquiry

2. The focus by sociologists on public, official, visible role players to the neglect of unofficial, supportive, private, and invisible spheres of social life and orga-nization that are equally important

3. The assumption in sociology of a "single society," in which generalizations can be made that will apply equally to men and women

---

[42]Stacey and Thorne, "The Missing Revolution," 309.

[43]Smith, *The Everyday World as Problematic*, 52.

[44]Smith, "Women's Perspective." 7. A similar criticism is made by Liz Stanley and Sue Wise in their book *Breaking Out: Feminist Consciousness and Feminist Research* (London: Routledge, 1983), 28.

[45]Shotter and Logan, "The Pervasiveness of Patriarchy." See also Dorothy Smith, "A Sociology for Women" in *The Prism of Sex*, ed. Julia Ann Sherman and Evelyn Torton Beck (Madison: University of Wisconsin Press, 1979), 135–188.

[46]Marcia Millman and Rosabeth Moss Kanter (eds.), *Another Voice: Feminist Perspectives on Social Life and Social Science* (New York: Octagon, 1976).

4. The neglect in numerous fields of study of sex as an important explanatory variable

5. The focus in sociology on explaining the status quo, which tends to provide rationalizations for existing power relations

6. The use of certain methodological techniques, often quantitative, and research situations that might systematically prevent the collection of certain kinds of data[47]

First, Millman and Kanter argue that sociologists' reliance on models of social structure and action has led to a "systematic blindness to crucial elements of social reality."[48] For example, they assert that the sociological focus on Weberian rationality as an explanation for human action and social organization effectively removes the equally important element of emotion from consideration. They also question the veracity of sociological models that do not focus on the individual and his or her subjective experience as the center of analysis and instead emphasize issues of agency.[49] Bernard had earlier made a distinction between "agency," which emphasizes variables, and "communion," which focuses on individuals:

> Agency operates by way of mastery and control; communion with naturalistic observation, sensitivity to qualitative patterning, and greater personal participation by the investigator.... The specific processes involved in agentic (sic) research are typically male preoccupations.... The scientist using this approach creates his own controlled reality. He can manipulate it. He is master. He has power. The communal approach is much humbler. It disavows control, for control spoils the results. Its value rests precisely on the absence of controls.[50]

Millman and Kanter make the point that research based exclusively on "agentic" quantitative methods fails to represent accurately crucial segments of the social world.[51]

Second, sociology overlooks important arenas of social life by focusing only on "official actors and actions" and ignoring private, unofficial, and local social structures, where women often predominate.[52] Millman, for example, posits that research on deviance and social control often emphasizes locations such as courtrooms and mental hospitals but fails to recognize "the importance of studying

---

[47]Ibid., ix–xvii.

[48]Ibid., ix.

[49]See Hochschild's essay "The Sociology of Feeling and Emotion: Selected Possibilities."

[50]Bernard, "My Four Revolutions," 785. For more discussion of agency and communion approaches to research, see David Bakan, "Psychology Can Now Kick the Science Habit," *Psychology Today* 5 (1972): 26, 28, 86–88 and Rae Carlson, "Sex Differences in Ego Functioning: Exploratory Studies of Agency and Communion," *Journal of Consulting and Clinical Psychology* 37 (1971):267–277.

[51]Millman and Kanter (eds.), *Another Voice*, x.

[52]Ibid., xi.

everyday, interpersonal social control and the subtle, continuous series of maneuvers that individuals use to keep each other in line during ordinary mundane activities."[53]

Third, the assumption by sociologists that all humans inhabit a "single society" runs counter to evidence collected by feminist sociologists such as Bernard and Oakley that men and women often inhabit their own social worlds.[54] Focusing on a more narrow issue, Thelma McCormack posits that voting studies have erroneously assumed that men and women inhabit a single political culture, with the result that women tend to appear more conservative or apathetic.[55]

Fourth, Millman and Kanter cite several studies that demonstrate the failure of social researchers to consider sex as an explanatory variable. They include Sarah Lightfoot's analysis of the sociology of education, in which she asserts that researchers do not consider issues raised by the fact that most teachers are women.[56]

Fifth, Millman and Kanter argue that by seeking to explain the status quo, sociologists need to be more sensitive to the ways in which their research might also legitimate existing social relations and institutions. They argue that researchers should focus more attention on social transformation.[57] Arlene Daniels goes further to assert that research on women should not only concern itself with revealing the sources of women's oppression but also engage in exploring the concrete ways in which their status and lives can be improved.[58]

Finally, Millman and Kanter point out that unquestioned methodological assumptions and techniques can adversely affect findings and conclusions. They cite David Tresemer's analysis of statistical studies on sex differences. Tresemer asserts that most of these studies are misleading because they improperly use bipolar, unidimensional continuous, normal distributions that have the effect of exaggerating differences.[59] Although this particular problem might best be corrected by adopting another, less biased quantitative method, Millman and Kanter claim that in many cases qualitative techniques might be more suitable and yield more balanced results than the standard quantitative approaches.[60]

Critical feminist theorists have developed several methodological approaches designed to address the topic of gender asymmetry and to avoid possible gender biases in standard sociological practices. Judith Cook and Mary Fonow assert that

---

[53]Ibid.

[54]Ibid. See also Bernard, *The Female World* and Oakley, *The Sociology of Housework*.

[55]Millman and Kanter (eds.), *Another Voice*, xiii. Also Thelma McCormack, "Toward a Nonsexist Perspective on Social and Political Change," in *Another Voice*, 1–33.

[56]Millman and Kanter (eds.), *Another Voice*, xiv.

[57]Ibid., xv.

[58]Ibid. See also, Arlene Daniels, "Feminist Perspectives in Sociological Research," in *Another Voice*, 340–380.

[59]Millman and Kanter (eds.), *Another Voice*, xv. See also David Tresemer, "Assumptions Made About Gender Roles," *Another Voice*, 308–339.

[60]Millman and Kanter (eds.), *Another Voice*, xvi.

feminist methodologies frequently employ the following seven research strategies and techniques:[61]

1. Visual techniques, such as photography and videotaping to collect or elicit data

2. Triangulation, or the use of more than one research technique simultaneously

3. The use of linguistic techniques in conversational analysis

4. Textual analysis as a means to identify gender bias

5. Refined quantitative approaches to measure phenomena related to sexual asymmetry and women's worlds

6. Collaborative strategies or collective research models to enhance feedback and promote cooperative, egalitarian relations among researchers

7. Situation-at-hand research practices that use an already existing situation as a focus for sociological inquiry or as a means of collecting data

Cook and Fonow stress that none of these techniques is explicitly or exclusively feminist; however, their innovative character is revealed in their application and in the degree to which they incorporate and are informed by five basic principles that govern the production of feminist knowledge.[62] Cook and Fonow identify these principles as follows:[63]

1. The necessity of continuously and reflexively attending to the significance of gender relations as a basic feature of social life, including the conduct of research

2. The centrality of consciousness-raising as a specific methodological tool and as a "way of seeing"

3. The need to challenge the norm of "objectivity" that assumes a dichotomy between the subject and the object of research

4. Concern for the ethical implications of research

5. An emphasis on the transformation of patriarchy and the empowerment of women

Feminist standpoint theories, as espoused by Dorothy Smith, Hilary Rose, Nancy Hartsock, and others, build on these epistemological and methodological principles by explicitly focusing on women and their direct experience as the center of analysis. Standpoint theorists argue that they can use women's experience to analyze social relations in ways that overcome the androcentric dichotomies of Enlightenment "positivism"—such as culture versus nature, rational mind versus irrational emotions,

---

[61]Judith Cook and Mary Fonow, "Knowledge and Women's Interests: Issues of Epistemology and Methodology in Feminist Sociological Research," *Sociological Inquiry* 56 (1986):2–29.

[62]Ibid., 14.

[63]Ibid., 2.

objectivity versus subjectivity, and public versus private—that have structured knowledge production in the social and natural sciences.[64] Smith asserts that "women's perspective discredits sociology's claim to constitute an objective knowledge independent of the sociologist's situation."[65]

Feminist standpoint theorists articulate a feminist methodology that at once privileges the feminist standpoint as more inherently objective, challenges "mainstream" sociological inquiry, and provides a paradigmatic alternative. Smith disputes that such a paradigm shift would entail a "radical transformation of the subject matter";[66] rather, she argues that what is involved is the restructuring of the relationship between the sociologist and the object of her research:

> What I am suggesting is more in the nature of a re-organization which changes the relation of the sociologist to the object of her knowledge and changes also her problematic. This re-organization involves first placing the sociologist where she is actually situated, namely at the beginning of those acts by which she knows or will come to know; and second, making her direct experience of the everyday world the primary ground of her knowledge.[67]

Critical theorists also suggest that a feminist standpoint methodology rooted in women's experience would elucidate the epistemological connections among the production of knowledge, everyday experiences, and political praxis that "positivistic" epistemologies often deny. Rose asserts in "Women's Work: Women's Knowledge" that human knowledge and consciousness "are not abstract or divorced from experience or 'given' by some process separate from the unitary material reality of the world. Human knowledge . . . comes from practice, from working on and changing the world."[68]

Viewed collectively, feminist empiricism—in the form of feminist methodologies, epistemologies, and standpoints—challenges key tenets of traditional empiricism embodied in "positivistic" science. Sandra Harding argues that feminist empiricism specifically questions three central assumptions:[69]

1. The assumption that the social identity of the observer is irrelevant to the "goodness" of the results of research, asserting that the androcentrism of science is both highly visible and damaging. It argues that women as a social group are more likely than men as a social group to select problems for inquiry that do not distort human social experience.

---

[64]Harding, *The Science Question in Feminism,* 136–162.

[65]Smith, "Women's Perspective," 11.

[66]Ibid.

[67]Ibid.

[68]Hilary Rose, "Women's Work: Women's Knowledge," in *What Is Feminism,* ed. Juliet Mitchell and Ann Oakley (New York: Pantheon, 1986), 161.

[69]Harding, 162.

2. The assumption that science's methodological and sociological norms are suf-ficient to eliminate androcentric biases by suggesting that the norms them-selves appear to be biased insofar as they have been incapable of detecting androcentrism.

3. The assumption that science must be protected from politics. Feminist empir-icism argues that some politics—the politics of movement for emancipatory social change—can increase the objectivity of science.

Critiquing the Critique: Challenges to Critical Feminist Theory. Feminist meth-odologies, epistemologies, and standpoint theories have received their own share of criticism. The most formidable of these have come from feminist critics themselves, who use feminist concepts and positions to, in effect, critique the "critique." What links many of these counter-critiques is an emphasis on the role of ideology in the structuring of feminist theory, epistemology, and practice.

The foundation for all critical feminist theory is the belief in the primacy of gen-der as a fundamental division that structures social relations. Sarah Matthews ques-tions the importance of gender dichotomy, arguing that "this dichotomy does not match social reality as closely as assumed."[70] The existence of gender identities coded masculine and feminine does not, she asserts, necessarily mean that gender is the critical variable determining social behavior:[71]

> All of these [feminist] critiques have in common as their beginning point the assumption that distinguishing between two genders is the appropriate founda-tion from which to build research questions and theory. To say that women have been excluded from sociological research; that research on women must be done to parallel research on men; that different methodologies must be uti-lized to understand women in society; that boys and girls are socialized differ-ently; and that women as a group are oppressed, is to accept and to re-enforce the taken-for-granted assumption that there are in fact two gender categories into which it is important to sort all human beings.[72]

Matthews goes on to argue that gender or sex is not "an immutable fact" and that feminist research and theory can be interpreted as supportive of this position. That this support has not been acknowledged, she asserts, is due to the ideological basis of feminism that is committed to seeing two genders.[73] She concludes by positing that sociologists can overcome sexual bias in research by developing paradigms "that do not include gender as having a priori significance."[74]

---

[70]Sarah Matthews, "Rethinking Sociology through a Feminist Perspective," *The American Sociologist* 17 (1982):29.

[71]Ibid.

[72]Ibid., 30.

[73]Ibid., 29.

[74]Ibid.

Attempts to construct feminist methods that espouse a privileged position for an independent "women's standpoint" have also been criticized by feminist critics such as Elizabeth Spelman. Spelman sees the phrase "as a woman" as "the Trojan horse of feminist ethnocentrism" because it embodies the assumption that "gender identity exists in isolation from race and class identity."[75] She argues that the feminist perspective or standpoint "obscures the heterogeneity of women"[76] and hence serves as little more than a methodological means of privileging white, middle-class women's experience. Spelman, in particular, challenges the following five assumptions inherent in feminist discussions of gender:[77]

1. Women can be talked about "as women."

2. Women are oppressed "as women."

3. Gender can be isolated from other elements of identity that affect one's social, economic, and political position, such as race, class, and ethnicity; hence, sexism can be isolated from racism and classism.

4. Women's situation can be contrasted with men's.

5. Relations between men and women can be compared with relations between other oppressor/oppressed groups, and hence, it is possible to compare the situation of women with the situation of blacks, Jews, the poor, and others.

Conclusion: Two or More Sociologies of Gender?

Critical feminism has been highly critical of specific forms of scientific theorizing[78] in sociology and, perhaps surprisingly, other forms of critical theorizing as

---

[75]Elizabeth Spelman, *Inessential Woman: Problems of Exclusion in Feminist Thought* (Boston, MA: Beacon, 1988), x.

[76]Ibid., ix.

[77]Ibid., 165.

[78]See, for example, the following essays in Paula England (ed.), *Theory on Gender/Feminism on Theory* (New York: Aldine de Gruyter, 1993): Lynn Smith-Lovin and J. Miller McPherson, "You Are Who You Know: A Network Approach to Gender," 223–251; Dana Dunn, Elizabeth M. Almquist, and Janet Saltzman Chafetz, "Macrostructural Perspectives on Gender Inequality," 69–90; Miriam Johnson, "Functionalism and Feminism: Is Estrangement Necessary?", 115–130; and Debra Friedman and Carol Diem, "Feminism and the Pro-(Rational-)Choice Movement: Rational-Choice Theory, Feminist Critiques and Gender Inequality," 91–114. Other works include Miriam Johnson, "Feminism and the Theories of Talcott Parsons," in *Feminism and Sociological Theory*, ed. R. C. Wallace (Newbury Park, CA: Sage, 1989), 101–118; Hochschild, "The Sociology of Feeling and Emotion: Selected Possibilities"; Paula England, "A Feminist Critique of Rational-Choice Theories: Implications for Sociology," *The American Sociologist* 20 (1989):14–28; and Paula England and Barbara Kilbourne, "Feminist Critique of the Separative Model of the Self: Implications for Rational Choice Theory," *Rationality and Society* 2 (1990):156–171.

well.[79] There are, of course, powerful scientific theories of gender dynamics[80] that explicitly seek to develop propositions that can explain gender discrimination and stratification. The development of these theories is driven by much the same motivation as critical theorizing: to understand the dynamics of gender stratification so that this understanding can be used to reduce, if not eliminate, gender inequalities. Yet these theories are not drawn from ideologies but from an assessment of the generic social processes that historically and today systematically generate gender inequalities.

For critical feminist theorizing, such scientific theories do not go far enough. They do not advocate change; and they assume that gender differences can be understood with the same tools as all other phenomena are to be understood, ignoring the differences in the social universes of men and women. Thus, in the end, critical and scientific theories of gender will remain at odds.

Critical Theories on Race and Ethnicity

From its very beginnings in the United States, sociology has been concerned with the pervasiveness of racial and ethnic discrimination; and indeed, the ameliorative thrust of much of early American sociology was devoted to documenting and then explaining racial and ethnic discrimination. Some of these explanations were

---

[79]In addition to the work cited at the beginning of this chapter, for Foucault and post-structuralism, see Caroline Ramazanoglu (ed.), *Up Against Foucault: Explorations of Some Tensions between Foucault and Feminism* (New York: Routledge, 1993) and Linda Alcoff, "Cultural Feminism versus Post-Structuralism: The Identity Crisis in Feminist Theory," in *Feminist Theory in Practice and Process,* ed. Micheline Malson, Jean O'Barr, Sarah Westphal-Wihl, Mary Wyer (Chicago, IL: University of Chicago Press, 1986), 295–326. For critical feminist analyses of Marxist theory and the connections between it and feminist theory, see Catherine MacKinnon, "Feminism, Marxism, Method, and the State: An Agenda for Theory," *Signs* 7 (1982):515–544; Mia Campioni and Elizabeth Grosz, "Love's Labours Lost: Marxism and Feminism," in *A Reader in Feminist Knowledge,* ed. Sneja Gunew (New York: Routledge, 1991), 366–397; Beth Anne Shelton and Ben Agger, "Shotgun Wedding, Unhappy Marriage, No-Fault Divorce? Rethinking Feminism-Marxism Relationship," in *Theory on Gender/Feminism on Theory,* 25–42; Zillah Eisenstein (ed.), *Capitalist Patriarchy and the Case for Socialist Feminism* (New York: Monthly Review Press, 1979); Heidi I. Hartmann, "The Unhappy Marriage and Marxism and Feminism: Towards a More Progressive Union," *Capital and Class* 3, (1979):1–33; Annette Kuhn and Ann Marie Wolpe (eds.), *Feminism and Materialism: Women and Modes of Production* (London: Routledge, 1978); Ben Agger, *Fast Capitalism: A Critical Theory of Significance* (Urbana: University of Illinois Press, 1989); and Alison Jagger, *Feminist Politics and Human Nature* (Sussex, UK: Harvester, 1983). Nancy Fraser and Linda Nicholson, "Social Criticism without Philosophy: An Encounter between Feminism and Postmodernism," in *The Postmodern Turn,* 242–264. Finally, additional works on feminist and postmodernism include Jane Flax, "Postmodernism and Gender Relations in Feminist Theory," in *Feminist Theory in Practice and Process,* 51–74 and Imelda Whelehan, *Modern Feminist Thought* (New York: New York University Press, 1995), 194–215.

[80]For examples, see Janel Saltzman Chafetz, *Gender Equity: An Integrated Theory of Stability and Change* (Newbury Park, CA: Sage, 1990). See also her *Feminist Sociology: An Overview of Contemporary Theories* (Itasca, IL: Peacock, 1988) and Rae Lesser Blumberg, *Stratification: Socio-Economic and Sexual Inequality* (Dubuque, IA: William C. Brown, 1978).

couched in more theoretical terms, others in explicitly ideological terms, but they were all "critical" in at least this sense: discrimination and inequality emerging from such discrimination are seen to be morally wrong and, moreover, dysfunctional for a society. Sociological knowledge should, therefore, be employed to expose racial oppression and to mount attacks on the institutional systems by which such oppression is carried out. In the modern era of sociology, this goal revolved around supporting the legal attack on ethnic discrimination, particularly discrimination against African Americans during the 1950s and later in the 1960s as the civil rights movement achieved at least one of its key goals: a series of civil rights acts in the federal codes that made discrimination on the basis of race and other categoric distinctions (e.g., gender and religious affiliation) illegal.

Critical Race Theory

Critical race theory emerged out of the critical approaches that developed in legal scholarship.[81] The basic conclusion was that the civil rights movement and the laws that it inspired were no longer effective in addressing long-term discrimination against "peoples of color" in the United States. The civil rights movement had lost its momentum, and compared with the feminist movement that was just gearing up in the 1970s, the civil rights movement seemed rather tame and uncritical of persisting ethnic/racial discrimination and stratification in America.

Some of the themes in critical race theory were similar to those emerging in the feminist movement. There was a parallel to feminist standpoint theorizing in the emphasis on the need to understand "the lived experiences" of people of color in their local circumstances as these were imposed upon them by patterns of institutionalized racism. The story of what people had to endure became a major preoccupation as ethnographic data, accounts, parables, and histories of people actually experiencing discrimination were assembled. It was implicit in this emphasis that whites and the more affluent sectors of America are in a very poor position to understand the plight of people of color. They should not, therefore, be at the vanguard of enacting and enforcing laws and establishing programs of amelioration because they could not understand what it was like to be living in circumstances created and sustained by prejudicial beliefs and overt as well as subtle patterns of

---

[81]Adalberto Aguirre, "Academic Storytelling: A Critical Race Theory Story of Affirmative Action," *Sociological Perspectives* 43 (2000):319–326; Kimberle Crenshaw, Neil Gotanda, Gary Peller, and Kendall Thomas (eds.), *Critical Race Theory: The Key Writings That Formed the Movement* (New York: New Press, 1995); Richard Delgado, "The Ethereal Scholar: Does Critical Legal Studies Have What Minorities Want?," *Harvard Critical Legal Studies Law Review* 22 (1987):301–322; Richard Delgado (ed.), *Critical Race Theory: The Cutting Edge* (Philadelphia, PA: Temple University Press, 1995); Mari J. Matsuda, Charles R. Lawrence, Richard Delgado, and Kimberle Crenshaw, *Words That Wound: Critical Race Theory, Assaultive Speech, and the First Amendment* (Boulder, CO: Westview Press, 1993); Carlos J. Nan, "Adding Salt to the Wound: Affirmative Action and Critical Race Theory," *Law and Inequality: A Journal of Theory and Practice* 12 (1994):553–572; and Enid Trucios-Haynes, "Why Race Matters: LatCrit Theory and Lantina/o Racial Identity," *La Raza Law Journal* 12 (2001):1–42.

discrimination. A number of important themes follows from this basic theme in much of critical race theory, including:[82]

1. Racism is normal, not an aberration. As a result, it is not so easy to eliminate racism because it not only is built into the way individuals categorize and respond to each other but is also part of a process by which prejudice and discrimination are built up in the culture and social structure of society.

2. Racism and the inequalities that it systematically generates persists because they promote the interests of whites, and whites only support "reform" when it is in their interests.

3. There is little incentive by whites in all classes to get rid of racism because it provides benefits, such as the following:
    A. Employers have a low-wage pool of desperate workers to exploit and to threaten working-class whites if their wage demands are too high
    B. Working-class whites, if they can split the labor market and confine people of color to a limited range of low-wage, low-benefit jobs, can protect their better-wage, better-benefit jobs.

4. Laws cannot be neutral when their enactment is constrained by 1, 2, and 3 above. Law is, therefore, inherently political and supportive of the interests of those with power and money.

5. Race is a "social construction" in this sense: it can be changed and adapted to new circumstances; and "racialization" of targeted subpopulations can be adjusted to sustain oppression.

6. Racialization is inherently "intersectional," which, in turn, fractures racial identities (and the potential for unified worldviews) because social categories, such as class, gender, sexual orientation, and politics, that partition a population all intersect with social constructions of race, making it less likely that all people of color will perceive that they have common interests in eliminating racism.

7. The seeming "fairness" of using "merit" and "credentials" as a means for sorting persons into various slots in society (carrying varying levels of resources) is a smokescreen for giving the middle classes a leg up in competition for jobs and other resources. Merit is defined by white culture and is supportive of their interests against the interests of people of color. For instance, standardized aptitude and achievement tests portray a white cultural world, making it difficult for those not exposed to this world to compete, thereby giving whites the false perception that the "playing field" of competition for life chances is level and that those who cannot meet these standards are less worthy. Continued racial oppression can occur because all peoples have had an "equal opportunity," again disadvantaging and stigmatizing those who have not grown up within white culture.

---

[82]Matsuda, Lawrence, Delgado, and Crenshaw, *Words That Wound.*

8. The call for "diversity" and the constant commentary of its benefits serve the interests of the whites (e.g., they qualify for research grants from the federal government) more than the interests of people of color, who are stigmatized by affirmative action programs as being less able to meet standards through normal recruitment routes. Moreover, this call for diversity does not generally meet the needs of people, while masking the fact that many people of color cannot qualify for many programs because of the barriers imposed by having to live under the conditions generated systematically by racism and patterns of discrimination. To have, for example, a diversity program for college students does little for those who have dropped out of high school and their parents, both of whom have different needs and interests from college students who qualify for diversity programs. Yet diversity programs offer the illusion that the effects of discrimination have been addressed, while stigmatizing those who have not qualified for such programs.

For at least these reasons, then, legal theory and social science theorizing, particularly that in sociology, have not adequately conceptualized the dynamics of racism. Of course, the points above represent assertions and, in many ways, fail to appreciate the explanatory power of many existing theories of ethnic and racial discrimination. Yet because these points are fueled by ideologies and are designed to criticize, if not inflame, they implicitly portray the existing state of theories of discrimination as never having considered the forces listed above. In actual fact, this assertion is not true,[83] but these lists mostly target law as an effective tool in eliminating racism.

Critical Theories of Race and Racism

Some scholars identified with critical race theory also seem to imply a variant and perhaps a somewhat less inflammatory alternative to critical race theory. As Bonilla-Silva emphasizes,[84] the notion of society becoming "color-blind" and only concerned with merit and accomplishment is a "smokescreen" to perpetuate subtle and invidious forms of discrimination. He proposes instead an assault on this kind of "new racism." There is a more academic flavor to these approaches. For example, Patricia Hill Collins,[85] who shares many of the precepts of critical race theory, offers a list of guidelines that critical theories of race and racism should follow. They are the following:

1. The focus theory should be on social inequalities rather than race, per se; emphasis should be on the processes by which social justice can be achieved by all those subject to discriminatory practices.

---

[83]See Adalberto Aguirre and Jonathan H. Turner, *American Ethnicity: The Dynamics and Consequences of Ethnic Discrimination,* 7th ed. (New York: McGraw-Hill, 2010), for a review of theories and for a more synthetic scientific theory that does take into account many of the points made by critical race theorists.

[84]Eduardo Bonilla-Silva, *Racism Without Racists: Color-Blind Racism and the Persistence of Racial Inequality in the United States* (Lanham, MD: Rowman and Littlefield, 2003).

[85]This list is taken from Collins's website and class syllabi.

2. Research and theorizing should be interdisciplinary.

3. The dynamics of intersectionality should be emphasized so that the relations among race, class, ethnicity, nation, and communities are examined.

4. The material basis of inequality as much as cultural processes, especially political and economic dynamics, should be central to the analysis of race and racism.

5. Race and racism in the global context should also be central to analysis.

6. The many manifestations of power and its dynamics in diverse settings should be emphasized in the analysis of race and racism.

Some of these points overlap with those listed under critical race theory, but there is an obvious difference in tone. Moreover, these points emphasize how the analysis of race and racism should proceed, rather than making a blanket critique of existing programs administered by law and social welfare programs.

Conclusion

Theorizing on the dynamics of discrimination has always been split between those theories that are more value-neutral and those that are explicitly ideological. At times, the same theorists have produced both kinds of theories, but there is— much like feminist theories—a significant difference between critical and scientific theories. In critical theories, there is often an indictment of scientific theories as "part of the problem," whereas in scientific theories the goal is to avoid the emotion-arousing effects of ideologies and, instead, to provide a more dispassionate analysis of the conditions under which prejudicial beliefs and institutionalized patterns of discrimination increase or decrease. Like all critical theories, one goal of critical race theories is to expose persistent and often invidious patterns of racism and discrimination; in so doing, plans of action (as opposed to explanation) to change social systems can be formulated. Scientific theorists often have the same goal, but critical theorists will generally see them as too sedate and as supporting the status quo. As in feminism, then, there will be at least "two sociologies" of race and ethnicity—a situation that has been part of American sociology since its beginnings and that clearly is not about to go away in the second decade of the twenty-first century.

Conclusions

There is an obvious difference in the emotional tone and subject matter of European and American critical theories. They often overlap, and Americans have contributed to the European canon probably more than the reverse because American critical theory tends to be somewhat nation-centric, especially critical race theory compared with critical feminist theory. European theory still focuses on the conditions and problems of modernity in all its manifestations, whereas feminism and race theories are about the dynamics revolving around unfairly devalued social categories of persons who have been the victims of discrimination, prejudices, and unjust treatment. European theories are clearly more academic and flow from academia to the lay intellectual world, whereas American critical theories are the result of social movements in the broader society that have been brought into academia and, in many respects, stay in academia.

It is clear that my biases—despite a substantial amount of activist work on my part, especially in my younger years—lie with science. I am much like Auguste Comte—only saner, I should hope—in my view that by discovering the laws of social dynamics, we can use these laws to make a better world. As I discovered in my own early work, when sociological analysis was driven by ideology, it became highly distorted by the emotion and passion about what I thought should and ought to be. Now, I am more circumspect; I try to figure out why certain social arrangements exist, not by positing evil but by trying to figure out, dispassionately, what forces are driving the formation and operation of these dynamics. The models and laws that emerge from such analysis will, I believe, provide better guidance to social amelioration than my earlier works that were driven by ideological fervor.

Critical theorists would disagree with my statements above, and often passionately so, as I have learned. And so the divide that has been woven through American sociology from its inception and, to a lesser extent, European sociology as well is still with us, with little chance of abating. In the end, each sociologist must discover which is the better path to take. I have taken both in my career, but even in the early, more activist period, I was disquieted by the fact that when doing science, I found that my conclusions came into conflict with my ideology. I wanted social arrangements that were often not attainable given the forces in play. To some, this is "to sell out" to the evil powers that be; and it is a justification of the status quo. To me, however, it is a better way to try to develop policies for change that actually have a chance of working rather than hurting people. Again, many would disagree. A book on contemporary sociological theory must accept the divide, unless we wish to have two types of contemporary theory books: those espousing the primacy of science and those espousing the primacy of doing something about the problems of the social world. And maybe there are two sociologies: scientific sociology and humanistic sociology. I do not think that these are a contradiction. But alas, some would disagree.

PART III

The State of Sociological Theory

CHAPTER 25

Elements of Scientific Theorizing in Sociology

Auguste Comte's original vision for sociology was that it could be both a science and useful in reconstructing societies.[1] Yet, since Comte's early advocacy, it has not been easy to reconcile the desire to make society better with the desire to study the social universe objectively. As illustrated in Figure 1.1 (p. 7), on various types of belief systems,[2] ideology and science are very different. One seeks to change the world through action driven by a moral view of what is good, while the other attempts to understand how the universe operates without making value judgments. As I will try to outline, this persistent split in sociology represents the biggest obstacle to developing coherent and cumulative theory in sociology. In many ways, matters are even worse because many simply do not believe that science is capable of capturing the nature of social reality,[3] for a wide variety of reasons, not all of them ideological. We have seen in earlier chapters that critical theorists generally see science as enhancing the interests of the powerful; Marxists conflict theorists

---

[1]Auguste Comte, *System of Positive Philosophy*, vol. 1 (Paris, France: Bachelier, 1830). Subsequent portions were published between 1831 and 1842.

[2]Talcott Parsons, *The Social System* (New York: The Free Press, 1951).

[3]For example, there is a growing conviction among some sociologists that science is much like any other thought system in that it is devoted to sustaining a particular vision, among a community of individuals called scientists, of what is "really real." Science simply provides one interesting way of constructing and maintaining a vision of reality, but there are other, equally valid views among different communities of individuals. Obviously, I do not accept this argument, but I will explore it in more detail in various chapters. For some interesting explorations of the issues, see Edward A. Tiryakian, "Existential Phenomenology and the Sociological Tradition," *American Sociological Review* 30 (October 1965):674–688; J. C. McKinney, "Typification, Typologies, and Sociological Theory," *Social Forces* 48 (September 1969):1–11; Alfred Schutz, "Concept and Theory Formation in the Social Sciences," *Journal of Philosophy* 51 (April 1954):257–273; Harold Garfinkel, *Studies in Ethnomethodology* (Englewood Cliffs, NJ: Prentice-Hall, 1967); and George Psathas, "Ethnomethods and Phenomenology," *Social Research* 35 (September 1968):500–520.

often view science as an implicit ideology legitimating the status quo;[4] many symbolic interactionists and others in diverse theoretical perspectives argue that humans have capacities for agency and, hence, can change the fundamental nature of the world;[5] and so the argument goes, as I will outline in Chapter 26.

This skepticism has intensified over the last thirty years. In fact, at one time, there was a plethora of books on science and theory construction in philosophy and sociology. Most of these books were highly flawed by a rather idealized view of how science operates and, more specifically, how scientists develop and test theories. As a result, they were easy targets for criticism. Now, there is the opposite problem; there are virtually no books on how to build theories, and thus, students today must find their own way.[6] In this chapter, I will finish what I started in Chapter 1 and provide a more detailed review on the nature of sociological theory and the various formats in which theorizing is expressed. As is evident, I have highlighted two approaches in the chapters of this book: (1) propositional schemes and (2) analytical models. But these are only two of a larger number of formats in which theory can be developed. Moreover, I have not indicated just what the elements of theory must be, and so, in this chapter, I will fill out the picture that I began to draw in Chapter 1.

Theory is a mental activity revolving around the process of developing ideas that explain how and why events occur. Theory is constructed with several basic elements or building blocks: concepts, variables, statements, and formats. Although there are many divergent claims about what theory is or should be, these four elements are common to all of them. In this chapter, I will examine each of these elements in

---

[4]Almost all Marxist-inspired critical theory holds this view. See Chapters 22, 23, and 24.

[5]Herbert Blumer, *Symbolic Interactionism: Perspective and Method* (Englewood Cliffs, NJ: Prentice-Hall, 1969). See also Anthony Giddens, *New Rules for the Sociological Method: A Positive Critique of Interpretative Sociology* (London: Hutchinson Ross, 1976).

[6]It is very difficult to find recent works in sociology on formal theory building because these kinds of works have fallen out of favor. There is some justification for this because these works tended to have an overly idealized view of how theories are built. Still, it is useful to read one or two such works, just to get an idea of the issues involved in developing formal theory. Though necessarily old, because no new works have been written, I have found the following useful references over the years: Paul Davidson Reynolds, *A Primer in Theory Construction* (Indianapolis, IN: Bobbs-Merrill, 1971; repr., New York: Macmillan); Arthur L. Stinchcombe, *Constructing Social Theories* (New York: Harcourt, Brace and World, 1968), 3–56; Karl R. Popper, *The Logic of Scientific Discovery* (New York: Harper and Row, 1959); David Willer and Murray Webster Jr., "Theoretical Concepts and Observables," *American Sociological Review* 35 (August 1970):748–757; Hans Zetterberg, *On Theory and Verification in Sociology*, 3rd ed. (Totowa, NJ: Bedminster Press, 1965); Jerald Hage, *Techniques and Problems of Theory Construction in Sociology* (New York: Wiley, 1972); Walter L. Wallace, *The Logic of Science in Sociology* (Chicago, IL: Aldine Publishing, 1971); Robert Dubin, *Theory Building* (New York: Free Press, 1969); Jack Gibbs, *Sociological Theory Construction* (Hinsdale, IL.: Dryden Press, 1972); Herbert M. Blalock Jr., *Theory Construction: From Verbal to Mathematical Formulations* (Englewood Cliffs, NJ: Prentice-Hall, 1969); Nicholas C. Mullins, *The Art of Theory: Construction and Use* (New York: Harper and Row, 1971); and Bernard P. Cohen, *Developing Sociological Knowledge: Theory and Method* (Chicago, IL: Nelson-Hall, 1989).

For my views on these controversial issues, see Jonathan H. Turner, "In Defense of Positivism," *Sociological Theory* 3 (Fall 1985):24–30 and Stephan Fuchs and Jonathan H. Turner, "What Makes a Science Mature?" *Sociological Theory* 4 (Fall 1986):143–150.

more detail and then, at the end, indicate which of the various formats in socio-logical theorizing is the most likely to built cumulative knowledge about the opera-tive dynamics of the social universe.

Concepts: The Basic Building Blocks of Theory

Theories are built from concepts. Concepts denote phenomena; in so doing, they isolate features of the world that are considered, for the moment at hand, important. For example, notions of atoms, protons, neutrons, and the like are concepts pointing to and isolating phenomena for certain analytical purposes. Familiar sociological concepts would include production, power, interaction, norm, role, status, and socialization. Each term is a concept that embraces aspects of the social world that are considered essential for a particular purpose.

Concepts are constructed from definitions.[7] A *definition* is a system of terms, such as the sentences of a language, the symbols of logic, or the notation of mathematics, that inform investigators as to the phenomenon denoted by a concept. For example, the concept *conflict* has meaning only when it is defined. One possible definition might be the following: *Conflict is interaction among social units in which one unit seeks to prevent another from realizing its goals.* Such a definition allows us to visual-ize the phenomenon that is denoted by the concept. It enables all investigators to "see the same thing" and to understand what it is that is being studied.

Thus, concepts that are useful in building theory have a special characteristic: they strive to communicate a uniform meaning to all those who use them. However, since concepts are frequently expressed with the words of everyday lan-guage, it is difficult to avoid words that connote varied meanings—and hence point to different phenomena—for varying groups of scientists. It is for this rea-son that many concepts in science are expressed in technical or more "neutral" languages, such as the symbols of mathematics. In sociology, expression of concepts in such special languages is sometimes not only impossible but also undesirable. Hence, the verbal symbols used to develop a concept must be defined as precisely as possible so that they point to the same phenomenon for all investigators. Although perfect consensus may never be attained with conventional language, a body of theory rests on the premise that scholars will do their best to define concepts unambiguously.

The concepts of theory reveal a special characteristic: *abstractness.*[8] Some con-cepts pertain to concrete phenomena at specific times and locations. Other, more abstract, concepts point to phenomena that are not related to concrete times or locations. For example, in the context of small-group research, *concrete concepts*

---

[7]For more detailed work on concept formation, see Carl G. Hempel, *Fundamentals of Concept Forma-tion in Empirical Science* (Chicago, IL: University of Chicago Press, 1952).

[8]For a useful and insightful critique of sociology's ability to generate abstract concepts and theory, see David and Judith Willer, *Systematic Empiricism: Critique of Pseudoscience* (Englewood Cliffs, NJ: Prentice-Hall, 1973).

would refer to the persistent interactions of particular individuals, whereas an *abstract* conceptualization of such phenomena would refer to those general properties of face-to-face groups that are not tied to particular individuals interacting at a specified time and location. Whereas abstract concepts are not tied to a specific context, concrete concepts are. In building theory, abstract concepts are crucial, although we will see shortly that theorists disagree considerably on this issue.

Abstractness, then, poses a problem: How do we attach abstract concepts to the ongoing, everyday world of events that we want to understand and explain? Although it is essential that some of the concepts of theory transcend specific times and places, it is equally critical that there be procedures for making these abstract concepts relevant to observable situations and occurrences. After all, the utility of an abstract concept can be demonstrated only when the concept is brought to bear on some specific empirical problem encountered by investigators; otherwise, concepts remain detached from the very processes they are supposed to help investigators understand. Thus, just how to attach concepts to empirical processes, or the workings of the real world, is an area of great controversy in sociology. Some argue for very formal procedures for attaching concepts to empirical events. Those of this persuasion contend that abstract concepts should be accompanied by a series of statements known as *operational definitions,* which are sets of procedural instructions telling investigators how to go about discerning phenomena in the real world that are denoted by an abstract concept.

Others argue, however, that the nature of our concepts in sociology precludes such formalistic exercises. At best, concepts can be only "sensitizing" devices that must change with alterations of social reality, and so we can only intuitively and provisionally apply abstract concepts to the actual flow of events. Moreover, among those making this argument, emulating the natural sciences in an effort to develop formal operations for attaching concepts to reality is to ignore the fact that social reality is changeable; it does not reveal invariant properties like the other domains of the universe.[9] Thus, to think that abstract concepts denote enduring and invariant properties of the social universe and to presume, therefore, that the concept itself will never need to be changed is, at best, naive.[10]

And so the debate rages, taking many different turns. We need not go into detail here, since these issues emerged again and again, in Chapters 2 through 24. Thus, for my purposes here, it is only necessary to draw the approximate lines of battle.

[9]For examples of this line of argument, see Herbert Blumer, *Symbolic Interaction: Perspective and Method* (Englewood Cliffs, NJ: Prentice-Hall, 1969) and Anthony Giddens, *New Rules of Sociological Method* (New York: Basic Books, 1977). For a more recent advocacy, see John Martin Levy, *The Explanation of Social Action* (New York: Oxford University Press, 2011).

[10]For the counterargument, see Jonathan H. Turner, "Toward a Social Physics: Reducing Sociology's Theoretical Inhibitions," *Humboldt Journal of Social Relations* 7 (Fall/Winter 1979–1980):140–155, "Returning to Social Physics," *Perspectives in Social Theory*, vol. 2 (1981):187–208. "Some Problematic Trends in Sociological Theorizing," *The Wisconsin Sociologist* 15 (Spring/Summer 1978):80–88, and *Theoretical Principles of Sociology,* vol. 1–3 (New York: Springer, 2010–2012).

Variables as an Important Type of Concept

When they are used to build theory, two general types of concepts can be distinguished: (1) those that simply label phenomena and (2) those that refer to phenomena that differ in degree.[11] Concepts that merely label phenomena would include commonly employed abstractions such as *dog, cat, group, social class,* and *star.* When stated in this way, none of these concepts reveals the ways in which the phenomena that they denote vary in terms of properties such as size, weight, density, velocity, cohesiveness, or any of the many criteria used to inform investigators about differences in degree among phenomena.

Those who believe that sociology can be like other sciences prefer concepts that are translated into variables—that is, into states that vary. We want to know the variable properties—size, degree, intensity, amount, and so forth—of events denoted by a concept. For example, to note that an aggregate of people is a group does not indicate what type of group it is or how it compares with other groups in terms of criteria such as size, degree of differentiation of roles, and level of cohesiveness. And so some concepts of scientific theory should denote the *variable* features of the world. To understand events requires that we visualize how variation in one phenomenon *is related to* variation in another. Others who are less enamored by efforts to make sociology a natural science are less compulsive about translating concepts into variables. They are far more interested in whether or not concepts sensitize and alert investigators to important processes than they are in converting each concept into a metric that varies in some measurable way. They are not, of course, against the conversion of ideas into variables, but they are cautious about efforts to translate each and every concept into a metric.

Theoretical Statements and Formats

To be useful, the concepts of theory must be connected to one another. Such connections among concepts constitute *theoretical statements.* These statements specify the way in which events denoted by concepts are interrelated, and at the same time, they provide an interpretation of how and why these events should be connected. When these theoretical statements are grouped together, they constitute a *theoretical format.* There are, however, different ways to organize theoretical statements into formats. Indeed, in sociological theory there is relatively little consensus over just how to organize theoretical statements; and in fact, much of the theoretical controversy in sociology revolves around differences over the best way to develop theoretical statements and to group them together into a format. Depending on one's views about what kind of science, if any, sociology can be, the structure of

---

[11]Reynolds, *Primer in Theory Construction,* 57; see also Stinchcombe, *Constructing Social Theories,* 38–47, for a discussion of how concepts point not only to the variable properties of phenomena but also to the interaction effects of interrelated phenomena. For an interesting discussion of the importance of variable concepts and for guidelines on how to use them, see Hage, *Techniques and Problems of Theory Construction.*

Figure 25.1 Elements of Theory and the Theoretical Formats

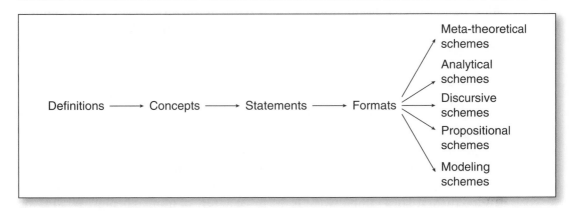

theoretical statements and their organization into formats differ dramatically. Let me review the range of opinion on the matter.

There are five basic approaches in sociological theory for generating theoretical statements and formats: (1) meta-theoretical schemes, (2) analytical schemes, (3) discursive schemes (4) propositional schemes, and (5) modeling schemes; Figure 25.1 summarizes the relations among these schemes and the basic elements of theory.

Concepts are constructed from definitions; theoretical statements link concepts together; and statements are organized into five basic types of formats. However, these five formats can be executed in a variety of ways, and so in reality there are more than just five strategies for developing theoretical statements and formats. Moreover, these various strategies are not always mutually exclusive, for in executing one of them, we are often led to another as a kind of "next step" in building theory. Yet—and this point is crucial—these various approaches are often viewed as antagonistic, and the proponents of each strategy have spilled a great deal of ink sustaining the antagonism. Moreover, even within a particular type of format, there is a constant battle over the best way to develop theory. This acrimony represents a great tragedy because in a mature science—which, sad to say, sociology is not—these approaches are viewed as highly compatible. Before pursuing this point further, we need to delineate in more detail each of these approaches.

Meta-theoretical Schemes

This kind of theoretical activity is more comprehensive than ordinary theory. Meta-theoretical schemes are not, by themselves, theories that explain specific classes of events; rather, they explicate the basic issues that a theory must address. In many sociological circles, meta-theory is considered an essential prerequisite to adequate theory building,[12] even though the dictionary definition of *meta* emphasizes

---

[12]For a review of different types of meta-theorizing, see George Ritzer, *Metatheorizing in Sociology* (Lexington, MA: Lexington Books, 1991).

"occurring later" and "in succession" to previous activities.[13] Furthermore, in most other sciences, meta-theoretical reflection has occurred *after* a body of formal theoretical statements has been developed. It is typically after a science has used a number of theoretical statements and formats successfully that scholars begin to ask these questions: What are the underlying assumptions about the universe contained in these statements? What strategies are demanded by, or precluded from, these statements and their organization into formats? What kind of knowledge is generated by these statements and formats, and conversely, what is ignored? In sociological theory, however, advocates of meta-theory usually emphasize that we cannot develop theory *until* we have resolved these more fundamental epistemological and metaphysical questions.

For those who emphasize meta-theory, several preliminary issues must be resolved: (a) What is the basic nature of human activity about which we must develop theory? For example, what is the basic nature of human beings? What is the fundamental nature of society? What is the fundamental nature of the bonds that connect people to one another and to society? (b) What is the appropriate way to develop theory, and what kind of theory is possible? For instance, can we build highly formal systems of abstract laws, as is the case in physics, or must we be content with general concepts that simply sensitize and orient us to important processes? Can we rigorously test theories with precise measurement procedures, or must we use theories as interpretative frameworks that cannot be tested by the same procedures as in the natural sciences? (c) What is the critical problem on which social theory should concentrate? For instance, should we examine the processes of social integration, or must we concentrate on social conflict? Should we focus on the nature of social action among individuals or on the structures of social organization? Should we stress the power of ideas, like values and beliefs, or must we focus on the material conditions of people's existence?

A great deal of what is defined as sociological theory in sociology involves trying to answer these questions. The old philosophical debates—idealism versus materialism, induction versus deduction, causation versus association, subjectivism versus objectivism, and so on—are re-evoked and analyzed with respect to social reality. At times, meta-theorizing has been true to the meaning of *meta* and has involved a reanalysis of previous scholars' ideas in light of these philosophical issues. The idea behind reanalysis is to summarize the metaphysical and epistemological assumptions of the scholars' work and to show where the schemes went wrong and where they still have utility. Furthermore, on the basis of this assessment, there are some recommendations for reanalyses as to how we should go about building theory and what this theory should be.

Meta-theorizing often gets bogged down in weighty philosophical matters and immobilizes theory building. The enduring philosophical questions persist because they are not resolvable—which is the reason why they are philosophical in the first place. One must just take a stand on the issues and see what kinds of insights can be generated. But meta-theory often stymies as much as stimulates theoretical activity

---

[13]Webster's *New Collegiate Dictionary* (Springfield, MA: G & C Merriman, 1976).

because it embroils theorists in inherently unresolvable and always debatable controversies. Of course, many sociologists reject this assertion, and so, for our present purposes, the more important conclusion is that a great deal of sociological theory is, in fact, meta-theoretical activity.

Yet not all meta-theorizing gets bogged down in unresolvable issues. Some meta-theorists, and I must include myself in this group, examine theories that have been stated in one format and try to convert it to another format, as has been evident throughout this book when I converted theories into analytical models and propositions. And so a theory stated discursively in just words and texts might be converted to more formal propositions so that the key theoretical ideas are highlighted; or the theory might be converted into an analytical model, where the variables or forces in play are visually arranged so as to highlight their causal relations to each other. Thus, as George Ritzer[14] has emphasized, there are several different types of meta-theorizing, with one of them being the analysis of existing theories to make them more formal and precise.

Analytical Schemes

Much of theoretical activity in sociology consists of concepts organized into a classification scheme that denotes the key properties, and interrelations among these properties, of the social universe. There are many different varieties of analytical schemes, but they share an emphasis on classifying the basic properties of the social world. The concepts of the scheme chop up the universe; then, the ordering of the concepts gives the social world a sense of order. Explanation of an empirical event comes whenever a place in the classificatory scheme can be found for the empirical event.

There are, however, wide variations in the nature of the typologies in analytical schemes, although there are two basic types: (1) *naturalistic schemes,* which try to develop a tightly woven system of categories that is presumed to capture the way in which the invariant properties of the universe are ordered,[15] and (2) *sensitizing schemes,* which are more loosely assembled congeries of concepts intended only to sensitize and orient researchers and theorists to certain critical processes. Figure 25.2 summarizes these two types of analytical approaches.

Naturalistic/positivistic schemes assume that there are timeless and universal processes in the social universe, just as there are in the physical and biological realms. The goal is to create an abstract conceptual typology that is isomorphic with these timeless processes. Talcott Parsons's version of functionalism (see Chapter 10) is, for example, a naturalistic scheme.

In contrast, sensitizing schemes are sometimes more skeptical about the timeless quality of social affairs. As a consequence of this skepticism, concepts and their linkages must always be provisional and sensitizing because the nature of human activity is to change those very arrangements denoted by the organization of concepts into

---

[14]George Ritzer, *Metatheorizing in Sociology* (see note 12).

[15]Talcott Parsons's work is of this nature, as we saw in Chapter 10.

Figure 25.2 Types of Analytical Schemes

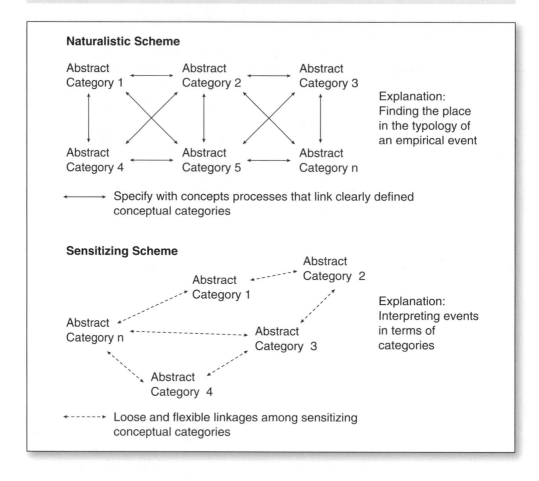

theoretical statements.[16] Hence, except for certain very general conceptual categories, the scheme must be flexible and capable of being revised as circumstances in the empirical world change. At best, then, explanation is simply an interpretation of events by seeing them as an instance or example of the provisional and sensitizing concepts in the scheme. Anthony Giddens's structuration theory (Chapter 20), for instance, is a sensitizing conceptual scheme.

Often it is argued that analytical schemes are a necessary prerequisite for developing other forms of theory. Until one has a scheme that organizes the properties of the universe, it is difficult to develop propositions and models about specific events. For without the general analytical framework, how can a theorist or researcher know what to examine? There is some merit to this position, but if the scheme becomes too complex and elaborate, it is not easily translated into other theoretical formats. Thus, analytical schemes can represent a useful way to begin

---

[16]Anthony Giddens's work represents this alternative. See his *The Constitution of Society* (Berkeley: University of California Press, 1984).

theorizing, unless they are too rigid and elaborate to stimulate theorizing outside the parameters imposed by the scheme itself.[17]

Discursive Schemes

Many theories are simply stated in words that are not highly formalized or ordered into propositions or other structured formats. They simply outline in everyday language key variables and forces, discursively suggesting the ways in which they affect each other. Indeed, it may be that the majority of sociological theories are stated in this way, without what their authors might think are the contrivances of formalization. Such theories are, of course, often subject to meta-theorizing as theorists try to extract the key arguments and formalize them in some manner.

The great strength of discursive schemes is that they are typically easier to understand than those that are more formal, but their great weakness can be that the variables and forces highlighted and the dynamic relations among them can sometimes be vague and imprecise. Such is often the case with meta-theorizing and analytical schemes, discussed above, and indeed, these may present more difficulty than discursive schemes in figuring out the causal connections or even the basic relationships among the forces theorized to operate. For example, a theory may be illustrated with so much historical detail that it is difficult to figure out what the more generic forces in play might be. Or the forces may be defined as a typology in which variations in the values and valences of the forces are not emphasized; as a result, it is difficult to understand how variations in the typologically defined forces cause variation in other forces. Yet when the theory is powerful, a meta-theorist can often make reasonable inferences about the range of variation in forces and thus connect them in analytical models or propositional schemes. When, however, the variables are not clearly defined and are used loosely in rambling text, meta-theorizing may not be able to isolate them and then connect their operation to other forces driving the social world. For example, it is relatively easy to convert the arguments of the founding theorists of sociology—say, Auguste Comte, Herbert Spencer, Karl Marx, Max Weber, Georg Simmel, Émile Durkheim, and George Herbert Mead—into propositions or laws, even if they themselves would not have agreed with such a meta-theoretical exercise. The arguments of some, like Spencer, Simmel, and Durkheim, are particularly easy to convert because they presented their discursive arguments in close-to-proposition formats, whereas a scholar like Weber did not. Still, it is not difficult to convert Weber's arguments, for all of their embeddedness in historical analysis and typologies (his "ideal types"), into causal models and propositions. For when a theorist is being a "good theorist," attention is paid to isolating key variables and forces and, in discursive text, connecting them to other forces. Even with a certain vagueness in language, it is still possible to discern the basic theoretical argument and convert it—if one is so disposed—into a more formal format like an analytical model or propositions scheme, as outlined below.

---

[17]For my best effort in using sensitizing schemes, see Jonathan H. Turner, *A Theory of Social Interaction* (Stanford, CA: Stanford University Press, 1988).

Propositional Schemes

A proposition is a theoretical statement that specifies the connection between two or more variables. It tells us how variation in one concept is accounted for by variation in another. For example, the propositional statement "Group solidarity is a positive function of external conflict with other groups" says that as group conflict increases, so does the internal sense of solidarity among members of the respective groups involved in the conflict. Thus, two properties of the social universe denoted by variable concepts, "group solidarity" and "conflict," are connected by the proposition that as one increases in value, so does the other.

Propositional schemes vary perhaps the most of all theoretical approaches. They vary primarily along two dimensions: (1) the level of abstraction and (2) the way propositions are organized into formats. Some are highly abstract and contain concepts that do not denote any particular case but all cases of a type (e.g., *group solidarity* and *conflict* are abstract because no particular empirical instance of conflict and solidarity is addressed). In contrast, other propositional systems are tied to empirical facts and simply summarize the relations among events in a particular case (e.g., "As World War II progressed, nationalism in America increased"). Propositional schemes vary not only in terms of abstractness but also by virtue of how propositions are laced together into a format. Some are woven together by very explicit rules; others are merely loose bunches or congeries of propositions.

By using these two dimensions, several different types of propositional schemes can be isolated: (a) axiomatic formats, (b) formal formats, and (c) various empirical formats. The first two (axiomatic and formal formats) are clearly theoretical, whereas various empirical formats are simply research findings that might be useful to test with more abstractly stated theories. But these more empirical types of propositional schemes are often considered theory by practicing sociologists, and so they are included in our discussion here.

Axiomatic Formats. An axiomatic organization of theoretical statements involves the following elements. First, it contains a set of concepts. Some of the concepts are highly abstract; others are more concrete. Second, there is always a set of existence statements that describe those types and classes of situations in which the concepts and the propositions that incorporate them apply. These existence statements make up what are usually called the *scope conditions* of the theory. Third—and mostly unique to the axiomatic format—propositional statements are stated in a hierarchical order. At the top of the hierarchy are *axioms,* or highly abstract statements, from which *all* other theoretical statements are logically derived. These latter statements are usually called *theorems* and are logically derived in accordance with varying rules from the more abstract axioms. The selection of axioms is, in reality, a somewhat arbitrary matter, but usually they are selected with several criteria in mind. The axioms should be consistent with one another, although they do not have to be logically interrelated. The axioms should be highly abstract; they should state the relationships among abstract concepts. These relationships should be law-like in that the more concrete theorems derived from them have not been disproved by empirical investigation. And the axioms should have an intuitive plausibility in that their truth appears to be self-evident.

The end result of tight conformity to axiomatic principles is an inventory or set of interrelated propositions, each derivable from at least one axiom and usually more abstract theorems. There are several advantages to this form of theory construction. First, highly abstract concepts, encompassing a broad range of related phenomena, can be employed. These abstract concepts do not have to be directly measurable since they are logically tied to more specific and measurable propositions that, when empirically tested, can indirectly subject the more abstract propositions and the axioms to empirical tests. Thus, by virtue of this logical interrelatedness of propositions and axioms, research can be more efficient since the failure to refute a particular proposition lends credence to other propositions and to the axioms. Second, the use of a logical system to derive propositions from abstract axioms can also generate additional propositions that point to previously unknown or unanticipated relationships among social phenomena.

There are, however, some fatal limitations to the use of axiomatic theory in sociology. In terms of strict adherence to the rules of deduction (the details of which are not critical for my purposes here), most interesting concepts and propositions in sociology cannot be legitimately employed because the concepts are not stated with sufficient precision and because they cannot be incorporated into propositions that state unambiguously the relationships between concepts. Axiomatic theory also requires controls on all potential extraneous variables so that the tight logical system of deduction from axiom to empirical reality is not contaminated by extraneous factors. Sociologists can create such controls, although in many situations, this kind of tight control is not possible.[18] Thus, axiomatic theory can be used only when precise definitions of concepts exist, when concepts are organized into propositions using a precise calculus that specifies relations unambiguously, and when the contaminating effects of extraneous variables are eliminated.

These limitations are often ignored in propositional theory building, and the language of axiomatic theory is employed (axioms, theorems, corollaries, etc.); but these efforts are, at best, pseudo-axiomatic schemes.[19] In fact, it is best to call them *formal propositional* schemes[20]—the second type of proposition strategy listed earlier.

Formal Formats. A formal format is, in essence, watered-down or loose versions of axiomatic schemes. The idea is to develop highly abstract propositions that are used to explain some empirical event. Some highly abstract propositions are seen as higher-order laws, and the goal of explanation is to visualize empirical events as instances of this "covering law." Deductions from the laws are made, but they are much looser, rarely conforming to the strict rules of axiomatic theory. Moreover, there is a recognition that

---

[18]For more details of this argument, see Lee Freese, "Formal Theorizing," *Annual Review of Sociology* 6 (1980):187–212 and Herbert L. Costner and Robert K. Leik, "Deductions from Axiomatic Theory," *American Sociological Review* 29 (December 1964):19–35.

[19]See, for example, Peter Blau's *Structural Context of Opportunities* (Chicago, IL: University of Chicago Press, 1994) and *Inequality and Heterogeneity: A Primitive Theory of Social Structure* (New York: Free Press, 1977).

[20]See Freese, "Formal Theorizing."

extraneous variables cannot always be excluded, and so the propositions usually have the disclaimer "other things being equal." That is, if other forces do not impinge, then the relationship among concepts in the proposition should hold true. For example, our earlier example of the relationship between conflict and solidarity might be one abstract proposition in a formal system. Thus, a formal scheme might say, "Other things being equal, group solidarity is a positive function of conflict." Then we would use this law to explain some empirical event—say, for instance, World War II (the conflict variable) and nationalism in America (the solidarity variable). And we might find an exception to our rule or law—such as America's involvement in the Vietnam War or, more recently, the wars in Iraq and Afghanistan—that contradicts the principle, forcing its revision or the recognition that "all things were not equal." In this case, we might revise the principle by stating a condition under which it holds true: when parties to a conflict perceive the conflict as a threat to their welfare, then the level of solidarity of groups is a positive function of their degree of conflict. Thus, in the end, the Vietnam War or the wars in Iraq and Afghanistan did not produce internal solidarity in America because, eventually, they were not defined as a threat to America's general welfare (whereas for the North Vietnamese or the Taliban, the threat posed by the American military did produce solidarity against an enemy, which in turn made the wars not only costly but difficult to win).

The essential idea here is that in formal theory, an effort is made to create abstract principles. These principles are often clustered together to form a group of laws from which we make rather loose deductions to explain empirical events. Much like axiomatic systems, formal systems are hierarchical, but the restrictions of axiomatic theory are relaxed considerably. Most propositional schemes in sociological theorizing are, therefore, of this formal type.

Empirical Formats. Much of what is defined as theory in sociology is more empirical. These empirical formats consist of generalizations from specific events in particular empirical contexts. For example, Golden's law states that "as industrialization increases, the level of literacy in the population increases." Such a proposition is not very abstract; it is filled with empirical content—industrialization and literacy, which have not existed in all times and places of human social organization. Thus, the law is not about a timeless process, since industrialization is only a few hundred years old and literacy emerged, at best, only 6,000 years ago. There are many such generalizations in sociology that are considered theoretical. They represent statements of empirical regularities that scholars think are important to understand. Indeed, most substantive areas and subfields of sociology are filled with these kinds of propositions.

Strictly speaking, however, these are not theoretical. They are too tied to empirical contexts, times, and places. In fact, they are generalizations that are *in need of a theory to explain them*. Yet many scholars working in substantive areas see their empirical generalizations as theory; so once again it is clear that there is no clear consensus in sociology as to what constitutes theory.

There are other kinds of empirical generalizations, however, that raise fewer suspicions about their theoretical merits. These are often termed *middle-range theories,* because they are more abstract than a research finding and because their empirical content pertains to variables that are also found in other domains of social reality.[21] For example, a series of middle-range propositions from the complex organization's literature might be stated:

> (a) Increases in the complexity (differentiation) of its structure, (b) reliance on formal rules and regulations, (c) decentralization of authority, and (d) span of control for each center of authority of a bureaucracy is a positive function of a bureaucracy's size and rate of growth.[22]

These principles (the truth of which is not at issue here) are more abstract than Golden's law because they denote a whole class of phenomena—organizations. They also deal with more generic variables—size, differentiation, centralization of power, spans of control, rules, and regulations—that have existed in all times and all places. Moreover, these variables could be stated more abstractly to apply to *all* organized social systems, not just bureaucratic organizations. For instance, a more abstract law might state,

> (a) Increases in levels of system differentiation, (b) codification of norms, (c) decentralization of power, and (d) spans of control for each center of power is a positive function of the size of the system and its rate of growth.

The truth or falsity of these propositions is not being asserted here; rather, these are illustrations of how empirical generalizations can be made *more abstract* and, hence, theoretical. The central point is that some empirical generalizations have more theoretical potential than others. If their variables are relatively abstract and if they pertain to basic and fundamental properties of the social universe that exist in other substantive areas of inquiry, then it is more reasonable to consider them theoretical.

In sum, then, there are three basic kinds of propositional schemes: axiomatic schemes, formal schemes, and various types of empirical generalizations. These propositional schemes are summarized in Figure 25.3. Although axiomatic formats are elegant and powerful, sociological variables and research typically cannot conform to their restrictions. Instead, we must rely upon formal formats that generate propositions stating abstract relations among variables and then make loosely structured "deductions" to specific empirical cases. Finally, there are empirical formats that consist of generalizations from particular substantive areas, and these are often considered theories of that area. Some of these theories are little more than summaries of research findings that require a theory to explain them. Others are more middle range and have more potential as theory because they are more abstract and pertain to more generic classes of variables.

---

[21]See Robert K. Merton's *Social Theory and Social Structure* (New York: Free Press, 1975), chap. 4.

[22]I have borrowed this example from Peter M. Blau's "Applications of a Macrosociological Theory," in *Mathematizche Analyse von Organisationsstrukktaren und Prozessen,* vol. 5 (Internationale Wissenschaftliche Fachkonferenz, March 1981).

Figure 25.3   Types of Propositional Schemes

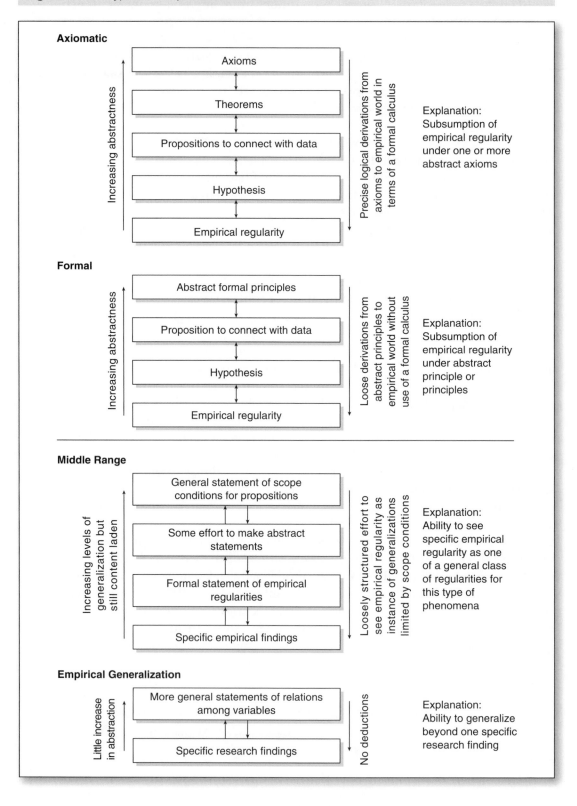

Modeling Schemes

At times, it is useful to draw a picture of social events, as I have done throughout the previous chapters. Some models are drawn with neutral languages such as mathematics, in which the equation is presumed to map and represent empirical processes.[23] In reality, such equations are propositions (formal statements of relations among variables) *unless* they can be used to generate a picture or some form of graphic representation of processes. There is no clear consensus on what a model is, but in sociological theory there is a range of activity that involves representing concepts and their relations as a "picture" that arrays in visual space what are considered the important elements of a social process.

A model, then, is a diagrammatic representation of social events. The diagrammatic elements of any model include (a) concepts that denote and highlight certain features of the universe, (b) the arrangement of these concepts in visual space so as to reflect the ordering of events in the universe, and (c) symbols that mark the connections among concepts, such as lines, arrows, vectors, and so on. The elements of a model may be weighted in some way, they may be sequentially organized to express events over time, or they may represent complex patterns of relations, such as lag effects, threshold effects, feedback loops, mutual interactions, cycles, and other potential ways in which properties of the universe affect one another.[24]

In sociology, most diagrammatic models are constructed to emphasize the *causal connections* among properties of the universe. That is, they are designed to show how changes in the values of one set of variables are related to changes in the values of other variables. Models are typically constructed when there are numerous variables whose causal interrelations an investigator wants to highlight.

Sociologists generally construct two different types of models, which can be termed *analytical* models and *causal* models. This distinction is somewhat arbitrary, but it is a necessary one if we are to appreciate the kinds of models that are constructed in sociology. The basis for making this distinction is twofold: first, some models are more abstract than others in that the concepts in them are not tied to any particular case, whereas other models reveal concepts that simply summarize statistically the relations among variables in a particular data set. Second, more abstract models almost always reveal more complexity in their representation of the causal connections among variables. That is, one will find feedback loops, cycles, mutual effects, and other connective representations that complicate the causal connections among the variables in the model and make them difficult to summarize with simple statistics. In contrast, the less abstract models typically depict a clear

---

[23]Actually, these are typically "regression equations" and would not constitute modeling as I think it should be defined. A series of differential equations, especially as they are simulated or otherwise graphically represented, would constitute a model. Computer simulations represent, I think, an excellent approach to modeling. See, for example, Robert A. Hanneman, *Computer-Assisted Theory Building: Modeling Dynamic Social Systems* (Newbury Park, CA: Sage, 1988).

[24]Good examples of such models are in my *Theoretical Principles of Sociology,* vol. 1: *Macrodynamics* (New York: Springer 2010). For examples of more empirical, yet still analytical, models, see Gerhard and Jean Lenski, *Human Societies* (Boulder, CO: Paradigm Press, 2011). See also the numerous analytical models in Randall Collins, *Theoretical Sociology* (San Diego, CA: Harcourt Brace Jovanovich, 1988).

causal sequence among empirical variables.[25] They typically reveal independent variables that affect variation in some dependent variable; and if the model is more complex, it might also highlight intervening variables and perhaps even some interaction effects among the variables.

Thus, analytical models are more abstract; they highlight the more generic properties of the universe; and they portray a complex set of connections among variables. In contrast, causal models are more empirically grounded; they are more likely to devote particular properties of a specific empirical case; and they are likely to present a simple lineal view of causality. These modeling strategies are summarized in Figure 25.4.

Figure 25.4 Types of Modeling Schemes

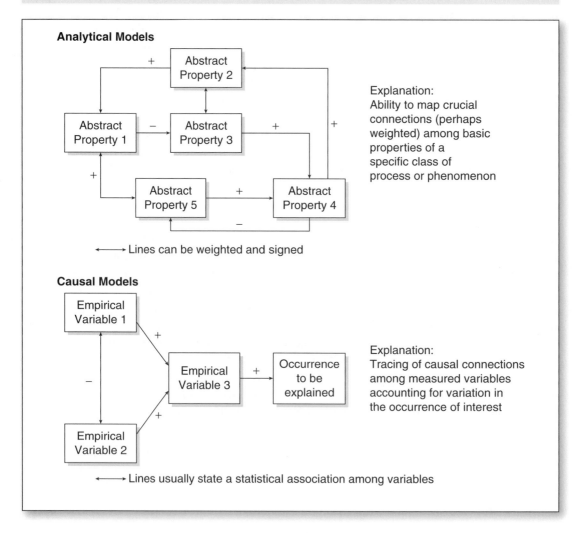

Analytical Models

Explanation: Ability to map crucial connections (perhaps weighted) among basic properties of a specific class of process or phenomenon

Lines can be weighted and signed

Causal Models

Explanation: Tracing of causal connections among measured variables accounting for variation in the occurrence of interest

Lines usually state a statistical association among variables

---

[25]The "path analysis" that was so popular in American sociology in the 1970s is a good example of such modeling techniques.

Causal models are typically drawn in order to provide a more detailed interpretation of an empirical generalization. They are designed to sort out the respective influences of variables, usually in some temporal sequence, as they operate on some dependent variable of interest. At times, a causal model becomes a way of representing the elements of a middle-range theory so as to connect these elements to the particulars of a specific empirical context. For example, if we wanted to know why the size of a bureaucratic organization is related to its complexity of structure in a particular empirical case of a growing organization, we might translate the more abstract variables of size and complexity into specific empirical indicators and perhaps try to introduce other variables that also influence the relationship between size and complexity in this empirical case. The causal model thus becomes a way to represent with more clarity the empirical association between size and complexity in a specific context.[26]

Analytical models are usually drawn to specify the relations among more abstract and generic processes. Often they are used to delineate the processes that operate to connect the concepts of an axiomatic or, more likely, a formal theory.[27] For example, we might construct a model that tells us more about the processes that operate to generate the relationship between conflict and solidarity or between size and differentiation in social systems. Additional concepts would be introduced, and their weighted, direct, indirect, feedback, cyclical, lagged, and other patterns of effect on one another would be diagrammed. In this way, the analytical model tells us more about how and why the properties of the universe are causally connected. In addition to specifying processes among formal propositions, analytical models can be used to describe processes that connect variables in the propositions of a middle-range theory. For example, we might use a model to map out how organization size and complexity are connected by virtue of other processes operating in an organization.

Of course, we can construct analytical models or causal models for their own sake, without reference to an empirical generalization, a middle-range theory, or a formal/axiomatic theory. We may simply prefer modeling to propositional formats. One of the great advantages of modeling is that it allows the presentation of complex relations among many variables in a reasonably parsimonious fashion. To say the same thing as a model, a propositional format might have to write complex equations or use many words. Thus, by itself, modeling represents a tool that many theorists find preferable to alternative theoretical schemes.

Conclusions: Assessing Diverse Theoretical Approaches

My belief is that theory should be abstract. That is, the less substantive the content in the concepts, the better they are. For if theories are filled with empirical referents, they are tied to specific contexts and, hence, are not as useful as those that view

---

[26]For an example of a model for these variables, see Peter M. Blau's "A Formal Theory of Differentiation in Organizations," *American Sociological Review* 35 (April 1970):201–218. See also Chapter 12.

[27]Ibid. is a good example.

specific empirical contexts as instances or examples of a more basic underlying process. Most theorists in sociology, however, would disagree with me on this score, and I will return to this point of contention shortly.

Theory should be stated in a way that allows empirical researchers to prove it wrong. As a general platitude, few would disagree with this statement. But as a more practical matter of how we should construct theories to be proved wrong, there is enormous disagreement. Theories must be sufficiently precise in their definitions of concepts and in their organization of concepts into statements so that they can be, in principle, measured and tested. It is only through the generation of precise theoretical statements and efforts at their refutation that scientific knowledge can be generated. What distinguishes good theoretical statements from the bad ones is that they *are created to be proved wrong*, and this makes scientific theory very different from other types of belief systems, such as ideologies and religious beliefs. A theory that, in principle, cannot be proved wrong is not very useful. It becomes a self-sustaining dogma that is accepted on faith. A theory must allow for understanding of events, and hence, it must be tested against the facts of the world. If a theoretical statement is proved wrong by empirical tests, science has advanced. When a theory is rejected, then one less possible line of inquiry will be required in search of an answer to the question "Why?" By successively eliminating incorrect statements, those that survive attempts at refutation offer, for the present at least, the most accurate picture of the real world. Although having one's theory refuted may cause professional stigma, refutations are crucial to theory building. It is somewhat disheartening, therefore, that some scientists appear to live in fear of such refutation. For in the ideal scientific process, just the opposite should be the case, as Karl Popper has emphasized:

> Refutations have often been regarded as establishing the failure of a scientist, or at least of his theory. It should be stressed that this is an inductive error. Every refutation should be regarded as a great success; not merely as a success of the scientist who refuted the theory, but also of the scientist who created the refuted theory and who thus in the first instance suggested, if only indirectly, the refuting experiment.[28]

Even statements that survive refutation and hence bring professional prestige to their framers are never fully proved. It is always possible that the next empirical test could disprove them. Yet if statements consistently survive empirical tests, they have high credibility and are likely to be at the core of a theoretical body of knowledge. As I have now phrased the issue, however, many sociological theorists would disagree. Moreover, most philosophers of science would argue that this process of refutation is idealized and, in fact, rarely occurs in the actual operation of science.

Despite these reservations, it is perhaps best to proceed *as if* we can develop theoretical statements that are highly abstract and, at the same time, sufficiently precise so as to be testable. Again, as has been evident in Chapters 2–24, many

---

[28]Karl R. Popper, *Conjectures and Refutations* (New York: Basic Books, 1962), 243.

social theorists disagree with this position. I have injected my personal views because it is important to understand the biases with which I have approached the review and analyses of social theory. Moreover, these biases are the central issue around which the debate over the best approach to developing theory and knowledge rages. So let me elaborate on them by assessing the merits of the various approaches that outlined in this chapter.

From my point of view, empirical generalizations and causal models of empirically operationalized variables are not theory at all. They are useful summaries of data that need a theory to explain them. Some would argue that theory can be built from such summaries of empirical regularities. That is, we can induce from the facts the more general properties that these facts illustrate. Yet induction is not a mechanical process of making empirical variables more abstract; often, a creative leap of insight is necessary, and so theory building that begins with total immersion in the empirical facts is, I believe, a barrier to rising above them and producing more abstract theory. Still, there are many instances in science where scholars have been able to make inductions, and so we should not be too quick to reject this approach out of hand. Still, there is almost always a creative leap here as one moves from empirical generalizations to more generic and abstract concepts, propositions, and models that can explain these generalizations.

At the other extreme, meta-theory is like empirical facts in that it often becomes difficult to move on to producing real theory. It is easy to get bogged down in enduring philosophical issues when producing meta-theory, with the result that scholars never get around to developing theory. Again, such is not always the case, but there is a clear tendency for theorists in sociology who practice meta-theorizing to remain meta-theorists and indeed to become hostile to formal theories and models or, if not hostile, to think of these as premature and as not fully exploring their implicit assumptions.

Analytical schemes often suffer from the same problems as meta-theory. Naturalistic schemes have a tendency to become overly concerned with their architectural majesty. In an effort to construct an orderly scheme that mirrors at an abstract level the empirical world in all its dimensions, naturalistic schemes get ever more complex; and as new elements are added to the scheme, efforts to reconcile new portions with the old take precedence over making the scheme testable. Moreover, the scheme as a whole is impossible to test because relations among its elements cover such a broad range of phenomena and are rarely stated with great precision. And when imprecision is compounded by the abstractness, then empirical tests are infrequent because it is not clear to researchers how to test any portion of the scheme. Yet, despite these problems, creators of analytical schemes view them as a necessary prerequisite for developing testable theoretical statements, and in this sense, they are much like meta-theoreticians.

In contrast, sensitizing schemes are typically constructed as a loose framework of concepts to interpret events and to see if they yield greater understanding of how and why these events occur. Even if such schemes are not considered science, they can be very insightful. Yet, much like naturalistic approaches, sensitizing schemes also become self-reinforcing because they are so loosely structured and so often vague (albeit suggestive and insightful) that the empirical facts can be bent to fit the scheme. Hence, the scheme can never be refuted or, I suspect, revised on the basis of actual empirical events. Sensitizing schemes as most useful, then, when they are used to orient us to important phenomena and, then, are elaborated upon with propositions and analytical models.

Discursive schemes vary in how useful they can be in generating explanations. If there is precision in the writing—that is, variables are clearly defined and their connection and effects on other variations are unambiguously stated—then a discursive format can offer a sound explanation. But if variables do not vary but are typologized in categories and if causal statements say things like "sometime has an effect on," "tends to influence," "is known to have an effect on," and the like, then the theory will lack precision, and it will be difficult to isolate the forces in play and their relation to each other. Unfortunately, much of discursive theorizing is imprecise, and even when highly provocative and interesting, the use of informal languages is filled with vagueness. As a result, a meta-theorist interested in formalizing the theory will have to make many inferences and, in the process, will not get the discursive stated argument as intended by the theorist. This weakness in much discursive theorizing is immediately noticeable once the reader seeks precise definitions of the concepts and the causal relations among the properties of the social universe supposedly denoted by these concepts.

Let me now turn to axiomatic/formal propositional formats, analytical models, and middle-range propositions. As already indicated, axiomatic theorizing is, for the most part, impractical in sociology. In my view, formal theorizing is the most useful approach because it contains abstract concepts that are linked with sufficient precision so as to be testable. Analytical models can be highly insightful, but they are hard to test as a whole. They contain too many concepts, and their linkages are too diverse to be directly tested. And so it is reasonable to ask in what sense they can be useful for sociological theorizing. My view is that an analytical model can best be used to specify the processes by which concepts in a formal proposition are connected.[29] For example, if a proposition states that the "degree of differentiation" is a function of "system size," the model can tell us why and how and through what processes size and differentiation are connected. That is, we can get a better sense of the underlying processes by which size increases differentiation (and perhaps vice versa). Alternatively, analytical models can also be a starting point for formal theorizing. By isolating basic processes and mapping their interconnections, we can get a sense of the important social processes about which we need to develop formal propositions. And although the model as a whole cannot be easily tested (because it is too complex to be subjected to a definitive test), we can decompose it into abstract propositional statements that are amenable to definitive tests.

Thus, analytical models are much more abstract, and so they can be the basis for developing formal propositional statements (in rare cases, perhaps even axiomatic), or they can specify at an abstract level the robust causal connections among the abstract variables stated in a formal proposition. Moreover, both analytical models and formal

---

[29]I have tried to illustrate this strategy in my *Theoretical Principles of Sociology.*

propositional schemes cover a wide range of phenomena without being too broad as to become difficult to test empirically. Let me illustrate further with the proposition presented earlier that conflict promotes increased solidarity. While this proposition specifies a fundamental relationship in the social universe, it does not tell us just *how* threat and conflict translate into solidarity. What are the processes by which conflict and threat generate solidarity? The answer to this question can often be stated in an abstract model that outlines the causal sequences—direct, indirect, and reverse—of events that move the parties to a conflict to form more cohesive structures revealing high solidarity. In fact, introducing the notion of threat (as I did earlier) could have come from an analytical model as a variable that is critical to transforming conflict into high levels of prolonged solidarity. And one might add other variables, such as (a) leader, who can frame the issues and articulate ideologies highlighting the threat, and (b) entrepreneurs, who can mobilize resources (including material and symbolic resources) to sustain the sense of threat and keep members of the conflict party mobilized and focused. Thus, an analytical model can "fill in" information that makes the basic relationship between conflict and solidarity more robust. One gets a better sense of why and through what processes conflict leads to solidarity and, of course, when it would not. Thus, there can be a synergy between formal propositional schemes and analytical models: the propositional scheme indicates the nature of the fundamental relationship (e.g., the basic relationships between conflict and solidarity), while the analytical model indicates how and through what basic processes this relationship is produced. Moreover, the key processes discovered in the analytical model can be converted into a propositional scheme—for instance, a proposition like the following (no claim is made about its accuracy or exhaustiveness):

> *The degree to which conflict generates solidarity among conflict parties is a positive and additive function of the level of threat posed, the availability of leaders to frame and formulate ideologies about the threat, and the capacity to mobilize symbolic, organizational, and material resources to pursue conflict.*

Analytical schemes are less likely to have this synergetic effect, even though they may be highly abstract and may incorporate a wide range of phenomena. Because they categorize phenomena rather than seeing them as variables and because they do not specify causal relations among these phenomena within categories, they are often difficult to convert to propositional schemes or analytical models. They describe, albeit at a very abstract level, the organization of a broad range of phenomena. Sensitizing schemes have the same problem. They are abstract, which is useful in building theory, but they do not specify in great detail the fundamental relations among phenomena. Rather, they denote phenomena, suggest how they might be related without great precision, and always hold out the possibility that the categories and variables in the scheme may be obviated by the agency of actors.

Middle-range propositions are, I feel, less useful as places to begin theory building. They tend to be too filled with empirical content, much of which does not pertain to the more basic, enduring, and generic features of the social universe.[30] For

---

[30]I doubt if this was Merton's intent when he formulated this idea, but my sense is that his advocacy became a legitimization for asserting that empirical generalizations were "theory."

example, a "theory of ethnic antagonism" is often difficult to translate into a more general proposition or model on conflict dynamics because it is loaded with empirical content about specific ethnic subpopulations at a particular time and place. Moreover, scholars working at this middle range tend to become increasingly empirical as they seek to devise ways to test their theories in specific empirical contexts. Their propositions become, I have found, ever more like empirical generalizations as more and more research content is added. There is no logical reason why substantive and empirical referents cannot be taken out of middle-range theories and the level of abstraction raised, but this has occurred only infrequently.

In Figure 25.5, I have summarized these conclusions in the right column. Meta-theory and naturalistic analytical schemes are interesting philosophy but poor theory. Sensitizing analytical schemes, formal propositional statements, and analytical models offer the best place to begin theorizing, especially if interplay among them is possible. Middle-range theories have rarely realized their theoretical potential,

Figure 25.5 Theoretical Formats for Building Testable Theory

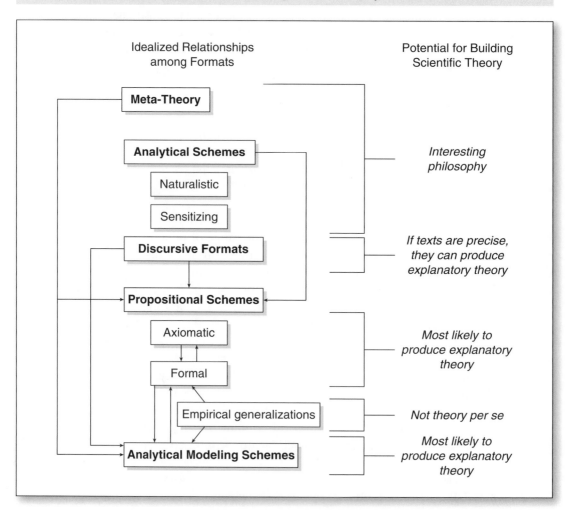

tending to move toward empirical generalizations as opposed to formal propositions. Causal models and empirical generalizations are useful in that they give theorists some sense of empirical regularities, but by themselves and without creative leaps in scope and abstraction, they are not theoretical. They are usually data in need of a theory.

In the left column, I have presented my idealized view of the proper place of each theoretical approach for generating knowledge.[31] If we begin to accumulate bodies of formal laws (perhaps on the basis of leads provided by a sensitizing scheme), then it is desirable to extract out the key concepts and look at these as the basic sensitizing and orienting concepts of sociology (much as magnetism, gravity, relativity, etc. were for early 20th-century physics). We may even want to construct a formal analytical scheme and ponder on the meta-theoretical implications of these. In turn, such pondering can help reformulate or clarify analytical schemes, which can perhaps help construct new, or reverse old, formal propositions. But without a body of formal laws to pull meta-theory and analytical schemes back into the domain of the testable, they become hopelessly self-sustaining and detached from the very reality they are supposed to help clarify.

For building theory, the most crucial interchange is, I believe, between formal propositions and analytical models. There is a creative synergy between translating propositions into models and vice versa. Theories that begin with analytical models or propositions will help improve each other. Analytical models will add robustness, which can be incorporated into propositions, whereas propositions will specify the beginning and end states of two phenomena—say, conflict, as the beginning state, leads to solidarity, the end state. They will inevitably lead theorists to ask this question: How and why does this beginning state lead to the end state? And once this question is asked, an analytical model can specify the flow of causality and, in this specification, introduce additional variables that are in play. In turn, these variables can be incorporated if theorists are so disposed, into propositional schemes.

---

[31]I should emphasize that this is not how things actually work in sociology; the diagram represents my *wish* for how sociological theory should be developed.

CHAPTER 26

Overcoming Roadblocks to Cumulative Explanatory Theory in Sociology

From its beginnings, sociology has had to defend itself as a useful enterprise. Sociology first treaded into the academic turf of well-established disciplines that, not surprisingly, viewed sociology as not only a nuisance but as a potential threat. It took over 100 years from Auguste Comte's naming of the discipline for it to penetrate a significant portion of universities in Europe and the United States; and outside Western Europe and North America, sociology has had virtually no presence in the rest of the world. The last seventy years have seen sociology successively penetrate academic institutions and academies of sciences all over the world, but there is always some question about the nature, goals, and usefulness of the discipline. This is surprising since most of the problems of the globe revolve around problems in social organization; and sociology is clearly the most relevant discipline for understanding these problems. Surface reasoning would say that sociology is relevant, and so there is a deeper concern about the character of the discipline.

I think that one cause of concern for outsiders, and indeed for insiders as well, is the scientific credentials of a discipline that seeks not only to explain social events but *to direct them*, typically from the perspective of left-leaning political ideologies (which I share but do not consider the goal of theorizing). From Comte's first pronouncement, he saw science as the key to creating better societies, but he mistakenly seemed to think that the solutions would be so obvious once sociology was established as a science that the problem of ideology would not arise. And this was from a scholar who would later write about political philosophy and proclaim himself to be the High Priest of Humanity. Karl Marx made it clear that his explanation of capitalism was both scientific and ideological, although he did not see himself as a sociologist (rather, sociology adopted him). Max Weber was most concerned about value-neutrality, but in reality his work is highly politicized with ideology. The same is true of Herbert Spencer's sociology because the specter of his moral philosophy hangs over his theories, which, despite their brilliance, are suspect because of his conception of morality. Émile Durkheim was much like Comte, seemingly believing that science will make clear the correct path, and so his sociology is also impregnated with a political ideology that was antireligious and heavily influenced by the moral reasoning of the French *philosophes,* writing before the French Revolution of 1789. Georg Simmel's sociology appears to be more neutral, but it is not hard to see his own personal situation of marginality by virtue of being a Jew as influencing his defense of modernity, markets, and differentiation. Mead was not a sociologist, but his synthesis of various philosophical traditions—Darwinism, behaviorism, utilitarianism, and pragmatism—produces a kind of moral philosophy of what is "good." And in the last century of sociological practice, this issue of value-neutrality and science has plagued sociology and sociologists as well as those looking at sociology from the outside. For if sociology cannot be value-neutral but, instead, "takes sides" in political and moral debates, those on "the other side" will cast aspersions on the utility of sociological knowledge. Thus, the first big problem for sociology, and especially for explanatory theories of how the world operates, is how to deal with the question of value-neutrality.

Value Neutrality: Is This Possible? Even Desirable?

There have been some fairly harsh critiques of sociology by prominent sociologists who questioned whether or not sociologists were on "the right side" morally and politically. Do sociologists care enough about the poor? The oppressed? The victims of discrimination? Or are sociologists content to hide in the ivory tower of academia and take the money of clients—government, patrons, foundations, and other sources of funding—no matter what their implicit agenda might be in making these funds available? Indeed, sociologists have had episodes of debate where they have beaten each other up over the issue. I personally have had fellow sociologists—and often very prominent and accomplished ones at that—accuse me, at worst, of supporting the "oppressors" (not clearly specified) or, at best, of being an apologist for the status quo by advocating a sociology that is as value-free as possible.

Indeed, academic departments of sociology have been known to go to war over this issue: Should sociology be activist, advocating moral goals and mobilizing its resources to realize these goals? Or are sociologists to explain why and how events occur and leave moralizing and action to the political sphere outside academia? Recent efforts by prominent sociologists such as Michael Burroway[1] to institutionalize a "public sociology" is an example of the call for a sociology that develops knowledge serving communities in need. By building a large tent and including diverse

---

[1]Michael Burroway, "For Public Sociology," *American Sociological Review* 70 (2005):4–28; see also his: "The Return of the Repressed: Recovering the Public Face of U. S. Sociology, 1000 Years On," *The Annals of the American Academy of Political and Social Science* (2006):68–78, and "Public Sociology: Populist Fad or Path to Renewal?" *British Journal of Sociology* 56 (2006):417–432.

sociologies, each can discipline the other and produce better and more useful knowledge that can be put to good use. As noble as this sounds, it does not take away the big issue that divides sociologists: neutral, value-free science versus activism, whether embracing or questing science. This issue will not go away, and it is often difficult for the protagonists to get along. Each adheres to a belief system—the canons of science and the moral righteousness of ideologies—and like all moral conflicts, they become intense and are not easily resolved.

It is not that activists cannot be good scientists—this conclusion is easily quashed by the power of the neo-Marxist theories summarized in Chapter 14. Nor is it that scientists are not activists. Indeed, many are or have been in their younger years, but they have at the same time tried to separate their science from their activism. This is certainly the path that I have taken over the last twenty-five years, but in my first twenty years, I mixed science with moral advocacy, which for me became less tenable and viable.

Since this divide is not likely to go away, it will continue to cause problems for the discipline internally. Conflict and lack of clarity over the mission and goals of sociology will also continue to arouse the suspicion of those who do not share the left-of-center ideologies of most sociologists, per se. Thus, sociologists will always have to overcome a certain skepticism from others about sociology generating useful knowledge.

One option would be to split the discipline into two departments—scientific sociology and activist sociology—but this would not be a clean line of division, because many activists are very good scientists and many scientists do some activism. Moreover, almost any time sociological knowledge of any sort is used, it is used to further the interests of a client that is not value-neutral. Companies want to make money, community organizers want to help the disenfranchised, government wants knowledge for its political goals, and so it would be for anyone for whom sociologists develop knowledge and/or to whom they give knowledge.

In Herbert Spencer's *The Study of Sociology*, he examines a long list of biases that always exist in creating knowledge (see Chapter 3). His solution—not as well practiced, as he advocated—is to be aware of these biases and work to mitigate them. Thus, theorists need to be aware of their biases and try, as best as possible, to keep them from influencing explanations on the dynamics of the social world. Of course, this is easier said than done, but I have found that by remaining very aware of what I would like to see and what I actually see when examining the data on social processes and trying to figure out the underlying forces driving the empirical processes being summarized as data, it is possible. Indeed, when I see forces operating in a way that I wish they would not, I become very aware of my biases and push them away mentally. So it is possible to achieve a certain degree of self-awareness and use this awareness to work at remaining value-free in developing explanations. Critics will rarely agree, but the burden falls on them to point out the biases, although I have found that positing the operation of dynamics that contradict the critics' biases will inevitably result in your being accused of having a bias. And so the debate continues.

What I have advocated in recent years is for sociology to develop an "engineering mentality" by formalizing knowledge and then bringing it to bear on problems that clients might have in organizing some facet of the social world.[2] By indicating what is possible and, equally important, what is not possible given the situation and the dynamics in play, sociologists can bring their knowledge to the real world. A client may have a bias—virtually all do—and the role of the engineer is to tell them if the goals implied by this bias are possible or not. If not, then the sociologist must indicate what is viable. This is a very different role for sociologists engaged in practice, where often the sociologists' biases drive their analysis. But a *theoretically* informed sociology of practice will have a discipline that an ideologically driven sociology of practice would not have. And if we sustain this engineering mentality with client after client over a sufficiently long period, perhaps some of the suspicion and, indeed, outright distrust of the public and potential clients of sociology may decline.

Still, let us not be too optimistic. The problem of values in sociology has been with the discipline since its founding; this problem will not vanish when a significant portion—perhaps a majority, but I do not know for sure about this—of sociologists are committed to a value-laden agenda in their work. But it will work against others' efforts to make sociology a mature science that is respected not only for its knowledge but also for the utility of this knowledge in addressing real problems in the real world.

Why Some Proclaim That Sociology Cannot Be a Natural Science

Apart from the roadblock thrown in the way of scientific theorizing, there are many other criticisms of sociology as a natural science. We have seen variants of the basic arguments throughout the chapters of this book, but let me boil these down to a few basic lines of attack:[3] (a) phenomenological solipsism, (b) hermeneutical dualism, (c) historical particularism, (d) scientific politics, and, finally, (e) critical discourse. Each of these is briefly reviewed below.

Phenomenological Solipsism

As we saw with Edmund Husserl's project, the basic argument is that conceptions of the world "out there" are mediated through the senses, which, in turn, are mediated through the human brain. All that we know is thus what the brain tells us, and in extreme form, nothing exists in the external world independently of consciousness. Hence, knowing about the exact nature of the social universe is impossible

---

[2]For my thoughts on applied sociology, see Jonathan H. Turner, "Social Engineering: Is This Really as Bad as It Sounds?" *Sociological Practice* 3 (2001):99–120, "The Practice of Scientific Theorizing in Sociology, and the Use of Scientific Theory in Practice," *Sociological Focus* 41 (2008):281–300, and "Is Public Sociology Really Such a Good Idea?" *The American Sociologist* 36 (2006):27–45.

[3]Jonathan H. Turner, "The Promise of Positivism," in *Postmodernism and Social Theory*, ed. D. G. Wagner and S. Seidman (New York: Basil Blackwell, 1990):371–391.

without first knowing how the dynamics of the brain filter impressions of the external world to consciousness.

For me, this line of criticism should alert us to the biasing effects of thought, consciousness, knowledge (including ideologies), and other sources of bias, but taken to the extremes, it puts us just where Husserl found himself: contemplating his navel in an exercise designed to discover the dynamics of the mind. Since the natural sciences appear to have learned a great deal about the biotic and physical universes, it does seem that it is possible to discover the fundamental properties of the world "out there." Moreover, hard scientists do not unduly worry about the distorting and biasing effects of thought and cognition; rather, they invent ways to extend the human senses into instruments that allow them to discover and learn about the properties of the universe.

I do not think that there is anything different about the social world. It exists as a thing "out there"—as Durkheim emphasized with his notion of "social facts." Systems of cultural beliefs and social structures are real things and can be discovered and understood in the same manner as the properties and dynamics of the physical and biological universes. When culture is shared among people and when they create social structures, these are real things, as anyone who violates cultural codes or tries to ignore the constraints of social structure knows. Thus, the criticism of phenomenology is no more valid for the social as for the hard sciences, and we should be very much like hard scientists, who generally ignore such philosophical ideas. True, we should be attuned to biases of culture and social structure, but we should not believe that these make social science impossible.

Hermeneutical Dualism

The basic criticism of hermeneutics is that the social world is symbolic in that actors engage in representations and interpretations of their situations, whereas the physical world is not this way. It exists external to human thoughts and representations. Anthony Giddens (see Chapter 20), for example, emphasizes that social sciences reveal a "double hermeneutic" in that beyond the basic hermeneutical critique, people are agents who can use the findings of science to change the fundamental properties of the social universe. This second hermeneutical capacity of human agents obviates the supposedly timeless laws that science develops about the social universe, because the social world is mutable in a fundamental way by the actions of agents.

It is true, of course, that people can change empirical realities at times by using social science knowledge; indeed, this was Comte's hope for positivism. But agents cannot obviate the underlying forces of social reality. Indeed, when people try to change the world around them and consistently fail, it is likely that they are bumping up against a fundamental force or forces driving the social universe. Critics like Giddens tend to conflate an empirical generalization that describes some empirical regularity with a sociological law that specifies the dynamic forces operating to create empirical regularities. As an agent, for example, I can change my eating routines, but I cannot change the fact that I need food. Thus, or to take a further example, the way in which a society organizes its economy and polity is changeable, but in a large society with many mouths to feed and people to coordinate, it cannot change the basic dynamics of production and power. These can be used to forge new empirical regularities, but the laws describing their operation cannot be obviated, no matter how hard agents might try.

Scholars who take this double hermeneutic seriously will generally develop sensitizing conceptual schemes that can be used to describe empirical events, and they will stop there because they believe that the scheme can eventually be made irrelevant as active agents change the fundamental nature of the social world. In my view, these agents have only changed the flow of empirical events, not the underlying forces driving these events; for example, an airplane temporarily defies the power of gravity, but unless the airplane goes into space (and not even then), gravity as a force of the physical universe is not eliminated by the actions of pilots.

Again, the social world is driven by forces like gravity as this physical force works to create the solar systems and galaxies of the universe, while keeping people and all physical matter pinned to the earth. Like gravity, social forces can be used to alter some empirical situations, but the forces themselves cannot be obviated by such actions. Even though social reality is composed of symbolic representations, these representations are driven by fundamental cultural forces, and these forces are just as real as gravity. One can change one's beliefs, but it would be difficult to suspend the biological and social forces driving belief formation as a basic reality of the social universe. Or people can forge a revolution and change political leaders and perhaps the form of government, but they cannot suddenly suspend the dynamics of power.

Historical Particularism

The historicist argument can be couched in hermeneutical terms: humans are constantly remaking their world; otherwise, there would be no history. Hence, it is not possible to have laws that apply to all times and places. A more muted version of this argument can be found in Marx, who argued that each historical epoch reveals its own laws of operation, but as I emphasized at the end of Chapter 4, Marx himself developed some laws about inequality, power, and conflict that apply to all of history and, if these are true laws, to all of the future.

There is a more sympathetic view of this critique provided by Weber. History is the confluence of historical events at times and places; and this is obviously a particular mode of explanation. That is, for some historical event to have occurred— say, the French Revolution—it had to be preceded by a series of events that, over time, led to the French Revolution. This is a historical explanation of a time-bound set of events; and it is one way to explain events in the social world. I am most sympathetic to these historical explanations because they often provide empirical descriptions that are useful in assessing the plausibility of scientific theories. Historical explanations are not wrong; they are just different from scientific ones. For a scientist, the French Revolution is an empirical event revolving around violent conflict; and for a scientist, the goal is to explain this event by reference to some general laws of conflict. The historian would be most dissatisfied with this kind of more deductive (from a law) explanation of the events (in this case, the French Revolution).

What historians find interesting is the sequences and flows of empirical events leading up to the big event to be explained; they want the details of history. The scientist is less interested in these historical details, except perhaps to use them to establish scope conditions that, in turn, can lead the scientist to the relevant theoretical principles. Again, it is just a matter of preference which type of explanation one prefers. Both are legitimate and useful, but they are different. But, and this is the important point, just because the empirical events leading up to another event in a historical account are often unique to a time and place, it does not mean that these events, along with many other historical events (societal conflicts in general), cannot be explained by an abstract set of principles on conflict, per se, that can be used to explain all historical conflicts in all times and places.

Scientific Politics

For a time, one of the most active research traditions in sociology and other social sciences was research on scientific organizations and the behaviors of scientists.[4] Some of this research ended up being a somewhat gleeful debunking of science with the discovery that the process of scientific investigation does not always follow the ideals of science and, indeed, is like any other endeavor and filled with bias, power plays, vested interests, and political influence. Such findings should not have been surprising to sociologists since science is organized like most human activities in bureaucracies, but, at least, the researchers acted surprised, which gave them the license to proclaim that science was not value-free, objective, and self-correcting, as the ideals of science would suggest.

The point made is sound, and then it is taken too far. It should not have been surprising to learn that scientists are indeed people who are organized in structures subject to external influences, which do bias inquiry at times. Yet scientific knowledge remains testable and, in the long run, is self-correcting. If it were not, none of the applied applications of science would work. Simply pointing out that scientists can be biased and self-interested is, quite frankly, to state the obvious, but the culture of science still demands that results be replicated and that any laws be subjected to rigorous empirical tests. Science still gives us the best representation of the world "out there" and the most objective explanation for this world's dynamics. Abstract theories about how the universe operates will, in the end, be assessed empirically and, as a result, will be rejected, revised, or replaced in a way that religion and ideologues would not allow. Thus, the criticisms that might be made from the empirical research on scientific research do not mean that laws of social organization are not

[4]Harry M. Collins and Steven Yearley, "Epistemological Chicken," in *Science as Practice and Culture*, ed. A. Pickering (Chicago, IL: University of Chicago Press, 1992), 301–326; Harry M. Collins, *Changing Order: Replication and Induction in Scientific Practice* (London: Sage, 1985); Bruno Latour, *Science in Action: How to Follow Scientists and Engineers Through Society* (Cambridge, MA: Harvard University Press, 1992); Andrew Pickering, *Constructing Quarks: A Sociological History of Particle Physics* (Chicago, IL: University of Chicago Press, 1984). For more sympathetic commentaries, see Stephan Fuchs and Jonathan H. Turner, "What Makes a Science Mature? Organizational Control in Scientific Production," *Sociological Theory* 4 (1986):133–150; Jonathan H. Turner, "The Failure to Institutionalize Cumulative Theorizing," in *Formal Sociology: Opportunity or Pitfall*, ed. J. Hage (Albany: SUNY Press, 1994): 41–51.

possible, any more than the laws of the hard sciences are obviated by the constraints of organizational activities.

Critical Discourse

I have already addressed this argument, and so let me only briefly summarize it here. Critical theorists, like Jürgen Habermas (see Chapter 23) argue that the creation of knowledge has a bias in supporting and legitimating the status quo.[5] Seeing current events and structures as manifestations of fundamental laws is, in his view, an ideology supporting those who have an interest in the status quo. For critical theorists, the goal is to expose oppressive social arrangements through discovery, proclamations, discourse, and potential action in order to develop plans for less restrictive and oppressive social arrangements. But like much of the criticism of the scientific prospects of sociology, there is a confusion between empirical generalizations and descriptions, on one side, and theories on the fundamental forces and dynamics that generate the empirical world, on the other. One does not have to support a particular form of economy and polity, for example, to discover the underlying forces and dynamics that drive the formation and operation of all economies and polities in all times and places. Indeed, if change is to be advocated in terms of some value premise, it is important to understand the dynamics of production and power as fundamental properties of the social world.

In fact, suggestions for less oppressive social arrangements will have more chances of success, if implemented, when they are built upon the foundation of scientific knowledge. Understanding the dynamics of production and power goes a long way in understanding how these dynamics can be channeled (not obviated) in directions for realizing the goals defined by some value premise. Ideologies are not a substitute for understanding the forces of the social universe; they blind people to reality and often cause them to pursue goals that are unattainable given the reality of the forces in play. For, as Comte emphasized, it will not be easy to change the social world until the dynamics driving its operation are known. Thus, the best critical theory would be one in which the laws of human social organization are used to make for more benign social arrangements—presuming that people can agree on what is benign (not so easily achieved, unfortunately).

Conclusions: Is a Natural Science of Society Possible?

This is A. R. Radcliffe-Brown's phrase,[6] which I have posed as a question. For me, as should be obvious, the answer is an unqualified "yes," whereas for many others the answer is "no" or perhaps "sort of." From the many theories and theorists summarized

---

[5]Jürgen Habermas, *Zur Logik der Sozialwissenschaften* (Frankfurt, Germany: Suhrkamp, 1970), *Knowledge and Human Interest*, trans. J. Shapiro (London: Heinemann, 1970).

[6]R. Radcliffe-Brown, *A Natural Science of Society* (Glencoe, IL: Free Press, 1957).

in this volume, all three answers are evident. I have tried to formalize some of the "no" and "sort of" answers to show that the dynamics examined in a theory can be converted to abstract models and principles that are amenable to empirical tests to assess their plausibility and validity. The key point for me is that there is nothing that would prevent sociology from being a natural science of society and all of its constituent processes; it is really a matter of will rather than an epistemological and ontological impossibility.

True, the substance of the social universe is different from that of the biotic and physical universes, but this does not mean that it cannot be studied and theorized scientifically. The obstacle is a skepticism that is pervasive in sociology, but it is a skepticism that often is simply too smug and self-assured. This smug skepticism holds the discipline back; it allows scholars to wage ancient wars of epistemology and metaphysics that are best left to philosophers. Sociology becomes a babble of discourse that has no end rather than a serious field that seeks to understand how the social world operates. We become useless to the real world that we all might want to change, and we remain isolated in our ivory towers, which only exacerbates our uselessness. I have stated these points in the extreme but they do reflect my intellectual biases, as has my review of theoretical sociology.

For all his obvious eccentricities, if not outright insanity, Comte had the right idea: science *is to be used* for the betterment of humans. There is nothing incompatible between value-free science (or at least sincere efforts to be value-free) and activism. Useful knowledge can be used to make a better social world, not perhaps the world we would want if we let our ideologies set our goals but a better world nonetheless. Theories will tell us what is possible and what is not; and given the constraints imposed by the forces driving the social universe, it is possible to use understandings of these forces to make social change. Utopias do us little good because they raise people's expectations for states of social organization that may not be viable. Much better is an engineering mentality where we take sociological knowledge, especially knowledge built around theories about fundamental properties of the social universe, and use this knowledge to argue for new sociocultural arrangements that improve the lot of humans. To be smug in rejecting such a view of how social change can occur is to close off humans' best hope for a better social life.

Index

About the Author

Jonathan H. Turner is Distinguished Professor of Sociology at the University of California at Riverside and University Professor of the University of California. He received his BS degree from the University of California at Santa Barbara in 1965 and his PhD from Cornell University in 1968. He has been a professor at the University of California at Riverside for forty-four years. In the field of sociology and more broadly, he is known as a general theorist, seeking to make sociology more like the natural sciences. He is the author of dozens of books and hundreds of articles on theory and many more substantive topics. This large book represents an effort to pull together and substantially add to his writings over the last forty years on theoretical sociology, from its very beginnings to the present day, with the hope that it can serve as a useful resource for professors and students interested in the development of theory in the discipline.